Economics, Law, and Institutions in Asia Pacific

The Asia Pacific region is expected to steadily enhance its economic and political presence in the world during the twenty-first century. At the same time, many serious economic and political issues remain unresolved in the region. To further academic enquiry and enhance readers' understanding about this vibrant region, the present series, Economics, Law, and Institutions in Asia Pacific, aims to present cutting-edge research on the Asia Pacific region and its relationship with the rest of the world. For countries in this region to achieve robust economic growth, it is of foremost importance that they improve the quality of their markets, as history shows that healthy economic growth cannot be achieved without high-quality markets. High-quality markets can be established and maintained only under a well-designed set of rules and laws, without which competition will not flourish. Based on these principles, this series places a special focus on economic, business, legal, and institutional issues geared towards the healthy development of Asia Pacific markets. The series considers book proposals for scientific research, either theoretical or empirical, that is related to the theme of improving market quality and has policy implications for the Asia Pacific region. The types of books that will be considered for publication include research monographs as well as relevant proceedings. The series show-cases work by Asia-Pacific based researchers but also encourages the work of social scientists not limited to the Asia Pacific region. Each proposal will be subject to evaluation by the editorial board and experts in the field.

More information about this series at http://www.springer.com/series/13451

Jerome A. Cohen · William P. Alford
Chang-fa Lo
Editors

Taiwan and International Human Rights

A Story of Transformation

Springer

Editors
Jerome A. Cohen
U.S.-Asia Law Institute
New York University
New York, NY
USA

Chang-fa Lo
Constitutional Court
Taipei, Taiwan
Republic of China

William P. Alford
Harvard Law School
Cambridge, MA
USA

ISSN 2199-8620 ISSN 2199-8639 (electronic)
Economics, Law, and Institutions in Asia Pacific
ISBN 978-981-13-0349-4 ISBN 978-981-13-0350-0 (eBook)
https://doi.org/10.1007/978-981-13-0350-0

Library of Congress Control Number: 2018939949

This Springer imprint is published by the registered company Springer Nature Singapore Pte Ltd.
The registered company address is: 152 Beach Road, #21-01/04 Gateway East, Singapore 189721, Singapore

Preface

In January 2017, one of the editors of this book, Jerome A. Cohen, delivered a public speech at National Taiwan University College of Law after he had served as a member of the international group of experts invited by the government of Taiwan to review its implementation of international human rights covenants. In his speech, he mentioned that based on his personal experience and his participation in the review, Taiwan has much to share with people in other parts of the world about its experiences in transforming itself from historically having had an authoritarian legal and political structure into what is now a vibrantly democratic society.

Spurred by this, we decided to put together a book to tell the story of Taiwan's performance in various fields of human rights from various perspectives. We are pleased that local and international scholars and other experts, many with a long history of writing about human rights, readily accepted our invitation to participate in this volume. They were enthusiastic about the opportunity to elaborate from a theoretical and/or practical vantage point areas of human rights protection with which they are familiar. In addition to the introductory chapter coauthored by the editors of this book, we have collected 37 chapters from authors representing a broad range of perspectives and topics, with some authors finding many developments to laud, while others instead emphasize the need for improvement.

Readers will find that there have been events, governmental decisions, and judicial decisions positively or adversely affecting human rights protection. Different views exist as to the proper way of achieving higher standards of protection. But one thing that is shared by all of the authors is that human rights treaties have played a key role in the case of Taiwan. There is a broad consensus among the authors in this volume that in the case of Taiwan, these treaties have contributed importantly to facilitating the transition from an authoritarian regime to a real democracy, even as Taiwan remains outside the "jurisdiction" of these treaties. We hope that this book will provide a useful example for the discourse of human rights protection in developing countries, for the discussion of practical and legal issues raised by human rights treaties, and for demonstrating how such treaties can help States Parties as well as nonparties to promote human rights.

The editors wish to thank the following institutes for their role in helping make this book possible:

- Asian Center for WTO and International Health Law and Policy, National Taiwan University College of Law
- Institutum Iurisprudentiae, Academia Sinica
- East Asian Legal Studies, Harvard Law School
- US-Asia Law Institute, New York University School of Law

We would also like to take this opportunity to thank Prof. Tzu-Yi Lin (Director of the Institutum Iurisprudentiae) for coordinating the resources, Prof. Chien-Chih Lin for his valuable role in editing several chapters, and many other members of the Institute for contributing to their chapters.

We would particularly like to thank Prof. Wen-Chen Chang for providing excellent ideas, especially in the initial stage of the editing process. We are grateful to all contributors for making efforts to contribute their chapters to enrich the volume.

Our extremely talented assistants Mao-wei Lo, Yi-tzu Chen and Hui-Heng Hong have taken the lead in coordinating a team of skilled assistants to help edit the book. The team members include Cheng-Kai Wang, Yun-Hsin (Cindy) Chen, Sheng-Chan Chen, Po-hsiang Liao, Jia-Jhen Liao, Ming-Hsi Chu, Arthur Wong, Ambra Minoli, Chia-Ying Chien, Angelique Saw, and Chi-Hsuan Liu. And we wish to acknowledge the superb editorial contribution of Nancy Hearst, librarian of the Fairbank Collection of the H.C. Fung Library at Harvard. Thank you very much for your excellent work!

New York, USA
Cambridge, USA
Taipei, Taiwan
July 2018

Jerome A. Cohen
William P. Alford
Chang-fa Lo

Contents

About the Editors

Jerome A. Cohen has been professor at NYU School of Law since 1990, Faculty Director of its U.S.-Asia Law Institute, and a leading American expert on Chinese law and government. A pioneer in the field, Prof. Cohen began studying and teaching about China's legal system in the early 1960s, and from 1964 to 1979 he introduced the teaching of Asian law into the curriculum of Harvard Law School, where he served as Jeremiah Smith Professor, Associate Dean, and Director of East Asian Legal Studies. In addition to his responsibilities at NYU, Prof. Cohen served for several years as C. V. Starr Senior Fellow and Director of Asia Studies at the Council on Foreign Relations, where he currently is an Adjunct Senior Fellow. He retired from the partnership of Paul, Weiss, Rifkind, Wharton & Garrison LLP at the end of 2000 after 20 years of law practice focused on China. In his law practice, Prof. Cohen represented many companies and individuals in contract negotiations as well as in dispute resolution in China. Professor Cohen has published several books on Chinese law, including *The Criminal Process in the People's Republic of China, 1949–63* (Harvard University Press, 1968), *People's China and International Law* (with Hungdah Chiu, Princeton University Press, 1974), *Contract Laws of the People's Republic of China* (with Yvonne Y. F. Chan and Ho Yuk Ming, Longman Group, 1988), and *Challenge to China: How Taiwan Abolished Its Version of Re-Education Through Labor* (with Margaret K. Lewis, Berkshire Publishing, 2013). In addition, he has published hundreds of scholarly articles on various topics as well as a book, *China Today*, coauthored with his wife, Joan Lebold Cohen, and a regular series of journalistic opinion pieces for various newspapers. Today, Prof. Cohen continues his research and writing on Asian law, specifically focusing on legal institutions, criminal justice reform, dispute resolution, human rights, and the role of international law relating to China and Taiwan.

William P. Alford is Jerome A. and Joan L. Cohen Professor of East Asian Legal Studies at Harvard Law School where he also serves as Vice-Dean for the Graduate Program and International Legal Studies, Director of East Asian Legal Studies, and Chair of the Harvard Law School Project on Disability. A scholar of Chinese law and society, his books include *To Steal a Book is an Elegant Offense: Intellectual*

Property Law in Chinese Civilization (Stanford 1995); *Raising the Bar: The Emerging Legal Profession in East Asia* (Harvard 2007), 残疾人法律保障機制研究 (A Study of Legal Mechanisms to Protect Persons with Disabilities) (Huaxia 2008, with Wang Liming and Ma Yu'er, in Chinese), and *Prospects for the Professions in China* (Routledge 2011, with William Kirby and Kenneth Winston). In addition, he has published dozens of articles concerning China, law and international affairs. Professor Alford's work has been recognized with an honorary doctorate from the University of Geneva in 2010 and honorary professorships at Renmin University of China and Zhejiang University. He is also the recipient of the inaugural O'Melveny & Myers Centennial Award, the Kluwer China Prize, an Abe (Japan) Fellowship, the Harvard Law School Alumni Association Award, an award from Special Olympics International recognizing his work on behalf of persons with intellectual disabilities, and several other fellowships and honors. He is a graduate of Amherst College (B.A.), the University of Cambridge (LL.B.), Yale University (M.A. in History and M.A. in Chinese Studies), and Harvard Law School (J.D.).

Chang-fa Lo has been Justice of the Constitutional Court of the ROC (Taiwan) since October 2011. Prior to his current judicial position, he was the Chair Professor and Lifetime Distinguished Professor at National Taiwan University (NTU); Dean of NTU College of Law; Founding Director of Asian Center for the WTO and International Health Law and Policy of NTU College of Law (ACWH); Founding Director of the Center for Ethics, Law and Society in Biomedicine and Technology of NTU; Commissioner of Taiwan's Fair Trade Commission; Commissioner of Taiwan's International Trade Commission; and legal advisor for Taiwan's GATT/WTO accession negotiations. In his capacity as Director of ACWH, Prof. Lo launched two English journals, namely, the *Asian Journal of WTO and International Health Law and Policy* (AJWH, an SSCI listed journal) and the *Contemporary Asia Arbitration Journal* (CAA) in 2006 and 2008, respectively. During his tenure as Dean of NTU College of Law, he also launched the English journal, the *NTU Law Review*. He was appointed by the WTO as a panelist for DS332 Brazil—Measures Affecting Imports of Retreaded Tyre in 2006, DS468 Ukraine—Definitive Safeguard Measures on Certain Passenger Cars in 2014, and a member of the Permanent Group of Experts under the SCM Agreement of WTO in 2008. He has also been Chairman of the Asia WTO Research Network (AWRN) since 2013. Prior to his teaching career, he practiced law in Taipei. He received his S.J.D. degree from Harvard University Law School in 1989. He is the author of 13 books (including *Treaty Interpretation under the Vienna Convention on the Law of Treaties—A New Round of Codification* published by Springer) and the editor of seven books (including this one), and he has authored more than 100 journal papers and book chapters. He was granted the "National Professorship Award" by the Ministry of Education and the "Outstanding Scholarship Chair Professorship Award" by the Foundation for Advancement of Outstanding Scholarship.

Part I
Introduction

Chapter 1
Introduction—An Overview

Jerome A. Cohen, William P. Alford and Chang-fa Lo

1 The Story Begins with the Lifting of Martial Law in 1987

Taiwan has gone through a number of important stages in its modern history. From the 17th century until 1895, Taiwan was under the governance of China's Ch'ing Dynasty before being ceded to Japan in the Treaty of Shimonoseki concluding the Sino-Japanese War (1894–1895). During the long period of Ch'ing rule and the subsequent half-century of Japanese colonialism, the concept and practice of rule of law as we know it today basically did not exist, although Japanese rule did introduce some Western legal notions that had recently been imported into Japan. In 1945, following World War II, China, through the Republic of China (ROC) or the Nationalist Kuomintang or KMT government, resumed governance on Taiwan, and in 1949, after the defeat of the Nationalist forces on the Mainland by the Chinese Communist Party, the Nationalist central government moved to Taiwan, making Taipei its capital. For four decades on Taiwan, the Nationalist government imposed martial law, "freezing" the application of many important rights and freedoms that had been guaranteed in the ROC Constitution of 1947. It was not until 1987 that the

J. A. Cohen (✉)
US-Asia Law Institute, New York University School of Law, New York, NY, USA
e-mail: Jerome.cohen@nyu.edu

J. A. Cohen
Council on Foreign Relations, New York, NY, USA

W. P. Alford
Harvard Law School, Cambridge, USA
e-mail: alford@law.harvard.edu

C. Lo
Constitutional Court, Taiwan, Republic of China
e-mail: lochangfa@gmail.com

J. A. Cohen et al. (eds.), *Taiwan and International Human Rights*, Economics, Law, and Institutions in Asia Pacific, https://doi.org/10.1007/978-981-13-0350-0_1

government abrogated martial law, finally allowing the people of Taiwan the autonomy needed to develop a democratic society and build a constitutional democracy able to protect their rights and freedoms.

Through visits to the island during the martial-law era, Jerome A. Cohen witnessed various aspects of the repression imposed by the Nationalists under the rule of President Chiang Kai-shek and his successors. In his chapter "Taiwan's Political-Legal Progress: Memories of the KMT Dictatorship," he illustrates Taiwan's human rights history through personal experience, beginning with his first visit in 1961 and including a few depressing but exciting and ultimately hopeful events that marked the long transition from Nationalist repression to constitutional democracy. This chapter concludes with a brief reference to Professor Cohen's service in both 2013 and 2017 as a member of the independent International Review Committees of Experts convened by successive contemporary Taiwan governments to evaluate progress in promoting the island's human rights transformation.

2 Human Rights Transition from Broader Perspectives

Part II of this volume focuses on Taiwan's human rights transition from historical, comparative and other perspectives. In the first chapter, Nigel Li examines "Asian Values, Confucian Tradition and Human Rights," explaining that when the Republic of China's first Constitution went into effect in 1947, it was still very much a nation of Confucian heritage without any recognized tradition of constitutionalism. He then reviews the obstacles that stood in the way of promoting constitutionalism when it was first transplanted to the distinctive soil of Taiwan. The chapter also examines how respect for constitutionalism gradually evolved and took root on the island in a setting in which the government was regarded as the ruler and was customarily understood as the people's parent. The fundamental notions of the rule of law, human rights, an independent judiciary, separation of powers, equality of individuals, and constitutionalism were all largely considered novel concepts.

Brad R. Roth explains in his chapter, "Human Rights and Transitional Justice: Taiwan's Adoption of the ICCPR and the Redress of 2/28 and Martial-Law-Era Injustices," the requirement in Article 2(3) of the International Covenant on Civil and Political Rights (ICCPR) to "ensure that any person whose rights or freedoms as herein recognized are violated shall have an effective remedy," which shall be "determined by competent judicial, administrative or legislative authorities, or by any other competent authority provided for by the legal system of the State," and enforced by "the competent authorities." He argues that Taiwan's adoption of the ICCPR raises issues about appropriate redress for injustices associated with the authoritarian period of KMT rule, including most prominently the atrocities committed in the aftermath of the 28 February 1947 uprising. According to Mr. Roth, coming to terms with the past is an indispensable component of the consolidation of a political order predicated on the irreducible dignity of the human person. This human rights obligation can be fulfilled, he believes, even when too much time has passed for criminal prosecutions to be undertaken, and even when the political party associated with the perpetrators retains a substantial political role.

Chun Hung Chen and Hung-Ying Yeh explain in their chapter, "The Battlefield of Transitional Justice in Taiwan: A Relational View," how Taiwan tackled the issue of transitional justice with a dynamic approach. When assessing the progress of transitional justice, instead of taking an exclusive top-down or bottom-up perspective, the authors argue that it is important to grasp the interactive nature of the relationship between state and society. That is to say, any transitional justice mechanisms that are implemented are the outcomes of interactions between government and grassroots actors. This chapter outlines achievements to date and discusses the structural factors that have shaped the present situation. The establishment of the National Human Rights Museum and the dispute over the nominations of Constitutional Court justices are taken as examples of the interactive nature of policy and institutional design. This chapter ends by demonstrating the implications of Taiwan's case for scholarship and practice.

Cheng-Yi Huang observes in his chapter "Frozen Trials: Political Victims and Their Quest for Justice" that, before the lifting of martial law in 1987, the Legislative Yuan passed the National Security Act prohibiting civilian cases tried by court martial from being appealed to the ordinary courts. The Constitutional Court affirmed this legislation in its notorious J.Y. Interpretation No. 272 in 1991, indicating that this was a very exceptional case, since the imposition of martial law had been maintained for some four decades. In its view, stability of the legal system came first and the court had to defer to the Legislative Yuan's decision. Later, a special statute authorized the government to reimburse the victims or their family members without overruling the original judgments. The government then dealt with 10,062 cases and issued monetary compensation amounting to over 19.6 billion New Talwan Dollars. However, the victims and their family members still continued to wait for rectified court judgments. This quest for justice after the start of Taiwan's democratic transition was delayed for thirty years. It was only in December 2017 that the Legislative Yuan passed new legislation in a further effort to confirm the value of transitional justice. In order to facilitate assessment of the progress thus far made, this chapter lays out the legal structure of the martial-law period and then reviews post-authoritarian governments' efforts to compensate victims. The chapter concludes with an innovative analysis of the critical shortcomings and potential benefits of Taiwan's model of transitional justice.

Chien-Chih Lin explains in his chapter "Towards an Analytical Framework of Constitutionalism in East Asia: The Case of Taiwan" that recent years have witnessed the reemergence of discussions on Confucian constitutionalism, communitarian constitutionalism, and Asian values. The author argues that, on the one hand, constitutionalism in East Asia is inevitably a blend of liberal constitutionalism and Confucian constitutionalism—that the differences between democracies and dictatorships in this regard in this region are often a matter of degree, not of kind. On the other hand, he claims, human rights are better protected in Taiwan than in most other Asian jurisdictions because human rights progress has taken place concomitantly with the decline of Confucianism on the island. From this perspective, he contends that it is plausible to say that Taiwan has become the only democracy in Greater China precisely because it has discarded Confucianism and Asian values, which, he suggests, served as a veneer of legitimacy for autocrats to justify dictatorship.

3 Institutional Setting and Voluntary Compliance with Human Rights Treaties

In Part II of this book, the discussions focus on two broad matters—the future institutional arrangements for human rights protection in Taiwan and the unique voluntary implementation of international human rights treaties by Taiwan's government.

Mab Huang raises a very important question in his chapter "A National Human Rights Commission for Taiwan?": why have sixteen years not been enough for the government to create a national human rights commission (NHRI) in Taiwan? It is puzzling to the author that, in light of the great strides Taiwan has been making in the promotion and protection of human rights over the past thirty-some years, and the current President's pledge that she will actively promote judicial reform and transitional justice, a NHRI based on the Paris Principles is nowhere in sight. He discusses the attitude and thinking of the political elite concerning a NHRI and how the bureaucracy has performed in the rapidly changing situation. He also comments that, through the years, several prominent human rights activists have been recruited into government service but then they quickly moved away from their previous views and supported instead government policies. This change of mind, he maintains, has been deeply demoralizing to their former colleagues in the NGO world, and has made for mistrust of the government.

Fort Fu-Te Liao addresses in his chapter "Establishing a National Human Rights Institution—Taiwan in Global Trends" a similar issue and explains that the United Nations has been promoting the establishment of independent NHRIs for several decades, with the Paris Principles as the relevant international standard. He discusses Taiwan's preparatory works in establishing a NHRI in line with global trends. His analysis focuses on three main issues—historical development, models, and accreditation results. It examines both global trends and Taiwanese endeavors. Professor Liao maintains that only two NHRI models—an independent human rights commission or a human rights ombudsman, the models most widely adopted—are proposed for Taiwan. He suggests that elements such as time, region and model are not key factors in accreditation.

Ernest Caldwell also deals with the national human rights institution issue in his chapter "The Control Yuan and Human Rights in Taiwan: Towards the Development of a National Human Rights Institution?" His approach is different from that in the preceding chapter, although he agrees that, despite decades of debate, Taiwan has never established a NHRI that complies with international human rights norms. At present, in his view, Taiwan confronts three viable options: the creation of an independent NHRI, the establishment of a national commission under the Office of the President, or reform of the Control Yuan into a NHRI. Here he focuses on the latter option. Specifically, he considers the historical relationship between the Control Yuan and human rights in Taiwan, and further considers the socio-legal, as well as constitutional, implications of reforming this branch of government into a NHRI that complies with international human rights norms.

Jacques deLisle addresses Taiwan's unique situation in implementing international human rights norms in his chapter "'All the World's a Stage': Taiwan's Human Rights Performance and Playing to International Norms." He observes that Taiwan's engagement with the international regime for human rights has been exceptional for reasons related to its unusual status in the world. Taiwan's precarious status has provided distinctive reasons to emphasize international human rights norms, including some of their more formal manifestations. In the 1980s and early 1990s, the improvement in Taiwan's human rights record became vital to maintaining U.S. support. In the late 1990s and 2000s, Taiwan's commitment to human rights norms and values continued to be an essential element in the island's efforts to preserve security and international stature. During the past decade, Taiwan has deepened its engagement with the UN-centered human rights regime, stressing compliance with that regime as if it were a member state, adopting domestic legislation to mirror the principal human rights covenants, and undertaking reports that parallel the requirements for States Parties to the major human rights conventions. Although this approach has benefited Taiwan's reputation internationally, as well as the lives of its citizens, Taiwan's human rights engagement strategy faces new and difficult challenges: internationally, the benefits of a relatively strong human rights record may be waning; domestically, discourse about human rights is turning to more intractable or controversial problems, including issues that resonate with economic, social and cultural dimensions of human rights, and issues of transitional justice.

Yu-Jie Chen also addresses the unique status of Taiwan in accepting the human rights treaties in her chapter "Isolated but Not Oblivious: Taiwan's Acceptance of the Two Major Human Rights Covenants." She observes that, despite Taiwan's isolation from the United Nations, in 2009 it still ratified the two major UN human rights covenants—the ICCPR and the International Covenant on Economic, Social and Cultural Rights (ICESCR). This development is a milestone in Taiwan's engagement with international human rights law. Although the government's attempt to deposit the instruments of ratification with the United Nations was rejected, it has committed itself to following the covenants by granting them the status of domestic legislation and instituting mechanisms to implement them. The efforts by Taiwan as a non-UN member state to adopt the two major human rights covenants are a shot in the arm for the international human rights system. This chapter examines how a state shut out of the UN human rights regime nevertheless became a strong supporter of the regime. With special attention to the relevant domestic advocacy campaigns and political discussions, this chapter seeks to identify the driving forces behind Taiwan's ratification.

Wen-Chen Chang discusses the issues of implementing human rights treaties in her chapter "Taiwan's Human Rights Implementation Acts: A Model for Successful Incorporation?" She explains that although Taiwan has been barred from accession to any human rights conventions, beginning in 2009 it has passed Implementation Acts in order to incorporate into domestic law fundamental rights and freedoms enshrined in the international human rights conventions. These Implementation Acts provide binding domestic legal effect for the rights enshrined in those human rights conventions. The Implementation Acts even oblige the government to issue state reports based on the requirements of those human rights conventions and to create a system of review of government implementation by independent international experts with prior experience serving on similar international panels. This chapter analyzes this innovative implementation mechanism and discusses its particular functions, challenges and difficulties in the context of Taiwan's unique international situation. It also addresses whether this model of an Implementation Act may be suitable for human rights incorporation and enforcement beyond Taiwan.

Yean-Sen Teng, in his chapter "The Problems with the Incorporation of International Human Rights Law in Taiwan," raises questions arising from internalizing international human rights law into the domestic legal system in with the Taiwan. His first question concerns the capacity to conclude international treaties and the legal effect of the government's unilateral acts in the context of international law. His second question deals with the status and effect of the international human rights treaties in the domestic legal order of Taiwan. Third is the question concerning the method of incorporating international human rights treaties by enacting implementing legislation designed especially to create the binding force of a treaty within the jurisdiction of Taiwan. His fourth question relates to the practice applied by the courts or in constitutional interpretations regarding the specific rights and freedoms prescribed in the human rights treaties. This chapter elucidates the legal implications of these questions and the related problems in an effort to offer possible solutions for the judiciary to consider as judges attempt to enforce the rights and fundamental freedoms involved.

Chang-fa Lo, in his chapter "The Approach of Introducing International Human Rights Treaties into the Interpretation of Constitutional Provisions in Taiwan," addresses a more specific issue concerning the introduction of international human rights norms into constitutional interpretations. He emphasizes the desirability and importance of ensuring a living constitution for the Republic of China by incorporating international human rights treaties and practices into the decisions made by the Constitutional Court. He suggests resort to the fundamental interpretation method of relying on textual interpretations to look for appropriate ordinary meanings of the constitutional text. But the "ordinary meaning" should not be the "ordinary meaning" at the time when the Constitution was adopted. Instead, it should be the "ordinary meaning" at the time when a provision is interpreted. The meaning should evolve by taking into consideration the subsequent development of international human rights treaties and practices. This approach is more in line with the duty entrusted by the Constitution to the Court to "interpret the Constitution" and also in line with the need to make sure that constitutional provisions will not become obsolete.

Yen-tu Su offers a unique discussion of the simulation of the Constitutional Court in his chapter "Rights Advocacy Through Simulation: The Genius of the Constitutional Court Simulation in Taiwan," drawing upon his experience in participating in a simulation case. He observes that the Constitutional Court Simulation (CCS) has received much attention and interest from the Constitutional Court as well as from the general public in recent years by tackling such salient issues as same-sex marriage, the death penalty, and transitional justice. He analyzes and assesses the workings of the CCS as a moot court education program, a shadow constitutional court, a deliberative forum, and a new approach to rights advocacy in Taiwan. Although the success of the CCS as a rights advocate would make it more difficult for the CCS to project itself as an impartial shadow court, the CCS enterprise attests to the ingenuity and enthusiasm of those who fight for liberal, progressive causes in civil society in Taiwan.

Song-Lih Huang and Yibee Huang look into the NGO aspect of Taiwan's human rights performance in their chapter "The Role of NGOs in Monitoring the Implementation of Human Rights Treaty Obligations." They observe that the ratification of the ICCPR and ICESCR through implementation legislation in 2009 has created a new model of operation for human rights NGOs. They are now able to engage with the government on human rights issues on a scale unprecedented in Taiwan's modern history. This chapter identifies three stages in the development of this model: (1) the influence of NGOs, although limited in number, on high officials during President Chen Shui-bian's two terms from 2000 to 2008; (2) the influence of core NGOs, particularly those participating in Covenants Watch, in shaping the format of state reports and their reviews; and (3) the involvement of a much larger number of NGOs and individuals in the review and follow-up processes. The chapter also identifies the limitations of this operation in reviewing state reports, especially when facing the institutional deficiencies of the government and in providing adequate training of civil servants, teachers, police, and judges.

To conclude Part III of this book, Manfred Nowak reflects on his personal experience in participating in the two international human rights reviews to date in his chapter "Personal Reflections on the Taiwan Human Rights Review Process." He relates how he was requested by the government of Taiwan to lead a group of highly distinguished international human rights experts entrusted with the task of reviewing Taiwan's compliance with the rights enshrined in the ICESCR and the ICCPR. The chapter contains reflections by the author on the review proceedings in 2013 and 2017. Particular emphasis is placed on the need to abolish the death penalty.

4 Protection of Civil and Political Rights

Part IV of this book discusses the protection of civil and political rights in Taiwan. Ming-Sung Kuo and Hui-Wen Chen discuss perhaps the most difficult issue—the death penalty—in their chapter "Killing in Your Name: Pathology of Judicial Paternalism and the Mutation of the 'Most Serious Crimes' Requirement in Taiwan." Their focus is on the legal issues arising from Article 6 of the ICCPR. They explain that although Article 6 falls short of banning the death penalty outright, it provides substantive and procedural requirements aimed at limiting the imposition of the death penalty before its abolition. Among them is the restriction of the death penalty to only the "most serious crimes." Drawing on the case law of Taiwan's Supreme Court, this chapter aims to shed socio-legal light on the role that the "most serious crimes" requirement has played in judicial rulings concerning the death penalty since the ICCPR became enforceable in Taiwan on 10 December, 2009. It argues that, in its translation into Taiwanese judicial practice, the "most serious crimes" requirement has been read together with the domestic legal provision requiring that individualized aggravating and mitigating circumstances be taken into account under the rubric of rehabilitability, and that this deviates from the jurisprudence of the UN human rights bodies. Under the "judge-civilizer" tradition prevalent in the Taiwanese judiciary, the idea of rehabilitability has gradually transformed judicial deliberation on whether to impose the death penalty into a valuation of the worth of the defendant's life, with a focus on the issue whether the defendant is an incorrigible offender. With its absorption into the individualizing idea of rehabilitability, the "most serious crimes" requirement of the ICCPR has thus become part of the pathology of judicial paternalism, suggesting a mutation of international human rights ideals in Taiwan.

Rong-Geng Li addresses the issue of the death penalty from a different perspective in his chapter "A Silent Reform of the Death Penalty in Taiwan (R.O.C.)." He notes the tension that exists between the general public, on the one hand, and most NGOs and scholars, on the other, on this issue. Without any revision of the statutes, he points out, Taiwan's Supreme Court has added several substantive and procedural requirements for any conviction and sentence of the death penalty. In addition, the Ministry of Justice has established two special organizations to review death penalty cases. Due to these practical developments, the author maintains, the threshold of the burden of proof in death penalty cases has been substantially raised. Thus, the author concludes, it is fair to say that the death penalty has been reformed, even though legislators are extremely unlikely to abolish it in the foreseeable future, and this reform is necessary and appropriate so as to reduce the possibility of wrongful execution.

Frederick Chao-Chun Lin examines personal liberty protection issues in his chapter "A Core Case for Judicial Review–Protecting Personal Liberty in Taiwan." In his view, Taiwan has made good progress in protecting personal liberty in the last three decades. One way to demonstrate this significant development is to use this experience to test some prominent academic theories, and the author believes that

Professor Jeremy Waldron's most recent attack on judicial review provides a valuable chance to demonstrate Taiwan's progress. This chapter therefore uses Taiwan's experience of protecting personal liberty to counter Professor Waldron's three major criticisms of judicial review. First, the author contends that Taiwan's experience shows that the text of a constitutional bill of rights does indeed strengthen the protection of rights. Secondly, Taiwan's case also reveals that it is in the cooperation between judicial review and the Legislative Yuan that rights are more fully able to be protected. Finally, it is suggested that Taiwan's lessons from protecting personal liberty prove that Professor Waldron's definition of the tyranny of the majority may be incomplete and even wrong.

Hui-chieh Su, in her chapter "From Suppression to Real Freedom of Expression in the Open and Plural Society of Taiwan—The Constitutional Court's Role in This Progress," discusses freedom of expression in Taiwan. She notes that freedom of expression in Taiwan was suppressed for 38 years prior to 1987. Yet, driven by an active civil society in the 1990s, the Taiwanese Constitutional Court has come to play a major role in deciding both classical and transformative freedom of speech disputes. However, she criticizes the Constitutional Court's reliance on American theories, since the Court often appears insensitive not only to a future of innovative communication technologies but also to the country's authoritarian past. She believes that although in an open and pluralistic society with an authoritarian past the Court has generally become more cautious, in its latest interpretations it nevertheless has created the most stringent scrutiny standards for prior restrictions of speech.

Jeffrey C. F. Li addresses the issues of freedom of movement in his chapter "Freedom of Movement in Taiwan—A Local Development to Meet International Standards." He explains that, under Article 12 of the ICCPR, freedom of movement includes at least three distinct rights, namely the right to enter one's own country, the right to leave any country, and the right to liberty of movement within the territory of a state. In Taiwan, the three rights are all covered by the Constitution and have been expanded by the Constitutional Court. The author introduces the concept of freedom of migration as it exists in Article 10 of the Constitution and how it corresponds to the freedom of movement under international treaties. He also discusses how the Constitutional Court has developed freedom of movement based on Article 22 of the Constitution.

Chih-hsing Ho discusses privacy issues in a comparative way in her chapter "Configuration of the Notion of Privacy as a Fundamental Right in Taiwan—A Comparative Study of International Treaties and EU Rules." She observes that, under the influence of new communications technologies, the traditional notion of the right to privacy has experienced a paradigm shift from a right to be left alone to respect for individual autonomy concerning the control of one's personal information. At the end of 2013, the United Nations General Assembly adopted Resolution 68/167 to address concerns about the potentially detrimental impact of electronic surveillance on human rights and liberal society. In the European Union, modernization of Data Protection Convention 108, as well as the recently enacted General Data Protection Regulation (GDPR), signal the kind of essential steps that should be taken to strengthen individuals' rights and autonomy with respect to data protection in the digital age. Thus, this chapter locates the development of the rights to privacy and personal data protection in Taiwan within the broader context of international and comparative analysis. The author also illustrates how the notion of privacy has been configured as a fundamental right in Taiwan, and explores the challenges arising from advances in information technology to privacy protection given Taiwan's legal and regulatory frameworks.

Margaret K. Lewis introduces the proposed transformation of Taiwan's criminal trial system in her chapter "Who Shall Judge? Taiwan's Exploration of Lay Participation in Criminal Trials." The ICCPR provides that "everyone shall be entitled to a fair and public hearing by a competent, independent and impartial tribunal established by law" but it does not dictate the composition of the tribunal. Lewis explains that international human rights law does not demand lay participation in criminal trials. But in recent years, Taiwan has tussled with the extent to which public access to observing trials should be transformed into direct public participation in the outcome of those trials. To date, however, the role that lay people will serve in the adjudication process remains contested on the island. As Taiwan moves towards formulating a specific plan for lay participation, Lewis questions whether proponents of lay participation are expecting too much of the proposed reforms and encourages greater focus on how lay participation might impact the rights of the accused.

5 Protection of Economic, Social and Cultural Rights

Part V of the book identifies a small number of areas in the broad group of rights covered by the ICESCR and examines the performance of Taiwan in these areas.

Chuan-Feng Wu discusses important right to health issues in his chapter "The Right to Health in Taiwan: Implications and Challenges." His observation is that although the right to health has been recognized as a fundamental right for everyone in Taiwan and universal National Health Insurance has been established to protect accessibility to healthcare, the right to health is still not comprehensively guaranteed because it is not explicitly stipulated in either the judicial or policy-making processes. This failure undermines the intrinsic values of the right to health and the importance of the individual's legal entitlements to health necessities, and it excuses the government's non-compliance with human rights obligations. In order to explore the implications and challenges of the realization of the right to health in Taiwan, he assesses Taiwan's commitment to the right to health from legal and public health perspectives through an analysis of constitutional and other domestic laws, health inequality, and the distribution of the underlying conditions of health. The notions of "accountability" and "participation" in regard to "social determinants of health" are also considered as important factors in the assessment.

Chun-Yuan Lin observes in his chapter, "The Evolution of Environmental Rights in Taiwan," that, in the last two decades, democratization has raised the rights consciousness of Taiwanese society and mobilized mass environmental movements and substantial legislation. In addition, the process of globalization has not only drawn Taiwan's attention to international environmental issues but also has pushed Taiwan to comply with international human rights standards. Yet, in spite of the growth in human rights consciousness, people in Taiwan still have limited understanding of their "environmental rights." The question of how to understand and conceptualize environmental rights within Taiwan's development is crucial for future generations. This chapter defines environmental rights as a collection of rights that provide legal protection against environmental problems. The author argues that environmental rights in Taiwan have evolved alongside political, social and economic development. During the process of democratization, massive enactment of, and progress on, environmental law has provided a legal basis for environmental claims and has transformed them into legal rights.

Wen-Chen Shih addresses a more specific environmental rights issue in her chapter "Human Rights and Climate Finance—How Does the Normative Framework Affect Taiwan?" She explains that climate change might affect certain specific human rights, such as right to life, right to adequate food, right to water, right to health, right to adequate housing, and right to self-determination. Climate change might also affect specific groups, in particular women, children, and indigenous peoples. However, it might be difficult for an individual to hold a particular state responsible for harm caused by climate change. A human rights-based approach to climate finance can help ensure that climate-financed activities comply with existing human rights obligations and principles. It is also desirable to establish institutional safeguard systems that prevent social and environmental harm and maximize participation, transparency, accountability, equity and rights protections. This chapter focuses on how the emerging normative human rights and climate finance framework will affect, and has already affected, Taiwan's climate finance, both in terms of the island's national climate finance and in terms of its foreign aid policy.

Ching-Fu Lin deals with important right to food issues in his chapter "Constitutional and Legal Dimensions of the Right to Food in Taiwan: The Long March toward Normative Internalization and Realization." He indicates that Taiwan has encountered various challenges in its efforts to normatively internalize and realize this right. Taiwan has incorporated numerous key elements of international human rights law into its domestic legal system through a myriad of approaches. But he argues that the manner in which Taiwan has opted to interact with international human rights law raises more questions than it answers. This chapter reviews the development of the right to food in the context of international human rights law and highlights the key elements constituting the current form and substance of this right. It further assesses the many faces of the right to food in Taiwan, from constitutional to legislative to executive practices, and identifies various challenges faced by the country in realizing the right to food. Noting the lack of rights-based discourse in constitutional and legal settings in Taiwan due to numerous underlying issues, this chapter proposes a framework law approach to address the normative challenges and to create an enabling environment for the progressive realization of the right to food.

People know that tobacco products are hazardous. But not many people in the local community look into the issue from a human rights perspective. This is what Tsai-Yu Lin discusses in her paper "Tobacco Investment and Human Rights: A Challenge for Taiwan's ICESCR Implementation in Its Foreign Investment Policy." She argues that the Taiwan government paid insufficient attention to its ICESCR obligations when it adopted an open permission policy for foreign tobacco industry investments in bilateral investment treaties. The Taiwan government has a duty to create conditions in which people can enjoy good health. The individuals' right to health in the ICESCR can never be "fully" respected and be "adequately" protected in the context of tobacco business activities. Neither can the government live up to its ICESCR duties when it encourages tobacco investment through BITs. To bridge the gaping hole between these two regimes, the ICESCR norms might accelerate the reform of Taiwan's tobacco investment policy and its bilateral investment treaty formulation. However, the success of these reforms ultimately depends on the willingness of Taiwan's government to effectively implement the ICESCR for its people.

Su-Hua Lee deals with human rights-related intellectual property issues in her chapter "Human Rights and Intellectual Property Protection: Their Interplay in Taiwan." She explains that the interplay between human rights and intellectual property has been at the center of important debates in recent decades and she argues that an over-protective IP system may be an obstacle in realizing human rights. If copyright is over-protected, it may guard the economic right of creative intellectual activity, but its enforcement might impede access to published works for persons with vision-related disabilities and lead to negative impacts on the right to information. In the public health field, without patents, existing medications and innovative pharmaceutical products which overcome diseases would not have been developed. Therefore, inadequate expansion and enforcement of IP protection might become a barrier to the accessibility and affordability of medications and adversely affect the implementation of the right to health. For this reason, the international community pursues a balance between human rights and IP protection. As a member of the international community, Taiwan closely follows new developments at the international level and introduces amendments of its IP laws accordingly. Regardless of Taiwan's unique international status, it still manages to establish relevant mechanisms that are consistent with international norms in its domestic IP legal framework.

6 Protection of Specific/Vulnerable Groups

There are certain groups of people who are disadvantaged in their economic and social positions and vulnerable in ensuring the proper protection of their rights. Part VI of the book identifies some potentially disadvantaged groups in Taiwan society and elaborates on the protection of their fundamental rights.

Chang-fa Lo addresses gender equality issues in his chapter "When Women's Human Rights Encounter Tradition in Taiwan." He explains that from time to time, when women's right to equality encounters some deeply embedded tradition, there are still struggles in Taiwan society and in the constitutional process to fully implement that right. The 2015 Constitutional Court case of J.Y. Interpretation No. 728 involved a typical gender equality issue, i.e., women being traditionally and continuously prevented from becoming a member of or successor in "ancestor worship guilds/associations." In this case, the protection of women's human rights and the protection of a long-established tradition, as well as freedom of contract, had to be properly balanced. He argues that, in the course of judicial balancing, the right of women to equal protection should have been prioritized because of the seriousness and the systemic and structural nature of such discrimination. He believes that the Constitutional Court should have declared the relevant law unconstitutional. Because it failed to do so, he urges the Legislative Yuan to correct the discriminatory situation by requiring equal status for female offspring, at least for successions that occur after the new legislation goes into effect.

Hsiaowei Kuan discusses the most recent Constitutional Court case on same-sex marriage in her chapter "LGBT Rights in Taiwan—The Interaction Between Movements and the Law." J.Y. Interpretation 748, issued on 24 May 2017 by the Constitutional Court regarding the constitutionality of the legal ban on same-sex marriages, was widely reported in other parts of the world. The Constitutional Court concluded that denying two persons of the same sex the right to marry violates both their right to equality and their right to marry. Although many factors such as Taiwan's robust democracy, judicial activism, and commitment to constitutionalism may have contributed to this landmark judicial triumph, Professor Kuan writes that Taiwan's vibrant LGBT communities paved the way for the progressive judicial and legislative atmosphere that finally led to this outcome. Because the constitutional and legal success in LGBT rights protection in Taiwan could not have been achieved without the long efforts by LGBT activism, this chapter explores the development of LGBT rights in Taiwan from the perspective of the interactions between LGBT rights movements and legislation. The discussion covers several important issues, such as destigmatization of same-sex sexual behavior, protection against discrimination based on sexual orientation and sexual identity in both education and employment, recognition of same-sex families, and articulation of the right to change legal gender identity. For these reasons, the author concludes, Taiwan deserves the attention of human rights observers.

Chih-Wei Tsai (Awi Mona) deals with the issues of indigenous rights in his chapter "National Apology and Reinvigoration of Indigenous Rights in Taiwan." He explains the huge debate that has taken place about the protection of indigenous rights in the context of legal reform. One of his focal points concerns how and to what extent the state's legal system and social transformation impact indigenous cultural development and needs. On 1 August 2016 President Tsai Ing-wen delivered a National Apology to Indigenous Peoples, which laid out a comprehensive scheme to provide historical and transitional justice for indigenous peoples. This chapter concentrates on the operation of law and legal pluralism amidst indigenous diversity. By way of empirical research, it seeks to demonstrate the interaction between the state's legal system and local indigenous communities, including how and to what extent indigenous customary laws have been incorporated into and implemented by the legal system.

Amy Huey-Ling Shee addresses children's rights issues in her chapter "Local Images of Global Child Rights: CRC in Taiwan." She emphasizes that the UN Convention on the Rights of the Child (CRC) is a manifestation of global law regarding children's rights, with 198 states participating. She reviews how the CRC has been integrated into Taiwan law and social practice since its promulgation in 1989. She observes the differences made by the 2014 CRC Enforcement Act to promote child rights in Taiwan and examines how the global law principles of the CRC are being implemented in a Confucian society. The author concludes that the development of global law calls for a new methodology for comparative study, requiring joint efforts by cross-border interdisciplinary experts.

William P. Alford, Qiongyue Hu and Charles Wharton address the protection of persons with disability in their chapter "People Over Pandas: Taiwan's Engagement of International Human Rights Norms with Respect to Disability." They argue that the area of disabilities is an especially illuminating one through which to consider Taiwan's engagement of the international human rights norms to which it is unable formally to adhere. Taiwan's embrace of international human rights instruments and the role of civil society are particularly salient, given both a tradition of citizen activism on Taiwan and the fact that the United Nations Convention on the Rights of Persons with Disabilities (CRPD) calls for more citizen participation than any previous international human rights instrument. The authors further argue that the exclusion of Taiwan from international human rights agreements such as the CRPD has produced the ironic result of accentuating the importance of Taiwan's adherence to those agreements and to the international human rights norms they embody.

Nai-Yi Sun also addresses disability in her chapter "On the Road to Equal Enjoyment of Human Rights for Persons with Disabilities: The Development of Domestic Laws in Taiwan and Their Dialogue with the CRPD." In 2014, Taiwan incorporated the CRPD into domestic law. Sun describes the development of domestic laws relating to the rights of persons with disabilities in Taiwan while analyzing the continuing discrimination occurring behind the façade of legislative progress. She further compares the distinct concepts of equal enjoyment of human rights as embodied in domestic law and the CRPD. She explains that the Convention takes an innovative approach to the principle of equality and non-discrimination, and presents a powerful vision of substantive equality designed to transform current social structures, systems and conceptions. The CRPD provides guidance on the changes required in domestic legislation, policy and jurisprudence. It can be used to broaden the domestic legislative framework, which to date has focused primarily on socio-economic rights for people with disabilities and the unilateral dimension of governmental obligations. The goal, however, is to enable equal enjoyment of civil, political, social, economic and cultural rights with regard to both government and the private sector.

Yi-Li Lee focuses on non-citizens' rights in her chapter "Constitutional Dynamics of Judicial Discourse on the Rights of Non-citizens: The Case of Taiwan." The author finds that the Constitutional Court's relevant decisions reveal two significant features. First, the Court has increasingly taken an inclusive approach towards the civil rights of non-citizens, which has facilitated the subsequent development of regulations regarding migrants. Second, the Court and the individual justices actively use international human rights instruments to address the rights of non-citizens while Taiwan has been taking steps to integrate itself with the international human rights regime. However, the Court's decisions on social and political rights drew scholarly criticisms when it took a rather deferential approach in reviewing cases involving national security and the allocation of limited social resources. Since non-citizens are usually regarded as "discrete and insular minorities," the author argues that the Constitutional Court should consider engaging in stricter scrutiny of the legal restrictions on the social and political rights of non-citizens. In addition, in order to guarantee human rights for non-citizens, the Court will likely find it necessary to develop special criteria for reviewing disputes that pertain to their social and political rights.

The editors of this book hope that its coverage is comprehensive enough to give readers a well-rounded picture of Taiwan's human rights performance and that readers will find appealing the story of Taiwan's efforts to achieve high standards of human rights protection even though the jurisdiction is barred from joining international human rights conventions.

Chapter 2
Taiwan's Political-Legal Progress: Memories of the KMT Dictatorship

Jerome A. Cohen

Abstract This brief memoir illustrates Taiwan's modern human rights history in broad strokes through my own experiences. It begins with a first visit in 1961, when the island was suffering under the harsh Chiang Kai-shek dictatorship. It ends with my participation in the unique recent reviews of Taiwan's immense human rights progress by leading international specialists. Along the way, I was privileged to witness and take part in a few depressing but exciting and ultimately hopeful events that marked the long transition from KMT repression to constitutional democracy.

Keywords Annette Lu · Chiang Ching-kuo · Chiang Kai-shek
Constitutional democracy · Dictatorship · Henry Liu · KMT · Ma Ying-jeou
Peng Ming-min

Nothing could be more satisfying for me than to mark the thirtieth anniversary of Taiwan's termination of martial law by recording my own occasional witness to the harsh dictatorship that preceded the island's immense political-legal progress.

1 The First Visit

My first visit to Taiwan was in 1961, sixteen years after Chiang Kai-shek's forces had occupied the island following Japan's surrender ending World War II. The island's capital, Taipei, was still a dilapidated, demoralized place. Economic conditions were poor, social conditions not much better and the "White Terror" that Chiang's forces had long imposed on Taiwan continued unchallenged.

J. A. Cohen (✉)
US-Asia Law Institute, New York University School of Law, New York, NY, USA
e-mail: jacohen@paulweiss.com

J. A. Cohen
Council on Foreign Relations, New York, NY, USA

J. A. Cohen et al. (eds.), *Taiwan and International Human Rights*, Economics, Law, and Institutions in Asia Pacific, https://doi.org/10.1007/978-981-13-0350-0_2

My heart went out to the gallant law professors and lawyers who, at a welcoming dinner, responded to the questions of a young, unsophisticated American law teacher by putting the best face on a sad situation. I still recall how impressed I was by the talent, resilience and humor of the group my wife, Joan Lebold Cohen, and I met on that first night on the island. Like me, some of the group were Yale Law School graduates and protégés of our prominent mentor, Professor Myres McDougal, who had alerted them to our impending arrival. It was a jolly, comforting reception for newcomers to Taiwan and Asia.

That opening dinner at Freedom House—its name as much a misnomer as the government's description of the island as "Free China"—set a tone for the extraordinary hospitality and warmth that lasted throughout a stimulating week. Yet one unusual aspect of our visit was the number of hosts and other new friends who asked to see us on our last day in Taipei, to take us to the airport or to meet us there to bid farewell. What a nice custom, we thought naively. Thus, departure day came as a shock when, one after another, many of our new friends took me aside and asked me to help them leave the island. Their inquiries came fast and furious: Can you find me a teaching post in America? Can you get me a research fellowship there? What about a scholarship to be a graduate student? Any chance of working in a law firm?

Our disillusionment at this unexpected farewell helped me grasp the reality of legal and personal life under the drab dictatorship of Generalissimo Chiang's Kuomintang (KMT) political party. As our plane flew toward Hong Kong, I reviewed what I had learned during the brief visit. The court system was said to be under strict KMT control. Judges were commonly believed to be so corrupt that lawyers joked that "honest" judges only kept the bribe given by the winning party. Especially in matters involving freedoms of expression, even lawyers backed by money and good political connections were limited in what they could do for their clients. Although the Party often used the courts to impose punishments, including the death penalty, upon certain political offenders as well as common criminals, the KMT also made full use of extra-legal measures, and the secret police, the Ministry of Justice's Investigation Bureau and the military's Garrison Command were widely and justifiably feared. Citizens could not voice their grievances in the heavily-censored media. Law professors themselves were under political constraints in both their teaching and publications and I noted how few Taiwanese law teachers I had met in comparison with the many who were relatively recent arrivals from the Mainland.

There seemed to be uncomfortable similarities between the KMT legal system and that of the Chinese Communist Party on the Mainland, which did not even permit me to visit until more than a decade later. I began to wonder whether any Chinese government could ever establish a democratic legal system, subject government officials and the ruling political party to a genuine rule of law and effectively protect political and civil rights. Were Chinese destined to remain prisoners of their authoritarian imperial past? This first visit to Taiwan strengthened my interest in comparative law, China's legal history and the enduring impact of the nation's distinctive political-legal culture.

2 An Exciting 1969 Visit

Several subsequent visits during the 1960s did not alter this picture. I especially recall our return to Taiwan in the summer of 1969, five years after I had moved from the University of California at Berkeley's law faculty to Harvard Law School. The American Council of Learned Societies and the Social Sciences Research Council had recently formed a Joint Committee on China. It organized a three-person delegation to visit Taiwan in order to acquire further information and insight in preparation for recommendations to be made concerning the need for a new American policy toward the Republic of China (ROC) on Taiwan and the People's Republic of China (PRC) on the Mainland, which was then still in the throes of the Cultural Revolution. The delegation was to consist of myself and Professor George Taylor, a well-known British political scientist at the University of Washington who was a strong supporter of Chiang Kai-shek, and Professor Martin Wilbur of Columbia University, a leading historian of China who was considered sympathetic to the KMT but moderate in outlook. I was known as an energetic advocate of seeking to normalize diplomatic relations between Washington and Beijing.

I was especially looking forward to the trip because I hoped to meet for the first time Professor Peng Ming-min, a rising international law expert on the faculty of National Taiwan University, whose promising career had been terminated the year before when it was discovered that he secretly supported Taiwan's independence from China. Peng's sentence to imprisonment had aroused a good deal of international protest, in which I had joined, and weeks before our scheduled visit, he was released from prison and placed under house arrest. In subsequent phone calls from Cambridge to friends in Taiwan I made clear that I hoped to meet Peng despite the obstacles.

Shortly thereafter, however, I was denied the then necessary visa to enter Taiwan. My calls to Taiwan had obviously been secretly overheard. I told this to my Harvard graduate students from Taiwan, including one named Tao Lung-sheng. I did not know that his father, Tao Hsi-sheng, was a famous and influential adviser to Chiang Kai-shek. Without telling me, Tao called his father and asked for his help to get me a visa. Mr. Tao then did the trick by guaranteeing my good behavior to the Generalissimo, who overruled the visa denial by the Investigation Bureau, reportedly telling them that "I hear he's open-minded. Maybe we can win him over."

Understandably, Mr. Tao was a bit anxious about having guaranteed my good behavior. He asked my favorite young Taiwan scholar, Chang We-jen, who had just returned from Harvard in the hope of finding an academic post as a budding legal historian, to greet me at the airport and ask me not to meet Peng Ming-min in order to avoid embarrassing Mr. Tao. Later in the day, however, Fox Butterfield, a part-time *New York Times* correspondent in Taiwan whom I had known during his Harvard graduate student days, told me he had arranged for Joan and me to secretly meet Peng at a house in the suburbs of Yang Ming Mountain later in the week. And, several days afterward, following our delegation's interesting 90-minute meeting with President and Madame Chiang and after some nerve-wracking automobile maneuvers required to throw the police off our trail, we did manage to meet Peng for a clandestine dinner at the home of an American missionary couple named Thornberry. I will go into detail about these exciting events in a future publication, but enough has been said to confirm why we believed that Chiang's Taiwan continued to be a police state more than two decades after martial law had been declared. Indeed, Joan was so rattled by the persistent, sometimes obvious, secret police surveillance that she vowed never to return to Taiwan until it attained political freedom, and she did not return until 1994, when democratization was well under way.

Not long after this memorable 1969 visit to Taiwan, Peng Ming-min escaped to Sweden, and some months later he turned up at Harvard Law School's East Asian Legal Studies Program. I was glad to see him, and we discussed his plan to stay in the United States until it was possible to return to Taiwan without again being criminally detained. Because of my interest in the international legal problems of East Asia—Hungdah Chiu, a recent Harvard doctoral recipient from Taiwan, and I were then working on a book entitled *People's China and International Law*—I was open to the possibility of inviting Peng to join our research effort if he decided to resume his interrupted scholarly career in public international law. But I made clear to him that, if he preferred instead to find a university base that would allow him to focus on political activities in support of Taiwan democracy and independence, a course that I would totally understand, it might be better for him to find a teaching opportunity in a political science department rather than to do research in a law school. He opted for teaching political science/international relations and managed to land a university post in Ohio that was consistent with his political ambitions.

3 Ted Kennedy and Taiwan Tensions of the 1970s

The exciting 1969 visit to Taiwan only enhanced my interest in promoting democracy there while at the same time advocating America's normalization of relations with Mainland China. Since 1966 I had been assisting Senator Edward "Ted" Kennedy in his efforts to persuade the United States Government to pursue a more open policy toward the People's Republic. For Kennedy, this controversial course not only represented enlightened foreign policy but was also personally attractive in terms of his desire to emulate two of his older brothers as a recognized leader of the Democratic Party and eventually a possible presidential candidate. The assassination of his brother Bobby in June 1968 and Richard Nixon's presidential victory a few months later served to enhance the younger Kennedy's ambition and hence his interest in China policy. Although Ted's 1969 auto accident at Chappaquidick on Cape Cod, resulting in the tragic death of a female staff assistant, proved a barrier to his immediate presidential prospects, it did nothing to diminish his interest in leading a new China policy.

Thus, in the spring of 1971, I arranged for Ted to secretly travel with me to Ottawa to meet with the recently-installed first PRC ambassador to Canada, Huang Hua. Beijing had evidently charged Huang, an able diplomat, to play a responsible role in the early stages of the process of normalizing relations between Washington and Beijing. Our goal in making the trip was to secure an invitation for Ted to visit China before any representative of the Nixon administration did. By that time, even before the July 1971 secret trip to Beijing of Henry Kissinger, Nixon's national security advisor, shrewd American political observers had anticipated that China policy might become a major issue in the 1972 presidential election, and Ted believed that being the first American politician to visit the People's Republic would give him widespread recognition as a wise and dynamic leader on foreign policy.

Our meeting with Ambassador Huang, conducted entirely in English, lasted almost three hours, and went very well. But Huang repeatedly sought to extract from Kennedy a commitment to the position that Taiwan was a part of China and should someday fall under the jurisdiction of the PRC. This Kennedy refused to give, even though we both inferred from Huang's words and demeanor that a Mainland visa might be granted if Ted would only utter the magic words. Sensing Huang's disappointment, at the end of the afternoon I tried to explain that, since the Senator might one day become president, he had to measure his language cautiously. This did little to placate Huang, and Nixon and Kissinger soon rode the Republican Party's new China policy to victory in Nixon's 1972 re-election campaign.

Because he refused to adopt Beijing's position regarding Taiwan, Kennedy did not get to visit the Mainland until the end of 1977. At that time, although Taiwan's *United Daily News* prominently criticized me for guiding the Senator on the trip, it forgave him, acknowledging that association with America's still evolving China policy was by that time essential for any future presidential candidate. Perhaps also by that time, in view of Ted's speeches and actions between 1971 and 1977, Taiwan's America-watchers had become convinced of the Senator's sincere continuing concern for Taiwan's security.

Because of the impending U.S. establishment of diplomatic relations with Beijing and withdrawal of formal relations from the ROC, the 1970s proved to be an excruciatingly difficult and tense period for the government and people of Taiwan. Moreover, the emergence on the island of a strong democratic movement that was increasingly marked by sympathy for the cause of Taiwan's independence, or at least its assured continuing security against a takeover by the Mainland, reinforced the KMT's incentives for ever harsher official repression. The death of Chiang Kai-shek in 1975 added to the KMT's perceived challenges. One experience that I recall from that period illustrates the situation.

To my surprise, I was invited to speak in Taipei at the 1975 biennial conference of Taiwanese and American specialists on Mainland affairs. Since I was asked to discuss PRC legal developments, I decided, somewhat mischievously, to compare the Mainland's criminal justice system with Taiwan's. Because of the sensitivity of the subject, instead of inflicting my labored Chinese on the audience, I accepted the host organization's offer to provide an interpreter for my talk. My theme emphasized the significant similarities between the Mainland's and Taiwan's Party-dominated Leninist legal systems. As the talk proceeded, I could sense the interpreter's increasing discomfort and, in the middle of the talk, he suddenly blurted out: "Professor Cohen is capable of delivering this speech in Chinese, and I am not going to continue." With that he stepped off the stage! The audience, apparently more aware than I of the local practice of punishing the messenger, did not seem as shocked as I was.

Although the Watergate scandal and Nixon's resignation gave the ROC several years' reprieve from Washington-Beijing normalization, the ax finally fell at the end of 1978, leading to an even more severe era of KMT oppression on the island. I did not personally witness it because, in view of my public support for normalization, my friends and former students in Taiwan urged me to delay any further visits until the situation stabilized and tempers cooled. Thus I was absent from Taipei from June 1978 until my unexpected return in late 1984.

4 Annette Lu, Ma Ying-Jeou and the Assassination of Henry Liu

Despite the advice to stay away from Taiwan for a period, I had been prepared to return in 1980 in order to be an observer at the criminal trial of my dear former Harvard Law School graduate student, Ms. Annette Lu Hsiu-lien. Annette, who was later destined to become Taiwan's vice-president, had become one of the persecuted "Kaohsiung eight." She and her colleagues had been arrested on 10 December 1979, International Human Rights Day, at an outdoor rally in support of freedom to publish the magazine of their budding anti-KMT political party. Yet each time I arranged to attend their trial by traveling from Beijing, where I was teaching and advising would-be foreign investors, the trial date was postponed. The KMT government finally settled on a date that my telephone conversations with Taiwan had indicated would be impossible for me to leave Beijing. I knew those telephone calls had been monitored, but I never learned whether the trial postponements were linked to the KMT's knowledge of my schedule. Although Timothy Gelatt, who was also my student and a good friend of Annette Lu, did manage to attend the trial, I have always felt guilty about my inability to join him in order to show my support for Annette and her co-defendants.

I subsequently published a long article in the *Asian Wall Street Journal* condemning the KMT's severe punishment of these courageous human rights activists, and through speeches and informal activities tried to add to pressures for their release. Nevertheless, the KMT, believing that harsh repression was the only way to deter further democratic activity and public unrest, remained adamant.

Yet, ironically, Annette, who had received a hideous twelve-year sentence for her exercise of freedom of speech, later proved to be the cause of my first post-normalization return to Taiwan. On 15 October 1984, Chen Chi-li, the leader of the Bamboo Union, Taiwan's largest criminal gang, and two of his assistants assassinated the Chinese-American writer Henry Liu (Liu Yi-liang) at his San Francisco home. Some of Liu's journalistic essays had offended the KMT by revealing embarrassing details about the family of the late Chiang Kai-shek and especially his son Chiang Ching-kuo, who by then had become Taiwan's president. Liu, whose pen name was Chiang Nan, was preparing to publish an entire book on the subject, and KMT efforts to persuade him from publication had failed. The international scandal that resulted from Liu's tragic assassination seemed to present a long-awaited opportunity to secure Annette's release.

I therefore quickly got in touch with another of my former Harvard students from Taiwan who later became famous, Ma Ying-jeou, then serving as President Chiang Ching-kuo's English-language interpreter. Ma and Lu had overlapped in the Harvard Law School graduate program, although their differing political views had kept them apart. After obtaining her Harvard master's degree in 1978, Annette chose the risky path of returning to Taiwan to work for political freedom and Taiwan independence. Ying-jeou, an unusually able student, stayed on several more years to obtain his law school doctoral degree before returning to Taiwan to join the KMT government. By late 1984 he had risen in rank to become a deputy secretary-general of the KMT and, as Chiang's interpreter, he was in daily contact with the President. Although he and Annette had not been friendly, he seemed the right person to ask for help to end her imprisonment.

I frankly told Ma that the recent brazen assassination on American soil had made the KMT dictatorship smell worse than ever in the United States, that Taiwan should take immediate steps on the long road to improve its reputation and that the release of Annette would be a wise first step. He saw the point and suggested that I return to Taiwan from Hong Kong, where I was then based, in ten days, giving him a chance to broach the idea with President Chiang. When I came back ten days later, Ying-jeou told me that he had arranged for the two of us to meet Annette the following day in the prison hospital, where she was undergoing treatment for cancer. That meeting, where I sat between my two best-known students from Taiwan, was probably the most emotionally draining I have experienced. Ying-jeou, a rising political star who was handsome in a three-piece suit, was on top of the world, whereas Annette, having already served five years of her sentence and weakened by both cancer and isolation, was at the opposite end of the spectrum.

I apologized to Annette for my failure to win her freedom as I had jokingly promised to do if she ever got locked up after returning from Harvard to Taiwan. She had forgotten that but remembered that, when we had discussed her career choices before she left Harvard, I had warned her about the risks of returning to political activism in Taiwan. I had cited former U.S. President Harry Truman's famous admonition to those contemplating a political career: "If you can't stand the heat, don't go in the kitchen." She looked at me ruefully and said: "I didn't realize how hot the kitchen could get!" Not long after this memorable meeting, thanks to

Ying-jeou's successful efforts, Annette was freed, on the understanding, to which I agreed, that she would leave Taiwan immediately to spend another year at Harvard, this time as a visiting scholar rather than a student agitator. This gave Annette time for recovery from her ordeal and allowed another year for Chiang Ching-kuo to move ahead with plans to gradually liberalize his regime, without suffering the renewal of Annette's powerful criticisms.

5 Prosecution of the Assassins

To be sure, Annette's belated release did not dispose of what became known in Taiwan as the "Chiang Nan *ming-an*"—the Henry Liu murder case. Because of U.S. government monitoring of communications with Taiwan, Washington knew the identity of the killers, who had returned to the island right after reporting by telephone the success of their mission. Despite the lack of an extradition treaty between the U.S. and the KMT government and indeed despite the total absence of official diplomatic relations between the two governments since 1979, Washington sought to persuade Taipei to extradite the killers for trial in California state courts. The KMT resisted, however, but finally agreed to put the gangster-killers on trial in Taiwan criminal court and the military officials who had conspired with them on trial in a court-martial prosecution.

In the interim, the widow of Henry Liu, Ms. Tsui Jung-chih, sought to hold the KMT government accountable in American federal court and consulted a San Francisco lawyer who had been my student at Harvard Law School. He in turn got in touch with me and asked whether my law firm, Paul, Weiss, Rifkind, Wharton and Garrison, and I would be willing to represent his client not only in the federal case but also in any necessary dealings with the KMT government. To my delight, Paul, Weiss, one of the foremost litigating firms in America, agreed to take the case on a "pro bono" basis. I hoped that the American lawsuit would provide Ms. Tsui with much-needed financial compensation for the wrongful death of her husband and also expose the KMT government's responsibility for committing the heinous assassination, so similar to others that it had previously carried out with impunity, even in the United States.

There were some challenging legal issues in bringing a wrongful death case against a foreign government, particularly one with which the U.S. no longer enjoyed diplomatic relations. But the most urgent problem was to acquire enough evidence to establish the KMT government's responsibility for inspiring the assassination. Knowing that Taiwan law permitted victims of criminal acts to bring civil suits for damages against the alleged perpetrators and that such suits were allowed to be joined together with criminal prosecutions of the perpetrators, in order to obtain the evidence we needed I decided to file a civil damage suit against the Bamboo Union killers in Taiwan court as the representative of Chiang Nan's widow and to attempt to have that suit joined with the criminal prosecution to which the KMT government had committed itself.

My first need was to find a competent Taiwan attorney who could serve as my counsel for this relatively innovative proceeding. Despite continuing official censorship in Taiwan, huge publicity had been attached to the murder, and whoever served as my lawyer was sure to be immersed in controversy. Because of the widespread belief that the killers had been in league with the Ministry of National Defense and perhaps even the office of President Chiang, my attorney was also certain to be placed in opposition to the KMT dictatorship, which could have been a career-threatening and even life-threatening situation.

Not surprisingly, my first attempts to find suitable counsel failed, but, finally, thanks to an introduction by another of my former students, the able legal historian Ms. Chang Fu-mei, I met Frank Hsieh Ch'ang-t'ing. Hsieh was then a dynamic member of the Taipei City Council known for his willingness to challenge the KMT. He obviously saw this case as an opportunity to enhance his political career. Frank seemed to be a very competent and energetic litigator, and I liked him. Once we agreed that the case had to be conducted solely in the interest of our client and not for the purpose of adding luster to his political resumé, Frank and I proved to be an effective team.

We were not permitted, however, to enter the initial trial of the Taiwan prosecution. The district court judge, perhaps under political orders to bar our participation, claimed that some technical error had occurred in the process of transmitting widow Tsui's authorization for me to act as her representative. But, after calling upon Chang Hsiao-yen, then the director of North American Affairs in the Ministry of Foreign Affairs and well known as one of the illegitimate twin sons of President Chiang Ching-kuo, I was at least allowed to observe the initial trial. As a supposed courtesy to me but apparently as a maneuver designed to raise doubts in the media about my seriousness, the Ministry assigned a very beautiful woman diplomat to be my escort to the trial, and, as we passed through the hundreds of armed guards and journalists surrounding the courthouse, she moved close to me as the cameras flashed! I quickly disengaged myself and thanked her for her assistance, which I said would no longer be required.

On television and in the press, I criticized the trial judge's refusal to allow us to enter the case but, on appeal, his decision was reversed, giving Frank and me a chance to obtain and introduce evidence and also question the witnesses and defendants in court as part of what was in effect a second public trial. Even though most of the targets of my Chinese-language cross-examination testified, in Watergate style, that they could not remember the key events in question, and Admiral Wang Hsi-ling, the government mastermind of the plot, actually lied about the facts, I thoroughly relished the experience.

More importantly, Frank's ability to learn about and obtain the transcript of the pre-trial interrogation of the accused by the police helped to verify the government's involvement in arranging the murder. It also brought out the literally intriguing detail that General Chiang Wei-kuo, younger brother of President Chiang Ching-kuo and then the third-ranking official in the Ministry of National Defense, had been guest of honor at a housewarming luncheon given by a famous film director where the leader of the Bamboo Union and Admiral Wang, the Ministry of

National Defense official in charge of orchestrating the assassination, met for the first time!

Although the government felt obliged to permit the media to report this extraordinary revelation, General Chiang's motive in attending the lunch never became clear. He told the media that he had attended the lunch "for purely social reasons," which, given the presence of movie starlets invited to enliven the festivities and General Chiang's reputation as a "ladies' man," may have been true. He claimed that there had been no discussion of the Chiang Nan problem at the lunch. Yet it appeared that, whatever his reason for attending, his presence demonstrated to the Bamboo Union chief, Chen Chih-li, that Admiral Wang was on very friendly terms with the president's brother, himself an influential figure. This demonstration proved useful when, the following week, Admiral Wang solicited the Bamboo Union chief to "teach a lesson" to Henry Liu, which would be seen as a patriotic act on behalf of the nation's highest officials.

Admiral Wang and his two closest aides were not prosecuted in the regular criminal courts, since they were military personnel. Instead they were subjected to court martial. Frank Hsieh and I were not allowed to take part in the court-martial proceedings but I was permitted to attend a public hearing of the case, which was itself unusual. Although there had certainly been public military trials of civilians, as in the Kaohsiung Eight case, I was told that Admiral Wang's may have been the first open hearing of a court martial in Taiwan history, a claim that I have never verified.

The most notable aspect of the hearing was the unusually bold defense made by Admiral Wang. He denied responsibility for Chiang Nan's murder and, to back up his claim, he boasted that, if his Defense Intelligence Bureau had done the job, the killers would never have been identified. With some pride he told the tribunal: "You know, your honors, we are professionals. Ten or twenty years ago we used to do things like this all the time and were never discovered." When he said that, a hush overcame the courtroom audience of perhaps one hundred shocked people.

Admiral Wang, like the principal defendant in the civilian trial, Bamboo Union chief Chen Chih-li, was found guilty and received a life sentence. But he was treated well while confined and, like Chen, managed to win release from prison some years later, a disappointing conclusion to what was said to have been Taiwan's most notorious criminal case up to that time.

Nevertheless, I have always believed that the Chiang Nan *ming-an*, coming as it did on the eve of Taiwan's political reform era, just before the elimination of martial law, played a helpful role in many aspects of Taiwan's history. It further exposed the lawless violence underlying the KMT dictatorship, demonstrated that restrictions on the media could be defied, promoted respect for human rights, and increased pressures for democratic progress and a genuine rule of law.

I hope that these brief personal recollections of some experiences encountered by a foreign lawyer and law teacher during the final three decades of KMT dictatorship may prove useful, especially to younger generations of Taiwanese who have known only the luxury of political freedom. Taiwan today deserves a proud position among the world's leading democracies, a fact brought home to me in recent years as a member of the international group of experts convened by the Taiwan government in 2013 and again in 2017 to review the island's impressive strides in implementing the world community's major human rights covenants. At a time when Mainland China, despite its growing wealth and power, maintains an increasingly repressive Leninist dictatorship that brainwashes its people to reject the universal values of constitutionalism, government under law, judicial independence and political democracy, Taiwan offers a vivid illustration that, whatever the challenges, citizens of predominantly Chinese ethnic origin and values are fully capable of sustaining a free society.

Jerome A. Cohen has been professor at NYU School of Law since 1990, Faculty Director of its U.S.-Asia Law Institute, and a leading American expert on Chinese law and government. A pioneer in the field, Prof. Cohen began studying and teaching about China's legal system in the early 1960s, and from 1964 to 1979 he introduced the teaching of Asian law into the curriculum of Harvard Law School, where he served as Jeremiah Smith Professor, Associate Dean and Director of East Asian Legal Studies. In addition to his responsibilities at NYU, Prof. Cohen served for several years as C. V. Starr Senior Fellow and Director of Asia Studies at the Council on Foreign Relations, where he currently is an Adjunct Senior Fellow. He retired from the partnership of Paul, Weiss, Rifkind, Wharton & Garrison LLP at the end of 2000 after 20 years of law practice focused on China. In his law practice, Prof. Cohen represented many companies and individuals in contract negotiations as well as in dispute resolution in China. Professor Cohen has published several books on Chinese law, including *The Criminal Process in the People's Republic of China, 1949–63* (Harvard University Press, 1968), *People's China and International Law* (with Hungdah Chiu, Princeton University Press, 1974), *Contract Laws of the People's Republic of China* (with Yvonne Y. F. Chan and Ho Yuk Ming, Longman Group, 1988), and *Challenge to China: How Taiwan Abolished Its Version of Re-Education Through Labor* (with Margaret K. Lewis, Berkshire Publishing, 2013). In addition, he has published hundreds of scholarly articles on various topics as well as a book, *China Today*, coauthored with his wife, Joan Lebold Cohen, and a regular series of journalistic opinion pieces for various newspapers. Today, Prof. Cohen continues his research and writing on Asian law, specifically focusing on legal institutions, criminal justice reform, dispute resolution, human rights, and the role of international law relating to China and Taiwan.

Part II
Human Rights Transition from Broader Perspectives

Chapter 3
Asian Values, Confucian Tradition and Human Rights

Nigel N. T. Li

Abstract The Republic that exists and operates now in Taiwan was originally founded in China in 1911. The Constitution which was promulgated in 1947, during the civil war in China, was a first for a nation of Confucian heritage without any recognized tradition of constitutionalism. This chapter reviews the obstacles that stood in the way of the value system of constitutionalism when it was first transplanted to the barren soil of Taiwan, including at various times cultural inertia, political resistance and hostility to the rule of a constitution. The chapter also examines how the non-native system gradually evolved and took root in a land dominated by Asian values, where the government or the ruler had customarily been pronounced as the people's parent, and the fundamental notions of the rule of law, human rights, independent judiciary, separation of powers, equality, and the constitution itself, were all considered novel, foreign concepts.

Keywords Absolute-power relationship · Asian values · Confucianism
Heavenly mandate · Rule of law · Rule of *li*

"Asian values" is a common term used with no universal academic definition. But, in the eyes of Professor William de Bary, the term denotes the value system of Confucianism prevailing in most major East Asian jurisdictions, including China, Japan, Korea, Singapore, Taiwan, and perhaps Vietnam.[1]

Confucianists' sacred documents are not devoid of fundamental constitutional questions, especially those about the legitimacy of the rulers, to which answers must be sought. A chapter in *Shangshu* (《尚書》, literally translated as High Book or the Book of Documents) entitled "Hong Fan" 〈洪範〉, translated as Grand Norms or Great Plan, tells of an event in which Emperor Wu (武王), the founding emperor of the Chou (周) dynasty, soon after overthrowing the Shang (商) dynasty,

[1]See de Bary (1998), pp. 2–4.

N. N. T. Li (✉)
Soochow University, Taipei, Taiwan
e-mail: nigelli@leeandli.com

J. A. Cohen et al. (eds.), *Taiwan and International Human Rights*, Economics, Law, and Institutions in Asia Pacific, https://doi.org/10.1007/978-981-13-0350-0_3

received a package of grand norms in Nine Provinces (九疇, or nine sets of general rules of thumb on the art of ruling)[2] from Ji-Tzu (箕子), a prince of the Shang (商) dynasty. The grand norms in Nine Provinces can be seen as analogous to a constitutional code addressing the issue of political legitimacy; they were teachings, or know-how, if not lessons, bestowed from above as a Mandate of Heaven (天命) upon a chosen ruler with high moral character. Theoretically, it is a form of divine right of monarchical power, but by no means without associated moral duties of being benevolent to his subjects under Heaven (天下). The ruler, empirically reigning–usually through force—with allegedly legitimate cause, who is considered or claims to be the one and only (予一人) Son of Heaven (天子), being carefully chosen by Heaven as a result of having garnered universal popular support owing to his high moral character (德), will, as he should, act as a parent-like governor to his subjects (曰天子作民父母,以爲天下王).[3] It is a textbook example of the notion that the nature of the heavenly mandate is virtuous.[4]

1 Subjecting the Head of State to the Rule of Law

Basing a ruler's legitimacy upon the Mandate of Heaven and his moral character persisted as a fundamental political theory in China for thousands of years, until the end of the Qing dynasty.[5] The Constitution of the Republic of China, when first promulgated, however, based its legitimacy on another power. Article 48 of the

[2]See Nylan (2001), p. 140. *The Nine Provinces of Great Plan* lists the sorts of resources available to the state; Sect. 1 cites the natural resources of the empire: water, fire, wood, metal and earth; Sect. 2 constructs a parallel between those physical and personal resources (cognitive and sensory) of the ruling elite; Sect. 3 turns to the kinds of institutional resources—from markets to diplomacy to armies—that together provide material security for one's subjects; Sect. 4 rests the prosperity of the state upon astronomical data, as the basis for the agricultural calendar; Sect. 6 considers the appropriate function of punishments in state rule, after which Sects. 7, 8 and 9 list three methods (divination, portent reading, and material verification or portent-outcome) by which the ruler may ascertain the best policy in a given situation, on the assumption that what is morally right will also be of greatest utility. (《尚書•洪範》:「初一、曰五行,次二、曰敬用五事,次三、曰農用八政,次四、曰協用五紀,次五、曰建用皇極,次六、曰乂用三德,次七、曰明用稽疑,次八、曰念用庶徵,次九、曰嚮用五福,威用六極。」)

[3]*Id.*

[4]Chan (1963), p. 3.

[5]See the last paragraph of the Imperial Edict of the Abdication of the Qing Emperor on 12 Feb 1912: "Today, … I realize that the whole nation is expecting the republic, and such expectation has been indicated by the new mandate of heaven…. I, the Empress Dowager, therefore, together with the Emperor, hereby hand over sovereignty to the possession of all the people, and declare that the constitution shall henceforth be Republican. May it comfort those who wish for times of peace and prosperity, and comport to the belief given by sages and men of virtue that the world is for the public and shared by all." (《宣統帝退位詔書》:朕欽奉隆裕皇太后懿旨,…今全國人民心理多傾向共和,…人心所向,天命可知。…特率皇帝將統治權公諸全國,定爲共和立憲國體,近慰海內厭亂望治之心,遠協古聖天下爲公之義。)

R.O.C. Constitution imposes a duty upon the Republic's President, a popularly elected head of state, to take a ritual vow to observe the Constitution upon taking the office, with a line of oath stipulated in the same provision reading, "before and toward the people of the entire nation,"[6] instead of declaring observance to heaven, or swearing on the Bible. This constitutional requirement marks the beginning of the rule of law. Article 48 established, for the first time, the idea that no one, not even the head of state, considered before then the only one who was above all others, is above the law.

The first judicial constraint placed upon the President's power, in Judicial Yuan Interpretation No. 262 (hereinafter J.Y. Interpretation),[7] arose from the Control Yuan's (監察院, which the author of this chapter considers translating more appropriately as Guardian Yuan) petition (proposed three decades before the lifting of martial law but lodged only afterward), and confirms the Control Yuan's constitutional power to impeach military officers, refuting a claim that the discipline of military personnel is by the President exclusively as the commander-in-chief.

A provision of the Constitution grants immunity from criminal prosecution proceedings, except for treason charges, to the President as the head of state. This provision is reminiscent of the one and only status claimed by the Son of Heaven and may lead the head of state to believe he is above the law. The Constitutional Court tackled this issue in an interpretation (Judicial Yuan Interpretation No. 388, hereinafter J.Y. Interpretation) in response to a petition to answer whether an incumbent President enjoys the same immunity during a campaign for reelection. The answer from the Constitutional Court was affirmative, with a caveat that the immunity stipulated in the Constitution is applicable only during the term of his office so as not to hinder his job.[8] This interpretation obliquely imposed substantial constraints upon presidential power and ushered the "one and only" beast quietly back into the cage of law.

Having written provisions of the Constitution does not necessarily lead to voluntary observance, particularly in the case of the head of state. Chiang Kai-shek (1886–1975) was the first president who found the need to have the Justices exercise their function in construing the Constitution in the 1950s. He did not file the petition in his own name or in any official capacity. Instead, he asked the then Secretary-General to the President to seek an interpretation from the Constitutional Court for him and obtained one subsequently (J.Y. Interpretation No. 76).[9]

---

[6]Zhonghua Minguo Xianfa (Constitution of the Republic of China) Art. 48 (1946) "On assuming office, the President shall take an oath, which shall read as follows 'I do solemnly and with all sincerity swear before the people of the whole country that I will observe the Constitution, faithfully perform my duties, promote the welfare of the people, and safeguard the security of the State so as not to betray the people's trust. Should I break my oath, I will submit myself to severe punishment by the State. This is my solemn oath."

[7]Si Fa Yuan Da Fa Guan Jie Shi Shizi Di 262 Hao [Justices of the Constitutional Court, Judicial Yuan, Interpretation No. 262] (11 June 1990) (R.O.C.). [hereinafter J.Y. Interpretation].

[8]J.Y. Interpretation No. 388 (27 Oct 1995).

[9]J.Y. Interpretation No. 76 (3 May 1957).

More than one president has followed suit. On one occasion President Lee Teng-hui (1923 ~) had his Secretary-General seek and obtain a constitutional interpretation from the Constitutional Court for him (J.Y. Interpretation No. 470).[10] Lee had failed to answer an earlier petition by a number of legislators for the Constitutional Court's Interpretation (J.Y. Interpretation No. 419) that challenged the constitutionality of his decision to reject his Vice-President's resignation from the prime minister's office, thereby allowing the Vice-President to remain as prime minister concurrently.[11] He twice refused to be present in the hearings before the Court.[12] The first time the head of state observed and acted as a party under the rule of law, voluntarily submitting himself to judicial review by the Court, came after Chen Shui-bian became President. Chen, like his predecessors, had his Secretary-General file a petition for him and received one interpretation from the Constitutional Court (J.Y. Interpretation No. 541) reminding him of his possible lack of standing and indicating that the Court would not ignore the standing issue the next time.[13] Thereafter, he submitted himself to the Court's jurisdiction, and in 2007, in his official capacity, signed off on a petition for the Constitutional Court's Interpretation (J.Y. Interpretation No. 627) of a matter where he had asserted his executive privilege to avoid the order to surrender certain files to the lower court.[14]

At that moment, constitutionalism could be seen to be functioning on the head of state. It was then that human rights and the political or social order were set on intersecting paths.

2 The Rule of *Li* and the Rule of Law

Instead of the rule of law, the universe of Confucianism functions under the rule of *li* (禮, or rites). *Li* is a set of norms that, inter alia, govern five fundamental human relations, that between father and son (父子), superordinate and subordinate (君臣), husband and wife (夫婦), elder and younger brother (兄弟), and friends (朋友), on

[10]J.Y. Interpretation No. 470 (27 Nov 1998).

[11]J.Y. Interpretation No. 419 (31 Dec 1996).

[12]See Ministry of Justice (1999), p. 3.

[13]Liu Tie Zheng Da Fa Guan Shizi Di 541 Hao Jie Shi Yi Bu Tong Yi Jian Shu [劉鐵錚大法官釋字第541號解釋一部不同意見書] (Justice Tieh-Chen Liu's partial dissenting opinion in Justices of the Constitutional Court, Interpretation No. 541) (4 Apr 2002) (R.O.C.). Hsieh Tsai Chuan Xie Zai Quan Da Fa Guan Shizi Di 541 Hao Jie Xie Shie Tong Yi Jian Shu [謝在全大法官釋字第541號解釋協同意見書] (Justice Tsai-Chuan Hsieh's concurring opinion in Justices of the Constitutional Court, Interpretation No. 541) (4 Apr 2002) (R.O.C.).

[14]J.Y. Interpretation No. 627 (15 June 2007), the Application filed by the "President" Shui-Bian Chen.

the basis of a patrilineal, class society.[15] The distinction between genders is emphasized to maintain the close family relationship of father and son, representing a divergence from the family of ancient matrilineal societies.[16] Hierarchical relations are thereby established to maintain a harmonious social order. Society under the rule of *li* is an oriental form of communitarian state. Families or patriarchal clans are considered the bedrock of the state (a notion literally expressed in the Chinese term for state, 國家 or "state family"). Equality between individuals is seldom emphasized; equality of man as a concept did not exist in China until the later part of the 19th century, as it falls outside of the Buddha's teachings.[17]

However, that individual citizens, irrespective of gender, religion, race, class, or party affiliation, shall be treated as equals before the law, has become a basic norm, being placed in the very first provision in the bill of rights of the R.O.C. Constitution by the framers,[18] predating the birth of the Universal Declaration of Human Rights, even if only marginally.[19] The society that was, to that point in time, accustomed to the rule-of-*li* then had to face the cultural, if not ideological, tests that the rules of the Constitution had set for it.

A number of the Constitutional Court's Interpretations coped with the challenges with a firm manner; however, the Constitutional Court sometimes regressed. An early interpretation (J.Y. Interpretation No. 365) found gender discrimination in a provision of the Civil Code that subordinated the mother's parental decision to the father's in the case of a conflict, and declared it to be unconstitutional.[20] In one of the five major relationships dealt with by Confucianist family ethics, it is taught that the wife shall follow the will of her husband (夫唱婦隨).

---

[15]The *Book of Documents, Zhong Yong* (translated as *The Mean*): "The universal Way of the world involves five relations, and practicing it involves three virtues. The five are the relations between ruler and minister, between parent and child, between husband and wife, between older and younger brother, and among friends. These five are the universal way of the world." (《禮記•中庸》:「子曰:『……君臣也、父子也、夫婦也、兄弟也、朋友之交也,舞者,天下之達道也。』」) See de Bary and Bloom (1999), pp. 336–337.

[16]*Guodian Chu Slips*: "If men are not distinct from women, father and son would not be close to each other. If father and son are not close to each other, there would be no righteousness between superordinate and subordinate. (《郭店楚簡》:「男女不別,父子不親;父子不親,君臣無義。」)

[17]The term ping-deng (平等) was not employed to depict equality until the late 19th century, except for the Buddhist idea that "all living beings are equal." (佛曰:「眾生平等。」) The rule of Li, as the core of social norms since ancient times in China, performed the critical role of distinguishing the nobility, civilians and slaves, as well as defining *guanxi* so that a social/political hierarchy may be established. See Li (2013), pp. 263–287.

[18]Zhonghua Minguo Xianfa (Constitution of the Republic of China) Art. 7 (1946) "All citizens of the Republic of China, irrespective of sex, religion, ethnic origin, class or party affiliation, shall be equal before the law."

[19]When the Universal Declaration of Human Rights was proclaimed by the United Nations General Assembly on 10 December 1948, the Constitution of the Republic of China had already been promulgated.

[20]J.Y. Interpretation No. 365 (23 Sept 1994).

The provision in the Civil Code was thus dismantled and gave way to the principle of equal protection.[21]

The Constitutional Court soon issued another interpretation (J.Y. Interpretation No. 372) reconstruing a legal provision in the Civil Code as allowing a spouse to sue for divorce after being the victim of domestic violence, and declaring a Supreme Court-selected precedent constitutional, only to the extent that it is understood in conformity with the intention of this interpretation.[22] The Constitutional Court's Interpretation relies upon an Amendment to the Constitution that requires the government authority to take proper and necessary action to proactively stamp out gender discrimination and to promote gender equality in everyday life. It implies that the selected precedent, if read so as not to outlaw domestic abuse in divorce litigation per se, would be omitting the obligation imposed by the Amendment. Again, the Court found a moderate judicial means to make clear that the absolute power traditional wedlock ethics gave husbands over their wives within the confines of the family, which often manifested itself in the form of physical violence and was long neglected if not endorsed implicitly by the Supreme Court, had to change and yield to the values championed by constitutionalism, that every person's human dignity, despite his or her gender, or contrary social culture, must be legally and rigorously protected in court.

Some years later, the Justices of the Constitutional Court, however, would find themselves in a serious debate over whether there is a constitutional limitation on the exercise of judicial power in urging or forcing other government branches to actively eradicate all forms of gender discrimination in the private sector. The Constitutional Court, at the end of the debate, delivered an interpretation (J.Y. Interpretation No. 728) which refused to strike down a statute that recognized the binding force among the clan members of common-place private regulatory regimes in traditional Taiwanese property guilds formed for the purpose of clan-ancestors worship. The issue at dispute was whether a common-place guild regulation that deprives all female offspring of membership can be recognized by law and enforced in court without violating the government's constitutional obligation of combating deeply rooted gender discrimination in the private sector. The majority in the Constitutional Court concluded that the statute's omission in outlawing the guild regulation does not constitute in-effect discrimination on the part of the government. Further, the judiciary is to restrain itself from crafting replacement programs and must pay deference to the legislators' discretion in devising appropriate corresponding means to intervene and overcome various gender discrimination practices in the private sector.[23]

---

[21]The concept of "Three Obediences and Four Virtues" (三從四德) neatly sums up the behavior that Confucians expected from women. "Three Obedience" indicates that a woman is under the authority of, or dependent upon, a male relative during all three stages of her life, reads as "Before marrying, she follows her father; after marrying she follows her husband; when her husband dies, she follows her son" (未嫁從父,既嫁從夫,夫死從子). "Four Virtues" are traits that every woman should develop, which are characterized as "wifely virtue" (婦德), wifely speech (婦言), wifely demeanor (婦容) and wifely work (婦功) as provided in Ban Zhao's Lessons for Woman (《班昭•女誡》).

[22]J.Y. Interpretation No. 372 (24 Feb 1995).

[23]J.Y. Interpretation No. 728 (20 Mar 2015).

The only legitimate explanation for the Constitutional Court's reluctance in declaring the statute as unconstitutional is perhaps that there were difficulties in finding a feasible way to sanction such practices through affirmative actions, which, in any event, would be beyond the reach of effective judicial enforcement efforts.

On a related note, an interpretation (J.Y. Interpretation No. 452) declared another civil code provision that required a married woman to take the husband's domicile as hers to be unconstitutional.[24] The Justices had not agreed with another petitioner when the law was first challenged on the grounds of gender discrimination (J.Y. Interpretation No. 413), but did not pass up the second chance to address the issue arising out of a case where a man sued his wife for divorce because she refused to move into his old domicile and change her job.[25] The wife was thereby declared to be under the protection of the Constitution and relieved from the duty to follow her husband physically. Equality now forms the basis of Taiwan's marriage law.

However, the Justices in a later interpretation (J.Y. Interpretation No. 554) found a criminal code provision that imposes criminal punishment for adultery if the spouse initiates the charge as being constitutional.[26] Although the freedom of sexual conduct is considered as inalienable from the concept of personal liberty by the Constitutional Court, family values cemented by the institution of monogamy and reinforced by criminal penalties were praised as compatible with the value system of fundamental human rights.

Fourteen years later, in another groundbreaking interpretation (J.Y. Interpretation No. 748) based on marriage equality, the Justices clarified that neither J.Y. Interpretation No. 554, nor any other interpretations previously issued regarding the legal institution of monogamy, had ever or implicitly answered the question of whether same-sex marriage should be lawfully recognized. Therefore, the Civil Code was said to be deficient constitutionally due to the lawmakers' omission in providing for parallel institutions to heterosexual marriage so as to make "intimately, exclusively, and permanently engaged same-sex union, or wedlock, legally possible." A grace period of two years was set forth in the interpretation for the legislators to adopt remedial legislation; failure to meet the deadline would necessitate immediate official recordation of same-sex marriage at the expiry of the two-year period.[27]

This interpretation followed its precedents and took marriage, not heterosexual marriage but marriage, as a fundamental human right, access to which should be guaranteed to individuals who have the same right to marriage but whose sexual orientation, as an immutable characteristic, is different from the majority in heterosexual marriages.[28] The tenet of this case may not be so much to deviate from or even to destroy conventional heterosexual marriage but to cement and enlarge

[24]J.Y. Interpretation No. 452 (10 Apr 1998).

[25]J.Y. Interpretation No. 413 (20 Sept 1996).

[26]J.Y. Interpretation No. 554 (27 Dec 2002).

[27]J.Y. Interpretation No. 748 (24 May 2017).

[28]*Id.*

the social base of the institution of marriage as an intimate, exclusive union between two consenting adults of the same-sexual orientation. Again, here the notion of equal protection of individuals becomes the focal point that illuminates a blind spot in conventional wisdom and makes all the difference.

3 Law Means Penalties v. Judiciary Means Independence

In the universe of Confucianism, litigation is considered an inauspicious exercise (訟必終凶) and it is only wise to shun it.[29] Litigation would be triggered upon deviation from the rule of *li* and is bound to result in criminal punishment (出禮入刑).[30] Law (法) in Chinese, therefore, is often used as a synonym for criminal punishment (刑). The mission of the judiciary is more to settle disputes (必也使無訟乎) than to deliver justice.[31] Although the main function of all punishments imposed by a judge is said to be "education" (汝作士,明于五刑,以弼五教) so that punishment will not be needed anymore (刑期無刑),[32] punishment is always imposed with an aim to help establish the harmonious universe of the rule of, although sometimes it is imposed to eliminate political enemies and thereby preserve the present regime.[33] An ancient teaching in the High Book is Emperor Wen's (文王) (Emperor Wu's father) wisdom in staying away from the business of dispute resolution. The only thing an emperor should do is find competent judges and let

[29]According to Chapter 12 of the *Analects*, the Master said: "In hearing lawsuits I am just like others. What is necessary is to see that there are no lawsuits." (《論語•顏淵》：「子曰:『聽訟,吾猶人也,必也使無訟乎!」) See Gardner (2007), p. 36.

[30]*The Volume of Chen-Chong in Hou Han-Shu* (or "*Book of the Later Han*"): "When the rule of *li* is insufficient, criminal punishment applies. That is the complementary relationship between the rule of li and criminal punishment." (《後漢書•陳寵傳》：「禮之所去,刑之所取;失禮則入刑,相爲表裡者也。」)

[31]*Supra* note 28.

[32]The *Book of Documents*, Yu-Shu (translated as the "*Book of Yu*"), Da-Yu-Muo (translated as "*the Great Counsel of Yu*"): " …Owing to you being the minister of Crime and your intelligence in the use of the five punishments to assist the inculcation of the five duties, with a view to the perfection of the government, there may come to be no punishments through punishment, but the people accord with the path of Mean." (《尚書•虞書•大禹謨》：「……汝作士,明于五刑,以弼五教,期于予治。刑期于無刑,民協于中,時乃功,懋哉。」)

[33]The *Book of Sayings of Confucius, Wu Shing Chieh* (translated as "*Understanding of the Five Offenses*"): "There are five severe offenses, and homicide is the least. Those who act against heaven would be punished along with their family for five generations. Those who slander King Wen and King Wu would be punished along with their family for four generations. Those who act against ethics and moralities would be punished along with their family for three generations. Those who seek for spiritual beings would be punished along with their family for two generations. Those who commit homicide would be punished alone. Accordingly, homicide is the least of the five severe offenses." (《孔子家語•五刑解》：「孔子曰:『大罪有五,而殺人爲下,逆天地者罪及五世,誣文武者罪及四世,逆人倫者罪及三世,謀鬼神者罪及二世,手殺人者罪及其身。故曰大罪有五,而殺人爲下矣。」)

them do their work, a piece of wisdom that still rings true in today's constitutional state.[34] While it would indeed be a virtue for an emperor to pay deference to the independent decision of a court, judges have, historically, seldom been independent nor distinguished from other administrative functions, and the emperor was always the one to whom the judges would eventually report,[35] as the unparalleled government ruling power must be unitary onto the emperor (人無有比德,惟皇作極).[36]

Not long after the Constitution took effect, the Constitutional Court, in its first decision, responded to a challenge initiated by the Guardian Yuan (監察院) with regard to a moderate form of unconstitutionality. The Constitutional Court announced an interpretation (J.Y. Interpretation No. 86) to the effect that the Judiciary Act must place all lower courts within the judiciary so as to be compliant with the Constitution's tenets.[37] The law at issue brought courts subordinate to the Supreme Court within the purview of the Ministry of Justice. Twenty years later, the law was amended to carry out the decision.

The Constitutional Court issued another monumental decision (J.Y. Interpretation No. 392) which clearly set forth that the prosecutors under the Ministry of Justice in the executive branch are distinct from the judges in the independent judiciary branch, as the latter is a reactive, independent branch while the former the opposite,[38] despite the fact that the law has made the prosecutor's

---

[34]The *Book of Documents, Lizheng* (translated as "Establishment of Government"): "(Emperor Wen would not himself appear for various notifications, in litigation, or in precautionary measures of the government.) Criminal affairs should be dealt with cautiously and carefully by appointing qualified officers and pastors, whose opinions bind the Emperor. This rule should not be breached. (《尚書•立政》:「庶獄、庶慎,惟有司之牧夫,是訓用違。」) This paragraph is now understood as the origin of judicial independence in ancient thought.

[35]The *Book of Sayings of Confucius, Shing Cheng* (translated as "*Criminal Affairs*"): "Penalties are preliminarily determined by Li (吏), who will report the tentative penalties to Cheng (正). After Cheng receives the report, he/she will report to Da Szu Kou (大司寇), who will then report to the emperor. The emperor will ask three ministers to comment on the tentative penalties and reduce the penalties if any doubts are raised. After the procedure, the emperor will finally decide the conviction and the sentence." (《孔子家語•刑政》:「成獄成於吏,吏以獄成告於正,正既聽之,乃告大司寇聽之,乃奉於王;王命三公卿士參聽棘木之下,然後乃以獄之成疑于王,王三宥之以聽命,而制刑焉,所以重之也。」) The paragraph shows the elaborate procedure leading to a conviction, the multiple instances, and the lack of real independence of the ancient judicial system.

[36]*Hongfan of Shangshu, The Nine Provinces of Great Plan*. See *supra* note 2.

[37]J.Y. Interpretation No. 86 (15 Aug 1960).

[38]Zhonghua Minguo Xianfa (Constitution of the Republic of China) Art. 80 (1946), "Judges shall be nonpartisan. They shall try cases independently, in accordance with law, and be free from any interference." Zhonghua Minguo Xianfa (Constitution of the Republic of China) Art. 81 (1946), "Judges shall hold office for life. No judge shall be removed from office unless he has been guilty of a criminal offense or subjected to disciplinary action, or declared to be under interdiction. No judge shall, except in accordance with law, be suspended from office, transferred, or liable to salary cuts."

office a part of the court.[39] It is hence incompatible with the separation-of-power scheme under which the then criminal procedure rules allowed the prosecutors to detain suspects while bypassing court review. However, a writ of habeas corpus cannot be issued by a prosecutor in lieu of a court judge. As a result, the due process of law guaranteed in the mechanism of judicial review in issuing the writ of habeas corpus has become a procedural trump card vis-à-vis prosecutors unilaterally pursuing collective values in the legal order established in criminal laws. These two interpretations are milestones in the process of drawing distinctions, and thereby bringing about actual separation, of the court from the executive branch, and have created the culture of judicial independence, which would not have existed in a conventional Confucianist society.

The Constitutional Court, for obvious reasons, is averse to striking down unconstitutional criminal law provisions unless there is no more appropriate way to read them in light of the Constitution.[40] In so doing, the Court treads the fine line between introducing constitutionalist values and the difficult task of preserving the traditional Confucian legal culture of relying on criminal law as the primary means of maintaining social order under the rule of *li*.

Being tolerant of the criminal sanctions against adultery is but one example of this. Another example is provided by a defamation case where the Constitutional Court adopted a modified version of the actual malice test established by the U.S. Supreme Court[41] in the case of *New York Times v. Sullivan* of 1964 in construing a law of criminal sanction (J.Y. Interpretation No. 509).[42] A chapter of the criminal code professing to protect the interest of reputation often charges the court to sanction abusive or indecent language, in fact making judges the enforcers of social moral codes.[43] The legal provision providing that a defendant is excused if proven to be stating the truth was read by the Constitutional Court in the context of the freedom of expression as not placing on the defendant the burden to prove the truth, nor aiming to punish defendants who have reasons to firmly believe their false statements to be true.[44] The Court, however, also confirmed that the Constitution

[39]J.Y. Interpretation No. 392 (22 Dec 1995).

[40]When disputes regarding the constitutionality of certain laws are raised before the Justices, if the disputed laws fall within the domain where legislators enjoy wide discretion and Justices could find multiple ways to interpret the laws, the Justices may choose to adopt an interpretation that permits the disputed laws to be read in harmony with the Constitution. See Xu Yu Xiu Da Fa Guan Shizi Di 582 Hao Jie Shi Xie Tong Yi Jian Shu [許玉秀大法官釋字第582號解釋協同意見書] (Justice Yu-Hsiu Hsu's concurring opinion in Justices of the Constitutional Court, Interpretation No. 582) (23 July 2004) (R.O.C.), which gives a clear explanation of the legal interpretation of constitutionality (Verfassungskonforme Auslgung, 合憲性解釋).

[41]New York Times Co. v. Sullivan, 1964 U.S. 1500, 376 U.S. 967, 84 S. Ct. 1130, 12 L. Ed. 2d 83 (1964).

[42]J.Y. Interpretation No. 509 (7 July 2000).

[43]Zhonghua Minguo Xingfa (Criminal Code) (Taiwan) Arts. 309 and 310.

[44]The Constitutional Court interprets Article 310 of the Criminal Code in the ways of constitutionality.

would allow criminal sanctions to be applied to deter defamation should the congress find monetary damages not a sufficient legal remedy.

The Constitutional Court has also construed a criminal provision that sanctions "obscene" materials in a way that does not impinge constitutional protection of the freedom of speech, while giving the term a carefully crafted and modified, but narrower, definition as developed and adopted by the U.S. Supreme Court in the case of *Miller v. California* of 1973.[45] The Taiwanese version (J.Y. Interpretation No. 617) breaks "hard-core obscenity" into three specific categories, all of which can be constitutionally prohibited by law, if the material bears no value in the respective realm of art, medicine or education; the rest falls within the Miller-type definition as "soft" obscenity, which cannot be prohibited by law if appropriate measures or devices are in place to bar access by minors.[46] A criminal offense on the abstinence list for "offending social morals" in a Confucianism state, existing since ancient times, is also finally circumscribed by the constitutional safeguards of an individual's fundamental human rights to express and receive messages of sexual desires.

A criminal provision that incorporates the age-old concept of retribution did not pass the Constitutional Court's review as it was not deemed to be an acceptable means of achieving the end set in a law. The law at issue is one that imposes upon an informant who falsely accuses others of drug trafficking the same criminal penalty reserved for the drug traffickers themselves.[47] The Constitutional Court struck it down as an unacceptably retributive punishment of an extent unrelated and thereby not suitable for the offensive conduct (J.Y. Interpretation No. 551). But, the Constitutional Court has, on more than one occasion, before and after martial law was lifted in the country, concluded that the death penalty is a constitutionally acceptable means of eradicating the rampant drug trafficking in Taiwan (J.Y. Interpretation No. 194 and J.Y. Interpretation No. 476).[48] The Constitutional Court passed on the issue of whether a drug user can be subject to the same punishment as a drug trafficker would,[49] maintaining that a healthy social life and order are considered as compelling government interests that eclipse the value of safeguarding individual human lives.[50] The Constitutional Court overwhelmingly supported, without even one dissenting opinion, the moralities and conventional values championed in the regime of capital punishment and did not budge in the face of the death penalty abolishment movements sweeping through the European community.

After J.Y. Interpretation No. 509, which delineated the constitutional limitations on the criminal sanctions for defamation, the Constitutional Court encountered another petition challenging a civil code provision which allowed the court to

[45]Miller v. California, 413 U.S. 15, 93 S. Ct. 2607, 37 L. Ed. 2d 419, 1973 U.S. 149 (1973).

[46]J.Y. Interpretation No. 617 (26 Oct 2006).

[47]J.Y. Interpretation No. 551 (22 Nov 2002).

[48]J.Y. Interpretation No. 194 (22 Mar 1985); J.Y. Interpretation No. 476 (29 Jan 1999).

[49]J.Y. Interpretation 476 (29 Jan 1999).

[50]*Id.*

demand the publication of an apology in newspapers to rectify the dissemination of defamatory remarks.[51] The demand for written public apologies can be seen as the signature relief commonly applied by the courts in Confucian jurisdictions. The Constitutional Court's Interpretation (J.Y. Interpretation No. 656) on the constitutionality of the legal regime of court-ordered public apologies is the third such judicial exercise in Asia on the topic, following those issued by Japan's supreme court in 1956 and Korea's constitutional court in 2003.[52] The Korean judiciary viewed the court-ordered public apology as an unconstitutional exercise undermining the freedom of conscience, a branch of fundamental rights not explicitly adopted in the constitutional documents of Taiwan as it is in Korea's. The Court refused to strike down the law to preserve the right to remain silent under the umbrella of the freedom of speech. The only restriction the Constitutional Court identified from the Constitution as applicable to any court-ordered public apology is that it does not offend the defendant's dignity when it is published in the vindictive plaintiff's name and at his expense.

On that score, Confucianism's emphasis on the virtue of moral self-reflection under the rule of *li*, as exemplified in the making of public apologies for one's misconduct, is able to beat back the antithetical constitutionalist value of individual autonomy in judging right and wrong, free from government compulsion by judicial powers. Interestingly, if not ironically, what the Constitutional Court has ignored is that this Confucian virtue not only underpins a voluntary exercise of self-reflection, but perhaps shapes the very history of the freedom of conscience, whose birth as a branch of human rights in the Universal Declaration of Human Rights of 1948 was an immediate result of discussions initiated by Peng-Chun Chang (張彭春 1892–1957), a scholar-diplomat, together with his deputy, John C. H. Wu (吳經熊 1899–1986), another world-renown legal philosopher. Chang led the delegation from the Republic of China to successfully insert the ancient, Eastern Confucianism-championed notion of humaneness (仁), translated in the document as the innate individual conscience (良知), into the draft Declaration, starting from the first provision.[53] There existed little reason for the Constitutional Court to find the freedom of conscience at odds with the bill of rights simply because the term was not in it.

4 Education as a Government Function

At the heart of "High Vows (泰誓)," a core chapter in the *High Book* (尚書), are messages in the following passage. "And Heaven so cares to protect all under Heaven that an emperor is chosen for them to be their teacher leader, the one and

[51]J.Y. Interpretation 656 (3 Apr 2009).

[52]See Oguri v. Kageyama, 10 Minshu 785 (Supreme Court, Japan 1956), the concurring opinion by Justice Kotaro Tanaka; See also 89 Hun-ma 160 (Constitutional Court, South Korea 1991) (decision on the constitutionality of law classified in file "e").

[53]Sun (2016), p. 209.

only able to assist Heaven to bring to them orderly peaceful life with care." (天佑下民 作之君 作之師 惟其克相上帝 寵綏四方.) It is said that Heaven, being like parents to all creatures, bestows a mandate upon the one and only chosen emperor to act as the parent to his subjects, because mankind is the foremost among all creatures, and the emperor the foremost among all man.[54] (惟天地萬物父母 惟人萬物之靈 亶聰明作元后 元后作民父母)

It is therefore no surprise that one major function of the government under the ruler, as expected by the Confucianists, is to educate the ruler's subjects (in Chinese 子民 "children subjects") as parent-like educators or teacher-like parents, while administering kindness and intervention in equal measure (恩威並施).[55] This image is innocuous until it becomes an issue, fulfilling the fundamental constitutionalist's assumption that the ruler would sooner or later act in his own interest and abuse the power placed in his hands, becoming a menace to his subjects. The Confucianist teachings are not short on warnings that the emperor may do harm to the people. Mencius has asked, "When a supposedly parent-like ruler becomes a beast-like leader devouring his subjects, where is the parent-like being in him?"[56] (爲民父母行政,不免於率獸而食人,惡在其爲民父母也?) But this corruption of a ruler may be considered an extreme case and is seldom an issue systematically addressed by the mainstream theories. After all, Heaven is considered infallible and would not erroneously choose one who is corruptible. It is therefore inconceivable that the carefully chosen ruler would descend into depravity, although in a pragmatist's eyes the descent, when it happens, must be confronted. So, an accountable, benevolent, model emperor can and will behave appropriately, and must play the role of an educator in all walks of life and through all aspects of his conduct. In sum, education is the main function of the government under the one and only chosen ruler.

The Constitutional Court started to review the boundary lines between the state and universities in terms of educational functions in the late 1990s. The first rule the Constitutional Court set in an interpretation (J.Y. Interpretation No. 380) is that without any clear statutory mandate, the Ministry of Education is not constitutionally allowed to impose mandatory course requirements for university students to receive college degrees, as such requirements intruded on the universities' self-governance which is guaranteed under the umbrella of academic freedom by the Constitution.[57] In the next interpretation, again for the sake of preserving

[54]The *Book of Documents,* Tai Shi (translated as the "*Great Vows*"). (《尚書,泰誓》).

[55]*Xunzi, Li-Lun* (translated as "*The Theory of Li*"): "The Book states that a man with noble character may be the parent of the people. The father is to give birth but not to foster. The mother is to foster but not to teach. A man with noble character is able to foster and to teach." (《荀子•禮論》:「詩曰:『愷悌君子,民之父母』。...父能生之,不能養之;母能食之,不能教誨之;君者,已能食之矣,又善教誨之者也。」)

[56]Mencius, King Hui of Liang: "Mencius replied to King Hui of Liang: ...It is only heard that a brutal man was killed. I had never heard that King of Zhou was killed unlawfully." (《孟子•梁惠王》:「...聞誅一夫紂矣,未聞弑君也。」)

[57]J.Y. Interpretation No. 380 (26 May 1995).

academic freedom, the Constitutional Court declared a law that required all universities to establish an office of military affairs in charge of military and medical training on campus as being unconstitutional (J.Y. Interpretation No. 450).[58] The intention of these interpretations, although not explicitly stated, is to promote a more liberated, liberal and diverse educational milieu without stifling or undue government control, something not uncommon in the traditional Confucian dynasties, but now considered incompatible with a constitutional democracy.

Meanwhile, the Constitutional Court revealed its view of the government's role in education in a case where it declared a court precedent denying a student's standing to sue a city-owned college for undue involuntary withdrawal as unconstitutional (J.Y. Interpretation No. 382).[59] As a more recent interpretation of the Constitutional Court confirmed (J.Y. Interpretation No. 736), all public schools are deemed equivalent to government agencies discharging educational functions, while all private schools are deemed as having been delegated governmental educational functions by law.[60] Wrongful discharge of a student is comparable to an illegal government act and therefore subject to challenge and is reviewable in an administrative court. The Constitutional Court failed to explain why the length of basic schooling guaranteed by the Constitution should be extended by the government, and all levels of formal education, both public and private schools, are taken as being a part of the government's educational function. Maybe in the mind of the Justices no explanation is needed, as judicial notice can be taken from the already prevalent understanding in a state with Confucian traditions.

Yet another interesting turn, propelled by the traditional concept of education, followed in a more recent interpretation by the Constitutional Court (J.Y. Interpretation No. 702).[61] It was a case where a legal provision was challenged for lacking the clarity as otherwise required in the Constitution, when applied by the school as the legal basis for disciplining one of its teachers for his misconduct in class. The law was found to be soundly composed and able to pass constitutional review. Its terms are superficially abstract and general but sufficiently specific for a teacher to understand the boundaries of occupational conduct as set for teachers, who are traditionally expected to follow the "teacher's way" (師道), and be a model for and earn high respect from students, without unfitting, abusive conduct while teaching.

[58]J.Y. Interpretation No. 450 (27 Mar 1998).

[59]J.Y. Interpretation No. 382 (23 June 1995). The author believes that the reason why the Constitutional Court took it for granted without any cited basis is due to the effect of traditional culture.

[60]J.Y. Interpretation No. 736 (18 Mar 2016).

[61]J.Y. Interpretation No. 702 (27 July 2012).

5 Transforming the Absolute-Power Relationship into Constitutional Relations

In the Confucian universe it is inconceivable for a son to sue his parents, a student to sue teachers or a subordinate to sue superordinates. The pre-World War I German theory of the special power relationship (*Das besonderes Gewaltverhältnis* or 特別權力關係, hereinafter "the SPR theory") is defined as an absolute obedience relationship between, inter alia, a public functionary and his superior, or a student and his teacher or school.[62] The SPR theory was easily transplanted into Taiwan during Taiwan's transition from a Confucian jurisdiction into a newly developing regime under the rule of law, with a carved-out turf under the rule of man.

On the eve of the lifting of martial law, the Constitutional Court took the first of many steps to dismantle the SPR theory in Taiwan. The first move was an interpretation (J.Y. Interpretation No. 187) where the past judicial practice was questioned.[63] A number of court decisions had adopted the SPR theory to dismiss on the grounds of lack of standing, with no statutory basis, any administrative action filed by a government functionary to challenge a decision or order made by his superiors, as well as any administrative action filed by a student against the school over a decision made by his teachers or the school authority. The petitioner was a military officer who sought to collect his full pension payment following an alleged wrongful denial and who had no access to court for the matter. He was vindicated on the issue in that his right to receive his pension upon retirement was a claim protected by constitutional litigation; the Constitutional Court concluded the claim could not be categorically barred simply because of his occupation or government affiliation alone. Thereafter, a series of interpretations followed (J.Y. Interpretation No. 201, 243, 298, 323, 338, and 382),[64] chipping away at the SPR theory until a new theory emerged with an interpretation (J.Y. Interpretation No. 430) on a case where a military officer was barred from lodging an action, again for lacking standing, over a disputed calculation of his pension-based years.[65]

J.Y. Interpretation No. 430 knocked down another Supreme Court-selected precedent as it unconstitutionally deprived the petitioner of his right to seek redress from the court. The Constitutional Court for the first time defined the relationship between the state and its public functionaries as a duty-oriented relationship under

[62]Wu (2015), p. 196. The SPR theory is defined as "legally adding special obligations through unilateral measures of executive power." Under the special power relationship, administrative power is not bound by any restriction set forth by law and thus has wider discretion, while individuals are required to obey administrative power and may not claim remedies. See J.Y. Interpretation No. 266 (5 Oct 1990) and J.Y. Interpretation No. 430 (6 June 1997).

[63]J.Y. Interpretation No. 187 (18 May 1984).

[64]J.Y. Interpretation No. 201 (3 Jan 1986); J.Y. Interpretation No. 243 (19 July 1989); J.Y. Interpretation No. 298 (12 Jun 1992); J.Y. Interpretation No. 323 (18 June 1993); J.Y. Interpretation No. 338 (25 Feb 1994); J.Y. Interpretation No. 382 (23 Jun 1995).

[65]J.Y. Interpretation No. 430 (6 June 1997).

public law (公法上職務關係). This interpretation was to rid Taiwan of the SPR theory, yet the new relationship does not quite constitute a public-law employment contract between two equal parties, as so deemed in some common-law jurisdictions that do not distinguish between the administrative courts' jurisdiction over administrative law cases and that of the ordinary courts over civil and criminal cases.

The theory of the duty-oriented relationship under public law supplanted the SPR theory in Germany, under a public-law doctrine of "high power in the hands of administration" (*schlichthoheiliche Verwaltung* 高權行政), a doctrine that the Constitutional Court found easier to adopt than the contractual theory, which supposedly applies to equals, because it is consonant with the Confucian concept of the unequal relationship between a superordinate and subordinate. In a dissenting opinion by Justices Pi-hu Hsu (1948∼) and Pei-Hsiu Yeh (1947∼) in J.Y. Interpretation No. 658, explanations were provided on the doctrinal difference between the two. The most notable difference is that the "high power in the hands of administration" doctrine is underpinned by an obligation-to-obligation relationship, instead of a right-to-obligation relationship, because monetary payment as a consideration under a contractual relationship is not what the public functionaries pursue in exchange for their services in government. This view in fact corresponds with traditional Confucianism, which takes as the core value in any significant relationship duty (義) instead of monetary gains (利). What the two Justices failed to address in their dissent, though, is the exchange of considerations for the fulfillment of a citizen's human right to participate in government and the services extended to the government by the public functionaries, which would in fact provide justification for the doctrine of contractual theory.

Following the chain of interpretations questioning the SPR theory that began with J.Y. Interpretation No. 187, which focused on the state-public functionary relationship,[66] J.Y. Interpretation No. 382 freed the student-school relationship from the theory. This interpretation, however, indicated that students are entitled to challenge any of the school's decisions that resulted in changing the student's status as a student, instead of all decisions that are allegedly illegal.

This decision was explicitly modified by a subsequent interpretation (J.Y. Interpretation No. 684). A graduate student filed an action against his university because his campaign poster on campus for a state presidential candidate in the popular election was banned by the school authority. The administrative court cited J.Y. Interpretation No. 382 to dismiss the action on the grounds that the student had no standing, that his student status had hardly been changed. The Constitutional Court accepted his petition for a new interpretation on the same issue and decided that a student is entitled to lodge an action against the university authority if significant human rights, such as freedom of speech in the case, are at stake, even if the student's status is not changed.[67] The interpretation encourages the

[66]J.Y. Interpretation No. 187 (18 May 1984); J.Y. Interpretation No. 382 (23 June 1995).

[67]J.Y. Interpretation No. 684 (17 Jan 2011).

establishment of on-campus pre-litigation due process mechanisms to resolve disputes between students and the school authority.

Now, the constitutionalist rule of law has found its way into educational institutions as well as other places, adding the concept of procedural due process to the conventional rule of li, thereby revising the fabric of substantive moral norms of conduct under it.

The concept of the rule of *li* may be seen as coinciding with that of the rule of law inasmuch as both govern the relationship between the emperor and his subordinates. However, the term special power relationship in its German literal meaning implies violence as it connotes absolute power that cannot be challenged, and authority in absolute power is force, or in Lord Acton's words, "Authority that does not exist for liberty is not authority but force." Or, "Absolute power demoralizes." It explains why absolute power relationships between the superordinate and subordinate or that between teachers and students, as without exception in the millennia preceding the Republic, cannot prevent the abusive exercise of violence.

What is relevant here is again the Constitutional Court's J.Y. Interpretation No. 388.[68] Before the interpretation was made, the provision in the Constitution that grants immunity to the President from criminal prosecution proceedings except for treason charges might be read under the SPR theory as giving the head of state, who is concurrently appointed by the Constitution as the commander-in-chief of the entire armed forces of the Republic, an absolute power to execute his enemies, subordinates or his subjects, at will, thus making him a serious threat to human rights. Without endorsing the SPR theory, J.Y. Interpretation No. 388 precluded any misreading for absolute immunity, banishing absolute power, along with the associated evil, from the rule of law. Interestingly, the Constitutional Court's J.Y. Interpretation No. 702 identified violence inflicted upon students as abuse in education and allowed disciplinary measures against teachers by the school authority, further stamping out the SPR theory while preserving the substance of the rule of *li* under the constitutionalist's state of the rule of law.[69]

References

Chan W-T (1963) A source book in Chinese philosophy. Princeton University Press, Princeton

de Bary WT (1998) Asian values and human rights: a Confucian communitarian perspective. Harvard University Press, Cambridge

de Bary WT, Bloom I (1999) Sources of Chinese tradition: from earliest times to 1600. Columbia University Press, New York

Gardner D (2007) The four books: the basic teachings of the later Confucian tradition. Hackett Publishing Co., Cambridge

[68]J.Y. Interpretation No. 388 (27 Oct 1995).

[69]J.Y. Interpretation No. 702 (27 July 2012).

Li N-T (2013) From obscurity to light—tracking equality's rise in the making of Chinese constitutions. J Leg Hist Stud 24:263–287

Ministry of Justice [法務部] (1999) Fu Zong Tong De Fou Jian Ren Xing Zheng Yuan Yuan Zhang Deng Shi Xian Xiang Guan Zi Liao Ji Yao [「副總統得否兼任行政院院長」等釋憲相關資料輯要] (Case Materials of the Interpretations of the Constitution: May the Vice-President hold the concurrent post of Premier of the Executive Yuan). Ministry of Justice, Taipei

Nylan M (2001) The five "Confucian" classics. Yale University Press, New Haven

Sun P-H (2016) Pengchun Chang's contributions to the drafting of the UDHR. J Civil Leg Sci 5:209–217

Wu G [吳庚] (2015) Xing Zheng Fa Zhi Li Lun Yu Shi Yong [行政法之理論與實用] (Administrative Law: the Theory and the Practices). Sanmin Publishing Co., Taipei

Nigel N. T. Li received his LL.M. degrees from Harvard in 1983 and National Taiwan University in 1980, after obtaining an LL.B. degree from Soochow University in 1977. In addition to his role as a practicing attorney specializing in dispute resolution and arbitration, media law, human and civil rights, international litigation and constitutional law, he is also an adjunct professor at both the Graduate School of Law of Soochow University and the Department of Political Science of National Taiwan University. He teaches Constitutional Law, Human Rights, ADR and International Arbitration. Nigel also served as Chairman of the Chinese Arbitration Association, Taipei from 2007 to 2014. He has made considerable effort in raising the quality of transnational arbitration and has contributed greatly to cross-Strait and international exchanges. Over the years, Nigel has dedicated himself to pro bono work. He has served as President of the Taipei Bar Association and now sits on the Board of the Judicial Reform Foundation. His determination to preserve human rights and justice has led to his involvement in numerous cases applying for the Constitutional Court's Interpretation of the Constitution and his appointment as a member of the Presidential Advisory Committee on Human Rights.

Chapter 4
Human Rights and Transitional Justice: Taiwan's Adoption of the ICCPR and the Redress of 2/28 and Martial-Law-Era Injustices

Brad R. Roth

Abstract Article 2(3) of the ICCPR obligates States Parties to "ensure that any person whose rights or freedoms as herein recognized are violated shall have an effective remedy," which shall be "determined by competent judicial, administrative or legislative authorities, or by any other competent authority provided for by the legal system of the State," and enforced by "the competent authorities." Taiwan's adoption of the ICCPR therefore raises issues about appropriate redress for injustices associated with the authoritarian period of Kuomintang rule, including most prominently the atrocities committed in the aftermath of the 28 February 1947 uprising. Coming to terms with the past is an indispensable component of the consolidation of a political order predicated on the irreducible dignity of the human person. This human rights obligation can be fulfilled even when too much time has passed for criminal prosecutions to be undertaken and even when the political party associated with the perpetrators retains a substantial political role.

Keywords International covenant on civil and political rights · Martial law Retrospective justice · Transitional justice · 2/28 incident

1 Introduction

On March 31, 2009, Taiwan's Legislative Yuan adopted the Act to Implement the International Covenant on Civil and Political Rights (hereinafter ICCPR) and the International Covenant on Economic, Social and Cultural Rights (hereinafter ICESCR).[1] Although the Legislative Yuan's simultaneous action to consent without reservation to the ratification of the treaties—originally signed on 5 October 1967

[1]Wang (2009); see also Huang (2009); see generally Shope (2012).

B. R. Roth (✉)
Wayne State University, Detroit, USA
e-mail: brad.roth@wayne.edu

J. A. Cohen et al. (eds.), *Taiwan and International Human Rights*, Economics, Law, and Institutions in Asia Pacific, https://doi.org/10.1007/978-981-13-0350-0_4

by a Republic of China (hereinafter ROC) government that still held China's United Nations seat[2]—is of no immediate international legal consequence (absent acceptance of the ratified instruments by the treaties' official depositary, the UN Secretariat), the implementing legislation operates as domestic law within Taiwan. The statute provides (rather obscurely) that:

> All levels of governmental institutions and agencies should take the responsibility for preparing, promoting and implementing human rights protection provisions in the two Covenants within their functions that are governed by existing laws and regulations.[3]

The legislation further establishes processes for amending laws to bring them into conformity with ICCPR and ICESCR obligations.[4] Moreover, since the Covenants have "domestic legal status,"[5] Taiwan's courts would appear to be empowered (if not necessarily willing)[6] to nullify prior statutory provisions inconsistent with the treaties' requirements.

Article 2(3) of the ICCPR obligates States Parties to "ensure that any person whose rights or freedoms as herein recognized are violated shall have an effective remedy," which shall be "determined by competent judicial, administrative or legislative authorities, or by any other competent authority provided for by the legal system of the State," and enforced by "the competent authorities."[7] Recent interpretations of these provisions, and of counterpart provisions of analogous human rights instruments, have trended toward greater insistence on thoroughgoing transitional justice processes, including criminal prosecution. Taiwan's adoption of the ICCPR therefore raises issues about appropriate redress for injustices associated with the authoritarian period of Kuomintang (hereinafter KMT) rule, including both the atrocities committed during the suppression of the 28 February 1947 rebellion (hereinafter the "2/28 Incident") and during the "White Terror" associated with the 1949–1987 martial-law period.

The 2016 elections yielded not only a strong mandate for a non-KMT President, Tsai Ing-wen, but also a first-ever legislative majority for her Democratic Progressive Party (hereinafter DPP) (which the 2000–2008 DPP administration of President Chen Shui-bian had lacked).[8] This development has raised expectations for new progress

---

[2]Wang, *supra* note 1.

[3]Act to Implement the International Covenant on Civil and Political Rights and the International Covenant on Economic, Social and Cultural Rights, art. 5 (2009), http://mojlaw.moj.gov.tw/NewsContentE.aspx?id=3.

[4]*Id.*, at art. 8.

[5]*Id.*, at art. 2.

[6]See, e.g., Activists urge ROC to comply with UN human rights covenants (2012) (although courts blocked prosecution of activist professor Lin Chia-fan for violations of the restrictive Assembly and Parade Act, they failed to nullify the Act itself, notwithstanding condemnations of the Act by human rights experts).

[7]International Covenant on Civil and Political Rights, art. 2(3), *opened for signature* 19 Dec 1966, 999 UN T.S. 171.

[8]See, e.g., Bush (2016). Tsai garnered 56.1% of the Presidential vote, to 30.1% for KMT candidate Eric Chu and 12.8% for James Soong of the People First Party (PFP), a party with its origins in the

on the transitional justice front. Taiwan's prior adoption of the ICCPR—all the more significant for having been effected by a KMT administration—inevitably adds greater impetus to the project of coming to terms with the residue of the repressive past.

Transitional justice in the Taiwanese context presents daunting puzzles. An extraordinary array of countries—covering the widest range of regions, cultures, and circumstances—have lately undergone "transition."[9] This ill-delimited phenomenon is typically associated with some combination of the following changeovers: from unmediated conflict to constitutional accord; from extemporary exercise of power to the rule of law; from authoritarianism to liberal-democratic electoral competition; and from systematic impositions upon civil liberty and physical integrity to the institutionalization of human rights.

In many instances, the prior regime fell in dramatic fashion, whether imploding suddenly, being overthrown by force, or surrendering power in the face of mass mobilization. Taiwan's transition—non-paradigmatically, though not uniquely so—was gradual, introduced and managed by officials of the authoritarian regime itself. This process led to the development of a competitive political system in which the former authoritarian ruling party has alternated in power with its one principal opponent. In the 2017 Freedom House index, Taiwan ranks as the second-freest country in Asia (trailing only Japan), and tied for 37th out of 195 nations globally (ahead of the United States).[10] Consequently, the post-transition "settling of accounts"[11] lacks a palpable urgency.

The second DPP presidency and first DPP legislative majority confront the transitional justice question three decades after the lifting of martial law, over two decades after the first genuine pluralistic elections, and more than a decade and a half after the first constitutional transfer of executive power to an opposition party. The most widespread and systematic atrocities occurred more than a half-century ago—over seventy years ago, in the case of the 2/28 massacres—leaving few residual targets of retrospective criminal prosecution for the most serious abuses. Yet the very absence of the prospect of criminal prosecution may plausibly open the way for the society to come to terms with its past, given that the abuses were perpetrated on behalf of a then-dictatorial party that retains a major political role in the democratic politics of the post-transition era.

KMT. The DPP and its allies also won a combined majority of the legislative vote, with the DPP winning a substantial absolute majority of the legislative seats.

[9]The vast literature on "settling accounts" in the wake of these transitions has adopted "transitional justice" as the term of art, following Teitel (2000).

[10]Freedom in the World (2017a); see generally Freedom in the World (2017b).

[11]This expression is the established term of art, but it is open to many serious substantive objections and is arguably offensive. Most obviously, the term implausibly connotes a commensurability of the proposed remedies with the harms and injustices to which they are supposed to correspond (which often include murder and torture). It also bears an unhappy resemblance to the term "settling scores," which suggests partisan revanchism rather than a political order refounded on the basis of universal principles.

The discussion below will address the implications of ICCPR Article 2(3) for the transitional justice question in the Taiwan context. It will offer some cautionary thoughts about the international legal order's present enthusiasm for the most robust versions of transitional justice. Finally, it will consider what lessons transitional justice experiments elsewhere might offer for Taiwan.

2 Previous and Current Efforts to Seek Redress of the 2/28 Incident and Martial-Law Abuses

The 2/28 Incident of 1947 and the White Terror of 1949–87 are well known among students of the history of ROC rule over Taiwan. Their details have been exhaustively elaborated elsewhere,[12] and will not belabored here.

In brief, "2/28" refers to the events following 28 February 1947, when substantial sectors of the local population began an uprising against the ROC forces that had come to rule Taiwan in the aftermath of the August 1945 Japanese surrender to the Allied Powers.[13] Although Taiwanese had not initially reacted negatively to the arrival of ROC forces, a series of harsh measures (including imposition of the Mandarin language) had generated antagonism, culminating in a violent rebellion. ROC military governor Chen Yi's first response was to indicate an openness to negotiation, but when reinforcements arrived from the Mainland, they proceeded to suppress the insurgents violently, enacting a bloody retribution. The 2/28 Incident death toll is estimated at between 18,000 and 28,000.[14]

The White Terror involved some 3,000 to 4,000 executions, the most extreme outcomes of the roughly 140,000 political trials conducted by ROC martial-law courts (including some 30,000 retrospectively deemed "improper").[15] Although by far the most serious repression occurred in the 1950s and 1960s, subsequent martial-law abuses notoriously included the events surrounding a 10 December 1979 International Human Rights Day demonstration in the city of Kaohsiung. The protest, associated with a critical journalistic outlet (lending "the Kaohsiung

---

[12]For an historical overview, see, e.g., Roy (2003).

[13]There remains vigorous dispute as to the legal status of Taiwan during the period immediately following Japan's defeat in World War II. The Chiang Kai-shek regime interpreted Allied proclamations during the war as establishing an immediate retrocession of Taiwan to China, thereby nullifying the transfer of sovereignty over Taiwan that the Treaty of Shimonoseki had effected as a consequence of China's military defeat at Japanese hands in 1895. The alternative view is that Taiwan, having been acquired by Japan at a time when forcible conquest was permissible in international law, remained legally a part of the Japanese Empire until Japan's formal renunciation of sovereignty over the island in the Treaty of San Francisco, 8 Sept 1951, 136 U.N.T.S. 46 (entry into force 28 Apr 1952). On that view, ROC forces in the late 1940s were occupiers acting as trustees of the Allied Powers.

[14]See, e.g., Chang et al. (2006).

[15]Hwang (2016), p. 170.

Incident" its other popular name, the "*Formosa Magazine* Incident"), was violently suppressed, and its leaders subjected to high-profile military trials that led to long prison sentences.[16] The "Kaohsiung Incident" is also taken to encompass the brutal murder of family members of one of the arrestees, in apparent retaliation for efforts to publicize the dissident's plight internationally.[17]

These two categories of KMT historical abuses fit into accounts of Taiwan's political development in distinct ways. The 2/28 Incident plays an iconic role in the narrative that animates the Independence Movement (the DPP-led "pan-Green" camp), a narrative that is to varying degrees contested by ROC loyalists (the KMT-led "pan-Blue" camp). From a pan-Green perspective, the suppression of the 2/28 rebellion represents the Mainland's forcible and ruthless imposition of an essentially foreign regime on a distinct political community. The rebellion's fallen thus figure not merely as victims of tragic internecine violence or of the excesses of a particular ruling apparatus born of its time, but as martyrs of the present-day cause of Taiwan independence.[18] Predictably, the pan-Blue camp, which continues to regard Taiwan as essentially Chinese and Chiang Kai-shek as a national hero of the Republic of China on Taiwan, has sought to downplay the Incident as a tragic episode attributable to lower-level wrongdoing.[19]

Retrospective treatment of the White Terror is less directly partisan in its implications, but beset by different complexities. Although actual and alleged Taiwan independence advocates were among its prominent victims, the largest number of victims (especially in the early period) were actual and alleged partisans of the People's Republic of China (PRC). As Vladimir Stolojan reports:

> Although since 1992 there had been a broad consensus as to the need to compensate the families of the 1947 victims, in 1997, the representative of the Ministry of Defence opposed the rehabilitation of all the victims of the White Terror. Although acknowledging that there may have been many who were convicted though innocent, and the severity of military justice, he asserted that martial law "had undeniable merits for the maintenance of national security in the face of pressure from Communist China."[20]

Among the consequences of the mixed composition of the White Terror's targets has been division between the leftist and the Independence Movement–oriented

---

[16]See Chen (2008), pp. 186–187.

[17]In February 1980, while dissident Li Yi-hsiung was in detention (where he was severely beaten), his mother and his young daughters were brutally murdered in their house immediately after his mother had sought to contact Amnesty International. As the house was under twenty-four police surveillance at the time, the authorities' claimed inability to solve the crime is inherently suspicious. Roy, *supra* note 12, at p. 169.

[18]See Fleischauer (2007), pp. 391–392.

[19]See Shih and Chen (2010), pp. 107–111; Chang (2010), p. 10 (noting the work of revisionist 2/28 historians Chu Hung-yuan and Huang Chang-chien, whose accounts are favorable to the Chiang regime); see also Hou (2015), pp. 60–62 (rendering a sympathetic account of the regime's reaction to the local uprising).

[20]Stolojan (2017), p. 32.

associations seeking justice for victims.[21] On the other hand, since some 40% of the White Terror victims were Mainlanders, assessment of these abuses may be less fraught a question than the conflicting interpretations of 2/28.[22]

Jau-Yuan Hwang complains that while progress has been made over the years on reparations to victims,[23] accountability for wrongdoers—whether by way of criminal or civil adjudication or by way of public exposure of their involvement through truth-seeking mechanisms—has been elusive.[24] Indeed, early measures at the conclusion of the martial-law period barred review by civilian courts of the lawfulness of military court convictions of dissidents. The reformist KMT administration of President Lee Teng-hui in the 1990s brought modest remediations, including apologies, restoration of personal rights and reputations where convictions could be specifically attributed to truncations of due process, and monetary compensation for the improperly convicted. Nonetheless, both the 1995 "Act Governing the Recovery of Damage of Individual Rights during the Period of Martial Rule" and the 1998 "Compensation Act for Improper Trials on Charges of Sedition and Espionage under the Martial-Law Period" operated from the premise of the legal validity of martial-law enactments and procedures (though not always of the actual proceedings), thereby shielding the repressive measures' authors and implementers from personal accountability.[25]

Efforts since the Tsai Administration's inauguration have focused on "four objectives: the opening of the archives, the restitution of goods wrongly acquired by the KMT …, the withdrawal of still visible symbols of the authoritarian regime, and the righting of injustices linked to the period of martial law."[26] Thus far, the Tsai Administration's most concrete achievement in the area of transitional justice has been the 10 August 2016 Act Governing the Handling of Ill-Gotten Properties by Political Parties and Their Affiliate Organizations, leading to the establishment of an Executive-appointed Ill-Gotten Party Assets Settlement Committee.[27] The statute targets all party assets not attributable to "party membership fees, political donations, election campaign contributions, government subsidies for elections, and interest generated from such funds," establishing a process for the return of such assets (or a monetary equivalent) to their rightful public or private owner.[28] With less than a third of the legislative seats, the KMT failed procedurally to trigger

[21] *Id.*, at p. 33.

[22] See Hwang, *supra* note 15, at p. 179.

[23] February 28 Incident Disposition and Compensation Act (2013), http://mojlaw.moj.gov.tw/NewsContentE.aspx?id=89 (initially promulgated on 7 April 1995, and amended repeatedly since).

[24] Hwang, *supra* note 15, at pp. 171–172.

[25] *Id.*

[26] Stolojan, *supra* note 20, at p. 35.

[27] Executive Yuan (2016), Clarifying the ill-gotten party assets act. http://english.ey.gov.tw/News_Hot_Topic.aspx?n=F80E27F3D7C30690&sms=D5327C4C848FEECB. Accessed 18 Oct 2017.

[28] *Id.*

a Constitutional Court abstract review of the statute, but the eventual application of the statute will undoubtedly occasion Constitutional Court evaluation of the statute.[29]

3 The Implications of ICCPR Article 2(3) for Transitional Justice

Taiwan's adoption of the ICCPR as domestic law provides an additional impetus to the project of transitional justice. In addition to establishing a domestic legal mandate for transitional justice measures, the ICCPR quasi-ratification places Taiwan in a position to distinguish itself in the international arena (consistent with its high "scores" in indexes of civil and political liberty) as maximally upholding human rights principles, definitively turning the page on the era when two structurally similar (even if not substantively equivalent) one-party dictatorships vied with each other for recognition as the legitimate government of One China. By authoritatively problematizing the Chiang Kai-shek regime's historical role in defining Taiwan's status—a role acquired and maintained over decades by distorting and constraining rather than authentically representing the entity's political expression—Taiwan can all the better present itself to the world as a distinct political entity ready to take its place as a leading member of the community of liberal-democratic states.

The project of exposing and repudiating the regime's ruthless and dictatorial conduct dovetails with human rights bodies' pronounced current tendency to demand the most vigorous retrospective scrutiny of past abuses. In its General Comment 31 of 2004, the Human Rights Committee emphasized the obligatoriness of effective remedial measures. These include, "where appropriate, … restitution, rehabilitation and measures of satisfaction, such as public apologies, public memorials, guarantees of non-repetition and changes in relevant laws and practices, as well as bringing to justice the perpetrators of human rights violations."[30] With respect to "those violations recognized as criminal under either domestic or international law, such as torture and similar cruel, inhuman and degrading treatment (Article 7), summary and arbitrary killing (Article 6) and enforced disappearance (Articles 7 and 9 and, frequently, 6)," a failure either to investigate or to bring perpetrators to justice constitutes an independent violation of the Covenant.[31] With particular relevance to transitional justice, the Committee opined that:

---

[29]Hwang et al. (2017) (provisional version available at https://papers.ssrn.com/sol3/papers.cfm?abstract_id=2926864).

[30]Human Rights Comm., General Comment no. 31 [80]: The nature of the general legal obligation imposed on States Parties to the Covenant, para. 16, UN Doc. CCPR/C/21/Rev.1/Add.13 (26 May 2004).

[31]*Id.*, at para. 18.

> [T]he States Parties concerned may not relieve perpetrators from personal responsibility, as has occurred with certain amnesties … and prior legal immunities and indemnities. Furthermore, no official status justifies persons who may be accused of responsibility for such violations being held immune from legal responsibility. Other impediments to the establishment of legal responsibility should also be removed, such as the defence of obedience to superior orders or unreasonably short periods of statutory limitation in cases where such limitations are applicable.[32]

The emergence of this hard-line attitude is traceable to the Human Rights Committee's 1992 General Comment on the ICCPR's prohibition of torture and cruel, inhuman, and degrading treatment or punishment. Replacing General Comment 7 on the same topic, which had not spoken to remedies or penal accountability, General Comment 20 invoked Article 2(3) to demand prompt and impartial investigation leading to "appropriate redress." It moreover cast most, if not all, amnesties as legally problematic:

> The Committee has noted that some States have granted amnesty in respect of acts of torture. Amnesties are generally incompatible with the duty of States to investigate such acts; to guarantee freedom from such acts within their jurisdiction; and to ensure that they do not occur in the future. States may not deprive individuals of the right to an effective remedy, including compensation and such full rehabilitation as may be possible.[33]

Although the Human Rights Committee's interpretations of ICCPR obligations are not themselves binding on the States Parties,[34] and display remarkably little methodological grounding for their elaborate assertions, this same hostility to impunity is reflected in developments in other international bodies,[35] and especially in the well-developed Inter-American human rights system. A series of rulings by the Inter-American Court of Human Rights has not only condemned but actually

---

[32] *Id.*

[33] Human Rights Comm., General Comment no. 20: Article 7 (Prohibition of torture, or other cruel, inhuman or degrading treatment or punishment), para. 15, UN Doc. HRI/GEN/1/Rev.9 (Vol. I), p. 200 (27 May 2008). This Committee soon thereafter reiterated the point in addressing an individual petition under the Convention's Optional Protocol. See Case of Hugo Rodríguez v. Uruguay, Human Rights Comm., Communication no. 322/1988, annex, paras. 12.3–12.4, UN Doc. CCPR/C/51/D/322/1988 (9 Aug 1994).

[34] Although General Comments have no specific status, the Committee has asserted that its determinations in Optional Protocol individual communication cases are "authoritative." Human Rights Comm., General Comment no. 33: Obligations of States Parties under the Optional Protocol to the International Covenant on Civil and Political Rights, para. 13, UN Doc. CCPR/C/GC/33 (5 Nov 2008). It is unclear whether States Parties accept that interpretation.

[35] The United Nations Secretary-General has asserted that "the peace agreements approved by the United Nations cannot promise amnesty for crimes of genocide, war, or crimes against humanity, or serious infractions of human rights." UN Secretary-General, *The Rule of Law and Transitional Justice in Societies That Suffer or Have Suffered from Conflict*, para. 10, UN Doc S/2004/616 (3 Aug 2004).

purported to nullify, post-conflict amnesties.[36] That Court has further held that even an amnesty "approved in a democratic regime and yet ratified or supported by the public, on two occasions, namely, through the exercise of direct democracy" is not automatically valid under international law.[37]

These rulings have, in turn, reverberated within the justice systems of the member states of the Organization of American States.[38] Perhaps most remarkably, after a generation of peace and stability following a brutal conflict, the Constitutional Chamber of the Supreme Court of El Salvador in July 2016 invalidated the General Amnesty Law for the Consolidation of Peace, adopted in March 1993 in the wake of the peace accords between the government and the insurgency.[39] This development in El Salvador is especially noteworthy because the peace accords had transformed an extraordinarily polarized political scene, to the point where constitutional processes endured not only a transfer of executive power between formerly warring factions but also a runoff election in 2014 in which a former guerrilla commander won the presidency with a bare 50.11% of the vote.[40] Unsurprisingly, the pursuit of prosecutions has since proceeded haltingly.[41]

This widespread enthusiasm within human rights bodies for retrospective criminal prosecutions is open to numerous objections, both practical and jurisprudential. A one-size-fits-all rejection of amnesties neglects the complexities of particular crises and sweepingly disparages a device that has frequently proved useful to conflict

---

[36]See Binder (2010), pp. 1208–1214 (citing Barrios Altos v. Peru, Merits, Judgment, Inter-Am. Ct. H.R. (ser. C) No. 75 (14 Mar 2001); La Cantuta v. Peru, Merits, Reparations and Costs, Judgment, Inter-Am. Ct. H.R. (ser. C) No. 162 (29 Nov 2006); Almonacid Arellano y otros v. Chile, Preliminary Objections, Merits, Reparations and Costs, Judgment, Inter-Am. Ct. H.R. (ser. C) No. 154 (26 Sept 2006).

[37]Gelman v. Uruguay, Merits and Reparations, Judgment, Inter-Am. Ct. H.R. (ser. C) No. 221, para. 238 (24 February).

[38]See *Id.*, at paras. 215–224 (invoking court decisions from Argentina, Peru, Uruguay, Chile, Honduras, Colombia, and El Salvador).

[39]Inter-American Commission on Human Rights [IACHR] (2016) IACHR hails determination of unconstitutionality of amnesty law in El Salvador. http://www.oas.org/en/iachr/media_center/PReleases/2016/098.asp. Accessed 18 Oct 2017.

[40]Salvadorean ex-rebel Sanchez Ceren wins vote—officials (2014). BBC News. http://www.bbc.com/news/world-latin-america-26556803. Accessed 18 Oct 2017.

[41]Curiously, notwithstanding that the overwhelming preponderance of atrocities had been committed on the government side, the first arrest warrants issued were against former insurgents who, after shooting down a United States Army helicopter that was ferrying weapons to the Salvadoran armed forces, killed two wounded U.S. soldiers. Lakhani (2017) El Salvador issues warrants for guerrillas who killed US soldiers during civil war. *The Guardian*. https://www.theguardian.com/world/2017/jul/25/el-salvador-guerrilla-fighters-us-soliders-helicopter-killings. Accessed 18 Oct 2017. Both sides are reportedly working to pass a new amnesty law to limit the scope of retrospective prosecutions. *Id.*

resolution.[42] Although many negotiated transitions seem to have withstood decisions in subsequent decades to renege on express or implied promises of impunity, it is hardly clear that these peaceful settlements would have been effectuated had they been held hostage in real time to demands for a settling of accounts. This concern is especially significant where the perpetrators, having operated with the tacit (or even express) approval of their faction's popular constituencies, cannot be regarded as rogue figures. Where complicity runs "all the way down," vilification of perpetrators is an attack on those constituencies' self-regard. And as a practical matter, where those constituencies do not stand defeated but have merely yielded to a compromise solution, agreement to disagree about heroes and villains may be indispensable (as, for example, in regard to the three-generations-long Israeli-Palestinian conflict).

Moreover, there seems to be a certain naïveté in the human rights community about the objectivity of legal processes where the reality is one of the winners of a political conflict imposing judgment on the vanquished adversaries. It is hardly clear that invocations of universal justice can be taken seriously in these contexts, nor is it clear why the international community ought to be affirmatively encouraging exercises of power that can easily amount to the dressing up of partisan grievances in international legal garb.

Philosophical problems run deeper still. The relationship of human rights law to criminal law reflects the supposed relationship of a wrong suffered to a wrong committed. Wrongs, after all, differ from mere harms by virtue of the indignity inherent in their infliction. A wrong suffered and a wrong committed thus appear as two sides of the same coin.[43] Such an unambiguous relationship, however, presupposes a morally ordered universe in which there cannot be genuine and irreconcilable contradictions between duties owed to those upon whom one acts and duties owed to those on whose behalf one acts. It is as though just order and tranquility constituted the baseline, a balance disturbed by the intrusion of human rights violations, such that redressing those violations restores to the universe its initial balance. Were the baseline to be reimagined as one of conflict and chaos, where struggle over the essential terms of public order exceeded institutional capacities for conflict management and where each side became convinced that the

[42]See Snyder and Vinjamuri (2003). The merits of post-transition amnesty remain hotly contested in almost every instance. For competing views of the post-Franco Spanish amnesty, which perhaps most closely resembles the non-prosecution of human rights violators in post–Chiang Kai-shek era Taiwan, compare Escudero (2014) (lamenting the amnesty) with Encarnacion (2012) (rendering a positive account of the amnesty's effects on Spain's democratic development).

[43]The relationship of human rights law to international criminal law is far more complicated than transitional justice enthusiasts, operating on the "two sides of the same coin" logic, tend to imagine. Illustratively, the term "*jus cogens* crimes," oft-repeated in the transitional justice literature, see, e.g., Sadat (2006), p. 966, n. 31, calculatedly elides the distinction between the legal status of certain human rights violations and the legal status of exercise of powers undertaken in the name of redressing those violations. Attribution of normative priority to the prohibitions does not necessarily imply attribution of normative priority to prosecutorial recourse in the face of countervailing norms of the international legal order (which may include *nullum crimen sine lege*, *ne bis in idem*, immunities, and other legal obstacles to effective prosecution).

other side respected no limits to the means of contestation, a different way of conceptualizing retrospective justice controversies might emerge.[44]

Penal accountability entails personal vilification. Such vilification presupposes not merely that the perpetrator's cause has been revealed in the course of recent history to have been a bad one, but that the perpetrator was on notice of the cause's illegitimacy and, perhaps, the invalidity—as a matter of natural law—of his or her regime's exculpatory enactments.[45] Where the prior regime did not purport to observe—at least not in emergent circumstances—currently prevalent interpretations of universal norms (which achieved their present global hegemony only very recently, and even then quite imperfectly and inconsistently), retrospective penal accountability may lack positive-law grounding (absent a penal norm previously established in the international legal order). Criminal prosecution may therefore be efficacious only through a retroactive expansion of the scope of criminal liability, in contradiction to the principle *of nullum crimen sine lege*. The imperatives of predictability and accountability in the exercise of power, requiring both notice of the line separating permitted from prohibited conduct and constraint on the exercise of discretionary judgment in the name of law, are thereby potentially compromised.[46]

Thus, an interpretation of the rights of victims that includes a right to see perpetrators criminally convicted may be regarded as both politically and jurisprudentially problematic. Characterization of the prior order as an invalid source of law—a criminal regime, rather than a regime in whose service some individuals committed crimes—may be impractical where the regime's supporters retain a viable role in liberal-democratic politics going forward, and may not be achievable in principle without recourse to an overtly partisan account of the legal norms applicable at the time and place of the conduct.

Accordingly, the nearly complete absence in the Taiwanese context of the prospect of retrospective penal accountability may actually be regarded as a feature, not a flaw: Taiwan is free to pursue Article 2(3) remedies without confronting the most pressing considerations that might countervail the most expansive interpretations of the norm.

4 Taiwan, Going Forward: Retrospective Justice Without Penal Accountability

The transitional justice question in Taiwan is essentially a question of retrospective justice. Apart from the lingering issue of the former ruling party's assets (as well as persistent problems of corruption that are not limited to the former ruling party), Taiwan's transition to a fully functioning liberal-democratic order is essentially

[44]See generally Roth (2014).

[45]For a critique of such thinking in the post-Cold War context, see Roth (2004).

[46]See generally Roth (2010).

complete. Taiwan's human rights performance is, by the most prominent gauges, exemplary, and there is no likelihood of regression to the repressive practices of the past. And with limited exceptions, such as the Kaohsiung Incident of 1979–80, the most serious abuses are too remote in time for criminal prosecutions to be contemplated, even were there the requisite political will.

The human rights community's insistence on prosecutions—the far end of the transitional justice spectrum—indicates that the full complement of measures short of penal accountability are obligatory *a fortiori*, and all the more imperative where criminal prosecution is not feasible due to the passage of time. Such measures need to include, above all, ascertainment of truth about violations and a memorialization of the past that both appropriately reaffirm the dignity of victims and bolster present and future human rights consciousness.

As Taiwan's unrecognized status excludes it from the process of Human Rights Committee evaluations of States Parties compliance with the ICCPR, the Taipei government has twice invited panels of international experts to review its human rights performance. On the topic of retrospective justice, the 2017 Review Committee spoke to the subject as follows:

> The Review Committee recognizes the fundamental value of transitional justice in the process of overcoming past wrongdoings. The Government's legislative proposals need to effectively and directly address the right to truth and the restoration of the access to justice after the lifting of martial law. In this regard, the effective access of victims and researchers to all archives should be guaranteed. The Review Committee strongly recommends that the Government, in a timely manner, initiate an inclusive truth and reconciliation process, involving also the security forces, to discuss and reflect on collective memory.[47]

Taiwan's transition thus poses centrally the question of what fidelity to human rights demands by way of memorializing past abuses. The minimum requisites should be taken to include, *inter alia*:

1. a determined effort to produce an unobscured (if not necessarily uncontroverted) factual account of the victims' sufferings and of the involvement of named regime officials and collaborators in their infliction;
2. legislative and judicial reforms designed to head off repetition of past abuses, even under what may be perceived as emergency conditions, and to establish prospectively both criminal and civil remedies for human rights violations;
3. a good-faith effort at reparation that, irrespective of the inevitable incommensurabilities, reaffirms the dignity of each individual victim, who in no case may be reduced to a mere object of the workings of historical forces (whatever else may be said about the latter); and

[47]Review of the second reports of the government of Taiwan on the implementation of the International Human Rights Covenants: Concluding observations and recommendations adopted by the International Review Committee, para. 17 (2017). http://www.humanrights.moj.gov.tw/HitCounter.asp?xItem=459857. Accessed 18 Oct 2017.

4. alteration of public monuments and scholastic practices so as to preclude state-sponsored romanticization of aspects of the past to which human rights violations were integral.[48]

In establishing a retrospective account of human rights violations and their implications, a careful distinction needs to be drawn between universal and partisan considerations. Remembering those who suffered at the hands of the dictatorship as victims, in consideration solely of their individual humanity—in isolation from, or even in spite of, any political role that they may have played on behalf of either Taiwan Independence or Chinese Communism—differs from remembering them as martyrs to a suppressed political aspiration. However valid and valuable the latter project may be in its own (partisan) right, its realization should not be confused with the fulfillment of (universal) rights obligations expressed or implied in ICCPR Article 2(3).[49] Nor is the worthy project of leveling the political playing field by stripping the former ruling party of its ill-gotten assets, strictly speaking, an implementation of ICCPR Article 2(3) obligations, except insofar as it relates to restitution of property wrongfully seized from persecuted individuals or to reparation payments for those injured by human rights violations ascribable to the KMT.

Taiwan has emerged from four decades of martial law and, over the ensuing three decades, has built a mature liberal-democratic governmental order, with repeated alternations of executive office between the parties of the dictatorship's successors and of its fierce opponents. Now that the latter party holds both

[48]The experience of the United States in the last quarter of the nineteenth century poses a cautionary tale. In the "Redemption" era that followed post-Civil War efforts by the victorious Union to restructure the politics and society of the defeated Confederate states (the 1865–1877 "Reconstruction"), a remarkable form of national reconciliation occurred, allowing the vanquished rebellion to be authoritatively remembered as co-patriotic rather than treasonous. Whatever may be said for its merits, this form of national (white) reconciliation came directly at the expense of the re-subjugation—for generations—of the Confederate order's (African-American) victims. Monuments to Confederate "heroes" have served the malign purpose not only of obscuring the flouting of human dignity inherent in the extolled "lost cause" but of rallying resistance to subsequent federal government efforts to disturb local patterns of racial subordination. See, e.g., Foner (2017).

[49]It might be noted, though, that even the human rights movement itself cannot easily strip away the political context of individual victimhood. With rare exceptions, human rights advocates and scholars make notably little effort to memorialize victims whose communities bore primary responsibility for a conflict's mass atrocities, such as German victims of World War II Allied firebombings. Additional examples included ethnic-German victims of post-World War II East-Central European "population transfers," see, e.g., Waters (2006), and Hutu victims of the Rwandan Patriotic Front's successful 1994 campaign against the genocidal Hutu Power regime, see, e.g., Human Rights Watch report: The Rwandan Patriotic Front (1999). https://www.hrw.org/reports/1999/rwanda/Geno15-8-03.htm. Accessed 18 Oct 2017. This neglect reflects justifiable concern about supplying aid and comfort to those who would rehabilitate unjust causes by relativizing or obfuscating a substantially greater pattern of atrocities. Yet the result is in tension with the orthodoxy about the unique dignity of each individual victim of human rights violations and with the idea that human rights stand above, rather than within, political contestation.

executive and legislative authority, and can draw additional impetus from ICCPR incorporation legislation passed under a KMT administration, Taiwan is in a favorable position to come to grips with the human rights violations of the past. Although the timing may seem anti-climactic, a carefully considered effort at truth and reconciliation may well benefit from the circumstance that the most severe human rights violations are now at some historical remove, and that the stakes of transitional justice at this late date exclude criminal liability for individuals respected (or even revered) by their partisans. ICCPR Article 2(3), by its specific terms and according to the object and purpose of the instrument as a whole, emphasizes the need to remediate the wrongs suffered. A single-minded pursuit of that goal, rather than of bolder objectives more naturally related to partisan advantage or revenge, may have the greatest potential to yield benefits to Taiwan's political and social development going forward.

References

Activists urge ROC to comply with UN human rights covenants (2012) Taiwan Today. http://taiwantoday.tw/news.php?unit=2,23,45&post=2264. Accessed 18 Oct 2017

Binder C (2010) The prohibition of amnesties by the Inter-American Court of Human Rights. German Law J 12:1203–1230

Bush RC (2016) Taiwan's election results, explained. Brookings Institute. https://www.brookings.edu/blog/order-from-chaos/2016/01/16/taiwans-election-results-explained/. Accessed 18 Oct 2017

Chang L (2010) A tragic beginning remembered: reflections on the dual history of the February 28 incident in post-martial law Taiwan (Institute of Chinese Studies, University of Heidelberg, Taiwan Lecture Series Working Papers Online No. 5)

Chang Y-H et al (2006) Research report on responsibility for the 228 massacre. The Memorial Foundation of 2/28, Taipei, http://www.228.org.tw/ResponsibilityReport/eng/index.htm

Chen KW (2008) Disciplining Taiwan: the Kuomintang's methods of control during the White Terror era (1947–1987). Taiwan Intl Stud Q 4(4):185–210

Encarnacion OG (2012) Justice in times of transition: lessons from the Iberian experience. Intl Stud Q 56(1):179–192

Escudero R (2014) Road to impunity: the absence of transitional justice programs in Spain. Hum Rights Q 36(1):123–146

Executive Yuan (2016) Clarifying the ill-gotten party assets act. http://english.ey.gov.tw/News_Hot_Topic.aspx?n=F80E27F3D7C30690&sms=D5327C4C848FEECB. Accessed 18 Oct 2017

Fleischauer S (2007) The 228 incident and the Taiwan independence movement's construction of a Taiwanese identity. China Inf 21(3):373–401

Foner E (2017) Confederate statues and "our" history. The New York Times. https://www.nytimes.com/2017/08/20/opinion/confederate-statues-american-history.html. Accessed 18 Oct 2017

Freedom in the World (2017a) Taiwan profile. Freedom House. https://freedomhouse.org/report/freedom-world/2017/taiwan. Accessed 18 Oct 2017

Freedom in the World (2017b) Table of country scores. Freedom House. https://freedomhouse.org/report/fiw-2017-table-country-scores. Accessed 18 Oct 2017

Hou K (2015) A tragic ethnic conflict in post-war Taiwan: reviewing the 228 uprising through the IMEP model as the primary analytical framework. East Asia 32(1):43–65

Huang P (2009) A breakthrough in human rights. Taipei Times. http://www.taipeitimes.com/News/editorials/archives/2009/04/08/2003440494. Accessed 18 Oct 2017

Human Rights Committee, Communication no. 322/1988, UN Doc. CCPR/C/51/D/322/1988 (9 Aug 1994)

Human Rights Committee, General Comment no. 20: Article 7 (Prohibition against torture, or other cruel, inhuman or degrading treatment or punishment), UN Doc. HRI/GEN/1/Rev.9 (Vol. I), p. 200 (27 May 2008)

Human Rights Committee, General Comment no. 31 [80]: The nature of the general legal obligation imposed on States Parties to the Covenant, UN Doc. CCPR/C/21/Rev.1/Add.13 (26 May 2004)

Human Rights Committee, General Comment no. 33: Obligations of States Parties under the Optional Protocol to the International Covenant on Civil and Political Rights, UN Doc. CCPR/C/GC/33 (5 Nov 2008)

Human Rights Watch Report: The Rwandan Patriotic Front (1999) https://www.hrw.org/reports/1999/rwanda/Geno15-8-03.htm. Accessed 18 Oct 2017

Hwang J-Y (2016) Transitional justice in postwar Taiwan. In: Schubert G (ed) Routledge handbook of contemporary Taiwan. Routledge, New York, pp 169–183

Hwang J-Y, Kuo M-S, Chen H-W (2017) The clouds are gathering: developments in Taiwanese constitutional law—the year 2016 in review. Intl J Const Law 15:753–762

Inter-American Commission on Human Rights [IACHR] (2016) IACHR hails determination of unconstitutionality of amnesty law in El Salvador. http://www.oas.org/en/iachr/media_center/Releases/2016/098.asp. Accessed 18 Oct 2017

Lakhani N (2017) El Salvador issues warrants for guerrillas who killed US soldiers during civil war. The Guardian. https://www.theguardian.com/world/2017/jul/25/el-salvador-guerrilla-fighters-us-soliders-helicopter-killings. Accessed 18 Oct 2017

Review of the second reports of the government of Taiwan on the implementation of the International Human Rights Covenants: concluding observations and recommendations adopted by the International Review Committee (2017). http://www.humanrights.moj.gov.tw/HitCounter.asp?xItem=459857. Accessed 18 Oct 2017

Roth BR (2004) Retrospective justice or retroactive standards? human rights as a sword in the East German leaders case. Wayne Law Rev 50:37–68

Roth BR (2010) Coming to terms with ruthlessness: sovereign equality, global pluralism, and the limits of international criminal justice. Santa Clara J Intl Law 8:231–288

Roth BR (2014) Just outcomes, overreaching rationales: how international criminal law's achievements augur flawed responses to political violence. Arizona J Intl Comp Law 31:55–80

Roy D (2003) Taiwan: a political history. Cornell University Press, Ithaca

Sadat LN (2006) Exile, amnesty, and international law. Notre Dame Law Rev 81(3):955–1036

Salvadorean ex-rebel Sanchez Ceren wins vote—officials (2014): BBC News. http://www.bbc.com/news/world-latin-america-26556803. Accessed 18 Oct 2017

Shih C, Chen M (2010) Taiwanese identity and the memories of 2-28: a case for political reconciliation. Asian Perspect 34(4):85–113

Shope ML (2012) The adoption and function of international instruments: thoughts on Taiwan's enactment of the act to implement the ICCPR and the ICESCR. Indiana Intl Comp Law Rev 22(1):159–192

Snyder J, Vinjamuri L (2003) Trials and errors: principles and pragmatism in strategies of international justice. Intl Secur 28(3):5–44

Stolojan V (2017) Transitional justice and collective memory in Taiwan: how Taiwanese society is coming to terms with its authoritarian past. China Perspect 2017(2):27–35

Teitel RG (2000) Transitional justice. Oxford University Press, New York

UN Secretary-General, The Rule of Law and Transitional Justice in Societies That Suffer or Have Suffered from Conflict, UN Doc S/2004/616 (3 Aug 2004)

Wang F (2009) Legislature ratifies UN rights treaties. Taipei Times. http://www.taipeitimes.com/News/taiwan/archives/2009/04/01/2003439900. Accessed 18 Oct 2017

Waters TW (2006) Remembering Sudetenland: on the legal construction of ethnic cleansing. Va J Intl Law 47(1):63–146

Brad R. Roth is Professor of Political Science and Law at Wayne State University in Detroit. He holds a J.D. from Harvard University (1987), an LL.M. in international and foreign law from Columbia University (1992) and a Ph.D. in jurisprudence and social policy from the University of California at Berkeley (1996). He is the author of *Governmental Illegitimacy in International Law* (Oxford University Press, 1999), *Sovereign Equality and Moral Disagreement* (Oxford University Press, 2011), and a wide range of book chapters, journal articles and commentaries dealing with questions of state sovereignty, human rights, and international criminal justice. He has authored several articles on Taiwan's international legal status and has served as a Visiting Professor of Law at National Taiwan University.

Chapter 5
The Battlefield of Transitional Justice in Taiwan: A Relational View

Chun-Hung Chen and Hung-Ling Yeh

Abstract This chapter describes how Taiwan tackles the issue of transitional justice with a dynamic approach. When assessing the progress of transitional justice, instead of taking a singular top-down or bottom-up perspective, we argue that it is important to grasp the interactive nature of the relationship between state and society. That is to say, any transitional justice mechanisms implemented are the outcomes of the interaction between government and grassroots actors. This chapter outlines the achievements so far and discusses the structural factors that have shaped the situation. The establishment of the National Human Rights Museum and the dispute over nominations for Constitutional Court Justices are taken as examples to show the interactive nature of policy and institutional design. This chapter ends by showing the implications of Taiwan's case in scholarship and praxis.

Keywords Lustration · Memory sites · State-society relations · Transitional justice

1 Introduction

The topic of transitional justice[1] has gained strong attention in academic studies and public policies at both the international and local levels since the 1980s. In the context of tackling human rights atrocities committed by prior regimes, scholars have developed different mechanisms to examine whether and how the states

[1]According to Teitel (2003), transitional justice can be defined as the conception of justice associated with periods of political change, characterized by legal responses to confront the wrongdoings of repressive predecessor regimes.

C.-H. Chen (✉)
Department of Political Science, Soochow University, Taipei, Taiwan
e-mail: cjh@scu.edu.tw

H.-L. Yeh
Department of Sociology, National Taiwan University, Taipei, Taiwan

J. A. Cohen et al. (eds.), *Taiwan and International Human Rights*, Economics, Law, and Institutions in Asia Pacific, https://doi.org/10.1007/978-981-13-0350-0_5

handle the issues of the perpetrators, the victims and the memories. These mechanisms can be classified into three main, overlapping groups: mechanisms of accountability for past crimes, including trials, truth commissions, and lustration policies;[2] victim-oriented restorative justice mechanisms, including reparations, construction of monuments, and public memory projects; and mechanisms of security and peace, including amnesties and pardons, constitutional amendments, and institutional reform.[3] However, after more than two decades, some central questions and presuppositions about the concept of transitional justice have changed. Hanson (2014) claims that the vertical and horizontal expansion of transitional justice is an important feature of the contemporary field. The state is no longer perceived as the only actor leading the transitional justice process. Debates about transitional justice have also occurred in contexts where there has been no regime change.[4] Yet in practice, local and international criminal justice systems still play a prominent role in redressing injustice. The promotion and reconstruction of "the rule of law" is still a key trend. As a result, most impact assessments of transitional justice projects have focused on institutional development.[5] Even for those who advocate a new paradigm of transitional justice, they still prioritize international law and international criminal systems.[6]

As a result, in recent years, some commentators have argued that a narrow, legalistic interpretation has impeded the potential and creativity of the concept and has been overly dominant in transitional justice. While these commentators did not assume a "simplistically rejectionist position" toward the traditional styles of transitional justice "from above," their arguments fall into two categories. In the first place, they objected to the "thin understanding" of transitional justice which tends to emphasize the formal or instrumental aspects of a legal system.[7] Subotic (2009) takes a similar view.[8] She traces the design and outcome of various mechanisms of transitional justice implemented in Serbia, Croatia, and Bosnia after the Yugoslav wars. She shows in full detail how these implementations lacked a broader consideration and understanding of post-conflict societies, partly because the international community has mainly emphasized only the arrest and trials of war crime suspects. Therefore transitional justice has been "hijacked" for very different political agendas by local politicians. Second, there are arguments that have called for more attention to be paid to practices "from below."[9] These researchers are

---

[2]Nalepa (2013) points out that lustration—a form of vetting—describes the broad set of parliamentary laws that restrict members and collaborators of former repressive regimes from holding a range of public offices, state management positions, or other jobs with strong public influence (such as in the media or academia) after the collapse of the authoritarian regime.

[3]Olsen et al. (2010), p. 1.

[4]Hanson (2014), p. 105.

[5]Merwe et al. (2009); Olsen et al., *supra* note 3.

[6]For example, Teitel (2014).

[7]Mcevoy (2008), p. 18.

[8]Subotic (2009).

[9]Mcevoy, *supra* note 7; Mcevoy and Mcgregor (2008).

interested in the actions taken by communities and organizations that have been directly affected by violent conflicts. Most of the cases can be seen in "weak states," where the corresponding mechanisms were absent due to limited state capacity. Their purpose is to broaden and to appreciate grassroots actions, since transitional justice projects and discourses should not be monopolized by the state. These commentators or actors with a "bottom-up" perspective are often critical in their evaluations of "top-down" approaches. However, in the opinion of the authors, the dichotomy of narrating transitional justice fails to adequately grasp the dynamics of the praxis of transitional justice. In analyzing cases with a strong state but slow progress in transitional justice such as Taiwan, a more dynamic viewpoint is needed.

In this chapter, a relational perspective in reviewing how Taiwan tackles the problem of transitional justice will be taken. Instead of evaluating the issues from the viewpoint of the state or of society, focus will be placed on the interactive nature of the relationship between state and society, and it will be argued that this is the core to grasping the changing reality of the field of transitional justice. That is to say, any implemented transitional justice mechanisms are the outcome of interactions between the state and grassroots organizations, even for mechanisms that seemingly came from the top. The experience in Taiwan provides evidence for this claim. Taiwan is a unique case among third-wave democratic states. While most of the new regimes have adopted a highly institutionalized way to redress historical injustice, the government in Taiwan has placed emphasis mainly on reparations for victims, while holding no one accountable. There have not been any trials or lustration law to identify or name any possible perpetrators, let alone any punishments. The same situation can be seen regarding the truth recovery mechanism. The pessimism of the government has led Taiwan to be a case with ten thousand victims but not a single perpetrator.[10] Meanwhile, some vibrant communities and civil society organizations have emerged, targeting the recovery of traumatic memory and justice. Relying on protests or policy initiatives, they have been able to attain their goals. The government has eventually endorsed some of their efforts.

It is contended that in the case of Taiwan it is the interaction between state and society that has shaped the situation of the victims and the collective memory of the masses. Consequently, instead of viewing various projects from above or from below, the boundary between "up" and "down," or between state and society, is not fixed. Instead, it is a dynamic result of the struggle among all parties involved in the field. Seeing the state-society relationship relationally rather than from a state-centric or society-centric perspective is crucial in reviewing the transitional justice achievements in Taiwan.

This chapter is organized in the following way. First, the background of transitional justice in Taiwan is discussed. After martial law was lifted in 1987, a series of appeals for rehabilitating old political cases emerged. Yet particular historical-political situations conditioned the approaches at hand. We trace the

[10]Wu (2005).

policies and attitudes of the governments, from Lee Teng-hui in the 1990s to the present day. Second, two restorative measures—the preservation of memory sites and the implementation of vetting are examined. These measures were launched by social forces and then acknowledged by the government. By investigating these current patterns of transitional justice implementation, it is concluded that a relational view is essential to grasp the changing reality of the transitional justice field. Finally, this chapter will conclude by illustrating the implications of this case study in scholarship and praxis.

2 Background: Transition Without Justice

When Japan was defeated in 1945, the government led by the Republic of China (ROC) replaced decades of colonialization in Taiwan. However, once the ROC administration was in place, the populace's joy at retrocession turned into disappointment, because people now suffered harsher political repression than during the colonial days. The Taiwanese people were repressed and silenced after the 28 February Incident and the reign of "White Terror" that followed. The temporary provisions and martial law prevented full constitutional democracy from taking effect on the island.[11] Thousands faced prosecution while some were executed for political reasons. Many Taiwanese citizens were frightened and became obedient, until the political liberalization process began in the late 1980s.

With this historical situation, Taiwan stands as a counterexample in the experience of democratization. Unlike many other countries in the third-wave democracies, Taiwan was able to carry along the process of authoritarian decomposition while avoiding economic disruptions and serious social conflicts. However, in tackling the problems of transitional justice, Taiwan is an anomaly among new democratic countries. Political scientist Naiteh Wu (2005) has shown in full detail how Taiwan's particular historical situation resulted in the phenomenon of "ten thousand victims without a single perpetrator."[12]

There is general agreement that the particular mode of democratic transition has crucial impacts on the new regime's approach to transitional justice.[13] In Taiwan's case, the previous ruling party, the Kuomintang, continued to rule Taiwan for more than a decade after the transition. Lee Teng-hui, the successor of the former dictator, Chiang Ching-kuo, launched a series of political reforms and finally led Taiwan to achieve his goal of a full-fledged democracy. Hand-picked by Chiang Ching-kuo, Lee did not have any incentive to blame Chiang and his father Chiang Kai-shek for the repression during the martial-law era. Besides, as chairman and a longstanding member of the KMT, Lee gradually took control of the

[11]Rigger (1999).

[12]Wu, *supra* note 10.

[13]Huntington (1991), Elster (2006).

party machine to confront pressures from opponents within the party and mass demonstrations by the public. The former authoritarian party and its leader transformed the country into a democracy but obstructed historical justice in the process.

In addressing the pattern of transitional justice in Taiwan, Wu argues that certain structural factors explain the Taiwanese path to transitional justice, including the type of former regime, the ethnic situation, the sustained power of the military, the performance of the authoritarian regime in economic development, and the "repression moment."[14] However, the need for brevity prevents further analysis of his theory in this chapter. Therefore, before more closely examining the confrontation between state and society, this chapter will briefly discuss the achievements and limitations of Taiwan's transitional justice.

Taiwan has over-emphasized compensation in its approach to transitional justice, while paying almost no attention to an investigation of the authoritarian system. The schemes for providing reparations for the 2/28 Incident and White Terror are markedly similar and, as of the end of 2017, the total amount of reparations was about NT$72 billion for the 2/28 Incident[15] and NT$194 billion for the White Terror.[16] While in regard to exposing the historical truth, the government has, as yet, failed to launch any official investigation mechanism. Thus, without experiencing social processes like public hearings held by a truth commission or wide dissemination of the results of research, the public's knowledge of the dark past is simplified and fragmented. Furthermore, with respect to dealing with the perpetrators, no institution has ever been initiated. This illustrates Taiwan's situation as a case of "transition without justice."

Overall, both the government and the public are not motivated to seek transitional justice and the institutional response toward the injustices of the past is lacking. The power to pursue historical justice comes directly from the victims themselves or from NGOs. The efforts on behalf of victims can roughly be divided into two periods. The promotion of rehabilitation and reparations in the 1990s resulted mostly from the struggles of the victims.[17] However, with the gradual decrease in the number of elderly victims, NGOs have become active in redressing past injustices since 2000. The NGOs devoted to transitional justice and human rights have not only cooperated with former political victims but also developed solidarity with, for example, judicial reform groups in different battlefields and the flexibility of their strategy has brought some reward. To ignore the confrontation between state and society is to misunderstand the interactive nature of any transitional justice project.

---

[14]Wu, *supra* note 10.

[15]The meeting minutes of the Memorial Foundation of 2/28. http://www.228.org.tw/recordinfo.aspx?v=D04D15D1180AF021. Accessed 9 Oct 2017.

[16]The 15th Anniversary Report of the Foundation for Compensating Improper Verdicts on Sedition and Communist Espionage Cases during the Martial-Law Period. Ni (2014).

[17]Ko (2011).

3 Battlefield of State and Society

The notion of transitional justice in Taiwan raises two distinct issues—the preservation of historical memory and small-scale lustration. To fully understand these two issues, a careful examination of the confrontation process between state and society is required.

3.1 *Preserving the Memory Sites: From Detention Centers to a National Human Rights Museum*

The first issue is the conservation of the sites of horror at two meaningful historical sites—Green Island prison and Jingmei detention center. Both were notorious during the White Terror years. Green Island prison is located on the northeast corner of Green Island, Taiwan's fourth largest offshore island, some 33 km to the east of Taitung City. The prison served as the Taiwan Provincial Security Command's Re-education Department (台灣保安司令部新生訓導處) from 1951 to 1965, and then as the Ministry of National Defense's Green Island Probation Training Prison (國防部綠島監獄感訓中心) from 1972 to 1987. The Jingmei detention center is located in the suburbs of Taipei. It was built on the original site of the Taiwan Garrison Command's Judge Advocate Office (台灣警備總司令部軍法處看守所) and operated from 1968 to 1992.[18] Thousands of political victims were prosecuted, tried and imprisoned here during the White Terror. After the lifting of martial law, some of the old buildings were abandoned while others were employed as prisons for ordinary criminals. Despite years of abandonment, the DPP government successfully transformed both sites into human rights memorial parks during the term of President Chen Shui-bian. The former prisons were reconstructed as human rights memorials to preserve and highlight the significance of Taiwan's dark past. Considering the fact that so many of the party's well-known politicians had been jailed in the 1980s, including Chen's vice-president, Annette Lu, it was reasonable for the DPP government to commemorate the traumatic events at these sites.

However, the KMT's resumption of power in 2008 caused a policy change. In February 2009, the authority of Human Rights Parks under the Council for Cultural Affairs (CCA) renamed these sites. The officials hoped to attract more visitors to the sites, but the action provoked widespread criticism and DPP politicians soon joined the chorus of objections. The spokesman of the party, Cheng Wen-Tsang (鄭文燦), accused the KMT government of wanting to wipe away history in the name of promoting culture. While the former DPP secretary-general, Wang Tuoh (王拓), who had been detained as a political prisoner, accused the KMT government of

[18]Introduction on the website of the Preparatory Office of the National Human Rights Museum. http://www.nhrm.gov.tw/Archive?uid=942. Accessed 9 Oct 2017.

"trying to erase its own ugly history."[19] However, the long-term antagonism between the KMT and DPP made the opposition party's objections look like just another contest shown on the daily news. Civil groups voiced their critical disapproval.

Several NGOs devoted to human rights and transitional justice immediately initiated protests. They were worried that the free use of the historic space would destroy the sites, and they contended that any renovation or usage should take the historical context of these sites into consideration. Their proposition received positive feedback, with hundreds of scholars, artists, and writers signing their petition, including Demos Chiang (蔣友柏), the grandson of Chiang Ching-kuo. Civil groups further mobilized the masses to attend the public hearings held by the CCA, organizing a protest surrounding the office of the CCA and calling for the minister's resignation. Among the crowd, gray-haired former victims held signs listing their sentences, creating a compelling scene.

These efforts led the CCA to reverse its decision. After collecting opinions from public hearings, the officials declared in June 2009 that they would rename the parks as "human rights cultural parks." At that time, the KMT government was conducting an organizational reform of the Executive Yuan (Cabinet) (行政院組織改造), with the purpose of streamlining the cumbersome bureaucracy. As such, most of the departments and ministers of the central government faced pressure to be downsized, merged or downgraded. However, in the case of the random transformation of the parks, human rights groups chose to argue for upgrading the legal status of the parks, as institutionalization of their names and purpose would ensure remembrance of the historical sites despite political changes. The Taiwan Association for Truth and Reconciliation took the lead to launch a petition in which it argued that the government should put more resources into the construction of the human rights parks to preserve the dark history of the island. Since both human rights parks were symbols of Taiwan's democracy, it was argued that the status of the parks should not be lower than that of the Chiang Kai-shek Memorial Hall, a symbol of the authoritarian regime which also fell under CCA jurisdiction. Considerable numbers of former political victims, human rights scholars and NGOs participated in the petition which forced the government, faced with public pressure, to make a compromise.

One month later, the new minister of the CCA, Emile Sheng (盛治仁), proclaimed that the Jingmei and Green Island human rights cultural parks would become part of the National Human Rights Museum institution that would focus solely on human rights-related exhibitions and research: "I am going to make it very clear that, from now on, human rights-related exhibitions and research on human rights issues will be a priority for the two parks."[20] While most of the cabinet positions were being downgraded and merged, the human rights museum was almost the only one that was upgraded.

---

[19]Council draws fire over human rights park plan, Taipei Times, 18 Apr 2009, at P1.

[20]Disputed parks to focus on human rights theme, Taipei Times, 23 July 2010, at P2.

This concrete measure not only secured the legal status of the parks but also ensured that a certain amount of resources would be devoted to this National Human Rights Museum each year. The preparatory office of the museum is now in full swing, working to build the collections and infrastructures, with the museum itself expected to be set up on International Museum Day in 2018.

The case of the human rights museum shows the forming of this memory project as the outcome of the battles between the government and NGOs, rather than of the good intentions of politicians or the ruling party. Reframing the ostensibly confrontational political disputes into the universal idea of human rights, the NGOs successfully achieved their goal under the KMT's conservative rule. Similar scenes occurred later in the transitional justice field. But the next battlefield involved the KMT and DPP governments.

3.2 Mini-lustration: The Recommendation and Nomination of Justices

The second issue concerns what can be called the mini-lustration. As mentioned earlier, holding no one accountable was a failure in tackling the historical injustices in Taiwan. No perpetrators were ever identified or named for their wrongdoing, let alone brought to court. No public servants were ever deprived of their official duties, since the government never implemented lustration or vetting projects. As Wu (2005) accurately points out, Taiwan's particular historical situation resulted in the phenomenon of "ten thousand victims without a single perpetrator."[21] Therefore, how perpetrators of the former regime are dealt with is a highly sensitive issue. Efforts to name names or bring perpetrators to trial are easily accused of staging witch-hunts or merely seen as part of a political power struggle. While opponents have often attacked such goals as nothing but the victor's justice, in the thirty years after martial law was lifted, none of the presidents has dared to handle this hot-button issue. However, some NGOs have raised the issue time and again in reaction to the nomination of high-ranking officials by the government. There have been two vigorous protests which have successfully obstructed nominations in recent years. Both candidates were related to the Kaohsiung Incident (高雄事件, 美麗島事件), a milestone in Taiwan's democratization of the 1980s.

On 10 December 1979, *Formosa Magazine*, published by *dangwai* (黨外, "outside the party," or independent) politicians opposing KMT rule, organized a pro-democracy rally in Kaohsiung. The crowds clashed violently with police and troops. However, opinions varied as to whether the police or the civilians should be held responsible for the clash, with the pro-government media blaming the pro-democracy side for the conflict. The next day, officials announced that they would arrest those who were responsible for the incident. The most influential

[21]Wu, *supra* note 10.

dangwai leaders, including Huang Hsin-Chieh (黃信介), Lin Yi-Hsiung (林義雄), Shih Ming-Te (施明德), Annette Lu (呂秀蓮), and Chen Chu (陳菊), were all arrested and eventually prosecuted for revolt, almost uprooting the democratic movement. The case attracted considerable media attention which prompted the KMT government, faced with public pressure at home and abroad, to hold a public trial. Even under the threat of heavy sentences, all the defendants were courageous and fearless in their statements. With the wide reporting of the process in the court, the defendants earned enormous respect and sympathy. Despite the fact that all the defendants were sentenced to years in jail, some of their wives gained tremendous victories in the following elections. The incident marked the rise of the opposition party and resulted in most of the defendants becoming heavy-weight politicians in Taiwan after being released from prison. It was widely seen as a landmark in the political liberalization of the eighties. In the 1990s, these former political prisoners received reparations and rehabilitation along with other White Terror victims. Their huge career successes also symbolized another type of reparation, paid by the people. It seems that transitional justice for the Kaohsiung Incident was to some extent achieved, but the issue of how to deal with the perpetrators did not begin to be addressed until more than twenty years later.

In recent years, nominations for Justices of the Constitutional Court have been interrupted twice because of disagreements about the background of the nominees, with two candidates faced boycotts stemming from their participation in the prosecutions of the Kaohsiung Incident. Surprisingly, the turmoil occurred not only during KMT rule, but also during the DPP government. In 2015, the Ministry of Justice was expected to recommend Lin Huei-Huang, the head of the academy for the Judiciary, as a justice of the Constitutional Court. But because Lin was one of the military prosecutors who indicted the defendants after the Kaohsiung Incident, several NGOs criticized Lin for never having shown any remorse over his role in the prosecution. The NGOs initiated a petition which claimed that Lin's accomplishments in the fields of human rights and democracy were in question and that Lin was inappropriate for such a prominent position.

The opposition party also harshly attacked the decision of the Ministry of Justice. Former Vice-President Annette Lu, who had been sentenced to a lengthy jail sentence after the incident, told the press that "Lin Huei-Huang represented the fiendish KMT. He indicted us and saw us as being guilty. His recommendation to serve as a justice of the Constitutional Court is an affront to democracy, the rule of law and human rights in Taiwan." DPP legislator Kuan Bi-Ling also charged that "Lin Huei-Huang was an accomplice of the authoritarian government. He hasn't even apologized for this incident."[22] Despite these criticisms, the Ministry of Justice still continued to defend the recommendation. In the end, however, Lin was not listed among the nominations by President Ma Ying-jeou. This outcome can be attributed to the efforts of the NGOs and DPP politicians.

[22]Justice Ministry slammed for recommending Martial-Law–era military prosecutor, Formosa News, 13 Mar 2005.

The case of the second justice candidate that faced boycott concerns, ironically, was an argument between NGOs and the DPP government. In July 2016, President Tsai Ing-wen (DPP) announced that she would nominate the Public Functionary Disciplinary Sanction Commission's Chief Commissioner Hsieh Wen-Ting (謝文定) to be Judicial Yuan president, and Judicial Yuan Secretary-General Lin Chin-Fang (林錦芳) to be vice-president. As senior officials in the judicial system, Hsieh and Lin were first seen as part of the conservative bureaucracy rather than as reformists. Soon after their nomination, however, the problems became more serious. Several NGOs committed to human rights, democracy issues and judicial reform indicated that Hsieh was a lead prosecutor in cases arising from the Zhongli Incident,[23] the Kaohsiung Incident and the murders of democracy activist Lin I-Hsiung's (林義雄) mother and twin daughters.[24] However, Hsieh didn't mention a word about these significant cases in his biography sent to the Legislative Yuan for review. The NGOs asked him to explain his role and participation in the cases, since what he had omitted was critical for transitional justice. In Hsieh's response he explained that, compared to his colleagues, his career was not as successful as the opponents had described. As for his role in the cases, he claimed that he merely tried to help his colleagues or to finish the cases apportioned to him. That is to say, he claimed not to have actively helped the authoritarian government prosecute the dissidents, insisting that he had done nothing more than show loyalty to his position.

The most astonishing moment, though, was yet to come. During a meeting with the NGOs to discuss the dispute, President Tsai questioned the criticism of Hsieh, asking "Isn't it normal that everyone chose to obey orders in the martial-law era?" Considering Tsai's commitment to transitional justice, the nomination and her response to the critics provoked a strong reaction. A wave of disapproval from civil groups like Taiwan Democracy Watch and pro-localization groups was directed at Tsai. This was especially damaging as NGOs with progressive tendencies had generally supported the DPP rather than the KMT. The NGOs did not slacken the attack, even unexpectedly comparing Tsai with her predecessor. "Former president Ma Ying-jeou (馬英九) drew heavy criticism by nominating a military judge involved in the Kaohsiung Incident as a justice. However, we were surprised that the Democratic Progressive Party administration nominated someone who held a high-level judicial position during the martial-law era to be president of the Judicial Yuan," said Chen Li-Fu (陳俐甫), director of the northern branch of the Taiwan Association of University Professors.[25] They asked Tsai to withdraw the nomination. Although Tsai had tried hard to secure the proposal, Hsieh and Lin were finally removed from consideration for the nomination.

---

[23]The Zhongli Incident was a demonstration in Novermber 1977 against ballot rigging in the Taiwanese town of Zhongli (now Zhongli District, Taoyuan City).

[24]Judicial Yuan nominee denies White Terror roles, Taipei Times, 20 July 2016, at P3.

[25]Groups slam picks for Judicial Yuan, Taipei Times, 25 July 2016, at P3.

As discussed above, the government has been reluctant to deal with the issues of transitional justice, not to mention the perpetrators. The discussion of accountability has constantly degenerated into political disputes and little attention has been given to the roles of the court or the lustration, both of which are typical transitional justice mechanisms when dealing with members of a former regime, including the core ruling elite and their personnel. The problem with these two approaches is the coercive force held by the state; sentencing perpetrators or depriving them of the right to work requires a highly institutionalized system to identify and expose their whereabouts. Therefore, dealing effectively with the issues of transitional justice requires solid coordination and operations among the administrative, judicial and legislative branches. These are inevitably top-down approaches, and it can be fairly certain that Taiwan has no such institutional foundation.

The failed recommendation and nomination of the justices proves this chapter's central argument—neither the top-down nor the bottom-up approach alone can achieve the results desired in each society's transitional justice process. It is the interaction of state and society that shapes the development of transitional justice. In the field of dealing with perpetrators in Taiwan, the state apparatus is absent and there are no other social organizations with corresponding powers at hand. That is to say, there is no mechanism to hold those who committed the historical injustices accountable. The line between memory and amnesia depends on the result of the confrontation between state and society. When the NGOs successfully revived the memory of the widely forgotten Kaohsiung Incident, the nomination of Lin Huei-Huang for justice of the Constitutional Court promptly lost its legitimacy. It can be said that the controversy symbolized a mini-lustration project launched from below, but in the end the outcome relied on the reaction of the state. This discussion shows the interactive nature of any transitional justice project. It can safely be assumed that were it not for the Kaohsiung Incident, the result might have been undecided. This example illustrates that holding a dynamic and relational perspective is essential when reviewing the implementation of transitional justice.

4 Conclusion

Transitional justice has gained global significance in the past thirty years. Local and international governing bodies have made many achievements in redressing past wrongs. While mainstream assessments of transitional justice and evaluations of their impact have exclusively focused on aspects of institution building, critical viewpoints focusing on grassroots projects have also emerged. Rather than taking a standpoint from above or from below, this chapter seeks to emphasize the relational view in reviewing the transitional justice process on Taiwan.

While Wu (2005) has already explored the structural factors that led to Taiwan being a case of transition without justice, this chapter highlights the confrontation between state and society. It is argued that the design and practice of transitional justice institutions can hardly be seen as the outcome of the goodwill or ambition of any politician or ruling party but that the results are inevitably the products of power struggles among various parties in the society. Taking the convoluted process of establishing the National Human Rights Museum and the dispute over the nominations of the Constitutional Court justices as instances, the authors have shown how the efforts of NGOs finally spurred policy changes. It is important to bear in mind the interactions between state and social actors during the making of policies or institutions and that contributions from above or below should not be downplayed or ignored. The most important lesson to bear in mind, however, is that considering only the state's or the society's perspective is insufficient for grasping the dynamics of the transitional justice process.

This discussion has some implications for both academia and practitioners. In academia, little attention has been paid to the social process behind the emergence of transitional justice projects, whereas much ink has been spent on the impact of the mechanisms. Failure to account for the interaction or confrontation between state and society may lead to a misinterpretation of the measures. The case of Taiwan shows that, although the boundary and the relations between state and society are not stable, it is the interaction between the powers from above and from below that structures the situation. Even in places like Taiwan, where robust institutions targeting past wrongs are absent, small steps toward transitional justice have been achieved. The institutional account obscures the fact that vigorous social activities are essential in dealing with the issues of transitional justice, as such, this chapter calls for greater examination of the social process in the transitional justice field.

As for practitioners, increasing resources are being invested in the establishment of institutions for globalized transitional justice. The increase in resources for transitional justice can be seen especially in the legal system whose institutions now include international courts, hybrid courts and the adoption and practice of international human rights law. In some countries, such institutions may only be a cynical way to collect international aid or to act as a tool for political antagonism. However, considering the complicated historical and political context of each post-conflict society or newly democratic regime, international forces must look more carefully in deciding what forms of intervention to take. The example from Taiwan makes it clear that the interaction between state and society shapes the outcome in the end. It seems reasonable to conclude that more resources and attention should be paid to the empowerment of local civil societies as a more robust and energetic civil society can foster more creative and productive interaction with the state.

References

Council draws fire over human rights park plan, Taipei Times, 18 Apr 2009, at P1
Disputed parks to focus on human rights theme, Taipei Times, 23 July 2010, at P2
Elster J (2006) Retribution and reparation in the transition to democracy. Cambridge University Press, Cambridge

Groups slam picks for Judicial Yuan, Taipei Times, 25 July 2016, at P3

Hansen TO (2014) The vertical and horizontal expansion of transitional justice: explanations and implications for a contested field. In: Buckley S, Beck TK, Braun C, Mieth F (eds) Transitional justice theories. Routledge, London, pp 105–124

Huntington S (1991) The third wave: democratization in the late twentieth century. University of Oklahoma Press, Norman

Introduction on the website of the Preparatory Office of National Human Rights Museum. http://www.nhrm.gov.tw/Archive?uid=942. Accessed 9 Oct 2017

Judicial Yuan nominee denies White Terror roles, Taipei Times, 20 July 2016, at P3

Justice Ministry slammed for recommending martial-law–era military prosecutor, Formosa News, 13 Mar 2005

Ko C (2011) Jieyan Shiqi Zhengzhifan Pingfanyundong De Chixu Yu Gonggonghua [戒嚴時期政治犯平反運動的持續與公共化] (The continuing and spreading of the rehabilitation of martial-law period political prisoners). In: Ho M, Lin H (eds) Shehui Yundong De Niandai: Wanjin Taiwan Ershinian Lai De Xingdongzhuyi [社會運動的年代:晚近台灣二十年來的行動主義] (Era of social movements: Taiwan's social activism in the past two decades). Socio, Taipei, pp 289–382

Mcevoy K (2008) Letting go of legalism: developing a "thicker" version of transitional justice. In: Mcevoy K, Mcgregor L (eds) Transitional justice from below: grassroots activism and the struggle for change. Hart Publishing, Oxford, pp 15–45

Mcevoy K, Mcgregor L (2008) Transitional justice from below: an agenda for research, policy and praxis. In: Mcevoy K, Mcgregor L (eds) Transitional justice from below: grassroots activism and the struggle for change. Hart Publishing, Oxford, pp 1–13

Meeting minutes of the Memorial Foundation of 2/28. http://www.228.org.tw/recordinfo.aspx?v=D04D15D1180AF021. Accessed 9 Oct 2017

Merwe HVD et al. (2009) Assessing the impact of transitional justice. USIP Press Books, Washington DC

Nalepa M (2013) Lustration. In: Stan L, Nedelsky N (eds) Encyclopedia of transitional justice. Cambridge University Press, Cambridge, pp 46–51

Ni Z (ed) (2014) Buchang Jijinhui Shiwu Zhounian Chengguo Jinian Zhuanji: 1998–2014 [補償基金會十五週年成果紀念專輯: 1998–2014] (The 15th anniversary report of the Foundation for Compensating Improper Verdicts on Sedition and Communist Espionage Cases During the Martial-Law Period: 1998–2014). Foundation for Compensating Improper Verdicts on Sedition and Communist Espionage Cases during the Martial-Law Period, Taipei

Olsen TD, Payne LA, Reiter AG (2010) Transitional justice in balance: comparing processes, weighing efficacy. USIP Press Books, Washington DC

Rigger S (1999) Politics in Taiwan: voting for democracy. Routledge, London

Subotic J (2009) Hijacked justice: dealing with the past in the Balkans. Cornell University Press, Ithaca

Teitel RG (2003) Transitional justice genealogy. Harv Hum Rts J 16:69–94

Teitel RG (2014) Globalizing transitional justice: essays for the new millennium. Oxford University Press, Oxford

Wu N (2005) Transition without justice or justice without history: transitional justice in Taiwan. Taiwan J Democracy 1(1):77–102

Chun-Hung Chen is professor in the Department of Political Science at Soochow University, and currently director of the National Human Rights Museum. He served as the director of the Chang Fo-Chuan Center for the Study of Human Rights, and the Human Rights Program at Soochow University (2015–2017). He also served as chairperson of the Taiwan Association for Truth and Reconciliation, an NGO advocating transitional justice in Taiwan (2011–2013). Dr. Chen received his Ph.D. from London School of Economics and Political Science (LSE). His current research focuses on human rights and transitional justice, with particular attention to the truth commission and memory politics.

Hung-Ling Yeh is a Ph.D. candidate in the Department of Sociology at National Taiwan University. Her research interests include political sociology, collective memory and transitional justice. Her most recent study, published in *Taiwanese Sociology* (Vol. 29, 2015), explores the institutionalization of traumatic memory in Taiwan. As chief executive officer of the Taiwan Association for Truth and Reconciliation, she also writes on transitional justice issues for a broader audience, having published in Taipei Times, China Times and many other journals in Taiwan.

Chapter 6
Frozen Trials: Political Victims and Their Quest for Justice

Cheng-Yi Huang

Abstract Before martial law was lifted in 1987, the Legislative Yuan passed the National Security Act prohibiting civilian cases tried in court martial from appealing to ordinary courts. In 1991, the Constitutional Court affirmed this legislation in its notorious J.Y. Interpretation No. 272, indicating that this was a very exceptional case, since the imposition of martial law had been maintained for over thirty-eight years. The stability of the legal system came first, and the Court had to defer to the Legislative Yuan's decision. Thereafter, the government passed a special statute to reimburse the victims or their family members without overruling the original judgments. The government had taken 10,062 cases and issued monetary compensation of over 19.6 billion NTD. However, over the years, the victims and their family members waited for rectified judgments from the courts. The quest for justice, despite the country's transition to democracy, has been delayed for thirty years. It was only in December 2017 that the Legislative Yuan passed new legislation to uphold the value of transitional justice. This chapter first articulates the legal structure of the martial-law period and then assesses the contours of the post-authoritarian government's endeavor to compensate the victims. Using the cases of the Simulated Constitutional Court, the chapter tries to analyze the critical shortcomings and potential benefits of Taiwan's model of transitional justice.

Keywords Act for promoting transitional justice · Judicial remedy National security act · Martial law · Political prisoner · Simulated Constitutional Court

C.-Y. Huang (✉)
Institutum Iurisprudentiae, Academia Sinica, Taipei, Taiwan
e-mail: chengyi@sinica.edu.tw

J. A. Cohen et al. (eds.), *Taiwan and International Human Rights*, Economics, Law, and Institutions in Asia Pacific, https://doi.org/10.1007/978-981-13-0350-0_6

1 Introduction

Reckoning with the legacy of authoritarian rule is one of the most difficult challenges for a new democracy like Taiwan.[1] As in Eastern Europe, Latin America and South Africa, the newly democratic Taiwanese government had to deal with the atrocities of past political oppression. However, what distinguished Taiwan from other transitional democracies was the fact that the authoritarian party, the KMT, a.k.a. the Chinese Nationalist Party, remained in power for a further thirteen years after martial law was lifted in 1987. From a legal perspective, a more deleterious move by the KMT is that right before martial law was lifted on 15 July 1987, the Legislative Yuan passed the National Security Act, Article 9 of which protects all the judgments rendered by court martial from appeal to ordinary courts for retrial. This legislation preempts the provisions in the Act of Martial Law, which had granted the defendants the right to appeal their cases to ordinary courts and would have taken effect immediately after martial law was lifted. By closing the door to judicial review of court-martial judgments just before opening up the government to democracy, the KMT emphatically expressed its unwillingness to resolve the issues of White Terror in the courtroom. It adopted an incomplete solution to the outcry for transitional justice, namely, monetary compensation for the victims and their families. As the result of the "compensation without appeal" policy, the political prisoners remained guilty of treason; however, they or their family members may be able to apply for reparations based on the penalty they received as a result of being court martialed.[2] They may also apply for reputational rehabilitation, which would reinstitute their entitlement to public services or pensions from the government without recognizing their innocence.

In November 2016, the Constitutional Court Simulation ("Simulation") reviewed two cases regarding political trials in the early 1950s and declared the Compensation Act for Improper Trials on Charges of Sedition and Espionage (戒嚴時期不當叛亂暨匪諜審判案件補償條例, hereinafter "White Terror Compensation Act") to be unconstitutional. Though the Simulation was not a real trial but rather a public event convened by civic groups (mainly the Taipei Bar Association and the Taiwan Association for Truth and Reconciliation), it was the first court-like process to respond to the outcry from victims' family members. Later, in December 2017, the Legislative Yuan passed the Act for Promoting Transitional Justice, which explicitly excludes the application of Article 9 of the National Security Act, nullifies the judgments of those who had already received monetary compensation, and bestows upon the Commission for Promoting Transitional Justice—an independent agency—quasi-judicial power to investigate the cases of those who had not yet received any compensation.

---

[1]Teitel (2000), p. 5.

[2]Wu (2015), p. 33.

This chapter first articulates the constitutional pathology of the White Terror and why the White Terror Compensation Act faced constitutional issues and difficulties reclaiming political justice for the victims. It then proceeds to discuss how legislation and judicial decisions post-democratization fail to deal with the political trials of the White Terror. Finally, this chapter discusses the latest legislation— the Act for Promoting Transitional Justice.

2 Institutional Background of Political Trials During the Cold War

The KMT government insisted that retrial of court-martial judgments made during 1949 and 1987 would be too costly in terms of time, effort, and money, given that martial law had been imposed on Taiwan for about four decades. For example, the government believed it would be impossible to collect the necessary evidence and testimony for cases tried by court martial in the 1950s. The government also argued that retrials would paralyze the judicial system after democratization, not only in terms of caseload but also in terms of public distrust in the judiciary. This position is worthy of some suspicion. During this time, the Ministry of Defense was trying to destroy—or hinder civil society from discovering—governmental records, documents and even private letters (like the diary Mr. Lei Chen [雷震] wrote in his cell, or the wills written by condemned prisoners).[3] Also, at the time of democratization, some notorious cases such as the political trials of the Kaohsiung Incident (美麗島事件) had taken place within the past decade. It would not have been impossible to re-collect those materials for retrial. However, going to court would, functionally, be putting the state on trial, which could shake the legitimacy of KMT rule on Taiwan. If and when the court found that the government had wrongfully convicted its political prisoners, that finding would open a Pandora's box and drive the demand for exposing more and more truth about the authoritarian government's rule.

The White Terror Foundation received 10,062 cases for monetary compensation, and as such needed to check the facts of each case by reviewing the relevant documents submitted by the applicants in order to determine the amount of compensation to be provided.[4] It took the Foundation fifteen years (1998–2014) to complete the process. If a government-funded organization could handle all these investigations and render decisions, it is very likely that a special court or a judicial commission could also have done the same job. The Court is constitutionally mandated to decide on both criminal culpability and state liability. Administrative procedures and delegated private entities, however, cannot annul the legality of

[3]Hu et al. (2015).

[4]Ni (ed.) (2014), p. 6.

judgments. Therefore, the political prisoners, even with grants of compensation, remained convicted of treason.

The thorny issue behind the rejection of judicial review is related to a complex set of dilemmas regarding loyalty, national security, political freedom, constitutional fidelity, and political identity. In the early 1950s, most political prisoners were convicted as underground members of the Chinese Communist Party (CCP). Their actions and organizations were tried in the name of sabotage against the Republic of China (ROC), since the civil war on Mainland China had recently ended with the founding of the People's Republic of China (PRC). The KMT government was extremely vigilant toward any threat to overthrow its rule in Taiwan. The CCP was, therefore, no longer regarded as a legitimate political party which could expect to be treated equally under the ROC Constitution. Instead, the CCP became a national enemy whose influence was to be eliminated from Taiwan. Even after the end of the Cold War, when the CCP and the KMT restarted political negotiations in the 1990s and despite the fact that the chairmen of the two parties met each other in Singapore in November 2015, the authoritarian regime's political prisoners are still being punished for having exercised their constitutional right to advocate communism back in the 1950s. Regardless of changes in the ruling party in 2000 and 2016, the ROC government as a whole has never admitted that its suppression of political dissidents was illegal or unconstitutional. In other words, from the government's perspective, the KMT-led government's tactics of self-preservation during 1949 and 1987 were fully justified in terms of the rule of law and constitutionalism.

The relationship between China and Taiwan makes the dilemma even more complicated since the CCP-KMT relationship has been drawn closer and the parties have intentionally chosen to ignore the issues of political suppression during the Cold War, which would have again made explicit their ideological conflicts. Officially, in 1991, the KMT-led government abolished the "Temporary Provisions Effective During the Period of National Mobilization for the Suppression of the Communist Rebellion" (動員戡亂時期臨時條款, hereinafter "Temporary Provisions"), holding that the CCP was no longer an unlawful party in Taiwan. Nevertheless, the rise of the political identity of Taiwan rather than that of China, especially after the start of the new millennium and the Sunflower Movement in 2014, called into question the KMT's authoritarian rule during the White Terror, since the younger generations wanted to know more about the KMT's past wrongdoings. Against this backdrop, the language of transitional justice appeared in President Tsai Ing-wen's inaugural speech in 2016, which announced the government's plan to submit a national report on the truth of the White Terror within three years; as such, the report is expected by May 2019. So far it is unclear how the Tsai administration, with a majority in the Legislative Yuan, will deal with political trials, the focal point of the White Terror. However, the implicit conflicts between political loyalty and political freedom continue to foster an ongoing debate surrounding not only cold cases from the past but also identity politics in the present.

3 Constitutional Pathology of White Terror

The KMT government used to claim that there were no political prisoners in Taiwan during the martial-law era.[5] Instead, the government claimed, those who had been convicted had committed treason, which was prohibited by criminal law. Thus, the government characterized itself as simply vindicating the rule of law rather than persecuting political dissidents. It is true that Article 100 of the Criminal Code, before 1992, provided that anyone who had committed an overt act with intent to destroy the republican regime, to seize the territory, or to use illegal means to change the constitution or to overthrow the government, should be sentenced to life imprisonment. Furthermore, the 1949 Suppressing Rebellion Act (懲治叛亂條例) increased the punishment to mandatory imposition of the death penalty. Therefore, positive law during the martial-law era did provide a legal basis for the government to prosecute and punish political dissidents.

However, the means and ends of these criminal statutes were highly problematic. According to the two statutes, defendants did not need to use any force or violence to carry out their plans; they could be convicted for writing or giving a speech on ideas inconsistent with the government's ideology—acts which should have enjoyed constitutional protection as freedom of expression and association.[6] Even though this kind of speech or organization can be properly limited by statute, the mandatory death penalty is not proportionate to its potential harm.[7]

Even crimes that did not trigger the mandatory imposition of the death penalty nevertheless triggered highly disproportionate penalties. For example, if convicted of joining a gathering such as a study group or a brownbag discussion that was later deemed to have been organized by a "betrayal group" (叛亂組織), one could be sentenced to life imprisonment or at least ten years in jail. These types of cases were reported to amount to 26.4% of the compensation cases.[8] Further, in 1950, the

---

[5]In the early 1970s, the Government Information Office in Taiwan still denied there were any "political prisoners." However, in October 1976, Amnesty International issued a report on the record of human rights violations by the KMT government. By then, the then president Chiang Ching-kuo admitted that there were about 254 persons convicted of sedition. In fact, a list of political prisoners had been collected and sent to the United States seeking support for freeing them in the 1970s. See Miles (2008), pp. 7–8.

[6]According to the ROC Constitution of 1947, all political parties enjoy the same constitutional protections, and the freedom of expression and association are enshrined in Articles 10 and 11. Although the Act of Suppressing Rebellions was passed after the constitutional ratification, it still inherited the essence of party rule and provided extreme and disproportionate punishment against political dissidents.

[7]Wang Tay-sheng points out that even though some judgments of court martial were based on the effective law of the day, the brutality and disproportionate punishment should be reconsidered today through the lens of the substantive rule of law. Moreover, some judgments were bluntly in violation of the effective law then, like the case of Mr. Lei Chen (雷震). These judgments should be vacated, since they represent the evil of lawlessness. See Wang (2017), pp. 11–12.

[8]Ni and Wu (2006), p. 210. There are 1,514 cases of this type among the 5,738 cases that received compensation from the Compensation Foundation.

Legislative Yuan passed the Communist Espionage Prevention Act (檢肅匪諜條例), which expanded the scope of rebellion to include those in touch with defendants under the Suppressing Rebellion Act. Citizens who knew about anyone suspected of rebellion had a duty to report to the government or face a sentence of up to seven years in prison (Articles 2 and 9). Anyone who reported on suspects of rebellion would be awarded money from the confiscated property of those convicted (Article 14).

On top of the Criminal Code, the Suppressing Rebellion Act, and the Communist Espionage Prevention Act, there were myriad laws and regulations contributing to the rise of the authoritarian state in the name of anti-communism or national security. In the heyday of martial law, the original procedural law for court martials (from 1949 to 1956) provided only two instances so the defendants could only appeal once. There was also no difference between prosecutors and judges; they performed their jobs alternately. After a thorough revision of the Code for Court Martial Procedure (軍事審判法) in 1956, there were three instances and judges had an independent role in the procedure. However, in both versions of the military tribunal procedure law, the military leaders and the commander-in-chief enjoyed the power of overrule. Once the commander-in-chief found the judgments unsatisfactory, he could order a retrial or a rewriting of the judgments.[9] Meanwhile, the jurisdiction of the court martial was extravagantly expanded to include civilians on various grounds. The Legislative Yuan amended Article 8 of the Act of Martial Law in January 1949, which provided that in the war zone (接戰地域), civilians who had violated the law of treason, espionage, social unrest, public threat, kidnapping and menace, or property damage could be tried by court martial. The governor of Taiwan, Mr. Cheng Chen, declared Taiwan a war zone and imposed martial law on May 19, 1949. However, according to the Act of Martial Law, a provincial governor did not have the power to impose martial law. Only the president had this power, and his decree had to be approved by the Legislative Yuan within one month. Therefore, the May 1949 decree of martial law by the governor of Taiwan was arguably unconstitutional but continued to be effective until 1987.

According to the legislative delegation, the Executive Yuan had announced in 1951, and later revised on several occasions, an administrative rule to solve the conflicts between court martial and ordinary courts, which gave the court martial a dominant role. No matter how the rule was amended, civilians who were charged with treason, espionage, or participating in Communist activities were all subject to a military tribunal. The legislation and administrative rules were in blatant violation of the ROC Constitution, in which Article 9 requires that "no person shall be subject to trial by a military tribunal, except those in active military service." In a 2006 report from the White Terror Foundation, 4,568 cases that had filed for compensation involved civilians as defendants, while the total number of cases receiving monetary compensation was 5,738 (i.e., as of 2006, 79.60% of monetary

[9]Su (2014), pp. 339–352.

compensation cases were filed by former civilian defendants).[10] The court martial process was the major mechanism for the government to apply severe criminal punishment against political dissidents.

In fact, the pervasive military control during the White Terror was a continuation of the pre-constitutional regime. Much of the legislation consisted of legal remnants from the military rule (軍政) or party rule (訓政) during the 1920s and 1940s. Although the Republic claimed to have entered the stage of constitutional rule (憲政), most pre-constitutional legislation was left intact, since the KMT government was not able to run periodic nationwide elections after 1948. As it turned out, the laws targeting Communist members were only changed with regard to titles and ideological language—for example, from "antirevolutionary" to the more neutral "national enemies." However, the purpose of these laws was still to secure the supremacy of KMT rule.[11]

The 1949 Suppressing Rebellion Act provided a vivid example of this model of legislative continuity and political maneuver. It was officially passed by the Legislative Yuan on 24 May 1949, in response to the collapse of political negotiations between the KMT and the CCP. However, this Act followed a long legacy of similar legislation dating back to 1928. Prior to 1949, there was a very similar piece of legislation which was effective between 25 December 1947 and 20 March 1949, entitled the Special Code for Crimes Against the State During the Communist Rebellion (戡亂時期危害國家緊急治罪條例, hereinafter "Special Code of 1947"). The Special Code of 1947 was abandoned in the hopes of making progress in the political negotiations between the KMT and the CCP. A similar piece of legislation existed before 30 January 1946, entitled the Special Code for Crimes Against the Republic (hereinafter "Special Code of 1931"), which was effectuated by the KMT's Central Executive Committee and the Legislative Yuan in March 1931 during the party-rule period.[12] The Special Code of 1931 did not use the term "counterrevolutionary" like its predecessor, the Temporary Provisions regarding Punishment for Counter-revolutionary Crimes (暫行反革命治罪法) of 1928, but it also imposed extreme punishment on those advocating opposition to the KMT government. The Special Code of 1931 was abandoned after the end of WWII, as the KMT and the CCP began political negotiations in 1945. The ebb and flow of anti-Communist legislation demonstrated that the law was used as a bargaining chip for political negotiation and was regarded as a weapon to fight against political rivals. Although it was targeted at CCP members, it could also be turned toward punishing advocates of Taiwan's independence movement or any other political activists against the KMT, like the case of the Kaohsiung Incident in 1979.

---

[10]While the White Terror Foundation ceased to function in November 2013, the total number of cases that received monetary compensation was 10,060.

[11]Lin (1992), pp. 14–17.

[12]According to the ROC's Basic Law under the party-rule period 中華民國訓政時期約法, the KMT Central Committee enjoyed the power to appoint key members in the government, including the Legislative Yuan and the Control Yuan, which were later regarded, together with the National Assembly, as Parliament in the ROC Constitution of 1947.

The controversial expansion of court-martial jurisdiction and the severe nature of anti-Communist legislation raised serious doubts about the government's use of martial law. Furthermore, based on the procedural law for court martial, the military leaders enjoyed judicial power to overrule cases. In many cases during the early 1950s, defendants were not sentenced to death in the original judgments but were later ordered by the commander-in-chief to be executed.[13] All of these cases were blocked from appeal or review after democratization.

4 Transitional Justice Legislation and Its Constitutional Issues

In the 1990s, the KMT government, under the presidency of Lee Teng-hui, passed two laws regarding political victims of the White Terror. The first one came in 1995, entitled the Act Governing the Recovery of Damage of Individual Rights During the Period of Martial Law (戒嚴時期人民受損權利回復條例). It provides a statutory basis for the reinstitution of political victims' rights to serve in public office and to receive pensions. In its 2000 amendment, victims who were taken into custody without warrants, judgments or any legal instruments also became entitled to request compensation from the government. The second bill, passed in the Legislative Yuan in May 1998 and effective from December 1998, was the Compensation Act for Wrongful Trials on Charges of Sedition and Espionage During the Martial Law Period (戒嚴時期不當審判暨匪諜審判案件補償條例, hereinafter, the Compensation Act).[14] The Compensation Act did not acknowledge the illegality of the trials by court martial but instead referred to these judgments as "wrongful" (or "improper"). The distinction between wrongful (or improper) and illegal (or unlawful, if taken from a procedural perspective) is not clear in this statute. According to the Compensation Act, whether a case was decided wrongfully would be investigated and determined by a reviewing committee consisting of scholars, experts, credible public figures, and representatives of the government. Article 8 Section 1 Paragraph 2, provides that the original judgment would not be regarded as wrongfully decided if it would also be sustained according to the current law. For example, Article 100 of the Criminal Code provides that individuals who carry out a plan of sedition with violence should be sentenced to life imprisonment, with a term of at least seven years. Therefore, if the defendants in

---

[13]Ni and Wu (2006), pp. 225–230.

[14]Jau-yuan Hwang translates the title as "improper" rather than "wrongful," which is more accurate to the original Chinese. He distinguishes the difference between the Act Governing the Recovery of Damage of Individual Rights during the Period of Martial Law [戒嚴時期權利回復條例] and the Compensation Act, claiming that the former "defends both the legality and the legitimacy of the martial-law regime," while "the [Compensation Act] allows the victims to challenge the political legitimacy of those 'formally lawful' court decisions, by calling such decisions 'improper' instead of 'unlawful.'" See Hwang (2016), p. 172.

court-martial judgments did use violence or weapons, they would not be eligible for compensation, since they would still be convicted as criminals in contemporary courts. However, the determination of whether a defendant was using violence or a weapon would be made by the reviewing committee, based on the evidence provided by the applicants and the documents collected from the martial law era. This requirement made the committee a pawn in the authoritarian apparatus. Most of the documents, such as voluntary confessions produced by secret agents or other forms of intelligence, were warrantless and probably coerced by threats of torture or other psychological pressures. These pieces of "evidence" were never properly examined through the due process of law but now operated as a baseline in the determination of wrongfulness. Even if the convicted actually was a Communist leader who organized militia and stored ammunition, the post-democratization state should have had a chance to decide the cases anew based on the values of a constitutional democracy. Otherwise, the same rationale may sustain a hypothetical scenario in which underground members of uMkhonto we Sizwe, the armed wing of ANC, should be held guilty after democratization, since they did try to use force to overthrow the apartheid government in South Africa. This approach simply ignores the legitimacy of the then government and the substance of its law. The extent to which the brutality of the KMT's authoritarian rule should be measured against the opposition camp's violent resistance is a question to be answered in a fair trial after democratic transition. However, the Compensation Act chose to silence these questions and doomed the cases to remain as they were during the White Terror.

4.1 *Underground Communist Members and Aboriginal Leaders*

During the Constitutional Court Simulation of 2016, a former Communist underground leader, Li Ma-tou, was featured in the petition raised by Legislator Huang Kuo-chang and his colleagues, which asked the court to review the constitutionality of Article 8 I (2), that excludes underground Communist Party members from the list of compensation. Mr. Li purportedly made a full confession without pressure or fear in the process of prosecution, admitting to his plot against the government as well as offering a list of his comrades. According to Article 100 of the 1935 Criminal Code and the Suppressing Rebellion Act, he was sentenced to death as a result of the court martial. When Li's daughter filed an application for compensation after democratization, the White Terror Foundation turned it down based on Article 8 I (2) of the Compensation Act, since Li had admitted to his use of force in his attempt to overthrow the government. Under the current criminal and evidentiary laws, this action remains criminal. However, according to the record compiled by Academia Historica in 2008, the intelligence agency used Mr. Li's girlfriend as a bargaining chip to elicit his confession. During the interrogation, Mr. Li promised to give sufficient information in exchange for the freedom of his girlfriend. Nevertheless, after Mr. Li made his confession and provided the list of comrades, his girlfriend, Ms. Chen Shu-duan, was executed on the same day as Mr. Li. Since democratization, there have been many memoirs and interviews of political victims revealing that the intelligence agency often used torture to elicit information and confessions. Although there is no evidence of abusive control on record (but remember, the record was created by the agency), it might not be wise to assume that the official record produced by the agency is accurate and offered due process of law. Legislator Huang and his colleagues therefore argued that Article 8 I (2) of the Compensation Act is in violation of the values of constitutional democracy based on the ROC Constitution as well as the doctrines of international human rights.

Meanwhile, Article 2 of the Compensation Act provides that only defendants charged with treason under the Criminal Code, all the crimes of the Suppressing Rebellion Act, or the Communist Espionage Prevention Act were eligible for application. In other words, the defendants charged with other crimes are not recognized as political victims and therefore are not eligible for compensation. However, as mentioned earlier, the web of the White Terror was not limited to only three statutes; it covered a myriad of regulations and legislation. For example, Voyʉe Toskʉ (Tu Hsiao-sheng, 杜孝生) was a doctor from the Tsou people, mostly living in the Ali Mountain area and his brother Uyongʉ’e Yatauyungana (Gao Yi-sheng, 高一生) was the chief administrator of Ali Township after 1945. Voyʉe and Uyongʉ’e were arrested in 1952 along with other leaders from aboriginal tribes, and were sent to the Division of Military Tribunal under the Taiwan Provincial Security Command (台灣省保安司令部) for investigation and trial by courts-martial. Later in 1954, Voyʉe was convicted of embezzlement, while Uyongʉ’e was convicted not only of embezzlement but also of treason. Voyʉe was sentenced to seventeen years imprisonment but was released two years later. However, Uyongʉ’e was not so fortunate. He was sentenced to death and executed immediately after the verdict. In fact, they were under surveillance by the intelligence department because the KMT government was afraid that the aboriginal people would assist Communist members to hide and develop their underground network in the area of Ali Mountain. Voyʉe had graduated from the Medical School of Taipei Imperial University (later renamed National Taiwan University after WWII) in 1945 and had returned to Ali Mountain to serve as the director of the local health bureau. According to the material presented in the courts-martial. He had not been heavily involved in his big brother’s business. The office of the district attorney in Chia-yi County was also investigating the case of embezzlement but dropped the charge for lack of evidence. The DA’s office had no jurisdiction over treason, so it did not investigate that charge.

Voyʉe Toskʉ lived the rest of his life mostly in silence and passed away in 2001. Family members of Uyongʉ’e Yatauyungana had successfully applied for monetary compensation after the Compensation Act went into effect. However, the application by the children of Voyʉe Toskʉ was rejected by the White Terror Foundation twice, because Voyʉe’s charge was not covered by the crimes listed in Article 2 of the Compensation Act. In fact, the whole case compiled by the intelligence department and courts marital not only labeled Uyongʉ'e Yatauyungana but also Voyʉe Toskʉ as well as the other defendants under one single case name, which had the result that they were all treated as one group. The action against the Tsou leadership in the early days of KMT rule in Taiwan successfully crushed the political elites left over from the Japanese colonial period and replaced them with a more collaborative group fostered by the KMT itself. The goal of the KMT's cleansing project in targeting Uyongʉ'e Yatauyungana and his colleagues and supporters is apparent. However, the statutory definition of political victim enshrined in the Compensation Act has misinterpreted and torn apart the full picture of political oppression carried out by the KMT. First of all, it unduly limited the scope of political prisoners to the defendants charged with the three statutes described above only. Secondly, it underestimated the pre-trial informal process of political oppression. Thirdly, it denied the facts that there were still many people who were not charged with the three statutes but were put into jails since they had challenged the government. Therefore, the Constitutional Court Simulation took the case of Voyʉe Toskʉ to solve these issues.

The Justices of the Constitutional Court Simulation consisted of a judge from the appeals court, two practicing lawyers, four law professors, and a scholar of philosophy.[15] During the two days of oral argument, the court also invited international jurists to serve as expert witness, including Richard Goldstone of South Africa, Marek Zubik of Poland, Javier Couso of Chile, and Susanne Karstedt of Germany, to discuss their experience and knowledge of transitional justice in their respective countries. Voyʉe Toskʉ's youngest son, Mr. Ming-che Tu, in front of the bench, gave his testimony about the diaspora and sufferings of their family, which was the most heart-wrenching moment during the oral argument. After one month of deliberation, the simulated court delivered a judgment declaring Article 2 and Article 8 I (2) of the Compensation Act and Article 9 of the National Security Act to be unconstitutional. It cited the testimony of three expert witnesses (Judges Goldstone, Zubik, and Dr. Couso) to reason that even during an emergency, the state cannot overstep the constitutional limits of the separation of powers. Once the state concentrates all constitutional powers in one single party without any effective checks and balances, it falls into the condition of an illegitimate state (*Unrechtstaat*). The court opined that the ultimate goal of constitutional democracy is to secure the fundamental promise of rights protection. In an illegitimate state, constitutional guarantees like separation of powers and rights protection are futile and law becomes a convenient machinery to serve one single party's political ideology. Based on the testimony of Wang Yun-ju, a professor of constitutional

[15]Originally, there were nine on the bench but a professor of modern Taiwan history was appointed as president of the 2/28 Compensation Foundation before the court heard the case so he resigned from the bench.

law, modern German history shows us that even with a functioning legal system (i.e., the Parliament passes laws and courts apply them), the law may fall prey to totalitarian dictatorship (*totalitäre Diktatur*) once it is shaped to serve a designated political ideology and the will and interest of certain political leaders.

4.2 Illegitimacy of the KMT Government and Its Laws

In response to the argument that the KMT government ruled in accordance with the ROC Constitution and the rule of law, the simulated court combed through the emergency powers of 1949 and the practice of the ROC Constitution in Taiwan before 1991. The ROC Constitution was passed by the constituent meeting of the National Assembly in December 1946 and went into effect the next December. The first meeting of the Inaugural National Assembly was convened in March 1948 when the CCP won several key victories in northern China. Owing to the deteriorating conditions in the country, members of the National Assembly passed the Temporary Provisions Effective During the Period of National Mobilization for Suppression of the Communist Rebellion (動員戡亂時期臨時條款, hereinafter the Temporary Provisions) before electing Chiang Kai-shek as the first president. The original design of the Temporary Provisions was very simple. It conferred emergency powers to the president without any oversight of the Legislative Yuan. However, it also provided that the exceptional conditions would only be effective for two and a half years. Therefore, the National Assembly would have to decide whether to renew or to abolish the Temporary Provisions before November 1950. However, the ROC government lost most of its territory and relocated to Taiwan in December 1949, while the CCP declared the founding of the PRC on 1 October 1949.

Among its 3,045 members, only a little more than a half (1,578) of the National Assembly moved to Taiwan with the KMT. However, the Constitution required at least two-thirds of the members to be present to revise the Constitution (Article 174), which would be necessary if they were to extend the Temporary Provisions. Also, the term limit of the National Assembly was six years, which meant that the first term of the National Assembly should have ended in December 1953. However, Article 28 of the Constitution provides that "the term of office of the delegates to each National Assembly shall terminate on the day on which the next National Assembly convenes." Therefore, President Chiang Kai-shek seized the loophole by issuing a statement to the National Assembly, "the election for the next term of the National Assembly is *de facto* implausible, so the delegates of the first term shall remain in office until the day on which the next National Assembly convenes."[16]

[16]Zong Tong Fu Gongbao [總統府公報] (Office of the President Gazette, Taiwan), no. 430 (September 1953), pp. 2–3.

However, the Constitution does not provide the same language for the Legislative Yuan and the Control Yuan, whose term limits are clearly defined as three years and six years respectively. Therefore, the Constitutional Court (i.e., the Justices collectively) weighed in, first to solve the reelection issue of the Legislative and Control Yuans in 1954 and then to solve the threshold issue of the National Assembly in 1960. In J.Y. Interpretation No. 31 of 1954, the Constitutional Court ruled, "owing to the national emergency, the election for the Legislative Yuan and the Control Yuan is physically implausible. However, if the two branches were to stop functioning for this reason, it would contradict the original intent of the Constitution to set up five branches. Therefore, members of the Legislative Yuan and the Control Yuan shall continue to fulfill their duty before the day when the second term can be legally elected and convened." Meanwhile, the Legislative Yuan passed a bill in 1953 to allow the substitution of the National Assembly's members. The statute invalidated the membership of those who stayed in Mainland China and allowed people from the same constituency to fill the vacuum.[17] By so doing, the second meeting of the first National Assembly could be successfully convened and could extend the effective period of the Temporary Provisions.

Furthermore, in J.Y. Interpretation No. 85 of 1960, the Justices came up with the reasoning that the "total number of National Assembly delegates" means those who were elected through a legal process and those who were able to attend the meeting at the location of the Central Government.[18] The Court explained that the framers did not foresee the tremendous political catastrophe that the Republic faced, so it had to interpret the Constitution so as to facilitate the functioning of the National Assembly and thereby maintain the Republic. Therefore, the Court constitutionalized the unlimited terms of the non-elected National Assembly members, which gave political leaders (i.e., Presidents) leeway to control the whole government, since the judicial branch had consolidated the non-democratic foundation of the KMT government. In fact, this scenario destroyed the check-and-balance mechanism enshrined in the Constitution, since both the Court and the representative institutions now only listened to the President. Within one month of J.Y. Interpretation No. 85, the National Assembly convened a second meeting and amended the Temporary Provisions to allow President Chiang Kai-shek to be reelected as President without any term limits. It was also the President who would decide when the "Period of Communist Rebellion" would end. The inaugural National Assembly, Legislative Yuan, and Control Yuan continued to play the role of sham "representative institutions" until the abolition of the Temporary Provisions in 1991.

Based on its historical analysis, the Constitutional Court Simulation concluded that the ROC constitution was substantively abandoned between 1949 and 1991. President Chiang Kai-shek had created a party-state which concentrated all state

[17]Di Yi Jie Guo Min Da Hui Dai Biao Chu Que Di Bu Chong Tiao Li [第一屆國民大會代表出缺遞充條例] (Act Governing Replacement of Any Vacant Seat on the First Term National Assembly) (abolished in 1988, Taiwan).

[18]Si Fa Yuan Da Fa Guan Jie Shi Shizi Di 85 Hao [Justices of the Constitutional Court, Judicial Yuan, Interpretation No. 85] (12 Feb 1960) (Taiwan).

power in himself, without any democratic checks. The President also set up the secret police and controlled the intelligence agency as well as the military. During the White Terror period, the military tribunal had to obey the President's final decision on sentencing. Therefore, the procedures and the judgments of courts-martial were apparently unconstitutional. The illegitimate state used the formal law as a tool to control the people in Taiwan rather than to confine state power as the constitution required. The simulated court wrote in a unanimous opinion that all the trials conducted during the White Terror period must be allowed to appeal to the ordinary courts. Articles 2 and 8 I (2) of the Compensation Act were held to be invalid since they obstructed these political victims' right to the truth and violated the constitutional values of a liberal democracy.

4.3 Act for Promoting Transitional Justice of 2017

In response to political pressure from civil society after the 2016 presidential election, the Legislative Yuan initiated legislation for promoting transitional justice in June 2016 and finally passed it in December 2017. The most prominent feature of this legislation is that it expressly mentions that Article 9 of the National Security Act will not be applied to any case conducted by court martial during the martial-law era. The political victims who had received money from the Compensation Foundation were to be acquitted immediately after the law entered into effect. For those who are not regarded as political victims by the Compensation Foundation, they and their family members may petition the newly established Commission for Promoting Transitional Justice, which will be an independent agency under the Executive Yuan. The Commission enjoys broad investigative powers and can search for related governmental dockets, if necessary. It can also invite relevant persons to give testimony about what happened during the martial-law period. If the petitioners receive unfavorable decisions from the Commission, they can appeal the cases to the Appellate Court. This is a great leap for the victims, but the KMT legislators intend to bring a suit to the Constitutional Court regarding the constitutionality of the Act. It remains unclear the fate of this Act and the operation of the Commission.

5 Concluding Remarks

According to the White Terror Foundation, there were 10,067 cases filed for monetary compensation after the Compensation Act went into effect.[19] Among these cases, 7,965 applicants were awarded monetary compensation totaling

[19]Ni (ed.) (2014), p. 36.

19.9 billion NTD (roughly 650 million USD).[20] Only 20% of the applications (2,036) were turned down (1,940 cases failed on procedural grounds, and 96 cases—less than 1% of all cases filed—failed on merit). Nevertheless, under the Compensation Act the government has unduly abstained from inquiring into the truth of the White Terror. Money cannot buy the truth, nor can money bury the ghosts of the past.

Thirty years after martial law was lifted, Taiwanese society is still on a quest for the full picture of what happened during the martial-law era. Although some victims eventually received monetary compensation, indicating that they had indeed been victimized, they are still formally convicted criminals, supposedly guilty of treason or espionage. But are they really betrayers of the state? And what has the state done to them? The KMT government has blocked their appeals, a right that had been granted to victims under the Act of Martial Law. These cases remain frozen in 2017, as the Constitutional Court upheld the constitutionality of Article 9 of the National Security Act in J.Y. Interpretation No. 272. However, the Constitutional Court also left a crack in the iron wall, as it mentioned its deference to legislative discretion. So only when the Legislative Yuan decides to reopen these frozen cases will the state endeavor to pursue rights protection and demonstrate the audacity to face the pathology of the authoritarian state, which was the very root of the White Terror.

References

Hu S-W [胡淑雯], Lu C-Y [吕蒼一], Chen Z-Y [陳宗延], Yang M-H [楊美紅], Lo Y-J [羅毓嘉], Lin Y-C [林易澄] (2015) Wu Fa Song Da De Yi Shu: Ji Na Xie Zai Kong Bu Nian Dai Shi Luo De Ren [無法送達的遺書:記那些在恐怖年代失落的人] (The letter never delivered: in memory of those who disappeared in the White Terror). Acropolis, Taipei

Hwang J-Y (2016) Transitional justice in postwar Taiwan. In: Schubert G (ed) Routledge handbook of contemporary Taiwan. Routledge, London, pp. 168–173

Lin S-T [林山田] (1992) Min Guo Cheng Li Zhi Jin Zhi Te Bie Xing Fa [民國成立至今之特別刑法] (Special criminal statutes since the founding of the Republic of China). Tai Da Fa Xue Lun Cong [臺大法學論叢] (NTU Law J) 22(1):1–32

Miles L (2008) Mei Xin Yi Ren Quan Xiang Guan Shu Xin Ji (1) [梅心怡人權相關書信集(1)] (Human rights as ends not means, human rights-related correspondence of Lynn Miles). Wu San-lien Taiwan Shi Liao Ji Jin Hui [吳三連臺灣史料基金會] (Wu San-lien Foundation for Taiwan Historical Materials), Taipei

Ni T-H [倪子修] (ed) (2014) Bu Chang Ji Jin Hui Shi Wu Zhou Nian Cheng Guo Ji Nian Zhuan Ji (1998–2014) [補償基金會十五週年成果紀念專輯 (1998–2014)] (The task report on the fifteenth anniversary of the Compensation Foundation). Cai Tuan Fa Ren Jie Yan Shi Qi Bu Dang Pan Luan Ji Fei Die Shen Pan An Jian Bu Chang Ji Jin Hui [財團法人戒嚴時期不當叛亂暨匪諜審判案件補償基金會] (Compensation Foundation for wrongful trials on charges of sedition and espionage during the martial-law period), Taipei

[20]*Id*., at p. 42.

Ni T-H [倪子修], Wu Z-C [吳祚丞] (2006) Jie Yan Shi Qi Chu Zhi Pan Luan Fan Zhi Te Bie Shi Ti Fa Ji Cheng Xu Fa [戒嚴時期處置叛亂犯之特別實體法及程序法] (Special substantive and procedural law for seditious criminals during the period of martial law). Cai Tuan Fa Ren Jie Yan Shi Qi Bu Dang Pan Luan Ji Fei Die Shen Pan An Jian Bu Chang Ji Jin Hui [財團法人戒嚴時期不當叛亂暨匪諜審判案件補償基金會] (Compensation Foundation for wrongful trials on charges of sedition and espionage during the martial-law period), Taipei

Su R-Q [蘇瑞鏘] (2014) Bai Se Kong Bu Zai Tai Wan: Zhan Hou Tai Wan Zheng Zhi An Jian Zhi Chu Zhi [白色恐怖在台灣:戰後台灣政治案件之處置] (White terror in Taiwan: political trials in post-WWII Taiwan). Daw Shiang Publishing Co., Ltd., Taipei

Teitel R (2000) Transitional justice. Oxford University Press, Oxford

Wang T-S [王泰升] (2017) Lun Taiwan De Zhuan Xing Zheng Yi: Guo Qu, Xian Zai, Yu Wei Lai Dui Hua [論台灣的轉型正義:過去、現在與未來的對話] (Transitional justice in Taiwan: a dialogue among the past, the present and the future). Taiwan Fa Xue Za Zhi [台灣法學雜誌] (Taiwan Law J) 315:1–24

Wu N-D [吳乃德] (2015) Guo Jia Dui Shou Hai Zhe De Pei Chang/ Bu Chang [國家對受害者的賠償/補償] (Compensation/reparation by the state for political victims). In: Taiwan Association for Truth and Reconciliation [臺灣民間真相與和解促進會] (ed), Ji Yi Yu Yi Wang De Dou Zheng (vol II) [記憶與遺忘的鬥爭(卷二)] (The struggle of memory against forgetting: a status report on transitional justice in Taiwan, vol 2). Acropolis, Taipei

Cheng-Yi Huang is Associate Research Professor at Institutum Iurisprudentiae, Academia Sinica. He mostly writes about and conducts research on constitutional theory, comparative administrative law, democratic theory, Taiwan legal history, and regulation. From 2016 to 2018, he served as chairperson of the Taiwan Association for Truth and Reconciliation, an NGO advocating transitional justice in Taiwan. Dr. Huang worked at Baker Mckenzie's Taipei Office after graduating from the College of Law, National Taiwan University. He received his J.S.D. from the University of Chicago Law School. His dissertation was awarded Honorable Mention for the Best Dissertation by the Law & Society Association in 2010. He has contributed to *Comparative Administrative Law* (Rose-Ackerman, Lindseth, and Emerson eds., 2017), *Comparative Law and Regulation* (Bignami and Zaring eds., 2016), and *Oxford Handbook on Comparative Administrative Law* (Cane et al., forthcoming). He is editing a book, *Constitutionalizing Transitional Justice* (Routledge), focusing on the role of the constitution and Constitutional Courts in the process of transitional justice in South Africa, Eastern Europe, Latin America and East Asia. His articles appear in *Law & Social Inquiry*, *NTU Law Journal*, *Taiwan Journal of Democracy*, etc. He is also a frequent contributor to local newspapers and online magazines on law and politics in Taiwan.

Chapter 7
Towards an Analytical Framework of Constitutionalism in East Asia: The Case of Taiwan

Chien-Chih Lin

Abstract Recent years have witnessed the reemergence of discussions on Confucian constitutionalism, communitarian constitutionalism, and Asian values. Despite the differences of these concepts, all reject Western liberal constitutionalism, emphasizing that Asian countries should prioritize social and economic rights over civil and political rights. Nevertheless, this dichotomy in fact does not hold in Taiwan and many other East Asian jurisdictions. This chapter suggests that, on the one hand, constitutionalism in East Asia is inevitably a blend of liberal constitutionalism and Confucian constitutionalism. Namely, in East Asia, the differences between democracies and dictatorships in this regard are often a matter of degree, not of kind. On the other hand, human rights are better protected in Taiwan than in most other Asian countries because the progress in human rights is taking place concomitantly with the decline of Confucianism. From this perspective, it is plausible that Taiwan will become the only democracy among societies that predominantly are comprised of people of Chinese descent precisely because it discards Confucianism and Asian values, which serve as a veneer of legitimacy for autocrats to justify dictatorship.

Keywords Confucian constitutionalism · China · East Asian constitutionalism Korea · Vietnam

Foreword

As a result of China's economic boom, arguments regarding Asian values, Confucian constitutionalism, or communitarian constitutionalism have reemerged in recent years. Despite the differences among these concepts, all reject Western liberal constitutionalism, emphasizing stability and meritocracy instead of liberty and democracy. In Cambodia, China, Malaysia, Singapore, and Vietnam, proponents of such arguments maintain that only a small number of elites should be at the helm of a country, since popular sovereignty may be short-sighted, overwhelmed

C.-C. Lin (✉)
Institutum Iurisprudentiae, Academia Sinica, Taipei, Taiwan
e-mail: chienchihlin@gate.sinica.edu.tw

J. A. Cohen et al. (eds.), *Taiwan and International Human Rights*, Economics, Law, and Institutions in Asia Pacific, https://doi.org/10.1007/978-981-13-0350-0_7

by short-term interest or frenzy. Given their different sociopolitical backgrounds, they continue, Asian countries should enshrine different paradigms of constitutionalism, prioritizing social and economic rights over civil and political rights, because the latter are luxuries that are not affordable in the face of poverty.[1] Nevertheless, this dichotomy does not hold in Taiwan. In fact, the contrast is misleading in the East Asian context in the sense that most countries in this region have been influenced historically both by Western liberal constitutionalism and Confucian constitutionalism, and so constitutional practices in these jurisdictions usually reflect an amalgam of both ideologies. Put differently, the difference between these various jurisdictions is a matter of degree, not of kind.

Yet the degree matters. This chapter suggests that human rights—be they negative or positive, social or political—are better protected in Taiwan than in most other East Asian countries precisely because Taiwan gradually discarded the notion of Confucian constitutionalism it had embraced during its authoritarian period. As one of the Four Asian Tigers, Taiwan has made great advances in protecting human rights after democratization. To give just a few examples: it has one of the best national health insurance systems in the world; cultural diversity is generally respected; intense political competition has led to three peaceful party turnovers; and same-sex marriage is publicly debated not only in the streets but also in the Constitutional Court, an issue that is still taboo in many Asian societies. Contrary to what proponents of Confucian constitutionalism have suggested, progress in human rights has been taking place concomitantly with the declining influence of Confucianism, which had impeded the implementation and advancement of fundamental rights in Taiwan. From this perspective, it is plausible that Taiwan will become the only democracy among the societies that are predominantly comprised of people of Chinese descent precisely because it has endeavored to discard Confucianism and Asian values, which often serve as a veneer of legitimacy for autocrats to justify dictatorship.

Constitutional development in this region prompts a broader theoretical debate on the concept of East Asian constitutionalism. When discussing different models of constitutionalism, much ink has been spilled over the contrasts between the American model and the European model.[2] However, scholars in comparative constitutional law have identified three kinds of constitutional practice in East Asia from different, and antithetical, angles. Some argue that after separating the chaff from the wheat, some elements of traditional Confucianism could become crucial ingredients of East Asian constitutionalism. By contrast, while rejecting Asian values, others suggest that constitutional development in East Asia possesses its own characteristics that do not mechanically mirror or transplant Western liberal constitutionalism. Still others aver that neither model can properly describe constitutional development in East Asia: on the one hand, Confucian constitutionalism is highly controversial and not largely prevalent in East Asian countries; on the

[1]See Bell (2015), at pp. 1–109.

[2]See e.g., Rosenfeld (2004), at p. 633.

other hand, the "characteristics" are not particular to constitutional development in this region. Intriguingly, all three camps refer to Taiwan as an example to buttress their stances.

Based on constitutional development in Taiwan in recent decades, the rest of this chapter proceeds as follows. After briefly introducing the aforementioned models of East Asian constitutionalism, Section 1 builds a matrix that illustrates a typology of constitutional practice in some East Asian countries, depending on the impacts of Confucian constitutionalism and liberal constitutionalism. This typology may provide a useful analytical framework for students of comparative constitutional law to study constitutionalism in East Asia. Section 2 turns to Taiwan, articulating the progress in human rights protection and its relationship with the rise and fall of Confucian influence. Influenced simultaneously by liberal constitutionalism and Confucianism, constitutional development in Taiwan has been a tug of war between the two ideologies, with the former eventually prevailing in most, but not yet all, cases. Section 3 concludes with some normative reflections, hoping to breathe new life into the debate on East Asian constitutionalism.

1 Towards a Typology of Constitutionalism in East Asia

In East and Southeast Asia, modern constitutionalism began to develop roughly after the end of the Second World War, when the specter of colonialization that had previously hovered over this region gradually dissipated. Many countries have since promulgated new constitutions, enshrined fundamental rights, and established new constitutional tribunals as the guardians of the constitution. This does not imply that constitutional development in this region has blossomed; instead, the progress is usually two steps forward, one step back. Despite (or perhaps because of) the arduous development in the past six decades, some scholars have started to ask whether there is a distinct model of constitutionalism in East Asian countries, or whether East Asia simply imports Western liberal constitutionalism, which stresses, *inter alia*, limited government, the separation of powers, checks and balances, protection of fundamental rights, and some sort of judicial review. Based on the experiences of three constitutional democracies, Professor Yeh and Professor Chang propose a model of East Asian constitutionalism that features instrumental constitutional state-building, textual and institutional continuity, reactive and cautious judicial review, and a wide range of rights.[3] This version of East Asian constitutionalism, they argue, departs from the typical understanding of liberal constitutionalism, transitional constitutionalism, and Asian values. While acknowledging that East Asian constitutionalism shares some similarities with Western liberal constitutionalism and Asian values, they maintain that constitutional developments in Japan, Korea, and Taiwan have demonstrated a variety of

[3]Yeh and Chang (2011), at p. 805.

characteristics not found in other models. Albeit illuminating, one obvious deficiency of this model is that it excludes constitutional implementation in all semi-democratic regimes in East Asia. Given that authoritarian constitutionalism is conceptually possible[4] and that many East Asian jurisdictions are not yet fully democratic, their argument is not comprehensive enough.[5]

Alternatively, there are various versions of Confucian constitutionalism—that is, constitutional practice influenced by Confucianism. Confucianism is the wellspring of legal thinking and has had a profound impact on legal developments in many countries.[6] Since the Han dynasty in 221 B.C., it has become the dominant socio-political ideology in China and with the expansion of the Chinese Empire it spread to neighboring countries, such as Japan, Korea, and Vietnam. Briefly, Confucianism stresses a hierarchical social structure to maintain an ordered and harmonious society.[7] To achieve this goal, it emphasizes the principles of patriarchy, meritocracy, and filial piety.[8] Not surprisingly, it "is often viewed as running counter to the liberal principle of treating people equally and impartially."[9] In the private domain, Confucianism undergirds patriarchy and reinforces gender inequality; in the public field, it has been used to justify illiberal regimes in which leaders are selected not by popular vote but by certain notions of "merit."

Despite all these factors repugnant to modern liberal constitutionalism, which prioritizes the separation of powers and the protection of human rights, a number of Confucian and constitutional scholars have endeavored to distill "constitutionalist" elements from Confucianism. Depending on the affinities they believe to exist between Confucianism and liberal constitutionalism, one may distinguish two kinds of Confucian constitutionalism: ideational Confucian constitutionalism and institutional Confucian constitutionalism.[10] The former includes but is not limited to the concepts of *li* (rules of decorum, rituals), *ren* (humaneness), *minben* (people as a basis), and *zheng ming* (the rectification of names), which are often cited as examples to indicate the compatibility of Confucianism and liberal constitutionalism.[11] For instance, the conception of *minben*—that people are the foundation of a country—emphasizes the democratic accountability of a government.[12] In practice, both politicians and judges in East Asia have invoked these ideas to support their stances. Lee Kuan Yew is the most well-known example, but he is not alone.

---

[4]See Tushnet (2015), at p. 391; Moustafa and Ginsburg eds. (2008), at pp. 1–2; Ginsburg and Simpser eds. (2014), at pp. 1–3.

[5]To be fair, they do not claim this. Neither do they reject the possibility that there may be other models of East Asian constitutionalism.

[6]Ginsburg (2012), at p. 88.

[7]Shin (2012), at p. 74.

[8]Tu et al. (1992), at p. 55.

[9]Shin, *supra* note 7, at p. 183.

[10]Ginsburg, *supra* note 6, at pp. 791–796.

[11]Hahm (2009), at p. 135; Kim (2016), at pp. 107–137; Son (2012), at pp. 152–209; Qing (2013), at pp. 27–43.

[12]But see He (2016), at p. 64.

At least one justice of the Korean Constitutional Court has also invoked, *inter alia*, the concept of righteousness, benevolence, and the feeling of commiseration in his personal opinions.[13]

Furthermore, other scholars have likened several modern political and legal institutions to the ancient practices of Confucianism. Judicial review, for example, has been compared to the remonstrance in some circumstances during the imperial period.[14] Specifically, apex courts in East Asia sometimes issue so-called "admonition decisions"—that is, a euphemistic way to declare potential unconstitutionality without directly challenging the political leaders. Other institutions include the meritocratic selection of state agents and bureaucratic hierarchies.[15] Among them, the most well-known examples are the Control Yuan and the Examination Yuan in Taiwan. Recently, there has been a call to establish a Control Yuan-like institution in the People's Republic of China, with an eye to combating corruption and reducing agency costs. All these suggest that constitutional development in East Asia is not completely immune from Confucian thinking. At first glance, a Confucian constitutionalism that has been institutionalized seems to be more durable as a result of path dependence. In reality, however, this is not necessarily the case, since the political salience of an institution may ebb and flow over time. By contrast, Confucian ideation, like other cultural traditions, may be deeply rooted in the mindset of a society and as a result be more resilient to social change.

All these arguments ring true in certain contexts, but scant attention has been paid to the dynamics of constitutional evolution in East Asian jurisdictions. As alluded to above, most if not all countries in this region have been influenced by both modern liberal constitutionalism and Confucian constitutionalism. Although most people, even those in authoritarian regimes, prefer liberal constitutionalism to Confucianism,[16] the latter has not been completely extinguished. Therefore, the issue is not whether constitutionalism and Confucianism are compatible or not as they have already coexisted with each other for decades.[17] On the one hand, this blend is reflected in a poll finding that "[i]n the minds of most people in Confucian Asia today, no strict choice has been made between meritocracy and democracy."[18] On the other hand, this by no means implies both ideologies are equally influential. As time goes by, the importance of the two ideologies may wax or wane, depending on the political, social, and economic environments. From this perspective, this chapter proposes a general framework of East Asian constitutionalism, two dimensions of which are respectively the impact of liberal constitutionalism and the

[13]UN Office High Comm'r for Human Rights, Conscientious Objection of Military Service Case, UN Doc HR/PUB/12/1, UN Sales No. E.12.XIV.3 (2004).

[14]Ginsburg (2002), at pp. 791–796.

[15]Ginsburg, *supra* note 6, at p. 19.

[16]Shin (2013), at p. 259.

[17]Admittedly, whether Confucianism and liberal constitutionalism are normatively compatible is still a debatable issue, which is beyond the scope of this chapter.

[18]Shin, *supra* note 16, at p. 282.

impact of Confucian constitutionalism. It is noteworthy that the strength (and weakness) of the impact in each jurisdiction is hard to measure with any degree of precision and therefore is used in a relative and impressionistic sense. Also, it should be emphasized that all societies are dynamic and the influence of any ideology may rise and fall over time. For instance, Korea is now less Confucian than it was in the past, but it may still be more Confucian than Taiwan currently is (Fig. 1).

Specifically, countries in the right-hand cells, such as South Korea and Taiwan, are strong constitutional democracies that champion individual rights, judicial review, and democracy. Simultaneously, Confucianism continues to shape the legal order in these countries as well, particularly in the domain of family law. Between the two jurisdictions, Confucianism has penetrated far more into South Korea than into Taiwan, to the extent that "Confucianism in Korea was intensified and became more Confucian than Confucius."[19] Intriguingly, this has not prevented South Korea from embracing liberal constitutionalism. One indicator is judicial performance: the South Korean Constitutional Court is arguably the most active constitutional tribunal in East Asia. In recent years, it has dissolved a political party, impeached a president, and declared a myriad of laws unconstitutional. In Taiwan, where liberal constitutionalism is equally entrenched, the legacy of Confucianism is embodied more in the form of government institutions than in societal ideals. Although Confucian concepts still persist in society,[20] Confucianism has lost much of its appeal in the contemporary constitutional domain, as will be articulated in the following section. The difference between the two models of constitutionalism is a matter of degree.

By contrast, both China and Vietnam reject Western liberal constitutionalism, but the Confucian impact on the two countries differs. Ironically, in China, the birthplace of Confucius, Confucianism may be the least influential in the four jurisdictions as a result of a number of ideological struggles after 1949, such as the Cultural Revolution. Meanwhile, China has consistently pursued so-called socialist constitutionalism or the rule of law with Chinese characteristics, vehemently denouncing liberal constitutionalism as pernicious to China. Likewise, Vietnam is another country where the Communist Party is still in power and rejects liberal constitutionalism, but where, unlike China, Confucianism has remained fairly influential since the imperial period.[21]

Two caveats are worth noting. First, the typology inevitably entails a certain degree of simplification and imprecision. Therefore, other East Asian countries may be included in this figure as well. Singapore, the most adamant advocate of Asian values, may arguably be grouped in the same category as Vietnam, while Japan can be grouped with Taiwan. Second, along with the evolution of constitutional implementation, a country may move from one cell to another over time. In Taiwan,

---

[19]Oh (2015), at pp. 91–92.

[20]Ma (1998).

[21]Son (2012), at p. 423; Son (2013), at p. 373.

		Impact of Liberal Constitutionalism	
		Weak	Strong
Impact of Confucianism	Weak	Socialist Constitutionalism (e.g., China)	Liberal Constitutionalism (e.g., Taiwan)
	Strong	Confucian Constitutionalism (e.g., Vietnam)	Hybrid Constitutionalism (e.g., South Korea)

Fig. 1 Constitutionalism in East Asia (*Source* Author)

for instance, many provisions of the civil code once reflected its Confucian heritage, such as the emphasis on patriarchy and paternalism, which meant that Taiwan was closer to South Korea in Figure I in the past. Most of these regulations have subsequently been declared unconstitutional and void. The following section articulates the controversies that bear witness to the paradigm shift of constitutionalism in Taiwan in both the private and the public domain.

2 The Decline of Confucianism in Taiwan

In Taiwan, a variety of institutions, including government branches and statutes, have been shaped in accordance with Confucianism. In the Constitution of the Republic of China (the Constitution), the supreme law of the land, there is a clear combination of liberal constitutionalism and Confucianism in terms of the institutional design of government branches. Ideationally, Confucianism was once enshrined in a draft constitution as the state religion of the young republic.[22] Although this proposal was eventually aborted in the process of drafting the Constitution, some of the Confucian legacies have persisted. Divergent from a typical Western constitutional model, there are five central branches prescribed in the Constitution: in addition to the tripartite separation of powers theory, the Examination Yuan and the Control Yuan are two other coequal branches, which are derived from the Confucian theory of good governance.[23] Roughly, the former aims to guarantee the impartiality and quality of the civil service system, while the latter, modeled on the imperial Censorate, is functionally equivalent to ombudsmen.[24]

Despite these lofty aims, several prominent constitutional law scholars in Taiwan have proposed repealing the two branches since the country's democratization,[25] partly because their tasks overlap with the executive and the Legislative Yuan to a

[22]Li (2014), at p. 845.

[23]He, *supra* note 12, at pp. 72–73.

[24]Caldwell (2017), at pp. 746–747.

[25]Lin et al. (2003), at pp. 634–637.

considerable extent. The overlapping and the appointments have spawned many constitutional and political quarrels, in addition to inefficiency and cronyism. Moreover, the Control Yuan has been deprived of many of its important powers as a result of a series of constitutional amendments: in particular, the power to consent was transferred to the Legislative Yuan and the power to impeach the president and vice-president to the Constitutional Court. Both revisions downplay the political salience of the Control Yuan and render it a "tiger with no teeth." In reality, it turned out that the government could function normally without the Control Yuan, when, in 2006, many vacancies were not staffed because of a political stalemate. Should the procedural threshold of constitutional amendments be overcome, the two institutions might be abolished.

Furthermore, the decline of Confucianism is even more evident in the revision of the Civil Code. Like early Roman law in which "the father was monarch and the head of the family,"[26] Confucian thinking declares that the husband is superior to the wife in a family.[27] Paternalism and primogeniture form the core of the Confucian family structure. Unfortunately, these features perpetuated and aggravated gender inequality in many provisions that were formally discriminatory against women until the Constitutional Court gradually struck them down. For instance, in J.Y. Interpretation No. 365 (1994), the Constitutional Court encountered the problem of the value of the superiority of fatherhood;[28] the old Civil Code prescribed that fathers would have the final say over mothers whenever there was a disagreement in exercising parental rights. This article was incorporated in 1930, when women were generally less educated and less likely to be in paid employment because of the traditional culture. Recognizing that times had changed, the Constitutional Court ruled that gender equality outweighed gender stereotypes and demanded statutory revision. Moreover, at one time the Civil Code prescribed that a wife's property belonged to her husband unless she could prove the property was acquired before marriage, since wives were supposed to have less property than husbands. In J.Y. Interpretation No. 410 (1996), the Constitutional Court demanded statutory revision as soon as possible on the grounds of equal protection.

Another example is found in J.Y. Interpretation No. 452 (1998), in which the Civil Code stipulated that the residence of the wife should be that of the husband if there is no agreement to the contrary. The location of residence is legally important because it involves many rights and obligations relevant to the couple. Similarly, such regulations reflected the fact that wives were expected to rely on their husbands because women back then were not encouraged to receive an education and therefore they had fewer opportunities to work outside the home. To eradicate male dominance, the Constitutional Court declared the article in question repugnant to equal protection and, therefore, void. Last but not least, the Constitutional Court legalized same-sex marriage in J.Y. Interpretation No. 748. Although it is arguable

[26]Friedman (1975), at p. 280.

[27]Hsieh (2015), at p. 6.

[28]Chen (2006), at pp. 80–90; Chen (2016), at pp. 122–129.

whether, or to what extent, Confucian thinking discriminates against same-sex marriage, entrenched ideas of filial piety, gender roles, family structure, and ancestor worship all render it unlikely that the ideology would accept or support gay rights. Indeed, maintaining Chinese traditional culture was one major argument used by conservative camps in the oral debate held in the Constitutional Court. Notwithstanding the fierce protest, the Constitutional Court declared the related Civil Code provisions that essentially prohibited same-sex marriage unconstitutional and void within two years.

Patriarchy was prevalent not only in the Civil Code but also in other administrative regulations. J.Y. Interpretation No. 457 is the paradigmatic example, in which the law in question prohibited married daughters of veterans from inheriting farmland distributed by the government. Part of the reason was that married daughters could rely on their husbands and thus did not need the benefits. By contrast, the regulation did not restrict sons' inheritance rights, married or not, because they were supposed to be the breadwinners of a family and needed greater financial resources. This definitely reinforced the gender stereotype and further exacerbated women's status in society. Unsurprisingly, the Constitutional Court declared it inconsistent with the Constitution, and required revision.

Even in issues irrelevant to family law or inheritance, some Justices have also publicly called for the rejection of Confucian culture in their separate opinions. In J.Y. Interpretation No. 702, the issue involved a teacher's professional dignity and status. Since Confucius himself is regarded as the greatest teacher in China, Confucianism puts special emphasis on the moral requirement and professional duties of teachers. This moralized high expectation placed on teachers is embodied in many laws that regulate and discipline teachers' activities. In his dissenting opinion, Justice Chen urged Taiwan to substitute the Confucian expectations of teachers with cultural diversity and the rule of law.[29] Another case relates to freedom of association, which was restricted during the authoritarian period. After political liberation, the composition and operation of occupational associations were still under the strict supervision of the government. In J.Y. Interpretation No. 724, Justice Su argued that this control mirrored the culture of Confucian paternalism and should be discarded.[30]

Furthermore, judicial review in Taiwan in recent years has been less "Confucian" as well. As mentioned above, it has been compared to remonstrance during the imperial era because the Constitutional Court was deferential even if it disagreed with the dictators during the authoritarian period. Hence, the Constitutional Court adopted a raft of interpretive methods to euphemistically nudge the political branches without nullifying the impugned laws. From the perspective of judicial politics, this cautiousness may be explicable and necessary to maintain judicial integrity and

---

[29]Dafaguan Shizi Di 702 Hao [大法官字釋第702號] (The Constitutional Court Interpretation No. 702) (27 July 2012) (Chen J dissenting) (Taiwan).

[30]Dafaguan Shizi Di 724 Hao [大法官釋字第724號] (The Constitutional Court Interpretation No. 724) (1 Aug 2014) (Su J concurring) (Taiwan).

secure implementation. Since democratization, this pro-dialogue style has gradually been replaced with a more decisive and clear-cut one.[31] Meanwhile, Justices are more assertive and unwilling to maintain the façade of judicial neutrality, in the sense that they promulgate many more separate opinions than their predecessors did. In this regard, the Constitutional Court functions in a way similar to the Supreme Court of the United States. In other words, the comparison to the remonstrance, albeit insightful in the past, may no longer be appropriate.

In the political domain, Confucianism emphasizes the concept of the sage king and *junzi* (those who are morally virtuous and knowledgeable).[32] At the risk of oversimplifying, it suggests that in theory a country should be led by those who are most capable instead of those who get the most votes. In practice, this leads to political meritocracy and elitism,[33] with Singapore being the best example on this front. Nonetheless, the constitutional development of Taiwan has not followed the same path. Scholars have suggested that grassroots organizations and students have played a significant role in the process of Taiwan's constitutional transformation.[34] One public opinion survey has further found that "people in Taiwan [are] much less likely to endorse the [Confucian] idea of excluding the masses from the political process."[35] It turns out that civil society in Taiwan has vigorously participated in the constitution-making process. The beginning of social participation is evidenced by the Wild Lily Student Movement in 1990; this voluntary student gathering called for national elections and eventually precipitated democratization. Since then, civil society has actively participated in the formation of constitutionalism through either political participation or public-interest litigation[36]—a development that has been acclaimed as civic constitutionalism.[37] In 2014, unsatisfied with the sloppy legislative process that tried to pass the Cross-Strait Service Trade Agreement, several students and social groups occupied the congressional assembly and stopped the Agreement. Many believed this "Sunflower Student Movement" resulted in the third party turnover and, more importantly, forged Taiwan's national identity. It is worth noting that the Movement was neither orchestrated nor anticipated by the opposition party.[38] In fact, this bottom-up self-empowerment has consistently been the defining feature of civil society in Taiwan over several generations. Although the occupiers were prosecuted, the district court ruled in favor of them on the grounds of civil disobedience.

Taiwanese people also participate in the formation of constitutional politics in a less dramatic way. Since the early 1980s, social groups such as the Awakening

---

[31]Yeh and Chang (2011).

[32]Kim (2014), at p. 126.

[33]Bell (2013), at pp. 1–7.

[34]Fan (2004), at p. 164.

[35]Shin, *supra* note 16, at pp. 259, 271.

[36]Chang (2011), at p. 136.

[37]Yeh (2016), pp. 244–246.

[38]For further introduction and analyses, see Jones and Su (2015), at p. 193; Yeh (2015), at p. 315.

Foundation have vigorously participated in constitutional transformation through political channels, giving birth to the revision and enactment of the family chapter of the Civil Code, the Act of Gender Equality in Employment, the Domestic Violence Prevention Act, and the gender quota for congressional seats. These statutes and constitutional amendments endeavored to dismantle gender discrimination in practice and successfully escalated the status of women not only in society but also in the political field. This suggests that Taiwan has deviated from the Confucian model of constitutionalism through both the judicial and political channels.

While manifesting the decline of Confucianism in Taiwan, these changes do not eradicate the legacy of Confucianism from Taiwan's constitutional practice. Instead, it has persisted in the domain of criminal law and inheritance. In terms of the former, Taiwan may be the only country outside of the Islamic world that still criminalizes adultery. Ostensibly, the provision constrains both sexes, but most husbands who commit adultery have been forgiven. In practice, the provision is wielded by wives as a weapon to undergird their crumbling marriages and punish their husbands' paramours. In J.Y. Interpretation No. 554, the Constitutional Court unanimously upheld the constitutionality of such punishment with an eye to maintaining marriage and the family system. This crime remains not only on the books but it is also enforced in practice, mainly because Confucianism stresses family values and social harmony, an ideology that affects both lay people and elites, including the legislators and the Justices. Another example is J.Y. Interpretation No. 728, in which the issue of whether the Act for Ancestor Worship Guilds can constitutionally exclude women's right to be the successors of guilds. Similarly, the provision in question is ostensibly gender-neutral, but in practice most female offspring are deprived of this right because of Confucian tradition. Unfortunately, the provision just managed to survive judicial review based on the principle of the autonomy of private law, notwithstanding five dissenting opinions. This state of affairs resonates with the observation in South Korea that traditional practices concerning the dead are more resilient than those regarding the living.[39] Whether this claim is accurate is beyond the scope of this chapter, but the inheritance of collective property does seem to be the last bastion of Confucianism in the guise of freedom of contract in both South Korea and Taiwan.

Furthermore, constitutional interpretation concerning the Control Yuan has rendered Taiwan's constitutional framework distinct from the traditional Western model. For instance, Taiwan once had three Parliaments—the National Assembly, the Legislative Yuan, and the Control Yuan—all of which shouldered and exercised different congressional duties and powers. Although this three-parliament arrangement was repealed through constitutional amendments, the interaction and division of labor between the Control Yuan and the Legislative Yuan in other domains still spawned two constitutional decisions: J.Y. Interpretation No. 325 and No. 729. Both interpretations involve the scope of the power to investigate, which is

[39]Kim (2013), at pp. 357, 373.

shared by both the Legislative Yuan and the Control Yuan. In short, the congressional power of investigation in Taiwan is slightly different from that in Western Parliaments, owing to the existence of the Control Yuan. Finally, legislators refused to exercise confirmation power because of political gridlock in 2006, and therefore the Control Yuan was paralyzed for several months. Encountering this issue, the Constitutional Court in J.Y. Interpretation No. 632 recognized that the Control Yuan was integral and indispensable for the operation of the separation of powers and it condemned the boycott as "jeopardizing the integrity of the constitutional system." Likewise, the Constitutional Court has reiterated that the Examination Yuan is also a constitutional agency coequal with the three traditional branches, predicated on the distinctive five-power constitutional framework. All these political dramas show the residual impact of Confucian thinking.

3 Normative Implications

Two implications may be distilled from constitutional development in Taiwan. First, if there is a so-called East Asian constitutionalism, it seems to be a blend of variant degrees of Confucianism and liberal constitutionalism. Despite its declining clout, there is no denying that Confucian concepts still play a role in the formation of constitutionalism in East Asia. In addition to the ideational dimension of Confucian constitutionalism, institutional Confucian constitutionalism embodied by the Control Yuan and the Examination Yuan also persists. In spite of the call to repeal the two branches, the procedural hurdle of constitutional revision renders them unlikely to be abolished in the near future. Namely, Confucian constitutionalism will still coexist with liberal constitutionalism for a long time. That said, Taiwan's experience refutes the argument that liberal constitutionalism is unsuitable or a luxury for East Asian countries. Nor can its constitutionalism be described as Confucian constitutionalism, since Confucianism has dissipated considerably in Taiwan to the extent that it may be the least Confucian jurisdiction in so-called Confucian Asia.[40] In fact, the protection of human rights has accelerated concomitantly with the decline of Confucianism. On the other hand, it also suggests that constitutionalism in Taiwan does not simply replicate or transplant Western liberal constitutionalism. Although modern liberal constitutionalism dominates the mainstream constitutional discourse in Taiwan, it is still susceptible to both institutional and ideational Confucian constitutionalism. A similar development has taken place in other East Asian jurisdictions as well. That is, "[i]n the light of a dynamic Asia, both universalism and particularism should understand their position in a humble way."[41]

[40]Shin, *supra* note 16, at p. 259.

[41]Dupre and Yeh (2013), at pp. 45, 51.

Secondly, Confucian elements, despite their undemocratic tendency, may in fact play a constructive role in bolstering liberal constitutionalism in Taiwan. To be specific, these Confucian elements serve as a constitutional irritant that galvanizes more dialogues and provides more opportunities for constitutional change.[42] This need not be surprising given the systemic effects of constitutional design.[43] In Taiwan, both ideational and institutional Confucian constitutionalism persist, despite the promulgation of a series of constitutional amendments after democratization. Many conflicting constitutional values thus coexist in Taiwan. These gaps between large-C and small-c constitutions do not indicate the triumph of Confucian constitutionalism in Taiwan. On the contrary, the inconsistency resulting from Confucian ideology actually stimulates more debates and reflections on constitutional practice on this island. In a sense, Taiwan may not have become one of the East Asian jurisdictions that best protects gender equality without these Confucian irritants that have repeatedly allowed the Constitutional Court to breathe new air into constitutional jurisprudence.

4 Conclusion

The case of Taiwan demonstrates the coexistence of modern liberal constitutionalism and Confucian constitutionalism. In fact, this may be one common characteristic of constitutional practice in East Asia. On the one hand, the declining influence of Confucianism in Taiwan disproves the Asian-values thesis that civil and political rights are luxuries unaffordable in East Asia countries; these rights are no more "Western" than Newtonian and quantum physics.[44] On the other hand, the fact that a Confucian legacy is still deeply rooted in Taiwan's constitutional structure and practice suggests that constitutionalism in Taiwan weaves together several threads of traditional culture, transnational legal order, and the colonial past.

References

Bell DA (2013) Introduction. In: Bell DA, Li C (eds) The East Asian challenge for democracy. Cambridge University Press, New York, pp 1–30

Bell DA (2015) The China model: political meritocracy and the limits of democracy. Princeton University Press, Princeton

Caldwell E (2017) Widening the constitutional gap in China and Taiwan. Univ Ill Law Rev 4:739–767

[42]Chang and Law (2017), pp. 37–42.

[43]Vermeule (2011), at pp. 3–37.

[44]Donnelly (1999), at pp. 60, 69; Sen (1999), at pp. 88, 97.

Chang W-C (2011) Public interest litigation in Taiwan. In: Yap P, Lau H (eds) Public interest litigation in Asia. Routledge, Abingdon, pp 136–160
Chang W-C, Law D (2017) Constitutional dissonance in China, Legal studies research paper series, Paper No. 17-03-03, Washington University Law
Chen C-J (2006) Mothering under the shadow of patriarchy: comparative constitutional theory. Natl Taiwan Univ Law Rev 1(1):45–96
Chen C-J (2016) The chorus of formal equality: feminist custody law reform and fathers' rights advocacy in Taiwan. Can J Women Law 28(1):116–151
Donnelly J (1999) Human rights and Asian values: a defense of "Western" universalism. In: Bauer J, Bell D (eds) The East Asian challenge for human rights. Cambridge University Press, New York, pp 60–87
Dupre C, Yeh J-r (2013) Constitutions and legitimacy over time. In: Tushnet M et al (eds) Routledge handbook of constitutional law. Routledge, Abingdon, pp 45–56
Fan Y (2004) Taiwan: no civil society, no democracy. In: Alagappa M (ed) Civil society and political change in Asia: expanding and contracting democratic space. Stanford University Press, Stanford, pp 164–190
Friedman LM (1975) The legal system: a social science perspective. Russell Sage Foundation, New York
Ginsburg T (2002) Confucian constitutionalism? the emergence of constitutional review in Korea and Taiwan. Law Soc Inquiry 27(4):763–799
Ginsburg T (2012) Constitutionalism: East Asian antecedents. Chicago-Kent Law Rev 88(1):11–34
Ginsburg, T, Simpser A (2014) Introduction: constitutions in authoritarian regimes. In: Ginsburg T, Simpser A (eds) Constitutions in authoritarian regimes. Cambridge University Press, pp 1–17
Hahm C (2009) Ritual and constitutionalism: disputing the ruler's legitimacy in a Confucian polity. Am J Comp Law 57(1):131–204
He B (2016) Confucianism and democracy. Taiwan J Democracy 12(2):59–84
Hsieh F-S (2015) Introduction: democracy, Confucian style? In: Hsieh JF (ed) Confucian culture and democracy. World Scientific Publishing Company, Singapore, pp 1–20
Jones BC, Su Y-T (2015) Confrontational contestation and democratic compromise: the sunflower movement and its aftermath. Hong Kong Law J 45(1):193–210
Kim MS-H (2013) In the name of custom, culture, and the constitution. Texas Intl J 48(3):357–392
Kim S (2014) Confucian democracy in East Asia. Cambridge University Press, New York
Kim S (2016) Public reason Confucianism. Cambridge University Press, New York
Li F-P (李富鵬) (2014) Gongshi Yu Zhengyi (共識與爭議). Peking Univ Law J 26(4):845–882
Lin T-Y et al (2003) Constitution: the separation of powers. Angle Publishing, Taipei
Ma H-P (1998) The rule of law in a contemporary Confucian society: a reinterpretation. Paper presented at Harvard Law School's East Asian legal studies program
Moustafa T, Ginsburg T (2008) Introduction: the functions of courts in authoritarian politics. In: Ginsburg T, Moustafa T (eds) Rule by law. Cambridge University Press, New York, pp 1–22
Oh J (2015) Adaptations in Korea: Confucianism, democracy, and economic development. In: Hsieh JF (ed), Confucian culture and democracy. World Scientific Publishing Company, Singapore, pp 85–110
Qing J (2013) A Confucian constitutional order. Princeton University Press, Princeton
Rosenfeld M (2004) Constitutional adjudication in Europe and the United States: paradoxes and contrasts. Intl J Constitution Law 2(4):633–668
Sen A (1999) Human rights and economic achievements. In: Bauer J, Bell D (eds) The East Asian challenge for human rights. Cambridge University Press, New York, pp 88–99
Shin DC (2012) Confucianism and democratization in East Asia. Cambridge University Press, New York
Shin DC (2013) How East Asians view meritocracy. In: Bell DA, Li C-Y (eds) The East Asian challenge for democracy. Cambridge University Press, New York, pp 259–287
Son BN (2012) The introduction of modern constitutionalism in the East Asian Confucian context: the case of Vietnam in the early twentieth century. Natl Taiwan Univ Law Rev 7(2):423–464

Son BN (2013) Confucian constitutionalism in imperial Vietnam. Natl Taiwan Univ Law Rev 8(2):373–436
Son BN (2016) Confucian constitutionalism in East Asia. Routledge, Abington
Tu W et al (1992) The Confucian world observed. University of Hawaii Press, Honolulu
Tushnet M (2015) Authoritarian constitutionalism. Cornell Law Rev 100(2):391–462
Vermeule A (2011) The system of the constitution. Oxford University Press, New York
Yeh J-R (2015) Marching towards civic constitutionalism with sunflowers. Hong Kong Law J 45(1):315–330
Yeh J-R (2016) The constitution of Taiwan. Hart Publishing, Taipei
Yeh J-R, Chang W-C (2011) The emergence of East Asian constitutionalism: features in comparison. Am J Comp Law 59(3):805–840

Chien-Chih Lin is currently Assistant Research Professor at Institutum Iurisprudentiae, Academia Sinica (Taiwan). He received B.A. and M.A. degrees from National Taiwan University and LL.M. and J.S.D. degrees from the University of Chicago. Before studying abroad, he was an attorney at law in Taipei for two years, working mainly on cases regarding administrative law and state compensation. His academic interests focus on comparative constitutional law in Asia, judicial politics, and judicial behavior. Chien-Chih Lin has published several articles and essays in the United States, Taiwan, and China. His articles can be found in both peer-reviewed and student-edited law journals as well as in edited volumes, including *Oxford Handbook of Constitutional Law in Asia, American Journal of Comparative Law, International Journal of Constitutional Law, University of Pennsylvania Asian Law Review, Georgetown Journal of International Law, National Taiwan University Law Review,* and *Asian Journal of Law & Society.* He is a co-editor of *Academia Sinica Law Journal*. For those who are interested in his work, he can be reached via chienchihlin@gate.sinica.edu.tw.

Part III
Institutional Setting and Voluntary Compliance of Human Rights Treaties

Chapter 8
A National Human Rights Commission for Taiwan?

Mab Huang

Abstract At a formal dinner held in the Presidential Office on 15 January 2017 for visiting scholars and experts from abroad before they settled down to review the second national report on implementation of the two international human rights covenants, the Vice-President announced that a decision on the creation of a national human rights commission will be forthcoming, no later than the end of the year. It came as no surprise that many human rights nongovernmental organizations (NGOs) had worked long and hard on this issue and several foreign offices in Taipei were encouraged by the news. However, the sense of impending success must be scrutinized against a dismal record of failure during a sixteen-year effort to bring about a national human rights commission, taking the year 2000 as year zero. The primary question of this chapter is why sixteen years were not enough for the government and civil society in Taiwan, with subtle but firm support from the international community, to come to a favorable decision. To be precise, this chapter asks: (1) Where did the initiative come from and what role did civil society play? (2) What were the responses of the Chen Shui-bian and Ma Ying-jeou administrations? (3) What role did mass media play? (4) What support came from the international community, and (5) What can be expected from the new administration of Tsai Ing-wen? It is indeed puzzling that, in light of the great strides Taiwan has been making in the promotion and protection of human rights over the past thirty-some years and President Tsai's pledge that she will actively promote judicial reform, transitional justice, as well as reform of the pension system, among other items on her agenda, a national human rights commission based on the Paris Principles is nowhere in sight. As of this writing, a promising hypothesis is that it is due to procrastination on the part of the political elite entangled in a tug of war among the different governmental branches, in particular, opposition from the Control Yuan. It needs to be noted in passing that the Control Yuan is quite unique in that it is one of the five branches of the government stipulated in the constitution that was designed by Dr. Sun Yat-sen, the founder of the Republic of China, as a creative improvement on modern Western theory and practice by taking advantage

M. Huang (✉)
Soochow University, Taipei, Taiwan
e-mail: mab@gm.scu.edu.tw

J. A. Cohen et al. (eds.), *Taiwan and International Human Rights*, Economics, Law, and Institutions in Asia Pacific, https://doi.org/10.1007/978-981-13-0350-0_8

of what are the best in the traditional Chinese governmental structure. As such, the Control Yuan has the power to supervise the performance of the government bureaucracy and to impeach them if and when the circumstances so warrant, thus the controversy over the investigatory power. More on that later. The literature relied on for this chapter includes both official documents and reports by civil society organizations as well as scholarly studies. It is supplemented by my observations as a member of the Presidential Human Rights Advisory Committee (PHRAC). I have learned a few things in regard to the attitudes and thinking of the political elite concerning a national human rights commission and how the bureaucracy performs in a rapidly changing situation. I have great admiration and respect for the tenacity and courage of the nongovernmental organizations that have worked hard and contributed much to bring Taiwan closer to international human rights standards. A caveat, however, needs to be addressed. Through the years, several prominent human rights activists have been recruited into government service and have quickly given up their previous positions to support government policies. This change of mind could not but be deeply demoralizing to their former colleagues in the NGOs and have led to mistrust of the government.

Keywords Civil society organizations · International human rights covenants National human rights commission · Presidential human rights advisory committee Investigatory power

1 Advocacy from Civil Society Organizations: A Simple Proposal

The initiative for establishing a human rights commission came from the academic community and civil society organizations. In October 1997, I was invited by the Institute for National Policy Research supported by the Chang Yung-fa Foundation to meet with a visiting delegation from the Council of Europe to brief them on the human rights situation in Taiwan. In my presentation, after a survey of the political changes in the previous decade, I proposed that it was time for Taiwan to declare its commitment to upholding international human rights standards by setting up a national human rights commission to coordinate its endeavors. This proposal was inspired in part by the Office of the United Nations High Commissioner for Human Rights which had been encouraging Asian states to do so.

This idea appealed to Mr. Peter Huang, the president of the Taiwan Human Rights Association. Mr. Huang was seeking a new direction for his Association after the end of the authoritarian government and he translated my statement from English into Chinese and circulated it among civil society organizations for discussion. However, it took more than a year for a coalition of some twenty organizations, including lawyers' associations, women's groups, the labor movement, environmental protection organizations and university professors to formally launch a campaign for setting up a national human rights commission.[1]

The NGO coalition quickly set up two working groups. The first group, chaired by Peter Huang, was charged with lobbying the presidential candidates to commit themselves to the idea of setting up a national human rights commission. Among the candidates, Lien Chan, then Vice President and running on behalf of the Chinese Nationalist Party, was the first to pledge his support. In a policy statement issued on 2 January 2000, he announced that he was committed to "a national human rights commission above any political interference." Peter Huang was highly pleased.[2]

The other group, chaired by myself, was given the task of compiling a draft proposed organic law for the national human rights commission. In this assignment, I was very fortunate to have the help of Professor Chen Lung-chu, law professor at New York Law School and advisor to Chen Shui-bian on human rights affairs, Professor Fort Fu-te Liao of the Academia Sinica, Mr. Lin Feng-jeng, a lawyer and human rights activist and Mr. Chen Chun-hung, a young instructor in the Political Science Department of Soochow University, among others. Suffice it to say that it took six months of hard work to get the job done. On 4 June 2000, a draft was presented at a press conference. This date was chosen with care to serve as a tribute to the young students and workers in the 1989 campaign for democracy and human rights in China, for which many of them paid with their lives, and as an urgent message to the government and society in Taiwan to move on vigorously with the task at hand.

The draft was based on the Paris Principles and the Commission was to be located in the Presidential Office. It was designed so the Commission would enjoy autonomy and independence in personnel and budget, while ensuring human rights organizations would be amply represented. The issue of investigatory power was heatedly debated within the drafting group, the dividing line being whether to claim investigatory power on individual complaints, and to what extent? Should the human rights commission enjoy investigatory power equal to or less than that of the Control Yuan? The argument had been made that part of the controversy was a language problem, for in Chinese usage investigation tended to be strictly separate from inquiry, survey and studies, while in English, it need not be so. In the end, the draft opted for self-discipline and deferred to the Control Yuan, the prosecutors and the courts. However, it would be empowered to study, inquire and assess important human rights situations concerning the well-being of the whole of society, such as those relating to indigenous peoples or migrant workers.

By September 2000, the NGO coalition ended its routine meetings. Even at this time, civil society organizations affiliated with the coalition were still very much divided on their conceptions of rights, not to mention the composition and power of the Commission. Nevertheless, the conclusions reached by the drafting group were

[1]Huang (2001).

[2]Huang (2000).

accepted as the coalition's position and Mr. Lin Feng-cheng, who had succeeded Peter Huang as the President of the Taiwan Human Rights Association, was appointed as its spokesman while Ms. Wang Shih-shi, the Executive Secretary of the Judicial Reform Council, was assigned to coordinate efforts vis-à-vis the Legislative Yuan.[3] However, no attempt to approach the legislators followed, and the draft bill was not formally introduced in the Legislative Yuan. It would seem that, in the excitement of witnessing the coming to power of the new administration, the NGO coalition had ceased all its activities.

2 The Multifaceted and Complicated Maneuvers During the Chen Shui-bian Administration

2.1 The First Draft Bill Debated in the Legislative Yuan

While the NGO coalition was drafting its bill, Ms. Hsiao Uan-u, a legislator for the Chinese Nationalist Party, quickly proposed a bill for setting up a national human rights commission. Mr. Ting Fu-hua, a former student of mine and one of Ms. Hsiao's research assistants, was given the task of helping draft the bill and I was consulted when it was being drafted. I made my comments on the draft known, saying that the nomination and selection processes of the Commission members were far too cumbersome, Ms. Hsiao of course had her reasons for this. The draft bill was eventually endorsed by seventy-eight of her colleagues. Yet when it was first debated, fellow legislators challenged her, arguing that by establishing the Commission in the Presidential Office, it was creating conflict among the President, the Legislative Yuan and the Executive Yuan. The criticism came from both political parties. The bill was withdrawn after Ms. Hsiao decided not to stand for re-election in late 2000.[4]

2.2 The Presidential Office, the Executive Yuan and the Control Yuan

In part due to its internal split, for the first time in the annals of the Republic of China, the Chinese Nationalist Party was defeated in a Presidential election in the year 2000 and a peaceful transfer of political power was secured. Apparently following the advice of the coalition pushing for the creation of a human rights commission, Chen Shui-bian, the Democratic Progressive Party candidate,

[3]Coalition for the Promotion of a National Human Rights Commission (2000).
[4]Su (2002).

promised, in his inaugural address on May 20, to abide by international human rights standards, among other things. To quote:

> The Republic of China cannot and will not remain outside global human rights trends. We will abide by the Universal Declaration of Human Rights, the International Convention for Civil and Political Rights, and the Vienna Declaration and Program of Action. We will bring the Republic of China back into the international human rights system.
>
> The new government will request the Legislative Yuan to pass and ratify the International Bill of Rights as a domestic law of Taiwan, so that it will formally become the "Taiwan Bill of Rights." We hope to set up an independent national human rights commission in Taiwan, thereby realizing an action long advocated by the United Nations. We will also invite two outstanding non-governmental organizations, the International Commission of Jurists and Amnesty International, to assist us in our measures to protect human rights and make the Republic of China into a new indicator for human rights in the 21st century.[5]

This declaration, as it turned out, was warmly welcomed by the international community and human rights NGOs in Taiwan. Hope rode high. How, then, would the Chen Shui-bian administration implement its pledge?

The new government proceeded to set up a Human Rights Advisory Committee in the Presidential Office chaired by Vice-President Annette Lu in October 2000. It was made up of scholars, lawyers and NGO representatives. One of its missions was to bring about a national human rights commission. The Committee at first decided to entrust the task of drafting a proposed organic law of the Commission to the then Research, Development and Evaluation Commission of the Executive Yuan. However, before long, it was engaged in a serious dispute with the Executive Yuan on the one hand, and the Control Yuan on the other. It would seem that the Executive Yuan was opposed to the creation of a national human rights commission, arguing officially that, since the government was in the midst of a move to streamline its structure, no new agency should be added. On a deeper level, the Ministry of Justice was obviously concerned about sharing investigatory power with the proposed commission, thinking that it would encroach on the domain of the prosecutors. It therefore, opted for an advisory committee. This position was clearly not acceptable to the NGO coalition, nor the PHRAC, yet it supported the position of the Control Yuan, though with different motives.

To break the deadlock, Mr. Su Yiu-chen, a well-known lawyer and member of the PHRAC, proposed that the Executive Yuan should study both the draft bill of the NGO coalition and that of Ms. Hsiao and come up with a compromise version for the Legislative Yuan. This recommendation was adopted by the Vice-President with the approval of the President. However, the Executive Yuan refused to compromise. It came up with a proposed bill in two parts, with the drafting of a proposed organic law entrusted to the Research, Development and Evaluation Commission and that concerning the use of investigatory power to the Ministry of Justice. They were then submitted to the PHRAC. Vice-President Annette Lu took

[5]Chen S-B (2000) Office of the President, Republic of China. http://english.president.gov.tw/NEWS/2643. Accessed 12 Aug 2017.

them seriously, convening eleven meetings between May 2001 and May 2002 to go over them article by article. In this endeavor, Su Yiu-chen and Professor Fort Fu-te Liao were Lu's closest aides. The Executive Yuan, nevertheless, still held its ground. The President was compelled, for the lack of a better word, to call in both sides to break the deadlock. In this meeting, the PHRAC was represented by Su Yiu-chen and Professor Liao, and the Executive Yuan by Professors Hsu Chih-hsiung and Hwang Jau-yuan, law professors at National Taiwan University and members of the Group for the Implementation of Human Rights Policy of the Executive Yuan. Mr. Su and Professor Liao argued successfully that their claims on behalf of the PHRAC draft bill regarding visitation, mediation, conciliation and arbitration were adapted from the United Nations handbook and did not violate individual freedoms or privacy, nor did they interfere with the judicial process as the Executive Yuan had asserted.[6] Chen Shui-bian sided with his Vice-President, and the draft prepared by her Committee was used as the text for further revision. The Executive Yuan finally submitted the bill to the Legislative Yuan in August 2002.

A month before the submission of the draft bill by the Executive Yuan, the Vice-President decided that she needed to accommodate the Control Yuan. The latter had charged that Article 2 Section 5 of the Organic Law Bill prepared by the PHRAC granting investigatory power in important human rights situations was unconstitutional and that Article 9 in the companion bill concerning the use of investigatory power infringed on its jurisdiction. Simultaneously, the press began to champion the position of the Control Yuan.[7] The Vice-President quickly gave in to the Control Yuan, after a dinner to which the President of the Control Yuan and some twenty members were invited to help resolve the dispute. It ended with the PHRAC endorsing the prime concerns of the Control Yuan in its exercise of investigatory power.[8]

The administration of Chen Shui-bian made no further move on the draft bill it had proposed.

2.3 *The NGO Coalition, the Control Yuan and the Press*

From the very beginning, the Control Yuan was opposed to the idea of a national human rights commission. Its basic position can be summed up as follows: the Control Yuan is the national human rights commission per se and it enjoys sole investigatory power. In May 2000, to strengthen its position, the Control Yuan proceeded to set up a human rights protection committee to take charge of investigation of human rights cases and to make recommendations for human rights laws.

[6]Su (2002).

[7]Cai (2002).

[8]Su (2002).

One month later, on 26 June 2000, a delegation from the NGOs coalition was invited to meet with selected members of the Control Yuan. The gathering apparently helped clarify the positions of both sides, yet it could not produce any meeting of the minds.[9] They barely managed a friendly parting.

In January 2001, the Control Yuan formally proposed that the management of human rights affairs should be divided into two divisions. The first division, which was primarily concerned with administration, would include the making of human rights policy, human rights education, the human rights index and international liaisons. This would be given to the national human rights commission set up either in the Presidential Office or in the Executive Yuan. The second division, concerned with supervision and investigation, would be the domain of the Control Yuan, and the human rights committee set up in May 2000 would be put in charge. This obviously was a compromise, well-thought-out and carefully calibrated. Yet it was not well received as it was judged not to be in accordance with the Paris Principles and posed the question whether a constitutional amendment would be needed to make it work. The Control Yuan retorted that since it was a constitutional organ, there was no need for a constitutional amendment, a position supported by a few scholars and experts.[10] Indeed, it is difficult, if not impossible, to speculate some sixteen years later what the result would have been had this proposal been taken seriously and its potential further explored.

As it was, the impasse continued. On 11 June 2002, the Secretary-General of the Control Yuan again returned to the dispute and openly branded the position of the NGO coalition unconstitutional, threatening to take it to the Constitutional Court for an interpretation. Taken by surprise and judging the reactions to be misleading, the coalition responded with a statement three days later that emphasized three points. First, as the proposed national human rights commission was designed to further promote and protect human rights and had been sanctioned by the United Nations, how could it be unconstitutional? Secondly, the domain and scope of the investigatory power enjoyed by the national human rights commission and the Control Yuan were clearly demarcated. The Control Yuan's role was to deal with the investigation of policy measures of government agencies and improper behavior of government officials and was endorsed by the Constitution, with the power of impeachment. The commission, on the other hand, would be concerned with the larger picture, such as the investigation of and inquiry into the situation of indigenous peoples and environmental protection. They could easily coexist. And thirdly, the commission would have many other functions, including human rights education and helping to shape human rights policy, which were beyond the reach of the Control Yuan.[11] In a letter to the coalition by the President of the Control Yuan, it was revealed that a meeting of the consultative committee of the Control Yuan had been held and that several scholars serving on the committee, including

---

[9]Huang (2002).

[10]Li (2012).

[11]*Id.*

Professor Hu Fu, a well-known constitutional law expert, were extremely sceptical about the need for a national human rights commission, viewing it as an aggrandizement of the power of the President, as both the draft bill of the NGO coalition and that of the PHRAC had opted to set up the commission at the Presidential Office. This information, as the NGO coalition saw it, explained the renewed confrontation.

Media commentary on the dispute between the NGO coalition and the Control Yuan tended to favor the status quo. Their arguments were, on the whole, banal. A few examples will suffice. As early as 6 January 2000, *China Times* came out with an editorial "The National Human Rights Commission should be located in the Control Yuan," making its position clear and straightforward. On 5 June, the same year, a *Liberty Times* editorial entitled "Do We Need a Super State Organ for the Protection of Human Rights?" pointedly questioned the motivations of the coalition. And on May 16, 2002, in an editorial entitled "The Human Rights Commission Must First Have a Legal Foundation in the Constitution," *United Daily News* argued that the NGO coalition draft bill violated the prerogatives of the investigatory power of the Control Yuan and encroached on the law-making power of the Legislative Yuan, thus setting up a higher state organ. Then, as if reaching for a compromise, in an editorial on 10 July 2002, entitled "The Important Point is Who Can Protect Human Rights, and Not Who has Investigatory Power," *China Times* asked why the national human rights commission sought investigatory power. For what purposes? The editorial ended up questioning the legal foundation of a national human rights commission and what it could do if it were to be set up in the Presidential Office.

It does not take much reflection to realize that behind the mass-media attack on the draft bill proposed by the NGO coalition there was a palpable fear of the expansion of the power of the President. The Control Yuan had been ineffective for decades and was primarily used by the authoritarian government as a reward for its supporters. It was for this reason that the Democratic Progressive Party had argued for its abolition. As for the press, it was hardly free during the era of Chiang Kai-shek and his son. Now some two decades after lifting the ban on the press, a dismal conclusion was unavoidable: Taiwan's most important newspapers were completely ignorant about the concept of human rights and its role in contemporary society.

3 The Administration of Ma Ying-Jeou: Falling on Deaf Ears?

In the Presidential election of 2008, Ma Ying-jeou led the Chinese Nationalist Party in a triumphant return to power. As I described his presidency elsewhere, his eight years in office presented a puzzling situation.[12] He was instrumental in the ratification of the two

[12]Huang (2017).

international human rights covenants, thus opening the way to the drafting of national reports and inviting experts to come to Taiwan to examine the reports. This, no doubt, was a great breakthrough. Yet he steadfastly refused to support the creation of a national human rights commission, arguing that the status of the Control Yuan should be kept intact.[13] His PHRAC, which was modeled on that of his predecessor, had done much work on setting up a national human rights commission, with encouragement and support from international society, especially the Canadian government. Yet the recommendations from the PHRAC were completely ignored.

The year 2013 was particularly busy for both the NGOs and the PHRAC. The expert group invited to Taipei to take part in the review of the initial national report of the two international human rights covenants urged in its concluding observations and recommendations, as had been expected, that a national human rights commission based on the Paris Principles should be set up without delay. Following this, the PHRAC decided to form four groups to handle the more important recommendations, i.e., the creation of a national human rights commission, human rights education and training, the review of laws and regulations incompatible with the obligations assumed under the covenants, and the making of an index for an assessment of the performance of the government agencies. I was assigned to chair the first and second groups. The former was referred to as the 5-member group, with Professor Chang Chueh, Ms. Wang Yu-ling, Professor Nigel N. T. Li and Professor Huang Chun-chie serving as my colleagues. From the beginning, the 5-member group decided that, for their recommendations to be legitimate and convincing, they should solicit the advice of all the stakeholders. Their invitations to the academic community, the foreign diplomats posted in Taipei, the five branches of the government and the NGOs were well received and the meetings held from September to December at the Ministry of Justice were well attended. The foreign diplomats posted in Taipei were highly supportive. The 5-member group was invited by the Canadian government to spend some time in that country that September. Professor Li unfortunately could not make it because he was taken ill on a trip to China, while Ms. Wang had to stay in Taipei for family reasons. Thus, the visiting group was made up of four people, that is, the three available members and Mr. Kuo Ming-li, the prosecutor who had coordinated the drafting of the initial national report. His participation turned out to be a great asset. He was diligent in preparing for meetings and quick in asking questions. The diplomats from Taipei posted in Canada were most friendly and courteous and took part in some of the meetings.

The visiting group had ample opportunity to meet with government officials, university professors and the NGO community, from whom they learned much about how the Canadians approached human rights issues, what their primary concerns were and what complaints their NGOs had against the government. Their encounters with the Canadian Human Rights Commission and the Canadian Human Rights Tribunal at the federal level as well as the British Columbia Human Rights Tribunal were especially useful. The visitors carefully examined how the human

[13]*Id.*

rights mechanism performed in that country and thus helped focus their attention and prepare them for their consultations with the stakeholders upon their return.

In August 2014, a report from the 5-member group was presented to the PHRAC. It proposed to set up the national human rights commission in the Presidential Office, an updated version of the NGO coalition draft bill of the year 2000. Given the constraints of the political dynamics, it was not possible to contemplate a free-standing national human rights commission, nor to proceed with a constitutional amendment. The report did not refer to the possibility of creating a commission under the Control Yuan, for through consultations, the 5-member group had learned that the Control Yuan would be making its own proposal. The Secretariat at the Ministry of Justice dutifully prepared all the necessary documents.

The presentation of the recommendations from the 5-member group did not stimulate much discussion. It was plain for all to see that the Convener of the PHRAC, then Vice-President Wu Den-yih, was determined to opt for a halting act. He had by that time, into his third year as the Convener, acquired the habit of lecturing the Committee on what it could not do as an advisory unit. Only the Executive Yuan had the power to implement policy, he reiterated time and again, while the PHRAC could only advise. For this reason, he did not earn much respect from the members of the Committee.

As anticipated, the Convener instructed that the Secretariat in the Ministry of Justice should again review all the proposals and make a comprehensive report at the next meeting. The Control Yuan was formally invited to present its revised proposal.

4 The Presidency of Tsai Ing-wen: Decision Postponed?

Tsai Ing-wen, the candidate running on behalf of the Democratic Progressive Party, was elected to the Presidency in a landslide victory in 2016, and the civil society organizations were electric, anticipating great progress not only in the promotion and protection of human rights, but expecting an ambitious restructuring of politics and the economy. Indeed Tsai, during her campaign and after the election, had promised as much. Among other things, she had openly criticized the Judicial Yuan and the courts, saying that they had lost the trust of the people and needed a complete overhaul. To this criticism, the then President of the Judicial Yuan replied in kind.[14] In conversation with representatives of the indigenous peoples, Tsai also said that she would redress the historical injustices that they had been made to suffer. It was not clear at that time if a specific committee on historical justice would be set up in her office as later turned out to be the case. As for establishing a national human rights commission, there could not be any doubt of her commitment. In early December 2015, Professor Huang Song-lih, a human rights activist then serving as the Convener of Covenants Watch, was invited to brief the President at a Central Executive Committee meeting of the Democratic Progressive Party

[14]Lin and Su (2016).

during which President Tsai again pledged not only to keep her promise but to move to the "next stage of constitutional amendment."[15]

Barely a year prior to the 2016 presidential election, the issue of a constitutional amendment was hotly debated. The impetus came from the NGO coalition and two legislators of the Democratic Progressive Party, Ms. Yu Mei-nu and Ms. Cheng Li-chiun. Ms. Yu, well-known for her long years of dedication to women's rights, had managed to form a bipartisan group for human rights in the Legislative Yuan. Yet given the lack of interest and the predominance of the Chinese Nationalist Party, she could not do much. More than thirty times within a two-year period, from 2014 to 2016, she failed to table a draft bill on a national human rights commission. Ms. Cheng was more focused on a constitutional amendment, including lowering the age of voting from 20 to 18, absentee ballots, and abolition of the Control Yuan. The young generation was highly enthusiastic, and a one-day workshop was held on May 2, 2015. But there was hardly an echo from the larger community or the government.

On taking over the government, President Tsai Ing-wen apparently quickly decided to work with the PHRAC, which had been appointed by Ma Ying-jeou and still had one year before its term would expire. Vice-President Chen Chien-jen was appointed as the Convener. In doing so, she inherited, among other things, the second national report on implementation of the two international human rights covenants. The Ma Ying-jeou administration had pointedly instructed that the second national report should be completed by May 20, 2016.

The new government quickly recruited several members to the PHRAC, including Professors Chang Wen-chen and Huang Sing-lih. At the first meeting of the PHRAC on 22 July 2016, a many-sided debate concerning a national human rights commission took up much of its time, and a vote was taken to indicate the degree of support for the alternative plans submitted by the 5-member group as well as the proposal of the Control Yuan. At this meeting, the proposal of the 5-member group for a national human rights commission under the Executive Yuan was formally abandoned.

It was widely known that the Control Yuan had been discussing several versions of its proposal, and what it formally presented was dubbed version C. According to this version, the members of the Control Yuan would serve simultaneously as members of the national human rights commission, with its President as the Convener and a member with human rights knowledge and background as the deputy convener (Article 3). As for the need for representation of civil society organizations, it was stipulated that a consultative committee would be formed with 11 to 15 members recruited from them, attention being paid to balancing the sexes, ethnic groups and specific professions (Article 6).[16]

After much deliberation, the proposal to set up the Commission in the Presidential Office garnered 16 votes, followed by 10 for the Control Yuan, and an

[15]Huang (2016).

[16]Presidential Advisory Committee on Human Rights ROC (2016a) Conclusion reached at the 20th meeting of the presidential advisory committee on human rights. Office of the President, Republic of China (Taiwan). http://www.president.gov.tw/Page/321/20/總統府人權諮詢委員會第二十次委員會議#. Accessed 11 Aug 2017.

independent commission coming last with 9 votes, again making it clear that the PHRAC realized the difficulty of a constitutional amendment.[17] The Convener promised to submit the results to the President for her decision, and it was anticipated that a national human rights commission would soon be announced.

While the PHRAC was waiting for the President to decide, without much warning in March 2017 she announced that she was recommending 11 candidates to take up the vacant seats in the Control Yuan. For years, as mentioned earlier, her Party had been agitating for the abolition of the Control Yuan and any effort for a constitutional amendment had to tackle this issue. By this move, the President clearly indicated that she was prepared to live with the Control Yuan. Has she chosen to postpone her decision?

5 Conclusions

The initiative for the creation of a national human rights commission no doubt came from the academic community and civil society organizations. It would not only be a new experiment, committing the government and society to new values and practices but with implications for Taiwan's position and visibility in the international community. Not surprisingly, the move was judged by many government agencies to have a serious impact on their power and interests, thus the entangled maneuvers without a final decision after 16 years. Two issues attracted much attention. First, where should the human rights commission be located? The choice seemed to be either the Presidential Office or the Control Yuan. There were two proposed bills in the Legislative Yuan in 2016: that of Yu Mei-nu and that of Wellington Li-hsiung Koo. Mr. Koo, a well-known lawyer and a legislator when he submitted his draft bill, is now a high-ranking government official in charge of handling the controversial dispute over what is referred to as the illegally owned property of the Chinese Nationalist Party. Yu's bill is modeled after the NGO coalition draft of 2000, and Koo's is an updated version of the Control Yuan's proposal. Mr. Koo stipulated that when the President nominated the members of the Control Yuan, 11 seats should be reserved for a human rights commission and that a minimum of half of them should have a background in human rights issues with NGO experience. They would be strictly separate from the other members of the Control Yuan, having different kinds of work.[18] This division is, on the face of it, an improvement on the Control Yuan proposal referred to above.

[17]Presidential Advisory Committee on Human Rights ROC (2016b) Conclusion reached at the 22nd meeting of the presidential advisory committee on human rights. Office of the President, Republic of China (Taiwan). http://www.president.gov.tw/Page/321/22/總統府人權諮詢委員會第二十二次委員會議. Accessed 11 Aug 2017.

[18]9th Legislative Yuan (2016a) Jianchayuan Guojia Renquan Weiyuanhui Zuzhifa Cao'an [監察院國家人權委員會組織法草案] (Draft proposed organic law for the Control Yuan–national human rights commission). 1st sess. 70委19440. 15 July 2016; 9th Legislative Yuan (2016b) Jianchayuan

Secondly, the controversy over investigatory power, I thought and still think, should be put to rest as a false issue. There are different kinds of investigatory powers enjoyed by different government agencies, the Ministry of Justice, the Control Yuan and a national human rights commission if it were to be created, among others. They are not in conflict. Instead, they are complementary. The delays and discussions about the investigatory power turned out to be an excuse on the part of the political elite. During the administration of Chen Shui-bian, the Executive Yuan was clearly against the creation of a human rights commission, giving the reason that in the effort to streamline the government structure, no new agency should be added. Then there was the opposition of the Control Yuan and the mass media. And for ideological reasons as the guardian of the legacy of the Chinese Nationalist Party, Ma Ying-jeou simply declined to have anything to do with a national human rights commission.

During the presidential campaign and after her election, Tsai Ing-wen repeatedly pledged to set up a national human rights commission, yet with proposals sitting on her desk awaiting her decision, she has declined to move on it. Assuming that Tsai's candidates for the vacant seats in the Control Yuan would be acceptable to the Legislative Yuan, could the decision be made by the end of the year? If the approval of the Legislative Yuan is secured, would President Tsai go ahead and support Mr. Koo and end the wrangling? By choosing to do so, she would have avoided facing the difficult issue of a constitutional amendment, and would seemingly accommodate all parties to the dispute. But in so doing, would she have not forfeited an opportunity to get on with a constitutional amendment for some years to come, thus contributing to the maintenance of the status quo in appearance if not in reality?

References

9th Legislative Yuan (2016a) Jianchayuan Guojia Renquan Weiyuanhui Zuzhifa Cao'an [監察院國家人權委員會組織法草案] (Draft proposed organic law for the Control Yuan–national human rights commission). 1st sess. 70委19440. 15 July

9th Legislative Yuan (2016b) Jianchayuan Zuzhifa Di San Tiao Zhi Yi Tiaowen Xiuzheng Cao'an [監察院組織法第三條之一條文修正草案] (Revision of Article 3 of the Control Yuan organic law bill). 1st sess. 70委19439. 15 July

Cai H-Z (2002) Hanwei Diaochaquan, Jianyuan Maoshang Zongtongfu [捍衛調查權,監院卯上總統府] (Defending investigatory power, the Control Yuan confronts the Presidential Office). China Times, 12 June

Chen S-B (2000) Office of the President, Republic of China. http://english.president.gov.tw/NEWS/2643. Accessed 12 Aug 2017

Coalition for the Promotion of a National Human Rights Commission (2000) Record for the meeting of the coalition for the promotion of a national human rights commission Taipei

---

Zuzhifa Di San Tiao Zhi Yi Tiaowen Xiuzheng Cao'an [監察院組織法第三條之一條文修正草案] (Revision of Article 3 of the Control Yuan organic law bill). 1st sess. 70委19439. 15 July 2016.

Huang M (2001) Drafting a bill for a national human rights commission: Taiwan, 2000. In: Paper presented at the international conference on the national human rights commission: promoting and protecting human rights, The Grand Hotel, Taipei, 2–4 Jan

Huang M (2002) Creating a national human rights commission: report from Taiwan. In: Paper presented at the international symposium on human rights in Taiwan, Howard Civil Service International House, Taipei, 16–18 Oct

Huang P (2000) Taiwan Jidai Sheli Guojia Renquan Weiyuanhui [台灣亟待設立國家人權委員會] (Taiwan needs to set up a national human rights commission). China Times, 4 Jan

Huang M (2017) After review, then what? In: Paper presented at the IAMSCU conference 2017, Universidad Madero, Puebla, Mexico, 27–31 May

Huang S-L (2016) Symposium on the 2016 new government and new Legislative Yuan: How to promote the establishment of the nhri? Taipei

Li N-T (2012) Lun Yi Bali Yuanze yu Jianchayuan Shezhi Guojia Renquan Weiyuanhui [論依巴黎原則於監察院設置國家人權委員會] (Locating a national human rights commission based on the Paris Principles at the Control Yuan). Taiwan Hum Rights J 1:125–143

Lin C-H, Su W-J (2016) Xieren Sifa Yuanzhang Lai Hao-Min, Pi Tsai Zongtong Daji Faguan Shiqi [卸任司法院長賴浩敏 批蔡總統打擊法官士氣] (Lai Hau-Min, retired president of the Judicial Yuan criticized president Tsai for damaging the morale of judges). United Daily News, 1 Nov

Presidential Advisory Committee on Human Rights ROC (2016a) Conclusion reached at the 20th meeting of the presidential advisory committee on human rights. Office of the President, Republic of China (Taiwan). http://www.president.gov.tw/Page/321/20/總統府人權諮詢委員會第二十次委員會議#. Accessed 11 Aug 2017

Presidential Advisory Committee on Human Rights ROC (2016b) Conclusion reached at the 22nd meeting of the presidential advisory committee on human rights. Office of the President, Republic of China (Taiwan). http://www.president.gov.tw/Page/321/22/總統府人權諮詢委員會第二十二次委員會議. Accessed 11 Aug 2017

Su Y-C (2002) Lun Guojia Renquan Weiyuanhui de Jiaose yu Diwei [論國家人權委員會的角色與地位] (The role and status of a national human rights committee). Natl Policy Q 1:1–32

Mab Huang Born and brought up in Xiamen, China, Mab Huang left for Taiwan with his parents in 1948. Having completed his first degree in Law at the National Taiwan University in 1955, he proceeded to the United States for further education, first at the University of Chicago taking up the study of International Relations and then at Columbia University in New York City majoring in political science. After teaching for almost three decades in the United States, Mab Huang returned to Taiwan and is now the Joseph K. Twanmoh Chair Professor at Soochow University, Taipei. He also served as the Director of Chang Fo-chuan Center for the Study of Human Rights (2000–2008), and the Human Rights Program (2006–2008), both of which he helped set up. Mab Huang's publications include Intellectual Ferment for Political Reforms in Taiwan, 1971–1973 (1976) and "Universal Human Rights and Chinese Liberalism," in Human Rights and Asian Values, Michael Jacobsen and Ole Bruun, eds. (2000). With Professor James D. Seymour, Professor Daniel Yu and Professor Theodore Orlin as co-editors, he is the editor-in-chief of a Chinese-English Bilingual Human Rights Dictionary (2007). He found and assumed in December 2010 the position of editor in chief of Taiwan Human Rights Journal. Through the years, Mab Huang also served as a member of the Presidential Human Rights Advisory Committee, from the Chen Shui-bian administration to the present time. He is particularly concerned with human rights education and the bringing of the international human rights regime to Taiwan, including the creation of a national human rights commission and the ratification of international human rights conventions.

Chapter 9
Establishing a National Human Rights Institution—Taiwan in Global Trends

Fort Fu-Te Liao

Abstract The UN has been promoting the establishment of independent NHRIs for several decades and the Paris Principles were passed as the international standards thereof. All treaty bodies believe that NHRIs are positive actors in the implementation of human rights treaties. There are currently 146 NHRIs, having been implemented in over 70% of the world's states. It can be observed that there have been two high tides of NHRI establishment between 1990 and 2009 during which 77% of the world's NHRIs were established. This chapter explores Taiwan's preparatory work in establishing a NHRI in line with global trends. The analysis focuses on three main issues, including historical developments, model types, and accreditation results. It examines both the global trends and Taiwanese endeavors. It explains that only two NHRI models, an independent human rights commission or a human rights ombudsman—the models adopted by most states, are proposed in Taiwan. It also observes that elements such as time, region and model are not key factors in accreditation. When Taiwan prepares to establish a NHRI, competence and responsibility, composition, independence and methods of operation are, in truth, the essential elements to be complied with.

Keywords Accreditation · Convention against torture and other cruel, inhuman or degrading treatment or punishment · Convention on the rights of persons with disabilities · Global alliance of national human rights institutions
National human rights institution

F. F.-T. Liao (✉)
Oxford University, Oxford, UK
e-mail: ftliao@sinica.edu.tw

F. F.-T. Liao
Institute of Law, Academia Sinica, Taipei, Taiwan

J. A. Cohen et al. (eds.), *Taiwan and International Human Rights*, Economics, Law, and Institutions in Asia Pacific, https://doi.org/10.1007/978-981-13-0350-0_9

1 Introduction

Discussion on the establishment of National Human Rights Institutions (hereinafter NHRI) was conducted by the Economic and Social Council of the United Nations (hereinafter UN) as early as 1946, two years earlier than the adoption of the Universal Declaration of Human Rights (hereinafter UDHR) in 1948. There were also unsuccessful endeavors to establish NHRIs in 1960 and 1978. It was not until 1991, however, that the first international conference on NHRIs was held in Paris. The conclusions of this conference included the passing of the Principles relating to the status and functioning of national institutions for the protection and promotion of human rights (hereinafter Paris Principles). The Paris Principles were then endorsed by the Commission on Human Rights and the General Assembly of the UN. The Paris Principles have since become the standard for establishing and measuring the effectiveness of NHRIs.

It should be emphasized that one of the reasons for the legitimacy and continuing influence of the Paris Principles stems from not being a document passed by UN agencies[1] represented by politicians or diplomats. The Paris Principles were passed by NHRIs themselves, that, in a professional sense, are independent and autonomous human rights institutions. It is also important that such professionally derived principles then became important standards followed by sovereign states.

A further development is that all international human rights treaties monitoring bodies believe that NHRIs are positive actors in the implementation of human rights treaties. Therefore, even in the situation that the provision of international human rights treaties does not specifically require it, all treaty bodies recommend that states establish and maintain an independent NHRI. For example, the Committee on the Rights of the Child emphasizes that Article 4 of the Convention on the Rights of the Child (hereinafter CRC) obliges States Parties to "undertake all appropriate legislative, administrative and other measures for the implementation of the rights recognized in the present Convention"; therefore NHRIs are an important mechanism in promoting and ensuring implementation of the Convention.[2]

Another important development includes incorporating NHRIs and the Paris Principles into international human rights treaties. While the early international human rights treaties of the 20th century did not do this, 21st century treaties have incorporated NHRIs and the Paris Principles. In 2002, an independent national preventive mechanism was included when the Optional Protocol to the Convention against Torture and other Cruel, Inhuman or Degrading Treatment or Punishment (hereinafter CAT Protocol) was adopted. Article 17 of the CAT Protocol requires that "each State Party shall maintain, designate or establish, at the latest one year after the entry into force of the present Protocol or of its ratification or accession, one or several independent national preventive mechanisms for the prevention of

[1]De Beco and Murray (2015), pp. 3, 146.

[2]Committee on the Rights of the Child (2002), para 1.

torture at the domestic level." Article 18 of the CAT Protocol provides further substantial requirements for states when establishing national preventive mechanisms. States are required to give due consideration to the Paris Principles and also to guarantee the functional and personnel independence of national preventive mechanisms.

In 2006, the independent mechanism for the rights of disabled people was included when the Convention on the Rights of Persons with Disabilities (hereinafter CRPD) was adopted. Article 33 paragraph 2 of the CRPD requires that states "shall, in accordance with their legal and administrative systems, maintain, strengthen, designate or establish within the State Parties, a framework, including one or more independent mechanisms, as appropriate, to promote, protect and monitor implementation of the present Convention." Further, when designating or establishing such a mechanism, states shall take into account the Paris Principles.

Judged from the strict view of international law, Taiwan, in being not able to deposit instruments of ratification to the Secretary-General of the UN, has not successfully adhered to international human rights treaties. It has been suggested that a NHRI may help in strengthening and complementing international human rights norms domestically. In Taiwan, the impetus for creating a NHRI is in fact coming from the bottom up, originating in civil society before being adopted by the Taiwanese government. Taiwan has been on a journey toward establishing a NHRI in line with global trends.

This chapter, therefore, explores Taiwan's preparatory work in establishing a NHRI. The analysis focuses on three main issues, including historical developments, model types, and accreditation results. Section 2 of this chapter is concerned with the historical development of NHRIs and rethinks what roles NHRIs should play. Section 3 conducts a comprehensive global review of current NHRIs to reveal their realities, while section 4 focuses on the results of the accreditation of NHRIs. This chapter examines both global trends and Taiwanese endeavors in these three sections. Concluding remarks are presented in Sect. 5.

2 Historical Developments

2.1 Two High Tides in Two Decades

It has been argued that the first NHRI was the French Commission Nationale Consultative des Droits de l'Homme which was established in 1947.[3] After seven decades of development, there are now more than one hundred NHRIs.[4]

---

[3]Livingstone and Murray (2004), p. 137.

[4]Kjærum (2015), p. viii.

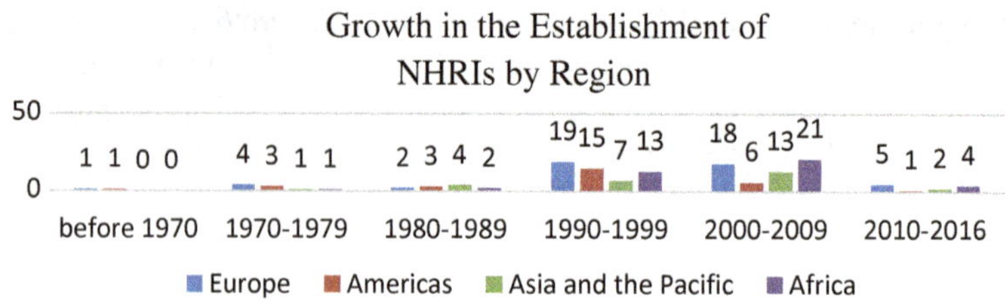

Fig. 1 The growth of NHRIs in the respective regions. (Except where otherwise indicated, all charts and tables used in this chapter are the work of the author.)

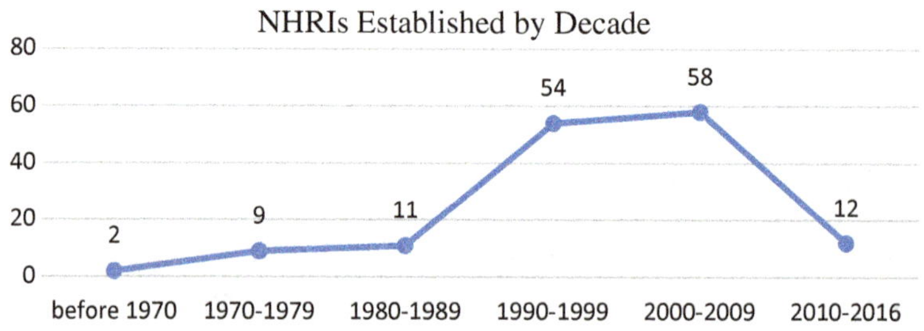

Fig. 2 The establishment of NHRIs by decade

According to the Global Alliance of National Human Rights Institutions (hereinafter GANHRI), by 17 January 2017 there were 146 NHRIs.[5] Among them, there are 49 NHRIs in Europe,[6] 27 in the Asia-Pacific region, 29 in the Americas and 41 in Africa. While currently about 70% of states have NHRIs, there are still 59 states which do not (Figs. 1 and 2).[7]

It is observed that there were two high tides in the establishment of NHRIs between 1990 and 2009. About 77% of NHRIs were established within these two decades, thanks in great part to international promotion. When most NHRIs were established, it should be mentioned that it was the international community that urged the state to establish such an institution. Also, when they were founded or modified, most NHRIs emphasized that they should comply with the Paris Principles.

---

[5]By 17 January 2017 GANHRI's website lists 147 NHRIs. But Tajikistan is repeated; therefore, the number of NHRIs listed at GANHRI should be 146.

[6]In GANHRI's website Armenia, Azerbaijan, Georgia, Kazakhstan and Kyrgyzstan are defined as European states. This definition is followed in this chapter.

[7]There are 9 in Europe, 28 in Asia-Pacific, 14 in Africa and 8 in America.

2.2 From NGOs to Government

As a result of Taiwan's isolation from the international human rights regime, there was little discussion of establishing a Taiwanese NHRI. It was not until the end of 1999 that establishing a NHRI in Taiwan began to be talked about when a group of nongovernmental organizations (hereinafter NGOs) set out to mobilize public opinion. In December 1999, a "Coalition for the Promotion of a national human rights commission in Taiwan"[8] was formed by 22 NGOs. It stated that the Paris Principles and the experiences of other countries would be consulted in designing a NHRI in Taiwan. The Coalition affirmed the principles of independence, effectiveness and reflection of the diversity of society.[9] The proposal, in fact, took place in the middle of the high tide of establishing NHRIs in the international arena.

The Coalition's idea was adopted by the Democratic Progressive Party (hereinafter DPP) in 2000 when the first ever partisan turn-over occurred. In his inaugural speech on 20 May 2000 former President Chen Shui-bian announced: "We hope to set up an independent national human rights commission in Taiwan, thereby realizing an action long advocated by the United Nations."[10] Therefore, the isolated island state, which is not a member of the UN, asserted its desire to follow international standards and trends. The Human Rights Advisory Commission in the Presidential Office proposed bills for a NHRI in 2003. However, such bills did not have the possibility of being passed in the Legislative Yuan (Parliament or Congress) by May 2008 when Chen's term ended. One key reason was that the DPP was a minority party in the Legislative Yuan during that time.

The Chinese Nationalist Party (hereinafter KMT) regained power in May 2008, also maintaining its majority in the Legislative Yuan. If the KMT government wished to establish a NHRI there would have been every possibility of doing so. However, former President Ma Ying-jeou did not focus on this issue during his terms between 2008 and 2016.

Taiwan has, however, incorporated several international human rights treaties, including the ICCPR, ICESCR, CEDAW, CRC and CRPD, in its own way. One special approach to monitoring is to invite independent human rights experts to review state reports. In March 2013, experts who reviewed initial reports on the implementation of the two International Human Rights Covenants recommended that "a specific time frame be set for the establishment of an independent national human rights commission in accordance with the Paris Principles as a priority objective."[11] The Review Committee of the CEDAW report also reiterated "the recommendations from the first CEDAW review in 2009 and the International

[8]Lin (2001), p. 2.

[9]Coalition for the Promotion of a National Human Rights Commission in Taiwan (1999), p. 1.

[10]Chen (2000).

[11]International Group of Independent Experts Taipei (2013) Review of the Initial Reports of the Government of Taiwan on the Implementation of the International Human Rights Covenants, para 9. http://www.humanrights.moj.gov.tw/cp-468-31488-75b0f-200.html. Accessed 20 Apr 2018.

Group of Independent Experts on the ICCPR and ICESCR to establish an independent national human rights institution in accordance with the Paris Principles."[12]

The Ma administration started to respond to these opinions in May 2013 when a team for the establishment of a NHRI was established in the Human Rights Advisory Commission in the Presidential Office. The team concluded several proposals for setting up a NHRI in either the Presidential Office, the Control Yuan (Ombudsmen) or the Executive Yuan (Administrative Government), and also a proposal for a Commission which did not fall under any current constitutional branch. However, no final decision was made by May 2016 when Ma's term ended.

Implementing Acts of the CRC and the CRPD were passed by the Legislative Yuan in May and August 2014, respectively. The Committee on the Rights of the Child emphasizes that NHRIs are an important mechanism for promoting and ensuring implementation of the Convention.[13] The Committee on the Rights of Persons with Disabilities also acknowledged the important role that NHRIs play, among others, in raising awareness of the CRPD's provisions and providing advice to authorities tasked with implementation of the treaty.[14] However, the domestication of the CRC and the CRPD did not accelerate the establishment of a NHRI. The CRC state report did not even mention independent monitoring institutions[15] while the CRPD state report merely described some details of the proposals made by the team for the establishment of a NHRI in the Human Rights Advisory Commission in the Presidential Office.[16]

Ms. Tsai Ing-wen of the DPP became the first female President of Taiwan in May 2016. During her first campaign in 2012 she stressed her support for an independent NHRI that complies with international standards.[17] During her second campaign in 2015 she again proposed an independent NHRI to review policies and laws and to prevent human rights violations.[18]

Again, in February 2017 the Review Committee of the second report on the Covenants recommended "establishing, without further delay, a completely independent and pluralistic national human rights commission in full compliance with the Paris Principles."[19]

As the DPP gained a stable majority in the Legislative Yuan in February 2016 and Tsai became President in May 2016, the DPP dominated both administrative and legislative branches. If the Tsai administration wished to establish a NHRI,

---

[12]Review Committee (2014).

[13]Committee on the Rights of the Child, supra note 2, at para 1.

[14]Committee on the Rights of Persons with Disabilities (2016), para 5.

[15]See Executive Yuan (2016).

[16]See Committee for the Promotion of the Rights of Persons with Disabilities (2016), para 306–307.

[17]*Epoch Times* (2011).

[18]See DPP press release on 9 December 2015.

[19]International Review Committee (2017), para 9.

there would have been a high probability of success. It was expressed by Vice-President Chen Chien-Jen that there would be a clear decision in this regard by the end of 2017.[20] It has to be noted that even if there is political confirmation of establishing a NHRI, a bill will need to be proposed in the Legislative Yuan, and estimating how much time the Legislative Yuan will take to pass such a bill is difficult. An optimistic estimate for passing the bill would be the end of 2018, however, pessimistically, there may be no achievement by May 2020 when Tsai's term ends.

When Taiwan proposed the idea of a NHRI in 1999, it was doing so during the first high tide of the global trend in establishing NHRIs, when 54 NHRIs were established. If Taiwan had established a NHRI at this time, it would have been among the first third of global states to do so. It is, therefore, regrettable that after 18 years, Taiwan still lacks a NHRI, placing it among the 30% of states that have yet to establish one.

3 Model Types

The Paris Principles do not require states to follow one specific NHRI model. The conclusions of the World Conference on Human Rights in 1993 also emphasized that states may decide their own NHRI models, depending on their specific need.[21] It can therefore be expected that different models of NHRIs will be formed.

3.1 Five Main Models

GANHRI has classified NHRIs into six categories, including human rights commissions, human rights ombudsman institutions, hybrid institutions, consultative and advisory bodies, human rights institutes and centers, and multiple institutions.[22] However, some points regarding human rights centers and hybrid institutions should be noted. First, some research institutes may, over time, change the nature of their role into a more positive one of monitoring and protecting human rights, which has been the case in Germany and some Scandinavian states.[23] Germany, Denmark and Norway have each turned their human rights research centers into different types of NHRIs. As a result, there are no NHRIs that are "pure" human rights research centers, and therefore there is no need to include human rights

[20]See Hung (2017).

[21]See UN Human Rights Office of the High Comm'n (1993), Part I, para 36.

[22]See website of GANHRI.

[23]See Liao (2011), p. 55.

research centers as a model type. Second, hybrid and multiple institutions have sufficiently similar characteristics that these two can thus be joined into one type of NHRI for the purposes of this chapter. This chapter therefore distinguishes NHRIs by five types: human rights advisory commissions, single function commissions, hybrid institutions, human rights ombudsmen and independent human rights commissions.

3.1.1 Human Rights Advisory Commission

Human rights advisory commissions can be regarded as the earliest NHRI type, as the French Commission Nationale Consultative des Droits de l'Homme, established in 1947, adopted this model. Despite being the earliest NHRI model, only six states can be found that have adopted an advisory commission as their NHRI model, namely: France, Luxembourg, Italy, Greece, Morocco and Algeria. Among these states, the commissions of France, Luxembourg, Greece and Morocco are accredited by GANHRI as A status.

Applying the UN's ideals and standards to advisory commissions, it is found that human rights advisory commissions can merely play the role of a promoter of human rights as they provide consultative opinions. Firstly, as advisory commissions can neither receive complaints nor be subject to, or conduct investigations, it is difficult to see how advisory commissions can act as protectors of human rights. There is also doubt as to whether advisory commissions can act effectively as a bridge between NGOs and the government as they need laws to guarantee their functions, including acting as a communication channel between NGOs, government and the international community. Fulfilling the function of offering recommendations necessitates being able to play the role of bridge effectively. Secondly, the ambit of the functions of an advisory commission cannot cover all that is required by the Paris Principles. Thirdly, some advisory commissions are regulated merely by administrative orders and none of them has constitutional status. Advisory commissions may not have a solid legal foundation.

3.1.2 Single Function Commission

Some NHRIs have only a single function, especially those concerning equality and anti-discrimination. In Europe, Belgium, Slovakia and Switzerland adopt this model, although Belgium and Slovakia have only one single function commission, whereas Switzerland has adopted two single function commissions which coexist as NHRIs. In addition to establishing commissions to address their own needs, European states establish equality bodies to comply with the European Union's racial[24] and employment equality[25] directives. Nonetheless, when the UN has urged states to establish NHRIs with broad mandates, some European states have adapted their single function commissions into comprehensive ones. Apart from the European states previously mentioned, only Hong Kong and Canada use an equality body (single function commission) as a NHRI.

A single function commission can act as a bridge as well as a promoter and protector which conforms to the expectations of the UN. However, the core problem with this model is that its function is too simplified. The Paris Principles have emphasized that NHRIs should be granted broad mandates. A single function commission can be very positive within one specific field of rights, especially anti-discrimination. Nonetheless, human rights promotion and protection should not be limited to only one field. However, if one commission were set up for each specific right, there would be an enormous number of commissions within the state, making coordination among them very complex. Therefore, there is a tendency for states to turn their single function commission into a comprehensive human rights commission.

3.1.3 Hybrid Institution

In recent years, some states, in order to comply with international standards, have created hybrid NHRIs. One example of how this is achieved is by integrating Ombudsman and human rights centers into a single NHRI. Finland has built a Human Rights Centre within the Ombudsman, while Uruguay combines the two into its National Human Rights Institution and Ombudsman.

A second example is produced through a combination of a human rights center and a single function commission. The Danish Institute for Human Rights, the Danish NHRI, was predominantly a research institution. In March 2004, the Danish Parliament passed Act No. 40 to amend the Act on Prohibition against Discrimination in Respect to Employment and to grant the Danish Institute for Human Rights power to receive complaints concerning racial discrimination. The Institute was also designed as an independent mechanism for promoting the rights of the disabled according to Article 33 of the CRPD.

The third example is that of human rights centers with multiple mandates. The German Institute for Human Rights (DIMR) started as a research center. However, the German government designated DIMR as an independent mechanism for promoting the rights of the disabled in line with the CRPD in 2009 and then as a CRC mechanism in 2015. But DIMR acts as an advisor and promotor, not a protector.

---

[24]Council Directive, 2000/43/EC of 29 June 2000, implementing the principle of equal treatment between persons irrespective of racial or ethnic origin.

[25]Council Directive, 2000/78/EC of 27 November 2000, establishing a general framework of equal treatment in employment and occupation.

A fourth type of hybrid model lists two separate institutions as NHRIs. For example, Bulgaria designates both the Ombudsman and the Commission for Protection against Discrimination, a single function commission, as a NHRI.[26]

3.1.4 Human Rights Ombudsman

Taking an ombudsman as a NHRI is prevalent on the Iberian Peninsula. Spain's Defensor del Pueblo was founded by Article 54 of the 1978 Constitutions, while Portugal passed Law nr. ° 9/91 to establish Provedor de Justiça in 1991. Owing to the influence of Spain and Portugal, most Central and South American states have also adopted the human rights ombudsman model.[27] Some Eastern European states have also adopted this type of NHRI.

A common feature in those states which have adopted ombudsmen as a NHRI is that these ombudsmen were comparatively newly founded institutions, mostly after 1990. Their approach is to follow both trends of establishing an ombudsman and a NHRI at the same time. As for its character, an ombudsman mainly exists to monitor the administrative branch of government. It can, therefore, act well as a protector of human rights, whereas it may not necessarily be a good promotor of rights, being unable to perform functions such as offering advisory opinions or conducting human rights education.

3.1.5 Independent Human Rights Commission

Expanding the remit of a single function institution to that of a comprehensive independent commission is an experience shared by the Commonwealth states. Both Australia's Human Rights and Equal Opportunities Commission[28] and New Zealand's Human Rights Commission[29] have developed from equality bodies into human rights commissions with broad mandates.[30] This has also been the experience in the United Kingdom. The Commission for Equality and Human Rights[31] was established in 2007 by merging the Equal Opportunities Commission,[32] the Commission for Racial Equality[33] and the Disability Rights Commission.[34]

[26]European Union Agency for Fundamental Rights (2012), p. 99.

[27]Elizondo and Aguilar (2000), pp. 209–210.

[28]von Doussa (2005), pp. 4–5.

[29]See Human Rights Act 2001, art 5 (NZ).

[30]Burdekin (2000), p. 831.

[31]O'Cinneide (2007), p. 142.

[32]See Neff and Avebury (2000), pp. 675–677.

[33]See Boothman (2000), pp. 691–732. Hadden (2000), p. 794. McCrudden (1987), pp. 227–266.

[34]See Suk (2006), pp. 439–454.

Many other Commonwealth states, such as Ghana,[35] Uganda,[36] South Africa,[37] Nigeria,[38] India,[39] Malaysia, Fiji,[40] Nepal,[41] and Sri Lanka, have also established independent human rights commissions as their model for NHRIs.

American states, however, do not adopt this model, while many states in Africa and the Asia-Pacific region prefer independent human rights commissions.

3.1.6 Comparative Characteristics

Two different comparative characteristics can be found among these NHRI models. One concerns different essences of the respective models. The other is in regard to their regional distribution.

- Different Essences

Some essential differences can be distinguished among these models. First, the main difference between single function commissions and independent human rights commissions is whether the mandate is limited to anti-discrimination, which is quite a narrow mandate. Mandates of an independent human rights commission may cover different generations of rights and include constitutional and international rights.

Second, an independent human rights commission differs from an advisory commission in that an independent human rights commission does not only act as a promotor of rights but also as a rights protector which may play a more active role through the power of investigation.

Third, a choice between an independent human rights commission and a human rights ombudsman is in fact a decision of structure of state mechanisms. A human rights ombudsman can merge ombudsman services and a NHRI into one institution. The choice of an independent human rights commission model can be quite easy for those states without ombudsmen. However, for those states that already have ombudsmen, choosing an independent human rights commission means establishing two separate organs with divided specializations. A human rights ombudsman can be a passive and ex-post protector, while an independent human rights commission may positively join in protecting human rights.

---

[35]Bossman (2005), pp. 57–86. International Council on Human Rights Policy (2000), pp. 9–20.

[36]Sekaggya (2005), pp. 165–178.

[37]Pityana (2000), pp. 627–638.

[38]Tabiu (2000), pp. 553–560.

[39]Sripati (2000), p. 1.

[40]Shameem (2005), pp. 43–56.

[41]Bahadur (2005), pp. 117–134.

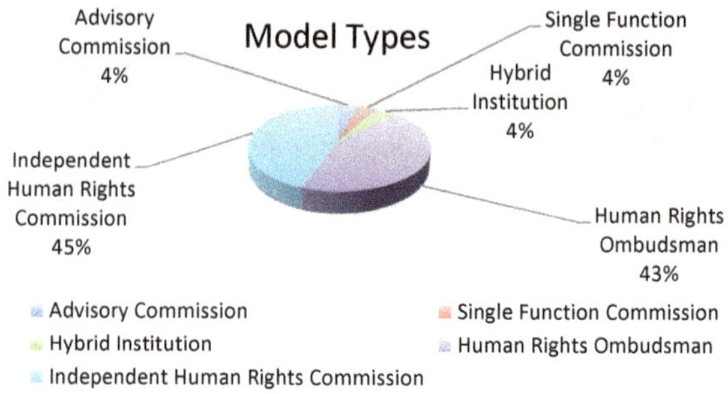

Fig. 3 Proportion of model types of NHRIs

The above five models are all recognized by the UN. However, if NHRIs are to be judged on the ability to fulfil the roles of bridge, promotor and protector as urged by the UN, some models are more acceptable than others. Human rights advisory commissions face difficulties in fulfilling the role of protector of rights, while single function commissions may only fulfil this role in a limited capacity. A human rights ombudsman may not intervene in issues between private parties, meaning that the role of acting as a bridge is unfulfilled. Therefore, independent human rights commissions appear to be the best model available to fully comply with the Paris Principles.

- Respective Distributions

It is found that the choice of which of the five models is adopted varies in respect to the region. In Europe 59% of states have adopted the human rights ombudsmen model; 15% of states prefer independent human rights commissions; 10% opt for hybrid institutions; 8% have adopted human rights advisory commissions and another 8% employ single function commissions. However, in the Americas as many as 86% of states adopt the human rights ombudsman model, whereas in Africa and the Asia Pacific, 80% and 85% of states, respectively, prefer independent human rights commissions.

In the global arena of NHRIs, the independent human rights commission is the most popular model, having been adopted by 45% of states, while the human rights ombudsman model has been adopted by 43% of states. The other three models, the human rights advisory commission, the single function commission and hybrid institutions, have each been adopted by 4% of states (Fig. 3).

3.2 *The Choice Between the Two Models and Approaches*

For Taiwan, the choice between NHRI models concerns two issues. One is about the legal approach, whether to amend the constitutional provisions so a NHRI will have constitutional status or simply to enact new laws. The other concerns regarding model is to be decided on raises questions about whether to abolish the Control Yuan or to which branch of government a NHRI will be subject.

3.2.1 Various Bills

NGOs in Taiwan have presented the "National Human Rights Organic Bill" three times, in 2000, 2009 and 2016. All these Bills proposed to establish a national human rights commission in the Presidential Office, choosing the independent human rights commission model.

The DPP government, during the Chen administration, presented a similar bill, wishing to establish a national human rights commission in the Presidential Office.[42] During the Ma administration, three proposals were put forward for consideration. All three proposals recommended establishing an independent human rights commission but each had different arrangements regarding how they would be subject to governmental branches. One proposal sought to establish a completely independent commission that did not belong to any current branch. A second proposed a commission in the Presidential Office, while the third aimed to establish a commission in the Executive Yuan. These proposals did not alter the status of the Control Yuan. However, there was no final decision by the end of Ma's term. The Tsai administration has not yet proposed a specific model at the time of this writing, the end of August 2017.

The Control Yuan has also proposed the establishment of a NHRI within itself. According to its proposal, a national human rights commission would become one of the specialized commissions in the Control Yuan, but the Control Yuan itself would not become a NHRI. The proposal expanded the mandate of the Control Yuan by including human rights issues, in addition to its original concerns such as impeachment and censure, within the Control Yuan's mandate. The details of this proposal in fact were not the same as those of a human rights ombudsman, as explored above.

3.2.2 Constitutional Amendments

All the above proposals were premised on not amending the Constitution. In 2005 there was a wave of provisions that amended the constitution. Although not all proposals at that time were successful, those proposals referred to human rights institutions and therefore deserve further examination.

The first type of proposal was to establish a human rights ombudsmen/ commission to replace the current Control Yuan. Proposal No. 15407 sought to amend Article 4 of the Additional Amendments of the Constitution to add three Human Rights Ombudsmen to the Legislative Yuan, who were to be nominated by

[42]See Liao, *supra* note 23, at pp. 353–357.

the President and approved by the Legislative Yuan. However, this proposal made reference to the experience of the Swedish ombudsmen, but not to the NHRIs. A second proposal brought forward by proposals No. 15906 and No. 17410 was to establish a national human rights commission in the Legislative Yuan; for this no similar model type from international development was referenced.

The second type of proposal sought the establishment of a national human rights commission with the co-existence of the Control Yuan. Both proposals, No. 17411 and No. 17636, state that "in order to effectively protect and promote human rights there should be established a National Human Rights Commission." This proposal adopted the approach of an independent human rights commission. Further laws had to be enacted to regulate the Commission's structures and mandates.

3.2.3 Options

Whereas five main types of NHRI can be found, proposals in Taiwan, whether from NGOs or governmental agencies, include only two types, i.e., an independent human rights commission or a human rights ombudsman. These two types are adopted by most other states. Therefore, the real decision that must be made in Taiwan is to choose between the two models, and the two legal approaches; constitutional amendment or new laws.

- Type and Affiliation

The first decision that needs to be made is to choose between the Control Yuan and a national human rights commission. This issue may be deliberated in several ways.

Firstly, a fundamental issue is whether to maintain the existence of the Control Yuan. The DPP has consistently advocated abolition of the Control Yuan, President Tsai has also argued for the abolition of the Control Yuan, retaining the Legislative Yuan as a single Parliament.[43] The proposals are in conflict as there are those seeking the abolition of the Control Yuan and those seeking the establishment of a human rights ombudsman/commission within the Control Yuan.

Secondly, observations from international developments show that new democratic states have established their ombudsmen and NHRIs at the same time, as a single body. However, the Control Yuan has already been operational in Taiwan for several decades. As such, the global tendency shows that states that already had ombudsmen have established their NHRIs separately. One of the reasons the UN has given for this is that a NHRI is an institution having "specially designed" mandates of promoting and protecting human rights.

[43]Su et al. (2016).

Thirdly, a NHRI may have a distinctly different nature from that of an ombudsman. One point is that they have different functions; an ombudsman focuses on monitoring administrative governments, while a NHRI focuses on human rights protection. A second point is that the Control Yuan has responsibilities for impeachment, rectification, correction and audit, with its ambit extending to all state organs of the Executive Yuan, Judicial Yuan, Examination Yuan and Control Yuan. There is, therefore, a doubt as to whether the Control Yuan will have sufficient capacity to take account of the promotion and protection of human rights. A third consideration is that a NHRI's mandate includes many human rights functions, such as education, generalization and recommendation. If a NHRI were to become only a part of the Control Yuan, it would be difficult for it to maintain its professional functions and fully achieve its endeavors.

Fourthly, the ambit of human rights is broad, covering many dimensions of human life, such as group labor rights in the event of factory closures and indigenous lands and cultures. Even with its responsibilities for impeachment, rectification, correction and audit, such issues do not fall within the scope of investigation of the Control Yuan;[44] therefore a national human rights commission capable of focusing on the protection of those rights is needed.

Even when an independent human rights commission is chosen, the second problem is to decide to which governmental branch this commission will be subject, the Presidential Office or the Executive Yuan, or whether it will have no affiliation at all.

In fact, there are examples of national human rights commissions being established that are completely independent from the three traditional separations of power, legislative, administrative and judicial. South Korea provides a good model. The National Human Rights Commission of the Republic of Korea is regarded as a quasi-international institution,[45] not being subject to any one of the legislative, administrative or judicial branches. Therefore, it can be suggested that in Taiwan a national human rights commission that is not subject to any of the current five Yuans would be an option. A second choice is, as argued by NGOs, to establish a national human rights commission in the model of Academia Sinica. The model provided by Academia Sinica shows that an independent institution can be established under the Presidential Office while still maintaining its independence. The last option would be a national human rights commission under the Executive Yuan.

- Legal Approach

A better legal approach to establish a national human rights commission in Taiwan would be to grant it constitutional status. The above-mentioned constitutional amendment proposals which sought to establish a national human rights commission

---

[44]See Huang (2003), pp. 4–10.

[45]Liu (2008), p. 129.

to replace the Control Yuan did not reflect the international standards of NHRIs. It should be emphasized that a comprehensive constitutional rule establishing a NHRI should include its independence, mandate and qualification as well as the selection method and the term of its members. Therefore, a new constitutional provision for the establishment of a national human rights commission is proposed, which reads:

1. *Mandates of the National Human Rights Commission (Commission) include*

    (1) *The drafting and reviewing of policies and laws for the purpose of promoting and protecting human rights.*
    (2) *Producing an annual national human rights report.*
    (3) *Conducting human rights education and promoting human rights ideas.*
    (4) *Implementing international human rights standards and promoting domestic and international human rights exchanges and co-operation.*
    (5) *Dealing with significant human rights events.*
    (6) *Visiting locations where serious violations of human rights may occur.*
    (7) *Other matters related to human rights promotion and protection.*

2. *There shall be 15 Human Rights Commissioners who are nominated by the President and approved by the Legislative Yuan. There shall be one Chief Human Rights Commissioner who is of political appointment rank and in charge of the affairs of the Commission, and a Deputy Chief Human Rights Commissioner who is of a rank equivalent to Grade 14 to assist the Chief Human Rights Commissioner. Other Human Rights Commissioners shall be of a rank equivalent to Grade 13.*
3. *The term of a Human Rights Commissioner is four years. When there is a vacancy, the term of the Human Rights Commissioner shall be completed by her/his successor.*
4. *A Human Rights Commissioner should have one of the following qualifications:*

    (1) *Having outstanding achievements in or contributing to the promotion and protection of human rights or disadvantaged groups.*
    (2) *Having outstanding publications or research in regard to human rights issues.*

5. *Human Rights Commissioners shall go beyond political parties and exercise their functions independently. They should not participate in any activities of political parties.*

Even without a constitutional amendment, a national human rights commission, whether under the Presidential Office or Executive Yuan or even with no affiliation, could be founded by enacting new laws which regulate its structures and mandates.

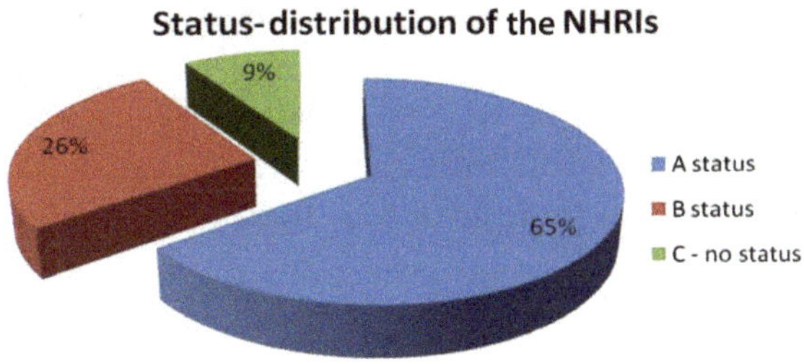

Fig. 4 *Source* National Human Rights Institutions and United Nations Treaty Bodies, GANHRI background paper, May 2016, p. 6

4 Accreditation Results

4.1 Comparative Outcomes

According to GANHRI's statistics in May 2016, among all NHRIs 65% of them are accredited as A status, 26% B status, 9% C status or without accreditation (Fig. 4).[46]

This section attempts to update the status of these NHRIs by reviewing factors such as time, region and model.

4.1.1 Time Factor

One key point to be considered is whether newly established NHRIs get better accreditations than longer established ones. There were only two states, France and Guyana, that had established their NHRIs by 1970; the French NHRI has been awarded A status, while Guyana's has not even been accredited. Among the nine NHRIs founded between 1970 and 1979, three have been awarded A status, two B, two C and two have no accreditation. There were fifty-four NHRIs established between 1990 and 1999. Among them, thirty have received A status, eleven B, five C, while eight have no accreditation. Among the fifty-seven NHRIs founded between 2000 and 2009, twenty-six have been awarded A status, eleven B, one C and nine have no accreditation. The number of NHRIs established between 2010 and 2016 is fourteen, of which six have received A status, three B and five have no accreditation (Table 1).

It can therefore be observed that time is not a key factor that affects the result of accreditations, as we can find that NHRIs established in each decade fall into different statuses and newly established NHRIs do not necessarily receive better accreditation statuses.

---

[46]According to GANHRI, there are currently three levels of accreditation: "A" voting member: complies fully with the Paris Principles, "B" observer member: does not fully comply with the Paris Principles or has not yet submitted sufficient documentation to make that determination, and "C" non-member: does not comply with the Paris Principles. See the website of the GANHRI.

Table 1 Number and proportion of accredited of NHRIs by decade

	A status Number/ Proportion		B status Number/ Proportion		C status Number/ Proportion		NO status Number/ Proportion		Total
Before 1970	1	50%	0	0%	0	0%	1	50%	2
1970–1979	3	34%	2	22%	2	22%	2	22%	9
1980–1989	6	60%	1	10%	2	20%	1	10%	10
1990–1999	30	56%	11	20%	5	9%	8	15%	54
2000–2009	26	46%	11	19%	1	2%	19	33%	57
2010–2016	6	43%	3	21%	0	0%	5	36%	14

4.1.2 Regional Distribution

A second possible factor affecting the accreditation status of NHRIs may be the regional distribution. It can be found that among the forty-nine European NHRIs, twenty-five have obtained A status, twelve B, three C and nine have no accreditation. In the Asia-Pacific, among the twenty-seven NHRIs fifteen have received A status, six B, two C and four have not been accredited. In the Americas, among the twenty-nine NHRIs fourteen have obtained A, two B, three C and ten have no accreditation. In Africa, there are forty-one NHRIs. Only eighteen have obtained A status, 8 have received B, two C, while there are thirteen that have not been accredited (Table 2).

It can also be found that the highest proportion of A status NHRIs is in the Asia-Pacific region, while the lowest proportion is in the Americas, where the highest proportion of NHRIs without accreditation can also be found. However, it does appear that there is an obvious regional distribution of accreditation outcomes.

For an overall picture of the world's 146 NHRIs, seventy-two have received A status, twenty-eight have received B, ten have obtained C, whereas thirty-six have no accreditation. This shows that less than half of the world's NHRIs are regarded as fully complying with the Paris Principles, and as many as 25% of all NHRIs have

Table 2 Number and proportion of accredited of NHRIs by region

	Europe		Asia Pacific		Americas		Africa		Total	
B status	12	25%	6	22%	2	7%	8	19%	28	19%
C status	3	6%	2	7%	3	10%	2	5%	10	7%
NO status	9	18%	14	15%	10	35%	13	32%	36	25%
Total	49	100%	27	100%	29	100%	41	100%	146	100%

not even been accredited. Therefore, the task is not only to urge the establishment of NHRIs but also to require them to fully realize their mandates and comply with the Paris Principles.

4.1.3 Model Difference

Model type may be taken as a third factor to account for differences in the accreditation results obtained by the NHRIs. Among the five models reviewed, human rights advisory commissions receive the highest proportion of A status accreditations. However, as there are only six NHRIs of this type and, as such, the sample size is insufficient to draw conclusions. Roughly half the NHRIs of the following three types; hybrid institution, human rights ombudsman and independent human rights commission, have obtained A status. While single function commissions have received the lowest rate of A status accreditation, it seems that GANHRI puts much more emphasis on whether a NHRI's mandate is broad and not limited to one particular right. As an overall review, it is reasonable to say that no one specific model receives better accreditations (Table 3).

4.2 Reminder for Taiwan

As has been noted, when a NHRI has been established does not affect its accreditation status and Taiwan should be reminded that a newly founded NHRI does not necessarily achieve a better accreditation result. Although the NHRIs in the Asia-Pacific receive the highest rate of A status accreditations, it does not follow that a NHRI in Taiwan, being a state in this region, will definitely obtain an A status. While about half of the two models of NHRI, human rights ombudsman and independent human rights commission, focused on by proposals in Taiwan receive A status accreditation, it should be noted that it does not mean that if Taiwan were to choose one of these NHRI models, it will be guaranteed an A status.

In fact, it should be emphasized that the GANHRI provides a checklist for assessing conformity with the Paris Principles, focusing on four areas including competence and responsibility, composition, independence and methods of operation. Therefore, it should be observed that elements such as time, region and model are not key factors when accreditation is considered. During Taiwan's preparations to establish a NHRI, competence and responsibility, composition, independence and methods of operation are the essential elements to be complied with.

Table 3 Number and proportion of accredited NHRIs by model

	Advisory Commission		Single Function Commission		Hybrid Institution		Human Rights Ombudsman		Independent Human Rights Commission		Total	
A status	4	67%	1	16%	3	50%	31	49%	33	51%	72	49%
B status	1	16%	1	17%	2	33%	10	16%	14	21%	28	19%
C status	0	0%	3	50%	0	0%	4	6%	3	5%	10	7%
NO status	1	17%	1	17%	1	17%	18	29%	15	23%	36	25%
Total	6	100%	6	100%	6	100%	63	100%	65	100%	146	100%

5 Concluding Remarks

The UN has been promoting the establishment and maintenance of independent NHRIs for several decades. The Paris Principles were passed by independent and autonomous NHRIs themselves and have been regarded as the international standards for establishing NHRIs. All treaty bodies believe that NHRIs are positive actors in the implementation of human rights treaties and as such NHRIs and the Paris Principles have been incorporated into international human rights treaties.

According to lists compiled by the GANHRI, as of 17 January 2017 there were 146 NHRIs, implemented in over 70% of the world's states. However, there were still 59 states without a NHRI. It can be observed that there were two high tides of NHRI establishment between 1990 and 2009, and about 77% of the world's NHRIs were established during these two decades. The justification for most NHRIs mentions international promotion of human rights and the Paris Principles.

As Taiwan was long isolated from the international human rights regime, it was not until the end of 1999 that some NGOs promoted the establishment of a NHRI. This proposal, in fact, came in the middle of the high tide of NHRI establishment in the international arena. The idea of establishing a NHRI was then adopted by President Chen Shui-bian in an attempt to bring the isolated island state of Taiwan, which is not a member of the UN, in line with international standards and trends. However, subsequent administrations did not focus much on this issue in the intervening years. Recently, however, there have been significant developments toward establishing a NHRI in Taiwan and it was expressed by the current Taiwanese government that a clear decision on this issue would be made by the end of 2017.

Neither the Paris Principles nor the Conclusions of the World Conference on Human Rights require states to follow one specific NHRI model. NHRIs can be distinguished by five types, including human rights advisory commissions, single function commissions, hybrid institutions, human rights ombudsmen and independent human rights commissions. Adoption of the five models varies in different regions. In Europe 59% of states have adopted human rights ombudsmen; in the Americas, as many as 86% of states have adopted the human rights ombudsman model, whereas in Africa and the Asia-Pacific, 80% and 85% of states, respectively, prefer independent human rights commissions. In the global arena of NHRIs, independent human rights commissions occupy the highest proportion, with 45% of states adopting this model, while the human rights ombudsman model is adopted by 43% of states. The other three models, human rights advisory commissions, single function commissions and hybrid institutions, have each been adopted by 4% of states.

For Taiwan, the choice between NHRIs models raises two issues. One issue is in regard to the legal approach; whether to amend the constitutional provisions so a NHRI will have constitutional status or simply to enact new laws. The other concerns which model is to be adopted, which raises questions of whether to abolish the Control Yuan or to which branch of government the NHRI will be subject. Only two

NHRI models, an independent human rights commission or a human rights ombudsman——the models adopted by most states—have been proposed in Taiwan.

It has also been shown that accreditation results do not depend on when the NHRIs are established. Newly established NHRIs do not necessarily receive better accreditations than older ones, nor does it appear that there is an obvious regional distribution of accreditation outcomes. As an overall review, it is reasonable to say that no one specific model gets better accreditations. It has further been shown that less than half of the NHRIs have been regarded as fully compliant with the Paris Principles and as many as 25% of NHRIs have not even been accredited. The task, therefore, is not only to urge for the establishment of NHRIs but also to require them to fully realize their mandates and comply with the Paris Principles.

The accreditation results remind Taiwan that a newly established NHRI does not necessarily obtain better accreditation results than an older one and that, although the NHRIs in Asia and the Pacific receive the highest rate of A status accreditation, it does not mean that a NHRI in Taiwan will definitely obtain an A status. While about half of the proposals in Taiwan focus on two models of NHRIs. Human rights ombudsman and independent human rights commission, achieve A status, it should be noted that it does not mean that if Taiwan were to choose one of these models that a Taiwanese NHRI would be guaranteed an A status. In fact, it should be emphasized that GANHRI provides a checklist for assessing conformity with the Paris Principles, focusing on four areas, including competence and responsibility, composition, independence and methods of operation. Therefore, it should be observed that elements such as time, region and model are not key factors for accreditation. When Taiwan does prepare to establish a NHRI, competence and responsibility, composition, independence and methods of operation are the essential elements that require compliance.

References

Bahadur N (2005) The protection role of the Nepalese Human Rights Commission. In: Ramcharan BG (ed) The protection role of National Human Rights Institutions. Martinus Nijhoff Publishers, Leiden, pp 117–134

Boothman C (2000) The Commission of Racial Equality. In: Kamal H et al (eds) Human Rights Commissions and Ombudsman Offices: national experience throughout the world. Kluwer Law International, Alphen aan den Rijin Frigen, pp 691–732

Bossman A (2005) The protection role of the Ghana Human Rights Commission. In: Ramcharan B (ed) The protection role of National Human Rights. Martinus Nijhoff Publishers, Leiden, pp 57–86

Burdekin B (2000) Human rights commissions. In: Kamal L et al (eds) Human Rights Commissions and Ombudsman Offices: national experience throughout the world. Kluwer Law International, New York, pp 827–835

Chen S (2000) Taiwan stands up: toward the dawn of a rising era, inauguration speech by President Chen S-B on 20 May 2000

Coalition for the Promotion of a National Human Rights Commission (1999) Press Release of the Coalition for the Promotion of a national human rights commission in Taiwan on 9 Dec

Committee for the Promotion of the Rights of Persons with Disabilities (2016) Implementation of the Convention on the Rights of Persons with Disabilities: initial report submitted under Article 35 of the Convention, Republic of China (Taiwan). https://www-ws.pthg.gov.tw/Upload/2015pthg/18/ckfile/eae93d5b-4225-4dbb-b1ea-e4120ec709a5.pdf. Accessed 20 Apr 2018

Committee on the Rights of Persons with Disabilities (2016) Draft guidelines on the establishment of an independent monitoring framework and participation in the work of the Committee. http://www.ohchr.org/Documents/HRBodies/CRPD/16thsession/DraftGuideline_establishment_independent_monitoring_frameworks.doc. Accessed 8 Dec 2017

Committee on the Rights of the Child, General Comment No. 2 (2002) The role of independent national human rights institutions in the promotion and protection of the rights of the child, November, CRC/GC/2002/2

De Beco G, Murray R (2015) A commentary on the Paris Principles on National Human Rights Institutions. Cambridge University Press, Cambridge

DPP press release "Tsai Ing-Wen: Establishing National Human Rights Commission Let Human Rights Values be implanted into Taiwanese Culture" on 9 December 2015. http://www.dpp.org.tw/news_content.php?kw=%E6%AD%A5&m1=12&y1=2022&menu_sn=7&sub_menu=43&show_title=%E6%96%B0%E8%81%9E&one_page=10&page=60&start_p=51&act=&sn=8529&stat=&order_type=desc&order_col=add_date&data_type=%E6%96%B0%E8%81%9E. Accessed 15 Dec 2017

Elizondo G, Aguilar I (2000) The ombudsman institution in Latin America: minimum standards for its existence. In: Lindsnaes B, Lindholt L, Yigen K (eds), National Human Rights Institutions articles and working papers. Danish Institute for Human Rights, Copenhagen, pp 209–220

Epoch Times (2011) Tsai Ing-Wen: support establishing National Human Rights Commission, 17 Dec 2011

European Union Agency for Fundamental Rights (2012) Handbook on the establishment and accreditation of National Human Rights Institutions in the European Union. European Union Agency for Fundamental Rights

Executive Yuan (2016) Implementation of the convention on the Rights of the Child: initial report submitted under Article 44 of the Convention, Republic of China (Taiwan). https://www.google.com.tw/url?sa=t&rct=j&q=&esrc=s&source=web&cd=1&cad=rja&uact=8&ved=0ahUKEwjkktq21PrXAhXEj5QKHT7pDFUQFggpMAA&url=http://crc.sfaa.gov.tw%2Fdownload_file.php%3Ff%3DrJ7QFjzfrT__iaTApv8NM3hPVnN2kciorfkCu4G9pSCWg2_cdsMd4g8YxhwkDzmgejSXZwDzUueXqmMWYgfYFw&usg=AOvVaw2FUjTDeAg-CwtunVJJqzOi. Accessed 8 Dec 2017

GANHRI (2017) http://nhri.ohchr.org/EN/AboutUs/Pages/RolesTypesNHRIs.aspx. Accessed 23 Aug 2017

Hadden T (2000) The role of a National Commission in the protection of human rights. In: Kamal H et al (eds) Human Rights Commissions and Ombudsman Offices: national experience throughout the world. Kluwer Law International, New York, pp 786–799

Huang M (2003) Promotion, arguments and prospects of Taiwan's "National Human Rights Commission": a view from a NGO. Taiwan Bar J 7:4–10

Hung Y-C (2017) National Human Rights Institution to be established, Chen Chien-Jen saying. Storm Media. http://www.storm.mg/article/213533. Accessed 8 Dec 2017

International Council on Human Rights Policy, Performance and Legitimacy: National Human Rights Institutions (2000) International Council on Human Rights

International Group of Independent Experts Taipei (2013) Review of the initial reports of the Government of Taiwan on the implementation of the international human rights covenants. http://www.humanrights.moj.gov.tw/cp-468-31488-75b0f-200.html. Accessed 20 Apr 2018

International Review Committee (2017) Review of the Second Reports of the Government of Taiwan on the Implementation of the International Human Rights Covenants. http://www.humanrights.moj.gov.tw/cp-487-31598-9616e-200.html. Accessed 20 Apr 2018

Kjærum M (2015) Foreword. In: De Beco G, Murray RA (eds) Commentary on the Paris Principles on National Human Rights Institutions. Cambridge University Press, Cambridge, pp i–viii

Liao F (2011) National Human Rights Commission. Wu-Nan, Taipei

Lin F (2001) The role of NGOs in setting up a National Human Rights Commission in Taiwan. In: Paper presented at the international conference on National Human Rights Commissions: promoting and protecting human rights. Taipei, Taiwan, 2–4 Jan

Liu N (2008) Human rights institutions and international communications: experience from the Republic of Korea. In: 228 memorial foundation, 2008 first Taiwan-Korea human rights forum proceedings, 2/28 Memorial Foundation, Taipei, pp 129–136

Livingstone S, Murray R (2004) The effectiveness of National Human Rights Institutions. In: Halliday S, Schmidt P (eds) Human rights brought home: socio-legal perspectives on human rights in the national context. Hart Publishing, Oxford, pp 126–137

McCrudden C (1987) The commission for racial equality: formal investigations in the shadow of judicial review. In: Baldwin R, McCrudden C (eds) Regulation and public law. Weidenfeld and Nicolson, London, pp 227–266

Neff S, Avebury E (2000) Human rights mechanisms in the United Kingdom. In: Hossain K et al (eds) Human Rights Commissions and Ombudsman Offices: national experience throughout the world. Kluwer Law International, New York, pp 670–684

O'Cinneide C (2007) The commission for equality and human rights: a new institution for new and uncertain times. Ind Law J 36(2):141–162

Pityana B (2000) The South African human rights commission. In: Hossain K et al (eds) Human Rights Commissions and Ombudsman Offices: national experience throughout the world. Kluwer Law International, New York, pp 627–638

Review Committee (2014) Review of Taiwan's second report on the implementation of the CEDAW. https://www.gec.ey.gov.tw/en/DL.ashx?u=/Upload/RelFile/2970/715274/Review%2520of%2520Taiwan%25e2%2580%2599s%2520Second%2520Report%2520on%2520the%2520Implementation%2520of%2520CEDAW%2520%2520%2520%2520%2520Conclusions%2520and%2520Recommendations%2520of%2520the%2520Review%2520Committee.pdf. Accessed 8 Dec 2017

Sekaggya M (2005) The protection role of the Uganda Human Rights Commission. In: Ramcharan B (ed) The protection role of National Human Rights Institutions. Martinus Nijhoff Publishers, Leiden, pp 165–178

Shameem S (2005) The protection role of the Fiji Human Rights Commission. In: Ramcharan B (ed) The protection role of National Human Rights Institutions. Martinus Nijhoff Publishers, Leiden, pp 43–56

Sripati V (2000) India's National Human Rights Commission: a shackled commission. Boston Univ Int Law J 18:1–46

Su F-H et al. (2016) Tsai reiterates position of abolishing the Control Yuan is not changed. Liberty Times. http://news.ltn.com.tw/news/politics/paper/1040796. Accessed 23 Aug 2017

Suk C (2006) Antidiscrimination law in the administrative state. University of Ill Law Rev. Spring:405–474

Tabiu M (2000) National Human Rights Commission of Nigeria. In: Hossain K et al (eds) Human Rights Commissions and Ombudsman Offices: national experience throughout the world. Kluwer Law International, New York, pp 553–560

UN Human Rights Office of the High Comm'n (1993) Vienna declaration and programme of action. http://www.ohchr.org/EN/ProfessionalInterest/Pages/Vienna.aspx. Accessed 8 Dec 2017

von Doussa J (2005) The protection role of the Australian Human Rights Commission. In: Ramcharan B (ed) The protection role of National Human Rights Institutions. Martinus Nijhoff Publishers, Leiden, pp 2–15

Fort Fu-Te Liao received his D.Phil. in Law from Oxford University. He is a research professor at the Institute of Law, Academia Sinica, Taiwan, with a joint appointment as a professor at the Graduate Institute of National Development of National Taiwan University. He also teaches at Chang Fo-Chuan Center for the Study of Human Rights of Soochow University and the College of Law of National Taipei University. His research interests focus on international human rights law and constitutional law. His main published books include *European Human Rights Law* (2003), *International Human Rights Law—Issues and Implementation* (2005), *Essays on Human Rights Law* (2007), *National Human Rights Commission* (2011), *International Human Rights Law's Domestic Impacts* (2012), The *United Nations and Human Rights Protections* (2013), and *Right to Private Life* (2014).

Chapter 10
The Control Yuan and Human Rights in Taiwan: Towards the Development of a National Human Rights Institution?

Ernest Caldwell

> *Taiwan has not yet decided whether it should establish a completely independent [human rights] institution or to subordinate it to either the Presidential Office or the Control Yuan.*
>
> (International Group of Independent Experts 2017).

Abstract This chapter contributes to the growing literature on international human rights and National Human Rights Institutions (NHRIs) in Taiwan. Despite decades of debate, Taiwan has never established a NHRI that complies with international human rights norms. At present, Taiwan is confronted with three viable options: the creation of an independent NHRI, the creation of a national commission under the Office of the President, or the reform of the Control Yuan into a NHRI. In this chapter, I focus on the latter option: the use of the Control Yuan as a NHRI. Specifically, I consider the historical relationship of the Control Yuan to human rights in Taiwan, and further consider the socio-legal as well as constitutional, implications of reforming this branch of government into a NHRI that complies with international human rights norms.

Keywords Control yuan · National human rights institution · Martial law

1 Introduction

In 2013, the Taiwanese government underwent its first ICCPR and ICESCR compliance review by an independent group of international experts in the field of human rights. Following that review, the group recommended, *inter alia*, that the government set a specific time frame "for the establishment of an independent

---

E. Caldwell (✉)
School of Law and Centre for Taiwan Studies, SOAS,
University of London, London, UK
e-mail: ec24@soas.ac.uk

J. A. Cohen et al. (eds.), *Taiwan and International Human Rights*, Economics, Law, and Institutions in Asia Pacific, https://doi.org/10.1007/978-981-13-0350-0_10

national human rights commission in accordance with the Paris Principles as a priority objective."[1] However, by the time of the second periodic review, conducted in January 2017, the group of experts still noted that despite their previous recommendation, Taiwan had yet to establish a National Human Rights Institution (hereafter "NHRI") that complies with the Paris Principles.[2] There are, of course, several reasons for the delay, but one primary reason is hinted at in the opening quotation of this chapter. What type of NHRI should Taiwan establish? The Paris Principles, which have become a set of international standards for establishing NHRIs, are written in broad and general language. Furthermore, although the Paris Principles enumerate specific functions and mandates, they do not define a NHRI by any specific structural form. Indeed, the list of NHRIs internationally accredited by the Global Alliance for National Human Rights Institutions (hereafter "GANHRI")[3] evidences a variety of acceptable institutional structures, ranging from single-member ombudsman offices to multi-member independent commissions. Therefore, in creating its own NHRI Taiwan can choose from several possible existing NHRI structures used in other jurisdictions or it can produce something unique, as long as the established institution conforms to the international norms provided by the Paris Principles.

In Taiwan, there has been little debate over whether the country needs a dedicated human rights institution or commission. However, the primary issue precluding the establishment of a NHRI to date has been the fact that the Taiwanese have yet to determine what type of NHRI best suits Taiwan's political and social landscape.[4] As the initial quote shows, Taiwan is currently confronted by three options for the establishment of a NHRI: a fully independent commission, a quasi-independent commission housed in the Presidential Office, or a commission housed within a reformed and repurposed Control Yuan. These options are not necessarily new and

[1]International Group of Independent Experts (2013) Review of the Initial Report of the Government of Taiwan on the Implementation of the International Human Rights Covenants: Concluding Observations and Recommendations Adopted by the International Group of Independent Experts, paras. 8–9. http://www.humanrights.moj.gov.tw/HitCounter.asp?xItem=385451&mp=205. Accessed 12 Sept 2017.

[2]The "Principles Relating to the Status and Function of National Institutions for the Protection and Promotion of Human Rights" (hereafter "Paris Principles") were drafted in 1991 by existing NHRIs and subsequently endorsed by the Commission on Human Rights in 1992 and the United Nations General Assembly in 1993. At present, they are internationally accepted as "the template against which to assess an NHRI." De Beco and Murray (2015).

[3]GANHRI, formerly known as the International Coordination Committee of National Institutions for the Promotion and Protection of Human Rights, has a Sub-committee on Accreditation (SCA). The SCA receives applications for accreditation from NHRIs and provides a ranking of "A"—fully compliant, "B"—partially compliant, or "C"—not compliant. This accreditation opens the door for various levels of participation in regional and UN-supported human rights events. Taiwan has not yet submitted an institutional application for accreditation. For more information, visit: Global Alliance of National Human Rights Institutions. http://nhri.ohchr.org/. Accessed 12 Sept 2017.

[4]Wei (2012), Huang (2014), Li (2012).

have been debated for decades.[5] Most recently, at a forum of NHRI experts held in the Legislative Yuan in Taipei from 24 to 28 July 2017, these three options were considered at length. In the end, the panelists recommended that of the three possible options for establishing a NHRI for Taiwan, the "rebranding" and transformation of the Control Yuan into a NHRI would be the most logical and cost-efficient option.[6] In this chapter I examine the Control Yuan's relationship to human rights in Taiwan, and then critically analyze the potential to transform the institution into a NHRI fully compliant with the Paris Principles. I argue that although the Control Yuan certainly appears to be the most logical choice, its successful transformation is by no means an easy task. Many of the alterations necessary to meet the compliance standards of the international human rights community require significant constitutional revisions, changes to legislation, and a bolstering of the Control Yuan's public image. Due to the procedural requirements for making constitutional changes and legislative revisions, such alterations, however minor, would require a great deal of cross-party cooperation as well as immense public support. It is hoped that the present chapter complements the other chapters on NHRIs in this volume written by Professors Mab Huang and Liao Fu-te.

This chapter consists of five sections. Following this introduction, Section 2 examines the Control Yuan as a constitutional branch of the national government and further considers the historical development of its role in the protection and promotion of human rights in Taiwan. Section 3 then provides a basic assessment of the Control Yuan vis-à-vis the Paris Principles. Section 4 turns to the steps highlighted by the recent forum at which participants discussed necessary options to transform the Control Yuan into a NHRI capable of receiving international accreditation, and critically assesses the feasibility of executing such changes. Finally, Section 5 concludes the chapter by considering the ongoing debates over the future of the Control Yuan and the potential impact of that future on human rights development and protection in Taiwan.

2 The Control Yuan and Human Rights: A Very Brief History

Those unfamiliar with the constitutional structure of Taiwan's national government may be forgiven for asking, *what is the Control Yuan?* or *what is the Control Yuan's relationship to human rights*? While the vast majority of the world's

---

[5]Su (2002), Liao (2001).

[6]Ren Quan Gong Yue Shi Xing Jian Du Lian Meng [Covenants Watch] (人權公約施行監督聯盟) (2017) Guo Ji Zhuan Jia Lai Tai Jin Xing Guo Jia Ren Quan Wei Yuan Hui Ping Gu Ren Wu Chu Bu Sheng Ming [Preliminary Report by International Specialists Assessing the Progress of a National Human Rights Institution] (國際專家來台進行國家人權委員會評估任務初步聲明). Ren Quan Gong Yue Shi Xing Jian Du Lian Meng [Covenants Watch] (人權公約施行監督聯盟). http://covenantswatch.org.tw/2017/07/28/preliminary_statement/. Accessed 12 Sept 2017.

constitutions divide government power via a tripartite government structure attributed to Montesquieu, the 1947 Republic of China Constitution (hereafter "1947 ROC Constitution") divides government power amongst five distinct branches of government.[7] Three of these branches correspond to the archetypical Executive, Legislative, and Judicial branches common throughout the world; however, two additional branches—drawing on China's imperial government institutions—complete the ROC's constitutional structure, the Control Yuan and the Examination Yuan.[8]

When first theorizing the five-power constitution, Sun Yat-sen (孫逸仙) showed great concern over both the dangers of maladministration and the potential for one branch of government to infringe on the powers of other branches. To deal with this problem, Sun took inspiration from the censorate (*yü shi* 御史), an institution of the former imperial government tasked with monitoring the conduct of officials throughout the empire, investigating claims of corruption or negligence, and further empowered to arrest or impeach officials in the name of the Emperor.[9] The modernized Control Yuan (Jian cha yuan 監察院) of Sun Yat-sen was thus designed to monitor and investigate government officials, impeach corrupt or negligent officials, provide consent for presidential appointments, and audit the government's expenditures.[10] Like its predecessor, the censorate, the modern institution's primary task was to ensure the government functioned efficiently. Thus, in its early manifestation, the Control Yuan had little influence on human rights. That said, one key function that would become important in later years is the Control Yuan's ability to receive and investigate individual petitions. At the time, these petitions were not necessarily articulated as human rights claims but were instead often claims against official corruption or negligence. In 1947, for example, the Control Yuan received over 14,000 individual petitions. During these early days of the institution, the individual petitions systems simply served as a means for the government, or at least its officials, to be monitored and to ensure it maintained the rule of law and lived up to the liberal democratic principles enshrined in the Constitution. This function would later become important as the individual petitions system of the Control Yuan now serves as one of the principal means for people to bring claims of human rights abuses against the government regarding official conduct or executive policy.

Like many other national-level institutions, the influence of the Control Yuan on government administration diminished greatly during the period of martial law (1949–1987). With the loss of the civil war on the Mainland to Communist forces, the Nationalist government transferred its operations to Taipei. Under the infamous Temporary Provisions and martial law, the majority of the liberal democratic elements of the Constitution were suspended, including numerous civil and political

[7]See generally, Vile (1998).

[8]See generally, Caldwell (2017a), Pan (1983).

[9]See generally, Walker (1947).

[10]See generally, Caldwell (2017b), Tung (1964).

rights.[11] Although the Control Yuan technically maintained its constitutional mandates, it was faced with the conundrum of attempting to act independently to investigate and potentially impeach officials of an authoritarian government. The martial-law period saw a drastic decline in impeachment cases; yet, despite its curtailed ambit of operations, the Control Yuan did manage to perform several beneficial acts for Taiwanese citizens and in some limited ways opened the door for increased awareness of citizens' rights vis-à-vis the government.[12] First, although the total number of individual petitions declined under martial law, several thousand citizens continued to file individual petitions each year. Most of these petitions related to corruption or abuse of power by lower-ranking officials. Second, prior to 1958, citizens lacked standing to petition the Judicial Yuan for a constitutional interpretation.[13] To circumvent this obstacle, citizens could submit individual petitions to the Control Yuan, which did have standing to request constitutional interpretations. Between 1950 and 1990, the Control Yuan requested thirty-nine interpretations, second only to the Executive Yuan. Many of these sought clarification over the constitutionality of the KMT government's actions and policies.[14] Lastly, although the number of impeachments dropped, the Control Yuan increasingly relied on a more politically safe power, its power to issue corrective measures (*jiu zheng* 糾正). These corrective measures were often written as critiques of specific government policies deemed unconstitutional, contrary to the law or detrimental to government efficiency. The use of these corrective measures allowed the Control Yuan to subtly challenge acts and policies of the authoritarian government.[15]

Although it can be demonstrated that the Control Yuan made some minor contributions under martial law, there were still significant limitations. For example, due to the policies of marital law, the Control Yuan could do very little for the thousands of political prisoners or those who had suffered from coercive land expropriation practices. It lacked the capacity to actively challenge the Taiwan Garrison Command or the courts-martial. Like the judiciary, the Control Yuan was unable to directly protect or promote the constitutional rights, and let alone the human rights, of the Taiwanese.[16] Furthermore, the Control Yuan's public reputation suffered greatly during martial law. The heavily constrained supplementary elections for Control Yuan members were fraught with claims by non-KMT candidates of corruption and undue influence over its candidates and voters. Due to its constrained constitutional powers and the contested nature of its membership, when martial law was finally lifted the Control Yuan was viewed by much of the public as an antiquated, nepotistic, and impotent branch of government. This would not seem, on the surface, to be

[11]Hsieh (2005), pp. 63–73.

[12]Caldwell, *supra* note 10, at pp. 757–759.

[13]Chen (2003), p. 7.

[14]*Id.*

[15]Caldwell, *supra* note 10, at pp. 757–758.

[16]Ma (1963).

an ideal candidate for a NHRI. However, as Taiwan democratized and human rights took center-stage in public and political debates, the Control Yuan needed to find a way to remain relevant within Taiwan's shifting constitutional landscape.

Martial law was lifted in 1987 and this was followed by abrogation of the Temporary Provisions in 1991. To better accommodate the social and political needs of the island of Taiwan, as opposed to the full population and territory of all of China, the 1947 ROC Constitution required a great deal of revision. Through a series of constitutional reforms, the national government reinstituted elections, reinstituted the civil and political rights enshrined in the constitution, and drastically reorganized several government offices.[17] While many look positively on this era of constitutional reform as a period of citizen empowerment, strengthening of the judiciary, and democratization, one branch of government, the Control Yuan, did not fare well. The Control Yuan was in many ways seen as a bargaining chip among the political parties, and via successive constitutional amendments the Control Yuan found itself stripped of many of its original powers and mandates.[18] With its most powerful constitutional duties reassigned to other representative institutions, such as the Legislative Yuan, questions arose over the continued need for the Control Yuan. Such questions were made more poignant by the increasingly active judiciary which, through several significant decisions and constitutional interpretations against government action and policy, greatly improved the judicial face of human rights protection in Taiwan.[19] As support for the Control Yuan steadily waned, there arose on the horizon a contested area of government jurisdiction and a potential source of new relevance for the institution: human rights protection.

In 2000, DPP candidate Chen Shui-bian (陳水扁) was elected president. This was the first time a non-KMT candidate had won the presidency since 1947. Chen and the DPP ran on a political platform that emphasized human rights promotion and protection in Taiwan. As president, Chen vowed to ratify the ICCPR and ICESCR, legislate a Human Rights Act and establish an independent human rights commission.[20] In 2001, after much debate the DPP government issued two draft laws for consideration that outlined the structure of the proposed human rights institution and provided key mandates, such as promoting human rights through education and awareness, advising the government on policies directly influencing human rights conditions in Taiwan, as well as providing investigatory powers for human rights violations.[21] This was of course heavily criticized by the KMT and the Control Yuan. The Control Yuan argued that providing a human rights institution with investigatory

[17]See generally, Fell (2012).

[18]Caldwell, *supra* note 10, at pp. 761–765.

[19]Chang (2015), Yeh and Chang (2014).

[20]Bowman (2012), pp. 499–502.

[21]*Id.*, at p. 501.

powers violated the constitution as it would infringe upon the Control Yuan's powers of investigation. To bolster its claim over a human rights protection mandate, the Control Yuan created its own Committee on Human Rights Protection.[22]

The Control Yuan Committee on Human Rights Protection (監察院人權保障委員會) is comprised of nine to eleven Control Yuan members serving a one-year term (Art. 4). The Committee is tasked with bolstering human rights protection via control powers, as well as research, planning, and organization of ministerial-level agencies to protect human rights (Art. 2). To accomplish these goals, the Committee is empowered to, *inter alia*, discover cases of human rights abuses on its own initiative, make legislative proposals related to human rights, promote and supervise the incorporation of international human rights conventions into domestic law, liaise with NGOs and international organizations, and promote human rights protection (Art. 3). The Committee meets once per month and has jurisdiction to consider and advise on any petition or investigation of the Control Yuan that has relevance to human rights. Although the existence of this Committee supports the Control Yuan's jurisdictional claim over human rights protection, it was, however, created via internal regulations of the Control Yuan, not statutory legislation. This raises questions about whether or not such a committee could provide the Control Yuan with enough credibility to claim the title of a NHRI.[23]

Due in part to Taiwan's semi-presidential system, which developed from successive constitutional reforms, Chen found his administration gridlocked by a divided government.[24] The DPP held the presidency and Executive Yuan, yet the Legislative Yuan remained in firm control of the KMT. As such, most of Chen's initiatives requiring legislative approval, including the Human Rights Act, ratification of the ICCPR/ICESCR, and the establishment of a NHRI, were all quashed by partisan politics and government gridlock.[25] On the one hand, the inability of the government to establish an independent NHRI certainly benefited the Control Yuan as it allowed the institution via its human rights committee to retain the title of "sole" investigator of human rights abuses, *de facto*. On the other hand, however, the Control Yuan found itself the political target of partisan politics under a divided government. From 2005–2008, the Control Yuan effectively ceased to exist.

As the end of the term of the third Control Yuan approached, President Chen announced his new nominees. These nominees, however, required consent from the KMT-dominated Legislative Yuan. Despite multiple requests, and a constitutional

[22]Jian Cha Yuan Ren Quan Bao Zhang Wei Yuan Hui She Zhi Bian Fa [Regulations on the Establishment of the Control Yuan Committee on Human Rights Protection] (監察院人權保障委員會設置辦法) (19 May 2000, amended 19 June 2013) (Taiwan).

[23]The Paris Principles require a NHRI to be established in a constitutional or legislative text. De Beco and Murray, *supra* note 2, at pp. 41–42.

[24]See generally, Huang (2006).

[25]See generally, Hawang (2016).

interpretation on the matter from the Constitutional Court, the Legislative Yuan refused to confirm the nominees.[26] For human rights protection, this certainly had a negative impact. Several thousand individual petitions were still filed each year for nearly four years, but the Control Yuan and its Committee on Human Rights Protection, lacking any members, had no way of investigating these claims.[27] Thus, partisan politics seriously undermined the legitimacy of the Control Yuan's claim as the "sole" investigator of human rights abuses in Taiwan. It wasn't until the election of KMT presidential candidate Ma Ying-jeou (馬英九) in 2008 that the Control Yuan was able to replenish its ranks and return to a functioning, albeit demoralized institution.

One does not readily associate Ma's administration with human rights promotion. During his presidency, many of the DPP's earlier human rights initiatives went inactive, and even the presidential Human Rights Advisory Committee "fell silent."[28] However, in 2009 the Legislative Yuan approved ratification of the ICCPR and ICESCR. This was followed later that year by the Act to Implement the ICCPR and ICESCR (2009), which embedded the provisions of these two international covenants into domestic law.[29] With these covenants now binding on the government, there arose a need to monitor and assess the government's compliance. Ma's administration expressed an interest in establishing a NHRI to fulfil that role, but once again the Control Yuan members cited the constitutional and jurisdictional overlap from empowering such an institution. In the end, the Control Yuan's arguments won the day as constitutional and legislative changes would have required too much political capital and resources. Therefore, Taiwan did not establish an independent NHRI under Ma's administration.

Under the present DPP-led administration of President Tsai Ing-wen (蔡英文), there are once again dual calls for the abolishment of the Control Yuan and the establishment of a NHRI. While Tsai originally advocated the abolishment of the Control Yuan, more recently there seems to be a trend towards retaining the institution, but recasting its role into that of a NHRI.[30] The remainder of this chapter considers what steps are necessary to effectively transform the Control Yuan into a NHRI capable of gaining international accreditation.

---

[26] Chen and Hsu (2016), pp. 161–163.

[27] Jian Cha Yuan [Control Yuan] (監察院) (2008).

[28] Ho (2014), pp. 110–11.

[29] Bowman, *supra* note 20.

[30] In her early campaigning, Tsai argued that the Control Yuan and Examination Yuan should be abolished and their remaining powers distributed among the three remaining branches (Ye 2014). However, recently she nominated several new members to the Control Yuan, many of whom have extensive human rights experience. Zhong (2017).

3 The Control Yuan as a NHRI

On 24–28 July 2017, a panel of international human rights specialists met in Taipei at the Legislative Yuan to discuss Taiwan's future options for establishing a NHRI.[31] Their discussions focused primarily on structural issues of establishment criteria and procedures. Overall, the panelists acknowledged that Taiwan had three viable options: to establish a fully independent NHRI; to establish a quasi-independent NHRI under the auspices of the Presidential Office; or to transform the Control Yuan into Taiwan's NHRI.

The first option, the establishment of a fully independent NHRI, was considered highly problematic. The panelists noted several significant issues that would likely impede the functionality of such an institution. As with the presidencies of Chen and Ma, the most difficult obstacle to overcome would be managing the overlapping jurisdiction of the Control Yuan. In effect, given the Control Yuan's existing jurisdiction and operations, Taiwan would be creating a multi-institutional human rights protection framework. While such arrangements do exist in other jurisdictions, most scholars highlight the practical and cost-effective benefits of single institution NHRIs.[32] Furthermore, the panelists noted that they had received little attention or positive responses from Taiwanese organizations that recommended the establishment of a stand-alone institution.

The second option considered the legislative establishment of a quasi-independent NHRI under the auspices of the Presidential Office. Such a practice had been common in the past and seems effective on paper. President Chen, for example, relied heavily on the presidential Human Rights Advisory Committee when his efforts to create a NHRI were thwarted. Such a practice would be particularly useful during periods of divided government. Yet such an arrangement likely would not comply with the independence criteria stipulated by the Paris Principles. NHRIs should be independent of all executive control and interference.[33] If part of the purpose of establishing a NHRI is to gain increased international recognition for human rights development in Taiwan, then such an institutional framework would not be the most effective choice.

For many, including the forum panelists, the Control Yuan represents the most logical and cost-effective pathway to establish a Taiwanese NHRI.[34] In its current status, however, the Control Yuan is not fully compliant with the NHRI criteria provided by the Paris Principles and the GANHRI. So how does the Control Yuan measure up? What are its deficiencies? And how can these be remedied?

At first glance, the Control Yuan already meets many of the basic criteria of the Paris Principles and the subsequent benchmarks of compliance formulated by the

[31]The panel included international participants, Rosslyn Noonan, Sushil Pyakurel, and Agantaranansa Juanda. Covenants Watch (人權公約施行監督聯盟), *supra* note 6.

[32]Carver (2011).

[33]Mertus (2012), p. 77.

[34]Li, *supra* note 4.

UN, the GANHRI, and other international organizations.[35] These benchmarks are divided into three broad categories of structure, mandate, and accountability.[36] Below I highlight a few of these benchmarks in each category to illustrate the Control Yuan's current level of compliance. Given the space constraints, I am unable to go into all the issues in detail.

3.1 *Structure*

The structural benchmarks of a NHRI require high levels of independence, establishment by constitutional or legislative texts, transparent appointment procedures, pluralism/diversity of membership, human rights skills of membership, constructive relations with civil society, and accessibility.[37]

The Control Yuan meets many of these requirements. It is a constitutionally established branch of the national government with a high level of independence from all other branches. Although appointments are based on presidential nomination, there are three factors that contribute to the institution's independence. First, nominees are not just selected by a single individual representing one party, but also require confirmation by another representative institution, the Legislative Yuan. Second, once confirmed, it is extremely difficult to impeach a Control Yuan member. This allows the Control Yuan to conduct investigations against the government without concern over retribution for its actions. Third, in order to avoid conflicts of interest, once members are confirmed they are not allowed to continue their professional or civilian occupations until their term has expired. Overall, the appointments procedure is quite public as the nominees are announced via the Office of the President and the debates and confirmation hearings for the nominees by the Legislative Yuan are open and published in the legislative gazettes. Finally, the Control Yuan is accessible to the public via conferences, workshops, and news releases, as well as by the individual petition system.

3.2 *Mandate*

The international benchmarks for NHRIs also require the mandate of the institution to be broad and general, including, but not limited to, the ability to comment on existing or draft laws, monitoring domestic human rights conditions, advising on

[35]This section utilizes the structural model of assessment for NHRIs, and relies heavily on the set of foundational benchmarks formulated by Carver (2005). This assessment model has been criticized, but remains valuable for the present chapter as it directly engages the current discourse in Taiwan (Mertus, *supra* note 33, at pp. 76–80).

[36]Carver (2005).

[37]*Id.*, at pp. 12–17.

compliance with international treaty obligations, educating in the field of human rights, receiving complaints, and monitoring government compliance with NHRI issued advice.[38]

Again, the Control Yuan meets many of the basic benchmarks for compliance. The Control Yuan has the capacity to discuss and recommend legislation or specific legislative changes that fall within its jurisdiction. The primary duty of the Control Yuan is to monitor the government (Constitution Art. 90) and it has a wide range of constitutionally enshrined investigatory powers. Furthermore, with the establishment of the Committee for Human Rights Protection and its related functions, the Control Yuan is now required to monitor and make recommendations related to the government's compliance with the ICCPR and ICESCR. Since 2000, the Control Yuan has received over 12,000 individual petitions from the public each year.[39] The vast majority of these petitions relate specifically to claims of human rights abuses.

One significant gap in the Control Yuan's mandate is the private sector. As mentioned above, the Control Yuan was originally designed to monitor the government. Although it now has a human rights mandate, its constitutionally provided powers are limited to investigations of the government, specifically the Executive, Judicial, and Examination Yuans. The Control Yuan does not have the authority to use its investigatory powers against private entities. Therefore, in its present status the Control Yuan only possesses a partial investigatory and quasi-judicial mandate.[40]

3.3 *Accountability*

The Paris Principles and the subsequent GANHRI accreditation criteria also require a NHRI to have a high level of public accountability.[41] This accountability is manifest in public reports of the institution, including reports on budgets, institutional activities, and advice/recommendations to the government.[42] Here too, the Control Yuan meets many of the international benchmarks. The Control Yuan produces numerous public reports each year, ranging from monthly gazette issues which include specific cases and communications with other branches of government, to annual reports on human rights. All of the Control Yuan reports are available to the public in print format, and most can be found online for free download on the Control Yuan website.[43]

---

[38] *Id.*, at pp. 17–22.

[39] Chen and Hsu, *supra* note 26, at p. 161.

[40] De Beco and Murray, *supra* note 2.

[41] *Id.*, at p. 141.

[42] Carver, *supra* note 36, at p. 23.

[43] Control Yuan of the Republic of China (Taiwan). http://www.cy.gov.tw. Accessed 12 Sept 2017.

4 Reforming for Compliance?

On the surface, the Control Yuan not only seems like the ideal candidate for a Taiwanese NHRI, but also appears to comply with many of the basic requirements of the international community. And yet, there are limitations to its compliance that could seriously jeopardize its ability to gain international accreditation should the Control Yuan be submitted for review in its current state. At the recent NHRI forum mentioned above, the panelists produced a list of suggestions on how the Control Yuan could be "re-packaged" as a NHRI. These include, among other things:

- Appointment of personnel should be public and engaged with civil society
- Nominees should have human rights qualifications and experience
- Membership should reflect the diversity of Taiwanese society
- Investigative powers should have jurisdiction over public and private claims
- Increased communications with Taiwanese civil society
- Being responsible to the Legislative Yuan

Such proposals, if acted upon, would certainly heighten the Control Yuan's conformity with the Paris Principles; however, to convert the Control Yuan into a NHRI along the lines suggested by the forum panelists would require some significant, and in some cases nearly insurmountable, alterations to Taiwan's constitutional structure as well as numerous revisions to key legislation related to the Control Yuan. In this section, I will highlight a few of the substantial obstacles to reforming the Control Yuan by examining the necessary steps involved in altering the appointments process. In doing so, I am *not* arguing against the possibility of transforming the Control Yuan into a NHRI, but I am merely articulating the significant obstacles which must be overcome in order to make the Control Yuan fully compliant with the Paris Principles.

4.1 Appointments

According to the Additional Articles of the 1947 ROC Constitution, the Control Yuan shall consist of 29 members appointed for six years, with nominees chosen by the President and confirmed by the Legislative Yuan (Additional Articles, Art. 7). Furthermore, the *Organic Law of the Control Yuan*[44] requires members to be at least 35 years of age and to meet one of a series of requirements, such as a period of civil service in provincial or national government, a distinguished career in a judicial role or as a university professor, or honesty and integrity with extensive political experience (Art. 3-1). Such requirements allow for great diversity in the educational and career backgrounds of appointees.

[44]Jian Cha Yuan Zu Zhi Fa [Organic Law of the Control Yuan] (監察院組織法) (31 Mar 1947, last amended 19 May 2010).

The NHRI forum panelists, however, highlighted several problematic elements of the Control Yuan appointment process that would need to be revised before the institution complies with the Paris Principles. It was noted that Control Yuan membership should be considered via an open and public process, in which all stakeholders may voice their opinions. This could include requirements to publicize vacancies (for each term), to mandate specific characteristics and human rights backgrounds for applicants, and to promote public consultation and participation in the application, screening, and appointment process.[45]

I do agree with the suggestions of the forum panelists; however, to accommodate such changes to the Control Yuan the Constitution and several pieces of legislation would need to be altered. For example, at present, the Constitution provides that nominees are chosen at the President's discretion without the need for public consultation (Additional Articles, Art. 7). To alter the nomination process, one would necessarily be required to revise the Constitution. In Taiwan, this has become an extremely difficult process. With the introduction of the 2005 Additional Articles, any constitutional revision requires a high level of bi-partisan cooperation and an extremely high level of direct popular support. For a constitutional revision to occur, it must first be passed by three-fourths of the Legislative Yuan members present at a meeting attended by at least three-fourths of the total membership. Then it must pass a public referendum in which the total number of valid votes in favor exceeds one-half the total number of electors (Additional Articles, Art. 12). All previously held public referenda have failed due to low voter turnout. Given the turbulent political climate in Taiwan and the necessary public support, it is doubtful that such a constitutional change could be effected.

On the other hand, however, there is a potential for altering membership requirements via statutory changes. One could "simply" revise the *Organic Law of the Control Yuan* and fulfil many of the Paris Principles' criteria for appointment. For example, to increase the diversity and pluralism of membership, Article 3-1 could provide that underrepresented groups hold a reserved number of seats, such as disabled persons, indigenous peoples, and women. This would fulfil the Paris Principles' requirements that the membership of a NHRI should reflect the diversity of Taiwanese society.[46] Furthermore, in revising the same article, one could establish criteria for membership which includes requirements for human rights experience. This could be gained through a career in activism, a judicial or legal career dealing with human rights cases, or an academic background in human rights teaching or promotion. By narrowing the eligibility criteria and including a greater emphasis on (a) diversity and (b) human rights experience, statutory changes could refine the acceptable applicant pool available to the President. This would not necessarily create a *requirement* that the President seeks nominees on the basis of consultations, but given the legislative majority currently held by the DPP, statutory changes of this nature would certainly be possible. By no means easy, but not impossible.

---

[45]De Beco and Murray, *supra* note 2, at p. 89.

[46]*Id.*, at pp. 67–80.

While this demonstrates the potential for providing a structural framework that would comply with the Paris Principles, the old dangers of Taiwan's hybrid semi-presidential system would remain. In echoing the warnings of Carver (2005), establishing a fully compliant NHRI does not necessarily correlate with the effective promotion and protection of human rights. In order to be effective, a NHRI must be designed with the local social and political contexts in mind.

Unless the Constitution were to be fully revised, the Control Yuan would always be a potential victim of government gridlock under a divided government. Just as Chen Shui-bian was unable to have his Control Yuan nominees confirmed by a KMT-led Legislative Yuan, so too could a future President find his or herself in a similar position. Yet, even in a period of unified government, for example, when the KMT held both the presidency with Ma Ying-jeou and the legislative majority, only eighteen of the President's Control Yuan nominees were confirmed.[47] Thus, instead of the normal twenty-nine members, during Ma's administration the Control Yuan functioned with a severely limited capacity. For human rights protection, this had significant ramifications for the Control Yuan. For example, in 2016 the Control Yuan received 13,615 individual petitions, of which 11,307 (83%) were specifically related to human rights claims.[48] The Control Yuan conducted a total of 273 investigations in 2016, and of those, 114 (41.8%) were human rights cases.[49] Yet, with eleven members not confirmed, the Control Yuan has limited time and resources to adequately review and investigate the increasing volume of human rights-related petitions it receives each year. Simply increasing diversity and selection criteria via statutory revision would not necessarily solve all the Control Yuan's problems. Nor would such changes necessarily benefit the protection and promotion of human rights in Taiwan.

5 Retain, Reform, or Retire: The Future of the Control Yuan and Its Role in the Protection and Promotion of Human Rights in Taiwan

In many ways, the discussion above leads to the all-important question of *whither the Control Yuan*? Should the institution be retained as it currently exists, reformed into a NHRI, or perhaps retired altogether? The answer to these questions impacts not only the Control Yuan's role as a core component of Taiwan's constitutional structure but also its continued role as part of Taiwan's developing human rights protection and promotion framework.

At present, there is no simple answer. The first option is to simply retain the Control Yuan in its current form and with its current mandate. Yet, what would this

[47]Lin (林楠森) (2014).

[48]Jian Cha Yuan (2017), p. 257.

[49]*Id.*

option mean for the advancement of human rights in Taiwan? Echoing the criticism of the 2017 human rights review committee, Taiwan would still lack a NHRI that complies with the Paris Principles. The Control Yuan would still be subject to the negative effects of the semi-presidential system that could severely limit its ability to effectively protect human rights. Furthermore, despite its Committee on Human Rights Protection, as several scholars have noted, the Control Yuan does not fully comply with the Paris Principles. In its current form, should the Control Yuan be submitted as a NHRI for international accreditation, it would certainly not receive an "A" rating, and it is questionable as to whether it would receive a "B" rating. An unaltered Control Yuan and a lack of a dedicated NHRI would not, therefore, likely prove to be a viable option for developing the Taiwanese human rights landscape.

The second option of substantially altering the Control Yuan would of course be the most beneficial pathway. As already mentioned, this would necessitate a great deal of constitutional revision, requiring public support and cross-party cooperation. Yet, one mustn't focus too closely on matching every single aspect of the Paris Principles. A great deal of attention must be paid to the actual social and political domestic issues that the NHRI must confront, engage, and contend with. As already shown, the Control Yuan currently suffers considerable downsides as an NHRI that go beyond the compliance issues mentioned by other scholars. Simply altering the appointments and eligibility requirements to provide greater pluralism and diversity as well as public engagement, would not be enough to ensure the Control Yuan functions effectively as a NHRI. The highly volatile political climate, and the way in which party politics play out within Taiwan's semi-presidential system, have the potential to seriously impede the Control Yuan's functionality. To be transformed into a successful and effective NHRI, the Control Yuan would certainly require not only a statutory overhaul but also a serious constitutional revision of its appointment process. Such changes would have significant implications for the constitutional structure of Taiwan and would be very difficult to carry out.

The final option is to retire the Control Yuan altogether. The DPP has long advocated the abolishment of this institution, and even President Tsai has in the past contemplated simply not re-appointing any new members once the current term expires. Yet, although the Control Yuan suffered a great downturn in public opinion since the martial-law era, there exists little support for fully abolishing the institution as was done with the National Assembly in 2005. Furthermore, given the current difficulties of constitutional reform in Taiwan, the possibility of altering the Constitution in such a drastic fashion is now highly unlikely. For decades, the Control Yuan has fought to preserve its role in human rights protection in Taiwan. Although it has many problems, by shuttering the Control Yuan Taiwan would leave an institutional void for human rights protection and promotion that would need to be immediately filled.

The futures of the Control Yuan and of human rights in Taiwan are inextricably linked. Given the options for reform and their requirements for bi-partisan cooperation and public support, the choice of direction forward is a matter for the Taiwanese people to determine.

References

Bowman D (2012) Righting the wrongs of the past? The human rights policies of Chen Shui-Bian and Ma Ying-Jeou. In: Blundell D (ed) Taiwan since martial law: society, culture, politics, and economy. Shung Ye Museum of Formosan Aborigines, Taipei, pp 485–526

Caldwell E (2017a) Chinese constitutionalism: five-power constitution. In: Grote R, Lachenmann F, Wolfrum R (eds) Max Planck encyclopedia of comparative constitutional law. Oxford University Press, Oxford

Caldwell E (2017b) Widening the constitutional gap in China and Taiwan: history, reform, and the transformation of the Control Yuan. Univ Illinois L Rev 2:739–766

Carver R (2005) Assessing the effectiveness of National Human Rights Institutions. International Council on Human Rights Policy. www.ohchr.org/Documents/Publications/NHRIen.pdf. Accessed 21 Sept 2017

Carver R (2011) One NHRI or many? How many institutions does it take to protect human rights? lessons from the European experience. J Hum Rights Pract 3(1):1–24

Chang W-C (2015) Courts and judicial reform in Taiwan: gradual transformations towards the guardian of constitutionalism and rule of law. In: Chang W-C, Yeh J-R (eds) Asian courts in context. Cambridge University Press, Cambridge, pp 143–182

Chen T-F (2003) Democracy and rule of law in Taiwan: the judiciary's authority and credibility. RCTED Working Paper Series No. 2003-0006, pp 1–18

Chen W-T, Hsu Jimmy C-S (2016) Horizontal accountability and the rule of law. In: Chu Y-H, Diamond L, Templeman K (eds) Taiwan's democracy challenged: the Chen Shui-Bian years. Lynne Rienner, Boulder, pp 145–171

Covenants Watch [人權公約施行監督聯盟] (2017) Guo Ji Zhuan Jia Lai Tai Jin Xing Guo Jia Ren Quan Wei Yuan Hui Ping Gu Ren Wu Chu Bu Sheng Ming [國際專家來台進行國家人權委員會評估任務初步聲明] (Preliminary Report by International Specialists Assessing the Progress of a National Human Rights Institution). Ren Quan Gong Yue Shi Xing Jian Du Lian Meng [人權公約施行監督聯盟] (Convenants Watch). 28 July. http://covenantswatch.org.tw/2017/07/28/preliminary_statement/. Accessed 11 Sept 2017

De Beco G, Murray R (2015) A commentary on the Paris Principles on National Human Rights Institutions. Cambridge University Press, Cambridge

Fell D (2012) Government and politics in Taiwan, 2nd edn. Routledge, London

Hawang S-D (2016) Executive-legislative relations under divided government. In: Chu Y-H, Diamond L, Templeman K (eds) Taiwan's democracy challenged: the Chen Shui-Bian years. Lynne Rienner, Boulder, pp 123–144

Ho M-S. (2014) The resurgence of social movements under the Ma Ying-Jeou government: a political opportunity structure perspective. In: Cabestan J-P, deLisle J (eds) Political changes in Taiwan under Ma Ying-Jeou: partisan conflict, policy choices, external constraints and security challenges. Routledge, London, pp 100–119

Hsieh C-T (2005) Zhonghua Minguo Xiuxian Shi [中華民國修憲史] (The history of revision to the ROC Constitution), 2nd edn. Polis, Taipei

Huang S-L (黃嵩立) (2014) Gong Min Tuan Ti Dui Guo Jia Ren Quan Wei Yuan Hui Zhi Yi Jian [公民團體對國家人權委員會之意見] (The opinions of Taiwanese civil society organizations on a National Human Rights Commission). Taiwan Ren Quan Xue Kan [台灣人權學刊] (Taiwan Journal of Human Rights) 2(3):81–95

Huang Thomas W-S (2006) The president refuses to cohabit: semi-presidentialism in Taiwan. Pac Rim L Policy J 15(2):375–402

International Group of Independent Experts (2013) Review of the initial report of the Government of Taiwan on the implementation of the international human rights covenants: concluding observations and recommendations adopted by the international group of independent experts. Taipei. http://www.humanrights.moj.gov.tw/mp205.html. Accessed 11 Sept 2017

International Group of Independent Experts (2017) Review of the second report of the Government of Taiwan on the implementation of the international human rights covenants: concluding observations and recommendations adopted by the international group of independent experts. Taipei. http://www.humanrights.moj.gov.tw/mp205.html. Accessed 11 Sept 2017

Jian Cha Yuan [監察院] (Control Yuan) (2008) Te Xu Yun Zhuan Yu Deng Dai——Jian Cha Yuan Mei You Jian Cha Wei Yuan Qi Jian Gong Zuo Ji Yao [特續運轉與等待——監察院沒有監察委員期間工作輯要] (Extraordinary Session Operations and Biding Time–A Summary of the Work for the Period in which the Control Yuan Had No Control Yuan Members). Control Yuan, Taipei

Jian Cha Yuan [監察院] (Control Yuan) (2017) Jian Cha Bao Gao Shu: Zhong Hua Min Guo 105 Nian [監察報告書:中華民國105 年] (Annual Report of the Control Yuan, 2016). Control Yuan, Taipei

Li N-T (李念祖) (2012) Lun Yi Ba Li Yuan Ze Yu Jian Cha Yuan She Zhi Guo Jia Ren Quan Wei Yuan Hui [論依巴黎原則於監察院設置國家人權委員會] (Establishing a National Human Rights Commission within the Control Yuan in Accordance with the Paris Principles). Taiwan Ren Quan Xue Kan [台灣人權學刊] (Taiwan Journal of Human Rights) 1(3):125–113

Liao Fort F-T (2001) Establishing a National Human Rights Commission in Taiwan: the role of NGOs and the challenges ahead. Asia-Pac J Hum Rights L 2(2):90–109

Lin N-S (林楠森) (2014) Taiwan Jian Cha Wei Yuan Ti Ming Ren Yu Shi Ren Wei Huo Tong Guo [台灣監察委員提名人逾十人未獲通過] (Over Ten Taiwanese Control Yuan Nominees Fail to be Confirmed). BBC Chinese Edition. 29 July. www.bbc.com/zhongwen/trad/china/2014/07/140729_tw_control_yuan_no rminations. Accessed 11 Sept 2017

Ma Herbert HP (1963) Chinese Control Yuan: an independent supervisory organ of the state. Wash Univ L Rev 4:401–426

Mertus J (2012) Evaluating NHRIs: considering structure, mandate, and impact. In: Goodman R, Pegram T (eds) Human rights, state compliance, and social change: assessing National Human Rights Institutions. Cambridge University Press, Cambridge, pp 74–92

Pan W-T (1983) The Chinese constitution: a study of forty years of constitution-making in China. Hyperion Press, Westport

Su Y-C (蘇友辰) (2002) Lun Guo Jia Ren Quan Wei Yuan Hui De Jiao Se Yu Di Wei [論國家人權委員會的角色與地位] (The Role and Status of a National Human Rights Commission). Guo Jia Zheng Ce Ji Kan [國家政策季刊] (Journal of National Policy) 1(2):1–32

Tung WL (1964) The political institutions of modern China. Martinus Nijhoff, The Hague

Vile MJC (1998) Constitutionalism and the separation of powers, 2nd edn. Liberty Fund, Indianapolis

Walker R (1947) The control system of the Chinese government. Far East Q 7(1):2–21

Wei C-F (魏千峯) (2012) Women Wei Shen Ma Xu Yao Guo Jia Ren Quan Wei Yuan Hui? [我們爲甚麼需要國家人權委員會?] (Why We Need a National Human Rights Commission?) Taiwan Ren Quan Xue Kan [台灣人權學刊] (Taiwan Journal of Human Rights) 1(3):97–123

Ye S-P (葉素萍) (2014) Tsai Ing-Wen Pan Bu Bu Ti Jian Wei [蔡英文盼不補替監委] (Tsai Ing-wen hopes not to supplement Control officials). Da Ji Yuan [大紀元] (Epoch Times) 30 Jul. www.epochtimes.com/b5/14/5/30/n4212718. Accessed 11 Sept 2017

Yeh J-R, Chang W-C (2014) A decade of changing constitutionalism in Taiwan: transitional and transnational perspectives. In: Chen AHY (ed) Constitutionalism in Asia in the early twenty-first century. Cambridge University Press, Cambridge, pp 141–168

Zhong L-H (鍾麗華) (2017) Jian Wei Bu Ti Ming Ren: Zuo Hao [Mo Dai Jian Wei] Xin Li Zhun Bei [監委補提名人:做好「末代監委」心理準備] (Supplementary Control Nominees: Prepared to Serve as 'Final Control Officials'). Zi You Shi Bao Dian Zi Bao [自由時報電子報] (Liberty Times Digital Edition). 2 March. http://m.ltn.com.tw/news/politics/breakingnews/1991307. Accessed 11 Sept 2017

Ernest Caldwell (B.A., M.A., LL.M., Ph.D.) is Lecturer (Assistant Professor) in Laws of China and Taiwan at the School for Oriental and African Studies, University of London, where he teaches courses on East Asian public law and environmental law. Caldwell's research has been published in a variety of journals and edited volumes including *Washington Journal of International Law, Chicago-Kent Law Review, Law and History Review, University of Illinois Law Review,* and *Max Weber Studies.*

Chapter 11
"All the World's a Stage": Taiwan's Human Rights Performance and Playing to International Norms

Jacques deLisle

Abstract Taiwan's engagement with the international regime for human rights has been exceptional for reasons related to Taiwan's unusual status in the world. Taiwan's precarious status has provided distinctive reasons to emphasize international human rights norms, including some of their more formal manifestations. In the 1980s and 1990s, the remarkable improvement in Taiwan's human rights record was vital to maintaining U.S. support. In the late 1990s and 2000s, Taiwan's commitment to human rights norms and values was an essential element in Taiwan's efforts to preserve security and international stature. More recently, Taiwan has deepened its engagement with the UN-centered human rights regime, stressing compliance with that regime as if it were a member state, adopting domestic legislation to mirror the principal human rights covenants, and undertaking reports that parallel the requirements for States Parties to the major human rights conventions. While this approach has benefited Taiwan internationally and the lives of Taiwan's citizens, Taiwan's human rights engagement strategy faces new and difficult challenges: internationally, the benefits of a relatively strong human rights record may be waning; domestically, discourse about human rights is turning to more intractable or controversial problems, including issues that resonate with economic, social and cultural dimensions of human rights, and issues of transitional justice.

Keywords International law · International status of Taiwan · United Nations

Taiwan's engagement with the international human rights regime has been exceptional. It has been so for much the same reason that Taiwan's position in the international system more generally has been exceptional. Taiwan's unusual—and precarious—place in the world has made its commitment to, and implementation of, international human rights laws and norms a resource in its persistent pursuit of

J. deLisle (✉)
Law and Professor of Political Science, University of Pennsylvania, Philadelphia, USA
e-mail: jdelisle@law.upenn.edu

J. deLisle
Asia Program, Foreign Policy Research Institute, Philadelphia, USA

J. A. Cohen et al. (eds.), *Taiwan and International Human Rights*, Economics, Law, and Institutions in Asia Pacific, https://doi.org/10.1007/978-981-13-0350-0_11

international status and security. A good record on human rights has offered a way to safeguard and enhance Taiwan's international standing. Undertakings to meet the demands of the major international treaties and the rules of customary international law for human rights have been a means to strengthen Taiwan's claim to state, or state-like, stature.

This is not to say that international status and the security it confers have been the most important consequences, or the principal motivations, for Taiwan's approach to, and progress on, human rights. But seeking maximal participation in the international human rights regime—despite formidable barriers to doing so—has held out a two-fold promise. By achieving a high level of human rights performance, especially for civil and political rights and particularly as measured by the international legal standards that set common obligations for states, Taiwan fares better on a metric that has mattered for the international stature of states and state-like entities in recent decades. By acting as if it were a member of major United Nations-centered international human rights treaties (and the broader international legal regime with which they are entwined), Taiwan acts the way that states (and, more specifically, responsible and accepted states) do in the international system, thereby supporting Taiwan's claim to state(-like) rights and status.

Engagement with the international human rights regime clearly has been no panacea for the chronic problem of Taiwan's besieged and contested international status. Still worse for Taiwan, the efficacy of such engagement may be in a phase of decline amid newly uncertain U.S. support for, and growing Chinese challenges to, the international human rights norms that Taiwan has embraced.

1 Prologue: The Rise of the International Human Rights Regime and Challenges for Taiwan

The international human rights regime has been transformed and strengthened during the last several decades. Although its roots are ancient and progenitors of some of its institutional and doctrinal features date to the period following the First World War, the contemporary international system for human rights began to emerge in the aftermath of the Second World War. Key developments included the adoption of the Universal Declaration of Human Rights and the establishment of the United Nations as an institutional locus for the new focus on human rights. The regime continued to undergo significant institutional and legal developments and gained normative clout thereafter. Major, relatively early, milestones included the adoption and entry into force of several major UN-centered human rights treaties—most prominently the International Covenant on Civil and Political Rights and the International Covenant on Economic, Social and Cultural Rights—and the empowering of international organizations to monitor and support their implementation.[1] Human rights also rose to greater prominence in the foreign policies of some major states, including the United States.

Of course, such phenomena were not limited institutionally to the United Nations system or nationally to the United States. Regional international organizations and other states were part of the growing human rights regime, but they were of limited relevance to Taiwan. Regional human rights organs and accords have been comparatively thin in East Asia. Although other states made human rights a major foreign policy concern, none mattered nearly as much for Taiwan as the United States did. Aside from the U.S., there was little overlap between states that adopted a significant human rights focus in foreign policy and states (mostly states in East Asia) that were most important (for good or for ill) to Taiwan's security.

Into the 1970s, the Republic of China had the international capacity to engage with the emerging human rights regime. The ROC participated in the drafting of the Universal Declaration of Human Rights in 1948 and signed both the ICESCR and the ICCPR in 1967.[2] Although its authority was in practice limited to Taiwan, the ROC held the Chinese seat at the United Nations until 1971. It was recognized as the government of a state and enjoyed widespread formal diplomatic relations (until 1979, in the case of the United States).[3]

During this period, the main impediments to Taiwan's engagement with the international human rights regime, and realization of the benefits it offered for Taiwan's international standing and security, lay elsewhere. Taiwan's human rights conditions fell short of the regime's evolving standards. During the height of the Cold War, the ROC loosely enjoyed human rights-related advantages with the U.S. and the West merely by being "free China" and an anti-Communist regime, in

[1]G.A. Res. 217 (III) A, Universal declaration of human rights, UN Doc. A/810, at 71 (10 Dec 1948) [hereinafter UDHR]; International Covenant on Civil and Political Rights, 16 Dec 1966, 999 U.N.T.S. 171 [hereinafter ICCPR]; United Nations Human Rights Committee: Introduction: Monitoring civil and political rights. United Nations Human Rights Office of the High Commissioner. http://www.ohchr.org/EN/HRBodies/CCPR/Pages/CCPRIntro.aspx. Accessed 15 Oct 2017; International Covenant on Economic, Social and Cultural Rights, 16 Dec 1966, 993 U.N.T.S. 3 [hereinafter ICESCR]; Committee on Economic, Social and Cultural Rights: Introduction: Monitoring the economic, social and cultural rights. United Nations Human Rights Office of the High Commissioner. http://www.ohchr.org/EN/HRBodies/CESCR/Pages/CESCRIntro.aspx. Accessed 15 Oct 2017; Gaer and Broecker (2013).

[2]Chang (2001), pp. 206–213, UN GAOR, 3rd Sess., 183rd plen. mtg. at. 119, UN Doc. A/PV. 183 (10 Dec 1948) (ROC affirmative vote on UDHR); International Covenant on Economic, Social and Cultural Rights. United Nations Treaty Collection. https://treaties.un.org/Pages/ViewDetails.aspx?src=IND&mtdsg_no=IV-3&chapter=4&clang=_en. Accessed 15 Oct 2017; International Covenant on Civil and Political Rights. United Nations Treaty Collection https://treaties.un.org/Pages/ViewDetails.aspx?src=IND&mtdsg_no=IV-4&chapter=4&clang=_en. Accessed 15 Oct 2017 (listing signatories to the two covenants).

[3]G.A. Res. 2758 (XXVI), Restoration of the lawful rights of the People's Republic of China in the United Nations (25 Oct 1971). For the ROC's final words to the General Assembly, see Garver (1997), p. 259.

contrast to (and at odds with) the People's Republic of China (which faced rejection by the U.S. and its allies for many reasons, including human rights abuses).

Events and developments during the 1970s and early 1980s meant that this was no longer enough. The U.S. rapprochement with the PRC was primarily in pursuit of Nixon-Kissinger policies of realpolitik, but it also entailed some de-demonization in U.S. politics and public opinion about the regime in Beijing. As a result, the longstanding view, particularly in the United States, of a stark human rights contrast between the PRC and the ROC eroded and, along with it, an important underpinning for Taiwan's international standing and security.[4] Washington's acquiescence in the PRC's assumption of the Chinese seat in the UN, progress toward normalization of U.S.-PRC relations, and growing expectations that Taiwan might soon fall under Beijing's rule were among the major markers of Taiwan's rising vulnerability. Washington no longer saw compelling reasons to overlook the repressive nature, and serious human rights violations, of the authoritarian Kuomintang regime in Taipei.

Abuses of human rights—especially the civil and political rights that have been preeminent in U.S. human rights discourse—under Chiang Kai-shek's and Chiang Ching-kuo's governments in Taiwan also became more visible and salient abroad, particularly in the United States. Accounts from members of the political opposition in exile (including in the United States) drew greater attention to the sometimes brutal suppression of dissent in Taiwan.[5] So, too, did the murder in California of the Chiang-criticizing journalist Henry Liu (Chiang Nan) by members of a Taiwanese criminal gang operating at the behest of government officials.[6] The most dramatic event was the Kaohsiung Incident of 1979; when pro-democracy and pro-reform protestors took to the streets on—tellingly—International Human Rights Day, they faced violent suppression by police and military forces. Leaders of the associated movement were subjected to politicized trials (in which future President Chen Shui-bian served as a defense lawyer).[7]

As Taiwan's human rights shortcomings were becoming more evident abroad, the foreign policy of Taiwan's indispensable ally was placing greater emphasis on human rights, both generally and with respect to Taiwan. Arguably the most distinctive element—and perhaps the most enduring feature—of the Carter administration's foreign policy was its emphasis on human rights, in pointed and intentional

---

[4]See Joint statement following discussions with leaders of the People's Republic of China, PUB. PAPERS 376 (27 Feb 1972). http://heinonline.org/HOL/Permalink?a=dXBlbm4uZWR1&u=http%3A%2F%2Fheinonline.org%2FHOL%2FPage%3Fhandle%3Dhein.presidents%2Fppp072000z%26size%3D2%26collection%3Dpresidents%26id%3D430. Accessed 15 Oct 2017; Suri (2015), pp. 111–112.

[5]Bush (2004), pp. 40–84; Howe (1986), p. A12; Exiles from Taiwan opposition, N.Y. TIMES, 25 Sept 1986, p. A4.

[6]Liu v. Republic of China, 642 F. Supp. 297 (N.D. Cal. 1986), rev'd, 892 F.2d 1419 (9th Cir. 1989); The plot to kill Henry Liu – Slayers confess details, L.A. TIMES, 3 Mar 1985, at 1; Kaplan (1992).

[7]Jacobs (2016), Bush (2004), pp. 76–82, 188–218.

contrast to the self-consciously amoral, power-focused doctrine of its predecessors.[8] This created a less hospitable international environment for the ROC, one in which Taiwan's human rights record was a significant liability. The Taiwan Relations Act (TRA) of 1979 made the point clearer still. Although the principal purpose and function of the landmark legislation was to provide a second-best substitute for the formal diplomatic ties, a mutual defense pact, and stature as a recognized government exercising the full rights and privileges of a state that the ROC lost in conjunction with the normalization of U.S.-PRC relations, the TRA also included a trenchant provision on human rights that implicitly criticized the ROC regime and suggested new, human rights-related conditions for continued U.S. support:

> Nothing contained in this Act shall contravene the interest of the United States in human rights, especially with respect to the human rights of all the approximately eighteen million inhabitants of Taiwan. The preservation and enhancement of the human rights of all the people on Taiwan are hereby reaffirmed as objectives of the United States.[9]

Taiwan urgently needed to shore up support from the United States in the wake of Washington's establishing ties with Beijing and severing formal diplomatic and defense relations with Taipei. Recognition that improving Taiwan's standing on "values" issues (including human rights) was a means to that end was reportedly a key reason why Chiang Ching-kuo adopted liberalizing political reforms and opened the door to Taiwan's democratic transition.[10] Taiwan thus took a major step forward in engaging with international human rights norms and did so partly to safeguard its increasingly imperiled international status and security.

Developments in the late 1980s and early 1990s set the stage for Taiwan to enjoy international stature and security gains from an improving human rights record. A global wave of democratization included Taiwan's political transformation and attendant progress in its human rights performance. The environment improved for Taiwan as the Soviet bloc and the Soviet Union itself crumbled, and as foreign policy thinking in the United States (and other democratic powers) came to be influenced by grand notions that democracy was ascendant and that undemocratic regimes were on the wrong, and losing, side of history.[11] Solidarity among

[8]Renouard (2015), pp. 146–148, Jimmy Carter, President's news conference of 30 June, 2 PUB. PAPERS 1200 (30 June 1997). http://heinonline.org/HOL/Permalink?a=dXBlbm4uZWR1&u=http%3A%2F%2Fheinonline.org%2FHOL%2FPage%3Fmen_tab%3Dsrchresults%26handle%3Dhein.presidents%2Fppp077002%26size%3D2%26collection%3Dpresidents%26set_as_cursor%3D%26id%3D50. Accessed 15 Oct 2017.

[9]Taiwan Relations Act, 22 U.S.C. §§ 3301–3316 (1979).

[10]Nathan and Ho (1993), pp. 31–61, Tucker (2011), p. 95.

[11]See generally Huntington (1993), Fukuyama (2006), Baker (1991) America and the collapse of the Soviet Empire: What has to be done. Address at Princeton University, 12 Dec 1991. http://heinonline.org/HOL/Page?handle=hein.journals/dsptch3&div=266&g_sent=1&collection=journals. Accessed 15 Oct 2017; End of the Soviet Union; Text of Bush's address to nation on Gorbachev's resignation, N.Y. TIMES, 25 Dec 1991; Clinton WJ (1995) Remarks at a Freedom House breakfast, 6 Oct 1995. http://www.presidency.ucsb.edu/ws/?pid=50612. Accessed 15 Oct 2017.

democracies became entrenched as an organizing principle in the U.S. and other like-minded states' approach to international relations.[12] Full international acceptance of the new states that emerged in post-Cold War Europe was made partly contingent on their conformity to norms (such as democracy and constitutionalism) related to human rights, and their commitment to international obligations (including human rights obligations). The European Union's Copenhagen Criteria for admission of new member states were the most formal and arguably the most consequential example.[13]

At the same time, China seemed to be headed in the opposite direction. In 1989, Chinese authorities launched a bloody military crackdown on protests at Tiananmen Square—protests that had resonated with the pro-democracy wave then sweeping the socialist world. The regime in Beijing drew international condemnation, including from the United States and from a major UN human rights body, for human rights violations committed in the course of crushing the pro-democracy movement.[14] In this environment, Taiwan's accomplishments in human rights—and contrast with the PRC's—mattered relatively a lot (and more than they did) for Taiwan's standing on international politics generally, and U.S. foreign policy more specifically.

---

[12]Transcript of the remarks by President W. J. Clinton to the People of Detroit. North Atlantic Treaty Website. http://www.nato.int/docu/speech/1996/s961022a.htm. Accessed 15 Oct 2017; Bush GW (2001) Address at Warsaw University, 15 June 2001. http://www.presidency.ucsb.edu/ws/?pid=45973. Accessed 15 Oct 2017; Remarks by President Obama, President Niinistö of Finland, and Prime Minister Solberg of Norway at the Nordic Leaders' Summit Arrival Ceremony (2016). The White House. https://obamawhitehouse.archives.gov/the-press-office/2016/05/13/remarks-president-obama-president-niinist%C3%B6-finland-and-prime-minister. Accessed 15 Oct 2017; Risse-Kappen (1995), Santiso (2001), Brown (2015).

[13]Presidency conclusions: Copenhagen European Council - 21-22 June 1993, SN 180/93. http://www.europarl.europa.eu/enlargement_new/europeancouncil/pdf/cop_en.pdf. Accessed 15 Oct 2017. For a supportive U.S. position, see Powell CL (2003) Remarks at Reception Hosted by the Ambassador of Greece to Celebrate the Signing of the European Union Accession Treaty by Ten New Member States, 16 Apr 2003. https://2001-2009.state.gov/secretary/former/powell/remarks/2003/19713.htm. Accessed 15 Oct 2017.

[14]UN Commission on Human Rights, Report of the Sub-Commission on Prevention of Discrimination and Protection of Minorities at its forty-first session, UN Doc. E/CN.4/1990/2 (13 Nov 1989). http://repository.un.org/handle/11176/181657. Accessed 15 Oct 2017; Maher and Weissbrodt (1990). In the U.S., the President criticized the Chinese government's behavior and Congress almost succeeded in stripping China of its favorable trading status. Efforts at hard line on China thwarted. CQ Almanac (1990). http://library.cqpress.com/cqalmanac/cqal90-1118657. Accessed 15 Oct 2017; Bush GHW (1989) Statement on the Chinese government's suppression of student demonstrations—3 June, 1 PUB. PAPERS 669 (3 June 1989). http://heinonline.org/HOL/Permalink?a=dXBlbm4uZWR1&u=http%3A%2F%2F0-heinonline.org.lola.law.upenn.edu%2FHOL%2FPage%3Fmen_tab%3Dsrchresults%26handle%3Dhein.presidents%2Fppp089001%26size%3D2%26collection%3Dpresidents%26id%3D691. Accessed 15 Oct 2017.

2 A Play in Many Acts: Accomplishments at Home and Engagement Abroad

As Taiwan's human rights record improved amid Taiwan's democratic transition and consolidation, and as human rights performance and commitments ascended as factors affecting a polity's standing in the international order, Taiwan began a long phase of growing engagement with the international human rights regime. This engagement has aided Taiwan's pursuit of status and security.

Hobbes famously said that when nothing else is turned up, clubs are trumps. As one would expect from a progenitor of the Realist school of international relations theory, Hobbes's dictum suggests a bleak prognosis for the security of Taiwan, as a lesser power that is the object of irredentist claims by an increasingly formidable great power with a rapidly improving military. Diamonds are not a very strong suit for Taiwan, either: although Taiwan's economic miracle, resulting per capita wealth, and outsized roles in international trade and investment are impressive, Taiwan's economics-based international clout is dwarfed by the PRC's, given China's rank as the world's second-largest economy, emergence as the top trading partner and increasingly important investment source for states in its region and beyond, and growing willingness to use its wealth—as carrots and sticks—to advance its foreign policy goals. Taiwan's best option, thus, has been to play hearts —to emphasize its high standing on "values" issues, including international human rights.[15] For Taiwan's human rights record to reach its potential in supporting Taiwan's international status and security, Taiwan also has had to do much spadework—touting its commitments and accomplishments to external audiences, emphasizing contrasts with human rights conditions across the Strait, and engaging as fully as possible with international human rights law, institutions, and norms.

The indispensable foundation for Taiwan playing the human rights card has been Taiwan's strong human rights performance at home. Taiwan's accomplishments have been impressive, all the more so because of the rapidity and smoothness with which Taiwan improved from its poor record during the ROC's early years on Taiwan. In less than a decade, Taiwan ended two generations of martial law, released political prisoners, instituted free and fair multiparty elections (which would soon lead to alternation of ruling parties), and saw the emergence of a Constitutional Court able and willing to strike down government actions and protect expansive civil and political liberties. Although broad-brush quasi-quantitative measures have their flaws, they do capture reasonably well contemporary Taiwan's positive record on human rights: Taiwan now scores at the high, or relatively high, end of such indexes and ranks far above the international medians.[16] More

[15]See generally deLisle (2014).

[16]See, for example, Freedom House (2017) Freedom in the world 2017: Taiwan. https://freedomouse.org/report/freedom-world/2017/taiwan. Accessed 15 Oct 2017 (giving Taiwan its highest ranking—"free"—and a score of 89 of 100 on a general index, and of 1 on a 7-point scale —where 1 is best—on civil and political liberties); Economist Intelligence Unit (2017) Democracy

qualitative assessments, including from leading NGOs and the U.S. State Department, paint a similar picture: although Taiwan still faces criticisms for some shortcomings, the overall record is acknowledged to be very good.[17]

With these domestic preconditions in place, Taiwan has addressed the international human rights regime in two complementary but distinct ways. Both have served to promote Taiwan's international stature and, thus, its security.

2.1 Emphasizing Conformity with International Norms

One mode has entailed touting Taiwan's record of embracing and implementing international human rights law and norms. Three features of the relationship between international human rights law and international legal status are relevant to understanding the contribution, or potential contribution, of domestic human rights performance to Taiwan's international standing—and, more specifically, to Taiwan's state-like stature—and, in turn, Taiwan's security.

First, international human rights obligations are primarily, although not exclusively, obligations *of states*. Stressing Taiwan's endorsement of, and conformity to, those obligations and related norms implies or supports the notion that Taiwan is entitled to a stature equaling or approaching that of a state in the international system. Second, the human rights metric for state and state-like actors is, in international political practice, a sliding scale, not a threshold or a determinative criterion for state status. Comparative assessments of human rights performance therefore are salient, and Taiwan accordingly has had reasons to showcase its own accomplishments and to emphasize the contrasts between the human rights conditions on opposite sides of the Strait.

Third, democracy and self-determination hold important but complex places in the relationship between internal human rights conditions and international status; democracy is an early-recognized and increasingly robust human right, but it remains more contested than many core civil and political rights. Its significance in terms of domestic human rights performance continues to rest partly—perhaps largely—on its long-recognized role as a vital underpinning for more traditional

index 2016: Revenge of the deplorables. https://www.eiu.com/Handlers/WhitepaperHandler.ashx?fi=Democracy-Index-2016.pdf&mode=wp&campaignid=DemocracyIndex2016. Accessed 15 Oct 2017 (ranking Taiwan 33rd in the world, with a score of 7.79, which puts Taiwan at the upper end of the "flawed democracy" category—the second highest of four categories).

[17]Taiwan 2016/2017 (2017). Amnesty International. https://www.amnesty.org/en/countries/asia-and-the-pacific/taiwan/report-taiwan/. Accessed 15 Oct 2017; Taiwan. Human Rights Watch. https://www.hrw.org/asia/taiwan. Accessed 15 Oct 2017; Country reports on human rights practices for 2016: Taiwan. U.S. State Department. http://www.state.gov/j/drl/rls/hrrpt/humanrightsreport/index.htm?year=2016&dlid=265374. Accessed 15 Oct 2017.

civil and political rights.[18] Self-determination is a venerable human right, but it is a right only of "peoples" (a contested category that is controversial in its application to Taiwan), and it is a right that may—or may not—entail a right to a separate state, or a political entity with state-like status, in the international system.[19]

The impact of Taiwan's human rights accomplishments in these aspects of human rights or human rights-related fields on Taiwan's international status has been correspondingly important and complicated. Several major examples illustrate broader patterns and trends that have emerged over the course of Taiwan's democratic era.

Under Taiwan's first democratically elected president, Lee Teng-hui, human rights accomplishments began to assume a prominent place in Taiwan's self-presentation to the outside world. Lee's government adopted the Guidelines for National Unification (GNU). The GNU were, inescapably, international audience-targeting in that they addressed prospects for resolving the fundamental issue in cross-Strait relations and the threat that Taiwan's contested status chronically posed to regional security and U.S.-China relations. The GNU invoked—albeit somewhat obliquely—Taiwan's achievements in human rights by declaring that "guaranteeing fundamental human rights" is an aim of unification, and establishing a "free" China is a task for a far-off final phase of consultation and unification.[20]

In speeches abroad, including an especially high-profile 1995 address at his alma mater Cornell University, Lee told his audience "human rights are respected and protected to a very high degree" in Taiwan. He particularly emphasized vigorous freedom of speech that "is in no way different from that enjoyed by people in the United States."[21] In his 1996 inaugural address following his victory in Taiwan's first fully democratic presidential election, Lee returned to such themes, asserting

[18]Franck (1992), Marks (2011), UDHR, *supra* note 1, art. 21 ("Everyone has the right to take part in the government of his country, directly or through freely chosen representatives" and "The will of the people shall be the basis of the authority of government; this will shall be expressed in periodic and genuine elections which shall be by universal and equal suffrage and shall be held by secret vote or by equivalent free voting procedures"); ICCPR, *supra* note 1, preamble, arts. 14, 21–22 (recognizing the "ideal of free human beings enjoying civil and political freedom" and its dependence on conditions of all enjoying human rights; restrictions on public trials, freedom of assembly and association limited to those necessary "in a democratic society" in the interests of national security, public safety, etc.); compare UDHR, *supra* note 1, art. 29.

[19]ICCPR, *supra* note 1, art. 1; ICESCR, *supra* note 1, art. 1 (right of all peoples to self-determination); Reference Re: Secession of Quebec, [1998] 2 S.C.R. 217 (Can.) (self-determination rights of the people of Quebec adequately protected by accommodation within the state of Canada), van der Vyver (2000), McCorquodale (1994).

[20]Mainland Affairs Council, Executive Yuan, Republic of China (1991) Guidelines for National Unification. https://law.wustl.edu/Chinalaw/twguide.html. Accessed 15 Oct 2017.

[21]Lee T (1995) Always in my heart. Olin Lecture at Cornell University. http://taiwantoday.tw/news.php?unit=4,29,31,45&post=3961. Accessed 15 Oct 2017.

that human rights (and democracy) are "universally adhered to values" that are "in full accord" with Taiwan's values.[22]

Lee's inaugural address began a pattern of Taiwan's presidents using this singularly—and, given the large number and prominence of foreign guests at such events and the extensive global media coverage—internationally high-profile opportunity to call attention to Taiwan's human rights (and related) accomplishments, and to link them to questions of Taiwan's international stature and standing. In 2000, the first president from the formerly opposition Democratic Progressive Party (DPP), Chen Shui-bian, recounted Taiwan's domestic political transformation, and then pledged "a more active contribution in safeguarding international human rights" by a Taiwan that "cannot and will not remain outside global human rights trends."[23] Chen reprised the point in his second inaugural, stressing Taiwan's achievements as "a completely free and democratic society" that collaborates with "other members of the global village" in advocating and defending human rights (as well as freedom and democracy), and that bases its "long-term friendship" with the U.S. and others on shared "core values" that include human rights (as well as freedom and democracy).[24] Near the end of his first term, Chen's speech upon receiving an international human rights award from the International League for Human Rights in New York characterized the award as "signif[ying] both affirmations and expectations" for Taiwan, as "representative of the international validation that the people of Taiwan have received" for their pursuit of human rights as well as democracy and freedom, and as a "reminder" of their "duty of protecting human rights and upholding international human rights principles."[25]

Chen's successors have offered variations on these themes on the occasion of their taking office. In his first inaugural speech in 2008, Ma Ying-jeou asserted that the people of Taiwan could "rely on the Constitution to protect human rights."[26] Beginning his second term, Ma spoke of Taiwan's "open society" and "climate of freedom," and expressed hope that cross-Strait exchanges on human rights and related matters would draw the Mainland closer to the levels that Taiwan had

---

[22]Lee T (1996) Presidential inaugural address. http://newcongress.yam.org.tw/Taiwan_sino/leespeec.html. Accessed 15 Oct 2017.

[23]President Chen's inaugural address (2000). http://english.president.gov.tw/NEWS/2643. Accessed 15 Oct 2017. [hereinafter Chen 2000 Inaugural Address.]

[24]President Chen's inaugural address "Paving the way for a sustainable Taiwan" (2004). http://english.president.gov.tw/NEWS/1726. Accessed 15 Oct 2017. [hereinafter Chen 2004 Inaugural Address.]

[25]Recognizing President Chen Shui-bian of Taiwan upon his reception of the International Human Rights Award, 149(158) CONG. REC. E2215-E2216 (4 Nov 2003) (speech by Chen). https://www.gpo.gov/fdsys/pkg/CREC-2003-11-04/html/CREC-2003-11-04-pt1-PgE2215-2.htm. Accessed 15 Oct 2004.

[26]President Ma's inaugural address (2008). http://english.president.gov.tw/NEWS/45. Accessed 15 Oct 2017. [hereinafter Ma 2008 Inaugural Address.]

achieved.[27] In her 2016 address, Taiwan's second president from the DPP, Tsai Ing-wen, echoed her predecessors on these issues. She pointed to Taiwan's "persiste[nce]," during its democratic era, in "upholding" human rights and other "universal values" and thereby serving as a "model citizen in global civil society."[28]

Proclaiming human rights performance has not been limited to the quadrennial ritual of presidential inaugurations. The speeches focusing on human rights made abroad by Presidents Lee and Chen (quoted earlier) are prominent examples. Less dramatically, Taiwan's presidents have used many meetings with international human rights groups, foreign media, and other events reaching global audiences to reiterate Taiwan's domestic human rights accomplishments and international human rights norm-consistent commitments.[29] Under Chen and Ma, international human rights initiatives in domestic law (including moves to ratify key UN human rights treaties, and to push for legislation to bring provisions of the two principal UN human rights covenants specifically into domestic law) provided additional high-profile occasions to highlight Taiwan's human rights successes.[30]

Throughout Taiwan's democratic era, the government has pointed to human rights issues and accomplishments in a context that has been especially relevant to state or state-like status: pushing for Taiwan's representation or participation in the United Nations or UN specialized organizations. Thus, the Lee government couched its bid for UN participation partly in terms of its contribution to promoting fundamental human rights. Repeated and unsuccessful motions for Taiwan's representation at the UN that were undertaken by Taiwan's diplomatic allies at Taiwan's instigation, and that were a hallmark of the Chen years with origins in the

[27]President Ma's inaugural address (2012). http://english.president.gov.tw/NEWS/3887. Accessed 15 Oct 2017. [hereinafter Ma 2012 Inaugural Address.]

[28]Inaugural address of ROC 14th-term President Tsai Ing-wen (2016). http://english.president.gov.tw/NEWS/4893. Accessed 15 Oct 2017. [hereinafter Tsai 2016 Presidential Inaugural Address.]

[29]The occasions have been numerous. A few examples suggest the breadth and frequency: President Chen meets world coalitions against death penalty founder Mario Marazziti (2007). http://english.president.gov.tw/NEWS/2634. Accessed 17 Nov 2017 (stating Chen's having "worked hard to create a nation based on human rights" and its commitment to enacting a "human rights basic law"); President Chen Shui-bian meets Dutch human rights expert Dr. Theodoor C. Van Boven (2007). http://english.president.gov.tw/NEWS/2682. Accessed 15 Oct 2017 (Chen's recounting to visiting human rights expert of "Taiwan's work and accomplishments in the area of human rights"); President Ma welcomes international experts to Taiwan to review the ROC's first national human rights report (2013). http://english.president.gov.tw/NEWS/4092. Accessed 15 Oct 2017 (welcoming international experts group to review Taiwan human rights report that "marks a milestone in the development of human rights in the ROC"); Ma highlights Taiwan's human rights efforts (2012) Taiwan Today. http://taiwantoday.tw/news.php?unit=2,23,45&post=2254. Accessed 17 Nov 2017 (meeting with the president of Youth for Human Rights International and noting Taiwan "has adopted human rights standards on par with those in leading democracies"); President Tsai meets delegation from Reporters without Borders (2017). http://english.president.gov.tw/News/5180. Accessed 15 Oct 2017 (welcoming organization's opening of its first Asian bureau in Taiwan as reflecting the "importance" that Taiwan places on freedom of the press and speech, and helping "Taiwan to contribute more to global human rights").

[30]These developments are discussed in detail in the next section of this chapter.

Lee era, closely linked human rights and UN representation for Taiwan: excluding Taiwan from representation deprived Taiwanese people of human rights, and Taiwan's strong record in respecting and implementing human rights (which are a core principle of the UN) warranted Taiwan's participation in the UN. In pressing for Taiwan's most successful post-ouster bid to participate in a major UN (specialized) organ, Ma argued that Taiwan's opportunity to participate in the World Health Assembly (WHA) was "a human rights issue." Tsai similarly asserted that participation in the WHA was vital to Taiwan's human rights development.[31]

Drawing contrasts between conditions in Taiwan and the Mainland has been another part of Taiwan's human rights-linked international status-enhancing external engagement, from the Lee administration on. This was a central element of Lee's GNU: by declaring unification to be a relatively far-off pursuit linked to goals of "fundamental human rights" (as well as democracy), this seminal directive on cross-Strait issues emphasized the gaps in human rights performance between Taiwan and the Mainland.

Lee's successors continued this theme, as illustrated in their inaugural addresses and other contexts. In his second inauguration speech, Chen emphasized the "very different political systems" on the two sides of the Strait and discerned "an opportune moment in history for China to move forward with democratization and liberalization." In a U.S. media interview, he contrasted Taiwan with China, which "lacks democratic elections, freedom of speech, freedom of the press, and freedom of religion."[32]

In his first inaugural address, Ma contrasted how "Sun Yat-sen's dream for a constitutional democracy"—a vision that subsumes a wide range of human rights—is "not yet realized on the Chinese Mainland but…has taken root, blossomed and borne fruit in Taiwan." In the speech marking the start of his second term, Ma's call for greater exchanges across the Strait on human rights and related matters cast Taiwan's role as one of improving conditions on the Mainland, thereby lessening the gap between the two sides.[33]

---

[31]Yang (1996), p. 122 (quoting Foreign Minister Frederick Chien); Request for the Inclusion of a Supplementary Item on the Agenda of the 57th Session: Question of the Representation of the Republic of China (Taiwan) in the United Nations, Letter dated 1 Aug 2002 from the representatives of Burkina Faso, Chad, El Salvador, the Gambia, Grenada, the Marshall Islands, Nicaragua, Saint Vincent and the Grenadines, Sao Tome and Principe, Senegal, Solomon Islands and Swaziland to the United Nations addressed to the Secretary-General, UN Doc. A/57/191 (20 Aug 2002); Ma optimistic over WHA participation, Taipei Times, 12 Dec 2008, at 3; President Tsai meets members of Taiwan's WHA action team (2017). http://english.president.gov.tw/NEWS/5152. Accessed 15 Oct 2017; Sehnálková and Kučera (2012), pp. 163–164.

[32]President Chen's Inaugural Address (2004); see also Cody E (2007) Interview with Chen Shui-bian, President of Taiwan. WASH POST, http://www.washingtonpost.com/wp-dyn/content/article/2007/07/07/AR2007070700929.html. Accessed 15 Oct 2017. See also President Chen's Inaugural Address (2000) (rejecting suggestion that "values of freedom, democracy and human rights" can be "ignored or changed in different contexts, including across the Strait).

[33]President Ma's Inaugural Address (2008); President Ma's Inaugural Address (2012).

Tsai's 2016 inaugural speech forewent drawing explicit human rights-related contrasts between Taiwan and the Mainland. But in other contexts Tsai has reprised Ma's practice of pointing to such differences when addressing issues that engage international audiences and interlocutors. For example, Ma regularly used the high-profile anniversary of the 4 June Tiananmen Incident to point to the contrast in human rights, democracy, freedom, and the rule of law between Taiwan and the Mainland. On 4 June of her first full year office, Tsai urged the PRC to "face" the Tiananmen Incident, much as Taiwan had faced dark episodes in its own political past, such as the 2/28 Incident and the Kaohsiung Incident.[34] For another example, Ma joined other international leaders in praising the awarding of the Nobel Peace Prize to Liu Xiaobo, characterizing it as significant for China's human rights development and expressing hope that China can make a "breakthrough" on "human rights issues," which will "win the recognition of Taiwanese people." When Liu died in 2017, Tsai expressed hope that China will realize Liu's dream of a country in which human rights (as well as the rule of law) are supreme, and offered Taiwan's assistance to China in achieving democracy (and in turn human rights)—an offer that implicitly asserted Taiwan's accomplishments in these areas and its contrast with circumstances in the PRC.[35]

Democracy—which international human rights discourse long has acknowledged as a vital underpinning for many human rights and which itself assumed a more core position in the pantheon of human rights during the 1990s—was a focal point for Lee Teng-hui in handling Taiwan's external relations. Lee's remarks directed at audiences abroad linked democracy to other human rights (specifically, civil and political rights) and to Taiwan's international status. In his 1995 speech at Cornell, for example, he declared "the institutions of democracy are in place....[and d]emocracy is thriving" in Taiwan, as evidenced by its free media and vibrant and critical political discourse. Moreover, Taiwan's recent political developments provided "a basis for defining the status of my country in the post-Cold War and post-Communist era" and made Taiwan a source of "tremendous hope for other developing nations."[36] In another prominent example, Lee's late 1999 article in *Foreign Affairs* extended these themes. He stressed that Taiwan had "attain[ed] full democracy" and argued that the "international community" needed to "update its perceptions of...Taiwan and the implications of [its] democratic development" and to "work ... to accord Taiwan the international status" that democratic Taiwan

[34]See, for example, President Ma issues statement on Tiananmen Square Incident (2011) Taiwan Today. http://taiwantoday.tw/news.php?unit=2,23,45&post=1843. Accessed 15 Oct 2017; Tsai urges China to face Tiananmen (2017) Taipei Times. http://www.taipeitimes.com/News/front/archives/2017/06/05/2003671928. Accessed 15 Oct 2017.

[35]See International reaction to Liu Xiaobo Nobel Peace Prize (2008) BBC News. http://www.bbc.co.uk/news/mobile/world-europe-11499931. Accessed 15 Oct 2017. (Ma's statement); Taiwan President mourns Liu Xiaobo, says China won't be great until it accepts his ideas (2017) The China Post. www.chinapost.com.tw/taiwan/2017/07/14/499421/taiwan-president.htm. Accessed 15 Oct 2017. (Tsai's statement).

[36]Lee, *supra* note 21; see also Kagan (2007).

deserved. He also criticized Beijing's "attack" on "the legitimacy of the democratic government" in Taiwan as an "affront" to "the prevailing values of the international community."[37]

In inaugural addresses by Lee's democratically elected successors, Taiwan's democracy—not surprisingly, given the nature of the occasion—has been a focus, often with articulated connections to Taiwan's broader accomplishments in human rights and to Taiwan's claims for international standing and stature. In his inaugural addresses and other contexts as well, Chen emphasized how his election, and the alternation in power that it heralded, represented a remarkable democratic breakthrough and made Taiwan a model for China, Asia, and other third-wave democracies in implementing the "universal values" of freedom and democracy. In his second inaugural speech, Chen pointed to the election that retained him in office as a reaffirmation of Taiwan's "exemplary success" with democracy and freedom. He also noted Taiwan's accomplishments and commitments reflected in the founding of the Pacific Democratic Alliance and the Taiwan Foundation for Democracy.[38] In a 2007 interview with the *Washington Post*, Chen recounted Taiwan's democratic progress since 1979, pledged the further "strengthening and deepening" of democracy in Taiwan, and declared democracy Taiwan's "most important asset" in pressing back against the PRC (and, in turn, securing Taiwan's international space).[39]

Ma began his presidency with an assertion that Taiwan's democracy had "matured," moving beyond the troubles of the preceding years, such that Taiwan had "rediscover[ed]" its values and become a "beacon of democracy to Asia and the world….respected by the international community." Ma returned to these themes in his second inaugural speech and in other statements reaching or targeting international audiences. He noted Taiwan's democratic "maturity" and "highly developed democratic mindset that [have] won praise from the international community."[40] In a wide-ranging *Washington Post* interview, he emphasized Taiwan's status as a "full-fledged democracy" that "cherish[es]" its "democratic system," "human rights safeguards," and "rule of law."[41]

Like Ma and Chen, in her inaugural speech Tsai stressed Taiwan's accomplishment of a peaceful transition of power to the previously out-of-power party. She praised "the people of Taiwan" for again "show[ing] the world" that they are "committed to the defense of … freedom and democracy."[42] Like her predecessors, she struck similar notes with the international media, for example, telling the *Wall*

[37]Lee (1999).

[38]President Chen's Inaugural Address (2000); President Chen's Inaugural Address (2004).

[39]Cody, *supra* note 32.

[40]President Ma's Inaugural Address (2008); President Ma's Inaugural Address (2012).

[41]Transcript: Post's interview with Taiwanese President Ma Ying-jeou, WASH POST, 17 Feb 2011.

[42]President Tsai's Inaugural Address (2016).

Street Journal that Taiwan's democratization is a "model of success" in pursuing "universal values" that include "democracy, freedom, and human rights."[43]

Among human rights, and among key political-institutional conditions for human rights, democracy is closely related to claims to state status, partly because of the connection between democracy and the human right of self-determination (of peoples), which sometimes can—but need not always—entail a right to separate statehood and which is presumptively implemented through democratic means (including referenda on statehood). The right to self-determination—with its uncertain yet, in many contexts (including the cross-Strait context), provocative linkage to a right to independent statehood—has had complex and evolving but durable significance in Taiwan's engagement with the international human rights regime and Taiwan's pursuit of international stature and security.

Any invocation of Taiwan's democracy inescapably points, at least obliquely, toward issues of self-determination and, in turn, international status. Taiwan's democratic progress has been inextricably entwined with the fact, regularly reflected in public opinion polling, that the preference of people living in Taiwan has been for at least *de facto* independence or—for many Taiwanese (and for many more under the counterfactual condition that Beijing would tolerate such an outcome)—*de jure* independent statehood.[44]

President Lee made such links explicit in a variety of contexts, including, for example, his 1995 Cornell speech. In this lecture to a foreign (and global) audience, he drew connections among democratization, popular sovereignty, and constitutional reforms that were leading to elections by the people "in the Taiwan area" of their own leaders. Lee took matters a step further when he later spoke of the "New Taiwanese" with a distinct "consciousness" and a sense of "common destiny," or a "Taiwanese society/*gemeinschaft/shengming gongtong ti*," eliding the Mainlander (*waishengren*) vs. Taiwanese (*benshengren*) distinction that had cut strongly against claims to a coherent Taiwanese people, distinct from the Chinese people of the Mainland, who are entitled—and already enjoyed—a state of their own. In Lee's account, that state was "the Republic of China [which] has been a sovereign state" since its founding in 1912—a bold if problematic assertion, in terms of application of relevant international legal principles of sovereignty, statehood, and self-determination.[45]

President Chen built on Lee's foundations in his inaugural addresses (and elsewhere), proclaiming the solidarity of a "New Taiwan" family that included Mainlanders and Taiwanese, and asserting that he had a mandate from the "people of Taiwan" to "defend the sovereignty of the nation" and its existence as a member

[43]Hutzler C and Hsu JW (2016) Taiwanese President Tsai: Taiwan won't succumb to China's pressure. The Wall Street Journal. https://blogs.wsj.com/chinarealtime/2016/10/05/taiwanese-president-tsai-taiwan-wont-succumb-to-chinas-pressure/. Accessed 15 Oct 2017.

[44]See, for example, Wang (2013), Hsieh and Niou (2005), Sobel et al. (2010).

[45]Lee, *supra* note 21; Lee (1999), p. 9; President Lee's message to the Taiwan retrocession day (1997). http://english.president.gov.tw/NEWS/1106. Accessed 15 Oct 2017; see also Hughes (2005), pp. 95–100, deLisle (2000), pp. 55–57.

of international society.[46] In more concrete moves, Chen pressed the point a good deal farther, with his successful effort to bring into Taiwanese politics and governance a referendum—a mechanism associated both with self-determination in international human rights law and with Taiwan independence in the DPP political tradition.[47]

Ma toned down these positions at his first inauguration, making only more muted and less clearly international status-implicating positive references to a distinctive, pluralist, and vigorous society that immigration (including by Ma himself) had produced in Taiwan. Tsai's inaugural address moved back in a pre-Ma direction, acknowledging the responsibility that she and her fellow Taiwanese bore to safeguard the sovereignty, democracy and freedom of the country.[48] Neither Ma nor, more clearly, Tsai abandoned the fundamental, enduring and self-determination-linked point that Taiwan's status vis-à-vis the PRC and Taiwan's international status more generally—and any change in that status—are matters for determination by the people of Taiwan through their uncoerced democratic processes.

Chen's government had insisted that Taiwan is "an independent sovereign nation" with sovereignty "vested in its 23 million people, and any change to Taiwan's future should be determined by these 23 million people."[49] In his reelection campaign, Ma had seemed, to critics, to cast doubt on that principle with his talk of a cross-Strait "peace accord." But facing considerable political blowback, he soon added preconditions that moved back toward established positions on self-determination and sovereignty, including a requirement of support by the public in the form of a plebiscite.[50] In interviews with high-profile international media (including the *Washington Post* and the *Wall Street Journal*), Tsai insisted that the people of democratic Taiwan and their democratically chosen leader would not accept conditions or deadlines from China that went against the "will of the people," and she expressed the hope that China would "respect Taiwan's democracy" and the fact that Taiwan would not relinquish its "insistence for freedom and democracy in the face of pressure from China."[51]

---

[46]President Chen's Inaugural Address (2004); cf. President Chen's Inaugural Address (2000).

[47]See generally Schubert and Braig (2011), deLisle (2004).

[48]President Ma's Inaugural Address (2008); President Tsai's Inaugural Address (2016).

[49]Mainland Affairs Council, Executive Yuan, ROC (2006) Position paper on the National Unification Council ceasing to function and the Guidelines for National Unification ceasing to apply. http://www.mac.gov.tw/en/News_Content.aspx?n=BEC36A4A0BB0663C&sms=BF821F021B282251&s=20C09FC2F3C10A1C. Accessed 15 Oct 2017.

[50]Ma attached three preconditions for a peace accord: that it be necessary for the ROC, that it be supported by the public (later adding that such support would be determined in a plebiscite), and that the process be subject to oversight by Taiwan's democratically elected legislature. President Ma holds press conference on "cross-strait peace agreement" (2001). https://www.mac.gov.tw/en/News_Content.aspx?n=FE07F9DA122E29D4&sms=3A4E63FA5107487D&s=CD5F7C3EB8CAD2E1. Accessed 15 Oct 2017; see also deLisle (2012).

[51]See Weymouth L (2016) Taiwanese President Tsai Ing-wen: Beijing must respect our democratic will, WASH POST, 21 July 2016; Hutzler and Hsu, *supra* note 43.

Taiwan's emphasis on human rights, democracy, and (to a more limited extent) self-determination has played effectively to, and received support from, the United States, which is of singular importance for Taiwan's security. From the Clinton administration on, senior U.S. officials have praised Taiwan's human rights record and democratic accomplishments and have cited them as a basis for Washington's resilient support for Taipei.[52] With formal and durable entrenchment in the TRA, Taiwan's human rights record has been a significant factor in U.S. support for Taiwan's international participation and status. With roots as far back as the Shanghai Communiqué, Washington has insisted that acceptability to the people of Taiwan—a democratic standard—is a precondition to any change in Taiwan's international status (in the direction of unification with the Mainland).[53]

Although generally wary of worsening frictions with Beijing and emboldening Lee, the Clinton administration framed its support for Taiwan during the 1995–96

[52]See, for example, Lord W (1994) Taiwan policy review: Statement before the Senate Foreign Relations Committee, Washington, DC, 27 Sept 1994. https://web.archive.org/web/20160914002741/http://ait.org.tw/en/19940927-taiwan-policy-review-by-winston-lord.html. Accessed 15 Oct 2017 (citing Taiwan's "dramatic strides toward democracy and the fulfillment of human rights" as bases for U.S. "friendship and ties with Taiwan"); Bush, RC (1998) The US role in the Taiwan Strait issue. http://www.taiwandc.org/nws-9867.htm. Accessed 15 Oct 2017 (characterizing Taiwan's democratization as "one of the most remarkable examples of political progress in our time"); Craner LW (2004) Briefing on supporting human rights and democracy: The U.S. record 2003–2004 report. https://2001-2009.state.gov/g/drl/rls/rm/32537.htm. Accessed 15 Oct 2017 (discounting criticism of Taiwan's not "perfect" 2004 election and citing the Taiwan example in support of U.S. policies of promoting democracy abroad); Campbell KM (2011) Testimony before the House Foreign Affairs Committee: Why Taiwan matters, Part II. https://2009-2017.state.gov/p/eap/rls/rm/2011/10/174980.htm. Accessed 15 Oct 2017 ("The foundation of our political ties with Taiwan is our common values and shared belief in democracy, and Americans have been deeply impressed by Taiwan's open, exuberant democratic polity and society," and characterizing the U.S. approach to its unofficial relations with Taiwan as an important part of U.S. strategy that includes promoting democratic values and human rights in Asia); Tong K (2016) Remarks: Taiwan's international role and the GCTF. https://2009-2017.state.gov/e/eb/rls/rm/2016/253915.htm. Accessed 15 Oct 2017.

[53]Text of Joint Communique, Issued at Shanghai, para. 12, 27 Feb 1972, 66 Department of State Bulletin [xxix], 458 (1972). http://heinonline.org/HOL/Permalink?a=dXBlbm4uZWR1&u=http%3A%2F%2Fheinonline.org%2FHOL%2FPage%3Fhandle%3Dhein.journals%2Fdsbul66%26collection%3Dustreaties%26id%3D491. Accessed 15 Oct 2017 (reaffirming U.S. "interest in a peaceful settlement of the Taiwan question by the Chinese [a group defined in the Communique to include the people on both sides of the Strait] themselves"); Lord, *supra* note 52 (U.S. will "welcome any evolution in relations between Taipei and Beijing that is mutually agreed upon and peacefully reached"); Remarks by the President to the Business Council, 24 Feb 2000, 1 PUB. PAPERS 296 (24 Feb 2000) ("issues between Beijing and Taiwan must be resolved peacefully and with the assent of the people of Taiwan"); Kelly J (2004) Assistant Secretary of State for East Asian and Pacific Affairs, The Taiwan Relations Act: The next 25 years, Hearing before the House International Relations Committee, 21 Apr 2004 (reiterating U.S. opposition to attempts by either side to unilaterally change the status quo); Rice SE (2015) Remarks on the U.S.-China Relationship at George Washington University, 21 Sept 2015. https://obamawhitehouse.archives.gov/the-press-office/2015/09/21/national-security-advisor-susan-e-rices-prepared-remarks-us-china. Accessed 15 Oct 2017.

cross-Strait crisis partly in terms of Taiwan's human rights and commitment to liberal rights.[54] U.S. administrations routinely include praise, and offer at least implicit support, for Taiwan's democracy (and, on occasion, other human rights-resonant values) in congratulatory messages to victors in Taiwan's presidential elections.[55]

In a pair of exceptions that largely prove the rule, the George W. Bush administration departed from customary (if somewhat anodyne) acclaim for Taiwan's democratic elections to criticize possible use of a new referendum law to address issues of national name or status (in 2004) and to seek support for an effort to join the United Nations under the name of Taiwan (in 2008).[56] These unprecedented and rare rebuffs confirmed that there were limits to Washington's deference to Taiwan's democratic processes (or possible self-determination rights) when the U.S. saw its interests (as well as Taiwan's) as needlessly imperiled (in this case by the prospect of an unnecessary crisis with a regime in Beijing that was very

[54]Lord W (1996) Testimony before the House International Relations Subcommittee on East Asia and the Pacific. http://dosfan.lib.uic.edu/ERC/bureaus/eap/960314LordTaiwan.html. Accessed 15 Oct 2017.

[55]Tyler PE (1996) Taiwan's leader wins its election and a mandate, N.Y. TIMES, 24 Mar 1996 (quoting White House spokesperson congratulating the people of Taiwan on the first democratic election of President and noting that no official congratulations from U.S. would be forthcoming); Clinton WJ (2000) Statement on the election of Chen Shui-bian as President of Taiwan - 18 Mar 2000, PUB. PAPERS 490, 490. https://www.gpo.gov/fdsys/pkg/WCPD-2000-03-27/pdf/WCPD-2000-03-27-Pg582.pdf. Accessed 15 Oct 2017 (congratulating Chen and stating that the election "clearly demonstrates the strength and vitality of Taiwan's democracy"); Office of the Press Secretary (2004) Statement on Taiwan elections: Announcement of election results on Taiwan. https://georgewbush-whitehouse.archives.gov/news/releases/2004/03/20040326-6.html. Accessed 15 Oct 2017 (congratulating Chen, congratulating the people of Taiwan on the successful conclusion of their election and praising reliance on legal mechanisms to address election dispute); Bush GW (2008) Statement on the presidential election in Taiwan, PUB. PAPERS 410, 411. https://georgewbush-whitehouse.archives.gov/news/releases/2008/03/20080322-4.html. Accessed 15 Oct 2017 (congratulating Ma and congratulating the people of Taiwan on the successful conclusion of their election and adding "Once again, Taiwan has demonstrated the strength and vitality of its democracy.... Taiwan is a beacon of democracy for Asia and the world."); Obama BH (2012) Statement on elections in Taiwan, PUB. PAPERS 43. https://obamawhitehouse.archives.gov/the-press-office/2012/01/14/statement-press-secretary-taiwan-s-elections. Accessed 15 Oct 2017 (congratulating Ma on reelection and the people of Taiwan on the successful conduct of their elections, stating that "Taiwan has again demonstrated the strength and vitality of its democratic system," and citing a "shared commitment to democracy and freedom" as a basis for the close relationship between the people of Taiwan and the people of the United States); Kirby J (2016) U.S. statement on Taiwan's presidential inauguration. https://2009-2017.state.gov/r/pa/prs/ps/2016/05/257465.htm. Accessed 15 Oct 2017 (congratulating Tsai and congratulating the "people on Taiwan for once again demonstrating the strength of their robust democratic system").

[56]President Bush and Premier Wen Jiabao remarks to the press (2003). https://georgewbushwhitehouse.archives.gov/news/releases/2003/12/20031209-2.html. Accessed 15 Oct 2017; Boucher R (2003) Daily press briefing. https://2001-2009.state.gov/r/pa/prs/dpb/2003/26776.htm. Accessed 15 Oct 2017; Christensen TJ (2007) A strong and moderate Taiwan. Speech to U.S.-Taiwan Business Council Defense Industry Conference, Annapolis, Maryland, 11 Sept 2007. https://2001-2009.state.gov/p/eap/rls/rm/2007/91979.htm. Accessed 15 Oct 2017; see also deLisle (2004).

wary of moves toward Taiwan independence or broader "desinicization" in Taiwan).

The extremity of the circumstances that prompted the rebuke—and the care U.S. officials took in framing their criticism—backhandedly confirmed a high level of U.S. respect for Taiwan's democracy (and, by implication, the human rights that it embodies and underpins) and the connection that the U.S. ordinarily draws to its support for Taiwan's international security. The Obama and Trump administration statements returned to the customary invocation of democracy and shared values (including those relating to human rights) as foundations for positive U.S.-Taiwan relations and U.S. policy toward Taiwan.[57] This has remained the pattern despite complaints from Beijing that Tsai has been returning to a path of "desinicization" and "creeping" or "soft" independence.[58]

2.2 *Acting like a State-Party to International Legal Treaties*

In a complementary, later-emerging, and more law-centered mode, Taiwan has engaged with international human rights norms and rules by behaving, as much as possible, as if it were a member of major components of the international legal regime for human rights. This approach dovetails with a broader pattern in Taiwan's strategy for international standing: acting "as if" it were a member in good standing of states-only (or states-primarily) regimes strengthens its claim to the status of a state (or status approaching that of a state)—and, specifically, a responsible state—in the international system.

A few characteristics of the international legal regime for human rights are significant in making sense of this "as if" dimension of Taiwan's behavior and its implications for Taiwan's international stature. First, Taiwan has had to adopt this approach because Taiwan has been unable to join the major treaty-based institutions

---

[57]See Obama, *supra* note 55; Remarks of President Obama to the People of Laos (2016). https://obamawhitehouse.archives.gov/the-press-office/2016/09/06/remarks-president-obama-people-laos. Accessed 15 Oct 2017 (praising Taiwan as an example of a thriving democracy in Asia and reaffirming the U.S. commitment to support universal human rights in the region); Russel DR (2016) Remarks at China's Growing Pains Conference, 22 Apr 2016. https://2009-2017.state.gov/p/eap/rls/rm/2016/04/256509.htm. Accessed 15 Oct 2017 (characterizing "support for democratic Taiwan and for universal values and human rights" as key elements in the Obama administration's Asia policy); Republican platform (2016), at p. 47. https://prod-cdn-static.gop.com/media/documents/DRAFT_12_FINAL[1]-ben_1468872234.pdf. Accessed 15 Oct 2017 ("We salute the people of Taiwan, with whom we share the values of democracy, human rights, a free market economy, and the rule of law"); Nomination of Rex Tillerson to be Secretary of State, Hearing before the Committee on Foreign Relations, United States Senate, 115th Congress, 1st Session, 11 Jan 2017. https://www.gpo.gov/fdsys/pkg/CHRG-115shrg24573/html/CHRG-115shrg24573.htm. Accessed 15 Oct 2017 (stating that the U.S. commitment to Taiwan is a "moral imperative" as well as a legal commitment, and characterizing "[s]tanding up for human rights and democracy" as a "moral imperative").

[58]Romberg (2017), pp. 3–6, deLisle (2016b), pp. 571–572.

of the international legal order for human rights. The simple and intractable reason is that the relevant treaties are primarily UN-based (all the more so, given the absence of a robust regional human rights treaty regime in East Asia), and Beijing's opposition to Taiwan's separate participation in the major relevant treaties has been an insurmountable barrier.

Second, an "as if" strategy toward the international human rights regime requires a record of good performance domestically. A state with a poor human rights record might be able to achieve some modest improvement in international standing by formally joining a human rights treaty even if the state severely shirks its responsibilities under the treaty.[59] For an entity that pursues an "as if" approach to the international human rights regime, however, there likely is no analogous gain to be had.

Third, human rights is an area of international law where an "as if" approach is comparatively likely to achieve some success. Many treaty-based international legal regimes are compatible with a non-member state acting in ways that would fulfill obligations if it were a member. Taiwan has taken this approach to several multilateral accords that it has not been able to join (on issues ranging from the environment to nuclear materials to the law of the sea).[60] Human rights treaty regimes, however, are especially amenable to an "as if" approach because the international legal obligations that these treaties impose predominantly govern how states treat their own citizens—something that is generally within a state's unilateral control. Relatedly, although state-to-state enforcement mechanisms are part of many human rights treaty regimes, they generally are not among the most central features of those regimes; breaches of obligations under human rights treaties are not primarily addressed by one state seeking to redress violations or to achieve compliance from another state through formal institutional mechanisms (whether specialized treaty bodies or more general-purpose international dispute resolution mechanisms) that are inaccessible to non-members. Rather, more informal pressure to comply focuses on a state's behavior at home.

Fourth, and relatedly, human rights is an area of international law where customary international law and treaty-based international law are deeply entwined. The demands that the two regimes impose are highly overlapping. The substantive provisions of the ICCPR and ICESCR are generally recognized as congruent with obligations that customary international human rights impose.[61] Rights embodied in other UN-based international human rights treaties that Taiwan has sought to engage in some cases have a somewhat less indisputable status as customary international law, but they very often do track or reflect elements of customary international law. Of special relevance to Taiwan, each of the two states that are most relevant for Taiwan's international security has yet to ratify one of the major covenants (the ICESCR in the case of the United States and the ICCPR in the case

---

[59]Compare, for example, Hathaway (2002).

[60]See generally deLisle (2007).

[61]Restatement (1987), Hannum (1996), Crawford (2012), pp. 642–643, Thrilway (2015).

of China) and thus accepts (and can invoke) the contents of one covenant only as customary international law.

When Taiwan proclaims to international audiences domestic conditions that constitute a strong record on human rights and dovetail with the behavior that is necessary to satisfy the obligations set forth in the large area of overlap between the customary international law of human rights and the major UN-centered human rights treaties, it is acting in accordance with an “as if” strategy toward both the customary and treaty-based elements of the international legal regime for human rights.

In relatively recent times, Taiwan has added a more focused and formal dimension to its “as if” approach to the treaty-based elements of the international human rights legal regime. Taiwan has adopted domestic legislative and policy measures of a type that would be undertaken by a responsible, obligation-fulfilling member of the major treaty regimes.

In his first inaugural address, President Chen pledged that Taiwan would abide by the UDHR, the ICCPR, and the Vienna Declaration and Program of Action on human rights. Chen established a presidential human rights advisory committee and called, unsuccessfully, for legislation to adopt a “Taiwan Bill of Rights” that would bring into Taiwan’s domestic law the “International Bill of Rights”—that is, the rights set forth in the two Covenants and the Universal Declaration.[62] Chen further promised to seek an independent national human rights commission, in keeping with UN human rights goals. Chen also promised to issue Taiwan’s first “human rights report”—an official analog to what Taiwanese human rights NGOs had been doing but that would provide an official assessment measuring Taiwan’s performance against the standards set forth in human rights treaty law, much as a member state of the treaty regimes would do under the ICCPR’s and ICESCR’s reporting requirements or other mechanisms, such as universal periodic reviews before the Human Rights Council.[63]

Under Ma (and single-party control of the presidency and the Legislative Yuan), Taiwan took significant additional steps in this direction. Ma established a human rights consultative committee in the Presidential Office. Taiwan adopted legislation to implement—and to bring into Taiwan’s domestic law—several major UN human rights treaties, including the ICCPR, the ICESCR, the Convention on the Elimination of All Forms of Discrimination Against Women, and the Convention

---

[62]Office of the United Nations High Commissioner for Human Rights (1996) Fact sheet no. 2 (rev. 1), the international bill of human rights. http://www.ohchr.org/Documents/Publications/FactSheet2Rev.1en.pdf. Accessed 15 Oct 2017.

[63]See President’s Chen’s Inaugural Address (2000); President Chen’s New Year’s Message (2001). http://english.president.gov.tw/NEWS/929. Accessed 15 Oct 2017; Recognizing President Chen Shui-bian of Taiwan upon his Reception of the International Human Rights Award, *supra* note 25; Neary (2005), pp. 116–117. The proposal for bringing international civil and political rights into domestic Taiwan law also echoed the approach adopted in Hong Kong, where the Bill of Rights Ordinance was adopted in the run-up to Hong Kong’s return to Chinese rule and drew a clear human rights contrast with the Mainland and sought to prevent post-reversion erosion of human rights in the Hong Kong SAR.

on the Rights of the Child. Ma stressed that Taiwan's "failure" (in reality, inability) to deposit instruments of ratification with the UN for the ICCPR and ICESCR (instruments that Ma signed in 2009 after the passage of relevant legislation, but which the UN refused to accept) "does not change the fact" that Taiwan's government is "now subject to the binding legal force of the content of these two UN human rights covenants."[64]

Under the auspices of a Human Rights Consultative Committee, the Ma government issued a first (in 2012) and second (in 2016) systematic report on Taiwan's human rights performance, specifically measured against the obligations of the ICCPR and ICESCR. The documents tracked the reporting that a state member in good standing would be expected to undertake pursuant to the two Covenants. In keeping with international practice for state members of the Covenants (and loosely echoing attributes of universal periodic reviews before the UN Human Rights Council), Taiwan invited international experts (as well as NGOs and domestic stakeholders) to participate in the human rights performance review process, and issued a government response to observations and recommendations by the committee of international experts.[65]

Tsai's government continued its predecessor's practices. It welcomed the report offering observations and recommendations by the group of international experts who reviewed the 2016 report. Tsai herself praised the review process as part of an effort to "develop a method for Taiwan to participate in the UN's human rights protection mechanism," and noted the legislation adopted under her predecessor to

[64]President Ma holds press conference on the release of Taiwan's second human rights report (2016). http://english.president.gov.tw/NEWS/4887. Accessed 15 Oct 2017. Relevant legislation included: The International Covenant on Civil and Political Rights and the International Covenant on Economic, Social and Cultural Rights Implementation Act (2009); The Convention on the Elimination of All Forms of Discrimination Against Women Enforcement Act, The Convention on the Rights of the Child Implementation Act, and The Convention on the Rights of Persons with Disabilities Implementation Act. See deLisle (2016b), pp. 567–568, deLisle (2014), p. 281.

[65]Implementation of the International Covenant on Civil and Political Rights, initial report submitted under Article 40 of the Covenant, Republic of China (Taiwan) (2012). http://www.humanrights.moj.gov.tw/ct.asp?xItem=385452&ctNode=40243&mp=205. Accessed 15 Oct 2017; Implementation of the International Covenant on Economic, Social and Cultural Rights, initial report submitted under Articles 16 and 17 of the Covenant, Republic of China (Taiwan) (2012). http://www.humanrights.moj.gov.tw/ct.asp?xItem=385452&ctNode=40243&mp=205. Accessed 15 Oct 2017; President Ma holds press conference on the release of Taiwan's first human rights report (2014). http://english.president.gov.tw/NEWS/3880. Accessed 15 Oct 2017; Implementation of the International Covenant on Civil and Political Rights, second report submitted under Article 40 of the Covenant, Republic of China (Taiwan), Apr 2016, Implementation of the International Covenant on Economic, Social and Cultural Rights, second report submitted under Articles 16 and 17 of the Covenant, Republic of China (Taiwan), Apr 2016; Response to the concluding observations and recommendations adopted by the International Group of Independent Experts on 1 Mar 2013, Republic of China (Taiwan). http://www.humanrights.moj.gov.tw/lp.asp?ctNode=43063&CtUnit=16034&BaseDSD=7&mp=205. Accessed 15 Oct 2017; President presided over the Second Report on ICCPR and ICESCR Press Conference (2016). http://www.humanrights.moj.gov.tw/ct.asp?xItem=431093&ctNode=40238&mp=205. Accessed 15 Oct 2017; Universal Periodic Review. United Nations Human Rights Office of the High Commissioner. http://www.ohchr.org/EN/HRBodies/UPR/Pages/UPRMain.aspx. Accessed 15 Oct 2017.

implement "major international human rights covenants." She stressed her government's commitment to "advance human rights protection" in Taiwan, to establish a National Human Rights Commission (a goal that had been set under Chen), and to undertake reviews and reports of Taiwan's performance of obligations set forth in other UN human rights conventions that Taiwan had pledged to implement beyond the ICESCR and ICCPR.[66]

3 Epilogue: Elegy for a Strategy?

Taiwan's engagement with international human rights norms, including the legal elements of the international human rights regime, always has had evident limits as a means to protect and promote Taiwan's international status and security. Even an exemplary record on human rights, punctilious conformity to the requirements of formal legal regimes for human rights, and deft presentation of accomplishments and commitments to the international community could only do so much for Taiwan's international stature and, in turn, security. Human rights matter in postwar and post-Cold War international politics, but they are often overshadowed in states' foreign policies by other factors, including calculations of national security, economic, and other interests. Although human rights commitments and performance can enhance—and their absence or weakness can erode—the international stature of a state or state-like entity, a good human rights record is not among the formal indicia of statehood, nor is it sufficient to overcome many other legal and practical impediments to enjoying the benefits that come with full acceptance as a state in the international system. For Taiwan, this simple truth is underscored by Taiwan's Beijing-driven exclusion from membership in the aspects of the international human rights regime that are most closely associated with state status: the major UN-linked treaties such as the ICCPR and the ICESCR.

Engagement with international human rights norms, laws, and institutions also may be in decline, at least temporarily, as an effective means to support status and security for Taiwan. Although human rights has always been a less-than-decisive factor in states' foreign policies, their importance has varied over time. Human rights are now in relative eclipse, especially in the foreign policy of Taiwan's long-indispensable patron, the United States. The Obama administration faced

[66]Review of the second report of the government of Taiwan on the Implementation of the International Human Rights Covenants, concluding observations and recommendations adopted by the International Review Committee (2017). http://www.humanrights.moj.gov.tw/lp.asp?ctNode=45412&CtUnit=18365&BaseDSD=7&mp=205. Accessed 15 Oct 2017; President Tsai hosts a luncheon for Members of International Review Committee for second national reports of ICCPR and ICESCR (2017). http://english.president.gov.tw/NEWS/5085. Accessed 15 Oct 2017.

reproach for what critics saw as underemphasizing human rights.[67] This critique may have reflected, in part, the disappointment of inflated expectations of a president who, as a candidate, had invoked inspirational ideals. The less assertive U.S. position on human rights in recent years may manifest a pragmatic recognition of the limits to the U.S.'s capacity for normative influence as a relatively declining power that had badly undermined its soft power during the George W. Bush administration's "war on terrorism." Or it may reflect a more considered ideological view about how the U.S. should exercise leadership and suasion in the world. Whatever the underlying reasons, the issue of human rights was less prominent in U.S. foreign policy under Obama than it had been—in various ways—under several of his predecessors, or than it had been expected to be in a Hillary Clinton administration.[68]

Donald Trump's presidency brought a qualitative downward shift in the place of human rights in U.S. foreign policy. In the foreign policy rhetoric of the Trump administration, internationalist concerns such as human rights have been dismissed or subordinated to a narrow definition of U.S. interests in an "America First" foreign policy. Economic issues—including a nationalist approach to trade—and security issues have taken clear precedence over "values" questions in Trump's otherwise often unclear foreign policy. Trump's temperamental affinity for authoritarian rulers, and testy relations with democratic ones, have offered potent confirmation to international audiences of a lack of emphasis on human rights in U.S. foreign policy.[69] The Department of State—traditionally the principal institutional locus of the human rights component in U.S. foreign policy—has been greatly overshadowed in Trump administration foreign policymaking by a national security team dominated by former generals. Within a marginalized, understaffed, and demoralized State Department, human rights have faded as a policy focus. Secretary Tillerson notably proclaimed that human rights concerns sometimes impeded the pursuit of U.S. foreign policy interests (and implied that they should

[67]Roth (2017), Dakwar (2016) President Obama, when it comes to human rights, we need more actions, not words. American Civil Liberties Union. https://www.aclu.org/blog/human-rights/president-obama-when-it-comes-human-rights-we-need-more-action-not-words. Accessed 15 Oct 2017; Crowley M (2015) Obama kowtows to China on human rights, critics say. Politico. http://www.politico.com/story/2015/09/xi-humanrights-213999. Accessed 15 Oct 2017; Carter J (2012) A cruel and unusual record. N.Y. TIMES. http://www.nytimes.com/2012/06/25/opinion/americas-shameful-human-rights-record.html?mcubz=0. Accessed 15 Oct 2017.

[68]Rubin J (2016) What is Clinton willing to do on human rights? WASH. POST. https://www.washingtonpost.com/blogs/right-turn/wp/2016/08/17/what-is-clinton-willing-to-do-on-human-rights/?utm_term=.853c87c7b24b. Accessed 15 Oct 2017; deLisle (2016a).

[69]Margon (2017), Sengupta (2016) Sworn in, UN next leader must factor Trump into approach to global crises, N.Y. TIMES, 13 Dec 2016, at A10; Watkins E (2017) Politicians knock Trump on human rights promotion. CNN. http://www.cnn.com/2017/05/21/politics/congress-saudi-arabia-human-rights/index.html. Accessed 15 Oct 2017; Remarks by President Trump to the 72nd Session of the United Nations General Assembly (2017). https://www.whitehouse.gov/the-press-office/2017/09/19/remarks-president-trump-72nd-session-united-nations-general-assembly. Accessed 15 Oct 2017; Rauhala E (2016) Trump just called Tiananmen Square a "riot." The Communist Party will be pleased, WASH. POST, 11 Mar 2016.

not do so), and the Department reportedly considered dropping democracy-promotion from its mission.[70]

Another problem for engagement with the international human rights regime as a path to greater international stature for Taiwan comes from mounting challenges posed by China. When the turn to human rights in U.S. foreign policy, the beginning in earnest of U.S.-PRC engagement, and a new age of peril for Taiwan's international status and security all coincided in the 1970s, the PRC was no more than a peripheral participant in the international human rights legal regime. Beijing had yet to accept officially the idea that there were universal human rights, and would not do so until faced with international opprobrium following the Tiananmen Incident. During the first three decades of China's post-Mao reform era, the PRC's trajectory (although uneven) was largely one of growing engagement. Beijing's posture toward international human rights came to be one of at least formal acceptance of universal status quo norms, and defensiveness concerning its own record—through denials of violations (often with weak factual basis), excuses for shortcomings (based on the level of economic development, the tragic legacy of the Cultural Revolution's assault on human rights, or the need to maintain social and political order), or assertions of subsidiarity-like principles of permissible national variation (on such bases as political system type or national culture) within the parameters of universal human rights obligations.

Since around the turn of the millennium, however, official Chinese positions once again have indicated skepticism about the universality of human rights norms, or interpretations of them—especially those that have been Taiwan's strong suit. Jiang Zemin's tenure as top leader brought a tepid flirtation with the hedged challenge to human rights universalism posed by the "Asian values" discourse. The Hu Jintao years and, especially, the Xi Jinping period have produced more pointed rejections of what Chinese sources see as subversive Western values masquerading as ostensibly universal values, including human rights.[71]

This shift in China's normative stance toward international human rights has been accompanied—and perhaps encouraged—by a rise in China's influence internationally. The mounting pushback against the conception of human rights endorsed by

---

[70]Tillerson RW (2017) Remarks to U.S. Department of State employees. https://www.state.gov/secretary/remarks/2017/05/270620.htm. Accessed 15 Oct 2017 (values can be "obstacles" to U.S. foreign policy); Piccone T (2017) Tillerson says goodbye to human rights diplomacy. The Brookings Institution. https://www.brookings.edu/blog/order-from-chaos/2017/05/05/tillerson-says-goodbye-to-human-rights-diplomacy/. Accessed 15 Oct 2017; Rogin J (2017) State Department considers scrubbing democracy promotion from its mission, WASH. POST, 1 Aug 2017.

[71]See Davis (1997). Hu Jintao warned against "international hostile forces [that] are intensifying the strategic plot of Westernizing and dividing China." Wong E (2012) China's President lashes out at Western culture, N.Y. TIMES, 3 Jan 2012. In Apr 2013, the General Office of the CCP Central Committee issued Document No.9, which criticized Western "universal values" including human rights, claiming that these values would "weaken the theoretical foundations of the Party's leadership," see Document 9: A ChinaFile translation (2013). China File. http://www.chinafile.com/document-9-chinafile-translation. Accessed 15 Oct 2017.

the U.S. and other critics of China's performance has been part of a broader Chinese criticism of international norms that PRC leaders see as not reflecting China's input and as at odds with China's interests and preferences. Beijing also has been moving beyond critiques of status quo norms to seek greater influence in shaping international rules.[72] In the international human rights regime, this has included the PRC's successful bid to be a member of the UN Human Rights Council when that body was established as a central institution for the ICCPR.[73] Beijing's growing will and capacity to affect international human rights norms and legal rules, and China's role in the principal, and Taiwan-excluding, UN body for civil and political human rights, threaten to weaken the linkage between Taiwan's human rights performance and commitments and Taiwan's international standing and security.

This is not to say that Taiwan would be wise to eschew a strategy of deeply engaging international human rights norms, laws, and institutions. A strong record on human rights is, of course, desirable and valuable for Taiwan for reasons other than its contribution to Taiwan's standing in the international community or Taiwan's security. The recent waning of the apparent effectiveness of human rights-based claims to international status and security has not been complete, and it very well may not be permanent. Even if the potential rewards of such an approach are modest and perhaps shrinking (at least for now), the risks remain very low. The human rights card remains one that Taiwan has shown it can play well from its weak hand in the high-stakes game of protecting Taiwan's security in an inhospitable world.

References

Baker J (1991) America and the collapse of the Soviet empire: What has to be done. Address at Princeton University, 12 Dec http://heinonline.org/HOL/Page?handle=hein.journals/dsptch3&div=266&g_sent=1&collection=journals. Accessed 15 Oct 2017

Boucher R (2003) Daily press briefing. https://2001-2009.state.gov/r/pa/prs/dpb/2003/26776.htm. Accessed 15 Oct 2017

Brown S (2015) Faces of power: constancy and change in United States foreign policy from Truman to Obama. Columbia University Press, New York

Bush GHW (1989) Statement on the Chinese government's suppression of student demonstrations 1 PUB. PAPERS 669 (3 June). http://heinonline.org/HOL/Permalink?a=dXBlbm4uZWR1&u=http%3A%2F%2F0-heinonline.org.lola.law.upenn.edu%2FHOL%2FPage%3Fmen_tab%3Dsrchresults%26handle%3Dhein.presidents%2Fppp089001%26size%3D2%26collection%3Dpresidents%26id%3D691. Accessed 15 Oct 2017

[72]See generally Friedberg (2011), Ikenberry (2008), Chan (2015), Potter (2017).

[73]General Assembly elects 47 members of new Human Rights Council; marks "new beginning" for human rights promotion (2006). https://www.un.org/press/en/2006/ga10459.doc.htm. Accessed 15 Oct 2017; Membership of the Human Rights Council 19 June 2006–18 June 2007 by year when term expires. http://www.ohchr.org/EN/HRBodies/HRC/Pages/Year20062007.aspx. Accessed 15 Oct 2017; China re-elected to the UN Human Rights Council (2009). Permanent Mission of the People's Republic of China to the UN. http://www.china-un.org/eng/hyyfy/t561953.htm. Accessed 15 Oct 2017; Potter (2008).

Bush GW (2001) Address at Warsaw University, 15 June 2001. http://www.presidency.ucsb.edu/ws/?pid=45973. Accessed 15 Oct 2017

Bush GW (2008) Statement on the presidential election in Taiwan, PUB. PAPERS 410. https://georgewbush-whitehouse.archives.gov/news/releases/2008/03/20080322-4.html. Accessed 15 Oct 2017

Bush RC (2004) At cross purposes: U.S.-Taiwan relations since 1942. Routledge, Abingdon, UK

Bush R (1998) The US role in the Taiwan Straits issue. http://www.taiwandc.org/nws-9867htm. Accessed 15 Oct 2017

Campbell KM (2011) Testimony before the House Foreign Affairs Committee: Why Taiwan matters, Part II. https://2009-2017.state.gov/p/eap/rls/rm/2011/10/174980.htm. Accessed 15 Oct 2017

Carter J (1997) President's news conference of 30 June, 2 PUB. PAPERS 1200. http://heinonline.org/HOL/Permalink?a=dXBlbm4uZWR1&u=http%3A%2F%2Fheinonline.org%2FHOL%2FPage%3Fmen_tab%3Dsrchresults%26handle%3Dhein.presidents%2Fppp077002%26size%3D2%26collection%3Dpresidents%26set_as_cursor%3D%26id%3D50. Accessed 15 Oct 2017

Carter J (2012) A cruel and unusual record. N.Y. TIMES. http://www.nytimes.com/2012/06/25/opinion/americas-shameful-human-rights-record.html?mcubz=0. Accessed 15 Oct 2017

Chan CW (2015) Human rights and democracy with Chinese characteristics. In: Chan CW (ed) China, state sovereignty and international legal order. Martinus Nijhoff, Leiden, Netherlands, pp 108–171

Chang P (2001) Chinese statements during deliberations on the UDHR (1948). In: Angel, S C and Svensson, M (eds) The Chinese human rights reader: Documents and commentary 1900–2000. M.E. Sharpe, Armonk, NY, pp 206–213

China re-elected to the UN Human Rights Council (2009) Permanent Mission of the People's Republic of China to the UN. http://www.china-un.org/eng/hyyfy/t561953.htm. Accessed 15 Oct 2017

Christensen TJ (2007) A strong and moderate Taiwan. Speech to U.S.-Taiwan Business Council Defense Industry Conference, Annapolis, Maryland, 11 Sept. https://2001-2009.state.gov/p/eap/rls/rm/2007/91979.htm. Accessed 15 Oct 2017

Clinton WJ (1995) Remarks at a Freedom House breakfast, 6 Oct. http://www.presidency.ucsb.edu/ws/?pid=50612. Accessed 15 Oct 2017

Clinton WJ (2000) Statement on the election of Chen Shui-bian as President of Taiwan - 18 Mar. PUB. PAPERS 490. https://www.gpo.gov/fdsys/pkg/WCPD-2000-03-27/pdf/WCPD-2000-03-27-Pg582.pdf. Accessed 15 Oct 2017

Cody E (2007) Interview with Chen Shui-bian, President of Taiwan. WASH. POST. http://www.washingtonpost.com/wp-dyn/content/article/2007/07/07/AR2007070700929.html. Accessed 4 July 2018

Committee on Economic, Social and Cultural Rights: Introduction: Monitoring the economic, social and cultural rights. United Nations Human Rights Office of the High Commissioner. http://www.ohchr.org/EN/HRBodies/CESCR/Pages/CESCRIntro.aspx. Accessed 15 Oct 2017

Country reports on human rights practices for 2016: Taiwan. U.S. State Department. http://www.state.gov/j/drl/rls/hrrpt/humanrightsreport/index.htm?year=2016&dlid=265374. Accessed 15 Oct 2017

CQ Almanac 1990 (1991) Efforts at hard line on China thwarted. https://library.cqpress.com/cqalmanac/document.php?id=cqal90-1118657. Accessed 15 Oct 2017

Craner LW (2004) Briefing on supporting human rights and democracy: The U.S. record 2003-2004 report. https://2001-2009.state.gov/g/drl/rls/rm/32537.htm. Accessed 15 Oct 2017

Crawford J (2012) Brownlie's principles of public international law. Oxford University Press, Oxford, UK

Crowley M (2015) Obama kowtows to China on human rights, critics say. Politico. http://www.politico.com/story/2015/09/xi-humanrights-213999. Accessed 15 Oct 2017

Dakwar J (2016) President Obama, when it comes to human rights, we need more actions, not words. American Civil Liberties Union. https://www.aclu.org/blog/human-rights/president-obama-when-it-comes-human-rights-we-need-more-action-not-words. Accessed 15 Oct 2017

Davis MC (1997) Constitutionalism and political culture: The debate over human rights and Asian values. Harv Hum Rts J 11:109–147

deLisle J (2000) The Chinese puzzle of Taiwan's status. Orbis 44(1):35–62

deLisle, J (2004) Reforming/Replacing the ROC Constitution: implications for Taiwan's State(-like) Status and U.S. policy. Woodrow Wilson Int Center Asia Program Spec Rep:12–18

deLisle J (2007) Eroding, not attacking, the "One China Policy": participating in international regimes without State membership, choosing symbolic struggles with substantive content, and getting help from U.S. law. In: Tkacik J Jr (ed) Reshaping the Taiwan Strait. Heritage Foundation, New York, pp 111–145

deLisle J (2012) Taiwan's 2012 presidential and legislative elections: winners, losers, and implications. FPRI E-Note. https://www.fpri.org/article/2012/01/taiwans-2012-presidential-and-legislative-elections-winners-losers-and-implications/. Accessed 15 Oct 2017

deLisle J (2014) Taiwan, China and soft power. In: Cabestan J, deLisle J (eds), Political changes in Taiwan under Ma Ying-jeou: Partisan conflict, policy choices, external constraints and security challenges. Routledge, Abingdon, UK, pp 265–295

deLisle J (2016a) Red state China? Why China (sort of) likes Trump. Foreign Policy Research Institute E-Note. https://www.fpri.org/article/2016/07/red-state-china-china-sort-likes-trump/. Accessed 15 Oct 2017

deLisle J (2016b) Taiwan's quest for international space: Ma's legacy, Tsai's options, China's choices, and U.S. policy. Orbis 60(4):550–574

Document 9: A ChinaFile translation (2013) China File. http://www.chinafile.com/document-9-chinafile-translation. Accessed 15 Oct 2017

Economist Intelligence Unit (2017) Democracy index 2016: Revenge of the deplorables. https://www.eiu.com/Handlers/WhitepaperHandler.ashx?fi=Democracy-Index-2016.pdf&mode=wp&campaignid=DemocracyIndex2016. Accessed 15 Oct 2017

End of the Soviet Union; Text of Bush's address to nation on Gorbachev's resignation, N.Y. TIMES, 25 Dec 1991

Exiles from Taiwan opposition (1986) N.Y. TIMES, 25 Sept at A4

Foreign Policy. Strategic Stud Q 7(2): 93–113

Franck TM (1992) The emerging right to democratic governance. Am J Int Law 86:46–91

Freedom House (2017) Freedom in the world 2017: Taiwan. https://freedomhouse.org/report/freedom-world/2017/taiwan. Accessed 15 Oct 2017

Friedberg A (2011) Hegemony with Chinese characteristics. National Interest. http://nationalinterest.org/article/hegemony-chinese-characteristics-5439. Accessed 15 Oct 2017

Fukuyama F (2006) The end of history and the last man. Free Press, New York

G.A. Res. 217 (III) (1948) A universal declaration of human rights, UN Doc. A/810, at 71 (10 Dec)

G.A. Res. 2758 (XXVI) (1971), Restoration of the lawful rights of the People's Republic of China in the United Nations (25 Oct)

Gaer FD, Broecker CL (eds) (2013) The United Nations High Commissioner for Human Rights: conscience for the world. Martinus Nijhoff, Leiden, Netherlands

Garver JW (1997) The Sino-American alliance: Nationalist China and American cold war strategy. Routledge, Abingdon, UK

General Assembly elects 47 members of new Human Rights Council; marks "new beginning" for human rights promotion (2006) https://www.un.org/press/en/2006/ga10459.doc.htm. Accessed 15 Oct 2017

Hannum H (1996) The status of the Universal Declaration of Human Rights in national and international law. Ga J Int Comp Law 15:287–397

Hathaway O (2002) Do human rights treaties make a difference? Yale Law J 111:1935–2025

Howe M (1986) Return is sought by Taiwan exiles, N.Y. TIMES, 19 Nov at A12

Hsieh JF, Niou EMS (2005) Measuring Taiwanese public opinion on Taiwanese independence. China Q 181:158–168

Hughes C (2005) Taiwan and Chinese nationalism: national identity and status in international society. Routledge, Abingdon, UK

Huntington SPH (1993) The third wave: democratization in the late twentieth century. University of Oklahoma Press, Norman

Hutzler C, Hsu JW (2016) Taiwanese President Tsai: Taiwan won't succumb to China's pressure. The Wall Street Journal. https://blogs.wsj.com/chinarealtime/2016/10/05/taiwanese-president-tsai-taiwan-wont-succumb-to-chinas-pressure/. Accessed 15 Oct 2017

Ikenberry JG (2008) The rise of China and the future of the West. Foreign Affairs 87(1):23–37

Implementation of the International Covenant on Civil and Political Rights, initial report submitted under Article 40 of the Covenant, Republic of China (Taiwan) (2012) http://www.humanrights.moj.gov.tw/ct.asp?xItem=385452&ctNode=40243&mp=205. Accessed 15 Oct 2017

Implementation of the International Covenant on Civil and Political Rights, second report submitted under Article 40 of the Covenant, Republic of China (Taiwan), Apr 2016

Implementation of the International Covenant on Economic, Social and Cultural Rights, initial report submitted under Articles 16 and 17 of the Covenant, Republic of China (Taiwan) (2012) http://www.humanrights.moj.gov.tw/ct.asp?xItem=385452&ctNode=40243&mp=205. Accessed 15 Oct 2017

Implementation of the International Covenant on Economic, Social and Cultural Rights, second report submitted under Articles 16 and 17 of the Covenant, Republic of China (Taiwan), Apr 2016

Inaugural address of ROC 14th-term President Tsai Ing-wen (2016) http://english.president.gov.tw/NEWS/4893. Accessed 15 Oct 2017.

International Covenant on Civil and Political Rights. United Nations Treaty Collection. https://treaties.un.org/Pages/ViewDetails.aspx?src=IND&mtdsg_no=IV-4&chapter=4&clang=_en. Accessed 15 Oct 2017

International Covenant on Economic, Social and Cultural Rights. United Nations Treaty Collection. https://treaties.un.org/Pages/ViewDetails.aspx?src=IND&mtdsg_no=IV-3&chapter=4&clang=_en. Accessed 15 Oct 2017

International reaction to Liu Xiaobo Nobel Peace Prize (2008) BBC News. http://www.bbc.co.uk/news/mobile/world-europe-11499931. Accessed 15 Oct 2017

Jacobs JB (2016) The Kaohsiung incident in Taiwan and memoirs of a foreign big beard. Brill, Leiden, Netherlands

Joint statement following discussions with leaders of the People's Republic of China (1972), PUB. PAPERS 376 (27 Feb), http://heinonline.org/HOL/Permalink?a=dXBlbm4uZWR1&u=http%3A%2F%2Fheinonline.org%2FHOL%2FPage%3Fhandle%3Dhein.presidents%2Fppp072000z%26size%3D2%26collection%3Dpresidents%26id%3D430. Accessed 15 Oct 2017

Kagan RC (2007) Taiwan's statesman: Lee Teng-Hui and democracy in Asia. Naval Institute Press, Annapolis, Maryland

Kaplan DE (1992) Fires of the dragon: politics, murder, and the Kuomintang. Atheneum, New York

Kelly J (2004) Assistant Secretary of State for East Asian and Pacific Affairs, Hearing before the House International Relations Committee: the Taiwan Relations Act: The next 25 years, 21 Apr 2004

Kirby J (2016) U.S. statement on Taiwan's presidential inauguration. https://2009-2017.state.gov/r/pa/prs/ps/2016/05/257465.htm. Accessed 15 Oct 2017

Lee T (1995) Always in my heart. Olin Lecture at Cornell University. http://taiwantoday.tw/news.php?unit=4,29,31,45&post=3961. Accessed 15 Oct 2017

Lee T (1996) Presidential inaugural address. http://newcongress.yam.org.tw/Taiwan_sino/leespeec.html. Accessed 15 Oct 2017

Lee T (1999) Understanding Taiwan: bridging the perception gap. Foreign Affairs 78(6):9–14

Lord W (1994) Taiwan policy review: statement before the Senate Foreign Relations Committee, Washington, DC, 27 Sept. https://web.archive.org/web/20160914002741/http://ait.org.tw/en/19940927-taiwan-policy-review-by-winston-lord.html. Accessed 15 Oct 2017

Lord W (1996) Assistant Secretary of State for East Asian and Pacific Affairs, Testimony before the House International Relations Subcommittee on East Asia and the Pacific. http://dosfan.lib.uic.edu/ERC/bureaus/eap/960314LordTaiwan.html. Accessed 15 Oct 2017

Ma highlights Taiwan's human rights efforts (2012) Taiwan Today. http://taiwantoday.tw/news.php?unit=2,23,45&post=2254. Accessed 15 Oct 2017
Ma optimistic over WHA participation (2008) Taipei Times, 12 Dec at 3
Maher RM, Weissbrodt D (1990) The 41st session of the UN Sub-Commission on Prevention of Discrimination and Protection of Minorities. Hum Rts Q 12:290–327
Mainland Affairs Council, Executive Yuan, Republic of China (1991) Guidelines for National Unification. https://law.wustl.edu/Chinalaw/twguide.html. Accessed 15 Oct 2017
Mainland Affairs Council, Executive Yuan, ROC (2006) Position Paper on the National Unification Council ceasing to function and the Guidelines for National Unification ceasing to apply. http://www.mac.gov.tw/en/News_Content.aspx?n=BEC36A4A0BB0663C&sms=BF821F021B282251&s=20C09FC2F3C10A1C. Accessed 15 Oct 2017
Margon S (2017) Trump's damning global retreat on human rights. Foreign Policy. http://foreignpolicy.com/2017/04/06/trumps-damning-global-retreat-on-human-rights/. Accessed 15 Oct 2017
Marks S (2011) What has become of the emerging right to democratic governance? Eur J Int Law 22:507–524
McCorquodale R (1994) Self-determination: a human rights approach. Int Comp Law Q 43(4): 857–885
Membership of the Human Rights Council 19 June 2006–18 June 2007 by year when term expires. http://www.ohchr.org/EN/HRBodies/HRC/Pages/Year20062007.aspx. Accessed 15 Oct 2017
Nathan AJ and Ho H (1993) Chiang Ching-kuo's decision for political reform. In: Leng S (ed) Chiang Ching-Kuo's leadership in the development of the Republic of China on Taiwan. University Press of America, Lanham, MD
Neary I (2005) Human rights in Japan, South Korea and Taiwan. Routledge, Abingdon, UK
Nomination of Rex Tillerson to be Secretary of State (2017) Hearing before the Committee on Foreign Relations, United States Senate, 115th Congress, 1st Session, 11 Jan. https://www.gpo.gov/fdsys/pkg/CHRG-115shrg24573/html/CHRG-115shrg24573.htm. Accessed 15 Oct 2017
Obama BH (2012) Statement on elections in Taiwan, PUB. PAPERS 43. https://Obamawhitehouse.archives.gov/the-press-office/2012/01/14/statement-press-secretary-taiwan-s-elections. Accessed 15 Oct 2017
Office of the Press Secretary (2004) Statement on Taiwan elections: Announcement of election results on Taiwan. https://georgewbush-whitehouse.archives.gov/news/releases/2004/03/20040326-6.html. Accessed 15 Oct 2017
Office of the United Nations High Commissioner for Human Rights (1996) Fact sheet no. 2 (rev. 1), the international bill of human rights. http://www.ohchr.org/Documents/Publications/FactSheet2Rev.1en.pdf. Accessed 15 Oct 2017
Piccone T (2017) Tillerson says goodbye to human rights diplomacy. The Brookings Institution. https://www.brookings.edu/blog/order-from-chaos/2017/05/05/tillerson-says-goodbye-to-human-rights-diplomacy/. Accessed 15 Oct 2017
Plot to kill Henry Liu–Slayers confess details (1985) L.A. TIMES, 3 Mar, at 1
Potter PB (2008) China and the international legal system: challenges of participation. In: Clarke DC (ed) China's legal system: new developments, new challenges. Cambridge University Press, Cambridge, UK, pp 145–166
Potter PB (2017) China and the international human rights legal regime: Orthodoxy, resistance, and legitimacy. In: deLisle J, Goldstein A (eds) China's global engagement: cooperation, competition, and influence in the 21st century. Brookings Institution Press, Washington DC, pp 291–324
Powell CL (2003) Remarks at Reception Hosted by the Ambassador of Greece to Celebrate the Signing of the European Union Accession Treaty by Ten New Member States, 16 Apr 2003. https://2001-2009.state.gov/secretary/former/powell/remarks/2003/19713.htm. Accessed 15 Oct 2017
Presidency conclusions: Copenhagen European Council - 21-22 June 1993, SN 180/93. http://www.europarl.europa.eu/enlargement_new/europeancouncil/pdf/cop_en.pdf. Accessed 15 Oct 2017

President Bush and Premier Wen Jiabao remarks to the press (2003) https://georgewbush-whitehouse.archives.gov/news/releases/2003/12/20031209-2.html. Accessed 15 Oct 2017
President Chen meets World Coalitions Against Death Penalty founder Mario Marazziti (2007) http://english.president.gov.tw/NEWS/2634. Accessed 15 Oct 2017
President Chen Shui-bian meets Dutch human rights expert Dr. Theodoor C. Van Boven (2007) http://english.president.gov.tw/NEWS/2682. Accessed 15 Oct 2017
President Chen's inaugural address (2000) http://english.president.gov.tw/NEWS/2643. Accessed 15 Oct 2017
President Chen's inaugural address "Paving the way for a sustainable Taiwan" (2004) http://English.president.gov.tw/NEWS/1726. Accessed 15 Oct 2017
President Chen's New Year's message (2001) http://english.president.gov.tw/NEWS/929. Accessed 15 Oct 2017
President Lee's message to the Taiwan retrocession day (1997) http://english.president.gov.tw/NEWS/1106. Accessed 15 Oct 2017
President Ma holds press conference on "cross-strait peace agreement" (2001) https://www.mac.gov.tw/en/News_Content.aspx?n=FE07F9DA122E29D4&sms=3A4E63FA5107487D&s=CD5F7C3EB8CAD2E1. Accessed 15 Oct 2017
President Ma holds press conference on the release of Taiwan's first human rights report (2014) http://english.president.gov.tw/NEWS/3880. Accessed 15 Oct 2017
President Ma holds press conference on the release of Taiwan's second human rights report (2016) http://english.president.gov.tw/NEWS/4887. Accessed 15 Oct 2017
President Ma issues statement on Tiananmen Square Incident (2011) Taiwan Today. http://taiwantoday.tw/news.php?unit=2,23,45&post=1843. Accessed 15 Oct 2017
President Ma welcomes international experts to Taiwan to review the ROC's first national human rights report (2013) http://english.president.gov.tw/NEWS/4092. Accessed 15 Oct 2017
President Ma's inaugural address (2008) http://english.president.gov.tw/NEWS/45. Accessed 15 Oct 2017
President Ma's inaugural address (2012) http://english.president.gov.tw/NEWS/3887. Accessed 15 Oct 2017
President presided over the Second Report on ICCPR and ICESCR Press Conference (2016) http://www.humanrights.moj.gov.tw/ct.asp?xItem=431093&ctNode=40238&mp=205. Accessed 15 Oct 2017
President Tsai hosts a luncheon for members of International Review Committee for second national reports of ICCPR and ICESCR (2017) http://english.president.gov.tw/NEWS/5085. Accessed 15 Oct 2017
President Tsai meets delegation from Reporters without Borders (2017) http://english.president.gov.tw/News/5180. Accessed 15 Oct 2017
President Tsai meets members of Taiwan's WHA action team (2017) http://english.president.gov.tw/NEWS/5152. Accessed 15 Oct 2017
President Tsai's inaugural address (2016) http://focustaiwan.tw/news/aipl/201605200008.aspx. Accessed 27 July 2018
Rauhala E (2016) Trump just called Tiananmen Square a "riot." The Communist Party will be pleased, WASH. POST, 11 Mar 2016
Recognizing President Chen Shui-bian of Taiwan upon his reception of the International Human Rights Award (2003) 149(158) CONG. REC. E2215-E2216 (4 Nov) (speech by Chen). https://www.gpo.gov/fdsys/pkg/CREC-2003-11-04/html/CREC-2003-11-04-pt1-PgE2215-2.htm. Accessed 15 Oct 2017
Remarks by President Obama, President Niinistö of Finland, and Prime Minister Solberg of Norway at the Nordic Leaders' Summit Arrival Ceremony (2016) The White House. https://obamawhitehouse.archives.gov/the-press-office/2016/05/13/remarks-president-obama-president-niinist%C3%B6-finland-and-prime-minister. Accessed 15 Oct 2017
Remarks by President Trump to the 72nd Session of the United Nations General Assembly (2017) https://www.whitehouse.gov/the-press-office/2017/09/19/remarks-president-trump-72nd-session-united-nations-general-assembly. Accessed 15 Oct 2017

Remarks by the President to the Business Council (2000) 24 Feb. 1 PUB. PAPERS 296 (24 Feb 2000)

Remarks of President Obama to the People of Laos (2016) https://obamawhitehouse.archives.gov/the-press-office/2016/09/06/remarks-president-obama-people-laos. Accessed 15 Oct 2017

Renouard J (2015) Human rights in American foreign policy: from the 1960s to the Soviet collapse. University of Pennsylvania, Philadelphia, PA

Republican platform (2016) https://prod-cdn-static.gop.com/media/documents/DRAFT_12_FINAL[1]-ben_1468872234.pdf. Accessed 15 Oct 2017

Request for the Inclusion of a Supplementary Item in the Agenda of the 57th Session: Question of the Representation of the Republic of China (Taiwan) in the United Nations, Letter dated 1 Aug 2002 from the representatives of Burkina Faso, Chad, El Salvador, the Gambia, Grenada, the Marshall Islands, Nicaragua, Saint Vincent and the Grenadines, Sao Tome and Principe, Senegal, Solomon Islands and Swaziland to the United Nations addressed to the Secretary-General, UN Doc. A/57/191 (20 Aug 2002)

Response to the concluding observations and recommendations adopted by the International Group of Independent Experts (2013) 1 Mar, Republic of China (Taiwan). http://www.humanrights.moj.gov.tw/lp.asp?ctNode=43063&CtUnit=16034&BaseDSD=7&mp=205. Accessed 15 Oct 2017

Restatement (Third) (1987) Foreign Relations Law of the United States § 702 Philadelphia, PA: Am. Law Inst.

Review of the second report of the government of Taiwan on the Implementation of the International Human Rights Covenants, concluding observations and recommendations adopted by the International Review Committee (2017). http://www.humanrights.moj.gov.tw/lp.asp?ctNode=45412&CtUnit=18365&BaseDSD=7&mp=205. Accessed 15 Oct 2017

Rice SE (2015) Remarks on the U.S.-China relationship at George Washington University, 21 Sept. https://obamawhitehouse.archives.gov/the-press-office/2015/09/21/national-security-advisor-susan-e-rices-prepared-remarks-us-china. Accessed 15 Oct 2017

Risse-Kappen T (1995) Cooperation among democracies: the European influence on U.S. foreign policy. Princeton University Press, Princeton

Rogin J (2017) State Department considers scrubbing democracy promotion from its mission, WASH. POST, 1 Aug 2017

Romberg AD (2017) Cross-Strait relations: skepticism abounds. China Leadership Monitor 54

Roth K (2017) Barack Obama's shaky legacy on human rights. Foreign Policy. https://foreignpolicy.com/2017/01/04/barack-obamas-shaky-legacy-on-human-rights/. Accessed 15 Oct 2017

Rubin J (2016) What is Clinton willing to do on human rights? WASH. POST. https://www.washingtonpost.com/blogs/right-turn/wp/2016/08/17/what-is-clinton-willing-to-do-on-human-rights/?utm_term=.853c87c7b24b. Accessed 15 Oct 2017

Russel DR (2016) Remarks at China's Growing Pains Conference, 22 Apr. https://2009-2017.state.gov/p/eap/rls/rm/2016/04/256509.htm. Accessed 15 Oct 2017

Santiso C (2001) International co-operation for democracy and good governance: Moving towards a second generation? Eur J Dev Res 13:154–180

Schubert G, Braig S (2011) How to face an embracing China? The DPP's identity politics and cross-Strait relations during and after the Chen Shui-bian era. In: Schubert G, Damm J (eds) Taiwanese identity in the 21st century: domestic, regional and global perspectives. Routledge, Abingdon, UK

Sehnálková J, Kučera O (2012) Taiwan's participation in international organizations: obstacles, strategies, patterns? In: Damm J, Lim P (eds) European perspectives on Taiwan. Springer, Wiesbaden, pp 163–164

Sengupta S (2016) Sworn in, UN's next leader must factor Trump into approach to global crises, N.Y. TIMES, 13 Dec 2016, at A10

Sobel R, Haynes W, Zheng Y (2010) The polls—Trends: Taiwan public opinion trends, 1992–2008: Exploring attitudes on cross-Strait issues. Public Opin Q 74(4):782–813

Suri J (2015) From isolation to engagement: American diplomacy and the opening to China 1969–1972. In: Hutchings R, Suri J (eds) Foreign policy breakthroughs: cases in successful diplomacy. Oxford University Press, Oxford, pp 101–120

Taiwan 2016/2017 (2017) Amnesty International. https://www.amnesty.org/en/countries/asia-and-the-pacific/taiwan/report-taiwan/. Accessed 15 Oct 2017

Taiwan. Human Rights Watch. https://www.hrw.org/asia/taiwan. Accessed 15 Oct 2017

Taiwan President mourns Liu Xiaobo, says China won't be great until it accepts his ideas (2017) The China Post. www.chinapost.com.tw/taiwan/2017/07/14/499421/taiwan-president.htm. Accessed 15 Oct 2017

Text of Joint Communiqué (1972) Issued at Shanghai, Feb, 1972, 66 Department of State Bulletin [xxix], 458 (1972) http://heinonline.org/HOL/Permalink?a=dXBlbm4uZWR1&u=http%3A%2F%2Fheinonline.org%2FHOL%2FPage%3Fhandle%3Dhein.journals%2Fdsbul66%26collection%3Dustreaties%26id%3D491. Accessed 15 Oct 2017

Thrilway H (2015) Human rights in customary law: an attempt to define some of the issues. Leiden J Int Law 28:495–506

Tillerson RW (2017) Remarks to U.S. Department of State employees. https://www.state.gov/secretary/remarks/2017/05/270620.htm. Accessed 15 Oct 2017

Tong K (2016) Remarks: Taiwan's international role and the GCTF. https://2009-2017.state.gov/e/eb/rls/rm/2016/253915.htm. Accessed 15 Oct 2017

Transcript of the remarks by President W. J. Clinton to people of Detroit. North Atlantic Treaty Website. http://www.nato.int/docu/speech/1996/s961022a.htm. Accessed 15 Oct 2017

Transcript: Post's interview with Taiwanese President Ma Ying-jeou (2011) WASH. POST, 17 Feb

Tsai urges China to face Tiananmen (2017) Taipei Times. http://www.taipeitimes.com/News/front/archives/2017/06/05/2003671928. Accessed 15 Oct 2017

Tucker NB (2011) Strait talk: United States-Taiwan relations and the crisis with China. Harvard University Press, Cambridge, MA

Tyler PE (1996) Taiwan's leader wins its election and a mandate, N.Y. TIMES, 24 Mar

UN Commission on Human Rights, Report of the Sub-Commission on Prevention of Discrimination and Protection of Minorities on its forty-first session (1989) UN Doc. E/CN.4/1990/2 (13 Nov). http://repository.un.org/handle/11176/181657. Accessed 15 Oct 2017

U.N. GAOR, 3rd Sess., 183rd plen. mtg. at. 119, UN Doc. A/PV. 183 (10 Dec 1948)

United Nations Human Rights Committee (1948) Introduction: Monitoring civil and political rights. United Nations Human Rights Office of the High Commissioner. http://www.ohchr.org/EN/HRBodies/CCPR/Pages/CCPRIntro.aspx. Accessed 15 Oct 2017

Universal Periodic Review. United Nations Human Rights Office of the High Commissioner. http://www.ohchr.org/EN/HRBodies/UPR/Pages/UPRMain.aspx. Accessed 15 Oct 2017

van der Vyver JD (2000) Self-determination of the peoples of Quebec under international law. J Transnat Law Policy 10:1–132

Wang Y (2013) Taiwan public opinion on cross-Strait security issues: implications for U.S

Watkins E (2017) Politicians knock Trump on human rights promotion. CNN. http://www.cnn.com/2017/05/21/politics/congress-saudi-arabia-human-rights/index.html. Accessed 15 Oct 2017

Weymouth L (2016) Taiwanese President Tsai Ing-wen: Beijing must respect our democratic will, WASH. POST, 21 July

Wong E (2012) China's president lashes out at Western culture, N.Y. TIMES, 3 Jan

Yang S (1996) The right to participate in the United Nations. In: Jean-Marie H (ed) The international status of Taiwan in the new world order: legal and political considerations. Kluwer, London, pp 117–132

Jacques deLisle is the Stephen A. Cozen Professor of Law, professor of political science, director of the Center for East Asian Studies, deputy director of the Center for the Study of Contemporary China, and co-director of the Center for Asian Law at the University of Pennsylvania, and director of the Asia Program at the Foreign Policy Research Institute. His writings, which appear in law reviews, foreign affairs journals, policy journals, edited volumes, and Internet and print media, focus on China's engagement with the international law and the international order, domestic legal reform and rule of law issues in China, and Taiwan's international status and external relations. He is co-editor of *China's Global Engagement* (with Avery Goldstein, 2017), *New Media, the Internet and a Changing China* (with Avery Goldstein and Guobin Yang, 2016), *Political Changes in Taiwan under Ma Ying-jeou* (with Jean-Pierre Cabestan, 2014), *China's Challenges* (with Avery Goldstein, 2014), and *China under Hu Jintao* (with T.J. Cheng and Deborah Brown, 2005).

Chapter 12
Isolated but not Oblivious: Taiwan's Acceptance of the Two Major Human Rights Covenants

Yu-Jie Chen

I wish to thank the many Taiwanese advocates, officials, legal practitioners and scholars for sharing their insightful observations, which have greatly informed this research. The interviewees are kept anonymous and identified by numbers (unless attribution is required to describe the development concerned, with the permission of the interviewee). I am particularly grateful to Jerome A. Cohen for his invaluable comments. All errors and omissions are my own.

Abstract Since the Republic of China on Taiwan (ROC or Taiwan) lost the seat of China in the United Nations (UN) to the People's Republic of China (PRC) in 1971, the ROC government has been excluded from the UN system, including its human rights treaty regime. Despite this isolation, Taiwan nevertheless ratified the two major UN human rights covenants in 2009—the International Covenant on Civil and Political Rights (ICCPR) and the International Covenant on Economic, Social and Cultural Rights (ICESCR). This development is a milestone in Taiwan's engagement with international human rights law. Although Taiwan's attempt to deposit the instruments of ratification with the UN was rejected, it is committed to following the covenants by granting them the status of domestic legislation and instituting mechanisms to implement them. The efforts of Taiwan as a non-UN member state to adopt the two human rights covenants are a shot in the arm for the international human rights system. This chapter examines how a state shut out of the UN human rights regime became a strong supporter of the regime. With special attention to the relevant advocacy campaigns and political discussions, this chapter seeks to identify the driving forces behind Taiwan's ratification. More broadly, the case study of Taiwan offers insight into the social, legal and political processes of a bottom-up ratification campaign as well as the obstacles in a contested political context.

Y.-J. Chen (✉)
Institutum Iurisprudentiae, Academia Sinica, Taipei, Taiwan
e-mail: yu-jie.chen@nyu.edu

Y.-J. Chen
U.S.-Asia Law Institute, NYU School of Law, New York, USA

J. A. Cohen et al. (eds.), *Taiwan and International Human Rights*, Economics, Law, and Institutions in Asia Pacific, https://doi.org/10.1007/978-981-13-0350-0_12

Keywords Civil society · International Covenant on Civil and Political Rights
International Covenant on Economic, Social and Cultural Rights
International isolation · Politics of ratification · Ratification campaign
International status · International norm diffusion · Norm intermediaries

1 Introduction

As human rights treaties have been criticized in recent years for offering "empty promises,"[1] the ratification by the Republic of China on Taiwan (hereinafter ROC, or Taiwan) of the two major human rights covenants—the International Covenant on Civil and Political Rights (hereinafter ICCPR) and the International Covenant on Economic, Social and Cultural Rights (hereinafter ICESCR)—shows that international human rights norms are still highly relevant to today's struggle for justice and rights, even for people in a place that has been excluded from the United Nations (hereinafter UN) and its human rights regime since 1971. In May 2009, Taiwan ratified the ICCPR and ICESCR, and enacted the Law to Implement the ICCPR and ICESCR[2] (hereinafter the Implementation Law), to grant the two covenants the status of domestic legislation and to require various implementation measures, including the setting up of a human rights report system in accordance with the two covenants and a review of inconsistent laws, regulations and government directives. This groundbreaking development marked the beginning of Taiwan's first systematic interaction with international human rights law since losing its UN membership decades ago.[3]

This chapter examines the processes that led to Taiwan's adoption of the two covenants. Special attention is paid to the advocacy initiatives that rallied for

[1]See e.g., Hathaway (2002), at p. 1935; Hafner-Burton and Tsutsui (2005), at p. 1373.

[2]Gongmin Yu Zhengzhi Quanli Guoji Gongyue Ji Jingji Shehui Wenhua Quanli Guiji Gongyue Shixing Fa [公民與政治權利國際公約及經濟社會文化權利國際公約施行法] Act to Implement the International Covenant on Civil and Political Rights and the International Covenant on Economic, Social and Cultural Rights (promulgated by the President, 22 April 2009, effective 10 December 2009) (Taiwan), http://law.moj.gov.tw/Eng/LawClass/LawAll.aspx?PCode=I0020028. This model of passing a short implementation law to grant international treaties domestic legal status in Taiwan has been applied to other treaties, including the Convention on the Elimination of All Forms of Discrimination against Women [hereinafter CEDAW] (ratified in February 2007; the Law to Implement the CEDAW effective 1 January 2012), the Convention on the Rights of the Child [hereinafter CRC] (the Law to Implement the CRC effective 20 Nov 2014), the Convention on the Rights of Persons with Disabilities [hereinafter CRPD] (the Law to Implement the CRPD effective 3 Dec 2014); the United Nations Convention against Corruption [hereinafter UNCAC] (the Law to Implement the UNCAC effective 9 December 2015).

[3]Prior to the ratification of the ICCPR and ICESCR, Taiwan had ratified the CEDAW in Jan 2007. However, the CEDAW did not command serious implementation until it was expressly incorporated into domestic law in Jun 2011 when the Legislative Yuan enacted an implementation law for the CEDAW. For a discussion of how the CEDAW successfully mobilized political support in 2007, see Liao (2010), at p. 31.

Taiwan's adoption of the human rights treaties and the political context in which the ratification efforts were mobilized, and at one point frustrated, before they could come to fruition. This chapter discusses the driving forces for ratification in three important stages: (1) the advocacy of local actors—especially individual leading advocates and nongovernmental organizations (NGOs)—to place international human rights on the national political agenda in the late 1990s; (2) the unsuccessful attempt of the new Democratic Progressive Party (DPP) administration, which took presidential power in 2000 for the first time, to adopt the two covenants during the period 2000–2002; and (3) the move by the Nationalist Party (hereinafter Kuomintang or KMT), after regaining the presidential office in 2008, to rapidly ratify the two covenants. As the case study demonstrates, the success of ratification should not be taken for granted. The diffusion of international human rights norms came as a result of tremendous social, political and legal processes. The chapter examines these processes, with the goal of understanding how a project of international norm diffusion is initiated and sustained and how it further mobilizes local civil society and political actors. It also cautions against the hurdles that can unexpectedly be created by partisan politics.

2 NGO Lobbying Leading up to the 2000 Presidential Election

Any organized attempt to promote the institutionalization of international human rights in Taiwan had been difficult during the KMT's oppressive rule, and it was further exacerbated by Taiwan's international isolation beginning in 1971. The martial-law regime in Taiwan (1949–1987), which was administered by Generalissimo Chiang Kai-shek and his son and heir Chiang Ching-kuo, was eventually lifted in 1987, heralding a new era. President Lee Teng-hui, who succeeded Chiang Ching-kuo in 1988, initiated a series of political reforms that facilitated the island's democratization. By the late 1990s, Taiwan had been transformed into a young democracy, with a growing, increasingly outspoken civil society. The year 2000 was about to see the second direct presidential election in which Taiwanese people could cast a vote for the candidate of their choice.

It was in this political-social context that a small number of advocates and scholars, along with their colleagues in the NGO community, took the lead to promote international human rights norms and institutions in Taiwan. Peter Wen-shiung Huang (黃文雄), an activist who had been in political exile for decades, returned to Taiwan in 1996. He assumed the leadership of the Taiwan Association for Human Rights (台灣人權促進會), a local independent human rights NGO known for rescuing political prisoners during the KMT's authoritarian era. In the 1990s, when the KMT government went through significant democratic changes, the Taiwan Association for Human Rights also faced the question of whether to transition from its traditional role of challenging authoritarian government oppression to a broader form of responsibility. The Association was confronted with, as one scholar puts it, "the need to transform or perish."[4]

When Peter Huang took the helm, he decided to transform the organization, envisioning a new capacity which would allow the Association to address a wider range of social problems in the young democracy. Having studied sociology in the US and participated in the civil rights movements and anti-Vietnam war protests in the 1960s, he was particularly sensitive to the challenge of how to mobilize civil society effectively. In his view, in contrast to non-generic (specialized) human rights NGOs, such as women's rights groups and labor groups, which had their own specialties and focuses, the Taiwan Association for Human Rights, as one of the few generic human rights organizations in Taiwan, should seek to play a somewhat different role. He wanted the Association to create an over-arching human rights framework, i.e., "tools" that could be used to benefit all NGOs across the board and the general public. To do this, one of his priorities was to introduce human rights legislation and institutions that were lacking in Taiwan. In his view, establishing international human rights norms ("norm setting") and institutions ("institution building") would create a wealth of resources that Taiwan could draw on to build a better human rights infrastructure for itself.[5]

Peter Huang also believed that Taiwanese politicians had a great number of incentives to commit to international human rights. As a savvy activist, he wanted to leverage the government's desire for international visibility and reputation. He believed that the NGOs should exploit the government's political orientation to pursue their own cause. This is what he called "mutual exploitation."[6]

In the late 1990s, despite the growing rights awareness of the public, engaging with international human rights law was still foreign to Taiwan, even to most civil society activists and scholars. To fill this gap as much as possible, Peter Huang reached out to international experts to provide training about the workings of the international human rights system for himself and other colleagues. Through these meetings many advocates learned about the system for the first time.[7] Peter Huang and his colleagues even tried to interact with the UN human rights bodies by submitting individual human rights complaints, but no response was received, and a few UN replies were reportedly sent to Beijing, instead of Taipei. These ad hoc efforts developed a more sustained momentum in 1998, when the Taiwan Association for Human Rights established a special project on human rights policies and legislation and persuaded a number of other Taiwanese NGOs to join.[8]

---

[4]Huang (2000).

[5]Interviews with Huang P W-s (former President of the Taiwan Association for Human Rights; former convener of Covenants Watch), in Taipei (4 Jan 2012) [hereinafter Huang P Interview (Jan)]; Interviews with Huang P W-s, in Taipei (17 Aug 2012) [hereinafter Huang P Interview (Aug)].

[6]Huang P Interview (Jan).

[7]Interview with #12, Human Rights Scholar; Former Vice-Chairman of the Taiwan Association for Human Rights, in Taipei (3 Aug 2012).

[8]Huang P Interview (Jan).

In the meantime, Mab Huang (黃默), a human rights scholar who had returned to Taiwan in 1995 after decades of teaching in the U.S. to promote human rights education on the island in response to the UN Decade for Human Rights Education (1995–2004), was also thinking about building the human rights institutions that he thought Taiwan needed. At the time, the UN had just begun to promote National Human Rights Institutions in the Asian region.[9] Inspired by this campaign, Mab Huang proposed the idea that Taiwan should establish a National Human Rights Commission (hereinafter NHRC) in accordance with international standards, first articulating it at a meeting with a delegation from the Council of Europe.[10]

Peter Huang liked Mab Huang's proposal and thought that there should be a concerted effort from the NGO community to thrust this onto the political agenda. Leading this endeavor, Peter Huang reached out to other civil society groups. In December 1999, under Peter Huang's stewardship, 22 NGOs, mostly advocacy groups, formed the "Alliance for the Establishment of a National Human Rights Commission" (hereinafter NHRC Alliance). They called for the government to set up a NHRC in accordance with the internationally recognized Paris Principles, which set forth the standards required for the independence and effective functioning of national human rights institutions.

The NHRC Alliance served two main functions—a "drafting" group that provided intellectual input to come up with a bill for the organization of a NHRC and a "mobilization and publicity" group that lobbied politicians.[11] Since the idea of setting up a NHRC in Taiwan was novel, Mab Huang was tasked with leading a small working team that consisted of colleagues in the academy and NGOs, a few of whom specialized in international law or European human rights law, to have weekly meetings to craft the bill for such an institution. Through this process, members of the drafting group, including Mab Huang, Peter Huang, Lung-chu Chen (陳隆志) and younger advocates such as Fort F.T. Liao (廖福特), Chun-hung Chen (陳俊宏) and Feng-cheng Lin (林峯正), conducted research about international human rights and learned from each other's specialties.[12] The learning process, however, was demanding, as the local stock of knowledge about human rights was inadequate and it was not as easy to do research online back then as it is in the current digital era. To collect UN materials, for example, the group had to ask the help of sympathetic groups in Hong Kong that had better access to the UN system.[13]

The other function was to lobby the five candidates running for the March 2000 presidential election. Although human rights was not a central theme in this contested election campaign, Peter Huang, using his good connections with the media,

[9]Interview with Huang M, in Taipei (13 Jan 2012) [hereinafter Huang M Interview].

[10]Huang M, The "Human Rights Diplomacy" Campaign of the Chen Shui-bian Administration, Address at the International Conference on Human Rights Protection and Practice (3 Oct 2008).

[11]Huang P Interview (Aug).

[12]Huang M Interview.

[13]Huang P Interview (Aug).

made it known that NGOs would try to raise the question about a National Human Rights Commission in the upcoming televised debate among the candidates. The strategy was effective. A number of candidates sent their aides to the Taiwan Association for Human Rights to learn about the NHRC Alliance's proposal, which was quickly endorsed by the major contenders, including the nominees of the KMT, Lien Chan (連戰), and the DPP, Chen Shui-bian (陳水扁).[14]

Despite this initial encouraging outcome, the challenges raised by a lack of knowledge and experience about international human rights law still imposed certain limitations on advocacy strategies. Most NGOs in the Alliance were not as familiar with international human rights as those core figures in the drafting group who were devoted to researching and learning. NGOs opted to work full force to promote a NHRC during the 2000 presidential campaign as a priority, rather than to press for human rights treaties, because, according to Peter Huang, to establish an organization such as a NHRC was a more "concrete" goal which would be relatively easier for them to work on than to adopt human rights treaties (they later found out that establishing a NHRC was also very challenging). The adoption of human rights treaties, in their view, would have required time-consuming detailed discussions among NGOs concerning each of the treaties, article by article. It would have also required at least some consensus on which approach to take and its implications, i.e., whether to simply ratify the treaties or enact a comprehensive human rights law. It was considered too difficult to proceed with such discussions while facing the pressing deadline of the 2000 presidential election.[15] Although human rights treaties were temporarily shelved as a part of the Alliance's agenda in the lead-up to the election, they later returned to the docket.

3 The DPP Government's Attempt to Ratify the Two Covenants

The result of the election was a surprise to many. Chen Shui-bian, who had launched his political career by defending a political dissident in the infamous 1979 Kaohsiung incident, scored a narrow victory, mainly due to internal friction in the KMT, which led to a third-party candidacy that split the votes of its supporters.[16] The DPP, whose precursor had been an underground party suppressed by the authoritarian KMT, for the first time became the ruling party.

Among the new President's initial tasks was drafting the inaugural address that he delivered two months after the election. This important speech, which set forth a groundbreaking international human rights project for Taiwan, established the foundation for Chen's stance on human rights and foreign policy for the following

---

[14] *Id.*

[15] Huang P Interview (Jan).

[16] Rigger (2001), at p. 194.

years, including the principles of "building the nation upon the principles of human rights" (人權立國) and "human rights diplomacy" (人權外交). Two people, Peter Huang and Lung-chu Chen, were particularly important in shaping this project from the beginning.[17]

Following the election on 18 March, Peter Huang continued to lobby the President-elect for a NHRC as well as international human rights norms and institutions more generally. Huang, widely known by many for his 1971 attempt to assassinate Chiang Ching-kuo in New York, was especially well known to Chen Shui-bian's inner circle of friends and advisors. Through a channel he would not specify, he managed to submit a memo he had prepared for Chen, in which he detailed a plan on how Taiwan could engage with international human rights, including establishing a NHRC, adopting international human rights standards and enhancing connections with international groups.[18] All of the ideas in the memo were later included in the inaugural speech.

Another important advisor of Chen Shui-bian was Lung-chu Chen, a Yale-trained international law professor and a vocal pro-independence advocate. He was the engineer of Chen Shui-bian's "Foreign Policy White Paper" during the 2000 presidential campaign, which emphasized the rise of "international civil society" and proposed, among other things, policies of "humanitarian diplomacy" and "all people's diplomacy," which aimed at gaining greater visibility for Taiwan by expanding the participation of Taiwanese NGOs in the international community.[19] Although Lung-chu Chen did not take part in the drafting of Chen Shui-bian's inaugural speech, these ideas were included in the speech in the context of discussing the new government's proposed foreign relations.[20]

President Chen's speech laid out three pillars for Taiwan's international human rights project: adopt international human rights norms (ratify the International Bill of Rights as a domestic law of Taiwan so that it would formally become the "Taiwan Bill of Rights"), establish an independent NHRC and strengthen cooperation with international nongovernmental organizations.[21] These new pledges received considerable attention (while other policies in the inaugural speech were considered more or less "predictable").[22] They guided the DPP administration's diplomatic efforts as well as human rights projects in later years. They also marked a turning point whereby international human rights norms were invoked as legal ideals and accepted as a national agenda in Taiwan for the first time.

[17]Huang (2011), pp. 131, 136–139.

[18]Huang P Interview (Jan); Huang P Interview (Aug).

[19]Chen L-c (2000), Xinshiji Taiwan de Guoji Jiaose (新世紀台灣的國際角色) [Taiwan's Role in the International Community in the New Century]. Address at National Taiwan University, 8 Apr.

[20]Huang, *supra* note 17, at p. 138.

[21]Office of the President, Republic of China (Taiwan) (2000).

[22]Huang P Interview (Aug).

To achieve these goals, the DPP administration set up a number of human rights task forces and retained those civil society activists and academics who advocated international human rights to advise the government. The DPP government relied heavily on the expertise of these advisors, as these bureaucrats had limited knowledge in this area to begin with.[23] Peter Huang, for example, served as Chen Shui-bian's National Policy Counselor for human rights matters until 2005 and had direct access to Chen in that capacity.

In October 2000, Chen Shui-bian created a Presidential Office Human Rights Consultative Task Force (which was renamed the Presidential Office Human Rights Consultative Committee in 2004), whose members were mainly scholars, lawyers and civil society advocates, including Lung-chu Chen, Peter Huang, Mab Huang and Fort F.T. Liao. Vice-President Annette Hsiu-lien Lu (呂秀蓮) served as the convener of the Presidential Office Human Rights Consultative Task Force and spent significant time and energy leading its projects, including spearheading the efforts to establish a NHRC.[24]

In addition, a Human Rights Promotion Task Force was set up in the executive branch—the Executive Yuan—in July 2001 to design and implement official human rights policies and coordinate and supervise all ministries and commissions in the executive branch.[25] The new DPP administration also had related ambitions to further human rights education, establish a human rights museum, and adopt human rights treaties.

These initiatives, for the most part, did not materialize. The KMT held a majority of seats in the Lesiglative Yuan throughout Chen Shui-bian's eight-year presidency, and Chen got off to a bad start. Five months into his rule, the pan-Blue (KMT) legislators filed a motion to remove Chen from office to fight his controversial plan to suspend the construction of a nuclear power plant. This bitter struggle between the two parties was exacerbated as time went by.

Chen's human rights projects were also viewed with suspicion. The KMT, for example, saw the establishment of the Presidential Office Human Rights Consultative Task Force and the plans to set up a NHRC, and even a human rights museum, as measures extending beyond the President's authority under the constitution and interpreted them as a plot to expand his own powers.[26] The pan-Blue-dominated Legislative Yuan was ready to do all it could to boycott many of Chen's policies and hamstring the administration. It stopped the administration's plan to establish a NHRC,[27] and also resolved in 2006 to disband a number of groups in the Presidential Office and remove their budget allocations, including those for the Human Rights Consultative Committee and the Preparatory Office of

---

[23]Huang P Interview (Jan).

[24]Interview with #28, Human Rights Scholar, Former Member of the Presidential Office Human Rights Consultative Task Force in the Chen Shui-bian era, in Taipei (3 Jan 2013).

[25]Huang, *supra* note 17, at pp. 141–142.

[26]Huang P Interview (Aug).

[27]Huang, *supra* note 17, at p. 145.

the National Human Rights Museum. The reason offered was that these groups had no legal basis to exist.

For the "norm setting" goal in Chen's inaugural speech, the initial plan of the new government was to pass a "Human Rights Protection Basic Law" (first named the "Human Rights Basic Law" and then renamed the "Human Rights Law") that would specify a comprehensive set of international human rights standards.[28] The Ministry of Justice was assigned to draft a bill, which would be evaluated and finalized by the Human Rights Promotion Task Force of the Executive Yuan.

As human rights policies were considered a priority for the Chen government, the bureaucrats prepared the draft of the Human Rights Basic Law quickly, presenting the first version in March 2001. Yet it was severely criticized by civic groups, which the bureaucrats had failed to consult in the drafting process. It was also thought to fall short in terms of quality because the haste with which it had been drafted led to inconsistencies throughout the bill.[29] A second draft was similarly deemed unsatisfactory. Although the Ministry of Justice seemed to have worked on the drafting process diligently, the government appeared to have lacked the necessary knowledge base and expertise to do the task well.[30]

Through Peter Huang's efforts, the International Commission of Jurists sent two expert missions, led by Professor Manfred Nowak, to Taiwan in August and November of 2003. They met with Peter Huang and the drafting group to revise the bill thoroughly.[31] The completed draft was then sent to the executive branch for further discussion.

However, the reactions from government agencies, which were said to be "still skeptical" about a human rights bill, were "most discouraging."[32] No consensus could be reached in terms of where such a Human Rights Law would be positioned in the legal hierarchy vis-à-vis domestic legislation and the constitution. In addition, some questions were particularly contentious, including whether to legalize same-sex marriages.[33] To accommodate the different opinions of various agencies, the final version contained many compromises that Peter Huang and his colleagues found unacceptable. The bill was then set aside and never submitted to the Legislative Yuan for approval. Perhaps the only virtue of this process, however,

[28]For a discussion of the process of drafting the "Human Rights Law," see Huang, *supra* note 17, at pp. 146–148.

[29]Huang P Interview (Jan).

[30]Huang, *supra* note 17, at p. 156.

[31]*Id.*

[32]*Id.*, at pp. 147–148.

[33]Huang P Interview (Jan); Interview with #15, Ministry of Justice Official Supervising the Implementation of the Two Covenants, in Taipei (8 Aug 2012); Interview #32, Former Member of the Human Rights Promotion Task Force of the Executive Yuan and Former Member of the Presidential Office Human Rights Consultative Committee, in Taipei (9 Jan 2013) [hereinafter #32 Interview].

was that a number of officials and advisors involved were given opportunities to learn about the meaning of a variety of international human rights standards.[34]

While the draft Human Rights Law was progressing slowly through the bureaucracy, another question arose as to whether to "ratify" the ICCPR and ICESCR. Even though Taiwan was not a member of the UN in its own right, it was not an easy question to answer. There had been some ad hoc efforts in 1998 and 1999 to discuss it, but the idea was soon aborted by the government at the time.[35]

This time, with the momentum from the new President's pledge in his inaugural speech, the administration decided in favor of ratification, offering the following reasons. First, Taiwan's political, economic and social development had already caught up with international standards, and therefore "Taiwan should also conform to international trends in fulfilling human rights protections." Second, although the UN would be expected to reject Taiwan's attempt to deposit the instruments of ratification, Taiwan would still "clearly declare its will and determination to comply with international human rights standards" by ratification and would prompt international society to acknowledge Taiwan's efforts to protect human rights.[36]

In preparation for ratification, the bureaucrats held several meetings to discuss whether all domestic legislation was compatible with the ICCPR and ICESCR. They found only a small number of laws that were considered to be inconsistent with the two covenants, which in the view of many civic groups was a gross underestimate of how much needed to be changed in response to the requirements of international human rights law. The administration was prepared to ratify the two covenants, either proposing amendments to possibly inconsistent laws or attaching relevant reservations to the covenants. It submitted the ratification proposal to the Legislative Yuan in April 2001, within the first year of the new President's term.

However, the ratification of the two covenants, like the other human rights initiatives of Chen Shui-bian, soon became an issue of political contention between the DPP and KMT, even though the two parties both purported to support human rights.[37] As a result, the proposal was blocked for months by KMT legislators in the

[34]#32 Interview.

[35]In 1998 and 1999, the Ministry of Foreign Affairs hosted three conferences to discuss with activists, scholars and government officials whether and how to ratify the two covenants. There was no consensus. The Executive Yuan then reached the conclusion that "the implications of the proposal [regarding ratification of the two covenants] are so broad and its influence so far-reaching" that the project of ratification should be postponed. See Xingzhengyuan Yanjiu Fazhan Kaohe Weiyuanhui [行政院研究發展考核委員會] (Executive Yuan Research, Development, and Evaluation Commission) (2002), at p. 45.

[36]Li Fa Yuan Gongbao (Legislative Yuan Gazette) (2001).

[37]The related legislative discussion can be found in the following: Li Fa Yuan Gongbao [立法院公報] (Legislative Yuan Gazette) 90, No. 52 (2001), p. 103; Li Fa Yuan Gongbao [立法院公報] (Legislative Yuan Gazette) 91, No. 51, 287 (2002); Li Fa Yuan Gongbao [立法院公報] (Legislative Yuan Gazette) 91, No. 78, 259 (2002); Li Fa Yuan Gongbao [立法院公報] (Legislative Yuan Gazette) 92, No. 2, 323 (2002); Li Fa Yuan Gongbao [立法院公報] (Legislative Yuan Gazette) 92, No. 3, 205 (2003); Li Fa Yuan Gongbao [立法院公報] (Legislative Yuan Gazette) 92, No. 5, 694 (2003).

preliminary procedural review. When it finally moved to substantive discussion, KMT legislators accused the DPP of having an ulterior motive for ratifying the covenants, namely to invoke the right of self-determination enshrined in each of the covenants in order to promote Taiwan's independence as a new sovereign country. The DPP legislators' denial was not enough to alleviate the skepticism.

Indeed, KMT politicians were worried about any move that could support the DPP's core political platform—Taiwan independence or self-determination. Their concerns were not without basis. Chen Shui-bian had been a contributor to the DPP's 1991 call for a referendum on Taiwan independence. In August 2002, Chen, as President, had just described Taiwan and China as "different countries on each side of the Strait," and later advocated a national referendum process.

In 2002, after several rounds of negotiation, KMT legislators at long last agreed to support ratification on the condition that the following declaration regarding the right of self-determination be made: "…The UN Assembly has never listed Taiwan as a dependent colony or a non-self-governing territory, and Taiwanese people are not colonial people or people under similar situations. Because the Republic of China has long been an independent sovereign, under existing treaties and international practice, it need not exercise the right of self-determination." DPP legislators accepted it, and the Legislative Yuan finally voted for ratification on 31 December 2002.[38] In addition to the above declaration, the Legislative Yuan further attached reservations to Article 6 (right to life) and Article 12 (freedom of movement) of the ICCPR and Article 8 of the ICESCR (right to form and join trade unions and right to strike).

However, mere days after that vote, leading DPP politicians and their advisors voiced their objection to the KMT's declaration, including the Vice-President Annette Lu. In her view, the KMT's declaration would "kill the DPP's platforms of Taiwan independence and referendum" and "the DPP would shoot itself in the foot if it accepted the KMT's declaration."[39] The DPP legislative caucus reversed its position and quickly filed a motion to request that the Legislative Yuan reconsider ratification, which blocked the ratification as modified by the declaration until it was reconsidered by the Legislative Yuan.[40]

The ratification proposal never had a second chance during Chen's presidency. Chen's second term (2004–2008) was plagued by controversies including corruption scandals involving his family and close associates.[41] In Jan 2006, amid contentious politics, the Presidential Office Human Rights Consultative Committee ceased to operate after its budget was removed by the Legislative Yuan. The

[38]Li Fa Yuan Gongbao [立法院公報] (Legislative Yuan Gazette) 92, No. 3, 205 (2003).

[39]Interview with Lu A, Former Vice-President of the Republic of China on Taiwan (2000–2008), in Taipei (16 Jan 2013).

[40]Li Fa Yuan Gongbao [立法院公報] (Legislative Yuan Gazette) 92, No. 5, 694 (2003).

[41]After leaving office in 2008, Chen was found guilty of corruption and is now released on medical parole.

Executive Yuan's Human Rights Promotion Task Force, which had fewer meetings after the first two years, seemed to have lost steam too.[42] Little momentum was generated to push Chen's human rights projects except for ratification of the CEDAW in 2007.[43] The CEDAW ratification—a unique success—did not generate similar energy for the ratification of other human rights treaties and other human rights initiatives by the, by now, lame-duck Chen administration.

4 Ratification by President Ma Ying-Jeou

The March 2008 presidential election brought about the second change of ruling party in Taiwan's history. Mr. Ma Ying-jeou of the KMT won a landslide victory over the candidate from the DPP. Just two months earlier, the KMT had achieved a great triumph in the Legislative Yuan, winning a two-thirds majority. In May, Ma assumed the Presidential Office as a highly popular politician with the strong backing of his fellow party members in the congress.

During the election campaign as well as in his inaugural speech,[44] Ma discussed human rights as part of his vision for Taiwan. But, compared with Chen Shui-bian, Ma at this point did not put forward any plan to adopt international human rights institutions, nor did he discuss human rights in the context of Taiwan's outreach efforts. Nevertheless, Ma, like Chen, supported the idea of "governing the nation based on the principles of human rights" (人權治國) (albeit with slightly different wording than Chen Shui-bian's policy of "building the nation upon the principles of human rights" [人權立國]).

Unexpectedly, on the first International Human Rights Day during his first term in office, 10 December 2008, Ma Ying-jeou announced that he would seek to ratify the ICCPR and ICESCR. He noted that the ROC was a signatory to both covenants but had been unable to ratify them over the past 40 years and that adopting the two covenants would demonstrate that international human rights norms had been realized in Taiwan.[45]

Ma Ying-jeou, a Harvard-trained international law scholar, showed a keen interest in overseeing the ratification process closely. He convened a meeting that gathered his advisors and government officials at the Presidential Office in February 2009. In the meeting, he gave the following instructions to move ratification up on the government agenda. First, there was no need to make any reservation to the

[42]Huang, *supra* note 17, at p. 142.

[43]See Liao, *supra* note 3, at p. 31.

[44]Bowman D, Towards a human rights state? A Comparison of Taiwan's Human Rights Policies under Chen Shui-bian and Ma Ying-jeou, at pp 57–58 (unpublished M.A. thesis, National Chengchi University) (on file with author); Ma (2008).

[45]Office of the President, Republic of China (Taiwan) (2008), President Ma Attends 2008 Asia Democracy and Human Rights Award Ceremony. http://english.president.gov.tw/NEWS/3053. Accessed 10 Dec 2008.

ICCPR and ICESCR, including to the right of self-determination because, based on UN practice, "ethnic minorities in a sovereign state are not allowed to invoke this provision to separate from the state." Second, once the two covenants were incorporated into domestic legislation, the Ministry of Foreign Affairs should send the instruments of ratification to the UN Secretary-General, and, even if such a request for deposit is rejected, the Ministry should ensure that there be a record of Taiwan's effort. Third, because deposit would be difficult due to Taiwan's unique international status, resulting in an incomplete procedure for the two covenants to become legally binding, to avoid any doubt, an "Implementation Law" for the two human rights covenants should be passed to grant the covenants the status of domestic legislation. Fourth, ratification should be completed before 20 May 2009 (the first anniversary of Ma's assumption of office) and the "Implementation Law" should come into effect no later than 10 December 2009.

The "Implementation Law" that Ma Ying-jeou referred to was actually a legacy of the DPP administration and the brainchild of Peter Huang and his colleagues. After the draft Human Rights Law had stalled for years, Peter Huang and his close colleagues in the administration decided to switch to a different approach. Instead, they adopted a minimalist approach and drafted a very simple law,[46] as opposed to the comprehensive approach of enumerating each of the human rights provisions as in the draft Human Rights Law they had previously prepared. The law they designed—the Law to Implement the ICCPR and the ICESCR—was sent to the Legislative Yuan in February 2008 (before the presidential election in March), but it was not passed. It was later picked up by the Ma administration and eventually passed on 31 March 2009.

The Legislative Yuan passed the Implementation Act and approved ratification at the same time; they worked so fast that many activists were surprised.[47] Unlike the previous debate surrounding ratification during 2000–2002, the legislative session this time did not provoke any discussion. There was also no reservation or declaration attached regarding the right of self-determination that KMT legislators

---

[46]This draft Implementation Law had only nine articles. The Implementation Law that was enacted in 2009 essentially followed the draft Peter Huang and his colleagues prepared. It states the purpose of the Act (Art. 1), grants the human rights provisions of the ICCPR and ICESCR domestic legal status (Art. 2) and refers to the legislative purpose of the Act and interpretations made by the two relevant UN treaty bodies as guidance to apply the two covenants (Art. 3). It also requires government agencies of all levels respect, protect and fulfill human rights (Art. 4) and calls for government agencies to coordinate among themselves and to cooperate with other governments, international NGOs and human rights mechanisms for the fulfillment of human rights protections (Art. 5). For concrete implementation measures, it requires the government to set up a human rights reporting system in accordance with the two covenants (Art. 6), to prioritize the budget for implementation (Art. 7) and to review all laws, regulations and administrative measures in order to correct those that are incompatible with the two covenants within two years after the Act goes into effect (Art. 8). Article 9 is the only provision different from that of the DPP version, which would have made the Act binding immediately upon promulgation. The provision in the final version allowed some buffer time, giving the Executive Yuan discretion to determine the effective date.

[47]Interview #13, NGO Activist, in Taipei (4 Jan 2012).

had objected to fiercely when blocking the DPP's proposal in 2002. Credit for this should go to Ma Ying-jeou and his ability to rally the support of his fellow KMT members in both the executive and legislative branches.

Ma signed the instruments of ratification on the eve of the first anniversary of his presidency. Like that of his predecessor, Ma's discourse on human rights clearly reflected a desire to improve Taiwan's international standing. At the signing ceremony, Ma stated: "Taiwan will become an equal of other countries throughout the world in human rights." He expressed the hope that ratification would let other countries know that the existence of Taiwan and the development of the ROC are in everyone's best interest.[48]

The instruments of ratification were delivered to the UN Secretariat in June 2009 through the help of four diplomatic allies of Taiwan.[49] Within a week, the UN Secretariat rejected Taiwan's attempt to deposit the instruments of ratification, on the basis of the 1971 UN General Assembly Resolution 2758 which expelled the representatives of the ROC government and declared that the representatives of the PRC are the only legitimate representatives of China to the UN. Despite this, the two covenants have been incorporated into Taiwan's domestic legal system through the Implementation Act, which went into effect on 10 December 2009.

5 Political Incentives, Social Processes and Contested Politics

The driving forces behind ratification of the two human rights covenants in Taiwan can be observed in two major respects. The first is the potent political incentives for Taiwanese political leaders to favor ratification, notably including internal concerns about the image of their political party in the eyes of the voters and external concerns about Taiwan's standing in the world.

In domestic politics, the adoption of international human rights standards can be regarded as a signal to the domestic audience of the government's intention to address human rights issues[50] (whether it is a credible signal or whether the government can deliver on the promise is another question). By actively pursuing the ratification of human rights treaties, a politician and his or her political party seek to build a domestic reputation for respecting human rights. Chen Shui-bian's government presented the attractive slogan, "building the nation upon the principles of human rights" (人權立國). Ma Ying-jeou's government came up with a similar slogan, "governing the nation based on the principles of human rights" (人權治國).

48Office of the President Republic of China (Taiwan) (2009), President Ma Signs Instruments of Ratification of Two Covenants on Human Rights. http://english.president.gov.tw/Default.aspx?tabid=491&itemid=19415&rmid=2355&sd=2009/05/01&ed=2009/05/30. Accessed 14 May 2009.

49Bowman, *supra* note 44.

50Simmons and Danner (2010), at pp. 225, 234.

As a human rights scholar shrewdly pointed out, the DPP and the KMT governments have engaged in a "human rights competition."[51] There is little room for dialing back the human rights policy in a robust democratic environment where political parties compete to project a favorable impression of themselves to the voters.

Ratification also sends a signal to the international audience.[52] In today's world, sovereignty can be understood as "status"—"the vindication of the state's existence as a member of the international system."[53] Status is an intangible asset valued by states for its own sake as well as for its potential to strengthen the state's political and economic relations with other countries.[54] The strong desire for good international standing is therefore not exclusive to states like Taiwan that are isolated from intergovernmental organizations and networks. States generally desire a strong reputation in order to increase their influence on the world stage. This is particularly true for states that are insecure about their influence, including those that have a marginalized role in international politics and those that are embroiled in domestic turmoil. Therefore, there is a powerful political incentive for prioritizing status concerns in their national agenda. The ratification of human rights treaties and taking their enforcement seriously help the state present a respectable vision of its role to international society.

The second crucial driving force was the successful initiative of a small number of leading advocates and scholars to mobilize the broader NGO community, which then acted collectively to put pressure on the government to adopt international human rights. Thanks to these bottom-up efforts of mobilization and political lobbying, the enterprise of institutionalizing international human rights norms was, for the first time, elevated to the level of a national political-legal agenda, which then commanded more investment in time, energy and resources both from within and outside the government towards the goal of ratification.

The context in which these efforts were made was Taiwan's democratic transition. There was no longer a martial-law regime to fight against, and the overriding belief was that society must advance to the next level in terms of pursuing social justice, good governance and a better life for its members. The goal of the NGO community was to use international human rights norms to strengthen Taiwan's transition, to instill human rights values in the society and to enhance rights protection. These efforts should also be viewed in the context of the changing role of NGOs from challenging the dictatorship in the martial-law era to addressing more comprehensive rights issues in the subsequent young democracy era. This new strategy helped civil society groups redefine their role, remain relevant in an evolving environment and fulfill their missions.

---

[51]Interview #2, Scholar, Former Vice-Chairman of the Taiwan Association for Human Rights, in Taipei (4 Jan 2012).

[52]Moore (2003), at pp. 879, 902–903.

[53]Chayes and Chayes (1998), p. 27.

[54]*Id.*

The individual advocates and NGOs began their campaigns by framing the challenges that confronted Taiwan's democratic transition, which was, in their view, seriously lacking in human rights laws, institutions and human rights culture. The lack of human rights development was, to a large extent, blamed on Taiwan's enduring isolation from the international human rights regime. The way the challenge is framed dictates how the challenge is addressed. The advocates and their organizations began to introduce new standards from the international realm.

Introducing new norms requires a variety of social, political and legal processes, which rely on individuals who can serve as "intermediaries" between the norms from the international sphere and the local sphere to which they are conveyed.[55] The intermediaries in Taiwan's case were savvy interlocutors. Knowing that there was a need for more intermediaries speaking on behalf of international human rights, they first recruited colleagues in the NGO community and persuaded them to take on international human rights as a new tool of advocacy. They started to educate themselves about the operation of the international human rights system and tried to connect with international actors to help them in this endeavor. Based on the acquired knowledge, they drafted policy papers and bills for lobbying purposes. They took advantage of the competitive political environment to lobby political leaders.

When lobbying politicians, Taiwanese NGOs spoke a language that shaped and satisfied the government's preferences for and interests in international recognition, political legitimacy and identity as a newly transitioned liberal democracy. They spoke of Taiwan's equal status to other states in terms of its ability to adopt and implement human rights treaties. They emphasized that Taiwan, as a member of the world community, should not refuse universal values. In this context, international human rights is framed within a political discourse that seeks to bolster state sovereignty, status and legitimacy, rather than in a discourse about its legal effects of restraining state power and adding to state obligations, although the latter was what essentially motivated civil society to promote international human rights.

However, Taiwan's case study offers a cautionary tale for promoting human rights during times of contentious politics. Beth Simmons finds that newly transitioned, but currently stable, democracies are generally more likely to ratify human rights treaties than are other governments.[56] Indeed, democratic transition may increase political motivations for ratification (to appeal to domestic and international audiences) as well as for civil society mobilization. On the other hand, new democracies may also be bogged down in fierce politics, upsetting the chance of institutionalizing human rights protection. Political parties that compete for legitimacy may try to discredit competitors that seek to ratify human rights treaties or adopt other international human rights institutions. They may not oppose such policies on the grounds that they disapprove of human rights values, which would hurt their popularity, but they may resort to other reasons, claiming that their

[55]Merry (2006), at p. 2.

[56]Simmons (2009), at pp. 82, 86.

competitors have ulterior motives behind these pro-human rights policies, such as illegitimate expansion of power. In Taiwan's case, this political struggle was further mired in the debate between the DPP and the KMT about the right of self-determination, which delayed Taiwan's ratification of the two human rights covenants from 2003 to 2009.

6 Conclusion

This chapter investigates the processes by which various actors in Taiwan—including leading advocates and scholars, civic groups and political leaders—promoted international human rights norms and eventually brought about ratification of the ICCPR and ICESCR. These processes were first launched by a small number of civil society actors, who were able to rally their colleagues in the wider NGO community to join their cause. Well aware of the political incentives for ratification, they used the run-up to the 2000 presidential election to get the international human rights project onto the national agenda. After the DPP won the election, they continued to work from within the government to try to put in place various international human rights mechanisms, including ratification of the two covenants. However, heated politics, exacerbated by the contention between the DPP and the KMT over the right of self-determination, put an abrupt end to the ratification campaign. But all was not lost. The legislative discussion and the draft Implementation Law for the two covenants prepared during this period laid the groundwork for the newly elected KMT administration to quickly mobilize the Legislative Yuan to ratify the two covenants and incorporate them into domestic law in 2009.

On the basis of the Taiwan case study, this chapter examines the driving forces behind the ratification of international human rights treaties and the social, legal and political processes involved. These forces have broader implications beyond Taiwan's case for understanding the processes of the diffusion of international human rights norms. International human rights norm diffusion depends on individual intermediaries who can convey the new norms from the international sphere to the local sphere. A bottom-up ratification campaign like the one examined in Taiwan requires these intermediaries to spread the ideals and knowledge of international human rights, to convince their colleagues to join the cause and to persuade and press the government to make it a priority. For the government, the political motivation to use ratification to send signals to the domestic and international audience is powerful. However, ferocious partisan battles in newly democratized regimes may also prove to be a great hurdle to the institutionalization of new norms.

References

Bowman D (2010) Towards a human rights state? A Comparison of Taiwan's Human Rights Policies under Chen Shui-bian and Ma Ying-jeou, at pp 57–58 (unpublished M.S. thesis, National Chengchi University) (on file with author)

Chayes A, Chayes AH (1998) The new sovereignty: compliance with international regulatory agreements. Harvard University Press, Cambridge

Chen L-c (2000), Xinshiji Taiwan de Guoji Jiaose (新世紀台灣的國際角色) [Taiwan's Role in the International Community in the New Century]. Address at National Taiwan University, 8 Apr 2000

Hafner-Burton E, Tsutsui K (2005) Human rights in a globalizing world: the paradox of empty promises. Am J So 110(5):1373–1411

Hathaway O (2002) Do human rights treaties make a difference? Yale Law J 111:1935–2042

Huang M (2000) Human rights NGOs of Taiwan: their rise, transformation and prospects. Paper presented at the Conference on "Taiwan NGOs: Marching Towards the 21st Century" 28–29 Jul 2000

Huang M (2008) The "Human Rights Diplomacy" Campaign of the Chen Shui-bian Administration, Address at the International Conference on Human Rights Protection and Practice (3 Oct 2008)

Huang M (2011) Human rights initiatives of the Chen Shui-bian administration: a sketch. In: Chou C-c (ed) Zaidi yu Guoji Renquan zhi Shijian yu Tiaozhan (在地與國際人權之實踐與挑戰) [Challenges and the Practice of Local and International Human Rights]. Perennial Culture 131–160

Li Fa Yuan Gongbao [立法院公報] (Legislative Yuan Gazette) 90, No. 52 (2001), p. 103

Li Fa Yuan Gongbao [立法院公報] (Legislative Yuan Gazette) 91, No. 51, 287 (2002)

Li Fa Yuan Gongbao [立法院公報] (Legislative Yuan Gazette) 91, No. 78, 259 (2002)

Li Fa Yuan Gongbao [立法院公報] (Legislative Yuan Gazette) 92, No. 2, 323 (2002)

Li Fa Yuan Gongbao [立法院公報] (Legislative Yuan Gazette) 92, No. 3, 205, 233 (2003)

Li Fa Yuan Gongbao [立法院公報] (Legislative Yuan Gazette) 92, No. 5, 694 (2003)

Liao F-T (2010) Partly virtual, partly real: Taiwan's unique interaction with international human rights instruments. Asian Yearb Intl Law 16:25–45

Ma Y-j (2008) Presidential inauguration speech, May 20. http://english.president.gov.tw/NEWS/45. Accessed 25 Dec 2017

Merry S (2006) Human rights and gender violence: translating international law into local justice. University of Chicago Press, Chicago

Moore D (2003) A signaling theory of human rights compliance. Northwest Univ Law Rev 97 (2):879–910

Office of the President, Republic of China (Taiwan) (2000) Chen Shui-bian, "Taiwan Stands Up: Presidential Inauguration Address," 20 May. http://english.president.gov.tw/NEWS/2643. Accessed 5 Nov 2017

Office of the President, Republic of China (Taiwan) (2008) President Ma Attends 2008 Asia Democracy and Human Rights Award Ceremony. http://english.president.gov.tw/NEWS/3053. Accessed 5 Nov 2017

Office of the President, Republic of China (Taiwan) (2009), President Ma Signs Instruments of Ratification of Two Covenants on Human Rights. http://english.president.gov.tw/Default.aspx?tabid=491&itemid=19415&rmid=2355&sd=2009/05/01&ed=2009/05/30. Accessed 14 May 2009.

Rigger S (2001) From opposition to power: Taiwan's democratic progressive party. Lynne Rienner, Boulder

Simmons B (2009) Mobilizing for human rights: international law in domestic politics. Cambridge University Press, New York

Simmons B, Danner A (2010) Credible commitments and the international criminal court. Intl Organ 64(2):225–256

Xingzhengyuan Yanjiu Fazhan Kaohe Weiyuanhui [行政院研究發展考核委員會] (Executive Yuan Research, Development, and Evaluation Commission) (2002). Human Rights Infrastructure-building for a Human Rights State—2002 human rights policy white paper of the Republic of China (Taiwan)

Yu-Jie Chen is a Post-Doctoral Scholar at the Institutum Iurisprudentiae of Academia Sinica and an Affiliated Scholar at the U.S.-Asia Law Institute of NYU School of Law. She received her J.S.D. and LL.M. degrees from NYU School of Law. She also holds an LL.M. and LL.B. from National Chengchi University in Taiwan. Chen has had extensive experience as a research scholar for the U.S.-Asia Law Institute of NYU School of Law. Prior to that, she served as a researcher and advocate for the nongovernmental organization Human Rights in China. She has also practiced in the Taipei-based international law firm of Lee and Li. Chen's research has focused on international and domestic law in relation to human rights in Mainland China and Taiwan. Her J.S.D. project, "Socialization in Isolation: Taiwan's Practice of Human Rights Treaties as a Non-UN Member State," is a socio-legal study of a particular phenomenon arising from Taiwan's acceptance of international human rights norms despite being excluded from the UN human rights regime. She has published journal essays and academic articles on human rights and rule of law issues in China, Taiwan and on cross-Strait relations.

Chapter 13
Taiwan's Human Rights Implementation Acts: A Model for Successful Incorporation?

Wen-Chen Chang

Abstract Owing to her contested statehood, Taiwan has been barred from accession to any United Nations-related mechanisms including international human rights conventions. Beginning in 2009, Taiwan passed Implementation Acts to incorporate the fundamental rights and freedoms enshrined in several international human rights conventions, including the International Covenant on Civil and Political Rights, the International Covenant on Economic, Social and Cultural Rights, the Convention on Elimination of All Forms of Discrimination against Women, the Convention on the Rights of the Child, and the Convention on the Rights of the Persons with Disabilities. These Implementation Acts provide binding legal effect for the rights enshrined in those human rights conventions in Taiwan's legal system, and stipulate a legal duty of the government—including the legislative, executive and judicial branches—for implementation and enforcement. The Implementation Acts even obliged the government to issue state reports based upon the requirements of those human rights conventions and created a system of review of government implementation by independent international experts with prior experience of serving on similar international panels. Perhaps the only matter that a domestic Implementation Act cannot stipulate is Taiwan's membership and international participation in those human rights conventions. This chapter is aimed at analyzing the special mechanism of the Implementation Acts, discussing their particular functions, challenges and difficulties in the context of Taiwan's special international situation. Drawing on these discussions, this chapter also explores whether the model provided for by the Implementation Acts may be suitable for human rights incorporation and enforcement beyond Taiwan.

Keywords CEDAW · CRC · CRPD · ICCPR · ICECER · Implementation Act International review

---

W.-C. Chang (✉)
College of Law, National Taiwan University, Taipei, Taiwan
e-mail: wenchenchang@ntu.edu.tw

J. A. Cohen et al. (eds.), *Taiwan and International Human Rights*, Economics, Law, and Institutions in Asia Pacific, https://doi.org/10.1007/978-981-13-0350-0_13

1 Introduction

The beginning of the twenty-first century witnessed a global trend in revitalizing and strengthening human rights protection with an unprecedented number of states acceding to core international human rights conventions under the United Nations (UN) and incorporating these conventions into their domestic legal systems through statutes or even constitutional amendments.[1] A convergence of international human rights and domestic legal systems has been widely observed.[2] Taiwan stands as no exception to this global trend despite its difficulty in joining the UN and related treaty mechanisms.

The half-century of Japanese colonization of Taiwan came to an end in 1945, followed by the rule of the Republic of China (ROC). In 1949, the ROC government under the Nationalist Party (Kuomintang, KMT) lost the civil war to the Communist Party and retreated to Taiwan while the Communist Party established the People's Republic of China (PRC) on the Chinese Mainland. The ensuing hostility between the PRC on the Mainland and the ROC on Taiwan has remained a feature of relations across the Taiwan Strait to this day. In 1971, the ROC government lost its UN seat to the PRC government,[3] and has since been confronted with international isolation. Meanwhile, the economic success in the 1970s, along with the subsequent democratization and constitutional reforms in the late 1980s and 1990s, have brought to Taiwan a vibrant civil society ready for global participation and a functioning democratic government that has vowed to observe democratic constitutionalism, the rule of law and universal human rights.[4] All of these factors have contributed to Taiwan's recent progress in its domestic incorporation of international human rights instruments.[5]

The ROC government was the signatory to the International Covenant on Civil and Political Rights (ICCPR) and the International Covenant on Economic, Social and Cultural Rights (ICESCR) in 1967, however, ratification of the two Covenants was not undertaken before the government was expelled from the UN in 1971. The democratization process of the 1990s brought back calls for ratifying the two Covenants and acceding to other international human rights conventions.[6] An initial move to ratify the two Covenants was made after the first transfer of government power from the KMT to the long-time opposition, the Democratic Progressive Party (DPP) in 2000. The DPP government's proposal for ratification of the two Covenants did not succeed in the parliamentary process in which the KMT held the majority. Nevertheless, a few years later, in 2007, the DPP government's proposal for acceding to the Convention on Elimination of All Forms of Discrimination

---

[1]Chang and Yeh (2012), p 1171.

[2]Yeh and Chang (2008), p 93.

[3]UN General Assembly Resolution 2758, A/RES/2758(XXVI) (25 Oct 1971).

[4]Yeh (2016), pp 1–2, Yeh and Chang (2014), p 143.

[5]Chang (2009a), p 221.

[6]Yeh (2016), pp 233–236.

against Women (CEDAW) was passed with a bipartisan majority vote. The government was not able to deposit the ratification instrument with the UN Secretary-General,[7] but that failure has not barred Taiwan from further ratifications or accessions.[8]

The KMT government returned to power in 2008. In 2009, a proposal to ratify the two Covenants, the ICCPR and the ICESCR, was made again, and this time passed by a bipartisan parliamentary majority. As in the case of the CEDAW, the ratification instruments of the two Covenants were not deposited with the UN Secretary-General. In order to provide the domestic legal effect of the two Covenants, an Implementation Act was passed and came into effect on 10 December 2009. Modeled on the Implementation Act of the two Covenants, the Implementation Act (or alternatively translated as "Enforcement Act")[9] of the CEDAW was passed in 2011 and went into effect on 1 January 2012. In June 2014, the Implementation Act of the Convention on the Rights of the Child (CRC) was passed, and became effective in November. In August 2014, the Implementation Act of the Convention on the Rights of Persons with Disabilities (CRPD) was enacted and went into effect in December. Accession to both the CRC and the CRPD was passed by the Parliament in 2016 and promulgated by the President in 2017, with retrospective effect dating back to 2014.

These Implementation Acts were primarily intended to provide domestic legal effect to the above-mentioned international human rights conventions to which Taiwan has unilaterally acceded. They obliged the government—including the legislative, executive and judicial branches—to implement the rights and freedoms of these conventions and to issue state reports examining their compliance. It remains to be seen whether—and how—these Implementation Acts have been effective in carrying out their functions and what challenges and difficulties they have confronted. To explore these issues, this chapter analyzes four key functions provided by the Implementation Acts, and identifies four leading actors that have substantially facilitated the Implementation Acts. It is concluded that the Implementation Acts alone would not have been as effective in carrying out the execution of the international human rights instruments without the relentless efforts made by those leading actors. Among those actors, human rights groups and their leaders have been particularly pivotal in advancing human rights advocacy and revitalizing human rights discourse through the variety of avenues, including litigation, that are available to them.[10]

---

[7]Citing UN General Assembly Resolution 2758, UN Secretary-General Ban Ki-moon returned Taiwan's instrument of accession to the CEDAW.

[8]Yeh (2016), pp 233–236.

[9]Gender Equality Committee of the Executive Yuan, https://www.ey.gov.tw/gec_en/News.aspx?n=98FF4D9BE97AB4B4&sms=5674ADAAA9DB9139. Accessed 28 Dec 2017.

[10]See also Chang (2009a), p 221.

2 Functions of the Implementation Acts

Thus far, there are four Implementation Acts that respectively incorporate the two Covenants, the CEDAW, the CRC and the CRPD into Taiwan's domestic legal system and stipulate their enforcement mechanisms. While specific details may vary from one Implementation Act to another, they all include five main functions: 1) providing domestic legal effect for the rights and freedoms guaranteed within the respective international human rights instruments, 2) reviewing and revising laws and regulations according to the respective international human rights instrument, 3) obligating the government to issue state reports for the respective international human rights instruments and conducting independent international reviews, and 4) providing human rights education and training.

2.1 Providing Domestic Legal Effect

In Taiwan, according to the Constitution, the President has the power to conclude treaties, the premier—the president of the Executive Yuan—and ministers must refer treaties that are to be sent to the Legislative Yuan to the Committee of the Executive Yuan for deliberation, but the Legislative Yuan retains the power to review and ratify treaties.[11] However, the Constitution does not specify the legal effect or status of the treaties that are duly acceded to according to the above procedures. Article 141 of the Constitution merely states that "the foreign policy of the Republic of China shall, …., respect treaties and the Charter of the United Nations, in order to protect the rights and interests of Chinese citizens residing abroad, promote international cooperation, advance international justice and ensure world peace."[12] The Constitutional Court in J.Y. Interpretation No. 329 has opined that treaties duly concluded in accordance with the procedures prescribed in the Constitution shall hold the same status as laws.[13] This constitutional interpretation has been understood as the Constitutional Court's adoption of a monist position, in which treaties duly concluded are given domestic legal effect upon legislative approval.[14]

Based upon the monist position adopted in J.Y. Interpretation No. 329, when the Legislative Yuan approved accession to the CEDAW in 2007, the treaty provisions should immediately have had domestic legal effect. Yet, because the CEDAW's accession instrument was not successfully deposited with the UN Secretary-General, doubts remained as to whether the process of the CEDAW accession was complete, and whether the CEDAW was ready for domestic application. In order to clarify any

[11]Zhonghua Minguo Xianfa (The ROC Constitution), arts. 38, 58(2), 63.

[12]Zhonghua Minguo Xianfa (The ROC Constitution), art. 141.

[13]Si Fa Yuan Da Fa Guan Jie Shi Shizi Di 329 Hao [Justices of the Constitutional Court, Judicial Yuan, Interpretation No. 329] (24 Dec 1993) (R.O.C.), Reasoning, para.1.

[14]Chang (2009a), pp 209–210.

doubts about domestic legal effect, the government decided to enact an Implementation Act when ratifying the two Covenants in 2009. The CEDAW's Implementation Act was also passed in 2011, followed by the Implementation Acts of the CRC and the CRPD in 2014.

Hence, the main purpose of the Implementation Acts was to provide domestic legal effect to these acceded international human rights instruments given (or notwithstanding) the failure to deposit the ratification instruments with the UN. Common Article 2 of these Implementation Acts was written for this purpose. To illustrate, Article 2 of the Implementation Act of the two Covenants states that the "human rights protection provisions in the two Covenants have domestic legal status." Article 2 of the the CEDAW's Implementation Act prescribes that "all terms and conditions specified in the Convention regarding protection to human rights of different genders and promotion of sexual equality shall have the same effect as domestic laws." Article 2 of the CRC's Implementation Act specifies that "the provisions of the Convention regarding the protection and promotion of the rights of the child and youth shall have the effect of domestic law." Article 2 of the CRPD's Implementation Act prescribes that "provisions in the Convention regarding the rights of persons with disabilities have domestic legal status."

To emphasize the domestic legal effect of international human rights treaties, Common Articles 4 and 5 of these Implementation Acts require that in carrying out their functions, all levels of governmental institutions and agencies—including the judiciary—conform to the human rights protection provisions enshrined in these acceded conventions. In addition, it is also stipulated that the government should cooperate with other national governments and international nongovernmental organizations and human rights institutions to realize the promotion and protection of the human rights provisions in these acceded conventions. Also, given the domestic legal effect of, and the obligations of the courts to protect the rights enshrined in these conventions, individuals whose rights are breached may sue in the courts, and judges should apply these acceded human rights instruments as part of Taiwan's domestic laws to examine if there is any government act or act of omission that fails to observe those rights.[15]

2.2 Reviewing and Revising Domestic Laws and Regulations

In addition to providing domestic legal effect, the Implementation Acts also obligate the government to review and revise the existing laws and regulations in accordance with these acceded human rights instruments. This requirement has given an unprecedented opportunity for a comprehensive overhaul of domestic laws and regulations to bring them into accord with international human rights standards.

[15]Chang and Lu (2011), pp 87–88.

Article 8 of the Implementation Act of the two Covenants reads that within two years of the Implementation Act coming into force, all levels of governmental institutions and agencies should review laws, regulations, directions and administrative measures within their functions according to the two Covenants, and revise those found to be incompatible so as to meet the requirements of the two Covenants. After the Implementation Act of the two Covenants went into effect on 10 December 2009, the Ministry of Justice began the review process. Eventually, the Ministry of Justice listed a total of 263 cases (including statutes, regulations, decrees or directives, among others) that required revision according to the two Covenants. By 31 August 2017, of those 263 cases, 228 of them have been revised, while 35 cases (13.3%) have not. Among the 35 cases waiting for revision, 8 cases involve statutory revisions, including the Assembly and Parade Act, the Criminal Procedure Law, the Industrial Group Act, the Juvenile Accident Act, the Detention Law, the Labor Insurance Act, the Act for Settlement of Labor-Management Disputes, and the Labor Union Act. Among the 8 cases lined up for revision, six have been sent for legislative deliberation; only the Act for Settlement of Labor-Management Disputes and the Labor Union Act are still under discussion.[16]

Like the two Covenants, the CEDAW's Implementation Act also requires a comprehensive review and revision of laws and regulations in Article 8. Because the process of review and revision in the case of the two Covenants took much longer than the required two-year period, the CEDAW's Implementation Act gives the government three years to complete its reviews and revisions following the Implementation Act's coming into force on 1 January 2012. In June 2012, the government launched a project for a comprehensive overhaul of the laws and regulations according to the CEDAW provisions, for which the Gender Equality Committee of the Executive Yuan served as the main steering force. Many legal experts, human rights groups and women's organizations were also invited to participate in the process. By the end of 2013, the laws and regulations that were found to be incompatible with the CEDAW totaled 228 cases. By May 2015, most of these incompatible laws and regulations had been amended or abolished, while some of them were still under review and deliberation by the Legislative Yuan.[17] In addition, a comprehensive guideline for a gender equality policy was also drawn up and revised in accordance with the CEDAW provisions.[18]

[16]Ministry of Justice, The progress of examining the law and administrative orders and regulations violating the two Covenants, https://www.humanrights.moj.gov.tw/ct.asp?xItem=283349&CtNode=32910&mp=200 (in Chinese), Accessed 22 Nov 2017.

[17]Gender Equality Committee of the Executive Yuan, The progress of examining the law and administrative orders and regulations violating the CEDAW, http://www.gec.ey.gov.tw/News.aspx?n=1662D3186C4B2F2D&sms=08DBC3A57A112D27 (in Chinese), Accessed 22 Nov 2017.

[18]Gender Equality Committee of the Executive Yuan, The Guidelines for Gender Equality Policy, http://www.gec.ey.gov.tw/cp.aspx?n=363DC330E476B467 (in Chinese), Accessed 22 Nov 2017.

The Implementation Act of the CRC went into force on 20 November 2014. Having reflected upon the previous experiences of the two Covenants and the CEDAW, the CRC Implementation Act came up with a rather sophisticated scheme. First, it stipulated that within one year of the Implementation Act becoming effective, the government must provide a priority review list of the laws and regulations that may not be compatible with the CRC provisions and that require further revision. For those laws and regulations that are on the priority list, their revision must be undertaken within three years. Those not on the priority list, their revision is to be completed within five years.[19] After the initial review, the government made a priority list that included 17 laws. One of those was a provision in the Protection of Children and Youth Welfare and Rights Act. The revision was quickly undertaken to affirm that every child and youth should have an equal right to participate in recreational and cultural activities and outlawed discrimination against children with special conditions to participate in recreational and cultural activities.[20]

A similar overhaul scheme with a longer time frame was adopted for the CRPD Implementation Act, which came into effect on 3 December 2014. The Implementation Act stipulates that the government must prepare a priority review list of the laws and regulations that may not be compatible with the CRPD provisions within two years of the Implementation Act becoming effective. Then, those laws and regulations on the priority list must be revised within three years, while the rest must be completed within five years. Most noteworthy is an added provision by which the government is obligated to consult and seek opinions from the organizations of persons with disabilities in the process of reviewing and revising laws and regulations according to the CRPD provisions.[21] After the initial review, more than 50 laws and regulations that were found to be incompatible with the CRPD provisions were placed on the priority list. By November 2015, 14 of such revisions were completed.[22] The revisions that have been completed thus far include an added obligation of the government to ensure barrier-free access of public transportation for persons with disabilities and to eliminate legal terminology for persons with disabilities that may have derogatory connotations.

---

[19]The Implementation Act of the CRC, art. 9.

[20]Zhonghua Minguo Weisheng Fuli Bu [中華民國衛生福利部] (Ministry of Health and Welfare), Lifa Yuan Sandu Tongguo Ertong Ji Shaonian Fuli Yu Quanyi Baozhangfa Xiuzheng Cao'an [立法院三讀通過兒童暨少年福利與權益保障法修正草案] (The amendment to the Protection of Children and Youth Welfare and Rights Act was passed by the Legislative Yuan), https://www.sfaa.gov.tw/SFAA/Pages/VDetail.aspx?nodeid=20&pid=4303. Accessed 17 Oct 2017.

[21]The Implementation Act of the CRPD, art. 10 (3).

[22]Zhonghua Minguo Weisheng Fuli Bu [中華民國衛生福利部] (Ministry of Health and Welfare), Lifa Yuan Sandu Tongguo Shenxin Zhang'aizhe Quanli Baozhangfa Xiuzheng Cao'an [立法院三讀通過身心障礙者權利保障法修正草案] (The amendment to the People with Disabilities Rights Protection Act was passed by the Legislative Yuan), https://www.sfaa.gov.tw/SFAA/Pages/VDetail.aspx?nodeid=20&pid=4432. Accessed 17 Oct 2017.

2.3 Issuing State Reports and Conducting Independent International Reviews

Because Taiwan cannot formally accede to international human rights conventions, the government is not obligated to issue state reports on the progress of its compliance with these conventions, let alone submit its state reports for periodic reviews by the respective committees of these conventions. The Implementation Acts, however, have sought to tackle this challenge.

Article 6 of the Implementation Act of the two Covenants obligates the government to set up a human rights report system in accordance with the two Covenants. After the Implementation Act became effective, the Advisory Committee of Human Rights under the Presidential Office[23] quickly decided that the report system under Article 6 must follow the state report system in the two Covenants, and that an independent panel of international experts with experience in reviewing state reports should be formed to review Taiwan's state reports and provide concluding observations and recommendations.[24] The initial state reports of the two Covenants were issued in 2012. A five-member panel of independent experts including one former member of the Human Rights Committee was formed to review Taiwan's initial state report concerning the ICCPR, and a five-member panel of independent experts including one current member and several former members of the Economic, Social and Cultural Rights Committee was formed to review the initial state report concerning the ICESCR.[25] The process of international review was designed to be open, transparent and dialogic, and human rights groups and social organizations were invited to participate by not only issuing shadow reports counter-balancing the views of the government but also by having direct access to dialogue with international experts on various issues.

The international review process of the two Covenants' initial state reports was deemed to be a success. The two panels of international experts commented that "the government and people of Taiwan have demonstrated exemplary commitment to the process of monitoring compliance with the relevant human rights obligations, and the government has provided valuable and detailed reports, following international precedents, and has engaged in a highly constructive manner with the international experts."[26] As to the participation of civil society, the experts praised the fact that they had seen the active engagement of a wide range of civil society

---

[23]It is also translated as the "Presidential Office Human Rights Consultative Committee," available at http://english.president.gov.tw/Page/225. Accessed 28 Dec 2017.

[24]It was decided at a meeting on 12 Apr 2012.

[25]The list of members and the process of the first international review is available at http://www.humanrights.moj.gov.tw/ct.asp?xItem=283761&ctNode=32959&mp=200. Accessed 28 Dec 2017.

[26]Concluding Observations and Recommendations Adopted by the International Group of Independent Experts, Review of the Initial Reports of the Government of Taiwan on the Implementation of the International Human Rights Covenants (1 Mar 2013), para. 4.

groups in all aspects of the review process, and that they received a large number of detailed alternative reports and they held focused hearings to enable non-governmental groups to provide input into the process.[27]

In April 2016, Taiwan issued the second state reports of the two Covenants, and the second international review by independent experts, most of whom had participated in the initial review,[28] took place in January 2017. The two panels of international experts in reviewing the second state reports of the two Covenants expressed once again their appreciation of Taiwan's exemplary commitment to the process of monitoring compliance, and the very active engagement of civil society groups.[29]

Based on the success of the two Covenants' reports and reviews, the CEDAW Implementation Act has adopted a similar process. It is stipulated that the government must establish a reporting system for eliminating all forms of discrimination against women, provide a national report every four years, and invite all relevant experts and representatives of non-government organizations to peruse such reports, and based on the comments and suggestions so provided, the government should endeavor to review the current circumstances and draw up subsequent resolutions.[30] The initial state report of the CEDAW was issued and reviewed in 2009, and the second state report was issued in 2013, with the international review in 2014. The third state report was released in December 2017.[31]

Article 7 of the CRC Implementation Act adopts a similar state report and review system, stipulating that the government should submit its initial state report within two years after the Implementation Act becomes effective, that state reports should be filed very five years, representatives from private organizations should be invited to review the reports, and the government should review and study subsequent policies based on their opinions. Taiwan's initial state report of the CRC was issued in November 2016, followed by an international review in November 2017.[32]

Having reflected on the previous experiences of state reports and reviews, the Implementation Act of the CRPD has a rather detailed provision regarding the CRPD state reports and international reviews. The initial state report should be submitted within two years after the Implementation Act becomes effective, and thereafter state reports should be filed every five years. For reviewing state reports,

---

[27] *Id.*, at para. 5.

[28] The list of members and the process of the second international review are available at http://www.humanrights.moj.gov.tw/ct.asp?xItem=445282&CtNode=44519&mp=200. Accessed 28 Dec 2017.

[29] Concluding Observations and Recommendations adopted by the International Review Committee, Review of the Second Reports of the Government of Taiwan on the Implementation of the International Human Rights Covenants (20 Jan 2017), para. 4 and 5.

[30] The CEDAW Implementation Act, art. 6.

[31] The state reports of the CEDAW and the process of the international review are available at https://www.gec.ey.gov.tw/news.aspx?n=D9EB035103686D4C. Accessed 28 Dec 2017.

[32] The initial state report of the CRC and the process of the international review are available at http://www.crcreview.org.tw/. Accessed 28 Dec 2017.

relevant academic experts and representatives from private organizations—particularly those who have had experience in affairs concerning the rights of persons with disabilities in the UN and related systems—are to be invited. After the international review, the government is obligated to review and study subsequent policies based on the opinions provided in the international reviews, and regularly check on the performance of the reporting system.[33] The initial state report of the CRPD was issued in December 2015, and the international review took place at the end of October.[34]

2.4 Providing Human Rights Education and Training

The recent accessions to these international human rights conventions have created unprecedented challenges for governmental institutions at all levels in terms of their capacity building for human rights implementation. Training and education are urgently needed. Yet, the Implementation Acts of the two Covenants and the CEDAW did not specify any provision for providing relevant training and education. Aside from obligating the government to prioritize funding for human rights implementation.[35] Having learned from past experiences, the Implementation Acts of the CRC and the CRPD specify the government's obligation to provide education and training and to prioritize financial resources for that purpose.[36]

For the two Covenants, the government has devoted efforts to provide the relevant training materials and to initiate training programs for civil servants, even without specific statutory requirements.[37] For the CEDAW, online courses have been developed,[38] and the Department of Gender Equality under the cabinet has been vigorous in developing various educational programs, including the gender Impact Assessment, gender accounting program, gender budget program, gender analysis, and the gender consciousness empowerment program.[39]

---

[33]The Implementation Act of the CRPD, art. 7.

[34]The initial state report of the CRPD and the process of the international review are available at https://www.sfaa.gov.tw/SFAA/Pages/Detail.aspx?nodeid=834&pid=6190. Accessed 28 Dec 2017.

[35]The Implementation Act of the two Covenants, art. 7; the Implementation Act of the CEDAW, art. 7.

[36]The Implementation Act of the CRC, art. 6 & 8; the Implementation Act of the CRPD, art. 6 & 9.

[37]Huang P, Liang Gongyue Shixingfa Jizhi Shixing [兩公約施行法機制實行] [The Implementation Act of the two Covenants and its Implementation], https://www.tahr.org.tw/files/newsletter/201003/013.pdf. Accessed 17 Nov 2017.

[38]Civil Servants online learning platform, https://elearn.hrd.gov.tw/mooc/index.php. (in Chinese). Accessed 22 Nov 2017.

[39]Gender Equality Committee of the Executive Yuan, Xingzhengyuan Suoshu Ge Jiguan Tuidong Xingbie Zhuliuhua Shishi Jihua (Nian 103–106) Shuominghui Jianbao Ziliao [行政院所屬各機關推動性別主流化實施計畫] (The materials of the press conference of the subordinate institutions of the Executive Yuan promoting the gender-mainstreaming project in the year 103–106), http://www.gec.ey.gov.tw/cp.aspx?n=02A3667FED9E6B98. Accessed 22 Nov 2017.

The Ministry of Health and Welfare is in charge of promotion of the CRC and the CRPD and their relevant education and training programs. With the specific requirement in both Implementation Acts, the Ministry has launched a five-year plan of promotion and training from 2014 to 2019. In order to promote both the CRC and the CRPD, the Ministry is planning to form a group of capable instructors and develop training programs aimed at capacity building in government and in society at large.

3 Leading Actors Facilitating the Implementation Acts

Beyond the above-discussed mechanisms provided by the Implementation Acts what has been pivotal to the success of implementation of these acceded human rights conventions is the relentless effort made by a few leading actors. Without them, the Implementation Acts alone would not have been as effective. These key leading actors include the Advisory Committee of Human Rights under the Presidential Office, the Ministry of Justice, the courts, and human rights groups.

3.1 The Advisory Committee of Human Rights Under the Presidential Office

Unlike most UN member states, Taiwan has not yet created an independent national human rights commission responsible for implementation of international human rights instruments in accordance with the Paris Principles. When the government decided to ratify the two Covenants in 2009, it decided to set up an advisory committee for human rights under the Presidential Office which would be responsible for the supervision of international human rights implementation before the establishment of a national human rights commission.[40] The Advisory Committee for Human Rights under the Presidential Office was established in 2010. The Committee consists of 15 to 21 members, appointed by the President from government representatives, nongovernmental organizations and human rights experts and scholars, with a term of two years.[41]

The first-term Committee was particularly critical to the success of the implementation of the two Covenants. One committee member, Professor Mab Huang of the Soochow University Human Rights Program, played a key role. In the first few

[40]The development of the committee is available at http://english.president.gov.tw/Page/225. Accessed 28 Dec 2017.

[41]The organic regulation of the committee is available at http://english.president.gov.tw/Page/231. Accessed 28 Dec 2017.

meetings of the Committee, it was decided that Taiwan's initial state reports of the two Covenants should be written in accordance with the rules and processes of state report submissions provided in the two Covenants. The Committee advised the government to submit the initial state reports to the UN and they were to be reviewed by the mechanism of the two Covenants, and if rejected, as a back-up plan, the review of the initial state reports were to be done by a group of independent international human rights experts with experience in UN-related mechanisms. A consensus was also reached that the process of reviewing state reports would heavily involve nongovernmental organizations and human rights groups, for example, having them submit shadow reports to counter-balance the government's views.[42]

It was the back-up plan that was eventually implemented and received acclaim. The committee watched the process of issuing state reports and conducting international reviews very closely and provided useful advice at each step of the process. Its hard work has certainly paid off. The initial doubts regarding the capacity of the Committee as a human rights institution, given its advisory nature, were soon dispelled, and a certain level of institutional trust and confidence in the Committee has gradually been built up.

3.2 *Ministry of Justice*

Under the ICCPR and ICESCR, state reports of member states are submitted to and reviewed by the Human Rights Committee and the Economic, Social and Cultural Rights Committee respectively. The technical assistance, however, is provided by their respective Secretariats, which should be neutral and independent in assisting member states in dealing with the issues brought up by member states, including the delivery of the files for member states, assisting the respective committees to order the List of Issues and Concluding Observations, and the delivery of the final decisions made by the Committees.[43]

Because Taiwan cannot submit its state reports for review by these international human rights conventions, it has to undertake international reviews by its own initiative. As decided by the Advisory Committee of Human Rights under the Presidential Office, invited international experts would serve as independent reviewers. Yet, deciding which institution or government agency would serve as a neutral Secretariat to help communications between the group of international experts and the government under review became quite a challenge.[44] It was suggested by human rights groups that the role of the Secretariat should not be

[42]The meeting records of the committee are available at http://www.president.gov.tw/Page/227/3/. Accessed 28 Dec 2017.

[43]ICCPR, art. 36; ICESCR, art. 16.

[44]Chang (2013a), p 141.

performed by government agencies but should be carried out by certain accredited and neutral institutions, such as a renowned international human rights organization, the bar association or a university human rights center, among others.[45] Regrettably however, it was still decided that the Ministry of Justice, which has served as the Secretariat for the Advisory Committee of Human Rights under the Presidential Office, would serve as the Secretariat for the international review of the two Covenants' initial state reports. To ease concerns as to the neutrality of the Ministry of Justice in the process of the international review, it was also decided that an advisory committee composed of four members from civil society and three members from the Advisory Committees of Human Rights under the Presidential Office would be formed to advise the Ministry of Justice.[46]

The problem of the Ministry of Justice serving as the Secretariat for the international review of the two Covenants' state reports can be illustrated by an incident related to death penalty executions at the end of 2012, just months before the international review of February 2013.[47] In November 2012, it was reported that there might be death penalty executions by the Ministry of Justice, drawing serious attention from international experts who urged the government not to take any action before the review. Yet, under public pressure, six death row inmates were executed in December. Tensions suddenly arose between the international experts and the Ministry of Justice which was serving as the Secretariat for the international review, gravely affecting the preparatory process.[48] Although the first international review of the two Covenants' initial state reports was eventually completed successfully, the challenge of having the Ministry of Justice as the Secretariat remained unresolved.[49]

Notwithstanding the perplexing role of the Ministry of Justice, many of its staff members have made substantial contributions to the issuance of state reports and the undertaking of international reviews. For example, one prosecutor, Mr. Ming-Li Kuo, who worked as a key staff member in the Secretariat, made enormous efforts in learning about the writing of state reports and the preparation of international reviews, and wrote to share his experiences.[50] Without these initial efforts made to support the process of state reports and reviews, as stipulated in the two Covenants, the processes of other human rights instruments including the CEDAW, the CRC and the CRPD would not have been as smooth.

[45] *Id.*, at p 143.
[46] *Id.*, at pp 143–144.
[47] *Id.*, at pp 144–145.
[48] *Id.*, at pp 144–145.
[49] *Id.*, at pp 145.
[50] See generally Kuo (2013).

3.3 The Judiciary

One strong indication that these human rights conventions have fully attained domestic legal status is the increase in judicial references, to the rights and freedoms enshrined in these conventions.[51] However, in the first international review of the two Covenants, the international experts observed that "the Covenants continue to be invoked only rarely in judicial decision-making."[52] Compared to judicial practices elsewhere, references to international human rights by Taiwanese courts are indeed very rare, but they have gradually been increasing since the recent accession to those international human rights conventions.

Prior to the implementation of the two Covenants, Taiwan's Constitutional Court made occasional references to international human rights instruments, mostly to the ICCPR and the CRC. Since the recent incorporations, the number of references to international human rights in the majority of opinions has not increased, but in separate opinions by individual judges the number of references has seen a drastic increase, not only in terms of quantity but also in terms of their quality and the depth of the discussions. The references to the ICESCR have also seen a significant increase compared to the number of references before the Implementation Act.[53]

Criminal cases—particularly death penalty decisions by the Supreme Court—have seen an increase in the number of references that are made to the provisions of the ICCPR. Some refer to Article 6 of the ICCPR to revoke the death penalty, while others may make reference to "the most serious crimes" in the same article to justify imposition of the death sentence. In addition, references to the guarantee of due process and the right to a fair trial, as guaranteed by Articles 14 and 15 of the ICCPR, have been frequently made. Most references were made to strengthen—rather than to contradict—domestic rules of procedure with human rights elements in those criminal cases.[54]

To the surprise of many, there has been an increase in the number of references to international human rights made by administrative courts. From 10 December 2009—when the Implementation Act of the two Covenants came into effect—to 31 August 2013, there were 39 decisions made by the Supreme Administrative Court which referenced the two Covenants, 65 decisions by the Taipei High Administrative Court, 3 decisions by the Taitung High Administrative Court, and 3 decisions by the Kaohsiung High Administrative Court.[55] These references, how-

[51]Chang (2011), p 593.

[52]Concluding Observations and Recommendations Adopted by the International Group of Independent Experts, Review of the Initial Reports of the Government of Taiwan on the Implementation of the International Human Rights Covenants (1 Mar 2013), para. 14.

[53]Chang (2009c), pp 253–272, Chang (2015), pp 20–21.

[54]Chang (2012b), pp 23–31.

[55]Liu (2016), p 83.

ever, were not at all critical to the decisions, and most references were actually made by the litigant parties rather than by the judges.[56] In addition, most references were made to the provisions, and only very few referred to the General Comments of the two Covenants.[57] Overall, however, references to international human rights in administrative litigation have been increasing. The steadiest rise has been seen in the decisions by the Supreme Administrative Court, while the rise in the decisions by other administrative courts has not been as evident. Also noteworthy is that more and more litigant parties are making reference to international human rights in their litigation.[58]

Most references have been made to the two Covenants and less to the CEDAW, the CRC and the CRPD. It may be because the two Covenants entail a wide range of rights whereas other conventions have many more specifically targeted groups. In addition, implementation of the two Covenants was earlier than that of the other international human rights conventions, and it is only natural that judges have become more familiar with the two Covenants than with other human rights conventions.[59]

3.4 Human Rights Groups and Strong Advocacy

Most pivotal in the implementation of these incorporated international human rights instruments is the strong advocacy by human rights groups. As soon as the Implementation Act of the two Covenants entered into force, a civil alliance including a wide range of human rights groups and social organizations was formed and named "Covenants Watch" to monitor the government's compliance with, and the progress of, the implementations.[60] Covenants Watch together with many other women's groups, children's rights advocacy groups and groups concerned with the rights of persons with disabilities have actively participated in the process of writing, submitting and reviewing state reports, preparing shadow reports counter-balancing the views of the government, and engaging in dialogues with international experts to understand human rights challenges in Taiwan.[61]

The advocacy of human rights groups has not been limited to the process of state reports and reviews, but it has been extended to other ventures as well. For example, immediately after the Implementation Act of the two Covenants became effective, the Taiwan Alliance to End the Death Penalty decided to test the legal

---

[56]Liao (2014), pp 4–5.

[57]*Id.*, at p 7.

[58]Liu (2016), pp 81–83.

[59]*Id.*, at p 84.

[60]Covenants Watch, English, http://covenantswatch.org.tw/english/. Accessed 28 Dec 2017.

[61]Chang (2013b), p 26.

applicability of the Covenants to the case of the death penalty and the rights of death row inmates.[62] Even though their petition was dismissed,[63] they successfully pressed the Constitutional Court to consider the legal applicability of the two Covenants—to which the Constitutional Court did not make any denial—and exposed the judicial shallowness by openly challenging the Court's understandings and interpretations of the Covenants' rights.[64] Such initial advocacy, and that which has followed it, have successfully created a discourse connecting death penalty issues and the ICCPR provisions, further generating an increase in references to the ICCPR provisions by the Supreme Court when confronting death penalty issues.[65]

Taiwan's women's groups have an even longer history of making references to the CEDAW in their advocacy. In the 1990s, the Awakening Foundation lobbied for an amendment to the Gender Equality in Employment Law by making reference to the CEDAW, though without detailed description.[66] In April 2004, the National Alliance of Taiwan Women's Associations together with other human rights groups participated in the Commission on the Status of Women Conference and made the first pledge to have the CEDAW become domestically applicable.[67] The lobby for acceding to the CEDAW succeeded in 2007, while the failure of depositing it with the UN was seen as a defeat. Nevertheless, women's groups continued to work on the passage of the CEDAW Implementation Act and have been actively engaged in the process of implementation, including writing and submitting shadow reports and holding alternative dialogues with international experts.[68]

In the case of the CRC, children's rights groups became involved as early as the drafting of the CRC Implementation Act. After the CRC Implementation Act became effective, these groups decided to form an alliance—Taiwan's NGO for the CRC—focusing on the CRC implementation. In 2014, the alliance took advantage of a local election to urge all candidates for municipal mayors and county magistrates to enhance children's rights, especially the right of participation.[69] In 2017, to counter-balance the initial state report of the CRC, the alliance issued its own

---

[62]Yeh (2016), p 237.

[63]The dismissal was made at the 1358th Council meeting on 28 May 2010 and the 1418th Council meeting on 6 Jun 2014.

[64]Chang (2009b).

[65]See *supra* note 54 and accompanying text.

[66]Chang (2012c), p 56.

[67]Awakening Foundation, "Minjian Tuidong Taiwan Luoshi CEDAW Lianmeng" Dashiji [「民間推動臺灣落實CEDAW聯盟」大事紀] (The Momentum of the Civil Alliance Promoting the CEDAW in Taiwan), http://www.awakening.org.tw/upload/uploadfile-665.pdf. Accessed 28 Dec 2017.

[68]See Chang (2012a), pp 3–4.

[69]Ertong Shaonian Quanli Weihu Wang [兒童少年權利維護網] (Children and Teenage Protection Website), Ershao Zhengjian Fushuhua Kongtonghua Xianjinhua! Xianshizhang Gei Wen Ma? [兒少政見附屬化、空洞化、現金化!縣市長給問嗎?] (Subordinates, Hollows, and Pork Bucket the Teenage Policies! Local Government Election Candidates, What's Your Opinion?), http://www.cylaw.org.tw/about/policy-promote/TWNGOsforCRC/178). Accessed 18 Nov 2017.

alternative report and actively engaged in the dialogue on the international review.[70]

The advocacy groups for the rights of persons with disabilities have also been deeply engaged in the implementation process of the CRPD. Three groups, including the Taiwan Community Living Consortium, the League for Persons with Disabilities, and Covenants Watch, have all submitted their individual parallel reports on the implementation of the CRPD and handed in their responses to the List of Issues during the international review of the initial state report on the CRPD.

All in all, Taiwan's human rights groups with their strong advocacy have substantially contributed to the successful implementation of international human rights conventions. These human rights groups through their regional or global networks have built up capacities not only in monitoring but also in executing domestic implementation of these international human rights conventions.[71] They are the key to rejuvenating human rights discourse and bridging the gap between the government and civil society.

4 Conclusion

Recent years have witnessed enactment of Implementation Acts for the domestic incorporation of international human rights conventions in Taiwan. These Implementation Acts have stipulated a few key functions. They are to provide domestic legal effect for the rights and freedoms guaranteed in those international human rights conventions, to make a comprehensive overhaul of laws and regulations incompatible with the respective international human rights conventions, to obligate the government to issue state reports under the respective international human rights conventions and conduct independent international reviews, and to provide human rights education and training.

However, as important as the mechanisms stipulated in the Implementation Acts are, they alone cannot guarantee the successful implementation of international human rights conventions. As this chapter has illustrated, key leading actors with their relentless efforts are more pivotal. Among these actors, the Advisory Committee of Human Rights under the Presidential Office was specifically created for steering the process of implementation, and it has certainly earned a substantial degree of institutional trust and confidence through its acclaimed performance. The Ministry of Justice, serving as Secretariat for both the Advisory Committee of Human Rights under the Presidential Office and the international review of the two Covenants, has a much more controversial role in the implementation process. Another key actor is the

[70]2017 Ertong Quanli Gongyue Zhixing Zhi Tidai Baogao [2017年兒童權利公約執行之替代報告] (2017 Backup Report on the CRC Implementation), http://www.cylaw.org.tw/about/policy-promote/TWNGOsforCRC/249. Accessed 28 Dec 2017.

[71]Chang (2012c), pp 65–66.

judiciary which, by making reference to these human rights conventions, consequently strengthens their domestic legal effects. All in all, most pivotal actors in the implementation of these incorporated international human rights conventions are human rights groups. Without them and their strong advocacy, implementation of these international human rights conventions would not have been as effective and the human rights discourse not as rejuvenating and energetic. Looking forward, the key to continued success in the implementation of international human rights lies in liaisons with these human rights groups and their continuing and effective advocacy.

Acknowledgments I would like to acknowledge the superb research assistance provided by Ms. Wan-Ni Lin and Mr. Hsiang-Yu Liu in writing this chapter. All errors of course remain mine.

References

2017 Ertong Quanli Gongyue Zhixing Zhi Tidai Baogao [2017 年兒童權利公約執行之替代報告] (2017 Backup Report on the CRC Implementation), http://www.cylaw.org.tw/about/policy-promote/TWNGOsforCRC/249. Accessed 28 Dec 2017

Awakening Foundation, "Minjian Tuidong Taiwan Luoshi CEDAW Lianmeng" Dashiji [「民間推動臺灣落實CEDAW聯盟」大事紀] (The Momentum of the Civil Alliance in Promoting the CEDAW in Taiwan), http://www.awakening.org.tw/upload/uploadfile-665.pdf. Accessed 28 Dec 2017

Chang W-C (2009a) An isolated nation with global-minded citizens: bottom-up transnational constitutionalism in Taiwan. National Taiwan Univ Law Rev 4(3):203–235

Chang W-C (2009b) Case dismissed: distancing Taiwan from the international human rights community. In: Chang W-C, Chang C-F (eds) My country kills: constitutional challenges to the death penalty in Taiwan. Taiwan Alliance to End the Death Penalty, Taipei, pp 47–68

Chang W-C (2009c) Xianfa yu Guoji Renquanfa de Huiliu: Jianlun Woguo Dafaguan Jieshi Zhi Shijian [憲法與國際人權法的匯流: 兼論我國大法官解釋之實踐] (The Convergence of Constitutions and International Human Rights: On the Practice of Taiwan's Constitutional Interpretations). In: Liao F F-T (ed) Xianfa Jieshi Zhi Lilun Yu Shiwu di 6 Ji [憲法解釋之理論與實務第 6 輯] (Constitutional Interpretation: Theory and Practice No. 6). Academia Sinica, Taipei, pp 223–272

Chang W-C (2011) The convergence of constitutions and international human rights: Taiwan and South Korea in comparison. N C J Int Law & Commercial Regul 36:593–624

Chang W-C (2012a) Guoji Renquanfa yu Neiguo Renquan Baozhang de Huiliu: Jiji yi CEDAW Lai Luoshi Funu Renquan Ji Xingbie Pingdeng [國際人權法與內國人權保障的匯流: 積極以CEDAW來落實婦女人權及性別平等] (The Influx of International Human Rights Law and the Protection of Domestic Human Rights: Actively Implement Women's Human Rights and Gender Equality). Taiwan Renquan Cujinhui Jikan [臺灣人權促進會季刊] (Taiwan Association for Human Rights Quarterly) 2012 (Spring): 3–4

Chang W-C (2012b) Liang Gongyue Shishi Liang Zhounian de Jiantao: Yi Sifa Shijian Wei Hexin [兩公約實施兩周年的檢討: 以司法實踐爲核心] (An Examination of the Implementation of the Two Covenants After Two Years: With a Focus on Judicial Practice), Si Yu Yan: Renwen Yu Shehui Kexue Zazhi [思與言: 人文與社會科學雜誌] (Thoughts and Words: J Humanities and Social Science) 50(4): pp 7–43

Chang W-C (2012c) NGO Yu Kuaguo Xianzheng Zhi Fazhan: Taiwan Jiaru Guoji Renquan Gongyue de Shijian Weili [NGO與跨國憲政之發展: 以臺灣加入國際人權公約的實踐爲例] (NGOs and the Development of Transnational Constitutionalism: Experience in the

Internalization of International Human Rights Law in Taiwan) Taiwan Guojifa Jikan [臺灣國際法季刊] (Taiwan Int Law Quarterly) 9(3): 47–72

Chang W-C (2013a) Liang Gongyue Guoji Shencha de Kunju: Fawubu Zuowei Mishuchu de Dingwei Shidang [兩公約國際審查的困局: 法務部作爲秘書處的定位失當] (The Pitfalls of the International Review of the Two Covenants in Taiwan: The Ill-defined Role of the Ministry of Justice as Secretariat) Taiwan Renquan Jikan [臺灣人權學刊] (Taiwan Human Rights Law J) 2(1):141–150

Chang W-C (2013b) Taiwan Zhengfu Neng Bu Cankui Ma? Fei Zhengfu Zuzhi Zai Liang Gongyue Guojia Baogao Guoji Shencha de Jiaose Yu Dìngwei [臺灣政府, 能不慚愧嗎? 非政府組織在兩公約國家報告國際審查的角色與定位] (Can the Taiwan Government not be Ashamed? The Position and Defined Role of NGOs in the International Review of the State Report). Sifa Gaige Zazhì [司法改革雜誌] (Judicial Reform Magazine) 95:26–27

Chang W-C (2015) Guoji Renquan Gongyue yu Xianfa Jieshi: Huiliu de Moshi Gongneng Ji Taiwan Shijian [國際人權公約與憲法解釋:匯流的模式、功能及臺灣實踐] (International Human Rights Covenants and the Interpretation of Constitutional Interpretation: The Models and Functions of the Influx and Practice of Taiwan). Paper presented at Sifayuan Dafaguan 104 Niandu Xueshu Yantaohui—Renquan Gongyue Yu Woguo Xianfa Jieshi [司法院大法官 104 年度學術研討會—人權公約與我國憲法解釋] (Seminar of the Constitutional Court: International Human Rights Law and Constitutional Interpretation), Taipei, 5 Dec 2015

Chang W-C, Lu S-Y (2011) Liang Gongyue Yu Huanjing Renquan Zhuzhang [兩公約與環環人境權主張] (The Two International Human Rights Covenants and the Claim to Environmental Rights. Taiwan Renquan Jikan [臺灣人權學刊] (Taiwan Human Rights Q) 1(1):69–102

Chang W-C, Yeh J-R (2012) Internationalization of constitutional law. In: Rosenfeld M, Sajó A (eds) Oxford handbook of comparative constitutional law. Oxford University Press, Oxford, pp 1165–1184

Civil Servants online learning platform, https://elearn.hrd.gov.tw/mooc/index.php. (in Chinese) Accessed 22 Nov 2017

Concluding Observations and Recommendations Adopted by the International Group of Independent Experts, Review of the Initial Reports of the Government of Taiwan on the Implementation of the International Human Rights Covenants (1 Mar 2013)

Concluding Observations and Recommendations Adopted by the International Review Committee, Review of the Second Reports of the Government of Taiwan on the Implementation of the International Human Rights Covenants (20 Jan 2017)

Covenants Watch, English, http://covenantswatch.org.tw/english/. Accessed 22 Nov 2017

Ertong Shaonian Quanli Weihu Wang [兒童少年權利維護網] (Children and Teenage Protection Website), Ershao Zhengjian Fushuhua Kongtong Hua! Xianjin Xian Shizhang Gei Wen Ma? [兒少政見附屬化、空洞化、現金化!縣市長給問嗎?] (Subordinates, Hollows, and Pork Bucket the Teenage Policies! Local Government Election Candidates, What's Your Opinions?), http://www.cylaw.org.tw/about/policy-promote/TWNGOsforCRC/178). Accessed 18 Nov 2017

Gender Equality Committee of the Executive Yuan, https://www.ey.gov.tw/gec_en/News.aspx?n=98FF4D9BE97AB4B4&sms=5674ADAAA9DB9139. Accessed 28 Dec 2017

Gender Equality Committee of the Executive Yuan, Guidelines for Gender Equality Policy, http://www.gec.ey.gov.tw/cp.aspx?n=363DC330E476B467 (in Chinese). Accessed 22 Nov 2017

Gender Equality Committee of the Executive Yuan, The progress of examining the law and administrative orders and regulations violating the CEDAW, http://www.gec.ey.gov.tw/News.aspx?n=1662D3186C4B2F2D&sms=08DBC3A57A112D27 (in Chinese). Accessed 22 Nov 2017

Gender Equality Committee of the Executive Yuan, Xingzhengyuan Suoshu Gejiguan Tuidong Xingbie Zhuliuhua Shishi Jihua (Nian 103–106) Shuominghui Jianbao Ziliao [行政院所屬各機關推動性別主流化實施計畫] (The Materials of the Press Conference of the Subordinate Institutions of the Executive Yuan Promoting the Gender-Mainstreaming Project in Year 103–106), http://www.gec.ey.gov.tw/cp.aspx?n=02A3667FED9E6B98. Accessed 22 Nov 2017

Huang P, Liang Gongyue Shixingfa Jizhi Shixing [兩公約施行法機制實行] [The Implementation Act of the Two Covenants and its Implementation], https://www.tahr.org.tw/files/newsletter/201003/013.pdf. Accessed 17 Nov 2017

Kuo M-L (2013) Chuci Guojia Renquan Baogao Zhi Zhuanxue yu Shencha de Chubu Jiantao yu Zhanwang [初次國家人權報告之撰寫與審查的初步檢討與展望] (A Preliminary Survey and Prospects for the Drafting and Review of the Nation's Initial Human Right Reports). Taiwan Renquan Jikan [臺灣人權學刊] (Taiwan Human Rights Law J) 2(1):73–105

Liao FF-T (2014), Sifa Shenpan yu Liang Gongyue Renquan Baozhang Siwei Suo Mianlin Zhi Tiaozhan: Xingzheng Fayuan Tongyong Liang Gongyue zhi Jianshi [司法審判與兩公約人權保障思維所面臨之挑戰—行政法院適用兩公約之檢視] (Court's Challenges When Applying the ICCPR and the ICESCR—Review of the Judgments of the Administrative Courts). Faxue Congkan [法學叢刊] (Law Review) 234:1–42

Liu T-C (2016) Guoji Renquan Gongyue Neiguofahua Dui Sifa Shiwu de Yingxiang Yi Xingzheng Fayuan de Zaipan Wei Guancha Zhongxin [國際人權公約內國法化對司法事務的影響: 以行政法院的裁判爲觀察中心] (The Impact of International Human Rights Treaties on Judicial Practices after Their Incorporation into Domestic Law – Focusing on the Judgments of the Administrative Courts in the R.O.C. [Taiwan]). Faling Yuekan [法令月刊] (The Law Monthly) 67(10):78–103

Ministry of Justice, The progress of examining the law and administrative orders and regulations violating the Two Covenants, https://www.humanrights.moj.gov.tw/ct.asp?xItem=283349&CtNode=32910&mp=200. Accessed 22 Nov 2017

Yeh J-R (2016) The Constitution of Taiwan: A Contextual Analysis. Hart Publishing, Oxford

Yeh J-R, Chang W-C (2008) The emergence of transnational constitutionalism: its features, challenges and solutions. Penn State Univ Int Law Rev 27(1):89–124

Yeh J-R, Chang W-C (2014) A decade of changing constitutionalism in Taiwan. In: Chen AHY (ed) Constitutionalism in Asia in the Early Twenty-first Century. Cambridge University Press, Cambridge, pp 141–168, p 247

Zhonghua Minguo Weisheng Fuli Bu [中華民國衛生福利部] (Ministry of Health and Welfare), Lifa Yuan Sandu Tongguo Ertong Ji Shaonian Fuli Yu Quanyi Baozhangfa Xiuzheng Caoan [立法院三讀通過兒童暨少年福利與權益保障法修正草案] (The Amendment to the Protection of Children and Youth Welfare and Rights Act was passed by the Legislative Yuan), https://www.sfaa.gov.tw/SFAA/Pages/VDetail.aspx?nodeid=20&pid=4303. Accessed 17 Oct 2017

Zhonghua Minguo Weisheng Fuli Bu [中華民國衛生福利部] (Ministry of Health and Welfare), Lifa Yuan Sandu Tongguo Shenxin Zhangaizhe Quanyi Baozhangfa Xiuzheng Cao'an [立法院三讀通過身心障礙者權利保障法修正草案] (The Amendment to the People with Disabilities Rights Protection Act was passed by the Legislative Yuan), https://www.sfaa.gov.tw/SFAA/Pages/VDetail.aspx?nodeid=20&pid=4432. Accessed 17 Oct 2017

Wen-Chen Chang received a LL.B. (National Taiwan University) in 1992, a LL.M. (National Taiwan University) in 1995, a LL.M. (Yale Law School) in 1998, and a J.S.D. (Yale Law School) in 2001. She is currently Professor at the College of Law, National Taiwan University and the Director of the Policy and Law Center for Environmental Sustainability at the College of Law. Professor Chang is a leading scholar on constitutional law and human rights in Taiwan and has published major scholarly works on comparative constitutional law, including *Asian Courts in Context*, with Jiunn-rong Yeh (Cambridge University Press, 2015) and *Constitutionalism in Asia: Cases and Materials*, with Kevin YL Tan, Li-ann Thio and Jiunn-rong Yeh (Hart Publishing, 2014). Her teaching and research interests lie in comparative constitutional law, international human rights, international environmental law, administrative law, and law and society. She has served on the editorial boards for leading academic journals, including the *International Journal of Constitutional Law*, *Cambridge Journal of Global Constitutionalism: Human Rights, Democracy and the Rule of Law*, *Asian Journal of Comparative Law*, and *National Taiwan University Law Review*, among others. She was awarded the Outstanding Research Award by the Ministry of Science and Technology in 2015, the Junior Research Investigators Award by the Academia Sinica in 2012, the Wu Ta-You Memorial Award by the National Science Council in 2010, and the Excellence in Teaching Award by National Taiwan University in 2007.

Chapter 14
The Problems with the Incorporation of International Human Rights Law in Taiwan

Yean-Sen Teng

Abstract Though Taiwan is not a member state of the United Nations, it is determined to incorporate some international human rights treaties in the same way a usual state does. In 2009, the Government made every effort to "ratify" the International Covenant on Civil and Political Rights, the International Covenant on Economic, Social and Cultural Rights and the Convention on the Elimination of All Forms of Discrimination against Women into the domestic legal system in accordance with the "treaty obligation." Unsurprisingly, none of the instruments of ratification were successfully deposited with the Secretary-General of the United Nations. Two years later, the Government submitted its initial reports under the two Covenants to a group of ten international independent experts for review in Taiwan. In this connection, the Government and people of Taiwan have come to recognize that international human rights law constitutes an integral part of the legal system of Taiwan. With this recognition, the courts have occasionally applied or referred to the two Covenants in their decisions and judgments in spite of the doubts and criticism as to the validity of the international human rights treaties' rules. Apparently, the determination to internalize international human rights law into the domestic legal system of Taiwan is beyond any doubt; however, several problems have emerged subsequent to the failure of completing the process of ratification under international law. The problems may be summarized as follows. First, the question concerning the capacity to conclude international treaties and the nature of the legal effect as regards the unilateral act by Taiwan in the context of international law. Second, the status and effect of international human rights treaties in the domestic legal order of Taiwan, Third, there are questions concerning the method of incorporating international human rights treaties by enacting the Implementing Act, which was specifically designed to create the binding force of the treaty law within the jurisdiction of Taiwan. Fourth, the practice applied by the courts or in constitutional

This chapter is based on a conference paper presented at the ILA-ASIL Asia-Pacific Research Forum in Taipei.

Y.-S. Teng (✉)
Soochow University, Taipei, Taiwan
e-mail: teng@scu.edu.tw

J. A. Cohen et al. (eds.), *Taiwan and International Human Rights*, Economics, Law, and Institutions in Asia Pacific, https://doi.org/10.1007/978-981-13-0350-0_14

interpretation as regards the rights and freedoms in the human rights treaties. Without proper theory and adequate practices concerning how to incorporate international human rights treaties in Taiwan, international human rights law is nothing but an unexpected and unwelcome international law that has caused an unpleasant disturbance in the domestic legal order. That said, this chapter intends to elucidate the legal implications of these questions and the problems therein and to deliberate a possible solution for the judiciary to take the rights and fundamental freedoms seriously.

Keywords Capacity · Incorporation · Legitimacy · Validity

1 Introduction

Since Taiwan is not admitted to the United Nations as a proper state, it has been a marginalized actor in the international arena. Even so, it is not ignorant of the significance of human rights protection with respect to good governance in domestic affairs. In 2009, the Government made every effort to try to incorporate the International Covenant on Civil and Political Rights (hereinafter ICCPR) and the International Covenant on Economic, Social and Cultural Rights (hereinafter ICESCR) respectively into the domestic legal system in accordance with the treaty rules. Two years later,[1] the Government submitted its initial reports in accordance with the Act to Implement the International Covenant on Civil and Political Rights and the International Covenant on Economic, Social and Cultural Rights (the Implementing Act)[2] to a group of ten independent experts for review.[3] The process of drafting the reports was based on the United Nations Human Rights Committee's rules and guidelines. "The Government and people of Taiwan have demonstrated exemplary commitment to the process of monitoring compliance with the relevant

[1]According to Article 40(a), The States Parties to the present Covenant undertake to submit reports within one year of the entry into force of the present Covenant for the States Parties concerned. Since the two Covenants have never been operative in Taiwan, the right time to submit the initial report is nonexistent in a legal sense.

[2]The Implementing Act was enacted for the sole purpose of overcoming the situation of the impossibility of ratifying the two Covenants. With the Implementing Act, the two Covenants were regarded as having domestic legal status. Some other international human rights treaties, namely, the Convention on the Elimination of All Forms of Discrimination against Women, the Convention on the Rights of the Child and the Convention on the Rights of Persons with Disabilities are all incorporated in Taiwan in an identical manner and are similar in their content. They are: the Enforcement Act of the Convention on the Elimination of All Forms of Discrimination against Women, the Implementation Act of the Convention on the Rights of the Child and the Act to Implement the Convention on the Rights of Persons with Disabilities.

[3]The ten independent experts included Philip Alston, Nisuke Ando, Virginia Bonoan-Dandan, Theodoor van Boven, Jerome Cohen, Shanthi Dairiam, Asma Jahangir, Manfred Nowak, Eibe Riedel and Heisoo Shin.

human rights obligations," said the independent experts.[4] In the Concluding Observations and Recommendations, some 44 specific issues relating to the two Covenants were presented to the Government and the public, acknowledging the deficits and violations of human rights protection in Taiwan.[5] This was the first time the Government and people of Taiwan had recognized that international human rights law constitutes an integral part of the normative framework of the legal system of Taiwan. With this recognition, a few local courts began to apply the two Covenants in their decisions and judgments in spite of some criticism on the question of the validity of the human rights law. Several constitutional interpretations by the Justices of the Constitutional Court have occasionally referred to international human rights law or have treated it as material or an indirect source of law, instead of positive law, in their reasoning on constitutional interpretations.

In fact, as a result of the determination to incorporate international human rights law into the domestic legal system of Taiwan in accordance with treaty rules under international law, several problems have emerged subsequent to the failure of completing the process of ratification under international law. The first problem concerns the issue of the capacity to conclude international treaties, such as the two International Covenants on Human Rights or the Convention on the Elimination of All Forms of Discrimination against Women (hereinafter CEDAW).[6] Since Taiwan is not a member of the United Nations, it lacks the *locus standi* to ratify the two Covenants and the CEDAW in accordance with Article 48 of the ICCPR, Article 26 of the ICESCR and Article 18 of the CEDAW respectively. Not surprisingly, Taiwan has not successfully deposited the instruments of ratification; as a result, the unilateral act of declaring its willingness to be bound by the two Covenants and the CEDAW has cast doubt on the effects of the international obligation attached thereto. The second problem concerns the method of incorporating the two Covenants and the CEDAW by enacting the Implementing Act and Enforcement Act, which were purposely designed to create the binding force of treaty law within the jurisdiction of Taiwan. With respect to the method of incorporation of an international treaty, Taiwan, presumably, adopts the formal process or the monistic approach of incorporation of an international treaty, thus, an international treaty once ratified by the President directly constitutes an integral part of the domestic

---

[4]Concluding observations and recommendations on the initial reports of Taiwan adopted by the international group of independent experts, Taipei, 1 Mar 2013, at para. 4. http://www.humanrights.moj.gov.tw/HitCounter.asp?xItem=385451. Accessed 30 Sept 2017.

[5]*Id.*, at paras. 36–80. Other points concern general issues which include the national commission for the protection and promotion of human rights; United Nations core human rights treaties; the Implementation Act Relating to the International Covenants; judicial implementation of the Covenants; human rights education and training; transparency and participation in decision-making; corporate responsibility; transitional justice; equality and non-discrimination based on gender and the rights of indigenous peoples.

[6]The instrument of ratification was deposited with the Secretary-General of the UN by the then President on 9 Feb 2007, two years earlier than the instruments of ratification to the Two Covenants. The result was rejection by the Secretary-General based on GA Resolution 2758 that states that the People's Republic of China is the sole representative of China. See also note 14.

legal system. Given that the human rights treaties have been incorporated into the domestic legal system, a theoretical question remains open. Can the two Covenants and the CEDAW become integral parts of the legal system of Taiwan by means of the Implementing Act or Enforcement Act, without successfully completing the process of ratification? Thus, if there is no legal obligation on the government, including the judiciary, to comply with international human rights law under domestic law, it is not clear whether the rights and freedoms stipulated in the human rights treaties are justiciable before the courts. This leads to the third problem: What is the methodology to be applied by the courts for recognizing those rights and freedoms contained within the human rights treaties under the domestic legal system? In addition, the problem is even more arduous considering that the process of ratification has not been completed.

In reality, these problems have caused some inconsistencies in court decisions with regard to the rights stipulated in the Covenants and the CEDAW. It is definitely detrimental to the inner morality of the law *stricto sensu* and the rule of law. Since the two Covenants and the CEDAW have been incorporated into the domestic legal system by Implementing Acts, the effect of direct applicability of the treaty is beyond any doubt. However, there is neither a clear rule as to the effect of a "ratified" treaty, nor is there any settled practice by the judiciary in this respect. The effect of direct applicability is thus open to doubt. In the absence of a proper process to incorporate international treaties, international human rights law is treated as an unexpected and unwelcome international law within the domestic legal order. It is generally held that constitutional law is sufficient to protect human rights.[7] The doubt is sometimes connected to the confusion between direct effect and direct applicability. Conceptually, direct applicability means that the ratified treaty per se constitutes an integral part of domestic law, therefore, it should be applied directly in domestic courts. Direct effect, on the other hand, concerns the rights protected by a treaty provision that is justiciable before a court without need of further legislation. Given that human rights treaties have been legalized in Taiwan by means of Implementing Acts the effect of direct applicability is beyond any doubt in terms of their legal status. The confusion has led to a skeptical approach in the application of international human rights treaty law in the decisions of the judiciary.

That said, this chapter endeavors to elucidate the legal implications of these problems and their consequences with respect to the two Covenants, especially in the practice of the judiciary.

[7]That is why the constitutional interpretation in Taiwan has deliberately ignored the status of human rights law in the domestic legal order. The deficit is discussed in part 5 of this chapter.

2 The Question of the Capacity to Conclude International Treaties

A state in international law has the capacity to enter into legal relations with other states and international organizations in accordance with the Montevideo Convention on the Rights and Duties of States of 1933.[8] In connection with this, a state has the capacity to conclude a bilateral agreement with another state or a multilateral treaty with other states. Thus, a state is a subject with full capacity under international law. However, the question remains, "what is the capacity of a subject in international law?" Before we answer this question, however, a predetermined question is, "who can be the subject?" In a domestic legal system, the word "subject" refers to persons including natural and artificial persons. A natural person by nature possesses the capacity to conduct all matters whether legal or non-legal. The capacity of a natural person is thus inherent and genuine, rather than derivative from some other authority. Human beings as natural persons are autonomous, free and capable of enjoying some inalienable rights that belong to human persons only. An artificial person or legal person created by law only has the capacity to enjoy certain rights, which are limited to the purpose and aims of the legal person. As a corollary, the capacity of a subject under a legal system is closely related to the policy of the system considering who should have the power or competence to act freely with respect to the creation of legal relations.[9] Thus, the subject under a given legal system has the capacity to create the legal relations as conferred by law. This is the traditional paradigm of civil law which treats natural persons as subjects with the capacity to enter into contracts with other parties, whether natural or legal persons.

In international law, however, the only subject which has the full capacity to enter into legal relations with another subject is a state.[10] Interestingly, a state is an artificial person in terms of the origin of its existence. In other words, it is created by its people. Thus, the capacity of states is in nature derivative and subjective. It is derivative because the capacity is conferred by the people who endow the entity with competence to enter into legal relations with other entities in the international community. With reference to the issue of its subjective nature, other than the conferral of capacity by its people, the capacity of a state requires approval from other states from an international perspective. The capacity needs to be verified by other states' approval, which is the outcome of the doctrine of recognition in

[8] Montevideo Convention on the Rights and Duties of States, art.1, 26 Dec 1933, 165 L.N.T.S. 19. The state as a person of international law should possess the following qualifications: capacity to enter into relations with the other states.

[9] Jennings and Watts (1996), p. 120.

[10] *Id.*

international law. The declaratory nature of recognition[11] in international law demonstrates, on the one hand, that the capacity of a state is derived from its people, rather than from other states. On the other hand, it is operative only after the fact of its existence has been recognized by other states that want to enter into relations with the state concerned. Given that the recognition is simply evidence that some requirements under international law have been satisfied, the existence of a state is not a social fact; rather, it is a legal fact because it meets the requirements under international law that mean that the state can legally be declared as existing.[12] Among the requirements, the most important one is the conferral of capacity on the entity. With the conferral of capacity, the state as a legal entity has the competence and power to act as a subject in the international community.

The question is whether Taiwan has the capacity to ratify an international human rights treaty. A negative answer may be found in Article 48 of the ICCPR and Article 26 of the ICESCR respectively. However, this answer does not address the question exactly. The answer to the question of whether or not Taiwan is endowed with the capacity is twofold. First, from the domestic perspective, the people in Taiwan must endow the state with capacity; secondly, the conferred capacity has to have been recognized by other states in the international community.

Viewing the function of the effective government in Taiwan, whether it is called the Republic of China or Taiwan, there is no doubt that the people of Taiwan have conferred on it the capacity to act as a state in the international arena. As regards the international perspective, General Assembly Resolution 2758 on the restoration of the lawful rights of the People's Republic of China in the United Nations[13] has literally denounced the capacity of Taiwan or the Republic of China to represent the whole of China in the UN system,[14] Taiwan, however, is not deprived of its capacity to act as a state in the international community as there are 20 states that recognize it. Taiwan, then, satisfies the criteria of being a state and is recognized as such by other states; in this connection, the truth of Taiwan as a state in the context of international law is beyond any doubt.

Following from that, one wonders whether the unilateral incorporation of human rights treaties into the domestic legal system of Taiwan can create international obligations in the absence of proper ratification. This is based on the rationale discussed in the Nuclear Test case.[15] The Court held, "[o]ne of the basic principles

---

[11]The declaratory theory is adopted by most writers in international law. The Arbitral Commission of the EC Conference on Yugoslavia was of the opinion that recognition was purely declaratory; however, it did confer certain rights and obligations under international law. See Arbitral Commission of the EC Conference on Yugoslavia, Opinion 8, 31 I.L.M. 1521 (4 July 1992).

[12]Jennings and Watts, *supra* note 9, at pp. 128–130.

[13]G.A. Res. 2758(XXVI), GAOR, 26th Sess., Supp. No. 29, UN Doc A/8429, at 2 (25 Oct 1971).

[14]On 15 June 2009, the Secretary-General of the UN rejected the instrument of ratification of the Government of Taiwan to the two Covenants by noting that the People's Republic of China was the only legal representative in the UN in accordance with G.A. resolution 2758.

[15]Nuclear Tests (Australia v. France), 1974 ICJ 253 (20 Dec); Nuclear Tests (New Zealand v. France), 1974 ICJ 457 (20 Dec).

governing the creation and performance of legal obligation… is the principle of good faith…Just as the very rule of *pacta sunt servanda* in the law of treaties is based on good faith, so also is the binding character of an international obligation assumed by unilateral declaration."[16] The legal effects of the unilateral act or declaration are even recognized as constituting a general rule of international law[17] and formulated by the International Law Commission in its Guiding Principles Applicable to the Unilateral Declaration of States Capable of Creating Legal Obligations 2006.[18] Point 2 states, "[a]ny State possesses capacity to undertake legal obligation through unilateral declaration." As Taiwan is not devoid of the capacity to act as a state under international law, in this regard the unilateral act of Taiwan to incorporate international human treaties is capable of incurring international responsibility to implement human rights obligations.

3 The Problem of Institutional Flaws in Incorporating a Treaty

How international law is incorporated into domestic legal systems is an issue of domestic law, since international law is devoid of any clear rule to that effect.[19] Without the acceptance of sovereign states, one wonders whether an international rule can exist. This is the traditional voluntarist point of view. Thus, the interaction and relationship of international law and national law generally suggest that they are two distinct legal systems. International law is not considered an integral part of national law directly. The dualism or different subject-matter theory is apt for the explanation of the relationship between international law and national law. The reasons, in summary, are twofold: (a) the paramount sovereignty of a state and (b) the doctrine of democratic legitimacy. The consensual nature of international law explains the supremacy of state sovereignty in this regard.[20] As to the doctrine of democratic legitimacy, it concerns the idea of constitutionalism that the congress or the Parliament is the only institution that is entrusted with the power to legislate for the people and the government. In that connection, the manner and method of incorporating international rules, especially treaty provisions, into the domestic legal order are subject to constitutional rules or national legislation, which provide the procedures for the incorporation of international laws.

However, general rules of international law or customary international law, which most states would not repudiate, are considered to be incorporated

[16]Nuclear Tests (Australia v. France), 1974 ICJ 253, para. 46 (20 Dec).

[17]Harris (2010), p. 50.

[18]Rep. of the Int'l Law Comm'n, 58 Sess., 1 May-9 June, 3 July-11 Aug 2006, UN Doc. A/61/10; GAOR, 61st Sess., Supp. No. 10, p. 367, quoted in Harris, *supra* note 17, at p. 51.

[19]See Denza (2014).

[20]Jennings and Watts, *supra* note 9, at pp. 14–15.

automatically into national law. Whatever has received the common consent of states in the international community must have received the assent of any state. That said, monism is apt for the manifestation of the relationship between international custom and national law.[21]

In practice, the methods of incorporation of treaty rules are either through the enactment of an *ad hoc* act in order for the treaty rules to be transformed into national rules or to approve the treaty as such without reformulating the treaty rules. Once a state assents to a treaty by ratification, the treaty shall have binding force upon the state. However, the treaty rules do not necessarily produce any legal effects within the domestic legal order of the ratifying state unless the treaty is transposed into domestic law. This is the process of substantive incorporation. Once the treaty has been transposed into domestic law, it then becomes an integral part of the domestic legal order. With regard to a state that does not transpose the ratified treaty but is able to apply it directly within its jurisdiction, the process is procedural.

The practice of the incorporation of international treaty law in Taiwan has never been one of substantive incorporation. In other words, a ratified treaty constitutes an integral part of domestic law without need for further legislation. Thereafter, the treaty can be applied directly.[22] Article 63 of the Constitution provides for the process of incorporation of international treaties. It states, "[t]he Legislative Yuan[23] shall have the power to decide by resolution upon statutory…bills or conclusion of …treaties." By this provision, a treaty which is to be constituted as an integral part of the domestic legal order must pass the resolution by the Legislative Yuan as a bill does. This process of internal ratification satisfies the doctrine of democratic legitimacy. After that, the President has the power to process the international ratification under Article 38 of the Constitution.[24] Thus, whenever there is a treaty to be passed by resolution by the Legislative Yuan under the Constitution the first thing to be resolved is that it is a treaty. Apparently, this is not a process most states follow, since the Vienna Convention on the Law of Treaties has defined the meaning of a treaty. It provides in Article 2.1(a), "[a]n international agreement concluded between states in written form and governed by international law, whether embodied in a single instrument or in two or more related instruments and whatever its particular designation." However, in the case of Taiwan, a marginalized actor in the international

[21]Klabbers (2013).

[22]The concept of direct applicability should not be confused with that of direct effect or that of a self-executing treaty. The former refers to the doctrine of sources of law. A ratified treaty therefore becomes a part of the formal sources of domestic law; however, the direct effect or self-executing treaty concerns the legal basis of a claimable right. The subject matter of direct applicability refers to the whole treaty concerned; however, the self-executing treaty concerns a specific provision in the treaty which is precise and unconditional in its meaning. No further legislation is needed for its application.

[23]The highest legislative organ in the constitutional law of Taiwan.

[24]Zhonghua Minguo Xianfa, art. 38 (Taiwan) ("The President shall, in accordance with the provisions of this Constitution, exercise the powers of concluding treaties, declaring war and making peace").

community, it is not clear as regards the meaning of a treaty when it lacks the *locus standi* to ratify treaties in the context of international law. In Judicial Yuan[25] Interpretation (hereinafter J.Y. Interpretation) No. 329,[26] it declares, "[w]within the Constitution, a treaty means an international agreement concluded between the Republic of China and other nations or international organizations whose title may apply to a treaty, convention or an agreement…Its content involves important subject matters of the state or directly concerns rights and obligations of the people and has the legal effects as law. Such agreements which employ the title of "treaty," "convention" or "agreement" with a ratification clause should be sent to the Legislative Yuan for deliberation." The criteria of substantive aspects were reiterated in the Act of Concluding Treaties, which was adopted by the Legislative Yuan on 1 July 2015. The criteria concern the effects of the treaty in question, namely, the subject matter must be significant or have sufficient legal force to affect people's rights and obligations. The criteria are *prima facie* related to the doctrine of democratic legitimacy. In this regard, the incorporation of the two Covenants and the CEDAW satisfied the criteria when the Legislative Yuan passed a resolution to approve them on 22 April 2009 and 5 January 2007, respectively. On the same day, the Legislative Yuan promulgated the "Act to Implement the International Covenant on Civil and Political Rights and the International Covenant on Economic, Social and Cultural Rights." The Enforcement Act of the Convention on the Elimination of All Forms of Discrimination against Women was not enacted until 20 May 2011.

Conceptually, the validity of start from here the Implementing Act or the Enforcement Act is based on that of the two Covenants and the CEDAW after they are properly incorporated. In the Act of Concluding Treaties, Article 11 expressly provides for the process, stating "[a]fter the treaties are approved by the Legislative Yuan, they should be processed as follows: (a) when a ratification, acceptance, assent or accession provision is required (in the treaties), the competent authority shall refer the treaties to the Executive Yuan, which shall submit them to the President to issue the instrument of ratification, acceptance, assent or accession…in accordance with the treaty provision to exchange or deposit the relevant instrument, and when they become effective, the competent authority shall refer the treaties to the Executive Yuan, which shall submit them to the President for promulgation." After the two Covenants and the CEDAW were approved by the Legislative Yuan, the President was required to deposit the instruments of ratification with the Secretary-General of the UN to complete the process of incorporation and ratification. Unsurprisingly, the two instruments of ratification were turned down by the Secretary-General on the

[25]The Judicial Yuan is the highest judicial organ in the constitutional law of Taiwan. It is in charge of civil, criminal, and administrative cases, and cases concerning disciplinary measures against civil servants.

[26]Sifayuan Jieshi [司法院解釋] (Judicial Yuan Interpretation) No. 329 (24 Dec 1993) (Taiwan).

grounds of a lack of *locus standi*.[27] For the purpose of rectifying the impossibility of ratifying an international treaty, the said Act provides a remedial process by stipulating that, "[i]n special cases when the exchange or deposit is not possible, the competent authority shall refer them to the Executive Yuan, which shall submit them to the President for promulgation." That said, another question emerges. Are the Implementing Act and the Enforcement Act still valid when the relevant treaties are not operative in the context of international law? Since the process of depositing the ratification documents has not been completed, the treaties are not effective with respect to the relevant treaty provision. Following from that, even if the Implementing Act or the Enforcement Act is valid in technical terms, there is an institutional flaw in the incorporation of the two Covenants in the context of constitutional law. For an international treaty to be operative within the domestic legal order, it requires the approval of the Legislative Yuan and the submission of the instrument of ratification to the relevant depositary. Consequently, when the process and procedure under the Constitution fails, appealing to the exceptional provision in the said Act is a convenient way to circumvent the process and procedure and is a serious institutional flaw in that regard. Without an adequate amendment in the Constitution to remedy the deficit, the Implementing Act or the Enforcement Act cannot be considered to possess the authority to validate international human rights law in Taiwan.

4 The Question Concerning the Application of Treaty Norms

The highly controversial aspect of both the Implementing Act and the Enforcement Act is, however, resorting to the explanations in its preamble. It expressly states that since it is impossible to ratify the two International Covenants, the Implementing Act will be a plausible method of incorporating human rights law into the legal system of Taiwan. Article 2 of the Act stipulates that the two Covenants have domestic legal status. As mentioned above, for a treaty to be incorporated into the domestic legal system, a resolution to approve it is the required procedure by the Legislative Yuan under the Constitution.[28] After the resolution, the power to conclude the treaty is vested in the President who deposits the instrument of ratification. When the whole process and procedure are completed, the treaty is incorporated and can have domestic legal effect. That said, it remains questionable whether international human rights law is valid in the legal system of Taiwan when there is no treaty operative from the perspective of international law. Consequently, the incorporation of international human rights treaties into the domestic legal

[27]See Harris (2010), *supra* note 17.

[28]The process and procedure of resolving a bill is different from that of an international treaty, as an international treaty is completed in the second reading. See Lifayuan Zhiquan Xingshifa [立法院職權行使法] (The Act of the Functions and Power of the Legislative Yuan), art.7 (Taiwan).

system of Taiwan by means of an Implementing Act will incur some problems thereafter. Interestingly, most people are unaware of the problem.[29] The authority of the two Covenants and the CEDAW is considered to be conferred by the Implementing Act and the Enforcement Act simply because it stipulates that they have domestic legal status. What does it mean that the two Covenants and the CEDAW have domestic legal status when they are in theory not in existence domestically? Are the human rights treaties positively valid as a legal basis for a claim before a court? What is the legal status of the treaty law in the domestic legal order? Do they rank within the constitutional hierarchy and prevail over ordinary legislation?

Without a clear rule to regulate the effect and status of an international treaty in the legal system of Taiwan,[30] these questions have stirred up theoretical debate and discussion.[31] Apparently, most people are of the opinion that human rights laws have the effect of ordinary legislation but rank higher in view of the effect of Article 8 of the Implementing Act.[32] It states that, "[a]all levels of governmental institutions and agencies should review laws, regulations, directions and administrative measures within their functions according to the two Covenants. All laws, regulations, directions and administrative measures incompatible with the two Covenants should be amended within two years after the Act enters into force by new laws, law amendments, law abolitions and improved administrative measures." Some, however, do not agree with that conclusion and are of the opinion that since the treaties are ordinary legislation, they are subject to the principle *Lex posterior derogat priori*.[33] Consequently, the Legislative Yuan can promulgate an act that purposely derogates from human rights norms. If this is the case, it contradicts the *ratio legis* of Article 8 to repeal any law or regulation that is in conflict with the Covenants.

[29]See generally Lin C-F (2010); Research, Development and Evaluation Commission, Executive Yuan, [行政院研究發展考核委員會] Policy research on the implementation of the two Covenants [落實兩公約施行法之政策研究] RES-099-034 (2011), https://www.ndc.gov.tw/News_Content.aspx?n=E4F9C91CF6EA4EC4&sms=4506D295372B40FB&s=549B97021773800B. Accessed 25 Dec 2017.

[30]The Act of Concluding Treaties passed on 1 July 2015 does not mention the legal status of an international treaty after it is resolved by the Legislative Yuan. A general discussion on the issue can be found in Lee (2014).

[31]During a forum organized by Judicial Yuan and the Ministry of Justice held on 11 Jan 2010 to celebrate the 65th Judicial Day a paper, "Some question and problems concerning the incorporation of the Two Covenants in Taiwan," was presented by Teng Y-S. Editorial, Implementing the Two Covenants on Human Rights Protection Forum in Celebrating the 65th Judicial Day Co-Organized by the Judicial Yuan and the Ministry of Justice [院部聯合慶祝第 65 屆司法節研討實踐兩公約之人權保障], JUDICIAL WEEKLY, 14 Jan 2010, http://www.judicial.gov.tw/jw9706/pdf/1475-1.pdf. Accessed 25 Dec 2017.

[32]Teng Y-S (2010) "Some question and problems concerning the incorporation of the Two Covenants in Taiwan" [两公约内国法化后相关问题之探讨]. Paper presented at the 65th Judicial Day Conference (11 January 2010); Hsu (2010); Lin, *supra* note 29, at p. 25.

[33]Liao (2011), Liao (2010), p. 52.

These unanswered questions have caused some problems in the application of the human rights treaties. A statistical review of court decisions in criminal matters demonstrates that more than 100 judgments have referred to the treaty provisions in the reasoning for decisions and judgments.[34] Most concern the right to life under Article 6 of the Covenant on Civil and Political Rights in relation to the death penalty. The other provisions referred to in the judgments can be found in Article 14, which addresses the right to a fair trial and covers issues such as the presumption of innocence,[35]

[34]Lin T-W (2013) "Implementation of the International Covenant on Civil and Political Rights, Article 6 and 7 in the Criminal Justice Practice of Taiwan: Focus of the Judgements of the Supreme Court Related to Right to Life". Paper presented at the Fourth International Conference on Human Rights Education: Global Convergence and Local Practice (21–26 November).

[35]Hualien Br, Prosecutors Office for Taiwan High Ct. v. Anon, 99 Tai Shang Zi No. 6259 [99 年度台上字第 6259 號判決] (S. Ct. [臺灣最高法院] 18 Oct 2010) (Taiwan); Anon. v. Kaohsiung Br, Prosecutors Office for Taiwan High Ct, 99 Tai Shang Zi No. 6287, [99 年度台上字第 6287 號判決] (S. Ct. [臺灣最高法院] 20 Oct 2010) (Taiwan); Anon. v. Prosecutors Office for Taiwan High Ct, 99 Tai Shang Zi No. 7167 [99 年度台上字第 7167 號判決] (S. Ct. [臺灣最高法院] 18 Nov 2010) (Taiwan); Prosecutors Office for Taiwan High Ct. v. Anon, 99 Tai Shang Zi No. 6251 [99 年度台上字第 6251 號判決] (S. Ct. [臺灣最高法院] 25 Oct 2010) (Taiwan); Tainan Br, Prosecutors Office for Taiwan High Ct. v. Anon, 99 Tai Shang Zi No. 6981 [99 年度台上字第 6981 號判決] (S. Ct. [臺灣最高法院] 10 Nov 2010) (Taiwan); Taichung Br, Prosecutors Office for Taiwan High Ct. v. Shao-Qiang Ji, 99 Tai Shang Zi No. 7287 [99 年度台上字第 7287 號判決] (S. Ct. [臺灣最高法院] 29 Nov 2010) (Taiwan); Tainan Br, Prosecutors Office for Taiwan High Ct. v. Kun-Li Zheng and Jin-Nan Guo, 99 Tai Shang Zi No. 7586 [99 年度台上字第 7586 號判決] (S. Ct. [臺灣最高法院] 13 Dec 2010) (Taiwan); Tainan Br, Prosecutors Office for Taiwan High Ct. v. Yan-Quan Lin et al., 99 Tai Shang Zi No. 8138 [99 年度台上字第 8138 號判決] (S. Ct. [臺灣最高法院] 30 Dec 2010) (Taiwan); Hualien Br, Prosecutors Office for Taiwan High Ct. v. Feng-Xing Xie, 100 Tai Shang Zi No. 319 [100 年度台上字第 319 號判決] (S. Ct. [臺灣最高法院] 24 Jan 2011) (Taiwan); Taichung Br, Prosecutors Office for Taiwan High Ct. v. Zhi-Cheng Chen, No. 487 [100 年度台上字第 487 號判決] (S. Ct. [臺灣最高法院] 27 Jan 2011) (Taiwan); Kaohsiung Br, Prosecutors Office for Taiwan High Ct. v. Ming-Jia Xu et al., No. 1399 [100 年度台上字第 1399 號判決] (S. Ct. [臺灣最高法院]. 24 Mar 2011) (Taiwan); Prosecutors Office for Taiwan High Ct. v. Shu-Fen Chen, No. 1716 [100 年度台上字第 1716 號判決] (S. Ct. [臺灣最高法院] 8 Apr 2011) (Taiwan); Prosecutors Office for Taiwan High Ct. v. Yi-Wei Wang and Guo-Jie Zhang, No. 2364 [100 年度台上字第 2364 號判決] (S. Ct. [臺灣最高法院] 12 May 2011) (Taiwan); Prosecutors Office for Taiwan High Ct. v. Shi-Ming Li et al., No. 3070 [100 年度台上字第 3070 號判決] (S. Ct. [臺灣最高法院] 9 June 2011) (Taiwan); Kaohsiung Br, Prosecutors Office for Taiwan High Ct. v. Chuan-de Xu, No. 3231 [100 年度台上字第 3231 號判決] (S. Ct. [臺灣最高法院] 16 June 2011) (Taiwan); Tainan Br, Prosecutors Office for Taiwan High Ct. v. Zhi-Dong Chen, No. 3618 [100 年度台上字第 3618 號判決] (S. Ct. [臺灣最高法院] 6 July 2011) (Taiwan); Tainan Br, Prosecutors Office for Taiwan High Ct. v. Jin-Hui Huang and Yu-Zhi Luo, No. 4036 [100 年度台上字第 4036 號判決] (S. Ct. [臺灣最高法院] 27 July 2011) (Taiwan); Prosecutors Office for Taiwan High Ct. v. Zhao-Feng Huang, No. 4761 [100 年度台上字第 4761 號判決] (S. Ct. [臺灣最高法院] 31 Aug 2011) (Taiwan); Prosecutors Office for Taiwan High Ct. v. Ming-Xiong Li, No. 5426 [100 年度台上字第 5426 號判決] (S. Ct. [臺灣最高法院] 5 Oct 2011) (Taiwan); Tainan Br, Prosecutors Office for Taiwan High Ct. v. Qin-Jie Huang, No. 6088 [100 年度台上字第 6088 號判決] (S. Ct. [臺灣最高法院] 9 Nov 2011) (Taiwan); Kaohsiung Br, Prosecutors Office for Taiwan High Ct. v. Zong-Yu Li, No. 6944 [100 年度台上字第 6944 號判決] (S. Ct. [臺灣最高法院] 14 Dec 2011) (Taiwan); Taichung Br, Prosecutors Office for Taiwan High Ct. v. Guang-Qing Xie, 101 Tai Shang Zi

detention,[36] the right to appeal[37] and the right to legal assistance.[38]

In reviewing those decisions and judgments which apply the human rights norms, one can find that the normative contents of the rights under the Covenant are not fully elaborated on in the reasoning for the decisions, in which only the article number or the provision per se is mentioned.[39]

The state is the sole duty-bearer of the human rights obligation and the possible remedy for its failure to comply with the obligation is to resort to the administrative courts to challenge either the validity of the administrative actions which cause damage to the applicant or the failure to take the necessary measures to protect the rights or interests of the applicant. As human rights obligations are, by nature, vertical, which means between an individual and the government or the state, in their legal relations, the application of human rights law in administrative matters is especially important as it relates to the question of whether human rights obligations have been fulfilled by the government.

One can find a similar deficit in the criminal courts' judgments and decisions with regard to the application of human rights law after the incorporation of the two

No. 577 [101 年度台上字第 577 號判決] (S. Ct. [臺灣最高法院] 15 Feb 2012) (Taiwan); Hualien Br, Prosecutors Office for Taiwan High Ct. v. Da-Xiong Wu et al., 101 Tai Shang Zi No. 720 [101 年度台上字第 720 號判決] (S. Ct. [臺灣最高法院] 22 Feb 2012) (Taiwan); Prosecutors Office for Taiwan High Ct. v. Ru-Bin Wang et al., 101 Tai Shang Zi No. 885 [101 年度台上字第 885 號判決] (S. Ct. [臺灣最高法院] 7 Mar 2012) (Taiwan); Kaohsiung Br, Prosecutors Office for Taiwan High Ct. v. Anon, 101 Tai Shang Zi No. 1072 [101 年度台上字第 1072 號判決] (S. Ct. [臺灣最高法院] 14 Mar 2012) (Taiwan); Taichung Br, Prosecutors Office for Taiwan High Ct. v. Mei-Ling Cai, 101 Tai Shang Zi No. 1690 [101 年度台上字第 1690 號判決] (S. Ct. [臺灣最高法院] 11 Apr 2012) (Taiwan); Hualien Br, Prosecutors Office for Taiwan High Ct. v. Zhi-Xin Lin, No. 101 Tai Shang Zi No. 1693 [101 年度台上字第 1693 號判決] (S. Ct. [臺灣最高法院] 11 Apr 2012) (Taiwan); Prosecutors Office for Taiwan High Ct. v. Li Chien, 101 Tai Shang Zi No. 1847 [101 年度台上字第 1847 號判決] (S. Ct. [臺灣最高法院] 18 Apr 2012) (Taiwan); Tainan Br, Prosecutors Office for Taiwan High Ct. v. He-Ping Huang and Zhong-Xian Li, 101 Tai Shang Zi No. 3100 [101 年度台上字第 3100 號判決] (S. Ct. [臺灣最高法院] 20 June 2012) (Taiwan).

[36]Cheng-Hao Hong et al., 100 Tai Kang Zi No. 113 [100 年度台抗字第113號] (S. Ct. [臺灣最高法院] 24 February 2011) (Taiwan); He-Shun Qin, 99 Tai Kang Zi No. 649 [99 年度台抗字第 649 號] (S. Ct. [臺灣最高法院] 12 August 2010) (Taiwan); Anon, 99 Tai Kang Zi No. 141 [99 年度台抗字第 141 號] (S. Ct. [臺灣最高法院] 10 February 2010) (Taiwan).

[37]Anon v. Prosecutors Office for Taiwan High Ct, 99 Tai Shang Zi No. 5087[99 年度台上字第 5087 號判決] (S. Ct. [臺灣最高法院] 12 August 2010) (Taiwan); Zong-Zhou Li v. Taichung Br, Prosecutors Office for Taiwan High Ct, 99 Tai Shang Zi No. 7060 [99 年度台上字第 7060 號判決] (S. Ct. [臺灣最高法院] 11 November 2010) (Taiwan); Yun-Long Wu v. Taichung Br, Prosecutors Office for Taiwan High Ct, No. 1045 [100 年度台上字第 1045 號判決] (S. Ct. [臺灣最高法院] 3 March 2011) (Taiwan).

[38]Anon. v. Prosecutors Office for Taiwan High Ct, 99 Tai Shang Zi No. 5079 [99 年度台上字第 5079 號判決] (S. Ct. [臺灣最高法院] 12 August 2010) (Taiwan); Anon. v. Taichung Br, Prosecutors Office for Taiwan High Ct, 99 Tai Shang Zi No. 5080 [99 年度台上字第 5080 號判決] (S. Ct. [臺灣最高法院] 12 August 2010) (Taiwan).

[39]See Lin, *supra* note 34.

Covenants, namely, ignoring arguments based on human rights law which have been raised by the applicants, and reasoning without sufficient elaboration on the human rights law pertinent to the case.[40] Some judgments even fail to consider relevant constitutional interpretations which have dealt with the issue. In this case, the court was of the opinion that there was no need to consider the relevant human rights norms.[41]

4.1 In the Context of Constitutional Interpretations, Similar Deficits Appear as Such and Are Summarized as Follows, Without Any Elaboration on the Normative Contents of the Relevant Human Rights Law

In J.Y. Interpretation No. 709[42] on the review and approval of urban renewal business summaries and plans, the issue was raised as follows: "[a]re the Urban Renewal Act's provisions governing the review and approval of urban renewal business summaries and plans constitutional?" The applicants claimed that the relevant act was unconstitutional for violating the right to property guaranteed under constitutional law. The majority opinion of the Interpretation held:

> Article 15 of the Constitution provides that the people's right to property shall be protected. The purpose of this Article is to guarantee each individual the freedom to exercise his rights to use, profit by, and dispose of his property during the existence of the property, and to prevent infringements by the government or any third party, so as to ensure that a person can realize his freedoms, develop his personality, and maintain his dignity… In addition, Article 10 of the Constitution stipulates that people shall have freedom of residence. This Article guarantees people the freedom to choose their residence and to enjoy their life in privacy without intrusion… However, in order to advance public welfare, a state may by law impose restrictions on the people's right to property or freedom of residence pursuant to the principle of proportionality under Article 23 of the Constitution….

In this regard, the restriction can be legitimate. "Urban renewal is a program of urban planning. Urban renewal promotes well-planned urban land redevelopment, revitalizes urban functions, improves the urban living environment, and advances public welfare. The Act was enacted for these purposes. The Act ensures that people can enjoy an adequate standard of living with safety, peace, and dignity (see Article 11(1) of the International Covenant on Economic, Social and Cultural Rights)."

Other than the reason of public welfare, the Interpretation does not answer the question of why the applicants who did not want to participate in the urban renewal program would not enjoy constitutional protection of their right to property. Surprisingly, the Interpretation introduces Article 11 of the ICESCR, the right to an

[40]See generally Liao (2014).

[41]*Id.*

[42]Sifayuan Jieshi [司法院解釋] (Judicial Yuan Interpretation), No. 709 (24 Apr 2013) (Taiwan).

adequate standard of living, as a justification for disregarding the applicant's unwillingness to participate in the renewal program. Whether the introduction of an economic and social right has the effect of curtailing the applicants' right to property is open to doubt when the normative contents of the right to an adequate standard of living need to be elaborated on in its reasoning.

4.2 *Taking Human Rights Norms as a Reference Rather Than the Positive Law*

Another example of a flaw is in J.Y. Interpretation No. 710,[43] which concerns the mandatory deportation and detention of people from Mainland China. One of the issues is as follows: "Is it constitutional that the Act Governing Relations between Peoples from the Taiwan Area and the Mainland Area provides no defense opportunity to a person from the Mainland Area prior to his mandatory deportation?" It holds,

> it is unconstitutional to mandatorily deport any person from the Mainland Area who has obtained permission to legally enter into the Taiwan Area without providing any defense opportunity to such person because it is in violation of the constitutional principle of due process of law and fails to comply with the meaning and purpose of the protection of migration freedom under Article 10 of the Constitution… Providing no prompt judicial remedy to a detainee who is under temporary detention for a reasonable period in order to enforce deportation and failing to subject an extension of the foregoing temporary detention to judicial review violate both the principle of due process of law under the Constitution and the meaning and purpose of protecting physical freedom guaranteed under Article 8 of the Constitution.

The right to a prompt judicial remedy when a person is detained is protected under Article 14 of the ICCPR and some basic rights provided in the article are also to be respected in relation to the state's obligation to protect the right to a fair trial. Nevertheless, the reasoning in the Interpretation deliberately ignores the normative contents of the human rights law.

The European Convention on Human Rights is simultaneously referred to in the reasoning of the Interpretation. It is not clear what the legal status of the Convention is in relation to the ICCPR, which has already been incorporated by the Legislative Yuan. It holds,

> The Cross-Strait Relations Act is the *sui generis* law enacted to regulate the rights and obligations between peoples from the Mainland Area and the Taiwan Area… Given that the two sides of the Taiwan Strait are currently governed by different political entities, restrictions are therefore imposed on the freedom of people from the Mainland Area to enter into the Taiwan Area….[A]fter formally obtaining permission from the competent authorities and having legally entered the Taiwan Area, the freedom of movement of people from the Mainland Area should in principle be protected by the Constitution (see Article 12

[43]Sifayuan Jieshi [司法院解釋] (Judicial Yuan Interpretation), No. 710 (5 July 2013) (Taiwan).

> and Paragraph 6 of General Comment No. 15 of the UN International Covenant on Civil and Political Rights)…[T]he mandatory deportation of a person from the Mainland Area who legally entered into the Taiwan Area must fulfil corresponding due process requirements (see Article 13 of the UN International Covenant on Civil and Political Rights; Article 1 of Protocol No. 7 to the European Convention on Human Rights). In particular, mandatory deportation of Mainland spouses who have been permitted to legally enter into the Taiwan Area requires extra caution because it significantly affects marriages and family relationships.

The institutional flaw, it seems, has caused the judiciary, including in the context of constitutional interpretation, to fail to recognize the legal effects of the Covenants which have the status of positive law in the domestic legal order. As a result, the normativity is not in reality internalized in judicial decisions. If this is the case, human rights law will be devoid of its internal point of view with regard to the rule of recognition in the legal system.[44]

4.3 *Purposely Deviated from Human Rights Law*

The state has obligations to ensure the free exercise of the rights to peaceful assembly and association at the national level. This freedom is especially fundamental to the right to participation in public affairs as guaranteed by Article 25 of the ICCPR. In that regard, the right to freedom of assembly and association should not be interfered with so as to be compatible with the idea of public participation in a democratic society. In J.Y. Interpretation No. 445,[45] before the incorporation of the two Covenants, the guarantee of the freedom of assembly as provided for in Article 14 of the Constitution is reiterated as a kind of freedom of expression that is considered to be the most important fundamental human right in a practicing democracy.[46] The said Interpretation rightly held that when restricting the rights of assembly and parade by law, the principle of clarity and definiteness of law, and the provisions of Article 23 of the Constitution must be complied with. In this regard, the provision under Article 11 (I) of the Assembly and Parade Act, which allows the competent authority to censor the contents of political speech, such as advocating communism or secession of territory prior to the approval of an assembly or a parade, is inconsistent with the protection of the freedom of expression under the Constitution. Other than the fact that the concept of advocacy is unclear, the advocacy of communism or secession of territory, to the extent that no right or freedom of another person is interfered with or infringed upon, should be protected under the right of freedom of expression. Sub-paragraph 2 of said article, which relates to the future possibility, instead of concrete evidence, of a danger to national

---

[44]See Hart (1997), p. 117.

[45]Sifayuan Jieshi [司法院解釋] (Judicial Yuan Interpretation) No. 445 (23 Jan 1998) (Taiwan).

[46]*Id.*

security, social order or public welfare is also held to be unconstitutional because it essentially denies the freedom of assembly.

The Interpretation was once praised as a huge step forward in the development of democracy in Taiwan. However, questions surrounding a controversial provision concerning the requirement to submit an assembly application for approval remains unanswered. The relevant issue is whether the provisions of the Assembly and Demonstration Act regarding applications for approval, which do not exclude urgent and incidental assemblies and parades, are unconstitutional.[47]

In answer to this question, the Interpretation held that the provisions under the Assembly and Demonstration Act, which regulate that holders of outdoor assemblies and demonstrations shall apply to the competent authority for approval and which does not exclude urgent and incidental assemblies and demonstrations, are contradictory to the proportionality principle of Article 23 of the Constitution and not in compliance with the spirit of the protection of freedom of assembly of Article 14 of the Constitution.

> To support the conclusion, the reasoning of this decision reiterates that,
>
> This freedom is based on the idea of sovereignty of the people, and is an important basic human right in the implementation of democracy as it facilitates thinking and debate, respects differences, and embodies the constitutional spirit of co-existence. To protect such freedom, in addition to providing suitable places for assemblies and adopting effective security measures to protect assemblies, the country should enact a law and formulate the system in such a way as to enable the participants in assemblies or demonstrations to exercise their freedom of assembly without fear.

No one would disagree with the legitimacy of the reasoning of the decision. However, Article 21 under the ICCPR which provides for the protection of the freedom in question was not mentioned at all.[48] Considering that the freedom of assembly is needed even more in the era of global pluralism in which state-centric interests in economic growth should be accommodated alongside the other interests of human persons, such as human rights and environmental protection,[49] the freedom of assembly should be elaborated on thoroughly so as to eliminate the controversy completely.

Another notorious example is Judicial Yuan Interpretation No. 618,[50] which was decided before the incorporation of the two Covenants. However, the relevant human rights treaty was the International Convention on the Elimination of All Forms of Racial Discrimination, which was the only human rights treaty signed and ratified by

[47]Sifayuan Jieshi [司法院解釋] (Judicial Yuan Interpretation) No. 718 (21 Mar 2014) (Taiwan).

[48]A similar deficit can be found in Judicial Interpretation No. 708 of 6 Feb 2013 on immigration detention of foreign nationals pending deportation, which relates to the protection under Articles 13 and 14 of the ICCPR.

[49]See Human Rights Council Res 24/5, Rep. on Rights to Freedom of Peaceful Assembly and of Association, 24th Sess., 9 Sept 3012–27 Sept 2013, UN GAOR, 69th Sess., A/69/365 (1 Sept 2014).

[50]Sifayuan Jieshi [司法院解釋] (Judicial Yuan Interpretation) No. 618 (3 Nov 2006) (Taiwan).

the Republic of China while it was a member of the United Nations.[51] The application for interpretation was initiated by the Taipei Administrative High Court on the unconstitutionality of the discriminatory measure of Article 21 (1) under the Statute on the Relations between Citizens Living in Taiwan and Mainland Regions.

The issue was whether the requirement that people who emigrated from the Mainland Area must hold a household registration in the Taiwan Area for at least ten years was unconstitutional. The applicant strongly claimed that the discriminatory measure flagrantly violated the prohibition of any discrimination based on national origin as provided for by Article 1(1) and was also incompatible with the equality principle stipulated in Article 7 of the Constitution. However, the Constitutional Court, in making its Interpretation, not only ignored the Convention, but also made a contrary interpretation based on the grounds of national security. It held,

> [G]iven the fact that a person who came from the Mainland Area but has had a household registration in the Taiwan Area for less than ten years may not be as familiar with the constitutional structure of a free democracy as the Taiwanese people, it is not unreasonable to give discriminatory treatment to such a person and not to the Taiwanese people of the Taiwan Area with respect to the qualifications to serve as a governmental employee, which is not in conflict with the principle of equality as embodied in Article 7 of the Constitution, nor contrary to the intent of Article 10 of the Amendments to the Constitution.

The Justices even went further to justify the institutional discrimination by declaring that, "it may also take a while for the Taiwanese people to place their trust in a person who came from the Mainland Area, if he or she served as a public functionary. If the review were to be conducted on a case-by-case basis, it would be difficult to examine an individual's subjective intentions and character, as well as his or her level of identification with the preservation of the constitutional structure of a free democracy. Besides, it would also needlessly increase the administrative costs to a prohibitive level with hardly any hope of accuracy or fairness. In conclusion, the ten-year period as specified by the provision at issue was held to be necessary and reasonable."

The obligation that governmental institutions and agencies at all levels respect, protect and fulfil human rights whenever they exercise their functions is expressly stipulated in the Implementing Act for the two Covenants.[52] However, what does "all levels of governmental institutions and agencies" mean? Is the judiciary

[51]The Republic of China signed it on 3 Mar 1966 and ratified on 14 Nov 1970 respectively.

[52]Lianggongyue Shixingfa [兩公約施行法] (The Implementing Act for the Two Covenants), art.4 (Taiwan), "Whenever exercising their functions, all levels of governmental institutions and agencies should conform to the human rights protection provisions in the two Covenants; avoid violating human rights; protect the people from infringement by others; positively promote the realization of human rights." Lianggongyue Shixingfa [兩公約施行法] (The Implementing Act for the Two Covenants), art. 5 (Taiwan), "All levels of governmental institutions and agencies should take responsibility for preparing, promoting and implementing the human rights protection provisions in the two Covenants within their functions that are governed by existing laws and regulations. When multi-functions are involved, distinct governmental institutions and agencies should contact and coordinate to carry out their responsibilities. The government should cooperate with other national governments and international nongovernmental organizations and human

included as one of the governmental institutions? In General Comment 31 adopted by the UN Human Rights Committee, it clearly advises,

> [t]he obligations of the Covenant in general and Article 2 in particular are binding on every State Party as a whole. All branches of government (executive, legislative and judicial), and other public or governmental authorities, at whatever level - national, regional or local - are in a position to engage the responsibility of the State Party.[53]

Accordingly, the judiciary is not excluded from the responsibility to fulfil the human rights obligations undertaken by a contracting state. In that regard, however, is the justice mandated for the constitutional interpretation also included in the institution of the judiciary? The answer must be positive, as there is no reason to regard the function of constitutional interpretation as non-judicial. That said, the reasoning employed in a constitutional interpretation should not disregard the human rights laws which have already been incorporated into the domestic legal system.

5 A Methodological Reflection

The question of whether Taiwan is a state in international law is different from the perspective of international politics. In international law, as mentioned above, the existence of a state is a legal fact.[54] This is a proposition of law rather than of politics. If statehood is based on international law by definition, then the question is, "On which international rule of law and by whom can an actor be endowed with statehood in the international community?" The truth is that there is no clear rule in international law to that effect. In this regard, the existence of a state and its capacity are thus relative, subjective[55] and a matter of national law. Following from that, that Taiwan does not have the required capacity to engage in international affairs and to conclude international treaties is a result of the manipulation of international politics rather than as a result of the international rule of law.

In view of this truth, one wonders whether there is any point to Taiwan incorporating international human rights treaties into its domestic legal system as most states do. Surely it is a must. The gesture of "ratifying" a human rights treaty can have the effect of demonstrating a state's political will to respect the human rights of its people. In addition, Taiwan's unilateral act of incorporating international

rights institutions to realize promotion and protection of the human rights provisions in the two Covenants."

[53]Human Rights Committee, General Comment No. 31, The Nature of the General Legal Obligation Imposed on States Parties to the Covenant, UN Doc CCPR/C/21/Rev.1/Add. 13 (26 May 2004).

[54]See Nuclear Tests (Australia v. France), 1974 ICJ 253 (20 Dec); Nuclear Tests (New Zealand v. France), 1974 ICJ 457 (20 Dec).

[55]This is the institution of recognition in international law that regulates the existence of a state. The prevailing international theory concerning recognition is declaratory in nature; however, in international politics, the doctrine of recognition is constitutive and relative.

human rights treaties, as previously mentioned, may impose treaty obligations upon it.[56]

From the realistic and positivist perspective, however, the methodology for the incorporation of international human rights law in Taiwan should apply the substantive process of incorporation. As such, the proper method of incorporation should be to enact a human rights act to incorporate international human rights law into the legal system of Taiwan. The law will provide the legal basis for those rights to be respected, protected and fulfilled. In addition, the corresponding obligations arising from those rights on all levels of government and its agencies should be defined clearly so that the relevant rights can have direct effect against the duty bearer concerned. Then, the protection of human rights in Taiwan may be deemed as legally recognizable.

However, this is only the first step to make international human rights law positively recognizable in the domestic legal system of Taiwan. There is more to be done to make human rights protection legally effective. As an old Chinese saying demonstrates, "Law alone is not to be operative."[57] Lawyers tend to focus on the formal validity of law which concerns the doctrine of legality. However, the distinction between legality and legitimacy should be maintained as it has been the subject of considerable discussion both in the past and today. The concept of legality, for the purpose of this chapter, concerns the validity of the treaty law in an institutional sense, namely, the ratification of an international human rights treaty. As to the concept of legitimacy, which is a broader concept than legality,[58] it can be defined as relating to the justification of the authority of legal rights or obligations. This, then, raises a question which must be answered, "What makes the authority of a human rights obligation binding upon the government of Taiwan even if it has not validly ratified the human rights treaty?" The key to answering this question lies in the understanding of the nature of the legal obligations in human rights law. The authority of human rights obligations which are binding on Taiwan is not related to the concept of legality; rather, it has to do with that of legitimacy. That said, the effect of the authority of human rights obligations binding upon Taiwan should not be considered as inferred from the formal incorporation of the human rights treaties; rather, it concerns the normativity of human rights law. As Bodansky correctly explains, "[l]egitimacy has a normative quality. It represents not merely a reason for action, but a justification."[59] The legitimacy of human rights law is thus concerning the normative nature of the obligation on the state to respect, protect and fulfil the dignity of human persons. Since the dignity of every person is equal, as stated in Article 1 of the Universal Declaration of Human Rights of 1948, the obligation in this regard is unconditional, objective and universal. As the notion that dignity is

[56]See Zhonghua Minguo Xianfa, art. 38 (Taiwan).

[57]"徒法不能自行." *The Sayings of Mencius*, Ch. 4, Li-Lou.

[58]*Id.*, at p. 3.

[59]Bodansky (2007).

held by everyone equally is a proposition a priori, thus, a human rights obligation to protect everyone's dignity is not positive in nature; instead, it is naturalistic and teleological. This is the ontological legitimacy of the human rights obligation. In other words, the validity of human rights obligations is not derived from the assent of the states that ratify the human rights treaty. In this regard, however, some are of the opinion that human rights law has become constituted as international custom. Consequently, it is immaterial whether a state has consented to the treaty or not. This ambitious assumption is not addressed in this chapter with respect to the idea of ontological legitimacy. International customs can make human rights norms valid in the context of international law; however, they cannot give human rights norms the effect of legitimacy. Following from this, Taiwan's unilateral declaration to incorporate the international human rights treaties may have created international obligations for it to protect human rights from the perspective of validity; however, the nature of the obligation to protect its people's human rights arises as a result of the ontological legitimacy of the human rights obligation.

That said, with regard to the deficit in the application of human rights law in judicial decisions and constitutional interpretations, one can find that the judiciary in Taiwan fails to recognize the ontological legitimacy of human rights.

Consequently, the judiciary should bear the responsibility to take judicial notice of human rights law in its decisions and judgments. The ontological legitimacy of human rights law in this respect serves as an interpretive principle so that the rule of law and justice can be satisfied with respect to the protection of the objective, universal and absolute value of human dignity. Thus, human rights are best understood as "a specific type of norm, namely, as standards of legitimacy," as one commentator urged.[60]

A further problem merits our attention with regard to the ontological legitimacy of human rights. Theoretically, human rights are individual rights that everyone should possess simply as a human person. However, third generation human rights —namely the right to development, the right to the environment and the right to peace—and second generation human rights—such as economic, social and cultural rights—are not normally regarded as invokable with respect to their abstract nature and contents. In fact, the argument on the nature of justiciability of human rights as claim rights has demonstrated its theoretical flaw with regard to the legal relationship therein.

Consequently, to avoid the theoretical flaw of treating human rights as claim rights and to recognize the legitimacy of human rights, we conclude by agreeing with the assertion that human rights should be considered as standards of legitimacy in relation to the validity of legal obligations. Thus, human rights constitute "higher-order norms that articulate the universal idea of rightness and serve as secondary rules to regulate institutional and legal change."[61]

---

[60]Chwaszcza (2010), p. 335.

[61]*Id.*

As such, human rights impact assessments with respect to the duties of the state in relation to the protection of human rights demonstrate the paradigmatic shift of human rights from the traditional doctrine of claim rights to the standards of legitimacy with respect to the functions of governmental institutions and agencies. Thus, a growing demand by various actors, states and corporations[62] that human rights impact assessments be undertaken before adopting and implementing policies has emerged in recent years. The process of conducting human rights impact assessments can raise awareness of the idea of human rights and empower the function of human rights in decision-making. They help to identify the impact of a policy, program or project on the enjoyment of human rights and help to voice concerns more effectively with respect to the realization of human rights.

Recalling the theoretical flaw of taking human rights as claim rights and recognizing the ontological legitimacy of human rights obligations owed by the state toward its people, we may conclude by saying that the incorporation of international human rights law into Taiwan's domestic legal system has the effect of recognizing the normative nature of human rights as mandatory and obligatory. Thus, the application of human rights law is the positive duty of the state to that effect.

6 Conclusion

The method of incorporating international treaties into a domestic legal system is mainly subject to the national law of the state concerned. Thus, the problem which emerges subsequent to the incorporation of a treaty is still a matter of national law. Normally, a state with the capacity to incorporate international treaties will encounter few problems. However, this is not true for Taiwan, which has not been admitted as a member of the United Nations. In this regard, the emerging problems mainly concern the issue of the validity of the treaty being incorporated, which is not properly ratified in terms of international law. Thus, the aforementioned problem is particular to Taiwan's situation. In the absence of a relevant law for incorporating international treaties in addition to a lack of sufficient practice to that effect, the application of international human rights law in the legal system of Taiwan, especially in the courts, becomes a question that merits deliberation.

The idea of human rights is exotic to most people in Taiwan due to its long isolation from the international community. Surprisingly, even with the experience of living under martial law for nearly 40 years,[63] the idea of human rights was not a

---

[62]See Götzmann N (2014).

[63]On 20 May 1950, the Nationalist Government issued A Martial Ordinance in Taiwan, which was not rescinded until 15 July 1987.

popular topic in public debate in Taiwan. It was not until the government became devoted to incorporating the two Covenants and the CEDAW into the domestic legal system of Taiwan in 2009 and 2007 respectively that human rights education for civil servants became a mandated task.[64] In fact, the real problem concerning human rights education and training in Taiwan lies in the fact that there are deep deficiencies of human rights expertise for education and training. The deficit can be blamed on the ignorance of human rights in schools and at universities. Hopefully, following the incorporation of international human rights treaties, the situation will have a chance to change.

Other than the problems particular to Taiwan, however, there are some other problems that are common to all states. The common problems in this regard are related to the doctrine of human rights. Traditionally and methodologically, human rights are treated as claim rights under institutional arrangements within a legal system. Thus, by treating human rights as claim rights, they are trapped in legal proceedings. If human rights can only be realized in legal proceedings, the proposition begs the question of what kind of human rights may be invoked in court. In practice, some human rights obligations are not so concrete that they can formulate a valid legal right in legal proceedings; in this regard, the right is not invokable. This is the fundamental flaw that distinguishes the normativity of human rights from the notion of invokable rights. It is unthinkable that some of the most important rights that should be enjoyed by every person are devoid of any legal effect simply because the obligation to protect those rights is obscure and conditional. Apparently, the flaw lies in the fact that human rights are embedded in the doctrine of subjective rights, as opposed to objective rights encapsulated in the Latin maxim *Ubi Jus Ibi Remedium*. If human rights are only valid for their subjectivity, namely, the law must confer on the specific person the rights that are claimable, it begs the question of how human rights are universally valid for all humans.

To take human rights seriously, one cannot take the obligation of human rights solely from the perspective of the concept and practice of legality. Bearing in mind that human rights exist for the sole purpose of protecting the dignity possessed by all, simply as a consequence of being human, the obligation to protect human rights is natural and teleological, rather than positive or pragmatic. The normative nature of human rights is thus related to the obligation a priori, namely, the obligation to protect human rights is inherent in the duty of the state. In this regard, the reason that makes the obligation a priori lies in the fact that the normativity of human rights possesses elements of ontological legitimacy. That said, methodologically,

[64]See Ministry of Justice, Human Rights in Taiwan on Human Rights Education and Training Arranged and Conducted, http://www.humanrights.moj.gov.tw/np.asp?ctNode=40301&mp=205. Accessed 23 Dec 2017. However, the concluding observations and recommendations noted a deficit relating to human rights education and training, Review of the Initial Reports, *supra* note 4, at paras. 17–19.

human rights are to be regarded as standards of legitimacy available for a rights-holder to evaluate the compliance and implementation of the obligation of normative nature, which is mandatory and obligatory on the state. From this perspective, the problems of incorporating human rights treaties in Taiwan appear less momentous.

References

Bodansky DM (2007) The Concept of Legitimacy in International Law (Univ of Georgia Sch of L, Research Paper No, 07-013), http://ssrn.com/abstract=1033542

Chwaszcza C (2010) The Concept of Rights in Contemporary Human Rights Discourse. Ratio Juris 23(3):333–364

Denza E (2014) The Relationship Between International and National Law. In: Evans MD (ed) International Law, 4th edn. Oxford University Press, Oxford, pp 412–440

Götzmann N (2014) Human Rights and Impact Assessment: Conceptual and Practical Considerations in the Private Sector (The Danish Institute for Human Rights, Matters of Concern for Human Rights Research Paper No. 2012/2)

Harris D (ed) (2010) Case and Materials on International Law, 7th edn. Sweet & Maxwell, UK

Hart HLA (1997) The Concept of Law, 2nd edn. Oxford University Press, Oxford

Hsu H-Y (2010) On the Normative Contents of the Covenant on Economic, Social and Cultural Rights—A Preliminary Inquiry on its Practice in Taiwan [論經濟、社會及文化權利國際公約中文化權之規範內涵我國實踐問題之初探]. Chinese (Taiwan) Review of International and Transnational Law [中華國際法與超國界法評論] 6(2):495–509

Jennings R and Watts A (eds) (1996) Oppenheim's International Law. Volume I: Peace. Longmans, London

Klabbers J (2013) International Law. Cambridge University Press, Cambridge

Lee C-L (2014) On the Legal Effects and the Status of International Treaty under Domestic Legal Order [論國際條約的國內法效力與法位階定位]. In: Liao F-T (ed) The Theory and Practice of Constitutional Interpretation [憲法解釋之理論與實務]. Academia Sinica Taipei, pp. 175–275. http://publication.iias.sinica.edu.tw/90501141.pdf

Liao F-T (2010) Should and How the Court Applies the International Covenant on Civil and Political Rights [法院應否及如何適用公民與政治權利國際公約]. Taiwan Law Journal [台灣法學雜誌] 163:45–65

Liao F-T (2014) Court's Challenges When Applying the ICCPR and the ICESCR-Review of Judgments of Administrative Courts [司法審判於兩公約人權保障思維所面臨之挑戰—行政法院適用兩公約之檢視]. China Law Journal [法學叢刊] 59(2):1–42

Liao T-S (2011) The Domestic Effects of the International Covenant on Civil and Political Rights in Taiwan: Focusing on the Criminal Judgments of the Supreme and High Court [公民與政治權利國際公約在我國的效力以最高及高等法院刑事裁判爲研究中心]. Chinese (Taiwan)

Lin C-F (2010) On the Supplementary Function of the Two Covenants to Human Rights Protection under Constitutional Law in Taiwan—An Inquiry into the Preliminary Framework [論兩公約對憲法人權保障的補充-一個初步架構的探討]. Journal of Taiwan Bar Association [全國律師] 14(3):23–41

Lin T-W (2013) Implementation of the International Covenant on Civil and Political Rights, Article 6 and 7 in the Criminal Justice Practice of Taiwan: Focus of the Judgements of the Supreme Court Related to Right to Life. Paper presented at the Fourth International Conference on Human Rights Education: Global Convergence and Local Practice (21–26 November)

Lin Y-H (2013) Criminal Procedural Law (1), 7th edn. New Sharing, Taipei

Ministry of Justice, Human Rights in Taiwan on Human Rights Education and Training Arranged and Conducted. http://www.humanrights.moj.gov.tw/np.asp?ctNode=40301&mp=205. Accessed 23 Dec 2017

Research, Development and Evaluation Commission, Executive Yuan [行政院研究發展考核委員會] (2011) Policy Research on the Implementation of the Two Covenants [落實兩公約施行法之政策研究]. https://www.ndc.gov.tw/News_Content.aspx?n=E4F9C91CF6EA4EC4&sms = 4506D295372B40FB&s = 549B97021773800B Accessed 26 Dec 2017

Review of International and Transnational Law [中華國際法與超國界法評論] 7(1):96–128

Review of the Initial Reports of the Government of Taiwan on the Implementation of the International Human Rights Covenants: Concluding Observations and Recommendations Adopted by the International Group of Independent Experts, Taipei, 1 Mar 2013, at para. 4. http://www.humanrights.moj.gov.tw/HitCounter.asp?xItem=385451. Accessed 30 Sept 2017

Teng Y-S. Editorial, Implementing the Two Covenants on Human Rights Protection Forum in Celebrating the 65th Judicial Day Co-organized by the Judicial Yuan and the Ministry of Justice [院部聯合慶祝第 65 屆司法節研討實踐兩公約之人權保障], JUDICIAL WEEKLY, 14 Jan 2010, http://www.judicial.gov.tw/jw9706/pdf/1475-1.pdf. Accessed 25 Dec 2017

Teng Y-S (2010) Some Questions and Problems Concerning the Incorporation of the Two Covenants in Taiwan 两公约内国法化后相关问题之探讨. Paper presented at the 65th Judicial Day Conference (11 Jan)

Yean-Sen Teng LL.B., LL.B., Soochow University; LL.M., MPhil, University of Nottingham, Professor of Law at the School of Law, Soochow University. He served as Director of Chung Fo-Chung Center for the Study of Human Rights and the Master's Program for Human Rights at Soochow University (2008–2010) in addition to Director of the Yuen-Li Liang International Law Centre at the School of Law (2006–2014). In 2009, following ratification of the International Covenant on Civil and Political Rights and the International Covenant on Economic, Social and Cultural Rights, Professor Teng was invited to deliver lectures on human rights at the Supreme Court, the Supreme Administrative Court, Taipei High Court, Taipei High Administrative Court and several district courts. Some of his important publications include: (1) "The Relationship between National Sovereignty and Human Rights in the Jurisprudence of the European Court of Human Rights" (in Chinese), *The Constitutional Review*, Vol. 27 (3), 2002; (2) "Human Rights and Rule of Law—A View from the Constitutional Interpretation in Taiwan" (in Chinese), *Soochow Law Review*, Vol. 15 (2), 2004; (3) "A Protean-Face of Human Rights in Taiwan," International Law Association, Asia-Pacific Regional Conference, Taipei, 31 May 2011; (4) "Human Rights: A Concept or an Idea, Human Rights Meet Legislation"—Cross Cultural and Legal Perspectives, Roundtable, University of Magdeburg, Germany, 15 January 2010; (5) "Who is Afraid of Human Rights? A Taiwanese Perspective," collected in Rainer Arnold (ed.) *The Universalism of Human Rights*, Springer, 2013; (6) *International Human Rights Law: Theory and Practice* (in Chinese), 2017, Angle Publishing.

Chapter 15
The Approach of Introducing International Human Rights Treaties into the Interpretation of Constitutional Provisions in Taiwan

Chang-fa Lo

Abstract The Constitution of the ROC contains a Bill of Rights Chapter which requires the fundamental rights of the people to be protected. Since it was drafted seven decades ago, an important issue arises concerning whether and how to keep the Bill of Rights in line with the development of international human rights treaties and practices. In this chapter of the book, the author argues for the desirability and importance of ensuring a living constitution for the Republic by incorporating international human rights treaties and practices into the decisions made by the Constitutional Court. The author suggests that the fundamental interpretative method of relying on textual interpretation should be employed to look for the appropriate ordinary meaning of the constitutional text. But the "ordinary meaning" should not be the "ordinary meaning" at the time when the Constitution was adopted. Instead, it should be the "ordinary meaning" at the time when a provision is interpreted; it should evolve by taking into consideration the development of international human rights treaties and practices. This approach would be more in line with the duty entrusted by the Constitution to the Court to "interpret the Constitution" and also in line with the desirability that the constitutional provisions will not become obsolete.

Keywords Constitutional Court · Constitutional interpretation · Evolutive interpretation · Living constitution · Ordinary or plain meaning · Textual interpretation

1 Introduction

The Constitution of the ROC was enacted seven decades ago. Many provisions in the Bill of Rights Chapter (i.e., Chapter II) of the Constitution are still up-to-date, but there are some important human rights issues that are not specifically addressed

C. Lo (✉)
Constitutional Court, Taipei, Taiwan, Republic of China
e-mail: lochangfa@gmail.com

J. A. Cohen et al. (eds.), *Taiwan and International Human Rights*, Economics, Law, and Institutions in Asia Pacific, https://doi.org/10.1007/978-981-13-0350-0_15

in the Constitution. Some constitutional provisions are not sufficiently clear as to whether the extent of protection is comparable with the level of protection required by related international human rights treaties and practices.

Notwithstanding that Taiwan is politically unable to join international human rights treaties, it has still substantively adopted some of them through its implementation legislation.[1] It must be noted, however, that implementation legislation only introduces the content of the treaties as "statutory norms" (not as "constitutional norms") for Taiwan. The Constitutional Court cannot "solely" depend on implementation legislation and declare some other legislation unconstitutional, just as it cannot depend on one piece of legislation to declare another piece of legislation unconstitutional.

Nor can the Constitutional Court depend "solely" on a human rights treaty to declare that a particular piece of domestic legislation is unconstitutional. There must be a certain "linkage" which connects a human rights treaty with the Constitution so as to enable the Constitutional Court to decide whether or not the legislation is unconstitutional when its content is in conflict with such a treaty.

There are three possible ways for the Constitutional Court to introduce international human rights treaties into its interpretation of the Constitution: to consider the content of the human rights treaties as natural law or of higher legal status, which would bind the Constitutional Court and mean that the Court would have to apply the content of the treaty directly; to consider human rights treaties as self-executing and as having a legal status that is the same as or higher than the Constitution so that the Constitutional Court can apply the treaty directly; and to take the human rights treaties into consideration so as to "read" the constitutional provisions as being consistent with the human rights treaties or to "read" the content in the treaties into the Constitution.

This chapter will argue that the last approach is the most feasible one and could ensure that the Constitution continues to be a living constitution.

The discussion will begin with an explanation of why it is desirable to have the constitutional decisions be in line with international human rights treaties. It will

---

[1]For instance, the following legislation has been enacted by the legislative body to implement international human rights treaties: GongMin Yu ZhengZhi QuanLi GuoJi GongYue Ji JingJi SheHui WenHua QuanLi GuoJi GongYue ShiXingFa [公民與政治權利國際公約及經濟社會文化權利國際公約施行法] (Act to Implement the International Covenant on Civil and Political Rights and the International Covenant on Economic, Social and Cultural Rights) (the English translation of this legislation can be found at http://law.moj.gov.tw/Eng/LawClass/LawAll.aspx?PCode=I0020028); ShenXinZhangAiZhe QuanLi GongYue ShiXingFa [身心障礙者權利公約施行法] (Act to Implement the Convention on the Rights of Persons with Disabilities) (the English translation can be found at http://law.moj.gov.tw/Eng/LawClass/LawAll.aspx?PCode=D0050194); ZhiDing ErTong QuanLi GongYue ShiXingFa [制定兒童權利公約施行法] (Implementation Act of the Convention on the Rights of the Child) (the English translation can be found at http://law.moj.gov.tw/Eng/LawClass/LawAll.aspx?PCode=D0050193); and XiaoChu Dui FuNu YiQieXingShi QiShi GongYue ShiXingFa [消除對婦女一切歧視公約施行法] (Implementation Act of the Convention on the Elimination of All Forms of Discrimination against Women) (the English translation can be found at http://law.moj.gov.tw/Eng/LawClass/LawAll.aspx?PCode=D0050175).

then compare the approaches taken to ensure that constitutional decisions are in line with the human rights treaties and explain why the "interpretation approach" is a more desirable one in the context of the Constitution of the ROC. The chapter will further elaborate on the general principles of constitutional interpretation and the ways to read international treaties into constitutional provisions.

2 Desirability of Having a Living Constitution

2.1 The Constitution Was Enacted 70 Years Ago

The ROC Constitution was enacted on 25 December 1946 in Nanjing (the capital of the Republic if China at that time) by the National Assembly for the Enactment of the Constitution. It was published on 1 January 1947 and implemented on 25 December 1947, making the Constitution 70 years old today.

The Constitution has 175 articles in 14 chapters: Chapter I (entitled "General Provisions"); Chapter II (entitled "Rights and Duties of the People"); Chapter III (entitled "The National Assembly"); Chapter IV (entitled "The President"); Chapter V (entitled "Administration"); Chapter VI (entitled "Legislation"); Chapter VII (entitled "Judiciary"); Chapter VIII (entitled "Examination"); Chapter IX (entitled "Control"); Chapter X (entitled "Powers of the Central and Local Governments"); Chapter XI (entitled "System of Local Government"); Chapter XII (entitled "Election, Recall, Initiative and Referendum"); Chapter XIII (entitled "Fundamental National Policies"); and Chapter XIV (entitled "Enforcement and Amendments to the Constitution"). Chapter II lists the fundamental rights that are supposed to be protected by the Constitution. Hence, it is most relevant to the discussion in this chapter.

In 1948, not long after the Constitution entered into force, the Nationalist Government moved to Taiwan (which had just been handed back to the ROC by Japan in 1945). The Constitution was designed to apply to the whole jurisdiction of the ROC in the Mainland; therefore when the constitution was enacted its jurisdiction covered the entire Mainland and Taiwan. However, the period during which the Mainland was under the jurisdiction of the Constitution was very short. Nevertheless, the Constitution has survived, even though there was a long period between 1949 and 1987 when many of the constitutional rights of the people were frozen.

Although there have been many different opinions about whether the Constitution appropriately fits the small geographical size of Taiwan, many people agree that after 1987 the Bill of Rights Chapter in the Constitution made very positive contributions to the enhancement of human rights protection and to the democratic development of the society.

The Constitution was amended a number of times in the period between 1991 and 2005. In those constitutional amendments, there were new provisions that required the direct election of the President of the Republic by the people;

practically eliminated the functions of the National Assembly; revised the interactive relations between the Executive Yuan and the Legislative Yuan; downsized the provincial government of Taiwan Province under the ROC, practically eliminating its functions; and required the legislative body to enact laws to govern relations between the people of Taiwan and the people from the Mainland, among other things.

Concerning human rights protection, the amendments only added two provisions, to protect women and handicapped people. Article 10, paragraph 5, of the Additional Articles of the Constitution of the Republic of China provides: "The State shall protect the dignity of women, safeguard their personal safety, eliminate sexual discrimination, and further substantive gender equality." Paragraph 6 of the same article provides: "The State shall guarantee insurance, medical care, obstacle-free environments, education and training, vocational guidance, and support and assistance in everyday life for physically and mentally handicapped persons, and shall also assist them to attain independence and to develop."

Aside from the addition of the two human rights-related provisions in the constitutional amendments, protection of the fundamental rights of the people in Taiwan basically still relies on the provisions in Chapter II of the Constitution—the Bill of Rights Chapter.

2.2 *The Bill of Rights Chapter in the Constitution Was Quite Advanced When It Was Enacted*

There is a relatively long list of rights included in Chapter II of the Constitution. The listed rights cover a wide range of human rights, including civil, political, social, and economic rights.

The main provisions in Chapter II include Article 7 which provides that all citizens, irrespective of sex, religion, race, class, or party affiliation, shall be considered equal before the law; Article 8 provides that personal freedom is guaranteed to the people; Article 10 provides that the people shall have freedom of residence and freedom of change of residence; Article 11 provides that the people shall have freedom of speech, teaching, writing and publication; Article 12 provides that the people shall have freedom of privacy of correspondence; Article 13 provides that the people shall have freedom of religious belief; Article 14 provides that the people shall have freedom of assembly and association; Article 15 provides that the right of existence, the right to work, and the right of property shall be guaranteed to the people; Article 16 provides that the people shall have the right to present petitions, lodge complaints, or institute legal proceedings; Article 17 provides that the people shall have the right of election, recall, initiative and referendum; Article 18 provides that the people shall have the right to take public examinations and to hold public offices; Article 19 provides that the duty of paying taxes must be provided by law; Article 21 provides that the people shall have the right and duty to receive a basic national education; Article 22 provides that all other freedoms and rights of the people that are not detrimental to social order or public welfare shall be guaranteed under the Constitution; and Article 23 provides that all the freedoms and rights enumerated in the preceding articles shall not be restricted by law except when as may be necessary to prevent infringement upon the freedoms of other persons, to avert an imminent crisis, to maintain social order or to advance public welfare.

Since Chapter II of the Constitution provides such wide coverage of the types of fundamental rights, the majority of human rights that are addressed by contemporary human rights treaties have already been included in the Constitution. The Bill of Rights provisions in the Constitution predate the adoption of the main human rights treaties and instruments, including the Universal Declaration of Human Rights of 1948; the Covenant on Civil and Political Rights (ICCPR) of 1966; the International Covenant on Economic, Social and Cultural Rights (CESCR) of 1966; the Convention on the Elimination of All Forms of Racial Discrimination (CERD) of 1965; the Convention on the Elimination of All Forms of Discrimination against Women (CEDAW) of 1979; the Convention against Torture and Other Cruel, Inhuman or Degrading Treatment (the Torture Convention) of 1984; the Convention on the Rights of the Child (CRC) of 1989; the Convention on the Protection of the Rights of All Migrant Workers and Members of Their Families (CMW) of 1990; and the Convention on the Rights of Persons with Disabilities (CRPD) of 2006. Considering the fact that the provisions in Chapter II of the Constitution were drafted in the 1940s, the constitutional ideas of the drafters of this Constitution were quite advanced for that period.

2.3 The Gaps Between the Bill of Rights Chapter and Human Rights Treaties

Having indicated that the Constitution is quite advanced in its human rights list, it must be said that there are still gaps between the contents of Chapter II of the Constitution and those provided in the contemporary human rights treaties and reflected in international human rights practice.

One of the notable gaps concerns the types of rights. There are many types of human rights listed in the various international human rights treaties that have not been included in the Constitution. This chapter will provide a few examples to illustrate this.

For instance, respect for human dignity is a fundamental type of human right. It is specifically provided for in many human rights treaties, including Article 10.1 of the ICCPR, which states that: "All persons deprived of their liberty shall be treated with humanity and with respect for the inherent dignity of the human person." Although it is possible to interpret the Constitution (as a whole) as also requiring the protection of the dignity of the people, the specific requirement to respect human dignity is not explicitly provided for in the Constitution.

Also, for instance, the prohibition of torture and of cruel/inhumane treatment should be a very important element in a democratic society and should be an essential right for all human beings. It is specifically provided for in the Torture Convention, which provides in Article 2.1 that: "Each State Party shall take effective legislative, administrative, judicial or other measures to prevent acts of torture in any territory under its jurisdiction." However, the prohibition of torture and cruel/inhumane treatment is not explicitly provided for in the Constitution, although it is possible to interpret the Constitution so that an act of torture is prohibited under the provisions of Article 8 in the Constitution which require personal freedom to be guaranteed to the people.

Some other examples include the right to family provided in Articles 17.1 and 23.1 of the ICCPR (that "No one shall be subjected to arbitrary or unlawful interference with his… family…" and that "The family is the natural and fundamental group unit of society and is entitled to protection by society and the State") and the right to health provided in Article 12.1 of the ICESCR (that "The States Parties… recognize the right of everyone to the enjoyment of the highest attainable standard of physical and mental health") and in the preamble of the WHO Constitution (that "The enjoyment of the highest attainable standard of health is one of the fundamental rights of every human being without distinction of race, religion, political belief, economic or social condition"). These are not explicitly provided for in the Constitution.

Another type of gap arises from the substantive meaning of the listed rights. There are many human rights provisions in international treaties that have been supplemented and interpreted by later instruments or decisions of international or regional courts. For instance, there are many "CCPR General Comments" which have been adopted by the Human Rights Committee and many "CESCR General Comments" which have been adopted by the Committee on Economic, Social and Cultural Rights to supplement the ICCPR and the ICESCR.

As a specific example, the right to an adequate standard of living (including the right to adequate housing) is provided in Article 11 of the ICESCR which states that "The States Parties to the present Covenant recognize the right of everyone to an adequate standard of living for himself and his family, including adequate food, clothing and housing, and to the continuous improvement of living conditions. The States Parties will take appropriate steps to ensure the realization of this right, recognizing to this effect the essential importance of international co-operation based on free consent." It is supplemented by CESCR General Comment No. 4,[2] which states in paragraph 18 that the "instances of forced eviction are *prima facie* incompatible with the requirements of the Covenant and can only be justified in the most exceptional circumstances, and in accordance with the relevant principles of international law." CESCR General Comment 7[3] also has similar provisions in paragraph 1.

[2]The text of General Comment 4 can be found at http://www.refworld.org/docid/47a7079a1.html.

[3]The text of General Comment 7 can be found at http://www.refworld.org/docid/47a70799d.html.

The Constitution of the ROC does not specifically address the right to adequate housing. Article 11 of the Constitution states in part that "The right of existence… shall be guaranteed to the people." From the wording, the specific content of this provision cannot be clearly perceived to cover the right to adequate housing. Considering Article 11 and General Comments Nos. 4 and 7 of the ICESCR, Article 11 of the Constitution should be understood as also including a guarantee of the right to an adequate standard of living, which in turn includes the right to adequate housing. The presumption of forced evictions as being incompatible with the right to adequate housing (as indicated in the above quoted General Comments) should be taken into consideration by the Constitutional Court when it interprets such rights in the Constitution so as to fill the gap of the substantive meaning in the constitutional provisions with that provided by international treaties.

2.4 The Need to Fill the Gap and the Desirability to Ensure a Living Constitution

The concept of a living constitution is about ensuring that the constitution is able to evolve in order to adapt to new circumstances or new developments without having to formally amend the constitutional provisions. An important way of ensuring that a constitution is able to adapt to new circumstances is through an appropriate approach to constitutional interpretation.

Different constitutional systems may have different needs regarding whether they have to adapt to their respective circumstances without formally amending the constitutional provisions. Even if a constitutional system needs to evolve so as to meet the new circumstances, an appropriate constitutional interpretation might not necessarily resolve all problems. This is especially true concerning whether to ensure the "government structure" provision in a constitution can be adapted to address new social and democratic developments. It may be difficult to rely on a constitutional interpretation to require a change in the government structure that is specifically provided in the constitution.

However, concerning human rights protection, it should be feasible to rely on constitutional interpretation to ensure that the constitutional protection of human rights is compatible and in line with the requirements of international human rights treaties and practices. Such an approach to constitutional interpretation would actually ensure a living constitution. Hence, the concept of a living constitution should be used to ensure the protection of fundamental rights.

The following reasons support the desirability of making the Constitution of the Republic of China a living one. First, the threshold of amending the Constitution is high. This high threshold became even more apparent when Article 12 of the Additional Articles of the Constitution of the Republic of China was included as a new requirement for constitutional amendments. It provides:

> Amendment of the Constitution shall be initiated upon the proposal of *one-fourth* of the total members of the Legislative Yuan, passed by at least *three-fourths* of the members present at a meeting attended by at least three-fourths of the total members of the Legislative Yuan, and sanctioned by electors in the free area of the Republic of China at a *referendum* held upon expiration of a six-month period of public announcement of the proposal, wherein the number of valid votes in favor exceeds *one-half of the total number of electors*. The provisions of Article 174 of the Constitution shall not apply. (Emphasis added)

Due to the high threshold of amending the Constitution and the difficulty of adding new provisions or changing existing ones in the Constitution, and also due to the premise that the constitutional provisions are supposed to be the fundamental norms and should not be subject to constant changes, it would be unrealistic and inappropriate to expect to have to constantly and continuously amend the Constitution so as to meet international human rights norms and practices.

Second, the stability of the constitutional framework should be an important element of any constitution. But this should not serve as a restriction to prevent the Constitution from becoming a living constitution. The protection of fundamental rights should not stand still and nor should it strictly follow the ideas and concepts of human rights protection held by the drafters of the Constitution many decades ago. If new norms and new developments cannot be integrated into the Constitution through certain appropriate methods, it is meaningless to conclude increasing numbers of international human rights treaties to address new human rights issues and to continually create new international human rights standards.

In short, it should be of high importance to ensure that the constitutional provisions for human rights protection are living provisions.

3 Comparing Different Approaches to Bring the Constitution in Line with Human Rights Treaties

3.1 Three Ways to Bring the Constitution in Line with Human Rights Treaties

There are three ways of ensuring the Constitution is in line with international human rights treaties and practices, and ensuring the Constitution continues to be a living constitution.

The first way (the "natural rights" approach) is to consider human rights as natural rights so that the Constitutional Court is required to apply them directly. Human rights are considered by many people as natural rights "held simply by virtue of being a person (human being). Such rights are natural in the sense that their source is human nature."[4]

This is, of course, an ideal way of directly incorporating human rights into the constitutional systems of all countries by requiring that all constitutions respect human rights, rights which are supposed to be held naturally by all human beings. However, in practice, it would be difficult to require all states to limit their sovereignty by admitting that all human rights are to directly govern their domestic constitutional systems, disregarding their existing constitutional provisions. Also, it could be very controversial concerning the scope of the rights to be considered as natural rights, especially in fields where states have made reservations on certain treaty provisions or where a human rights provision only requires states to progressively realize the expected standards.

The second way (the "higher norm" approach) is to consider human rights treaties as self-executing and as having a legal status equal to or higher than the Constitution. Taking this approach would bind the Constitutional Court and require the Court to directly apply the treaty provisions. In this regard, Article 141 of the Constitution provides:

> The foreign policy of the Republic of China shall… *respect* treaties and the Charter of the United Nations, in order to… promote international cooperation, advance international justice and ensure world peace. (Emphasis added)

One possible interpretation of this constitutional provision is that the whole Republic (including the Legislative Yuan and the Constitutional Court) is required to respect international treaties, including human rights treaties. Hence, any legislation should not be drafted in such a way as to be in violation of the relevant human rights treaties so as to *respect* them. The Constitutional Court should also interpret the Constitution in a way to realize human rights treaties so as to *respect* them.

This way of ensuring that the Constitution is in line with international human rights treaties would encounter some practical problems. First, it is suggested that controversies would arise concerning whether the entire Republic should *respect* a treaty that is not signed or accessed by it. Second, there could also be different views about whether the term "respect" should be interpreted in a broad manner. If it were, the legislative body would be required to enact laws to implement human rights treaties, while inconsistent legislation or the lack of needed legislation would be considered "unconstitutional." Third, there could also be human rights provisions that are reserved by certain contracting states or that merely require states to progressively realize certain standards. It would be very controversial whether the Republic would be required to *respect* these kinds of provisions in the human rights treaties to the same degree as other provisions in the human rights treaties.

The third way (the "interpretation" approach) is to rely on constitutional interpretation to take human rights treaties into consideration, to "read" human rights treaties in a way that is consistent with constitutional provisions or to "read" the contents of the human rights treaties into the constitutional provisions. Below, the

[4]Donnelly (1982), p. 391.

author of this chapter will explain why the "interpretation" approach is the most appropriate way of maintaining a living constitution.

3.2 The "Interpretation" Approach Is a Desirable Way

The following reasons support the use of constitutional interpretation (instead of considering human rights as natural rights or treating human rights treaties as higher norms to bind the Constitutional Court) to ensure a living constitution and that the international treaties will be systemically taken into serious consideration by the Constitutional Court:

First, if the "natural rights" approach or the "higher norm" approach were adopted, it would actually disregard the provisions of the Constitution and replace them with the relevant provisions from human rights treaties or other international instruments (such the General Comments mentioned above). This would create a serious problem as to whether the constitutional provisions could be disregarded on a case-by-case basis or even systemically.

Second, Article 78 of the Constitution provides, in part, that "The Judicial Yuan shall interpret the Constitution…" Article 79, paragraph 2, provides, in part, that "The Judicial Yuan shall have a certain number of Justices [i.e., the "Constitutional Court"] to take charge of matters specified in Article 78 of this Constitution." Hence, the Constitutional Court's responsibility is to apply and interpret the Constitution. It would be beyond its role to disregard the constitutional provisions and solely or directly apply international human rights treaties or practices. A more desirable approach would be to interpret the Constitution in such a way as to ensure that its human rights provisions are fully in line with international human rights treaties and practices. This would not only ensure the full protection of human rights in Taiwan but would also ensure that the Constitutional Court was fulfilling the duties entrusted to it by the Constitution.

4 Some General Principles for Constitutional Interpretation

There are no codified principles for constitutional interpretation provided for by the Constitution or other legislation. Basically, constitutional interpretation should be guided by the plain meaning or ordinary meaning of the text, and the context of the interpreted norm should also be taken into consideration. There is no difference between constitutional interpretation and other kinds of legal interpretation (including statutory interpretation and treaty interpretation) in that they all begin with the textual wording as a basis from which to find the plain meaning or ordinary meaning and that the interpreted provision should be understood in its context. However, constitutional interpretation is different from other kinds of legal interpretation in many ways.

The drafting history, the drafters' intention or the preparatory work may all be important factors which affect a "statutory" interpretation of a piece of legislation. When it comes to constitutional interpretation, the situation could be quite different. The Constitution is both a legal and political document. It serves to reflect the collective will of the people. Hence, it would be inappropriate to totally disregard the drafting history. However, this does not mean that the drafters' intention should always strictly guide the interpretation of the Constitution. After the Constitution comes into effect, it should have its own life and should be able to evolve. Hence, when interpreting the Constitution, different significance should be given to the drafting history, the drafters' collective intention or the preparatory work in regard to the interpretation of the constitutional provisions governing the government structure and in regard to the interpretation of the human rights provisions in the Constitution.

If the interpreted constitutional provision concerns human rights protection, the drafting history, the drafters' intention and the preparatory work should not be given too much weight or be emphasized too much. Otherwise, the level and extent of human rights protection for the people will be fixed to the standards that were set forth many decades ago, which is definitely an undesirable outcome.

In this regard, the author would argue that constitutional interpretation should be subject to an "evolutive interpretation" so as to be able to give new meaning, as it becomes necessary, to an aged constitutional provision concerning human rights protection. In a separate book, the author of this chapter has indicated that:[5]

> This is particularly important if there are new contents of fundamental rights being developed or recognized at the international level (such as a treaty recognizing a new kind of human rights being concluded) and if the contents of such rights are in contradiction with the intent of the drafter of the constitution, the new element must be brought into the process of constitutional interpretation. This approach will help a constitution adapt to new circumstances in the society of the State and will make sure that the constitution will not hinder the progress of the society. This approach will also ensure that a constitution will evolve and improve over time and will also reduce the need to amend the text of a constitution.

5 The Way of Reading International Treaties into the Constitutional Provisions

After having argued that the human rights provisions in the Constitution should be subject to an "evolutive interpretation" so as to ensure a living constitution and to ensure its adaptation to new developments in international human rights protection and new situations faced by the society, a further question to be asked is: what should be the specific method of interpreting these provisions?

The author's argument is that the interpreter of the Constitution should still resort to the textual interpretation and give "appropriate plain or ordinary meaning" to its human rights provisions. The plain meaning or ordinary meaning of the constitutional

---

[5]Lo (2017), p. 25.

provisions should not be the "ordinary meaning" at the time when the Constitution was drafted. The ordinary meaning should evolve with the development of the concept of human rights protection and the progress of the society. The constitutional provisions should be given contemporary meaning (i.e., the ordinary meaning at the present time). International human rights treaties and practices can shed light on the wording used in the Constitution to help the Constitutional Court find their contemporary ordinary meaning. In other words, when understanding the contemporary meanings of the constitutional provisions, the Constitutional Court must take international human rights treaties and practices into consideration and read the exact same meaning within human rights treaties as it does in constitutional provisions or read the contents of the human rights treaties into the constitutional provisions.

The attitude of taking international human rights treaties into consideration is in line with the expectation provided in the above-quoted provision in Article 141 of the Constitution, which requires that international treaties are respected. It also meets the requirement that the Constitutional Court is discharging its function of interpreting the Constitution and ensuring its implementation.

The author of this chapter has submitted many separate opinions (either concurring or dissenting opinions) to the Constitutional Court as one of its members. In a number of these opinions, arguments were made that the Court should systemically consider international human rights treaties and practices so as to read these treaties and practices into the meaning of the constitutional provision. For instance, in the Concurring Opinion that the author submitted to the Court on J.Y. Interpretation No. 696, he indicated the following:

> The Universal Declaration of Human Rights of 1948 provides in Article 16 that the family is the natural and fundamental group unit of society and is entitled to protection by society and the State. Article 10 of the International Covenant on Economic, Social and Cultural Rights (ICESCR) also emphasizes various rights that should be accorded to the family. Article 23 of International Covenant on Civil and Political Rights (ICCPR) further states that the family is the natural and fundamental group unit of society and is entitled to protection by society and the State. The European Convention on Human Rights has even wider protection to marriage and family, including Article 8.1 (which provides that "Everyone has the right to respect for his private and family life, his home and his correspondence") and Article 12 (which provides that "Men and women of marriageable age have the right to marry and to found a family, according to the national laws governing the exercise of this right").... Although the Constitutional Court cannot directly apply these human rights instruments as the sole basis to make its decisions, this does not affect the universal nature of the rights and the values recognized in these international instruments. Neither should it prevent the Court from taking into serious consideration these international instruments when interpreting the Constitution and trying to understand the essence of its provisions.[6]

[6]Lo Chang-fa Da Fa Guan Shizi Di 696 Hao Jie Shi Xie Tong Yi Jian Shu [羅昌發大法官釋字第696號解釋協同意見書] (Justice Chang-fa Lo's concurring opinions among the Justices of the Constitutional Court, Interpretation No. 696) (20 Jan 2012) (R.O.C.). This concurring opinion can be found at http://www.judicial.gov.tw/constitutionalcourt/uploadfile/C100/696協同意見書_羅昌發_pdf.

In previous interpretations, the Constitutional Court has cited human rights treaties or documents as "references" from time to time. For instance, in J.Y. Interpretation No. 710 concerning the mandatory deportation and detention of people from Mainland China,[7] the Constitutional Court cited Article 12 of the ICCPR and paragraph 6 of General Comment No. 15 to rule that the freedom of movement of people from Mainland China within Taiwan needs to be protected by the Constitution. The Court also cited Article 13 of the ICCPR and Article 1 of Protocol No. 7 to the European Convention on Human Rights to support the notion that the mandatory deportation of a person from Mainland China who legally entered Taiwan must fulfill corresponding due process requirements, except where immediate actions are otherwise required in response to a threat to national security or social order. It is clear that both international and regional treaties are taken into consideration by the Constitutional Court when interpreting the constitutional provisions.

Also, in J.Y. Interpretation No. 756 which was recently issued concerning prisoners' rights,[8] there is an endnote included in the interpretation, quoting paragraph 5 of the Basic Principles for the Treatment of Prisoners adopted by the United Nations General Assembly (A/RES/45/111) as a reference. The quoted paragraph states that: "Except for those limitations that are demonstrably necessitated by the fact of incarceration, all prisoners shall retain the human rights and fundamental freedoms set out in the Universal Declaration of Human Rights, and, where the state concerned is a party, the International Covenant on Economic, Social and Cultural Rights, and the International Covenant on Civil and Political Rights and the Optional Protocol thereto, as well as such other rights as are set out in other United Nations covenants." Apparently, the Constitutional Court even reads the international human rights practice (in addition to the human rights treaties) into the textual language of the Constitution.

6 Concluding Remarks

This chapter discusses the desirability and importance of ensuring a living constitution for the Republic. A very important aspect of ensuring a living constitution is to introduce or incorporate international human rights treaties and practices into the decisions made by the Constitutional Court.

---

[7]Si Fa Yuan Da Fa Guan Jie Shi Shizi Di 710 Hao [Justices of the Constitutional Court, Judicial Yuan, Interpretation No. 710] (5 July 2013) (R.O.C.). The translation of J.Y. Interpretation 710 can be found at http://www.judicial.gov.tw/constitutionalcourt/EN/p03_01.asp?expno=710.

[8]Si Fa Yuan Da Fa Guan Jie Shi Shizi Di 756 Hao [Justices of the Constitutional Court, Judicial Yuan, Interpretation No. 756] (1 Dec 2017) (R.O.C.). The Chinese version of J.Y. Interpretation 756 can be found at http://www.judicial.gov.tw/constitutionalcourt/p03_01_1.asp?expno=756. The translation was not available when the author prepared this chapter.

This chapter suggests that although there may be different approaches to the introduction or incorporation of international treaties and practices into the operation of the Constitution, the most feasible way is to resort to the fundamental interpretation method of relying on textual interpretation to look for appropriate plain meanings or ordinary meanings for the interpreted term. The ordinary meaning should, however, not be the "ordinary meaning" at the time when the Constitution was drafted. The ordinary meaning of the human rights protection provisions should evolve by taking into consideration the developments of international human rights treaties and practices. This approach would be more in line with the duty entrusted to the Court by the Constitution and would also make sure that the constitutional provisions do not become obsolete.

References

Donnelly J (1982) Human rights as natural rights. Hum Rights Q 4(3):391–405

Lo C-f (2017) Treaty interpretation under the Vienna Convention on the Law of Treaties: a new round of codification. Springer, Berlin

United Nations Human Rights Office of the High Commissioner, Women's Human Rights and Gender Equality, http://www.ohchr.org/EN/Issues/Women/WRGS/Pages/WRGSIndex.aspx. Accessed 19 Dec 2017

Chang-fa Lo has been Justice of the Constitutional Court of the ROC (Taiwan) since October 2011. Prior to his current judicial position, he was Chair Professor and Lifetime Distinguished Professor at National Taiwan University (NTU); Dean of NTU College of Law; Founding Director of Asian Center for WTO and International Health Law and Policy of NTU College of Law (ACWH); Founding Director of the Center for Ethics, Law and Society in Biomedicine and Technology of NTU; Commissioner of Taiwan's Fair Trade Commission; Commissioner of Taiwan's International Trade Commission; and legal advisor for Taiwan's GATT/WTO accession negotiations. In his capacity as Director of the ACWH, Prof. Lo launched two English journals, namely, the *Asian Journal of WTO and International Health Law and Policy* (AJWH, an SSCI listed journal) and the *Contemporary Asia Arbitration Journal* (CAA) in 2006 and 2008, respectively. During his tenure as Dean of NTU College of Law, he also launched the English journal, the *NTU Law Review*. He was appointed by the WTO as a panelist for DS332 Brazil—Measures Affecting Imports of Retreaded Tyre in 2006, DS468 Ukraine—Definitive Safeguard Measures on Certain Passenger Cars in 2014, and appointed as a member of the Permanent Group of Experts under the SCM Agreement of WTO in 2008. He is also Chairman of the Asia WTO Research Network (AWRN) since 2013. Prior to his teaching career, he practiced law in Taipei. He received his S.J.D. degree from Harvard University Law School in 1989. He is the author of 13 books (including *Treaty Interpretation under the Vienna Convention on the Law of Treaties—A New Round of Codification* published by Springer) and the editor of seven books (including this one), and he has authored more than 100 journal papers and book chapters. He was granted the "National Professorship Award" by the Ministry of Education and the "Outstanding Scholarship Chair Professorship Award" by the Foundation for Advancement of Outstanding Scholarship.

Chapter 16
Rights Advocacy Through Simulation: The Genius of the Constitutional Court Simulation in Taiwan

Yen-tu Su

Abstract As a fledgling civic institution in Taiwan, the Constitutional Court Simulation (CCS) has received much attention and interest from the Taiwan Constitutional Court as well as the general public in recent years by tackling such salient issues as same-sex marriage, the death penalty, and transitional justice. This chapter analyzes, explains and assesses the workings of the CCS as a moot court education program, a shadow constitutional court, a deliberative forum, and as a new approach to rights advocacy in Taiwan. Though the success of the CCS as a rights advocate would make it more difficult for the CCS to project itself as an impartial shadow court, the CCS enterprise attests to the ingenuity and enthusiasm of those who fight for liberal progressive causes in civil society in Taiwan.

Keywords Civic deliberation · Civil society · Constitutional Court Simulation (CCS) · Moot court · Rights advocacy · Shadow court · Taiwan Constitutional Court (TCC)

The author participated in the Constitutional Court Simulation (CCS) in 2016 as a CCS Justice. The author would like to express his deepest appreciation to Professor Hsu Yu-hsiu and to all the other participants in the CCS. The author would also like to thank Mr. Huang Jen-hsien (黃任顯) for sharing his insights, and Mr. Hsieh Zong-en (謝宗恩) for his research assistance.

Y. T. Su (✉)
Institutum Iurisprudentiae, Academia Sinica, Taipei, Taiwan
e-mail: yentusu@sinica.edu.tw

J. A. Cohen et al. (eds.), *Taiwan and International Human Rights*, Economics, Law, and Institutions in Asia Pacific, https://doi.org/10.1007/978-981-13-0350-0_16

1 Introduction

On 24 May 2017, the Taiwan Constitutional Court (hereinafter TCC) issued J.Y. Interpretation No. 748, a landmark ruling that paves the way for Taiwan to become the first Asian country to recognize same-sex marriage.[1] Many groups and individuals played a role in helping to bring about this milestone achievement in marriage equality in Taiwan, and the Constitutional Court Simulation (模擬憲法法庭; hereinafter CCS) can surely be counted as one of them. Before the legendary LGBT activist Chi Chia-wei (祁家威) filed his latest petition to the Court in August 2015, a few lawyers on Mr. Chi's side had been able to test the constitutional arguments for marriage equality in a pilot case before the CCS. The CCS held an oral argument for its hypothetical same-sex marriage case in June 2014. This first-ever public simulation of a Constitutional Court oral argument drew a packed audience and was webcast by an online news media affiliated with the Public Television Service in Taiwan. The CCS issued its mock ruling on the case in August 2014, holding that the ban on same-sex marriage and adoption violates the Constitution, and that same-sex couples should be entitled to marriage and adoption even before the law is changed.[2] The opinion of the CCS was published in a widely-circulated law journal, and was submitted to the Constitutional Court. Soon thereafter, the real Constitutional Court decided to hold oral arguments on the issue of same-sex marriage in March 2017 for cases brought to the Court by Mr. Chi and the Taipei City Government. Though much had changed in Taiwan since the TCC dismissed Mr. Chi's previous same-sex marriage petition in 2001 for "lack of merits,"[3] the mock ruling of the CCS appears to have not only encouraged LGBT activists to seek out constitutional adjudication once again but it also encouraged the Constitutional Court to take on the issue as a serious matter of constitutional law.

The first CCS, a harbinger of Taiwan's same-sex marriage ruling of 2017, was primarily a graduate course taught by former TCC Justice Hsu Yu-hsiu (許玉秀) at National Chiao Tung University School of Law.[4] Under Professor Hsu's vision and leadership, the CCS has since been transformed into a collective enterprise that aspires to serve as a shadow Constitutional Court of, by, and for civil society in Taiwan. Sponsored by the Taipei Bar Association and organized according to the unofficial Constitutional Court Simulation Act (模擬憲法法庭法) as drafted by Professor Hsu, the second CCS was formed in 2015 as an independent entity to

[1]Dafaguan Shizi Di 748 Hao [大法官釋字第748號] (Judicial Yuan Interpretation No. 748) (24 May 2017) (R.O.C.). The official English translation of this decision is available at: http://www.judicial.gov.tw/constitutionalcourt/EN/p03_01.asp?expno=748.

[2]Constitutional Court Simulation Judgment No. 2 (2014).

[3]Dismissal Resolution No. 2 of the 1166th Conference of the Taiwan Constitutional Court (2001). http://www.judicial.gov.tw/constitutionalcourt/p10_02.asp?id=381. Accessed 2 Nov 2017.

[4]For an introduction to the origin and evolution of the CCS in Chinese, see Huang and Wu (2015); see also Hsu (2015) [hereinafter interview with Professor Hsu].

address another cultural war issue of the day: the constitutionality of the death penalty. During the two-day oral argument for the simulated death penalty case, the CCS, once again, drew much attention from the media and the public alike by channeling moving or thought-provoking statements made by attorneys, expert witnesses, and a few friends of the court—including three who spoke as members of the victims' families. The CCS moved swiftly to grant a mock stay for all pending executions.[5] Ultimately, it rendered a mock ruling, by a vote of 5–4, that deemed the very use of the death penalty as constitutionally impermissible.[6] Professor Chang Wen-chen (張文貞) of the National Taiwan University wrote a meticulous opinion that cited various authorities in international human rights law and comparative constitutional law for the simulated court, and all other eight CCS Justices filed concurring and/or dissenting opinions. It is merely a matter of time before the real Constitutional Court in Taiwan will revisit its jurisprudence on capital punishment, and when it does so, its decision is bound to be compared to and measured against the precedent set by its counterpart that works in the shadows.

The third CCS convened in 2016 to hear two cases concerning issues of transitional justice in Taiwan, and, for the first time, there was a professor of philosophy and a high court judge sitting on the simulated bench.[7] As the CCS has grown into a notable actor in Taiwan's civil society, the boundary between the fictional and the real has become more permeable and less clear-cut. Whereas the simulated same-sex marriage case was brought to the CCS by purely fictional legislators, the simulated legislative petition this time was signed by three members of the Legislative Yuan, and the lead petitioner Legislator Huang Kuo-chang (黃國昌) attended the oral argument to argue for the simulated petition, which was inspired by the true story of Li Ma-dou (李媽兜), a Taiwanese Communist who was convicted and executed for treason in 1953. The third CCS expanded its rules of access to hear the simulated case brought by Du Ming-jhe (杜銘哲), who in real life could not be compensated for the wrongs suffered by his late father Dr. Du Siao-sheng (杜孝生). Dr. Du, an aboriginal elite, was politically framed and persecuted in the 1950s for embezzlement but not for the specific political crimes eligible for reparation under the existing law. Once again, the CCS held a two-day oral argument that attracted great interest from the public. Later, the simulated court unanimously held that a myriad of laws central to the issue were unconstitutional for violating human rights when the R.O.C. regime was an *Unrechtstaat*, or for failing to meet the basic needs of transitional justice after Taiwan democratized. It also overruled two TCC precedents (J.Y. Interpretation Nos. 272 and 477) and exhorted the

---

[5]Constitutional Court Simulation Temporary Order No. 1 (2015).

[6]Constitutional Court Simulation Judgment No. 3 (2015). The official English translation of this decision is available at: https://sites.google.com/site/simulateconstitutionalcourt/judgement/ccs-j-003.

[7]Originally the third CCS also included a professor of history, Professor Hsueh Hua-yuan (薛化元), but Professor Hsueh resigned from the CCS after he was appointed president of the Memorial Foundation of 2/28 (財團法人二二八事件紀念基金會), a government-funded organization and one of the respondents to the case under review.

political branches to take certain steps to right the wrongs of transitional injustice.[8] It remains to be seen whether and to what extent the TCC and the unified government of the Democratic Progressive Party (DPP) will follow the footsteps of the CCS in pursuing the agenda of transitional justice, but at least many more people in Taiwan have come to know the true stories of Li Ma-dou and Dr. Du Siao-sheng thanks to the play performed by the CCS.

It is correct to think of the CCS activities as a series of plays that took place in the civil society of Taiwan. These plays were directed and produced by the visionary Professor Hsu, while she and many other individuals and NGOs worked voluntarily and tirelessly on stage and/or behind the scenes to make the constitutional court simulation one of the most remarkable developments in civic constitutionalism in Taiwan in recent years.[9] This chapter court simulation one of the most remarkable developments to help outsiders understand and appreciate the plays put forth by the participants on the CCS. In addition to recounting how the CCS has worked thus far, this chapter seeks to interpret what the CCS has meant to Taiwan by assessing its performance against four possible objectives of the simulation. With certain degrees of success, the CCS has met its goals in serving as (i) a moot court education program, (ii) a shadow court experiment for judicial reform, and (iii) a forum for civic deliberation. This chapter further contends that the entire CCS simulation play that begins with the inception of the petition and ends in a CCS decision can be considered (iv) an innovation for rights advocacy in Taiwan. Though the success of the CCS as a rights advocate makes it more difficult for the CCS to project itself as an impartial shadow court for all, the unyielding quest to live up to such noble aspirations is arguably what makes it possible for the CCS to become an even more powerful "engine of liberty" than traditional modes of rights advocacy.[10]

2 A Moot Court Education

Moot courts and mock trials have long been part of legal, civics, or liberal arts education in many countries, and the CCS can certainly be viewed as a newcomer to this venerable tradition.[11] Justice Hsu Yu-hsiu had thought about teaching the first-ever simulation course on constitutional adjudication in Taiwan for some time, and she managed to put the idea into action after she left the TCC upon the conclusion of her 8-year term as an associate Justice in 2011. Professor Hsu first taught the Constitutional Court Simulation as a professional course at the Taipei

---

[8]Constitutional Court Simulation Judgments Nos. 4 and 5 (2016). https://sites.google.com/site/civilconstitutionalcourt/judgement/scc45. Accessed 2 Nov 2017.

[9]On the recent development of civic constitutionalism in Taiwan, see Yeh (2017); see also Chang (2009).

[10]On the idea of "engine of liberty," see Cole (2016).

[11]On the educational uses of moot courts and mock trials, see, e.g., Milstein (2001), Spader (2002) and Finneran (2017).

Bar Association in the spring of 2013.[12] Later, she taught a graduate course with the same title at National Chiao Tung University School of Law in the spring of 2014. About 10 mid-career and graduate students took the course with Professor Hsu when it was listed on the law school's curriculum. With the wholehearted devotion of these students, who had to play the roles of Justices and law clerks at the same time, and with help from prominent academics and practicing lawyers who filled the vacancies on the bench, the course gave birth to the blockbuster play of simulated adjudication concerning same-sex marriage in 2014.[13] Since early 2015 the CCS has turned into an extracurricular project, but this only makes it more effective as an educational program for training more and more constitutional lawyers as well as virtuous citizens. For many participants on the CCS, what the CCS has meant to them is first and foremost a learning experience.

The CCS is not a typical moot court, however. Whereas moot courts in the American mold usually aim at preparing and training law students with practical skills for appellate advocacy, the CCS is centered on role play of constitutional judges. It is a training program not just for those who want to argue cases before the TCC, but also for those who want to be in the shoes of Constitutional Court judges in Taiwan.[14] The CCS Justices wear robes only when the simulated court is in session, but even when they do not wear robes, they play the roles assigned to them throughout the term of the simulated court. During the term, which lasts for about 6 months, the CCS Justices have to convene frequently and exchange tens of thousands of emails just for the sake of handling the simulated case(s) on its docket. At the insistence of Professor Hsu, they address one another as "Justice" even in their closed conferences, email exchanges, and private conversations. They study, deliberate, and vote on the case(s) before them; they also have to write opinions to justify and elaborate their collective or individual positions. Although the CCS hears merely one or two cases each term, playing the role of the CCS Justices is as demanding a *pro bono* work as one can think of.[15] The intensive training of the CCS Justices is simply impossible without the devotion of those who play important supporting roles, such as counsels, expert witnesses, and law clerks. Their CCS experiences, too, are shaped by countless moments of teaching and learning.[16]

Legal education in Taiwan has been known for putting significant emphasis on training students to think like judges, but the predominant model is about training students to see things and approach legal issues like a career judge in a single-judge court. The CCS is not only the first moot court exercise in Taiwan that focuses on constitutional adjudication but also the first one that simulates appellate judging in a collegial court. As the director and the producer of the simulation play, Professor

[12]See interview with Professor Hsu.

[13]See Huang and Wu (2015), at pp. 7–8.

[14]See interview with Professor Hsu.

[15]For a few CCS Justices' reflections on their experiences on the CCS, see Chang (2015) and Li (2015).

[16]See, e.g., Huang and Wu (2015) and Shih (2015).

Hsu would share her experiences in the TCC with the CCS Justices, and would make some comments and suggestions with respect to the administration of the simulated court, but she also would do her best to refrain from intervening in the CCS Justices' deliberation and decision making. The outcome of the simulated case is by no means scripted, and each and every CCS Justice has wide latitude to act and improvise throughout the course of the simulation. Under these circumstances, the CCS Justices have ample opportunities to learn from each other, which helps them gain a much deeper appreciation of how constitutional law is interpreted and constructed through human interactions in the real world than they otherwise would have.[17] It is too early to tell whether the CCS could serve as an unofficial orientation for future TCC Justices; however, Professor Hsu would certainly love to see that in the future.[18] Although few, if any, CCS Justices have ever expected or dreamed that one day they would sit on the real Constitutional Court, what they have learned from their experiences on the CCS may well have helped them to become better constitutional lawyers who know more about how judges think and how judicial politics shapes the law. We may soon be able to observe the ripple effect of CCS education when these fortunate few pass on what they have learned to their colleagues, friends, and students.

3 A Shadow Court Experiment

One cannot tell the story of the CCS without also telling the story of the Taiwan Constitutional Court, and not merely because the CCS is the brainchild of former TCC Justice Professor Hsu. As one of the oldest Constitutional Courts in the world, the TCC has been transformed from a weak court in an authoritarian regime into a powerful guardian of constitutionalism over the past three decades.[19] Armed with a jurisprudence of judicial supremacy, the TCC has played a major role in updating and rewriting the old constitutional order of the ROC for the new democracy in Taiwan. The judicialization of politics is such a notable trend in Taiwan that some commentators mistakenly believe that constitutional interpretation is the sole purview and responsibility of the TCC. The high expectations people have for the Court, however, often turn into disappointment. Composed of 15 Justices appointed by the President and confirmed by the Legislative Yuan, each year the TCC issues, at a deliberate pace, very few merit decisions, known as J.Y. Interpretations. Its plenary docket even shrank to single digits in 2013, 2015, and 2016.[20] The low productivity

---

[17]See Huang and Wu (2015), at pp. 9–10.

[18]See interview with Professor Hsu.

[19]For an introduction to the TCC and its changing roles throughout the constitutional development of Taiwan, see Yeh (2016), pp. 167–174.

[20]Dafaguan Jieshi Anjian Shoujie Qingxing [大法官解釋案件收結情形] (The Constitutional Court cases commenced, terminated, and pending) (2017) Judicial Yuan. http://www.judicial.gov.tw/juds/report/sa-2.htm. Accessed 18 Nov 2017.

of the Court has much to do with how it conducts its business. Organized as a council and hearing all of its cases *en banc*, the TCC is extremely selective in choosing cases to hear, and it is even more discerning in deciding whether to hold oral arguments. Most of the petitions in the rolling docket of the Court are summarily dismissed for lack of merit, as determined by the majority of the TCC Justices. While majority rule is also applied to certain types of J.Y. Interpretations, the TCC can "interpret" the Constitution or rule on the constitutionality of a statutory law only with a vote of 2/3 supermajority. All J.Y. Interpretations are *per curiam* in form as in substance, but they have been accompanied by more and more concurring and/or dissenting opinions issued by individual Justices since the late 2000s. Though the reform of the TCC has been discussed for nearly 2 decades, the Legislative Yuan has yet to revise and replace the Constitutional Interpretation Procedure Act (司法院大法官審理案件法) of 1993.

It is against this backdrop that the CCS has developed its identity as a shadow Constitutional Court—that is, a private, unofficial Constitutional Court that seeks to influence the real one by showing what the simulated court would do if it were in power.[21] The purpose of the simulation, in other words, is less about imitating and celebrating what the TCC has been doing thus far and more about envisioning and enacting a realistic utopia of constitutional adjudication in Taiwan.[22] By taking on those hot-button issues the TCC has dodged or squandered in the past, and by producing alternative outcomes that are more progressive and more persuasive than what the TCC would make in light of its existing jurisprudence, the CCS certainly hopes to "shame those in power into doing better" and thereby fits the bill of a reform-minded shadow institution as generalized and commended by Dean Heather Gerken of Yale Law School.[23] Furthermore, the CCS adopts several organizational and procedural measures that were proposed initially for the reform of the TCC.[24] The CCS is organized as a court rather than a council. In addition to reviewing the constitutionality of all sorts of norms, it is authorized to scrutinize the constitutionality of judicial decisions on specific cases. All of the CCS decisions are made by majority rule. Its merit decisions are formatted as court opinions as opposed to interpretations, and they are signed by the authoring CCS Justice(s). By serving as a laboratory for testing a new institutional design for the constitutional court, the CCS not only enables the TCC reformers to think through and work out the details of their reform proposals, but also helps them to showcase the benefits and feasibility of the proposed reforms.

The social standing of the CCS as a shadow Constitutional Court is much dependent on the men and women who sit on the CCS bench. The first CCS that heard the simulated same-sex marriage case was composed of 15 CCS Justices, 11

---

[21]On the idea of shadow institutions, see generally Gerken and Kang (2011), at pp. 91–93. For an instance of shadow court experimentation in the United States, see Foley (2010).

[22]See Kao (2015).

[23]Gerken and Kang (2011), at p. 92; see also Gerken (2008).

[24]See Li (2015) and Tsai (2015).

of whom were mid-career or graduate students who took the course with Professor Hsu. While these students had proved themselves as competent CCS Justices, the credibility of the first CCS was further enhanced by the participation of 4 legal celebrities in Taiwan, including prominent constitutional lawyer Nigel N. T. Li (李念祖), who guest-starred as the Chief CCS Justice and presided over the oral argument of the case at the request of Professor Hsu. The identity of the CCS as a shadow Constitutional Court has become more and more pronounced after it became independent and was reorganized into a 9-member court in 2015. According to the unofficial CCS Act, CCS Justices are publicly nominated and selected by a committee formed by the outgoing CCS Justices.[25] The selection process places significant emphasis on the composition diversity of the simulated court, as the CCS Act requires that no more than 2/3 of the CCS Justices be of the same gender and that legal academics, bar associations and civic groups be equally represented on the CCS.[26] Thanks in part to the TCC, which has made the act of constitutional judgment worth emulating but has meant that the legal profession and civil society in Taiwan are less occupied with works related to real constitutional cases, the CCS has managed to host an impressive list of notable names to serve as CCS Justices. So far, all except two CCS Justices have been trained in law. However, the extraordinary performance of the two non-lawyers—writer Chang Chuan-fen (張娟芬) and philosophy professor Chen Jau-hwa (陳瑤華)—has made a strong case for breaking up the lawyers' monopoly over constitutional judging. Most of the CCS Justices are not senior enough in the profession to be qualified to serve on the TCC,[27] but they are reputable in their respective fields; some even have public profiles as human rights lawyers and/or public intellectuals. The CCS, therefore, could build its collective reputation as a shadow constitutional court upon the individual reputation of those who have served as CCS Justices.

As part of its experiments in the institutional design of constitutional adjudication, the CCS welcomes interested third parties or concerned citizens to take part in its proceedings as *amici curiae*, i.e., friends of the court. *Amici* are invited to submit their briefs to the CCS, and they are given the opportunity to speak before the CCS Justices during oral arguments. All *amicus* briefs are listed and published on the CCS website, and some have been cited in the opinions of the simulated court. The unofficial CCS Act does not institutionalize the participation of *amici*, but it does not stop the CCS from engaging with them, either. To a certain extent, this open policy helps the CCS to establish itself and be recognized as a shadow Constitutional Court not just for some, but for all.[28] The CCS also considers itself to be a friend of the TCC, and it submitted its mock opinion on same-sex marriage to

---

[25]Moni Xianfa Fatingfa [模擬憲法法庭法] (Constitutional Court Simulation Act), arts. 5–6 (2015) (Taiwan).

[26]*Id.*, arts. 2–3.

[27]For the qualifications of the CCS Justices, see *id.*, art. 7. For the qualifications of the TCC Justices, see Sifayuan Zuzhifa [司法院組織法] (The Judicial Yuan Organization Act), art. 4 (2015) (Taiwan).

[28]See Huang and Wu (2015), at pp. 10–11.

the TCC as an *amicus* brief when the TCC decided to hear oral arguments for the same-sex marriage petitions on its docket. But unlike the CCS, the TCC declines to accept or acknowledge help from any *amicus curiae* in the absence of *ex ante* rules regarding *amici* participation.[29] The CCS's lack of formal recognition from the TCC, however, belies the close ties between the two and whatever influence the former may have on the latter. During the confirmation hearings for the seven TCC nominees in 2016, the CCS was mentioned by a few legislators,[30] and at least two TCC nominees were reported to have expressed their agreement with CCS jurisprudence in their written responses to the questionnaires sent to them.[31] The TCC may not like the pressure of being compared to the CCS, but the Court should be thankful for having a true friend like the CCS, which, after all, has run a myriad of institutional experiments for the sake of its betterment.

4 A Deliberative Forum

The oral arguments of the CCS, in many ways, resemble a large seminar or symposium held in public for the purpose of fostering civic deliberation on an important issue of the day. Taking place in an auditorium capable of seating a large audience, the oral arguments for a CCS case may continue for as long as two whole days for two consecutive weeks. On the day of the oral arguments, the counselors representing the petitioner(s) and the respondent(s) take turns to argue their cases before the CCS Justices, who let the counselors finish their presentations as prepared and

[29]The TCC treated all of the *amicus* briefs it received in the same manner as the grievance letters it commonly received and circulated them among the Justices who participated in the same-sex marriage case; see Sifayuan Zhendui Minjiantuanti Jiu 106 Nian 3 Yue 24 Ri Xianfa Fating Xiangguan Chengxu Yijian zhi Shuoming [司法院針對民間團體就 106 年 3 月 24 日憲法法庭相關程序意見之說明] (The response of the Judicial Yuan to the opinions of the civic groups regarding the procedural issues in the TCC oral argument scheduled for 24 Mar 2017) (2017). Judicial Yuan. http://jirs.judicial.gov.tw/GNNWS/NNWSS002.asp?id=259355. Accessed 20 Mar 2017.

[30]See Chen Lai Su-Mei Weiyuan Fayan [陳賴素美委員發言] (Statement by Legislator Su-Mei, Chen Lai), Li Fa Yuan Gongbao [立法院公報] (Legislative Yuan Gazette) 105, no. 70 (2016), p. 488; Ceng Ming-zong Weiyuan Shumian Yijian [曾銘宗委員書面意見] (Legislator Ming-zong Ceng's written opinion), Li Fa Yuan Gongbao [立法院公報] (Legislative Yuan Gazette) 105, no. 74 (2016), p. 191; Wang Hui-Mei Weiyuan Fayan [王惠美委員發言] (Statement by Legislator Hui-Mei Wang) Li Fa Yuan Gongbao (Legislative Yuan Gazette) 105, no. 74 (2016), p. 409.

[31]See Li (2016) Huang rui ming ting tong xing hun, chan sen lin zan cheng fei chu sixing [黃瑞明挺同性婚, 詹森林成廢除死刑] (Huang Jui-min endorses same-sex marriage, and Chan Sen-lin supports abolishing the death penalty). Kairos News. https://kairos.news/54243. Accessed 2 Nov 2016; Huxley (2016) Duiyu Tongxing Hunyin, Tongjian Chuzui, Feisi ji Yuanzhumin Yiti, Dafaguan Men Zenme Kan? [對於同性婚姻, 通姦除罪, 廢死及原住民議題, 大法官們怎麼看?] (What are the TCC nominees' stances on same-sex marriage, decriminalization of adultery, abolition of the death penalty, and issues concerning aboriginals?). The News Lens. https://www.thenewslens.com/article/52100. Accessed 2 Nov 2017.

ask questions later on during the Q&A session. As important as these men and women in robes may be, their acting on that day usually pales in comparison to the performance of those who appear and speak before the simulated court as expert witnesses or friends of the court. In collaboration with attorneys from both sides, the CCS has managed to appoint several prominent jurists, historians and social scientists in Taiwan to serve as expert witnesses or court-appointed *amici* for each case that has come before it. In 2015 and 2016, the CCS also took advantage of other international events concurrently held in Taiwan and heard expert opinions from former Justices Albie Sachs and Richard Goldstone of the South African Constitutional Court, Justice Marek Zubit of the Constitutional Tribunal of Poland, and four acclaimed scholars from the United States, the United Kingdom, Australia, and Chile. The live testimony by these domestic and international experts occupied a large portion of the CCS oral arguments. Their participation not only lent credence to the CCS as an activity that should be taken seriously but also made the CCS oral arguments session one of the most informative and sought-after civic events in Taiwan in recent years. Many people have attended the CCS oral arguments just to learn the thought-provoking or well-researched views as provided by these leading intellectuals from a myriad of perspectives, and what they said during the CCS oral arguments has been webcast and extensively covered in the news media in Taiwan.[32]

The seminar-like oral arguments epitomize the efforts by the CCS to serve as a deliberative forum for civil society in Taiwan. These events alone may hold the potential to facilitate and/or initiate a national conversation about a constitutional issue worthy of discussion. By providing easy access to the relevant information and different viewpoints on a given issue, they may also help concerned citizens make an informed judgment for themselves. However, the CCS has a more ambitious goal: It hopes that by striving to be as fair and impartial as a constitutional court should be under the due process of law, it can create a common space for people with different convictions on a given issue to sit down together, argue with reason, and hear each other out. The judgments and opinions of the CCS are further hoped to obtain a certain persuasive authority from this deliberative process

---

[32]See, e.g., Qiu and Chang (2015) Moni Xianfa Fating Tang Ying-Shen An Shengsibian [模擬憲法法庭湯英伸案生死辯] (The CCS heard arguments for and against the death penalty in the Tang Ying-shen case). PTS News Network. https://pnn.pts.org.tw/main/2015/05/01/. Accessed 2 Nov 2017; Qiu and Kuan (2015) Sixing Fei Bu Fei? Liang Beihairen Jiashu Butong Diao [死刑廢不廢?兩被害人家屬不同調] (Victims' families do not agree on death penalty issues). PTS News Network. https://pnn.pts.org.tw/main/2015/05/11/. Accessed 2 Nov 2017; Ho (2016) Dang Guojia Yudao Jinji Zhuangtai, Zhexie Yuanze Yiran Yao Zunshou [當國家遇到緊急狀態, 這些原則依然要遵守] (Even in times of emergency, the state should stick to these principles). PTS News Network. https://pnn.pts.org.tw/main/2016/11/15/. Accessed 2 Nov 2017; Qiu (2016) Zhanshi Tizhi Huo Bufa Guojia? Moxianfating Bian Weiquan Benzhi [戰時體制或不法國家? 模憲法庭辯威權本質] (Wartime government or *Unrechtstaat*? The CCS questioned the nature of authoritarian rule). PTS News Network. http://pnn.pts.org.tw/main/2016/11/22/. Accessed 2 Nov 2017.

so that they can move the constitutional dialogue to the next level.[33] This is a noble cause, and Professor Hsu and the CCS crew she leads have worked very hard to make it a reality. The problem, though, is that, as a self-appointed shadow constitutional court, the CCS is not able to compel the government to appear before it to defend the law at issue as the respondent or an *amicus*.[34] The CCS also has a hard time inviting those who publicly oppose the petitioner's cause to take part in the simulation play as the respondent. The first CCS invited a few lawyers associated with social conservative circles in Taiwan to make their case against same-sex marriage; however they pulled out at the last minute because they thought the deck was stacked against them.[35] The second and third CCS ended up having to rely on a few enthusiastic lawyers to play the role of Devil's Advocate.[36] However, by structuring its oral arguments in a less adversarial manner and by inviting those who support the law at issue to address the simulated court as expert witnesses or *amici*, the CCS may have been able to function as a more inclusive deliberative forum than the kind of adversarial forum it aspired to be, but in reality could never have been.

5 A New Approach to Rights Advocacy

For the CCS to work as a shadow Constitutional Court, someone needs to initiate its process by bringing a case to it in the first place. Professor Hsu knew from very early on that the ideal party responsible for filing a petition to the CCS would be an NGO known for advocating a certain matter of rights in Taiwan.[37] By reaching out to the leading NGOs for certain causes and coaching them to develop solid petitions to the CCS, Professor Hsu has worked behind the scenes to make sure that, for each term, the CCS not only has a simulated case that interests and matters to many people in Taiwan but that it can also hear arguments from those activists who are most passionate about, and fully prepared for, their advocacy on behalf of the Team Petitioner. The CCS play, in this regard, can be seen as a joint venture between the

---

[33]See Huang and Wu (2015), at p. 9; Hsu (2014) Dachanghua Luntan Yu Moni Xianfa Fating [大腸花論壇與模擬憲法法庭] (The Dachanghua forum and the Constitutional Court Simulation). PTS News Network. http://pnn.pts.org.tw/main/2014/05/31/. Accessed 2 Nov 2017.

[34]The 2/28 Memorial Foundation was by this time the only government-related organization that had appeared before the CCS as a respondent. A few government officials, though, had attended the CCS oral arguments as audience.

[35]See Qiu and Su (2014) Moni Xianfa Fating: Fanfang Linshi Tuichu, Zhengfang Pi Jujue Duihua [模擬憲法法庭: 反方臨時退出, 正方批拒絕對話] (Constitutional Court Simulation: The team respondent abruptly quit and drew criticism from the team petitioner for refusing to talk). PTS News Network. http://pnn.pts.org.tw/main/2014/07/02/ccstj14_1/. Accessed 2 Nov 2017.

[36]See Shih (2015).

[37]Professor Hsu's decision to solicit CCS petitioners from existing NGOs was arguably driven by her ambition to establish the CCS as a deliberative forum for civil society in Taiwan.

CCS and the NGOs that work on the CCS petition so that, in truth, the play has begun months before the petition is filed to the CCS. Through the coordination of Professor Hsu, the CCS partnered with the Awakening Foundation (婦女新知基金會) in 2014, with the Taiwan Alliance to End the Death Penalty (台灣廢除死刑推動聯盟) in 2015, and with the Taiwan Association for Truth and Reconciliation (TATR; 台灣民間真相與和解促進會) in 2016. These NGOs deserve a lot of credit for the success of the CCS plays. They chose and framed the specific issues to be deliberated and adjudicated by the CCS. They invented the characters of the fictitious petitioners based on true stories, or they found real persons to petition the CCS.[38] They assembled the legal teams and orchestrated the written and oral arguments for the petitioners. Last but not the least, they poured many resources into promoting the CCS plays.[39]

The tacit alliance works to the benefit of the partnering NGOs as well. To the extent that the CCS serves as a deliberative forum, initiating the simulation process may help to raise the public's interest and awareness of the issues they care about most. Since the CCS is the only shadow Constitutional Court in town and only hears one set of issues at a time, setting its agenda may hold some promise to advance the partnering NGO's cause in the larger political agenda in Taiwan. The partnering NGOs are beneficiaries of CCS education, too. The CCS provides them with a rare opportunity to test the waters of constitutional adjudication, and throughout the course of the simulation they receive a lot of feedback that may help them make stronger constitutional cases. Their lawyers can use the CCS training to hone their skills in appellate advocacy and get ready for real court battles in the future. The NGOs may also use this opportunity to recruit and train the next generation of cause lawyers, and this is arguably what the TATR did in 2016.[40] Moreover, to the extent that the CCS functions as a shadow Constitutional Court, its jurisprudence carries some weight in the legal-political discourse in Taiwan and may have the ears of those in power, including the TCC Justices. Although the composition of the CCS may have made it more sympathetic to liberal progressive causes than the TCC, the endorsement of the CCS still means something, as the message comes from a messenger who is proud of being independent and is not a

[38]For instance, the simulated death penalty case that the CCS heard in 2015 was adapted from the real case of Tang Ying-shen [湯英伸], a young aboriginal man whose execution in 1987 shook the conscience of many people in Taiwan. The TATR brought two cases concerning issues of transitional justice to the CCS in 2016, and one of the petitions was filed on behalf of a real victim, Du Ming-jhe, who would not have appeared before the CCS if not for the great effort by the TATR.

[39]The TATR, for instance, created an impressive website (https://www.bookrep.com.tw/activeimg/const160909/page01-01.html) and published a nice booklet to promote the third CCS play.

[40]A list of the TATR legal team for the third CCS play is available at: https://www.bookrep.com.tw/activeimg/const160909/page01-04.html.

familiar face for advocating the rights at issue. It is therefore worth the effort to seek victory in the simulated court, which is more likely than not to become an ally of the partnering NGO in its pursuit of justice.

Skeptics of the CCS suspect that its simulation plays have liberal progressive overtones. They have a point. When situated in the larger context of the socio-political development in Taiwan, what the CCS and its partners have done arguably presents a new approach to rights advocacy: persuade your friends who sit on the simulated bench and they will help you translate the mock victory you win today into a real one in the future. As a shadow institution, the CCS offers not only a new site for advocating rights, but also a new voice of rights advocacy which will be heard by many more people in Taiwan. The strength of this strategy hinges on the extent to which the CCS can establish itself as a shadow Constitutional Court for all of civil society in Taiwan. The more the CCS can function and be perceived of as a shadow court for all, the more influential it will be as an advocate of rights. But, conversely, the more success the CCS achieves in terms of rights advocacy, the more difficult it will be for the CCS to attract support from the conservatives. As a result, the CCS has tended to act as a liberal shadow court and has become known as such. However, the CCS has and will continue to act in the manner of a shadow Constitutional Court under the due process of law. Though doing so may not allay the suspicion and distrust the conservatives harbor toward the CCS, it is essential to the success of the simulation play as a liberal project of rights advocacy. The development along with the fine execution of this approach is a testament to the ingenuity and vitality of the liberal-progressive forces in the legal profession and civil society in Taiwan. The prospects for the CCS enterprise, though, are ultimately contingent on which side—the liberal or the conservative—will win over the hearts and minds of the people in Taiwan.

6 Conclusion

The CCS is still in its infancy. However, thanks in no small part to the dedication of those who have volunteered in its simulation plays, this fledgling civic institution has managed to tackle such salient issues in Taiwan as same-sex marriage, the death penalty, and transitional justice, and it has received a significant amount of attention and interest from the TCC as well as from the general public during the short period between 2014 and 2016. While there is no crystal ball available to predict the future of the CCS, and it might still be too early to assess how it has influenced law and society in Taiwan, many practicing and academic lawyers, law students, scholars, human rights activists and citizens in Taiwan have played various roles in the CCS plays, and most (if not all) of them have considered their CCS experiences rewarding and meaningful. Their stories certainly need to be told. This chapter tells their stories by describing and analyzing how, and how well, the CCS has worked as a moot court education program, a shadow Constitutional Court, a deliberative forum, and as a new approach to rights advocacy in Taiwan. In short, the CCS enterprise attests to the ingenuity and enthusiasm of those who fight for liberal progressive causes in civil society in Taiwan, though part of the CCS's success may also be attributed to some contextual and historical factors—such as the high expectations people have for the TCC, the tradition of judge-oriented legal education, and the underused support structure for rights litigation in Taiwan.

On the website of the CCS, one can find the CCS logo that contains the following message both in English and Chinese: "Embracing everyone into the Constitution with an equal mind" (用平等的心 把每一個人擁入憲法的懷抱).[41] This is a solemn pledge, and the CCS has taken it seriously. The forms and functions of the CCS may evolve over time, but the spirit will live on—or let's hope so.

References

Ceng Ming-zong Weiyuan Shumian Yijian [曾銘宗委員書面意見] (Legislator Ming-zong Ceng's written opinion), Li Fa Yuan Gongbao [立法院公報] (Legislative Yuan Gazette) 105, no. 74 (2016)

Chang W-C (2009) An isolated nation with global-minded citizens: Bottom-up transnational constitutionalism in Taiwan. Natl Taiwan Univ Law Rev 4(3):203–235

Chang W-C (2015) Sixing Shixian: Yinling Gonggong Bianlun ji Gongshi Xingcheng de Moni Xianfa Fating [死刑釋憲: 引領公共辯論及共識形成的模擬憲法法庭] (Adjudicating the constitutionality of the death penalty: Initiating public deliberation and building consensus via Constitutional Court Simulation). Taiwan Bar J 6:13–19

Chen Lai Su-Mei Weiyuan Fayan [陳賴素美委員發言] (Statement by Legislator Su-Mei, Chen Lai), Li Fa Yuan Gongbao [立法院公報] (Legislative Yuan Gazette) 105, no. 70 (2016)

Cole D (2016) Engines of liberty: The power of citizen activists to make constitutional law. Basic Books, New York

Constitutional Court Simulation Judgment No. 2 (2014). Taiwan Law J 253:91–145

Constitutional Court Simulation Judgment No. 3 (2015). Taiwan Law J 273:71–106

Constitutional Court Simulation Judgments Nos. 4 and 5 (2016). https://sites.google.com/site/civilconstitutionalcourt/judgement/scc45. Accessed 2 Nov 2017

Constitutional Court Simulation Temporary Order No. 1 (2015). Taiwan Law J 273:65–70

Constitutional Court Simulation. https://sites.google.com/site/civilconstitutionalcourt/. Accessed 2 Nov 2017

Dafaguan Jieshi Anjian Shoujie Qingxing [大法官解釋案件收結情形] (The Constitutional Court cases commenced, terminated, and pending) (2017). Judicial Yuan. http://www.judicial.gov.tw/juds/report/sa-2.htm. Accessed 18 Nov 2017

Dismissal Resolution No. 2 of the 1166th Conference of the Taiwan Constitutional Court (2001). http://www.judicial.gov.tw/constitutionalcourt/p10_02.asp?id=381. Accessed 2 Nov 2017

Finneran RE (2017) Wherefore moot court? Wash Univ J Law Policy 53:121–134

Foley EB (2010) The McCain v. Obama simulation: A fair tribunal for disputed presidential elections. N Y Univ J Legislation Public Policy 13:471–521

[41]Constitutional Court Simulation. https://sites.google.com/site/civilconstitutionalcourt/. Accessed 2 Nov 2017.

Gerken HK (2008) An intriguing institutional design question: Shadow redistricting commissions. Balkinization. https://balkin.blogspot.tw/2008/05/intriguing-institutional-design.html. Accessed 19 Oct 2017

Gerken HK, Kang MS (2011) The institutional turn in election law scholarship. In: Gerken HK, Kang MS, Charles GE (eds) Race, reform, and regulation of the electoral process: Recurring puzzles in American democracy. Cambridge University Press, New York, pp 86–100

Ho Y-H (2016) Dang Guojia Yudao Jinji Zhuangtai, Zhexie Yuanze Yiran Yao Zunshou [當國家遇到緊急狀態, 這些原則依然要遵守] (Even in times of emergency, the state should stick to these principles). PTS News Network. https://pnn.pts.org.tw/main/2016/11/15/. Accessed 2 Nov 2017

Hsu Y (2014) Dachanghua Luntan Yu Moni Xianfa Fating [大腸花論壇與模擬憲法法庭] (The Dachanghua forum and the Constitutional Court Simulation). PTS News Network. http://pnn.pts.org.tw/main/2014/05/31/. Accessed 2 Nov 2017

Hsu Yu-hsiu Qian Dafaguan Caifang Baodao [許玉秀前大法官採訪報導] (An interview with former Justice Hsu Yu-hsiu) (2015). Taiwan Alliance to End the Death Penalty. http://www.taedp.org.tw/story/2833. Accessed 19 Oct 2017

Huang J-H, Wu H-T (2015) Moni Xianfa Fating: Qidian yu Zhanwang [模擬憲法法庭—起點與展望] (The Simulation Constitutional Court: The start and prospects). Taiwan Bar J 6:6–12

Huxley (2016) Duiyu Tongxing Hunyin, Tongjian Chuzui, Feisi ji Yuanzhumin Yiti, Dafaguan Men Zenme Kan? [對於同性婚姻、通姦除罪、廢死及原住民議題, 大法官們怎麼看?] (What are the TCC nominees' stances on same-sex marriage, decriminalization of adultery, abolition of the death penalty, and issues concerning aboriginals?). The News Lens. https://www.thenewslens.com/article/52100. Accessed 2 Nov 2017

Kao Y-H (2015) Miaohui Xianfa Fating de dianfan tuxiang [描繪「憲法法庭」的典範圖像] (Envisioning an ideal Constitutional Court). Taiwan Bar J 6:2–5

Li C-H (2015) Cong Moni Xianfa Fating Zhi Canyu Jingyen Kan Dafaguan Zhidu de Jige Wenti [從模擬憲法法庭之參與經驗看大法官制度的幾個問題] (Institutional issues of the Taiwan Constitutional Court: From the perspective of a Constitutional Court Simulation participant). Taiwan Bar J 6:20–23

Li Y-P (2016) Huang Rui ming ting Tong Xing hun, Zhan sen lin Zan cheng fei chu Si Xing [黃瑞明挺同性婚, 詹森林贊成廢除死刑] (Huang Jui-min endorses same-sex marriage, and Chan Sen-lin supports abolishing the death penalty). Kairos News. https://kairos.news/54243, Accessed 2 Nov 2016

Milstein ES (2001) Clinical legal education in the United States: In-house clinics, externships, and simulations. J Leg Educ 51(3):375–381

Qiu Y-Y (2016) Zhanshi Tizhi Huo Bufa Guojia? Moxianfating Bian Weiquan Benzhi [戰時體制或不法國家? 模憲法庭辯威權本質] (Wartime government or *Unrechtstaat*? The CCS questioned the nature of authoritarian rule). PTS News Network. http://pnn.pts.org.tw/main/2016/11/22/. Accessed 2 Nov 2017

Qiu Y-Y, Chang F-T (2015) Moni Xianfa Fating Tang Ying-Shen An Shengsibian [模擬憲法法庭湯英伸案生死辯] (The CCS heard arguments for and against the death penalty in the Tang Ying-shen case). PTS News Network. https://pnn.pts.org.tw/main/2015/05/01/. Accessed 2 Nov 2017

Qiu Y-Y, Kuan H-C (2015) Sixing Fei Bu Fei? Liang Beihairen Jiashu Butong Diao [死刑廢不廢?兩被害人家屬不同調] (Victims' families do not agree on death penalty issues). PTS News Network. https://pnn.pts.org.tw/main/2015/05/11/. Accessed 2 Nov 2017

Qiu Y-Y, Su P-C (2014) Moni Xianfa Fating: Fanfang Linshi Tuichu, Zhengfang Pi Jujue Duihua [模擬憲法法庭: 反方臨時退出, 正方批拒絕對話] (Constitutional Court Simulation: The team respondent abruptly quit and drew criticism from the team petitioner for refusing to talk). PTS News Network. http://pnn.pts.org.tw/main/2014/07/02/ccstj14_1/. Accessed 2 Nov 2017

Shih H-C (2015) Moni Xianfa Fating Canyu Zaxiang [模擬憲法法庭參與雜想] (Reflections on my experience with the Constitutional Court Simulation). Taiwan Bar J 6:32–36

Sifayuan Zhendui Minjiantuanti Jiu 106 Nian 3 Yue 24 Ri Xianfa Fating Xiangguan Chengxu Yijian zhi Shuoming [司法院針對民間團體就 106 年 3 月 24 日憲法法庭相關程序意見之說明] (The response of the Judicial Yuan to the opinions of the civic groups regarding the procedural issues of the TCC oral argument scheduled for 24 Mar 2017) (2017). Judicial Yuan. http://jirs.judicial.gov.tw/GNNWS/NNWSS002.asp?id=259355. Accessed 20 Mar 2017

Spader DJ (2002) Two models and three uses for mock trials in justice education. J Criminal Justice Educ 13(1):57–86

Tsai C-Y (2015) Moni Xianfa Fating Xuni yu Xian Shi Jianping Sifayuan Dafaguan Shenli Anjianfa Xiuzheng Cao'an Xiangguan Guiding [模擬憲法法庭虛擬與現實兼評司法院大法官審理案件法修正草案相關規定] (The fiction and the truth of the Constitutional Court Simulation, and some comments on the draft revision of the Constitutional Interpretation Procedure Act). Taiwan Bar J 6:24–31

Wang Hui-Mei Weiyuan Fayan [王惠美委員發言] (Statement by Legislator Hui-Mei Wang) Li Fa Yuan Gongbao (Legislative Yuan Gazette) 105, no. 74 (2016)

Yeh J-R (2016) The Constitution of Taiwan: A contextual analysis. Hart Publishing, Oxford

Yeh J-R (2017) Marching towards constitutionalism with sunflowers. In: Jones, BC (ed) Law and politics of the Taiwan Sunflower and Hong Kong Umbrella movements. Routledge, New York, pp 49–61

Yen-tu Su is Associate Research Professor at the Institutum Iurisprudentiae, Academia Sinica (IIAS) in Taiwan. He also serves as Deputy Director of the Center for Empirical Legal Studies at the IIAS. His research interests include the law of democracy, democratic theory, constitutional theory, judicial politics, and comparative constitutional law. Su has sought to bridge and extend interdisciplinary dialogues among doctrinal jurisprudence, comparative law, and institutional design on the one hand, and democratic/political theory on the other. He also has tried to integrate normative discourse with legal-political history and empirical studies. Su received his S.J.D. from Harvard University in 2010.

Chapter 17
The Role of NGOs in Monitoring the Implementation of Human Rights Treaty Obligations

Song-Lih Huang and Yibee Huang

Abstract The ratification of the Covenants through the enactment of the "Act to Implement the International Covenant on Civil and Political Rights and the International Covenant on Economic, Social and Cultural Rights" in 2009 brought a new model of operation for human rights NGOs, in particular taking advantage of the review of the state human rights reports and the follow-up of the Concluding Observations and Recommendations. NGOs are now able to engage with the government on human rights issues on a scale unprecedented in Taiwan's modern history. This chapter gives an account of three stages in the development of this model: (1) the influence of NGOs, although limited in number, on high officials during President Chen Shui-bian's terms from 2000 to 2008; (2) the influence of core NGOs, particularly those participating in Covenants Watch, in shaping the format of the state reports and its reviews; (3) the involvement of many more NGOs and individuals in the review and follow-up processes. The chapter also identifies the limitations of this operation around the review of the state reports, especially when facing the institutional deficiencies of the government, and in providing adequate training of civil servants, teachers, the police, and judges.

Keywords Consultative committee · Civil society · NGOs · Mobilization President's Office human rights consultative committee · State human rights reports

This chapter describes the role of civil society in facilitating the implementation of the human rights conventions in Taiwan after 2009, when the Parliament brought the human rights Covenants into the domestic legal order. However, the story would be incomprehensible without a brief account of the historical milestones in Taiwan's politics, and how those factors affected the introduction of human rights norms to the political and legal systems.

Taiwan was under an authoritarian government ruled by a single political party (the Nationalist Party, or Kuomintang, hereinafter KMT) between 1945 and 1987,

S.-L. Huang (✉) · Y. Huang
Covenants Watch, Taipei, Taiwan
e-mail: songlih@gmail.com

J. A. Cohen et al. (eds.), *Taiwan and International Human Rights*, Economics, Law, and Institutions in Asia Pacific, https://doi.org/10.1007/978-981-13-0350-0_17

the year when martial law was lifted. The KMT continued to enjoy considerable dominance in the political system, including executive, judicial, and legislative powers. The major opposition party (the Democratic Progressive Party, hereinafter DPP) was only allowed to officially register in 1986. Before that, dissidents formed various types of organizations with informal networks, collectively recognized as "*dangwai*" (literally, outside the Party) organizations which functioned as a quasi-political party by fielding candidates and establishing campaign groups. The "*dangwai* movement" was essentially a democracy and human rights movement pursuing, of course, civil and political rights; however, it might also have been focused on labor, environmental, and consumer issues.[1] The KMT regime did not cease employing the language of human rights in an effort to secure international support and maintain its own legitimacy in the Cold War context, but human rights violations took place in everyday life. Thus, the human rights movement and the *dangwai* (and later, the DPP) had a common goal to establish a new government, necessarily through the realization of civil and political rights.

1 NGO's Advisory Roles During President Chen's Terms

In the 2000 presidential election, DPP candidate Chen Shui-bian was among the lawyers who defended political dissidents arrested in the *Formosa Magazine* incident. The DPP won the election over a divided KMT, resulting in the first peaceful power transition in Taiwan. It is quite understandable that the DPP government was more receptive to ideas of human rights from civil society. A paragraph in President Chen's inauguration speech indicated the influence of human rights activists: "The new government will urge the Legislative Yuan to ratify the International Bill of Rights as a domestic law of Taiwan, so that it will formally become the 'Taiwan Bill of Rights.' We hope to set up an independent National Human Rights Commission in Taiwan, thereby realizing an action long advocated by the United Nations."[2]

One way the government maintained a close yet informal connection among human rights activists and high-level officials was to invite them to act as consultants. Some key players in the human rights movement, including NGO activists,

[1]Lin (2003).

[2]According to an interview with Mr. Peter Wen-shiung Huang in 2012, Mr. Huang, a human rights advocate serving as President of the Taiwan Association for Human Rights (hereinafter TAHR) from 1998–2000, submitted a memo to President-elect Chen and suggested these policies and received a positive response from Chen. Mr. Wen-shiung Huang also served as National Policy Advisor on human rights issues from 2000 to 2005. The interview (in Chinese) is available from TAHR at http://www.digitaltahr.org.tw/pages/db/collection/human-rights-oral-metadata.jsp?id=10608. President Chen's Inauguration Address, 20 May 2000, is available at the US-China Institute, University of Southern California. http://china.usc.edu/chen-shui-bian-%E2%80%9Ctaiwan-stands-presidential-inauguration-address%E2%80%9D. 20 May 2000.

lawyers, and independent scholars, were offered advisory positions in the government. Two committees were of particular importance in shaping human rights policies: the "President's Office Human Rights Consultative Group" (which was later renamed the President's Office Human Rights Consultative Committee, hereinafter POHRCC)[3] and the "Executive Yuan Human Rights Protection and Promotion Group" (hereinafter HRPPG),[4] chaired by the Vice-President and Premier, respectively. Human rights advocates on these committees tried to lay out a human rights infrastructure plan for the government, but their roles were only advisory. The government faced substantial difficulties since the DPP government inherited a steadfast bureaucratic system accustomed to the former authoritarian regime and, even more decisively, a KMT majority in Parliament. In fact, the KMT and its allied political parties held an effective majority in Parliament (the Legislative Yuan) until 2016.

Two objectives of fundamental significance early in President Chen's term were to establish a National Human Rights Institution (hereinafter NHRI), and to incorporate international human rights laws into the domestic legal system by enacting a "Human Rights Act" and ratifying the International Covenants on Civil and Political Rights (hereinafter ICCPR) and the International Covenant on Economic, Social and Cultural Rights (hereinafter ICESCR). Both proposals were extensively discussed by these two committees during President Chen's terms and draft bills were produced, but these efforts did not eventuate in legislation. The two committees have survived subsequent power transitions and remain a channel for NGOs, albeit a very limited number contribute their suggestions to the top levels of government.[5]

[3]Guidelines for the establishment of the President's Office Human Rights Consultative Group are available at http://www.rootlaw.com.tw/LawArticle.aspx?LawID=A030030001011000-0950519. The group was chaired by the vice-president and composed of 15 civilian members and three high officials: vice-president of the Judicial Yuan, vice-president of the Control Yuan, and the vice-premier. The group met every 3 months. The missions of the POHRCC were to: domesticate the international human rights bills, facilitate establishment of a National Human Rights Commission, review human rights policies, promote participation in international human rights activities, and propagate human rights education.

[4]Guidelines for the establishment of the Executive Yuan Human Rights Protection and Promotion Group are available at http://www.humanrights.moj.gov.tw/ct.asp?xItem=283222&ctNode=37809&mp=200. The group was chaired by the Premier (currently chaired by a Minister without portfolio), deputy ministers from nine ministries, and 10–16 experts or scholars. The group meets every 6 months.

[5]The President's Office Human Rights Consultative Group was expanded and renamed the POHRCC in 2004. During President Chen's second term, the KMT legislators claimed that the POHRCC was unlawful and ended its operations in 2006. Ironically, after President Ma took office, the POHRCC was reinstated in 2010.

2 The Act to Implement the Covenants

Starting in President Chen's first term, the President's Office and the Executive Yuan separately prepared drafts for the proposed human rights act. The two drafts underwent several rounds of discussion and were combined into the "Human Rights Basic Law" by the Executive Yuan HRPPG in 2003. This draft was subjected to scrutiny by a special committee; after 22 extensive meetings stretching over almost a year, the draft bill for the "Human Rights Act" was completed in October 2004.[6] It is worth noting that the special committee was led by a member of the HRPPG, himself a human rights lawyer and an active member in human rights NGOs, demonstrating the influence of NGOs in a semi-official setting. The bill for the Human Rights Act was influenced by international human rights conventions (ICCPR, ICESCR, CRC, and CEDAW), regional human rights instruments (European Convention on Human Rights and Charter of Fundamental Rights of the European Union), and constitutions of some countries (USA, Japan, and Germany).

When the draft bill for the Human Rights Act was finally ready to be sent to Parliament in 2006, governmental agencies were not ready to handle the many tasks associated with the new act. The HRPPG decided, in January 2007, that the Executive Yuan should shift emphasis from enacting the Human Rights Act to an "Act to implement the ICCPR and ICESCR" (hereafter the Implementation Act).[7] The decision narrowed the scope of human rights for the Executive Yuan; it was hoped this might reduce resistance to the bill in the KTM-majority Parliament. The Implementation Act was designed not only to serve the function of conveying the Covenants; it also imposed positive duties on the government, including to "take responsibility for preparing, promoting and implementing human rights protection provisions in the two Covenants within their functions" (Article 5), to "set up a human rights reports system in accordance with the two Covenants" (Article 6), and to "review laws, regulations, directions and administrative measures within their functions according to the two Covenants" (Article 8).[8] The draft of the

---

[6]Meeting minutes of the 9th Committee Meeting of the Executive Yuan HRPPG, 28 Oct 2004. The Executive Yuan expressed appreciation to the "Human Rights Protection Basic Law Research Group" and the participating governmental agencies led by attorney Wellington Koo for their efforts in the process. Available (in Chinese) at http://www.humanrights.moj.gov.tw/ct.asp?xItem=283,224&ctNode=37809&mp= 200.

[7]Meeting minutes of the 12th Committee Meeting of the Executive Yuan HRPPG, 12 Jan 2007. "Regarding the two bills in file, i.e., the Bill for Human Rights Act and the Bill for the Act to Implement the ICCPR and ICESCR, the committee adopts the opinion of Mr. Wen-Shiung Huang and others to prioritize the domestication of the two Covenants. The Ministry of Justice is to submit the draft bill of the "Act to Implement the ICCPR and ICESCR" to the Executive Yuan. As for the Human Rights Act, it is better to be dealt with at the constitutional level, i.e., to amend the Constitution and enrich its human rights provisions. Minutes (in Chinese) available on the website in the preceding note.

[8]The content of the Implementation Act is available from the Ministry of Justice at http://law.moj.gov.tw/Eng/LawClass/LawContent.aspx?PCODE=I0020028.

Implementation Act was submitted to Parliament in October 2007, but it was not reviewed until President Ma Ying-jeou began his term in 2008.

President Chen's plea for Parliament to ratify the two Covenants, which the government had signed before it withdrew from the United Nations, did cause some discussion among the parliamentarians. In 2002, the KMT majority decided that it could ratify the Covenants with reservations about Articles 6 and 12 of the ICCPR and Article 8 of the ICESCR, the articles concerning the death penalty, permitting political dissidents to travel across the border, and the right to form labor unions, respectively.[9] The Parliament also attached a declaration to Article 1 of the ICCPR (but peculiarly not to the same article of the ICESCR), claiming that there was no need to exercise the right to self-determination as the ROC had always been an independent state. The Parliament also attached a declaration to Article 1 of the ICCPR (but peculiarly not to the same article of the ICESCR), claiming that there was no need to exercise the right to self-determination as the ROC had always been an independent state.[10] The DPP minority counteracted with a motion for reconsideration on the reservation and declaration but the KMT did not respond. Discussion of the ratification was discontinued until President Ma took office in 2008. The Covenants were ratified without any reservation or declaration, and, indeed, without any comment by the legislators, on 31 March 2009. The Implementation Act was passed the same day, bringing the Covenants into the domestic legal system.[11]

During President Chen's terms, an important channel which allowed NGOs to exert their influence was the human rights consultative committees in the President's Office and the Executive Yuan. Admittedly, only a small number of NGOs and scholars had access to this channel. Nevertheless, they used their initiative and knowledge to bridge the gap between Taiwan and the international human rights system. These NGOs tried to direct the government's efforts toward complying with international human rights standards and toward the establishment of a National Human Rights Institution. Although the DPP government was not able to witness any concrete progress in this regard, President Chen's government paved the way to implementing the Covenants in Taiwan.

3 Implementing the Covenants: Expansion of NGO Participation

Ma and the KMT won the presidential and Parliament elections by a significant margin in 2008. Despite an emphasis on themes of anti-corruption and economic growth during the campaign, Ma did pledge to uphold the International Bill of

[9]Kenneth Huang-chuen Chiu, The background and implementation of the ICCPR and the ICESCR. TAHR Newsletter, March 2010 (in Chinese).

[10]Liao (2014).

[11]Article 2 of the Implementation Act: "Human rights protection provisions in the two Covenants have domestic legal status."

Human Rights. The KMT's reservations toward democracy and human rights had not changed over the eight years of Chen's presidency, therefore Ma's pledge, although welcomed by the NGOs, was bewildering. Whether it was a "strategic ratification" or otherwise, a level of consistency in the main framework of human rights policy was maintained despite the power transition.[12] The Executive Yuan HRPPG resumed operations in 2008 and the PHORCC in 2010. Compared to President Chen's administration, relations between high officials and NGOs during President Ma's administration were less enthusiastic; the members of these committees were mostly scholars and lawyers.

Of the positive duties prescribed in the Implementation Act, the duty to establish a human rights reporting system had the greatest potential to set the stage for civil society organizations to engage with the government. The following discussion will focus on the preparation and review of the state human rights reports to illustrate the role of civil society in animating the Covenants.

Reviews of the state human rights report are one of the mechanisms by which the treaty body monitors the States Parties on the fulfillment of its treaty obligations. Since the instrument ratifying the Covenants could not be deposited with the UN Secretary-General, Taiwan's ratification remained domestic and the government had to decide the shape and form of the reports as well as to devise a mechanism to review them. This task was assigned to the POHRCC, which resumed in December 2010 and was chaired by Vice-President Vincent Wan-Chang Siew.

At the third meeting of the POHRCC on 12 April 2011, a decision was made to prepare the state human rights report in accordance with the requirements laid out in the "Compilation of guidelines on the form and content of reports to be submitted by States Parties to the international human rights treaties" (HRI/GEN/2/Rev.6, 3 June 2009). This critical decision laid the ground work for further development along this line. Originally, the government decided to prepare the report according to a generic guideline which would divide the report into a general report and a special report covering themes such as the death penalty, indigenous rights, and migrant workers' rights. The guideline, therefore, ran the risk of being arbitrary and not comprehensive.

For NGOs, the enactment of the Implementation Act brought high expectations and ignited a new model for the human rights movement. A NGO coalition named Covenants Watch (hereinafter CW) was founded on 9 December 2009, to monitor the fulfillment of government obligations imposed by the Covenants. The CW, composed of more than 40 NGOs whose work involved human rights issues, was convened by a well-respected human rights veteran, Mr. Wen-Shiung Huang. CW held a series of reading clubs and workshops to study UN human rights mechanisms and practices, aiming to urge the government to achieve a level of human rights protection no less than that of formal States Parties. Most NGOs were just beginning to collect and digest the huge amount of information scattered in numerous UN

[12]The term "strategic ratifiers" describes governments that trade off the short-term certainty of positive ratification benefits against the long-term, uncertain risk that they may face compliance costs in the future. They may ratify for diplomatic rewards, to avoid criticism, or to ingratiate themselves with domestic groups or international audiences. Simmons (2009), p. 58.

documents when CW learned that the government had decided to deviate from the UN guideline. An emergency letter was issued to the President and the POHRCC in early April, asking the government to follow the UN reporting guidelines and to consult the NGOs during the drafting of the state reports.[13] The letter might have had some impact on the POHRCC decision in April, as mentioned earlier, because the members of the POHRCC during Ma's terms were less militant, but they included independent scholars who were well-versed in human rights principles. While during President Chen's two terms in office it was the cooperation between the POHRCC/HRPPG and the government that shaped the outlook on human rights policies, during President Ma's terms it was the relationship between the POHRCC and the NGOs that facilitated implementation of the human rights policies.

The Ministry of Justice served as Secretariat for both the POHRCC and the Executive Yuan HRPPG, and it was assigned the task of coordinating all governmental departments and agencies in drafting the state reports. The first draft by the agencies was completed in May, and dozens of consultation meetings took place between June and August 2011 to discuss the reports, article by article. This model established a new platform whereby NGOs and independent scholars confronted representatives of government agencies on human rights issues in meetings chaired by POHRCC members.[14] This opposition was fueled by the government's own reports, which were filled with data and information about how much had been done, but without any reflections on the deficiencies in the processes or outcomes. The encounters between the NGOs and the government agencies during these consultation meetings were not pleasant, with occasional statements of contempt and hostility.

4 The Format of the Review on the State Reports on the Covenants

The next point of contention was how to conduct the review on the state reports. Many of the initiatives in designing the format of the reviews came from CW, which met on a weekly to bi-weekly basis and was eager to communicate its ideas to the POHRCC and the Ministry of Justice.[15] Covenants Watch requested to meet with the POHRCC in October 2011 to convey several messages.[16] First, that members of the review committee should include experts with UN treaty body

[13]Letter submitted to the POHRCC by CW, April 2011.

[14]The meetings to review the drafts of the state reports were chaired by civilian members of the POHRCC. There were 15 civilian members, but only 6 of them took turns in chairing.

[15]It should be stressed that it was the Division of Legal Systems in the Ministry of Justice that served as the Secretariat for the POHRCC. Prosecutor Guo Ming-Li was recruited by the division in April 2011 and played important roles in the review of the Initial Reports.

[16]Four POHRCC members met with four CW representatives on 25 Oct 2011.

experience and those who possess expertise on issues of particular importance to Taiwan, such as indigenous people's rights and transitional justice, and that membership of the review committee should take into account geographical considerations and should be comprised of an equal number of male and female members. Secondly, the Secretariat should be independent and neutral. CW recommended inviting organizations of international reputation to come to Taiwan and set up temporary offices.

The government initially decided to designate the Ministry of Justice as the Secretariat for the review of the initial state report; however, following the demand by NGOs to have an independent Secretariat, the POHRCC decided to form a supervisory committee to oversee the operation of the review process. A seven-member committee was established, with three members drawn from the civilian members of the POHRCC and four from the NGOs. The supervisory committee set the tone for the review: it decided that there should be two panels (one review committee for each Covenant), finalized the members of the review committees, and determined the format of the review, including such items as the time allocation and the participation by the NGOs. Because there was no precedent to use as a reference, the supervisory committee had to improvise along the way. During this period, there were intensive communications with the review committees, and a delegate from the International Commission of Jurists went to Taipei to explain the procedures of the treaty bodies. One of the authors of this piece, representing CW, was a member of the supervisory committee, and CW contributed many ideas to the final format of Taiwan's unique review system.[17] The supervisory committee was committed to designing a review system "better than the UN." Decisions by the supervisory committee were executed quite faithfully by the Secretariat, with minimal interference from the government, except in applying stringent budget limitations.

In the review system's final form there would be three days of review, divided into 6 sessions; the fourth day would allow a recess for the preparation of the concluding observations and recommendations (hereinafter COR), with a ceremony on the fifth day for the government to officially receive the COR.[18] One decision by the supervisory committee of particular importance was to allocate one full hour for the NGOs to present their views in each of the six sessions.[19] This model was followed by the reviews of the CEDAW, CRC, and CRPD.

[17]CW's suggestions included: having two review committees rather than one, having at least five members who would be physically present in Taipei on each review committee, gender and geographical considerations of the committee members, sufficient time for NGOs, the rules for NGOs present at the meeting, on-line broadcasting of all sessions, inviting embassies and representatives from foreign offices in Taipei to the review, inviting international NGOs to the review, and a one-hour summary statement by the NGOs following the opening ceremony.

[18]The COR for the review of the initial state reports (Review of the initial reports of the government of Taiwan on the implementation of the international human rights covenants concluding observations and recommendations adopted by the International Group of Independent Experts), Taipei, 1 March 2013 [hereinafter COR 2013]) is available at the Ministry of Justice website http://www.humanrights.moj.gov.tw/ct.asp?xItem=298633&ctNode=37008&mp=200.

[19]For the review of the initial reports, NGOs took a total of 5.5 hours.

5 Participation of NGOs in the Review of State Reports

The notion that there could be opportunities for direct interactions with human rights experts with UN experience was encouraging to the NGOs, which for a long time felt that the government was ignoring their concerns and reluctant to take action. There was also an expectation that there would finally be a fair judge between the two sides of the argument; this was a compelling sentiment because the court was not perceived to be fair.[20]

For governmental agencies, the review of the initial state report on the Covenants in 2013, starting from the preparation of the report to the actual dialogue with the international panels, was a top-down process that widely spread the concept of international human rights. During the three days of actual review, hundreds of civil servants were present in the meeting room during the review period and many more stood by, ready to send in supplementary information to the delegates. The review was endorsed by the President and the international human rights community, making it one of the most distinguished human rights events in decades.[21] It should also be remembered here that what happened in 2013 was the blossoming of seeds planted by NGOs even before President Chen took office.

The review of the state report was made meaningful by the participation of NGOs, which brought insights into human rights violations. For NGOs which were already occupied with dealing with the daily challenge of fighting for clients' rights, spending time on writing up a shadow report for an unfamiliar (and perhaps fruitless) process did not appear to be a reasonable investment. Much mobilization and coordination was carried out by CW, which held numerous workshops aided by countless personal communications to help the NGOs understand the purposes and processes of the state report review, prepare shadow reports, and draft alternative replies to the list of issues. The list of issues quoted the shadow reports submitted by CW dozens of times, testifying to the significance of its contribution. During the actual review, more than one hundred NGOs from all corners of Taiwan came eagerly to tell their stories of suffering to the review committees. In addition to human rights NGOs that were more involved from the start, many civil society groups came for their own causes, most prominently indigenous groups, disabled people's organizations, LGTBI groups, and grassroots organizations of victims of forced evictions.

The mobilization around the review of state reports did not terminate when the review ended. The government held a series of meetings to discuss each paragraph of the concluding observations. Again, based on the request of civil society, these meetings, chaired by POHRCC members, invited relevant NGOs to engage in dialogues. Even if these dialogues did not result in policy changes in the short term, these activities had the effect of making government agencies aware of the NGOs' appeals. In short, the review of the state report demanded by the Implementation

[20]Wu and Huang (2004).

[21]Huang (2013).

Act provided a rare opportunity for NGOs to engage with the government on a scale never seen before.

Although it is a more complex task to evaluate the direct effects of this process, a number of victories have given human rights NGOs enough reason to continue their endeavors. The period between the two reviews, as a result of the suggestions of the 2013 COR, saw the ratification of the Act to Implement the CRC and the Act to Implement the CRPD, granting medical parole to former President Chen Shui-bian a partial amendment to the Habeas Corpus Act, amendment of the Immigration Act granting the rights of defense for Chinese immigrants, and the repeal of the HIV Infection Control and Patient Rights Protection Act to allow aliens with HIV infections to remain in Taiwan and receive medical treatment.[22]

To explain the relatively prompt response of the government, one should consider the role of the international human rights community. Risse and Sikkink have pointed out that the transnational advocacy networks could serve to put norm-violating states on the international agenda, to empower and legitimate the claims of domestic opposition groups, and to challenge norm-violating governments by creating a transnational structure pressuring such regimes.[23] In the case of Taiwan, however, the transnational advocacy network provided a weak structure, as the experts were invited to Taiwan on a relatively short-term basis and members of the review committee clearly expressed that they were independent experts working in their personal capacities.[24] Therefore, sustained pressure from the international community seems an unlikely answer, while domestic pressure from civil society groups working on human rights issues legitimized by the international experts could be a more reasonable explanation. The formation and success of the social and political movements were linked to political, legal, organizational, or social changes that reduced the costs of mobilization and improved the likelihood of success.[25] It can be concluded that the review of state reports increased the probability of success as well as reduced some of the problems of collective action by providing, though temporarily, a common goal and platform for multiple actors.

[22]Although the review cycle for the ICCPR was four years and for the ICESCR five years, the supervisory committee suggested, and was later agreed to by the government, that the two reviews should be synchronized at intervals of four years. In both the first review in 2013 and the second review in 2017, the first day was allocated to common issues. Some review committee members regarded the simultaneous review of the ICCPR and the ICESCR as beneficial (personal communication with Professor Eibe Riedel).

[23]Risse and Sikkink (1999).

[24]COR 2013, para 2.

[25]Jenkins (1983) and Simmons (2009).

6 More Than the Review of State Reports

Despite these opportunities and developments, there are serious limitations to this model of action in the review of the state reports. Although social mobilization increased the visibility of some human rights issues and legitimized their pursuits, the governmental institutions for human rights protection and promotion seemed beyond the reach of the NGOs.

Firstly, human rights NGOs formed an alliance to urge the government to establish a NHRI as early as 1999, and for almost 20 years the government has never regarded a NHRI as a priority. NGOs have continued to work with legislators and have put forward several bills for an NHRI, but this has had little effect because for most of Taiwan's modern history the President has also been the leader of the ruling party, thereby influencing Parliament. On the other hand, establishing an NHRI was always on the POHRCC's agenda during the terms of Presidents Chen Shui-bian, Ma Ying-jeou, and Tsai Ing-wen; yet despite unanimous support from the POHRCC, the government paid little more than lip service to the agenda. The lack of progress drew the attention of the second Covenants review in 2017, whose comment provides an accurate summary: "In 2013, the Review Committee recommended the establishment of an independent national human rights commission in accordance with the Paris Principles as a priority objective. Despite various initiatives taken in the period under review, Taiwan has not yet decided whether it should establish a completely independent institution or subordinate it to either the Presidential Office or the Control Yuan. The Committee recommends establishing, without further delay, a completely independent and pluralistic national human rights commission in full compliance with the Paris Principles."[26]

Secondly, according to Article 8 of the Implementation Act, all levels of governmental institutions and agencies should review the laws, regulations, and directions and administrative measures within their functions according to the two Covenants, and those incompatible with the Covenants should be amended within two years of the Act entering into force. The review of domestic laws was arguably the most critical step in ensuring compliance with the Covenants, but it was done sporadically, with the responsibility being handed to agencies that were accustomed solely to the application of laws and therefore unlikely to detect their shortcomings. The NGOs advocated a regular (continuing after the two-year deadline) and systematic process of reviewing the law, and a specialized department in the Executive Yuan to develop expertise and professionalism on human rights issues, but the government never responded.

---

[26]Review of the second reports of the government of Taiwan on the implementation of the international human rights covenants concluding observations and recommendations adopted by the International Review Committee, Taipei, 20 January 2017, para 9. The COR is available at the Ministry of Justice website. http://www.humanrights.moj.gov.tw/ct.asp?xItem=464124&ctNode=45414&mp=200.

Thirdly, the Implementation Act would not make much difference unless all governmental agencies were made aware of its obligations through adequate training for civil servants, teachers, the police, prosecutors, and judges. This responsibility lies in the hand of the government, but few mechanisms exist for the officials, even those designing the training, to learn international human rights laws and mechanisms. Despite repeated appeals by NGOs to improve the quality of training, the government's response was sluggish to the point that the COR of the second review stated: "The appropriateness and effectiveness of human rights education and training continue to be a serious concern. There appears to be little improvement since the initial review in 2013, when the Review Committee noted the 'over-emphasis on quantity rather than quality' in the relevant programmes."[27]

Enlisting human rights concerns in the COR would be meaningless if the recommendations in the COR were not implemented. Based on the experience of 2013, CW made two suggestions to the follow-up mechanism of the CORs, which were adopted by the POHRCC.[28] The first was that governmental agencies should develop an action plan based on the recommendations in the COR. The second was that the follow-up meetings should be chaired by officials, preferably ministers-without-portfolio, rather than by POHRCC members. As the process is still on-going, we can only hope that there will be more concrete results from the second COR. CW also organized two events that aimed to facilitate implementation of the recommendations. First, through FORUM ASIA, CW invited Mrs. Rosslyn Noonan to Taipei for a week-long exploratory mission to identify possible factors and arrangements which will encourage the government to set up a NHRI. Second, CW, in collaboration with the NGOs, invited two experts on the ICESCR review committee, Professors Eibe Riedel and Miloon Kothari, to return to Taiwan to provide training on two themes emphasized in the COR: application of the ICESCR in the judicial system, and policies regarding forced evictions.[29] A series of training workshops will also be designed for judges, lawyers, and officials. In the meantime, many NGOs continue to work on other issues mentioned in the COR, for example the Taiwan Association for Human Rights is working on the Refugee Act and the Assembly and Parade Act, the Alliance to End the Death Penalty is arranging grassroots deliberations on alternatives to the death penalty, and gender groups are working diligently on human rights education and equal marriage rights.

The enactment of the Act to Implement the CEDAW (2011), the Act to Implement the CRC (2014), and the Act to Implement the CRPD (2014) further spread the UN human rights mechanism to more NGOs that have become motivated to learn rights-based reasoning and advocacy. These Implementation Acts were the result of the review of the initial state reports, but the ripple effect based on

---

[27]*Id.*, at para 14.

[28]The convener of CW, also the author of this chapter, was invited to be a member of the POHRCC when President Tsai took office in May 2016.

[29]In collaboration with the TAHR, Legal Aid Foundation, Taiwan Alliance of Anti-Forced Eviction, Taipei Bar Association, and Foundation for Judicial Reform.

the knowledge acquired through the "Act to Implement the Covenants" was not limited to the scale of mobilization. The Act to Implement the CRPD, for example, was more sophisticated in enforcing government obligations, thanks to the collaboration between NGOs and legislators.[30] However, the lack of involvement of high officials in the implementation of other human rights conventions seems to have undermined the momentum.

Interestingly, some misconceptions about international human rights laws were aggravated by the Implementation Act. Several court decisions on manslaughter and murder cases cited the ICCPR when the judges refrained from death sentences. These judges annoyed citizens who believed that the death penalty was the only approach to counter injustices, and the Covenants became the target of attacks. It is common to find in social media opinions claiming that the two Covenants interfered with state sovereignty and the independence of judges. The reaction was so predictable that one KMT legislator sent in a formal proposal to amend the Implementation Act, intending to postpone implementation "until the Republic of China becomes a formal State Party to the Covenants," so that the courts may have the freedom to use the death penalty.[31] During the 2015–16 gender equality movement which fought for marriage equality for gay and lesbian persons, the claim for equal rights was again linked to the Covenants, and some conservative and religious groups accused human rights advocates of disturbing "traditional values," be they Confucian, Asian, or Christian. Ironically, some groups against equal rights cited ICCPR Article 23 and argued that the Covenants never meant to protect equal marriage rights. Parents who insisted that LGBT education in schools conflicted with their moral values cited ICESCR Article 13 and asserted that teaching materials should be approved by parents "to ensure the religious and moral education of their children is in conformity with their own convictions." These debates indicate that the rhetoric of human rights has spread to many corners of society. The next step should be to move from rhetoric to public reasoning.

In summary, the Implementation Act has brought about a new form of human rights movement since 2009. The positive duties prescribed by the Implementation Act, particularly the review of the state human rights reports, provide a unique channel allowing direct dialogues between government agencies and civil society. The endorsement by the President's Office and the international human rights community legitimized human rights pursuits and encouraged effective social mobilization by

---

[30]For example, the Act to Implement the CRPD included a new article: "Persons with disabilities protected by the Convention and the relevant regulations that have their rights infringed, which cannot or may only with difficulty be implemented shall make an appeal, file a claim or other way of petitioning to protect their rights. … When persons with disabilities appoint an attorney to exercise the rights in the preceding paragraph, the government shall provide legal aid according to the act." The Act to Implement the CRPD is available at http://law.moj.gov.tw/Eng/LawClass/LawAll.aspx?PCode=D0050194.

[31]Liwei Yao Xiu Liang Gongyue Shixingfa, Rang Faguan Ke Pan Sixing [立委要修兩公約施行法 讓法官可判死刑] (Legislator to amend the Act to Implement the Covenants; Judges allowed to use death penalty) (2017). Liberty Times. http://news.ltn.com.tw/news/politics/breakingnews/2065871. Accessed 10 Dec 2017.

human rights NGOs. The widespread participation by civil society was key to the enforcement of the Implementation Act. However, it is to be noted that long before 2009, advocacy NGOs paved the way for the Act during President Chen's terms through their efforts in the semi-official committees. The process of social mobilization, as measured by the number of NGOs involved and the number of governmental agencies called upon to directly answer the challenges of civil society, can be viewed as a long and winding road. The destination could be glimpsed only by visionaries at first, but as people have traveled along it, it has become almost reachable.

References

Chiu, KH-c (2010) The background and implementation of the ICCPR and the ICESCR. TAHR Newsletter, Mar (in Chinese).

Huang S-L (2013) Cong Gongmin Shehui de Jiaodu Guancha Chuci Guojia Renquan Baogao de Zhuanxie he Shencha [從公民社會的角度觀察初次國家人權報告的撰寫和審查] (Observing the proposing and reviewing of the initial Taiwan national human rights report from the view of civil society). Taiwan Hum Rights J 2(1):123–131

Jenkins JC (1983) Resource mobilization theory and the study of social movements. Annu Rev Sociology 9(1):527–553

Liao F-T (2014) Liang Gongyue zhi Lishi Fazhan ji Taiwan Canyu [兩公約之歷史發展及台灣參與] (Historical development of the Covenants and Taiwan's participation). In: Liao F-T (ed) Lianheguo Renquan Liang Gongyue—Gongmin yu Zhengzhi Quanli Guoji Gongyue, Jingji Shehui Wenhua Quanli Guoji Gongyue [聯合國人權兩公約—公民與政治權利國際公約, 經濟社會文化權利國際公約] (The United Nations Covenants: International Covenant on Civil and Political Rights and International Covenant on Economic, Social and Cultural Rights). Xin Xue Lin [新學林], Taipei, pp 1–23

Lin, S.-f. (2003). "Democratization" in Taiwan and its discontents: transnational activism and Human Rights Movement as a critique. In: A. Uhlin and N. Piper (eds). Transnational activism in Asia: Problems of power and democracy, Routledge, London.

Liwei Yao Xiu Liang Gongyue Shixingfa, Rang Faguan Ke Pan Sixing [立委要修兩公約施行法讓法官可判死刑] (Legislator to amend the Act to Implement the Covenants; Judges allowed to use the death penalty) (2017). Liberty Times. http://news.ltn.com.tw/news/politics/breakingnews/2065871. Accessed 10 Dec 2017

Review of the initial reports of the government of Taiwan on the implementation of the international human rights covenants concluding observations and recommendations adopted by the International Group of Independent Experts, Taipei, 1 March 2013

Review of the second reports of the government of Taiwan on the implementation of the international human rights covenants concluding observations and recommendations adopted by the International Review Committee, Taipei, 20 January 2017

Risse T, Sikkink K (1999) The socialization of international human rights norms into domestic practices: introduction. In: Risse T, Ropp SC, Sikkink K (eds) The power of human rights: international norms and domestic change. Cambridge University Press, Cambridge, pp 1–38

Simmons BA (2009) Mobilizing for human rights: international law in domestic politics. Cambridge University Press, New York

Wu C-l, Huang C (2004) Politics and judiciary verdicts on vote-buying litigation in Taiwan. Asian Surv 44(5):755–770

Song-Lih Huang was trained in medicine and public health, and has been working with NGOs for 17 years. He has been a core member of Covenants Watch (CW) since its initiation in 2009. CW is an umbrella organization composed of human rights NGOs in Taiwan to monitor the government's fulfillment of its obligations imposed by the international human rights treaties. He is now serving as the President of CW's Board of Directors. CW has been providing NGOs with various background and appeals to prepare parallel reports and advocacy papers, international human rights instruments. CW has participated extensively in the advocacy and debate on national policies to build up the mechanisms for human rights protection and promotion in Taiwan, including the procedures of the review of the state reports on the ICCPR and the ICESCR by international experts, and the establishment of the National Human Rights Institute. He is a professor at the Institute of Public Health, National Yang Ming University. He is also the founder of the International Health Program at Yang Ming University. His research interests in recent years mostly focus on the living and working conditions of vulnerable groups in different societies using the mixed research method, for example, street vendors in Burkina Faso, expectant mothers in the Gambia, and children with disabilities looking for education in Aceh, Indonesia. Another area of interest is the application of quantitative methods to measure the government commitment and progress on the realization of human rights, such as the development of human rights indicators for the general public as well as specific indicators for persons with disabilities.

Dr. Yibee Huang is a full-time human rights NGO worker and currently the Chief Executive Officer of Covenants Watch, an umbrella organization that monitors the government on its obligations prescribed by the Covenants and other international human rights conventions. She is also a researcher at Taiwan International Medical Alliance (TIMA), which is one of the founding members of Covenants Watch. She studied psychology, and law, and holds a Ph.D. degree in public health from National Yang Ming University. Her dissertation is on developing human rights indicators for future application in Taiwan, especially indicators for the right to work and the rights of persons with disabilities. She works on advocacy of several institutional issues, including the establishment of a National Human Rights Institution, capacity building for NGOs, and awareness raising for the public, and she collaborates extensively with the legal community to facilitate the application of human rights conventions in litigation and judicial decisions.

Chapter 18
Personal Reflections on the Taiwan Human Rights Review Process

Manfred Nowak

Abstract The author was requested by the government of Taiwan to lead a group of highly distinguished international human rights experts entrusted with the task of reviewing Taiwan's compliance with the rights enshrined in the International Human Rights Covenants (ICESCR and ICCPR). This chapter contains some personal reflections by the author on the review proceedings in 2013 and 2017. Particular emphasis focuses on the need to abolish the death penalty.

Keywords Death penalty · International human rights · State reporting procedure UN covenants on human rights · United Nations

In November 2003, I led a human rights mission of the International Commission of Jurists to Taiwan. We provided advice to the Government of Taiwan on the draft Human Rights Act. When I met President Chen Shui-bian on 20 November, we also discussed the idea of ratifying major United Nations (hereinafter UN) human rights treaties in order to show to the international community that Taiwan, despite being prevented from joining the UN, was willing to comply with the obligations deriving from the two International Covenants and other core UN human rights treaties.

The Government of Taiwan followed our advice and ratified the International Covenant on Civil and Political Rights (hereinafter ICCPR) and the International Covenant on Economic, Social and Cultural Rights (hereinafter ICESCR) in 2009; however, the UN did not formally recognize these ratifications as Taiwan was not a UN member state. This also meant that the respective UN treaty monitoring bodies, such as the Human Rights Committee and the Committee on Economic, Social and Cultural Rights, were prevented from reviewing reports submitted by the Government of Taiwan.

M. Nowak (✉)
University of Vienna, Vienna, Austria
e-mail: manfred.nowak@univie.ac.at

M. Nowak
European Inter-University Centre for Human Rights and Democratisation (EIUC), Venice, Austria

J. A. Cohen et al. (eds.), *Taiwan and International Human Rights*, Economics, Law, and Institutions in Asia Pacific, https://doi.org/10.1007/978-981-13-0350-0_18

In November 2011, I was again invited to Taiwan, this time to deliver various lectures. I was accompanied by my assistant at Vienna University, Tina Hofstätter. At National Taiwan University, I delivered the 1st Lei Chen Memorial Lecture on "Torture: Perspectives from the UN Special Rapporteur on Torture" and another lecture on the creation of a "World Court of Human Rights." At Soochow University, I led a workshop on the "Dialogue with Taiwan NGOs," and finally I delivered another Lei Chen Memorial Lecture on "The Implementation of the International Covenant on Civil and Political Rights." During the ensuing discussions, we also spoke about implementation of the Covenant in Taiwan. Following my visit to Mr. Chiou Ho-shun at the Taipei Detention Centre, who had been sentenced to death and had spent a total of 23 years in prison, I also raised my concerns about the continuing application of the death penalty in Taiwan. If the Government of Taiwan wished to show to the international community that it was willing to comply with international human rights standards, which it had voluntarily adopted as a matter of domestic law, in my opinion it was high time to abolish the death penalty.

At this time, the Government of Taiwan under President Ma Ying-jeou invited me to put together a group of highly respected human rights experts willing to review the initial reports submitted by the Government in accordance with the two UN Covenants. During 2012, I was able to recruit ten leading human rights experts from the Asia-Pacific region, Europe and the US: Philip Alston (Australia), Nisuke Ando (Japan), Virginia Bonoan-Dandan (Philippines), Jerome Cohen (USA), Shanthi Dairiam (Malaysia), Asma Jahangir (Pakistan), Eibe Riedel (Germany), Heisoo Shin (South Korea) and Theo van Boven (Netherlands). The Government of Taiwan had appointed Prosecutor Ming-Li Kuo to act as contact person for the Government, who coordinated the overall endeavor in a highly efficient manner. From the side of the independent experts, Ms. Karolina Januszewski, who was at that time my assistant at Vienna University, coordinated our input and was also invited by the Government of Taiwan to accompany us to Taipei. In summer 2012, we received the initial reports for both Covenants as well as a core document explaining the constitutional and legal system of Taiwan and the status of both Covenants in the domestic legal system. On the basis of these documents and a considerable number of "shadow reports" submitted by Nongovernmental Organizations (hereinafter NGOs), we prepared a comprehensive list of issues which we submitted to the Government in autumn 2012. Although we were one joint "International Group of Independent Experts," we created two sub-committees, one on the ICESCR, led by Eibe Riedel, the other on the ICCPR, led by myself. In February 2013, we spent a full week in Taipei, meeting with a large number of high government officials representing the various departments as well as representatives of the Office of the President, the Legislative, Executive, Examination and Control Yuans, partly in plenary, partly in our two sub-committees. We also held animated discussions with a large group of NGO representatives. Since our meetings were public and webcast live, civil society and the population at large could follow our discussions. At the end, we jointly drafted and adopted a number of Concluding Observations and Recommendations, which we submitted to the Government and President Ma on 1 March 2013.

Unfortunately, the review meetings were overshadowed by the fact that the Government of Taiwan had decided to resume executions of death row prisoners shortly before our arrival in Taipei. On 21 December 2012, six death row convicts were executed. These were the first executions after quite a long period during which no executions had taken place. Since we had raised serious concerns on our list of issues about the continuing existence of capital punishment, the International Group of Independent Experts considered these executions, which took place only two months before our scheduled review process, as a provocation. We had a serious discussion among ourselves whether we should cancel the entire review process. But we finally decided to continue and hoped that we could convince the Government of Taiwan that the death penalty constituted inhuman punishment in violation of the right to personal integrity and dignity in Article 7 of the ICCPR. I also raised this issue personally with President Ma during an official lunch in the Presidential Palace on 1 March. But, unfortunately and despite fairly strong recommendations to at least implement a moratorium on executions in accordance with various resolutions of the UN General Assembly, executions continued during the following years.

In 2016, I was again requested by the Government to chair a group of experts, now called the "International Review Committee," for a review of the second periodic reports. I agreed again, as did the majority of the members of our original group of experts. Nevertheless, we had to replace some of the members and invited a number of new members. The Committee on Economic, Social and Cultural Rights was again chaired by Eibe Riedel (Germany) and was now composed of Virginia Bonoan-Dandan (Philippines), Miloon Kothari (India), Jannie Lasimbang (Malaysia) and Heisoo Shin (South Korea). The Committee on Civil and Political Rights was again chaired by me and consisted of Jerome Cohen (USA), Shanthi Dairiam (Malaysia), Peer Lorenzen (Denmark) and Sima Samar (Afghanistan). This time, our contact person in the Government was Prosecutor Wen-Hsiang Chou who was as efficient as his predecessor. The same is true for Anna Zenz, my assistant at the European Inter-University Centre for Human Rights and Democratisation (EIUC) in Venice, who was invited by the Government of Taiwan to accompany me and to coordinate our input. During the summer of 2016, we received the second periodic reports as well as the Core Document and Responses to our Concluding Observations and Recommendations of 2013. On the basis of these documents and a considerable number of NGO reports, we again drafted a list of issues and submitted them to the Government. The review took place in January 2017 and followed the same procedure as that in 2013. On 20 January we presented our Concluding Observations and Recommendations at a public meeting in the Ministry of Justice, followed by an official lunch with the new President, Tsai Ing-wen, in the Presidential Palace.

In my opinion, the review process initiated by the Government of Taiwan in accordance with the two International Covenants constitutes best state practices. The reports and other documents submitted by the Government and the NGO community of Taiwan follow the practices of the UN treaty monitoring bodies. But the discussions with representatives of the Government and civil society in Taipei are much more detailed, as we spend more time than the UN treaty monitoring bodies can afford. Since the review takes place in Taiwan, rather than on UN premises in Geneva, many more representatives of both the Government and the NGO community are able to participate. This also means that the review attracts much more media attention than most of the reviews of the UN treaty monitoring bodies in Geneva. Both the reports of the Government and the "shadow reports" of the NGOs are very frank and critical, and the discussions touch upon all relevant human rights issues and problems. The Government responds to all questions raised by the independent experts in a highly open and professional manner.

On the basis of the review of the initial reports in 2013, the "International Group of Independent Experts" adopted Concluding Observations and Recommendations on many different human rights issues. We recommended that the Government of Taiwan establish a National Human Rights Institution in full accordance with the Paris Principles of 1993, put economic, social and cultural rights on the same legislative level as civil and political rights, improve human rights education and training, pay due attention to the issue of corporate responsibility, reveal the full truth about the gross human rights violations during the years of the "White Terror," enact comprehensive legislation covering all fields of gender equality, and better respect the rights of indigenous peoples, most notably in relation to a planned nuclear waste site. With respect to the ICESCR, we recommended to increase the employment rate of women, to make basic labor protection legislation more inclusive so as to also cover migrant workers, domestic workers and dispatched workers, to bring the rights of trade unions in line with international standards, to better care for homeless people and to stop forced evictions unless alternative housing is provided to families living in informal settlements, to combat discrimination against lesbian, gay, bisexual, transgender and intersex (LGBTI) persons and to improve sex education programs in order to decrease the high pregnancy and abortion rates amongst female adolescents. With respect to the ICCPR, the experts, above all, strongly recommended that the Government of Taiwan intensify its efforts towards abolition of capital punishment. We also recommended to establish torture as a separate crime with adequate penalties in the Criminal Code, to respect the principle of non-refoulement and to adopt a Refugee Act including this principle, to address the serious problem of prison overcrowding by, inter alia, liberalizing the harsh policy of the Government of Taiwan on drug use and by introducing less restrictive provisions on pre-trial bail and parole, to apply the right to habeas corpus to foreigners and Mainlanders placed in immigration detention, to amend the "Speedy Trial Act" in order to drastically reduce the maximum period of eight years for pre-trial detention and to also reduce the excessive length of criminal trials, to abolish wide-scale restrictions by administrative and tax authorities with respect to the right of Taiwanese citizens to travel abroad, to abolish mandatory HIV testing requirements and other restrictions on aliens living with HIV, to abolish the crime of adultery, to introduce vigorous judicial oversight of telecommunications and other forms of surveillance, to combat media concentration, to insert a crime of advocacy of national, racial or religious hatred into the Criminal Code, to change the approval system to a registration system in the Assembly and Parade

Act, to abolish differences in the age of marriage between men and women, to better address domestic violence and other forms of violence against women, and to amend abortion legislation so as to enable pregnant women to decide on abortion based on their own free will.

The Concluding Observations and Recommendations of the International Review Committee adopted in January 2017 resembled to a certain extent our earlier recommendations, since many of our recommendations had not yet been implemented. This applies, most importantly, to the non-abolition of the death penalty and the continuing practice of carrying out executions despite the strong call by the UN General Assembly to introduce a moratorium. Rather than raising public awareness against this cruel and inhuman punishment, the Government of Taiwan continued to justify its retentionist attitude by referring to opinion polls. The same argument was put forward with respect to the failure of the Government to abolish the crime of adultery. The International Review Committee had to stress "that it is the responsibility of the Government to bring its legal system in line with international human rights law and to take the lead, by means of awareness raising and other initiatives, to dispel concerns among the general public" (para. 70). Other recommendations which, unfortunately, needed to be reiterated because of non-compliance, were to establish a completely independent National Human Rights Institution, to make the ICESCR directly applicable before domestic courts (the Supreme Administrative Court in August 2014 had even effectively ruled out its applicability), to hold Taiwanese and foreign companies accountable for human rights violations, to improve the situation for migrant and domestic workers, to stop forced evictions, to find a solution to radioactive waste disposal that would not jeopardize indigenous communities, to enact a specific crime of torture in the Criminal Code, to respect the principle of non-refoulement and to enact a Refugee Act, to reduce the maximum period of eight years of pre-trial detention authorized in the "Speedy Trial Act" and to reduce the overall length of criminal trials, to address the overcrowding of prisons (which the Government had even tried to excuse by a lack of human resources and financial constraints), and to amend the Assembly and Parade Act.

The International Review Committee also added a number of new concerns and recommendations. For example, it expressed serious concern about the growth of income inequality in Taiwan, which "threatens the social stability, democratic coherence and the general realisation of human rights" (para. 18). We also expressed concerns regarding the accountability of the Government of Taiwan to effectively enforce its laws on Taiwanese-flagged fishing vessels that are reportedly engaged in illegal, unreported and unregulated (IUU) fishing, which has serious impacts on the labor rights of workers, on the environment and the survival of endangered marine species. With respect to the right to housing, the Review Committee expressed a number of additional concerns, including that the thrust of Taiwan's economic policies is dictating a "market" solution to the housing and land crisis, resulting in a lack of available and affordable housing and speculation in the field of housing, property and land. With respect to the ICCPR, we expressed, for instance, concern about the comparatively high rate of recent deaths in custody and about the uncontrolled measures of surveillance by intelligence agencies.

On the other hand, we also recognized a number of positive initiatives undertaken by the Government of Taiwan and improvements in accordance with our earlier recommendations. For example, we welcomed Taiwan's acceptance, without reservations, of the obligations contained in six of the core UN human rights treaties, the measures taken to implement the Gender Equality Education Act and to combat domestic violence, the historic apology to indigenous peoples by President Tsai Ing-wen in August 2016 and various initiatives undertaken to protect the rights of indigenous peoples, the prohibition of all forms of corporal punishment in all sectors of society, including the police, the military, in schools, in the family and as judicial or disciplinary sanctions, the significant progress that has taken place in expanding the scope of habeas corpus, and initiatives taken to raise the minimum age of marriage of women to 18. Finally, the Review Committee noted "with appreciation the initiatives taken by the Government of Taiwan aimed at introducing same-sex marriage into Taiwanese law. The full realisation of these legislative changes would be a manifestation of Taiwan as a pioneer in the Asia-Pacific region, in combating discrimination on the basis of sexual orientation and gender identity" (para. 77).

The overall assessment of the review process of the Government of Taiwan's compliance with obligations deriving from its voluntary acceptance of the two International Human Rights Covenants is, therefore, mixed. On the procedural level, the Taiwanese example certainly represents best practices, both in terms of the quality of the reports submitted by the Government and by the NGOs and in terms of the quality of the dialogue between independent human rights experts, high representatives of various government departments as well as members of the legislative and judicial powers, civil society, academia and the media. On the substantive level, many initiatives have been undertaken by the Government of Taiwan, and partially also by the Legislative Yuan, to implement our recommendations and to comply with international human rights standards. In this context, we should also recognize the dramatic progress that has been made in Taiwan under different governments since 1987, when Taiwan began to emerge from a long and dark period of martial law. Today, Taiwan certainly belongs to the countries with the best human rights records in the Asia-Pacific region.

On the other hand, there are a number of areas where the human rights situation in Taiwan does violate international human rights standards and where our recommendations were not taken seriously. The most striking example is, of course, the continued application of the death penalty and the fact that Taiwan is among only a few remaining countries in the world, including the People's Republic of China, the USA, Japan and certain Islamic countries, where executions still take place. If Taiwan wishes to show that it takes its international human rights obligations seriously and that it wishes to prove that it is the "better China" in terms of human rights compliance, then it needs to swiftly abolish capital punishment and, as a first step, immediately implement a moratorium on executions. I have a certain hope that President Tsai Ing-wen, in line with our conversation after the last review, might be willing to take decisive action in this respect. But there are also other serious flaws in the administration of criminal justice, including the length of proceedings, the excessive use of pre-trial detentions, the deplorable state of overcrowded prisons and the lack of a specific crime of torture and respective independent investigations of torture allegations. There are also problems in relation to the right to privacy, such as excessive surveillance without proper judicial control and the continued application of the crime of adultery. Despite certain progress, there also remain serious problems with respect to the labor rights of migrant and domestic workers, the rights of indigenous peoples to their lands and respect for their traditional way of life, and the right to housing for the homeless and those living in informal settlements. Finally, Taiwan needs to pay attention that its free market economy does not lead to a further increase in economic inequality which, as in many other countries, threatens to undermine social coherence and the values of a democratic society based upon equality, social security, human rights and the rule of law.

Manfred Nowak. Since January 2016, Manfred Nowak has been the Secretary-General of the European Inter-University Center for Human Rights and Democratisation (EIUC) in Venice. He is Professor for Human Rights Law at the University of Vienna, and head of the Research Center on Human Rights (Vienna University). He is also founder and co-director of the Austrian Ludwig Boltzmann Institute for Human Rights. In October 2016, he was appointed as an independent expert leading the UN Global Study on Children Deprived of Liberty. He acted as Chair of the International Review Committee on the International Covenant on Civil and Political Rights (ICCPR) appointed by the Government of Taiwan (Republic of China) from 2012 to 2013 and 2016 to 2017. Manfred Nowak graduated from Vienna Law School (Dr. iur. 1973) and from Columbia University, New York (LL.M. 1975). He has been professor at the Institute of Constitutional and Administrative Law at the University of Vienna since 1986. He was a member of the Austrian Delegation to the UN Commission on Human Rights (1986 and 1993). He coordinated NGO-parallel events during the 1993 UN Conference for Human Rights in Vienna while he also was Professor of Law at the Austrian Federal Academy of Public Administration in Vienna until 2002. As a UN expert on missing persons in the former Yugoslavia he started a process aimed at identifying missing persons through exhumation of mortal remains between 1994 and 1997. From 1996 to 2003, Manfred Nowak was a judge in the Human Rights Chamber in Bosnia. From 2000 to 2012 he was head of an independent human rights commission at the Austrian Interior Ministry. From 2002 to 2003 he was Visiting Professor at the Raoul Wallenberg Institute of Human Rights and Humanitarian Law at the University of Lund. From 2004 to 2010, he was UN Special Rapporteur on Torture and other Cruel, Inhuman or Degrading Treatment. From 2009 to 2014, he was head of the interdisciplinary Ph.D. Research School "Empowerment through Human Rights" (University of Vienna). In 2014, he held the Austrian Visiting Chair at Stanford University. Manfred Nowak has published more than 600 books and articles on international, constitutional, administrative and human rights law, including the standard commentary on the International Covenant on Civil and Political Rights. He was awarded the UNESCO Prize for the Teaching of Human Rights in 1994 and the Bruno Kreisky Prize for Human Rights in 2007.

Part IV
Protection of Civil and Political Rights

Chapter 19
Killing in Your Name: Pathology of Judicial Paternalism and the Mutation of the "Most Serious Crimes" Requirement in Taiwan

Ming-Sung Kuo and Hui-Wen Chen

Abstract Although Article 6 of the International Covenant on Civil and Political Rights (ICCPR) falls short of banning the death penalty outright, it provides for substantive and procedural requirements aimed at limiting imposition of the death penalty before its abolition. Among them is the restriction on the "most serious crimes" in jurisdictions where the death penalty remains lawful (ICCPR Article 6 (2)). Drawing on the case law of the Taiwanese Supreme Court (TSC), this chapter aims to shed socio-legal light on the role that the "most serious crimes" requirement has played in judicial rulings concerning the death penalty since the ICCPR rights became enforceable in Taiwan on 10 December 2009. It is argued that in its translation into Taiwanese judicial practice, the "most serious crimes" requirement has been read together with the domestic legal provision for individualized aggravating and mitigating circumstances under the rubric of rehabilitatibility (教化可能性), deviating from the jurisprudence of the UN human rights bodies. Under the judge-civilizer tradition prevalent in the Taiwanese judiciary, the idea of rehabilitatibility has eventually turned the judicial deliberation on whether to impose the death penalty into a valuation of the worth of the defendant's life, with a focus on the discovery of the incorrigible offender. With its absorption into the individualizing idea of rehabilitatibility, the "most serious crimes" requirement of the ICCPR has thus become part of the pathology of judicial paternalism, suggesting a mutation of international human rights ideals in Taiwan.

M.-S. Kuo (✉) · H.-W. Chen
University of Warwick School of Law, Coventry, UK
e-mail: M-S.Kuo@warwick.ac.uk

H.-W. Chen
e-mail: H-W.Chen@warwick.ac.uk

J. A. Cohen et al. (eds.), *Taiwan and International Human Rights*, Economics, Law, and Institutions in Asia Pacific, https://doi.org/10.1007/978-981-13-0350-0_19

Keywords Death penalty · ICCPR (International Covenant on Civil and Political Rights) · Judge-civilizer · Judicial paternalism · Most serious crimes Rehabilitatibility

1 Introduction

Since the statutory adoption of the International Covenant on Civil and Political Rights (hereinafter ICCPR) and the International Covenant on Economic, Social and Cultural Rights (hereinafter ICESCR) in 2009,[1] the death penalty has been at the center of public debate as to whether and, if so, how international human rights law as provided for in both treaties has enhanced the protection of human rights in Taiwan, especially through judicial rulings. Although Article 6 of the ICCPR falls short of banning the death penalty outright, paragraph 6 thereof stipulates that "[n]othing in this article shall be invoked to delay or to prevent the abolition of capital punishment by any State Party to the present Covenant," pointing in the direction of its eventual abolition.[2] In the meantime, the rest of Article 6 provides for substantive and procedural requirements aimed at the limitation of the imposition of the death penalty before its abolition. Among them is the restriction of the "most serious crimes" in jurisdictions where the death penalty remains a lawful punishment (ICCPR, Article 6 (2)). The role that the "most serious crimes" requirement has played in death sentences since ICCPR rights became enforceable in Taiwan on 10 December 2009 is the focus of this chapter.[3]

Among Taiwanese scholars and commentators, it is widely perceived that Article 6 of the ICCPR has effectively narrowed imposition of the death penalty by way of the restrictive application of the "most serious crimes" requirement in judicial proceedings.[4] The sentencing court is obliged to address the international human rights law–derived condition in its judgment in death penalty cases. For this reason, the ICCPR (together with the ICESCR and other statutorily adopted international human rights treaties) has been credited with adding impetus to the judicial protection of human rights and the creation of a new human rights culture in Taiwan. Whether and to what extent the case law bears out such a positive appraisal requires further scrutiny. Moreover, it remains to be determined whether the perceived narrowing of the death sentences, if there has been any at all, has resulted from the

[1] Statutory adoption here refers to the citation to the ICCPR and the ICESCR in Taiwan's ICCPR and ICESCR Implementation Act of 2009, without taking a stance as to whether the ICCPR and the ICESCR have been duly ratified in terms of international law or given direct effect as ratified treaties in terms of Taiwanese domestic treaty law.

[2] Hood and Hoyle (2008), pp. 21–22.

[3] The ICCPR and ICESCR Implementation Act, which put the domestic application of the ICCPR and the ICESCR on a statutory basis, was promulgated on 22 Apr 2009 but did not come into force until 10 Dec 2009.

[4] See, e.g., Liao (2014), p. 927.

adoption of the ICCPR or has simply continued with the trend set out in judicial practice before its entry into force.[5]

Instead of focusing on the question of whether the statutory adoption of the ICCPR has actually resulted in an improvement in the condition of human rights in Taiwan, this chapter looks at Article 6 from a different vantage point. Drawing on the case law of the Taiwanese Supreme Court (hereinafter TSC), this chapter aims to shed socio-legal light on the actual role that the "most serious crimes" requirement has played in judicial rulings concerning the death penalty. In contrast to the positive image perceived in current literature, the role of the "most serious crimes" requirement in case law is ambiguous, as this chapter will show.

In this chapter, it will be argued that in its translation into Taiwanese judicial practice, the "most serious crimes" requirement has been read together with the domestic legal provision for individualized aggravating and mitigating circumstances under the rubric of rehabilitatibility (教化可能性). This is a deviation from the approach taken by the jurisprudence of the UN human rights bodies in the interpretation of the "most serious crimes," which has centered on legislation instead of individualized sentencing. As a result, it is the idea of rehabilitatibility that has played the decisive role in the death penalty cases. Yet, under the judge-civilizer tradition prevalent in the Taiwanese judiciary, the idea of rehabilitatibility has eventually turned the judicial deliberation on whether to impose the death penalty into a valuation of the worth of the defendant's life, with a focus on the discovery of the incorrigible offender. As it has become absorbed into the individualizing idea of rehabilitatibility, the "most serious crimes" requirement of the ICCPR has become part of the pathology of judicial paternalism in Taiwan. The TSC jurisprudence on Article 6 of the ICCPR indicates that the judge has not only evaluated the defendant's behavior in moralistic terms but has also valued the worth of his or her life in terms of rehabilitatibility in death penalty cases. This development represents nothing less than a mutation of international human rights ideals. To proceed, this chapter first notes the variegated criminological rationales for the death penalty in Taiwanese judicial practice. Following the discussion on how the "most serious crimes" requirement of Article 6 of the ICCPR has been applied in TSC case law, the chapter provides a critique of the pathology of judicial paternalism and the resulting mutation of Article 6 of the ICCPR.

2 The Image of the Killing Leviathan: A Chimera of Incapacitator, Rehabilitator, and Retributor

Paralleling the development of criminal punishment in Western history, the death penalty played a major role in traditional Chinese criminal law thinking and practice in which it was associated, with the manifestation of the powers of dynastic

[5]See generally Wang (2011).

emperors.[6] That cultural register cast a long shadow on Taiwanese legal thinking and judicial practice after the Republic of China Criminal Code (hereinafter Criminal Code) was imposed on Taiwan following the surrender of the Imperial Japanese Army to Chinese troops at the behest of the Allied Forces on 25 October 1945.[7] In the following decades, Taiwan was placed under a quasi-military dictatorship powered by draconian martial-law measures and emergency decrees until its gradual transformation into a constitutional democracy from the late 1980s on.[8] During the period of martial-law rule, the number of capital crimes grew exponentially. Apart from the Criminal Code, manifold special statutes were enacted to address criminalities that were considered to be a threat to national security or public order. Under the martial-law regime, civilians were also charged and punished according to the Military Criminal Code for some serious crimes. As a result, offenses such as sedition, corruption, smuggling, gang robbery, drug trafficking, to name just a few, were met with much harsher criminal punishment (including the death penalty) than those already stipulated in the Criminal Code. With the provision for capital punishment continuing to expand, numerous non-homicidal crimes became punishable by death. Moreover, despite a limited number of crimes incurring the mandatory death penalty in the Criminal Code, the scope of the mandatory death sentence was greatly broadened because of the push for harsher punishment by means of special criminal codes and the extended application of the Military Criminal Code.

Against that backdrop, the death penalty was frequently imposed by the courts as a deterrence to prevent the committing of capital crimes. Deterrence and incapacitation were the principal rationales behind the judicial imposition of the death penalty when the Taiwanese people lived under the Chinese Nationalist-dominated dictatorship.[9] The death penalty was then considered the ultimate form of "punitive segregation" by way of which the "incorrigible offenders" of the legal order, or rather, the enemies of the state, were to be incapacitated.[10] Under martial-law rule, the Taiwanese state was not only an authoritarian state but also acted like a "killing leviathan."[11] That said, the retributivist rationale for capital punishment, which had

---

[6]See generally Kim and LeBlang (1975); cf. Cheng (1948), p. 463. For the role of capital punishment and law enforcement in medieval Europe, see Foucault (1990), pp. 137–138; Garland (2001), p. 29.

[7]Wang (2002), pp. 537–538.

[8]Peng (1973), pp. 163–168; see also Yeh (2016), pp. 28–38.

[9]Hsu (2006), p. 31; cf. Johnson and Zimring (2009), pp. 197–199.

[10]Garland (2001), pp. 142–145. For a discussion on how the idea of the incorrigible offender has been tied to modern penological policies under both totalitarian regimes and liberal democracies, see, e.g., Eghigian (2015). How the idea of the incorrigible offender plays out in Taiwanese judicial rulings on the death penalty will be further discussed in Sects. 3 and 4.

[11]According to Professor Jaw-Perng Wang (2011), p. 146, over fifty different offenses still required mandatory imposition of the death penalty in the 1990s. The term "killing leviathan" is an adaptation of what Austin Sarat observes in the United States as a "killing state." Sarat (2001), p. 46.

pervaded the Chinese legal tradition for centuries, did not disappear from legal thinking and judicial practice in post-war Taiwan. The conventional wisdom that, to redress the homicidal offense, the loss of the killer's life should be demanded as compensation, had found its way into Taiwan's modernist criminal law that subscribed to theories of retributivism and just deserts alongside other Western philosophies of punishment.[12] Taken as a whole, retribution, together with deterrence and incapacitation, underlay the judicial policy on the imposition of the death penalty when Taiwan was under martial law.

It has been noted in the literature that Taiwan's embrace of legal modernity has been a gradual process, which started with the replacement of the Great Qing Code by a modern legal system under Japanese colonial rule from 1895 to 1945.[13] Taiwan's transition to a constitutional democracy in the late 1980s marked another stage in her adoption of legal modernity.[14] Echoing bourgeois calls for the abolition of the death penalty in modern Europe during the late eighteenth century,[15] the question of how to tame the killing leviathan has drawn much attention from Taiwanese activists and reformers in the post-martial-law era. Activists and reformers indeed gained some political ground in the pushback against the killing leviathan, resulting in the stipulation on the abolition of the death penalty as a state goal in the draft Human Rights Law Bill of 2003.[16] Yet that victory proved to be short-lived. The draft Human Rights Law Bill was shelved soon after its publication and populist voices in support of the death penalty have since effectively drowned out the continuing calls for its abolition.[17] Even so, the movement to curtail the statutory provision for the death penalty and restrict its imposition in sentencing has gradually gained currency. In 2002, capital crimes were substantially reduced, with the amendment or repeal of many of the draconian special criminal codes. Furthermore, all the statutory provisions for a mandatory death penalty, whether in the Criminal Code or special legislation, were amended in 2006 to allow for discretion as to the imposition of the death penalty in sentencing.[18] Apart from legislative reform, the movement to curtail capital punishment has had an impact on the judicial practice of sentencing. Since 2002, the courts have effectively restricted

---

[12]For the retributivist character of Chinese traditional criminal law, see Cheng (1948), p. 468.

[13]Wang (2002), pp. 532–535.

[14]*Id.*, at pp. 538–539. The martial-law decree was lifted in 1987, ending the prosecution of civilian crimes under the Military Criminal Code.

[15]For a balanced, brief discussion of the relationship between the emergence of Enlightenment humanitarianism and the abolition movement in Western history, see Shoemaker (2001), pp. 19–27; cf. Foucault (1990), p. 138.

[16]Hood and Hoyle (2008), pp. 90–91.

[17]For a discussion of how the draft Human Rights Law Bill lost political momentum, see generally Kuo and Chen (forthcoming).

[18]Wang (2011), p. 147.

the death sentence only to murders.[19] Taken together, and in spite of the setback for the abolition movement, the killing leviathan has been considerably tamed by legislative reform and judicial constraints since Taiwan's transformation from a quasi-military dictatorship into a constitutional democracy.

In the meantime, the function of criminal law has been reconsidered in Taiwan's latest reception of legal modernity at the end of authoritarian rule. No longer is it viewed as a tool for the deterrence or suppression of political dissidents. Nor is it aimed at the preservation of the reigning regime's power by incapacitating its enemies. Instead, progressive theories of rehabilitation and reformation have emerged as the guiding philosophy for criminal punishment since Taiwan's liberation from the yoke of martial law.[20] To be clear, the adoption of the progressive rehabilitative ideal does not mean its automatic translation into correctional practices. Nor does it completely displace established theories of retribution, incapacitation, or deterrence from Taiwan's post-martial law penological policy. Rather, the legacies of retributivism and preventionism still linger on, although rehabilitation has emerged as the dominant idea in judicial judgments and other discourses on penology.[21]

Particularly pertaining to our present purposes, the same array of penological ideas has also applied to imposition of the death penalty in the judicial practice of sentencing.[22] Much to the bafflement of criminologists and philosophers of punishment,[23] rehabilitation has since been invoked by Taiwanese courts in judgments on the death penalty alongside the ideas of just deserts and incapacitation.[24] Apparently, justification for the death sentence in rehabilitative terms is problematic, as will be further discussed in Sec. 4. And that seemingly self-contradictory discursive manuever needs to be situated in the broader socio-legal context. Viewed thus, invocation of the rehabilitative ideal and the debate surrounding the rehabilitatibility of convicts in death penalty cases is part of the progressive development of Taiwan's revamping of her draconian legal system in the transition to a constitutional democracy. The point for present purposes is that paralleling the rehabilitative trend in general penological policy, the judicial debate about the imposition of the death penalty in individual cases has centered on rehabilitation,

---

[19]According to Professor Jaw-Perng Wang, out of the ninety-three death sentences in the period 2000–2009, only three were imposed on non-homicidal crimes. Moreover, those three outliers occurred before 2002. *Id.*, at p. 162.

[20]See Hsu (2006), p. 33; cf. Lo (2006), p. 57; Jan (1988). For the linkage of the rehabilitative ideal and modernity, see Garland (2001), pp. 40–41.

[21]Hsu (2006), p. 33.

[22]E.g., Hsieh Y-h et al. v. Republic of China, 105 Tai Shang Zi Di 1856 Hao Panjue [105 台上字第 1856 號判決] (Supreme Ct. [最高法院刑事庭] 27 July 2016) (Taiwan).

[23]It has been noted that the rehabilitative ideal in Western history has pointed in the direction of abolition. Hammel (2010), pp. 173–175; cf. Eghigian (2015), p. 49.

[24]Hsieh (2013), p. 10.

although the terms of retribution and incapacitation are still employed.[25] In sum, becoming a tamer beast, the image of the Taiwanese killing leviathan turns out to be a chimera of incapacitator, rehabilitator, and retributor. That chimerical image has spelled out efforts to continue to curtail imposition of the death penalty by virtue of the "most serious crimes" requirement in Article 6 of the ICCPR.

3 "Most Serious Crimes," "Rehabilitatibility," and Presentation of the Incorrigible Offender

It should be noted that in the continuing battle against the death penalty before the court, Taiwanese activists have invoked the ICCPR on two fronts. With respect to constitutional petitions, they have turned to Article 6 and other provisions of the ICCPR to challenge the legal procedures governing imposition of the death penalty and its execution, but to no avail.[26] The Taiwan Constitutional Court (hereinafter TCC) has yet to grant leave for any constitutional petition resulting from imposition of the death penalty following statutory adoption of the ICCPR. Even so, the ICCPR has not been totally missing from TCC jurisprudence with respect to issues concerning the death penalty. In J.Y. Interpretation No. 582 (2004), which resulted from a case concerning a death sentence, albeit prior to the statutory adoption of the ICCPR, the TCC tightened the rules of evidence in criminal procedures with reference to the ICCPR.[27] Nevertheless, the TCC made its ruling on constitutional grounds. For this reason, the extent to which the requirement of the ICCPR contributed to the enhancement of the procedural safeguards in that case was not easy to pin down. Activists have also opened a second front outside the TCC in the fight against the death penalty. The TSC has since become the main theater where the judicial battle against the death penalty has been fought. The "most serious crimes" requirement as stipulated in paragraph 2 of Article 6 of the ICCPR has been invoked to add substantive constraints on imposition of the death penalty.[28] To see how that strategy can possibly be conceived and deployed, a closer look at the "most serious crimes" requirement will be helpful.

Noticeably, the "most serious crimes" requirement is abstract. In the negotiations leading up to the adoption of the ICCPR, the substantive requirement of "most

---

[25]*Id.*, at pp. 12–13.

[26]Chang (2012), pp. 22–23.

[27]In the *ratio decidendi*, the TCC refers to Article 14 of the ICCPR. Da Fa Guan Shi Zi Di 582 Hao [大法官釋字第582號] (J.Y. Interpretation No. 582) (23 July 2004) (R.O.C.). http://www.judicial.gov.tw/constitutionalcourt/EN/p03_01.asp?expno=582. Accessed 25 Oct 2017.

[28]It has been argued that Article 6 of the ICCPR has enhanced the procedural rules in cases of the death penalty to the extent that the TSC has held oral hearings for those cases more often than it did prior to the statutory adoption of the ICCPR. Cf. Hsieh (2013), p. 10. That may be true. Yet, it is hard to establish the causation between the increasing frequency of the TSC's holding of oral hearings and the adoption of the ICCPR, as the TSC rarely explained why it granted a request for oral hearings in its rulings.

serious crimes" was preferred to more specific terms so that the draft ICCPR could satisfy those countries that demanded that the death penalty be imposed in more stricter terms before its eventual abolition and to accommodate those countries that upheld the death penalty at the same time.[29] Undergoing the process of dynamic interpretation as conceived of by its drafters,[30] the "most serious crimes" requirement has "progressively restrict[ed] the number of offenses for which capital punishment might be imposed."[31] As it stands, the jurisprudence of the UN human rights bodies on the "most serious crimes" requirement puts emphasis on "intention" and on "lethal or other extremely grave consequences," excluding many non-homicidal offenses.[32] Though it seems to imply that to qualify as most serious crimes, "the offences should lead to loss of life or be life-threatening, in the sense that death is a very likely consequence of the action,"[33] Professor Philip Alston has interpreted that line of jurisprudence even more narrowly. In his capacity as the UN Special Rapporteur on extrajudicial, summary, or arbitrary executions, Professor Alston explicitly confined "the most serious crimes" to "[the] cases where it can be shown that there was an intention to kill which resulted in the loss of life."[34] And it is that reading that has underlain the invocation of the "most serious crimes" requirement in cases of the death penalty before the TSC.

Before proceeding to the interpretation of the "most serious crimes" requirement in TSC case law, it merits special mention that a fundamental distinction has been drawn between the validity of the mandatory death penalty and the restriction of the death penalty to the "most serious crimes" in the jurisprudence of the UN human rights bodies in Article 6 of the ICCPR. The jurisprudence on the former centered on the stipulation that "[n]o one shall be arbitrarily deprived of his life" under paragraph 1 of Article 6.[35] Specifically, it requires "weighing factors that will not be

[29]Alston (2007), paras 44–47.

[30]Hood and Hoyle (2008), pp. 130–131. It should be noted that with respect to the dynamic interpretation of the "most serious crimes" requirement, the body of law comprises statements, resolutions, communications, and other documents issued or adopted by various institutions. Among the institutional co-interpreters of the ICCPR are the UN Economic and Social Council, the Human Rights Council (replacing the Commission on Human Rights), the Human Rights Committee, the UN General Assembly as well as the Secretary-General (through reports by several Special Rapporteurs).

[31]This is indicated in paragraph 1 of the Safeguards Guaranteeing Protection of the Rights of Those Facing the Death Penalty (Safeguards), which was adopted by a resolution of the Economic and Social Council of the United Nations. *Id.*, at p. 131; see also *Id.*, at pp. 21–22 (discussing GA Resolutions 28/57 (1971) and 32/61 (1977). Notably, failing to recognize the unique dynamic process of how international law and the ICCPR in particular have developed and mistaking the Human Rights Committee as the ICCPR treaty body for the authoritative interpreter of the ICCPR, the TSC in Peng C-y v. Republic of China, 103 Tai Shang Zi Di 3062 Hao Panjue [103 台上字第 3062 號判決] (Supreme Ct. [最高法院刑事庭] 2 Sept 2014) (Taiwan) dismissed the relevance of the foregoing Safeguards outright for they were not issued by the Human Rights Committee.

[32]*Id.*, at pp. 131–132.

[33]*Id.*, at p. 131.

[34]Alston (2007), paras 53, 65.

[35]*Id.*, at para 55.

taken into account in the process of determining whether a defendant is guilty of committing a 'most serious crime.'"[36] As "[t]hose extenuating factors can only be taken into account in the context of individualized sentencing by the judiciary in death penalty cases," the validity of a mandatory death penalty requires a "case-by-case approach."[37] In contrast, as suggested in the foregoing discussion, the jurisprudence on the "most serious crimes" indicates an objective approach under which the focus is on the nature of the offense as proscribed in legislation, not the context of the individualized sentencing. That fundamental distinction will place the distinctiveness of the Taiwanese approach to the "most serious crimes" requirement of Article 6 into stark relief.[38]

As noted above, no convict could receive a mandatory death penalty for a crime of which he was found guilty in Taiwan after 2006, three years before the statutory adoption of the ICCPR. Moreover, although some non-homicidal crimes are still punishable by death, the death penalty has, for the most part, only been pursued by public prosecutors and has been imposed by the courts in murder cases since 2002. Thus, there seems to be no grounds for raising the issue of the "most serious crimes" in death sentences before the TSC as that requirement applies to the statutory provision for capital crimes in terms of international human rights law. In practice, however, it has been invoked to set the stage for the TSC's consideration of the aggravating and mitigating factors for meting out the punishment. In response to such invocation, the TSC has tackled the "most serious crimes" requirement time and again in the context of individualized sentencing. Let us take a closer look at how the TSC applied the general "most serious crimes" requirement to individual sentencing. Under Taiwanese law, the court must take into account the ten factors stipulated in Article 57 of the Criminal Code in its sentencing.[39] In the

---

[36] *Id.*

[37] *Id.*, at paras 54–55.

[38] In a different context, Justice Stevens of the United States Supreme Court noted that "[s]erious as this defendant's crime was, I believe it is irrational to conclude that every similar offender is wholly incorrigible," suggesting the distinction between the determination of the crimes and the individualized sentencing. *Harmelin v. Michigan*, 501 U.S. 957, 1028 (1991) (Stevens J, dissenting).

[39] Criminal Code of the Republic of China, art. 57 (2016), http://law.moj.gov.tw/Eng/LawClass/LawAll.aspx?PCode=C0000001. Accessed 25 Oct 2017 [hereinafter the Criminal Code].

Sentencing shall be based on the liability of the offender and take into account all the circumstances, and special attention shall be given to the following items:

[1] The motive and purpose of the offence.
[2] The stimulation perceived at the moment of committing the offence.
[3] The means used for the committing of the offence.
[4] The offender's living conditions.
[5] The disposition of the offender.
[6] The education and intelligence of the offender.
[7] Relationship between the offender and the victim.
[8] The seriousness of the offender's obligation violation.
[9] The danger or damage caused by the offence.
[10] The offender's attitude after committing the offence.

case of murder, the court has discretion in sentencing as to the statutory punishment of the death penalty, life imprisonment, or fixed-term imprisonment of not less than ten years (Article 271 of the Criminal Code). Once the court reaches a verdict and finds the defendant guilty of murder, it is obliged to take into account all the factors provided for in Article 57 before deciding on the specific sentence. It is at this point that the TSC has tackled the "most serious crimes" requirement following adoption of the ICCPR.

It should be noted that whether or not the sentencing court has fully fulfilled its obligation under Article 57 has long been the focus of the appellate review of capital cases in the TSC. Thus, the "most serious crimes" requirement, at first glance, seems to have been invoked as a legal interpretive rule to read the condition of premeditation into the definition of the restricted category of murder that is punishable by death,[40] mirroring the jurisprudence of the UN human rights bodies. Seen in this light, the "most serious crimes" requirement has been treated as if it were a prior and separate question before the TSC could proceed to review the death sentence in terms of Article 57. Yet, TSC case law does not bear this reading out. Instead, immediately following invocation of the "most serious crimes" requirement and the corresponding jurisprudence of the UN human rights bodies, the TSC did not answer the question of what would constitute the "most serious crimes" in terms of the case before it but simply noted that the sentencing court must instead look beyond the objective factors. Given that Article 57 includes both subjective and objective factors, the TSC seemed to suggest that the objective requirement of the "most serious crimes" amounted to the placeholder of all objective factors under Article 57. To meet the legal requirement under Article 57, the sentencing court must consider all the subjective and objective factors thereunder to the full in individual sentencing. Taken as a whole, the "most serious crimes" requirement of Article 6 of the ICCPR has been absorbed into the TSC's appellate review under Article 57 of the Criminal Code.[41]

More importantly, in a death sentence, the TSC has taken an aggregate approach to Article 57. Instead of being explicit about its considerations and findings as to

---

[40]Article 271 of the Criminal Code fails to make such a distinction.

[41]X v. Republic of China, 102 Tai Shang Zi Di 5251 Hao Panjue [102 台 上字第 5251 號判決] (Supreme Ct. [最高法院刑事庭] 30 Dec 2013) (Taiwan) is exemplar of the absorption of the "most serious crimes" requirement into the individualized sentencing criteria under Article 57 of the Criminal Code. See also Chen C-f v. Republic of China, 104, Tai Shang Zi Di 1171 Hao Panjue [104 台 上字第 1171 號判決] (Supreme Ct. [最高法院刑事庭] 30 Apr 2015) (Taiwan). A caveat to the method is due. Although the analysis of the judicial approach to the "most serious crimes" requirement in this chapter is based on the canvassing of TSC case law in the database of the Taiwan Judicial Yuan with the keywords covenant (公約), death penalty (死刑), and rehabilitation (教化), this chapter focuses on the issues indicated in individual cases without claiming to present the *gestalt* of TSC case law concerning the death sentence.

each of the ten factors under Article 57, the TSC tends to address all the aggravating and mitigating circumstances in a case indistinctively. In line with the progressive rehabilitative ideal in Taiwan's post-authoritarian penological policy, the TSC has aggregated all the factors under the rubric of rehabilitatibility.[42] For example, whether the convict showed remorse, whether he reconciled with the victim's family, and whether he paid the victim's family reparations all contributed to the judicial determination of his rehabilitatibility. Given that the determination of rehabilitatibility focuses on the selfhood of the defendant, it must be an individualized judgment based on strict scrutiny of his mental status and personal history alongside the foregoing considerations. Only those who were found to be beyond rehabilitation needed to be subject to incapacitation in the ultimate form of the "punitive segregation," i.e., death, which is also their just deserts.[43] To put it another way, if the convict was judged unrehabilitatible, the death penalty would ensue as he must be dealt with by means other than mere imprisonment.[44]

In the final analysis, it is in the context of individualized sentencing that the "most serious crimes" requirement of Article 6 of the ICCPR has been invoked and debated in TSC case law on the death penalty, deviating from the approach of the UN human rights bodies.[45] As a result, the objective "most serious crimes" requirement has been relegated to the process of an individualized judgment of the convict's rehabilitatibility and his incapacitation, if need be, as well as just deserts in the context of sentencing.[46] The restrictive "most serious crimes" requirement of Article 6 of the ICCPR is thus tied to the construction and presentation of the incorrigible offender in an individual sentencing.[47]

[42]E.g., X v. Republic of China, 105 Tai Shang Zi Di 2337 Hao Panjue [105 台 上字第 2337 號判決] (Supreme Ct. [最高法院刑事庭] 14 Sept 2016) (Taiwan) [hereinafter 105 Tai-Shang No. 2337].

[43]Cheng C v. Republic of China, 105 Tai Shang Zi Di 984 Hao Panjue [105 台 上字第 984 號判決] (Supreme Ct. [最高法院刑事庭] 22 Apr 2016) (Taiwan), which resulted from a murder case concerning a stabbing frenzy on a Taipei underground train in 2014, is an outlier. The convict Cheng Chieh (鄭捷) was sentenced to death based on the theory of just deserts and the TSC rejected the request for a psychiatric evaluation of the convict's rehabilitatibility.

[44]Under Taiwanese law, life imprisonment means indefinite imprisonment with a sentence of twenty-five years. Criminal Code, art. 77.

[45]E.g., 105 Tai-Shang No. 2337.

[46]See Packer (1964), pp. 1080–1081 (discussing incapacitation and rehabilitation as parts of the individualizing trend in punishment)

[47]It is noteworthy that in the cases where the death sentence was upheld, the TSC did respond to whether the particular crime before it constituted one of the "most serious crimes" in the affirmative, whereas in those rulings in which the convicts were saved from the death penalty, the "most serious crimes" requirement was mentioned but left unaddressed. See, e.g., X v. Republic of China, 105 Tai Shang Zi Di 3424 Hao Panjue [105 台 上字第 3424 號判決] (Supreme Ct. [最高法院刑事庭] 28 Dec 2016) (Taiwan).

4 Towards a Pathology of Judicial Paternalism: When the ICCPR Meets the Judge-Civilizer Tradition

It is not the purpose of this chapter to judge the deviation in Taiwanese judicial practice from the jurisprudence of the UN human rights bodies on the "most serious crimes" of Article 6 of the ICCPR in terms of international law. Nor is it intended to take a normative stance on that Taiwanese exceptionalism, if you will. Yet, as will become clear, the deployment of the "most serious crimes" requirement in the context of an individualized sentencing of death in Taiwan has led to its reframing under the guiding rationales behind the imposition of the death penalty and further to its falling prey to the leviathanian chimera of incapacitator, rehabilitator, and retributor. To be precise, the linkage of the requirement of the "most serious crimes" and the individualized consideration of rehabilitatibility in the death sentence in Taiwan has ridiculed the concept of human dignity, which lays the foundation for all the rights enshrined in the ICCPR,[48] reflecting on the statutory adoption of the ICCPR in an ironic light.

While the rehabilitative ideal is considered the embodiment of progressive penological policies in Western history and traces its roots back to the Enlightenment, the Chinese translation of its core ideas, including rehabilitation (*jiao hua* 教化) and rehabilitatibility (*jiao hua ke neng xing* 教化可能性), connotes something else and it is disconcerting. In contemporary penology, the rehabilitative ideal has been associated with reformation. In other words, through a correction of what went wrong, the offender will be able to be restored to the moral standing expected of all community members and thus return to society.[49] Yet, in its Chinese translation, rehabilitation has the opposite connotation. Historically, it was used in the civilizing mission of the Chinese Empire towards the "barbarians" living on the frontiers of China proper.[50] That civilization-oriented register of rehabilitation was transplanted to Taiwan with the Han Chinese settlers, manifesting itself in the attitude of the successive settler regimes towards Taiwanese aborigines. To be rehabilitated meant leaving barbarity for civilization through submission to the cultural hegemony of the political center. To resist submission meant inhabiting barbarity, which had to be segregated from civilization. Thus, considered a threat to civilization, unrehabilitated or unrehabilitatible barbarians had to be either closely watched or permanently incapacitated, i.e., annihilated.[51] Only through the lens of this cultural register of rehabilitation as civilization can the justification for the death sentence in rehabilitative terms in Taiwan be understood.

---

[48] Preamble to the ICCPR. See McCrudden (2008), pp. 656, 669.

[49] Garland (2001), pp. 34–40.

[50] Brindley (2015), pp. 117–118.

[51] This paralleled the civilization-annihilation dialectic in the Spanish conquest of America. For an excellent analysis of that dialectic, see generally Todorov (1984); see also Fitzpatrick (2001), pp. 153–161.

To be sure, the invocation of rehabilitation (*jiao hua* 教化) and rehabilitatibility (*jiao hua ke neng xing* 教化可能性) may suggest that the seemingly rehabilitative discourse on the death sentence is different from the rehabilitative ideal guiding the employment of other penological measures, such as imprisonment, probation, and reformatory treatment for non-capital offenses.[52] Upon closer inspection, however, justification for the death sentence in rehabilitative terms in Taiwanese judicial discourse turns out to be indicative of the general moralistic attitude of the judiciary towards convicts and delinquents. As noted above, in reaching the conclusion as to the (un)rehabilitatibility of the convict of capital crimes, the TSC has taken account of the factors of remorse, apology, reparations, and reconciliation with the victim's family in its appellate review under Article 57 of the Criminal Code. In short, the assessment of the convict's rehabilitatibility was conducted in terms of atonement. The showing of atonement has become a necessary condition for deciding on rehabilitatibility.

Notably, the rehabilitative justification for the death sentence corresponds to the emphasis that the Taiwanese judiciary has put on the moralistic conception of atonement in settling legal disputes.[53] Without going into too much detail, it suffices to say that the Taiwanese judiciary remains oriented towards the preservation of conventional moralities,[54] despite the progressive development in the past decades of democratic reform. Although freedom of speech has been seen as the epitome of Taiwan's transformation into a constitutional democracy,[55] for example, slanderous insult, libel, and other defamatory acts are still punishable by fine or imprisonment. It is true that no one has been condemned to prison for committing a defamatory offense since Taiwan's metamorphosis into a constitutional democracy. Nevertheless, the courts have continued to enforce those criminal proscriptions. In a typical slanderous insult case, the court hinges its verdict on whether the slanderous remarks have caused reputational harm to the "victim." Furthermore, the court has approached the convention-embedded issue of reputational harm by looking up whether the slanderous remarks are obscene in the Chinese lexicon. Taking such a pedantic approach, the judge has acted more like the enforcer of moral discipline than the interpreter of the law, revealing a trait of judicial paternalism.

To be sure, judicial paternalism is not necessarily wicked and in some instances it is even benevolent.[56] Yet, when judicial paternalism is mediated by the Chinese traditional cultural register, the judge is not only a moral discipline enforcer but becomes a righteous civilizer with the potential to inflict tormenting pain on those

[52]Hsieh (2013), p. 13; cf. Bottoms (1983), p. 179.

[53]For the moralistic character of atonement, see Eddy and Beilby (2006), p. 18.

[54]Cf. Shapiro (1981), pp. 191–192.

[55]Yeh (2016), pp. 208–213.

[56]See, e.g., West (1990) (regarding judicial paternalism as judicial regulation or mitigation of private desires/ preferences for social interest); Daly (1989) (discussing judicial paternalism in the context of gendered relations); Sefton-Green (2011) (associating judicial paternalism with solidarity in the pursuit of social justice).

who break conventional moralities. The prevalence of a court-ordered public apology as the remedy in civil torts of defamation, which was upheld by the TCC,[57] illustrates the problem of the judge-civilizer. Granted that an unwilling apology would fail to reconcile the plaintiff with the defendant, the court-ordered apology has been given new meaning. Although a public apology is not necessary to clear up the falsehood to which the damage to the plaintiff's social standing is attributed, it has been contended that the court-ordered public apology helped to heal the plaintiff's wound by making the defendant experience public humiliation.[58] Under the view that extends retribution from criminal justice to civil cases, the judicial decree to grant healing by humiliating is nothing less than a pathology of judicial paternalism.

The consistent emphasis that the court has placed on apology and atonement in various areas, as noted above, is a symptom of the pathology of judicial paternalism. Manifested in the death sentence, the pathology of judicial paternalism becomes fatal.[59] Mediated by the cultural register of rehabilitation as civilization, the paternalistic judge-civilizer organizes his life-or-death judgment on the convict around the rehabilitative ideal. Judged unrehabilitatible, the convict is doomed as he does not belong to the world of living human beings.[60] To the extent that unrehabilitatibility is a function of psychiatric evaluation and individualized aggravating and mitigating circumstances, the judgment of (un)rehabilitatibility also is seen as an assessment of whether the convict is worthy of living. When the convict's life is characterized in terms of worth, he is subject to a process of dehumanization. Such a retribution-mediated dehumanization inadvertently links the Taiwanese judicial discourse on the death penalty to pathological modernity, as manifested in the killing regime of the Nazis rather than the progressive rehabilitative ideal in modern penology.[61] As expressed in TSC case law, the death penalty, the most brutal punishment, has been determined in terms of rehabilitation and correction. With rehabilitation weaved into brutality, the focus of the sentencing court has been on the distinction between the corrigible and the incorrigible. The presentation of the incorrigible offender becomes indispensable to the rehabilitation-mediated death sentence, evoking the criminal justice system under Nazi Germany.[62]

As discussed above, the "most serious crimes" requirement of Article 6 of the ICCPR has been absorbed as part of the TSC appellate review of the death sentence under the rubric of rehabilitatibility. When the "most serious crimes" requirement

[57]Da Fa Guan Shi Zi Di 656 Hao [大法官釋字第 656 號] (J.Y. Interpretation No. 656) (3 Apr 2009) (R.O.C.).

[58]Yeh (2015), pp. 32–33; see also Chang et al. (2014), pp. 738–739; cf. van Dijck (2017) and Choi (2000). For a critique, see generally Smith (2014).

[59]Cf. Kobiel (2007), pp. 48–49.

[60]See generally Sarat and Shoemaker (2011).

[61]See generally Bauman (1989).

[62]Eghigian (2015), pp. 49–52.

meets the judge-civilizer tradition in the death sentence, it becomes clear that "[g]uilt goes from referring to a guilty deed to [referring to] a guilty way of life."[63] Given that the rehabilitative ideal has been mediated by the civilization-oriented cultural register, the increasing invocation of the "most serious crimes" requirement does not so much suggest a reorientation of the judicial discourse towards international human rights law as it indicates the co-optation of the ICCPR by the pathological judicial paternalism in Taiwan. Absorbed into the assessment of rehabilitatibility, the "most serious crimes" requirement as set out in the ICCPR has failed to add much legal constraint to cases in which the convict was spared the death penalty. Rather, it has mutated into a convenient endorsement when the death penalty has been imposed. Invocation of the "most serious crimes" requirement as it is amounts to lending the ICCPR's name to judicial killing.

5 Conclusion

In this chapter, the dilemma facing the Taiwanese abolition movement is exposed through a critique of how the "most serious crimes" requirement of Article 6 of the ICCPR, a treaty constraint on the statutory provision for capital punishment, has been absorbed into the traditional dehumanizing, paternalistic discourse by the Taiwanese judiciary. In light of the judicial rulings on the death penalty, it is argued that the judicial debate over imposition of the death penalty has not been a discourse on the underlying rights and values of Article 6. Rather, the judicial discourse has focused on determining the worth of the convict's life in terms of rehabilitatibility. Under the rehabilitative ideal that is seen through the lens of the civilization-oriented cultural register, the increasing invocation of the "most serious crimes" requirement is testimony to the pathology of judicial paternalism in Taiwan. Invoked by the judge-civilizer, the "most serious crimes" requirement mutates and is thus rendered instrumental to the discursive strategy of dehumanization whereby the worth of the convict's life is valued. As a result, the lines becomes blurred between punishment by judicial killing and a cleansing of the incorrigible offenders. The idea of human dignity underpinning ICCPR rights has thus eventually been lost in the Taiwanese judicial discourse. Confronted with the co-optation of the ICCPR by pathological judicial paternalism in Taiwan, the fight against the death penalty will not progress very far by simply framing the death sentence in the language of international human rights law. Leaving the civilization-mediated conception of rehabilitation in the imposition of the death penalty untouched, invocation of the "most serious crimes" requirement testifies to the mutation of the ICCPR in Taiwan.

---

[63] *Id.*, at p. 51.

Acknowledgments This article is part of the results of the research project "Unmoored from International Legality: Rights Internationalism and Taiwan's Embrace of International Human Rights Law" that Dr Ming-Sung Kuo has conducted under the auspices of the Chiang Ching-kuo Foundation for International Scholarly Exchange (Project Number: RG005-U-15).

References

Alston P (2007) Civil and political rights, including the questions of disappearances and summary executions: report of the Special Rapporteur on extrajudicial, summary, or arbitrary executions, UN Doc. A/HRC/4/20 (29 Jan 2007)

Bauman Z (1989) Modernity and the holocaust. Polity, Cambridge

Bottoms A (1983) Neglected features of contemporary penal systems. In: Garland D, Young P (eds) The power to punish: contemporary penality and social analysis. Gower, Aldershot, pp 166–202

Brindley EF (2015) Ancient China and the Yue: perceptions and identities on the southern frontier, c. 400 BCE-50 CE. Cambridge University Press, Cambridge

Chang W-C (2012) An examination on the implementation of the two covenants after two years: with a focus on judicial practice. Thought Words J Hum Soc Sci 50(4):7–43 (in Chinese with English title and abstract)

Chang W-C et al (2014) Constitutionalism in Asia: cases and materials. Hart, Oxford

Cheng C-Y (1948) The Chinese theory of criminal law. J Cri Law Criminology 39:461–470

Choi D-K (2000) Freedom of conscience and the court-ordered apology for defamatory remarks. Cardozo J Int Law Com Law 8:205–224

Daly K (1989) Rethinking judicial paternalism: gender, work-family relations, and sentencing. Gender Soc 3:9–36

Eddy PR, Beilby JK (2006) The atonement: an introduction. In: Beilby JK, Eddy PR (eds) The nature of the atonement: four views. InterVarsity Press, Downers Grove, IL, pp 9–66

Eghigian G (2015) The corrigible and the incorrigible: science, medicine, and the convict in twentieth-century Germany. University of Michigan Press, Ann Arbor

Fitzpatrick P (2001) Modernism and the grounds of law. Cambridge University Press, Cambridge

Foucault M (1990) The history of sexuality, volume 1: an introduction. Hurley R (trans). Vintage, New York

Garland D (2001) The culture of control: crime and social order in contemporary society. University of Chicago Press, Chicago

Hammel A (2010) Ending the death penalty: the European experience in global perspective. Palgrave Macmillan, Basingstoke

Hood R, Hoyle C (2008) The death penalty: a worldwide perspective, 4th edn. Oxford University Press, Oxford

Hsieh Y-W (謝煜偉) (2013) Jianping Jinnianlai Youguan Sixing Anjian zhi Zuigao Fayuan Panjue (簡評近年來有關死刑案件之最高法院判決) [A Commentary on the TSC's Recent Rulings on the Death Penalty]. Quanguo Lüshi (全國律師) [National Bar Review] 17:5–21

Hsu H-F (2006) State power and penal rhetoric: a historical analysis of the prison system in Taiwan. Asian J Criminology 1:21–36

Jan L-J (1988) Corrections in Taiwan (Republic of China). Int J Com Appl Crim Justice 12:95–100

Johnson DT, Zimring FE (2009) The next frontier: national development, political change, and the death penalty in Asia. Oxford University Press, Oxford

Kim C, LeBlang TR (1975) The death penalty in traditional Chine. Ga J Int Com Law 5:77–105

Kobiel DT (2007) Should mercy have a place in clemency decisions. In: Sarat A, Hussain N (eds) Forgiveness, mercy, and clemency. Stanford University Press, Palo Alto, pp 36–63

Kuo M-S, Chen H-W (forthcoming) The Brown moment in Taiwan: making sense of the law and politics of the Taiwanese same-sex marriage case in a comparative light. Colum J Asian Law 31
Liao FF-T (2014) Impact of domestication of the ICCPR: review of death penalty related cases of the supreme court. NTU Law J 43:911–956 (in Chinese with English title and abstract)
Lo C-F (2006) The legal culture and system of Taiwan. Kluwer, Alphen aan den Rijn
McCrudden C (2008) Human dignity and judicial interpretation of human rights. Eur J Int Law 19:655–724
Packer HL (1964) Making the punishment fit the crime. Harv Law Rev 77:1071–1082
Peng M-M (1973) Political offences in Taiwan: laws and problems. Akron Law Rev 6:163–187
Sarat A (2001) Killing me softly: capital punishment and the technologies for taking life. In: Sarat A (ed) Pain, death, and the law. University of Michigan Press, Ann Arbor, pp 43–70
Sarat A, Shoemaker K (eds) (2011) Who deserves to die: constructing the executable subject. University of Massachusetts Press, Amherst
Sefton-Green R (2011) A vision of social justice in French private law: paternalism and solidarity. In: Micklitz H-W (ed) The many concepts of social justice in European private law. Edward Elgar, Cheltenham, pp 237–256
Shapiro M (1981) Courts: a comparative and political analysis. University of Chicago Press, Chicago
Shoemaker K (2001) The problem of pain in punishment: historical perspectives. In: Sarat A (ed) Pain, death, and the law. University of Michigan Press, Ann Arbor, pp 15–41
Smith N (2014) Justice through apologies: remorse, reform, and punishment. Cambridge University Press, Cambridge
Todorov T (1984) The conquest of America: the question of the other. University of Oklahoma Press, Norman, Okla
van Dijck G (2017) The ordered apology. Oxf J Leg Stud 37:562–587
Wang J-P (2011) The current state of capital punishments in Taiwan. NTU Law Rev 6:143–175
Wang T-S (2002) The legal development of Taiwan in the 20th century: toward a liberal and democratic country. Wash Int Law J (formerly Pac Rim Law Policy J) 11:531–559
West R (1990) Taking preferences seriously. Tulane Law Rev 94:659–703
Yeh J-R (2015) Court-ordered apology: the function of courts in the construction of society, culture and the law. In: Yeh J-R (ed) The functional transformation of courts: Taiwan and Korea in comparison. National Taiwan University Press, Taipei, pp 21–37
Yeh J-R (2016) The Constitution of Taiwan: a contextual analysis. Hart, Oxford

Ming-Sung Kuo is a tenured associate professor of law at the University of Warwick (UK). His research interests are in the fields of constitutional and legal theory, comparative constitutional law, administrative law and regulatory theory, and public international law. He has also written on global constitutionalism and global administrative law, European constitutionalism and integration, and judicial review in Taiwan. His publications have appeared in leading law journals, including *Modern Law Review*, *International Journal of Constitutional Law*, *European Journal of International Law*, *International and Comparative Law Quarterly*, *Ratio Juris*, and *Oxford Journal of Legal Studies*. He earned his J.S.D. and LL.M. from Yale and his LL.B. and his LL.M. from National Taiwan University. Dr. Kuo previously held a Max Weber Fellowship at the European University Institute in Florence (Italy), a visiting fellowship at the Max Planck Institute for Comparative Public Law and International Law in Heidelberg (Germany), and a visiting associate professorship at National Taiwan University.

Hui-Wen Chen earned her LL.B. and LL.M. from National Taiwan University. After receiving her LL.M. from Harvard Law School, she continued with her S.J.D. study at Harvard where she was awarded a Chayes International Public Service Fellowship. Her research interests include constitutional law, law and society, transitional justice, international human rights law, and feminist legal theories. She is currently a research assistant at the University of Warwick School of Law (UK) and works on several projects, including implementation of international human rights law in domestic courts and constitutional politics in Taiwan.

Chapter 20
A Silent Reform of the Death Penalty in Taiwan (R.O.C.)

Rong-Geng Li

Abstract There is great tension among the general public, most NGOs and scholars. The death penalty is in line with the ICCPR and the Constitution. Without any revision of the statutes, the Supreme Court has added several substantive and procedural requirements to the death penalty. In addition, the Ministry of Justice has established two special organizations to review death penalty cases. Due to practical developments, the burden of proof in death penalty cases has been substantially raised. It is fair to say that the death penalty has been reformed even though legislators are extremely unlikely to abolish it in the foreseeable future. Reform of the death penalty is necessary and appropriate because it should be the common ground for people who are both for and against the death penalty to reduce the possibility of wrongful execution.

Keywords Constitutional Court · Death penalty · ICCPR · Judicial reform Supreme court

1 Introduction

The death penalty is a form of punishment available in Taiwan's criminal justice system. For a long time, whether to abolish the death penalty has been a controversial issue in Taiwan. People who oppose the death penalty have been vocal in social movements and in lobbying the legislative process. However, the general public opposes the abolition of the death penalty.

Without any revisions to the Code of Criminal Procedure (hereinafter CCP), the Supreme Court and the Ministry of Justice (hereinafter MOJ) have carried out a reform of the death penalty in the current criminal justice system, even though whether the death penalty should be abolished is still in question. The reform has proceeded in silence, attracting almost no attention as no provisions have been

R.-G. Li (✉)
National Taipei University Law School Taiwan (R.O.C), Taipei, Taiwan
e-mail: rgli@mail.ntpu.edu.tw

J. A. Cohen et al. (eds.), *Taiwan and International Human Rights*, Economics, Law, and Institutions in Asia Pacific, https://doi.org/10.1007/978-981-13-0350-0_20

revised. However, this silent reform of the death penalty is significant because it has substantially changed the death penalty law. This chapter seeks to examine the reform of the death penalty made by the Supreme Court and the MOJ, in particular, how the reform changes the current death penalty law and whether the changes effectively protect people's rights. First, this chapter will explain the death penalty in the criminal justice system, especially whether the death penalty is in violation of international human rights treaties and the Constitution (Part 2). This chapter will also describe the tensions surrounding the death penalty among the general public, NGOs, and scholars (Part 3). Following this, the reform introduced by the Supreme Court will be discussed (Part 4) and finally, this chapter will analyze how the special organizations established by the MOJ work (Part 5).

2 The Death Penalty in the Criminal Justice System

According to the Criminal Code and other provisions of criminal punishment in other statutes, the death penalty is a form of criminal punishment in Taiwan. The death penalty is in line with the international human rights treaty which was ratified and incorporated into domestic law. In addition, according to the Interpretations held by the Justices of the Constitutional Court, the death penalty is not in violation of the Constitution.

2.1 International Covenant on Civil and Political Rights

Taiwan devotes itself to the advancement of human rights protection for its people and aligns itself with international standards, even though Taiwan is unable to participate in many international affairs or organizations. Taiwan signed both the International Covenant on Civil and Political Rights (hereinafter ICCPR) and the International Covenant on Economic, Social and Cultural Rights (ICESCR) in 1967, however, it was unable to deposit instruments of ratification with the UN after having lost its UN seat. However, on 31 March 2009, the Legislative Yuan ratified the two covenants at the insistence of then-President Ma Ying-Jeou. Moreover, it enacted the "Act to Implement the International Covenant on Civil and Political Rights and the International Covenant on Economic, Social and Cultural Rights." The act was promulgated on 14 May 2009 and entered into effect on 10 December of the same year. Following ratification of the two covenants, international human rights have been directly enforced through the national courts.

Art. 6 sec. 2 of the ICCPR provides: "In countries which have not abolished the death penalty, a sentence of death may be imposed only for the most serious crimes in accordance with the law in force at the time of the commission of the crime and not contrary to the provisions of the present Covenant and to the Convention on the Prevention and Punishment of the Crime of Genocide. This penalty can only be carried out pursuant to a final judgment rendered by a competent court." ICCPR General Comment No. 6 explains that according to Articles 6 (2) to (6), States Parties are not obliged to abolish the death penalty. They are only restricted in the use of the death penalty. The death penalty can be imposed only for the most serious crimes and what constitutes "the most serious crimes" must be read strictly.[1] ICCPR General Comment No. 32 explains that the death penalty can only be imposed through trials which comply with the fair trial doctrine required by Article 14 of the ICCPR.[2] Imposition of the death penalty constitutes a violation of Article 6 (right to life) of the ICCPR if the trial is unfair. Therefore, the Supreme Court takes the position that the provisions concerning the death penalty and judgments imposing the death penalty are not in violation of the ICCPR as long as they comply with the substantial and procedural limitations required by the ICCPR.[3]

2.2 *National Framework—Constitution*

There are several interpretations with respect to the death penalty held by the Constitutional Court. All of them consider the death penalty to be constitutional and not in violation of any provisions of the Constitution.

J.Y. Interpretation No. 194 holds that the mandatory death penalty does not violate the proportionality requirement, Article 23 of the Constitution, or the Equal Protection Principle, Article 7 of the Constitution. J.Y. Interpretation No. 263 also holds the mandatory death penalty is not in violation of the Constitution. J.Y. Interpretation No. 476 is about the death penalty, not the mandatory one. In that interpretation, the Court explains that the death penalty does not violate Article 8 (right to life) and Article 23 (the proportionality requirement) of the Constitution as long as the statute conforms with people's expectations and the law. Accordingly, courts take the position that the death penalty is constitutional. For instance, the Supreme Court held that Article 23 of the Constitution provides that constitutional freedoms and rights may be restricted by law as long as it is necessary to prevent infringement upon the freedoms of other persons, to avert an imminent crisis, to maintain social order or to advance public welfare. Art. 23 of the Constitution does not limit the period of the restriction on freedoms and rights, meaning they may be

[1]United Nations Human Rights Committee (1982).

[2]United Nations Human Rights Committee (2007).

[3]Huang Lin Kai v. Prosecutor of the Taiwan High Court Prosecutors Office, 106 Tai Shang Zi No. 810 [106 台上字第 810 號判決], lines 705–776 (Supreme Ct. [最高法院] 3 July 2017) (Taiwan).

restricted permanently. The death penalty is the permanent restriction of rights and freedoms and therefore is constitutional.[4] In addition, the Supreme Court holds that the death penalty does not conflict with the purposes of criminal punishment. The Court holds that the purposes and functions of criminal sanctions include retribution, deterrence, and rehabilitation, in other words, deterrence and rehabilitation, retribution; imposing punishments on offenders according to their offenses is one of the purposes of criminal punishment. Therefore, one cannot argue that, as the death penalty does not serve a rehabilitative function, it is not an acceptable criminal punishment.[5]

Like the Constitutional Court, the general public has consistently been found to be in favor of the death penalty. While abolition of the death penalty has never been a mainstream demand, calls to end the death penalty have never ceased. The death penalty, therefore, is a huge controversy in society.

3 Tensions with Respect to the Death Penalty

The death penalty has long been controversial in Taiwan. There is serious tension among the general public, NGOs, and scholars. People who support and oppose the death penalty hold strong opinions against one another and it seems that they cannot reach a consensus.

Polls conducted by the government and nongovernmental organizations have consistently showed that people oppose the abolition of the death penalty. In 2007, a poll announced by the Ministry of Justice showed that more than 80% of people support the death penalty[6] while a 2015 poll conducted by TVBS (a TV company) indicated that 82% of people opposed abolition of the death penalty. Only 11% of people were in support of abolishing the death penalty.[7] In 2016, a poll announced by the National Development Council showed that about 60% of people took the position that whether to abolish the death penalty should be decided on a country-to-country basis. In other words, there is no unified standard applied to all countries; 88% of people opposed abolition of the death penalty because they

[4]Zheng Jie v. Prosecutor of the Taiwan High Court Prosecutors Office, 105 Tai Shang Zi No. 984 [105 台上字第 984 號判決] (Supreme Ct. [最高法院] 22 Apr 2016) (Taiwan) [hereinafter 105 Tai Shang Zi No. 984].

[5]*Id.*

[6]Fawubu Taiwan Diqu Sixing Cunfei Wenti zhi Minyi Diaocha Baogaoshu [法務部台灣地區死刑存廢問題之民意調查報告書] (The Ministry of Justice, Report on the Survey of the Death Penalty in Taiwan) (2007). https://www.moj.gov.tw/dl-26073-81b326a6d0df4ebb92322add728a3a14.html.

[7]Sixing Zhengyi! TVBS Mindiao: 8 Cheng 2 Minzhong Bu Zancheng Feisi [死刑爭議！TVBS民調: 8 成 2 民眾不贊成廢死] (Death Penalty Dispute! TVBS Poll: 82% Oppose Abolishing the Death Penalty) (2015) TVBS. http://news.tvbs.com.tw/local/602428. Accessed 27 July 2017.

consider that having no death penalty will lead to a deterioration of social order. Only less than 5% of people supported abolition of the death penalty.[8]

Poll numbers consistently demonstrate that people are in favor of the death penalty. Abolition of the death penalty is supported by relatively few in the population and has never been the mainstream opinion. However, many NGOs and scholars persist in urging for the abolition of the death penalty,[9] leading to the conclusion that the majority of NGOs and scholars are against the death penalty. The death penalty, therefore, remains a controversial topic and periodically causes serious tensions among social activists, scholars and the general public.

4 The Reform of the Death Penalty

While the Constitutional and Supreme Courts have never doubted its constitutionality, and the majority of society is against its abolition, the Criminal Code and the CCP do not have special provisions with respect to the death penalty. Legislators treat the death penalty merely as one of many forms of criminal punishment and do not support revising any statutes. However, a silent movement has been undertaken by the Supreme Court to change the death penalty law in essence.

4.1 Extra Substantive Requirements of the Death Penalty

In several cases, the Supreme Court held that the death penalty can only be imposed for the most serious crimes. The death penalty cannot be imposed on those defendants who have opportunities for rehabilitation. Furthermore, the Supreme Court has indicated a number of factors that should not be considered when determining whether to impose the death penalty. The substantive requirements of the death penalty are not explicitly provided for in the Criminal Code.

4.1.1 The Most Serious Crimes

In many cases, the Supreme Court has emphasized that the death penalty can only be imposed for the most serious crimes because of the provisions in the ICCPR,

---

[8]8 Cheng 8 Minzhong Bu Zancheng Feichu Sixing [八成八民眾不贊成廢除死刑] (Press: 88% of People Oppose the Abolishment of the Death Penalty) (2016) The National Development Council. https://www.ndc.gov.tw/News_Content.aspx?n=114AAE178CD95D4C&sms=DF717169EA26F1A3&s=A65BDE8C237B201C. Accessed 27 July 2017.

[9]Many NGOs in Taiwan are devoted to the abolition of death penalty, e.g., the Taiwan Alliance to End the Death Penalty, the Taiwan Association for Human Rights, the Judicial Reform Foundation, the Taipei Bar Association, the Fu-Jen Catholic University John Paul II Peace Institute, and Soochow University Chang Fe-Chuan Center for the Study of Human Rights.

Article 6 sec. 2. The Supreme Court, therefore, has added an extra material element, the most serious crimes, to the death penalty.

The Court explained that, according to art. 1 of "Safeguards Guaranteeing Protection of the Rights of Those Facing the Death Penalty," which was approved by the UN Economic and Social Council on 25 May 1984, "the most serious crimes" must be intentional and with lethal or other extremely grave consequences.[10] The Court also indicated deprivation of lives is not a material element of "the most serious crimes." In other words, an offender could commit a most serious crime even if his/her conduct does not cause anyone's death. However, not all crimes depriving victims' lives constitute "the most serious crimes." Only those crimes in which the offenders' motives are most ethically condemnable, the offenders' conduct is especially brutal, the circumstances are extremely cruel, and the results are highly destructive and dangerous, constitute "the most serious crimes."[11]

4.1.2 Rehabilitation

Another substantive requirement the Court has added to the death penalty is the possibility of rehabilitation. Courts that seek to impose the death penalty on defendants must meet all the conditions provided by Criminal Code art. 57 to decide whether the defendants are flagrant, their offenses are severe, and they have no opportunities for rehabilitation. Only if these conditions are met may the death penalty be imposed on defendants, in order to isolate them from society and maintain social order and public security.[12] It is undeniable that assessing the possibility of rehabilitation and correction is a rather vague requirement to apply to cases and courts have difficulties determining whether defendants have the opportunity of rehabilitation. Perhaps because of this difficulty, the court has developed certain procedural standards concerning that requirement.

4.1.3 Factors Which Should not Be Considered

The Supreme Court has also indicated some additional factors that should not be considered when deciding whether to impose the death penalty. Specifically, the Court has held that the effectiveness of correction and the availability of alternate punishment or sanctions for the defendant should not be considered when determining whether to impose the death penalty. According to the Criminal Code, an

---

[10]E.g., Liu Zhi-Ming v. Prosecutor of the Taiwan High Court Prosecutors Office, 105 Tai Shang Zi No. 1627 [105 台上字第 1627 號判決] (Supreme Ct. [最高法院] 30 June 2016) (Taiwan) [hereinafter 105 Tai Shang Zi No. 1627].

[11]105 Tai Shang Zi No. 984.

[12]E.g., Shen We-Bin & Shen Wen-Xia v. Prosecutor of the Taiwan High Court Prosecutors Office, 104 Tai Shang Zi No. 3631 [104 台上字第 3631 號判決] (Supreme Ct. [最高法院] 30 Nov 2015) (Taiwan) [hereinafter 104 Tai Shang Zi No. 3631].

inmate sentenced to life imprisonment, after having served twenty-five years in prison can be considered for parole.[13] Moreover, life imprisonment without parole is not available in the current criminal justice system, meaning an inmate sentenced to life imprisonment may be released after twenty-five years. However, the Supreme Court has held that the provisions concerning parole and life imprisonment are irrelevant when imposing the death penalty. In other words, a court cannot impose the death penalty simply because otherwise the defendant could be paroled after serving twenty-five years of a life sentence.

In addition, the effectiveness of a correction cannot be taken into account when deciding whether to impose the death penalty. The death penalty should not be imposed on an individual for the reason that correction organizations are ineffective in the rehabilitation of sentenced people and therefore the risk of recidivism is high. Imposition of the death penalty, in such a situation, is in violation of the proportionality requirement.[14]

4.2 Extra Procedural Requirements of the Death Penalty

Besides substantive requirements, the Supreme Court also added several procedural requirements to the imposition of the death penalty. Some of them are relevant to the aforementioned substantive requirements.

4.2.1 Reasoning

The death penalty can only be imposed for the most serious crimes. Courts imposing the death penalty must, in the judgment, elaborate on what grounds the offense constituted the most serious of crimes.[15] Moreover, as capital punishment deprives the convicted of life and isolates him from society permanently, it is distinguished from life imprisonment or imprisonment which is imposed on the convicted who have a chance of being released. Courts should consider the circumstances of the offense, the unlawfulness of the crime, the aggravation of the liability, and the attitude of the convicted after the committing of the offense. Courts should especially take into account why the convicted should be permanently isolated from society in order to realize justice and maintain social security.[16] The above considerations should be elaborated upon in judgments imposing the

[13]Criminal Code, art. 77, section 1 (Taiwan).

[14]105 Tai Shang Zi No. 1627.

[15]*Id.*

[16]Prosecutor of the Taiwan High Court Prosecutors Office v. Xie Yi-Han, 104 Tai Shang Zi No. 483 [104 台上字第 483 號判決] (Supreme Ct. [最高法院] 12 Feb 2015) (Taiwan) [hereinafter 104 Tai Shang Zi No. 483].

death penalty.[17] The reasoning is incomplete and in violation of the requirement of the Code of Criminal Procedure if the courts do not fully and properly explain the imposition of the death penalty on those defendants.[18]

4.2.2 Expert Witness

The opportunity for rehabilitation is an extra substantive requirement for the death penalty. How to determine the opportunity, therefore, is a significant procedural matter. In many cases, courts have tended to send defendants subject to the death penalty to expert witnesses (e.g., hospitals and psychologists) to evaluate the defendants' possibility of rehabilitation and correction. The possibility of rehabilitation cannot be determined by the courts alone. Moreover, the courts' determination of the possibility of rehabilitation must be in line with the opinions given by the expert witnesses. Otherwise, the reasoning of the judgment may be contradictory and inconsistent.[19]

In death penalty cases, courts must examine whether the defendant is able to be rehabilitated by criminal punishment. In order to do so, courts are obliged to confirm whether psychiatrists or psychotherapists may be helpful in the decision on the defendant's rehabilitation opportunities.[20]

The Supreme Court does not explicitly hold that the opportunity for rehabilitation can only be decided by expert witnesses. However, in most cases, if not all, courts have sent defendants to hospitals or psychologists to be evaluated. This has become a common method in practice and an extra-procedural requirement for the death penalty. To send defendants to expert witnesses to evaluate the possibility for rehabilitation is more appropriate than determination by the courts alone. However, the courts may ignore the fact that only the courts and the public prosecutors have the authority to select expert witnesses.[21] Defendants may not retain their own expert witnesses to prove that rehabilitation is possible. The protection for defendants' expert witnesses, therefore, is rather limited. However, sending defendants to expert witnesses for evaluation is preferable to requiring that the courts carry out the evaluation themselves. The use of expert witnesses is an improvement in the death penalty law, as disproving the possibility of rehabilitation is a requirement for the death penalty.

[17]105 Tai Shang Zi No. 1627.

[18]Code of Criminal Procedure, art. 379(14) (Taiwan).

[19]104 Tai Shang Zi No. 483.

[20]104 Tai Shang Zi No. 3631.

[21]Code of Criminal Procedure, art. 198 (Taiwan).

4.2.3 Courts' Obligation to Provide Information

According to the Supreme Court, courts are obliged to provide necessary information to expert witnesses to evaluate the defendants' opportunities for rehabilitation and correction. This is, of course, highly relevant to the rehabilitation requirement.

In almost all cases, the reasonable possibility of rehabilitation and correction was evaluated by expert witnesses. All information concerning personality formation and developmental background, which may help expert witnesses make an accurate analysis of the defendant for the courts, should be provided for the expert witnesses. The next question is: who has the obligation to gather that information or to provide that information to the courts?

The Supreme Court takes the position that it is the courts, in sending defendants to expert witnesses for evaluation that are obliged to gather the information for the expert witnesses. Relevant information is anything that may help the expert witnesses prepare proper evaluation reports for the courts and enhance their validity and accuracy. Therefore, academic transcripts, working status, performance in detention centers, written statements from the defendants' mothers, and interviews with the defendants' friends and family members should be provided by the courts for the expert witnesses, if they think they will contribute to the evaluation of those defendants. A judgment imposing the death penalty is illegal if the court fails to provide such information.[22]

4.2.4 Supreme Court Oral Arguments

Before 2012, the Supreme Court rarely heard oral arguments. From the 1970s to 2012, the Supreme Court heard oral arguments in only four criminal cases.[23] In other words, all cases in the third instance were tried by written data and documents. Parties in the third instance do not stand before the judge from the beginning of the proceedings to the end, even in death penalty cases. In 2012, the Supreme Court resolved that in all death penalty cases, oral arguments should be heard. That resolution totally altered the procedure for death penalty cases.

The Supreme Court Rarely Proceeds with Oral Arguments

CCP art. 389 sec. 1 provides that the court of third instance may be tried without an oral argument, provided that the court may order arguments if necessary. According

[22]Xie Yi-Han v. Prosecutor of the Taiwan High Court Prosecutors Office, 104 Tai Shang Zi No. 3630 [104 台上字第 3630 號判決] (Supreme Ct. [最高法院] 27 Nov 2015) (Taiwan).

[23]The four cases are: the *Feng Shu-Ping* case (attempted murder on the high seas, 1978), the *Chen Cong-Ming* case (negligent homicide while performing occupational duties, 1980), the *Li Yue-bo* case (murder, 1997), and the *Ke Ju-Cai* case (perjury, 2012).

to that provision, the Supreme Court does not have to proceed with oral arguments if it thinks that it is unnecessary. In other words, oral arguments are exceptional at the Supreme Court. That provision might mislead people into thinking that provision resulted in the Supreme Court rarely hearing oral arguments. However, the rare oral arguments at the Supreme Court did not result from that provision.

Compared with Civil Procedure, the Code of Civil Procedure provides that the judgment of the court of third instance shall be based on oral arguments, except where the court considers it unnecessary to conduct oral arguments (art. 474 sec. 1). According to that provision, in civil cases the Supreme Court must hear oral arguments unless the Court thinks it is unnecessary. That provision is just the opposite of the CCP. In civil cases, the Supreme Court should thus have proceeded with more oral arguments than in criminal cases. However, in the last decade, the Supreme Court has only heard oral arguments in two cases. Therefore, in both criminal and civil cases, it is normal not to have oral arguments at the Supreme Court.

The reasons that the Supreme Court has seldom heard oral arguments are that the CCP does not adopt the certiorari system and because of the sheer volume of the caseload. Firstly, only where cases are felonious and the original judgments are in violation of the law and regulations may appeals be filed with the Supreme Court.[24] Parties may file appeals with the Supreme Court and the Court has no discretion to decide whether those cases involve significant theories and they must hear all appeals as long as they are felonious and the original judgments violate the laws and regulations.

Due to that provision, the Supreme Court tries a large number of cases annually. From 2007 to 2016, the Court accepted an average of 6,910.6 civil cases and 10,460.6 criminal cases a year, meaning the Court hears 6,910.6 + 10,460.6 cases in an average year.[25] The heavy caseload makes hearing oral arguments at the Supreme Court extremely difficult, if not impossible. For the Court, hearing more oral arguments means more cases will be delayed, allowing less time for other cases. Almost all cases in the third instance, therefore, are tried without an oral argument.

The Court's Resolution Concerning Oral Arguments in Death Penalty Cases

In 2012, an internal meeting was held in the Supreme Court resolving that, in order to express due caution and respect for life, beginning from December 2012 in all death penalty cases appealed to the Supreme Court, an oral argument will be heard. The Court explained both whether the indicted facts are accurate and whether the sentencing has had great impact on the defendants. In addition, the death penalty is the deprivation of the defendants' life and cannot be reversed after execution. Therefore, the parties, including public prosecutors, defendants, and defense

---

[24]Code of Criminal Procedure, arts. 377, 379 (Taiwan).

[25]Judicial Yuan (2017) State of filing and dispositions in civil cases in the Supreme Court. In: 2016 judicial statistics yearbook. http://www.judicial.gov.tw/juds/year105/03/02.pdf. Accessed 26 July 2017.

lawyers, should have the opportunity to debate the sentencing. The Court, then, may comprehend the entire import of the oral arguments, along with the opinions of the victims' family to make proper decisions with respect to sentencing, which is in line with the proportionality requirement.[26]

After the resolution of the Supreme Court, the first case in which the Court heard oral arguments was the *Wu Min-Cheng* case.[27] In 1993, Wu stabbed his girlfriend to death. Wu was convicted of murder and sentenced to eight years' imprisonment. In 2009, Wu shot his girlfriend on a public street. The trial court sentenced Wu to life imprisonment while the appeals court applied the death penalty. The case was appealed to the Supreme Court and became the first case in which oral arguments were heard following the resolution of the Court. In that case, the defendant admitted killing the victim and committing the murder. What was disputed was the sentencing of the death penalty. Before the oral argument, the Court listed three issues to be argued in advance.[28]

The CCP does not require the Supreme Court to proceed with oral arguments in certain cases. The Court has full discretion as to whether an oral argument is necessary[29] and parties cannot argue that their rights are infringed upon if the Court decides not to order an oral argument. In other words, an oral argument is not mandatory even in death penalty cases. However, the 2012 resolution by the Supreme Court made a material change. According to the Court's resolution, an oral argument must be proceeded with in death penalty cases. The parties, then, have the opportunity to fully explain their reasons with respect to the death penalty and the reasons for or against imposing the death penalty on the defendant. The oral argument allows the Court to listen directly to the parties' statements and reasons and helps the Court better understand the parties' arguments and issues regarding the death penalty. Therefore, the Court is able to make a more thorough decision on the death penalty. In addition, through an oral argument, the society may better

---

[26]Zuigao Fayuan Jueding Sixing Anjian Yihou Yilu Xing Yanci Bianlun [最高法院決定死刑案件以後一律行言詞辯論] (All Death Penalty Cases Heard with an Oral Argument) (2012) Judicial Yuan. http://jirs.judicial.gov.tw/GNNWS/download.asp?sdMsgId=28148. Accessed 26 July 2017. In Dec 2012, the Court made another resolution that stated that other than death penalty cases, in all cases appealed to the Supreme Court and with significant meaning in legal principle, an oral argument will also be heard. Zuigao Fayuan Guanyu Yanci Bianlun Xinwengao [最高法院關於言詞辯論新聞稿] (Supreme Court, Press Report Regarding Oral Arguments) (2012). http://jirs.judicial.gov.tw/GNNWS/download.asp?sdMsgId=28337. Accessed 26 July 2017.

[27]Prosecutor of the Taiwan High Court Prosecutors Office v. Wu Min-Cheng 台灣, 101 Shang Zhong Geng Er Zi 第 2号 判決 [101 上重更(二)字第 2 號判決] (Taiwan High Ct. [台北高等法院] 29 June 2012) (Taiwan).

[28]Wu Min-Cheng v. Prosecutor of the Taiwan High Court Prosecutors Office, 102 Tai Shang Zi 第 170号 判決 [102 台上字第 170 號判決] (Supreme Ct. [最高法院] 10 Jan 2013) (Taiwan). The issues included: 1. The public prosecutor asked the court to impose life imprisonment on the defendant and the trial court did so. However, the public prosecutor appealed and asked the court to sentence the defendant to the death penalty. Were the public prosecutors in violation of estoppel? 2. Is the death penalty in violation of the ICCPR? 3. Was the sentencing of the death penalty in line with the sentencing factors listed in art. 57 of the Criminal Code?

[29]Code of Criminal Procedure, art. 389 (Taiwan).

understand how the Court has proceeded with the trial, formed its beliefs, and made its own judgments because oral arguments are open to the public.[30] People may realize the reasons why the death penalty is or is not imposed in some cases as a result of the oral arguments.

As an oral argument is now mandatory in all death penalty cases appealed to the Supreme Court, improvements are needed within the courts to ensure that practitioners have the necessary experience and skills to ensure the utility of these arguments. Without competent defense lawyers, oral arguments may become a mere formality with no substantial effects. However, there are no rules governing defense lawyers in death penalty cases. Defendants' rights to counsel, therefore, are not properly protected. In addition, there are no rules governing oral arguments at the Supreme Court. In each case, the presiding judge announces its own rule and decides whether the preliminary proceeding will be held and how to proceed with the oral argument. Defense lawyers and public prosecutors know how to proceed with the argument only after the presiding judge announces the rules for the individual case. The defendants' presence, however, is another issue. In the oral argument at the Supreme Court, all defendants are absent. The Court never summones any defendant to present an oral argument as the Court takes the position that the third instance is a trial of law, not of facts so the defendants need not be summoned at the oral argument. Moreover, the defense lawyers' presence at the oral argument may effectively safeguard the interests of the defendants. However, to be present throughout the criminal process is part of the defendants' important procedural rights to defend themselves and to provide opinions. Whether the process is a trial of law or of facts is irrelevant; the right to counsel is not a substitute for a defendant's right to be present at the trial. The Court, therefore, should allow the defendants in death penalty cases to be present during the oral argument.

In conclusion, the mandate of an oral argument allows the Court to make proper and cautious decisions on imposition of the death penalty, resulting in decisions that are more convincing to society as a whole. One cannot deny that the Court's resolution represents a landmark in the development of the law regarding the death penalty, even though there is still much room for improvement.

5 Special Organizations for Death Penalty Reviews Within the Public Prosecutors System

In addition to the requirements added to the death penalty by the Supreme Court, the MOJ established two special organizations to review death penalty cases. The establishment of the two special organizations, in essence, raises the standard of evidence in death penalty cases.

---

[30]Organic Law of Courts, art. 86 (Taiwan).

5.1 The Small Group for Reviewing Death Penalty Cases in Dispute

In 2016, the Ministry of Justice asked the Supreme Prosecutors Office to establish a small group for reviewing death penalty cases in dispute (hereinafter the small group).[31] The MOJ expounded that there are still significant controversies over evidence and fact-determination in some death penalty cases, even though the MOJ has dealt with examination of their execution with great caution. Moreover, as execution of the death penalty is non-reversible, new evidence that the courts were not aware of may come to light which, in other circumstances, could be used for a retrial, but which is obviously impossible in death penalty cases. In order to prevent wrongful convictions, public prosecutors will examine the cases in which the defendant denies the indictments or in which the evidence and the fact-determination are in great dispute. Public prosecutors may file motions for retrial or file extraordinary appeals through the chief prosecutor.

According to the MOJ's announcement, the review of final death penalty cases is initiated by the small group, which is an internal organization, and the convicted and third parties cannot apply for a review of death penalty cases. How outside information and opinions may reach the small group is unclear, nor did the MOJ explain who the small group consists of or how the review is carried out. However, the establishment of the small group is a very significant step in the reform of the death penalty. The establishment of the small group shows that the government treats death penalty cases more cautiously than others. A higher standard for death penalty cases has been set.

5.2 The Review Committee on Final Convicted Cases

In June 2017, the Ministry of Justice promulgated the "Rules Governing Prosecutors Offices Reviewing Final Convicted Cases" (hereinafter RGPORFCC). The Review Committee on Final Convicted Cases (hereinafter RCFCC), consequently, was established in the High Prosecutors Office. The RCFCC consists of chief prosecutors, head prosecutors designated by the chief prosecutor, prosecutors, forensic medical examiners, forensic experts, criminal scholars, lawyers, and retired judges and prosecutors.[32] Opinions may be provided to the chief prosecutor of the High Prosecutors Office by the Taiwan Bar Association, district bar associations, and human rights NGOs admitted by the chief prosecutor of the High Prosecutors

---

[31]Fawu Buzhang Zhishi Zuigaojian Chengli Zhengyi Sixing Anjian Jiuji Shencha Xiaozu [法務部長指示最高檢成立爭議死刑案件救濟審查小組] (Minister of the MOJ asks the Supreme Prosecutors Office to establish a small group for reviewing Disputed Death Penalty Cases) (2016) Ministry of Justice. https://www.moj.gov.tw/cp-21-50414-5aef5-001.html. Accessed 28 July 2017.

[32]The Rules Governing Prosecutors Offices Reviewing Final Convicted Cases, art. 3 (Taiwan).

Office. The opinions of the convicted may also be provided through the aforementioned NGOs.[33] The chief prosecutor may convene the RCFCC if necessary.[34] The RCFCC should make a review decision with clear reasoning. That review decision should be sent to the head prosecutor or the Prosecutor General if the RCFCC considers it is necessary to file a motion for retrial or extraordinary appeal; if it is considered unnecessary, the decision should be sent to the opinion providers.[35] That decision is unappealable and there are no remedies for the decisions of the RCFCC. That is to say that the NGOs and the defendants have no right to apply for reviews of certain final cases, even though they are allowed to provide opinions to the RCFCC.

The RCFCC follows the example of conviction integrity units in the U.S. and is an internal organization within the public prosecutor's system, much like the death penalty small group.[36] At trial, public prosecutors and defense lawyers oppose each other, yet neither party wants innocent citizens to be incarcerated or even executed. Similarly, establishment of the RCFCC shows that the government is eager for certainty in criminal punishment.

In practice, most cases reviewed by the RCFCC are death penalty cases, even though the RGPORFCC does not provide that only final convicted death penalty cases may be reviewed. This result is quite predictable because death penalty cases most attract people's attention. Society's response is also the greatest if the defendant is wrongfully convicted, which is the last thing public prosecutors want to go through. Compared with other cases, death penalty cases, therefore, are more likely to be reviewed by the RCFCC. The establishment of the RCFCC, consequently, requires a higher standard for the death penalty. The procedure for death penalty cases, in fact, is stricter than others, even though the CCP has common provisions for all cases regardless of criminal sanctions.

5.3 *Interim Summary*

The public prosecutor system established the death penalty small group and the RCFCC, which are special remedies for the death penalty not provided in the CCP. The CCP has no provision for either the trial of death penalty cases or remedies for them. Moreover, the CPP does not have any rules for death penalty cases after they are finalized. The establishment of the death penalty small group and the RCFCC have additional remedies for the death penalty without any legislative revision of the relevant statutes. This constitutes a substantial reform of the death penalty.

[33] *Id.*, at art. 4.

[34] *Id.*, at art. 7.

[35] *Id.*, at 11.

[36] E.g., Chandler (2016).

First, the additional mechanism for the death penalty raises the accuracy requirement of death penalty cases. With respect to the death penalty small group and the RCFCC, the MOJ does not explicitly explain the standard for reviewing final convicted cases. However, according to the MOJ description, the death penalty small group may examine a final convicted death penalty case as long as it is in great dispute. The RGPORFCC provides that the RCFCC may be convened as long as the chief prosecutor of the High Prosecutors Office considers it is necessary. There is no extremely strict standard for the two special organizations to review death penalty cases, which means that the accuracy requirement for death penalty cases has been advanced.

The CCP does not provide the standard required for guilty judgments. Courts, however, consistently hold that a court may enter a guilty judgment only when an ordinary man would have no doubt and would be convinced the facts are true. A court must pronounce a not-guilty judgment if the facts have not been thus proven and reasonable doubt exists.[37] In other words, in order to validate a guilty judgment, the indicted facts have to be proved beyond a reasonable doubt. A not-guilty judgment must be pronounced if the prosecution is not proved to the extent that a reasonable person has no reason to doubt that the defendant is guilty.[38] That standard of evidence applies to all criminal cases, according to the CCP. Establishment of the aforementioned mechanisms, however, sets a substantially higher standard of proof for death penalty cases because they may be re-examined if there is a significant dispute or if it is deemed necessary. That is to say, in order to enter a guilty judgment in a death penalty case the burden of proof (persuasion) is "beyond doubt," "no doubt," or "not a single doubt," instead of "beyond a reasonable doubt." The higher standard of proof may effectively prevent wrongful convictions and wrongful impositions of the death penalty on innocents.

Second, according to the RGPORFCC and the MOJ's statement, the convicted have no right to apply for a review of their final cases. Both the RCFCC and the death penalty small group initiate reviews at their own discretion. However, defendants may still provide opinions to the High Prosecutors Office through certain NGOs. The additional mechanism for the death penalty still reserves certain room for defendants in death penalty cases to express their arguments.

Third, there are still many theoretical and practical problems with respect to the RCFCC and the death penalty small group that should be resolved. For example, it is unimaginable how the adversarial system works without revising the current CCP if the RCFCC or the death penalty small group decide to file a motion for a retrial which is granted by the competent court. According to the CCP, a public prosecutor should still be against the convicted at the retrial. However, public prosecutors are the ones who file the motions for a retrial in the interest of those convicted. How can public prosecutors act as plaintiffs and still oppose the convicted's argument? Obviously, the current CCP should be revised to be in line with these special circumstances.

---

[37] 76 Tai Shang Zi No. 4986 (precedent) [76 台上字第 4986 號判例] (Supreme Ct. [最高法院] 30 July 1987) (Taiwan).

[38] Wang et al. (2015), pp. 158–159.

In sum, the death penalty small group and the RCFCC have substantially raised the burden of proof in death penalty cases to beyond a doubt. In addition, the additional mechanisms also provide defendants in final convicted death penalty cases with the opportunity to ask public prosecutors to review their cases. Thus, it is convincing to say that the establishment of the death penalty small group and the RCFCC has, in essence, reformed the current death penalty law and may have a significant impact on the death penalty law.

6 Conclusion

It is clear that although the death penalty is in line with the ICCPR and the Constitution, as well as with the expectations of the general public, most NGOs and scholars oppose the death penalty. Without any revision of the statutes, the Supreme Court has added several substantive and procedural requirements to the death penalty, such as applying it only to the most serious crimes, the opportunity of rehabilitation, the courts' reasoning obligation, the courts' obligation to provide information, and oral arguments. The MOJ, moreover, established two special organizations to review death penalty cases. These developments have substantially raised the burden of proof in death penalty cases and have also reduced the possibility of wrongful convictions. Owing to the general public's expectations, legislators are extremely unlikely to abolish the death penalty in the foreseeable future, leaving it as an available form of criminal punishment. However, the reforms of the death penalty made by the Supreme Court and the MOJ are practical and appropriate because the possibility of wrongful reducing of executions should be a common ground for people who are both for and against the death penalty. People who are for the death penalty do not want to execute innocents even as people who are against the death penalty want to make the death penalty more difficult to be imposed.

References

Chandler IH (2016) Conviction Integrity Review Units. Criminal Justice 36:14–16. https://wwwamericanbar.org/content/dam/aba/publications/criminal_justice_magazine/v31/chandler.authcheckdam.pdf. Accessed 28 July 2017

Cheng 8 Minzhong Bu Zancheng Feichu Sixing. [八成八民眾不贊成廢除死刑] (Press: 88% of People Oppose Abolishment of the the Death Penalty) (2016) The National Development Council. https://www.ndc.gov.tw/News_Content.aspx?n=114AAE178CD95D4C&sms=DF717169EA26F1A3&s=A65BDE8C237B201C. Accessed 27 July 2017

Fawu Buzhang Zhishi Zuigaojian Chengli Zhengyi Sixing Anjian Jiuji Shencha Xiaozu [法務部長指示最高檢成立爭議死刑案件救濟審查小組] (Minister of the MOJ asks the Supreme Prosecutors Office to Establish a Small Group for Reviewing Disputed Death Penalty Cases) (2016) Ministry of Justice. https://www.moj.gov.tw/cp-21-50414-5aef5-001.html. Accessed 28 July 2017

Fawubu Taiwan Diqu Sixing Cunfei Wenti zhi Minyi Diaocha Baogaoshu [法務部台灣地區死刑存廢問題之民意調查報告書] (The Ministry of Justice Report on the Survey of the Death Penalty in Taiwan) (2007). https://www.moj.gov.tw/dl-26073-81b326a6d0df4ebb92322add728a3a14.html. Accessed 27 July 2017

Judicial Yuan (2017) State of filing and dispositions in civil cases in the Supreme Court. In: 2016 judicial statistics yearbook. http://www.judicial.gov.tw/juds/year105/03/02.pdf. Accessed 26 July 2017

Sixing Zhengyi! TVBS Mindiao: 8 Cheng 2 Minzhong Bu Zancheng Feisi [死刑爭議!TVBS民調:8成2民眾不贊成廢死] (Death Penalty Dispute! TVBS Poll: 82% Oppose Abolishing the Death Penalty) (2015) TVBS. http://news.tvbs.com.tw/local/602428. Accessed 27 July 2017

United Nations Human Rights Committee, CCPR General Comment no. 6: Article 6: Right to life (30 Apr 1982)

United Nations Human Rights Committee, General Comment no. 32: Article 14: Right to equality before courts and tribunals and to a fair trial, UN Doc. CCPR/C/GC/32 (23 Aug 2007)

Wang J-P et al (2015) Xingshi Susongfa (Xia) [刑事訴訟法(下)] (Criminal procedure vol 2), 3rd edn. [瑞興]: Taipei

Zuigao Fayuan Guanyu Yanci Bianlun Xinwengao [最高法院關於言詞辯論新聞稿] (Supreme Court Press Report Regarding Oral Arguments) (2012) http://jirs.judicial.gov.tw/GNNWS/downloadd.asp?sdMsgId=28337. Accessed 26 July 2017

Zuigao Fayuan Jueding Sixing Anjian Yihou Yilu Xing Yanci Bianlun [最高法院決定死刑案件以後一律行言詞辯論] (All Death Penalty Cases Heard with an Oral Argument) (2012) Judicial Yuan. http://jirs.judicial.gov.tw/GNNWS/download.asp?sdMsgId=28148. Accessed 26 July 2017

Rong-Geng Li is Professor of Criminal Law and Criminal Procedure at National Taipei University Law School, Taiwan (R.O.C.). He has been teaching criminal law and criminal procedure at the law school since 2008. He received his first LL.M. degree from Soochow University in 2002, and his second from Indiana University in Bloomington in 2006. In 2008, Li obtained his S.J.D. degree from Indiana University in Bloomington. Li participated in many revisions of the law, such as the Criminal Procedure and the Communication Protection and Security Law. He was one of the founders of the Taiwan Innocence Project and is a director of the board. Li has published more than 50 articles with respect to criminal justice and books with other well-known scholars.

Chapter 21
A Core Case for Judicial Review–Protecting Personal Liberty in Taiwan

Frederick Chao-Chun Lin

Abstract Taiwan had made huge progress in protecting personal liberty in the last three decades. One of the best ways to demonstrate this significant development is to use this experience to test some prominent academic theories. Coincidentally, Professor Waldron's most recent attack on judicial review provides a valuable chance to demonstrate Taiwan's progress. This chapter uses Taiwan's experience of protecting personal liberty to counter Professor Waldron's three major criticisms of judicial review. First of all, Taiwan's experience shows that the text of a constitutional bill of rights does indeed strengthen the protection of rights. Secondly, Taiwan's case also reveals that it is in the cooperation between the judicial review and the Legislative Yuan that rights are more fully protected. Finally, Taiwan's lessons from protecting personal liberty prove that Professor Waldron's definition of the tyranny of the majority may be incomplete or even wrong.

Keywords Constitutional bill of rights · Constitutional texts · Jeremy Waldron Judicial review · Personal liberty

1 Introduction

One of the most significant contributions that the Constitutional Court has made to Taiwan is protection of personal liberty. In several landmark cases dealing with issues of personal liberty, the work of the Constitutional Court has consolidated the protection of personal liberty in various fields. It goes without saying that protecting personal liberty, among other various fundamental rights, is one of the most significant achievements in Taiwan. Therefore, to understand the development of human rights in Taiwan it is essential to understand the development of the protection of personal liberty.

F. C.-C. Lin (✉)
National Taipei University, Taipei, Taiwan
e-mail: fredcc.lin@msa.hinet.net

J. A. Cohen et al. (eds.), *Taiwan and International Human Rights*, Economics, Law, and Institutions in Asia Pacific, https://doi.org/10.1007/978-981-13-0350-0_21

No less importantly, the significance of Taiwan's development of human rights lies not only in the jurisprudence created for particular rights per se but also in the relationship of the jurisprudence of particular rights to other constitutional issues, for example issues regarding judicial review. The experience of protecting personal liberty in Taiwan can be used to rebut some theories against judicial review. As such, Professor Jeremy Waldron's doctrine of judicial review is pertinent to the issue at hand.

There is no doubt that in terms of comparative law, judicial review (or more precisely constitutional review) has become an integral part of modern constitutional governments around the world.[1] Even the motherland of constitutionalism, the United Kingdom, after some years of resistance embraced judicial review in some form[2] following the adoption of the Human Rights Act in 1998. As the practice of judicial review is applied in most countries, it is remarkable that scholars would still be debating this institution today. The debate originated in the birthplace of judicial review, the United States. From the 1960s onward, many prominent US constitutional scholars[3] developed doctrines with American characteristics in dealing with judicial review from a diversified perspective, e.g., the legitimacy of judicial review, judicial supremacy, and constitutional interpretation etc., which have greatly affected constitutional jurisprudence in the rest of the world.[4]

Despite the outstanding academic research already achieved in this field, Professor Jeremy Waldron's paper "The Core of the Case against Judicial Review"[5] broke new ground on old turf and brought us into a new, fascinating world of judicial review, arguing that legislatures are better than judicial review in identifying rights. The significance of this paper not only lies in its delicate and exquisite analyses, but also in the wave of new studies and debates following it. The paper has not only been frequently cited, many leading scholars have joined the debate and have issued direct responses to it,[6] either to support or to oppose his arguments.

Whether judicial review can contribute to identifying fundamental rights is certainly not only an issue of abstract theory but also a question of practice. Since Waldron's prime argument is that judicial review is inferior to the legislature in protecting rights, how to prove this in practice poses a serious question. Fortunately, development of the protection of personal liberty in Taiwan over the

---

[1]According to Professor Stone Sweet, judicial review is one basic formula among the three formulas found in new constitutionalism. See Sweet (2012), p. 816.

[2]Various scholars have coined different terms to reflect the characteristics of the model of judicial review in the UK. Most recently, Stephen Gardbaum categorizes this pattern of judicial review as the "commonwealth model of constitutionalism;" see Gardbaum (2013).

[3]To name just two of the most well-known and cited pieces: Bickel (1962) and Ely (1980).

[4]For example, Alexander Bickel's classic term "the counter-majoritarian difficulty" has appeared in many textbooks on constitutional law in Taiwan. This would mean that many law students in Taiwan have become familiar with this idea from their first year of legal study.

[5]Waldron (2006).

[6]Kumm (2007), Fallon (2008), Harel and Kahana (2010), Tushnet (2010) and Harel and Shinar (2012).

last three decades can be used to review some major arguments submitted by Waldron in his paper. In at least three of the main arguments advocated by Professor Waldron, Taiwan's development of protecting personal liberty provides different perspectives on those arguments, i.e., Waldron's definition of the tyranny of the majority, Waldron's ideas towards constitutional texts, and Waldron's main thesis that the legislature is in a better position than judicial review to protect rights.

This chapter aims to achieve more than simply introducing the development of protection of personal liberty in Taiwan. It aims to use the development of protecting personal liberty as a core case for judicial review. In short, this chapter will evince that judicial review does protect rights in a practical way that is ignored by Waldron. To do this, the chapter will proceed as follows: Section II will introduce Waldron's theory against judicial review, Section III will evince the development of protecting personal liberty in Taiwan, and Section IV will discuss the implications of Taiwan's experience in endorsing judicial review.

2 Waldron's Theory Against Judicial Review

Probably the most distinct feature (or paradox?) of Waldron's paper "The Core of the Case against Judicial Review" is that he asserts that he will develop abstract arguments against judicial review, but these arguments have four underlying conditions.[7] With the four conditions in mind, Waldron attacks judicial review for three reasons, those relating to outcome, process and, that everlasting issue, "the tyranny of the majority."

2.1 A Sketch of Waldron's Arguments

Waldron first gives three reasons for attacking the conventional wisdom that judicial review performs more effectively than legislatures in implementing rights in terms of the outcome, the position held by many prominent scholars in the past.[8] First of all, for Waldron, the current practice of judicial review, especially at the stage of the final court, only focuses on the abstract legal issue, which has quite often cut its ties with the original facts and therefore loses the advantage of developing law in an individualized case.[9] Secondly, he asserts that in delivering opinions, courts adhere too closely to the text of the constitutional bills of rights,

[7]This would probably act as the most serious blow to Professor Waldron's arguments. Further detail will be given in Section 3 below.

[8]For instance, the late Ronald Dworkin is one example.

[9]Waldron (2006), at p. 1359.

which may "distort judicial reasoning."[10] Waldron's final reason is that the reasoning in most judicial cases is based on analogy or disanalogy. Meaning that rather than engaging in true reasoning, judges develop their analysis based on doctrines rather than the issue itself, and therefore the law at issue is usually not resolved from true moral reasoning.[11]

Waldron then goes on to discuss the process-related reasons by advancing two relatively innovative attacks on judicial review, reminding us of the deficiency of judicial review in identifying rights. First, Waldron poses a question that has rarely been asked: why are judges entitled to employ a simple-majority decision, normally the reserve of democratic institutions, to decide the constitutionality of a particular statute? Is there any legitimate foundation for this "judicial majoritarianism"?[12] Second, Waldron addresses an old issue, the manner in which constitutional judges are selected, by asking a new question: why can a small number of judges alone be endowed with the privilege to overturn decisions determined by a democratic institution?[13] Particularly in cases where the public lacks the opportunity to review judicial performance, how can judges who are without a democratic endorsement be allowed to gain such immense power and determine issues with such high stakes?[14]

Finally, Waldron addresses the old but significant idea that the function of judicial review is to guard against the so-called "tyranny of the majority," safeguarding so-called "discrete and insular minorities." Deconstructing the conventional wisdom by clarifying the distinction between the topical minority and the decisional minority Waldron argues that only when the topical minority is also the decisional minority can the tyranny of the majority take place.[15] However, if this situation were to occur in a society, that society would no longer be in what he has defined as a core case situation, becoming instead a non-core case society,[16] where the rights of the minority have not been well respected by the majority.

2.2 *Questions regarding Waldron's Arguments*

The significance of Waldron's paper consists in its transnational characteristics. As Waldron has asserted in the paper, he would like to make arguments against judicial review by "boiling the flesh off the bones," putting aside the historical background

[10] *Id.*, at p. 1382.
[11] *Id.*, at pp. 1383–1385.
[12] *Id.*, at pp. 1391–1393.
[13] *Id.*, at p. 1391.
[14] *Id.*
[15] *Id.*, at pp. 1397–1398.
[16] *Id.*, at p. 1398.

or development of judicial review in any particular country.[17] More importantly, scholars who have joined the debate nearly all follow in his footsteps, discussing issues not confined to a particular jurisdiction.[18] However, if Waldron's theory cannot be sustained after a review based on the practices of constitutional frameworks, his theory cannot but be a context-based one.

Of the three varieties of attack Waldron employs against judicial reviews, this chapter focuses on the outcome-related attacks and Waldron's definition of the tyranny of the majority. This chapter will make the following three arguments: Taiwan's experiences in developing the protection of personal liberty will show that Waldron's definition of the tyranny of the majority is defective, that constitutional texts have played an important role in Taiwan, and cooperation between the judicial and legislative branches does improve the protection of personal liberty in Taiwan. Before elaborating on these points, a brief introduction to the development of protecting personal liberty in Taiwan is necessary.

3 Protecting Personal Liberty in Taiwan

As mentioned earlier, personal liberty is probably the most important right in the caseload of the Constitutional Court Justices. The cases include the constitutionality of the following issues: police detention, preventative detention of hooligans, pretrial detention in criminal procedure, the detention of people failing to pay taxes, quarantines, and immigration detention. Overall, the Constitutional Court has presided over most of the landmark cases in Taiwan's Justice Jurisprudence. As such, this chapter will introduce these influential cases sequentially.

3.1 The Prelude

The voyage of the Constitutional Court to protect personal liberty began from two cases relevant to the power of the police to detain people. As early as 1980, in J.Y. Interpretation No. 166, the Constitutional Court held that executive detention and forced labor regulated in the then Act Governing the Punishment of Police Offenses amounted to the kinds of restrictions on physical freedom that must be reviewed by judges, according to Article 8 paragraph 1 of the ROC Constitution. Since the Act governing the Punishment of Police Offenses allowed the police to impose

[17] *Id.*, at pp. 1351–1353.

[18] See the literature cited in footnote 6.

detention and forced labor without being reviewed by judges, the Constitutional Court declared the law at issue unconstitutional.[19]

Although the relevant articles of the Act Governing the Punishment of Police Offenses have been held to be unconstitutional, since the Justices did not declare them invalid, the relevant articles were still in operation. Therefore, the Justices were compelled to revisit the Act Governing the Punishment of Police Offenses ten years later in J.Y. Interpretation No. 251. This time the Justices not only declared the laws stipulating executive detention and forced labor in the Act Governing the Punishment of Police Offenses unconstitutional, the Justices also specified a period of time (roughly one and one-half years) as the sunset regulation for these articles.[20]

3.2 *The Leading Case*

Although the above-mentioned cases have made a huge contribution to the protection of personal liberty in Taiwan, owing to their isolated characteristics and the fact that the judicial reasoning does not refer to any grand theories, these two cases are not normally regarded as pioneering in the protection of personal liberty in Taiwan. The landmark case recognized as the turning point is J.Y. Interpretation No. 384.

In terms of establishing general principles, J.Y. Interpretation No. 384 has been widely recognized as the leading authority. Most importantly, this Interpretation established the two foremost principles regarding physical freedom. Firstly, this case invokes the US constitutional doctrine of due process of law as the premise to protect personal liberty. Secondly, the Interpretation stresses that due process protection is extended to criminals as well as to non-criminals.

Some thirty years ago, in an effort to control crime, the Taiwanese Legislative Yuan transformed an executive regulation traceable to the period of Japanese colonial rule into the "Hooligan Law," or the "Liumang Act."[21] This act formally consolidated the *de facto* power of the police,[22] although most of the regulations for detaining hooligans in this law can be found in various similar articles in Taiwan's Criminal Code or they already existed in other special criminal statutes. More importantly, by borrowing the term "hooligan" from everyday life and transforming

---

[19]Dafaguan Shizi Di 166 Hao [大法官釋字第 166號] (J.Y. Interpretation No. 166) (17 Nov 1980) (R.O.C.).

[20]Dafaguan Shizi Di 251 Hao [大法官釋字第 251 號] (J.Y. Interpretation No. 251) (19 Jan 1990) (R.O.C.).

[21]For an introduction to the development of the Hooligan Law in Taiwan in English, see generally Cohen and Lewis (2013), pp. 24–36. See also Lu (2011), pp. 693–694.

[22]To put it another way, the Hooligan Law empowered the police to control crimes without undergoing the normal procedures required by the law of criminal procedure.

it into a legal concept[23] and a basis for detention, and by designing a special institution and a simplified procedure,[24] which lessened the elements of due process to their bare minimum, the Taiwanese government launched a new wave of crime control under the "Hooligan Law."

Similarly, to circumvent the normal criminal law and the criminal procedure law, the "Hooligan Law" introduced the concept of "hooligan," which had not appeared in law before, placing huge powers in the hands of the police to crack down on crimes. This law provided the police with the power, in investigations, to approach judges directly, without going through prosecutors, to get warrants to detain people (hooligans).[25] The act further allowed the police to circumvent prosecutors and send detainees directly to trial.[26] During the trial, the procedure as set out in the "Hooligan Law" was not only ex parte,[27] but it also allowed for the so-called "secret witness" to testify. The "secret witness" could not be cross-examined by detainees or their counsel,[28] giving less procedural protection to "hooligans" than normal criminal procedure. Under this system, in addition to maintaining the normal powers provided for by the criminal procedure, the police at the same time also assumed the powers of prosecutors. When the law was challenged for the first time in Taiwan's Constitutional Court, the Court delivered J.Y. Interpretation No. 384 and emphasized that the characteristic of this system was executive.[29] Thus, there is an irony here: the police are granted more power in the process of executive detention than in normal criminal procedure.

3.3 *Later Developments*

After J.Y. Interpretation No. 384, various cases regarding physical freedom came onto the docket of the Constitutional Court. First of all, a few months after J.Y. Interpretation No. 384, the Justices delivered another landmark case, J.Y. Interpretation No. 392, which declared that only judges, not prosecutors, have the power to decide on pretrial detention.[30] Afterwards, in J.Y. Interpretation No. 588, when addressing the constitutionality of the detention of non-compliant taxpayers,

[23]For a discussion on the definition of hooligan or *liumang*, see Cohen and Lewis, at pp. 37–52.

[24]*Id.*, at pp. 53–61.

[25]Jiansu Liumang Tiaoli [檢肅流氓條例] (Hooligan Law), art. 6, section I (Taiwan). (The law was abolished on 21 Jan 2009).

[26]*Id.*, at art. 11.

[27]*Id.*, at art. 13, section I.

[28]*Id.*, at art. 12, section I.

[29]Dafaguan Shizi Di 384 Hao [大法官釋字第 384 號] (J.Y. Interpretation No. 384) (28 July 1995) (R.O.C.) [hereinafter J.Y. Interpretation No. 384].

[30]Dafaguan Shizi Di 392 Hao [大法官釋字第 392 號] (J.Y. Interpretation No. 392) (22 Dec 1995) (R.O.C.).

the Justices added to the principle crafted in J.Y. Interpretation No. 384, stressing that although non-criminals can also enjoy due process protection, the due process elements for a non-criminal are different from those for a criminal.[31] Further, in J.Y. Interpretation No. 690, as the decisions in quarantine cases are based on medical expertise and are expected to be made quickly to avoid the spread of disease, the standard of due process protection in this situation may be lowered and thus does not require a prompt review by the judges.[32] Finally, in J.Y. Interpretation No. 708, the Constitutional Court held that the minimum due process standard to protect immigration detainees is to allow a prompt review by a judge.[33]

4 A Core Case for Judicial Review

Development of protecting personal liberty in Taiwan has been extremely significant over the last twenty-five years. The experience gained by studying this development can be used to rebut the three arguments against judicial review as put forward by Professor Waldron: the function of a constitutional bill of rights, the prevalence of the legislature over judicial review in protecting rights and the tyranny of the majority that can be protected by judicial review.

4.1 The Significant Function of the Text of a Bill of Rights

One of Waldron's prime, innovative arguments against the design of judicial review is his downgrading of the significance of the text of a constitutional bill of rights, one of the outcome-related reasons against judicial review. Waldron asserts that the text of a constitutional bill of rights is inclined to "encourage a certain textual formalism" and may "distort judicial reasoning," placing judicial review in a position that is not necessarily superior to the legislature in terms of protecting rights. In this section, the status, role and function of the text of a constitutional bill of rights combined with judicial review in protecting rights will be discussed. In terms of protecting physical freedom in Taiwan, it will be argued that Professor Waldron has failed to fathom the complex matters involved in this issue. It will be argued that the text of a constitutional bill of rights makes the following three major contributions: establishing a valuable basis to challenge the law, strengthening the

[31]Dafaguan Shizi Di 588 Hao [大法官釋字第 588 號] (J.Y. Interpretation No. 588) (28 Jan 2005) (R.O.C.).

[32]Dafaguan Shizi Di 690 Hao [大法官釋字第 690 號] (J.Y. Interpretation No. 690) (30 Sep 2011) (R.O.C.).

[33]J.Y. Interpretation No. 384.

stability and certainty of jurisprudence, and providing a direct means for seeking remedies.

It is interesting and significant that rather than obstructing the creativity of judges, Taiwan's constitutional bill of rights can proffer an example that a longer text of a constitutional bill of rights can contribute tremendously to the protection of rights.[34] Although most articles in Taiwan's constitutional bill of rights are short and abstract, there are two important exceptions: Article 7 (equal protection) and Article 8 (personal liberty, due process and habeas corpus). Among these two exceptions, Article 8 is more complex: not only longer but more specific.[35] In reviewing various cases pertinent to Article 8, it will be shown that a more detailed article in a constitutional bill of rights can have the following two, far-reaching advantages: firstly, providing a more precise and solid basis for challenging the constitutionality of ordinary statutes, and secondly, making the relevant constitutional jurisprudence more predictable and stable.

One of the merits of the more comprehensive texts of a constitutional bill of rights is that due to the focus on a specific text, a more stable and predictable constitutional jurisprudence can be built. In particular, this situation is evinced in Taiwan, where constitutional judges have referred to foreign jurisprudence in their own reasoning, especially in assenting and dissenting opinions, from time to time. An advantage of the predictability that a detailed text would provide is that by forcing parties to focus on a particular section, clause or term in a specific article of the constitution, the discretion of judges will be curbed. Narrow judicial discretion will result in a more solid foundation for constitutional jurisprudence, allowing people a greater degree of accuracy in what they can expect. For example, if the content of Article 8 were prescribed in a way similar to the other articles in Taiwan's Constitution; only stipulating that "People have a right to personal liberty," or "People have a right to the protection of procedural due process…," it is doubtful whether the result would be the same. Regarding the advantage of stability, this can be demonstrated by a series of cases dealing with the same rights issue.

For example, since the above-mentioned J.Y. Interpretation No. 384, several important cases have developed their constitutional jurisprudence by engaging in a

---

[34]Another advantage of a longer text is that it allows scholars to engage in what Professor Amar designates as intratextualism. See Amar (1999).

[35]There are four sections in Article 8 of Taiwan's Constitution. Section 1 may be used as an example to show the detailed wording of the article:

> Personal freedom shall be guaranteed to the people. In no case except that of flagrante delicto, which shall be separately prescribed by law, shall any person be arrested or detained other than by a judicial or police organ in accordance with the procedure prescribed by law. No person shall be tried or punished other than by a law court in accordance with the procedure prescribed by law. Any arrest, detention, trial or punishment not carried out in accordance with the procedure prescribed by law must be resisted.

dialogue with the legislature and, as such, explicating the meaning of Section I as well as Section II of Article 8 and constructing a strong basis for protecting personal liberty.[36] It would be hard to imagine that without the specificity of content relating to personal liberty and due process in Article 8 that the outcome could be the same. In J.Y. Interpretation No. 384, after parsing the contents of Article 8, the Justices made the following two momentous conclusions. Firstly, relying on the first clause in Section I of Article 8, the Constitutional Court declared that the constitutional protection of personal liberty is not limited to criminal matters but also includes civil matters.[37] Secondly, centering on the second clause of the same section of Article 8, the Constitutional Court proclaimed that any procedural regulation must contain the element of due process before it may be declared constitutional.[38]

In the aforementioned cases, it was the longer text of Article 8 that inspired people to challenge a particular facet of the law, creating a strong basis for many to challenge the law generally. Thus, from the perspective of judicial reasoning, the text of a constitutional bill of rights is probably like two sides of a coin. On the one side, Professor Waldron is right to declare that the text of a particular right could have a negative impact on judicial reasoning. On the other side, the text, particularly a longer text, could give people the foundation on which to build arguments that are more precise, coherent, and powerful.

4.2 *Cooperation Between Judicial Review and the Legislature to Protect Rights*

To date, the most forceful counterattack to Professor Waldron's theory against judicial review is, probably, that put forward by Professor Richard Fallon. Despite the fact that his colleague at Harvard, Professor Mark Tushnet, delicately analyzed his arguments and countered that the differences between Professor Fallon's and Professor Waldron's arguments are very limited,[39] this chapter maintains that Professor Fallon's doctrine does demonstrate substantial dimensions of judicial review that Professor Waldron does not deal with. Among Fallon's arguments, the one that is most convincing and crucial, as well as being the most relevant to the main thesis of the current chapter, is that rather than choosing one in a zero-sum game between judicial review and the legislature in protecting human rights, we should ask whether rights protection would be better if there were cooperation between judicial review and the legislature.[40] For Professor Fallon, the real question is not whether judicial review or the legislature alone can carry out the

[36]For more detail, see section 4.2 below.

[37]J.Y. Interpretation No. 384.

[38]*Id.*

[39]Tushnet (2010).

[40]Fallon (2008), at p. 1695.

responsibility of protecting rights, but whether these two institutions working together can promote the protection of rights.[41]

This chapter holds that Professor Fallon's argument is quite persuasive and indeed the experience of protecting personal liberty in Taiwan, which shows several rounds of dialogue between judicial review and the legislature in specifying the contents of rights, can be used to endorse this theory.

Further, to properly specify the contents of an individual right in a particular case, judicial review must go further to look for other similar cases at the same time and, more importantly, establish a systematic protection of that particular right. Also, the opinions of the Court in a specific case will inspire others to challenge similar laws in different cases, either strengthening the arguments submitted before or distinguishing further the categories of the same rights. Consequently, judicial review can be conducive to constructing the overall protection of a specific right.

As previously mentioned, the main goal of the special system established by the "Hooligan Law" was to crack down on crime. However, when Taiwan proceeded into the democratic era, this authoritarian-style mechanism became obsolete, raising questions about the constitutionality of such legislation. In total, three cases[42] dealt with the constitutionality of the Hooligan Law: the aforementioned J.Y. Interpretation No. 384, J.Y. Interpretation No. 523 and J.Y. Interpretation No. 636. In J.Y. Interpretation No. 384, appealing to US due process jurisprudence, the Constitutional Court not only declared the regulations in various articles unconstitutional but indicated to the legislature the way to reform the old law at issue.[43] Following the instructions from the Justices, the legislature carried out a large-scale overhaul of this law; however, the basic structure was maintained. Consequently, people designated as hooligans were still not satisfied with the new regulations and attempted to challenge the constitutionality of the law once again, resulting in a similar outcome. Again, in J.Y. Interpretation No. 636,[44] many of the articles in this law were declared by the Justices to be unconstitutional, despite having been modified following J.Y. Interpretation No. 384. Finally, one year after the delivery of J.Y. Interpretation No. 636, the government proclaimed that it would not only abandon the chance to modify the law but would completely abolish the law immediately.[45]

Therefore, Taiwan's experiences in protecting personal liberty reveal that cooperation between judicial review and the legislature can make a better contribution to the protection of rights than would be achieved by one of the institutions acting alone. Importantly, the merits lie in the several rounds of dialogues between

---

[41]*Id.*, at p. 1705.

[42]J.Y. Interpretation No. 384; Dafaguan Shizi Di 523 Hao [大法官釋字第 523 號] (J.Y. Interpretation No. 523) (22 Mar 2001) (R.O.C.); Dafaguan Shizi Di 636 Hao [大法官釋字第 636 號] (J.Y. Interpretation No. 636) (1 Feb 2008) (R.O.C.) [hereinafter J.Y. Interpretation No. 636].

[43]J.Y. Interpretation No. 384.

[44]J.Y. Interpretation No. 636.

[45]For literature in English, see Cohen and Lewis (2013), at pp. 197–200.

the two branches in exchanging their opinions on the same or similar issues. It is hard to imagine the outcome if there had only been one institution engaged in protecting rights on this very serious and difficult matter. The issue here is not whether the legislature or the courts can perform better in enforcing rights but whether it is superior to have the legislature and judicial review working together to modify the law. Thus, in assessing the historical development of the structure of preventative detention of hooligans in Taiwan, it is clear that it has taken cooperative efforts by two or even three (including the executive power) branches to achieve the current situation. In the context of this series of cases, Professor Fallon's argument to enlist judicial review in collaboration with the legislature in protecting rights does make sense.

4.3 The Tyranny of the Majority Protected by Judicial Review but Neglected by Waldron

To show the protection of rights by judicial review in practice necessitates an analysis of Professor Waldron's seminal, as well as powerful, attack on the conventional wisdom regarding the tyranny of the majority. Perhaps Professor Waldron's definition of the tyranny of the majority, which inflicts the most serious blow to the well-accepted conventional wisdom, is the most potent assault on judicial review. According to Professor Waldron, one longstanding justification for judicial review lies in its function to counter the tyranny of the majority, which, as yet lacks a precise definition.[46] However, Professor Waldron makes a ground-breaking argument, underscoring that decisional minorities in a democratic process are not necessarily the victims of the tyranny of the majority, except when this decisional minority is at the same time the topical minority.[47] In other words, only when what he has termed the topical and decisional minorities are merged will the tyranny of the majority occur. However, if this situation were to occur, it would mean that people did not respect other people's (the minority) rights and, therefore, would not meet his third assumption regarding people respecting other's rights, and therefore such a society would belong to the category of non-core case societies.[48] Based on this seminal distinction between topical and decisional minorities, Professor Waldron attacks the longstanding idea that judicial review plays a role in defeating the tyranny of the majority.

Professor Waldron's definition of the tyranny of the majority is beautifully simple, but, nevertheless, it is unsound in one very important aspect. Sometimes, in practice, a topical minority is not determined during the legislative process of a law,

---

[46]Waldron (2006), at p. 1396.

[47]*Id.*, at p. 1397.

[48]*Id.*, at p. 1398.

but may be formed afterwards in the process of applying that law.[49] To put it another way, when the law at issue was passed, the potential topical minority may not yet have existed, but, following the enforcement of that law, some people, probably only a very minor percentage of the population, ended up suffering through the application of that law. The later injustice caused by the enforcement of the law makes some people become a sort of "topical minority" that deserves help from judicial review. We can call this group of people an "applied minority." Moreover, paradoxically, in practice even some of this applied minority might have belonged to the decisional majority when the law at issue was passed. Under this circumstance, the question we should ask is not whether there exists a superficial combination of the topical and decisional minorities in the legislative process but whether the application of the law at issue has created a "minority group" that deserves to be protected by judicial review. In this situation, again, Professor Waldron's definition of the tyranny of the majority is seemingly incomplete.

The experience of protecting personal liberty in Taiwan has seen, in attempting to represent the people's desire to maintain social or national security, an unprecedented system of preventative detention, in particular, a special procedure with the power of issuing indefinite detention[50] has been established to cope with possible serious threats to society. Under these circumstances, owing to inadequate procedures and as an outcome of indefinite detention, the situation of hooligans may actually be worse than that of average criminal defendants.

The crux is that the detainees under the Hooligan Law certainly belong to the category of the topical minority as defined by Waldron, but they are not necessarily, and probably mostly not, a decisional minority. This is simply because when the law at issue was enacted, most or probably all hooligans had not been identified as such or even did not in fact exist. The inferior treatment of hooligans is the product of the notorious decision-making process crafted by the law at issue. Unlike the situation for topical minorities with unalterable traits, most people later identified as hooligans did not achieve that status when the law at issue was enacted. What's more, ironically, most people later identified as hooligans would have endorsed the law during the legislative process, supporting the government's policy in cracking down on organized crime and defeating foreign threats, never thinking about the possibility of the law being applied to them in the future. Therefore, most hooligans not only did not belong to the topical minority when the law at issue was enacted but they may even have been on the side of the decisional majority in the process of legislation. Since what Waldron calls a "topical minority" did not exsit at the time the law was passed, there was no possibility of the tyranny of the majority as defined by Waldron.

---

[49]The term "topical minority" was invented by Waldron, and it seems to me that Waldron has not defined precisely what "topical minority" means. Thus, a topical minority can be arrived at through any number of possible situations.

[50]In the Hooligan Law (Article 19, section 1), the period of indefinite detention is up to 3 years.

It seems to me that Professor Waldron's theory would make most sense only when the topical minority is based on what American constitutional jurisprudence calls "unalterable traits or immutable characteristics." In other words, there is a non-stated premise in Professor Waldron's idea of the tyranny of the majority, i.e., both the topical and decisional minorities must be a group of people with unalterable traits. This is simply because when the idea is only based on the classification of unalterable traits can we easily identify whether a topical minority in the legislative process of a particular statute is also the minority (decisional minority). However, the problem is that any topical minority that has been affected by a particular law, regardless of whether their minority status is a result of unalterable traits (not to mention whether or not they are a decisional minority), could be qualified to be protected by judicial review. In other words, the question we should ask is not whether the superficial combination of the topical and decisional minorities exists, but whether a particular group of the minority deserves protection.

Professor Waldron's theory on the tyranny of the majority is not complete in an important dimension, therefore, to a large extent his arguments against judicial review fail.[51]

5 Conclusion

Taiwan has made huge progress in protecting personal liberty in the last three decades. One of the best ways to demonstrate this significant development is to use this experience to test some prominent academic theories. Coincidentally, Professor Waldron's most recent attack on judicial review provides a valuable chance to demonstrate Taiwan's progress. This chapter has used Taiwan's experience of protecting personal liberty to counter Professor Waldron's three major criticisms of judicial review. First of all, Taiwan's experience shows that the text of a constitutional bill of rights does indeed strengthen the protection of rights. Secondly, Taiwan's case also reveals that it is in the cooperation between judicial review and the Legislative Yuan that rights are more fully protected. Finally, Taiwan's lessons from protecting personal liberty prove that Professor Waldron's definition of the tyranny of the majority may be incomplete or even wrong.

[51]All in all, the above analysis reveals that Waldron's idea of the tyranny of the majority is a formalistic one. In particular, in terms of the practice, the evils that can only be rectified by judicial review are by no means confined to the situation described by Waldron, therefore the concept of the tyranny of the majority should be a functional one.

References

Amar A (1999) Intratextualism. Harv. Law Rev 112:747–827

Bickel A (1962) The least dangerous branch. Bobbs-Merrill, New York

Cohen J, Lewis M (2013) Challenge to China: how Taiwan abolished its version of re-education through labor. Berkshire, Great Barrington, MA

Ely J (1980) Democracy and distrust: a theory of judicial review. Harvard University Press, Cambridge

Fallon R (2008) The core of an uneasy case for judicial review. Harv Law Rev 121:1693–1736

Gardbaum S (2013) The new commonwealth model of constitutionalism: theory and practice. Cambridge University Press, Cambridge

Harel A, Kahana T (2010) The easy core case for judicial review. J Leg Anal 2(1):227–256

Harel A, Shinar A (2012) Between judicial and legislative supremacy: a cautious defense of constrained judicial review. Intl J Constitutional Law 10(4):950–975

Kumm M (2007) Institutionalising Socratic contestation: the rationalist human rights paradigm, legitimate authority and the point of judicial review. Eur J Leg Stud 1(2):1–32

Lu I (2011) Judicial impacts on social change: a study on anti-hooligan cases in Taiwan's Constitutional Court. NTU Law Rev 6:673–704

Sweet AS (2012) Constitutional Courts. In: Rosenfeld M, Sajo A (eds) The Oxford handbook of comparative constitutional law. Oxford University Press, Oxford, pp 816–830

Tushnet M (2010) How different are Waldron's and Fallon's core cases for and against judicial review? Oxf J Leg Stud 30:49–70

Waldron J (2006) The core of the case against judicial review. Yale Law J 115:1346–1406

Professor Frederick Chao-Chun Lin, former Dean of National Taipei University College of Law, specializes in constitutional law and criminal procedure. In particular, Professor Lin focuses on the following areas: the design of constitutional review, the system of the judiciary, and various issues regarding due process. Furthermore, Professor Lin has been a member of the committees established in the Judicial Yuan, the highest judicial institution in Taiwan, responsible for modifying Taiwan's Habeas Corpus Act and Code of Criminal Procedure. Additionally, Professor Lin has been invited several times by the Constitutional Court in Taiwan to testify as an expert witness in formal hearing procedures or in inquiry panels. Finally, Professor Lin has also been invited several times by various committees in the Legislative Yuan, the Congress in Taiwan, to offer testimony on major issues.

Chapter 22
From Suppression to Real Freedom of Expression in the Open and Plural Society of Taiwan—The Constitutional Court's Role in This Progress

Hui-chieh Su

Abstract Freedom of expression is the most essential fundamental right in a democratic state, developing an individual's personality, forming public opinion, and facilitating the control of government powers by allowing the person to express himself or herself freely. Regrettably, the freedom of expression in Taiwan had been suppressed for exactly these reasons for 38 years, the longest martial-law regime in human history. Under the legal framework of both the mobilization for the suppression of the Communist Rebellion (1948–1991) and martial law (1949–1987), the KMT government not only controlled mass media, assemblies, and associations by means of prior restraints but persecuted speech supporting communism and Taiwanese independence with strict penalties. Although under the domination of the KMT, the Press Law, Article 100 of the Criminal Code (old version) and other speech suppressions were abolished during times of democratic transition, many remained in force. Driven by an active civil society in the 1990s, the Taiwanese Constitutional Court has come to play a major role in deciding both classical and transformative freedom of speech disputes. Since the earliest Constitutional Court's Interpretations on the freedom of expression, the Court has referred to American free speech jurisprudence, especially the two-tiered theory (J.Y. Interpretations Nos. 407, 414, 577, 617, and 623) and the two-track theory (J.Y. Interpretations Nos. 445, 644, and 734). Compared to other Taiwanese fundamental rights argumentations that are deeply influenced by German fundamental rights theory and dogma, this approach makes freedom of expression a quite unique field. However, the Constitutional Court's reliance on American theories does not necessarily guarantee free speech a high level of protection since the Court often appears insensitive not only to a future of innovative communication technology but also to the country's authoritarian past. With regard to freedom of the media, or more precisely, freedom of broadcasting, the Court's majority failed to pay particular attention to the characteristics and significance of the respective media in the communication system, not to mention the impact of media convergence, which

H. Su (✉)
College of Law, National Taiwan University, Taipei, Taiwan
e-mail: huichiehsu@ntu.edu.tw

J. A. Cohen et al. (eds.), *Taiwan and International Human Rights*, Economics, Law, and Institutions in Asia Pacific, https://doi.org/10.1007/978-981-13-0350-0_22

could subject TV broadcasters to out-of-date restrictions. In addition, although not surprising but definitely dangerous is the Court's inattention to the unbearable White Terror history in dealing with prior restraints of expression in the 1990s. Knowing that political speech was at stake, the Constitutional Court in its J.Y. Interpretation No. 445 still insisted on holding the prior restrictions on the time, place, and manner of speech in the pursuit of public order and traffic safety as constitutional. The presumptive priority of spatial and social order undermined the significance of political expression in the context of intertwining social activities, and eventually expelled political dissidents from the focus of public attention. Fortunately for Taiwan, an open and plural society with an authoritarian past, the Court has become more cautious and has created the most stringent scrutiny standards for prior restrictions of speech in its latest J.Y. Interpretation No. 744.

Keywords Civil culture · Post-authoritarian · Prior censorship
Stalking · Two-tiered theory · Two-track theory

1 Introduction: Challenges from New Communications Technology, Taiwan's Authoritarian Past and China

Freedom of expression is the most essential fundamental right in a democratic state, developing an individual's personality, forming public opinion, and facilitating the control of government powers by allowing the person to express himself or herself freely. Within "a democratic republic of the people, to be governed by the people and for the people,"[1] it is natural and essential for the Taiwanese Constitution to protect the freedom of speech, teaching, writing, publication, assembly and association for its people.[2] Despite its explicit wording, the constitutional protection of freedom of expression is not limited to these mentioned forms but extends to all forms (speech, words, sounds, pictures, videos, actions, etc.) and all media (newspapers, radio, television and the Internet) being used to convey messages. Every communicated message is covered by freedom of expression, whether it is true, rational, valuable or of public interest.

Regrettably, Taiwanese people had no chance to exercise the freedom of expression enshrined in the 1947 Constitution from the very beginning. Under the legal framework consisting of the Temporary Provisions Effective during the Period of National Mobilization for Suppression of the Communist Rebellion (1948–1991) and Martial Law (1949–1987), the party-state system of the KMT not only controlled mass media, assemblies, and associations (especially political parties) by

[1]Zhonghua Minguo Xianfa (Taiwan) [hereinafter Taiwanese Constitution], Art 1.

[2]Article 11 of the Taiwanese Constitution: "The people shall have freedom of speech, teaching, writing and publication." Article 14 of the Taiwanese Constitution: "The people shall have freedom of assembly and association."

means of prior restraints but persecuted speech supporting communism and Taiwanese independence with strict penalties. Such suffocating control and its resulting intergenerational (lack of) practice of freedom of expression have left a great influence upon the attitudes of the young democracy toward regulating (new) communications technologies and social conflicts, those regarding Taiwan-China relations in particular. In order to clarify the reality of freedom of expression in Taiwan, this chapter will shed light on the dark shadow of the White Terror, the achievements the Taiwanese Constitutional Court has accomplished and has yet to accomplish, and the challenges of the new technologies, social conflicts, and the China factor.

2 Practice of Freedom of Expression Under the Martial-Law Regime and the Civil War Between the "Two Chinas"

2.1 Meaning and Scale of Freedom of Expression

The freedom of expression, from its very nature as a communicative freedom,[3] does not protect monologues with oneself but rather transmissions among people, i.e., between speakers and their audiences.[4] From this perspective, the freedom of expression is understood as being a dual dimensional and cornerstone of democracy[5] that should be highly protected: "Given that freedom of speech carries the functions of self-fulfillment, communication of viewpoints, pursuing truth, gratification of the people's right to know, formation of public opinion and promotion of all kinds of rational political and social activities, thus constituting an essential mechanism in the maintenance of normal development in a democratic and diverse society, the state must endeavor to provide protection to the maximum extent."[6]

The freedom of expression—essential for individual self-realization, democratic self-government and truth-searching—is guaranteed in the Taiwanese Constitution according to Article 11: "The people shall have freedom of speech, teaching, writing and publication" and Article 14: "The people shall have freedom of assembly and association." Obviously, the Taiwanese Constitution did not adopt the brief and general wording of the First Amendment of the U.S. Constitution: "Congress shall make no law … abridging the freedom of *speech*[.]."[7] Taking the

---

[3]See Solum (1988), p. 111.

[4]See Brugger (2007), p. 517.

[5]See Si Fa Yuan Da Fa Guan Jie Shi Shizi Di 364 Hao [Justices of the Constitutional Court, J.Y., Interpretation No. 364] (23 Sept 1994) (R.O.C.), Reasoning recital 1 [hereinafter J.Y. Interpretation].

[6]J.Y. Interpretation No. 734, Reasoning recital 3.

[7]Emphasis added by the author.

two freedoms "created" in the constitutional practice into account, the constitutionally protected freedom of expression encompasses eight sub-freedoms in light of the form (freedom of speech, freedom of writing, freedom of assembly and freedom of association), the content (freedom of teaching and freedom of the press)[8] or the medium (freedom of publication and freedom of broadcast media).[9] The freedom of speech, otherwise understood as a synonym of the generic term freedom of expression,[10] protects the expression of opinion in spoken form or, in other words, verbal communication. The freedom of writing protects the expression of opinion in the forms of words, pictures, videos, music, etc.[11] The freedom of assembly guarantees the expression of opinion in the form of the physical presence of a group of people in the same place at the same time.[12] The freedom of association guarantees the expression of opinion in the form of continuous organization.[13] The freedom of teaching, divergent from its wording, protects not only teaching activities but all relevant expressive activities and institutions aiming to pursue truth.[14] The freedom of the press protects relevant activities producing and transmitting news reports.[15] The freedom of publication protects the expression of opinion in printed form.[16] The freedom of broadcast media protects the expression of opinion via radio and television.[17] All eight freedoms shape the landscape of the freedom of expression in the Taiwanese Constitution.

[8]J.Y. Interpretation No. 689 derives freedom of the press from Article 11 of the Taiwanese Constitution.

[9]J.Y. Interpretation No. 364 derives freedom of the broadcast media from Article 11 of the Taiwanese Constitution.

[10]See J.Y. Interpretation Nos. 364, 644, 656, and 678.

[11]The concept of "writing" has not found a unanimous definition among constitutional justices and lawyers. The Interpretations of J.Y. No. 445 define writing as expression in written form, while some scholars understand writing in a broader sense as encompassing words, pictures, videos, music, etc. See Wu and Chen (2017), p. 232; Lee (2015), p. 211; Chen (2015), p. 297.

[12]Lee (2015), p. 235; Wu and Chen (2017), p. 229.

[13]Lee (2015), p. 236; Wu and Chen (2017), p. 230.

[14]J.Y. Interpretation No. 380 defines freedom of teaching broadly as academic freedom, which encompasses the freedom of research, the freedom of study and the institutional guarantee of the self-government of universities.

[15]In the official English translation of J.Y. Interpretation No. 407, the freedom of publication has been translated as freedom of the press. However, in a later decision, J.Y. Interpretation No. 689, the freedom of the press is defined as the right to provide contents of news reports that encompass news gathering and verification.

[16]See J.Y. Interpretation Nos. 407 and 617.

[17]See J.Y. Interpretation Nos. 364, 613 and 678.

2.2 *Speech Regulations Under the Legal Framework of the Mobilization for the Suppression of Communist Rebellion (1948–1991) and Martial Law (1949–1987)*

Although written in black and white, the freedom of expression remained a mirage for the four decades following the promulgation of the Constitution in 1947. The reason for this was the legacy of the Civil War between the two Chinas—the People's Republic of China founded in 1949 and the Republic of China that has not ruled "Mainland China" since then—and its consequence, the longest martial-law regime in human history. By the Temporary Provisions Effective during the Period of National Mobilization for the Suppression of the Communist Rebellion (1948–1991), which in fact served to "invalidate" the Constitution, the party-state regime of the KMT not only repeatedly expanded presidential powers and broke the mechanism of checks and balances[18] but suffocated civil society by strictly suppressing individual rights, especially the freedom of expression.

Under the Legal Framework of the Mobilization for the Suppression of Communist Rebellion and Martial Law, the KMT regime imposed strict controls on free speech, primarily by means of censorship (of textbooks, mass media, assembly and the establishment of political associations), severe punishment for expressing specific political viewpoints and patriotic education, including military training at schools.

2.2.1 Comprehensive Censorship of Mass Media, Assemblies, Political Parties and Textbooks

Considering the suggestive effects of mass media, the KMT regime imposed comprehensive censorship throughout media operations.[19] (Potential) newspaper operators were subject to a prior license restriction for entering the market,[20] prior censorship for every publication,[21] a three-page restriction on the length of newspapers[22] and a regional restriction [23] for the distribution of newspapers. [24] If articles violating the Three Principles of the People, the public order or defaming the head of state were going to be or had been published, these publications were to be

[18]Chang (2017), pp. 254–278.

[19]See National Mobilization Act, art. 22.

[20]See Publication Act, art. 9.

[21]See Publication Act, art. 14.

[22]See Enforcement Rules for the Publication Act, art. 27.

[23]See Publication Act, arts. 9 and 10.

[24]For an Introduction to censorship imposed upon newspapers, see Yang H-C (2002) Regulation of the Press in the Martial-Law Era (unpublished master's dissertation, National Chengchi University, College of History), pp. 61–64, 78–82, 85–93.

seized and the owner might lose his or her license and face criminal charges.[25] On the other hand, the broadcasting branch faced even stricter control. Under the martial-law regime, not only were licenses limited to a small number of operators, but most radio and television stations were operated by the KMT directly or indirectly; for instance, the three licensed television stations were owned by the Ministry of Defense, the government of Taiwan Province and the KMT.[26] Beyond that, if a radio or television operator broadcast a program or a commercial committing or inciting other persons to commit a civil disturbance, treason or crimes in the Statute for the Punishment of Treason, his or her license was to be revoked.[27] Naturally, the press never acted as the fourth estate but rather as a propaganda machine for the party-state system.[28]

Due to scarce access to mass media, political dissidents could have their voices heard only by taking to the streets.[29] However, prior and subsequent censorship measures applied to outdoor assemblies and parades as well.[30] With this idea of thorough control of public opinion, censorship also extended to the formation of civil organizations (in particular political parties),[31] the writing of school textbooks[32] and curriculum design of higher education.[33]

2.2.2 Content-Based Restrictions and Severe Punishments

Another measure that was used to effectively suppress free speech between 1948 and 1991 was severe punishment for expressing unwelcome viewpoints, such as speech in favor of communism and the independence of Taiwan.

According to the notorious Statute for the Punishment of Treason, any person committing the crimes of Article 100, Paragraph 1 of the Criminal Code[34] was to be

[25]See Regulations for the Publication of Newspapers, Magazines and Books during the Period of Martial Law, arts. 2, 3, 4, 8, and 9 (since the Revision in 1970 see the Regulations of Publications during the Period of Martial Law). See also Yang (2002), pp. 94–103; Lin (2005), pp. 281–283.

[26]See Yang (2002), pp. 94–103; Lin (2005), pp. 268–281; Liu et al. (2014), pp. 11–15.

[27]See Radio and Television Act §45 I (1).

[28]See Liu et al. (2014), p. 15.

[29]See Hung (2006), p. 9.

[30]See Martial Law, art. 11 I and Assembly and Parade Act during the Period of National Mobilization for the Suppression of the Communist Rebellion, arts. 8 I, 9, 11, 14, 15 and 25.

[31]See Civil Organization Act during the Unusual Period, art. 13.

[32]See Citizen Education Law, art. 8 II.

[33]Until the unconstitutional announcement of J.Y. Interpretation No. 380, military training and nursing were obligatory courses at every college and university.

[34]Criminal Code, art. 100 I: "Any person by violence or threats committing an overt act with intent to destroy the organization of the State, seize State territory, or, using illegal means, change the Constitution or overthrow the Government shall be sentenced to imprisonment for not less than seven years; the ringleader shall be sentenced to life imprisonment."

sentenced to death,[35] any person participating in seditious organizations or gatherings would face a life sentence or imprisonment of over ten years,[36] any person spreading rumors or untrue information capable of harming public security or unsettling people would face a life sentence or imprisonment of over seven years[37] and any person favoring traitors by conducting propaganda in the form of writings, images or speech was to be imprisoned for more than seven years.[38] In order to discover traitors, the authorities could make an arrest and check his or her posts, telegrams, printed matter, propaganda materials, etc.[39]

2.3 *The Long, Dark Shadow of the White Terror*

The aforementioned restrictions built a comprehensive controlling mechanism that extended to every dimension of freedom of expression: First, with controls over media ownership and management, the issuance of licenses and program content, the KMT regime cultivated a state capitalist and authoritarian-clientelist culture in the field of mass media and successfully blocked an effective fourth estate.[40] The freedom of assembly and the freedom of association, another two freedoms in a democracy, suffered strict prior and content-based restrictions as well. Beyond the obstruction of effective channels, severe punishment for expressing unpopular viewpoints further ensured a chilling effect on political dissidents; mind control via curricula and textbooks, on the other hand, was aimed at destroying "improper" speech from birth.

This multilayered mechanism cast a long, dark shadow upon civil society in Taiwan. The longstanding White Terror caused general political indifference, which is so deeply engrained in social memory, that the civil culture in Taiwan is still struggling thirty years after the end of the martial-law regime.

3 The Constitutional Court's Role in the Process of Democratization

By the termination of the martial-law regime and the Civil War between the "Two Chinas," Taiwan joined the third wave of democratization. However, the KMT, then the ruling party, passed the so-called Three Acts regarding National Security as

---

[35]See Statute for the Punishment of Treason, art. 2 I.

[36]See Statute for the Punishment of Treason, art. 6.

[37]See Statute for the Punishment of Treason, art. 7.

[38]See Statute for the Punishment of Treason, art. 8.

[39]See Statute for the Eradication of Communist Espionage, art. 6(2).

[40]See Hung (2006), p. 9.

the quid pro quo for democratization, based on which Taiwanese civil society remained tamed to an extent. In the first decade of democratization, therefore, it was the Constitutional Court rather than the Congress that paved the way toward a society that fostered wide-open discourse and robust debate.

3.1 Partial Deregulation of Free Expression by the Legislative Yuan

3.1.1 Mass Media

In view of the mass media's decisive influence upon public opinion, the opposing powers demanded the liberation and deregulation of the mass media in the process of democratization.[41] On the one hand, by the repeal of the Publication Act of 1997, prior and subsequent censorship of newspapers, magazines and books was finally consigned to history. As for the operation of radio and television, the Cable Radio and Television Act of 1993 opened the market, and the revised provisions of the so-called Three Acts of Radio and Television in 2003 explicitly prohibited political parties, the government and the army from controlling the media.[42]

3.1.2 The Three Acts Regarding National Security

At the dawn of democratization, the KMT passed the National Security Act, the Assembly and Parade Act and the Civil Associations Act, the so-called Three Acts regarding National Security, to protect the national policy objectives of anti-communism and reunification with Mainland China from being challenged in the new democracy.[43] According to §2 I of the National Security Act of 1992, any assembly or association that advocates communism or secession of national territory is not permitted. On this basis, §11 (1) of the Assembly and Parade Act of 1992 provides that advocacy of communism or secession of national territory during an assembly or a parade constitutes one of the essential conditions for which the competent authority may deny an application for an outdoor assembly. Likewise, §53 I of the Civil Associations Act provides that no permission shall be granted for applicants/civil associations that advocate communism or secession of national territory. In this regard, both the Assembly and Parade Act and the Civil Associations Act adopted twofold protection for national security: prior censorship, i.e., the approval system, and content-based prohibitions.

[41]See Liu et al. (2014), pp. 17–18.

[42]See Radio and Television Act, art. 5-1, Cable Radio and Television Act, arts. 20(2), (3) and Satellite Broadcasting Act, art. 9.

[43]See Liu (2009), p. 25; Yeh (1991), pp. 199–213.

3.2 Theorization of Free Speech Protection by the Constitutional Court

In comparison to the limited deregulation at the legislative level, the Taiwanese Constitutional Court has played a major role in increasing the level of protection given to freedom of expression since the 1990s, though one case at a time. In an overview of its performance, the Constitutional Court has theorized and improved free speech protection by reference to the two-tiered theory and two-track theory of American free speech jurisprudence.

3.2.1 Two-Track Theory

Ever since Justice Oliver Wendell Holmes took the "free marketplace of ideas" as the very basis of the jurisprudence of the First Amendment of the U.S. Constitution, the U.S. Supreme Court has seen the neutrality of the state toward the content of speech as a fundamental principle of free speech: "If there is a bedrock principle underlying the First Amendment, it is that the government may not prohibit the expression of an idea simply because society finds the idea itself offensive or disagreeable."[44] Content-based regulations, which restrict specific viewpoints, subject matters, speakers or communicative impacts,[45] are therefore to be strictly scrutinized.[46] That is to say that a content-based restriction can only be constitutionally justified if it is the least restrictive means possible to protect a compelling interest from a clear and present danger.[47] On the other hand, content-neutral regulations that restrict merely the time, place and manner of expression and do not distort public discourse are constitutional, if they are "narrowly tailored to serve a significant governmental interest, and they leave open ample alternative channels for communication of the information."[48]

Strict Scrutiny for Content-Based Regulations: J.Y. Interpretations Nos. 445 and 644

As mentioned, the Assembly and Parade Act of 1992, one of the Three Acts regarding National Security, provides that the competent authority may deny an application for an outdoor assembly if participants will advocate communism or secession of national territory during this assembly. To deal with this textbook

---

[44]*Texas v. Johnson*, 491 U.S. 397, at 414.

[45]See Harward Law Review (1989), pp. 1906–1907.

[46]See *Turner Broadcasting System, Inc. v. FCC*, 512 U.S. 622, 641–42 (1994); *Sable Communications of Cal., Inc. v. FCC*, 492 U.S. 115, 126 (1989).

[47]See Stone (1986), p. 476.

[48]*Ward v. Rock Against Racism*, 491 U.S. 781 (1989), at 791.

case of discrimination of political viewpoints, the Constitutional Court issued J.Y. Interpretation No. 445.

Within this Interpretation, the Constitutional Court not only recognizes freedom of expression as "the most important fundamental human right in practicing democracy,"[49] but emphasizes the significance of the freedom of assembly as a form of collective expression of opinions between the people and the government through action, "for the general public who do not have easy access to the media."[50] This leads to a positive obligation of the state to "actively provide appropriate places for assembly and to protect the safety of assemblies and parades so as to facilitate their smooth proceedings."[51] Any restriction on such a highly protected freedom, in the absence of a clear and present danger to the public interest, will then be seen as unconstitutional discrimination.[52]

As for freedom of association, the Constitutional Court in its J.Y. Interpretation No. 644 found that non-approval of the establishment of civil associations, the most severe restriction on freedom of association, cannot be justified on the grounds that it advocates communism or the partition of national territory.[53]

Intermediate Scrutiny for Time, Place, Manner Regulations: J.Y. Interpretations Nos. 445 and 718

As a leading case in the field of freedom of assembly, J.Y. Interpretation No. 445 also discusses the constitutionality of important content-neutral regulations in the Assembly and Parade Act, such as restricted areas (§6) and the approval system (§11).

In dealing with the constitutionality of restricted areas, the Constitutional Court shows a relatively lenient attitude toward the issue. The Constitutional Court recognizes the priority of preserving "the functions of the head of state, constitutional organs and adjudicative body, unhindered flow of traffic and communications, and security of important military facilities"[54] and accepts an unexceptional prohibition as "necessary to maintain social order or to advance public interests."[55] This holding about the priority of non-communicative spatial and social order over free speech is also reflected in the Court's opinion regarding the constitutionality of the approval system: provided that the prior review of an application for an assembly or a parade focuses exclusively on their formalities, such as time, place and manner

---

[49]J.Y. Interpretation No. 445, Reasoning, recital 7.

[50]*Id.*

[51]*Id.*

[52]See J.Y. Interpretation No. 445, Reasoning recital 10.

[53]See J.Y. Interpretation No. 644, Reasoning.

[54]J.Y. Interpretation No. 445, Reasoning recital 8.

[55]*Id.*

rather than their purposes or contents, the Court says, there should still be no infringement on freedom of expression.[56] On this basis, J.Y. Interpretation No. 445 holds the approval system to be constitutional.[57] The presumptive priority of spatial and social order undermines the significance of political expression in the context of intertwining social activities, and eventually expels political dissidents from the focus of public attention. Noteworthy here, however, is the Constitutional Court's acceptance of the one exception to the approval system: incidental assemblies.[58] According to J.Y. Interpretation No. 718, urgent and incidental assemblies enjoy exceptionally prioritized protection, while the Constitutional Court re-emphasizes the legislative prerogative in protecting the non-communicative social order over freedom of assembly.[59]

3.2.2 Two-Tiered/Three-Tiered Theory

In reference to American free speech jurisprudence,[60] the Constitutional Court differentiates speech types in accordance with their value. Therefore, low-valued expressions such as obscenities enjoy less protection under the Constitution. Restrictions on political and other self-fulfilling speech are, on the other hand, presumed unconstitutional.

Rational Scrutiny for Restrictions on Low-Valued Speech: J.Y. Interpretations Nos. 407 and 617

In J.Y. Interpretations Nos. 407 and 617, the Constitutional Court not only decides the scrutiny standards for restrictions on low-valued speech, but also the definition of obscene publications: Obscene publications are defined as "obscene material whose content includes violence, sexual abuse or bestiality but is lacking in artistic, medical or educational value … or … is so sexually stimulating or gratifying from an objective standpoint that an average person will either find it not publicly presentable or find it so intolerable as to be repulsive."[61] Based on their lower value and offensiveness, their criminal prohibition can be easily justified in the name of maintaining sexual morality and social decency.[62]

---

[56]*Id.*

[57]*Id.*

[58]See J.Y. Interpretation No. 445, Reasoning recital 15.

[59]See J.Y. Interpretation No. 718, Reasoning recital 1–2.

[60]See Tribe, American Constitutional Law, §§ 12–17, 12–18, pp. 920–44; *R. A. V. v. City of St. Paul, Minnesota*, 505 U.S. 377 (1992), Stevens, J., concurring, at 422; Tribe (1988).

[61]J.Y. Interpretation No. 617, Holding recital 3.

[62]*Id.*

Intermediate Scrutiny for Restrictions Commercial Speech: J.Y. Interpretations Nos. 414, 577, 623, 634 and 744

According to the Constitutional Court in J.Y. Interpretation No. 414, commercial speech is of such little value in the formation of public opinion, fact-finding, and expression of beliefs that its restriction—a prior restraint in this very case—can be easily justified in the pursuit of the public interest, such as the health of nationals.[63] However, this underestimation of commercial speech has been abandoned. In later cases such as J.Y. Interpretations Nos. 577, 623, 634 and 744, the Court has now come to understand commercial speech as being "helpful to consumers in making their rational economic choices" and having "the same function of promoting self-realization" given that its content is not false or misleading. In this regard, restrictions on commercial speech are justified, if they are qualified as a substantially related means for the protection of substantial public interests.

Strict Scrutiny for Restrictions on High-Valued Speech: J.Y. Interpretations Nos. 445, 644 and 734

There can be no democracy without freedom of speech. In light of its constitutive significance for a functioning democracy, freedom of expression must include the freedom to criticize the government and to express public opinions. On the basis of the adopted two-track theory, restrictions on high-valued, political expressions are only justified inasmuch as they are the least restrictive means for protecting compelling interests from a clear and present danger.

Remarkably, the Constitutional Court also takes the high value of political expressions into account in cases regarding incidental restrictions. When the Constitutional Court in J.Y. Interpretation No. 734 considered the question of whether the official notice authorized by the Waste Disposal Act was to be applied to two hanging slogans of a religious group, they underlined the evaluation of political expression in the process of their ad hoc balancing: "Even though the official notices at issue were not published for the purpose of restricting people's freedom of speech …, such restrictions imposed on people's freedom of speech … may occur when, in individual cases, the competent authority disapproves of the placing of advertisements after reviewing the context thereof and the time, place and manner of the placement. Hence, when the competent authority amends the official notices at issue according to this interpretation, the necessity and appropriateness of the possible constraint imposed on people's freedom of speech or other fundamental rights guaranteed by the Constitution shall be comprehensively and thoroughly considered."[64]

[63]See J.Y. Interpretation No. 414, Reasoning recital 1.

[64]J.Y. Interpretation No. 734, Reasoning recital 3.

3.2.3 Constitutionality of Criminal Defamation: J.Y. Interpretation No. 509

In terms of the conflict between free speech on one side and personal reputation and privacy on the other, the Constitutional Court drew two conclusions in J.Y. Interpretation No. 509. First, it was acknowledged that criminalizing defamation was necessary to protect personal reputation, privacy and other public interests under a comprehensive consideration of relevant factors, such as the civil culture, civil respect, the validity of civil remedies and the professional ethics of the media, etc. Without criminal defamation, according to the majority opinion, it would be tantamount to issuing anyone capable of paying monetary compensation a license to defame.[65] Second, as long as the speaker has reasonable grounds to believe the truthfulness of the relevant statement, he is deemed to have fulfilled the burden of proving the truth and should be found innocent.[66]

3.2.4 The Freedom to Withhold Expression: J.Y. Interpretations Nos. 577 and 656

Similar to the active freedom of expression, the passive freedom to withhold expression is a performance of self-determination in society.[67] As to what extent a person shall not be coerced to express, the Constitutional Court held in J.Y. Interpretations Nos. 577 and 656 that it depends on the linkage between the message to be expressed and the free development of personality. The issue in J.Y. Interpretation No. 577 is, for instance, whether tobacco companies can be coerced into expressing their products' contents. According to the majority opinion, the labeling obligation does not coerce the company to express its ethical, moral or religious beliefs, therefore it is justified if this labeling obligation is qualified as the reasonably necessary and proper means to serve significant public interests in safeguarding the health of the people and providing necessary trade information to consumers.[68] In contrast to a mere issue of product labeling, the contentious point in J.Y. Interpretation No. 656 is about a public apology, which was directly related to the self-determination of a natural person. Given that the Constitutional Court in this case saw a public apology as a necessary means to protect the social reputation of the offended persons, and such coercion can be justified as long as the public apology does not constitute self-humiliation or a violation of human dignity for the offender.[69]

---

[65] See J.Y. Interpretation No. 509, Reasoning recital 1.

[66] See J.Y. Interpretation No. 509, Reasoning recital 2.

[67] See J.Y. Interpretation No. 656, Reasoning recital 2.

[68] See J.Y. Interpretation No. 577, Reasoning recital 3.

[69] See J.Y. Interpretation No. 656, Reasoning recital 3.

3.2.5 Future of Prior Restraints: J.Y. Interpretation No. 744 as a Turning Point?

To this point, we have seen the Constitutional Court's achievement as a guardian of free speech in the progress of democratization by theorizing the freedom of expression on the basis of U.S. free speech jurisprudence: First of all, the Constitutional Court declared content-based restrictions (especially on political expression) to be strictly scrutinized, i.e., to be presumed unconstitutional (J.Y. Interpretation No. 445). Second, it accords different levels of protection to different values of relevant expression. The interpretation and application of incidental regulations should take the high value of political speech into account (J.Y. Interpretation No. 734). Third, the close relationship between reputation-dignity (J.Y. Interpretation No. 509) and expression-dignity (J.Y. Interpretation No. 734) should have a great influence on the process of ad hoc balancing. What remains to be discussed here is the future of prior restraints, which remain valid in the so-called Three Acts regarding National Security and have been recognized as constitutional twice (J.Y. Interpretations Nos. 445 and 718). The situation, however, is somewhat different after J.Y. Interpretation No. 744.

On the face of it, J.Y. Interpretation No. 744 relates to regulation of commercial speech. But the Constitutional Court in fact focused its argumentation on the issue of prior restraints and brought forward the strictest standard for scrutinizing free speech restrictions:[70] "Prior censorship … constitutes a severe intervention of the freedom of speech, therefore it is to be presumed unconstitutional. A speech regulation is only deemed to be in compliance with the constitutional principle of proportionality and the protection of free speech if relevant legislative material proves that the prior censorship for the advertisement of cosmetic products is directly connected to and absolutely necessary for the protection of the most important public interests, such as protection of human life, physical integrity and health, from a direct, immediate and irreversible danger, and if the person concerned is granted the possibility of immediate judicial relief."[71]

It remains unclear whether all restrictions on drug commercials should be strictly scrutinized in the future.[72] Nonetheless, even in strict adherence to the principle of "one case at a time," J.Y. Interpretation No. 744 will inevitably have an impact on

---

[70]See Hwang Jau-yuan Da Fa Guan Shizi Di 744 Hao Jie Shi Xie Tong Yi Jian Shu [黃昭元大法官釋字第744號解釋協同意見書] (Justice Jau-yuan Hwang's concurring opinion in Justices of the Constitutional Court, Interpretation No. 744) (6 Jan 2017) (R.O.C.). Lo Chang-fa Da Fa Guan Shizi Di 744 Hao Jie Shi Xie Tong Yi Jian Shu [羅昌發大法官釋字第744號解釋協同意見書] (Justice Chang-fa Lo's concurring opinion in Justices of the Constitutional Court, Interpretation No. 744) (6 Jan 2017) (R.O.C.).

[71]J.Y. Interpretation No. 744, Reasoning recital 3. See also Liu (2017), pp. 198–201.

[72]See Hwang Jau-yuan Da Fa Guan Shizi Di 744 Hao Jie Shi Xie Tong Yi Jian Shu [黃昭元大法官釋字第744號解釋協同意見書] (Justice Jau-yuan Hwang's concurring opinion in Justices of the Constitutional Court, Interpretation No. 744) (6 Jan 2017) (R.O.C.). Hsu Tzong-li Da Fa Guan Shizi Di 744 Hao Jie Shi Xie Tong Yi Jian Shu [許宗力大法官釋字第744號解釋協同意見書] (Justice Tzong-li Hsu's concurring opinion in Justices of the Constitutional Court, Interpretation No. 744) (6 Jan 2017) (R.O.C.).

future argumentation regarding prior censorship, especially the approval system prescribed in the Assembly and Parade Act.[73]

4 The Constitutional Court's Responses to Challenges of New Communication Technologies and Social Conflicts

The above section portrays the role of the Taiwanese Constitutional Court in the process of democratization. However, as we all know, the Court is confronted not only with the shadow from the past but also with the possibilities contained in the future.

4.1 De-regulation and Re-regulation of Mass Media and the Right of Access to the Media

During the period of the Suppression of the Communist Rebellion, most mass media were directly or indirectly controlled by the KMT, which led to a state capitalist culture and corrupted the fourth estate. On this ground, the media reform during the time of transition was mainly focused on deregulation, i.e., the liberation of the media market during the early phase of democratization. Regrettably, the removal of political influence from the management of the media has created a power vacuum and made the media vulnerable to a neo-liberal economic order.[74]

4.1.1 Fair and Reasonable Distribution of Radio Wave Frequencies and Bandwidths: J.Y. Interpretation No. 364 and 678

Not unlike the Congress, the Constitutional Court has neither been future- nor technology-sensitive in dealing with the freedom of radio and television in J.Y. Interpretations 364 and 678. In consideration of the fair and reasonable distribution of radio wave frequencies and bandwidths, the constitutionality of the prior approval system for broadcasting and punishment for the unapproved use, the Court's arguments are mainly based on the scarcity of radio wave frequencies, while overlooking the development of new technologies and the trend of media convergence.[75]

---

[73]*Id.*

[74]Liu (2009), pp. 13–16; Hung (2006), pp. 8–11; Liu et al. (2014), p. 9.

[75]See Hsu Tzong-li Da Fa Guan Shizi Di 678 Hao Jie Shi Xie Tong Yi Jian Shu [許宗力大法官釋字第678號解釋協同意見書] (Justice Tzong-li Hsu's concurring opinion in Justices of the

4.1.2 Right of Access to Media: J.Y. Interpretation No. 364

With respect to the relationship between individuals and media owners/managers, J.Y. Interpretation No. 364 acknowledges the individual's right of access to the media, by which an individual is entitled to offer a response or request to the media to revise their reports or commentary if his or her right is infringed upon due to wrongful media reports or commentary.[76]

4.2 Freedom of the Press and the Right to the Free Development of Personality: J.Y. Interpretation No. 689

Quite surprisingly, the Taiwanese Constitutional Court had not mentioned freedom of the press until dealing with the conflict between freedom of the press and the right of personality in J.Y. Interpretation No. 689. In this case, the Court reviewed the constitutionality of the Social Order Maintenance Act §89 II that restricts the act of stalking. Though, to be exact, this regulation only imposes an incidental burden on the freedom of the press when a journalist follows someone to conduct news gathering or interviews.[77]

The purpose of §89 II of the Social Order Maintenance Act is to protect a person's liberty to be free from physical and emotional harm, freedom of movement, freedom from intrusion into one's private sphere and an individual's autonomy over his personal information. One part of the importance of J.Y. Interpretation No. 689 lies in the Court's acknowledging that the protection of an individual's aforementioned liberties will not be undermined simply by entering into the public sphere; interferences shall be tolerated to a reasonable extent, and only intrusions into an individual's private sphere and the autonomy to control his personal information within the scope of social expectations will be prohibited by §89 II of the Social Order Maintenance Act.

On the other hand, because freedom of the press is an indispensable mechanism by which to maintain the normal development of a democratic and pluralistic society, the significance of freedom of the press shall be taken into consideration in the process of ad hoc balancing.[78]

Constitutional Court, Interpretation No. 678) (2 July 2010) (R.O.C.); Lin Tzu-Yi yu Li Chen-Shan Da Fa Guan Gong Tong Ti Chu De Shizi Di 678 Hao Jie Shi Yi Bu Xie Tong Yi Bu Fen Bu Tong Yi Jian Shu [林子儀大法官與李震山大法官共同提出的釋字第678號解釋部分協同、部分不同意見書] (Justice Tzu-Yi Lin and Chen-Shan Li's concurring opinions in Justices of the Constitutional Court, Interpretation No. 678) (2 July 2010) (R.O.C.). General Comment, see Shyr (2011), pp. 25–49.

[76]Introduction to the right of access to the media, see Lin (2002), pp. 246–256.

[77]See J.Y. Interpretation No. 689, Reasoning recital 10.

[78]See J.Y. Interpretation No. 689, Reasoning recital 10.

4.3 Freedom of Expression in a Split Society: The China Factor

In past years, the aggravation of political, social and economic differences has triggered many social protests: the Sunflower Movement in 2014, the protest against courts-martial in peacetime in 2013, the parade against the amendment of the Labor Standards Law in 2017, demonstrations pro/against same-sex marriage, etc.

All these assemblies and parades should have their chance to be heard, for this reason J.Y. Interpretation No. 445 has imposed an obligation on the state to provide appropriate places for assemblies and parades and to protect their safety. Having said this, governments at different levels are still used to an authoritarian mentality and are always inclined to suppress the public sphere. Therefore, the approval system for outdoor assemblies and parades remains valid until today, thirty years after the termination of the martial-law regime; and the space for assemblies and parades often is minimized or displaced in the name of free speech or media zones.[79]

In addition to the controversy over space regulation, China has recently become a significant factor in the field of freedom of expression. Since advocacy of communism is no longer prohibited, there are many assemblies that use the national symbols of the People's Republic of China. As long as these assemblies and parades are not in violation of legal norms, there will be no legal issue. However, when the assembly somehow relates to China or to national identity, violent conflicts can easily occur as these issues relate to the very basis of Taiwanese civil society.

5 Conclusion: Consolidation of Civil Culture in a Post-authoritarian Information Society Threatened by China

If we were only to look to the text of the Taiwanese Constitution and the numerous constitutional interpretations written by the Constitutional Court with reference to U.S. free speech jurisprudence, we may have the impression that freedom of expression has been and always will be preciously protected in this island country. This impression is of course false, or at least incomplete. In order to avoid these biases and to provide overall knowledge, this chapter begins with a history of the suppression of speech that lasted for four decades. The second part introduces and analyzes the achievements the Constitutional Court has accomplished, one case at a time over the past thirty years, while the legislative branch has not done much in this regard. By connecting these two parts, we can clearly identify the long, dark

[79] See Liu (2009), pp. 16–21.

shadow of the White Terror. This historical experience has left such a great influence not only upon civil society but also upon the constitutional branches that it has forced the Constitutional Court to vote for J.Y. Interpretation No. 744 to challenge prior censorship of political assemblies. The third part deals with the challenges of future developments. In the face of new communication technologies and social conflicts, the future jurisprudence of free speech shall be capable of analyzing the influences of technologies upon information flows, social actions, as well as social institutions and the impacts of social opposition upon the public sphere, the strength of civil society and the culture of human rights. In the end, the only valid theory of free speech is the one that can secure the consolidation of civil culture in a post-authoritarian, modern society threatened by China.

In short, comprehensive and exact insights into the performance of freedom of expression in Taiwan demand sensibility towards the authoritarian past, towards the innovative future and towards the nearby rising power.

References

Brugger W (2007) Kants System der Redefreiheit. Der Staat 46:515–540

Chang M-W (2017) The party-state ruling under the constitution [憲法下的訓政]. Angle, Taipei

Chen S-M (2015) Constitutional law [憲法學釋論]. Vanity Press, Taipei

Harvard Law Review (1989) The content distinction in free speech analysis after "Renton." Harv Law Rev 102:1904

Hung C-L (2006) Whose media? whose freedom of speech? the right of access to media in the post-martial-law era. Taiwan Democracy Q 3(4):1–36

Lee H-T (2015) Constitutional law [憲法要義]. Angle, Taipei

Lin C-F (2005) An exploration into the banning of non-nationalist political magazines in Taiwan in the late and early 1980s. Bull Acad Hist 5:253–325

Lin T-Y (2002) The right of access to the media. In: Lin T-Y (ed) Freedom of speech and the press [言論自由與媒體自由]. Angle, Taipei, pp 229–259

Liu C-Y (2009) The unfulfilled promise of human rights protection: an analysis of freedom of speech and freedom of assembly and parade in Taiwan's democratic transition. Taiwan Democracy Q 6(3):1–46

Liu C-Y (2017) Why prior restraints? a brief comment on interpretation no. 744 of the Judicial Yuan. Taiwan Law Rev 267:194–201

Liu J-W, Lai C-M, Kuo C-H (2014) An analysis of Taiwan's licensing policy relationship between media and the state. Chin Public Adm Rev 20(3):1–26

Shyr S-H (2011) On radio wave regulation and prior restraints on freedom of speech: an analysis of interpretation no. 678 of the Judicial Yuan. Law Monthly 62(3):25–49

Solum L (1988) Freedom of communicative action: a theory of the first amendment freedom of speech. NW Univ Law Rev 83:54–135

Stone R (1986) Anti-pornography legislation as viewpoint-discrimination. Harv J Law and Public Policy 9:461–480

Tribe L (1988) American constitutional law, 2nd edn. Foundation Press, New York

Tsai S-C (2010) The suppressed publications in the 1950s. Bull Acad Hist 26:75–130

Wu G, Chen C-W (2017) Constitutional theories and the system of government [憲法理論與政府體制]. San Min, Taipei

Yang H-C (2002) Regulation of the press in the martial-law era. National Chengchi University dissertation

Yeh J-R (1991) Normalization of the civil associations act for the period of the Communist Rebellion. In: Taiwan Law Society (ed) Legal reconstruction and prospects for rule of law at the end of the period of the Communist Rebellion. Taiwan Law Society, Taipei, pp 199–213

Hui-chieh Su is Assistant Professor at the College of Law, National Taiwan University. Her interests in scholarship include constitutional theory and freedom of expression. In addition to her recent project on the justification for transitional justice under a liberal-democratic constitution, she is dedicated to the analysis and comparative study of constitutional argumentations on speech restrictions in Germany, the US, and Europe. Hui-chieh Su received her Doctor Juris from the University of Heidelberg in 2012. Before joining National Taiwan University in 2017, she was an Assistant Research Fellow at the Institute of European and American Studies (IEAS), Academia Sinica, Taiwan.

Chapter 23
Freedom of Movement in Taiwan—A Local Development to Meet International Standards

Jeffrey C. F. Li

Abstract According to Article 12 of the ICCPR, the freedom of movement includes at least three distinct rights: (1) the right to enter one's own country; (2) the right to leave any country; and (3) the right to liberty of movement within the territory of a state. In Taiwan, the three rights are all covered by the Constitution and have been expanded on by the Constitutional Court. Article 10 of the Constitution states that people should have the freedom of migration and the Constitutional Court has declared a series of interpretations that elaborate on the freedom of migration. In addition to the traditional freedom of movement, the Constitutional Court has also developed a freedom of movement in Article 22 of the Constitution. Therefore, further observation and analysis is required regarding the actual scope of the freedom of movement in Article 22 of the Constitution as developed by the Constitutional Court. By observing the constitutional interpretations in Taiwan, the author intends to introduce the freedom of migration as it exists in the Constitution and how it corresponds to the freedom of movement under international treaties.

Keywords Freedom of migration · Freedom of movement · Freedom to leave any country · Freedom to travel · Right to enter one's own country

1 Introduction

The scope and definition of "freedom of movement" seem to be consistent under the various world human rights treaties. For instance, Article 13 of the Universal Declaration of Human Rights (hereinafter UDHR) reads: "(1) Everyone has the right to *freedom of movement* and residence within the borders of each state. (2) Everyone has the right to leave any country, including his own, and to return to his country."[1]

[1]G.A. Res. 217 (III) A, Universal Declaration of Human Rights (10 Dec 1948) [hereinafter Universal Declaration of Human Rights]. http://www.refworld.org/docid/3ae6b3712c.html. Accessed 10 Oct 2017.

J. C. F. Li (✉)
Soochow University Law School, Taipei, Taiwan
e-mail: jeffreyli@leeandli.com

J. A. Cohen et al. (eds.), *Taiwan and International Human Rights*, Economics, Law, and Institutions in Asia Pacific, https://doi.org/10.1007/978-981-13-0350-0_23

Article 12 of the International Covenant on Civil and Political Rights (hereinafter ICCPR) has a similar definition.[2] The article bestows on an individual the following freedoms:

1. Everyone lawfully within the territory of a State shall, within that territory, have the right to liberty of movement and freedom to choose his residence (Paragraph 1).
2. Everyone shall be free to leave any country, including his own (Paragraph 2).
3. No one shall be arbitrarily deprived of the right to enter his own country (Paragraph 4).

Together, the freedoms under Article 12 are known by the Human Rights Committee as "freedom of movement."[3] We may summarize the freedom presented by Paragraph 1 of the ICCPR as the "freedom of movement within a country," Paragraph 2 as the "freedom to leave any country" and Paragraph 4 as the "right to enter one's own country." Interestingly, an individual's freedom to enter a foreign country is not explicitly protected by either the UDHR or the ICCPR. A fair reason is that the states are reserved for border sovereignty.

Paragraph 3, Article 12 of the ICCPR provides that necessary restrictions may be imposed by law on the freedom of movement within a country and the freedom to leave any country if the purpose is to "protect national security, public order (*ordre public*), public health or morals or the rights and freedoms of others, and are consistent with the other rights recognized in the present Covenant."[4] However, the restrictions in Paragraph 3 of Article 12 are not applicable to Paragraph 4.[5] In other words, the right to enter one's own country may not be restricted. The Human Rights Committee emphasizes in General Comment No. 27 that "[i]n no case may a person be arbitrarily deprived of the right to enter his or her own country."[6]

To understand the scope of the "right to enter one's own country" as presented in paragraph 4, Article 12 of the ICCPR it is important to determine who enjoys this right. The Human Rights Committee pointed out in General Comment No. 27 that "[t]he scope of 'his own country' is broader than the concept 'country of his nationality'"[7] and "it embraces, at the very least, an individual who, because of his or her special ties to or claims in relation to a given country, cannot be considered to be a mere alien."[8] The Human Rights Committee thus adopted a substantive view in finding "his own country" under Paragraph 4, Article 12 of the ICCPR.

---

[2]International Covenant on Civil and Political Rights, 16 Dec 1966, 999 UN T.S 171 [hereinafter ICCPR]. http://www.refworld.org/docid/3ae6b3aa0.html. Accessed 9 Oct 2017.

[3]See UN Human Rights Committee [HRC], CCPR General Comment No. 27: Article 12 (freedom of movement), para 11, UN Doc. CCPR/C/21/Rev.1/Add.9 (2 Nov 1999) [hereinafter General Comment No. 27]. http://www.refworld.org/docid/45139c394.html. Accessed 9 Oct 2017.

[4]ICCPR, at art. 12, para 3.

[5]See General Comment No. 27, at para 11.

[6]*Id.*, at para 21.

[7]*Id.*, at para 20.

[8]*Id.*

As to "freedom of movement within a country" and "freedom to leave any country," the Human Rights Committee stressed that once a person is lawfully within a state he/she should not suffer differential treatment regarding the freedom without justifiable reason under paragraph 3, Article 12 of the ICCPR.[9]

Taiwan's Constitution also contains an article to protect freedom of movement, and the Constitutional Court has rendered a number of interpretations to illustrate its scope and content. Although freedom of residence is also provided by paragraph 1, Article 12 and interpreted by the Human Rights Committee in General Comment No. 27,[10] in order to limit the analysis of this article, focus will be given to the "freedom of movement within a country," the "freedom to leave any country" and the "right to enter one's own country" as provided for by the Constitution and the Constitutional Court Interpretations in parts 2 and 3.

2 Freedom of Migration Under the Constitution

Article 10 of the ROC Constitution reads: "The people shall have freedom of residence and migration." In Chinese, Article 10 of the Constitution uses "遷徙" (*qian xi*), which incorporates meanings of moving from one place to another and change of status.[11] Due to the wide range of meanings contained in the word "遷徙," there are various options for an English translation. The English translator of J.Y. Interpretation No. 265 chose "freedom of migration,"[12] while the English translator of J.Y. Interpretation No. 443 chose "to move freely."[13] The English translation of J.Y. Interpretation No. 558 uses "freedom of movement,"[14] and the English translation for

[9]*Id.*, at para 4.

[10]*Id.*, at paras 4–7.

[11]Re-codified Chinese dictionary by Ministry of Education. http://dict.revised.moe.edu.tw/cgi-bin/cbdic/gsweb.cgi?ccd=b57j_o&o=e0&sec=sec1&op=v&viev=5-1. Accessed 12 Nov 2017.

[12]Dafaguan Shizi Di 265 Hao [大法官釋字第265號] (J.Y. Interpretation No. 265) (5 Oct 1990) (R.O.C.) [hereinafter Interpretation No. 265]. http://www.judicial.gov.tw/constitutionalcourt/EN/p03_01.asp?expno=265. Accessed 15 Nov 2017; see also Dafaguan Shizi Di 454 Hao [大法官釋字第454號] (J.Y. Interpretation No. 454) (22 May 1998) (R.O.C.) [hereinafter Interpretation No. 454]. http://www.judicial.gov.tw/constitutionnalcourt/EN/p03_01.asp?expno=454. Accessed 15 Nov 2017; Dafaguan Shizi Di 542 Hao [大法官釋字第542號] (J.Y. Interpretation No. 542) (4 Apr 2002) (R.O.C.) [hereinafter Interpretation No. 542]. http://www.judicial.gov.tw/constitutionalcourt/EN/p03_01.asp?expno=542. Accessed 15 Nov 2017.

[13]Dafaguan Shizi Di 443 Hao [大法官釋字第443號] (J.Y. Interpretation No. 443) (26 Dec 1997) (R.O.C.) [hereinafter Interpretation No. 443]. http://www.judicial.gov.tw/constitutionalcourt/EN/p03_01.asp?expno=443. Accessed 15 Nov 2017.

[14]Dafaguan Shizi Di 558 Hao [大法官釋字第558號] (J.Y. Interpretation No. 558) (18 Apr 2003) (R.O.C.), available at: http://www.judicial.gov.tw/constitutionalcourt/EN/p03_01.asp?expno=558. Accessed 15 Nov 2017.

Article 10 available at the ROC laws and regulations database website uses "change of residence."[15]

Since the Constitutional Court has developed an independent "freedom of movement" in Article 22 of the Constitution through its Interpretations,[16] in order to distinguish between Article 10 and Article 22, the translations of "to move freely" or "freedom of movement" will not be used for the translation of "遷徙." Further, "遷徙" is not necessarily limited to "change of residence" and the Constitutional Court has declared Article 10 to include one's right to depart from or to enter Taiwan, whether changing residence or not.[17] Therefore, in this chapter "freedom of migration" will be used to represent "遷徙自由" under Article 10 of the Constitution.

Unlike ICCPR Article 12, Article 10 of the Constitution does not specify the exact content of freedom of migration. From a textual reading of "freedom of migration," it may include people's freedom to move freely inside Taiwan, freedom to leave Taiwan, and freedom to enter Taiwan (without differentiating a national or a foreigner), corresponding to and even broader than freedom of movement under Article 12 of the ICCPR.[18]

The Constitutional Court has issued the following Interpretations to elaborate on the meaning of "freedom of migration" under Article 10 of the Constitution.

2.1 *J.Y. Interpretation No. 265 (5 October 1990)*[19]

The National Security Act During the Period of National Mobilization for Suppression of the Communist Rebellion (hereinafter NSA during the Period) was enacted in 1987 and was abolished and replaced by the National Security Act in 1992.[20] Article 3, Paragraph 2, Subparagraph 2 of the NSA during the Period provides that entry into and exit from the country may not be permitted if, judging

---

[15]English translation of the Constitution, on the ROC laws and regulations database website, available at: http://law.moj.gov.tw/Eng/LawClass/LawAll.aspx?PCode=A0000001.

[16]See *infra* Section 3.

[17]See, e.g., J.Y. Interpretations Nos. 454 and 558.

[18]See e.g., Fa and Dung (2006), p. 214 (recognizing freedom of migration may include people's freedom to move and reside within a state, foreigners' freedom to enter a state, and people's freedom to go abroad); Wu (2015), pp. 314–315 (agreeing that freedom of migration includes people's freedom to move freely inside Taiwan, freedom to leave Taiwan, and freedom to enter Taiwan); Chen (2005), p. 235 (pointing out that freedom of migration may refer to a people's general freedom of movement as the broader meaning, or may refer to freedom to change residence as the narrower meaning, and concluding that freedom of migration under the Constitution should be understood as the broader meaning. Also, he concludes that freedom of migration may include freedom of migration within a state and freedom to go abroad).

[19]J.Y. Interpretation No. 265.

[20]Legislative History of the National Security Act. Laws and Regulations Database of the ROC. http://law.moj.gov.tw/Eng/LawClass/LawHistory.aspx?PCode=A0030028vggb. Accessed 12 Nov 2017.

from the facts, it may be reasonably suspected that the applicant may pose a threat to national security or social stability. Further, Article 12 (6) of the Enforcement Rules of the NSA during the Period further specifies that those from Mainland China may not be permitted to enter Taiwan if they fail to reside in the free area continuously for five years.

In this case, the petitioner's wife was from Mainland China, having moved from China to Hong Kong on 10 February 1987 and having applied for residency in Taiwan on 17 February of the same year.[21] The immigration agency, based on the NSA during the Period and its Enforcement Rules, rejected the petitioner's wife's application because she had not resided in Taiwan continuously for five years.[22] The petitioner resorted to complaint, administrative appeal, and administrative suit to remedy his wife's case, and he finally petitioned the Constitutional Court after those remedies had failed.[23]

The Constitutional Court announced J.Y. Interpretation No. 265 on 5 October 1990. The Court first pointed out that a law such as Article 3, Paragraph 2, Subparagraph 2, of the NSA during the Period is a regulation on immigration and restricts people's freedom of residence and migration.[24] However, the Court also indicated that such restrictions "were necessary to maintain the country's social order and therefore not in conflict with the Constitution."[25] Further, Article 12 (6) of the Enforcement Rules of the NSA during the Period provided the government with criteria for finding facts, and because the Enforcement Rules only provide that the application "may" not be permitted instead of "should" not be permitted, such Rules are consistent with the intent of the NSA during the Period to ensure national security and social order.[26] The Court, nonetheless, stated that "the said Enforcement Rules should be reviewed and amended from time to time after taking into account the purposes of Article 3, Paragraph 2, Subparagraph 2 of the NSA during the period so as to meet the needs as dictated by social developments."[27]

The case of J.Y. Interpretation No. 265 seems to regard the restriction on people's right to enter a foreign country (or a foreigner's right to enter a state) as a right that is not explicitly emphasized by Article 12 of the ICCPR and Article 13 of the UDHR. Although the restriction on a citizen's freedom of migration was upheld by J.Y. Interpretation No. 265, there are still a few lessons to learn from this Interpretation. First, a foreigner's right to enter Taiwan is protected by freedom of migration under Article 10 of the Constitution, though such freedom may be

[21]See the Petition of J.Y. Interpretation No. 265, available at: http://www.judicial.gov.tw/constitutionalcourt/P03_01_detail.asp?expno=265&showtype=%AC%DB%C3%F6%AA%FE%A5%F3.

[22]*Id.*

[23]*Id.*

[24]Reasoning of J.Y. Interpretation No. 265, para 1.

[25]Holding of J.Y. Interpretation No. 265.

[26]Reasoning of J.Y. Interpretation No. 265, para 2.

[27]*Id.*

restricted with justifiable reason. Second, protection of the freedom of migration under Article 10 of the Constitution does not distinguish between local or foreign citizens.

2.2 *J.Y. Interpretation No. 443 (26 December 1997)*[28]

In 1993, the petitioner was a draftee who intended to go abroad. According to the Regulations for the Exit of Draftees, draftees are, in principle, restricted from departure and need to apply for exceptional permission. The petitioner's application was denied, leading to a challenge of the constitutionality of such a restriction under the Regulations for the Exit of Draftees.[29]

J.Y. Interpretation No. 443 is well known as the Interpretation which established the structure and system for the principle of "Vorbehalt des Gesetzes."[30] However, as this article focuses on freedom of migration, the principle of "Vorbehalt Gesetzes" as derived from J.Y. Interpretation No. 443 will not be explored.[31]

The Court first explained that freedom of residence and migration refer to "the freedom [of people] to choose their residences, to enjoy their lives without intrusion, and *the right to move or travel around based on their free will*."[32] The Court then cited Article 23 and Article 22 of the Constitution[33] to conclude that without a law or a regulation explicitly authorized by law, people's freedom and rights shall not be limited, and major matters concerning the military service of draftees shall not be regulated.[34] The Court therefore found the Regulations to limit the right of draftees to freely leave the country are in violation of the Constitution.[35]

[28]J.Y. Interpretation No. 443.

[29]See Petition of J.Y. Interpretation No. 443, available at: http://www.judicial.gov.tw/constitutionalcourt/P03_01_detail.asp?expno=443&showtype=%AC%DB%C3%F6%AA%FE%A5%F3.

[30]See. e.g., Wu (2007), pp. 103–106; Chen (2013), pp. 159–160. The principle of "Vorbehalt des Gesetzes" originated in Germany. A similar principle in U.S. law would be the non-delegation principle. See, e.g., Hwang (2004), pp. 1–45.

[31]See Reasoning of J.Y. Interpretation No. 443, para 1.

[32]*Id.*, at para 2.

[33]Article 22 of the ROC Constitution reads: "All other freedoms and rights of the people that are not detrimental to social order or public welfare shall be guaranteed under the Constitution." Article 23 of the ROC Constitution reads: "All the freedoms and rights enumerated in the preceding Articles shall not be restricted by law except by such as may be necessary to prevent infringement upon the freedoms of other persons, to avert an imminent crisis, to maintain social order or to advance public welfare."

[34]Reasoning of J.Y. Interpretation No. 443, para 2.

[35]*Id.*

In addition to underscoring that the freedom of migration may not be restricted without a law or a regulation authorized by law, J.Y. Interpretation No. 443 recognizes that freedom of movement within a country and freedom to leave any country are covered by the articles of the Constitution.

2.3 J.Y. Interpretations No. 454 (22 May 1998)[36]

The petitioner in this case was from Hong Kong and had applied for a long-term residency permit, which was granted by the government. However, based on the Guidelines for Nationals' Temporary Entry into Long-term Residence in, and Listing on, the Household Registry of the Country (hereinafter the Guidelines), the immigration agency subsequently decided to revoke the long-term residency permit. The immigration agency sought to revoke the permit based on reports that the petitioner was involved in criminal activities in Hong Kong. After exhausting the administrative litigation remedies, the petitioner challenged the constitutionality of the Guidelines.[37]

The Constitutional Court first pointed out that the Guidelines to "refuse to grant long-term residency permits, cancel such permits, or cancel or deregister household registration to nationals not listed on the household registry of Taiwan" are "major restraints on the people's freedom of residence and migration, and thus must be authorized by law or by the authorities legally empowered to do so."[38] The Constitutional Court therefore declared part of the Guidelines to be unconstitutional owing to a lack of legal authority.[39]

When expounding on the freedom of residence and the freedom of migration under Article 10 of the Constitution, the Court stated that the freedom "is to protect the people's freedom *to select their residence, to change their residence and to travel, including the right to exit or enter the country*."[40] However, the Court also indicated that:

> The degrees of restriction on the right of entry and residence for nationals listed on Taiwan's household registry, *those residing overseas or residing in Hong Kong or Macau may differ reasonably*, provided such restriction conforms to the principle of necessity stipulated in Article 23 of the Constitution, and is provided for by law or by rules prescribed by administrative bodies with the express authorization from the legislative bodies.[41]

---

[36]J.Y. Interpretation No. 454.

[37]See Petition of J.Y. Interpretation No. 454, available at: http://www.judicial.gov.tw/constitutionalcourt/p03_01.asp?expno=454.

[38]Holding of J.Y. Interpretation No. 454.

[39]See *id.*

[40]Reasoning of J.Y. Interpretation No. 454, para 1.

[41]*Id.* (Emphasis added.)

Although part of the Guidelines were held to be unconstitutional by the Constitutional Court, the Court based its reasoning mainly on the principle of "Vorbehalt des Gesetzes," meaning that the Guidelines restricted people's freedom of migration without legal authority.

Although the Court recognized the right of foreigners to enter Taiwan, the Court also considered it justifiable for the Legislative Yuan to differentiate between nationals listed on Taiwan's household registry and those residing overseas, and that stricter and reasonable limitations may be applied on the latter's freedom of entry. Regarding the right to enter one's own country, the Court allows differential treatment based on whether an individual appears on Taiwan's household registry, which is not consistent with ICCPR Article 12 and General Comment No. 27.

2.4 *J.Y. Interpretation No. 497 (3 December 1999)*[42]

The petitioner, in this case, applied on behalf of his wife for a permit to stay and reside in Taiwan China in December 1994. The petitioner's wife had visited Taiwan in July 1995 and had failed to depart until October of that year as the result of an error by her of travel agency. For this reason, the immigration agency rejected the petitioner's application and issued an order to the petitioner's wife prohibiting her from entry into Taiwan in 1996. After exhausting the administrative judicial remedies, the petitioner filed the case with the Constitutional Court, challenging the constitutionality of the Regulations Governing Permission to Enter the Taiwan Area for People from Mainland China and the Regulations Governing Permission for Permanent or Temporary Residence for People from Mainland China.[43]

The Constitutional Court first stated that although people's freedom of migration is protected by Article 10 of the Constitution, "such freedoms may be restricted by law in order to prevent infringement upon the freedoms of other persons, to avert an imminent crisis, to maintain the social order or to advance the public welfare pursuant to Article 23 thereof."[44] Citing Article 10 of the Amendment to the Constitution (presently Article 11 of the prevailing Amendment to the Constitution), reading, "Rights and obligations between the people of the Chinese Mainland area and those of the free area, and the disposition of other related affairs may be specified by law," the Court found the Act Governing Relations between People of the Taiwan Area and the Mainland Area "is a special law governing the

[42]Dafaguan Shizi Di 497 Hao [大法官釋字第 497 號] (J.Y. Interpretation No. 497) (3 Dec 1999) (R.O.C.), available at: http://www.judicial.gov.tw/constitutionalcourt/EN/p03_01.asp?expno=497. Accessed 15 Nov 2017.

[43]See Petition of J.Y. Interpretation No. 497, available at: http://www.judicial.gov.tw/constitutionalcourt/uploadfile/C100/497.pdf.

[44]See Reasoning of J.Y. Interpretation No. 497.

rights and obligations between the people of the Taiwan area and the Mainland Area to ensure the security and public welfare of the Taiwan area before the reunification of the nation."[45] The relevant regulations were therefore found as being authorized by law and, as such, constitutional.[46]

Owing to Article 11 of the Amendment to the Constitution, the Constitutional Court seems to have adopted a rational scrutiny regarding whether the relevant restriction on freedom of migration of people from Mainland China is authorized by law.

2.5 *J.Y. Interpretation No. 542 (4 April 2002)*[47]

J.Y. Interpretation No. 542 deals with freedom of movement within a country.

The area in which the petitioner in this case lived was designated as the reservoir catchment area for the establishment of Feitsui Reservoir. Since the area would be endangered by the construction of the Feitsui Reservoir, and the residents would also pollute the water source, the government announced the "Implementation Plan for the Relocation of Residents in Bi Shan, Yun An and Ge To Villages of Shediang County, Feitsui Reservoir Catchment Area" (hereinafter the Plan) forcing the residents to migrate. According to the Plan, compensation would only be issued to those who had household registry records from before 1 January 1980, and who were actually residents in the area. Since the petitioner did not have household registry records in the area until August 1980, his application for compensation was rejected. The petitioner therefore exhausted the judicial remedies and petitioned for a constitutional interpretation, challenging the Plan.[48]

Citing J.Y. Interpretations No. 443 and No. 454, the Constitutional Court first confirmed that the "restriction on this freedom shall not exceed the degree of necessity required by Article 23 of the Constitution and must be mandated by the law."[49] Since the Plan was to "preserve the water quality and quantity in the protected water supply region, and the means it adopts are necessary," the Court therefore concluded "[a]lthough the Plan places a restriction on the people's freedom of residence and migration, it cannot be said to have infringed upon Article 10 of the Constitution since the means of relocation conforms to the principle of proportionality when considering the end—the protection of the water resources."[50]

---

[45] *Id.*

[46] *Id.*

[47] J.Y. Interpretation No. 542.

[48] See Summary of Facts of J.Y. Interpretation No. 542, available at: http://www.judicial.gov.tw/constitutionalcourt/P03_01_detail.asp?expno=542&showtype=%AC%DB%C3%F6%AA%FE%A5%F3.

[49] Holding of J.Y. Interpretation No. 542, para 1.

[50] Reasoning of J.Y. Interpretation No. 542, para 2.

As to the provision of compensation, the Court indicated that as the Plan used household registry records as the sole determinant of actual residence in the water supply region, it excluded residents who had actually been residing in and had vacated the water supply region from receiving the benefit of relocation compensation. Though such an exclusion did not necessarily violate the principle of equality under the Constitution, the Court still requested the administrative agency to amend the Plan to consider other factors in determining residence in the area.[51]

2.6 *J.Y. Interpretation No. 558 (18 April 2003)*[52]

Mr. Huang, a national of Taiwan, entered Taiwan in 1996 without obtaining a permit and was found to be in violation of the National Security Act. The judges of the Taiwan High Court found the application of Paragraph 1, Article 3 of the National Security Act, reading, "People exiting or entering the country shall apply to the Ministry of the Interior Entry and Exit Service Bureau to be granted permission, and those who are not granted permission are prohibited from exiting or entering the country" as unconstitutional and therefore petitioned the Constitutional Court for an interpretation.[53]

The Constitutional Court reaffirmed that the freedom of residence and immigration under Article 10 of the Constitution includes "*people's freedom to choose and change their residence and to travel, including the right to exit or enter the country*,"[54] which had already been reiterated by prior constitutional interpretations.[55] The Court further stated that "[i]f *the nationals choose their domicile and have a household registry in the Taiwan Area, they can return to the homeland at any time without asking to be granted permission*."[56] Like the general human right, the right of the people to exit or enter the country may be restricted if such a restriction is provided by law and is in accordance with the proportionality principle under Article 23 of the Constitution.[57]

As to the constitutionality of Article 3, Paragraph 1 of the National Security Act, a similar article of the NSA during the Period was upheld by the Constitutional

---

[51]See Reasoning of J.Y. Interpretation No. 542, para 3.

[52]Dafaguan Shizi Di 558 Hao [大法官釋字第 558 號] (J.Y. Interpretation No. 558) (18 Apr 2003) (R.O.C.), available at: http://www.judicial.gov.tw/constitutionalcourt/EN/p03_01.asp?expno=558. Accessed 13 Nov 2017.

[53]See Summary of Facts of J.Y. Interpretation No. 558, available at: http://www.judicial.gov.tw/constitutionalcourt/P03_01_detail.asp?expno=558&showtype=%AC%DB%C3%F6%AA%FE%A5%F3.

[54]Reasoning of J.Y. Interpretation No. 558, para 2.

[55]See, e.g., J.Y. Interpretations No. 443 and No. 454.

[56]Reasoning of J.Y. Interpretation No. 558, para 2.

[57]See *id.*

Court in J.Y. Interpretation No. 265.[58] The Court did not choose to overrule J.Y. Interpretation No. 265; instead, it admitted that the NSA during the Period was intended to meet the country's needs that were specific to the period and necessary for the Suppression of the Communist Rebellion, therefore not in conflict with the Constitution.[59] However, the Court also pointed out that after the end of the Period of National Mobilization for Suppression of the Communist Rebellion and martial law, the Legislative Yuan enacted the Immigration Act, which became effective on 21 May 1999. Although the National Security Act was amended in 1992, Article 3, Paragraph 1 of the Act:

> *[M]aking no distinction between those people who chose their domicile and thus have a household registry in the Taiwan Area and those who do not,* uniformly requires that people apply with the governing authority to be granted permission to enter the country and prohibits those people who are not granted permission from entering the country.[60]

Also, given that the Act imposed a punishment clause on people who entered the country without being granted permission, the Court therefore concluded the provision "is in violation of the principle of proportionality as elaborated on in Article 23 of the Constitution and *the freedom of people to return to the homeland at any time.*"[61]

The Court also indicated two special groups of people, whose freedom to enter Taiwan may be subject to further legal restrictions. One group is people living in Mainland China. Citing Article 11 of the Amendments to the Constitution[62] and J.Y. Interpretation No. 497, the Court found the restriction imposed on the people from the Chinese Mainland from entering Taiwan is consistent with the rationale of the Constitution.[63] Another group is citizens of Taiwan, residing outside the country and who have no domicile but have a household registry in the Taiwan Area, for whom the relevant provisions of the Immigration Act should also be applicable.[64]

In J.Y. Interpretation No. 558 the court emphasized for the first time that people's freedom to return to the homeland at any time is protected by Article 10 of the Constitution. However, the freedom enjoyed by those nationals who have a domicile and are on the household registry in Taiwan seem to receive more protection. The reason why Article 3, Paragraph 1 of the National Security Act was

---

[58]Subparagraph 2, Paragraph 2, Article 3 of the NSA during the Period provides that entry into and exit from the country may not be permitted if, judging from the facts, it may be reasonably suspected that the applicant may pose a threat to national security or social stability.

[59]Reasoning of J.Y. Interpretation No. 558, para 3.

[60]*Id.* (Emphasis added.)

[61]*Id.* (Emphasis added.)

[62]Article 11 of the Amendments to the Constitution reads: "Rights and obligations between the people living in the free area and those of the Chinese Mainland Area, and the disposition of other related affairs may be specially prescribed by law."

[63]Reasoning of J.Y. Interpretation No. 558, para 2.

[64]*Id.*

declared unconstitutional was not merely because it created a permit system for entry into Taiwan but because it failed to distinguish between people who have a domicile and are on the household registry in Taiwan and those who are not.

Justice Liu Tieh-Cheng pointed out in his dissenting opinion that J.Y. Interpretation No. 558 seemed to recognize Article 3, Paragraph 1 of the National Security Act's constitutionality in asking for a permit if the national has only a household registry in Taiwan without having a domicile.[65] However, citing Article 13, Paragraph 2 of the UDHR[66] and Article 14, Paragraph 4 of the ICCPR,[67] both of which recognize an individual's right to freely return to his country, Justice Liu doubted the justifiability for the Legislative Yuan to choose a domicile as the condition upon which to restrict people's freedom of migration, since a domicile is not like a nationality which connects people with a nation.[68]

Based on Justice Liu Tieh-Cheng's doubt as to the justifiability of using a domicile as a standard for determining whether people should obtain a permit before entering Taiwan, one could also ask why a national on the household registry should be exempt from requiring a permit. Unfortunately, J.Y. Interpretation No. 558 failed to provide ample reasoning for requiring a national to have a domicile and a household registry if he/she desires to freely return to his/her own country. The conclusion of J.Y. Interpretation No. 558 regarding the right to enter one's own country is not consistent with the ICCPR or the Human Rights Committee's General Comment No. 27, which does not narrow the scope of protection in one's own country.

2.7 J.Y. Interpretation No. 710 (5 July 2013)[69]

The petitioner in this instance was from Mainland China, having married a Taiwanese citizen in 2003. Thereafter, the petitioner frequently traveled between Taiwan and China as a Taiwanese spouse. In 2007, the fourth time the petitioner

[65] See Dissenting Opinion of Justice Liu Tieh-Cheng of J.Y. Interpretation No. 558, available at: http://www.judicial.gov.tw/constitutionalcourt/p03_01.asp?expno=558.

[66] Paragraph 2, Article 13 of the Universal Declaration of Human Rights reads: "Everyone has the right to leave any country, including his own, and to return to his country."

[67] Paragraph 4, Article 14 of the ICCPR reads: "No one shall be arbitrarily deprived of the right to enter his own country."

[68] *Id.*

[69] Dafaguan Shizi Di 710 Hao [大法官釋字第 710 號] (J.Y. Interpretation No. 710) (5 July 2013) (R.O.C.), available at: http://www.judicial.gov.tw/constitutionalcourt/EN/p03_01.asp?expno=710. Accessed 15 Nov 2017.

was permitted to enter Taiwan as a citizen's spouse, the National Immigration Agency found significant discrepancies in the statements of the petitioner and her husband during their interviews. Therefore, the National Immigration Agency revoked the petitioner's Entry and Exit Permit in accordance with the relevant laws. At the same time, the National Immigration Agency imposed a mandatory deportation on the petitioner according to the Cross-Strait Relations Act Governing Relations between Peoples from the Taiwan Area and the Mainland Area, and also temporarily detained the petitioner in accordance with the Rules Governing Enforced Deportation of People from Mainland China, Hong Kong, and Macau. The petitioner was detained for a total of 126 days, and then she was mandatorily deported from Taiwan. The petitioner thereafter filed a lawsuit for national compensation based on the detention. The court's final decision was to reject the petitioner's claim. The petitioner therefore applied for an interpretation.[70]

Before the announcement of J.Y. Interpretation No. 710, a group of petitioners with similar case backgrounds had petitioned and obtained from the Constitutional Court J.Y. Interpretation No. 708, dated 6 February 2013.[71] The petitioners of J.Y. Interpretation No. 708 had been temporarily detained and mandatorily deported from Taiwan. The Constitutional Court in J.Y. Interpretation No. 708 found the laws regarding "the temporary detention of a foreign national for a reasonable period in order to complete repatriation does not provide the detainee with prompt judicial relief" and "an extension of the aforementioned temporary detention is also not subject to judicial review."[72] The laws of temporary detention and mandatory deportation were thus declared to be "in violation of the meaning and purpose of the protection of physical freedom guaranteed under Article 8 of the Constitution, and shall be null and void no later than two years from the issuance of this Interpretation."[73]

The conclusion of J.Y. Interpretation No. 710 is similar to that of J.Y. Interpretation No. 708. The relevant laws were found to be in violation of due process of law.[74] However, J.Y. Interpretation No. 710 added that the laws

[70]This paragraph is summarized from the Summary of Facts of J.Y. Interpretation No. 710.

[71]Dafaguan Shizi Di 708 Hao [大法官釋字第 708 號] (J.Y. Interpretation No. 708). (6 Feb 2013) (R.O.C.), available at: http://www.judicial.gov.tw/constitutionalcourt/EN/p03_01.asp?expno=708. Accessed 15 Nov 2017.

[72]Holding of J.Y. Interpretation No. 710.

[73]*Id.*

[74]See Holding of J.Y. Interpretation No. 708.

endorsing mandatory deportation "without providing any defense opportunity to such person," in addition to immediate actions required in response to a threat to national security or social order, were in violation of Article 10 of the Constitution and due process of law.[75] The Court expounded in its reasoning that the restrictions imposed on the freedom of people from Mainland China, owing to the particular political factors between the two sides of the Taiwan Strait,[76]

> [A]fter formally obtaining permission from the competent authorities and having legally entered the Taiwan Area, *the freedom of migration of people from the Mainland Area should in principle be protected by the Constitution* (see Article 12 and Paragraph 6 of General Comment No. 15 of the UN International Covenant on Civil and Political Rights),

and:

> Except where immediate actions are otherwise required in response to a threat to national security or social order, the mandatory deportation of a person from the Mainland Area who legally entered the Taiwan Area must fulfill the corresponding due process requirements (see Article 13 of the UN International Covenant on Civil and Political Rights; Article 1 of Protocol No. 7 of the European Convention on Human Rights).[77]

Therefore, J.Y. Interpretation No. 710 seems to suggest that after entry into Taiwan, freedom of migration, including one's freedom of movement within Taiwan and freedom to leave any country, shall be equally protected. Further, since J.Y. Interpretation No. 710 cites the ICCPR and its General Comments, it can be fairly concluded that the content of freedom of movement under the ICCPR and the international covenants is recognized by the Constitutional Court and has become part of Article 10 of the Constitution via the interpretations made by the Constitutional Court.

3 Freedom of Movement Created by the Constitutional Court Under Article 22 of the Constitution

Article 22 of the Constitution reads: "All other freedoms and rights of the people that are not detrimental to social order or public welfare shall be guaranteed under the Constitution." The Constitutional Court has used this article many times to

75 *Id.*

76 See J.Y. Interpretations Nos. 497 and 558.

77 Reasoning of J.Y. Interpretation No. 710, para 2.

recognize human rights that are not listed in Articles 7–21 of the Constitution, including the right of privacy,[78] freedom of marriage,[79] freedom to adopt children,[80] the right to reputation,[81] the right to establish paternity,[82] etc.

---

[78]J.Y. Interpretation No. 603 reads:

> Although the right of privacy is not among those rights specifically enumerated in the Constitution, *it should nonetheless be considered as an indispensable fundamental right and thus protected under Article 22 of the Constitution* for purposes of preserving human dignity, individuality and moral integrity, as well as preventing invasions of personal privacy and maintaining self-control of personal information.

[79]J.Y. Interpretation No. 748 reads:

> Unspoused persons eligible to marry shall have their freedom of marriage, which includes the freedom to decide "whether to marry" and "whom to marry" (see J.Y. Interpretation No. 362). Such decisional autonomy is vital to the sound development of personality and to the safeguarding of human dignity, *and therefore is a fundamental right to be protected by Article 22 of the Constitution.* The creation of a permanent union of intimate and exclusive nature for the purpose of living a common life by two persons of the same-sex will not affect the application of those provisions on betrothal, conclusion of marriage, general effects of marriage, matrimonial property regimes, and divorce, as provided for in Sections 1 through 5 of the Marriage Chapter to the union of two persons of the opposite sex. Nor will it alter the social order established upon existing opposite-sex marriages. Furthermore, the freedom of marriage for two persons of the same-sex, once legally recognized, will constitute the bedrock of a stable society, together with opposite-sex marriages.

[80]J.Y. Interpretation No. 712 reads:

> The family system is based on the free development of personality and is essential for ensuring the functions of inheritance, education, the economy and culture. It is vital for an individual's growth in society and is the foundation for the creation and development of our society. Adoption is part of our country's family system. It is an action that establishes a parent-child relationship with a view to creating an identity. In this way, it forms human relationships between the adopter and the adoption of education, nurturing, support, belonging and inheritance of property. It plays an important role in developing the mind and body and molding the personality of both adopter and adopted. The people's freedom to adopt children, *in particular the freedom of development of personality for both adopter and adopted, is protected under Article 22 of the Constitution.*

[81]J.Y. Interpretation No. 656 reads: "The right to reputation, necessary in the realization of human dignity, aims to maintain and protect individual sovereignty and moral integrity. *It is guaranteed under Article 22 of the Constitution* (see J. Y. Interpretation Nos. 399, 486, 587 and 603)."

[82]J.Y. Interpretation No. 587 reads:

> A child's right to identify his/her blood filiations is declared by Article 7, Section 1, of the UN Convention on the Rights of the Child, validated on 2 Sept 1990. *The right to establish paternity is concerned with a child's right to personality and shall be protected under Article 22 of the Constitution.*

Although the Constitutional Court had already opined on the freedom of migration under Article 10 of the Constitution to include the right or freedom to travel,[83] the Court seemed to consider the right of freedom to travel as encapsulated by Article 10 to be limited, and thus established a further "freedom of movement" (一般行動自由) from a reading of Article 22 of the Constitution.

The freedom of movement was referred to by the Constitutional Court for the first time in J.Y. Interpretation No. 535, announced on 14 December 2011.[84] The Court found that the police stop-and-check powers under the Police Service Act, including searches, street checks, and interrogations, "may have a great effect upon personal freedom, freedom of [movement],[85] property rights and the right of privacy, and therefore found that such checks must be in accordance with the rule of law as well as the legal principles guiding police functions and legal enforcement."[86] However, in its reference to freedom of movement, the Constitutional Court failed to specify the exact content of such a freedom and how such a freedom was inferred from the Constitution. The reason for this failure might be because the rights of privacy and property were referred to together in J.Y. Interpretation No. 535. The critical point of J.Y. Interpretation No. 535 is, however, to depict due process of law as being required for the police to stop and check.[87]

---

[83]See, e.g., J.Y. Interpretations Nos. 443 and 454.

[84]Dafaguan Shizi Di 535 Hao [大法官釋字第 535 號] (J.Y. Interpretation No. 535) (14 Dec 2001) (R.O.C.), available at: http://www.judicial.gov.tw/constitutionalcourt/EN/p03_01.asp?expno=535. Accessed 15 Nov 2017.

[85]The English translation of J.Y. Interpretation No. 587 uses "right to travel," however, to distinguish the right to travel under Article 10 of the Constitution; I choose "freedom of movement" as a more correct English translation of "一般行動自由."

[86]Holding of J.Y. Interpretation No. 587, para 1.

[87]Holding of J.Y. Interpretation No. 535 reads:

> The relevant provisions concerning police checks in the aforementioned Act never delegate police unlimited authority to exercise any check, law enforcement or interrogation without due consideration of time, place, manner and subjects. Unless prescribed otherwise in the law, the police shall limit their checking authority to public transportation, public places, or other places where danger exists or may exist according to reasonable and objective judgments. Among these places, some places may be private residences that must be protected to the same extent as any homes. Police shall not exercise checking authority over any persons unless there is a reasonable belief that actions taken by such persons have caused or may cause danger; and in so doing, police must abide by the principle of proportionality and not go beyond the degree of necessity. Before conducting any checks, police must immediately inform the involved persons of the reasons for exercising such checks and identify themselves clearly as law enforcement officers. Any police checks must be conducted on the spot. If police do not obtain the consent of the persons to be checked and, with no alternative to identify the persons to be checked or to conduct on-the-spot checks, and they still conduct such checks, this may have harmful effects or may impede traffic flows and interfere with social tranquility. Moreover, police are not permitted to ask checked persons to go to a police station for further interrogation. After the identification of such persons has been confirmed, police should permit them to leave without delay unless they are suspected of having committed a crime, in which case criminal law procedures should be followed.

"Freedom of movement" appeared again in J.Y. Interpretation No. 689, dated 29 July 2011.[88] Article 89, Paragraph 2 of the Social Order Maintenance Act punishes stalking behavior, which has been urged to end, yet has continued without any legitimate reason. The court found that this provision "does not violate the principle of clarity and definitiveness of law."[89] Further, the Court pointed out that "a journalist following a person shall be considered to have legitimate reasons and shall not be subject to penalty… if judging from the facts a specific event is of concern to the public, of public interest, and newsworthy, it is not intolerable under the general social standard."[90] The Court therefore found the provision to be constitutional. When elaborating on the purpose of Article 89, Paragraph 2 of the Social Order Maintenance Act, the Court referred to "a person's freedom of movement, freedom from bodily and mental harm, freedom from intrusion with reasonable expectation in public space and the right to autonomous control of personal information, and to punish stalking behavior that has been urged to end, yet has continued without any legitimate reason."[91] The Court further opined on the freedom of movement in the reasoning of J.Y. Interpretation No. 689 as follows:

> Based on respect of human dignity, we believe that one's autonomy and the free development of personality shall be safeguarded by the Constitution (see J. Y. Interpretation Number 603). In addition to the various freedoms already protected by the Constitution, for the protection of individual autonomy and the free development of personality, *an individual's freedom of action, including willful action or inaction, shall also be safeguarded in Article 22 of the Constitution*, under the premise of not jeopardizing public order and interests. *The freedom of movement guaranteeing a person's willful move toward or stay in a place* (see J. Y. Interpretation Number 535) *shall be protected within the scope of freedom of action*. Nevertheless, the freedom of movement is not an absolute right that cannot be appropriately restrained by laws or administrative regulations clearly authorized by laws, for instance if the restriction is necessary for preventing the obstruction of another person's freedom or for preserving social order. (Emphasis added.)[92]

The scope of the freedom of movement is therefore clear from reading J.Y. Interpretation No. 689, being the freedom to move to another place or stay in any place. Such freedom is protected and inferred by the general freedom of action under Article 22 of the Constitution. However, if freedom of movement is one's freedom to move around or to stay in a place, then it should be asked: what is the difference between the freedom of movement in Article 22 and the right to travel under Article 10 of the Constitution? Why would the Constitutional Court neglect

---

[88]Dafaguan Shizi Di 689 Hao [大法官釋字第 689 號] (J.Y. Interpretation No. 689) (29 Jul 2011) (R.O.C.), available at: http://www.judicial.gov.tw/constitutionalcourt/EN/p03_01.asp?expno=689. Accessed 15 Nov 2017.

[89]Holding of J.Y. Interpretation No. 689.

[90]*Id.*

[91]*Id.*

[92]Reasoning of J.Y. Interpretation No. 689, para 5.

the right to travel or freedom of migration and choose to infer freedom of movement from the general freedom of action?

Freedom of movement was further expounded upon in J.Y. Interpretation No. 699, dated 18 May 2012.[93] The Interpretation dealt with the constitutionality of the Road Traffic Management Penalties Regulation, requiring that the government to suspend a motor vehicle operator's driver's license, prohibiting such a driver from taking/receiving a driver's license for three years, and suspending all classes of vehicle licenses if the driver refuses to participate in a test of blood alcohol concentration or a sobriety test.[94] The Court found that the Regulation exists to "strengthen the ban on driving under the influence and to ensure traffic safety,"[95] and to "avert any loopholes when controlling driving under the influence and to effectively deter driving under the influence,"[96] and therefore the relevant provisions under the Regulation "do not contravene the principle of proportionality of Article 23 of the Constitution and do not violate the constitutional safeguards for people's freedom of movement and right to work."[97] Regarding the freedom of movement, the court indicated that:

> Under the premise of not offending the social order of the public interest, people shall have the freedom of movement to arbitrarily head to another location at any time or to remain at a certain premise, as is protected under Article 22 of the Constitution (with reference to J. Y. Interpretation Nos. 535 and 689). *This freedom of movement shall include the freedom of operating a motor vehicle or any other transportation vehicle.*[98] (Emphasis added.)

The Court expanded the freedom of movement to include an individual's freedom to operate a motor vehicle or any other transportation vehicle. The expansion, however, does not help in understanding the difference between the right to travel and the freedom of movement. It may be fairly concluded that the Constitutional Court to a certain extent relocated the right to travel and the freedom of migration under Article 10 of the Constitution to Article 22 of the Constitution. Freedom of movement seems also to be broader than the right to travel; whenever there is a restriction on an individual's freedom of action (e.g., stops and checks, stalking, or a mandatory test of alcohol concentration), freedom of movement may enter into the discussion.

---

[93]Dafaguan Shizi Di 699 Hao [大法官釋字第 699 號] (J.Y. Interpretation No. 699) (18 May 2012) (R.O.C.), available at: http://www.judicial.gov.tw/constitutionalcourt/EN/p03_01.asp?expno=699. Accessed 15 Nov 2017.

[94]Holding of J.Y. Interpretation No. 699.

[95]Reasoning of J.Y. Interpretation No. 699, para 4.

[96]*Id.*

[97]Holding of J.Y. Interpretation No. 699.

[98]Reasoning of J.Y. Interpretation No. 699, para 1.

4 Conclusion

Under Article 12 of the ICCPR, freedom of movement includes freedom of movement within a country, freedom to leave any country, and the right to enter one's own country.

The ICCPR has already been cited by the Constitutional Court in J.Y. Interpretation No. 710. The Taiwanese government further enshrined the ICCPR when it enacted the Act to Implement the International Covenant on Civil and Political Rights and the International Covenant on Economic, Social and Cultural Rights in 2009. It may be fairly concluded that the ICCPR is an explanatory tool for the Constitutional Court to interpret the Constitution and has binding effect in Taiwan.

Regarding the three distinct rights contained within the freedom of movement under the ICCPR and the freedom of migration under Article 10 of the Constitution, the following conclusions may be drawn:

1. The freedom of movement within a country, the freedom to leave any country, and the right to enter one's own country are all covered by Article 10 of the Constitution (Interpretations Nos. 443 and 558). Differing from the ICCPR and the UDHR, the Constitutional Court seems to recognize a foreigner's right to enter Taiwan (J.Y. Interpretation Nos. 265 and 454). However, such freedoms may be restricted with justifiable reason (J.Y. Interpretation No. 265).
2. The Constitutional Court will tolerate more in regard to restrictions on the freedom of migration of people from Mainland China, as evidenced by Article 11 of the Amendments to the Constitution (Interpretations Nos. 497 and 558).
3. The Court allows differential treatment regarding the right to enter one's own country based on whether an individual appears in the Taiwan household registry. This is not consistent with ICCPR Article 12 and General Comment No. 27 (J.Y. Interpretation No. 454), and the restrictions on those nationals who have a domicile and appear on the household registry in Taiwan require stricter scrutiny (J.Y. Interpretation No. 558). The necessity test under Article 23 may be applicable to the right to enter one's own country, which also differs from ICCPR Article 12.
4. Once a foreigner has legally entered Taiwan, his freedom of movement within the country and freedom to leave Taiwan should be protected by Article 10 of the Constitution, and due process of law must be followed (J.Y. Interpretation No. 710).
5. In regard to the freedom of movement within a country, in addition to the right to travel under Article 10 of the Constitution, the Constitutional Court has also inferred "freedom of movement" to be derived from Article 22 of the Constitution. However, the Court has not elaborated on the differences between these rights.

References

Chen M (2013), Xing Zheng Fa Zong Lun [行政法總論] (The General Administrative Law). New Sharing, Taipei

Chen X-M (2005) Xian Fa Xue Shi Lun [憲法學釋論] (Constitutional Law Commentary). San Min, Taipei

Fa J-P, Dung B-T (2006) Xian Fa Xin Lun [憲法新論] (Novel Commentary on Constitutional Law). Angle, Taipei

G.A. Res. 217 (III) A, Universal Declaration of Human Rights (10 Dec 1948). http://www.refworld.org/docid/3ae6b3712c.html. Accessed 10 Oct 2017

Hwang S (2004) Falu Baoliu Yuanze zai Deguo Fazhixu xia de Yihan yu Tezheng [法律保留原則在德國法秩序下的意涵與特徵] (The Principle of "Vorbehalt des Gesetzes" in the Context of the German Legal Tradition). Chung Yuan Financ Econ Law Rev 13:1–45

Legislative History of the National Security Act. Laws and Regulations Database of the ROC. http://law.moj.gov.tw/Eng/LawClass/LawHistory.aspx?PCode=A0030028vggb. Accessed 12 Nov 2017

Re-codified Chinese Dictionary by Ministry of Education. http://dict.revised.moe.edu.tw/cgi-bin/cbdic/gsweb.cgi?ccd=b57j_o&o=e0&sec=sec1&op=v&viev=5-1. Accessed 12 Nov 2017

UN Human Rights Committee, CCPR General Comment No. 27: Article 12 (freedom of movement), UN Doc. CCPR/C/21/Rev.1/Add.9 (2 Nov 1999). http://www.refworld.org/docid/45139c394.html. Accessed 9 Oct 2017

Wu G (2007) Xing Zheng Cheng Xu Fa Zhi Li Lun Yu Shi Yong [行政程序法之理論與實用] (The Practice and Theory of Administrative Law). San Min, Taipei

Wu X-H (2015) Xian Fa Shi Lun [憲法釋論] (The Constitution Commentary). San Min, Taipei

Jeffrey C. F. Li obtained his LL.M. degrees from Harvard in 2013 and National Taiwan University in 2010. He is now a senior associate in the litigation department of Lee and Li in Taiwan. His practice focuses on administrative and constitutional litigation, domestic and international commercial arbitration, and civil litigation. Jeffrey was a member of the attorneys group for the petition of the Judicial Yuan Constitutional Interpretations No. 737 and 740. He is also an adjunct lecturer at Soochow University Law School. Jeffrey constantly publishes papers and articles regarding comments and analyses on the constitutional interpretations.

Chapter 24
Configuration of the Notion of Privacy as a Fundamental Right in Taiwan—A Comparative Study of International Treaties and EU Rules

Chih-hsing Ho

Abstract The rapid development of information technology has introduced numerous innovative challenges into the arena of privacy protection. Under the influence of new communications technologies, such as the Internet and social media, the traditional notion of the right to privacy has experienced a paradigm shift from a *right to be let alone* to respect for individual autonomy with regard to the control of one's personal information. At the end of 2013, the United Nations General Assembly adopted Resolution 68/167 to address concerns over the potentially detrimental impacts of electronic surveillance on human rights and liberal society. In addition, the Resolution includes a statement affirming that the rights people hold offline shall also be protected online. Similarly, in the European Union, the modernization of Data Protection Convention 108, as well as the recently enacted General Data Protection Regulation (GDPR), signal the kind of essential steps that need to be taken to strengthen individuals' rights and autonomy with respect to data protection in the digital age. This chapter aims to locate the development of the rights to privacy and personal data protection in Taiwan within the broader context of international and comparative analysis. By examining the Constitutional Court's Interpretations and the rationale behind its reasoning, this chapter illustrates how the notion of privacy has been configured as a fundamental right in Taiwan, and explores the challenges arising from advances in information technology to the privacy protection given by Taiwan's legal and regulatory frameworks.

Keywords Data Protection Convention 108 · EU general data protection regulation (GDPR) · Information privacy · Mass surveillance · Right to privacy UN Resolution 68/167

C. Ho (✉)
Institute of European and American Studies, Academia Sinica, Taipei, Taiwan
e-mail: chihho@sinica.edu.tw

J. A. Cohen et al. (eds.), *Taiwan and International Human Rights*, Economics, Law, and Institutions in Asia Pacific, https://doi.org/10.1007/978-981-13-0350-0_24

1 Introduction

Rapid developments in information technologies, especially digital communications technologies, have increased the capacities of both public and private sectors to conduct data collection and electronic surveillance. In recent years, growing concerns about the threats posed by *Big Brother* have moved increasingly beyond areas of national jurisdiction. In 2013, Edward Snowden's revelations demonstrated how collaboration between the US National Security Agency (NSA), Northern Ireland, and the UK's General Communications Headquarters made unlimited mass digital surveillance and interception possible through the establishment of a transnational network of government agencies and private IT companies.[1]

Although we lack a concrete definition of the term, mass surveillance is normally understood as a form of widespread, systematic interference with the right to privacy.[2] It usually involves the systematic collection, interception or generation of data relating to unspecific and non-targeted individuals.[3] Such broad surveillance operations easily generate chilling effects on society when the scope of those with a reasonable expectation of being observed by the state is not limited to individuals subject to a legal warrant but extends to the general population. The growing, yet unaccountable, power of the state makes such surveillance activity worrisome, for unfettered by appropriate and precautionary public supervision the surveillance apparatus may evolve to give rise to serious privacy concerns. Thus, mass surveillance is both harmful to the fundamental rights of individuals and the foundations of liberal democracy, which include the freedom of expression and the free development of one's personality.

In fact, mass surveillance is far from a recent phenomenon. According to research carried out by civil rights groups—Privacy International and Amnesty International—national databases are one of the oldest forms of surveillance.[4] Historical surveillance techniques include censuses of administrative data used for registration purposes or in order to understand better the population of a kingdom, and denoting individuals' physical characteristics or otherwise categorizing people on the basis of race or features noted on identification documents. As these databases are usually rich in identifiable personal information, they are easily transformed into powerful investigative tools if adequate supervision is not in place. In order to better govern data collection, several principles have been developed in the international legal frameworks to guide the safeguarding of privacy and data protection. These principles include purpose limitation, proportionality, transparency, accountability, etc. Purpose limitation, for example, emphasizes that detailed administrative data collected on individuals should not be used for secondary purposes, such as criminal investigations without legal grounds or statutory

[1]Ball et al. (2013).

[2]Rule (2013), p. 4.

[3]*Id.*

[4]Two years after Snowden: Protecting human rights in an age of mass surveillance (2015).

obligations clearly prescribed in law. In addition, any identifying use of databases shall be limited to specific purposes and governed by mechanisms to safeguard against prejudicial outcomes such as discrimination or stigmatization.[5]

Mass surveillance techniques have developed rapidly alongside technological advances such that electronic surveillance, which focuses on intercepting and monitoring communications, is now easier to carry out, while mobile surveillance tools have been developed that make it possible for governments to identify devices within a specific geographic area, for instance at the site of political protests. These tools help governments retain the contents of communications and trace the electronic footprints of devices to particular individuals. Legally, the question has arisen as to how the right to privacy is to be protected and how the emergence of an unaccountable surveillance state can be avoided?

2 International Human Rights Frameworks

2.1 UN Resolution 68/167

Considering the detrimental impact of these surveillance operations on human rights, the General Assembly of the United Nations adopted Resolution 68/167 in December 2013, calling upon member states to respect the individual's right to privacy in the digital age.[6] The Resolution requires the Office of the High Commissioner for Human Rights (OHCHR) to submit a report to the UN Human Rights Council, as well as to the General Assembly, on its reflections and recommendations for the protection of privacy in the face of mass data collection and digital communications.[7] As UN Resolution 68/167 demonstrates, international human rights law provides fundamental legal frameworks for protecting the right to privacy. Article 12 of the Universal Declaration of Human Rights, for instance, states: "No one shall be subjected to arbitrary interference with his privacy, family, home or correspondence, nor to attacks upon his honour and reputation." Recognition of the role the right to privacy plays in providing shelter from unlawful interference is echoed in other international and regional legal provisions. These include the International Covenant on Civil and Political Rights (ICCPR, Art 17), the International Convention on the Protection of All Migrant Workers and

---

[5]For more information, see the introduction page for mass surveillance on the Privacy International website: What is mass surveillance? Privacy International. https://www.privacyinternational.org/node/52. Accessed 22 Oct 2017.

[6]UN Human Rights Council, *The Right to Privacy in the Digital Age—Report of the Office of the United Nations High Commissioner for Human Rights*, UN Doc A/HRC/27/37 (30 June 2014) [hereinafter UN Human Rights Council Report].

[7]*Id.*

Members of Their Families (Art 14), and the European Convention on Human Rights (ECHR, Art 8).[8]

Despite the widespread recognition of privacy as a fundamental right which underpins such core values as human dignity and the right to freedom of expression, challenges remain as the content of the right to privacy lacks explicit articulation. This ambiguity arises mainly from difficulties in interpreting what constitutes the private sphere and the so-called public interest when one tries to strike a balance between the two.[9] In the modern information age, the content of the right to privacy extends to one's ability to decide how much personal information he or she would like to share with others, and how such information may be used. The right to privacy, under these circumstances, is no longer a passive one which mainly focuses on avoiding interference with, or from, others. Instead, it emphasizes an affirmative decision from an individual with regards to one's control over his or her personal information.

UN Resolution 68/167 reemphasizes the right to privacy in the digital age and highlights the principles of legality, necessity and proportionality.[10] It aims to examine the exercise of state power to ensure that any limitations imposed on individual privacy be clear and precise in law.[11] In addition, the UN report points out that as big data enables new and innovative modes of data usage, focusing exclusively on controlling the collection and retention of personal data may no longer be sufficient to protect privacy. It argues that any capture, including the interception and collection of communications data, constitutes a potential point for privacy interference, and therefore some proportionate means of ensuring that only legitimate aims are pursued is required.[12] In responding to the growing electronic surveillance conducted by states for national security purposes, Resolution 68/167 argues that even though surveillance for the prevention of terrorism may constitute a legitimate aim, there remains a need to assess the necessity of the measure, and the degree of interference, to determine whether the proposed means to that end is proportional, and if preference is being shown for the least intrusive option.[13] According to the report, the *use limitations* requirement is essential in national legal frameworks. In addition, the state must ensure that any interference with the right to privacy is authorized by laws with sufficiently precise measures tailored to specific legitimate aims and that effective safeguards are in place.[14]

[8] *Id.*, at p. 6.

[9] Fraser (1990), pp. 56–80.

[10] GA Res 68/167, UN Doc A/RES/68/167 (21 Jan 2014), http://undocs.org/A/RES/68/167.

[11] UN Human Rights Council Report, *supra* note 6, at p. 8.

[12] *Id.*, at p. 6.

[13] *Id.*, at pp. 8–9.

[14] *Id.*, at p. 10.

2.2 *Data Protection Convention 108 and the GDPR*

In the European Union, the Council of Europe has also started the process of modernizing its Personal Data Protection Convention 108 in order to respond to new technological challenges.[15] Drafted in 1981, Convention 108, named the Convention for the Protection of Individuals with regard to Automatic Processing of Personal Data, remains the only legally binding international treaty in the field of data protection.[16] Originally, the Convention aimed to ensure that the processing of personal data was consistent with Article 8 of the European Convention of Human Rights, in particular by guaranteeing the right to respect one's private life, family life, home and correspondence.[17] However, as Convention 108 is open for signature to any country in the world, it has substantial potential for providing a universal standard of data protection rules beyond Europe.[18]

In consideration of growing threats to privacy posed by innovative uses of new information and communications technologies, a plan for the modernization of Data Protection Convention 108 was proposed in 2010. In the later phase of this modernization process in 2016, the goal was that a final consensus be reached and that the modernized Convention would be able to meet the new challenges of big data technologies while being consistent with the newly enacted EU General Data Protection Regulation (hereinafter GDPR). Based on Article 17 of the Statute of the Council of Europe, an ad hoc intergovernmental Committee on Data Protection (CAHDATA) was established to be responsible for public consultations and modernization works.[19] The drafted provisions of the Convention offer several principles according to which states may implement their individual data protection rules, such as a stronger consent requirement, a privacy by design approach, proportionality with regards to data processing and data minimization, as well as transparency and accountability (required for data controllers and processors).

In early 2017, the Convention's Consultative Committee (T-PD) published written guidelines responding to big data applications of the Signatory States,

[15]For more information on the modernization of Data Protection Convention 108, see the introduction on the Council of Europe's website: Modernisation of Convention 108 (CAHDATA). Council of Europe Portal. https://www.coe.int/en/web/data-protection/convention108/modernisation. Accessed 22 Oct 2017.

[16]Greenleaf (2013).

[17]Article 8 of the European Convention of Human Rights states that "1. Everyone has the right to respect for his private and family life, his home and his correspondence. 2. There shall be no interference by a public authority with the exercise of this right except such as is in accordance with the law and is necessary in a democratic society in the interests of national security, public safety or the economic well-being of the country, for the prevention of disorder or crime, for the protection of health or morals, or for the protection of the rights and freedoms of others." Convention for the Protection of Human Rights and Fundamental Freedoms, art. 8, 4 Nov 1950, E.S.T. 5.

[18]Greenleaf (2016).

[19]Greenleaf (2013), *supra* note 16.

requiring them to apply appropriate measures to effectively implement the Convention.[20] Addressing primarily the responsibilities of data controllers and processors,[21] the Guidelines highlight the protection of personal autonomy and the rights of individuals to control their personal data, including awareness of the use of data and real freedom of choice as to the context of big data usage. According to the Guidelines, data protection legal resolutions proposed by states need to take into account the asymmetrical nature of the information shared between data controllers and individual data subjects, and should be tailored to fit particular social and technological contexts.[22] The Guidelines also suggest that, given the nature of big data applications, it would be easier for the re-identification of data subjects. Data controllers are therefore required to carry out a more thorough impact assessment of risks in order to provide better protection of the individuals' control and use of data and to safeguard fundamental freedoms.

In addition to Data Protection Convention 108, the newly enacted GDPR plays another essential role in data protection in the EU. In 2012, the European Commission initiated its data protection reform to harmonize EU data protection rules for the digital age. The GDPR aims at facilitating data processing within the EU by forming a functional Digital Single Market while at the same time strengthening citizens' fundamental rights through the establishment of a harmonized legal framework for data protection.[23] The proposed GDPR provides several innovative provisions to bolster the rights of individuals, including the following rights: to inquire about information relating to personal data processing, to object to data being processed for direct marketing purposes, to portability, to erasure (right to be forgotten), and to notification in cases of a data breach. In addition, the proposed GDPR requires that Data Protection Officers (DPO) be established in circumstances in which sensitive data processing is being conducted, and permits class actions proposed by public interest privacy groups before the Data Protection Authorities (hereinafter DPA) or the courts. After more than four years of discussions, the proposed Data Protection Regulation was approved by the European Parliament's Civil Liberties Committee and the Council in April 2016. Unlike the

---

[20]Guidelines on the Protection of Individuals with regard to the Processing of Personal Data in a world of Big Data (2017). https://rm.coe.int/t-pd-2017-1-bigdataguidelines-en/16806f06d0. Accessed 23 Oct 2017 (published by the Consultative Committee of the Convention for the Protection of Individuals with regard to Automatic Processing of Personal Data).

[21]According to the definition provided in Section III of the Guidelines, data controller refers to the natural or legal person, public authority, service, agency or any other body which, alone or jointly with others, has the decision-making power with respect to data processing. Data Processor is a natural or legal person, public authority, service, agency or any other body which processes personal data on behalf of the controller. *Id.*, at p. 2.

[22]*Id.*, at p. 3.

[23]For more information on the EU General Data Protection Regulation (GDPR), see its official website for a detailed introduction: The European Union legislative process: The Ordinary Legislative Process as it relates to Privacy and Data Protection Legislation. The EU General Data Protection Regulation. http://www.eugdpr.org/the-process.html. Accessed 22 Oct 2017.

existing EU Data Protection Directive, which requires adoption and implementation by member states via national legislation, the GDPR applies directly to member states and took effect in May 2018.

3 The Right to Privacy in Taiwan

3.1 *The Constitutional Court's Interpretations*

In Taiwan, the right to privacy is not enumerated in the Constitution. Rather, it is conveyed through Constitutional Court interpretations on privacy as an indispensable fundamental right. Back in 2004, J.Y. Interpretation No. 585 illustrated the need to consider privacy as a fundamental right, and thus one that ought to be protected under the general clause of Article 22 of the Constitution, which guarantees a person's liberty and rights so long as they are not detrimental to social order or public welfare.[24] In J.Y. Interpretation No. 585, the Justices of the Constitutional Court emphasized the importance of recognizing the right to privacy in order to preserve human dignity and the completeness of personal development. The Interpretation demonstrates the Court's position on respecting autonomy, which it treats as a fundamental value for a liberal democracy.

In 2005, the Constitutional Court further elaborated on the notion of information privacy. Focusing on informational rather than the physical or spatial dimensions of privacy, J.Y. Interpretation No. 603 consolidates the notion of information privacy by affirming one's autonomous control over his or her personal information. The Interpretation is intended to guarantee that people are entitled to decide whether or not to disclose their personal information, and if so, to whom and to what extent, in what manner, as well as how much information they would like to disclose. Respect for the free development of personality, in the view of the Court, is an essential value of the constitutional structures of liberal democracies. In other words, recognizing the right to privacy, especially information privacy, means that the surveillance power of the state will have to be limited to avoid the dangers posed by a surveillance state. Jeremy Bentham introduced his innovative "Panopticon" as a means of encouraging prisoners to discipline themselves even though they did not know when, exactly, they were being observed.[25] Today, the mass collection of personal data for unspecific purposes by governments poses a similar threat, not to prisoners but to the general population; this constitutes the main context of J.Y. Interpretation No. 603.

In J.Y. Interpretation 603, the issue is the constitutionality of the relevant provisions of Article 8-II and 8-III of the Household Registration Act (1997) which

---

[24]Article 22 of the ROC Constitution states that all other freedoms and rights of the people that are not detrimental to social order or public welfare shall be guaranteed under the Constitution.

[25]Bentham (1791); see also Chesterman (2010), p. 34.

stipulate that every applicant over the age of fourteen shall be fingerprinted for record keeping when applying for a new R.O.C. identity card.[26] As Article 8-III provides that fingerprinting an applicant is a necessary condition for the issuance of an identity card pursuant to Article 8-II, it makes fingerprinting compulsory. However, the Constitutional Court has found that the provisions of the Household Registration Act fail to specify any particular major purpose for keeping fingerprint records. The administrative purposes listed by the Ministry of the Interior for use of an identity card, such as anti-counterfeiting activities and the prevention of false claims, or the verification of the identity of unconscious persons on the roadside or unidentified corpses, nonetheless, in the view of the Constitutional Court, have not yet reached the threshold of being major public interests. Furthermore, even if mandatory fingerprinting satisfies the purposes as claimed, it fails the principle of proportionality, "using excessively unnecessary means" and failing "to achieve the balance of losses and gains."[27]

3.2 *The Rationale Behind J.Y. Interpretation No. 603*

Along with the rapid development of biometric technologies, the collection and storage of physiological and behavioral characteristics of individuals have become easier than ever before. These physiological characteristics may include biometric data, such as DNA profiles and fingerprints, which are unique means of personal identification. For this reason, the collection of biometric data increases the potential for turning biometric technologies into tools of mass surveillance if proper safeguards or legal mechanisms are not in place when these technologies are applied. J.Y. Interpretation 603 recognizes that fingerprints are part of an individual's abstract personality and a form of personal data that requires protection.[28] It also points out that the disclosure and provision of such information must be determined at the discretion of that person, and that the inviolability of such decisions should be guaranteed by the Constitution under the right to privacy and the right to autonomous control of personal information. According to the Court,

[26]Article 8-II stipulates that: "While applying for an ROC identity card pursuant to the preceding paragraph, the applicant shall be fingerprinted for record keeping; provided that no national who is under fourteen years of age will be fingerprinted until he or she reaches fourteen years of age, at which time he or she shall then be fingerprinted for record keeping." Article 8-III stipulates that: "No ROC identity card will be issued unless the applicant is fingerprinted pursuant to the preceding paragraph."

[27]Dafaguan Shizi Di 603 Hao [大法官釋字第 603 號] (J.Y. Interpretation No. 603) (28 Sept 2005) [hereinafter Interpretation No. 603].

[28]Interpretation No. 603 states that: "Fingerprints are biological features of an individual's person, which are characterized by personal uniqueness and lifetime unchangeability. As such, they will become a form of personal information that is highly capable of performing the function of identity verification once they are connected with one's identity."

compulsorily taking fingerprints to establish databases not only trespasses on individuals' privacy and thus infringes on their rights, but also imposes unnecessary restrictions on the rights of individuals to control their personal information.

3.2.1 The Principle of Proportionality

In analyzing the legislative purposes behind the requirement for taking fingerprints stated in Article 8-II of the Household Registration Act, the Court argues that the Act fails to specify substantially important purposes for the compulsory fingerprinting of all nationals over the age of fourteen. The claimed purposes, particularly identification verification, although legitimate are overly generalized and broad, and are not the least intrusive means available to achieve such purposes, and therefore violate the principle of proportionality. The Constitutional Court adopted the principle of proportionality as its standard in reviewing the case. J.Y. Interpretation No. 603 shows that in order to pass such a standard of judicial review, the Household Registration Act not only needs to fulfill major public interests, but also must be narrowly tailored to the means it employs to achieve such purposes.

According to the Interpretation, for the state to engage in the mass collection of personal information and to establish databases, for instance to store people's fingerprints, it requires *specific purposes* enacted by law and assurances that such collection, storage and use of the data are *necessary and relevant* to the achievement of the claimed statutory purposes. In addition, the Court requires that the competent authority engage in the collection in a manner that is sufficient to ensure the accuracy and safety of the information, and that the authority take necessary protective measures, both procedurally and organizationally, to protect the individual's right to information privacy.

3.2.2 The Principle of Legal Reservation and Purpose Limitation

Compulsory fingerprinting and the establishment of databases for record keeping, according to the Interpretation, is an exercise in governmental power substantially affecting people's constitutional rights, and therefore should be clearly prescribed by law to satisfy the principle of legal reservation.[29] Without a clear statutory obligation, the provisions of Article 8 of the Household Registration Act, which enable an administrative agency to collect fingerprints, are in violation of the due process of law requirement. The Court argues that as there is insufficient linkage between taking fingerprints and the issuance of an ROC identity card, the refusal to issue an identity card on the basis of an individual refusing to submit to fingerprinting violates the principle against an irrational basis. To achieve the purposes

[29]Interpretation No. 603, *supra* note 27.

for which fingerprints are taken, there are less intrusive means available that would cause less inconvenience and inflict less damage on those affected.

It is worth noting that even though the Court considers privacy a fundamental right, it recognizes that the Constitution does not make the right absolute. As a result, the state may impose appropriate restrictions on the right to privacy by enacting clear and unambiguous laws, if necessary, given a compelling public interest and if consistent with the principle of proportionality as stipulated by Article 23 of the Constitution.[30]

4 The Right to Information Privacy

J.Y. Interpretation No. 603 provides crucial legal grounds for the recognition of the right to information privacy in Taiwan. According to the Constitutional Court, the essence of the right to information privacy refers to individual autonomy and control over personal information. This Interpretation is intended to guarantee that individuals have the right to decide whether or not to disclose their information (and if so, to what extent, at what time, in what manner, and to whom), and also that people have the right to control how their information is used. The latter includes the right to know as well as the right to correct inaccurate entries with regards to their recorded personal information. Moreover, as the right to information privacy is fundamental, yet not absolute in the view of the Court, one should take into consideration the public interests to be served by the collection of data and the possible infringement upon the individual, when evaluating whether the trade-off between the two is proportionate.

4.1 The Standard of Scrutiny

In setting a standard of scrutiny regarding the right to information privacy, the Court has suggested that different standards should apply in different cases. In practice, the application of a standard requires evaluating the situation by looking into whether the personal information to be collected is of a sensitive or confidential nature, or whether the information may make it easier to profile a particular individual in combination with other information, even if such information is not, itself, sensitive or confidential. In the context of big data, identification of individuals is easier than anticipated when aggregating information from different databases even when anonymized. As a result, a proper appreciation of the potential risks of data

[30]Article 23 of the Constitution (1947) stipulates that "all the freedoms and rights enumerated in the preceding Articles shall not be restricted by law except by such as may be necessary to prevent infringement upon the freedoms of other persons, to avert an imminent crisis, to maintain social order or to advance public welfare."

collection requires a more comprehensive assessment and evaluation. In J.Y. Interpretation No. 603, as the data that were to be collected were fingerprints, the Court required that the mass collection should be conducted through "less intrusive means substantially related to the achievement of a compelling public interest," which also ought to be clearly prescribed by law.

4.2 Purpose of Limitation and Precautionary Measures

The purpose of limitation is essential in data protection. According to the Interpretation, the state shall ensure that any information legitimately collected by the state is used only for the specified purposes, which shall be clearly prescribed by law. Any use outside of the original collection purposes requires the consent of the subjects from whom the data were collected, or must satisfy the statutory obligation in order to ensure that the secondary use of the data is legitimate. The rationale behind this purpose of limitation is to respect the autonomy of individuals and their control over their own personal information, allowing subjects of data collection to learn in advance the reasons for the collection of their information, how it will be collected, stored, and used.

Moreover, in the Interpretation, the Court points out that the Ministry of the Interior's claim that the purpose of fingerprint collection—crime prevention—should not be covered by the statutory purposes of the Household Registration Act. The Court finds that the separation of the two systems—household administration and police administration—has been assured since the end of martial law, as stated in J.Y. Interpretation No. 575. In addition to the requirement of purpose limitation, adequate precautionary measures, such as space for data storage and a secured IT environment, must both necessarily be taken into account when assessing whether the collection and storage of personal data are justified.

4.3 The Personal Data Protection Act

While closely linked, as Bygrave argues, the notions of "privacy" and "data protection" are not completely identical.[31] In the European context, data protection has been increasingly treated as a set of norms and rights that focus mainly on the informational rather than the physical or spatial dimensions of privacy, and therefore can be separated from the traditional right to respect for privacy or private life.[32] In Taiwan, the Personal Data Protection Act (hereinafter PDPA) was enacted in 2010 to replace and enhance the protections offered at the time under the

[31]Bygrave (2014), p. 3.

[32]*Id.*, at pp. 3–8.

Computer-processed Personal Data Protection Act (CPPDPA). The PDPA aims to regulate the collection, processing and use of personal data. The PDPA implements several data protection principles adopted by the EU's Data Protection Directive (95/46/EC). These include the principles of minimum collection, fair and lawful process, sensitive data protection, and direct marketing opt-out.[33] In addition, in order to protect the autonomy of individuals, the PDPA gives assurances regarding several of the rights of data subjects that comprise the right of access (such as the right to review, copy, supplement or correct data subjects' personal data), the right to object to processing, and the right to request the deletion of their personal data.

According to the PDPA, data subjects can request that data controllers cease collecting, processing and using their personal data. If their personal data have been used for marketing purposes by a private sector data processor, data subjects can also object to the use of their personal data for such purposes. Even though the PDPA aims to enhance the protection of individual autonomy by following the EU data protection framework, there is a lack of a single and independent DPA for the enforcement of privacy and data protection rules in Taiwan. Instead, both central government and local government agencies share responsibility for implementation of the PDPA for those industries and sectors that they regulate. Without a national regulator for overall data protection enforcement, it remains to be seen how successfully the PDPA will function in safeguarding information privacy.

5 Conclusion

In order to make the most of big data applications, many states have begun to establish computerized local or national databases to store and retrieve citizens' data for secondary uses. This mass collection of personal data and the recent advances in algorithms have put individuals in a more vulnerable position with respect to growing electronic surveillance and intrusive data mining. Although mass surveillance is far from a new phenomenon, the rapid development of information and communications technologies has transformed such databases into a threat to privacy and liberal democracy. In Taiwan, the right to privacy has been configured as one of the fundamental rights via the Constitutional Court interpretations. Viewing privacy as an essential value of the constitutional structures of liberal democracies, the Court adopted strict scrutiny in its review and constructed the notion of information privacy in J.Y. Interpretation No. 603. As a guardian of human rights, the Constitutional Court's Interpretation reflects the Court's efforts to limit the growing potential power of state surveillance, echoing recent developments in international legal frameworks on privacy and data protection. In addition, both the EU Data Protection Convention 108 and Taiwan's PDPA stress the

[33]Directive 95/46, 1995 OJ (L 281) 31 (EC), http://ec.europa.eu/justice/policies/privacy/docs/95-46-ce/dir1995-46_part1_en.pdf. Accessed 23 Oct 2017.

protection of personal autonomy and the right of individuals to control their personal data. However, the right to control personal data should also include a right to be informed of the use of the data, and real freedom of choice in the context of big data applications. Taking account of the asymmetrical information relationship between data controllers and individual data subjects, how to design an appropriate legal framework to enhance transparency and accountability remains a challenge for Taiwan in the implementation of its information privacy and data protection rules.

References

Ball J, Borger J, Greenwald G (2013) Revealed: how US and UK spy agencies defeat internet privacy and security. https://www.theguardian.com/world/2013/sep/05/nsa-gchq-encryption-codes-security. Accessed 23 Oct 2017

Bentham J (1791) Panopticon or the inspection house. T. Payne, London

Bygrave LA (2014) Data privacy law: an international perspective. Oxford University Press, Oxford

Chesterman S (2010) Privacy and surveillance in the age of terror. Survival 52(5):31–46

Directive 95/46, 1995 OJ (L 281) 31 (EC). http://ec.europa.eu/justice/policies/privacy/docs/95-46-ce/dir1995-46_part1_en.pdf. Accessed 23 Oct 2017

Fraser N (1990) Rethinking the public sphere: a contribution to the critique of actually existing democracy. Soc Text 25(26):56–80

GA Res 68/167, UN Doc A/RES/68/167 (21 Jan 2014). http://undocs.org/A/RES/68/167

Greenleaf G (2013) "Modernising" data protection convention 108: a safe basis for a global privacy treaty? Comput Law Secur Rev 29(4):430–436

Greenleaf G (2016) Renewing Data Protection Convention 108: the COE's "GDPR lite" initiatives. Priv Laws Bus Int Rep 142:14–17

Guidelines on the protection of individuals with regard to the processing of personal data in a world of Big Data (2017). https://rm.coe.int/t-pd-2017-1-bigdataguidelines-en/16806f06d0. Accessed 23 Oct 2017

Modernisation of Convention 108 (CAHDATA). Council of Europe Portal. https://www.coe.int/en/web/data-protection/convention108/modernisation. Accessed 22 Oct 2017

Rule J (2013) The limits of privacy protection. In: Goold BJ, Neyland D (eds) New directions in surveillance privacy. Routledge, Abingdon, pp 3–17

The European Union legislative process: the ordinary legislative process as it relates to privacy and data protection legislation. The EU General Data Protection Regulation. http://www.eugdpr.org/the-process.html. Accessed 22 Oct 2017

Two years after Snowden: protecting human rights in an age of mass surveillance (2015). https://www.amnestyusa.org/wp-content/uploads/2017/04/ai-pi_two_years_on_from_snowden_final_final_clean.pdf. Accessed 23 Oct 2017

UN Human Rights Council, The right to privacy in the digital age—report of the Office of the United Nations High Commissioner for Human Rights, UN Doc A/HRC/27/37 (30 June 2014)

What is mass surveillance? Privacy international. https://www.privacyinternational.org/node/52. Accessed 22 Oct 2017

Chih-hsing Ho is Assistant Research Fellow at the Institute of European and American Studies (IEAS) at the Academia Sinica, Taiwan. She holds a Ph.D. in law from the London School of Economics (LSE), where she was an Olive Stone Scholar. She obtained her first law degree in Taiwan, and later received her LL.M. from Columbia Law School and her J.S.M. from Stanford University. Her research focuses on issues of privacy, data protection and the nexus of law and medicine in general, with particular attention to the governance of newly emerging information technologies and biotechnologies, such as big data and biobanks. She is currently a Co-principal Investigator for a health cloud project in Taiwan and is responsible for designing an adequate regulatory framework for the secondary use of personal data and health-related data linkages. Before returning to Taipei in 2014, she worked at the Centre for Medical Ethics and Law (CMEL) at the University of Hong Kong.

Chapter 25
Who Shall Judge? Taiwan's Exploration of Lay Participation in Criminal Trials

Margaret K. Lewis

Abstract International human rights law does not demand lay participation in criminal trials. The International Covenant on Civil and Political Rights provides that "everyone shall be entitled to a fair and public hearing by a competent, independent and impartial tribunal established by law" but it does not dictate the composition of the tribunal. In recent years, Taiwan has tussled with the extent to which public access to observing trials should be transformed into direct public participation in the outcome of those trials. To date, however, the role that lay people will serve in the adjudication process remains contested. As Taiwan moves towards formulating a specific plan for lay participation, this chapter questions whether proponents of lay participation are expecting too much of the proposed reforms and encourages greater focus on how lay participation might impact the rights of the accused.

Keywords Criminal procedure · ICCPR · Jury · Lay participation
Trial

1 Introduction

Guilty or not guilty: in every criminal trial, someone needs to decide. International human rights law does not dictate who this someone must be. The International Covenant on Civil and Political Rights (hereinafter ICCPR) provides that "everyone shall be entitled to a fair and public hearing by a competent, independent and impartial tribunal established by law" (Article 14.1), but it does not specify the composition of that tribunal.[1]

[1]UN Human Rights Comm., General Comment No. 32, Article 14: right to equality before courts and tribunals and to a fair trial, para 18, UN Doc. CCPR/C/GC/32 (23 Aug 2007).

M. K. Lewis (✉)
Seton Hall University, School of Law, Newark, NJ, USA
e-mail: Margaret.Lewis@shu.edu

J. A. Cohen et al. (eds.), *Taiwan and International Human Rights*, Economics, Law, and Institutions in Asia Pacific, https://doi.org/10.1007/978-981-13-0350-0_25

Taiwan has for years tussled with the extent to which public access to observing trials should be transformed into direct public participation in the outcome of those trials. To date, however, the role that lay people will serve in the adjudication process remains hotly contested. Is a consultative body of lay people who lack a vote in the verdict a proverbial "half a loaf" that is better than none (聊勝於無)? Alternatively, should Taiwan choose to maintain the current use of solely professional judges shift dramatically to an American-style jury, or fall somewhere in between with a German-style mixed bench? This chapter takes stock of the ongoing debate and encourages focusing greater attention on how the proposed reforms may support, or undermine, Taiwan's energetic commitment to international human rights.

The story of legal reforms in Taiwan has been interwoven with a deepening commitment to human rights. Taiwan's Constitutional Court, for example, has served a crucial role in giving heft to rights in the Republic of China (hereinafter ROC) Constitution.[2] The other branches of government have likewise vocally supported human rights norms since the lifting of martial law. In 2009, then President Ma Ying-jeou signed the ratification instruments of the ICCPR and the International Covenant on Economic, Social and Cultural Rights.[3] Taiwan could not actually deposit those instruments due to its unusual international status, but the Legislative Yuan incorporated the contents of the covenants into domestic law. How criminal suspects are treated is a critical test of a government's commitment to the ICCPR, and Taiwan is at a moment when it is directly confronting that test.

Section 2 of this chapter briefly explains efforts to introduce lay participation in criminal trials. It ends with the uncertainty of the reform efforts at the time of the writing of this chapter. Section 3 looks to the future and first questions whether proponents of lay participation are expecting too much from the proposed reforms. Deep doubts remain whether lay participation at trials will bring about the widespread, positive change in public opinion that the judiciary seeks. In need of a more concrete explanation is the web of complementary criminal procedure reforms that are necessary to support a successful shift towards lay participation. In closing, this chapter encourages greater focus on the interplay between lay participation and the rights of the accused.

2 Efforts to Introduce Lay Participation in Criminal Trials

Whatever criticism might be levied against efforts to introduce lay participation in criminal trials, the ROC government, having contemplated reforms for several decades, has certainly not made any rash decisions. The protracted debate exemplifies the openness with which Taiwanese officials and scholars look abroad for

[2] Lewis (2015).

[3] Chen (2016).

inspiration. Years of rumination have not only failed to yield a consensus but perhaps have even left more pronounced lines between factions than originally existed. Nor has the debate crystallized what exactly is the problem that lay participation is meant to fix, let alone whether lay participation is the right prescription for the perceived ill. For instance, one Taiwanese criminal procedure scholar has questioned whether the government's stated aim of "'responding to the expectations of the people' [is] an appropriate goal of Taiwan's court reform" because it is "neither clear nor directive."[4]

The "expectations of the people" were of little judicial concern for much of Taiwan's history. Authoritarian-era courts were instruments to control the people rather than to support human rights.[5] The current debate has its roots in the wave of criminal justice reforms following the end of martial law in 1987. Initial reforms that shifted power away from the military and toward civilian authorities were followed by a deep rethinking of how to structure criminal procedure in a newly democratic Taiwan. One aspect of these changes was to welcome people into courtrooms by largely ending the closed-door hearings,[6] but lay people were not given any direct role in deciding outcomes at trial.

The first post-martial-law push for citizen participation in the form of a mixed bench combining professional and lay judges lost momentum by 1994 when the Executive Yuan declined to endorse it.[7] This initial proposal for incorporating non-professionals into the judging process was not totally without precedent; at the end of the 1920s, when the ROC government was still based on the Mainland, certain charges related to instigating revolution included lay judges.[8] Such carefully controlled, politically motivated trials were a far cry from a system that is meant to shift power away from the professional judiciary to the broader citizenry.

Since democratization, debates about lay participation have been but one piece of a multifaceted discussion of legal reforms. No country's criminal justice system fits entirely the stylized "adversarial" or "inquisitorial" model but Taiwan's system is a particularly pronounced hybrid of features from disparate legal traditions. The pivotal 1999 Judicial Reform Conference ushered in a "modified adversarial system" (改良式當事人進行主義).[9] This innovation was an uncomfortable fit for Taiwan's existing system that was largely modeled on a Continental-style inquisitorial model. One goal was to elevate the roles of prosecutors and defense attorneys at trial and, concomitantly, lessen reliance on judge-led questioning of witnesses. Nonetheless, judges retained a role in directly investigating evidence in

[4]Su (2017), p. 237.

[5]Wang (2002), p. 554.

[6]Republic of China (2012). Providing exception for open hearings in limited situations such as cases involving national safety or juveniles.

[7]Judicial Yuan (2016).

[8]See generally Chin (forthcoming).

[9]Gailiangshi Dangshiren Jinxing Zhuyi [改良式當事人進行主義] (Modified Adversarial System). http://www.judicial.gov.tw/work/work02/work02-01.asp. Accessed 5 Oct 2017.

court.[10] Reforms on paper also did not fit how judges and prosecutors had long viewed their joint role as "judicial officers" (司法官). Nor did it change the education system in which new civil servants become judges and prosecutors only after lengthy combined training by the Ministry of Justice, which cultivates a sense of a shared role of prosecutors and judges rather than placing prosecutors on par with defense lawyers in the courtroom.

The reform momentum following the 1999 Judicial Reform Conference inspired a renewed push to infuse people's voices into the judging process, this time with a proposal to introduce non-judge legal experts. Like the reform debates that preceded and followed this wave, the conversation was limited to using non-professional judges in certain types, usually the most serious, criminal cases. Discussions regarding the possible incorporation of legal experts, who were not career judges, quieted by 2006 when the Executive Yuan again declined to endorse reforms.[11]

By the mid-2000s, reform discussions had shifted away from using non-judge legal experts towards exploring a mixed-bench system, as has long been seen in Germany and more recently in Japan. This system empowers both professional judges and lay people to vote on the verdict (often referred to as the "trial participation system" or 參審制), thus taking a less extreme approach than an American-style jury (陪審制) where the decisional reins are handed from judge to jury. Critics of the mixed-bench approach raised concerns whether lay people would too readily defer to professional judges rather than express their own opinions,[12] as well as whether it is even constitutional to have non-professional judges in criminal cases.[13]

Other reformers sought a middle ground between handing lay people a vote in the outcome and retaining the current system. This compromise position would avoid constitutional concerns, provide a voice for citizenry in serious criminal cases and yet leave final decision-making power in the hands of professional judges. This option, literally named a "trial observation system" (觀審制), was touted as an elegant win-win solution by some but roundly criticized by others as creating the mere appearance of reform without any real heft. Under this lay observer system, people would be limited to expressing to the judges opinions that the judges could ultimately reject.

The past decade has witnessed a protracted and spirited debate regarding the merits, and pitfalls, of the three main proposals for citizen participation: lay observer (two-rounds of voting—first by lay participants and then by judges who maintain final decision-making power), lay judge (joint voting of lay participants with judges in a mixed-bench format), and jury (only lay participants voting on whether to convict). Supporters of these various positions agree insomuch that they all recognize a lack of public confidence in the judicial system. Scholars at

[10]Lewis (2009).

[11]Judicial Yuan (2016), *supra* note 7.

[12]Wu et al. (2017).

[13]Lou (2014), pp. 120–121.

Academia Sinica have noted, "It is clear that the most important driving force for Taiwan's Judicial Yuan to adopt lay participation is to promote citizens' trust in the judicial system rather than to democratize its judicial decision making."[14] One Taiwanese criminal procedure scholar describes Taiwan's judiciary as facing a "serious crisis of confidence."[15] The judiciary's response has been an emphasis on transparency, with lay participation seen as a crucial component:

> The key step of the Judicial Yuan's judicial reform policy is to allow the people to participate in the core of judicial power, i.e., trial procedure, and increase the transparency of court activities through lay participation. This would provide an opportunity for the people to participate in the decision-making process, and thus understand the judiciary, trust the judiciary.[16]

Greater contact between judges and non-judges is hence seen as a means towards the end of increasing public confidence. High-profile incidents like the bribery conviction in 2011 of several judges,[17] and perceived lenient sentencing of a convicted pedophile,[18] undercut already shaky public support. A public survey conducted by the Judicial Yuan in 2015 found that 71.6% of respondents reported not understanding the legal system (12.5% answered "totally unfamiliar" and 59.1% answered "unfamiliar").[19] Only 22% agreed with the statement that "most judges can decide cases independently" and 38.5% agreed that "judges will usually try to impose appropriate sentences."[20] A majority of respondents cited the media as the source of their negative perceptions, as compared with negative personal experiences or those of a friend/relative. The Judicial Yuan is pushing to reduce the "gap" (距離) between people and the courts in hopes of directly shaping people's views of the judiciary. To this end, the Judicial Yuan created a website devoted to explaining proposed lay participation at trial.[21]

From 2012 to 2016, the Judicial Yuan held moot courts in various district courts in the hopes of forming a sounder basis for recommending which type of system Taiwan should pursue. All three models—lay observer, lay judge, and jury—were tested. The Judicial Yuan concluded that people who participated in moot courts showed greater support for the judiciary than those who had not participated. Participation in the selection process alone had a positive effect, even if not chosen

[14]Huang and Lin (2013), p. 547.

[15]Su (2017), *supra* note 4, p. 239.

[16]Judicial Yuan (2016), *supra* note 7, at slide 9.

[17]*Corrupt judges handed lengthy prison sentences*. Taipei Times. http://www.taipeitimes.com/News/taiwan/archives/2011/07/01/2003507146. Accessed 5 Oct 2017.

[18]*Judges incur fury over pedophile sentencing*. The China Post. http://www.chinapost.com.tw/taiwan/national/national-news/2010/08/26/270104/Judges-incur.htm. Accessed 5 Oct 2017.

[19]Judicial Yuan (2016), *supra* note 7.

[20]*Id.*

[21]Guomin Canyu Xingshi Shenpan Wangzhan [國民參與刑事審判網站] (Website for Citizen Participation in Criminal Trials). http://www.judicial.gov.tw/LayParticipation/intro08.asp. Accessed 5 Oct 2017.

for participation at trial: "[T]he more involved, the more understanding, thus, the more trust."[22]

What remains murky is the extent to which proponents of lay participation think the judiciary is currently doing a good job and the problem that lay participation is aimed at correcting is erroneous public perception. In other words, if people could have first-hand experience with the criminal trial process (other than participation as a defendant), they would realize that judges are actually fair and just. Alternatively, reforms could be motivated by the view that lay participation will improve the system by aligning verdicts more closely with the public's sense of justice and/or making the outcomes more factually accurate. Based on this view, the current system of judging in criminal cases is problematic and lay participation will improve not only the perception of the judiciary but the actual quality of the judging itself. Reforms may also be motivated by some combination thereof: the public both (1) has an inaccurate negative perception of the judiciary that can be improved by closer contact, and (2) lay participation will also change court decisions for the better, such as by adding the new perspective of immediate citizen oversight when scrutinizing evidence.

Further fueling reform efforts is the increasing global prevalence of including non-professional judges in criminal trials. The Judicial Yuan has cited this "world trend" towards lay participation.[23] Scholars at Academia Sinica have posited that, of the "wave of jury resurgence for the past two decades around the world, the Asian countries' embrace of lay participation in the adjudicatory process is the most significant both in terms of latitude and magnitude."[24] In 2008, South Korea introduced an advisory jury system that, like Taiwan's contemplated lay observer system, allows lay participants to express opinions but not to have a binding vote on the outcome.[25] In 2009, Japan began using a mixed-bench system for serious criminal cases in which six lay judges—called "saiban-in" (裁判員)—join three professional judges, with each of the nine having an equal vote.[26]

Tempering enthusiasm for increasing lay participation is an awareness that adding greater complexity to trial processes will likely increase costs and further strain an already burdened court system. There are aspects of lay participation that may alleviate some judicial tasks. Over thirty years ago, John H. Langbein praised how "German mixed [lay and professional judge] courts discharge their caseloads with enviable dispatch."[27] In particular, a shift to a jury system with a simple guilty/not-guilty verdict relieves the presiding judge from writing a detailed opinion, as is currently required. Supporters in Taiwan of a more radical shift to an American-style jury system have cited the potential cost savings of simple guilty/

[22]Judicial Yuan (2016), *supra* note 7, at slide 41.

[23]*Id.*

[24]Huang and Lin (2014), *supra* note 14.

[25]Kwon (2016); Kim (2015); Lee (2010).

[26]Plogstedt (2013); Fukarai (2013); Fukurai (2007).

[27]Langbein (1981).

not-guilty verdicts.[28] Both the proposed lay observer and lay judge models, however, would retain detailed written opinions. Moreover, the time for deliberations is expected to increase if lay participation means additional layers of discussions among the "citizen judges" (國民法官), followed by joint discussions with the professional judges. And any system involving non-judges will require time and resources for selecting lay participants. All told, lay participation is projected to require greater expenditures per trial than the current system.

President Tsai Ing-wen entered office against this backdrop of widespread calls for changes to the judging process and widespread disagreement regarding what those changes should be.[29] In her May 2016 inaugural remarks, President Tsai highlighted "social fairness and justice" ("社會的公平與正義") as a key area for her administration to address and asserted that people feel the current judicial system is unable to fight crime effectively.[30] She further announced the creation of a National Affairs Conference on Judicial Reform (司法改革國是會議).[31] The sprawling Conference included over one hundred participants composed of an eclectic mix of representatives from government, academia, legal practice, and civil society. Public participation at trial was a central, albeit far from the sole, focus of the Conference. A companion issue was a potentially greater role for the public in prosecutorial decisions not to bring charges. The extensive agenda also included whether to bring cameras into the courtroom to broadcast proceedings.

The Fourth Sub-Committee was charged with examining lay participation and transparency so as to eliminate the gap between the judicial system and the people (消弭司法體系與人民之間的距離).[32] The group met six times between February and May 2017 and was composed of a diverse mix of twenty members. In keeping with the theme of increasing transparency, the proceedings of all sub-committees were recorded and made accessible online, including written documents and video feeds. Links encouraged the public to leave comments and share the information on a variety of social media platforms.

The Fourth Sub-Committee ultimately failed to reach a consensus on the recommended direction for the reforms, nor did the overall Conference adopt a specific proposal at its closing meeting. The concluding document summarizing the results on the main issues (大項重點議題) begins with "promoting people's participation in the judicial system" ("推動人民參與司法制度").[33] It notes that lay participation is a priority judicial reform and that although the Judicial Yuan should consider Taiwan's specific circumstances, it should also look to the experience of various

[28]Wu et al. (2017) *supra* note 12.

[29]Pan (2017), Sun (2016b).

[30]Tsai (2016).

[31]*President Tsai launches judicial reform in Taiwan*. Taiwan Today. http://taiwantoday.tw/news.php?unit=2,6,10,15,18&post=3923. Accessed 5 Oct 2017.

[32]Disi Fenzu: Canyu Touming Qinjin De Sifa [第四分組:參與透明親近的司法] (Fourth Sub-Committee: Participatory, Transparent, and Close Justice). https://justice.president.gov.tw/meetinggroup/4. Accessed 5 Oct 2017.

[33]Judicial Reform Conference (2017).

countries in formulating the reforms. The issue was once again sent back to the Judicial Yuan for further study and formulation of a proposal to the Legislative Yuan.

3 The Promise and Perils of Lay Participation in Criminal Trials

At the time of this writing, the prospects for either a lay observer (non-binding vote) or jury (binding lay-participants-only vote) appear slim. A mixed-bench system in which lay participants and judges share voting power appears most likely, though the reform debate is far from over and may ultimately result in retention of a solely-professional-judge system. Sun Chen-hua, a lawyer who previously served as a judge and prosecutor, has cautioned, "But in a bid to improve public trust, the government needs to ask itself whether it is necessary to introduce an entirely new system, or should it focus on making major amendments to the current one?"[34]

As the Judicial Yuan formulates a concrete proposal for transmission to the Legislative Yuan, this chapter raises three cautions: (1) Avoid overpromising the benefits of the proposed reforms: it remains uncertain to what extent, if at all, proximity will promote greater affinity among the populace for the courts. (2) Pull back the perspective to encompass the entire reform ecosystem; a number of accompanying changes to the courts have been raised during the debate over lay participation. As the Judicial Yuan formulates a detailed proposal, the web of interrelated reforms needs to come into sharper relief. (3) Refocus the debate on how the proposed reforms might impact the rights of the accused. The ROC Criminal Procedure Code, the ROC Constitution, and international human rights law as incorporated into domestic law all contain robust protections for the defendants. A more searching discussion is overdue on how the various forms of lay participation might undermine, or perhaps conversely shore up, these rights.

3.1 Maintain a Skeptical View of Lay Participation's Influence in Shifting Public Perceptions

Reform advocates should avoid overselling the ability of lay participation to improve the courts' image. Initial indications are that Taiwanese citizens who engaged with the Judicial Yuan's moot courts came away with an improved view of the system. Nonetheless, whether greater familiarity with the judicial system will indeed create an affinity in all, or even most, cases is uncertain, especially if lay participation is focused on the most serious and controversial criminal cases. For instance, will the "citizen judges" agree if the professional judges decide to exclude

[34]Sun (2016a).

inculpatory evidence in a case where a child or another sympathetic victim was killed because the evidence was obtained in an illegal manner? For some citizens, absence from the judicial process could actually make the heart grow fonder.

Any roll-out of a lay participation system should thus proceed with close oversight by scholars trained in empirical research who can provide an objective analysis of the reforms and identify any unintended consequences. For example, the introduction of a "plea bargaining" type of procedure over a decade ago was seen as a way to partially alleviate caseload pressure but it had little impact in practice.[35] Likewise, the reputational benefits of lay participation remain largely speculative.

Assuming participation at trial—or at least in the selection process for lay judges despite not ultimately serving at trial—in fact increases respect for the judiciary, there is a further question of how widespread this positive influence will be. If, as currently envisioned, only a small percentage of criminal cases include lay participation, then only a limited segment of the populace will interact directly with the system. For a broader effect, the argument needs to be that the very existence of lay participation will markedly improve public perceptions. In other words, simply knowing that other citizens are participating will make people feel better about the courts. Those people who are not actual lay judges will not receive any immediate educational benefit and, instead, their information will be through an intermediary, whether that be through personal accounts by acquaintances who serve as lay judges, the media, government information campaigns, and/or formal civics education in schools. The contentious relationship between the courts and the media suggests that journalists may continue to take a critical view of any reform efforts.

3.2 *View Lay Participation in the Context of a Larger Reform Ecosystem*

Lay participation is but one strand in a complex web of interrelated reforms. Accordingly, reforms should avoid a myopic focus on lay participation as a panacea for the judicial system's woes. The root cause of public dissatisfaction is not that people are unhappy about being left out of court. Accordingly, the solution is not merely to inject people into the judging process. Certainly, few people celebrate in the United States when a jury summons arrives in the mail. Even as a law professor who believes deeply in the jury system despite all its flaws, I must admit that I experienced a certain sense of relief when my time in Taipei excused me from jury service in New Jersey.

One empirical study in Taiwan found "although the great majority of Taiwanese citizens support introducing lay participation, [that] only 55% of respondents express willingness to serve is worrisome."[36] Even if people are willing to serve,

[35]Lewis (2009), *supra* note 10.

[36]Huang and Lin (2013), *supra* note 14, at p. 562.

the Judicial Yuan noted that participants in moot courts had limited tolerance for the actual length of service. Of the people who participated, 59% said "within 3 days" was a reasonable legal obligation, whereas only 11% responded "as long as it takes."[37] A 2016 article on Japan's experience reported that many eligible citizens are opting out of service in large part because of family and work commitments.[38] A 2017 case from Japan involving intimidation of lay judges raises a more serious concern that all jurisdictions with lay participation face: how to ensure the safety and impartiality of those citizens who actually participate.[39]

As many people in Taiwan's reform debate recognize, lay participation is not a stand-alone reform but rather one piece in a larger puzzle. Lay participation raises complex issues regarding rules of evidence, discovery by the defense, sentencing guidelines, and other fundamental criminal procedure issues. For example, lay participation will require a careful rethinking of evidence law to determine what information will be shared with the lay judges. Will the professional judges first cull any illegally obtained evidence as would be done in a pretrial suppression hearing in the United States? If so, will the lay judges be told that they are proceeding with a more limited view of available information than the professional judges who, based on their training, are deemed more able to disregard tainted evidence?[40] Or, if all information is brought before the mixed bench and only then the professional judges tell the lay judges that they must disregard certain information because it was collected illegally, will the lay judges readily accept this determination even if the excluded information is a damning confession or other emotionally compelling information? In short, the narrative that simply reducing the "gap" between judges and the public will improve the judicial system's reputation masks a complex range of interrelated issues.

Even if a suite of reforms is introduced in tandem to support lay participation, improving the perception of the courts will likely require additional reforms that are not directly related to lay participation. A number of factors contribute to public dissatisfaction with the judiciary, such as that young "baby" (娃娃) judges lack broad experience because they are selected through a highly competitive exam process shortly after law school. Another derogatory term is "dinosaur" (恐龍) judges, to describe judges who are out of touch with the concerns of contemporary society. Neither of these critiques will automatically disappear by adding lay judges to the mix. Instead, there needs to be a larger discussion about how judges are selected and trained.

How judges are selected and trained was addressed at the National Affairs Conference on Judicial Reform but it has not yet generated concrete reforms. At

---

[37]Judicial Yuan (2016), *supra* note 7.

[38]Ryall (2016).

[39]Two men found guilty of intimidating lay judges in yakuza trial but walk free. The Japan Times. http://www.japantimes.co.jp/news/2017/01/07/national/crime-legal/two-men-found-guilty-intimidating-lay-judges-yakuza-trial-walk-free/. Accessed 5 Oct 2017.

[40]However, research has demonstrated the prevalence of bias even among well-intentioned, highly qualified experts. Dror (2016).

present, prosecutors, who have a similar civil servant status, can shift to becoming judges,[41] though this is still relatively uncommon. It is also rare for a practicing lawyer or other non-career civil servants to join the bench, thus limiting the infusion of fresh views from people who have actually defended clients. Moreover, given the substantial pay cut that successful practicing lawyers often take by becoming judges (without necessarily an off-setting increase in prestige and job satisfaction), there are doubts about the quality of those lawyers who are willing to become judges. Further, to my knowledge, there has been no serious study of whether the diversification of the judges' backgrounds improves the Taiwanese public's view of the judiciary.

Regardless of the backgrounds of those serving as judges, Taiwan continues to grapple with questions regarding how best to balance judicial independence with meaningful oversight once those people are on the bench. Taiwan took steps to increase scrutiny of judges in the wake of bribery scandals but to limited effect in changing public opinion. The government reported as follows during its second review of its implementation of the ICCPR:

> Between 2006 and 2015, a total of 5 judges were disciplined for involvement in bribery. The Judges Act, passed in 2011, introduces disciplinary measures such as removal from judgeship duties, dismissal, suspension, transfer to a position other than judgeship for those who have been deemed incompetent for the role.[42]

The Judges Act further introduced new committees under the Judicial Yuan to oversee disciplinary measures and safeguard judicial independence. It is possible that once lay people participate in the trial process, they will form a more positive opinion of these prior reforms. The extent to which people will see these prior reforms as sufficient—and that any positive evaluation will seep far beyond individual participants at trial—is, however, uncertain.

Lay participation also will not necessarily improve the relationship between the judiciary and the media. A persistent concern is leaks by government officials that tend to fuel negative media reports. When reviewing Taiwan's implementation of the ICCPR in 2013, the international experts recommended that the government "take effective administrative and criminal measures to punish officials who release information about criminal cases to the media in violation of the laws and regulations designed to safeguard the presumption of innocence."[43] Adding lay people to the adjudication process will create more opportunities for leaks. As with any country that uses lay participation in the judging process, the hope is that people will heed warnings about the confidentiality of the process. Of concern is that lay participation is expected to be used for particularly serious and high-profile cases, which could increase the media's incentives to seek inside information. Creating an atmosphere that both respects freedom of the press and the need for confidentiality of ongoing criminal proceedings will require a serious, and likely protracted, conversation regarding the role of legal rules and ethics.

---

[41] Republic of China (2016).

[42] *Id.*, at para 233.

[43] ICCPR Review (2013).

3.3 Refocus the Debate on How the Proposed Reforms will Impact the Rights of the Accused

Leaks to the media not only can sully the judiciary's reputation but also can harm the rights of the accused. International experts evaluating Taiwan's performance expressed concern over "trial by the media" in violation of ICCPR Article 14(2), which provides that everyone charged with a criminal offense shall have the right to be presumed innocent until proved guilty according to law.[44] That lay judges might be influenced by media reports despite efforts to shield them is but one of the concerns for the rights of the accused. Accordingly, in closing, this chapter encourages a reframing of the lay participation debate to more overtly address its importance for defendants.

Taiwan made a formal legal commitment to the rights in the ICCPR by incorporating the Covenant's contents into domestic law. As part of this commitment, Taiwan initiated a self-imposed review process that mirrors what would occur if it were a formal state party.[45] As noted above regarding the presumption of innocence, the concluding observations of the initial review by international experts published in March 2013 addressed several aspects of the "Administration of Justice" under Articles 9, 10, and 14.[46] The 2013 report did not, however, address proposals for lay participation in criminal trials, nor did the second report published in March 2017[47] or do either of the reports by the Taiwan government address this issue.[48] The review committee made clear that the concluding observations "do not deal with all of the very large number of issues presented to it."[49] Further, the committee had more than enough current issues to examine without pre-emptively addressing the possible human rights implications of the reform proposals. Nevertheless, as lay participation moves from abstract ideas towards a more concrete legislative proposal, the time is ripe to evaluate the potential impact on the accused.

The 2017 National Affairs Conference on Judicial Reform addressed the connection between various proposed reforms and defendants, such as reforms to evidence rules.[50] Yet with respect to lay participation, public trust in the judiciary and resource constraints have dominated the debate. For example, a Judicial Yuan summary of the moot courts cites four functions of lay participation: (1) reinforcing transparency of the judicial system and increasing trust, (2) reflecting the values of the people and reducing the gap between the judiciary and society, (3) educating the public and nurturing citizens, and (4) facilitating court activity and avoiding trials

[44]*Id.*

[45]Chen (2016), *supra* note 3.

[46]ICCPR Review (2013), *supra* note 43.

[47]ICCPR Review (2017).

[48]Relevant documents are available at the Ministry of Justice's website. http://www.humanrights.moj.gov.tw/mp200.html. Accessed 5 Oct 2017.

[49]ICCPR Review (2017), *supra* note 47, at para 7.

[50]Judicial Reform Conference (2017), *supra* note 33, at item 6.

on paper.[51] The first three of these functions focus on benefits to people other than the defendant. The fourth could benefit the defendant by emphasizing the in-court adversarial process instead of prejudging the outcome based on court filings. Whether this occurs will depend on whether lay participants do at least as good of a job as professional judges in evaluating evidence and withholding judgment until the trial is complete.

Ensuring that an objective, unbiased evaluation of the evidence determines the verdict is a universal issue. Indications from studies of other countries' systems are that a "diversity of viewpoints and the opportunity to deliberate increase the likelihood that trial evidence will be thoroughly evaluated. …"[52] It is similarly possible (though not guaranteed) that infusing lay participants into the deliberation process in Taiwan will encourage more meaningful scrutiny of evidence. Taiwan's Innocence Project has taken the lead in exposing wrongful convictions and pursuing reforms that will reduce the likelihood that people other than the actual perpetrator will be convicted.[53] Of critical concern is how lay participation will support or impede these efforts.

One mock jury study in Taiwan "indicat[ed] that deliberation can ameliorate the problem of most Taiwanese citizens not viewing a wrongful conviction as more undesirable than a wrongful acquittal."[54] This study involving a total of 279 people —largely divided into seven-member juries—provides an initial view of the importance of how deliberation procedures are structured. Whatever form of lay participation that Taiwan ultimately adopts, the shift from moot courts to real defendants will mean that some defendants will need to be the first people subject to the new system. The extent to which evidence is being carefully considered in accordance with the legal procedures should be under the microscope as a fledging system works out any kinks. For comparison, a *New York Times* article on early implementation of the South Korean lay participation system noted that the "novelty of the system has contributed to confusion among the public and judicial authorities alike and has produced sometimes-awkward moments in courtrooms."[55]

Nor are concerns limited to the influence on defendants who have lay participants help determine their fate: defendants who remain subject to professional-judge-only processes may also be affected. Specifically, the resources needed for trials incorporating lay participation could have externalities. If, as expected, lay participation increases the resources needed per trial, this could intensify pressures to further simplify procedures in cases that do not use lay participation. As I have argued elsewhere, Taiwan is far from alone in using streamlined trials and guilty pleas to resolve cases.[56] Efficiency-driven reforms should, however, be pursued with an

---

[51]Judicial Yuan (2016), *supra* note 7, at slide 54.

[52]Hans (2007), pp. 307–308.

[53]Taiwan Innocence Project. http://twinnocenceproject.org/index.php. Accessed 5 Oct 2017.

[54]Huang and Lin (2014), p. 367.

[55]Lee (2008).

[56]Lewis (2009), *supra* note 10.

abundance of caution so as to avoid an assembly-line criminal process that fails to protect the rights of the accused.

In addition to potential pressures to spend less time actually adjudicating seemingly straightforward cases, there is also the potential that diverting resources towards lay participation might cause other cases to languish and actually take longer to be cleared through the system. Delays already occur, in part because of the ability of both the defense and the prosecutors to appeal and the tendency for cases to be remanded to lower courts for further handling. The international experts evaluating Taiwan's compliance with Article 14(3)(c) of the ICCPR expressed concern over the length of time needed for criminal cases to reach a final resolution.[57] This is all to say that it is unclear what effects lay participation will have on those cases still adjudicated by judges alone. Without the allocation of new resources, there is the potential for a backlog of cases combined with undue haste in addressing a case's merits, both of which are problematic from the perspective of the rights of the accused.

Another simmering issue is the extent to which lay people's opinions will be taken into account when sentencing. If Taiwan adopts a mixed-bench system, will lay participants have a vote not only with respect to whether the defendant is guilty but also with respect to what sentence he shall receive? So long as the sentences meted out remain within legislatively prescribed limits—and those limits do not violate prohibitions on cruel, inhuman, or degrading punishment—giving lay participants a say in sentencing is not overtly problematic from a human rights perspective. Nonetheless, lay participation might ratchet up sentences, particularly in highly emotional cases such as crimes against children: "[M]ock trials indicated that citizen jurors gave heavier sentences than professionals, including judges and even law school students."[58] Lay participation might also result in greater sentencing disparities than if repeat-player professional judges decide sentences on their own. Although the detailed implications of including lay participants in sentencing are a major issue beyond the scope of this chapter, they are yet another aspect of the lay-participation puzzle that deserves more extensive consideration.

To be clear, lay participation is not only about the rights of the accused. In the United States, for example, the Constitution explicitly gives the defendant a right to a jury trial for non-petty criminal offenses. Yet the Constitution does not give the defendant a right to a bench trial; the government can insist on use of a jury over the defendant's wishes because other interests are at stake. Likewise, how lay participation may impact defendants is but one viewpoint from which to evaluate the proposed reforms in Taiwan. It is, however, an essential one. That the National Affairs Conference on Judicial Reform brought together disparate views from the judiciary, academia, legal practice, and civil society is a testament to the current government's efforts to broaden the debate. The Judicial Yuan is now tasked with

[57]ICCPR Review (2013), *supra* note 43.

[58]Trial by jury not a cure-all for judiciary pains. The China Post. http://www.chinapost.com.tw/editorial/taiwan-issues/2016/10/06/480277/Trial-by.htm. Accessed 5 Oct 2017.

the challenge of reconciling the various views into a cohesive legislative proposal, no easy task indeed. As an American academic looking in on Taiwan, the hope of this chapter is to raise some cautions as the Judicial Yuan takes the next steps in moving lay participation from theory to practice.

References

Chen Y (2016) Socialization in isolation: Taiwan's practices of human rights treaties as a non-UN member state and transnational educational networks. Unpublished J.S.D. dissertation, New York University School of Law, New York

Chin M (forthcoming) Adopting a lay participation system in Taiwan, in Judicial Reform in Taiwan: institutionalising democracy and the diffusion of law, Routledge (draft on file with the author)

Corrupt judges handed lengthy prison sentences. Taipei Times (1 July 2011). http://www.taipeitimes.com/News/taiwan/archives/2011/07/01/2003507146. Accessed 5 Oct 2017

Disi Fenzu: Canyu Touming Qinjin De Sifa [第四分組:參與透明親近的司法] (Fourth sub-committee: participatory, transparent, and close justice). https://justice.president.gov.tw/meetinggroup/4. Accessed 5 Oct 2017

Dror I (2016) A hierarchy of expert performance. J Appl Res Mem Cogn 5(2):121–127

Fukarai F (2013) A step in the right direction for Japan's judicial reform: impact of the justice system reform council recommendations on criminal justice and citizen participation in criminal, civil, and administrative litigation. Hastings Int Comp Law Rev 36(2):517–567

Fukurai H (2007) The rebirth of Japan's petit quasi-jury and grand jury systems: a cross-national analysis of legal consciousness and the lay participatory experience in Japan and the U.S. Cornell Int Law J 40(2):315–354

Gailiangshi Dangshiren Jinxing Zhuyi [改良式當事人進行主義] (Modified adversarial system). http://www.judicial.gov.tw/work/work02/work02-01.asp. Accessed 5 Oct 2017

Guomin Canyu Xingshi Shenpan Wangzhan [國民參與刑事審判網站] (Website for citizen participation in criminal trials). http://www.judicial.gov.tw/LayParticipation/intro08.asp. Accessed 5 Oct 2017

Hans V (2007) Introduction: citizens as legal decision makers: an international perspective. Cornell Int Law J 40(2):303–314

Huang K, Lin C (2013) Rescuing confidence in the judicial system: introducing lay participation in Taiwan. J Empirical Leg Stud 10(3):542–569

Huang K, Lin C (2014) Mock jury trials in Taiwan: paving the ground for introducing lay participation. Law Hum Behav 38:367–377

ICCPR Review (2013) Review of the initial reports of the government of Taiwan on the implementation of the international human rights covenants: concluding observations and recommendations adopted by the International Group of Independent Experts. http://www.humanrights.moj.gov.tw/HitCounter.asp?xItem=385451. Accessed 5 Oct 2017

ICCPR Review (2017) Review of the second reports of the government of Taiwan on the implementation of the international human rights covenants: concluding observations and recommendations adopted by the International Review Committee. https://www.ly.gov.tw/pages/ashx/File.ashx?FilePath-File/Attach/37315/File. Accessed 5 Oct 2017

Judges incur fury over pedophile sentencing. The China Post (26 Aug 2010). http://www.chinapost.com.tw/taiwan/national/national-news/2010/08/26/270104/Judges-incur.htm. Accessed 5 Oct 2017

Judicial Reform Conference (2017) Sifa Gaige Guoshihuiyi Fenzu Jueyi Guina Shuoming (12 Daxiang Zhongdian Yiti) [司法改革國是會議分組決議歸納說明[12 大項重點議題]] (National Affairs Conference on Judicial Reform: summary of Sub-Committee Resolutions [12 Important Main Topics]). https://drive.google.com/file/d/0B6gni5Xwp9QwVW9JRFU3Vk12Qzg/view. Accessed 5 Oct 2017

Judicial Yuan (2016) Introducing lay participation in Taiwan: focusing on lay participation in moot courts. http://social.judicial.gov.tw/LayJudge.Accessed 5 Oct 2017

Kim R (2015) A benchmark in Asian judicial reform: the new Korean jury system. Suffolk Transnational Law Rev 38(2):281–324

Kwon S (2016) Toward democracy in criminal procedure: the significance & limitation of citizen participation in criminal trials in an attempt to accomplish democracy in criminal justice in Korea. North Ill Univ Law Rev 37(1):101–125

Langbein J (1981) Mixed court and jury court: could the continental alternative fill the American need? Am Bar Found Res J 1981(1):195–219.

Lee J (2010) Korean jury trial: has the new system brought about changes? Asian-Pacific Law Policy J 12(1):58–71

Lee S (2008) South Korea struggles to incorporate a young jury system (7 July 2008). The New York Times. http://www.nytimes.com/2008/07/07/world/asia/07iht-jury.2.14299454.html. Accessed 5 Oct 2017

Lewis M (2009) Taiwan's new adversarial system and the overlooked challenge of efficiency-driven reforms. Va J Int Law 49(3):651–726

Lewis M (2015) Constitutions across the strait. In: Chen T, Chen D (eds) International engagement in China's human rights. Routledge, Abingdon, pp 134–156

Lou Y (2014) Establishing a suitable lay participation system for the Taiwanese criminal justice system. Indiana University Maurer School of Law, Bloomington

Pan J (2017) Campaigners advocating jury trial system protest at presidential office. Taipei Times (25 Feb 2017). http://www.taipeitimes.com/News/front/archives/2017/02/25/2003665660. Assessed 5 Oct 2017

Plogstedt A (2013) Citizen judges in Japan: a report card for the initial three years. Indiana Int Comp Law Rev 23(3):371–428

President Tsai launches judicial reform in Taiwan. Taiwan Today (12 July 2016). http://taiwantoday.tw/news.php?unit=2,6,10,15,18&post=3923. Accessed 5 Oct 2017

Republic of China (2012) Implementation of the International Covenant on Civil and Political Rights: initial report submitted under Article 40 of the covenant. http://www.humanrights.moj.gov.tw/HitCounter.asp?xItem=385452&ixCuAttach=119792. Accessed 5 Oct 2017

Republic of China (2016) Implementation of the International Covenant on Civil and Political Rights: second report submitted under Article 40 of the covenant. http://www.humanrights.moj.gov.tw/HitCounter.asp?xItem=453796. Accessed 5 Oct 2017

Ryall J (2016) Japanese opting out of serving as lay judges. Deutsche Welle (4 June 2016). http://www.dw.com/en/japanese-opting-out-of-serving-as-lay-judges/a-19328332. Accessed 5 Oct 2017

Su K (2017) Criminal court reform in Taiwan: a case of fragmented reform in a not-fragmented court system. Wash Int Law J 27(1):203–240

Sun H (2016a) Society, system not equipped for jury trials: experts. The China Post (30 Sept 2016). http://www.chinapost.com.tw/taiwan/national/national-news/2016/09/30/479802/Society-system.htm. Accessed 5 Oct 2017

Sun H (2016b) Judicial Yuan nominee urged to support fully jury system. China Post. http://www.chinapost.com.tw/taiwan/national/national-news/2016/10/13/480962/Judicial-Yuan.htm. Accessed 5 Oct 2017

Taiwan Innocence Project. http://twinnocenceproject.org/index.php. Accessed 5 Oct 2017

Trial by jury not a cure-all for judiciary pains. The China Post (5 Oct 2016). http://www.chinapost.com.tw/editorial/taiwan-issues/2016/10/06/480277/Trial-by.htm. Accessed 5 Oct 2017

Tsai I (2016), Tsai Ing-wen Zongtong Jiuzhi Yanshuo Zhong Ying Wen Quanwen [蔡英文總統就職演說中英文全文] (Inaugural address, complete Chinese and English text). http://www.cna.com.tw/news/firstnews/201605205012-1.aspx. Accessed 5 Oct 2017

Two men found guilty of intimidating lay judges in yakuza trial but walk free. The Japan Times (7 Jan 2017). http://www.japantimes.co.jp/news/2017/01/07/national/crime-legal/two-men-found-guilty-intimidating-lay-judges-yakuza-trial-walk-free/. Accessed 5 Oct 2017

UN Human Rights Committee (2007). General Comment no. 32, Article 14: right to equality before courts and tribunals and to a fair trial. UN Doc. CCPR/C/GC/32 (23 Aug 2007)

Wang T (2002) The legal development of Taiwan in the 20th century: toward a liberal and democratic country. Pac Rim Law Policy J 11(3):531–559

Wu Z, Chen W, Xiang C et al. (2017) "Zhaohui Minzhong Xinlai": Minjian Sigaihui Tui Peishenzhi [「找回民眾信賴」民間司改會推陪審制] (Restore the trust of the people: judicial reform foundation promotes jury system). Liberty Times Net (26 Mar 2017). http://news.ltn.com.tw/news/politics/paper/1089026. Accessed 5 Oct 2017

Margaret K. Lewis is Professor of Law at Seton Hall University. Professor Lewis has been a Fulbright Scholar at National Taiwan University, a Term Member of the Council on Foreign Relations, a Public Intellectuals Program Fellow with the National Committee on United States-China Relations, and a Delegate to the U.S.-Japan Leadership Program. She is also a Non-Resident Affiliated Scholar of NYU School of Law's U.S.-Asia Law Institute. Her publications have appeared in the *Virginia Journal of International Law*, *Vanderbilt Journal of Transnational Law*, *Columbia Journal of Transnational Law*, *NYU Journal of International Law and Politics*, and other academic journals. She is also the co-author, with Jerome A. Cohen, of the book *Challenge to China: How Taiwan Abolished Its Version of Re-Education Through Labor.*

Part V
Protection of Economic, Social and Cultural Rights

Chapter 26
The Right to Health in Taiwan: Implications and Challenges

Chuan-Feng Wu

Abstract Even though the right to health has been recognized as a fundamental right of everyone in Taiwan and universal National Health Insurance has been established to protect the accessibility of healthcare, the right to health is still not comprehensively guaranteed because the right is not explicitly stipulated in either the judicial or policy-making process. The ignorance then undermines the intrinsic values of the right to health and the importance of the individual's legal entitlements to health necessities, and excuses the government's non-compliance with human rights obligations. In order to explore the implications and challenges of the realization of the right to health in Taiwan, this chapter assesses Taiwan's commitments to the right to health from legal and public health perspectives through an analysis of constitutional and domestic laws, health inequality status, and the distribution of underlying conditions of health. The notions of "accountability" and "participation" in regard to "social determinants of health" are also considered as important factors in the assessment.

Keywords National Health Insurance (NHI) · Right to health · Social determinants of health

Taiwan has recognized health as the most fundamental asset for everyone regardless of age, gender, socio-economic, or ethnic background and has excelled in promoting and maintaining the health of its population. The implementation of comprehensive healthcare policies and the construction of nationwide medical networks, including National Health Insurance (hereinafter NHI), generally guarantees citizens' access to basic healthcare facilities and services and their enjoyment of a minimum standard of health. However, it should be noted that, even though significant progress has been made on selected health indicators, the right to health is still not formally guaranteed in Taiwan because the right is not explicitly stip-

C.-F. Wu (✉)
Academia Sinica, Taipei, Taiwan
e-mail: cfw@sinica.edu.tw

J. A. Cohen et al. (eds.), *Taiwan and International Human Rights*, Economics, Law, and Institutions in Asia Pacific, https://doi.org/10.1007/978-981-13-0350-0_26

ulated in either the judicial or policy-making process, and the aims and principles of realizing the right have not been well established.

1 The Right to Health in Taiwan

In Taiwan, the right to health is not explicitly listed in the Constitution. The only health issues that can be found in the Constitution are stated as part of national policy (rather than as constitutional rights) in Articles 155 and 157 and amendment Article 10, which argue that the government should provide adequate and sufficient medical care to promote national health, especially among the elderly, women, children, and the handicapped.[1] However, the restrictive interpretation of the right to health that falls within the category of the "evidence-based medical model"[2] would exclude certain essential elements of the right to health, such as health promotion and disease prevention (which partially go beyond the scope of "medical care")[3] and underlying preconditions for health (including health education, social support, improved nutrition, sanitary facilities, environmental hygiene, etc.).[4] Furthermore, because the state's responsibility is limited to the implementation of national policy rather than to the respect for, protection, and fulfillment of the right to health,[5] the court generally considers that the public has only "reflective interests" as passive receivers of the welfare provided by the government and has no legal entitlement requiring government performance.[6]

Therefore, Lin Ming-Hsin proposed that the right to health should be derived from Article 22 of the Constitution,[7] which states that "[a]ll other freedoms and rights of the people that are not detrimental to social order or public welfare shall be guaranteed under the Constitution." Lin's proposal expands the possibilities for justiciable recourse for violations of the right to health in Taiwan[8] because individuals' claims to the right to health can be made stronger as an indispensable fundamental right, even though it is not clearly enumerated under the Constitution.[9]

[1]Wu (2016), pp. 206–207.

[2]*Id.*, at p. 207.

[3]Toebes (1999), p. 247.

[4]*Id.*, at pp. 247, 254–258.

[5]In the framework of the Taiwanese Constitution, Articles 155 and 157 are listed under "Chapter XIII: Fundamental National Policies," not "Chapter II: Rights and Duties of the People."

[6]Sun (2016), p. 1187.

[7]Lin (2005), pp. 26–36.

[8]Li (2005a), pp. 132–134.

[9]For example, the Taiwan Constitution also does not contain the word "privacy," but the right to privacy has been upheld on numerous occasions by the Constitutional Court and has been recognized as a constitutional right based on Article 22 of the Constitution. Recognition of the right then provided a solid foundation for developing a preferable strategy of judicial review involving privacy. Chen (2010), pp. 21, 44–45.

Recently, the Constitutional Court seemed to support Lin's argument and regarded the right to health as a "non-enumerated right" under Taiwan's Constitution.[10] For example, Justice Chen Shin-Min stated in Judicial Yuan (J.Y.) Interpretation No. 701 that the right to health under Article 22 of the Constitution refers to the entitlement to appropriate, prompt, and fair healthcare.[11] In the same case, Justice Lo Chang-Fa also cited Article 22 of the Constitution and international human rights documents to confirm the state's obligations to respect, protect, and fulfil the individual's right to the highest attainable standard of health.[12] Furthermore, in J.Y. Interpretation No. 753 the Constitutional Court clearly declared the right to health to be a constitutional right and argued that, if the right to health is implicated by regulations affecting individuals' access to decent healthcare, such regulations must be carefully evaluated under constitutional scrutiny.[13] In other words, Taiwan's Constitutional Court agreed that the right to health could be recognized as a legally enforceable constitutional right under Article 22 of the Constitution because it is necessary to preserve human dignity, individuality, and the wholeness of personality development,[14] as well as to safeguard an individual's fair opportunity to pursue his or her life plans.[15]

Additionally, the International Covenant on Civil and Political Rights (hereinafter ICCPR), accompanied by the International Covenant on Economic, Social and Cultural Rights (hereinafter ICESCR), were ratified in Taiwan in 2009, through the Act to Implement the International Covenant on Civil and Political Rights and the International Covenant on Economic, Social and Cultural Rights (Implementation Act). According to Article 2 of the Act, the protection of human rights (including the right to health) under the two Covenants has status in domestic law.

2 Follow-up Challenges: Ignorance of the Right to Health

Even though the Constitutional Court has tried to play a more important role in a contentious policy process over healthcare reform, the top-down judicial rulings have not substantially changed the administration's attitudes towards the right to

[10]Wu, *supra* note 1, at p. 209.

[11]See Chen Xin Min Da Fa Guan Shizi Di 701 Hao Jie Shi Xie Tong Yi Jian Shu [陳新民大法官釋字第701號解釋協同意見書] (Justice Chen Shin Min's concurring opinions in J.Y. Interpretation No. 701) (6 July 2012) (R.O.C.).

[12]See Lo Chang Fa's Da Fa Guan Shizi Di 701 Hao Jie Shi Xie Tong Yi Jian Shu [羅昌發大法官釋字第701號解釋協同意見書] (Justice Lo Chang Fa's concurring opinions in J.Y. Interpretation No. 701) (6 July 2012) (R.O.C.).

[13]Si Fa Yuan Da Fa Guan Shizi Di 753 Hao Jie Shi [司法院大法官釋字第753號解釋] (J.Y. Interpretation No. 753) (6 Oct 2017) (R.O.C.).

[14]Li (2005b), pp. 33–40.

[15]Daniels et al. (1996), p. 20.

health. The administration seems to insist that the protection of individuals' health and the accessibility of healthcare should be regarded as "reflective interests" provided by social beneficence and public policy rather than a constitutional right which people can claim. It is because the government is afraid that recognizing the right to health as a constitutional right would lead healthcare costs to spiral out of control and undermine attempts to promote public health through health plans and rational priority setting,[16] guided by government officials or experts. The ignorance then undermines the intrinsic value of the right to health and the importance of the individual's legal entitlements to health necessities, and excuses the government's non-compliance of human rights obligations.

For example, through the centralized, universal NHI program, the Taiwanese government is quite committed to looking after the population's health. However, in 2012 nearly 200,000 insured persons were suspended[17] because the state refused to provide basic payments for medical care when individuals failed to pay his or her NHI premiums. Even though in J.Y. Interpretation No. 472 the Constitutional Court explicitly stated that the temporary suspension of NHI benefits should be revised because the government "shall give appropriate assistance and relief and shall not refuse to pay benefits, in order to fulfill the constitutional purposes of promoting national health insurance, protecting senior citizens, the infirm and the financially disadvantaged,"[18] the government refused to lift the suspension entirely until 2016.[19] In another example in regard to the compulsory hospitalization of persons suffering from mental illness, the review procedure for involuntary commitment is undertaken by the Ministry of Health and Welfare's (MHW's) Mental Illness Mandatory Assessment and Community Treatment Review Committee (hereinafter Review Committee) in Taiwan. The government admitted in the 2012 initial state report on the ICCPR that the relief procedure was not comprehensive enough to protect patients' right to health (especially the right to control one's health and body)[20] because the Review Committee does not often have access to the patient during the investigation process.[21] However, the human rights burdens remain, and the government fails to respond to human rights groups' criticism of the malfunctions of the Review Committee, the absence of a mental health court for review purposes, and ignorance of a comprehensive review of alternative treatments.[22]

In addition to the administration's negative attitudes toward the right to health, the administrative court's stance is also strict and conservative about applying the

---

[16]Gloppen and Roseman (2011), p. 1.

[17]Covenants Watch (2012), p. 95.

[18]Si Fa Yuan Da Fa Guan Shizi Di 472 Hao Jie Shi [司法院大法官釋字第472號解釋] (J.Y. Interpretation No. 472) (29 Jan 1999) (R.O.C.).

[19]Central News Agency (2016).

[20]See Comm Econ Soc Cultural Rights, General Comment No. 14, para. 8, 22nd Sec, 25 Apr–12 May 2000, UN Doc E/C.12/2000/4 (11 Aug 2000) [hereinafter General Comment No. 14].

[21]Ma (2012), p. 62.

[22]League for Persons with Disabilities (2017), pp. 7–8.

right to health framework to assess human rights burdens imposed by healthcare policies and regulations. For example, the People with Disabilities Rights Protection Act imposes obligations on the government to create a public environment with barrier-free access to persons with disabilities. The requirements are consistent with paragraph 9 of CESCR General Comment No. 14 ("the right to health must be understood as a right to the enjoyment of a variety of facilities, goods, services and conditions necessary for the realization of the highest attainable standard of health"). But in the public healthcare system in Taiwan, medical services are still provided without considering the needs of persons with disabilities[23] because most clinics or hospitals have failed to create a barrier-free environment with auxiliary aids and services, such as sign language interpretation services or medicine dispensing bags that enable visually impaired patients to identify their medications.[24] The government argued that the "barrier-free accessibility" requirements in the Act are merely a part of social policy and fall under governmental discretion rather than constitutional rights claims.[25] The administrative courts, firmly embedded in the civil-law tradition, seemed to concur with the government's perspective and argued that the Act does not grant people the right to appeal against the government's failure to ensure the access of people with disabilities, on an equal basis with others, to the physical environment.[26]

However, this maximum regard for governmental discretion and ignorance of the right to health in healthcare policymaking is inconsistent with the Constitutional Court's position and might have the serious consequence of giving wide latitude to limitations on the right to health. *First*, it is important to notice that the objectives of the right to health are not always the same as the objectives of social policy. For example, advocating on behalf of health-related information is extremely important in the right to health framework[27] because individuals need such information to make well-considered decisions about their healthcare affairs. But the right to access health-related information might be regarded as trivial in terms of social policy. Therefore, treating protection of the right to health as "reflective interests" under social/welfare policy might overlook the essential functions of the right to health.

Second, the government's and the administrative court's unwillingness to admit individuals' right to health claims would substantially devalue the independent legal status of the right to health, undermine the intrinsic value of the right, and excuse the government's non-compliance with its human rights obligations. For example, restricting individuals' right to health claims in the administrative court

---

[23]Covenants Watch (2012), *supra* note 17, at p. 102.

[24]Covenants Watch (2016), pp. 109–110.

[25]Sun (2016), *supra* note 6, at p. 1187.

[26]____ v. Kaohsiung County Stadium et al. 98 Su Di 186 Hao Panjue [98訴第186號判決] (Kaohsiung Admin. High Ct. [高雄高等行政法院] (17 Aug 2010) (Taiwan). See also Chen J-W & Chen M-S v. The Government of Kaohsiung City et al., 100 Pan Zi Di. 1454 Hao Panjue [100判字第1454號判決] (Supreme Admin. Ct. [最高行政法院] (18 Aug 2010) (Taiwan).

[27]See e.g., General Comment No. 14, para 12(b) ("… accessibility includes the right to seek, receive and impart information and ideas concerning health issues").

would substantially deprive their right to seek remedies whenever they believe their rights have been infringed upon by the government. It is hard to imagine that the right to health, which the Constitutional Court recognizes as a constitutional right, can be fairly protected without legal claims pursuant to the right to health standards. Studies have also shown that right to health litigation can help to make human rights a reality, giving meaning to a state's longstanding commitment to realize the highest attainable standard of health for all.[28]

3 Follow-up Challenges: Lack of Social Determinants Perspectives

Furthermore, except for forcing the contested issue of the right to health into public policy discussions, the Constitutional Court has failed to develop a comprehensive framework for the right to health. Therefore, the nature and content of the right to health under the Constitution remain vague. One problem is that healthcare policies in Taiwan remain centered on medical subsidies and the establishment of medical facilities/services, neglecting crucial social determinants of health,[29] which are closely linked to the human rights approach to health.[30]

3.1 Social Determinants and the Right to Health

According to the model of pathways of social influences on health,[31] the unequal distribution of avoidable factors that cause health risks, disability and death can be attributed not only to an individual's health behavioral factors (such as smoking, physical activity, and diet) but also to socio-economic factors. For example, it is difficult to argue that females who have had circumcisions have an actual choice in this procedure because they are often influenced by social customs and peer pressures from their family, community, and even doctors and midwives.[32] Since health can be influenced by social determinants (such as socio-economic inequality),[33] when fulfilling the right to health, in addition to sufficient supplies of medical products/services and the protection of individual physical and mental conditions (which are the immediate precursors of healthcare), social determinants should also be taken into consideration. In other words, social determinants of health, which

[28]Meier and Yamin (2011), p. 81.

[29]Covenants Watch (2016), *supra* note 24, at p. 103.

[30]Chapman (2010), p. 17; Alston (2005), p. 755.

[31]Marmot (2006), p. 49.

[32]Steiner and Alston (2000), p. 411.

[33]Adler et al. (1993), pp. 3140–3145; Lynch et al. (1997), p. 809.

involve an individual's ability to perform socially allocated roles, as part of social normality, free from physical or mental limitations, should be regarded as important contents of the right to health.[34]

In order to respond to the importance of social determinants in the right to health framework, the World Health Organization (WHO) Commission on Social Determinants of Health (hereinafter CSDH) proposed that, in addition to recognizing that the Universal Declaration of Human Rights (UDHR) "points to the interdependence of civil, cultural, economic, political, and social rights—dimensions of social exclusion highlighted in the social determinants of health framework"—there are also clear links between a rights approach to health and the social determinants of health approach to health equity.[35] In the CSDH's framework, protection of the right to health should not be limited to health distribution or healthcare accessibility; the causes of health inequality, which can span from unfair healthcare distribution to deeper social structural determinants and conditions (such as economic inequalities and dysfunctional political structures) should also be regarded as a human rights violation.

More specifically, there are two important dimensions in the CSDH's framework regarding the social determinants of health (Fig. 1): (A) Daily living and working conditions, including equity from the start; health practices; fair employment and a decent work environment; universal healthcare; and social protection across the course of life. (B) Structural drivers (meaning equitable distribution of power, money, and resources), including health equity in all policies, systems and programs; fair financing; market responsibility; gender equality; political empowerment; and good global governance. In this framework, violations of the right to health might be systematic, produced by social norms, policies, and practices that tolerate or actually promote unfair distribution of and access to power, wealth, and other necessary social resources; it then evaluates health inequality at the macro level (such as living and working conditions) rather than at the micro, individual level. In other words, individuals are not randomly distributed into healthy and unhealthy social conditions[36] and it is important for the government to remove the unfair influences of social conditions on health.

3.2 Examining Taiwan's Healthcare Policy with respect to Social Determinants

In Taiwan, the low level of health of the poor, the social gradients in health, and the marked health inequities between different areas are also partly caused by

[34]WHO (2008), p. 6.

[35]*Id.*, at p. 173.

[36]Braveman and Egerter (2008), p. 53.

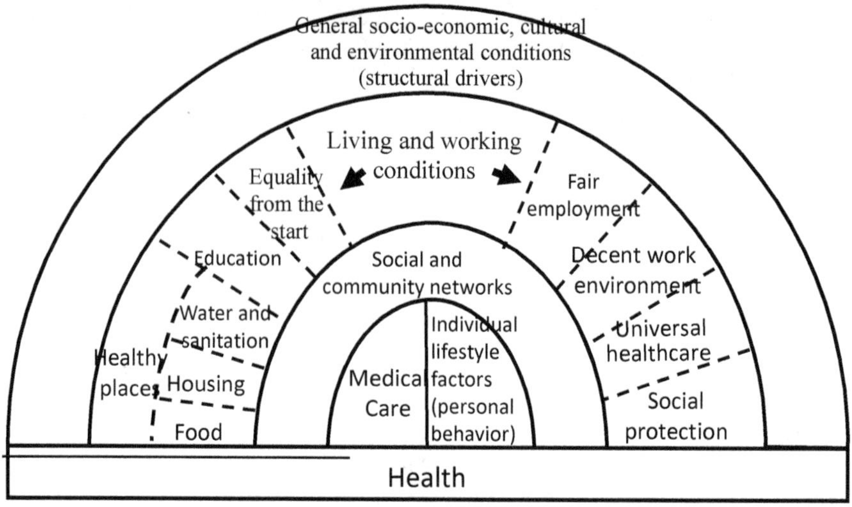

Fig. 1 Conceptual framework of the social determinants of health. This figure is a slight variation of that proposed by the WHO and scholars. WHO (2008), p. 43; Braveman and Egerter (2008), *supra* note 36, at p. 81; Whitehead et al. (2001), p. 314

differences in the social determinants of health,[37] such as the immediate, visible circumstances of people's lives (their access to healthcare, schools and education their conditions of work and leisure, their homes and communities, and financial resources),[38] their concomitant chance of leading flourishing lives, and political empowerment.[39] For example, studies show that individuals' physical and mental health coincides with the social organism's functions in terms of social concerns.[40] In Taiwan, studies also show that, given the same health conditions, income-related healthcare utilization inequities increase and tend to be pro-rich as age increases.[41] Additionally, infant mortality in rural areas was 112% more than that in urban areas in 2000, and it later increased to 126%.[42] Indigenous people's participation/coverage rate (80.19%) in NHI is lower than the average (96.20%).[43]

However, the Taiwan government constantly ignores social determinants in its healthcare policymaking process. This narrow focus bypasses the fact that the absence of social determinants of health imposes restrictions on individuals' underlying essential capabilities related to health and causes potential violations of

[37]WHO (2008), p. 1.

[38]Chapman (2010), *supra* note 30, at p. 19.

[39]Schulz and Northridge (2004), p. 457.

[40]Patrick and Erickson (1993), pp. 93–95; Broadhead et al. (1983), pp. 521–537; Thoits (1982), pp. 324–336.

[41]Chen et al. (2012), p. 58.

[42]Liu (2004), p. 9.

[43]Lin et al. (1998), p. 6.

the right to health. For example, in order to prevent waste and abuse, the National Health Insurance Act (NHI Act) authorizes the National Health Insurance Administration (NHIA) to review the medical necessity of healthcare prospectively (especially care that involves high technology and/or high risk or expensive medications).[44] The problem is that the NHIA usually limits its reimbursements to cost-beneficial healthcare on the basis of biomedical models, regardless of the influence of social determinants. The fulfillment of the highest attainable standard of "health" then falls within the "physical and mental" notion,[45] regardless of the influence of social contingencies (such as class or economic status) and environmental factors on individuals' normal functioning.[46] But paragraph 11 of CESCR General Comment No. 14 states that the right to health should be regarded as "an inclusive right extending not only to timely and appropriate healthcare but also to the underlying determinants of health, such as access to safe and potable water and adequate sanitation, an adequate supply of safe food, nutrition and housing, healthy occupational and environmental conditions, and access to health-related education and information, including information on sexual and reproductive health." In another example regarding civic empowerment, which is an important social determinant of health[47] because it helps arm individuals with the necessary information and capabilities with which to protect themselves from violations of the right to health,[48] Wen-May Rei found that the NHIA generally overlooks the need to communicate with the public and makes its coverage and reimbursement decisions without a public deliberative process or explanation of its rationale.[49] But, "the participation of the population in all health-related decision-making at the community, national and international levels" is also regarded as an important aspect of the right to health in accordance with paragraph 11 of CESCR General Comment No. 14.

The courts in Taiwan also fail to play a more active role in ensuring that the healthcare authorities take social determinants of health into consideration in these decisions. For example, in one case the physician recommended that the claimant

[44]Article 51 of the National Health Insurance Act, "Expenses arising from the following service items are not covered in this Insurance: … 12. Other treatments and drugs as stipulated by the Insurer, reviewed by the Board, and promulgated by the Competent Authority." Article 53, "No insurance benefits shall be paid by the Insurer for any one of the following events: … 3. Treatment and drugs which are not medically necessary according to the pre-examination …" In addition, Article 41.1 of the Act also argues that, "The Fee Schedule and Reference List for Medical Services shall be established jointly by the Insurer and the relevant agencies, experts, beneficiaries, employers, and contracted medical care institutions, and shall be reported to the Competent Authority for approval." Article 41.2, "Drug dispensing and fee schedules should be established jointly by the Insurer and the relevant agencies, experts, beneficiaries, employers, and contracted medical care institutions; drug providers and relevant experts as well as patients should also be invited to voice their opinions and they shall be reported to the Competent Authority for approval."

[45]Toebes (1999), *supra* note 3, at p. 23.

[46]Daniels (1995), pp. 26–27, 34.

[47]WHO (2008), p. 18.

[48]Nnamuchi (2014), p. 126.

[49]Rei (2011), p. 132.

use Tarceva for his cancer treatment because he had no positive response to Irressa. The NHIA, however, refused to reimburse the claimant's healthcare costs because, according to NHIA's indications list, Tarceva is not regarded as a more efficacious agent than Irressa and thus Tarceva cannot be used if Irressa has been proven to be ineffective. The Taipei High Administrative Court ruled in favor of the NHIA because, based upon the NHIA's own evaluation, treating the claimant with Tarceva would neither significantly prolong the claimant's life nor be a cost-effective use of healthcare resources.[50] But the court failed to note that the NHIA's indication list is made on the basis of an economic model only and that, in addition to cost-effectiveness, the securing of a fair opportunity (a slim but important chance that using both Rituximab and chemotherapy could possibly prolong the claimant's life) should also have been taken into consideration in the NHIA's decision-making processes. In other words, even though applying only a cost-effectiveness analysis in the NHIA's reimbursement decisions is not rational[51] and should be regarded as a violation of the right to health, the court still takes a passive, conservative stance and has unconditionally respected NHIA's decisions in which social determinants of health are missing. It is consistent with Rei's findings that after reviewing 19 cases related to NHI reimbursement decisions brought to Taiwan's administrative courts between 1995 and 2010,[52] the courts directly cited the NHIA's reimbursement reference list to deny the claimants' appeals in 13 cases, without examining whether the list was justified.[53]

4 Conclusion

After reviewing Taiwan's situation in light of the right to health, we find that the significance of the right to health in Taiwan's healthcare policy and judicial approaches to human rights is seriously underestimated. This chapter proposes that, in order to ensure more effective implementation, a right-to-health-based strategy which includes the right to health as a concrete legal right rather than as a soft moral right, should be established to monitor the fulfillment and protection of the right to health in Taiwan.

Additionally, because the unfair distribution of the social determinants of health can result in very large numbers of preventable deaths, disabilities, unnecessary suffering, and injustices and inequalities in each country, the social determinants of health should be regarded as essential contents of the right to health.[54] Thus, failing

[50]Taipei High Administrative Court 2009 Ruling No. 388 Precedent.

[51]Otley, R v. Barking & Dagenham NHS Primary Care Trust, [2007] EWHC 1927 (Admin), para. 26 (Eng.).

[52]Rei (2011), pp. 184–188.

[53]*Id.*, at p. 161.

[54]Venkatapuram et al. (2010), p. 8.

to take social determinants into consideration when developing healthcare policy can be regarded as the denial of the right to health. However, social determinants of health are still ignored in the right to health framework in Taiwan. The rights-based approaches to health in Taiwan, with some notable exceptions, have not engaged with the growing body of research that demonstrates the significant impact of the social determinants of health and health inequalities on the population's health in a meaningful way.[55] Therefore, this chapter proposes that the notions of "availability," "accessibility," "acceptability," and "quality" in regard to the "biomedical model" as well as the notions of "accountability" and "participation" in regard to the "social determinants of health" are all considered to be important indicators or benchmarks in human rights impact assessments.[56]

References

Adler NE et al (1993) Socioeconomic inequalities in health: no easy solution. J Am Med Ass'n 267:3140–3145

Alston P (2005) Ships passing in the night: the current state of the human rights and development debate seen through the lens of the millennium development goals. Hum Rights Q 27:755–829

Braveman P, Egerter S (2008) Overcoming obstacles to health: report from the Robert Wood Johnson Foundation to the commission to build a healthier America. http://www.rwjf.org/files/research/obstaclestohealth.pdf. Accessed 12 Oct 2017

Broadhead WE et al (1983) The epidemiologic evidence for a relationship between social support and health. Am J Epidemiol 117:521–537

Central News Agency (2016) National health insurance restores coverage to defaulters. Taiwan News, 7 June 2016. https://www.taiwannews.com.tw/en/news/2934510. Accessed 21 Oct 2017

Chapman AR (2010) The social determinants of health, health equity, and human rights. Health Hum Rights 12(2):17–30

Chen C (2010) In search of a new approach of information privacy judicial review: Interpretation No. 603 of Taiwan's Constitutional Court as a guide. Ind Int Comp L Rev 20:21–45

Chen WY et al (2012) Health equality and equity of healthcare utilization in different age-groups given the trend of an aging population. Taiwan J Public Health 31(1):58–70

Covenants Watch & Taiwan Association for Human Rights (2012) 2011 Taiwan human rights report: parallel report on the implementation of the International Covenant on Economic, Social and Cultural Rights. Covenants Watch & Taiwan Association for Human Rights, Taipei

Covenants Watch & Taiwan Association for Human Rights (2016) 2016 Taiwan human rights report: parallel report on the implementation of the International Covenant on Economic, Social and Cultural Rights. Covenants Watch & Taiwan Association for Human Rights, Taipei

Daniels N (1995) Just health care. Cambridge University Press, Cambridge

Daniels N et al (1996) Benchmarks of fairness for health care reform. Oxford University Press, New York

Gloppen S, Roseman MJ (2011) Introduction: can litigation bring justice to health? In: Yamin AE, Gloppen S (eds) Litigating health rights: can courts bring more justice to health? Harvard University Press, Cambridge, Massachusetts, pp 1–16

[55]Chapman (2010), *supra* note 30, at p. 17; Alston (2005), *supra* note 30, at p. 755.

[56]Hunt (2009), pp. 1757–1759.

Hunt P (2009) Missed opportunities: human rights and the commission on social determinants of health. Glob Health Promot 16(1):36–41

League for Persons with Disabilities (2017) Parallel report on the Convention on the Rights of Persons with Disabilities

Li C (2005a) Xian Fa Wei Lie Ju Zhi Gu You Quan: Sheng Ming, Shen Ti, Zong Yan Yu Ren Ge [憲法未列舉之固有權:生命、身體、尊嚴與人格] (Non-enumerated constitutional inherent rights: right to life, body, dignity and personality) In: Li C (ed) Duo Yuan, Kuan Rong Yu Ren Quan Bao Zhang: Yi Xian Fa Wei Lie Ju Quan Zhi Bao Zhang Wei Zhong Xin [多元、寬容與人權保障—以憲法未列舉權之保障爲中心] (Plurality, tolerance, and the protection of human rights: focusing on the protection of non-enumerated rights). Angle, Taipei, pp. 93–148

Li C (2005b) Xian Fa Wei Lai Zhi Quan Li Bao Zhang Zhi Du Mian Mao: Yi Xian Fa Di 22 Tiao Wei Zhong Xin [憲法未來之權利保障制度面貌:以憲法第22條爲中心] (The multiple dimensions of non-enumerated constitutional rights: focusing on Article 22 of the R.O.C. constitution) In Li C (ed) Duo Yuan, Kuan Rong Yu Ren Quan Bao Zhang: Yi Xian Fa Wei Lie Ju Quan Zhi Bao Zhang Wei Zhong Xin [多元、寬容與人權保障—以憲法未列舉權之保障爲中心] (Plurality, tolerance, and the protection of human rights: focusing on the protection of non-enumerated rights). Angle, Taipei, pp. 18–53

Lin M (2005) Jian Kang Quan: Yi Guo Jia Zhi Bao Hu Yi Wu Wei Zhong Xin [健康權:以國家之保護義務爲中心] (The right to health: based on the protective obligation of the state) Fa Xue Jiang Zuo [法學講座] (Law Forum) 32:26–36

Lin Y et al. (1998) Feasible strategies for universal coverage of the national health insurance program (Research Project, National Health Insurance Bureau)

Liu C (2004) Inequality in Taiwan: from the perspectives of the differences of infant mortality between cities/towns. Master Thesis, National Taiwan University

Lynch J et al (1997) Why do poor people behave poorly? variations in adult health behaviour and psychosocial characteristics by stages of the socioeconomic lifecourse. Soc Sci Med 44:809–819

Ma Y (2012) Foreword by the ROC President implementation of the International Covenant on Civil and Political Rights: initial report submitted under Article 40 of the Covenant (Taiwan)

Marmot M (2006) Social causes of social inequalities. In: Anand S et al (eds) Public health, ethics, and equity. Oxford University Press, New York, pp. 37–61

Meier BM, Yamin AE (2011) Right to health litigation and HIV/AIDS policy. J Law Med Ethics 39:81–84

Nnamuchi O (2014) Millennium development goal, human rights, and maternal health in Africa: possibilities, constraints, and future prospects. Annals Health L 23:92–140

Patrick D, Erickson P (1993) Health status and health policy: quality of life in health care evaluation and resource allocation. Oxford University Press, Oxford

Rei WM (2011) Si Fa Shen Cha Jian Bao Gei Fu Jue Ce De Zheng Dang Xing Ji Qi Jie Xian: Quan Min Jian Bao Gao Ke Ji Zhen Liao Xiang Mu Pan Jue Fen Xi [司法審查健保給付決策的正當性及其界限?—全民健保高科技診療項目判決分析] (Judicial review of medical necessity coverage decisions? an analysis of court decisions in prospective reviews of national health insurance). In: Huang CY (ed) 2010 Xin Zheng Guan Zhi Yu Xing Zheng Zheng Song [2010 行政管制與行政爭訟] (2010 administrative regulation and judicial remedies). Academia Sinica, Taipei, pp. 129–193

Schulz A, Northridge ME (2004) Social determinants of health: implications for environmental health promotion. Health Educ Behav 31(4):455–471

Steiner H, Alston P (2000) International human rights in context: law, politics, morals. Oxford University Press, New York

Sun N (2016) Wu Zhang Ai/Ke Ji Xing, He Li Tiao Zheng Yu Ping Deng Bu Qi Shi Yuan Ze: Cong Shen Xin Zhang Ai Zhe Quan Li Gong Yue Jian Shi Wo Guo Xian Fa Ji Shen Xin Zhang Ai Zhe Quan Yi Bao Zhang Fa Zhi Ping Deng Yuan Ze Nei Han [無障礙/可及性、合理調整與平等不歧視原則:從身心障礙者權利公約檢視我國憲法及身心障礙者權益保障法之平等原則內涵] (Accessibility, reasonable accommodation and non-discrimination principle: a legal review of consistency between the CRPD and equal treatment regulations in the

Constitution and the Rights Protection Act for Persons with Disabilities in Taiwan). Guo Li Taiwan Da Xue Fa Xue Lun Cong [國立臺灣大學法學論叢] National Taiwan University Law Rev 45:1163–1128

Thoits P (1982) Conceptual, methodological, and theoretical problems in studying social support as a buffer against life stress. J Health Soc Behav 22:324–336

Toebes BC (1999) The right to health as a human right in international law. Hart, Amsterdam

Venkatapuram S et al (2010) The right to sutures: social epidemiology, human rights, and social justice. Health Hum Rights 12(2):3–16

Whitehead M et al (2001) Developing policy response to inequities in health: a global perspective. In: Evans T et al (eds) Challenging inequities in health: from ethics to action. Oxford University Press, Oxford, pp. 309–322

WHO (2008) Closing the gap in a generation: health equity through action on the social determinants of health. http://apps.who.int/iris/bitstream/10665/43943/1/9789241563703_eng.pdf. Accessed 12 Oct 2017

Wu C (2016) The emergence of the right to health in Taiwan: transplantation from the West and its implementation. In: Lo C et al (eds) Legal thoughts between the East and the West in the multilevel legal order. Springer, Singapore, pp. 199–214

Chuan-Feng Wu serves as Associate Research Professor at the Institutum Iurisprudentiae, Academia Sinica, and has a joint appointment as Associate Professor at the College of Public Health, National Taiwan University and the Institute of Health and Welfare Policy, National Yang-Ming University. He received his J.S.D. from U.C. Berkeley and LL.M. from Harvard Law School. In addition to degrees in law, he also holds a master's degree in health and welfare policy and a bachelor's degree in public health. His specialty fields of study include healthcare laws and ethics, international human rights and the right to health, and healthcare distributive justice. Dr. Wu's recent works include The Emergence of the Right to Health in Taiwan: Transplantation from the West and Its Implementation: An Analysis of Taiwan's Pharmaceutical Affairs Act Amendment Regarding Data Exclusivity of Pharmaceutical Products, with an Emphasis on Pharmaceutical New Indications (in Chinese), The Right to Health and Health Equality under the ICESCR—With an Analysis of the Human Rights Burdens of NHI's Reimbursement Policy (in Chinese), Can Compulsory Health Insurance Be Justified? An Examination of Taiwan's National Health Insurance, and Transnational Pharmaceutical Corporations' Legal and Moral Human Rights Responsibilities in Relation to Access to Medicine.

Chapter 27
The Evolution of Environmental Rights in Taiwan

Chun-Yuan Lin

Abstract Without constitutional provisions on environmental rights, democratization and globalization have significantly promoted human rights related to environmental issues. In the last two decades, democratization has raised the rights consciousness of Taiwanese society and mobilized massive environmental movements and legislation. In addition, the process of globalization has not only drawn Taiwan's attention to international environmental issues but also pushed Taiwan to comply with international human rights standards. Taiwan enacted the Act to Implement the ICCPR and ICESCR in 2009, attempting to provide more comprehensive protection of human rights in Taiwan. Yet, in spite of this growth in human rights consciousness, people in Taiwan have little, and very differentiated, understanding of "environmental rights." The question of how to understand and conceptualize environmental rights within Taiwan's development is crucial for future generations. This chapter defines environmental rights as a collection of rights that provide legal protection against environmental problems. By analyzing environmental rights within the dynamics of environmental threats, the social/political context, and laws, it is argued in this chapter that the substance of environmental rights is evolving within these contexts and the times. In Taiwan, environmental rights have evolved alongside political, social and economic development. From personal injury to legal rights and human rights, the evolution of environmental rights in Taiwan can be divided into three distinct periods that coincide with the country's democratization. In the pre-democratic period, environmental harm remained a personal grievance and did not generate legal claims. During the process of democratization, massive enactment of, and progress on, environmental law provided a legal basis for environmental claims and transformed them into legal rights. Following democratic consolidation, however, privatization and climate change have brought new challenges to environmental rights in

C.-Y. Lin (✉)
Department of Financial and Economic Law, Chung-Yuan Christian University, Taoyuan City, Taiwan
e-mail: chunyuanlin@cycu.edu.tw

J. A. Cohen et al. (eds.), *Taiwan and International Human Rights*, Economics, Law, and Institutions in Asia Pacific, https://doi.org/10.1007/978-981-13-0350-0_27

Taiwan. Yet, this period has seen the introduction of international human rights jurisprudence and an increasing emphasis on procedural rights in Taiwan that may provide opportunities to further enrich environmental rights in Taiwan.

Keywords Democratization · Environmental rights · ICCPR · ICESCR

1 Introduction: Changing Environmental Rights in Context

There has been a call to legalize environmental rights in Taiwan, yet the meaning of environmental rights has never been clear. Constitutionalizing environmental rights was the main agenda during democratization in the 1990s; however, it was not adopted successfully. Article 10 of the failed Constitutional Amendment stated that "[en]vironmental and ecological protection shall be given equal consideration with economic and technological development." In 2011, in his third inaugural speech, President Ma Ying-Jeou stressed "sovereignty, human rights and environmental rights" as his policy goals. However, President Ma said nothing about the concept of the right and only stated that "economic development with the cost of environment degradation is not generational justice." In 2016, President Tsai In-Wen stated in her inaugural speech that "as we pursue economic development, we must not forget our responsibility to the environment. Our New Model for Economic Development will be fully integrated with national land-use planning, regional development and environmental sustainability." This basically repeats the ideology of Article 10 of the Constitutional Amendment and the rhetoric of President Ma's speech, only removing the phrase "environmental rights." These examples indicate that although rights in regard to the environment are frequently mentioned, they remain solely as a slogan for civic groups to challenge pollution and as rhetoric for government policy.

The enactment of the Act to Implement the International Covenant on Civil and Political Rights and the International Covenant on Economic, Social and Cultural Rights (hereinafter Act to Implement the ICCPR and the ICESCR) in 2009 has brought new life to the discussion of environmental rights. Due to the anxiety of international isolation, the Taiwanese government has been keen to demonstrate to international society that Taiwan is a "civilized" country that should be recognized. Since the first partisan turnover, the government has been expressing to the international community that Taiwan is a democratic country with high human rights standards and is different from China. After several failed attempts to become a party to the ICCPR and ICESCR, the Legislative Yuan passed the Act to Implement the ICCPR and ICESCR in 2009. Several other important human rights conventions, such as the CEDAW, were also adopted as domestic law. The internalization of international human rights standards has prompted Taiwanese society to talk and think about human rights in a deeper way, especially as two rounds of international reviews on Taiwan's Human Rights Report exposed various human rights issues and generated significant public debate. Among the issues exposed by the reports, how environmental degradation and land exploitation infringe upon human rights has become a salient issue. Despite the lack of a specific article protecting environmental rights, the framework and jurisprudence developed by the ICCPR and the ICESCR are useful tools to analyze and evaluate Taiwan's performance with respect to the protection of environmental rights.

In discussions on environmental rights, however, people have very different understandings and perspectives. In order to better delineate the dynamics, this chapter defines environmental rights in a more abstract and inclusive way, referring to various legal claims that can be exercised in the face of environmental degradation. In other words, environmental rights in this chapter refer to a collection of rights that provide legal protection against environmental problems. With this definition, it is argued that the substance of environmental rights changes within different contexts and over time. By analyzing environmental rights within the dynamics of environmental threats, the social/political context, and the laws, this chapter attempts to present the evolution of environmental rights in Taiwan. From the Japanese colonial period to the present, environmental rights in Taiwan have evolved from personal losses to legal rights to fundamental human rights and may still expand further.

2 Environmental Rights as Victims' Cry: 1945–1980s

The history of environmental degradation in Taiwan can be traced back to the modernization that began in 1895 during the Japanese colonial period. However, it was the policy of the Nationalist government after 1945 that exacerbated the environmental problems in Taiwan.

2.1 Political Background: De-Colonization and a Base for National Salvation

Japan colonized Taiwan from 1895 to 1945 and initiated a policy of modernization in Taiwan. The infrastructure, roads, harbors, railroads, power plants, and factories built by the Japanese government set a basis for later economic development. Like other colonies, Taiwan's resources were exploited to benefit the Japanese, not the Taiwanese. Therefore, environmental sustainability was of no concern in Japan's development policy in Taiwan. When the Nationalist government took over Taiwan following World War Two, Taiwan soon became "the base for national salvation," in which natural resource exploitation had to be maximized to achieve the goal of "rescuing China from the Communists." The Taiwanese government adopted a planned economy policy which prioritized the development of industry in Taiwan. Planning bureaucrats consciously regarded natural resources as resources solely to be exploited for economic growth. Concerns about environmental protection were not mentioned until the late 1970s.[1]

When, in 1971,[2] the UN replaced the ROC (Taiwan) with the People's Republic of China (China) as the only official representative of the Chinese government in the UN, President of Taiwan, Chiang Kai-shek, withdrew Taiwan's membership from the UN. The Taiwanese government then started to put more effort into its domestic infrastructure and economic policy. Yet the obsession with fast economic growth at any cost left public health and the environment unprotected. During this period, the state and leading industrialists formed a powerful coalition and dominated the market, leading to environmental degradation.

2.2 Legal Framework and State Performance

The law had little function in protecting environmental rights in this period. It was not until 1972 that the first law governing environmental matters, the Drinking Water Management Act, was enacted. The Legislative Yuan continued to pass several important environmental laws during this period, including the Clean Air Act (1975), the Water Pollution Control Act (1974), the Waste Disposal Act (1974) and the National Park Law (1972). The early enactment of environmental laws, however, did not necessarily represent progress in environmental protection in Taiwan. The regulations adopted relatively low standards, with no specific government agency responsible for the execution of environmental laws until the establishment of the Bureau of Environmental Protection in 1982, which was a low-level agency acting under the Department of Health with few resources.

The narrow ideology of economic development and the close relationship between government and big business made the execution of environmental regulation difficult. The government suppressed many environmental controversies, which on some occasions were resolved through political rather than legal means. Since laws provided neither regulations nor dispute-resolution mechanisms for environmental conflicts, discontented people protested on the streets and usually approached legislators or city councilors to negotiate compensation. It is fair to say that environmental law had only a very limited function in the period of economic blooming.

Throughout the period of economic development, the government was the major contributor to environmental degradation. On the one hand, government-owned enterprises, such as China Steel and the Chinese Petroleum Corporation, produced serious pollution. On the other hand, the state allowed, encouraged, and even

---

[1]See Hsiao (1987). According to Hsiao, some local scientists and scholars tried to warn the public about the danger of environmental pollution, yet their voices went largely unheard. See Hsiao (1990), pp. 163–179.

[2]G.A. Res. 2758 (1971).

facilitated industries to exploit the natural environment for economic profit. Major polluters nowadays are either originally state-owned enterprises or state-facilitated industries. For example, thermal power plants contribute 30% of total greenhouse gas emissions, while petrochemical and iron industries continue to produce serious air and water pollution. The 2014 gas blast in Kaohsiung, which caused 33 deaths and thousands of injuries, was a legacy of the petrochemical industry established in the 1970s.[3] Recent movements against illegal industrial waste disposal, the anti-nuclear movement and the movement to reclaim indigenous people's lands are also actions against the legacy of the developmental state.[4]

Without concern for the environment, unrestrained economic growth brought disastrous consequences for the ecological and natural resources of Taiwan.[5] The ideology of economic growth without regard for the environment remains the dominant ideology in Taiwan and continues to determine the direction of policy. It was not until the 1980s, when environmental awareness grew, that restraints were placed on the environmental impacts of economic growth.

2.3 *Victims' Claims Without a Legal Basis*

During the period of economic growth, the state's development strategy and construction projects directly produced pollution and caused damage to citizens and the environment. If some environmental scandals did not generate public outrage it was because the authoritarian martial-law regime suppressed information against the government, leading to an underdevelopment of rights consciousness among the public. Only when an environmental problem caused serious damage to the property or the health of citizens would it trigger resistance. Yet resistance seldom went through legal mechanisms since the law provided little protection for victims. Victims' injuries remained a personal issue or a reason for political mobilization.

Undoubtedly, the government was the direct polluter and should have been held responsible. Yet, interestingly enough, the government was seldom the direct target of protestation. In the early years of the environmental movement in Taiwan, victims primarily expressed their complaints directly against big factories or industrial parks. Governments, especially local governments, were only secondary targets.[6]

It is worth mentioning the infringement of indigenous people's rights in the process of Taiwan's economic development. The land of indigenous people was easily exploited under the guise of development, because their land was less

---

[3]On 31 July 2014, a series of gas explosions occurred in Kaohsiung, the second largest city in Taiwan. At least thirty-three people were killed, and 321 others were injured. The accident is attributed to the petrochemical factory, LCY Chemical Corp, which was founded in 1965 as part of the planned economy policy.

[4]For details on the indigenous lands claim movement, see Lo (2013a).

[5]Grano (2015), p. 40.

[6]*Id.*, at pp. 46–47.

populous, and linguistic and cultural differences deterred indigenous people from effectively exercising their legal rights. The Asia Cement Company in Shoulin Township, Hualian, is a prime example. In the 1970s, as major members of the company were top officials in the central government, the central authority and local government made it easy for the company to "rent" indigenous land without informed consent.[7] The land of the Taroko tribe was largely exploited for cement production, resulting in a loss of land and property as well as damage to the community and traditional culture that was closely connected to the land.[8] The stories of harm to indigenous people in the 1970s–1980s were seldom heard, indicating an underdeveloped rights consciousness among indigenous communities at that time.

It was not until the 1980s that environmental awareness grew in Taiwan's civil society. On the one hand, environmental degradation became too serious to ignore; on the other hand, Taiwanese citizens who had traveled abroad were becoming aware of the importance of environmental protection and tried to inform the public about environmental issues. While rarely articulated using the language of rights, the main concern of the environmental movement in the 1980s was personal health and one's immediate living environment. According to Hsiao, environmental movements in Taiwan in the 1980s were mostly generated from environmental concerns about their immediate homes and from a "victim consciousness."[9] In other words, people initiated protests mostly out of concern for their own property or health, not out of concern for the environment.

3 Environmental Rights as Legal Rights: 1987–2000

Democratization and international pressure are the two primary driving forces that have contributed to the progress of Taiwan's environmental law and the protection of environmental rights since the 1980s. People who suffered from environmental pollution were able to find a legal basis to transform their losses into exercisable legal rights. The claims for the environment went beyond personal health or property damage, extending to natural resources and the future.

3.1 Political Background: Democratization and International Pressures

Since the 1980s, as discontent with the degree of environmental degradation increased, several movements initiated by grassroots organizations and intellectuals

---

[7]According to Articles 44 and 45 of the Mining Act (礦業法), a mineral rights-holder can legally rent or buy private land for mining purposes, and the landowners cannot refuse.

[8]For details on the case of Asia Cement Company, see Lo (2013b), pp. 7–8.

[9]See Hsiao (1982).

started to draw attention to environmental problems and challenge the government and industries. The lifting of martial law in 1987 released further energy in civil society, with the establishment of important grassroots environmental groups, such as the Taiwan Environmental Protection Union and the Wild Bird Federation of the Republic of China. Such organizations were capable of organizing and leading discussions and movements on environmental issues. The growth of environmental NGOs demonstrates that environmentalism was no longer restricted to middle-class professionals; focusing on educating the public about nature conservation issues, it became a cross-class collaboration. Moreover, environmentalists were able to shift their targets from industries to the government, blaming it for promoting economic development over ecological protection. Criticism of the authorities developed into the political power of the opposition party: the Democratic Progressive Party (hereinafter DPP).[10] As Ho has pointed out, "environmentalism, using both protests and newly opened institutional venues, became institutionalized as a vital component of political life" in the process of democratization.[11] The environmental movement contributed to Taiwan's democratization, and democratization, in turn, also legitimized the environmental protests. The importance of grassroots organizations in Taiwan's democratization can be seen by the Wide Lily Student Movement and Constitutional Court J.Y. Interpretation No. 261 which in 1990 successfully demanded that the government hold national elections for representatives, thus transforming Taiwan into a democratic country.[12]

Aside from the momentum gained domestically through the course of Taiwan's democratic transition, pressure from the global community also contributed to the growth of Taiwan's environmentalism. The very first event in which the international community exerted pressure on Taiwan out of environmental concerns was a result of local environmental NGOs. Taiwanese society had a long tradition of practicing Chinese medicine that used not only herbs but also animal parts, such as rhino horns or tiger bones, which were regarded as precious materials. In the early 1990s, local environmental groups announced opposition to the use of endangered animals in Chinese medicine, and soon the British Environmental Investigation Association and several other international environmental groups came to Taiwan to conduct an investigation. International environmental groups later announced that Taiwan had not adopted any measures to protect endangered species, and was thus in

---

[10]The DPP is the current ruling party in Taiwan. Before 2000, the DPP was the major opposition party that regarded environmental protection as one of its main tenets.

[11]Ho (2011), pp. 283–314.

[12]During the Martial Law period, the government suspended the election of national representatives. The Constitutional Court J.Y Interpretation No. 31 confirmed the constitutionality of the decision. The Wild Lily Student Movement urged the restoration of national elections and created significant pressure on the government. The Constitutional Court then made J.Y. Interpretation No. 261, holding the practice unconstitutional, and mandated that the government hold a nationwide second-term election of national representatives. See Dafaguan Shizi Di 31 Hao [大法官釋字第 31 號] (J.Y. Interpretation No. 31) (29 Jan 1954), Dafaguan Shizi Di 261 Hao [大法官釋字第 261 號] (J.Y. Interpretation No. 261) (21 June 1990).

violation of the Convention on International Trade in Endangered Species of Wild Fauna and Flora (hereinafter CITES, also known as the Washington Convention). Taiwan soon realized that, though not a contracting party to any environmental conventions and thus under no international obligation concerning environmental protection, it did not necessarily follow that Taiwan was, in reality, exempt from consequences. In 1994, under the urging of CITES authorities and pressures from domestic environmental groups, the U.S. applied the Pelly Amendment to impose trade sanctions on Taiwan. This amendment allows the U.S. President to impose trade restrictions on countries that engage in trade that diminishes the effectiveness of international programs to protect threatened or endangered species. Because most of Taiwan's economic growth depended on international trade, the sanctions significantly affected Taiwan's economy. Although the trade sanctions were lifted in 1996, the experience taught Taiwan a precious lesson about the importance of catching up with the international community in terms of the development of environmental norms. In the years after the trade sanctions were lifted, Taiwan's government has been paying greater attention to international environmental issues.

3.2 *Strong Environmental Legislation with Weak Implementation*

It was under the dual pressures of internal and international protests that Taiwan made significant progress on environmental legislation since the 1980s. Some of the most important environmental laws were passed, or considerably revised, during this time, such as the enactment of the Noise Control Law and the Toxic Chemical Substances Control Act, and the revision of the Clean Air Act and the Water Pollution Control Act. Mostly using the command-and-control model, environmental legislation since the 1980s has established a more comprehensive system of environmental regulations to deter and mitigate environmental degradation. Pressure from international society has also contributed to the environmental legislation in Taiwan. The above-mentioned CITES case, for example, pushed Taiwan to revise the Wild Animal Protection Act in order to meet international standards. The increase in environmental legislation has restrained pollution and facilitated the development of legal mechanisms to address environmental controversies.

By the end of the 1980s, the increasing number of regulatory tasks had gone far beyond the capacity of the low-level Bureau of Environmental Protection at that time. In 1988, the government established the Environmental Protection Agency (hereinafter EPA), reflecting the growing importance of environmental policy on the government's agenda. The establishment of the EPA further promoted a more comprehensive environmental law plan, including four dimensions of preventative, regulatory, remedial, and organizational laws.[13] As environmental regulations in

[13]Yeh (1994), pp. 73–132, 119 (Chapter 3: "Massive Legislation on Environmental Law: Taiwan's Model, Issues and Solutions") (confirmed).

Taiwan became stricter, local enterprises sought overseas investment opportunities. By the end of the 1990s, many local factories had closed in order to relocate to markets with weak environmental regulations and cheap labor. The majority of these enterprises re-invested in China and Southeast Asian countries, making Taiwanese industries a source of global pollution.

During this period, the narrative of economic growth remained the dominant ideology in Taiwan. Reflecting the preferences of the majority, the government prioritized economic growth as the highest goal on its agenda and marginalized environmental value. Despite huge amounts of environmental regulations, during this period Taiwan still stood in the shadow of the developmental state model, only subject to more legal restraints. The function of the environmental regulatory system was undermined because of the lack of a strong motive and inadequate resources for enforcement.

The prevailing ideology also weakened the effectiveness of environmental regulation. The administrations responsible for environmental regulation received far fewer resources and, as such, were not able to develop a long-term, comprehensive plan for environmental protection or sustainable development. Therefore, the interests of environmental protection had to be evaluated against other values, resulting in piecemeal degradations. While victims and environmental NGOs turned to the courts for redress, they found it difficult in environmental cases, since the requirement of legal standing, the burden of proof, the strict rule of causation and even the ideology of the judges all became obstacles to judicial remedies.

3.3 *Beyond Personal Injuries*

Democratization and the development of environmental legislation gradually changed the understanding of environmental rights in Taiwan. The first change was to transform environmental claims into legal claims, and the second was to extend protection of the environment and natural resources to future generations.

3.3.1 From Protestation to Legal Rights

One obvious change has been the legalization of environmental claims. Environmentalism is no longer a matter of political struggle; it is a matter of law. In the past, victims of pollution preferred to protest on the streets or to seek political bargaining, but now environmental legislation has empowered victims and NGOs to transform environmental claims into legal rights. Regulations have prescribed the standards which determine illegal pollution, which, in turn, have empowered civil society to seek redress from polluters or to demand that the government provide better policies and execution. In addition to regulatory laws, enactment of the Public Nuisance Dispute Mediation Act (hereinafter PNDMA) in 1992, the Environmental Impact Assessment Act (hereinafter EIAA) in 1994, and creation of citizen-suits clauses in 1999 have contributed the most to transform environmental claims into legal rights.

The enactment of the PNDMA created a legal mechanism to effectively respond to environmental conflicts. Due to the incompetence of the courts, public nuisance controversies in the 1980s usually resulted in protests or political negotiations. This proved to be extremely inefficient as the political resolution of public nuisance cases took a significant amount of time and money, yet provided no guidance for future controversies. In 1992, the PNDMA was enacted as an alternative dispute resolution mechanism for environmental controversies. By providing a lower threshold and more flexible resolutions, more people initiated the public nuisance mediation process, reducing the social and political costs of resolving environmental conflicts and also accumulating legal doctrines for future guidance.

Yet the rights-based judicial system took direct rights-infringements to be contingent on a judiciable case, leaving many natural resources cases unresolved. The Administrative Litigation Law, since its 1999 revision, has provided a legal basis for citizen suits. Article 9 of the revised Administrative Litigation Act provides that citizens can file a lawsuit in the public interest. This signifies a break from the traditional thinking of rights in Taiwan. Now a citizen need not be a direct rights holder or a victim to sue the government; she can sue for the cause of environmental protection. Environmental regulatory laws, more often than not, include citizen suit clauses. In recent years, concerned citizens or environmental groups have frequently initiated citizen suits to address environmental concerns, reflecting an understanding of environmental protection that goes beyond personal injury and covers degradation of the natural environment.

The EIAA of 1992 introduced the mechanism of the Environmental Impact Assessment (EIA) as a "prevention rather than a cure." The Act requires that the government consider possible environmental costs in the decision-making process of major construction projects or policies. The EIAA was the first attempt not only to establish an ex ante procedural requirement to include environmental value in the decision-making process but it also created space for public discussion and participation. The citizen suits clause of the EIAA makes the EIA crucial in Taiwan's environmental conflicts.[14]

The growth of environmental law has enabled victims of pollution and NGOs to develop rights claims through specific legal mechanisms. Those who have suffered as a result of environmental degradation can be identified and their losses can be transformed into legal rights. The growth of citizen suits and environmental laws has also reshaped the state's role in and obligations toward environmental protection. They clearly prescribe the responsibility of the government to regulate, execute and supervise, ways through which victims and NGOs may more easily make claims when the government fails to fulfill its responsibilities, and to seek remedies through the courts.

[14]Section 8, Article 23 of the EIAA provides that, after paper notification, public interest groups may directly file a lawsuit against the government for its negligent behavior in fulfilling its implementation duties in order to seek a ruling ordering the competent authority to carry out implementation. As a result, the EIA and the courts have become the most important battlefield for environmental controversies in contemporary Taiwan.

3.3.2 Environmental Concerns Beyond Personal Interests

During this period, environmental claims began to go beyond immediate personal concerns of health and property. The movement against a fourth nuclear power plant in Taiwan is a salient example marking the transformation of environmental rights. When a fourth nuclear power plant was proposed in 1980, several international nuclear accidents such as Chernobyl in Ukraine attracted the attention of Taiwanese intellectuals who raised environmental concerns about a fourth nuclear power plant. With the lifting of martial law, residents of Gongliao and environmental groups joined intellectuals and initiated an anti-nuclear movement. The claim of the movement transcended individual harm and local problems to encompass environmental and ecological issues concerning the entire nation and beyond.[15]

Protesters, especially intellectuals and NGOs, did not claim personal compensation but instead extended their claim to the natural environment and ecology, going beyond individual concerns. As such, an awareness of "a right to the environment" was developed to protect the natural environment for present and future generations. A rights-claim related to the environment can include compensating for past pollution and preserving the environment for future generations; it can even transcend local damage to consider damage to national or global ecological systems. The implementation of National Health Insurance may also have contributed to the transformation. Since citizens now have easy access to medical services, concerns about injuries to health from pollution may have shifted to concerns about the natural environment.[16]

Moreover, by targeting the state, the anti-nuclear movement also inquired into the obligations of the government in environmental protection. The government was believed to have obligations to make regulations to prevent and control pollution and to make policies to preserve the natural environment for future generations. In this way, the government is regarded as having a preemptive role in protecting citizens from possible environmental harm, rather than a reactive role of mediating conflicts or providing remedies for damage.

4 Environmental Rights as Human Rights: 2000–Present

After the second partisan turnover, Taiwan became a consolidated democratic country. Unfortunately, the government seems incapable of dealing with new environmental threats. The emerging jurisprudence on human rights, however, may further deepen and widen the understanding and function of environmental rights in Taiwan.

---

[15]Ho (2003).

[16]Taiwan started its compulsory NHI in 1995 and reached population coverage of 99% in 2014.

4.1 Democratic Consolidation and New Threats

In 2000, the opposition DPP won the presidential election and created the first partisan turnover in Taiwan's political history. In 2008, the KMT won the presidential election and accomplished the second partisan turnover. According to Huntington's two-turnover test, Taiwan has survived two turnovers of power and should be recognized as a consolidated democratic country.[17] Taiwan is further changing, in line with the trend towards globalization. Perhaps unexpectedly, new threats to the environment have emerged following Taiwan's democratization and globalization.

The newly adopted policies of privatization and deregulation brought new threats. When the planned economy policy was seriously questioned during the process of democratization, proposals for privatization and deregulation were introduced into Taiwan on agendas for regulatory reform.[18]

Deregulation released a new market for private citizens and enterprises, inviting new threats to the natural environment,[19] for example, Qingjing Farm which was established in 1961. The farm was exclusively managed by the Veterans Affairs Council of the Executive Yuan and became a popular tourist destination. In 1992, the government decided to deregulate Qingjing, allowing citizens to buy and sell its land, resulting in unrestrained development. Over 147 hotels and hostels, of which only 4 are legal, are now located on Qingjing, occupying over 5,000 hectares of the mountain's area. Without proper regulation, commercial development of Qingjing has destroyed the beautiful scenery and threatened the ecological and natural environment.

Privatization, including the outright distribution of shares to the general public and "contracting out" and inviting the private sector to carry out publicly organized and financed activities, was believed to be a symbol of liberty and efficiency, but now, as it turns out, may be a new source of environmental degradation.[20] Due to financial difficulties, local governments in Taiwan have preferred to take advantage of private capital and private contractors for public construction projects. The expectation is that privatization introduces not only capital but also incentivizes the maximization of profits. A notable approach to public-private cooperation in Taiwan can be seen in the Build-Operate-Transfer (hereinafter BOT) scheme. Numerous cases, such as the

---

[17]Huntington (1993), p. 267.

[18]Some politicians and scholars see government regulation as inefficient, costly and undemocratic, proposing to reduce government involvement in the market and civil society. Moreover, they also believe that private enterprise may provide better products and services than the government, suggesting more involvement of private entities in public services and construction.

[19]According to the OECD, deregulation is a subset of regulatory reform and refers to complete or partial elimination of regulation in a sector to improve economic performance. Khemani and Shapiro (1993).

[20]Privatization refers to the transfer of ownership and control of government or state assets, firms and operations to private investors. Organisation for Economic Co-operation and Development (OECD) (1997), p. 11.

Taidong Beautiful Bay Resort[21] and the Taoyuan Aerotropolis Project,[22] as well as the controversy surrounding the Taipei Dome,[23] are all vivid examples which show that, in fulfilling their contractual obligations, the private sector is more than willing to sacrifice environmental protection for the sake of profit.

In addition to threats from the market, the development of climate change has also brought new challenges. The uncertain and large-scale nature of climate change makes it a global environmental issue that requires collective global action and cooperation. International society started to combat climate change through treaties with the United Nations Framework Convention on Climate Change (hereinafter UNFCCC) of 1992, and continued to make various agreements and rules to regulate as well as to empower states in climate change mitigation and adaptation. The UNFCCC recognizes climate change as a global environmental problem and requires all parties to take common but differentiated responsibility. The Kyoto Protocol (1997) established a regulatory framework to impose on so-called Annex 1 Parties a compulsory legal obligation to reduce greenhouse gas emissions. The enactment of the UNFCCC and the Kyoto Protocol emphasized the legal obligation of states to protect their own citizens as well as the global environment. Although Taiwan has been deprived of the opportunity to participate in global law making and to receive resources from the global community, climate change has already caused disastrous property loss, injury and death in Taiwan. Answering the question of how to deal with the environmental threats coming from the market and climate change is the most crucial task for contemporary Taiwan.

4.2 *Legal Change and State Performance*

During democratization there was a proposal to amend the Constitution to include "a right to the environment." Unfortunately, the ambiguous content of the proposal led to divisions within environmental groups and thus it failed to gain enough support during the process of political negotiation. Environmental groups that failed to constitutionalize an environmental law then sought legislative possibilities.

[21]Taidong Beautiful Bay Resort case was a BOT project involving the illegal operation of the Environmental Impact Assessment process since 1994. For details on the case, see Sect. 4.3.1 of this chapter.

[22]Taoyuan Aerotropolis Project seeks to promote the Taoyuan Airport as a hub for East Asia and to enhance the competitive advantage of Taiwan. It will allegedly create NT$7 trillion in revenue. Phased commercial, industrial and residential development will expropriate an area totaling over 3700 ha, including specific high-quality farmland and 15,000 houses with 46,000 residents. This project invites serious resistance from residents and NGOs for its over-ambitious public interests and flawed procedures.

[23]The Taipei Dome is also a BOT project for the establishment of a stadium in Taipei. It was originally scheduled to start construction in 2007. The project involves many controversies, including the improper inclusion of commercial facilities, the destruction of old trees and historical sites, and concerns about public safety and transportation.

In 2002, the Legislative Yuan passed the Basic Environment Act which set up fundamental principles for Taiwan's environmental policy. Article 1 of the Basic Environment Act requires the government pursue sustainable development by promoting environmental protection, while Article 3 further emphasizes the priority of environmental value, stating that "in the event that economic, technological or social development has a seriously negative impact on the environment or endangers the environment, the protection of the environment shall prevail." The law prescribes the government's obligations in environmental protection, including pollution prevention, compensation, environmental education, law and policy making, as well as their implementation. If a competent authority fails in its obligations, persons or public interest groups may file lawsuits to the administrative courts. The Basic Environmental Law also legalizes some important policies, such as the "nuclear-free homeland" policy in Article 23.

In 2009, the Legislative Yuan passed the Act to Implement the ICCPR and ICESCR, making international human rights law a part of Taiwan's domestic law. As mentioned above, the enactment of the two human rights treaties has again animated discussions of human rights in Taiwan. Administrative agencies and the courts increasingly refer to the ICCPR and ICESCR in making decisions.[24] These developments have made environmental protection one of the highest values in Taiwan's legal system and have enriched discussions on environmental rights in Taiwan.

4.3 *State Performance*

In the face of coming threats, the performance of the government is disappointing.

4.3.1 Privatization and Forced Evictions

Due to the recession in the global economy, competition from China and the East Asian countries as well as the inherent limits of economic growth, the economic growth rate in Taiwan has slowed since 1992 and has dropped below its average growth rate since 2011. The government thus initiated several large-scale projects for industrial or economic redevelopment, many of which required land-use changes, land acquisitions or the exploitation of natural resources.

Democratization may have awoken environmentalism in Taiwan, but it has not changed the ideology of economic development. The policies of privatization and deregulation have invited market forces to chase economic profits at the cost of natural resources. Unfortunately, the government has, so far, managed the new

[24]From 2009 to 2016, there were at least 1,541 judicial rulings citing the ICCPR or ICESPR in their judgments. The Constitutional Court refers to the two Covenants in 21 Interpretations.

market extremely poorly. Taitung Beautiful Bay provides an example of the government's poor management. In December 1994, the Taitung County Government signed a BOT contract with the Beautiful Bay Resort Co., according to which the company would "renovate" and operate existing facilities on Sanyuan beach in Taitung. In 2005, the Beautiful Bay Resort Co. separated 9,997 m^2 of land from the total 59,956 m^2 of property in order to shield itself from the legal requirements of EIA procedures and to maximize its profits. The Taitung County Government did not safeguard the natural environment by requiring the project to undergo an EIA. Instead, the county government allowed the Beautiful Bay Resort Co.'s circumvention, going on to facilitate the passing of EIAs on the remaining parts of the project. The Taitung County Government even refused to suspend construction when the court ruled the EIA illegal.[25] Although the court ruled in favor of the environmental NGOs, making this the first victory of citizen suits in Taiwan's history, the harm to the environment and indigenous people may be irreversible.[26]

In addition to the harm to natural resources, some public-private cooperation projects lead to forced evictions, Take Taoyuan Aerotropolis Project (hereinafter TAP) as an example. In order to advance the capacity of Taoyuan airport and make Taiwan more competitive in the changing global market, the Taiwanese government initiated the TAP.[27] The initial project was to construct a third air strip in order to increase the capacity of the airport. Yet the project has enlarged its scope several times to include a residential area, a commercial area, and a specific zone for industries, in addition to the airport itself. The project currently covers 4,687 ha, yet only 1,700 hectares are used by the airport, with 945 hectares for other public construction. The project will result in more than 46,000 residents being forced to move from their homes. Similar to the case of Taitung Beautiful Bay, the private investors in the BOT saw an opportunity to make greater profits through the expanded residential and commercial zones. Yet even if the construction of a third air strip is justified as being in the public interest, the legitimacy of the land acquisitions for the sole benefit of commercial companies is questionable. The large-scale land acquisitions not only involve many residents' rights and property; some of the lands are high-quality farmland that is crucial for Taiwan's food self-sufficiency ratio. The project and decisions relating to private land acquisitions may not survive careful constitutional review.

[25]There are several court rulings on this case. The first one is TEPU v. Taitung County Government, 96 Nian Suzi Di 647 Hao Panjue [96 年訴字第 647 號判決] (Kao-Hsiung Admin. High Ct. [高雄高等行政法院] 23 Jan 2007) (Taiwan).

[26]The court first confirmed the standing of the environmental group as a public interest group to file a citizen suit. The court emphasized the purpose of the EIA is to lessen and prevent possible adverse environmental impacts by major construction projects and then ruled that to merge-and-re-segment the land in order to avoid the EIA process violated the legal requirement of the EIA. TEPU v. Taitung County Government, 96 Nian Suzi Di 647 Hao Panjue [96 年訴字第 647 號判決] (Kao-Hsiung Admin. High Ct. [高雄高等行政法院] 23 Jan 2007) (Taiwan).

[27]For an official introduction to the Taoyuan Aerotropolis Project, visit its official website. Taoyuan Aerotropolis http://taoyuan-aerotropolis.com/en_content/index.aspx (last visited 17 Nov 2017).

Deregulation and privatization releases market forces that may sacrifice the natural environment for private interests, yet the government does little to properly regulate market forces in the public domain, leaving natural resources to be damaged piece by piece. On many occasions, the government has invited private capital but has failed to guard the public interest and human rights. The decision-making processes are usually flawed and not fully participatory. The cases of Taitung Beautiful Bay and TAP reflect only a small part of a systemic problem.

4.3.2 Gesture Politics on Climate Change

Taiwan's response to climate change began in May 1992, yet most policies remain ineffective political slogans.

The Executive Yuan established a Working Group for Global Environmental Change, renaming it the Working Group Guiding Global Environmental Change Policy to cope with the normative demands of the 1992 UNFCCC. In August 1997, the Executive Yuan re-organized it as the National Council for Sustainable Development of the Executive Yuan (hereinafter NCSD). One working group under the NCSD is in charge of mitigating greenhouse gas emissions and promoting energy efficiency.[28] In 1999, the Council was further elevated and chaired by the Vice-Premier, indicating gradual awareness of climate change in the government.

The Ministry of Economy and the EPA held a National Energy Conference for the first time in 1998, reaching a consensus on the target and agenda of reducing greenhouse gas emissions.[29] The conference also confirmed the need for a fourth nuclear power plant. In 2005, in response to the coming into force of the Kyoto Protocol, the Task Force for Responding to the UNFCCC and the Kyoto Protocol was founded, with similar offices later established in relevant agencies in the central and local governments to deal with the issue of carbon reduction.[30] The government again set out to work on policies concerning the mitigation of the environmental impact, holding national conferences including the National Energy Conference of 2005, the National Sustainable Development Conference of 2006, and the Conference on Sustaining Taiwan's Economic Development of 2006. The focus of these discussions was on policy for the post-Kyoto Protocol era and the strategies for industrial sectors. In this wave of deliberation, however, the earlier proposed

---

[28]Human Rights Council Res. 7/23, UN Doc. A/HRC/7/78 (28 Mar 2008).

[29]The 1998 National Energy Conference proposed implementation measures which were approved by the Executive Yuan on 11 June 1998. It emphasized energy conservation and called for an accelerated transformation of the energy structure. The goal was to reduce CO_2 emissions from fuel combustion to 2000 levels before year 2020, and to increase renewable energy to 3% of the total energy supply by year 2020.

[30]According to official reports, Taiwan's total carbon dioxide emissions nationwide are more than 277 million tons per year, with an average growth of 124% every year. The energy conversion industry contributed 7% of the emissions; heavy industry contributed 52%; the transportation sector contributed 14%; the commercial sector 6% and private households 12%.

goals of mitigation were found to be difficult to implement and the government proposed to adjust the agenda. Since then, no consensus has been reached on this issue and greenhouse gas emissions have increased at an annual rate of 2.94%.[31]

The Legislative Yuan passed the Long-Lingering Greenhouse Gas Reduction and Management Act some months ahead of the 2016 Paris Conference of the Parties (COP). The Act set up the basic principles for the legal response to climate change. The primary principle is to reduce dependence on fossil fuels, aiming at promoting low-carbon growth. The Act sets a 50% emissions reduction target for 2050, compared to the 2005 greenhouse gases (GHG) levels. The Act also announces a nuclear-free policy, the development of renewable energy and implementation of a tax mechanism on imported fossil fuels.[32] These articles reflect past efforts of both the Conference of Parties of the UN Framework Convention on Climate Change and Taiwanese society. However, the government has still, so far, been passive in making effective policy and taking measures on GHG emissions. As such, there has been little progress on the development of renewable energy and green infrastructure.[33]

In the government's strategy to address the problems of climate change, the latest development is the National Guideline for Climate Change Adaptation Policy (hereinafter Adaptation Guideline) proposed in 2010, the goal of which is to implement a comprehensive set of policies for adapting to the impact of climate change.[34] Although the Adaptation Guideline provides detailed evaluations on the impact of climate change in eight fields, it fails to provide frameworks and organizational or procedural reforms for later programs and actions.

The sluggish progress in climate change mitigation and adaptation has been criticized as merely "gesture politics" intended to comfort domestic NGOs and international society.[35]

4.4 *Human Rights for the Future*

In the face of growing threats, environmental rights have evolved accordingly. Implementation of the human rights treaties and the procedural turn of rights are

[31]Taiwan Environmental Protection Administration (2015).

[32]Wenshi Qiti Jianliang ji Guanlifa [溫室氣體減量及管理法] (Greenhouse Gas Reduction and Management Act), arts. 5–6 (Taiwan).

[33]Taiwan imports over 97% of its energy supply from foreign countries due to its limited energy resources. The effort to develop renewable energy started in 2003 when the government guaranteed the price of electricity generated from renewable energy. In 2009, the government passed the Renewable Energy Development Act (REDA), aiming to increase the installed renewable energy capacity in Taiwan to 9.95 GW by 2030. Yet the use of renewable energy has been lower than 5%; solar and wind are two major forms of renewable energy in Taiwan.

[34]For an English introduction, see Kuo (2013). See also Council for Economic Planning and Development (2012).

[35]Lin and Yeh (2016).

two of the most important developments in environmental rights in Taiwan. In addition, the human rights approach to climate change may also inform the future development of environmental rights.

4.4.1 Greening Human Rights

It is not clear how the implementation of the ICCPR and the ICESCR changes the substance of environmental rights in Taiwan. Yet the emerging human rights jurisprudence may shed some light on the discussion of environmental rights.

First, the ICCPR and the ICESCR provide a list of rights that are believed to be inherent to all human beings. Although the ICCPR and the ICESCR make no specific reference to protection of the environment,[36] it is generally accepted that human rights provisions can apply to environmental problems.[37] For example, in 1994 the Ksentini Report prepared for the UN Human Rights Commission argued that all persons have a right to a secure, healthy, and ecologically sound environment.[38] Christopher Weeramantry stated in his separate opinion in the Gabčíkovo-Nagymaros Project case, "the protection of the environment is likewise a vital part of contemporary human rights doctrine, for it is a sine qua non for numerous human rights such as the right to health and the right to life itself."[39]

The Human Rights Committee (hereinafter CHR) and the Committee on Economic, Social and Cultural Rights (hereinafter CESCR) have published General Comments on the ICCPR and the ICESCR, expressing their interpretations of certain provisions. The CHR and CESCR have already developed a series of general comments, demonstrating an emerging jurisprudence on greening human rights. These General Comments confirm that recognition of environmental rights is fundamental to the inherent dignity of the human person and indispensable to the fulfillment of other human rights. If serious environmental degradation undermines the rights to life, health, adequate standard of living, food, water, family or the right to culture, the state has an obligation to protect the environment to the degree that citizens can fully exercise their human rights. For example, the ICCPR General

[36]Principle 1 of the 1972 Stockholm Declaration on Environment and Development (New York, 1973) declares, "Man has the fundamental right to freedom, equality and adequate conditions of life, in an environment of a quality that permits a life of dignity and well-being, and he bears a solemn responsibility to protect and improve the environment for present and future generations."

[37]The ICESCR, Article 12(2)(b), for example, directs states to adopt measures as may be necessary for the "improvement of all aspects of environmental and industrial hygiene" in order to fully realize the right to health.

[38]Final Rep. Prepared by Fatma Zohra Ksentini, Spec. Rapporteur, UN Sub-Commission on the Prevention of Discrimination and the Protection of Minorities, UN Doc. E/CN.4/Sub.2/1994/9 (6 July 1994).

[39]Gabčíkovo-Nagymaros Project (Hung. v. Slovk.), Judgement, 1997 I.C.J. Rep. 7, 88, 91 (25 Sept), http://www.icj-cij.org/docket/files/92/7383.pdf (separate opinion by J. Weeramantry).

Comment No. 31 affirms that the right to life includes threats to life caused by health risks as well as dangers emanating from nuclear waste. CESCR General Comment No. 14 suggests that the right to health includes "the requirement to ensure an adequate supply of safe and potable water and basic sanitation; the prevention and reduction of the population's exposure to harmful substances such as radiation and harmful chemicals or other detrimental environmental conditions that directly or indirectly impact upon human health."[40] CESCR General Comment No. 12 especially recognizes the relation between the environment and the right to food, noting that the right to adequate food requires the state to make "appropriate economic, environmental and social policies."

Secondly, the General Comments suggest that if a state fails to respect, protect or fulfill a citizen's rights against environmental degradation, the state violates its obligations under the two covenants. The state is obliged not only to refrain from degrading the environment but also to protect citizens from environmental harm done by other private entities or natural disasters. For example, CESCR General Comment No. 12 suggests that states should take active measures to ensure that even vulnerable groups can fulfill their human rights in a proper environment.[41] On some occasions, states are obliged to take active measures and implement policies to fulfill human rights. In other words, the obligations of a state depend on the extent to which citizens can fully enjoy and exercise their human rights.

The ICCPR and ICESCR have re-interpreted existing human rights provisions to cope with environmental harm, resulting in a human rights law that is "greened" and able to deal with environmental problems. The greening of human rights has substantially enlarged the understanding and application of existing human rights. Nowadays, the resolution of environmental problems is no longer limited to regulation and implementation of environmental law; environmental problems have become human rights issues. People are asking, what rights are infringed upon by environmental degradation? As a result, the human rights of disadvantaged groups, such as indigenous people, women and children, have been taken more seriously. For example, General Comment No. 12 underscores the special needs of the vulnerable population, stating that "even where a state faces severe resource constraints, whether caused by a process of economic adjustment, economic recession, climate conditions or other factors, measures should be undertaken to ensure that the right to adequate food is fulfilled especially for vulnerable population groups and individuals." While the General Comments have resulted in a greening of existing human rights legislation, they have also led to an emphasis on procedural rights to adequate information and participation.

---

[40]UN Committee on Economic, Social, and Cultural Rights, General Comment No. 14: The right to the highest attainable standard of health, UN Doc. E/C.12/2000/4 (11 Aug 2000).

[41]UN Committee on Economic, Social and Cultural Rights, General Comment No. 12: The right to adequate food (art. 11), UN Doc. E/C.12/1999/5 (12 May 1999).

4.4.2 The Demand for Procedural Rights

Social movements against forced evictions and improper land use have enriched procedural-rights protection in Taiwan.

A series of environmental controversies have directly brought into question the due process of decision-making. When environmental controversies involve complex, professional knowledge and conflicts of values, the courts are reluctant and perhaps incapable of making judgments on substantive issues. The administrative agencies have started to realize that, in such situations, unilateral opinions are no longer able to persuade concerned citizens.

Through constitutional interpretations and court decisions, a right to due process in decision-making is gradually being developed in Taiwan. J.Y. Interpretations 709 and 732 are the two most important interpretations establishing the constitutional requirement of due process in administrative procedures.[42] In J.Y. Interpretation 709, the Constitutional Court declares that due process in administrative procedures includes the existence of an appropriate organization, information disclosure and the opportunity to present opinions. With regard to decisions that might greatly affect people's rights directly, the competent authority should hold official hearings publicly. In J.Y. Interpretation 732, the Court suggests that any official hearing for expropriation should be necessarily required for public construction and for public use, owing to the serious impact on the freedom of residence and citizens' property rights.[43]

In addition to the court's decisions, and as a result of public pressure, administrative agencies have also put efforts into improving the decision-making process. Evidence of progress in this area can be seen in the above-mentioned TAP case. Complicated cases such as this require an inclusive and deliberative process through which the voices of concerned parties, such as residents and human rights groups, can be heard and the issues involved can be fully debated. In recognition of this need, the Ministry of Transportation and Communication (MOTC) and the Taoyuan City Government held 12 preliminary hearings and 6 formal hearings to allow concerned parties to voice their opinions. Observers still criticized these hearings' failure to clarify key issues and to allow for deliberation of the flawed institutional arrangements.[44] However, this experience demonstrates significant progress in the decision-making process and has triggered an action on rule-making in hearings by the Ministry of Interior.[45]

---

[42]Dafaguan Shizi Di 709 Hao [大法官釋字第 709 號] (J. Y. Interpretation 709) (26 Apr 2013) (R.O.C.). English translation is available at http://www.judicial.gov.tw/constitutionalcourt/en/p03_01.asp?expno=709.

[43]Dafaguan Shizi Di 732 Hao [大法官釋字第 732 號] (J. Y. Interpretation 732) (25 Sept 2015) (R.O.C.). English translation is available at http://www.judicial.gov.tw/constitutionalcourt/en/p03_01.asp?expno=732.

[44]Abraham (2017).

[45]Operational directions for holding a hearing (2016).

5 Changing Environmental Rights in Taiwan

The meaning and function of environmental rights are not fixed and universal. They are dependent on context and they change with time. In Taiwan, environmental rights have evolved within the political and social contexts as well as within the corresponding legal framework. From personal injury to legal rights to human rights, the evolution of environmental rights in Taiwan can be divided into three periods. In the first period, before democratization, the development agenda caused serious threats to Taiwan's natural environment, while the law provided almost no protection for victims. Victims of environmental degradation may have suffered losses for which they sought to blame the polluter. However, the blame seldom transformed into a legal claim. The law failed to set up standards to determine illegal pollution and corresponding responsibilities. Victims of environmental degradation in this period did not expect the government to take a primary role in environmental protection, nor did they trust the courts to prioritize environmental protection. In this period, claims against environmental degradation were predominantly prompted by victims who had suffered personal damage to either property or health. Under the framework of the ICCPR and the ICESCR, these claims could be understood as premature claims of the right to health and property.

The second period from the late 1980s to 2000 has been categorized as early democratization. This period not only saw vibrant environmental movements contribute to Taiwan's democratization, but these movements also triggered the implementation of specific environmental legislation. Regulatory laws from this period provided standards to regulate pollution, imposing on the government the responsibility to control pollution. In addition to regulations, the enactment of the PNDMA, EIAA and the emergence of citizen suits clauses made environmental claims enforceable legal rights. Citizens could take advantage of legal mechanisms to resolve public nuisance disputes, participate in and supervise the environmental impact of major construction projects, and bring suits against the government in the interest of the environment, without personal rights infringements. The new legal framework not only enabled the transformation of victims' grievances into legal rights but also enlarged the understanding of the "environment" in general. With the development of the anti-nuclear movement, legalized environmental rights began to be applied to environmental damages beyond personal injuries, such as natural resource degradation and the need to maintain a sustainable environment for future generations.

The third period, since 2000, has seen the development of deregulation, privatization and climate change, all of which have brought new threats to Taiwan's environment. However, the introduction of international human rights law into the domestic legal system may yet promote environmental rights. The policies of deregulation and privatization have generated new motives for the private sector to take advantage of natural resources, while the government has little experience in protecting the environment from the piecemeal degradation threatened by the newly opened market. The development of climate change has provided further challenges to the government's capacity to protect the environment which, as yet, has provided no effective policy regarding energy structure, greenhouse gas emissions and climate change adaptation. Despite that, environmental rights have become more profound with the progress on procedural rights and international human rights. The introduction of international human rights law has helped to further emphasize environmental rights as inherent conditions for human rights. Moreover, the emerging jurisprudence on environmental rights extends human rights protection to environmental issues and highlights the future face of environmental rights.

The development of environmental rights in Taiwan can be better illustrated by the following table.

Period	Political/social context	Environmental threats	Legal framework and state performance	Environmental rights in reality
Before 1980s	Japanese colony Developmental state	State-owned or state-run enterprises	Development strategy No environmental law	Personal damage rights to health and property rights
1987–2000	Democratic state in transition	State-owned or state-run enterprises	Legislation on environmental law	Environmental rights as legal rights; a right to the environment
2000–present	Democratic consolidated state	Private sector and climate change	Higher environmental law and human rights law	Environmental rights as human rights Generational justice

6 Conclusion

Determining the kinds of rights people can exercise in the face of environmental degradation is crucial for preserving the environment and human dignity. Given the fact that scholars have not reached a consensus on the definition of environmental rights, this chapter has chosen to define these rights broadly to better delineate the changing face of environmental rights in Taiwan.

It is argued in this chapter that while the process of democratic transition has shaped the face of environmental rights in Taiwan, environmental rights can only be fully understood within the dynamics of environmental threats, legal frameworks and social and political contexts. Taiwan's democratic transition can be divided into three periods, each with distinct political and social contexts as well as legal frameworks, and it is only in the dynamics among these factors that we may understand the development of environmental rights in Taiwan. As the scope of environmental rights in Taiwan increases with the development of environmental rights as human rights, the obligations of the state and the legal consequences of violations become ambiguous and diluted. The next question is how to prevent environmental rights from becoming simple rhetoric. On this point, whether the courts and government can effectively respond to the increasing importance of environmental rights may be the key for their realization.

References

Abraham G (2017) Taoyuan housing project figures misleading: groups. Taipei Times. http://www.taipeitimes.com/News/taiwan/archives/2017/07/30/2003675593. Accessed 21 Nov 2017

Council for Economic Planning and Development (2012) Adaptation strategy to climate change in Taiwan. Council for Economic Planning and Development, Taipei

Final Rep. Prepared by Fatma Zohra Ksentini, Spec. Rapporteur, UN Sub-Commission on Prevention of Discrimination and Protection of Minorities, UN Doc. E/CN.4/Sub.2/1994/9 (6 July 1994)

G.A. Res. 2758 (1971)

Grano SA (2015) Environmental governance in Taiwan: a new generation of activists and stakeholders. Routledge, Oxon

Ho M-S (2003) The politics of anti-nuclear protest in Taiwan: a case of party-dependent movement (1980–2000). Mod Asian Stud 37:683–708

Ho M-S (2011) Environmental movement in democratizing Taiwan (1980–2004): a political opportunity structure perspective. In: Broadbent J, Brockman V (eds) East Asian social movements. Springer, New York

Hsiao H-H (1982) Ziran Baoyu yu Huanjing Yundong: Bi Jiao She Hui Xue Zhong Mei She Hui Zhi Bi Jiao Yan Tao Hui 自然保育與環境運動-比較社會學, 中美社會之比較研討會。

Hsiao H-H (1987) Women Zhiyou Yige Taiwan—Fanwuran, Shengtai Baoyu yu Huanjing Yundong [我們只有一個台灣—反污染、生態保育與環境運動] (We have only one Taiwan). Yuanshen [圓神], Taipei

Hsiao MH-H (1990) Emerging social movements and the rise of a demanding civil society in Taiwan. Aust J Chin Aff 24:163–179

Human Rights Council Res. 7/23, UN Doc. A/HRC/7/78 (28 Mar 2008)

Huntington SP (1993) The third wave: democratization in the late twentieth century. University of Oklahoma Press, Norman

Khemani RS, Shapiro DM (1993) Glossary of industrial organisation economics and competition law. OECD Publishing, Paris

Kuo F-Y (2013) The national climate change adaptation policy guideline and local adaptation plan (in Chinese) Taipei. http://www.apectyphoon.org/sdt175/img/img/3865/ppt/21020306_FeiYu%20Kuo.pdf. Accessed 18 Nov 2017

Lin C-Y, Yeh J-R (2016) The Paris agreement and the transformation of global climate law: Taiwan's perspective. Paper presented at an international seminar, Republic of Korea, 28–30 Apr 2016

Lo Y-C (2013a) Accessing indigenous land rights through claims in Taroko area, eastern Taiwan. Ph.D. dissertation, Leiden University

Lo Y-C (2013b) Making indigenous lands into "concrete": land grabbing and the embeddedness of the cement industry in the Taroko area of eastern Taiwan. Paper presented at the conference on Legal Ground: Land and Law in Contemporary Taiwan and the Pacific, Institute of Ethnology, Academia Sinica 11–12 Sept 2013

Operational directions for holding a hearing (2016) Ministry of the Interior, R.O.C. (Taiwan). https://www.moi.gov.tw/chi/chi_legal/points.aspx. Accessed 15 Nov 2017

Organisation for Economic Co-operation and Development (OECD) (1997) Regulatory reform: a synthesis. OECD, Paris

Taiwan Environmental Protection Administration (2015) 2015 Taiwan greenhouse gas inventory: executive summary. http://unfccc.saveoursky.org.tw/2015nir/uploads/00_abstract_en.pdf. Accessed 17 Nov 2017

Taoyuan Aerotropolis. http://taoyuan-aerotropolis.com/en_content/index.aspx. Accessed 17 Nov 2017

UN Committee on Economic, Social and Cultural Rights, General Comment No. 12: The right to adequate food (art. 11), UN Doc. E/C.12/1999/5 (12 May 1999)

UN Committee on Economic, Social, and Cultural Rights, General Comment No. 14: The right to the highest attainable standard of health, UN Doc. E/C.12/2000/4 (11 Aug 2000)

Yeh Y-R (1994) Huanjing Zhengce yu Falu [環境政策與法律] (Environmental policies and law). Yuedan [月旦], Taipei

Chun-Yuan Lin With his Ph.D. degree from National Taiwan University, School of Law, Chun-Yuan Lin is now Associate Professor in the Department of Financial and Economic Law, Chung-Yuan Christian University, Taiwan. He is also a director of the Environmental Jurist Association. His academic research mainly focuses on constitutional law, environmental law, climate change law, and international human rights law. Recent publications include: (1) "An Unprincipled Principle? A Comparative Study on the Application of the Principle of Proportionality in Environmental Cases in Taiwan and the EU," Academia Sinica Law Journal, pp. 99–158 (2016); (2) "Climate Change Adaptation Through Administrative Litigation? The Experience of Taiwan," in Climate Change Liability and Beyond (Jiunn-rong Yeh ed.), NTU Press (2017); (3) "Bring Human Rights to Climate Change Adaptation—From International Law to Domestic Policy," presented at the North American Taiwan Studies Association 22nd Annual Conference (2016/6/9–2016/6/11, Canada); (4) "The Paris Agreement and the Transformation of Global Climate Law: Taiwan's Perspective," presented at the International Seminar on the Paris Agreement: Key Elements and Implementations (2016/4/28–2016/4/30, Republic of Korea); (5) "Beyond Social Rights—Changing Constitutionalism in the Face of Economic Crisis and Climate Change," at the 9th World Congress of the International Association of Constitutional Law (2014/6/16–2014/6/20, Norway).

Chapter 28
Human Rights and Climate Finance—How Does the Normative Framework Affect Taiwan?

Wen-Chen Shih

Abstract According to a study on the relationship between climate change and human rights conducted by the Office of the United Nations High Commissioner for Human Rights (OHCHR) in 2009, the effect of climate change might affect certain specific human rights, such as the right to life, the right to adequate food, the right to water, the right to health, the right to adequate housing, and the right to self-determination. The effects of climate change might also affect specific groups, in particular women, children, and indigenous peoples. This study, however, points out that it might be difficult for an individual to hold a particular state responsible for harm caused by climate change. Human rights law provides more effective protection with regard to the measures taken by states to address climate change and their impact on human rights, such as access to information and participation in decision-making. The OHCHR made a submission to the 21st Conference of Parties of the UNFCCC in 2015 entitled: "Understanding Human Rights and Climate Change." The submission presents ten key messages on human rights and climate change, one of which is "to mobilize maximum available resources for sustainable, human rights-based development." This key message is crucial as the financial demands of climate change mitigation and adaptation have been increasing rapidly with the rise of the environmental, social and economic costs of global warming and their associated environmental catastrophes on an unprecedented scale. A human rights-based approach to climate finance can help ensure that climate-financed activities comply with existing human rights obligations and principles. It also requires the establishment of institutional safeguard systems that prevent social and environmental harm and maximize participation, transparency, accountability, and equity and rights protections. Guiding principles such as consistency with international human rights obligations, doing no harm, transparency and accountability, public participation in decision-making, and equity and non-discrimination have been proposed to guide the development and implementation of climate finance policies and activities. This chapter focuses on human rights and climate finance, and how this emerging normative framework will affect

W.-C. Shih (✉)
Department of International Business, National Cheng-chi University, Taipei City, Taiwan
e-mail: wcshih@nccu.edu.tw

J. A. Cohen et al. (eds.), *Taiwan and International Human Rights*, Economics, Law, and Institutions in Asia Pacific, https://doi.org/10.1007/978-981-13-0350-0_28

or has affected Taiwan's climate finance both in terms of Taiwan's national climate finance and in terms of Taiwan's foreign aid policy.

Keywords Climate finance · Climate change financial mechanism Foreign aid · Rights-based approach

1 Introduction

According to a study on the relationship between climate change and human rights conducted by the Office of the United Nations High Commissioner for Human Rights (hereinafter OHCHR) in 2009, the effect of climate change might affect certain specific human rights, such as the right to life, the right to adequate food, the right to water, the right to health, the right to adequate housing, and the right to self-determination. The effects of climate change might also affect specific groups, in particular women, children, and indigenous peoples.[1] This study, however, points out that it might be difficult for an individual to hold a particular state responsible for harm caused by climate change. Human rights law provides more effective protection with regard to the measures taken by states to address climate change and their impact on human rights, such as access to information and participation in decision-making.[2] The OHCHR made a submission to the 21st Conference of Parties (hereinafter COP) of the UN Framework Convention on Climate Change (hereinafter UNFCCC) in 2015 entitled: "Understanding Human Rights and Climate Change."[3] The submission presents ten key messages on human rights and climate change, one of which is "to mobilize maximum available resources for sustainable, human rights-based development."[4]

This key message is crucial as the financial demands of climate change mitigation and adaptation have been increasing rapidly with the rise of the environmental, social and economic costs of global warming and the associated environmental catastrophes on an unprecedented scale. A human rights-based approach to climate finance can help ensure that climate-financed activities comply with existing human rights obligations and principles. It also requires the establishment of institutional safeguard systems that prevent social and environmental harm and maximize participation, transparency, accountability, equity and rights protections. Guiding principles such as consistency with international human rights obligations, doing no harm, transparency and accountability, public participation in decision-making, and equity and

[1]Office of the United Nations High Commissioner for Human Rights, Report of the United Nations High Commissioner for Human Rights on the Relationship Between Climate Change and Human Rights, pp. 8–18, UN Doc. A/HRC/10/61 (15 Jan 2009) [hereinafter 2009 OHCHR report].

[2]*Id.*, at p. 24.

[3]Office of the United Nations High Commissioner for Human Rights (2015) [hereinafter 2015 OHCHR submission].

[4]*Id.*, at p. 3.

non-discrimination have been proposed to guide the development and implementation of climate finance policies and activities.[5]

This chapter will focus on human rights and climate finance, and how this emerging normative framework will affect or has affected Taiwan's climate finance both in terms of Taiwan's national climate finance and in terms of Taiwan's foreign aid policy. After this introduction, Part 2 will briefly look at the relationship between climate change and human rights. Part 3 will focus on climate finance and human rights and will present a rights-based approach to climate finance. Part 4 will first introduce Taiwan's climate finance framework and, based on the findings of Parts 2 and 3, conduct a preliminary analysis of whether Taiwan's climate finance fits into the model of the rights-based approach to climate finance. Part 5 concludes with some policy suggestions as to how Taiwan can reorient its climate finance framework toward a more rights-based approach.

2 Climate Change and Human Rights

Linkages between the environment and human rights have long been debated. The core international human rights treaties do not recognize a stand-alone right to a clean environment.[6] However, it is recognized that a clean, healthy and functional environment is integral to the enjoyment of human rights, such as the rights to life, health, food and an adequate standard of living. In short, environmental protection protects human rights. At the same time, adherence to human rights—such as those that ensure public access to information and participation in decision making—contributes to more just decisions about the utilization and protection of environmental resources and protects against the potential for abuse under the auspices of environmental action.[7] In terms of climate change, far-reaching environmental impacts have already taken place. These impacts, together with direct harm to people, property, and physical infrastructure, pose a serious threat to the enjoyment and exercise of human rights across the planet. Furthermore, measures undertaken to mitigate greenhouse gas (GHG) emissions and to adapt to climate change, such as hydroelectric and biofuel projects, can themselves adversely affect the enjoyment of human rights.[8]

Drawing from the findings of the 5th Assessment Report of the Inter-governmental Panel on Climate Change (hereinafter IPCC AR5), specifically the contribution of Working Group II on Impacts, Adaptation, and Vulnerability, an United Nations Environment Programme (hereinafter UNEP) report identified how the impacts of climate change affect specific human rights that are incorporated into

---

[5]Johl and Lador (2012), at pp. 4–6.

[6]United Nations Environment Programme (2015), at p. 12.

[7]*Id.*, at p. 1.

[8]*Id.*, at p. 1.

the core international human rights treaties.[9] These impacts and the affected human rights are summarized in Table 1.

As can be seen in Table 1, the effects of climate change will affect a wide range of human rights that are protected under the core international human rights treaties. As a result, efforts have been undertaken in the international human rights regime to address the issues of climate change. Two events sparked a search for international dialogue on human rights and climate change. First, in December 2005, the Chair of the Inuit Circumpolar Conference submitted a petition to the Inter-American Commission on Human Rights requesting relief for human rights violations resulting from the impacts of global warming and climate change. Second, in November 2008, the Small Island Developing States adopted the Male' Declaration on the Human Dimension of Global Climate Change. The Male' Declaration was the first international instrument to explicitly recognize that "climate change has clear and immediate implications for the full enjoyment of human rights." That same month, OHCHR issued a public statement for the UNFCCC COP 13 in Bali, acknowledging that "climate change can adversely affect the fundamental human rights of present and future generations." The public statement reminded the COP that governments have both moral and legal obligations to protect and promote basic human rights when tackling climate change.[10] Responding to the Male' Declaration, the UN Human Rights Council (hereinafter UNHRC) issued Resolution 7/23 in 2008 and directed the OHCHR to conduct "a detailed analytical study of the relationship between climate change and human rights." The OHCHR released a report in 2009 describing how the observed and projected impacts of climate change have implications for the enjoyment of human rights and for the obligations of states under international human rights law.[11] Since the issuance of this report, UNHRC has issued four resolutions recognizing the linkages between climate change and human rights: Resolution 10/4 (March 2009), Resolution 18/22 (September 2011), Resolution 26/27 (July 2014), and Resolution 29/15 (July 2015).[12]

As the UNHRC in its Resolution 26/27 emphasizes, "climate change is an urgent global problem requiring a global solution." It is now widely recognized that climate change has profound impacts on a wide variety of human rights, including the rights to life, self-determination, development, food, health, water and sanitation and housing. Simply put, climate change is a human rights problem and a human rights framework must be part of the solution.[13] Many have advocated to incorporate human rights references into the international climate change regime. The

[9] *Id.*, at p. 3.

[10] *Id.*, at p. 13.

[11] 2009 OHCHR Report.

[12] United Nations Environment Programme (2015), at p. 14.

[13] 2015 OHCHR Submission, at p. 6.

Table 1 Effects of climate change on human rights[a]

		Affected rights
Impacts on ecosystems and natural resources	Freshwater resources	Right to water and sanitation, right to health, right to life, right to food, right to an adequate standard of living
	Terrestrial ecosystems	Right to food, right to an adequate standard of living, right to health
	Coastal systems and low-lying areas	Right to life, right to health, right to housing, right to an adequate standard of living, right to food, right to water, right to property, right to self-determination
	Ocean systems	Right to food, right to an adequate standard of living, right to health
	Food security and production systems	Right to food, right to health, right to life, right to an adequate standard of living
Impacts on physical infrastructure and human settlements	Urban areas	Right to life, right to housing, right to health, right to water and sanitation, right to an adequate standard of living, right to property
	Rural areas	Right to life, right to health, right to housing, right to food, right to water and sanitation, right to an adequate standard of living, right to property
	Key economic sectors and services	Right to health, right to an adequate standard of living, right to food, right to water
Impacts on livelihood, health, and security	Livelihood and poverty	Right to an adequate standard of living, right to health, right to life, right to food, right to water, right to property
	Human health	Right to health, right to life
	Human security	Right to life, right to an adequate standard of living, right to a nationality, right to self-determination, right to mobility, right to property

[a] United Nations Environment Programme (2015), at pp. 2–8

2010 Cancun Agreements,[14] a series of decisions adopted at COP 16, was the first instrument in the international climate change regime where references to human rights were explicitly mentioned. Recital 8 of this COP decision states: "Noting resolution 10/4 of the United Nations Human Rights Council on human rights and climate change, which recognizes that the adverse effects of climate change have a

[14]UNFCCC Conference of the Parties, Decision 1/CP.16: The Cancun Agreements: Outcome of the Work of the Ad Hoc Working Group on Long-term Cooperative Action under the Convention, UN Doc. FCCC/CP/2010/7/Add.1 (15 Mar 2011). See also the Cancun Agreements. http://unfccc.int/cancun/. Accessed 14 Dec 2017.

range of direct and indirect implications for the effective enjoyment of human rights and that the effects of climate change will be felt most acutely by those segments of the population that are already vulnerable owing to geography, gender, age, indigenous or minority status, or disability…." In addition, paragraph 8 of the Cancun Agreements states that Parties "should, in all climate change-related actions, fully respect human rights as enunciated in the outcome of the sixteenth session of the Conference of the Parties to the Convention."[15] Similar language can be found in UNHRC Resolutions 18/22 and 26/27.[16] Since then, more pledges have been made to insert human rights references into the international climate change regime, including, and especially, into the Paris Agreement.[17] After intense negotiations, references to human rights were explicitly incorporated into the Preamble to the Paris Agreement: recital 12 of the Preamble states: "*Acknowledging* that climate change is a common concern of humankind, Parties should, when taking action to address climate change, respect, promote and consider their respective obligations on human rights, the right to health, the rights of indigenous peoples, local communities, migrants, children, persons with disabilities and people in vulnerable situations and the right to development, as well as gender equality, empowerment of women and intergenerational equity…." Apart from this reference in the preamble, no other provisions in the Paris Agreement specifically mention human rights. However, scholars identify several provisions in the Paris Agreement as well as several paragraphs in the COP decision adopting the Paris Agreement that "relate, broadly, to the advancement of human rights, ranging from gender equality and participation to sustainable development and poverty eradication."[18]

These developments demonstrate the growing consensus in both the international human rights regime and the international climate change regime that human rights and climate change impact each other and should no longer be addressed separately.

On another front, human rights mainstreaming[19] advocates the harmonization or integration of human rights norms and practices with social justice issues, such as development, environmental protection, health, education, business, safety, government and labour. It is a process-based strategy that tries to integrate human rights norms into all levels of political, legislative and regulatory decision-making. Mainstreaming human rights means making sure that human rights are integrated and considered at all stages of development and delivery of actions, programs and

[15]*Id.*

[16]Human Rights Council Res. 18/22, Human rights and climate change, UN Doc. A/HRC/Res/18/22 (17 Oct 2011); Human Rights Council Res. 26/27, Human rights and climate change, UN Doc. A/HR/Res/26/27 (15 July 2014).

[17]Mayer (2016), at pp. 111–112.

[18]*Id.*, at pp. 115–117.

[19]The concept of "mainstreaming" is a "paradigm that seeks to understand the interrelationships between diverse societal strata, such as the arts, business, education, environment, faith, finance, government, labour, gender, media, public safety, public health and science." Olawuyi (2016), at p. 144.

policies, and by everyone involved in such program delivery.[20] Human rights mainstreaming provides a practical framework through which human rights principles and standards can be integrated and reflected in decision-making processes to ensure coherence, harmonization and effectiveness.[21] In other words, human rights can be integrated into climate change-related actions by applying a "rights-based approach" to policy and development, as called for by the Declaration on the Right to Development and agreed to in the UN Common Understanding of a Human Rights-Based Approach to Development Cooperation.[22]

OHCHR submitted a document entitled "Understanding Human Rights and Climate Change" to COP 21 in 2015.[23] The key message on human rights and climate change was the call to take several issues into consideration in all climate actions, including the agreement to be negotiated at COP 21. One of the issues was to mobilize the maximum available resources for sustainable, human rights-based development. Another issue was international cooperation. It was advised that international assistance for climate change mitigation and adaptation should be added to existing ODA commitments.[24] Protecting human rights from harm resulting from businesses was also called for. The UN Guiding Principles on Business and Human Rights[25] affirm that states have an obligation to protect human rights from harm by businesses, while businesses have a responsibility to respect human rights and to do no harm. Where states incorporate private financing or market-based approaches to climate change within the international climate change framework, the compliance of businesses with these responsibilities is especially critical.[26] The next parts of this chapter will look more closely at climate finance and human rights, especially from a rights-based approach.

3 Climate Finance and Human Rights: A Rights-Based Approach

Climate finance has many definitions. For example, the UNFCCC Standing Committee on Finance, in its 2014 report, defines climate finance as: "Climate finance aims at reducing emissions and enhancing sinks of greenhouse gases and aims at reducing vulnerability of, and maintaining and increasing the resilience of,

---

[20] *Id.*, at p. 145.

[21] *Id.*, at p. 149.

[22] 2015 OHCHR Submission, at p. 9.

[23] *Id.*

[24] *Id.*, at p. 3.

[25] Full text available at: http://www.ohchr.org/Documents/Publications/GuidingPrinciplesBusinessHR_EN.pdf.

[26] 2015 OHCHR Submission, at p. 4.

human and ecological systems to negative climate change impacts."[27] Climate finance usually comprises public and private finance for climate change mitigation and adaptation, often understood to mean money flows from developed to developing countries.[28] Climate change financing can be effective, efficient, and equitable only when policy coherence—both with respect to the institutions involved in channeling money flows as well as in the use of funding for concrete mitigation and adaptation measures—is observed.[29] Climate finance has been an important element in the international climate change regime. However, it is also one of the most controversial issues in terms of the enormous scale of finance that will be needed to support mitigation and in terms of adaptation and in terms of the evident lack of resources to fulfil the need.

Human rights may provide a justification for funding the mitigation and adaptation responses to climate change. The proponents of this approach have emphasized the liability and responsibility of developed countries for the current and projected human rights violations arising from human-induced climate change. However, there are reasons to think a strong or exclusive focus on the potential of human rights responsibility for the impacts of climate change may not form the best legal foundation for the response to climate change.[30] The OHCHR has identified that it is less than clear that the invocation of state responsibility for human rights violations arising from climate change finds strong support in existing international human rights law.[31] Conditioning climate finance on liability may undermine the obligations of shared responsibility of all states for the realization of human rights included in the ICESCR and may create arbitrary distinctions between environmental disasters or change based on whether or not they can be linked to the consequences of climate change.[32]

In short, human rights may be unable to justify funding for the mitigation and adaptation response to climate change. Nevertheless, climate finance and human rights have another more straightforward and urgent relationship; that is, the concern that certain types of mitigation/carbon projects undertaken to reduce or sequester GHGs can adversely affect human rights. Hydroelectric projects and biofuel policies and projects are two types of such mitigation projects.[33] The human rights impacts of carbon finance schemes include: forced displacement and the right to property, loss of the benefits of culture and tradition, loss of subsistence rights, loss of life, health concerns, inequality and discrimination against minority communities and vulnerable groups, and loss of consultative/participatory rights such as

[27]UNFCCC Standing Committee on Finance (2014), at p. 5.

[28]Ryan et al. (2012), at p. 10.

[29]Schalatek (2010), at p. 8.

[30]Jodoin (2010), at p. 4.

[31]2009 OHCHR Report, at para 70.

[32]Jodoin (2010), at pp. 4–5.

[33]Columbia Law School Sabin Center for Climate Change Law, Re: Comments on the rules, modalities, and procedures for the SDM, at 1–2 (5 Oct 2016).

the right to information, project review/complaints procedures and access to justice.[34] Such concerns about the high incidence of human rights violations and risks from carbon projects have led to increased expectations and calls for a more transparent, accountable and human rights-based approach to the design, approval and execution of carbon projects.[35] A human rights-based approach to climate finance will help to ensure that countries avoid or minimize the human rights impacts of mitigation and adaptation measures and promote sustainable and equitable low-carbon development.[36] In this context, four key legal challenges have emerged. First, international and national climate finance laws and policies need to be based on a recognition of the human rights impacts of climate change, particularly the rights to life, an adequate standard of living, culture, health, food, and water. Second, international climate finance laws and policies have to be linked to the shared obligation of all states to ensure the realization of economic, social and cultural rights, including through the provision of international funding and assistance by developed countries to developing countries. Third, international and national climate finance laws and policies have to respect, protect and fulfil the full range of human rights, taking into account the adverse consequences of certain response measures on vulnerable and disadvantaged groups potentially affected by the response measures. Fourth, they need to scale up the use of rights-based approaches at the project level to design effective and equitable climate finance frameworks and mechanisms at the international, national and sub-national levels.[37]

On another note, market-based mechanisms such as emissions trading or carbon taxes have been widely used by international and national climate change laws and policies as potential means to provide sources of climate finance. One of the theoretical critiques of the human rights mainstream paradigm is that market-based mechanisms are incentive-based mechanisms that should not be diluted by conduct-based instruments such as human rights.[38] However, human rights mainstreaming theorists suggest that social justice issues such as the environment are far too important to be left to market distortions. In addition, markets have been criticized for fostering discrimination and inequities.[39] Markets, however, are not the biggest problem. The biggest problem is an unregulated or ineffectively governed market, that is, a market without adequate rules that prevent oppression and injustice. It is thus important not to throw away markets but rather to ask how new policy measures can be designed to achieve the two-pronged goals of maintaining

[34]Olawuyi (2016), at pp. 90–138.

[35]*Id.*, at p. 14.

[36]Johl and Lador (2012), at p. 3.

[37]Jodoin (2010), at p. 6.

[38]Olawuyi (2016), at p. 185.

[39]*Id.*, at pp. 186–187.

the market outlook of the international climate change regime, while establishing stricter regulations that respond to the injustices of the carbon market.[40]

All of the above-mentioned debates on climate finance and human rights point to the importance of a rights-based approach to climate finance. A human rights-based approach is "a conceptual framework for the process of human development that is normatively based on international human rights standards and operationally directed to promoting and protecting human rights."[41] The international climate finance architecture has significant implications for the enjoyment of human rights. However, as has been mentioned, inadequate attention has been given to the positive and negative impacts of climate-financed activities on individuals and communities around the world. A human rights-based approach provides for consideration of these human impacts in the institutions, policies, and measures that enable climate finance.[42] Several guiding principles in applying a rights-based approach to climate finance have been suggested, such as consistency with international human rights obligations, doing no harm, transparency and accountability, public participation in decision-making, equity and non-discrimination, etc.[43]

The principle of "doing no harm," for example, can act to filter the types of projects that should or should not receive climate finance. The principle of "doing no harm" is important in providing policy coherence in public climate change finance. Several "don'ts" for climate change financing are suggested, such as do not invest in largely business-as-usual fossil fuel projects in oil, gas and mining, do not invest in nuclear power generation, do not invest in export production of agrofuels and oil plants, do not invest in a "new green revolution" based on genetically modified organisms, do not invest in the building of large hydro dams, do not support monoculture reforestation efforts under the reducing emissions from deforestation and forest degradation (REDD) financing schemes.[44]

Another example is the principle of transparency and accountability. Transparency and accountability in public climate finance are important core democratic principles and procedural rights in public climate finance, which should be applicable across all three elements of any climate change financial mechanism, i.e., the generation, distribution and governance of the financial mechanism.[45] These principles include the rights to information, participation in decision-making, and access to justice in the form of redress mechanisms to provide for restitution or guarantees of non-repetition. These rights and standards are well established under both human rights law and international environmental law and policy.[46] When

[40]*Id.*, at pp. 189–190.

[41]Office of the United Nations High Commissioner for Human Rights (2006), at p. 15.

[42]Johl and Lador (2012), at pp. 3–4.

[43]*Id.*, at pp. 4–6.

[44]Schalatek (2010), at pp. 25–28.

[45]For climate change financial mechanisms, see Shih (2011).

[46]Schalatek (2010), at p. 29.

they apply to the mobilization of public climate change finance, the need for more transparency and accountability in the discussion is the measurement of the amount of climate finance that flows from developed to developing countries, the reporting of these finance flows to the global public, and the verification of the completeness and accuracy of the reported data (the "MRV").[47] When the principles apply to the governance of climate change public finance, transparency refers to making all information on climate change public finance publicly available, accurate and timely. A redress mechanism is also paramount.[48] When the principles apply to disbursement, national ownership is crucial, including applying MRV to the disbursement of funds. Whether in-country civil society can independently monitor and verify government disclosures on climate finance spending and hold their own governments accountable is also important.[49]

All these principles under the rights-based approach to climate finance should be carefully taken into consideration in any climate change financial mechanisms. An important means for advancing rights considerations is through an institutional safeguards system within a climate change financial mechanism that effectively prevents social and environmental harm and promotes sustainable development.[50] In fact, most of the major climate change financial mechanisms have already adopted rules aimed at protecting the rights of affected stakeholders, but these rules vary in terms of the degree and adequacy of the protection afforded.[51] For example, the Council of the Global Environment Facility, one of the financial mechanisms of the UNFCCC, approved the Policies on Environmental and Social Safeguards and Gender Mainstreaming in 2011,[52] which are similar to the World Bank safeguard policies. The Board of the Adaptations Fund, another financial mechanism under the UNFCCC, approved an Environmental and Social Policy in 2013 and revised it in 2016.[53] These principles explicitly require that all projects supported by the Adaptation Fund respect and, where applicable, promote human rights.[54] The latest financial mechanism set up under the UNFCCC, the Green Climate Fund (GCF), also adopted, on an interim basis by its Board, the Environmental and Social Performance Standards of the International Finance Corporation (hereinafter IFC) for GCF-funded projects.[55] These standards are explicitly tied to human rights obligations. They also recognize that businesses as well as government actors have

---

[47]*Id.*, at p. 30.

[48]*Id.*, at pp. 31–32.

[49]*Id.*, at pp. 33–34.

[50]Johl and Lador (2012), at p. 14.

[51]Columbia Law School Sabin Center for Climate Change Law (2016), at p. 3.

[52]GEF policies on environmental and social safeguards and gender mainstreaming, GEF/C.40/10/Rev.1 (26 May 2011).

[53]Adaptation Fund Board, Environmental and Social Policy (Approved in Nov 2013; Revised in March 2016).

[54]*Id.*, at para. 15.

[55]Green Climate Fund, Decisions of the Board—Green Climate Fund, Annex III, GCF/B.07/11 (19 June 2014).

an obligation to respect human rights.[56] The GCF Board also created a Monitoring and Accountability Framework and an "Independent Redress Mechanism."[57] On the national front, some national development banks, for example the Netherlands Development Finance Company and the German Investment Corporation, apply a set of environmental and social guidelines as drafted by the IFC in their 2012 Environmental and Social Performance Standards by virtue of being members of the Equator Principles Framework.[58]

In addition to several core principles concerning the procedural rights of transparency and accountability as mentioned above, relevant substantive principles for the mobilization, governance and disbursement of public climate change financial mechanisms have also been suggested, as Table 2 summarizes.[59]

After surveying 19 multilateral and bilateral dedicated public climate funding initiatives, including the Adaptation Fund and the GEF, against these principles, it is suggested that most of the funding approaches remain "top-down," ignoring the need for subsidiarity and strengthened national/local ownership. All current climate finance mechanisms show a lack of procedural rules and mechanisms that would guarantee more effective involvement of relevant stakeholder groups and better and more active public participation in decision-making. None of these mechanisms have redress mechanisms. Overall, full transparency, accountability, and with it public oversight, are still lacking in most funding mechanisms to varying degrees, although public information efforts are made. Most climate funding mechanisms fall short even of the basic requirements for good overseas development aid (hereinafter ODA), as defined and widely accepted by the international community in the Paris Declaration on Aid Effectiveness[60] and the Accra Action Agenda.[61]

What can be observed from these discussions? First, the need for a rights-based approach to climate finance is apparent as there is an observed intrinsic relationship between human rights protection and climate finance activities. Second, having an institutional safeguard mechanism seems to be an appropriate means to incorporate the rights-based approach into a climate change financial mechanism. This can already be seen from current practices of several international climate change financial mechanisms. Last but not least, experiences have shown that current practices in many international and bilateral climate change financial mechanisms seem to be failing to implement a rights-based approach. This is probably one of the reasons why negative impacts on human rights from mitigation/carbon projects are still on-going phenomena. Nevertheless, the need and urgency for a rights-based

---

[56]Columbia Law School Sabin Center for Climate Change Law (2016), at p. 6.

[57]For the GCF's independent redress mechanism, see https://www.greenclimate.fund/independent-redress-mechanism.

[58]Perez et al. (2016), at p. 10.

[59]Schalatek (2010), at pp. 34–51.

[60] Paris Declaration and Accra Agenda for Action, OECD. http://www.oecd.org/dac/effectiveness/parisdeclarationandaccraagendaforaction.htm. Accessed 15 Feb 2017.

[61]Schalatek (2010), at p. 52.

Table 2 Relevant substantive principles for the mobilization, governance, and disbursement of public climate change finance

Mobilization	Polluter pays principle
	Respective capability
	New and additional
	Adequacy and precaution
	Predictability
Governance	Under the authority and guidance of the UNFCCC
	Equitable representation
	Public participation in decision-making
Disbursement	Subsidiarity, devolution and national/local ownership
	Precaution and timeliness
	Appropriateness
	Direct access and vulnerability focus
	Gender equity

approach to climate finance is essential to address the increasing overlapping common concerns of both the international climate change regime and the international human rights regime. How does this emerging normative framework affect Taiwan's climate finance?

4 Taiwan's National Climate Finance and Overseas Development Aid: A Reorientation of Climate Finance?

There are two dimensions of Taiwan's climate finance: internal and external. The internal dimension refers to Taiwan's national climate finance framework that provides financial support for domestic mitigation and adaptation policies and projects. The external dimension refers to Taiwan's climate finance framework that provides international financial support for mitigation and adaptation policies and projects abroad. This part of the chapter will introduce Taiwan's climate finance framework first, and then proceed to provide a preliminary review from the perspective of a rights-based approach to climate finance.

4.1 Taiwan's Climate Finance Framework

In terms of Taiwan's internal climate finance framework, Taiwan adopted the "Greenhouse Gases Reduction and Management Act" (hereinafter GHG Act) in July 2015, after more than 15 years of controversial deliberations. The GHG Act provides the most comprehensive regulations on Taiwan's GHG mitigation policies. Article 19 of the GHG Act establishes the "GHG Management Fund," which is currently the most relevant internal climate finance mechanism. Regarding use of the "GHG Management Fund," Article 19.2 of the GHG Act presents 9 different types of use, such as to facilitate GHG emissions reduction, to inspect emission sources and to provide them with assistance, subsidies and grants for voluntary reductions, to provide administrative support to the National Registry, auctions, sales and allowance trading, to coordinate, plan and implement adaptation, and to carry out international cooperation, etc. The "GHG Management Fund" does not provide funding for mitigation projects. It mainly provides funding for policy and program research and planning.[62] Therefore, the kinds of controversies surrounding the human rights impact of mitigation/carbon projects funded by climate finance mechanisms are less observable in the operation of Taiwan's internal climate finance. As a result, the following analysis will focus only on the external dimension of Taiwan's climate finance.

In terms of Taiwan's external climate finance framework, most relevant is Taiwan's ODA as Taiwan has not set up dedicated bilateral climate change financial mechanisms[63] to support developing countries in mitigation and/or adaptation projects and programs. Taiwan adopted the "International Cooperation and Development Act" (hereinafter the ICD Act) on 18 May 2010 to serve as the legal basis for conducting Taiwan's ODA activities. In addition, as mandated by Article 11 of the ICD Act, the "International Cooperation and Development Fund" is commissioned to carry out ICD affairs. Accordingly, the "Act for the Establishment of the International Cooperation and Development Fund" (hereinafter ICDF Act) was adopted on 15 June 2010. The Ministry of Foreign Affairs (hereinafter MOFA), the agency in charge, subsequently issued 6 regulations in December 2011 to implement the ICD Act. According to Article 5 of the ICD Act, one of the goals of Taiwan's international cooperation and development is to "ensure human security and to safeguard such universal values as peace, democracy, human rights, humanitarian care and sustainable development." Article 6 presents several principles to be followed in carrying out international cooperation and development affairs, such as to promote the economic and social development of partner countries in line with international development trends and key issues and to help partner countries in formulating development strategies, ensuring the welfare of their people and promoting sustainable development. Article 7 states that

[62]See, for example, Attachment to the First Meeting of the GHG Management Fund Committee of 7 Apr 2017 where specific items for the use of the Fund are listed at 76-81. Available at: https://www.epa.gov.tw/public/Data/741413413071.pdf (in Mandarin).

[63]Several countries such as the UK, Germany, Australia, Japan, and Norway have set up bilateral climate change financial mechanisms to support developing countries in carrying out mitigation projects. For a summary of these bilateral climate change financial mechanisms, see http://www.climatefundsupdate.org/listing.

the scope of international cooperation and development affairs shall include participation in bilateral or multilateral cooperation and development projects to promote sustainable development. The issue of climate change is not specifically mentioned in the Act. However, it is now widely recognized that climate change is an important component of sustainable development. In the "White Paper on Foreign Aid Policy,"[64] published by the MOFA in May 2009, sustainable development is one of the two main strategies for Taiwan's foreign aid. Promoting environmental sustainability falls within one of the issue areas of sustainable development. "Meeting the special demands of small island countries" is also mentioned as another issue area and the White Paper commits Taiwan to assist these small island countries in the areas of energy and climate change, amongst others.[65]

Taiwan's foreign aid is, according to Article 11 of the ICD Act, mainly carried out by the "International Cooperation and Development Fund" (hereinafter ICDF). One of the five sectors that receives assistance from the ICDF is the environment. "Climate change and natural disasters" and "energy efficiency and the introduction of clean energy" have been identified as amongst the list of global challenges and opportunities. Accordingly, the objectives and assistance from the ICDF will include assisting partner countries to develop green energy via investments of financing and to implement pilot projects involving renewable energy technologies.[66] In addition to providing project financing and technical assistance, the ICDF also invested in the Green Energy Special Fund of the European Bank for Reconstruction and Development (hereinafter EBRD). Amongst the 16 projects listed under the "environment" heading, four projects are related to climate change. For example, the ICDF funded, via its investment in the Green Energy Special Fund, two projects: one concerning the financing of a landfill gas recovery system at a solid waste landfill facility in Amman, Jordan,[67] and another concerning the financing of the rehabilitation of major streets and the modernization of public lighting in the center of Chisinau, Moldova.[68]

According to Article 8 of the ICD Act, Taiwan's ODA can be provided in various ways, including technical assistance and capacity building, investment, lending, guarantees, grants, and others. From the projects supported by the ICDF, it can also be observed that Taiwan's external climate finance supports mitigation projects. Is the current climate finance framework following a rights-based approach? If not, what can Taiwan's climate finance framework learn from the emerging normative framework on a rights-based approach to climate finance?

---

[64] Ministry of Foreign Affairs (2009).

[65] *Id.*, at p. 51.

[66] See the official website of the ICDF at: Environment. http://www.icdf.org.tw/ct.asp?xItem=12408&ctNode=29857&mp=2. Accessed 2 Nov 2017.

[67] For the project description, see: Lending and Investment. http://www.icdf.org.tw/ct.asp?xItem=31234&CtNode=29824&mp=2. Accessed 2 Nov 2017.

[68] For the project description, see: Lending and Investment. http://www.icdf.org.tw/ct.asp?xItem=24882&CtNode=29824&mp=2. Accessed 2 Nov 2017.

4.2 An Evaluation of Taiwan's Climate Finance Framework from the Perspective of a Rights-Based Approach to Climate Finance

During the Second International Covenant on Economic, Social and Cultural Rights (ICESCR) Report Review, Taiwan's ODA operation was subject to the question of "…is there a human rights impact assessment process before, during and after providing the ODA?"[69] The response from the MOFA is as follows:

> The Ministry of Foreign Affairs commissions TaiwanICDF to execute ODA missions.
>
> TaiwanICDF follows a Project Cycle and has adopted a Design and Monitoring Framework, with indicators designed to measure project impacts, outcomes, and outputs, to show the correlation between such results (including impacts, outcomes, and outputs) and project inputs, to highlight the role of project stakeholders, and to evaluate possible risks in advance that may affect a project during its implementation so as to ensure project effectiveness. The projects currently underway (such as agricultural, forestry, fishery, public health, and educational projects) have been and will be put to assessments before, during, and after their implementation according to the aforementioned framework to ensure that we meet our ODA goals, promote social development, and make progress on the condition of human rights.[70]

From this above-quoted response, it is apparent that Taiwan's ODA does not undertake a human rights impact assessment process before, during and after providing the ODA. As the previous sub-section points out, Taiwan's external climate finance framework relies on its ODA assistance. As a result, it seems fair to state that Taiwan's climate finance framework has not adopted a rights-based approach. Nevertheless, a more detailed analysis of the overall legal and institutional framework of Taiwan's ODA serving as a climate finance framework against several principles of the rights-based approach to climate finance might provide a more comprehensive evaluation.

From the discussion in Part 3, several guiding principles in applying a rights-based approach to climate finance have been suggested, such as consistency with international human rights obligations, doing no harm, transparency and accountability, public participation in decision-making, equity and non-discrimination, etc. In addition, several core principles concerning the procedural rights of transparency and accountability, as well as the relevant substantive principles for the mobilization, governance and disbursement of public climate change financial mechanisms, have also been suggested in the literature,[71] as Table 3 summarizes. All these principles

---

[69]The list of issues submitted by the Review Committee for the Second ICESCR Report, as well as the response from the agencies, in charge of the issues can be downloaded from: http://www.humanrights.moj.gov.tw/lp.asp?ctNode=44633&CtUnit=17115&BaseDSD=7&mp=200. Accessed 26 December 2017.

[70]*Id.*

[71]Schalatek (2010), at pp. 29–51.

Table 3 Procedural and substantive principles in the mobilization, governance and disbursement of public climate change financial mechanisms

Mobilization	Polluter pays principle
	Respective capability
	New and additional
	Adequacy and precaution
	Predictability
	MRV
Governance	Under the authority and guidance of the UNFCCC
	Equitable representation
	Public participation in decision-making
	Climate finance information should be publicly available, accurate and timely
	Redress mechanism
Disbursement	Subsidiarity, devolution and national/local ownership
	Precaution and timeliness
	Appropriateness
	Direct access and vulnerability focus
	Gender equity
	In-country civil society can independently monitor and verify government disclosures on climate finance spending and hold their own governments accountable

will be used as yardsticks to evaluate the legal and institutional framework of Taiwan's ODA.

First of all, a rights-based approach to climate finance needs to make sure that funded projects and activities are consistent with international human rights obligations. Article 6 of the ICD Act provides several guiding principles for conducting Taiwan's ODA. None of the guiding principles relate to the consistency of international human rights obligations. This implies that the legal framework of Taiwan's external climate finance has not yet committed to complying with international human rights conventions.

Second, in terms of the principle of "doing no harm," several "don'ts" for climate change financing are suggested, such as do not invest in largely business-as-usual fossil fuel projects in oil, gas and mining, do not invest in nuclear power generation, do not invest in export production of agrofuels and oil plants, do not invest in a "new green revolution" based on genetically modified organisms, do not invest in the building of large hydro dams, and do not support monoculture reforestation efforts under REDD financing schemes. The climate change-related projects, as mentioned in the previous sub-section, that have received or are receiving Taiwan's foreign aid are not these types of projects. In addition, another sector that receives ICDF assistance relates to agriculture; four main objectives under this heading are: to increase the production of crops and animal protein through technical cooperation, to promote the development of the agricultural sector in partner countries, to provide short- to medium-term financing for farmers and microbusinesses, and to promote aid for trade by improving animal and plant disease prevention and quarantine measures.[72] Projects funded under this heading also do not include the types listed as "don'ts" projects.

Third, several core principles concerning the procedural rights of transparency and accountability as well as relevant substantive principles for the mobilization, governance and disbursement of public climate change financial mechanisms have been identified. Does Taiwan's ODA framework, which serves as Taiwan's climate finance, comply with these principles?

In terms of mobilization of climate finance, six principles are identified: the polluter pays the principle, respective capability, new and additional, adequacy and precaution, predictability, and MRV. In Article 14 of the ICD Act, the funds available for Taiwan's ODA "shall depend on the government's financial position, as well as in consideration of international foreign aid standards." In Article 5 of the ICDF Act, it is more specifically stated that the source of financing for the ICDF shall consist of the following: budget allocations from the government, interest accrued from bank deposits, loans, donations, and other types of income. During the Second ICESCR Report Review, Taiwan's ODA operation was asked, as "Taiwan's 2014 budget for international cooperation was 0.05% of GNI. In order to meet the international commitment of 0.7% of GNI, is there any plan to increase Taiwan's ODA?" The MOFA responded that: "Due to fiscal constraints, the Zero-Based Budgeting System has been applied to government budgets for the past few years. Under these circumstances, our ODA/GNI ratio has been maintained at 0.05%. At present, it is unlikely that an increase in the ODA budget will be seen unless our fiscal condition improves."[73] It seems that the source of funding mainly comes from the government budget, which will depend on the government's financial position. As the current situation indicates, Taiwan's ODA/GNI ratio will not be able to reach the international commitment of 0.7% in the near future. Thus, the principles of "polluter pays," "adequacy and precaution," and "predictability" might not be complied with in the mobilization of Taiwan's climate finance. But the principle of "respective capability" might be complied with as the government will evaluate the resources available depending on its financial position. As Taiwan does not have a dedicated climate finance mechanism, the principle of "new and additional" is, of course, not complied with. Regarding MRV, Art. 13 of the ICD Act requests the agency in charge to "plan, evaluate, supervise and assess the implementation of all related matters." The "Regulation Governing the Planning, Appraisal, Implementation, Supervision and Performance Evaluation of International Cooperation and Development Affairs" was issued by the MOFA in 2011 to deal with this task. Article 5 of the Regulation states that, when implementing development projects, the agency in charge or other responsible agencies/institutions "shall carry out

[72]See: Agriculture. http://www.icdf.org.tw/ct.asp?xItem=12410&ctNode=29859&mp=2. Accessed 4 Nov 2017.

[73]The list of issues submitted by the Review Committee for the Second ICESCR Report as well as the response from the agencies, in charge of the issues can be downloaded from: http://www.humanrights.moj.gov.tw/lp.asp?ctNode=44633&CtUnit=17115&BaseDSD=7&mp=200. Accessed 26 Dec 2017.

regular supervision of such projects with partner countries to ensure alignment between the implementation results and project objectives." And, within six months after completion of a development project, the responsible agency "shall work with partner countries to determine whether project effectiveness was achieved and prepare a project completion report." Within two to five years after completion of a development project, Article 6 of the Regulation requests the responsible agency to "conduct a performance evaluation based on the status and requirements of each individual case." It seems that an MRV system is included in the overall ODA framework.

In terms of the governance of climate finance, five principles have been identified: the UNFCCC is the source of authority and guidance, there should be equitable representation, there should be public participation in decision-making, climate finance information should be publicly available, accurate and timely, and there should be a redress mechanism. As the first principle mainly refers to international climate finance, it might be inapplicable in Taiwan's climate finance. Article 12 of the ICD Act requires the agency in charge to "actively coordinate with local governments, nongovernmental organizations or public/private enterprises to participate in international cooperation and development affairs, and provide necessary assistance." To encourage our citizens to participate in international cooperation and development affairs, the same article also requires the agency in charge to "make public through its website, or other suitable channels, details of the latest international cooperation and development projects, except for classified information." Article 15 of the ICD Act also states that a report on Taiwan's ODA shall be submitted to the Executive Yuan and forwarded to the Legislative Yuan for reference. The ICDF, the main operator of Taiwan's ODA, consists of a board of directors, 3–5 supervisors, a Secretariat and a consultative committee. Article 8 of the ICDF Act provides that the Board of Directors shall have 11–15 directors, including 6 government representatives from relevant ministries and "specialists, scholars, and representatives from national industrial and commercial groups." Directors from the latter categories shall constitute no less than one-third of the board. Article 12 of the ICDF Act sets up a consultative committee with 7–11 members. These committee members "shall be nominated by the chairman of the board and consist of staff of concerned government agencies, specialists, and scholars," and shall be subject to approval by the board of directors. Article 16 of the ICDF Act also requires the ICDF to present reports of its work to the Legislative Yuan on a periodic basis. All the projects funded by the ICDF can find a project summary on the ICDF's website. From these provisions and practices, it may be concluded that the principles of "equitable representation" and "climate finance information should be publicly available, accurate and timely" are complied with. As for the principle of "public participation in decision-making," the ICD Act only "encourages" the participation of Taiwan's ODA. How the public can actually participate in the process is not legalized or institutionalized. Lastly, it seems that no redress mechanism is available under the overall legal framework.

In terms of disbursement of climate finance, six principles have been identified: subsidiarity, devolution and national/local ownership, precaution and timeliness, appropriateness, direct access and vulnerability focus, gender equity, and in-country civil society can independently monitor and verify government disclosures on climate finance spending and hold their own governments accountable. Article 8 of the ICD

Act establishes several methods to deliver Taiwan's ODA: technical assistance and capacity building, investments, loans, guarantees, financial donations, gifts in kind, dispatch of personnel, development strategy consultations, and other feasible methods. According to Article 13 of the ICD Act, if ODA is funding public construction projects that cost more than US$5 million and that fulfil one or more of the following conditions, "an objective and impartial opinion on project feasibility from a third party" shall be provided if the project is: funded entirely by Taiwan, handled by the MOFA, and procurement takes place in Taiwan at the request of the recipient country's government. As for other project types, it seems that no additional requirements are specifically established in the ICD Act. In the context of MRV, as mentioned in the preceding paragraphs, Article 5 of the "Regulation Governing the Planning, Appraisal, Implementation, Supervision and Performance Evaluation of International Cooperation and Development Affairs" states that, within six months after completion of a development project, the responsible agency "shall work with partner countries to determine whether project effectiveness was achieved and to prepare a project completion report." The "Regulation Governing Development Strategy Consultations for International Cooperation and Development Affairs" was issued by the MOFA in 2011. Article 3 of the Regulation states that when development strategy consultations are provided by the MOFA, the following principles shall be complied with: "(1) Respect the leadership of diplomatic allies or friendly countries regarding their own development strategies; (2) Review the development strategies of diplomatic allies or friendly countries and use relevant local mechanisms for distributing aid resources; (3) Establish harmonized, collaborative relations with diplomatic allies or friendly countries, their government agencies, intergovernmental organizations, international nongovernmental organizations and other stakeholders in the development strategy; (4) Assist diplomatic allies or friendly countries to establish a results-focused development strategy; and, (5) Reach a consensus with diplomatic allies or friendly countries on mutual accountability with respect to the effectiveness of development strategies." Article 5 of the Regulation also states that the planning of the MOFA's ODA shall be made "in accordance with the consensus reached with diplomatic allies or friendly countries through development strategy consultations." From all these relevant provisions relating to disbursement, it seems fair to conclude that the principle of "subsidiarity, devolution and national/local ownership" is complied with when Taiwan's ODA is provided in the form of development strategy consultations. It is not clear whether the ICDF-funded projects need to undergo such requirements. The principle of "direct access" might be met as the ICDF does not rely on implementing agencies to make disbursements, apart from in one operation. As mentioned in the sub-section, the ICDF has invested in the EBRD's Green Energy Special Fund. Projects funded by this Special Fund will receive co-financing from the EBRD and ICDF. The EBRD will submit project proposals to the ICDF for approval before committing to implementation.[74] Thus, direct access to the ICDF is not possible

[74]See: Lending and Investment. http://www.icdf.org.tw/ct.asp?xItem=6776&CtNode=29824&mp=2. Accessed 5 Nov 2017.

Table 4 Compliance of Taiwan's climate finance with a rights-based approach

Rights-based approach to climate finance		Does Taiwan's climate finance comply with these principles
Consistent with international human rights conventions		X
Do no harm		O
Mobilization of climate finance	Polluter pays principle	X
	Respective capability	?
	New and additional	X
	Adequacy and precaution	X
	Predictability	X
	MRV	O
Governance of climate finance	Under the authority and guidance of the UNFCCC	Inapplicable
	Equitable representation	O
	Public participation in decision-making	?
	Climate finance information should be publicly available, accurate and timely	O
	Redress mechanism	X
Disbursement of climate finance	Subsidiarity, devolution and national/local ownership	O, only in development strategy consultations
	Precaution and timeliness	?
	Appropriateness	?
	Direct access and vulnerability focus	O
	Gender equity	X
	In-country civil society can independently monitor and verify government disclosures on climate finance spending and hold their own governments accountable	X

if projects are funded by the Green Energy Special Fund. Regarding the principles of "precaution and timeliness" and "appropriateness," the legal framework of Taiwan's ODA provides insufficient information in this regard. As for gender equity, it seems that there are no general guidelines as to, for example, which priority group can receive funding. As a result, the principle of "gender equity" might not be fulfilled. Lastly, for the principle of "in-country civil society can independently monitor and verify government disclosures on climate finance spending and hold their own governments accountable," it will depend on, for example, the extent to which ODA information is disclosed. Although Article 12 of the ICD Act mandates the disclosure of ODA affairs, it also authorizes the agency in charge to withhold information if it is classified. Furthermore, as has been mentioned in the preceding paragraph, there is no redress mechanism in Taiwan's ODA framework. Therefore, it might be difficult for the domestic civil society to independently monitor and verify government disclosures on climate finance spending and to hold the government accountable.

Table 4 provides a summary as to whether Taiwan's ODA framework, which serves as Taiwan's external climate finance framework, has complied with a rights-based approach.

5 Conclusion

This chapter seeks to explore the question of whether Taiwan's climate finance follows a rights-based approach. Part 2 and Part 3, respectively, present a strong foundation for the linkage between climate change and human rights, and the importance of incorporating human rights considerations into climate finance. Part 3 further identifies several principles for a rights-based approach to climate finance. Part 4 excludes Taiwan's internal climate finance from the analysis, as Taiwan's national climate finance rarely funds specific mitigation projects. Part 4 then points out that Taiwan does not have a dedicated external climate finance. Instead, the overall ODA framework is used as Taiwan's external climate finance. Part 4 proceeds to analyze Taiwan's ODA legal and institutional framework against the set of principles relating to a rights-based approach to climate finance, as identified in Part 3. As can be seen from Table 4, Taiwan has a mixed compliance record. There are of course many qualifications in this analysis and conclusion, the most important one is that this analysis is conducted based on the overall legal framework of Taiwan's ODA. Climate finance constitutes only a minor part of ODA operations. Nevertheless, this analysis might bring about two policy recommendations. Firstly, it points out the failure of Taiwan's overall ODA operations to follow a rights-based approach, which is a serious impediment to Taiwan's implementation of the relevant international human rights conventions. Therefore, the government might consider taking stock of ODA operations from a human rights perspective and contemplate a progressive reform of ODA operations. Second, Taiwan should consider setting up a dedicated climate finance scheme to fund the most vulnerable small island countries, some of which happen to be Taiwan's important and few diplomatic allies. Under these circumstances, principles relating to the rights-based approach to climate finance, as pointed out in this chapter, can guide the government in the design of its climate financial mechanisms.

References

Agriculture: http://www.icdf.org.tw/ct.asp?xItem=12410&ctNode=29859&mp=2. Accessed 4 Nov 2017

Cancun Agreements. http://unfccc.int/cancun/. Accessed 15 Dec 2017

Columbia Law School Sabin Center for Climate Change Law, Re: Comments on the rules, modalities, and procedures for the SDM. 5 Oct 2016

Environment: http://www.icdf.org.tw/ct.asp?xItem=12408&ctNode=29857&mp=2. Accessed 2 Nov 2017

GEF policies on environmental and social safeguards and gender mainstreaming, GEF/C.40/10/Rev.1. 26 May 2011

Green Climate Fund, Decisions of the Board—Green Climate Fund, Annex III, GCF/B.07/11. 19 June 2014

Human Rights Council Res. 18/22, Human rights and climate change, UN Doc. A/HRC/Res/18/22. 17 Oct 2011

Human Rights Council Res. 26/27, Human rights and climate change, UN Doc. A/HR/Res/26/27. 15 July 2014

Jodoin S (2010) Rights-based frameworks for climate finance. CISDL, Italy

Johl A, Lador Y (2012) A human rights-based approach to climate finance. Friedrich-Ebert-Stiftung, Germany

Lending and Investment. http://www.icdf.org.tw/ct.asp?xItem=24882&CtNode=29824&mp=2. Accessed 2 Nov 2017

Lending and Investment. http://www.icdf.org.tw/ct.asp?xItem=31234&CtNode=29824&mp=2. Accessed 2 Nov 2017

Lending and Investment. http://www.icdf.org.tw/ct.asp?xItem=6776&CtNode=29824&mp=2. Accessed 5 Nov 2017

Mayer B (2016) Human rights in the Paris Agreement. Clim Law 6:109–117

Ministry of Foreign Affairs (2009) Partnership for progress and sustainable development: white paper on foreign aid policy. https://www.mofa.gov.tw/Upload/RelFile/2173/80233/%E5%A4%96%E4%BA%A4%E9%83%A8%E6%8F%B4%E5%A4%96%E6%94%BF%E7%AD%96%E7%99%BD%E7%9A%AE%E6%9B%B8%E8%8B%B1%E6%96%87%E7%89%88%EF%BC%88PDF%EF%BC%89.PDF. Accessed 2 Nov 2017

Office of the United Nations High Commissioner for Human Rights (2006) Frequently asked questions on a human rights-based approach to development cooperation. OHCHR, Geneva

Office of the United Nations High Commissioner for Human Rights (2015) Understanding Human Rights and Climate Change, submission of the Office of the High Commissioner for Human Rights to the 21st Conference of the Parties to the United Nations Framework Convention on Climate Change

Office of the United Nations High Commissioner for Human Rights, Report of the United Nations High Commissioner for Human Rights on the relationship between climate change and human rights, UN Doc. A/HRC/10/61. 15 Jan 2009

Olawuyi DS (2016) The human rights-based approach to carbon finance. Cambridge University Press, Cambridge

Paris Declaration and Accra Agenda for Action, OECD. http://www.oecd.org/dac/effectiveess/parisdeclarationandaccraagendaforaction.htm. Accessed 15 Feb 2017

Perez BF et al (2016) Rethinking the role of development banks in climate finance: Panama's Barro Blanco CDM project and human rights. Law Environ Dev J 12(1):1–17

Ryan L et al (2012) Plugging the energy efficiency gap with climate finance: the role of international financial institutions and the Green Climate Fund to reduce the potential of energy efficiency in the developing countries. OECD/IEA, France

Schalatek L (2010) A matter of principle(s): a normative framework for a global compact on public climate finance. Heinrich Böll Foundation, Germany

Shih WC (2011) Financial mechanisms for climate change mitigation and adaptation: what lessons can be learned from the reform experiences of the IMF? NTU Law Rev 6(2):581–617

UNFCCC Conference of the Parties, Decision 1/CP.16: The Cancun Agreements: Outcome of the Work of the Ad Hoc Working Group on Long-term Cooperative Action under the Convention, UN Doc. FCCC/CP/2010/7/Add.1. 15 Mar 2011

UNFCCC Standing Committee on Finance (2014) 2014 biennial assessment and overview of climate finance flows report. UNFCC, Germany

United Nations Environment Programme (2015) Climate change and human rights. UNON Publishing Services Section, Nairobi

Wen-Chen Shih is Professor of Law in the Department of International Business, National Cheng-chi University. She obtained her LL.B. degree from National Taiwan University, her LL.M. degree from the London School of Economics and Political Science, and her Ph.D. degree from the School of Oriental and African Studies, University of London. Her area of specialty includes international economic and trade law, and international environmental law. She has published, both in Mandarin and in English, journal articles and book chapters on trade and the environment, trade and climate change, energy tax, climate change legislation, climate change financial mechanisms, emissions trading, good governance, animal welfare, and marine-protected areas. She has also published two books (both in Mandarin): "Greening the WTO," and "WTO, Climate Change and Energy." She teaches international economic law, international trade law, legal issues on emissions trading, international environmental law, and seminars on trade and the environment at both the undergraduate and post-graduate levels. She has been carrying out research projects funded by the Ministry of Science and Technology since 2000. She serves as legal consultant on international trade law and international environmental law issues for Taiwan's Bureau of Foreign Trade, Ministry of Economic Affairs, Forestry Bureau, Council of Agriculture, and Environmental Protection Administration. In this capacity, she has assisted the government to draft position papers on trade and environment issues under the Doha Round, and she attended several sessions of the Conference of the Parties to the Convention on Biodiversity Diversity. She is currently the Commissioner of the International Trade Commission, Ministry of Economic Affairs, and a Committee Member of the Wildlife Conservation Advisory Committee, Council of Agriculture. She also lectures on WTO law at various training programs organized by the Ministry of Economic Affairs and the Ministry of Foreign Affairs, such as the Academy of International Economic Affairs, the training program for high-level and mid-level civil servants on international economic and trade negotiations and litigation. She has been invited by the Ministry of Industry and Trade of Vietnam to give several lectures on trade and environment issues at the APEC Seminar on Facilitating Trade and Environmental Protection.

Chapter 29
Constitutional and Legal Dimensions of the Right to Food in Taiwan: The Long March Toward Normative Internalization and Realization

Ching-Fu Lin

Abstract The right to food has long been recognized in a number of international instruments. Faced with the evolving form and substance of the right to food, Taiwan has nonetheless encountered various challenges in its efforts to normatively internalize and realize this right. Because the country has been unable to formally participate in most international human rights treaties, Taiwan has incorporated numerous key elements of international human rights law into its domestic legal system through a myriad of approaches. Yet the manner in which Taiwan has opted to interact with international human rights law arguably raises more questions than it answers. This chapter reviews the development of the right to food in the context of international human rights law and highlights the key elements constituting the current form and substance of this right. It further assesses the many faces of the right to food in Taiwan, from constitutional to legislative to executive practices, and it identifies various challenges faced by the country in realizing the right to food. Noting the lack of a rights-based discourse in constitutional and legal settings in Taiwan due to numerous underlying issues, this chapter proposes a legal framework approach to address the normative challenges and to create an enabling environment for the progressive realization of the right to food.

Keywords Constitutional law · ICESCR · Framework law · Rights-based approach · Right to food

C.-F. Lin (✉)
National Tsing Hua University, Hsinchu, Taiwan
e-mail: chingfulin@mx.nthu.edu.tw

J. A. Cohen et al. (eds.), *Taiwan and International Human Rights*, Economics, Law, and Institutions in Asia Pacific, https://doi.org/10.1007/978-981-13-0350-0_29

1 Introduction

First recognized in the 1948 the *Universal Declaration of Human Rights* (hereinafter UDHR) as an integral aspect of the right to an adequate standard of living,[1] the right to food is enshrined as a legally binding norm in the 1966 *International Covenant on Economic, Social and Cultural Rights* (hereinafter ICESCR)[2] and has subsequently been embraced by other international and regional human rights instruments.[3] Article 11 of the ICESCR requires States Parties to take appropriate steps to realize the right to "adequate food"[4] and to adopt measures and engage in necessary international cooperative activities in recognition of "the fundamental right of everyone to be free from hunger."[5] The essence of the right to food therefore denotes that all human beings, regardless of their race, color, sex, religion, political or other opinions, birth, national or social origin, property, or other conditions, have the right to adequate food

[1]Universal Declaration of Human Rights, G.A. Res. 217 (III) A, UN Doc A/810, at 76, art. 25.1 (10 Dec 1948) [hereinafter Universal Declaration of Human Rights], which reads "[e]veryone has the right to a standard of living adequate for the health and well-being of himself and of his family, including food, clothing, housing and medical care and necessary social services, and the right to security in the event of unemployment, sickness, disability, widowhood, old age or other lack of livelihood in circumstances beyond his control."

[2]International Covenant on Economic, Social and Cultural Rights, art. 11, *opened for signature* 16 Dec 1966, 6 I.L.M. 360, 993 U.N.T.S. 3 [hereinafter ICESCR].

[3]For instance, the Convention on the Elimination of All Forms of Discrimination Against Women recognizes the right of pregnant and lactating women to nutrition in Article 12(2); the Convention on the Rights of the Child in Article 24 recognizes children's right to adequate nutrition and calls for actions to address disease and malnutrition. More recently, the Convention on the Rights of Persons with Disabilities, which entered into force in 2008, recognizes the right to food in Articles 25(f) and 28(1) in different contexts. The Convention on the Elimination of All Forms of Discrimination Against Women, art. 12, *opened for signature* 18 Dec 1979, 1249 U.N.T.S. 13; The Convention on the Rights of the Child, arts. 24, 27, *opened for signature* 20 Nov 1989, 1577 U.N.T.S. 3; The Convention on the Rights of Persons with Disabilities, arts. 25, 28, *opened for signature* 28 June 1952, 210 U.N.T.S. 131. At the regional level, examples of recognizing or incorporating the norm of the right to food include the African Charter on the Rights and Welfare of the Child (Article 14) and the Additional Protocol to the American Convention on Human Rights in the Area of Economic, Social and Cultural Rights (Article 12).The African Charter on the Rights and Welfare of the Child, art. 14, *opened for signature* 11 July 1990, OAU Doc. CAB/LEG/24.9/49; Additional Protocol to the American Convention on Human Rights in the Area of Economic, Social and Cultural Rights, art. 12, *opened for signature* 17 Nov 1988, 28 I.L.M. 156 (1989). For more discussion, see International Development Law Organization (2015), pp. 17–18.

[4]ICESCR, art. 11.1.

[5]ICESCR, art. 11.2. More specifically, Article 11.2(a) states that States Parties shall take measures to advance approaches to producing, conserving, and distributing food through the use and sharing of scientific and technical knowledge, agrarian system development or reform, and efficient utilization of natural resources. Article 11.2(b) requires States Parties to ensure an "equitable distribution of world food supplies in relation to need," considering the interests and difficulties of both importing and exporting countries.

and the right to be free from hunger.[6] Premised in such fundamental legal instruments, the right to food has evolved in recent decades—in terms of its normative implications—in the context of the changing demographic, political, social, economic, and environmental landscapes.

Faced with the evolving form and substance of the right to food, Taiwan has encountered various challenges in its efforts to normatively internalize and realize this right. Although the country may not be able to formally participate in any of the relevant international instruments, Taiwan has incorporated numerous key elements of international human rights law into its domestic legal system through a myriad of approaches. However, does the incorporation of international human rights law through the use of the Implementation Act result in effective implementation on the ground? How is the right to food respected, protected, and fulfilled in Taiwan? What have the practices of the Constitutional Court and the lower courts been in relation to the right to food? Given the broad scope and multiple facets of this right, how would responsible government agencies perceive and react to relevant aspects oriented toward the right to food in Taiwan? What are the normative challenges faced by Taiwan in realizing the right to food? What represents the optimal institutional design to address such challenges? All of these questions have a theoretical and practical bearing on the constitutional and legal dimensions of the right to food in Taiwan.

This chapter endeavors to review the right to food in the context of international human rights law and to discuss whether—and if so, why—there is a governmental duty to take legislative and regulatory action. It further assesses the many facets of the right to food in Taiwan—its recognition and realization via legal protections at the national level through constitutional provisions and interpretations, national legislation and regulation, and the direct applicability of international law. Premised upon a preliminary analysis, this chapter identifies the various challenges faced by Taiwan in realizing the right to food. In particular, a rights-based discourse has been missing in the constitutional and legal settings, and this is attributable to a myriad of reasons linked to constitutional practices, the Implementation Act, and misperceptions about the nature of the right to food and the ICESCR. This chapter concludes by proposing the use of a legal framework approach that promises to address the normative challenges and to create an enabling environment for the progressive realization of the right to food.

2 Evolution of the Right to Food in International Human Rights Law

As Article 11 of the ICESCR does not elaborate on the nature, scope, and substance of the right to food, the 1996 World Food Summit, which was organized by the Food and Agriculture Organization of the United Nations (hereinafter FAO), called

[6] UN Office High Comm'r for Human Rights [hereinafter OHCHR] (2010).

for further clarification of the obligations arising from such a right as provided for under the ICESCR and, more broadly, international human rights law.[7] In 1999, the Committee on Economic, Social and Cultural Rights (hereinafter CESCR) issued *General Comment No. 12*,[8] which defines the right to food and serves as the cornerstone for its future normative development. In 2000, the General Assembly adopted the *United Nations Millennium Declaration*, in which states committed to reducing by one-half the number of people suffering from hunger by 2015.[9] In 2004, the FAO adopted the *Voluntary Guidelines to Support the Progressive Realization of the Right to Adequate Food in the Context of National Food Security*,[10] which further elucidates practical implementation guidance to states with regard to the right to food.[11] The trajectory of the normative development of the right to food sheds critical light on the discussion regarding how the right is perceived and realized in Taiwan.

Of crucial relevance and importance is *General Comment No. 12*,[12] which elaborates on ICESCR Article 11 by defining the right to food as "the right of everyone to have physical and economic access at all times to food in adequate quantity and quality or to means of its procurement."[13] The CESCR further categorizes the right to food into two distinct forms: the right to adequate food, and the right to freedom from hunger. The right to adequate food, as provided for in paragraph 1 of Article 11, has three normative dimensions: adequacy,[14] availability,[15] and accessibility.[16] Because the term "adequate" indicates a relative standard, the right to adequate food cannot be narrowly and specifically interpreted to require a minimum level of calories or particular nutrients, but it can be realized in a progressive manner.[17] Yet the right to be free from hunger, as provided for in

---

[7]*Id.*, at p. 9.

[8]UN Econ. & Soc. Council, Comm. on Econ., Soc. & Cultural Rights [hereinafter CESCR], *General Comment 12: The Right to Adequate Food (Art. 11)*, UN Doc. E/C.12/1999/5 (12 May 1999) [hereinafter *General Comment No. 12*].

[9]United Nations Millennium Declaration, G.A. Res. 55/2, at para 19, UN Doc. A/55/L.2 (18 Sept 2000).

[10]Food and Agriculture Organization of the United Nations [hereinafter FAO] (2005).

[11]OHCHR (2010), *supra* note 6, at p. 1.

[12]Many have discussed the implications of ICESCR Article 11 as well as the relevant General Comments (in particular *General Comment No. 12*). See, e.g., Söllner (2007); Haugen (2007), at p. 154; Seatzu (2011); Ziegler et al. (2011), at pp. 15–22.

[13]*General Comment No. 12*, at para. 6.

[14]*Id.*, at para. 7.

[15]*Id.*, at paras. 8, 12.

[16]*Id.*, at paras. 8, 13.

[17]*Id.*, at para. 6. *See also* Haugen (2007), *supra* note 12, at p. 154.

paragraph 2 of Article 11, constitutes a core, absolute, and indispensable element of the right to food from which no state may deviate, "even in times of natural or other disasters."[18]

The two forms of the right to food are different in nature and may therefore be subject to different potential restrictions, as governed by Article 4 of the ICESCR, as well as by *General Comment No. 14* of the CESCR. ICESCR Article 4 allows States Parties to restrict some rights in certain contexts, if "such limitations … are determined by law … compatible with the nature of these rights and solely for the purpose of promoting the general welfare in a democratic society."[19] *General Comment No. 14*, however, underscores the importance of limiting the use of Article 4 to "protect[ing] the rights of individuals."[20] Nevertheless, there has been little consensus among scholars and practitioners as to whether the right to food may be subject to Article 4 restrictions. Some argue that the right to food as a whole is, by nature, not subject to any limitations.[21] Others claim that restrictions on the right to adequate food may be justified under some circumstances, but the fundamental right to be free from hunger shall not be subject to any restrictions.[22] Because the CESCR emphasizes States Parties' core obligations to ensure a minimum, essential level of satisfaction with regard to all of the rights enshrined in the ICESCR,[23] the right to be free from hunger, which is by its very nature indispensable to the realization of the right to food, should not be restricted under any circumstances. To better realize the right to food, any restriction on the right to adequate food should be limited to strictly necessary situations and policed by clearly defined, specific, and narrowly interpreted laws.[24]

Human rights are not self-contained; rather they are interrelated and interdependent systems. Indeed, realization of the right to food is inherently linked to human dignity and social justice and is oftentimes indispensable to the fulfillment of other human rights.[25] The right to food, for instance, is inextricably tied to the right to life (Article 6 of the International Covenant on Civil and Political Rights, hereinafter ICCPR) as well as to the right to health (ICESCR Article 12), among others. The CESCR explicitly refers to the right to food as closely related to—and therefore necessary to be read in conjunction with—the non-derogable right to life

[18]*Id.*, at para. 6. To realize the latter right, the CESCR notes that States Parties have the obligation to take necessary actions to mitigate and alleviate hunger even under the circumstances of natural disasters and the like.

[19]ICESCR, art. 4.

[20]CESCR, *General Comment No. 14: The Right to the Highest Attainable Standard of Health (Article 12 of the International Covenant on Economic, Social and Cultural Rights)*, at para. 28, UN Doc. E/C.12/2000/4 (11 Aug 2000) [hereinafter *General Comment No. 14*].

[21]Hutter (2015), at p. 56.

[22]*Id.*

[23]CESCR, *General Comment No. 3: The Nature of States Parties' Obligations (Art. 2, Para. 1, of the Covenant)*, UN Doc. E/1991/23 (14 Dec 1990) [hereinafter *General Comment No. 3*].

[24]Sepulveda (2003), at p. 279.

[25]*General Comment No. 12*, at para. 4.

in *General Comment No. 6*.[26] The right to be free from hunger cannot be derogated, since its minimum satisfaction is essential to the protection of the right to life, even under circumstances of emergency or armed conflict.[27] Hence, the arbitrary denial by a States Parties to provide humanitarian assistance in times of crisis may potentially violate both ICCPR Article 11 and ICCPR Article 6. In a similar fashion, the right to health, to a large extent, depends on realization of the right to food. Such a normative connection is underscored by the CESCR in *General Comment No. 14*,[28] as well as in *General Comment No. 12*.[29] Finally, ICESCR Article 2.2 prohibits any discrimination when States Parties implement the Covenant, as non-discrimination and equality are of fundamental importance to the exercise and enjoyment of all human rights.[30] A violation of the ICESCR takes place when there is "any discrimination in access to food as well as to means and entitlements for its procurement."[31]

All in all, States Parties bear three obligations to realize the right to food—the obligation to respect, the obligation to protect, and the obligation to fulfill (i.e., to facilitate and provide)—on a non-discriminatory basis.[32] Further, while the notion of progressive realization applies, States Parties shall "move as expeditiously and effectively as possible" toward the full realization of all ICESCR rights (including the right to food) and refrain from taking retrogressive steps.[33] Importantly, the Reports by the Special Rapporteur on the Right to Food have, in past years, propelled the normative development of the right to food to cover contemporary issues

---

[26]The Committee rejected a widespread narrow interpretation of the right to life merely as a safeguard against arbitrary killing and encouraged States Parties to take "positive measures" to protect the right to life in a broader sense, which includes "measures to eliminate malnutrition and epidemics." Human Rights Comm., *General Comment No. 6*, at para. 5, UN Doc. A/37/40(1982) (30 Apr 1982).

[27]See Cotula and Vidar (2003), at pp. 6–7; Ziegler et al. (2011), *supra* note 12.

[28]The CESCR notes that the fulfillment of the right to health includes access to food: "[T]he right to health embraces a wide range of socio-economic factors that promote conditions in which people can lead a healthy life, and extends to the underlying determinants of health, such as food and nutrition, housing, access to safe and potable water and adequate sanitation, safe and healthy working conditions, and a healthy environment." *General Comment No. 14*, at para. 4.

[29]When articulating the notion of "adequacy," the CESCR points to a diet containing "a mix of nutrients for physical and mental growth, development and maintenance, and physical activity…." *General Comment No. 12*, at para. 11.

[30]ICESCR, art. 2.2.

[31]*General Comment No. 12*, at para. 18.

[32]*Id.*, at para. 15. "The obligation to respect existing access to adequate food requires States Parties not to take any measures that result in preventing such access. The obligation to protect requires measures by the State to ensure that enterprises or individuals do not deprive individuals of their access to adequate food. The obligation to fulfil (facilitate) means the State must proactively engage in activities intended to strengthen people's access to and utilization of resources and means to ensure their livelihood, including food security. Finally, whenever an individual or group is unable, for reasons beyond their control, to enjoy the right to adequate food by the means at their disposal, States have the obligation to fulfil (provide) that right directly."

[33]*General Comment No. 3*, at para. 9. For relevant discussions, see Desierto (2015), at pp. 87–88.

surrounding its respect, protection, and fulfillment. The first Special Rapporteur, Jean Ziegler, provides a refined definition of the right to food, namely "the right to have regular, permanent and unrestricted access, either directly or by means of financial purchases, to quantitatively and qualitatively adequate and sufficient food corresponding to the cultural traditions of the people."[34] Ziegler also rightly identifies the scope of the right to food and areas of concern covered by it, such as farmland, irrigation, financing, technology, markets, sufficiency of income, safe drinking water, and access to social welfare assistance.[35] Olivier De Schutter, who succeeded Ziegler as Special Rapporteur, further elaborates on the normative latitude of the right to food toward the availability and accessibility of not only "sufficient and adequate" food but also toward "culturally acceptable food that is produced and consumed sustainably, preserving access to food for future generations."[36] The current Special Rapporteur, Hilal Elver, in turn, emphasizes that the States Parties have a primary obligation to "ensure its progressive realization [of the right to food] through ratification of international treaties and the development of supportive domestic and national legislation."[37]

3 The Right to Food in Taiwan: The (Lack of) Constitutional and Legal Dialogues

Against this well-nourished setting of legalization and normative discourse on the right to food at the international level, those in Taiwan have faced a rather barren landscape. Since Taiwan was replaced in the United Nations by the People's Republic of China in 1971,[38] it has been unable to join treaty regimes under the auspices of the United Nations. Along with the country's trajectory of democratization, a handful of human rights organizations urged the Taiwanese government to join and/or ratify important human rights treaties in the late 1990s.[39] In 1993, the

[34]UN Commission on Human Rights, *The Right to Food: Report by the Special Rapporteur on the Right to Food, Mr. Jean Ziegler, Submitted in Accordance with the Commission on Human Rights Resolution 2000/10*, at para. 14, UN Doc. E/CN.4/2001/53 (7 Feb 2001); see also Human Rights Council, *Promotion and Protection of All Human Rights, Civil, Political, Economic, Social and Cultural Rights, Including the Right to Development: Report of the Special Rapporteur on the Right to Food, Jean Ziegler*, at para. 17, UN Doc. A/HRC/7/5 (10 Jan 2008); Ziegler et al., (2011), *supra* note 12, at p. 18.

[35]Human Rights Council (2012), *supra* note 34, at para. 18; see also *General Comment No. 12*, at paras. 7, 11.

[36]Human Rights Council, *Report of the Special Rapporteur on the Right to Food, Olivier De Schutter*, at para. 2, UN Doc. A/HRC/25/57 (24 Jan 2014) [hereinafter Report of Olivier De Schutter].

[37]G.A. Res. 71/282, at para. 21 (3 Aug 2016).

[38]G.A. Res. 2758 (XXVI), at p. 2 (25 October 1971); see also Wang (2002), p. 537; Huang (2003), p. 81.

[39]Chang (2011), p. 598.

government made its first formal declaration to voluntarily comply with the Convention on the Rights of the Child and subsequently revised domestic laws accordingly.[40] On 31 March 2009, Taiwan's Legislative Yuan ratified the ICCPR and the ICESCR, but the ratification instruments were later rejected by the Secretary-General of the United Nations.[41] On the same day, despite the international political realities, the Legislative Yuan enacted the *Act to Implement the International Covenant on Civil and Political Rights and the International Covenant on Economic, Social and Cultural Rights* (Implementation Act) to incorporate all of the rights under the two Covenants and ensure their applicability in the domestic legal system.[42] According to the Implementation Act, government agencies at all levels are required to conform to the human rights protection provisions of the two Covenants, avoid violations, protect the people from infringements by others, and actively promote the realization of all of the delineated human rights while exercising their respective functions.[43]

Owing to the failed accession to the ICCPR and the ICESCR and the underlying political realities, Taiwan has not been able to participate in the national reporting and review mechanisms. At the domestic level, however, the Taiwanese government is required by Article 6 of the Implementation Act to establish a national human rights reporting and review system in accordance with the two Covenants.[44] Accordingly, the government issued its first official state report in April 2012 and invited a group of independent international experts for the first compliance review in February 2013.[45] The second official state report was issued in April 2016, while the second review was undertaken in January 2017.[46] During the two sessions, experts with experience and formal roles in various international human rights institutions reviewed the national reports, consulted with civil society groups, and made recommendations covering a wide range of issues. Based on the expert reviews, the Ministry of Justice has also hosted consultation meetings to advance enhanced implementation with relevant government agencies and has urged them to provide responses or to take appropriate actions vis-à-vis the experts' recommendations.

---

[40]*Id.*, at p. 223.

[41]*Id.*; see also Wang (2009).

[42]Gongmin Yu Zhengzhi Quanli Guoji Gongyue Ji Jingji Shehui Wenhua Quanli Guoji Gongyue Shixingfa [公民與政治權利國際公約及經濟社會文化權利國際公約施行法] (Act to Implement the International Covenant on Civil and Political Rights and the International Covenant on Economic, Social and Cultural Rights) (2009) (Taiwan) [hereinafter the Implementation Act]. Article 2 of the Implementation Act states that "[h]uman rights protection provisions in the two Covenants have domestic legal status." Article 8 further stipulates that "[a]ll levels of governmental institutions and agencies should review laws, regulations, directions and administrative measures within their functions according to the two Covenants … [those] incompatible to the two Covenants should be amended within two years …."

[43]*Id.*, art. 4.

[44]*Id.*, art. 6; International Covenant on Civil and Political Rights [hereinafter ICCPR], art. 40, *opened for signature* 16 Dec 1966, 999 U.N.T.S. 171; ICESCR, arts. 16–17.

[45]Ministry of Justice (Taiwan) (2012b).

[46]Ministry of Justice (Taiwan) (2016b).

While full realization of the two Covenants remains a significant challenge, the government and civil society groups have learned through the joint process of national reports and external reviews and have also gained valuable experience regarding pseudo international United Nations human rights practices in which they had previously not been versed.[47] The growing institutionalization of government self-assessments, reporting and corrective measures, civil society involvement, and independent external reviews have also played important roles in cultivating and familiarizing a varied array of actors in the country with all of the rights protected under the Covenants as part of a gradual internalization process.

However, the right to food has not been a core consideration in the national reports and external reviews, and this, in part, reflects the fundamental lack of constitutional and legal discourses regarding this right in Taiwan (see the discussion below). During the first review process, the Review Committee considered the initial ICESCR report submitted by the government and listed a number of issues to which relevant agencies were expected to respond, including food supply in disaster management, welfare support for the homeless, and basic labor protection, including migrant workers' right to food.[48] The government report also referred to its efforts in the areas of food safety, food prices, and food assistance to the disadvantaged.[49] Covenants Watch, a representative civil society group, in its shadow report highlighted the problems of food safety, food self-sufficiency, and industry seizure of water designated for agricultural irrigation.[50] The second review process did not go beyond the issues scrutinized in the first review—food self-sufficiency, local food banks and coupons, and food safety.[51] While repeating its concerns regarding the expropriation of special agricultural districts and the implications for food self-sufficiency and safety,[52] Covenants Watch urged the government to assess the impact of trade and investment agreements on human rights, although the right to food was not specifically referenced.[53]

---

[47]See Severson (2013).

[48]See Review Meeting on Taiwan's initial reports under the ICCPR and ICESCR: Consideration of reports submitted by States Parties under Articles 16 & 17 of the Covenant: List of issues submitted by the Review Committee for the initial ICESCR report, at pp. 11–12 (21 Jan 2013). http://www.humanrights.moj.gov.tw/HitCounter.asp?xItem=294736. Accessed 30 Sept 2017; see also Review of the initial reports of the Government of Taiwan on the implementation of the International Human Rights Covenants: Concluding observations and recommendations adopted by the International Group of Independent Experts, Taipei, 1 Mar 2013, at paras. 38–39, 50. http://www.humanrights.moj.gov.tw/HitCounter.asp?xItem=385451. Accessed 30 Sept 2017 [hereinafter Concluding Observations and Recommendations].

[49]Ministry of Justice (Taiwan) (2012a).

[50]Covenants Watch (2012), pp. 65–73.

[51]Ministry of Justice (Taiwan) (2016a), at paras. 198–201.

[52]Covenants Watch (2016).

[53]*Id.*, at p. 245. Interestingly, Covenants Watch cited the Guiding Principles on Human Rights Impact Assessments of Trade and Investment Agreements (A/HRC/19/59/Add.5), which were prepared by United National Special Rapporteur Olivier De Schutter on the right to food.

Apart from the rather thin external scrutiny on implementation of the right to food, this right has received limited attention in the domestic Constitution and legal settings. To be sure, there have been a few occasions when the judiciary has referred to the right to food, albeit in a very limited fashion. At the constitutional level, while there exists a rich body of literature on the legal status and effect of the ICCPR and the ICESCR in Taiwan, as well as their relationship with the respective provisions of the Constitution,[54] the right to food is clearly an overlooked issue. First, at the time of this writing, the Constitutional Court has cited and referred to different provisions of the ICCPR,[55] but it has rarely mentioned the ICESCR. Indeed, J.Y. Interpretation No. 709 represents the first and only instance to date in which the Court explicitly refers to the ICESCR in its holding and reasoning, although there are a number of references to the ICESCR by individual Justices in their concurring or dissenting opinions.[56] The right to food, unsurprisingly, has not at all been discussed in the setting of the Constitutional Court. Second, as pointed out by prominent scholars in Taiwan, the Constitutional Court tends to cite international human rights treaties to serve a myriad of purposes, such as serving as a benchmark by which to instruct the Legislative Yuan or the executive in revising existing laws or regulations; as a justification to sustain a law or regulation; as the basis to expand the list of constitutionally protected rights; or as a reinforcement or supplement to its reasoning regarding constitutionally protected rights.[57] The Constitutional Court has not yet revealed a tangible contour of how it approaches international human rights law in general, and the ICCPR and the ICESCR in particular. It is no surprise then that there exists no consensus on the legal status of the two Covenants in Taiwan's constitutional order. Some argue that given the normative significance and universal recognition of the two Covenants in the arena of international human rights law, the ICCPR and the ICESCR shall enjoy the same legal status as the Constitution.[58] Others observe that the ICESCR may, by nature, differ from the ICCPR, and many social and economic rights are expressed in the Constitution as "Directive Principles of State Policy" that involve democratic accountability and distributional justice. Hence, they do not enjoy justiciability.[59] Faced with such an uncertain and unstable state of affairs, we have little guidance from the practices of the Constitutional Court with regard to constitutional, rights-based protection of the right to food and the appropriate ways to protect and realize it.

[54]See, e.g., Hsu (2014), at pp. 842–43; Chen (2015), at pp. 341–42; Huan (2010), at pp. 5, 19–20; Chang (2015); Liao (2011), at p. 5.

[55]For more discussion, see Chang (2011), *supra* note 39.

[56]More specifically, the Constitutional Court cited Article 11 of the ICESCR when underscoring people's right to enjoy an adequate standard of living with safety, peace, and dignity. See Dafaguan Shizi Di 709 Hao [大法官釋字第709號] (J.Y. Interpretation No. 709) (26 Apr 2013) (Taiwan).

[57]See generally Chang (2011), *supra* note 39; Hwang (2015), at pp. 59–60.

[58]Chang (2011), *supra* note 39.

[59]Yeh (2015).

Outside the Constitutional Court, an increasing number of lower courts have made reference to the ICESCR in addition to the General Comments issued by the CESCR, and the right to food has been discussed on some occasions. For example, the Supreme Administrative Court cites Article 11.1 of the ICESCR in its discussion on adequate living standards.[60] The Taipei District Court cites Articles 11 and 12 of the ICESCR, as well as *General Comment 15*, in recognizing the right to water as a fundamental human right, highlighting the obligation of courts to apply the relevant provisions of the two Covenants in light of the Implementation Act.[61] The Kaohsiung High Administrative Court responded to a plaintiff's claim that some urban development projects may undermine the right to food as per the ICESCR, granting a provisional injunction without examining the normative substance of the right to food.[62] The Nantou District Court made explicit references to the ICESCR, Articles 11 and 12, *General Comments No. 4, 14, and 15*, and relevant domestic laws in holding that the right to access to sunlight is a legally protected right under the Civil Code, Article 184.1, first paragraph.[63] However, it should also be noted that a common misunderstanding about the right to food is also found in a judgment of the Taipei High Administrative Court. The Court, in response to a plaintiff's claim that the government bears an obligation to ensure that the priority of the agricultural use of water is not deprived, notes that the ICESCR is primarily about the protection of rights in developing countries and hence is of limited relevance here.[64] Such a misperception about the right to food—that it concerns primarily developing countries—arguably reflects the normative atmosphere vis-à-vis economic rights in Taiwan and may result in ramifications that perpetuate rather than alleviate the lack of constitutional and legal discourses regarding the right to food.

More recently, some lawmaking initiatives by the Legislative Yuan and the executive branches have direct or indirect implications on the right to food. In addition to the amendments, proposed by two legislators, to the Food Administration Act to list national food security as one of the purposes stipulated in Article 1 in light of the

---

[60]Kuoyi Industrial Co., Ltd. v. Ministry of Interior, 105 Nian Du Pan Zi Di 162 Hao [105年度判字第162號] (Sup. Admin. Ct. [最高行政法院] 14 Apr 2016) (Taiwan).

[61]Wu Youyāo v. Lai Qingli et al., 102 Nian Du Zhong Su Zi Di 957 Hao [102年度重訴字第957號] (Taiwan Taipei Dist. Ct. [台北地方法院] 29 May 2015) (Taiwan).

[62]Lin Shuling et al. v. Taitung County Government, 102 Nian Du Ting Zi Di 7 Hao [102年度停字第7號] (Kaohsiung Admin. High Ct. [高雄高等行政法院] 28 June 2013) (Taiwan).

[63]Liao Biyun v. Wang Yingxue, 104 Nian Du Su Zi Di 169 Hao [104年度訴字第169號] (Taiwan Nantou Dist. Ct. [台灣南投地方法院] 17 Aug 2016) (Taiwan).

[64]Chen Zhengzong et al. v. Environmental Protection Administration, Executive Yuan, 99 Su Zi 1882 Hao Pan Jue [99訴字1882號判決] (Taipei Admin. High Ct. [台北高等行政法院] 15 Sept 2011) (Taiwan). While the Supreme Administrative Court later remanded the case, it did not express its opinions about the Taipei High Administrative Court's flawed interpretation of the right to food and more broadly about the nature of the ICESCR. See Chen Zhengzong et al. v. Environmental Protection Administration, Executive Yuan, 102 Nian Pan Zi Di 70 Hao [102年判字第70號] (Sup. Admin. Ct. [最高行政法院] 7 Feb 2013) (Taiwan).

changing economic, social, demographic, and climatic conditions,[65] there are also revisions proposed by the Ministry of Health and Welfare to the Public Assistance Act regarding the provision of food and social support[66] as well as recent reforms to the Food Safety and Sanitation Act.[67] Furthermore, some have proposed new laws to address the issues of food banks and social support,[68] food waste,[69] food and agricultural education,[70] and the promotion of better nutrition and healthy diets.[71] While the legislative proposal for the promotion of better nutrition and healthy diets cites the first half of Article 25.1 of the UDHR and notes that everyone shall enjoy "a standard of living adequate for the health and well-being of himself and of his family, including food, clothing, housing and medical care, and necessary social services,"[72] the notion of the "right" to these necessities is omitted in the translated quote and is not incorporated into any of the proposed provisions.[73] Remarkably, while it appears that the above-mentioned proposed laws and amendments touch upon various aspects relevant to the realization of the right to food, none of them explicitly refers to the right or to the ICESCR. Rights-based discourse on different facets of the right to food has remained absent throughout the entire law- and policy-making process, which reflects the overall constitutional and legal realities, as noted above. Without the normative anchor of the right to food in the ICESCR and the relevant General Comments and Reports of the Special Rapporteurs, legislative initiatives can only be undertaken in a fragmented, piecemeal manner.

---

[65]http://misq.ly.gov.tw/MISQ/IQuery/misq5000QueryBillDetail.action?billNo=1051110070202100. Accessed 30 Sept 2017.

[66]http://www.mohw.gov.tw/dl-13263-4857e204-22a2-409d-a760-b4318ba97b67.html. Accessed 30 Sept 2017.

[67]Legislative History. http://law.moj.gov.tw/Eng/LawClass/LawHistory.aspx?PCode=L0040001. Accessed 30 Sept 2017; see also Lin (2016).

[68]http://misq.ly.gov.tw/MISQ/IQuery/misq5000QueryBillDetail.action?billNo=1050325070201400. Accessed 30 Sept 2017.

[69]http://misq.ly.gov.tw/MISQ/IQuery/misq5000QueryBillDetail.action?billNo=1050225070200300. Accessed 30 Sept 2017.

[70]http://misq.ly.gov.tw/MISQ/IQuery/misq5000QueryBillDetail.action?billNo=1050304070200700. Accessed 30 Sept 2017.

[71]http://misq.ly.gov.tw/MISQ/IQuery/misq5000QueryBillDetail.action?billNo=1060316070200800. Accessed 30 Sept 2017.

[72]Universal Declaration of Human Rights, art. 25.1.

[73]Weisheng Fuli Bu [衛生福利部] (Health Promotion Administration) (2017) Guomin Yingyang ji Jiankang Yinshi Cujin Fa Casan Zong Shuoming [國民營養及健康飲食促進法草案總說明] (General Information on the Proposed National Nutrition and Healthy Diet Promotion Act), https://www.hpa.gov.tw/Pages/ashx/File.ashx?FilePath=~/File/Attach/7466/File_7017.pdf. Accessed 30 Sept 2017.

4 Conclusion: The Call for a Legal Framework Approach to the Right to Food and Its Normative Implications

The right to food is not merely about the ample supply of food. Rather, it is a multi-faceted human rights issue with a broad scope of application encompassing a myriad of issues, including *inter alia* food safety, the environment and eco-systems, agricultural policy, social welfare, food waste, malnutrition, and even noncommunicable diseases (hereinafter NCDs). In addition, there are cross-border dimensions to this right, where countries bear an obligation to respect, protect, and fulfill the right to food in extraterritorial settings. Given the unique international circumstances faced by Taiwan, the country has not been able to become a States Party to the ICESCR and many other human rights treaties. Indeed, Taiwan has arguably opted for a path dependence approach toward the realization of the right to food—in light of its constitutional practices, the Implementation Act, and its narrow interpretation and understanding of social, economic, and cultural rights—which in turn has resulted in a lack of constitutional and legal discourses as well as the absence of a rights-based approach. The uncertain and unstable relationship between the ICESCR (and the right to food in particular) and the domestic constitutional and legal order effectively serves as a shield that excuses the government from taking concrete measures. For the same reason, while recent legislative proposals on aspects of the right to food seem to be moving in the right direction of constructive government action, they involve multiple agencies and remain fragmented and piecemeal in nature, lacking comprehensive, systematic, and coherent logic.

In light of the discrepancies and the many challenges identified above, a *legal framework approach* may be desirable to serve as a normative anchor for rights-based discourse and actual progress toward the realization of the right to food in Taiwan.[74] A legal framework approach may serve to bridge the gap between the treatment of this critical right as simply an issue of the directive principles of national policy and a human right that requires protection of the law by handing the government the responsibility, as well as the necessary enforcement tools, to take concrete action, under clear, guiding principles. A rights-based, legal framework approach helps shift the focus from political decisions to the legal duties of the government so as to ensure a better distribution of power and resources with regard to aspects of the right to food.[75] This would in turn empower those who are underrepresented to enjoy the right to food in the long run. An overarching law passed by the Legislative Yuan may more effectively address the substantial demand for democratic accountability and distributional justice when the government acts to implement the ICESCR. While it might not address the problem of circularity caused by the uncertain status of the right to food (or more broadly, the

[74]See generally Coomans and Yakpo (2004); FAO (2009).

[75]FAO (2009), *supra* note 74, at p. 174.

ICESCR) in the domestic constitutional order, a legal framework approach may well serve to reinforce the effectiveness of both internal and external scrutiny by civil society and expert international reviews. Furthermore, a legal framework approach may provide a set of comprehensive, systematic, and coherent principles and rules for government action in various subsectors related to the right to food—nutrition, food safety, the environment, agriculture, social welfare, and so on.

In designing this legal framework approach to the right to food, the government must look to references beyond the explicit text of the ICESCR, which offers very vague language with limited guidance. Rather, the drafting endeavor should incorporate key elements as provided in the relevant General Comments issued by the CESCR, reports submitted by the UN Special Rapporteurs, and guidelines prepared by the FAO, among others. This chapter does not seek to exhaust all such key elements (about which the *FAO Guide on Legislating for the Right to Food* provides comprehensive details),[76] but merely aims to highlight two seemingly overlooked aspects of the right to food in Taiwan, i.e., the international dimensions of the right to food as well as the issues of overnutrition and NCDs. With regard to the international dimensions, while a state is primarily responsible for the realization of the right to food within its national boundaries, it should actively address the extraterritorial spillover of its actions, especially in our interdependent world with a globalized food supply chain.[77] The government of Taiwan should therefore pay sufficient attention to those policies that may affect the right to food of migrant workers and foreigners, and should conduct adequate impact assessments when it enters into international trade and investment agreements. International cooperative mechanisms should also be promoted to assist other countries to progressively realize the right to food.[78] With regard to overnutrition and NCDs, while there has been a growing number of national, regional, and international endeavors to address the relevant problems, a right to food perspective must be embraced by both developed and developing countries.[79] A right to food approach to the issue of NCDs may help the state shift from an oversimplified model of food charity to a more effective and accountable solution that ensures not only the supply of food but also optimal nutrition.[80]

There may be critics who discourage the proposal for a legal framework approach to the right to food because it does not promise to solve the issue of constitutional uncertainty. This chapter acknowledges the fact that the legal framework approach is largely silent regarding the status of the right to food in the domestic constitutional order, but this is not necessarily a disadvantage. The adoption of a legal framework

[76]*Id.*

[77]See OHCHR (2010), *supra* note 6, at pp. 22–23.

[78]See G.A. Res. 71/282, at para. 21 (3 Aug 2016).

[79]Report of Olivier De Schutter, at paras. 5, 9, 12; Human Rights Council, *Report Submitted by the Special Rapporteur Olivier De Schutter on the Right to Food*, at paras. 9–12, 26–35, UN Doc. A/HRC/19/59 (26 Dec 2011).

[80]Silvasti and Riches (2014), at pp. 206–208.

approach that creates detailed rules for legal protections does not prevent the Constitutional Court from providing additional constitutional protections to address the right to food in the future, and such an overlap should not be regarded as a problem. The citizens of Taiwan, and civil society as a whole, can enjoy multiple venues and tools to hold the government accountable—especially in light of the fact that Taiwan's unique international status often results in limited external scrutiny. Further, even if the right to food is subsequently incorporated into Article 22 of the Constitution by the Constitutional Court as part of the "other constitutionally protected rights," specifics about covered issues, essential requirements, policy options, appropriate means of redress or remedy, coordination among multiple agencies, and government accountability still must be spelled out by the Legislative Yuan. In addition, a legal framework approach will not conflict with the Implementation Act, but, rather, will complement it. Given the differences in nature between ICCPR and ICESCR rights, the Implementation Act—by simply bringing the two Covenants into the domestic legal system in a wholesale fashion—inevitably favors the former. ICCPR rights primarily ask the government not to passively violate them, while ICESCR rights—usually perceived by the Taiwanese government as rights that are not self-executing[81]—heavily rely on the government to actively take specific actions to respect, protect, and fulfill them through various supportive measures.[82] Yet the Implementation Act provides no further guidance and specific requirements in this regard, and the judiciary has been puzzled as to whether and how to move forward. The legal framework approach can be employed to address such concerns and articulate the appropriate means of execution, with adequate democratic accountability for the government to utilize in its efforts to realize the right to food.

All in all, given the existing weak constitutional and legal infrastructure in support of respect for and protection and fulfilment of the right to food in Taiwan, a legal framework approach promises to create an enabling, normative environment. It may help facilitate a rights-based discourse about the right to food and identify optimal institutional designs and legal and policy means toward the faithful internalization and realization of this right in Taiwan. The benefits of a legal framework approach should not be limited to the context of the right to food or the setting of developing countries. Rather, it should be considered as a way to uphold the social, economic, and cultural rights enshrined in the ICESCR in all corners of the world.

[81]Concluding Observations and Recommendations, at paras. 14–15.

[82]Key concepts on ESCRs—Can economic, social and cultural rights be litigated at courts? http://www.ohchr.org/EN/Issues/ESCR/Pages/CanESCRbelitigatedatcourts.aspx. Accessed 30 Sept 2017.

References

Chang W (2011) The convergence of constitutions and international human rights: Taiwan and South Korea in comparison. NC J Int Law Commercial Regul 36(3):593–624

Chang W (2015) Guoji Renquan Gongyue Yu Xianfa Jieshi: Huiliu De Moshi, Gongneng Ji Taiwan Shijian [國際人權公約與憲法解釋:匯流的模式、功能及台灣實踐] (International human rights treaties and constitutional interpretations: The modes and functions of convergence and the experiences of Taiwan). Paper presented at Sifayuan Dafaguan 104 Niandu Xueshu Yantaohui—Renquan Gongyue Yu Woguo Xianfa Jieshi [司法院大法官104年度學術研討會—人權公約與我國憲法解釋] (The Justices of the Constitutional Court annual conference: human rights treaties and constitutional interpretations in Taiwan, Judicial Yuan), Judges Academy, Taipei, 5 Dec 2015

Chen Y (2015) Application of international human rights law in Taiwan's court: case studies on the death penalty on mentally retarded persons. Const Rev 40(3):311–359

Coomans F, Yakpo K (2004) A framework law on the right to food—an international and South African perspective. Afr Hum Rights Law J 4(1):17–33

Cotula L, Vidar M (2003) Right to adequate food in emergencies. Food and Agriculture Organization of the United Nations, Rome

Covenants Watch (2012) Taiwan human rights report: parallel report on the implementation of the International Covenant on Economic, Social and Cultural Rights. https://drive.google.com/file/d/0B6XXC2kUbbLDaTY1X2o1Y2RScWs/view. Accessed 30 Sept 2017

Covenants Watch (2016) Shadow report 2016 on the implementation of the International Covenant on Economic, Social and Cultural Rights. http://covenantswatch.org.tw/wp-content/uploads/2017/01/ICESCR_Shadow-Report__final.pdf. Accessed 30 Sept 2017

Desierto D (2015) Public policy in international economic law: the ICESCR in trade, finance and investment. Oxford University Press, Oxford

Food and Agriculture Organization of the United Nations (2005) Voluntary guidelines to support the progressive realization of the right to adequate food in the context of national food security. Food and Agriculture Organization of the United Nations, Rome

Food and Agriculture Organization of the United Nations (2009) Guide on legislating for the right to food. Food and Agriculture Organization of the United Nations, Rome

G.A. Res. 2758 (XXVI) (25 October 1971)

G.A. Res. 71/282 (3 Aug 2016)

Haugen HM (2007) The right to food and the TRIPs agreement: with a particular emphasis on developing countries' measures for food production and distribution. Brill, Leiden

Hsu HY (2014) A study on the application of the Supreme Court and the Supreme Administrative Court to the International Covenant on Civil and Political Rights and the International Covenant on Economic, Social and Cultural Rights. Natl Taiwan Univ Law J 43(special issue):839–909

http://misq.ly.gov.tw/MISQ/IQuery/misq5000QueryBillDetail.action?billNo=1051110070202100. Accessed 30 Sept 2017

http://misq.ly.gov.tw/MISQ/IQuery/misq5000QueryBillDetail.action?billNo=1050325070201400. Accessed 30 Sept 2017

http://misq.ly.gov.tw/MISQ/IQuery/misq5000QueryBillDetail.action?billNo=1050225070200300. Accessed 30 Sept 2017

http://misq.ly.gov.tw/MISQ/IQuery/misq5000QueryBillDetail.action?billNo=1050304070200700. Accessed 30 Sept 2017

http://misq.ly.gov.tw/MISQ/IQuery/misq5000QueryBillDetail.action?billNo=1060316070200800. Accessed 30 Sept 2017

http://www.mohw.gov.tw/dl-13263-4857e204-22a2-409d-a760-b4318ba97b67.html. Accessed 30 Sept 2017

Huan J (2010) Constitutional law. Natl Taiwan Univ Law J 39(2):5–30

Huang ET (2003) Taiwan's status in a changing world: United Nations representation and membership for Taiwan. Annu Surv Int Comp Law 9:55–99

Human Rights Committee, *General Comment No. 6*, UN Doc. A/37/40(1982) (30 Apr 1982)

Human Rights Council, Promotion and Protection of All Human Rights, Civil, Political, Economic, Social and Cultural Rights, Including the Right to Development: Report of Special Rapporteur Jean Ziegler, on the Right to Food, UN Doc. A/HRC/7/5 (10 Jan 2008)

Human Rights Council, Report of the Special Rapporteur, Olivier De Schutter, on the Right to Food. UN Doc. A/HRC/25/57 (24 Jan 2014)

Human Rights Council, Report Submitted by the Special Rapporteur Olivier De Schutter, on the Right to Food. UN Doc. A/HRC/19/59 (26 Dec 2011)

Hutter S (2015) Starvation as a weapon: domestic policies of deliberate starvation as a means to an end under international law. Brill, Leiden

Hwang S (2015) Guoji Ji Quyu Renquan Gongyue Zai Xianfa Jieshi Zhong Banyan De Jiaose: Jianping Sifayuan Shixian Shiwu Dui Guoji Ji Quyu Renquan Gongyue Zhi Kandai Yu Yinyong Fangshi [國際及區域人權公約在憲法解釋中扮演的角色:兼評司法院釋憲實務 對國際及區域人權公約之看待與引用方式] (The role of international and regional human rights treaties in constitutional interpretation: an analysis of the Constitutional Court's Interpretation practices in referring to and citing international and regional human rights treaties). Paper presented at the Sifayuan Dafaguan 104 Niandu Xueshu Yantaohui—Renquan Gongyue Yu Woguo Xianfa Jieshi [司法院大法官104年度學術研討會—人權公約與我國憲法解釋] (The Annual Conference of the Justices of the Constitutional Court: human rights treaties and the constitutional interpretation in Taiwan's Judicial Yuan), Judges Academy, Taipei, 5 Dec 2015

International Development Law Organization (2015) Realizing the right to food: legal strategies and approaches. International Development Law Organization, Rome

Key concepts on ESCRs—Can economic, social and cultural rights be litigated at courts? http://www.ohchr.org/EN/Issues/ESCR/Pages/CanESCRbelitigatedatcourts.aspx. Accessed 30 Sept 2017

Legislative History. http://law.moj.gov.tw/Eng/LawClass/LawHistory.aspx?PCode=L0040001. Accessed 30 Sept 2017

Liao FF (2011) Should and how courts apply the ICESCR. Taiwan Hum Rights J 1(1):3–25

Lin CF (2016) The limit of regulatory borrowing: "cocktail therapy" reforms of the food safety law in Taiwan. In: Lo C, Li NT, Lin T (eds) Legal thoughts between the East and West in the multilevel legal order. Springer, Singapore, pp 409–422

Ministry of Justice (Taiwan) (2012a) Implementation of the International Covenant on Economic, Social and Cultural Rights: initial report submitted under Articles 16 and 17 of the Covenant. http://www.humanrights.moj.gov.tw/ct.asp?xItem=283640&ctNode=32921&mp=200. Accessed 30 Sept 2017

Ministry of Justice (Taiwan) (2012b) Initial state reports on the ICCPR and the ICESCR. http://www.humanrights.moj.gov.tw/ct.asp?xItem=385452&ctNode=40243&mp=205. Accessed 30 Sept 2017

Ministry of Justice (Taiwan) (2016a) Implementation of the International Covenant on Economic, Social and Cultural Rights: second report submitted under Articles 16 and 17 of the Covenant. http://www.humanrights.moj.gov.tw/ct.asp?xItem=431257&ctNode=43060&mp=200. Accessed 30 Sept 2017

Ministry of Justice (Taiwan) (2016b) The second national reports on the ICCPR and the ICESCR. http://www.humanrights.moj.gov.tw/lp.asp?ctNode=43063&CtUnit=16034&BaseDSD=7&mp=205. Accessed 30 Sept 2017

Review Meeting on Taiwan's initial reports under the ICCPR and ICESCR: consideration of the reports submitted by States Parties under Articles 16 & 17 of the Covenant: List of issues submitted by the Review Committee for the initial ICESCR report (21 Jan 2013). http://www.humanrights.moj.gov.tw/HitCounter.asp?xItem=294736. Accessed 30 Sept 2017

Review of the initial reports of the government of Taiwan on the implementation of the International Human Rights Covenants: Concluding observations and recommendations adopted by the International Group of Independent Experts, Taipei, 1 Mar 2013. http://www.humanrights.moj.gov.tw/HitCounter.asp?xItem=385451. Accessed 30 Sept 2017

Seatzu F (2011) The UN committee on economic, social and cultural rights and the right to adequate food. Anuario Español De Derecho Internacional 27:573–590

Sepulveda M (2003) Nature of the obligations under the International Covenant on Economic, Social and Cultural Rights. Intersentia, Antwerpen

Severson D (2013) Taiwan offers a model for advancing human rights. East Asia Forum. http://www.eastasiaforum.org/2013/08/23/taiwan-offers-a-model-for-advancing-human-rights/. Accessed 30 Sept 2017

Silvasti T, Riches G (2014) Hunger and food charity in rich societies: what hope for the right to food? In: Silvasti T, Riches G (eds) First world hunger revisited: food charity or the right to food? Palgrave Macmillan, Hampshire, pp. 191–208

Söllner S (2007) The "breakthrough" of the right to food: the meaning of *General Comment No. 12* and the voluntary guidelines on the interpretation of the human right to food. Max Planck Yearbook United Nations Law Online 11(1):391–415

UN Commission on Human Rights, The Right to Food: Report by Special Rapporteur Mr. Jean Ziegler on the Right to Food, submitted in accordance with the Commission on Human Rights Resolution 2000/10, UN Doc. E/CN.4/2001/53 (7 Feb 2001)

United Nations Economic and Social Council, Committee on Economic, Social and Cultural Rights, *General Comment No. 12* (1999): The Right to Adequate Food (Art. 11), UN Doc. E/C.12/1999/5 (12 May 1999)

United Nations Economic and Social Council, Committee on Economic, Social and Cultural Rights, *General Comment No. 14* (2000): The Right to the Highest Attainable Standard of Health (Article 12 of the International Covenant on Economic, Social and Cultural Rights), UN Doc. E/C.12/2000/4 (11 Aug 2000)

United Nations Economic and Social Council, Committee on Economic, Social and Cultural Rights, *General Comment No. 3* (1990): The Nature of States Parties' Obligations (Art. 2, Para. 1, of the Covenant), UN Doc. E/1991/23 (14 Dec 1990)

United Nations Office of the High Commissioner for Human Rights (2010) The right to adequate food, Fact Sheet No. 34. United Nations, Geneva

Universal Declaration of Human Rights, G.A. Res. 217 (III) A, UN Doc. A/810 (10 Dec 1948)

Wang F (2009) Legislature ratifies UN rights treaties. Taipei Times. http://www.taipeitimes.com/News/taiwan/archives/2009/04/01/2003439900. Accessed 30 Sept 2017

Wang T (2002) The legal development of Taiwan in the 20th century: toward a liberal and democratic country. Pac Rim Law & Policy J 11:531–560

Weisheng Fuli Bu [衛生福利部] (Health Promotion Administration) (2017) Guomin Yingyang ji Jiankang Yinshi Cu Jin Fa Cao'an Zong Shuo Ming [國民營養及健康飲食促進法草案總說明] (General Information on the Proposed National Nutrition and Healthy Diet Promotion Act). https://www.hpa.gov.tw/Pages/ashx/File.ashx?FilePath=～/File/Attach/7466/File_7017.pdf. Accessed 30 Sept 2017

Yeh J (2015) Jingji Shehui Wenhua Quanli Gongyue Yu Sifa Shencha: Shuangzhong Zhiyue Xia De Duihua Sifa [經濟社會文化權利公約與司法審查:雙重制約下的對話司法] (The ICESCR and judicial review: the dialectic judiciary under dual constraints). Paper presented at Sifayuan Dafaguan 104 Niandu Xueshu Yantaohui—Renquan Gongyue Yu Woguo Xianfa Jieshi [司法院大法官104年度學術研討會—人權公約與我國憲法解釋] (The Justices of the Constitutional Court annual conference: human rights treaties and constitutional interpretations in Taiwan, Judicial Yuan), Judges Academy, Taipei, 5 Dec 2015

Ziegler J, Golay C, Mahon C, Way S (2011) The fight for the right to food: lessons learned. Palgrave Macmillan, Hampshire

Ching-Fu Lin is Assistant Professor of Law at National Tsing Hua University (NTHU), where he teaches international health law, food law and policy, and international law and global governance. Professor Lin received his LL.M. and S.J.D. degrees from Harvard Law School, with the honors of the John Gallup Laylin Memorial Prize (best paper in public international law) and the Yong K. Kim Memorial Prize (best paper in East Asian legal studies). He also holds a dual degree in law (LL.B.) and chemical engineering (B.S.) from National Taiwan University. Before joining NTHU in 2015, Professor Lin served as Visiting Fellow at the Graduate Institute of International and Development Studies in Geneva, Switzerland. He has also been Peter Barton Hutt Student Fellow at the Petrie-Flom Center for Health Law Policy, Biotechnology, and Bioethics as well as Visiting Scholar Coordinator at the East Asian Legal Studies Program, Harvard Law School. Active in legal academia, Professor Lin has been invited to lecture in many academic settings, such as the Summer Academy in Global Food Law and Policy in Spain, Brescia University School of Law in Italy, and the World Food Law Program and the United Nations Food and Agriculture Organization in the United States. His legal scholarship has appeared in numerous journals and edited collections, including *Virginia Journal of International Law*, *Columbia Science and Technology Law Review*, *Food and Drug Law Journal*, and *Journal of World Trade*.

Chapter 30
Tobacco Investment and Human Rights: A Challenge for Taiwan's ICESCR Implementation in Its Foreign Investment Policy

Tsai-Yu Lin

Abstract Corporate businesses can enhance human rights protection. The formulation of investment treaties can also be supportive in implementing the ICESCR. However, the life-threatening nature of tobacco businesses will pose a significant impact upon the enjoyment of the right to health. From the perspective of policy coherence, granting market access to tobacco industry investment through bilateral investment treaties (BITs) presents a particular challenge for ICESCR compliance. The Taiwan government paid insufficient attention to its ICESCR obligations when it adopted an open permission policy for foreign tobacco industry investment in BITs. As argued in this chapter, the Taiwan government can achieve little to redress this problematic market access commitment. In the case of withdrawing market access commitments through treaty amendments, for instance, existing tobacco investors' rights would still remain intact and continue to be protected. The Taiwan government has a duty to create a condition in which people can enjoy good health. Individuals' right to health in the ICESCR can never be "fully" respected and be "adequately" protected in the context of tobacco business activities. Nor can the government live up to its ICESCR duties while it still encourages tobacco investments through BITs. To bridge the gaping hole between these two regimes, the ICESCR norms might accelerate the reform of Taiwan's tobacco investment policy and its BIT formulation. However, the success of these reforms ultimately depends on the Taiwan government's willingness to effectively implement the ICESCR for its people.

Keywords BIT · ICESCR · Market access · Right to health · Tobacco industry investment · Treaty amendment

T.-Y. Lin (✉)
National Taiwan University College of Law, Taipei City, Taiwan
e-mail: tylinkry@ntu.edu.tw

J. A. Cohen et al. (eds.), *Taiwan and International Human Rights*, Economics, Law, and Institutions in Asia Pacific, https://doi.org/10.1007/978-981-13-0350-0_30

1 Introduction

Human rights and foreign investment protections have long evolved under separate treaty regimes. Human rights protection is principally built on various human rights treaties. States Parties under the International Covenant on Economic, Social and Cultural Rights (hereinafter ICESCR),[1] for instance, are bound to provide individuals with economic, social, and cultural rights (e.g., labor rights, the right to health and an adequate standard of living). In contrast, the protection of foreign investors and their investments is primarily realized through a web of bilateral investment treaties (hereinafter BITs). States Parties in BITs might commit to liberalize investments and provide protection to investors, such as non-discrimination treatment, fair and equitable treatment (hereinafter FET) and justified compensation for an expropriation. Foreign investors are often entitled to recourse under international arbitration for dispute resolution.

To what extent transnational corporations might be able to influence human rights implementation has been a growing concern. As recognized by the Committee on Economic, Social and Cultural Rights (hereinafter CESC) under the ICESCR, businesses can contribute to the fulfillment of economic, social and cultural rights of individuals. At the same time, however, businesses can also deeply impact the enjoyment of specific human rights of people, for instance, rights relating to health, housing, water, social security and the right to work and just and favorable conditions of work.[2] Likewise, alleviating the adverse effects on the public interest associated with foreign investments have been widely discussed by the investment law community. An increasing number of BITs have provided protection for certain preeminent interests, such as health, safety, the environment and labor rights.[3] Fostering foreign investors' respect for human rights protection in their business activities has also been addressed in some BITs.[4] With respect to

[1]The ICESCR together with the Universal Declaration of Human Rights and the International Covenant on Civil and Political Rights constitutes the International Bill of Human Rights.

[2]See *infra* Section II of this chapter.

[3]For instance, the U.S.–Rwanda BIT sets out a specific provision on investment and labor in Article 13.2, which reads: "For purposes of this Article, 'labor laws' means each Party's statutes or regulations, or provisions thereof, that are directly related to the following internationally recognized labor rights: (a) the right of association; (b) the right to organize and bargain collectively; (c) a prohibition on the use of any form of forced or compulsory labor; (d) labor protections for children and young people, including a minimum age for the employment of children and the prohibition and elimination of the worst forms of child labor; and (e) acceptable conditions of work with respect to minimum wages, hours of work, and occupational safety and health." Treaty Between the Government of the United States of America and the Government of the Republic of Rwanda Concerning the Encouragement and Reciprocal Protection of Investment, US–Rwanda, art 13.2, 19 Feb 2008, http://investmentpolicyhub.unctad.org/Download/TreatyFile/2241.

[4]For instance, Article 16 (Corporate Social Responsibility) of the Canada–Benin FIPA reads: "Each Contracting Party should encourage enterprises operating within its territory or subject to its jurisdiction to voluntarily incorporate internationally recognized standards of corporate social responsibility in their practices and internal policies, such as statements of principle that have been

investment jurisprudence, human rights-based claims in the interest of the general public (e.g., rights relating to water, health, labor and culture) have occasionally occurred.[5]

Generally, treaty states have the duty to ensure that transnational corporations in their jurisdiction respect and protect individuals' human rights in the context of business activities under the ICESCR. Besides the business interests of foreign investors, host states' regulatory powers to protect public interests are also recognized by BITs. To this extent, it can be said that BITs can supplement and support the realization of the universal human rights values protected by the ICESCR. However, on the other hand, BITs might be applied as an instrument that undermines fundamental human rights while protecting foreign business. In this regard, foreign investments by the tobacco industry can serve as a notable example. Tobacco products are lethal to human life.[6] This characteristic makes tobacco businesses and investments inherently harmful. As tobacco industry investment is boosted and protected through BITs, more production, consumption and possible deaths associated with tobacco in host states are likely to occur. From the perspective of human rights, the individuals' right to health will therefore be adversely and irreparably affected.

The ICESCR has been incorporated into Taiwan's domestic law since 2009. Implementation of the ICESCR requires Taiwan's government to address many important issues.[7] To date, however, the ICESCR has seemingly yet to figure prominently in the government's formulation of economic and business-related policies. In contrast, as argued in this chapter, the Taiwan government has created an obstacle for the realization of the right to health of its people by granting market access to Japanese tobacco investments under the Taiwan–Japan BIT, which was concluded in 2011. This problematic market access commitment has limited Taiwan in its ability to fully protect the right to health of its population, which is inconsistent with the ICESCR. A relevant discussion follows.

---

endorsed or are supported by the Contracting Parties. These principles address issues such as labor, the environment, human rights, community relations and anti-corruption." Agreement Between the Government of Canada and the Government of the Republic of Benin for the Promotion and Reciprocal Protection of Investments, Can–Benin, art 16, 8 Jan 2013, http://internationall.gc.ca/trade-commerce/trade-agreements-accords-commerciaux/agr-acc/benin/fipa-apie/index.aspx?lang=eng#a19.

[5]See generally Kube and Petersmann (2016), Lo (2015).

[6]Notably, tobacco is lethal in nature, killing up to one-half of its users. As estimated by the WHO, more than 7 million deaths result from tobacco-related illnesses each year, which include direct tobacco users and non-smokers who are exposed to second-hand smoke. See Tobacco. WHO. http://www.who.int/mediacentre/factsheets/fs339/en/. Accessed 24 Sept 2017.

[7]The International Review Committee of Independent Experts on the ICESCR was created subsequently to oversee the government's compliance with the obligations it has undertaken.

2 States Parties' Obligations Associated with Business Activities and the Right to Health: An Overview

Article 2.1 of the ICESCR provides that States Parties must take steps, "to the maximum of available resources," "with a view to achieving progressively the full realization of the rights recognized in the present Covenant by all appropriate means."[8] Therefore, States Parties to the ICESCR have the duty to adopt appropriate measures, including legislative and other means to progress toward the fulfillment of the rights of individuals enshrined in the ICESCR.

There have been several instruments concerning corporate activities and human rights. In 2011, the CESC made a statement on States Parties' obligations with regard to corporate activities and economic, social and cultural rights.[9] In this statement, corporations' contributions to implementing ICESCR rights through their inputs to economic development, employment and investment are recognized. However, potential adverse effects on the enjoyment of ICESCR rights brought about by corporate activities also raised concern. It is stated that the range of related problems which may occur include child labor, unsafe working conditions, harmful impacts on the right to health and the natural environment.[10]

In 2011, the UN Human Rights Council endorsed the "Guiding Principles on Business and Human Rights: Implementing the United Nations 'Protect, Respect and Remedy' Framework."[11] In accordance with the Guiding Principles, State Parties should ensure that enterprises governed by business-related laws and policies respect human rights.[12] States Parties also need to maintain adequate domestic policy space to meet their human rights obligations through investment treaties.[13] Additionally, as stated in the commentary attached to the Guiding Principles, "the terms of international investment agreements may constrain states from fully implementing new human rights legislation, or put them at risk of binding international arbitration if they do so. Therefore, States Parties should ensure that they

[8]Article 2.1 states that "Each State Party to the present Covenant undertakes to take steps, individually and through international assistance and co-operation, especially economic and technical, to the maximum of its available resources, with a view to achieving progressively the full realization of the rights recognized in the present Covenant by all appropriate means, including particularly the adoption of legislative measures." International Covenant on Economic, Social and Cultural Rights, art. 2.1, *opened for signature* 16 Dec 1966, http://www.ohchr.org/EN/ProfessionalInterest/Pages/CESCR.aspx (entered into force 3 Jan 1976). Regarding the historical development and interpretation of the ICESCR, see generally Desierto (2015), pp. 70–150.

[9]UN Econ. & Soc. Council, Comm. on Econ., Soc. & Cultural Rights, Statement on the Obligations of States Parties Regarding the Corporate Sector and Economic, Social and Cultural Rights, UN Doc. E/C.12/2011/1 (12 July 2011).

[10]*Id.*

[11]See Human Rights Council Res. 17/4, UN Doc, A/HRC/RES/17/4 (6 June 2011).

[12]*Id.*

[13]*Id.*

retain policy and regulatory ability adequate for the protection of human rights under the terms of such agreements, while providing the necessary investor protection."[14]

The UN Human Rights Council in 2011 also issued the "Guiding principles on human rights impact assessments of trade and investment agreements."[15] These Guiding Principles purport to provide guidance which may render trade and investment agreements consistent with human rights instruments. States Parties are therefore encouraged to undertake human rights assessments of "investment treaties." In cases where a problematic provision makes the realization of human rights difficult, it is suggested to remove such a provision or apply safeguard provisions so as to properly reflect human rights obligations. It is suggested that the relevant policies be designed and implemented through the human rights impact assessment.[16]

In 2017, the CESC held a general discussion on the draft "General Comment on State Obligations in the Context of Business Activities" (to be No. 24).[17] This new draft General Comment seeks to clarify the duties of States Parties under the ICESCR so as to ensure business activities contribute to and do not hinder the enjoyment of economic, social and cultural rights. For instance, as indicated in the draft General Comment, if a State Party facilitates businesses' breaches of ICESCR rights, it will constitute a violation of its "obligation to respect" under the ICESCR. If a State Party's incentive measures provided to businesses lead to a restriction or hindrance of the enjoyment of ICESCR rights, it will be considered to be against the "obligation to protect" States Parties under the ICESCR. The draft General Comment also deals with issues of investment agreements and domestic investment regimes. As stated, investment instruments should be designed in a manner that increases investment flows rather than risking undermining ICESCR rights.[18] Also, there is a need for States Parties to identify any potential conflict between their ICESCR obligations and subsequent investment agreements. They are to refrain from concluding agreements where conflicts exist.[19]

---

[14] *Id.*

[15] See Olivier De Schutter (Special Rapporteur on the Right to Food), Report on the right to food: Addendum on guiding principles on human rights impact assessments of trade and investment agreements, UN Doc. A/HRC/19/59/Add.5 (19 Dec 2011).

[16] *Id.*

[17] UN Econ. & Soc. Council, Comm. on Econ., Soc. & Cultural Rights, General Comment on State Obligations under the International Covenant on Economic, Social and Cultural Rights in the Context of Business Activities: draft prepared by Olivier De Schutter and Zdzislaw Kedzia, Rapporteurs, UN Doc. E/c.12/60/R.1 (17 Oct 2016). General Comments serve as an important legal instrument reflecting the reading of treaty rights and obligations by the supervisory human rights bodies in the various conventions. Although the General Comments do not constitute an authentic interpretation of the relevant treaties, they are believed to represent considerable authority for States Parties to consider in good faith.

[18] *Id.*

[19] *Id.*

On a different level, the right to health is protected in Article 12 of the ICESCR. States Parties recognize "the right of everyone to the enjoyment of the highest attainable standard of physical and mental health"; and to ensure "steps to be taken by the State Parties… to achieve the full realization of this right." Regarding the normative content of "the improvement of all aspects of environmental and industrial hygiene" under Article 12.2(b), General Comment No. 14 (The Right to the Highest Attainable Standard of Health, Art. 12) further illustrates[20] that Article 12.2(b) includes "[discouraging]…the use of tobacco…and other harmful substances."[21] If state policies or laws contravene the standards of Article 12 and are likely to result in bodily harm, unnecessary morbidity and preventable mortality,[22] then a violation of "the obligation to respect" would arise. The failure of States Parties to take into account obligations regarding the right to health when concluding bilateral or multilateral agreements with other states is considered to be one example of such a violation.[23]

More importantly, in relation to violations of "the obligation to protect" the right to health, General Comment No. 14 notes:

> Violations of the obligation to protect follow from the failure of a State to take all necessary measures to safeguard persons within their jurisdiction from infringements of the right to health by third parties. This category includes… the failure to protect consumers and workers from practices detrimental to health, e.g., by…*the failure to discourage production, marketing and consumption of tobacco*.... (Emphases added.)[24]

In summary, States Parties must take appropriate steps to ensure that all ICESCR rights (including the right to health) are fully realized in the context of business activities. To this end, business-related laws and policies in particular should not constrain but rather should foster business respect for human rights. States Parties are not allowed to facilitate a violation of ICESCR rights by the business sector. Nor can they adopt policies to incentivize businesses to restrict or impede the enjoyment of the ICESCR rights of individuals.

The above relevant ICESCR instruments raise specific concerns regarding the investment regime and tobacco respectively. On the investment regime, States Parties are called on to maintain adequate domestic policy room and regulatory ability to protect human rights under investment treaties. The formulation of investment treaties should ensure that increased investments enhance, rather than undermine, human rights protection. Additionally, States Parties are to abstain from signing investment treaties that contradict their human rights obligations. On the right to health and the issue of tobacco, States Parties are bound to take

---

[20]UN Econ. & Soc. Council, Comm. on Econ., Soc. & Cultural Rights, Substantive Issues Arising in the Implementation of the International Covenant on Economic, Social and Cultural Rights, UN Doc. E/C.12/2000/4 (11 Aug 2000).

[21]*Id.*, at paras. 15, 44(c).

[22]*Id.*, at para. 50.

[23]*Id.*

[24]*Id.*, at para. 51.

"all necessary measures" to protect all of the population from interference by corporations so as to fulfill their "obligation to protect" the right to health. Discouraging the use of tobacco constitutes part of the obligation in Article 12.2(b). More specifically, failure to discourage production, marketing or consumption of tobacco would trigger States Parties' liability as breaching the protection of the right to health.

3 Taiwan's Unilateral Market Access Commitment Granted to Tobacco Industry Foreign Investment under the Taiwan–Japan BIT

This chapter argues that Taiwan's government has unilaterally offered a market access commitment in favor of tobacco industry investments under the Taiwan–Japan BIT. The Japanese investors are therefore entitled to enter the Taiwan market under national treatment conditions. In fact, Japan Tobacco International (hereinafter JTI), the world's third-largest tobacco company, has also been permitted to invest in Taiwan and is protected by the BIT.

3.1 The Tobacco Industry Is Subject to Taiwan's Market Access Commitment

Investment liberalization or market access operates through pre-establishment provisions. That is, if a host state has the will, it can grant foreign investors the right to establish an investment on a national treatment basis, unless explicitly excluded. National treatment requires a host state to treat foreign investors and/or their investments no less favorably than it would treat its domestic investors in similar circumstances. Article 3 of the Taiwan–Japan BIT reads:

1. Investors of either Side and their investments shall within the Area of the other Side be accorded treatment no less favorable than the treatment accorded in like circumstances to investors of the other Side and to their investments with respect to investment activities.
2. Notwithstanding paragraph 1, it is understood that special formalities may be prescribed in connection with investment activities of investors of the other Side, provided that such special formalities do not impair the substance of the treatments which both Sides consider under this Arrangement to be accorded to such investors.

As such, investors from the other contracting party shall be accorded treatment no less favorable than the treatment accorded to the host state's own domestic investors in like circumstances with respect to investment activities. Without laying down specific conditions and terms, this type of national treatment clause can be read as states making liberal and positive commitments for national treatment in the pre-establishment and post-establishment phases of an investment. The legal implication will be that the host state should treat foreign investors and their investments in like situations on a non-discriminatory basis with respect to investment activities, unless otherwise provided in reservations[25] or exceptions.

With regard to tobacco industry investments, in accordance with Article 10 of Taiwan's Tobacco and Alcohol Administration Act, companies, partnerships or wholly-owned enterprises are eligible to file an application with the central competent authority to be incorporated as a tobacco manufacturer. The applicant will not be allowed to begin its production, manufacture and business operations as a tobacco producer until the permission and license have been granted by the relevant authority. As such, Taiwan's domestic investors are entitled to request an investment permit to engage in tobacco production and business under the required screening and licensing procedure. As a result of applying the national treatment obligation under the BIT, Taiwan's government is bound by the open admission policy to screen and determine whether a proposed foreign tobacco investments can be granted a license and be permitted to operate. From this perspective, Japanese tobacco companies would be able to benefit from the same market access opportunities in the manufacture of tobacco as Taiwan's domestic tobacco companies at the pre-establishment phase. The Taiwan government's power in regulating or controlling foreign tobacco investments would therefore be subject to greater limitations. Unless justifications can otherwise be established, denying or restricting foreign tobacco investments will likely trigger the government's liability under the BIT. More importantly, for the purposes of the Taiwan–Japan BIT, Taiwan does not list the manufacture of tobacco products in its annexed reservations, to which the obligation to provide national treatment does not apply. In contrast, Japan has reserved some items in its obligations from national treatment under Article 3, which includes the manufacture of tobacco products. The Japanese government, therefore, does not offer an equivalent market access commitment for Taiwan's tobacco companies to invest in the tobacco industry in Japan.[26]

Granting foreign investors a right to market access with national treatment conditions may constrain the host state's regulatory ability to control foreign

---

[25]The U.S. Model BIT, for instance, refers to certain activities or matters in its Annex, to which the obligations to provide national treatment and most-favored-nation do not apply.

[26]In Annex II of the Taiwan–Japan BIT, Japan provides that "[i]n the event where the supply of telegraph services, postal services and betting and gambling services, *manufacture of tobacco products*, which are restricted to designated enterprises or governmental entities, are liberalized to those other than the designated enterprises or governmental entities, or in the event where such designated enterprises or governmental entities no longer operate on a noncommercial basis, any measure relating to those activities may be adopted or maintained" (emphasis added). Arrangement Between the Association of East Asian Relations and the Interchange Association for the Mutual Cooperation on the Liberalization, Promotion and Protection of Investment, Taiwan–Japan, annex II of the Interchange Association, 22 Sept 2011, http://www.moea.gov.tw/CWS/tji/content/wHandMenuFile.ashx?menu_id=6694.

investments. If the Taiwan government wishes to deny market access to foreign tobacco investments, it must apply it on a non-discriminatory basis.

3.2 Japan Tobacco International's (JTI) Investment Project in Taiwan

A recent foreign investment project in Taiwan's tobacco industry involved JTI. In 2013 JTI claimed to have invested more than US$300 million to establish a tobacco manufacturing unit in Tainan, a southern city of Taiwan.[27] After approval by the Ministry of Economic Affairs, JTI began its plant construction on 7.6 ha of land in the Tainan Technology Industrial Park. Meanwhile, JTI was eligible to receive financial benefits from tax exemptions as it had agreed to locate its plant within the industrial park. This investment project was expected to bring about 300–400 jobs and promote local development.

While the government reviewed the investment project, JTI encountered opposition from domestic anti-smoking advocates, which attracted public attention in Taiwan. For instance, in 2015 anti-smoking groups attacked Tainan City Government for approving JTI's plan to build its tobacco plant in the industrial park.[28] In 2016, the group further claimed that the Ministry of Finance should not have issued an operating license to JTI's new tobacco plant. Additionally, it urged the Executive Yuan to revoke the operating license that had been granted. According to the anti-smoking groups, establishment of the tobacco plant would increase tobacco use in Taiwan.[29] Consequently, the overall health of Taiwan's people would be left to suffer.

Certain issues relating to both domestic and international law were raised in this case. For instance, some argued that the JTI investment was an illegal investment due to its inconsistency with Article 7.1 of Taiwan's "Statute for Investment by Foreign Nationals." In their view, the tobacco industry should be considered an industry that brings adverse impacts to national health, falling into the sector which

[27]Regarding discussion of the JTI case in Taiwan, see Complaint filed over JTI's planned plant in Taiwan. Tobacco Reporter. https://www.tobaccoreporter.com/…/complaint-filed-over-jtis-planned-p. Accessed 24 Sept 2017; Plans for JTI plant in Taiwan meeting opposition. Tobacco Reporter. https://www.tobaccoreporter.com/2015/07/plans-for-jti-plant-in-taiwan-meeting-opposition/. Accessed 24 Sept 2017.

[28]JTI had been considered a high-tech company located within a technological industrial park for not polluting and for the involvement of a technical tobacco production process, thereby it could benefit from the use of the land with lower costs and tax preferences specifically granted to the high-tech industry (Liao et al. (2015)). Ironically, the tobacco company had been considered to be an eligible technological company because it was non-polluting and it introduced a new technology in the tobacco production process. *Id.*

[29]See Gerber (2016).

shall be prohibited from foreign investments as required by the Statute.[30] Moreover, some claimed that the investment permission granted and the subsidies provided to JTI constituted a violation of the WHO Framework Convention on Tobacco Control (FCTC).[31] Some also criticized that the Taiwan government's unilateral market access commitment granted to Japanese tobacco companies under the Taiwan–Japan BIT was an unwise decision.

Additionally, the anti-smoking groups proposed forming a task force that aimed to revoke the building licenses granted to the tobacco plants that were still under construction. It was suggested that the Ministry of Economic Affairs should explicitly include the tobacco industry on the list of foreign investments prohibited by law and that the relevant domestic laws (e.g., the Tobacco and Alcohol Administration Act, Tobacco and Alcohol Tax Act, and Tobacco Hazards Prevention Act) should be amended so as to comply with international treaties.

In the view of this author, modifying domestic law or withdrawing an already granted license would not genuinely address the source of the problem. Admission or denial of market access to Japanese tobacco investment is no longer purely a domestic matter. Instead, properly addressing the problem will involve Taiwan's obligations concerning the BIT and the ICESCR. To this extent, the regulatory power of Taiwan's government is constrained if it wishes to reverse Japanese tobacco investments.

4 A Problematic Market Access Commitment to Tobacco Industry Investments Under BITs: A Perspective from the ICESCR

The Taiwan government has adopted a liberal policy concerning market access of the tobacco industry's investments under the Taiwan–Japan BIT. As a result, tobacco companies from Japan are able to apply for investment permission and to benefit from tax preferences in the same way as domestic tobacco companies on the basis of national treatment. Obviously, Taiwan's negotiators had neither placed much emphasis on the tobacco business's harmful nature nor seriously considered protecting the Taiwanese people's right to health.

---

[30]Article 7.1 of the "Statute for Investments by Foreign Nationals" provides that "the investor is prohibited from investing in the following industries: Those which may negatively affect national security, public order, good customs and practices, or national health." Wai Guo Ren Tou Zi Tiao Li (Statute for Investments By Foreign Nationals), art. 7.1 (1997) (Taiwan). The Ministry of Economic Affairs has classified the tobacco manufacturing sector as an industry in which foreign investors are restricted from investing, not prohibited from investing.

[31]In the foreword to the FCTC, the WHO recognizes that "foreign direct investment" is one of the various complex factors with cross-border effects, which facilitate the spread of the tobacco epidemic. Tobacco companies' investment activities would aggravate the globalized tobacco epidemic. See Lin (2013).

Indeed, investing in foreign markets to expand their business operations or gain greater market presence has been a strategy recently pursued by transnational tobacco companies. Outbound investment activities can help tobacco companies overcome the costs caused by higher tariffs. Associated tax preferences and exemptions granted by host states can make tobacco companies more competitive by reducing prices and increasing sales of tobacco products. It is generally accepted that this increased level of tobacco industry investments will lead to a higher level of tobacco consumption in the host states.[32] As a result, the population in the host states will face heightened health risks.

From the perspective of human-rights protection, granting market access benefits to tobacco industry foreign investments is problematic. The main reason is that such harmful investments will hinder, rather than enhance, enjoyment of an individual's right to health in the host state. More specifically, looking to the ICESCR and its General Comment No. 14, it is stated that the States Parties' policy violating Article 12 and resulting in "bodily harm, unnecessary morbidity and preventable mortality" will be a breach of the "obligation to respect" the right to health of individuals. A failure to "discourage" production, marketing or consumption of tobacco will violate an "obligation to protect" the right to health. As argued above, granting market access to tobacco industry investments is likely to bring about more production, marketing or consumption of tobacco in the host states. The health risks of bodily harm and mortality associated with tobacco use may be increased as a result.[33] Consequently, a liberal tobacco industry investment commitment under BITs might impede a state's fulfilment of its duty to protect the individual's right to health under the ICESCR.

A state's incentive program linked to tobacco industry investments might arguably contravene the ICESCR.[34] Draft General Comment No. 24 states that a state's business incentive program "should not lead to restrict or hinder" enjoyment of the ICESCR rights. As shown in the case of Taiwan, foreign tobacco companies are able to receive the same tax preferences and economic incentives as domestic investors. JTI has benefited from the use of land with lower costs and tax preferences specifically granted to high-tech industries, and has been permitted to establish its tobacco plant within a technological industrial park. To the extent that a state's incentive programs are used to encourage investments by foreign companies, these programs might "restrict or hinder" fulfillment of the right to the health of the people due to the increase in tobacco production and consumption.

[32]See Lo (2010), at pp. 310, Mcgrady (2012), at pp. 83–98.

[33]Tobacco use remains the leading preventable cause of premature death in the United States. The WHO states that tobacco use is "the single most preventable cause of death in the world today." See U.S. Department of Health and Human Services (2010), at p. 647.

[34]FCTC Article 5.3 guidelines provide that "the tobacco industry should not be granted incentives, privileges or benefits to establish or run their businesses." WHO Framework Convention on Tobacco Control, art. 5.3, *opened for signature* 21 May 2003, 2302 U.N.T.S. 166, http://apps.who.int/iris/bitstream/10665/42811/1/9241591013.pdf?ua=1.

Additionally, under the ICESCR, States Parties have a duty to enable or foster corporations to respect and protect human rights in the context of business-related policy. Foreign investment policy relates to the establishment and operation of transnational companies in a host state. Therefore, encouraging foreign companies to respect human rights has been the subject of widespread concern under the recent BITs. In fact, a state's attempts to enable or enhance "foreign tobacco companies" to respect the right to health of the people (e.g., tobacco users) might raise a particular concern. The fundamental issue is that the harmful nature of tobacco business operations frustrates enjoyment of the right to health of the people. It is the tobacco industry that is supposed to be held directly accountable for tobacco users' deaths, in which case it seems unlikely that tobacco companies can be enabled to "fully" realize protection of the right to health of individuals. It is the view of this author that, although tobacco companies may undertake other commitments or activities to support and promote human rights (e.g., labor protection), this does not offset a failure to respect the right to health of people due to their harmful operations. A state, by granting market access to tobacco investments under BITs, hinders the right to health of individuals by supporting the tobacco industry. As identified in draft General Comment No. 24, such an action would be in breach of the "obligation to respect" under the ICESCR.

The ICESCR instrument offers some specific guidance on the design and implementation of BITs in relation to human rights. For instance, States Parties should retain adequate domestic policy room and regulatory ability to satisfy their human rights obligations through investment treaties. Investment treaties should ensure that increases in investments improve ICESCR rights. States Parties should not conclude investment treaties that conflict with their ICESCR obligations. As argued, a state's commitment to grant market access to tobacco investments under BITs might run counter to the core of ICESCR guidance. First, under the market access commitment, a state will not be able to liberally deny or control foreign tobacco investments in order to protect its population's right to health from interference by tobacco companies. Second, the increased tobacco investments would undermine enjoyment of the right to health, in particular for tobacco users and non-smokers who are exposed to second-hand smoke. Third, the provision of granting market access to tobacco investments under BITs exposes an inherent conflict with a state's ICESCR obligations to protect the right to health of individuals, and such a conflict should be averted to the greatest extent possible.

States Parties should bear the duty to preclude tobacco industry investments from undermining fulfillment of the ICESCR rights of individuals when drafting investment treaties. In other words, States Parties are obliged to ensure that their investment treaties will be compatible with their obligations under the ICESCR. As such, in the view of this author, there are solid grounds for Taiwan to change its policy regarding foreign tobacco industry investments.

5 Aligning with the ICESCR: Is it Possible for Taiwan to Deny Market Access to Tobacco Industry Investments under the Existing BITs?

The Taiwan government has, through its domestic legislation, demonstrated its willingness to be bound by its ICESCR obligations. Therefore, on the part of the Taiwan government, the issue of tobacco industry investments involves not only market access commitments made under the Taiwan–Japan BIT but also relates to fulfilling its ICESCR obligations. Granting market access to tobacco industry investments is likely to frustrate people's right to health, resulting in a breach of the ICESCR. As such, whether or under what conditions a host state is likely to reverse tobacco industry investments under the BIT to protect the right to health of its population requires further discussion. The Taiwan local community has proposed some options for discouraging tobacco industry investments. Examples include withdrawing the previously granted operating licenses and cancelling the tax preferences. From the perspective of the BIT, these proposals will likely involve the host state's obligations regarding national treatment, FET or indirect expropriations. In the case of indirect expropriations, Article 12.3 of the Taiwan–Japan BIT reads:

> The determination of whether an action or a series of actions by the authorities of either Side, in a specific fact situation, constitutes an indirect expropriation requires a case-by-case, fact-based inquiry that considers, among other factors: (a) the economic impact of the action, although the fact that such action by the authorities has an adverse effect on the economic value of an investment, standing alone, does not establish that an indirect expropriation has occurred; (b) the extent to which the action interferes with distinct, reasonable expectations arising out of investment; (c) the character of the action; and (d) the objectives of the action, including whether such action is taken for legitimate public objectives, such as protecting the public welfare, safety and health, and protecting and preserving the environment.[35]

A host government withdrawing an operating license which was granted to a company would, arguably, completely frustrate the future business of the invested company. This would result in a substantial or permanent deprivation of market access rights and the economic value of the investment. In a case where a specific market access commitment has been made by a host state, it seems difficult to argue that an investor could reasonably have expected that the permitted business entry would have been cancelled subsequently through the revocation of an already granted license. Therefore, even if a state's withdrawal of the operating license is justified by the protection of the right to health of the people and that such a withdrawal can be considered reasonable in relation to this goal, the deprivation of market access rights and the legitimate expectations of an investor still seem

---

[35]Arrangement Between the Association of East Asian Relations and the Interchange Association for the Mutual Cooperation on the Liberalization, Promotion and Protection of Investment, Taiwan–Japan, art. 12.3, 22 Sept 2011, http://www.moea.gov.tw/CWS/tji/content/wHandMenuFile.ashx?menu_id=6692 [hereinafter Taiwan–Japan BIT].

questionable. One might argue that the significant negative economic impact imposed on the investor will not be proportional to the human rights protection sought to be realized. In this view, the withdrawal of an operating license seems likely to be treated as an indirect expropriation. Additionally, with respect to the FET obligation, Article 5.1 of the Taiwan–Japan BIT provides that "[i]nvestments of investors of either Side shall within the Area of the other Side be accorded treatment in accordance with international law, including fair and equitable treatment …."[36] Granting an operating license represents a host state's binding written commitment to an investor contemplating investment. An investor is entitled to rely on such a specific express guarantee from the government to run its business in the host state. In terms of the specific commitment, a host state would refrain from denying its prior assurance leading to a nullification of the legitimate expectation of an investor. A violation is also likely to be inconsistent with the FET requirement.

A host state might try invoking some exceptional clauses provided in the BITs to justify the denial of its market access commitment. In the case of indirect expropriation, for instance, one might argue that the withdrawal of an operating license which was granted to a tobacco investor will be exempt from an indirect expropriation since it is acting in consideration of public health. Annex B, 13(1)C of the Canada Model BIT provides an example,[37] which reads

> [e]xcept in rare circumstances, such as when a measure or series of measures are so severe in the light of their purpose that they cannot be reasonably viewed as having been adopted and applied in good faith, non-discriminatory measures of a Party that are designed and applied to protect legitimate public welfare objectives, such as health, safety and the environment, do not constitute indirect expropriation.

In light of this provision, non-discriminatory regulations with essential public purposes will likely be exempted from the determination of indirect expropriation. Hence, it is possible that a non-discriminatory bona fide regulation that is aimed at protecting the health of the people would generally not constitute an indirect expropriation. To the extent that the health of the general public is protected, enjoyment of the right to health of individuals under the ICESCR can be realized. However, the bona fide exception might be dynamically applied and the concept is not absolute. The tribunal in *El Paso v. Argentina* held that if general regulations are "unreasonable," i.e., arbitrary, discriminatory, disproportionate or otherwise unfair, they can be considered to be indirect expropriations if they result in a neutralization of the foreign investor's property rights.[38] Applying this principle to Taiwan's case, it seems doubtful that the specific withdrawal of an operating license or a general denial of market access to tobacco industry investments would be treated as a non-compensable lawful act. The main reason is that there is already an

---

[36] *Id.*, art. 5.1.

[37] Canada Model BIT, annex B.13(1)(c) (2004), http://investmentpolicyhub.unctad.org/Download/TreatyFile/2820.

[38] El Paso Energy International Co. v. The Argentina Republic, ICSID Case No. ARB/03/15, Award, para. 241 (31 Oct 2011).

established state-owned tobacco company (i.e., Taiwan Tobacco and Liquor Corporation) running the tobacco business domestically. In practice, tobacco companies from other countries have also been permitted to invest in Taiwan.[39] Therefore, in such cases, a discriminatory measure resulting in a nullification of the market access right of an investor might arguably amount to indirect expropriation.

Additionally, Article 18.1(a) of the Taiwan–Japan BIT states that none of the provisions in the BIT shall prevent states from taking measures to protect public health. It reads:

> [i]t is understood that the following measures may be adopted or enforced in the Area of either Side, to the extent that such measures are not applied in a manner which would constitute a means of arbitrary or unjustifiable discrimination against the investor of the other Side, or a disguised restriction on investments of the investor of the other Side; (a) measures necessary to protect human, animal or plant life or health….[40]

A violation of the BIT can be justified if it constitutes a measure "necessary" to protect human, animal or plant life or health. If such a general health exception can provide valid grounds to support a breach of national treatment or FET with respect to a denial of market access to tobacco industry investment generally, or indeed, a specific license withdrawal also invites discussion, in the view of this author, it seems inconsistent that a host government is able to offer specific market access commitments to foreign investments in the first place, but is not able to defend the cancellation of such market access as "necessary" owing to the life-threatening nature of such investment businesses that threaten to undermine public health. If the government considers the nature of an investment operation vital, especially in regard to the right to health, it should not have made a market access commitment to such an investment through a treaty negotiation. In fact, whether or not to grant market access and liberalize investment should be left to the discretion of the treaty parties. If the general health exception can be used as a justification in this case, it might increase the legal uncertainty associated with market access commitments. Moreover, as previously mentioned, Taiwan has its own tobacco company and other permitted foreign tobacco companies running tobacco businesses within its territory. These facts might increase the difficulty of effecting a denial of market access to Japanese companies while taking account of good faith.

For the purposes of this chapter, the issue of whether or not a host state can rely on the ICESCR to establish the legitimacy of a denial of a market access commitment

---

[39]In 2007, the Britain-based Imperial Tobacco Group, the world's fourth-largest tobacco company, began construction of a tobacco manufacturing and logistics center in Miaoli county, in the central part of Taiwan. The plant was built on 1.9 ha of land at the Kuan-Yuan Science Park in Zhunan and construction was completed in 2008, starting mass production the same year. Reportedly, the total cost of this tobacco investment amounted to US$85 million, which was expected to create around 300 job opportunities. According to a more recent report, the Imperial Tobacco investment project did not create as many jobs as expected. Instead, Imperial Tobacco engaged in unlawful promotional activities, such as delivering free samples and lotteries at night markets and shrimp finishing pools in Taiwan.

[40]Taiwan–Japan BIT (2011), *supra* note 35, art. 18.1(a).

to tobacco industry investments merits discussion. Generally, for the purpose of interpreting BITs, an investment arbitral tribunal can refer to Article 31.3. (c) of the Vienna Convention on the Law of Treaties (VCLT)[41] as an interpretative aid when giving a specific meaning to the provision of BITs. A non-BIT treaty, as an external rule of law, could be considered through a legal avenue such as a treaty interpretation if an investment arbitral tribunal deems it appropriate. Therefore, a host state's human rights obligations from the ICESCR can become relevant for the purpose of interpreting BIT provisions. To this extent, protecting the right to health of people in a host state might be taken into account when interpreting the relevant obligations, such as national treatment or FET. Despite this, it should be noted that as an external treaty, the ICESCR cannot replace or redress some textual limitations within BITs. Even if the ICESCR rights of individuals can be given more weight in specific investment disputes, it seems less likely that respecting the obligations under the ICESCR should completely prevail over the obligations under a BIT in the case of inconsistency, unless otherwise provided for by the BIT.

In summary, a host state's reversal of market access commitments to tobacco industry investments might involve a breach of BITs. Recourse to exceptional clauses or treaty interpretations might not ensure a desirable solution to redress the conflict between the BIT and the ICESCR obligations with respect to tobacco industry investments. In this regard, cancelling a problematic market access commitment through a treaty amendment might offer another possible option. It is stated in Article 26.5 of the Taiwan–Japan BIT that "[e]ither Side may at any time request consultations with the other Side for the purpose of amending this Arrangement."[42] Under this provision, states are free to request consultations for amending the existing BIT at any time. This formulation does not explicitly specify the effective conditions of an amendment, such as through mutual consent of the treaty parties or in the form of a written agreement.[43] Nor does it place limits on an amendment. For the Taiwan government, implementing its duty to protect the right to health of its

[41]VCLT Article 31(3)(c) provides that "[t]here shall be taken into account, together with the context: […] any relevant rules of international law applicable in the relations between the parties." Vienna Convention on the Law of Treaties, art. 31(3)(c), *opened for signature* 23 May 1969, 1155 U.N.T.S. 331.

[42]Taiwan–Japan BIT (2011), *supra* note 35, art. 26.5.

[43]Article 11 of the Czech and Malaysian BIT states: "This Agreement may be amended by mutual consent of both Contracting Parties at any time after it is in force. Any alternation or modification of this Agreement shall be done without prejudice to the rights and obligations arising from this Agreement prior to the date of such alternation or modification until such rights and obligations are fully implemented." Agreement Between the Czech Republic and Malaysia for the Promotion and Protection of Investments, Czech–Malay, art. 11, 9 Sept 1996, http://investmentpolicyhub.unctad.org/Download/TreatyFile/957. The Ghana and Malaysia BIT states: "Any alteration or modification of this agreement shall be done without prejudice to the rights and obligations arising from this Agreement prior to the date of such alteration or modification until such rights and obligations are fully implemented." Agreement Between the Government of the Republic of Ghana and the Government of Malaysia for the Promotion and Protection of Investments, Ghana–Malay, art. 11, 8 Nov 1996, http://investmentpolicyhub.unctad.org/Download/TreatyFile/1456.

population as required by the ICESCR seems to be valid grounds to negotiate the removal of its false unilateral market access commitment to Japanese tobacco companies. As the Japanese government is also a state party to the ICESCR, and it did not offer equivalent market access to tobacco industry investments from Taiwan, there seems to be no particular barriers which will prevent the achievement of an agreement.

Normally, an amendment to an existing treaty is presumed to operate prospectively so that after an amendment enters into force, Taiwan will have full discretion to deny harmful tobacco investments from Japan. But whether such a revision will impact the existing tobacco investments (e.g., JTI) remains a point worthy of contemplation. In this regard, the tribunal in *Sempra Energy Int'l v. Argentine Republic* held that "[s]tates are of course free to amend the Treaty by consenting to another text, but this would not affect rights acquired under the Treaty by investors or other beneficiaries. In fact, Article XIV of the Treaty provides that in case of termination, the investment will continue to be protected under its provisions 'for a further period of ten years.' So too, with reference to rights protected under the Energy Charter Treaty, the tribunal in Palma has held that any denial of advantages to which an investor might have rights 'should not have retrospective effect,' as such a situation would result in making legitimate expectations false at a much later date."[44] A withdrawal of market access commitments in the case of a treaty amendment would nullify the advantages afforded to investors and negate their legitimate expectations. Such an amendment would not apply on a retrospective basis. Market access rights of existing investors would therefore not be affected. The entitlement to implement their acquired rights under the BIT would remain unchanged. As such, a treaty amendment cannot genuinely redress the gaping hole between the BIT and the ICESCR in relation to tobacco industry investments. Consequently, for existing tobacco investors, a host state's granting of market access might persist as an "irrevocable" commitment as long as it has been included in BITs.[45]

6 Conclusion

Corporate businesses can enhance human rights protection. The formulation of investment treaties can also be supportive in implementing the ICESCR. However, the life-threatening nature of tobacco businesses has a significant impact upon enjoyment of the right to health of people. From the perspective of policy

---

[44]See Sempra Energy Int'l v. Argentine Republic, ICSID Case No. ARB/02/16, Award, para. 386 (28 Sept 2007), https://www.italaw.com/sites/default/files/case-documents/ita0770.pdf.

[45]Notably, the acquired rights of investors in the case of treaty termination can only exist for another 10 or 15 years. But in the case of a treaty amendment, the period of protection of acquired rights seems unlimited until it has been fully implemented.

coherence, granting market access to tobacco industry investments through BITs presents a particular challenge for ICESCR compliance.

The Taiwan government paid insufficient attention to its ICESCR obligations when it adopted an open permission policy for foreign tobacco industry investments in BITs. As a result, BIT-based investment commitments have turned out to frustrate the fulfillment of the human rights of its population. As argued in this chapter, little can be achieved by the Taiwan government to address the human rights concerns arising from its problematic market access commitment in relation to tobacco investments under the BIT. The withdrawal of market access commitments through a treaty amendment can provide the government with more regulatory power to prevent and control future tobacco industry investments; however, such an amendment would not affect the existing investors' acquired rights under the current BIT. As a result, existing tobacco investors' rights remain intact and continue to be protected.

The Taiwan government has a duty to create conditions in which people can enjoy good health. An individual's right to health in the ICESCR can never be "fully" respected nor "adequately" protected in the context of tobacco business activities. Nor can the government live up to its ICESCR duties while it encourages tobacco investments through BITs. To bridge the gaping hole between these two regimes, the ICESCR norms might accelerate the reform of Taiwan's tobacco investment policy and its BIT formulation. However, the success of these reforms ultimately depends on the Taiwan government's willingness to effectively implement the ICESCR for its people.

References

Complaint filed over JTI's planned plant in Taiwan. Tobacco Reporter. https://www.tobaccoreporter.com/…/complaint-filed-over-jtis-planned-p. Accessed 24 Sept 2017

De Schutter O (2011) (Special Rapporteur on the Right to Food), Rep. on the right to food: Addendum on guiding principles on human rights impact assessments of trade and investment agreements, UN Doc. A/HRC/19/59/Add.5 (19 Dec 2011)

Desierto DA (2015) Public policy in international economic law: the ICESCR in trade, finance, and investment. Oxford University Press, Oxford

Gerber A (2016) Protests call for tobacco operating license reversal. Taipei Times. http://www.taipeitimes.com/News/taiwan/archives/2016/08/05/2003652492. Accessed 24 Sept 2017

Human Rights Council Res. 17/4, UN Doc, A/HRC/RES/17/4 (6 June 2011)

Kube V, Petersmann EU (2016) Human rights law in international investment arbitration. Asian J WTO & Int Health Law Policy 11(1):65–113

Liao P et al (2015) Wei Shi Wei Gong Yue Yan Shang She Chang Kong Sheng Bian (The Tobacco Plant Project is Likely to Change Because of Its Breach in the WHO FCTC). China Times. http://www.chinatimes.com/newspapers/20150717000404-260102. Accessed 24 Sept 2017

Lin T (2013) Preventing tobacco companies' interference with tobacco control through investor-state dispute settlement under the TPP. Asian J WTO & Int Health Law Policy 8(2):565–582

Lo C (2010) FCTC guidelines on tobacco industry foreign investment would strengthen controls on tobacco supply and close loopholes in the tobacco treaty. Tob Control 19:306–310

Lo C (2015) Normative and operational linkages between human rights law and BITs—building a firmer status of human rights in investor-state arbitration. Contemp Asia Arbitr J 8(1):1–28

Mcgrady B (2012) Confronting the tobacco epidemic in a new era of trade and investment liberalization, commissioned by the World Health Organization. Tobacco Free Initiative

Plans for JTI plant in Taiwan meeting opposition. Tobacco Reporter. https://www.tobaccoreporter.com/2015/07/plans-for-jti-plant-in-taiwan-meeting-opposition/. Accessed 24 Sept 2017

Tobacco. WHO. http://www.who.int/mediacentre/factsheets/fs339/en/. Accessed 24 Sept 2017

UN Econ. & Soc. Council, Comm. on Econ., Soc. & Cultural Rights (2000) Substantive Issues Arising in the Implementation of the International Covenant on Economic, Social and Cultural Rights, UN Doc. E/C.12/2000/4 (11 Aug 2000)

UN Econ. & Soc. Council, Comm. on Econ., Soc. & Cultural Rights (2011) Statement on the Obligations of States Parties Regarding the Corporate Sector and Economic, Social and Cultural Rights, UN Doc. E/C.12/2011/1 (12 July 2011)

UN Econ. & Soc. Council, Comm. on Econ., Soc. & Cultural Rights (2016) General Comment on State Obligations under the International Covenant on Economic, Social and Cultural Rights in the Context of Business Activities: Draft Prepared by Olivier De Schutter and Zdzislaw Kedzia, Rapporteurs, UN Doc. E/c.12/60/R.1 (17 Oct 2016)

U.S. Department of Health and Human Services (2010) How tobacco smoke causes disease: the biology and behavioral basis for smoking-attributable disease: a report of the surgeon general. U.S. Government Printing Office, Washington, DC. https://www.ncbi.nlm.nih.gov/books/NBK53017/pdf/Bookshelf_NBK53017.pdf

Tsai-Yu Lin is Professor at National Taiwan University's (NTU) College of Law and Director of its Asian Center for WTO & International Health Law and Policy (ACWH). Professor Lin has actively published books and articles in the areas of WTO laws, international investment law and international health law. She is also the executive secretary of the Asian WTO Research Network (AWRN); commissioner of Taiwan's International Trade Commission; a senior member of the Editorial Committees of *Asian Journal of WTO & International Health Law and Policy* and *Contemporary Asia Arbitration Journal*; and a member of the Indicative List of Governmental and Nongovernmental Panelists for resolving WTO disputes. Professor Lin currently advises Taiwan's government on trade and related health law and policy issues.

Chapter 31
Human Rights and Intellectual Property Protection: Their Interplay in Taiwan

Su-Hua Lee

Abstract The interplay between human rights and intellectual property has been at the center of important debates in recent decades. This chapter includes three major sections to elaborate on Taiwan's efforts to implement human rights in its intellectual property regime. The first section introduces the interplay between human rights and intellectual property. Section 2 explores implementation of the right to information in copyright law. Section 3 addresses the interaction between the right to health and intellectual property protection. The chapter concludes by indicating that an over-protected IP system may be an obstacle in realizing human rights. If copyright is over-protected, it may guard the economic rights of creative intellectual activity, but its enforcement might impede access to published works for persons with print disabilities and lead to negative impacts on the right to information. In the public health field, without patents, existing medications and innovative pharmaceutical products which overcome diseases would not have been developed. Therefore, inadequate expansion and enforcement of IP protection might become a barrier to the accessibility and affordability of medications and adversely affect implementation of the right to health. For this reason, the international community pursues a proper balance between human rights and IP protection. As a member of the international community, Taiwan closely follows new developments at the international level and introduces amendments to its IP laws accordingly. Regardless of Taiwan's unique international status, it still manages to establish relevant mechanisms, consistent with international norms, in its domestic legal framework.

Keywords Compulsory license · Copyright · Patent · Right to health
Right to information

S.-H. Lee (✉)
College of Law, National Taiwan University, Taipei City, Taiwan
e-mail: leesh@ntu.edu.tw

J. A. Cohen et al. (eds.), *Taiwan and International Human Rights*, Economics, Law, and Institutions in Asia Pacific, https://doi.org/10.1007/978-981-13-0350-0_31

1 Introduction

Since the 1990s, intellectual property (hereinafter IP) protection has become increasingly important to the economic development and international competitiveness of Taiwan. In order to follow the rapid pace of technological change and meet societal needs, there have been frequent amendments to statutory IP laws.[1] Furthermore, the "Intellectual Property Rights Action Plan"[2] was launched in 2002 to facilitate a more comprehensive IP legal system and strengthen the enforcement of IP rights and border control measures. In July 2008, the IP Court[3] was established to expedite and improve the quality of court judgments on IP-related cases. Apart from the improvement in IP protection regulations, policy makers in Taiwan have also included human rights norms in the implementation of IP laws. Both the legal framework and legal practice have been updated to match international developments.

This chapter elaborates on Taiwan's efforts to implement human rights in its IP regime. Section 2 of the chapter introduces the interplay between human rights and IP protection. Sections 3 and 4 focus on the right to information and the right to health, while exploring international developments and how they have been realized in the IP regime in Taiwan. Finally, Section 5 concludes this chapter.

2 Interplay Between Human Rights and IP

The interplay between human rights and IP has been at the center of important debates in recent decades. In principle, human rights norms can interact with IP in two ways. First, the right to IP protection is a human right, as recognized in Article 27(2) of the Universal Declaration of Human Rights (hereinafter UDHR)[4] and Article 15(1)(c) of the International Covenant on Economic, Social and Cultural

---

[1]Taiwan's Copyright Act was enacted and entered into effect in 1928. Over the past nine decades, the Copyright Act has been amended 19 times, with an average life cycle of 4.7 years for each amendment. The Trademark Act and the Patent Act were enacted and entered into effect in 1930 and 1944 respectively. To date, the Trademark Act has been amended 15 times and the Patent Act has been amended 14 times. A major revision of IP law was the amendment in 2003, when Taiwan acceded to the WTO and aligned its IP legal system with the requirements of the TRIPS Agreement (Agreement on Trade-Related Aspects of Intellectual Property Rights).

[2]For details about the Intellectual Property Rights Action Plan (智財戰略綱領), see https://www.ipsp.org.tw/index.aspx (in Chinese). Accessed 28 Dec 2017.

[3]For details about the mission of the IP Court, see http://ipc.judicial.gov.tw/ipr_english/. Accessed 28 Dec 2017.

[4]Art. 27 of the UDHR provides: Everyone has the right freely to participate in the cultural life of the community, to enjoy the arts and to share in scientific advancement and its benefits (para 1). Everyone has the right to the protection of the moral and material interests resulting from any scientific, literary or artistic production of which he is the author (para 2).

Rights (hereinafter ICESCR).[5] That is to say, products of the human mind and creativity should be protected by law, regardless of whether or not they are products of scientific or cultural fields. Corresponding to international norms, Article 15[6] and Article 23[7] of the Constitution of the Republic of China (Taiwan) guarantee the right of property, including IP protection. To protect intangible property resulting from intellectual activity, the legal frameworks of copyright[8] and cultural rights,[9] rights related to unfair competition,[10] and industrial property rights[11] were established in 1928, 1930 and 1944 respectively. Thus, the right holder can either license or make use of his/her own creativity and invention and realize substantial economic gains.

The second way in which these rights interact is that human rights norms can be used to interpret IP protection. The above-mentioned international treaties, namely Article 27(1) of the UDHR and Article 15(1)(b) of the ICESCR, also emphasize the right to participate in cultural life and to enjoy the arts and the benefits of scientific progress. Articles 11,[12] 15 and 23 of Taiwan's Constitution explicitly stipulate that the exclusivity of IP rights has to be constrained to a certain extent. For example, after taking the right to life and the right to health into consideration, the enforcement of a pharmaceutical patent should be limited so that it does not interfere with access to medication. Also, the effect of IP rights shall not extend to

---

[5]Art. 15 of the ICESCR provides: The States Parties to the present Covenant recognize the right of everyone: (a) To take part in cultural life; (b) To enjoy the benefits of scientific progress and its applications; (c) To benefit from the protection of the moral and material interests resulting from any scientific, literary or artistic production of which he is the author (para 1). The steps to be taken by the States Parties to the present Covenant to achieve the full realization of this right shall include those necessary for the conservation, the development and the diffusion of science and culture (para 2). The States Parties to the present Covenant undertake to respect the freedom indispensable for scientific research and creative activity (para 3). The States Parties to the present Covenant recognize the benefits to be derived from the encouragement and development of international contacts and co-operation in the scientific and cultural fields (para 4).

[6]Zhonghua Minguo Xianfa, art. 15 (1947) (Taiwan) provides: The right of existence, the right of work, and the right of property shall be guaranteed to the people.

[7]Zhonghua Minguo Xianfa, art. 23 (1947) (Taiwan) provides: All the freedoms and rights enumerated in the preceding Articles shall not be restricted by law except by such as may be necessary to prevent infringement upon the freedoms of other persons, to avert an imminent crisis, to maintain social order or to advance public welfare.

[8]It is worth noting that the neighboring right is not recognized in Taiwan. All kinds of creative work, including databases, photographic work, audiovisual work, sound recordings, and performance, are protected by copyright.

[9]Apart from copyright, Taiwan introduced the Protection Act for the Traditional Intellectual Creations of Indigenous Peoples in 2007 to provide protection to the traditions and culture of indigenous people.

[10]Rights related to unfair competition cover the protection of trademarks and trade secrets.

[11]Industrial property rights include patent rights on inventions, utility models and designs, circuit layout rights and plant variety rights.

[12]Zhonghua Minguo Xianfa, art. 11 (1947) (Taiwan) provides: People shall have freedom of speech, teaching, writing and publication.

acts that are necessary for the purpose of teaching, sharing knowledge and conducting research and development. In compliance with the human rights norms for the interpretation of IP rights, exclusions to IP protection,[13] limitations on enforcement and exceptions to infringement,[14] and compulsory licensing[15] are included in Taiwan's IP laws.

Since Taiwan acceded to the WTO in 2002, the requirements for protection and enforcement of IP rights have principally complied with the TRIPS Agreement (Agreement on Trade-Related Aspects of Intellectual Property Rights) and other international treaties. The following sections of this chapter focus on the right to information and the right to health, and they explore their implementation in the IP regime.

3 Right to Information and Copyright

The law of copyright, on the one hand, protects the economic right of creative intellectual activity while, on the other hand, provisions for limitations and exceptions of copyright guarantee the freedom to teach, share knowledge and access information. Among these exceptions, the accessibility of published works for persons with a print disability seems to be a minor issue, yet it is indispensable for the realization of humanitarian principles and the right to information.

3.1 Development of Access to Published Works for Persons with a Print Disability at the International Level

The general principle of equality and non-discrimination is a fundamental element of international human rights law, as recognized in Article 2 of the UDHR[16] and

[13]For details, see section 24 of the Patent Act (ineligible subject matter), section 9 of the Copyright Act (ineligible subject matter) and section 30 of the Trademark Act (absolute and relative grounds for refusal of trademark registration).

[14]For details, see sections 59–61 of the Patent Act, sections 44–65 of the Copyright Act and section 36 of the Trademark Act.

[15]For details, see sections 87–91 of the Patent Act and sections 69–71 of the Copyright Act.

[16]Art. 2 of the UDHR provides: Everyone is entitled to all the rights and freedoms set forth in this Declaration, without distinction of any kind, such as race, colour, sex, language, religion, political or other opinion, national or social origin, property, birth or other status. Furthermore, no distinction shall be made on the basis of the political, jurisdictional or international status of the country or territory to which a person belongs, whether it be independent, trust, non-self-governing or under any other limitation of sovereignty.

Article 2(2) of the ICESCR.[17] This human rights principle guarantees that those in equal circumstances are dealt with equally in law and practice. To implement the principle of equality and non-discrimination, states in certain circumstances have to take affirmative actions to diminish or eliminate conditions that cause or help perpetuate discrimination. When persons with disabilities are involved, adapting legal frameworks in some areas might be necessary so that they can effectively exercise their rights. With regard to persons who are blind, visually impaired or otherwise print disabled, accessibility to published works is indispensable. Despite pressure from the publishing industry, a guarantee of the right to information for persons with print disabilities and other related limitations on copyright have been recognized by international norms in recent years.

For example, the most important international IP organization, the World Intellectual Property Organization (hereinafter WIPO) recently initiated the first copyright treaty including a clear perspective on human rights. On the basis of humanitarian principles outlined in the United Nations Convention on the Rights of Persons with Disabilities (UNCRPD), the Marrakesh VIP Treaty (Marrakesh Treaty to Facilitate Access to Published Works for Persons Who Are Blind, Visually Impaired, or Otherwise Print Disabled) was adopted on 28 June 2013 and entered into effect on 30 September 2016.[18] Its main goal is to benefit blind, visually impaired and otherwise print disabled people and to ensure their right to information. The Marrakesh VIP Treaty creates a set of mandatory norms for countries that ratify this treaty to introduce an exception in copyright law to allow the creation, import and export of accessible versions of books and other copyrighted works for persons with a print disability.

3.2 *Realization of the Right to Information for Persons with a Print Disability in Taiwan*

Article 7 of Taiwan's Constitution emphasizes that all citizens shall be equal before the law. Thus, persons with all types of disabilities must enjoy all human rights and fundamental freedoms. In order to guarantee the right to information for persons with a print disability, Taiwan's Copyright Act has adopted a limitation on the enforcement of copyright since the 1980s.

[17]Art. 2(2) of the ICESCR provides: The States Parties to the present Covenant undertake to guarantee that the rights enunciated in the present Covenant will be exercised without discrimination of any kind as to race, colour, sex, language, religion, political or other opinion, national or social origin, property, birth or other status.

[18]WIPO (2013).

3.2.1 Initiative to Implement the Right to Information in Copyright Law

Apart from provisions for protecting the results of creative activities, there are also limitations and exceptions in Taiwan's Copyright Act, for instance, oral and written journalism with the sole intention to communicate facts should not be the subject matter of copyright, as set forth in section 9 of the Copyright Act. Furthermore, sections 44–65 of the Copyright Act adopted limitations on enforcement of copyrights and the Fair Use Doctrine.

Regarding the right to information for persons with a print disability, the Copyright Act of 1985 introduced a provision allowing published works to be reproduced in Braille.[19] Also, under certain conditions, it is permitted to use published works to create sound recordings exclusively for the use of visually impaired people. The amendment to section 53 of the Copyright Act of 2003 was a major step forward in the realization of the right to information for persons with a print disability.[20] This provision not only ensures that the interests of the visually or hearing impaired are protected, but also that those with a learning or a perceptual disability are equally protected. Furthermore, the permitted use of published works is not limited to reproduction in Braille and sound recordings. Taking the development of digital formats and electronic production into consideration, computers, verbal imagery, accompanying sign language and other necessary methods to exploit the published works are also legally allowed by copyright law.

3.2.2 Implementation of the Marrakesh VIP Treaty in 2014

Given its unique international status, Taiwan is not entitled to participate in global IP organizations or agreements, such as the WIPO, the Paris Convention, the Marrakesh VIP Treaty and the Patent Cooperation Treaty (PCT). For this reason, Taiwan is not in principle obliged to conform to the Marrakesh VIP Treaty. However, Taiwan's Intellectual Property Office (hereinafter TIPO) began a review of copyright law following the treaty's adoption on 27 June 2013. As of 12 October

[19]Section 30 of the Copyright Act of 1985 provides: Works that have been publicly released may be reproduced in Braille (para 1). Legally accredited organizations aiming at promoting the welfare of visually impaired people may, by means of sound recordings, exploit works that have been publicly released exclusively for the purpose of use by visually impaired people (para 2).

[20]Section 53 of the Copyright Act of 2003 provides: Works that have been publicly released may be reproduced in Braille or with accompanying sign language translation or text for the visually impaired, learning disabled, the hearing impaired or other persons with perceptual disabilities (para 1). Legally accredited non-profit organizations aimed at promoting the welfare of the visually impaired, learning disabled, the hearing impaired or other persons with perceptual disabilitise may, by means of sound recordings, computers, verbal imagery, accompanying sign language or otherwise, exploit works that have been publicly released, exclusively for the purpose of use of visually impaired, learning disabled, hearing impaired or other persons with perceptual disabilities (para 2).

2017, 31 contracting parties had ratified the Marrakesh VIP Treaty. The Republic of India was the first country that ratified this treaty on 24 June 2014, and the European Parliament reached an agreement to implement the treaty on 6 July 2017. Presently, it is still controversial in some countries whether to include the Marrakesh VIP Treaty in domestic copyright law and to what extent the limitations and exceptions of copyright should be included. By comparison, the amendment to Taiwan's Copyright Act of 2014, which implemented the Marrakesh VIP Treaty and provided support for persons with a print disability, was promulgated on 22 January 2014, while the treaty was not ratified by any contracting party.

Section 53 of the Copyright Act of 2014 further extends the scope of the limitations.[21] To facilitate accessibility, non-profit organizations, local and central government agencies, legally established schools, and disabled persons and their guardians are allowed to exploit published works exclusively for the purpose of use by the visually impaired, learning disabled, hearing impaired and other persons with a perceptual disability. Regarding the means by which the copyrighted works may be exploited, this provision further allows distribution or public transmission of reproduced copies among disabled persons, local or central government agencies, non-profit organizations and legally established schools.

Furthermore, the amendment to the Copyright Act of 2014 introduced two provisions to realize the right to information for persons with a print disability. Namely, print-disabled persons may invoke the above-mentioned section 53 of the Copyright Act to circumvent the technological protection measures adopted by copyright holders, according to section 82*ter* of the Copyright Act. Also, to enhance the sharing of resources, section 87*bis* prescribes that persons with a print disability may import and circulate copies of works reproduced by means of translation, Braille, sound recordings, digital transformation, verbal imagery, accompanying sign language or otherwise, provided that such copies are used in compliance with the provisions set forth in section 53 of the Copyright Act.

To sum up, even though Taiwan is not a WIPO member, its Copyright Act has still implemented the humanitarian principles that are recognized by the international treaty.

---

[21]Section 53 of Copyright Act 2014 provides: For the purpose of exclusive use by the visually impaired, learning disabled, hearing impaired or other persons with a perceptual disability, works that have been publicly released may be exploited by local or central government agencies, non-profit organizations and all levels of legally established schools, by means of translation, Braille, sound recordings, digital transformation, verbal imagery, accompanying sign language or otherwise (para 1). The preceding paragraph shall be applied *mutatis mutandis* to the disabled persons or their guardians referred to in the preceding paragraph for personal and nonprofit use by the disabled (para 2). The copies reproduced in accordance with the preceding two paragraphs may be distributed or publicly transmitted among the disabled persons, local or central government agencies, non-profit organizations and all levels of legally established schools as prescribed in the preceding two paragraphs (para 3).

4 Right to Health and IP Protection for Medications

The enjoyment of the highest attainable standard of health is fundamental to human rights, and medications play a crucial role in maintaining the health and well-being of people.

4.1 Confrontation Between the Right to Health and IP Protection at the International Level

On 16 December 1966, the General Assembly of the United Nations adopted the ICESCR. Article 12(1) of the ICESCR recognizes "the right of everyone to the enjoyment of the highest attainable standard of physical and mental health." This is the first time that the "right to health" was identified by international norms. To guarantee the right to health and medications, in particular innovative medicines, is indispensable. However, the nature of the pharmaceutical industry is research-based. The research and development of new pharmaceutical products is, in most cases, expensive and full of risks, and can continue for decades before the first dollar invested in the search for a new medication results in the first dollar returned from that investment. Effective IP protection for the development of pharmaceutical products is thus an important incentive to promote innovation. Conversely, the over-protection of IP for medications and improper enforcement of IP rights might prevent further research and development, and delay market entry of cheap generic drugs. Consequently, negative impacts on the accessibility and affordability of pharmaceutical products at reasonable prices might occur.

With the widespread effects of acquired immune deficiency syndrome (hereinafter AIDS) and other deadly pandemics, the international community has been forced to face the greatest tensions between the right to health and IP protection. Issues such as whether IP protection for pharmaceutical products is a facilitating or inhibiting factor for the realization of the right to health have been the subject of considerable debate. In 2001, the Commission on Human Rights of the United Nations adopted a resolution that recognized that access to medication in the context of pandemics such as HIV/AIDS is a fundamental element for the full realization of the right to health.[22] Furthermore, the Doha Declaration (Declaration on the TRIPS Agreement and Public Health)[23] was adopted by the Doha WTO Ministerial on 14 November 2001. The Doha Declaration recognized that IP protection is indispensable for the development and innovation of medications. However, it also reaffirmed that the TRIPS Agreement can and should be

[22]UN Commission on Human Rights, Access to Medication in the Context of Pandemics such as HIV/AIDS, 1, UN Doc. E/CN.4/RES/2001/33 (20 Apr 2001).

[23]World Trade Organization, Ministerial Declaration on the TRIPS Agreement and Public Health, WTO Doc. WT/MIN(01)/DEC/2 (2001).

interpreted and implemented in a manner to support WTO members' right to protect public health and, in particular, to promote access to pharmaceutical products for all.

It might appear that there is an antagonistic relationship between the right to health and IP protection for medications. Yet, fair and effective IP protection for pharmaceutical products will raise people's standard of living, which will benefit public health and development of the right to health. Issues of accessibility and affordability of medications at reasonable prices cannot be solved by denying IP protection or applying the "one-size-fits-all" approach. Every country faces different challenges under different domestic circumstances, including healthcare systems,[24] pricing mechanisms for medications,[25] domestic market scale, and development of the domestic pharmaceutical industry. Given these differences, each country will have different desires for IP protection of medications and will take different approaches to realizing the fundamental right to health.

4.2 Balance Between the Right to Health and IP Protection in Taiwan

4.2.1 The Domestic Public Health System and the Pharmaceutical Market

In comparison with other Asian countries or developing countries, the affordability of medication does not seem to be a major issue in Taiwan, since the National Health Insurance (hereinafter NHI) program was launched in March 1995 and every citizen is required to join the program and pay monthly NHI premiums. When seeking medical care, citizens merely pay the registration fee, from 150 to 450 NT Dollars (ca. 5 to 15 US Dollars). Patients need only cover the co-payment costs for some innovative pharmaceutical products not listed on the NHI program. For this reason, all citizens in Taiwan can access and afford basic healthcare at reasonable or even relatively low prices.

With regard to the pharmaceutical industry, since the 1980s Taiwan has designated biotechnology and pharmaceuticals as key development areas, and has sought to establish a domestic industry. Following the "Action Plan for Strengthening the Biotechnology Industry" in 1995, government agencies introduced the "Biotech and New Pharmaceutical Development Statute" in 2007 and implemented the

[24]Taking countries in Asia as examples, everyone has public health insurance in Japan, Singapore and Taiwan. However, national healthcare is still developing in India, so a certain proportion of the population has to purchase medications with their own money.

[25]For instance, in Japan, Singapore and Taiwan, the price of medication is mainly determined or influenced by the public sector, regardless of whether or not there is a mechanism for patient co-payment for pharmaceutical products.

"Taiwan Diamond Action Plan for Biotech Takeoff" in 2009 in order to promote R&D results and increase assistance through venture funds.

The domestic pharmaceutical industry has developed steadily but slowly, so the majority of domestic pharmaceutical companies are solely capable of manufacturing generic drugs.[26] The country's demand for innovative medications is mainly satisfied by imports, with Germany and the USA as the most important countries for providing new pharmaceutical products to Taiwan.[27] Nevertheless, it is worth mentioning that domestic companies have been undertaking R&D in recent years and trying to establish patent portfolios, and some of them are now capable of launching new dosage forms of existing drugs.[28]

The scale of the domestic pharmaceutical market is relatively small,[29] and Taiwan might not be targeted by foreign manufacturers as a priority market for launching new medications. To ensure the accessibility of innovative pharmaceutical products, IP protection plays an indispensable role in providing incentives to encourage foreign manufacturers to introduce new medications to Taiwan's market. Yet, the over-protection of IP might delay market entry of generic drugs and lead to a heavy financial burden for the national healthcare system. For this reason, it is apparent that Taiwan's IP laws try to maintain a balance between brand-name and generic companies.

4.2.2 IP Protection for Medications

Patent Rights

Since 1986, in compliance with the policy goal of promoting the biotechnology and pharmaceutical industries, chemical and pharmaceutical products have been eligible subjects of patent rights. Remarkably, neither the Paris Convention nor the TRIPS Agreement impose an obligation on contracting members to adopt patent term extensions or similar mechanisms[30] to strengthen the protection of patents on pharmaceuticals that require market approval prior to being sold, or on innovative methods of using or manufacturing pharmaceuticals. Countries have latitude to determine whether, and to what extent, patent law should allow the extension of

---

[26]Biotechnology and Pharmaceutical Industries Promotion Office of the Ministry of Economic Affairs (2017), p. 52.

[27]*Id.*, at p. 54. Notably, there is a growing trend in imported medications. For instance, in 2015 and 2016 the growth rates were 11.15% and 6.84% respectively. *Id.*, at p. 53.

[28]*Id.*, at p. 57.

[29]Global spending on medications reached 1.1 trillion in 2016. Among that, spending on medications in the USA, Japan, South Korea and China were 461.7, 90.1, 13.0 and 116.7 billion US Dollars respectively. By comparison, spending on medications in Taiwan was 5.33 billion US Dollars. *Id.*, at p. 50; IMS, Outlook for Global Medicines through 2021 (2016), at p. 9.

[30]For example, some European countries adopt the mechanism of the SPC (Supplementary Patent or Supplementary Protection Certificate) to strengthen protection of pharmaceutical patents.

patent terms to pharmaceutical inventions.[31] To encourage innovation and the introduction of new drugs in the Taiwan market, the Patent Act of 1994 established patent term extensions.[32]

Pharmaceutical inventions can be patented in Taiwan for three decades and until now the majority of patent assignees have been foreign companies. However, according to TIPO's annual reports from 2003 to 2016, there is a growing trend in the number of domestic patent assignees, which reveals that the domestic pharmaceutical industry is aware of the importance of IP protection and is attempting to accumulate patents (Figs. 1 and 2).

It is worth mentioning that based on the growing trend of pharmaceutical patents filed by domestic inventors, Taiwan's Food and Drug Administration (TFDA) and the TIPO believe an early resolution mechanism for avoiding disputes about pharmaceutical patents[33] is in compliance with knowledge-based economic development and the goal of encouraging innovations and increasing the competitiveness of the domestic industry. For this reason, the Legislative Yuan[34] is now reviewing an amendment to the Pharmaceutical Affairs Act, which introduces a drug approval-patent linkage (patent linkage)[35] with the aim of establishing a statutory competitive environment for the pharmaceutical industry.

According to the amendment to the Pharmaceutical Affairs Act, the patent linkage in Taiwan includes four main mechanisms, namely (i) disclosure of patent information by branded drug makers, (ii) patent certificates and notices, (iii) stays of ANDA approval for a period of 12 months, and (iv) 12 months of market exclusivity for the first qualified ANDA filer. The mechanisms of "patent certificates and notices" and the "stay of ANDA approval" provide branded drug makers an opportunity to resolve patent disputes before generic drugs are launched. At the same time, generic drug makers benefit from the identification of relevant patents

[31]Taking Asian countries as examples, patent term extensions have been adopted in Japan, Singapore and Taiwan, but not in China, India and Malaysia.

[32]According to section 53 of the Patent Act of 2017, invention patents related to pharmaceuticals and the manufacturing process thereof are eligible for patent term extensions, to compensate patent holders for time lost while awaiting regulatory market approvals.

[33]In recent years, the importance of early resolution mechanisms for avoiding disputes about pharmaceutical patents has emerged during the negotiations of the Free Trade Agreements (FTAs). Countries entering into FTAs with the USA, including Australia, Canada, Singapore and South Korea, have created a drug approval-patent linkage or a similar system to strengthen intellectual property protection for pharmaceuticals.

[34]The Legislative Yuan is equivalent to a Parliament in other democracies.

[35]It is well known that the USA is the first country that established a complex patent linkage system, which was introduced by the Drug Price Competition and Patent Term Restoration Act of 1984 (Pub. L. No. 98-417), commonly called the "Hatch-Waxman Act." It is noteworthy that the Hatch-Waxman Act on the one hand enhanced intellectual property protection and enabled branded drug makers, which conducted innovations and filed a New Drug Application [hereinafter NDA] to benefit from the mechanisms of patent term extensions and data exclusivity. On the other hand, it accelerated the introduction of generic drugs into the market and allowed generic drug makers to take advantage of a simple approval process, called the Abbreviated New Drug Application [hereinafter ANDA] and statutory research exemptions (the "Bolar provisions").

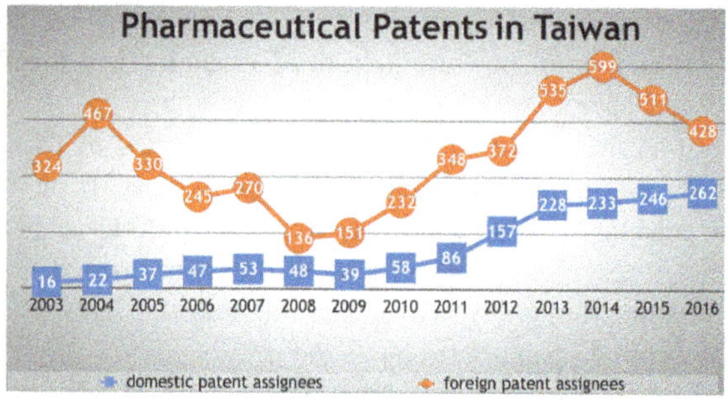

Fig. 1 Pharmaceutical patents in Taiwan. *Source* TIPO annual report

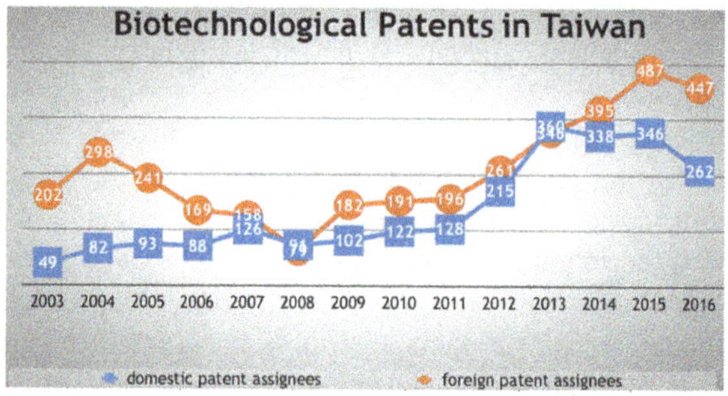

Fig. 2 Biotechnological patents in Taiwan. *Source* TIPO annual report

by the "disclosure of patent information." In addition, the first ANDA filer, which successfully challenges the validity of a pharmaceutical patent, enjoys 12 months of market exclusivity.[36]

Data Exclusivity of New Drugs

Apart from patent protection, Article 39 of the TRIPS Agreement preserves the right of states to adopt proper measures to protect undisclosed information resulting from considerable efforts contributed to governmental agencies, and the conditions for approving the marketing of pharmaceuticals. In 2005, to encourage the innovation and introduction of new drugs into the Taiwan market, the Pharmaceutical Affairs Act adopted data exclusivity protection for new drugs that qualified as a new chemical entity (NCE).[37]A right holder of data exclusivity is entitled to prohibit third parties (normally generic manufacturers) from relying on the undisclosed test

[36]For details about patent linkages in Taiwan, see Lee and Wu (2016), pp. 163–177; Lee (2016), pp. 5–28.

[37]According to section 40*ter*(2) and (3) of the Pharmaceutical Affairs Act of 2017, NCE drugs enjoy five years of data exclusivity. Yet, after three years of issuance of the new drug's approval, other pharmaceutical companies are entitled to file for market approval and to rely on the undisclosed test data concerning the safety and efficacy of the reference drug.

data, including information regarding the safety and efficacy of the new drug (the reference drug), when a third party applies for market approval for the same or a similar drug without the right holder's consent.

Furthermore, new indication drugs may have a five-year data exclusivity if local clinical trials are conducted by the drug manufacturers, according to section 54 of the Regulations for Registration of Medicinal Products. It is noteworthy that the TFDA is currently considering providing a three-year data exclusivity for other kinds of qualified new drugs, such as new combination drugs, drugs with a new route of administration, and new dosage forms.

4.2.3 Limitations on Patent Rights of Medications

To provide foreign companies incentives to launch new pharmaceutical products in the Taiwan market and to encourage the domestic industry to undertake R&D, IP protection is essential. However, proper limitations on patent rights are vital to ensure the accessibility and affordability of medications. Following the discretion of Article 30 of the TRIPS Agreement reserving the right of states to introduce reasonably foreseeable exceptions of patent rights, Taiwan's Pharmaceutical Affairs Act and Patent Act adopted experimental use exemptions (so-called "Bolar provisions") in 2005 and 2013 respectively, which allow researchers to use the patented invention without the patentee's consent in the course of research and tests preparing for market regulatory approval of pharmaceuticals.[38] Remarkably, the scope of the "Bolar provisions" set forth in section 60 of the Patent Act of 2017[39] includes circumstances in which the patented invention is used as a research tool.

Furthermore, limitations on patent rights extend to dispensing medicine as recognized in section 61 of the Patent Act of 2017. Namely, the effect of the patent rights for a pharmaceutical invention manufactured by mixing two or more medicines or for the invention of a process thereof shall not extend to the preparation of medicines in accordance with a prescription from a physician, or for medicines so prepared.[40] Dispensation of medicines acts as an important mechanism for ensuring the accessibility and affordability of drugs.

[38]Experimental use exemptions have been stipulated in many Asian countries, including China, India, Japan, Malaysia, Singapore and Taiwan.

[39]Section 60 of the Patent Act of 2017 provides: The effects of the patent right shall not extend to research and trials, including their practical requirements necessary for obtaining registration and market approval of drugs under the Pharmaceutical Affairs Act or obtaining market approval of pharmaceuticals from a foreign country.

[40]It is noteworthy that the dispensation of medicine is not recognized in some countries. For instance, the effects of patent rights extend to the preparation of medicine or medicines in the USA.

4.3 Compulsory Licensing of Tamiflu Vaccine in 2005

Traditionally, compulsory licenses have been granted very rarely. However, in recent years this mechanism has played an important role in guaranteeing the accessibility and affordability of medications and implementation of the right to health. For instance, Ecuador issued compulsory licenses on medications for the treatment and prevention of HIV/AIDS in 2009 and 2012 respectively.[41] Also, governments in Indonesia and India lifted patent protections on drugs used to treat HIV, Hepatitis B and cancer by granting compulsory licenses in 2012.[42] It is also noteworthy that in July 2017 the German Federal Supreme Court (Bundesgerictshof, BGH) agreed with the decision adjudicated by the German Patent Court (Bundespatentgericht, BPatG) to grant a compulsory license for a HIV/AIDS drug.[43] Apart from developments at the international level, in 2005 Taiwan faced an influenza pandemic public health crisis, and a compulsory license was granted to access the Tamiflu vaccine.

4.3.1 Background

In autumn 2005, the H5N1 influenza pandemic was on the verge of breaking out, according to WTO warnings; 133 incidences of infection and 68 cases of death were reported in China and the Southeast Asia region. Even though there was no incident of an avian influenza infection reported in Taiwan, the threat of an influenza pandemic was imminent owing to Taiwan's geographical location. Taiwan is in the direct path of migratory birds and there are frequent travels between Taiwan, China and the Southeast Asian region. Under these circumstances, the Department of Health (hereinafter DOH), now renamed the Ministry of Health and Welfare (MOHW), had to be fully prepared for this potential emergency. At that time, the Tamiflu vaccine had been expected to be effective for the treatment of the H5N1 influenza. Yet the Tamiflu vaccine, patented by Gilead Science Inc., was protected by patent rights in Taiwan,[44] with Roche Holding AG holding the exclusive license.

Following the WTO's suggestion that each country's stockpile of Tamiflu should be 10% of the total population, Taiwan placed orders for the vaccine with Roche, since its stockpile was only 0.7% at that time. Due to the large number of

[41]Ecuador Issues a Compulsory License on Abacavir/Lamivudine (2012).

[42]MSF Responds to Indonesia's Intent to Issue Compulsory Licences on 7 HIV Drugs (2012) and Estavillo (2012).

[43]Bundesgerichtshof [BGH] (Federal Court of Justice) 11 July 2017, X ZB 2/17, https://www.jurion.de/urteile/bgh/2017-07-11/x-zb-2_17/.

[44]In contrast, Tamiflu is not patented in Indonesia, the Philippines and Thailand. The pharmaceutical industry is free to manufacture generic versions of Tamiflu in those countries. Tamiflu Compulsory License not Necessary, Roche Tells Three Asian Nations (2005).

orders from many countries, Roche could not meet Taiwan's demand immediately and only agreed to supply 2.3 million treatments of Tamiflu by the end of June 2006. The DOH, as well as experts in public health and disease control, believed the number of treatments supplied by Roche would still put people in Taiwan at risk, especially if an earlier than expected outbreak of the influenza pandemic were to take place or the delivery timelines could not be met by Roche. Furthermore, since Taiwan is not a WHO member, Taiwan would not receive any of the Tamiflu stockpiled by the WHO if a regional or global pandemic were to take place. In light of the need for disease control and prevention, and taking into consideration that Roche might not supply an adequate amount of Tamiflu in time as well as Taiwan's unique international situation, the DOH believed Taiwan faced a state of urgency and emergency. In order to stockpile anti-virus medication and to prevent the spread of an influenza pandemic, in October 2005 the DOH applied for a compulsory license for the Tamiflu patent.

4.3.2 Compulsory Licensing Granted by the TIPO

Section 76 of the Patent Act of 2010,[45] which is in compliance with Article 31 of the TRIPS Agreement, sets forth that the TIPO may grant a compulsory license to allow government agencies or third parties to use a patented invention without the authorization of the right holder in the case of a national emergency or other circumstances of extreme urgency. After scrutinizing the facts and reasoning behind the DOH's application and holding two public hearings, the TIPO reached the decision to grant a compulsory license under the following conditions:[46]

(i) The compulsory license is valid only until 31 December 2007.
(ii) Pharmaceuticals manufactured under this compulsory license should be supplied exclusively for the purpose of domestic disease control and prevention.
(iii) Only if the Tamiflu supplied by Roche cannot meet the demand required by the DOH may the generic version of Tamiflu manufactured under this compulsory license be used.
(iv) If the DOH, Gilead and Roche reach a voluntary licensing agreement, the TIPO may annul the decision regarding this compulsory license.
(v) The DOH shall negotiate with Gilead and Roche for adequate remuneration, and the TIPO will render a final decision on the remuneration if an agreement cannot be reached.

[45]Section 76 of the Patent Act of 2010 is equivalent to Section 87 of the current patent law, the Patent Act of 2017.
[46]TIPO, Decision Zhi Fa Zi Di 09418601140 Hao (智法字第 09418601140 號), 8 Dec 2005.

Apart from the above-mentioned conditions, the TIPO further ordered that the DOH should take full responsibility for implementation of this compulsory license and ensure the interests of the right holders.

The first time the international community faced a significant risk of an outbreak of the avian influenza was when the global spread of H5N1 in birds occurred in 2005. Given its unique international status and circumstances, Taiwan was the first country to issue a compulsory license for the manufacture of a generic version of Tamiflu to ensure sufficient reserves of the medication and the right to health. The compulsory license was granted under strict conditions to safeguard the interests of the rights holders. The patent system has never been one-sided and has never been intended to provide unlimited protection to patents and patentees per se. Its true purpose consists of striking a balance between public and private interests. With regard to the circumstances of a national emergency or other circumstances of extreme urgency and the protection of the right to health, compulsory licenses are an indispensable tool for striking such a balance. Taiwan endorsed this principle by granting compulsory licensing for Tamiflu in 2005.

4.4 Compulsory Licensing for the Export of Medication

4.4.1 Developments at the International Level

As mentioned, IP protection is needed in order to provide incentives to sustain long-term investments and recoup the high costs of R&D in the pharmaceutical industry. However, this exclusive right can make medications prohibitively expensive for people in developing and less-developed countries. To recognize that IP protection should not prevent countries from taking measures to protect public health, WTO members adopted the Doha Declaration in 2001. Paragraph 5 of the Doha Declaration stresses that each country has the right to grant a compulsory license when facing a national emergency or other circumstances of extreme urgency, including public health crises relating to HIV/AIDS, tuberculosis, malaria and other epidemics. With a compulsory license, countries with manufacturing capacity, such as India and Brazil, can legally manufacture generic drugs to ensure domestic accessibility and affordability of medications.

However, the mechanism of the compulsory license provides less help to countries with insufficient or no manufacturing capability in the pharmaceutical sector. These countries cannot import affordable generic drugs from countries with manufacturing capacity because a compulsory license cannot be granted if the products are primarily supplied to foreign markets. To overcome this difficulty, "Implementation of Paragraph 6 of the Doha Declaration on the TRIPS Agreement and Public Health"[47] was adopted in 2003, which allows countries facing a national emergency or other circumstances of extreme urgency and lacking a production capacity the ability to notify the Council of the TRIPS Agreement of its intention to import essential medications. Meanwhile, countries with manufacturing capability can grant a compulsory license to generic suppliers exclusively for the purpose of manufacturing and exporting the pharmaceutical products.

Furthermore, WTO members unanimously decided to remove an important obstacle to the import of affordable drugs by waiving the limitation in the TRIPS Agreement to predominantly supply the local market. The Protocol amending the TRIPS Agreement[48] was adopted in 2005, which introduces Article 31*bis* and establishes a permanent mechanism to help countries access life-saving medications produced in other countries under a compulsory licensing arrangement. On 23 January 2017, the Amendment of the TRIPS Agreement entered into force. It was not only the first time that WTO accords were amended since the WTO started to operate in 1995, but also a remarkable milestone for striking a balance between the right to health and IP protection at the international level. Article 31*bis* of the TRIPS Agreement provides a secure and sustained legal basis for countries with limited or no production capacity to import affordable medications from countries where pharmaceuticals are protected by patent rights.

4.4.2 Implementation in Taiwan

The Doha Declaration and its implementation ensure greater access to life-saving medication for resource-poor countries. After the Protocol amending the TRIPS Agreement was adopted in March 2006, the TIPO proposed the introduction of new provisions allowing the granting of compulsory licenses and facilitating access to essential medicines in foreign countries. The Legislative Yuan passed the amendment to the Patent Act in 2011, thus assisting countries with limited domestic capacity to obtain the pharmaceutical products needed to treat HIV/AIDS, tuberculosis, malaria and other epidemics. The TIPO may, upon request, grant the requestor a compulsory license to exploit patented inventions exclusively for the purpose of producing and exporting medications to countries without production capability. The prerequisites for granting compulsory licenses, procedures and adequate remuneration, set forth in sections 90 and 91 of the Patent Act of 2017, are entirely in compliance with international norms.

Taiwan, as a member of the international community, is obligated to implement the right to health. Compulsory licensing for exporting medication may only be applied in extremely exceptional circumstances and Taiwan immediately made a commitment to comply with international norms.

[47]World Trade Organization, Implementation of Paragraph 6 of the Doha Declaration on the TRIPS Agreement and Public Health, WTO Doc. WT/L/540 (2003).

[48]World Trade Organization, Amendment of the TRIPS Agreement, WTO Doc. WT/L/641 (2005).

5 Conclusion

IP protection plays a decisive role in implementing the right to benefit from advances in science and technology, which is emphasized by international human rights norms. However, an over-protected IP system may be an obstacle in realizing human rights. If copyright is over-protected, it may guard the economic rights of creative intellectual activity, but its enforcement might impede access to published works for persons with print disabilities and lead to negative impacts on the rights to information. In the public health field, without patents existing medications and innovative pharmaceutical products that overcome diseases would not have been developed. Therefore, inadequate expansion and enforcement of IP protection might become a barrier to the accessibility and affordability of medications and adversely affect implementation of the right to health.

For this reason, the international community pursues a proper balance between human rights and IP protection. As a member of the international community, Taiwan follows new developments at the international level closely and introduces amendments of its IP laws accordingly. Regardless of Taiwan's unique international status, it still manages to establish relevant mechanisms, consistent with international norms, in its domestic legal framework.

References

Biotechnology and Pharmaceutical Industries Promotion Office of the Ministry of Economic Affairs [經濟部生技醫藥產業發展推動小組] (2017) Biotechnology Industry in Taiwan [生技產業白皮書]. Ministry of Economic Affairs, Taipei

Ecuador issues a compulsory license on Abacavir/Lamivudin (2012) Tumblr. http://msf-utw.tumblr.com/post/35774074899/ecuador-issues-a-compulsory-license-on. Accessed 12 Oct 2017

Estavillo M (2012) India grants first compulsory licence, for Bayer cancer drug, intellectual property watch. I-P Watch. http://www.ip-watch.org/2012/03/12/india-grants-first-compulsory-licence-for-bayer-cancer-drug/. Accessed 12 Oct 2017

IMS, Outlook for global medicines through 2021 (2016) http://static.correofarmaceutico.com/docs/2016/12/12/qiihi_outlook_for_global_medicines_through_2021.pdf. Accessed 12 Oct 2017

Lee S-H (2016) Patent protection of pharmaceutical products in Taiwan: reflections on the establishment of patent linkages [我國藥品專利保護之現況與未來——從專利連結制度之研擬談起]. Intellectual Property Rights [智慧財產權月刊] 216:5–28

Lee S-H, Wu C-F (2016) An introduction to the amendment to the Pharmaceutical Affairs Act and the establishment of patent linkage [初探藥事法增訂專利連結專章之立法芻議]. Taiwan Law Rev. [月旦法學] 258:163–177

MSF responds to Indonesia's intent to issue compulsory licences on 7 HIV drugs (2012) Tumblr. http://msf-utw.tumblr.com/post/35769102223/msf-responds-to-indonesias-intent-to-issue. Accessed 12 Oct 2017

Tamiflu compulsory license not necessary, Roche tells three Asian nations (2005) The Pharma Letter. https://www.thepharmaletter.com/article/tamiflu-compulsory-license-not-necessary-roche-tells-three-asian-nations. Accessed 10 Oct 2017

WIPO (2013) Main provisions and benefits of the Marrakesh Treaty. http://www.wipo.int/edocs/pubdocs/en/wipo_pub_marrakesh_flyer.pdf. Accessed 12 Oct 2017

Su-Hua Lee received her Bachelor of Law degree from National Taipei University, her Master of Law (Magister iuris comparativi, M. iur. Comp.) degree from Rheinischen Friedrich-Wilhelms-Universität Bonn, and earned a Doctor of Law (Ph.D.) from National Taiwan University in 2006. As a scholarship holder of the German DAAD Program for Ph.D. students and the Max Planck Institute for Innovation and Competition in Munich, she was a Visiting Researcher at the Max Planck Institute for Innovation and Competition from 2005 to 2007. Lee has been Professor of Law at National Taiwan University since 2016 and previously served on the law faculties at National Tsing Hua University and National Taipei University. Lee's principal teaching and research interests are in the fields of intellectual property, patent protection of biotechnology and pharmaceutical products, civil law (contracts and torts) and competition law. Over the years, she has published articles in various journals in Chinese as well as in English. Lee has conducted research projects funded by public and private sectors. Since 2015 she has been leading a research team to help the government draft a bill on drug approval-patent linkages. Lee is a member of governmental expert groups relating to intellectual property and pharmaceutical affairs. She participates in Asian academic groups focusing on current and emerging issues regarding Asian intellectual property law.

Part VI
Protection of Specific/Vulnerable Groups

Chapter 32
When Women's Human Rights Encounter Tradition in Taiwan

Chang-fa Lo

Abstract Taiwan is generally considered to be a good example of how gender equality can be widely respected and implemented. But from time to time when women's rights to equality encounter some deeply embedded traditions, there are still struggles in the society and in the constitutional process to fully implement the rights to gender equality. The 2015 case of J.Y. Interpretation No. 728 involves a typical gender equality issue, i.e., women continuously prevented from serving as members or successors of "ancestor worship guilds/associations" for traditional reasons. In this case, the protection of women's human rights and the need to protect the long-established traditions and the freedom of contract should be properly balanced. This chapter argues that protection of the tradition of systemically discriminating against women's ancestor-worship status and the rights and freedoms associated with such discrimination are of minimal constitutional value. Women's right to equal protection should be prioritized because of the seriousness and the systemic and structural nature of such discrimination. The Constitutional Court should have declared the law unconstitutional. Although the Constitutional Court failed to declare the challenged law to be unconstitutional, the legislative body still has a chance to correct the discriminatory situation by requiring equal status for female offspring, at least for the successions that are to occur after the new legislation.

Keywords Ancestor worship guilds/associations · Constitutional complaint Constitutional Court · Gender equality · Women's human rights

C. Lo (✉)
Justice, Constitutional Court, Taiwan, Republic of China
e-mail: lochangfa@gmail.com

J. A. Cohen et al. (eds.), *Taiwan and International Human Rights*, Economics, Law, and Institutions in Asia Pacific, https://doi.org/10.1007/978-981-13-0350-0_32

1 Introduction

Gender equality is widely considered to be at the "very heart of human rights and United Nations Values."[1] In line with this worldwide recognition of the importance of women's human rights protection (especially women's rights to equality), Taiwan has been generally regarded as making good progress concerning the promotion of women's human rights in the political, economic, cultural and social arenas and concerning securing women's status in gender equality.

However, from time to time, when women's rights to equality encounter some deeply embedded traditions, there are still difficulties in society and in the constitutional process to fully implement the rights to gender equality. In 2015, the Constitutional Court of the ROC issued a controversial interpretation (i.e., J.Y. Interpretation No. 728), which was considered by many people to be against the general requirement of gender equality and to fail to strike a proper balance between protection of women's human rights on the one hand, and the need to protect the long-established traditions and the freedom of contract on the other hand. This is considered by some people to conflict with the general image of the Constitutional Court (which is the first of this type of court in Asia), which is relatively liberal, active and progressive in ensuring the enjoyment and protection of human rights within its jurisdiction.

This chapter explains the problems of conflicting interests and considerations involved in this case and suggests that a new balance needs to be reached when women's human rights encounter local traditions.

The discussion begins with an introduction to the background of the case in the second part of this chapter. It will then introduce J.Y. Interpretation No. 728 as issued by the Constitutional Court. The chapter will further identify the ignorance of the "systemic discrimination" arising from or facilitated by the "seemingly" neutral legislation and also point out the imbalance in the case leading to stereotyping women as not being able to play certain traditional roles and functions in society. It will conclude by suggesting a new balance that should be reached in future legislative actions adopted by the Congress.

2 Background of the 2015 Case of J.Y. Interpretation No. 728

In Taiwan society, there are still many "Ancestor Worship Guilds/Associations," most of which were founded by the male members of their respective family clans in earlier times in Taiwan. Many of them were created more than one hundred years ago when Taiwan was in the Qing Dynasty and the Japanese colonial periods. Many founders of such guilds/associations were at that time new immigrants from

---

[1]United Nations Human Rights Office of the High Commissioner (2017).

Mainland China. They cherished the memory of their ancestors back in their homeland. The guilds/associations could be composed of one male member individually or several male members jointly who donated his/their real estate to such guilds/associations for the specific purpose of worshiping their common ancestors. The guilds were created to show that the descendants cared about their deceased parents and ancestors. They used some of the donated land to build an ancestral hall to conduct daily and periodic worship activities and used the remaining donated land for profit-making purposes so that there would be regular and continuous proceeds arising from the estates. The proceeds from these estates serve as a financial source by which to administer the guilds' affairs, to maintain the ancestral hall and to support the worship activities. The whole idea of creating a guild was to unify the descendants of the founders with the expectation that they would be bound together forever through such as everlasting arrangement.[2]

The traditional practice has been that only male descendants are allowed to inherit membership status and therefore the associated property rights. Such descendants are called successors or members of the guild. This discriminatory practice of only allowing male descendants to be successors is maintained through the "internal regulations" of the guilds, regulations that were drafted by the founders when they first established the guilds.

The dispute involved in the case of J.Y. Interpretation No. 728 concerns discrimination against a female descendant and her son. The factual background of the case is summarized below:[3]

> The petitioner Lu Pi-Lien (in an uxorilocal marriage) is the eldest daughter of Lu Chin-Jung, who is one of the successors to the Ancestor Worship Guild of Lu Wan-Chun. The other petitioner, Lu Chia-Sheng, is Lu Pi-Lien's son (he carries his mother's surname). Lu Chin-Jung's living was maintained by the petitioners and he had three sons, none of whom has a male child. When Lu Chin-Jung and two of his sons passed away, only the youngest son, Lu Hsueh-Chuan, remained. The forepart of Article 4 of the Internal Regulations Governing the Management of the Ancestor Worship Guild of Lu Wan-Chun… provides that "In a case where the registered successor has died, the lineal heirs have the right to appoint a representative to assume the status of successor, provided, however, that a woman has no right of inheritance pursuant to the relevant government regulations." Consequently, succession to Lu Chin-Jung's registered membership in the Ancestor Worship Guild of Lu Wan-Chun was inherited only by Lu Hsueh-Chuan. The petitioners thus initiated litigation to claim their right to inherit the status of successor but the case was dismissed by the … District Court … The petitioners then appealed but it was dismissed both in the civil judgment of the Taiwan High Court … and in the civil judgment of the Supreme Court … All above-mentioned civil judgments applied the forepart of Paragraph 1 of Article 4 of the Statutes Governing Ancestor Worship Guilds, which

[2]Department of Civil Affairs, Ministry of Interior (R.O.C.), Ji Si Gong Ye Ji Shen Ming Hui [祭祀公業及神明會] (Ancestor Worship Guilds/Associations) (2017).

[3]Si Fa Yuan Da Fa Guan Jie Shi Shizi Di 728 Hao [Justices of the Constitutional Court, Judicial Yuan, Interpretation No. 728] (20 Mar 2015) (R.O.C.) [hereinafter J.Y. Interpretation No. 728]. The English translation of the summary of the case background is quoted from the official website of the Judicial Yuan. It can be found at http://www.judicial.gov.tw/constitutionalcourt/EN/p03_01.asp?expno=728. Accessed 19 Dec 2017.

> stipulates: "For the guilds that existed before the promulgation of the Statutes, whether a person is a qualified successor to a guild should be determined by its internal regulations" and referred to the foregoing Internal Regulation which indicates that "only the male lineal heirs are qualified to inherit the status of successor" as the reasoning. Consequently, the petitioners then requested an interpretation on the grounds that the disputed provision applied in the final judgment was unconstitutional under Article 7 of the Constitution.

Briefly, the law (i.e., the forepart of paragraph 1 of Article 4 of the Statutes Governing Ancestor Worship Guilds) provides that the qualification of successorship/membership of a guild may be decided by the "internal regulations" of the specific guild. And the specific "internal regulations" of the guild in this case required that only the male lineal heirs are qualified to inherit the status of successor of the guild members. Because of such "internal regulations," the ordinary courts decided that the petitioners (one of whom was the daughter of a deceased member and the other one was her son) were not qualified to be the successors/members of the guild. The petitioners argued that the provision in the Statute violated the equal protection provision in Article 7 of the Constitution, which states that "All citizens of the Republic of China, irrespective of sex, religion, race, class, or party affiliation, shall be equal before the law."

The current system of the Constitutional Court is that a petitioner can only file an application to the Constitutional Court to ask the Court to declare a *provision in a law or regulation* to be in violation of the Constitution. The "constitutional complaint" (or "*verfassungsbeschwerde*" in German) created by the German constitutional system had not yet been adopted in Taiwan when this chapter was prepared in 2017, although it can reasonably be expected that there will be such a system introduced in the operation of Taiwan's Constitution in the near future when the judicial reform plan is put into force.

Hence, the current law does not make it possible for individuals to assert that their rights, as guaranteed by the Constitution, have been directly infringed upon by a decision of an ordinary court, merely as a result of the views adopted in it. Petitioners can only file a petition to the Constitutional Court asking it to interpret, in an abstract way, whether a provision in a piece of legislation or in a regulation (which has been applied by a court as the basis of its final judgment) is in violation of any constitutional provision or principle. Accordingly, Article 5, paragraph 1(2), of the Constitutional Interpretation Procedure Act[4] provides:

> The grounds on which the petitions for interpretation of the Constitution may be made are as follows: … 2. When an individual, a legal entity, or a political party, whose constitutional right was infringed upon and remedies provided by law for such infringement had been exhausted, has questions on the constitutionality of the statute or regulation relied thereupon by the court of last resort in its final judgment…

---

[4]Si Fa Yuan Da Fa Guan Shen Li An Jian Fa (Constitutional Interpretation Procedure Act) (1993). The English translation of the law can be found at: http://www.judicial.gov.tw/constitutionalcourt/en/p07_2.asp?lawno=73. Accessed 19 Dec 2017).

In this case, the Constitutional Court could only focus on whether the challenged legislation (i.e., Paragraph 1 of Article 4 of the Statutes Governing Ancestor Worship Guilds) contradicts the equality requirement provided in Article 7 of the Constitution by not protecting women's right to be successors/members of a guild.

3 The Main Content of J.Y. Interpretation No. 728

The Constitutional Court in this case basically supported the position held by the ordinary courts and declared that the challenged legislation was "constitutional." The Constitutional Court held in its J.Y. Interpretation No. 728[5] that:

> The forepart part of paragraph 1 of Article 4 of the Statutes Governing Ancestor Worship Guilds stipulates: "For guilds that existed before the promulgation of the Statutes, whether a person is a qualified successor to a guild should be determined by its internal regulations." It does not use gender as a criterion for determining the status of a successor. In general, most, if not all, of the related internal regulations of guilds follow the traditional perception of clans in restricting succession to male offspring (including adopted children) only. As a result, female offspring are prohibited from being successors in most circumstances. However, the enactment of the internal regulations for the guilds is an act performed by the founders and their descendants to form an association and dispose of their property under private law. Therefore, based on the principle of the autonomy of private law, the internal regulations shall be respected for the preservation of the stability of the law. The foregoing provision which stipulates whether a person is a qualified successor to a guild should be determined by the internal regulations of the guild and should not be in conflict with the gender equality guaranteed by Article 7 of the Constitution, nor should it damage women's property rights.

The reasoning of the Constitutional Court's Interpretations is mostly short and concise. This is also the situation in the case of J.Y. Interpretation No. 728. The main reason provided for this Interpretation is included in paragraph 2 of its Reasoning. It states in part that:

> An ancestor worship guild is an association formed by the properties donated by the founders for the purpose of providing services for ancestor worship or other forms of worship. … The establishment and existence of an ancestor worship guild involves the freedom of association, property rights and freedom of contract of the founders and also of their descendants. The disputed provision constitutes differential treatment in substance in cases where the relevant internal regulations follow the traditional perception of clans in restricting succession to male offspring (including adopted children) only. Thus, female offspring are prohibited from becoming successors in most cases. However, the disputed provision does not provide gender as a criterion in form for determining the status of the successor and the objective is to preserve the stability of the law and the principle of the prohibition of retroactive law. Furthermore, the enactment of internal regulations for guilds is an act performed by their founders and their descendants by which an association is formed and property disposed of under private law. This should, in principle, be respected

[5]J.Y. Interpretation No. 728. The English translation of this interpretation is quoted from the Judicial Yuan's official website. It can be found at http://www.judicial.gov.tw/constitutionalcourt/EN/p03_01.asp?expno=728. Accessed 19 Dec 2017.

> based on the protection of the freedom of association in Article 14 of the Constitution, the protection of property rights in Article 15 of the Constitution, and the protection of freedom of contract and the autonomy of private law in Article 22 of the Constitution. Therefore, even though such a disputed provision may constitute differential treatment in substance, since it is not arbitrary, it is not in conflict with the principle of gender equity as embodied in Article 7 of the Constitution nor does it infringe upon women's right to property.

In essence, the Constitutional Court considers that the actual discriminatory practice is maintained through the "internal regulations" of the guilds adopted by the founders when the guilds were established, not because of the challenged law that requires discrimination against women. Since the law does not prohibit women from being qualified successors/members of guilds, it does not violate the equal protection provision in the Constitution, even though common practice in almost all guilds has followed the long tradition of preventing women from becoming qualified successors/members.

4 The Problems with J.Y. Interpretation No. 728

4.1 The "Systemic" Discriminatory Effect Arising from the "Seemingly" Neutral Legislation

It is true that the challenged legislation does not formally include gender as an "element" or a "criterion" for determining the status of the successor or membership of a guild. However, such a provision has an adverse effect on gender equality in practice. The challenged provision basically implies that the founders of guilds are permitted to discriminate against their female offspring. In other words, it is because of the challenged provision that the guild founders can discriminate against women.

The above-mentioned result of maintaining and continuing the historical discriminatory practice was clearly predictable when the Statutes Governing Ancestor Worship Guilds were enacted in 2007 and were implemented in 2008. The wide practice of excluding women from being successors or members of guilds had been in place for more than one hundred years, so the fact that the legislation allows the founders to decide their own qualifications for successorship/membership of a guild implies that the law passively encourages society to continue such discrimination. The legislative body collectively, and its members individually, can reasonably expect that the discriminatory practice will certainly be carried on because of the law.

Clearly knowing that the discriminatory tradition will continue, the current law still provides that if there are "internal rules" for a guild to decide the qualifications of successorship or membership, the "internal rules" shall govern. Hence, the maintenance and continuation of such a discriminatory practice is actually made possible by the challenged legislation.

The Constitutional Court's assertion is that the challenged law is neutral because it merely recognizes the "internal regulations" of the guilds. However, from factual and practical perspectives, it is not neutral. The law makers knew that the existing practice (with virtually no exception) was discriminatory against women. However, they still formulated a legal provision which permitted or even legalized such discrimination, therefore the law has already taken an obvious position in favor of the discrimination. Hence, the question has become whether the challenged legislation has provided a legal ground for discrimination or has even facilitated such systemic discrimination. If this is the case, the answer should clearly be "yes."

The majority view in this case has been that it is the guild's "internal regulations" themselves that are discriminatory; not the challenged legal provision. It is true that the guild's "internal regulations" were clearly discriminatory, however, this does not mean that such discrimination has not been "contributed" to, "made possible" or "facilitated" by the challenged legal provision.

In the dissenting opinion[6] that I presented in this case, I argued that since the tradition of only allowing male offspring to perform the ancestor-worship role is firmly rooted among the guilds, its practice is so widespread and since virtually all "internal regulations" of such guilds reaffirm such tradition, there is systemic and structural discrimination against women in this regard. The law, by recognizing such a tradition and allowing the "internal regulations" to serve as the basis for deciding the successorship or membership of the guilds, has turned the issue into whether the law itself is also discriminatory against women. Such discrimination is similar to direct discrimination by legislation.

4.2 The Need to Weigh and Balance Relevant Rights and the Involved Public Interests

Under the Constitution, when there is an infringement of a constitutionally guaranteed right by a law, the Constitutional Court will have to conduct a "necessity" analysis so as to decide whether such infringement is justified. This requirement is provided in Article 23 of the Constitution, which reads:

> All the freedoms and rights enumerated in the preceding Articles shall not be restricted by law except by such as may be necessary to prevent infringement upon the freedoms of other persons, to avert an imminent crisis, to maintain social order or to advance public welfare.

Under this constitutional provision, any restriction on the protection or enjoyment of any constitutional right or freedom must be examined to see whether its purpose is "to prevent infringement upon the freedoms of other persons, to avert an imminent crisis, to maintain social order or to advance public welfare." These purposes can be collectively called "public interest purposes." If the answer is no, then such a restriction would never be considered to be necessary. On the other

[6]Lo Chang-fa Da Fa Guan Shizi Di 728 Hao Jie Shi Bu Tong Yi Jian Shu [羅昌發大法官釋字第728 號解釋不同意見書] (Justice Chang-fa Lo's dissenting opinion in Justices of the Constitutional Court, Interpretation No. 728) (20 Mar 2015) (R.O.C.) (in Chinese).

hand, if the answer is positive, then the Constitutional Court needs to further decide whether it is really necessary. Hence, the analysis is a two-step process, i.e., to decide whether there is any public interest involved and whether the challenged restriction is necessary to achieve such a public interest.

The necessity assessment is a process of weighing and balancing a series of factors, including the relative importance of "the freedom of other persons to be prevented from infringement, the crisis to be averted, and the social order and public welfare to be maintained or advanced," the existence and extent of the contribution to achieving the purposes through the challenged restriction, and the extent or level of infringement on the restricted constitutional rights. After having weighed and balanced these factors, the Constitutional Court needs to further consider whether there exists any measure that is less restrictive on the constitutional rights but can still achieve similar purposes.

4.3 The Relative Importance of Infringed Constitutional Rights and the Public Interest

In this case, there are two groups of opposing rights and public interests involved. From the perspective of the discriminated women, their right to property inheritance[7] and their right to equal protection are apparently infringed upon. The discrimination is *systemic* and *structural* in nature. It reflects the whole society's deeply rooted idea of the son being the one to carry on and continue the family line. Although fewer and fewer people firmly hold this idea, it is still a prevailing concept in rural areas and in traditional villages and it still affects the daily practices of many people. Hence, the discrimination is not merely about an individual woman's rights to property being infringed upon or her status being the target of discrimination. It is actually, in this case, the entire gender which is being systemically discriminated against. Hence, if we are talking about the seriousness of the infringement by the challenged law, such discrimination in this case is much more serious than that experienced by an individual woman being sporadically discriminated against.

From the perspective of local tradition, there are the following freedoms and rights as well as potential public interests involved: First, the freedom of contract is involved in this case, because the founders are supposed to be free to enter into contractual relations to govern their associations and guilds. The freedom of contract is admitted by the Constitution of the Republic under the property protection clause in Article 15. Second, the freedom of disposing of one's own property is also involved in this case. Article 15 of the Constitution not only explicitly admits the

[7]Zhonghua Minguo Xianfa (Constitution of the Republic of China), Art. 15 reads: "The right of existence, the right of work, and the right of property shall be guaranteed to the people." The right to property inheritance falls within the scope of the constitutional protection of property rights.

right to property, but also implies the inclusion of the freedom of disposing of one's own property. The founders should be able to decide the way in which their donated estates are used. Third, the freedom of association provided in Article 14[8] is also involved. It is because the particular practice of creating a guild is about establishing a private association to play certain worship roles. Fourth, the public interest of maintaining the stability of legal relationships is also involved. In Taiwan, there have been many thousands of such associations, under which numerous numbers of legal relationships were established, some more than one hundred years ago; any retroactive change to such relations could create unimaginably chaotic consequences.

4.4 The Majority View Failed to Prioritize Gender Equality Over Tradition and Other Rights

The majority view of the Constitutional Court apparently gave more weight to the freedom of contract, the freedom of association and the right to dispose of one's own property and prioritized maintenance of the stability of legal relationships. But I would argue that the Court failed to give appropriate weight to, and to prioritize, the gender equality requirement in the Constitution. In my opinion, our Court should be in a proper position to (in fact, should be obligated to) invalidate the law based on the above-quoted constitutional provision in Article 7 for the following reasons:

First, the discrimination has been of a systemic and structural nature, as explained above. Hence the infringement of women's constitutional rights should be considered to be of a very serious nature.

Second, Article 10.6 of the Constitutional Amendment provides: "The State shall protect the dignity of women, safeguard their personal safety, eliminate sexual discrimination, and further substantive gender equality." Hence the State has an obligation to progressively and actively promote gender equality. This provision is also applicable to this case. This means that the State has an obligation to invalidate a legal provision which admits traditional and systemic discrimination against women. This Constitutional Amendment actually puts more weight on the importance of gender equality.

Third, Articles 2 and 5 of the Convention on the Elimination of All Forms of Discrimination against Women ("CEDAW") also requires the State to take all appropriate measures to eliminate discrimination against women by any person, organization or enterprise; to take all appropriate measures to modify or abolish existing laws, regulations, customs and practices which constitute discrimination against women; and to modify the social and cultural patterns of conduct of men and women, with a view to achieving the elimination of prejudices, customs and all

[8]Zhonghua Minguo Xianfa (Constitution of the Republic of China), Art. 14 reads: "The people shall have freedom of assembly and association."

other practices that are based on the idea of the inferiority or the superiority of either of the sexes or on stereotyped roles for men and women.

In my view, the traditional practice of ancestor worship guilds is a discriminatory customary practice based on the superiority of men and based on stereotypical roles of men and women. The treaty provisions in the CEDAW can definitely help us understand that the local tradition of discriminating and stereotyping women regarding the worship of ancestors is of no real value from a human rights perspective. These treaty provisions can also help interpret and apply Articles 7 and 23 of the Constitution to require that more weight should be given to the importance of gender equality.

Fourth, the freedom of contract and freedom of disposing of ones' own property relate to the engagement in economic relations and the exercise of property rights. The freedom of association is about entering into a group or a collective relation. No one can suggest that these rights are not important. But compared with the structural and long-standing tradition of discrimination against women, such freedoms should give way to gender equality which is the cure to the tradition of discrimination.

Also, if the Constitutional Court is to declare the challenged law as unconstitutional, it does not need to retroactively require full recovery of the successor status for *all female offspring in the entire history of a guild* or *all female offspring of a guild after implementation of the Constitution in Taiwan*. Such retroactive recovery would be technically impossible and practically unnecessary because there would not be sufficient and correct information to allow the family line to be traced back one hundred years or several decades. Even if the information were sufficient and accurate, such recovery would create complicated and intertwined relations among the existing successors and newly admitted successors. The Constitutional Court can simply require that the law should cease its application prospectively so that the "internal regulations" of guilds will have to be modified within a certain time limit to allow female offspring to become successors/members.

5 Concluding Remarks—Prioritizing Women's Human Rights in a Future Amendment

When we decide whether the restriction of women's rights to inheritance and to participation in the guilds has exceeded the necessary limitation, we have to weigh and balance all related rights and interests.

My conclusion, after having weighed and balanced various rights and interests, is that the tradition of systemically discriminating against women in regard to their ancestor-worship status and the rights and freedoms associated with such discrimination are of minimal constitutional value and ought not be protected when encountering women's right to equality. Women's right to equal protection should be prioritized because of the seriousness and the systemic and structural nature of such discrimination. The Constitutional Court should have declared the law unconstitutional.

Of course, there must be a transitional mechanism to resolve the discrimination arising from the long tradition, such as providing state assistance to the associations, their members, and female offspring to clarify the family lines and to establish appropriate procedures and a reasonable time frame for the proper handling of the matter.

In my opinion, this is an appropriate balance to strike between the protection of women's rights (especially their right to equality) in regard to the undesirable, long tradition and the avoidance of chaotic legal relations.

Although the decision has already been made by the Constitutional Court, the legislative body still has a chance to correct the discriminatory situation by requiring equal status for female offspring at least for successions that will occur after the new legislation.

References

Department of Civil Affairs, Ministry of the Interior (R.O.C.), Ji Si Gong Ye Ji Shen Ming Hui [祭祀公業及神明會] (Ancestor Worship Guilds/Associations) (2017) https://www.moi.gov.tw/dca/02sacrifices_001.aspx. Accessed 19 Dec 2017

United Nations Human Rights Office of the High Commissioner (2017) Women's Human Rights and Gender Equality. http://www.ohchr.org/EN/Issues/Women/WRGS/Pages/WRGSIndex.aspx. Accessed 19 Dec 2017

Chang-fa Lo has been Justice of the Constitutional Court of the ROC (Taiwan) since October 2011. Prior to his current judicial position, he was Chair Professor and Lifetime Distinguished Professor at National Taiwan University (NTU); Dean of NTU College of Law; Founding Director of the Asian Center for WTO and International Health Law and Policy of the NTU College of Law (ACWH); Founding Director of the Center for Ethics, Law and Society in Biomedicine and Technology of NTU; Commissioner of Taiwan's Fair Trade Commission; Commissioner of Taiwan's International Trade Commission; and legal advisor for Taiwan's GATT/WTO accession negotiations. In his capacity as Director of ACWH, Professor Lo launched two English journals, namely, the *Asian Journal of WTO and International Health Law and Policy* (AJWH, an SSCI listed journal) and the *Contemporary Asia Arbitration Journal* (CAA) in 2006 and 2008, respectively. During his tenure as Dean of NTU College of Law, he also launched an English journal, the *NTU Law Review*. He was appointed by the WTO as a panelist for DS332 Brazil—Measures Affecting Imports of Retreaded Tyre in 2006, DS468 Ukraine—Definitive Safeguard Measures on Certain Passenger Cars in 2014, and appointed a member of the Permanent Group of Experts under the SCM Agreement of the WTO in 2008. He has also been also Chairman of the Asia WTO Research Network (AWRN) since 2013. Prior to his teaching career, he practiced law in Taipei. He received his S.J.D. degree from Harvard University Law School in 1989. He is the author of 13 books (including *Treaty Interpretation under the Vienna Convention on the Law of Treaties—A New Round of Codification* published by Springer) and the editor of seven books (including this one), and has authored more than 100 journal articles and book chapters. He was granted the "National Professorship Award" by the Ministry of Education and the "Outstanding Scholarship Chair Professorship Award" by the Foundation for Advancement of Outstanding Scholarship.

Chapter 33
LGBT Rights in Taiwan—The Interaction Between Movements and the Law

Hsiaowei Kuan

Abstract On 24 May 2017, the world was impressed by the decision made by the Justices of the Constitutional Court in Taiwan regarding the constitutionality of the legal ban on same-sex marriages. The decision of the Constitutional Court concludes that denying the marriage of two persons of the same-sex violates both their right to equality and the constitutional right to marry. Although many factors such as Taiwan's robust democracy, judicial activism, and commitment to constitutionalism may have contributed to this landmark judicial triumph, the existence of the most vibrant LGBT communities in its civil society must have paved the way for the progressive judicial and legislative atmosphere that finally led to this outcome. The constitutional and legal success in LGBT rights protection in Taiwan could not have been achieved without the long-term efforts made by LGBT activism. It is essential to determine how the LGBT rights movement in Taiwan affected and expedited the changes in legislation regarding LGBT rights. This chapter explores the development of LGBT rights in Taiwan from the perspective of the interaction between the LGBT rights movements and legislation. The discussion covers specific yet important issues, such as the destigmatization of same-sex sexual behavior, anti-discrimination based on sexual orientation and sexual identity in both education and employment, recognition of same-sex families, and the right to change legal gender identity, which are relevant concerns for human rights observers.

Keywords Anti-discrimination · Legal gender identity · LGBT rights Same-sex couple family · Same-sex marriage · Social movements and law

H. Kuan (✉)
College of Law, National Taipei University, New Taipei City, Taiwan
e-mail: hwkuan@mail.ntpu.edu.tw

J. A. Cohen et al. (eds.), *Taiwan and International Human Rights*, Economics, Law, and Institutions in Asia Pacific, https://doi.org/10.1007/978-981-13-0350-0_33

1 Introduction

On 24 May 2017, the world was impressed by the decision made by the Constitutional Court in Taiwan regarding the constitutionality of the legal ban on same-sex marriages. The decision, Judicial Yuan Interpretation No. 748 (hereinafter J.Y. Interpretation No. 748), concludes that denying two persons of the same-sex the equal right to marry violates both their equality and the constitutional right to marry.[1] The Justices gave the Legislative Yuan 2 years to amend the current law or to enact a new law to allow same-sex couples to marry; otherwise, same-sex couples will automatically be allowed to register their marriages under the current framework. The international media praised Taiwan as the most progressive country in Asia due to its attempt to safeguard the human rights of lesbians, gay men, bisexual people, and transgender people (hereinafter LGBT).[2] International observers may wonder how this small island became the first country in Asia to legalize same-sex marriage. Although many factors such as Taiwan's robust democracy, judicial activism, and commitment to constitutionalism may have contributed to this landmark judicial triumph, the existence of vibrant LGBT communities in its civil society must have paved the way for the progressive judicial and legislative atmosphere that finally led to this outcome.[3]

The constitutional and legal success in LGBT rights protection could not have been achieved without the long-term efforts made by LGBT activism. It is essential to determine how the LGBT rights movement in Taiwan affected and expedited the changes in legislation regarding LGBT rights. Taiwan's LGBT rights movement can be traced back to over 30 years ago, when martial law was lifted. During the repressive era of authoritarian rule, Chi C-W, who was also the petitioner of the landmark judicial case in 2017, had already begun his long journey to fight for the right for gay couples to marry in the late 1980s.[4] Organized gay and lesbian activism began in the early 1990s, when the first lesbian organization, "Between Us," was established in February 1990. Early gay and lesbian activism in Taiwan focused more on developing cultural and identity confidence in the community and eliminating the social stigma against LGBT people. The first preliminary discussion on gay and lesbian rights and equality was at a public hearing held in the Legislative Yuan in 1993. At this hearing, LGBT groups advocated for gay and lesbian people's equal rights in employment, education, and other fields, asserting

[1]The English version of the ruling can be found at Judicial Yuan (2017) Press Release on the Same-Sex Marriage Case. http://www.judicial.gov.tw/constitutionalcourt/p10_02.asp?id=267570. Accessed 25 Aug 2017.

[2]Taiwan's same-sex marriage ruling raises hopes across Asia (2017).

[3]Sutton and Harding (2017).

[4]In 1986, Chi sent a petition letter to the Legislative Yuan to demand the legalization of same-sex marriage; he later filed a petition with the Ministry of Interior and the Ministry of Justice in 1994. Chi's effort to fight for marriage equality was summarized in the Reasoning of J.Y. Interpretation No. 748, see Si Fa Yuan Da Fa Guan Jie Shi Shi Zi Di 748 Hao [司法院大法官解釋釋字第 748 號] (J.Y. Interpretation No. 748) (24 May 2017) (Taiwan).

that their equality should be protected by anti-discrimination laws. Henceforth, the priority of rights advocacy groups was on the agenda of the gay and lesbian movement. Comprehensive LGBT anti-discrimination legislation had yet to be realized. However, this was close to occurring when a draft of a progressive human rights act prepared by the Ministry of Justice and the Human Rights Consultative Committee of the Presidential Office was released in July 2003. Article 24 of the Human Rights Basic Law declares that the State shall respect the rights of homosexual people, and they shall be legally permitted to form a family and to adopt children.[5] This draft was never sent to the Legislative Yuan for further review as the Act covered far too many controversial issues for it to gain support within the cabinet.

This chapter provides a discussion of the development of LGBT rights in Taiwan from the perspective of the interaction between the LGBT rights movements and legislation. The discussion covers specific yet important issues that are relevant concerns for human rights observers.

2 Destigmatization of Same-Sex Sexual Behavior

International human rights observers interested in LGBT rights in a certain state first establish whether sex between two same-sex adults is considered a criminal offense. Currently, in at least 76 countries, discriminatory laws criminalize same-sex sexual behavior, exposing millions of individuals to the risk of arrest, prosecution, and imprisonment—and even the death penalty.[6] However, consensual same-sex sexual behavior was never included as a crime in Taiwan's criminal codes after World War II. Therefore, unlike many other countries where the decriminalization of same-sex sexual behavior was a long struggle for those advocating LGBT rights, it was never on the agenda of the gay and lesbian movement in Taiwan.

However, this does not mean that sex between same-sex people was deemed to be moral or legal. Gay bars, saunas, sports clubs, or other places considered to be gathering places for gay men were viciously and constantly raided by police in the 1990s under the charge of public obscenity, which is punishable both under the Social Order Maintenance Act and the criminal codes.[7] LGBT groups protested against these discriminatory practices of law enforcement and called for a reexamination of the overly broad legal definition of obscenity. The discriminatory raids gradually subsided after the Justices announced in 2001 that arbitrary raids were

[5]Yang (2001).

[6]United Nations for LGBT Equality: Free & Equal (2017).

[7]For instance, on 31 July 1997, 15 armed policemen blocked Chang-der Street, a street where gays often socialize, and arrested forty gay men without due process. On 20 December 1998, police stormed AG Gym, also a gay sports club, and forced gay members to pose in obscene positions in order to arrest them on the charge of public obscenity. See generally Wang (1999).

unconstitutional, and any raid or check should follow due process of law and the principle of proportionality.[8]

In addition to places where same-sex intimate behavior was deemed to occur, bookstores containing gay and lesbian literature were susceptible to police raids and harassment. Chingching Bookstore, a bookstore mainly serving gay customers in Taipei, was constantly raided by the police from the nearest precinct. In a raid in 2003 commanded by the prosecutor, Chingching Bookstore, which represents a rebellious cultural base in Taipei's LGBT history, was raided and 500 magazines aimed toward gay men were deemed to be obscene materials and seized. The bookstore owner, Lai C-J, was charged and found guilty of selling obscene materials in 2006. LGBT groups assisted Lai to file a constitutional petition against the Department of Justice, asserting that the definition of "obscene" in Article 235 of the Criminal Code is too vague and incomprehensible, and therefore violates an individual's freedom of speech. The petition also argued that the purpose of the punishment is said to protect sexual morality and social decency, which, if interpreted inappropriately, may only allow mainstream explicit sex materials to be distributable and leaves materials involving sexual minorities unequivalently punishable. In October 2006, the Justices rendered an interpretation affirming the constitutionality of Article 235 of the Criminal Code.[9] This stated the following:

> In order to maintain sexual morality and social decency, the constitutional interpreters should, in principle, give due respect to the lawmakers in respect of the latter's judgment on the common values held by the majority of the society where the legislative organ designs a law to regulate the subject.

LGBT groups were certainly discouraged by this decision. On the one hand, the Justices used the term "sex minority cultural group" in this decision to refer to the LGBT community, as if the LGBT lifestyle is merely a type of subculture. On the other hand, the decision allowed lawmakers to impose restrictions through law if "it is necessary to maintain the common sexual values and mores of the majority."[10] LGBT groups held a joint press conference to express their disappointment with this judicial decision.

J.Y. Interpretation No. 617 was an embodiment of the negative attitude toward LGBT people in the legal field. Several years after homosexuality ceased to be considered a mental disease, homosexual sexuality was still considered obscene and was prevented from explicitly being mentioned in a legal decision.

[8]See Si Fa Yuan Da Fa Guan Jie Shi Shi Zi Di 535 Hao [司法院大法官解釋釋字第 535 號] (J.Y. Interpretation No. 535) (14 Dec 2001) (Taiwan).

[9]See Si Fa Yuan Da Fa Guan Jie Shi Shi Zi Di 617 Hao [司法院大法官解釋釋字第 617 號] (J.Y. Interpretation No. 617) (26 Oct 2006) (Taiwan).

[10]J. Y. Interpretation No. 617.

3 Anti-discrimination in Education and Employment

3.1 The Prohibition of Discrimination in the Realm of Education

The first affirmative legal protection for LGBT rights was in the educational realm. In June 2004, the enactment of the Gender Equity Education Act explicitly prohibited discrimination against students based on their sexual orientation. The success of the enactment was an achievement that resulted from the combined efforts of women's groups and LGBT groups initially formed as a result of the tragic death of Yeh Y-C. On 20 April 2000, Yeh was discovered lying in his own blood in a school bathroom, and he died the following day. His death drew media attention, and the Ministry of Education assigned an investigative group to explore the cause of death and how he was treated while he was alive. The report concluded that Yeh was a victim of gender discrimination and bullying. As a boy who had a soft voice and thin figure, Yeh was different from other boys due to his feminine appearance and expressions. Teachers and classmates were aware that he was constantly being bullied in school and after class but they chose to ignore it. Yeh's story triggered heated discussions about how discrimination harms LGBT students and those who have distinct gender temperaments. Women's groups and LGBT groups contended that gender is not a binary choice of male or female; rather, it is diverse and located on a fluid spectrum. The educational authority accepted this idea and transformed its gender equity policy from focusing on "equity between the two sexes" to "gender diversity."[11]

Thus, when the Gender Equity Education Act was passed in 2004, the purpose of gender equality in this law was no longer simply to promote equality between men and women but among people with different gender characteristics, temperaments, identities, and sexual orientations. Under this law, each school has an obligation to provide a safe campus and a gender-friendly environment for all students, faculty, and staff of different genders, gender temperaments, gender identities, and sexual orientations.[12] In addition, the act states that a school shall not discriminate against a prospective student during recruitment or the evaluation of admission applications on the basis of his or her gender, gender temperament, gender identity, or sexual orientation.[13] The prohibition against discrimination also applies to instruction, activities, assessments, rewards and penalties, benefits, and services provided to current students.[14] In 2011, the legal definition of gender equity education was formally revised to be a form of education that would generate respect for "gender diversity," eliminate gender discrimination, and promote substantive gender equality through

[11]Bi (2000).

[12]Gender Equity Education Act, art. 12 (2004) (Taiwan).

[13]*Id.,* art. 13.

[14]*Id.,* art. 14.

education. In the same year, the concept of sexual bullying, which was defined as ridicule, attacks, or threats directed at another person's gender characteristics, gender temperament, sexual orientation, or gender identity by using verbal, physical, or other forms of violence, was introduced in this law and became punishable. The Enforcement Rules for the Gender Equity Education Act promulgated in June 2006 further demand that schools shall include a curriculum related to gender equity education that covers courses on affective education, sex education, and gay and lesbian education in order to enhance students' gender equity consciousness.[15]

3.2 *The Prohibition of Discrimination in the Realm of Employment*

On 4 September 2000, LGBT rights activists and representatives of LGBT groups met with President Chen Shui-bian to express their demands on behalf of the LGBT community, namely "safety and human rights," "the right to education," and "the equal right to work," as well as to urge the President to become a leading model for respecting lesbians and gay men.[16] Although gender discrimination in the workplace had been prohibited since 2001, the law only addressed discrimination based on sex, failing to cover discrimination based on sexual orientation. In 2003, the Department of Labor of the Taipei City Government for the first time recognized that the termination of employment based on an employee's sexual orientation constitutes gender discrimination and is prohibited by law.[17] Following this, there were continuing calls for explicit legal protection for the LGBT community and the prohibition of discrimination based on sexual orientation and gender identity. However, full realization of this legal recognition did not occur until 2007, when the original Act of Equality between Men and Women in Employment was amended to become the Act of Gender Equality in Employment. The purpose of the revision in 2007 was to broaden the scope of the definition of gender discrimination to include discrimination based on sexual orientation.[18] From job recruitment, hiring, assignment, promotion, and payment of wages to discharge and termination, the law prohibits employers from discriminating against applicants or employees based on their gender or sexual orientation.

Whether the new law covers discrimination against transgender or transsexual workers later became an issue because the new law again omits significant needs of the LGBT community. In 2010, a transgender technician, Chou Y-R, was dismissed by the hospital where he worked due to an excessive number of unexcused

[15]Enforcement Rules for the Gender Equity Education Act, art. 13 (2006) (Taiwan).

[16]Taiwan Association for Human Rights (2001), pp. 143–144.

[17]Huang (2003).

[18]Article 5 of the Employment Service Act was also revised in the same year to include sexual orientation as a new classification in its anti-discrimination provision.

absences. Chou sued the hospital for committing discrimination in the workplace based on his gender identity. He claimed that he had been transferred to another post and had been assigned trivial tasks to avoid his coming into contact with others since he began to dress in women's clothes. He was surrounded by unfriendly colleagues, which caused him to change his seating position to work with friendly colleagues in the library. The court found that the transfer and dismissal of Chou by the hospital resulted from a motive to intentionally discriminate against him based on his gender identity and that the hospital should be subjected to punishment.[19] The court decision never questioned whether discrimination based on gender identity constitutes gender discrimination; it considered gender to be a concept broad enough to cover gender temperaments as well as gender identity.

4 Recognition of Same-Sex Families

LGBT activists' efforts toward the destigmatization of homosexual sexuality and the legislative realization of anti-discrimination laws in education and in the workplace have all helped to pave the way toward a friendlier environment for those in the LGBT community. An increasing number of LGBT people are willing to "come out" in public; some even enthusiastically participate in gay pride parades. Taiwan is famous for holding its carnival-style LGBT pride parade annually in Taipei. From its beginning with a group of 2,000 people in 2003, the LGBT pride parade is now the largest annual gay pride event in Asia, attracting 80,000 participants from all over the world.

After gaining various rights in terms of education, employment, and other fields, activists for the rights of lesbians and gay men focused on securing the right to marry and the right to form a family. The first legislative attempt was proposed in 2006 by Legislator Hsiao B-K. A public hearing was held, but the bill, which proposed allowing same-sex couples to register as partners, did not pass the threshold that would have allowed it to be on the agenda for a committee review. A second attempt was made by Legislator Yu M-N at the end of December 2012.

However, it was the third attempt that stirred heated national debate. For the first time, a comprehensive bill was drafted, and LGBT activism was the driving force behind the legislative drafting and lobbying. In 2009, several women's groups and LGBT groups established a platform to draft a bill to revise the current Civil Code in order to address the different needs of various forms of contemporary families.[20] A few months later, those groups affiliated with the platform decided to establish an organization, the Taiwan Alliance to Promote Civil Partnership Rights (hereinafter TAPCPR),

---

[19]MacKay Memorial Hospital v. The Government of Taipei City, 101 Jian Zi No. 164 [101 簡字 164 號] (Taipei District Ct. [臺北地方法院] 2 Jan 2012) (Taiwan).

[20]The participants included the Awakening Foundation, the Taiwan Tongzhi Hotline Association, the Tong-Kwang Light House Presbyterian Church and Taiwan LGBT Family Rights Advocacy.

which had a single mission: to advocate for the legal recognition of diverse forms of families. The original bill contains three parts: (1) the first part intends to legalize same-sex marriage by expanding the existing marriage relationship to include same-sex couples, replacing all of the legal terms representing "husband" and "wife" with "spouses"; (2) the second part entails creating a new category of marriage—a civil partnership—by adding a new chapter to the Civil Code; and (3) the third part recognizes multiple-person families by adding more protection to the already existing provisions. The TAPCPR bill was proposed by Legislator Cheng L-C in October 2013. However, only the first part of the same-sex marriage bill was officially proposed in the Legislative Yuan. The other two parts could not obtain enough signatures because the ideas of both a nonmarital partnership and a multiple-person family were unprecedented concepts among the public at that time.

The proposal to legalize same-sex marriage soon encountered a social obstacle from those with opposing viewpoints. Those in opposition to the proposal rapidly mobilized through a network of churches and other religious groups. On 30 November 2013, tens of thousands of people rallied on the streets to demonstrate against the same-sex marriage bill. After this demonstration, same-sex marriage supporters realized that they were witnessing the emergence of a counter-movement against LGBT rights. Under tremendous pressure from the opposing side, both the ruling party and the opposition party decided to retreat, taking marriage equality off their political agendas.

Realizing that the legislative path may not have been viable at that time due to a lack of sufficient political support, the TAPCPR embarked on a path of legal mobilization, challenging the current Civil Code through case litigation and constitutional petitions. On 1 August 2014, the TAPCPR recruited 30 same-sex couples to enter the district registrar, demanding to be registered as married couples. Three couples agreed to become parties of the following test cases for constitutional petitions. The subsequent legal actions on these cases drew considerable public attention. However, none of these cases reached the phase of a constitutional petition. In Taiwan, a petition to challenge the constitutionality of a law must be a case that has exhausted every level of judicial remedy, which may take several years. Therefore, the case of Chi C-W fulfilled the first requirement of the exhaustion of judicial remedies, when the highest administrative court overruled his request to marry in September 2014. The TAPCPR then recruited lawyers to work on Chi's constitutional petition. The petition was finally filed and accepted by the Constitutional Court on 20 August 2015, Chinese Valentine's Day. A constitutional petition in Taiwan can also take years; the Justices have total power in determining whether to grant a certiorari, whether to convene a public court, and when to publish their opinions. When Chi's petition was filed, half of the incumbent Justices had only 1 year of service remaining until the end of their terms. During this year, the President and the legislators would be reelected, the President would nominate candidates to be new Justices, and the Legislative Yuan would review and approve the nominations. Regardless of the results, concluding a term with a controversial case such as Chi's would have been a political risk for those seeking reelection.

Until the end of the reelection process, the Justices of the previous term took no action in regard to this case.

When the Democratic Progressive Party won the presidential and legislative elections, Legislator Mei-nu Yu organized representatives of several LGBT groups to redraft a marriage equality bill focusing solely on the inclusion of same-sex couples in the current framework of marriage by revising the Civil Code. Instead of changing the legal terms of "husband," "wife," "mother," and "father" to "spouse" and "parent," Yu's draft expanded the application of a marital relationship to same-sex couples by simply amending several provisions, leaving most of the articles unchanged. This tactic was crucial in Taiwan's context because a change of relational terms in law causes unease among the public. The opponents of marriage equality often argue that "if same-sex marriage is to be legalized, the terms father and mother, or grandfather and grandmother will be gone." In Taiwanese culture, the loss of kinship names is assumed to result in the misplacement of the fixed role of each family unit, which will then cause a decline in traditional family values. Hence, expanding this definition to include same-sex couples as an addendum and leaving the original legal terms unchanged may persuade more opponents to change their minds.

In October, Professor Jacques Picoux, who was deeply affected by his partner's illness and death, committed suicide. His failure to marry his partner and thus handle the burial of his partner and his affairs after his death caused him considerable distress. The tragedy galvanized the public to empathize with same-sex couples who, under the current legal framework, enjoyed no right to form their own families. It seemed like a perfect time to propose a bill for marriage equality. Since President Tsai I-W had expressed her support for marriage equality before the election, the ruling party then had no excuse to ignore the bill proposed by their own colleague. Without hesitation, three bills proposed by cross-partisan legislators were submitted for review in the Legislative Yuan. However, this does not mean that the bill faced less opposition than previously. The opposition's support grew even larger, particularly from the southern and rural parts of Taiwan, where LGBT lifestyles may still be considered by some to be "abnormal." However, realizing that a total denial of legal protection for same-sex couples was now no longer an option, the opposition accepted the enactment of a special law for same-sex relationships by creating a separate institution similar to the German concept of life partnership. Furious with this proposal, marriage equality supporters criticized the "Special Law Camp" that reinforced discrimination by creating a separate but unequal system. Both supporters and opponents of marriage equality mobilized their adherents on the streets to express their viewpoints.[21] On 26 December 2017, the judicial committee concluded the review process and at the time of this writing, the bills are currently awaiting further partisan consultation. The timeline for completion of this consultation has also not yet been confirmed. The leaders of the ruling party, nevertheless, seemed to have chosen to pause and observe.

[21]Lee (2016).

After 2 months, the newly elected Justices suddenly announced that an open court would be convened on 24 March 2017, to hear Chi C-W's pending case. LGBT groups were optimistic about the outcome, as five out of the seven newly nominated Justices exhibited positive attitudes toward marriage equality during the nomination process. The Justices announced that they would hear the petitioners and the relevant authorities debate the following issues: (1) does the current Civil Code deny two persons of the same-sex the right to be legally married; (2) if the answer to the former question is yes, does this denial violate the constitutional protection of people's freedom to marry? (3) does this denial violate the constitutional protection of people's equal rights? (4) does the creation of a nonmarital institution solely for same-sex couples violate people's freedom to marry and their equal rights? The representatives of the petitioners and the Minister of the Department of Justice debated these issues. Six legal scholars were also invited to express their opinions as expert witnesses. To hear more opinions from the public and viewpoints from those in other professional fields, the Justices for the first time informally accepted a dozen "amici curiae" (friends of the court), comprising experts and members of professional groups. On 24 May 2017, the Justices announced that preventing same-sex couples from marrying under the current law is unconstitutional:

> The provisions of Chapter 2 on Marriage of Part IV on Family of the Civil Code do not allow two persons of the same sex to create a permanent union of intimate and exclusive nature for the committed purpose of managing a life together. The said provisions, to the extent of such failure, are in violation of both the people's freedom of marriage as protected by Article 22 and the people's right to equality as guaranteed by Article 7 of the Constitution.

The Justices further demanded that both the legislative and administrative authorities amend or enact laws to allow same-sex couples to marry within 2 years. The Justices stated that if the authorities fail to do so in 2 years,

> Two persons of the same sex who intend to create the said permanent union shall be allowed to have their marriage registration effectuated by the authorities in charge of household registration, by submitting a written document signed by two or more witnesses in accordance with the said Marriage Chapter. And any such two persons, once registered, shall be accorded the status of a legally recognized couple, and then enjoy the rights and bear the obligations arising for couples.

In effect, this declaration confirms that same-sex marriage is to be legalized in Taiwan within a maximum period of 2 years. The Justices, in this interpretation, succeeded in striking a balance between the judiciary and the political establishment. The interpretation avows that the insufficient protection afforded to same-sex couples in the current law violates the Constitution, while at the same time provides discretion to the administrative and legislative powers to decide how exactly the freedom of marriage shall be protected. It specifies that the formality, such as the revision of the chapter on marriage, the enactment of a special chapter in the Civil Code, the enactment of a special law, or other formalities, is within the discretion of the authorities concerned. It also emphasizes that allowing same-sex couples to marry will not affect the existing provisions regarding the obligations and rights of heterosexual spouses.

This interpretation emphasizes that the scope of the judicial review is limited to the chapter regarding marriage. This limitation omits other facets of a same-sex family's relationship, particularly the relationship of the same-sex parents and their children. This is a reasonable outcome because the legal protection of parentage was not included in the petition documents or the assigned issues prepared by the Justices. Consequently, it is likely that the authorities will avoid examining legal parentage issues, such as adoption, marital presumption, artificial reproduction, and surrogacy, in the next round of legislation. The issue of legal protection of same-sex parentage will surely be the focal point of the forthcoming legislative debate.

5 The Right to Change Legal Gender Identity

In the 1990s, the term "*tongzhi*" was solely used to refer to lesbians and gay men, but perception of the term was so positive and inclusive that it gradually became a term that included every category of sexual minority, including transgender people. Transgender activism in Taiwan dates back to the year 2000 when the first transgender group, the Taiwan Transgender Butterfly Garden (hereinafter TG Garden), was established. In May 2003, a transsexual woman, Lin K-H, committed suicide as a result of being surrounded by a society that was hostile and cruel toward transgender people. LGBT groups held a large memorial for Lin K-H to raise social awareness for transgender people's rights and equality.

In 1988, the Ministry of the Interior permitted the change of legal gender with the requirement of a medical diagnosis of primary transsexualism, signed by two psychologists, and medical proof demonstrating that sex reassignment surgery, including the removal of the sexual organs and reconstruction of the genitals, had been completed. The process of sex reassignment surgery is expensive and dangerous; therefore, authorities sometimes approved the application for change of legal gender even when the applicants had not undergone the reconstructive surgery. As a result of the efforts of TG Garden and other LGBT groups, this practice finally became legal after the Ministry of the Interior issued a directive in 2008 that explicitly stated the prerequisites for a change of legal gender: (1) for both male-to-female and female-to-male applicants: medical opinions on a diagnosis of primary transsexualism, signed by two psychologists; (2) for female-to-male applicants: medical proof confirming the removal of the female sex organs, including the breasts, uterus, and ovaries; (3) for male-to-female applicants: medical proof confirming the removal of the male sex organs, including the penis and testicles. However, this achievement was not the end point for transgender activism.

This requirement still implies that transsexuality is a mental disease, which has been refuted since it was finally depathologized in 2013 by the American Psychiatric Association.[22] Furthermore, transgender people who are in the process of transitioning must choose whether to endure surgery to remove their sexual organs if they wish their legal identity to be consistent with their gender identity. In 2012, another transgender group, the Intersex, Transgender and Transsexual People Care Association (hereinafter ITTCA), began to advocate for the removal of surgery as a requirement for a gender identity change. In December 2013, the ITTCA and the Department of Health reached an agreement that "gender identity is a basic human right and that it is not necessary to force or require extirpation of the reproductive organs."

In June 2014, the ITTCA and other transgender groups submitted a shadow report during the review process of the National Report of the Convention on the Elimination of all Forms of Discrimination against Women (CEDAW).[23] These groups criticized this current oppressive requirement of legal gender recognition, stating that it violates the right to health and human dignity of transgender people. The review's conclusions and recommendations accepted the argument and recommended that the government take appropriate action to abolish this discriminatory requirement.[24] In 2015, the Ministry of the Interior convened three meetings with different departments, experts, and transgender groups to discuss how to change one's legal identity if removal of sexual organs is not a requirement. A draft of a new administrative ordinance was proposed during this discussion. It adopted an alternative approach for transgender people who have no intention of having their sexual organs removed. These transgender people can apply to change their gender assigned at birth if they provide the diagnosis of gender dysphoria signed by two psychologists, proof of their nonmarital status or the approval of the spouse, and an affidavit attesting that the applicants will not return to their original gender. However, issuance of the new ordinance was postponed because the draft was strongly opposed by anti-LGBT rights groups.[25]

[22]In 2013, the American Psychiatric Association published the *Diagnostic and Statistical Manual of Mental Disorders* (DSM-5), which redefined the diagnosis by eliminating the misleading term "Gender Identity Disorder" and recognized that appropriately evaluated transgender and gender variant individuals can benefit greatly from medical and surgical gender transition treatments. See American Psychiatric Association (2013).

[23]Convention on Elimination of all Forms of Discrimination against Women Information (2017) http://www.cedaw.org.tw/tw/en-global/download/index/1. Accessed 25 Dec 2017.

[24]Conclusions and Recommendations of the Review Committee, Review of Taiwan's Second Report on the Implementation of the CEDAW [消除對婦女一切形式歧視公約 (CEDAW) 中華民國 (臺灣) 第 2 次國家報告審查委員會總結意見與建議] (2014) para 34. http://www.cedaw.org.tw/tw/en-global/download/downloadFile/149. Accessed 25 Dec 2017.

[25]See Intersex, Transgender and Transsexual People Care Association [性別不明關懷協會] (2015).

6 Conclusion

Taiwan has proven, through its attitude toward LGBT rights, that it is in every respect one of the most progressive countries in Asia, not just due to its recognition of same-sex marriages. The active LGBT rights movements constitute one of the main contributors toward this achievement. LGBT rights activists have worked extensively on issues relating to LGBT people's rights and equality to create a more liberal and equal environment for LGBT people. In recent years, however, Taiwan has also witnessed a strong backlash against LGBT rights, similar to that in many countries during the past few decades. In 2011, an anti-LGBT rights organization, the True Love Coalition, initiated a mass petition movement demanding that the education authorities exclude gay and lesbian education from the school curriculum.[26] The anti-LGBT campaign circulated false information and misleading and libelous accusations in order to appeal to the public for support.[27] After the TAPCPR bill of marriage equality was proposed, two coalitions of anti-LGBT groups were established in 2013: one was the Taiwan Family Guardian Coalition, and the other was the Coalition for the Happiness of Our Next Generation. Through grassroots networks of different religious groups and parent organizations, these anti-LGBT forces rapidly gathered and effectively mobilized. The aim of this backlash was not only to delay the prospective legal advancement for the protection of LGBT rights but also to undermine the existing progress that LGBT activism had worked for decades to achieve. The government was torn between the two opposing viewpoints held by its citizens and thus remained silent on many policies it had formerly vowed to support. The rise of certain right-wing ideologies has also caused setbacks to many human rights achievements in Western countries, such as France, Austria, and the United States.[28] Similarly, due to the emergence of anti-LGBT movements in Taiwan, the time frame for the advancement of the protection of LGBT rights has become indefinite.[29] Whether the right-wing forces will decline because of the 2017 constitutional decision on marriage equality still remains to be observed. One certainty is that the road toward steady advancement in LGBT rights will probably be a bumpy one for the next several years.[30]

---

[26]See Taiwan Gender Equity Education Association (2013).

[27]Authors of the gay education materials decided to sue the True Love Coalition for libel in 2012. The prosecutor dismissed the case in the following year.

[28]Joffe (2017).

[29]See Rauhala (2017).

[30]*Id.*

References

American Psychiatric Association (ed) (2013) The Diagnostic and Statistical Manual of Mental Disorders (DSM-5), 5th edn. American Psychiatric Association, Washington, DC

Bi H (2000) From equality between two sexes to gender equality [從兩姓平等到性別平等]. Gender Equity Education [性別平等教育季刊] 13:125–132

Conclusions and Recommendations of the Review Committee, Review of Taiwan's Second Report on the Implementation of the CEDAW [消除對婦女一切形式歧視公約 (CEDAW) 中華民國(臺灣)第 2 次國家報告審查委員會總結意見與建議] (2014) http://www.cedaw.org.tw/tw/en-global/download/downloadFile/149. Accessed 25 Dec 2017

Convention on the elimination of all forms of discrimination against women information (2017) http://www.cedaw.org.tw/tw/en-global/download/index/1. Accessed 25 Dec 2017

Huang JH (2003) For the first time the Taipei city sex equality committee fined the employer for discrimination against gay, CAN News, 27 Nov 2003

Intersex, Transgender and Transsexual People Care Association [性別不明關懷協會] (2015) Public Records of the Meetings regarding Gender Recognition [研商性別變更認定及登記程序相關事宜會議記錄]. http://www.istscare.org/gender-recognition-opendoc/. Accessed 20 Sept 2017

Joffe J (2017) The right is rising and social democracy is dying across Europe—but why? The Guardian. https://www.theguardian.com/commentisfree/2017/sep/29/right-social-democracy-dying-europe-afd-far-right-germany. Accessed 25 Dec 2017

Judicial Yuan (2017) Press release on the same-sex marriage case. http://www.judicial.gov.tw/constitutionalcourt/p10_02.asp?id=267570. Accessed 25 Aug 2017

Lee W (2016) Pro- and anti-gay marriage demonstrators rally in Taipei. Taiwan News. https://www.taiwannews.com.tw/en/news/3031855. Accessed 20 Oct 2017

Rauhala E (2017) A backlash against same-sex marriage tests Taiwan's reputation for gay rights. The Washington Post. https://www.washingtonpost.com/world/asia_pacific/a-backlash-against-same-sex-marriage-tests-taiwans-reputation-for-gay-rights/2017/04/19/f855c8b8-2004-11e7-bcd6-6d1286bc177d_story.html?utm_term=.ea45f1a21f03. Accessed 24 Oct 2017

Sutton T, Harding B (2017) Why Taiwan's gay marriage ruling matters. The Diplomat. http://thediplomat.com/2017/06/why-taiwans-gay-marriage-ruling-matters/. Accessed 25 Aug 2017

Taiwan Association for Human Rights (2001) LGBT Rights [同志人權]. In Taiwan Association for Human Rights (ed) Taiwan Human Rights Report of 2000 [二千年人權報告]. Taiwan Association for Human Rights, Taipei, pp 139–146. https://issuu.com/digitaltahr/docs/a012-012

Taiwan Gender Equity Education Association (2013) Chronicle of the True Love Coalition event. http://www.tgeea.org.tw/download/voice_130131-2.pdf. Accessed 20 Oct 2017

Taiwan's same-sex marriage ruling raises hopes across Asia (2017) The Strait Times. http://www.straitstimes.com/asia/east-asia/taiwans-same-sex-marriage-ruling-raises-hopes-across-asia. Accessed 25 Aug 2017

United Nations for LGBT Equality: Free & Equal (2017) Fact sheet: criminalization. https://www.unfe.org/system/unfe-43-UN_Fact_Sheets_-_FINAL_-_Criminalization_(1).pdf. Accessed 20 Sep 2017

Wang YG (1999) Gay equality movement in Taiwan [台灣男同志平權運動史]. Kaixin Yangguang [開心陽光], Taipei

Yang MY (2001) Taiwan enacts human rights law to protect homosexuals [台灣立法保護同性戀權益]. BBC Chinese. http://news.bbc.co.uk/chinese/trad/hi/newsid_1400000/newsid_1409100/1409122.stm. Accessed 20 Sep 2017

Hsiaowei Kuan is Associate Professor of Law and Director of the Center for Jurisprudence Studies at the College of Law, National Taipei University, Taiwan. She received her S.J.D. from the University of Pennsylvania School of Law. Her work addresses gender and law, legal mobilization, women's rights and LGBT rights. She co-edited a textbook on the Convention on the Elimination of All Forms of Discrimination against Women (with Wen-Chen Chang 2015) and has served as a member of the board of directors of the Awakening Foundation and a board member of Taiwan LGBT Family Advocacy.

Chapter 34
National Apology and Reinvigoration of Indigenous Rights in Taiwan

Chih-Wei Tsai (Awi Mona)

Abstract There has been a huge debate about the protection of indigenous rights in the context of legal reform. One of the focal points of the debate is how and to what extent the state's legal system and social transformation construct indigenous cultural development and needs. On 1 August 2016 Taiwan's President Tsai Ing-wen delivered a National Apology to Indigenous Peoples, which laid out a comprehensive scheme to restore historical and transitional justice for indigenous rights. In brief, this chapter focuses on the deliberation of law and legal pluralism amongst indigenous diversity. By way of empirical research, this chapter demonstrates the legal web of the state's legal system and its influence on local indigenous communities. Also, it explores how and to what extent indigenous customary laws have been incorporated and implemented through the state's legal system. To conclude, the theoretical emphasis on ontology framing distinctive bodies and processes of indigenous jurisprudence, together with the possibility of collaboration and translation between indigenous knowledge and academic disciplines, will create space for postcolonial indigenous legal consciousness, ongoing dialogues and relationship-building of self-determination and indigenous justice paradigms.

Keywords Historical and transitional justice · Indigenous peoples
Legal pluralism · National apology · Self-determination

Foreword

The reinvigoration of indigenous rights, such as self-government, traditional territory, traditional intellectual creations, and tribal public juristic figures, has received considerable attention in recent years in Taiwan. Despite all this attention, the conceptualization of indigenous rights is an issue that remains little understood by the general public. Who are indigenous peoples? What is meant by indigenous rights? Why has President Tsai Ing-wen apologized to the indigenous groups?

C.-W. Tsai (Awi Mona) (✉)
National Dong Hwa University, Shoufeng, Taiwan
e-mail: awimona@gms.ndhu.edu.tw

J. A. Cohen et al. (eds.), *Taiwan and International Human Rights*, Economics, Law, and Institutions in Asia Pacific, https://doi.org/10.1007/978-981-13-0350-0_34

Prior to contact with colonial settlers, indigenous territories were under the sole control of Taiwanese indigenous nations. Indigenous territorial governance depended upon traditional indigenous regulatory rules and spiritual ties. Since the arrival of the Dutch settlers in the 1600s, the dispossession of traditional lands and territories has been one of the major problems facing the indigenous peoples in Taiwan. In retrospect, the non-recognition of aboriginal titles and the absence of national reconciliation with indigenous peoples have gradually devastated the indigenous rights foundation embedded in the Constitution and constructed by the Indigenous Peoples Basic Act of 2005. Legislatively, the Indigenous Peoples Basic Act has broken new ground in the government's relationship with indigenous people. However, Taiwan's history of law-making and policy implementation has caused significant bitterness and frustration for indigenous peoples. Although Taiwan's President Tsai Ing-wen delivered the National Apology to Indigenous Peoples on 1 August 2017, which laid out a comprehensive scheme to restore historical and transitional justice for indigenous rights, the prospect that indigenous peoples will find remedies for their problems under the Indigenous Peoples Basic Act is not promising. Accordingly, this chapter views indigenous human rights based on a comparative study approach, which aims at exploring whether the existing legal design of indigenous rights corresponds to the cultural conceptualization of traditional tribal governance, and conforms with the constitutionally entrenched value of cultural diversity. This research argues that until this issue is substantially resolved, the existing uncertainties about the restoration of indigenous justice and the reinvigoration of indigenous rights will continue.

The reinvigoration of indigenous rights consists of two interlocking parts: the realization of indigenous historical and transitional justice and the implementation of aboriginal title jurisprudence. First, this chapter endeavors to discover the effects of indigenous movements on comprehensive land claims. Second, this research attempts to establish the fundamental legitimacy of aboriginal titles within the legal framework of Taiwan. I reason that identifying and affirming the legitimacy of indigenous historical and transitional justice is the keystone for the realization of indigenous rights of self-government in Taiwan.

In Taiwan, there are sixteen officially recognized indigenous nations. The population of these groups comprises roughly 2.4% of Taiwan's population. Throughout the Japanese occupation and Taiwan (Republic of China) rule, government officials continued to profess a desire to protect indigenous peoples, while also attempting to persuade them to shift from their traditional life to one of a modern-state civic member. In actual practice, indigenous communities were dispossessed of their traditional territory and mostly relocated to areas considered undesirable by the non-indigenous population. In general, a number of key social and economic indicators have shown a huge gap in development between indigenous peoples and the Taiwanese general population. Despite the extensive natural resources situated within their traditional territories, indigenous peoples are the most impoverished minority groups in Taiwan. The combination of indigenous social, cultural, and economic deficiencies and the abundance of valuable resources within their traditional lands is absurdly ironic to the indigenous peoples. Academic empirical studies have attributed these indigenous deficiencies to two critical factors. One is the non-recognition of an inherent right to land for indigenous peoples. Another factor is the general lack of indigenous control over, and effective participation in, their own affairs, such as primary education programs and indigenous land governance. The complaints by various indigenous communities conform with these studies.

In 1999 Mr. Chen Shui-bian, then the presidential candidate of the Democratic Progressive Party, signed a partnership agreement with the leaders of the Taiwan indigenous tribes as an important part of his campaign. After his election, President Chen signed another agreement with these leaders and reconfirmed his administration's intention to honor the commitments in the earlier agreement. The government pledged to ensure that indigenous peoples would have the tools to become self-sufficient and self-governing by recognizing indigenous rights to land and self-government. After his reelection for a second term in 2004, President Chen declared that the government would commit to a government-to-government relationship with the indigenous tribes and add a special indigenous chapter to the R.O.C. Constitution.

These actions opened up a new indigenous rights dialogue between the indigenous peoples and the Taiwan government. During the first 50 years under the Chinese Nationalist Party, the Taiwan government engaged in a series of inappropriate policies designed to control, subjugate, and assimilate the indigenous peoples. After President Chen assumed office, the government took some positive steps. The Indigenous Peoples Basic Act stipulates that the government should recognize indigenous land rights and assist the development of self-government based on the will of each tribe. However, despite policy developments and emerging indigenous legislation, indigenous rights still lack substantiation.

Indigenous self-government has always been an important channel through which to reconstruct the special relationship between indigenous peoples and the nation-state. Now, however, the Taiwanese government is flaunting its pledge to restore indigenous historical and transitional justice. This is a serious issue facing implementation of the indigenous right to self-government. Apart from unsuccessful specialized legislation, the Indigenous Peoples Basic Act, on the other hand, reflects the principles of self-governance and of the participatory informed consent mechanism, which conceive multi-models of indigenous self-government. Nevertheless, an important revision has been added to the Indigenous Peoples Basic Act, i.e., *buluo* (部落) can now act as a public juristic person with ratification by the central authority. This research dwells upon avoiding the national legal framework which may place indigenous self-government in a structure of uniformity and homogenization, and act to further the termination of the *sui generis* nature of indigenous rights.

To elaborate, this research embraces two primary goals: (1) to understand the unique status of indigenous rights in Taiwan and to discover whether indigenous peoples can establish aboriginal title claims within the legal framework of Taiwan; (2) to explore the relationship between the National Apology and the reinvigoration of indigenous rights. The basis of my argument is that indigenous peoples' rights will continue to be undermined and subsumed into a Han ideology of discrimination and assimilation unless the National Apology to indigenous people is recognized and strengthened.

1 A Reconceptualization of Indigenous Peoples' Rights in an International Context

Everything about indigenous peoples is inextricably interwoven with, and connected to, the land. The indigenous struggle for land rights has largely been defined by the common law doctrine of "discovery and conquest" and the doctrine of "*terra nullius*."[1] The United States used the discovery doctrine to justify the takeover of Indian lands. In a similar fashion, Australian law used the concept of *terra nullius*, the legal myth that Australia had no previous owners.[2] However, classical international law held that only vacant land could be claimed by discovery, not land that was owned and occupied by indigenous peoples. The U.S. courts have been inconsistent in characterizing indigenous rights, employing rationales based on a limited interpretation of Indian sovereignty as well as reasoning based on the concept of the original Indian title.[3]

In actuality, the discovery doctrine is one of the most misunderstood concepts of international law. This principle was manipulated by Europeans to rationalize their presence in the New World and elsewhere on lands previously inhabited by indigenous peoples. Because most lands had inhabitants and the traditional legal doctrine hindered expansion, the term *terra nullius* was expanded to include lands that were uncultivated according to European standards, i.e., where the inhabitants had no fixed residence and roamed the territory like a "wild beast in a forest."[4] Additionally, under the doctrine of discovery, the discoverer gained title good against all other Europeans, but it was not a perfect title as against original

[1]Tully (1994b), pp. 158–169.

[2]Milirrpum v. Nabalco Pty Ltd and the Commonwealth of Australia, (1971) 17 FLR 141 [hereinafter the Gove Land Rights Case]; Mabo v. Queensland (No. 2), (1992) 175 CLR 1. The *Gove Land Rights Case* reinforced the conservative legal position that before colonization Australia was *terra nullius* and that aboriginal titles could not be enforced in the common law of Australia. It was not until the *Mabo* decision that the principle of *terra nullius* was implemented.

[3]Early well-noted cases, known as the 'Marshall Trilogy,' established the foundations for the development of the U.S. Federal Indian Law and Policy. See Johnson v. McIntosh, 21 U.S. (8 Wheat) 543 (1823); Worcester v. Georgia, 31 US (6 Pet.) 515 (1832) [hereinafter *Worcester v. Georgia*]; and Cherokee Nation v. Georgia, 30 U.S. 1 (1831).

[4]Robert Gray, A Good Speed to Virginia, quoted by Porter (1979).

inhabitants.[5] The lands "discovered" by Europeans were in fact already owned by indigenous peoples and governed by the laws and traditions of indigenous societies. The discovery doctrine, according to Michael C. Blumm, "was a principle of international law which sought to reconcile European notions of land ownership and sovereignty with aboriginal possession."[6] However, the most that discovery could do was to grant priority to the discovering state vis-à-vis other potential colonizers in pursuing trade with or purchasing land from the indigenous nations.

Thus, the doctrine of discovery, inasmuch as it has been used to justify claims of sovereignty over indigenous lands, is a legal fiction without justification. Its purported justification is the prejudicial treatment of indigenous peoples simply based on the fact that they were not Christians at the time of the European arrival. By stripping indigenous peoples of most of their lands and the power to govern themselves, the discovery doctrine stands as a monumental violation not only of the most fundamental human rights of indigenous peoples but also of the "natural rights" of humankind.

Perhaps the most fundamental justification for indigenous rights is that indigenous peoples lived on and occupied the land before the arrival of the colonial settlers. A claim of prior occupancy suggests that, all other things being equal, a prior occupant of land possesses a stronger claim to that land than subsequent settlers.[7] Aboriginal title stems from this prior occupancy. Hence, aboriginal title is "a right to the land itself" which is proprietary in nature.[8]

Along with the ongoing development of indigenous rights in the international regime, aboriginal title as an indigenous inherent right creates a *sui generis* form of property within a number of national legal systems.[9] Furthermore, this form of

---

[5]*Worcester v. Georgia*. In Marshall's decision, "This principle, acknowledged by all Europeans, because it was the interests of all to acknowledge it, gave to the nation making the discovery, as its inevitable consequence, the sole right of acquiring the soil and of making settlements on it. It was an exclusive principle which shut out the right of competition among those who had agreed to it; not one which could annul the previous rights of those who had not agreed to it (namely, the indigenous peoples). It regulated the right given by discovery among the European discoverers; but could not affect the rights of those already in possession, either as aboriginal occupants or as occupants by virtue of a discovery made before the memory of man."

[6]Blumm (2004), p. 714.

[7]Macklem (2001), p. 78.

[8]Delgamuukw v. British Columbia, [1998] 1 C.N.L.R. 14 (S.C.C.).

[9]Guerin v. The Queen, [1984] 2 S.C.R. 335. (It is true that the *sui generis* interest that the Indians have in the land is personal in the sense that it cannot be transferred to a grantee, but it is also true that the interest gives rise upon surrender to a distinctive fiduciary obligation on the part of the Crown to deal with the land for the benefit of the surrendering Indians.) *Mabo, supra* note 2. (Native title has its origins in and is given its content by the traditional customs observed by the indigenous inhabitants of a territory. The nature and incidents of native title must be ascertained as a matter of fact by reference to those laws and customs.) *Begay v. Keedah*, 19 Indian L. Rep. 6021 (Navajo Supreme Court 1991). (Traditional Navajo land tenure is not the same as English common law tenure, as used in the United States. The Navajo have always occupied land in family units, using the land for subsistence. Families and subsistence residential units [as they are sometimes called] hold land in the form of communal ownership.)

property has been complemented by a number of international instruments to protect indigenous interests in land over the past three decades. The international initiative has been spearheaded by the International Labour Organization (ILO), which expressly safeguards aboriginal title in its groundbreaking Convention No. 169 of 1989.[10] In Robert A. Williams Jr.'s words, it is "international law's most concrete manifestation of the growing recognition of indigenous peoples rights to property in lands."[11] In the inter-American sphere, indigenous rights to land are strengthened in the American Declaration on the Rights of Indigenous Peoples.[12] Additionally, indigenous peoples have a deep relationship with the land on which they live. Thus, indigenous rights to land, territory, and resources cannot be separated from traditional indigenous forms of property and cultural survival. As Article XXV of the American Declaration states:

1. Indigenous peoples have the right to maintain and strengthen their distinctive spiritual, cultural, and material relationship with their lands, territories, and resources and to uphold their responsibilities to preserve them for themselves and for future generations.
2. Indigenous peoples have the right to the lands, territories and resources which they have traditionally owned, occupied or otherwise used or acquired.
3. Indigenous peoples have the right to own, use, develop and control the lands, territories and resources that they possess by reason of traditional ownership or other traditional occupation or use, as well as those which they have otherwise acquired.
4. States shall give legal recognition and protection to these lands, territories and resources. Such recognition shall be conducted with due respect to the customs, traditions and land tenure systems of the indigenous peoples concerned.

One of the most important international initiatives for indigenous peoples is the United Nations Declaration on the Rights of Indigenous Peoples,[13] which provides

---

[10]International Labour Organization Convention No. 169 Concerning Indigenous and Tribal Peoples in Independent Countries, 27 Jun 1989 (entered into force 5 Sept 1991). Detailed provisions for the protection of indigenous land rights are framed in Part II of Convention. In particular, Article 14(1) provides that, [t]he rights of ownership and possessions of the peoples concerned over the lands which they traditionally occupy shall be recognized. In addition, measures shall be taken in appropriate cases to safeguard the rights of the peoples concerned to use lands not exclusively occupied by them, but to which they have traditionally had access for their subsistence and traditional activities. Particular attention shall be paid to the situation of nomadic peoples and shifting cultivators in this respect.

[11]Robert A. Williams, Jr., *Amicus Curiae Brief* (presented by the National Congress of American Indians in the case of the Mayagna (Sumo) Community of Awas Tingni), Inter-American Court of Human Rights Case No. 11.577.

[12]American Declaration on the Rights of Indigenous Peoples, AG/RES. 2888 (XLVI-O/16) (15 June 2016).

[13]United Nations Declaration on the Rights of Indigenous Peoples, G.A. Res. 61/295, UN Doc. A/RES/61/295 (13 Sept 2007), 46 I.L.M. 1013 (2007) [hereinafter UN Declaration on the Rights of Indigenous Peoples].

further evidence of the increasingly international recognition of indigenous peoples' land property rights. Article 26 of the Declaration reads:

1. Indigenous peoples have the right to the lands, territories and resources which they have traditionally owned, occupied or otherwise used or acquired.
2. Indigenous peoples have the right to own, use, develop and control the lands, territories and resources that they possess by reason of traditional ownership or other traditional occupation or use, as well as those which they have otherwise acquired.
3. States shall give legal recognition and protection to these lands, territories and resources. Such recognition shall be conducted with due respect to the customs, traditions and land tenure systems of the indigenous peoples concerned.[14]

In short, aboriginal title as indigenous peoples' inherent right is inextricably interconnected with international instruments. We can observe a pattern of activity by the UN bodies and other international organizations, such as the OAS, in conjunction with numerous state practices. According to Robert A. Williams Jr., "The international norms that recognize rights based on indigenous peoples traditional landholdings and resource use are increasingly incorporated and reflected in the domestic legal practice of states throughout the American region and the world."[15] These activities demonstrate a steadily broadening consensus that aboriginal title is a rule of customary international law.[16]

2 Indigenous Peoples Rights in Contemporary Taiwan

Historically, indigenous peoples have been excluded from having any meaningful input into how, when, and why governmental policies concerning their affairs are implemented. This situation changed somewhat after the establishment of the Council of Indigenous Peoples, Executive Yuan, in 1996. The new indigenous policy finally opens the door to communications and negotiations between indigenous peoples and the Taiwan government. Since the Council was established, indigenous people have had some influence on legislation affecting their rights.[17]

In the contemporary era, indigenous Zìrán Zhǔquán (自然主權, inherent sovereignty) and self-determination have become major issues on the national and

[14]UN Declaration on the Rights of Indigenous Peoples. Relevant provisions are Article 25 and Article 27.

[15]Williams, *supra*, note 11.

[16]Wiessner (1999), p. 109. As Wiessner concludes, "Today, many of these proposed or actual prescriptions, coinciding, as they do, with domestic state practice … have created a new set of shared expectations about the legal status and rights of indigenous peoples that has matured and crystallized into customary international law."

[17]For examples, the Indigenous Peoples Basic Law, the Indigenous Peoples Employment Rights Protection Act, the Status Act For Indigenous Peoples, and the Indigenous Peoples Education Act.

international stages. Since the 1990s, the indigenous movements in Taiwan have concentrated on two interlocking goals related to inherent sovereignty and self-determination: self-government rights and traditional territorial claims. In the first changeover of power in 2000–2004, Taiwan President Chen Shui-bian signed and reconfirmed the semi-official alliance treaty, "A New Partnership between Aborigines and the Taiwanese Government,"[18] with indigenous representatives. This alliance treaty purported to foster indigenous self-determination and economic development. In 2004, the Taiwan government, under Chen's presidency, further announced that it would structure its relations with indigenous tribes on a Guó yu Guó (國與國, Nation-to-Nation) basis. Finally, a milestone accomplishment for indigenous rights was reached when President Chen signed the Yuánzhùmínzú Jīběnfǎ (原住民族基本法, the Indigenous Peoples Basic Act) in January 2005, which is designed to implement a new policy of indigenous human rights.

The Indigenous Peoples Basic Act, however, is seen as being out of step with the bulk of Taiwanese traditional law because it singles out a segment of the society on the basis of race. The Basic Act removes significant portions of indigenous property from the commercial mainstream and gives the Council of Indigenous Peoples and other government officials a degree of discretion that is not only intrusive but also offensive to other members of the society. For example, the exercise of indigenous hunting rights within the national parks has created tensions between groups advocating the preservation of indigenous culture and environmental conservation groups. Furthermore, the Basic Act requires that any economic or development activity within Yuánzhùmínzú Chuántǒng lǐngyù (原住民族傳統領域, indigenous traditional territory) proposed by the government or a non-indigenous party must be approved by, and share its benefits with, the local indigenous community. The Basic Act has been criticized in every respect. The majority of opponents tend to be non-indigenous citizens who demand the Basic Act be abolished because it violates normative standards of equality. Even the National Apology to Indigenous Peoples delivered by current President Tsai emphasizes the following:

> After the democratic transition, the country began to respond to the appeals of indigenous movements. The government made certain promises and efforts. Today, we have an Indigenous Peoples Basic Act that is quite advanced. However, government agencies have not given sufficient weight to this law. Our actions have not been fast enough, comprehensive enough or sound enough. For this, I apologize to the indigenous peoples on behalf of the government.

---

[18]The New-Partnership between Aborigines and the Taiwanese Government was signed on 10 September 1999 among 11 major Aboriginal representatives and the DPP presidential candidate, Mr. Chen Shui-bian. These electoral promises were further refined and discussed in the *Yuanzhuminzu zhengce baipishu* [原住民族政策白皮書] [2000 DPP] White Paper on Aboriginal Policy). On 19 October 2002, President Chen reconfirmed the treaty which thus became an official document highlighting the guiding principles of the government's platform.

In an effort to achieve self-government, indigenous peoples have sought constitutional, legislative, and policy reforms. Adoption of the Indigenous Peoples Basic Act is the most significant development in the past decades. However, indigenous peoples maintain that any form of delegated authority is inconsistent with indigenous inherent rights of land and self-government. While the existing Indigenous Peoples Basic Act is landmark legislation that has frightened the Han majority, it fails to address the fact that indigenous peoples still have serious limitations, namely, a reduced land base and restrictions on indigenous self-government.

The historical examination of Taiwan illustrates that colonial experiences imposed on the indigenous peoples manifested some similarities with the colonization experienced by the aboriginals in the New World, including "indigenous land dispossessions and colonizers' settlements," "imposed legal systems upon tribal societies," and "integrationist and assimilationist policies towards indigenous peoples."[19] However, while the principle of recognizing aboriginal title had become well-entrenched in common law jurisprudence before the end of the 19th century, after nearly two centuries it has not achieved the same recognition in Taiwan.

Nevertheless, the Taiwan government has repeatedly stated its commitment to protect indigenous human rights in a number of official pronouncements, as well as through negotiation and legislation, which aim to satisfy indigenous interests of self-government while safeguarding the integrity of the state's sovereign power. The aforementioned Indigenous Peoples Basic Act is built upon two vital issues that are the focus of this chapter, namely the rights of indigenous peoples to land and to self-government. Yet, the Indigenous Peoples Basic Act merely provides abstract recognition of these rights. The actual content and application of these rights remain uncertain and open to interpretation. The most infamous case is the promulgation of Yuánzhùmínzú Tǔdì Huò Bùluò Fànwéi Tǔdì Huàshè Bànfǎ (原住民族土地或部落範圍土地劃設辦法, Regulation on Demarcating Indigenous Peoples' Land or Tribal Land Area) issued by the Council of Indigenous Peoples in February 2017.

There has been a huge debate on the protection of indigenous rights in the context of legal reform. One of the focal points has been how and to what extent the state's legal system and social transformation construct indigenous cultural development and needs. This deliberation is embedded with academic and practical values that are not simply matters of legal history. In actuality, from a wider research framework based on law and society and law and cultures, the above-mentioned regulation is significant because it triggers the involvement of the academic community in legal transformations within the post-colonial discourse following legal reception of Western ideas of state law. A number of issues have been examined and widely discussed over the past year, such as traditional indigenous organization, conceptualizations of indigenous dispute resolution, and the establishment of a relational cultural/legal pluralistic-based judicial system.

[19]McHugh (2004), pp. 124–127, Russell (2005).

Although formal recognition of indigenous rights to land and self-government has occurred with the enactment of the Indigenous Peoples Basic Act, the issue remains controversial within Taiwan. Domestic normative and structural difficulties reduce the likelihood that the principles of indigenous self-determination, collective land rights, and self-government rights will be internalized and institutionalized within the legal framework of Taiwan.

3 Recognition of Indigenous Laws

Taiwan's Indigenous Laws are embedded in two basic theories and principles. One is cultural integrity and self-government, and the other is effective participation. Comprehensively, the core of the Indigenous Peoples Basic Act was constructed upon the concepts of Yuánzhùmínzú (原住民族, indigenous peoples) and Bùluò (部落, tribal community). Furthermore, formal recognition of aboriginal title contributes to at least two goals. First, recognition of aboriginal title affirms indigenous peoples' distinct interests in land, which are based on prior occupation and culturally and spiritually specified rights and responsibilities. Second, recognition of indigenous entitlements to land enhances indigenous peoples' right to self-determination.[20] Paradoxically, the current Taiwanese regulatory mechanisms for recognition of indigenous land entitlements fail to recognize certain aspects of indigenous interests in land, especially the collectivity of indigenous title to land.

Traditionally, the special relationship of indigenous people to land has various social, cultural, spiritual, economic and political dimensions which are collective in nature. This collective dimension is significant to traditional indigenous land tenures. In contrast, the existing Taiwanese land rights regime focuses on private, individual title and is premised on commercial, monetary values, which are "alien to the collective social organization of indigenous communities." Although the Indigenous Peoples Basic Act affirms that the government should "recognize indigenous peoples' right to land," it is unclear whether indigenous communities have the right to own land or have the right to own land collectively. The failure of the Taiwanese government to accord appropriate legal rights to traditional indigenous interests to land probably accounts for the overwhelming majority of human rights problems affecting indigenous peoples in Taiwan.

In the context of aboriginal title common law, James Tully argues for proper recognition of the distinct and pre-existing set of relations with land enjoyed by indigenous peoples before expropriation.[21] Further, Tully emphasizes the need to

[20]Daes (2001), Macklem (2001), pp. 104–106.

[21]Tully (ed) (1994a).

avoid seventeenth- to nineteenth-century cultural biases in understanding both the nature of aboriginal nations and the characteristics of the property systems of those peoples.[22] As mentioned above, a recognition of aboriginal title enhances the indigenous right of self-determination. Clearly, indigenous self-government requires that it be "indigenous peoples" who identify and articulate the interests of aboriginal title—recognition of indigenous legal authority and indigenous traditional laws.

Recognition of indigenous legal authority and indigenous traditional laws has also found strong support in international human rights laws. ILO Convention No. 169 declares that indigenous peoples must be consulted in good faith prior to the establishment of any policies that concern them and stresses that states must take into account aboriginal customary laws.[23] There is also a broad recognition of indigenous traditional laws in the UN Declaration on the Rights of Indigenous Peoples (UNDRIPs). It views the recognition, preservation and promotion of customary indigenous laws as a key element for advancing the indigenous right of self-government.[24] In particular, the UNDRIPs affirms that indigenous peoples have the right to "own, use, develop, and control the lands, territories and resources that they possess by reason of traditional ownership or other traditional occupations or use" and accords full recognition of their laws, traditions and customs, land-tenure systems and institutions for the development and management of resources.[25]

Similarly, important aspects regarding the principle of recognition of indigenous customary laws are set out in Article 34 of the UNDRIPs:

> Indigenous peoples have the right to promote, develop and maintain their institutional structures and their distinctive customs, spirituality, traditions, procedures, practices and, in the cases where they exist, juridical systems or customs, in accordance with international human rights standards.

In terms of the legitimacy and cultural "match" of the Indian tribal government, Joseph P. Kalt comments that, "governance depending on the consent of the governed hinges critically upon shared conceptions of legitimacy in the use of power and authority."[26] Legitimacy in this context means that "the governed have confidence in, and support the government."[27] Hence, indigenous peoples are

---

[22]*Id.*

[23]ILO Convention No. 169, Article 8, states, "1. In applying national laws and regulations to the peoples concerned, due regard shall be had to their customs or customary laws. 2. These peoples shall have the right to retain their own customs and institutions, where these are not incompatible with fundamental rights defined by the national legal system and with internationally recognized human rights."

[24]The preamble to the UN Declaration on the Rights of Indigenous Peoples states, "*Recognizing also* that respect for indigenous knowledge, cultures and traditional practices contributes to sustainable and equitable development and proper management of the environment."

[25]Article 26 of the UN Declaration on the Rights of Indigenous Peoples.

[26]Kalt (2006), p. 197.

[27]Chartrand (2006).

entitled to develop institutions of self-government appropriate to their circumstances and to match the reality of their contemporary indigenous cultures.

The close interdependence of indigenous peoples, their lands and their customary laws has been recognized in international law.[28] It is also evident that the recognition of indigenous traditional laws can lead to effective implementation of both indigenous rights of self-determination and self-government, two core objectives of the UNDRIPs. Since the 2000s, ethnic relations in Taiwan have changed from an assimilationist framework to a new multicultural approach based on the partnership between the indigenous peoples and the Taiwan government. Indigenous rights are not constitutionally recognized nor are their own traditional governance authorities, which form the political and legal barriers that prevent indigenous peoples from full realization of the right to self-government. In addition, disparities continue to exist between the indigenous and non-indigenous populations with regard to employment, income, health, education, and access to the court system. In the course of indigenous empowerment, nothing illustrates this process better than the complex issue of indigenous land rights. I see the economic aspect as the short-term goal and social justice empowerment as an interim measure. By securing the financial capacity and consolidating the institutional measures, indigenous peoples in Taiwan may have a better chance of achieving self-government.

4 Conclusion

More than 540,000 people living in Taiwan are descendants of the Austronesian people who had a rich, self-sufficient culture on the island until Europeans started arriving 400 years ago. These indigenous peoples established their own sovereignty and operated a constitutional regime. In 1895, these independent political entities were conquered by the Japanese Empire, and fifty years later they were annexed by the Republic of China. The successive change in colonial regimes has taken its toll on the indigenous peoples and has resulted in the loss of most of their lands. Furthermore, during some periods of colonial rule, indigenous people were prohibited from speaking their language and discouraged from practicing their cultural traditions. Ever since Taiwan became a part of the R.O.C. in 1945, and particularly

[28]World Commission on Environment and Development (The Brundtland Commission) (1987). According to the report of the Brundtland Commission, "The starting point for a just and humane policy for such groups is the recognition and protection of their traditional rights to land and other resources that sustain their way of life—rights they may define in terms that do not fit into standard legal systems. These groups' own institutions to regulate rights and obligations are crucial for maintaining harmony with nature and the environmental awareness characteristic of the traditional way of life. Hence, the recognition of traditional rights must go hand in hand with measures to protect the local institutions that enforce responsibility in resource use. And this recognition must also give local communities a decisive voice in the decisions about resource use in their areas."

beginning in the 1970s, an indigenous movement has been underway, and indigenous peoples now want to regain control over their land and their right to govern themselves.

The protection of indigenous rights and traditional cultures, from 1980 onward, along with the UN advocacy for international indigenous human rights, have received considerable attention in recent years both domestically and internationally. On 2 February 2005 enactment of the Indigenous Peoples Basic Act signified a new milestone for the legalization and justification of indigenous rights and traditional cultures. A preliminary study of the Indigenous Peoples Basic Act shows that the legislative foundations of contemporary indigenous rights are built upon the following principles: (1) Indigenous historical and transitional justice; (2) Realization of multiculturalism and substantial equality; and (3) Effectuation of indigenous autonomy, self-government, and self-determination.

Paragraphs 11 and 12 of Additional Article 10 of the ROC Constitution, which affirms existing indigenous rights and multiculturalism, have acquired constitutional status of basic rights by virtue of the adoption of the ICCPR, the ICESCR and its Implementing Act. In addition, the relationships and connections to the land and natural resources are the bases for indigenous identity and their spiritual and cultural distinctions within indigenous traditional society. Therefore, land and natural resources are widely recognized as the core elements of indigenous cultures, which have been substantiated through the Indigenous Peoples Basic Act into a bundle of indigenous cultural rights, including rights to land, natural resources, self-government, customary laws, traditional knowledge, and free, prior, and informed consent.

The paradigm within which the Taiwanese government addresses indigenous issues is, for the most part, consistent with that endorsed by the UNDRIPs and other UN international human rights instruments. However, this chapter has shown that states with superior political, economic and military power have control over the norms and rules of international law and can selectively control their implementation. As currently enacted, Yuánzhùmínzú Tǔdì Huò Bùluò Fànwéi Tǔdì Huàshè Bànfǎ (原住民族土地或部落範圍土地劃設辦法, Regulation of Demarcating Indigenous Peoples Land or Tribal Land Area) has impaired the ability of indigenous peoples to enjoy their right of self-government.

The modern legal system in Taiwan is based upon the Westernized idea of individual liberalism. This individualized-focused regime cannot accommodate indigenous traditional cultural habitus, nor can it realize indigenous community life rules. From the standpoint of cultural relativism and indigenous self-determination, the main concern of this chapter is how to harmonize the constitutionality of individual rights and the cultural integrity and identity of indigenous collective rights within the liberal multiculturalist structure.

To conclude, the questions surrounding the Taiwanese indigenous peoples rights to land and self-government, which originated from historical and transitional justice, are problematic primarily for three different reasons. First, the legislation about the concept is unclear; second, the rights depend on historical relationships; and third, the rights are a source of conflict. This chapter begins with the active development and presentation of indigenous rights in the international and domestic regime. Next, taking the view of indigenous human rights based on a comparative study approach, it aims to explore whether the existing legal design of indigenous rights corresponds to the cultural conceptualization of traditional tribal governance is in conformity with the constitutionally entrenched value of cultural diversity.

President Tsai Ing-wen stressed in the National Apology to Indigenous Peoples that,

> I know that even now, there are some around us who see no need to apologize. But that is the most important reason why I am representing the government to issue this apology today. To see what was unfair in the past as a matter of course, or to treat the pain of other ethnic peoples as an unavoidable part of human development, this is the first mindset that we, standing here today, resolve to change and overturn.

Rather than seeking formal statehood, however, indigenous peoples seek legitimacy and authority as juridical subjects within the Taiwanese state. In reviewing the state's relationship with indigenous peoples, the core issue remains: how can, and how should, the state empower the autonomy and effectiveness of indigenous governance in the relationship between indigenous peoples and cultural integrity? Overall, the goal of this chapter is to study how indigenous communities come to be imagined as a "nation," creating a society in which such independent nations within postmodern states can share power in a spirit of mutual respect.

References

Blumm MC (2004) Retracing the discovery doctrine: aboriginal title, tribal sovereignty, and their significance to treaty-making and modern natural resources policy in Indian country. Vermont Law Rev 28:713–777, at 714

Chartrand P (2006) International expert group meeting on the millennium development goals. In: Lah, P. (ed) Indigenous participation and good governance (UN Permanent Forum on Indigenous Issues) PFII/2006/WS.3/4. New York, 11–13 Jan 2006

Daes EI (2001) Prevention of discrimination and protection of indigenous peoples and minorities. In: Indigenous peoples and their relationship to land (Final working paper E/CN.4/Sub.2/2001/21)

Kalt JP (2006) Constitutional rule and the effective governance of native nations. In: Lemont ED (ed) American Indian constitutional reform and the rebuilding of native nations. University of Texas Press, Texas, pp 184–219, at 197

Macklem P (2001) Indigenous difference and the constitution of Canada. University of Toronto Press, Toronto, p 78

McHugh PG (2004) Aboriginal societies and the common law: a history of sovereignty, status, and self-determination. Oxford University Press, Oxford, pp 124–127

Porter RG (1979) A good speed to Virginia, quoted by Harry C. Porter in The inconstant savage: England and the North American Indian 1500–1660. Duckworth, London (Southwest Books Services)

Russell PH (2005) Recognizing aboriginal title: the Mabo case and indigenous resistance to English-settler colonialism. University of Toronto Press, Toronto

Tully J (ed) (1994a) Philosophy in an age of pluralism: essays in honour of Charles Taylor. Cambridge University Press, Cambridge

Tully J (1994b) Aboriginal property and Western theory: recovering a middle ground. In: Paul EF, Miller FD Jr., Paul J (eds) Property rights. Cambridge University Press, Cambridge

Wiessner S (1999) Rights and status of indigenous peoples: a global comparative and international legal analysis. Harv Hum Rights J 12: 57–128

World Commission on Environment and Development [The Brundtland Commission] (1987) Our common future. Oxford University Press, Oxford

Chih-Wei Tsai (Awi Mona) is the first indigenous person in the country to obtain a doctoral degree in Law. He is now Associate Professor at the National Dong Hwa University Institute of Financial and Economic Law. He teaches primarily in the areas of Indigenous Law, Aboriginal Title Law, and Cultural Law. Since 2007, he has continuously worked on extensive collaborations on indigenous rights movements with local communities in Taiwan, as well as providing legal and policy advice on a wide variety of indigenous law and related issues. Tsai is a member of the Seediq Nation.

Chapter 35
Local Images of Global Child Rights: CRC in Taiwan

Amy Huey-Ling Shee

Abstract Globalization has brought about cross-border socio-cultural, politico-economic and technological exchanges while instantaneous communications have allowed knowledge and culture to be shared around the world simultaneously. Thus "global law" denotes the cross-border development of legal norms that involve a transnational legal culture of a pluralistic nature. In the trend of globalization, general rules of international conventions and treaties are adopted as local laws to accelerate national development. Socio-legal research has observed that global legal rules and concepts function in radically different ways in various local contexts. This draws our attention to how international rules are enforced by national legislation in books vis-à-vis the living law in local practice. The UN Convention on the Rights of the Child (CRC) is a manifest of global law on children's rights with 198 state members. Although Taiwan is not a UN member, the "Enforcement Act of the Convention on the Rights of the Child" (the Act) of 20 November 2014 has mandated self-executory effects of the CRC provisions on child rights as national laws. This chapter aims to review how the CRC has been integrated into Taiwan's laws and social practices since its promulgation in 1989. It also attempts to observe the differences made by the 2014 CRC Enforcement Act to promote the rights of children in Taiwan and to examine how the global law principles of the CRC can be implemented in an East Asian, Confucian society. The development of global law calls for a new methodology for comparative study that requires joint efforts by cross-border interdisciplinary experts.

Keywords Convention on the rights of the child · Enforcement act of the convention on the rights of the child · Exclusion · Globalization
Global law · Glocalization · Inclusion · Socio-legal studies

A. H.-L. Shee (✉)
Taiwan Legal Information Institute, National Chung Cheng University, Chiayi, Taiwan
e-mail: lawamy@ccu.edu.tw

J. A. Cohen et al. (eds.), *Taiwan and International Human Rights*, Economics, Law, and Institutions in Asia Pacific, https://doi.org/10.1007/978-981-13-0350-0_35

1 Prelude

If human rights are granted to every person on an equal basis, should the civil, political, economic, gender and development rights of a person diverge simply because of one's nationality? In theory, it is easy for human rights advocates to stand for inclusion against exclusion. In reality, however, the global human rights discourse invokes the term "state party" to exclude countries not recognized by the United Nations. Debates over whether Taiwan is part of China have appeared in the daily media around the world. The PRC is the sole recognized Chinese state party to the UN Conventions. However, Taiwan has *de facto* independent administrative, legislative and judicial organs under the governance of the UN de-recognized Republic of China (UN Resolution 2758, 1971). This makes Taiwan a unique case in the realization of international treaties. Despite this political reality, international human rights treaties do not allow any kind of discrimination to be imposed upon Taiwan's people. Over the decades, Taiwan (ROC) has mandated various paths to enter global society as an active member, including the WTO. In recent years, the ROC government has unilaterally recognized the UN's major human rights conventions by passing the Enforcement Acts to mandate compliance at the central and local levels. Consequently, national reports have been published to invite international reviews, after which legislative, administrative and judicial changes have been made in response.

It is therefore worthwhile to observe how Taiwan manages to bypass the walls and borders created by international politics. This chapter tells the story of Taiwan's attempt to join the global human rights network by using the example of the UN Convention on the Rights of the Child (hereinafter CRC). The CRC is the most popular of the UN Conventions, having 196 parties. Out of these parties, 192 are UN-recognized states and the 4 others are political entities, excluding Taiwan. Despite its political exclusion, Taiwan authorities and civil society are committed to realizing the CRC. Although Taiwan's children's rights issues still cannot be heard at official UN meetings, the CRC "initial report" of Taiwan (ROC) has been completed according to UN Guidelines.[1] Legislative amendments are on the way to meet the Convention without reservations.[2] Administrative measures at all government levels are geared toward implementing the CRC.[3]

---

[1]See the Taiwan government website of the Social and Family Affairs Administration, Ministry of Health and Welfare for the Report: Guojia Baogao [國家報告]. http://www.sfaa.gov.tw/SFAA/Pages/List.aspx?nodeid=606. Accessed 6 Apr 2017.

[2]See the Taiwan government website of the Social and Family Affairs Administration, Ministry of Health and Welfare for the review on laws: Fagui Jianshi [法規檢視]. http://www.sfaa.gov.tw/SFAA/Pages/List.aspx?nodeid=582. Accessed 6 Apr 2017.

[3]The Executive Yuan (Cabinet) of Taiwan has set up a Child Rights and Welfare Committee to coordinate the relevant work of the CRC in all concerned authorities, including the judiciary and the legislature. See Xingzhengyuan Ertong ji Shaonian Fuli yu Quanyi Tuidong Xiaozu [行政院兒童及少年福利與權益推動小組]. http://www.sfaa.gov.tw/SFAA/Pages/List.aspx?nodeid=800. Accessed 6 Apr 2017.

Based on Article 2 of the CRC, which manifests the principle of non-discrimination, this chapter considers the following questions: What justifies the exclusion of Taiwanese children in the UN review process of the CRC national reports? Can human rights arguments work to supersede political walls and sovereign borders and let the voices of children in Taiwan be heard in global society?

In order to elaborate on and discuss the above questions, this chapter first gives an historical account of the evolving status of Taiwan vis-à-vis the UN conventions. Mechanisms concerning the protection and promotion of children's rights in Taiwan will then be introduced to show a unique case of the CRC in terms of its global recognition and local realization.

2 Localization of Global Human Rights Laws

Under modernization theory, developing countries translated and borrowed foreign laws to achieve internationalization. At the turn of this century, globalization brought about global law which has generated cross-border legal norms that are to be transplanted into local laws and practice.[4] In the 21st century, the world has witnessed the trend of globalization. It has influenced the nature and methods of comparative studies. Socio-legal research has observed that global legal rules and concepts function in dramatically different ways in various local contexts. A global rule may function or dysfunction differently because of local beliefs, conditions, needs, and so on. This draws our attention to the needs of observing how international rules are enforced by national legislation vis-à-vis the living law in various localities. The CRC has been a manifest of global law. Although Taiwan is not a UN member, the Parliament passed the "Implementation Act of the Convention on the Rights of the Child" (the Act), which entered into force on 20 November 2014 and mandates the self-executory effects of the CRC provisions on children's rights as national laws. However, the CRC provisions have been translated and incorporated into various laws of Taiwan since 1989. So why was the Act still needed?

This study aims to review how the CRC has been adopted by Taiwan's laws and social practices since its promulgation in 1989. It also attempts to observe the differences due to the 2014 CRC Implementation Act to promote children's rights in Taiwan.

2.1 *Bridging the Sovereign Walls and Political Borders*

Formerly being among the jurisdictions that promoted the "transplant" model of comparative studies under globalization, Taiwan is now moving from simple copies

[4]See Hong and Song (2010), Michaels (2013).

of black-letter laws to an approach that gives more and more consideration to local needs.[5] Local initiatives are taken into account by law makers and practitioners to challenge the mainstream theories of globalization that emphasize modernization theory. Foreign black-letter laws and cases may have been borrowed instrumentally to help with the modernization and internationalization of Taiwan before the 1980s. However, since the lifting of martial law in 1987, social campaigns and civil group activities have brought about legislative efforts to reflect upon the localities of socio-legal conditions.[6] The story of the CRC and its enforcement law is the most self-evident example of this development.

For a country like Taiwan, to follow the currents of modernization and globalization is an inevitable tactic for survival in both the political and economic spheres. Local elites in the socio-legal disciplines have worked together to lead grassroots campaigns for human rights since the late 1980s. The advanced black-letter laws of foreign origins have been borrowed as learning models to review local laws and practices. The argument that Taiwan is a country which promotes human rights is becoming well accepted at the international level. This chapter will demonstrate how Taiwan has been implementing the UN Convention on the Rights of the Child despite political walls and boundaries.

2.2 The Unique Case of Taiwan (Republic of China)

Under the promotion of globalization, general rules of international treaties are transplanted into local laws to accelerate national development. However, it is becoming a matter of socio-legal common sense that the mere duplication of global law does not bring about local development.[7] In the realization of the UN Human Rights Conventions, contextual issues are always tackled by individual laws and societies before a state ratifies or accedes to international treaties. However, it has also been established that globalization has brought about cross-border socio-cultural, politico-economic and technological exchanges due to instantaneous communications that allow knowledge and culture to be shared around the world.[8] Therefore, the methodology of glocalization has been developed to assist global law studies. Together with socio-legal studies, glocal law looks for the contextual elements of a global legal principle.[9] In other words, local realities and socio-cultural factors are taken into consideration in the legislative process and

---

[5]See Gerber (2001), Gutteridge (1947).

[6]See Droria et al. (2014).

[7]See Halliday and Osinsky (2006).

[8]For detailed discussions, see Giddens (ed) (2001).

[9]See Roudometof (2015), p. 1.

enforcement of laws.[10] In other words, contextual information is the real essence of a human rights treaty or covenant, not the black-letter provisions.

The Republic of China (Taiwan) has, since its establishment in 1911, borrowed legislation and corresponding measures from advanced countries to achieve better development.[11] The fact that Taiwan has been denied a position in the international arena for political reasons since 1971 has pushed the ROC government in Taiwan to reinforce global conventions. At the same time, the influences of law and society studies have made dynamic changes to Asian comparative studies.[12] As the law-in-context methodology is promoted among the East Asian countries, the black-letter comparative law has been gradually redressed by local needs and considerations. This chapter thus argues that the political walls created by the traditional international-law regimes in which the members should be UN-recognized states may also be torn down like the Berlin Wall.

The position of the Republic of China (Taiwan) in the United Nations was replaced by the People's Republic of China.[13] Since then, the legitimate status of the ROC as a state party in any UN Convention has also been replaced by the PRC. The unique case of Taiwan may challenge, if not change, the conventional approach of East Asian comparative law, which has since the late 19th century looked up to the so-called "advanced" countries to search for benchmark legislation to copy. In the eyes of the United Nations, as well as those countries that have recognized the PRC as the sole legitimate government of China, Taiwan is part of the PRC. Thus, when the PRC enforces UN Conventions, the effectiveness shall cover Taiwan. When the PRC prepares a national report on any Convention, observations on Taiwan shall be included. However, this is not the case in reality as there has been independent legislation and a court system in Taiwan since 1949 when the PRC was established in Mainland China and the ROC was expelled from the Mainland.[14]

3 Practical Operations of the UN Convention on the Rights of the Child

The unique status of Taiwan in international politics has further reinforced the determination of the ROC government to enforce important global conventions on human rights, including the CRC. Globalization has also brought global law to

[10]See Deflem (2006).

[11]See details in Wang (2015), Wang (2013).

[12]See Twining (1999), p. 217.

[13]On 25 Oct 1971, the UN General Assembly passed United Nations Resolution 2758 (XXVI) which states that the People's Republic of China is the only legitimate government of China. The resolution replaced the ROC with the PRC as a permanent member of the Security Council in the United Nations. See Restoration of the lawful rights of the People's Republic of China in the United Nations. http://www.un.org/documents/ga/res/26/ares26.htm. Accessed 25 Feb 2017.

[14]See Michaels (2013).

Taiwan, which has generated social dynamics that have transferred cross-border legal norms into local laws and practices. The general belief of the people in the legitimacy of human rights laws has further accelerated this development.[15]

3.1 *Legitimacy of the CRC Enforcement Law*

Despite the fact that Taiwan is not a UN member, it has become policy for our national President to initiate the enforcement of major UN human rights laws, including the CRC. As a result, the "Implementation Act of the Convention on the Rights of the Child" came into force on 20 November 2014, which mandates the self-executing effects of the CRC provisions on children's rights as national laws (Article 2). It also requires the government to complete a CRC national report within 2 years (Article 7), to propose a priority revised list of laws within 1 year, and to amend all national and local laws according to the CRC within 5 years of the enforcement of the Implementation Law (Article 9). However, doubts have been raised as to how the CRC may be implemented in Taiwan with the semi-self-executory Enforcement Law. An interdisciplinary study may be helpful to find possible solutions.

Researchers on public and private laws as well as experts in the fields of international politics, history, criminology, and field studies have been assembled to conduct an interdisciplinary CRC study. Based on the methodologies of global law and glocalization, as opposed to the legal transplant of aspects of comparative law, a consensus has been reached that human rights should not give way to political considerations. For the unique case of Taiwan, the traditional debates between monism and dualism[16] may not apply to decide the effects of UN Conventions.

3.2 *The Page for Children's Rights in Taiwan's Legislation*

When the Declaration of the Rights of the Child was adopted by the United Nations in 1959, the ROC was one of the original signatories. The Declaration was then incorporated to initiate domestic social welfare legislation. The 1973 Child Welfare Act was enacted to convince international society that ROC legislation complied with the UN Declaration and that the Taiwan government was willing to carry out certain child and juvenile development programs, financially supported by UNICEF. It did not signal a real recognition by the ROC decision-makers themselves that the rights of the child had to be materialized in law or that the protection

[15]See Hong and Song (2010).

[16]See Shaw (2008), pp. 31–32, Henkin et al. (1993), pp. 153–154.

of children from abuse and neglect had become so important as to deserve a specific law. The effects of the law on providing welfare for children were marginal.

Stimulated by the adoption of the UN Convention on the Rights of the Child in 1989, the Taiwan government was again motivated to implement a law in line with world trends. Again, the law was based on foreign models taken from Japan, Korea, the USA, England, Germany, France, and so on. Some principles of the UN Convention were also emphasized and incorporated as guidelines. This time, however, civil groups took the lead in the lobbying process. Armed with Western welfare laws, child protection professionals stated that the traditional functions of the Chinese family were withering and all Western developed modern legislation had extended state intervention into family lives for the purpose of child protection. At the same time, Western ideas of "childhood" were introduced to justify a separate sphere of children in law and society.[17]

In general, the 1993 Child Welfare Act was a hybrid of idealist measures derived from several foreign welfare systems balanced by solutions to local problems. The scale of welfare services was also adjusted by the practical concerns of tight governmental budgets. Although the UN Declaration and Convention have been highlighted in the ROC child welfare legislation, the state's regulation of parental rights and childcare is still legally expressed in terms of child-saving, rather than children's rights, language. Such discourses were reconfirmed in the 1989 Juvenile Welfare Act, which was intended to deal with delinquency problems in welfare-oriented programs.

An innovative legal principle was adopted in the 1993 Child Welfare Act—the parameter of the first and paramount consideration of the best interests of the child. Article 4 of the Law states, "[w]hen child related matters are dealt with by governments of all levels and governmental as well as nongovernmental institutions or organisations, the first consideration should be the best interest of the child; in addition, cases concerning children's protection, rescue and assistance shall be preferentially admitted and attended to." Although this is only a moral principle, it is significant in terms of law as an instrument of education. In 2003, a Child and Juvenile Welfare Law was promulgated to promote the rights of children under the age of 18 in a unified law. Many of the UN Convention's principles were reinforced in black letters and put under the protection of the Child Welfare Bureau hand-in-hand with a booming civil society; children's rights have thus become a fashion in practice, though not equally shared among social classes and cultural divisions.

With regard to the law-making process, it used to be a legislative tradition to translate foreign laws and distribute them among law-makers to ensure the progressiveness of domestic law. This tradition has prevailed in civil society. Lobbying groups for women's and children's rights are functionalists who worship the power of the law to eliminate discrimination and to protect rights. Legislative bills are proposed with reference to international instruments and the laws of developed countries, although some room has been made to accommodate local solutions.

[17]For details, see Shee (1999).

In short, NGOs have been established as a result of concerns over local problems, but solutions have been found in the knowledge and expertise received from Western training which has helped to make definitions, explain causes and locate solutions. It is noticeable that with ever-growing body and power, civil society has acted to propagate the adoption of Western (mainly US) children's rights, ideologies and disciplinary expertise.

As previously mentioned, the CRC has become a clear example of how global law has been implemented in Taiwan. The Taiwan Parliament has passed the "Implementation Act of the Convention on the Rights of the Child" (the Act) which came into force on 20 November 2014 to adopt the CRC as national law. However, one must not forget that, since the late 1980s, most of the CRC provisions had already been translated and gradually integrated into various Taiwan laws. The legislative bridge of the CRC started construction in 1989, after which the CRC principles and provisions were incorporated into Taiwan's laws and social practices. It is also important to observe the differences made by the 2014 CRC Implementation Act to the promotion of children's rights in Taiwan and to examine how global law principles of the CRC can be implemented in an East Asian Confucian society.

The realization of global children's rights in Taiwan's socio-legal environment has distinctive political and social backgrounds. It is worthwhile to examine how the CRC has, since 1993, affected local legislation despite the fact that Taiwan is not a State Party to the CRC. Throughout the years, from the amendment of the Child Welfare Law in 1993 to the enactment of the Law to Protect the Rights and Welfare of Children and Juveniles in 2011, and more recently the Law to Enforce the Convention on the Rights of the Child which entered into force on 20 November 2014, the CRC had been cited in all legislative materials, including the official legislative backgrounds of concerned pieces of laws.[18]

3.3 *Local Efforts Before and After the CRC Enforcement Law*

3.3.1 Before the Enforcement Law

It is interesting to see how Taiwan society has used the global principles of children's rights to meet local realities. Traditional comparative law in Taiwan adopts the transplant model which copies foreign or international black-letter laws directly into domestic legislation. Therefore, when a global legal concept is transplanted into national laws, the statutes and case laws of advanced countries, such as Japan, Germany, USA, or the EU, are taken as legislative and judicial models. As a result, Taiwan has adopted the parameters of the "advanced" jurisdictions to govern issues

[18]Mccorquodale (2013).

of children's rights while ignoring local needs. The major CRC concept—the best interests of the child—was thus copied and pasted onto the 1993 Child Welfare Act as a guiding principle. Since then, the children's rights provisions of the CRC have been gradually inserted into amendments of laws concerning children and juveniles. Taiwan society has thus habitualized the CRC principles into local practices.

The global principle of "the best interests of the child" (Art. 3 of the CRC) has been incorporated into Taiwan's laws to influence the nature of the transplanted concept of "parental authority" from Japan, shifting the emphasis from denoting the power and authority of a father to an equal sharing of duties and responsibilities over children. Historically, both the Korean and the Chinese-Taiwanese laws were transplanted from Japanese law. Therefore, the first Chinese Civil Code took the Japanese term of 親権. In the process of modernization, the legal concept was translated to mean parental rights and duties. Through internationalization the concept developed into a "duty-right" and was further influenced by the 1989 UN Convention on the Rights of the Child. The concept of "parental right" thus became "parental responsibilities," and Taiwan law gradually took on the global concept of "the best interests of the child" to reinforce the notion of "parental responsibility."[19]

Therefore, although the Taiwan Civil Code still shares the Japanese term 親権, the translation of its meaning to parental authority is no longer appropriate. In view of this, we may suggest that translations for comparative studies should move from linguistic translations to conceptual and contextual translations. In order to understand the essence of "the best interests of the child" under the Confucian idea of a "parental right" that was traditionally employed in Taiwan, local contextual elements for the incorporation of the global legislative principle need to be carefully studied.

The first wave of children's rights movements started in the early 1990s when a Child Welfare League was founded under the leadership of a legislator in collaboration with high-profile academics, practitioners and lawyers to lobby for an amendment of the 1973 Child Welfare Act. The second wave was initiated at the end of 1994 by a coalition of children's rights volunteer groups under the slogan of "Ratify the UN Convention on the Rights of the Child." It was, of course, a rather political statement, but the aim was to make the government realize the Convention in local laws. With the support of a few prominent legislators from all political parties, the government finally made an official statement on 23 Sept 1995, to commit itself to the realization of the Convention. The statement was later distributed among international governmental and nongovernmental organs.

At the dawn of this century, the Child Bureau, the state authority for policy and enforcement of children's rights, further decided to appeal to all governments in the world for the equal protection of children in Taiwan despite the political

[19]親権 (Kanji) or 親權 (traditional Chinese) is a common term in family law of the East Asian countries. Though the laws of Japan, Korea, Taiwan and Mainland China (CJKT) share the same Chinese characters, the notion is translated into different English terms. In Japan and Korea it translates as "parental authority" but in Taiwan and Mainland China it is translated as "parental rights and duties\obligations."

considerations of the United Nations. The "Official Statement for the Realization of the United Nations Convention on the Rights of the Child," published in both English and Chinese, was thus formally presented to all governments. It is celebrated as a children's rights manifesto in this new era of globalization. It states:

> The 1989 United Nations Convention on the Rights of the Child (hereinafter the Convention) is the basic source of international human rights law for the protection of children. The Convention consolidates the achievements of international society working on children's livelihood and development since the beginning of the 20th century. The basic spirits of the Convention are to call on the human society to pay attention to the needs of the child, and that children should be taken care of and respected by the State and the family. Accordingly, it is the purpose of the Convention to have as many contracting States as possible, so as to fulfill the requirement of Article 2, Section 1 of the Convention, which states that States Parties shall respect the rights of each child within their jurisdiction without discrimination of any kind, irrespective of the child's race, color, sex, language, religion, political or other opinion, national, ethnic or social origin, property, disability, birth or other status.... Nevertheless, certain international political reasons have barred the Republic of China on Taiwan (hereinafter Taiwan) from becoming a member of the United Nations. As a result, Taiwan is not allowed to sign and join the Convention. And in order to express our determination for realizing the Convention, the government of Taiwan made an official announcement on 27 Sept 1995 that it should respect the spirit and principles of the Convention. Yet, such a unilateral declaration does not automatically give the children in Taiwan equal protection under the international human rights law, not to mention fulfilling the constitutional requirement of promoting international cooperation and advancing international justice. Since the lifting of martial rule in 1987, various kinds of human rights movements can be found in Taiwanese society. Improper treatments of children (such as abuse and exploitation etc.) are no longer permitted and are seriously condemned. The legislative organ, under the pressure of society and the government's self-consciousness, has thus passed different kinds of law for the protection of children. For this purpose, a special administrative organ, with an independent budget has also been established to train experts, implement relevant measures, and subsidize non-governmental organizations. In addition, facing the adverse international situation, the Taiwan government and the non-governmental organizations have worked together to participate in international activities regarding child protection. Our Ministry of Foreign Affairs, as mentioned above, has formally declared Taiwan's determination to observe the Convention. All these are evidence of Taiwan's determination and efforts.
>
> As a mature democracy and an active participant in internationalization and globalization, Taiwan being excluded from the Convention is not only a loss for international society, but also reflects the lack of courage on the part of international society to fight for justice. Therefore, we urge every State in the world to accept Taiwan as a member of the Convention, so as to let our government effectively protect the basic rights of the child. This has nothing to do with international politics or power struggles. Our concern is simply to realize what the Charter of the United Nations requires every State to do: respect human rights and take special care of the child'. The Statement was then delivered to relevant governmental and non-governmental organs to further highlight the determination of Taiwan to become a qualified member of the global society for children's rights.

Such determination, while politically oriented in its discourse, gave civil society an effective warrant for the making and enforcement of law. The Child and Juvenile Welfare Act 2003 has not only combined the existing Child Welfare Act and the Juvenile Welfare Act, which had governed children under age 12 and juveniles under age 18 separately but also has taken on most legislative principles of the

Convention considered applicable in Taiwan. Under the auspices of children's rights movements, children became a legal subject in the family under a law which was the first to challenge parental authority and then to supersede parental rights with the claim for the best interests of the child. While the Convention may be celebrated as being the most popular human rights commitment shared by the global village, Taiwan is still not on the official map. But it does not make too much difference now, at least in theory. Under Article 2 of the Convention, a Taiwanese child is to be equally protected wherever he is on the planet and vice versa if a child of another identity comes to Taiwan.

In consideration of children as a legal subject, Judicial Yuan Interpretation No. 587 (2004) is clear. It launched its children's rights statement under the auspices of the UN Convention on the Rights of the Child. It first holds that the present law of establishing paternity "is intended to balance the maintenance of a stable status order and the protection of a child's interests." However, the "law has inappropriately restricted the right of a child to litigation, and is thus insufficient in defending the right to personality. Within this ambit, such law is inconsistent with the Constitutional principle of protecting the right to personality and the right to litigation."

It is then elaborated on in the reasoning that "(a) child's right to identify blood filiations is declared by Article 7, Section 1 of the UN Convention on the Rights of the Child validated on 2 Sept 1990. The right to establish paternity is concerned with a child's right to personality and shall be protected under Article 22 of the Constitution." Therefore, it was recommended that the law be amended to protect "the best interests of the child that the Civil Code governing the parent-child relationship has been abided by."

3.3.2 After the Implementation Act

Major provisions of the Enforcement Law of the Convention on the Rights of the Child read:

Article 1: This Act is made to implement the 1989 Convention on the Rights of the Child (hereinafter the Convention), to fulfill the physical and mental development of children and youths and to substantiate the protection and promotion of the rights of the child and youth.

Article 2: The provisions of the Convention regarding the protection and promotion of the rights of the child and youth shall have the effect of domestic law.

Article 3: The laws and administrative measures to which the provisions of the Convention apply shall be in reference to the purpose of the Convention and the interpretation of the Convention by the United Nations Committee on the Rights of the Child.

Article 7: (1) The government shall establish a reporting system regarding the rights of the child and youth and shall submit its first national report within two years from the implementation of this Act. (2) Thereafter, national reports shall be filed every five years. Relevant academic experts and representatives from private organizations shall be invited to review the reports. The government shall review and study subsequent policies based on their opinions.

Article 9: Each level of government authority shall provide a priority review list regarding the legislation and administrative measures under its jurisdiction based on the provisions of the Convention within one year from the implementation of this Act. Any laws and regulations inconsistent with the provisions of the Convention shall be corrected by addition, amendment or abolition, and administrative measures shall be improved within three years from the implementation of this Act. The legislation (amendment), revision or cancellation of the remaining laws and regulations, and improvement of administrative measures shall be completed within five years from the implementation of this Act.

Article 10: This Act shall be implemented from 20 November 2014.

As mentioned above, Taiwan cannot be qualified as a State Party of any UN Convention, and thus the CRC national reports cannot be accepted by the United Nations, nor can they follow the review procedures carried out by the Children's Committee. The political walls and sovereign borders against Taiwan do not affect the determination of the ROC government to bridge the obstacles to the implementation of the CRC. Under the CRC Implementation Act, Taiwan assumes two major obligations of a "State Party," namely, to prepare national reports according to the UN guidelines[20] and to review and amend the national laws that breach the CRC.[21] The authority responsible for working on the implementation of the CRC is the "Social and Family Affairs Administration, Ministry of Health and Welfare."[22]

[20]According to Article 7 of the CRC Implementation Act, "(1) The government shall establish a reporting system regarding the rights of the child and youth and shall submit its first national report within two years from the implementation of this Act. (2) Thereafter, national reports shall be filed every five years. Relevant academic experts and representatives from private organizations shall be invited to review the reports. The government shall review and study subsequent policies based on their opinions." Source of information: Weisheng Fulibu Shehui ji Jiatingshu [衛生福利部社會及家庭署]. http://www.sfaa.gov.tw/SFAA/. Accessed 2 Mar 2017.

[21]According to Article 9 of the CRC, "Each level of government authority shall provide a priority review list regarding the legislation and administrative measures under its jurisdiction based on the provisions of the Convention within one year from the implementation of this Act. Any laws and regulations inconsistent with the provisions of the Convention shall be corrected by addition, amendment or abolition, and administrative measures shall be improved within three years from the implementation of this Act. The legislation (amendment), revision or cancellation of the remaining laws and regulations, and improvement of administrative measures shall be completed within five years from the implementation of this Act." Source of information: *Id.*

[22]The Social and Family Affairs Administration (SFAA), Ministry of Health and Welfare, was established on 23 July 2013. The primary focus of the SFAA is to formulate and promote policies and services relating to the welfare of senior citizens, people with disabilities, women, children and youths, and to provide family support. Source of information: Social and Family Affairs Administration, Ministry of Health and Welfare. http://www.sfaa.gov.tw/SFAA/Eng/. Accessed 2 Mar 2017.

3.3.3 The CRC "National Report"[23]

Taiwan published the initial national report of the CRC[24] on 17 November 2017 and started a two-day symposium on the CRC's implementation. Deputy Minister of Health and Welfare Lu Pau-ching, who also served as a member and executive secretary of the Welfare and Rights of Children and Youth Promotion Group under the Executive Yuan, spoke on the release of the report at a press conference at the Civil Service Development Institute in Taipei.

At the symposium, child rights experts were invited to speak and share their experiences. These experts included Professor Jaap E. Doek from the Netherlands, who served as chairperson of the UN Committee on the Rights of the Child from 2001–2007, Sanphasit Koompraphant, founder of the Centre for the Protection of Children's Rights in Thailand, Professor Trond Waage, a former Ombudsman for Children of Norway, and Meas Samnang, secretary-general of the NGO Coalition on the Rights of the Child in Cambodia.

The release of the initial national report on the status of children's rights in the country two years after the adoption of the Convention is stipulated in the Implementation Act of the Convention on the Rights of the Child introduced in November 2014. The Ministry of Health and Welfare (hereinafter MOHW), as the Secretariat of the Executive Yuan's Child Welfare and Right Promotion Group, began compiling the report in July 2015. With the cooperation of various government agencies, the report was completed after 33 review meetings with experts, academics and civic groups.

The MOHW lists and explains the measures Taiwan has taken to recognize children's rights and the progress made in the enjoyment of such rights in the initial report, which contains eight chapters covering the general principles of the convention, civil rights and freedoms, family environment and alternative care, basic health and welfare, education, leisure and cultural activities, and special protection measures. The ministry expects the report to demonstrate the Taiwanese government's efforts to protect and promote child rights.

The first step was to study the Initial National Reports of the CRC States Parties to sum up what constitutes the "basic information" required for each right of the child. A comprehensive list attached with examples from other countries may then be used for reference. Therefore, ten CRC Initial National Reports were carefully studied, including those of Japan, Korea, Singapore, the People' Republic of China, Hong Kong, Macau, Canada, France, Finland and Sweden.

[23]The relevant information is published on the website of the Ministry of Health and Welfare, Source of information: Taiwan publishes initial national report under UN Convention on the Rights of the Child (CRC). http://www.sfaa.gov.tw/SFAA/Eng/Pages/Detail.aspx?nodeid=235&pid=5509. Accessed 2 Mar 2017.

[24]For the English version of the report, see file:///C:/Users/admin/Downloads/File_167934.pdf, published on 20 Nov 2017 at Weisheng Fulibu Shehui ji Jiatingshu [衛生福利部社會及家庭署]. http://www.sfaa.gov.tw/SFAA/. Accessed 2 Mar 2017.

The second step was to develop a standard format to provide a structured outline and instructions for related government authorities to fill in the information required by the UN Guidelines for Writing CRC National Reports. If some standard sentences such as "(t)he purpose of the new legislation is to promote …." are used, the information so provided will offer the relevant information in a compact way. The third step is to create a network to translate the basic information in a timely manner. The fourth is to develop a human network to respond to inquiries.

Meanwhile, the two-day symposium was held to raise awareness of the UN Convention on the Rights of the Child. International experts, civic groups and academics and government officials in the fields of social services, immigration, legal affairs, crime prevention and public education were expected to exchange their views and look at possible challenges facing child rights protection in Taiwan through speeches and discussions at the symposium.

A panel of five international children's rights experts was formed to examine Taiwan's initial national report under the CRC and to release their concluding observations in 2017, which the government would take into consideration to further enhance the protection of children's rights in the country, according to the ministry.[25] The government also welcomes CRC reports made by civil groups.[26] This will bring the national report of Taiwan closer to the human rights standards of international society.[27]

[25]Ministry of Health and Welfare welcomes international human rights groups and related international organizations to participate in the review meetings of the ROC's Initial Report under the Convention on the Rights of Persons with Disabilities (CRPD) and the Convention on the Rights of the Child (CRC). www.roc-taiwan.org/id_en/post/1693.html. Accessed 26 Dec 2017.

[26]Source of information: Feizhengfu Zuzhi Baogao [非政府組織報告]. http://www.sfaa.gov.tw/SFAA/Pages/List.aspx?nodeid=783. Accessed 2 Mar 2017.

[27]In June 2014, the Legislative Yuan of the Republic of China (Taiwan) passed the Implementation Act of the Convention on the Rights of the Child ("Implementation Act"). The Act came into force on 20 Nov 2014 and provides the framework for domestic harmonization of the CRC. On 22 Apr 2016 Taiwan's Legislative Yuan passed a bill to support the adoption of the CRC, paving the way for the President to sign the Instrument of Accession to the CRC in May 2016. The Executive Yuan, according to the Implementation Act, published the initial state report in Nov 2016 and its English version was made available in Mar 2017. In order to review its initial state report, the government of Taiwan invited five independent international children's rights experts to form an International Review Committee ("Review Committee"). They were Jaap Doek (Chairperson) (The Netherlands), Judith Karp (Israel), Nigel Cantwell (United Kingdom/Switzerland); Laura Lundy (Northern Ireland) and John Tobin (Australia). The Review Committee examined the initial report of Taiwan which was submitted to the Review Committee in Mar 2017. The Review Committee received reports from civil society organizations, including children's organizations and groups of children. The Review Committee submitted a List of Issues to Taiwan in June 2017 and received detailed written replies in Sept 2017. The Review Committee also received a number of additional reports from civil society in response to the List of Issues and the state's replies to the List of Issues. As part of the review on 20 Nov 2017 the Review Committee held private meetings with children and members from civil society. On 21 and 22 Nov 2017, the Review Committee engaged in a public dialogue with the Government delegation. The Review Committee adopted the present Concluding Observations and presented them on 24 Nov 2017. The Review Committee acknowledges the serious and sincere efforts of the Government of

4 Prospects

This chapter endeavors to observe Taiwan as a unique case of human rights development. UN Human Rights Conventions have constructed and reconstructed manhood followed by womanhood and childhood and so on. Human civilization has moved toward an ideology of human rights over political, economic, racial, gender and age walls to extend the boundaries of the definition to reach all corners of the global village. The 1989 UN Convention on the Rights of the Child is a crucial manifestation of this development, which covers not only 192 UN-recognized countries (except the USA) but also 4 non-state "parties." We have witnessed a similar socio-legal construction and reconstruction of childhood under the Enforcement Act of the Convention on the Rights of the Child in Taiwan. It may thus be argued that Taiwan may come to be recognized as the 5th non-state party to the CRC.

In Taiwan, the socio-legal construction of childhood under the ideology of children's rights (the best interest of the child principle) has been a major topic for interdisciplinary studies for decades. In order to respond to the 1989 UN Convention on the Rights of the Child, childhood is being reconstructed in the law and society of Taiwan despite its political exclusion from the United Nations. Taiwan is not an UN member, but it still passed the 2014 CRC Enforcement Act to implement the Convention as a national law. The Enforcement Act also stipulates the obligation to complete the first national report within 2 years as well as to review and amend all existing laws that may have violated the Convention. Further, various administrative measures have been taken by central and local governments to facilitate realization of the CRC. In view of efforts to be part of the CRC, Taiwan deserves to be included as a party to the UN Convention on the Rights of the Child.

As a law professional and human rights activist who has been heavily involved in this development process, I have frequently criticized Taiwanese developments in order to provoke or accelerate reform. This chapter is thus to be shared by those who are concerned about global justice with a sensitive perception and due respect for the individuality and integrity of a legal culture at the periphery. Taiwan may not avoid the political obstacles against sending in our national reports of the UN

Taiwan to implement the CRC. The Review Committee greatly appreciates the constructive dialogue with the government during the review, which was attended by representatives from all relevant ministries and government bodies. The active participation of civil society and in particular children was also essential to the review process. The Review Committee expresses its appreciation to the Ministry of Health and Welfare, and particularly its CRC team, for providing the Review Committee with substantive and logistical support. Source of information: Concluding Observations on the Initial Report of the Republic of China/Taiwan on the Implementation of the UN Convention on the Rights of the Child. file:///D:/user/Downloads/%E5%85%92%E7%AB%A5%E6%AC%8A%E5%88%A9%E5%85%AC%E7%B4%84%E9%A6%96%E6%AC%A1%E5%9C%8B%E5%AE%B6%E5%A0%B1%E5%91%8A%E5%9C%8B%E9%9A%9B%E5%AF%A9%E6%9F%A5-%E7%B5%90%E8%AB%96%E6%80%A7%E6%84%8F%E8%A6%8B-%E8%8B%B1%E6%96%87%E7%89%88.pdf. Accessed 26 Dec 2017.

Conventions. It may also be difficult to avoid the sovereign borders when presenting Taiwan as a country that respects the rule of law in global society. As shown in this chapter, however, practical bridges have been built to channel international human rights laws into Taiwan society.

Taiwan's laws may have been evidentially analyzed or criticized as a state tool to achieve economic growth or political survival; however, its context and effects on the family qualify for a separate study. Foreign legal discourses such as the best interests of the child may have been translated and adopted in law books, but they have been applied and interpreted in ways that take local contexts into consideration. Case studies of Taiwan's children's rights law[28] have shown the inter-communicating cross-border progress among and between law, culture, ideas, values, institutions and processes during which foreign elements interact with local conditions to reproduce and transform domestic law and society. The dynamics of legal reforms and practices concerning child (and juvenile) rights and welfare will serve as a bridge to take Taiwan over the political walls and sovereign borders.

It was asked at the beginning of this chapter: If human rights are granted to every person on an equal basis, should the civil, political, economic, gender and development rights of a person diverge simply because of one's nationality? Human rights advocates may urge for inclusion against exclusion, but the reality that international human rights law invokes the "party state" to justify exclusion must still be recognized. Political walls and sovereign borders may thus deprive the people under an unrecognized government of the chance to be the subject of an UN Convention. Debates over whether Taiwan is part of China thus affect the status of Taiwanese children in the CRC, though Taiwan's civil groups have been active in all kinds of global activities involving children's rights. The Taiwan government further passed a 2014 CRC Enforcement Act to enable the "national" implementation of the Convention, and the CRC "National Report" of Taiwan was officially published on 20 November 2016 for international review. This chapter thus asks the global human rights network to consider: Can the development of children's rights break down the political walls, pass over the sovereign borders and provide a bridge so that the voices of children in Taiwan can be heard in global society?

References

Deflem M (2006) Global rule of law or global rule of law enforcement? Ann Am Acad Political Soc Sci 603:240–251

Droria GS, Höllererb MA, Walgenbachc P (2014) Unpacking the globalization of organization: from term, to theory, to analysis. Eur J Cultural Political Sociology 1(1):85–99

Fagui Jianshi [法規檢視]. http://www.sfaa.gov.tw/SFAA/Pages/List.aspx?nodeid=582. Accessed 6 Apr 2017

[28]See publications in English, for example, Liu (2001), pp. 185–225, Liu (2004a), pp. 224–305, Liu (2004b), pp. 85–103.

Feizhengfu Zuzhi Baogao [非政府組織報告]. http://www.sfaa.gov.tw/SFAA/Pages/List.aspx?nodeid=783. Accessed 2 Mar 2017
Gerber DJ (2001) Globalization and legal knowledge: implications for comparative law. Tulane Law Rev 75:949–975
Giddens A (ed) (2001) The global third way debate. Polity Press, Cambridge, UK
Guojia Baogao [國家報告]. http://www.sfaa.gov.tw/SFAA/Pages/List.aspx?nodeid=606. Accessed 6 Apr 2017
Gutteridge HC (1947) Comparative law: an introduction to the comparative method of legal study and research. Modern Law Rev 10(2):224–229
Halliday T, Osinsky P (2006) Globalization of law. Ann Rev Sociol 32:447–470
Henkin L, Richard C, Schachter O (1993) International law: cases and materials. West Publishing, St Paul, MN
Hong PYP, Song IH (2010) Glocalization of social work practice: global and local responses to globalization. Intl Soc Work 53:656–670
Liu HE (2001) Mother or father: who received custody? The best interests of the child standard and judges' custody decisions in Taiwan. Intl J Law Policy Family 15:185–225
Liu HE (2004a) Custody decisions in social and cultural contexts: in-depth and focus group interviews with nineteen judges in Taiwan. Columbia J Asian Law 17(2):224–305
Liu HE (2004b) Postdivorce single-mother families in difficulties and the need to reform the current policy—reflections on two empirical socio-legal studies of Taiwanese Child Custody Law. Cross-Strait Law Rev 5:85–103
Mccorquodale R (2013) Pluralism, global law and human rights: strengthening corporate accountability for human rights violations. Glob Constitutionalism 2:287–315
Michaels R (2013) Globalisation and law: law beyond the state. In: Banakar R, Travers LM (eds) Law and social theory, 2nd edn. Hart, Oxford, pp 287–304
Restoration of the Lawful Rights of the People's Republic of China in the United Nations. http://www.un.org/documents/ga/res/26/ares26.htm. Accessed 25 Feb 2017
Roudometof V (2015) Theorizing globalisation: three interpretations. Eur J Soc Theory 19(3):1–18
Shaw MN (2008) International law. Cambridge University Press, Cambridge
Shee A (1999) Legal protection against sexual exploitation of children in Taiwan: a socio-legal study. Dartmouth Publishing Ltd., UK
Social and Family Affairs Administration, Ministry of Health and Welfare. http://www.sfaa.gov.tw/SFAA/Eng/. Accessed 2 Mar 2017
Taiwan publishes initial national report under UN Convention on the Rights of the Child (CRC). http://www.sfaa.gov.tw/SFAA/Eng/Pages/Detail.aspx?nodeid=235&pid=5509. Accessed 2 Mar 2017
Twining W (1999) Globalization and comparative law. Maastricht J Eur Comp Law 6:217–243
Wang T (2013) The modernization of civil justice in colonial Taiwan, 1895–1945. J Jpn Law (Germany) 36:95–116
Wang T (2015) Legal reform in Taiwan under Japanese colonial rule, 1895–1945: the reception of Western law. University of Washington Press, Seattle
Weisheng Fulibu Shehui ji Jiatingshu [衛生福利部社會及家庭署]. http://www.sfaa.gov.tw/SFAA/. Accessed 2 Mar 2017
Xingzhengyuan Ertong ji Shaonian Fuli yu Quanyi Tuidong Xiaozu [行政院兒童及少年福利與權益推動小組]. http://www.sfaa.gov.tw/SFAA/Pages/List.aspx?nodeid=800. Accessed 6 Apr 2017

Amy Huey-Ling Shee obtained her LL.M. at LSE and her Ph.D. in law from Warwick University in 1995, and has since been affiliated with National Chung Cheng University (CCU) in Taiwan. Apart from being a full-time Professor at the College of Law, Professor Shee also serves as Director of CCU's Taiwan Legal Information Institute (Taiwan LII, http://www.taiwanlii.ccu.edu.tw/), chairperson of the Human Research Committee, coordinator of the Aging Society Legal Studies, and the director of the Fundamental Law Research Centre. Her research interests are mainly Family Law, Children Rights, Sociology of Law, Legal Education, and Law & Literature. After receiving a governmental appointment in 2012, Prof. Shee has led a research team to work on drafts of the Enforcement Act of the UN Convention on the Rights of the Child (CRC) and the CRC National Report. She has now been appointed as advisor to child rights committees of governmental and nongovernmental organs. She received the honor of the "Child Protection Angel National Award 2010" from the national president.

Chapter 36
People Over Pandas: Taiwan's Engagement of International Human Rights Norms with Respect to Disability

William P. Alford, Qiongyue Hu and Charles Wharton

Abstract Taiwan's early law (1980) regarding disability presumed a medical model —i.e., seeing disability as an individual problem rather than a societal responsibility. Facing considerable discrimination and inspired by the social model embodied elsewhere, including in the United Nations Convention on the Rights of Persons with Disabilities (CRPD), citizen activists, including disabled persons organizations, have pressed for legislative reform. Following the earlier support of the administration of President Ma Ying-jeou for incorporation of the United Nations Human Rights Covenants into domestic law (owing to Taiwan's being barred from formal accession), the Legislative Yuan in 2014 passed a bill designed to incorporate the CRPD into Republic of China (R.O.C) law. That measure not only retained all key provisions of the CRPD but also called on the Executive Yuan to conduct a comprehensive review of existing legal measures for compliance and pro-actively to engage persons with disabilities in implementing the new law, while also establishing innovative reporting and monitoring mechanisms intended to parallel the requirements of the CRPD. Much progress has been achieved but serious challenges remain regarding discrimination, especially with respect to employment and reasonable accommodations, while some scholars have questioned the suitability of a highly individual-focused rights-based model for Taiwanese society. Disabled persons organizations continue to play an active role both in policy and legal advocacy and in seeking to educate the public more broadly about disability.

Keywords Disability · United Nations Convention on the Rights of Persons with Disabilities (UN CRPD) · Citizen activism · Disabled persons organizations (DPOs) Discrimination · Reasonable accommodation · Executive Yuan

---

W. P. Alford (✉) · Q. Hu · C. Wharton
Harvard Law School, Cambridge, USA
e-mail: alford@law.harvard.edu

Q. Hu
e-mail: qhu@jd17.law.harvard.edu

C. Wharton
e-mail: charlesgwharton@gmail.com

J. A. Cohen et al. (eds.), *Taiwan and International Human Rights*, Economics, Law, and Institutions in Asia Pacific, https://doi.org/10.1007/978-981-13-0350-0_36

1 Introduction

The area of disability is an especially illuminating one through which to consider Taiwan's engagement of international human rights norms to which it is unable formally to adhere. Not only are issues that course through Taiwan's embrace of other international rights instruments, such as the importance of efforts to distinguish itself from the Chinese Mainland, evident here, but others—most notably that of the role of civil society—are particularly salient, given both a tradition of citizen activism on Taiwan[1] and the fact that the United Nations Convention on the Rights of Persons with Disabilities (hereinafter CRPD) calls for more citizen participation than any previous international human rights instrument.[2] After commencing with a quick review of the treatment in law of disability on Taiwan, this chapter will examine the impetus for Taiwan to give domestic effect to the CRPD, the measures through which implementation is occurring (including judicial responses thereto), challenges that remain for its full implementation, and the manner in which civil society suggests these challenges should be met.

2 Historical Background

As one of the co-authors of this chapter has shown elsewhere, the treatment of disability in imperial Chinese history was appreciably more nuanced than conventional wisdom would have it, albeit still deeply concerning viewed from a 21st century vantage point.[3] That noted, the first disability law of the Republic of China (hereinafter R.O.C.)—the 1980 Law on the Welfare of Disabled Citizens[4]—very much adhered to a "medical" or "charitable" model. That is, the law, in effect, envisioned disability as a problem for the individual rather than one resulting from the way in which society was constructed, and it consequently sought to advance the situation of persons with disabilities through special set-asides (such as separate schools and sheltered employment) rather than through integration and societal transformation.[5] Interestingly, in relying on a medical model, R.O.C. authorities were already emulating global human rights norms to which Taiwan was not a party

[1]See, e.g., Winckler (1992).

[2]See, for instance, the Convention on the Rights of Persons with Disabilities arts. 3–4, 29, 33, 36, 13 Nov 2006, 2515 U.N.T.S. 3 [hereinafter CRPD] as well as Stein and Lord (2010).

[3]Alford (2014).

[4]We intentionally use the translation provided by the Ministry of the Interior throughout this chapter.

[5]For more on the various models of disability law, see Stein (2007).

—in this instance, the United Nations General Assembly's Declaration on the Rights of Disabled Persons of 1975.[6]

The 1980 law did not sit well with many in the disability community on Taiwan,[7] generating citizen activism (particularly after the 1987 cessation of martial law),[8] which by 1997 yielded both an amendment to the R.O.C. Constitution and a major revision of the national disability law. The former, at Article 10, specifically provided that "the State shall guarantee insurance, medical care, obstacle-free environments, education and training, vocational guidance and support and assistance in everyday life for physically and mentally handicapped persons, and shall also assist them to attain independence and to develop." And the latter, inching toward a social model (in the sense of seeing disability as a societal responsibility more than an individual misfortune), expanded both the range of persons covered and the scope of state attention. But this was only a start—and less than a decade later heightened popular involvement, exemplified by the emergence of groups such as the League for Disabled Persons of the R.O.C. (hereinafter the League), led to the 2007 People with Disabilities Rights Protection Act,[9] which, as its name suggests, took on a more rights-oriented coloration, although still appreciably less than advocates had wished.

Not long thereafter, under the leadership of newly elected President Ma Ying-jeou, a Harvard-trained lawyer, the government took steps to incorporate international human rights standards more generally into domestic law.[10] Specifically, Ma announced his intention on the first International Human Rights Day of his presidency—10 Dec 2008—that Taiwan move expeditiously to ratify and implement the International Covenant on Civil and Political Rights (hereinafter ICCPR) and the International Covenant on Economic, Social and Cultural Rights (hereinafter ICESCR). Within months, the Legislative Yuan enacted the necessary legislation, and although the United Nations, unsurprisingly, rebuffed Taiwan's attempts to deposit the necessary instruments of ratification, implementation on Taiwan of the Covenants proceeded apace. In 2010, President Ma established a Presidential Office Human Rights Consultative Committee to facilitate implementation. Contemplating a comprehensive project on domesticating all major international human rights treaties, the Ma administration considered opinions from civil society as to which treaties should follow the ICCPR and ICESCR,[11] and in 2011, the President proposed and the Legislative Yuan adopted measures to implement

[6]Hu (2017).

[7]*Id.*

[8]Taiwan's democratization is chronicled in Chu and Lin (2001).

[9]Again, the translation is that of the Ministry of the Interior.

[10]This paragraph draws from the very fine doctoral dissertation by Chen Yu-jie (2016).

[11]Interview with Liao YH, Professor, National Chengchi University (3 Aug 2017) [hereinafter Liao Interview].

the UN Convention on the Elimination of All Forms of Discrimination Against Women (hereinafter CEDAW).[12]

As another co-author of this paper has shown elsewhere,[13] while these efforts by the government to align Taiwan with the Covenants and the CEDAW were underway, disability activists and scholars continued to make the case for both immediate reform in state measures concerning disability as well as deeper and more thoroughgoing change. One galvanizing point for the former involved the refusal of UNI Air, a subsidiary of the major carrier EVA Air, to honor the ticket of a would-be passenger who was a wheelchair user on the grounds that it "had no experience in assisting people in wheelchairs."[14] That UNI Air's refusal came not long after the airline had praised itself for transporting pandas from the Mainland prompted outrage, with some activists publicly demanding to know why animals received better treatment than people. Spurred on by the so-called Thousand Coalition and activist Sleeve Yu (known as "the Angel in a Wheelchair"), among others, legislative allies such as Yu Chung-hsiung were able to secure amendments to the 2007 national disability law intended to limit such discriminatory behavior.[15]

At the same time, inspired in important part by the CRPD's embrace of a social model of disability, by the array of specific rights it articulated, and by its call for more citizen engagement, activists and scholars, such as the League of Welfare Organizations for the Disabled, Wang Kuo-yu, Chang Heng-hao, Tsai I-lun, Ho Ming-sho, and Chou Yueh-ching, called for yet more fundamental change regarding the 2007 law and the overall approach to disability on Taiwan.[16] Specifically, they attacked the law for its continued embodiment of dimensions of a medical model, its absence of provisions clearly setting out a requirement for reasonable accommodations and anti-discrimination provisions, and its lack of an independent monitoring mechanism. These features and particularly the requirement of meeting somewhat rigid state definitions of what constituted a disability had led, it was suggested, to a very serious undercounting of persons with a disability. Indeed, the official count of less than 5% of the population[17] was drastically below the figure estimated by the World Health Organization and the World Bank, in an authoritative 2011 report, that 15% of the world's population has a disability.[18] The incorporation of the CRPD itself would be necessary, many argued, to bring Taiwan's domestic law up to international standards.

[12]*Id.*

[13]Hu (2017).

[14]Qiu and Li (2009).

[15]Hu (2017).

[16]See, e.g., Wang (2008), Chang (2007), Tsai and Ho (2010), Chou and Zhu (2011).

[17]Covenants Watch (2017), p. 1.

[18]World Health Organization and World Bank (2011).

The effort to go beyond the Covenants and to make the CRPD itself part of Taiwan law quickly gained momentum. Drawing upon the logic of arguments advanced internationally to justify a disability-specific convention, scholars such as Wang and Chou made the case that, worthy though the Covenants were, many vital gaps remained in domestic disability law and policy that could only effectively be addressed through domestication of the CRPD and that adoption of the CRPD would, inter alia, hasten the move from an approach toward disability still largely premised on government good-will toward a more rights-based model that would empower individuals and, hence, would enhance dignity.[19] Soon thereafter in 2011, Lee Hung-bing, a visually impaired lawyer, developed the first draft of implementing legislation, offering the rationale, inter alia, that this would create more of a rights-based foundation for disability law on Taiwan; would provide a clearer yardstick for reviewing the completeness of current legislation pertinent to access to the physical and virtual environments, voting rights, and the justice system; would result in more government accountability; and would, symbolically, constitute an important statement regarding Taiwan's commitment to its citizens with a disabilities.[20] Many disabled persons organizations (hereinafter DPOs), as well as human rights groups that were not disability-specific, rallied behind incorporation (without necessarily being deeply steeped in its implications, which, in any event, had yet to have fully unfolded anywhere).[21]

As one scholar and former member of the Presidential Office Human Rights Consultative Committee has pointed out, initially some in the government focused their attention more on other human rights instruments, thinking that Taiwan's domestic law on disability approximated the standards of the CRPD. However, in time the aforementioned advocacy and scholarly work persuaded the Ma administration of the need to incorporate the CRPD as a central component of its plan to have Taiwan embrace the corpus of international human rights law.[22]

Movement toward incorporation was further advanced in 2013 by recommendations from the so-called International Group of Independent Experts that had been appointed by President Ma's Human Rights Consultative Committee to review that Committee's Initial Report on Implementation of the International Human Rights Covenants (a process established to emulate the international processes from which Taiwan had been excluded by virtue of its diplomatic status).[23] Specifically,

---

[19]See Wang (2008), p. 13.

[20]Hu (2017).

[21]See, e.g., the work of the League which, in time, gathered the support of more than 127 groups. See also Interview with Chang HH, Professor, National Taipei University (7 July 2017) [hereinafter Chang Interview].

[22]Liao Interview.

[23]Hu (2017), Chen (2016).

the Independent Experts Group put forward the idea that the government commence a process that might lead to the domestic incorporation of the CRPD. This, in turn, eventuated in hearings on the implications of CRPD adoption, several different legislative proposals building on the earlier efforts by Lee Hung-bing, and further lobbying by an array of groups. Finally, in August 2014, the Act Implementing the Convention on the Rights of Persons with Disabilities (hereinafter CRPD Implementing Act, or implementing legislation) was passed, with ratification coming two years later.

3 Incorporating the CRPD

The CRPD Implementing Act is noteworthy for its thoroughgoing embrace of the UN Convention. Not only does Article 2 state unambiguously that provisions of the CRPD "regarding the rights of persons with disabilities have domestic legal status" but further provisions read as intended to ensure that Taiwan's incorporation of the Convention be a deep and dynamic one, notwithstanding the sizable shift that would entail in prevailing approaches to disability and, indeed, rights vindication more generally. "Each level of government" is required to review legislation and regulation for which it is responsible for possible inconsistency with the CRPD in order to make needed changes while, more pro-actively, all governmental institutions are called upon to "prepare, promote and implement" measures needed to realize those rights set out in the CRPD. And, according to Article 3 of the implementing legislation, they are to carry out their application of the law in a manner that will be informed by both the original "legislative purposes" of the CRPD and interpretations that the UN Committee on the CRPD might make.

To facilitate this, the implementing legislation, reflecting the CRPD's unprecedented call for citizen engagement, directs the Executive Yuan not only to "seek the opinions" of persons with disabilities but also to invite representatives of DPOs, along with academic experts, to join with government to establish mechanisms to make this tangible. Specifically, the law, at Article 6, calls for the formation of a committee to oversee the promotion of training about the CRPD and its implementation as well as to foster research on the situation of persons with disabilities, submit national reports, and receive complaints. Reflecting the CRPD's innovative monitoring provisions and given that Taiwan is frozen out of the official UN reporting system, the implementing legislation also mandates, at Article 7, the production of national reports (with the first due in two years) to be reviewed by academic experts "experienced in the affairs of the rights of persons with disabilities in the United Nations," with the idea that the government should take seriously their recommendations. And, again in the spirit of the CRPD's focus upon rights and citizen participation, the implementing legislation, at Article 8, calls on the state to ease the way for claims of rights infringement, to provide legal aid, and to conduct training for judicial personnel about the CRPD.

To ensure that these provisions would not be simply hortatory, the government soon thereafter promulgated several detailed documents intended to guide governmental entities and others in giving force to the implementing legislation. In the Plan to Facilitate the Implementation of the CRPD, the Executive Yuan spelt out precise steps that would need to be taken between 2014 and 2019 with respect to the revision or abrogation of laws and regulations, reporting requirements, efforts to promote the training of officials, and the dissemination of publicity (regarding the new rights and their implications).[24] Lest there be any question about the first of these tasks, these steps complemented by the Standard Procedures for Reviewing Domestic Legislation and Regulations, complete with elaborate flow charts.[25] To be sure that the CRPD's requirements regarding the voices of the citizenry were heeded, the Executive Yuan also promulgated Guidelines on the Participation of Disabled Persons' Organizations and Civil Society Organizations in the Work of the Committee that were called for by the implementing legislation. And as an important first step in that undertaking, the Ministry of Health and Welfare commissioned (or, in the words of some who questioned the government's choice not to lead the meeting directly, "outsourced") the convening of an international conference designed to help foster understanding on Taiwan of best practices with respect to the CRPD.[26] Scholars have noted that for both the government and civil society, the process of developing an understanding of international legal language in the area of disability has been a significant element in moving toward the effective interpretation and implementation of the Convention.[27]

Not surprisingly, given the nature of Taiwan's civil law system, the courts have not been the primary locus of activity in the effort to give vibrancy to the implementing legislation.[28] Nonetheless, it is worth noting that as of July 2017, Taiwan's courts had decided some 20 cases involving that legislation. Interestingly, save for two at the Taipei High Administrative Court,[29] these cases have taken place at the

---

[24]Executive Yuan (2017).

[25]*Id.*, at p. 8, annex 1 (Fagui Jianshi Zhuzhou Jihua [法規檢視主軸計畫] (Standard Procedures for Reviewing Domestic Legislation and Regulations).

[26]Interview with Shi SJ, Professor, National Taiwan University (18 July 2017) [hereinafter Shi Interview]. One of the co authors of this piece, Charles Wharton, was a keynote speaker at this conference.

[27]Chang Interview; Shi Interview.

[28]For an excellent study of the courts and the role of the Constitution on Taiwan, see Yeh (2016).

[29]Liu NP. The Government of New Taipei City, 105 Jian Shang Zi Di 170 Panjue [105簡上字第170號判決] (Taipei Admin. High Ct. [臺北高等行政法院] 11 Oct 2016) (Taiwan) and Pu T-s [蒲桃松] v. Government of New Taipei City [新北市政府] et al., 104 Jian Kang Zi Di 33 Hao Cai Ding] [104簡抗字第33號裁定] (Taipei Admin. High Ct. [臺北高等行政法院] 13 Apr 2016) (Taiwan).

district court level (and predominantly in Hsinchu District), perhaps reflecting the greater activism and familiarity with the CRPD of younger judges and/or the likelihood that it is more probable that they, rather than more senior judges, have been exposed to the training that the court system has promised to provide to members about the CRPD. Those judges have applied the law in a purposive manner (as the implementing legislation directed), heeding what they understood to be the CRPD's underlying rationale and core principles even in the absence of provisions specifically on point, while also at times grounding their reasoning on the R.O.C.'s general provisions regarding disability, which they saw as being given new meaning by virtue of the force and intention of the CRPD implementing legislation. Several such cases, for instance, have involved guardianship and specifically, questions of whether sufficient due process has been provided to meet the right of access to justice provided for in Article 13 of the CRPD (as effectuated by Articles 1 and 2 of the implementing legislation)—which ought not to be surprising, given the difficulty of addressing guardianship in so many jurisdictions.[30] One notable case, in the Taipei High Administrative Court, addressed the issue of whether the government provided reasonable accommodations, while the other case in that court focused on the question of whether certain units of government had adequately discharged their obligation to review all measures for consistency with the CRPD. Nonetheless, given the nature of Taiwan's civil law system, notwithstanding calls by some for more use of litigation,[31] the disability community continues to look more toward executive and legislative action as the chief governmental avenues for driving deeper engagement of the CRPD,[32] although some human rights lawyers hope to make greater use of impact litigation in the future.[33]

4 Domesticating the CRPD

As elsewhere in the world, making the CRPD a part of one's law is not the end, but rather is better thought of as the beginning of bringing it to bear on changing one's society to meet the broad aspirations its specific provisions are intended to promote. On Taiwan, DPOs and other activists moved quickly to educate their constituencies about the CRPD (for even though it enjoyed wide support, that did not necessarily

[30]See, e.g., Fiala-Butora (2016).

[31]Readers should also see Professor Sun's piece in this volume. Sun (2017).

[32]See, e.g., Covenants Watch (2017); and League (2017).

[33]Interview with Huang YB, Chief Executive Officer, Covenants Watch (19 July 2017) [hereinafter Huang Interview].

equate with a deep understanding of it—again, a universal phenomenon). One particular vehicle was to use the requirement of the implementing legislation (mirroring CRPD Article 35) that the government produce a report within two years of its entry into force and every four years thereafter on progress made in giving effect to the Convention and the opening that this, in turn, gave to civil society to produce so-called shadow or parallel reports. Groups—most notably the League and Covenants Watch—made effective use of this. The former, for instance, both held many meetings to hear complaints and convey information and also developed citizen expertise around a half-dozen different specific areas of the CRPD in order to generate a targeted shadow report,[34] while the latter ultimately put together a coalition of 17 quite varied groups to produce a finely textured, almost 100-page parallel report in June 2017.[35]

An examination of the Executive Yuan's official report[36] and of the various shadow reports, as well as academic and advocacy literature since the passage of the CRPD Implementing Act, yields much insight into the status of thinking and action about disability on Taiwan, some of it general and conceptual—if, at times, more implicitly than directly stated—and some of it quite detailed as to specific areas warranting improvement. Perhaps the broadest of concerns has to do with the belief that paradigm shifts are needed to give full effect to the legislative wish to have the CRPD meaningfully be effectuated on Taiwan—shifts regarding how disability should be understood, the role of citizens vis-à-vis government, and the place of rights in this equation. While grateful for the CRPD Implementing Act and appreciative of concrete steps taken and not wanting to lose existing benefits, the parallel reports, in the words of the opening paragraph of the Covenants Watch report, clearly convey the sense that "[o]ur government continues to view persons with [a] disability through the lens of charity or medical treatment…[t]his fails to realize the meaning of 'enabling persons with [a] disability to enjoy the same foundation for rights as other people' under the…CRPD. Not only is the government unable to advance policies that promote equal rights, but it also ignores the participation of persons with disabilities in the policy process."[37]

[34]The League's intricate strategy is discussed in an Interview with its Secretary-General Emma Teng (11 July 2017).

[35]Participating groups ran the gamut from "traditional" DPOs, such as the Taiwan Association for Disability Rights, to newer disability-oriented organizations, such as Hand Angel (the mission of which is "advocating sex rights of the…disabled"), to entities with a general mandate, such as the Taiwan Alliance to End the Death Penalty.

[36]Executive Yuan (2017).

[37]Covenants Watch (2017), p. 1.

In essence, as also noted by Sun Nai-Yi among other scholars,[38] attitudes persist that have real-world consequences, including treating persons with disabilities as passive recipients of largesse rather than as rights-bearers having both the capacity and entitlement to participate fully in decisions concerning their lives. An important challenge will be how to change such attitudes and associated policies without jeopardizing the continuation of benefits provided by the state.[39]

Given the power of the administrative state in Taiwan's legal system, in the view of the parallel reports, training at both the central and local levels is imperative but not sufficient. First, the state itself needs to take many more measures, starting with accurately counting the number of persons with disabilities (still listed as approximately one-third of the world average as recently as 2016), and also including comprehensively assessing "policies, laws and social services" to gauge their full effect (as is required by the implementing legislation), providing barrier-free access to all public buildings (for its own sake and for the example it sets), and committing adequate resources to this undertaking (scarcely more than one-half of 1% of the budget was devoted to disability as of 2016).[40]

But reliance on state action alone, the parallel reports argue, is insufficient, given the lingering stigma and its impact. Echoing CRPD provisions about raising public awareness, the Covenants Watch report calls for the cleansing of derogatory terms such as "retarded" from the legal lexicon and for a more nuanced approach on the part of media such that "the general public… [no longer] regards them [i.e., persons with a disability] as a child or an incapacitated person who is in need of protection."[41] And given the emphasis in the Convention on access to justice, it is crucial that legal aid, procedural accommodations and other steps be taken so that persons with disabilities will be able as fully as possible to exercise their legal rights, both for the particular grievances that may be addressed through this and for the sense of empowerment and inclusion in society that such an exercise of one's rights may help instill.

One particular focus of such a concern has been what Covenants Watch's report describes as Taiwan's "lack of integral [i.e., integrated] anti-discrimination laws"[42] and the League terms as the "scattered" nature of "channels of grievance against discrimination."[43] Notwithstanding January 2017 recommendations by the International Committee of Experts that reviewed Taiwan's compliance with the obligations it

---

[38]Sun (2017).

[39]See Huang Interview.

[40]Covenants Watch (2017), p. 1.

[41]*Id.*, at p. 17.

[42]*Id.*, at pp. 7–8.

[43]League (2017), p. 1.

undertook in incorporating the ICCPR and ICESCR, the failure of the R.O.C. to enact or develop judicially an overarching anti-discrimination statute concerning "all types of grounds listed in International Human Rights Law, such as gender, race, national origin, religion and disability," or at least to have a unified view and consistent approach to discrimination across subject areas, has impaired opportunities to "promote public awareness about the elimination of prejudice and discriminatory behavior, attitude and speech."[44] According to Covenants Watch, the right to equality (or the absence of discrimination)—enshrined in the Constitution and reiterated in specific legislation—calls out for such a law which should also "stipulate…the positive duties that the government and other duty-bearers should bear to achieve substantive equality."[45]

This noted, not all advocates of adoption of the CRPD saw its rights emphasis as an unalloyed good. Some, such as Professor Wang Kuo-yu of National Chung Cheng University,[46] have noted that, for all its positive dimensions, the CRPD's framing in terms of the rights of persons with disabilities poses challenges for the concerns of others, such as family members. Family members and caretakers have also voiced concerns about unforeseen effects of the CRPD's decision-making provisions on disability rights self-advocates engaging in public training,[47] and child advocacy groups have raised questions about how to protect children's welfare in unsafe or unstable homes, including when a parent may be affected by mental illness.[48] Given this context, suggests Wang, there may be tension between the CRPD and core traditional dimensions of Chinese society, at least raising the question of whether, in time, there might be an approach to these issues that is able to meld the benefits of the CRPD with the contributions of societies outside the West. Others, such as Professor Bruce Liao Yuan-Hao of National Chengchi University, are concerned that the characteristics of Taiwan's civil law system (e.g., limited recognition of punitive damages in torts) and its unique market composition (i.e., comprised chiefly of small- and medium-sized private companies) will likely frustrate the purpose of integrated anti-discrimination laws, even were they to be legislated.[49] Again, the argument is not to disregard the value of the CRPD, for

[44]Covenants Watch (2017), p. 1.

[45]*Id.*

[46]Interview with Wang KY, Professor, National Chung Cheng University (28 June 2017).

[47]Interview with Chang G, Secretary, Taiwan Association for Disability Rights (6 June 2017).

[48]Interview with Chien YH, Senior Supervisor, Department of Social Work, Child Welfare League Foundation and Li HW, Director of Advocacy Center, Child Welfare League Foundation, National Taiwan University (17 Mar 2017).

[49]Interview with Liao YH, Professor, National Chengchi University (11 Jan 2016).

which Wang and Liao were champions, or that of rights more broadly, but to advance the idea that the realm of what might be possible has yet to be exhausted.

One area in particular where this tension appears to be playing out has been that of legal capacity and guardianship—an area, to be sure, that was contentious in the drafting of Article 12 and remains so in several national settings.[50] The Executive Yuan's report, at Paragraphs 75–79, addresses the issue as largely settled through the law of trusts, treating it as principally involving financial management—an approach that comes in for criticism in key shadow reports. The League's report takes issue with "a severe lack in procedures, assessment tools and protection" in proceedings to commence guardianship and decries the absence of any provision "for participation by persons other than psychiatrists" (presumably including, but not limited to, family members).[51] The Covenants Watch report also takes issue with the Executive Yuan's depiction—noting that the impact of being subject to guardianship "extends to all types of legal activity requiring expression of intent, such as marriage, leaving a will…disposition of property, expressing consent to medical procedures…election rights, etc." and it calls, therefore, for the development of "an 'assisted decision-making system'" so as to repose autonomy with the individual or with an "independent representative" thereof.[52]

The particular impact of disability on women has also been a focal point of shadow reports and scholars. Both the League report and that of Covenants Watch point out what they believe is the possibility of coerced abortion and sterilization found in Taiwan's Genetics Health Act and its inconsistency with the CRPD. And in keeping with the CRPD's recognition that women with disabilities have been the subject of even more discrimination than their male counterparts, the Covenants Watch report stresses the "multiple and intersectional discrimination faced by women with disabilities in public and private sectors" and makes the case that this can only be addressed if general measures designed to foster greater gender equality (in areas from education to employment and beyond) engage specifically with the rights of women with disabilities.

The issue of what might constitute a reasonable accommodation—which also is one of considerable controversy elsewhere[53]—is another area with respect to which the parallel reports have taken the authorities to task. To be sure, there is appreciation both for those areas of R.O.C. law that call for "appropriate assistance" and for the state's acknowledgment that an overall definition is not yet forthcoming.

---

[50]Freeman et al. (2015).

[51]League (2017), pp. 3–4.

[52]Covenants Watch (2017), p. 33.

[53]See, e.g., Stein (2003).

But, even with that, there remains a lack of clarity as to "what the duties and who their bearers should be with regard to 'reasonable accommodation'" as well as a lack of "objective criteria of the term 'reasonable'" and no stipulated penalties for a failure to comply—with consequences especially in the areas of education and employment.[54]

Some progress appears to have been made with respect to education, with a growing recognition by the authorities of findings from other parts of the world of the benefits of inclusive education and a concomitant move toward mainstreaming, rather than isolation, for children with disabilities. Yet much remains to be done to make possible an inclusive environment both with respect to physical barriers and with respect to academic supports tailored to the differing needs of individual students.[55] Training in special education, whether for general or specialized teachers, needs be ramped up, as does sign language. Opportunities for tertiary education need to be opened. College admissions procedures may contain implicit or even explicit barriers to the entrance of students with disabilities in certain programs, which is a continuing area of scholarly attention.[56] And, observes the Covenants Watch report, particular attention needs to be focused on the education of girls and women with disabilities who, whether because of official inaction, family preferences or social expectations generally, have been left farther behind than their male counterparts with disabilities.[57]

Even with a more developed approach toward reasonable accommodations than other areas, employment remains a deeply troubling area on Taiwan, as elsewhere. According to official statistics, labor market participation by persons with disabilities is only one-third that of persons without disabilities[58]—and those numbers fail to adequately convey problems of inadequate support, insufficient training, underemployment and more, especially for persons with intellectual or socio-psychological disabilities. Hence, there is a call in the various parallel reports for the development of more vocational training programs, for greater efforts to acquaint employers with ways in which jobs could be re-cast so as to facilitate greater employment for persons with disabilities, and for a drastic re-think of sheltered workplaces.[59]

---

[54]Covenants Watch (2017), p. 8.

[55]*Id.*, at p. 33.

[56]Chang Interview.

[57]Covenants Watch (2017), pp. 8–10.

[58]Executive Yuan (2017), p. 76.

[59]League (2017), pp. 19–21 and Covenants Watch (2017), pp. 75–82.

Beyond these, there are several other important issues that the shadow reports and scholars have identified as needing to be addressed in order for Taiwan to meet the international standard it set for itself in the Implementing Act. These include, but are not limited to, much greater access to health services responsive to the needs of persons with disabilities, significantly upgraded disaster notification and relief services, and improved housing without sacrificing the possibilities for independent living.[60] The Covenants Watch report accords particular prominence to the situation of indigenous persons (who make up approximately 2% of the population) with disabilities, taking the government to task for not specifically addressing this issue or heeding the impact of culture or language.[61]

And finally, and pertinent to all of the foregoing issues, there is the question—underscored in the Covenants Watch report and by many commentators—of the establishment of a National human rights commission.[62] In incorporating the CRPD into its domestic law, the government obligated itself to establish an independent monitoring body to promote, protect and monitor its actions in implementation.[63] The Covenants Watch report points out that the Control Yuan, empowered by the Constitution to independently exercise monitoring power over the executive branch to protect the rights of citizens, "does not meet the requirements set under the 1993 United Nations Paris Principles on National Institutions for the Promotion and Protection of Human Rights, in both the composition of personnel and its functions."[64] Other human rights advocates have expressed the same concerns.[65] In their view, having an independent monitoring institution would advance scrutiny of the government's compliance with the CRPD, as well as the process of reviewing domestic legislation and regulations for any possible inconsistency with the CRPD.[66] Some commentators have suggested that questions remain as to the appropriate location of such a monitoring institution, including whether it should be a committee in the Presidential Office or the Executive Yuan, or completely independent from any government agency, but there is a broad support in civil society for its establishment.[67]

[60]See, e.g., Taiwan Community Living Consortium (2017).

[61]Covenants Watch (2017).

[62]*Id.*, at p. 91.

[63]Article 33 of the CRPD specifies national implementation and monitoring.

[64]Covenants Watch (2017).

[65]Shih (2014), Huang (2015).

[66]*Id.*

[67]Huang (2015).

5 Conclusion

An argument can be made that the exclusion of Taiwan from international human rights agreements such as the CRPD has had the ironic result of accentuating the importance of Taiwan's adherence to those agreements and to the international human rights norms they embody. The standards set by the CRPD were clearly in mind as scholars and activists, a decade ago, critiqued and worked to improve Taiwan's own laws concerning disability. The affirmation of Taiwan's stature as a law-abiding member of the international community of states provided by incorporation into domestic law was undoubtedly a factor both in the priority that President Ma accorded their early adoption and in the subsequent measures taken by the Executive Yuan to translate such adoption into practice. The authority of the Implementing Act has been used by at least some in the judiciary to buttress claims based in part on the Constitution and other legislation. And the example of the CRPD as effectuated by many states has been a powerful instrument in the hands of DPOs, many activists, and scholars in pressing the government to meet its full obligations and to push for more profound transformations in the ways in which both state and society on Taiwan conceive of and treat disability.

To be sure, as evidenced in the initial round of parallel reports, much work remains to be done. But as Professor Sun Nai-Yi has underscored, it is work with pertinence not only to improve the situation of persons with disabilities but, as well, work with the potential to contribute to Taiwan's broader development by fostering a greater respect more generally for the rule of law and for a more humane, civic-minded and responsible society.[68]

Acknowledgments The authors wish to thanks Lee Yi-li, Michael Stein and Cui Fengming for their insights. We remain responsible for opinions expressed and errors contained in this chapter.

References

Alford WP (2014) Rehabilitating history: a revisionist perspective on the treatment of disability in Chinese history. Paper presented at a lecture in honor of Grand Justice Ma Han-bao, National Taiwan University College of Law, 19 Dec 2014

Chang HH (2007) Special education and sociology of disability: a theoretical reflection. Formosan Edu Soc 13:71–94

Chen YJ (2016) Socialization in isolation: Taiwan's practice of human rights treaties as a non-UN member state (unpublished J.S.D. dissertation, New York University School of Law)

Chou YC, Zhu YZ (2011) Jianshi Taiwan shenxin zhang'ai fuli zhengce yu fa'an zhi lishi jincheng yu biange [檢視台灣身心障礙福利政策與法案之歷史進程與變革] (A review of disability and social welfare law and policy reform in Taiwan). Paper presented at Shehui fuli moshi—cong chuancheng dao chuangxin yantao hui [社會福利模式—從傳承到創新研討會] (Seminar on the social welfare model—from tradition to innovation), Beijing, 15–19 Apr 2011

[68]Sun (2017).

Chu YH, Lin JW (2001) Political development in 20th century Taiwan: state-building, regime transformation and the construction of national identity. Chin Q 165:102–129

Covenants Watch (2017) Parallel report on the implementation of the Convention on the Rights of Persons with Disabilities. http://covenantswatch.org.tw/wp-content/uploads/2017/07/2017_CW_CRPD_Parallel_Report_Eng.pdf. Accessed 6 Oct 2017

Executive Yuan (2017) Luoshi shenxin zhang'ai quanli gongyue tuidong jihua [落實身心障礙者權利公約推動計畫] (The plan to facilitate implementation of the Convention on the Rights of Persons with Disabilities). http://www.sfaa.gov.tw/SFAA/Pages/ashx/File.ashx?FilePath=*/File/Attach/5908/File_168109.pdf. Accessed 6 Oct 2017

Fiala-Butoro J (2016) Reconstructing personhood. (Unpublished S.J.D. dissertation, Harvard Law School)

Freeman MC et al (2015) Reversing hard won victories in the name of human rights: a critique of the General Comment on Article 12 of the UN Convention on the Rights of Persons with Disabilities. Lancet Psychiatry 2(9):844–850

Hu QY (2017) The incorporation of the CRPD in Taiwan: motivation and impact. (Unpublished paper, Harvard Law School)

Huang YB (2015) Shijie Renquan Ri, Qing Chengli Guojia Renquan Weiyuan Hui [世界人權日, 請成立國家人權委員會] (On Human Rights Day, please establish a National Human Rights Institution). Apple Daily Net. http://www.appledaily.com.tw/realtimenews/article/new/20151209/749865/. Accessed 26 Aug 2017

League for Persons with Disabilities ROC (2017) Parallel report on the Convention on the Rights of Persons with Disabilities. http://www.sfaa.gov.tw/SFAA/Pages/ashx/File.ashx?FilePath=*/File/Attach/5928/File_169107.pdf. Accessed 6 Oct 2017

Qiu S, Li W (2009) Shangxia ji mei ren bei lirong ju zaishen zhang zhe [上下機沒人背 立榮拒載身障者] (Uni Air prevented a passenger with a disability from boarding a flight after staff were unable to carry the passenger onto the plane). Liberty Times Net. http://news.ltn.com.tw/news/life/paper/321515. Accessed 26 Aug 2017

Shih YS (2014) Mo rang shenxin zhang'ai zhe quanli gongyue chengwei renquan kongtou zhipiao [莫讓身心障礙者權利公約成爲人權空頭支票] (Don't let the UN Convention on the Rights of Persons with Disabilities become an empty human rights promise). Taiwan Association for Human Rights. https://www.tahr.org.tw/node/1516. Accessed 26 Aug 2017

Stein MA (2003) The law and economics of disability accommodations. Duke Law J 53:79–191

Stein MA (2007) Disability human rights. Calif Law Rev 95:75–121

Stein MA, Lord J (2010) Monitoring the Committee on the Rights of Persons with Disabilities: innovations, lost opportunities, and future potential. Hum Rights Q 31:689–728

Sun NY (2017) The right to accessibility for people with disabilities: a legal analysis of enforcing the governmental obligation to construct a barrier-free environment through litigation. Const Interpretation Theor Pract 9:437–512

Taiwan Community Living Consortium (2017) Taiwan Community Living Consortium shadow report to the UN Convention on the Rights of Persons with Disabilities. http://www.sfaa.gov.tw/SFAA/Pages/ashx/File.ashx?FilePath=～/File/Attach/5930/File_169449.pdf. Accessed 6 Oct 2017

Tsai IL, Ho MS (2010) An institutionalist explanation of the evolution of Taiwan's disability movement: from the charity model to the social model. J Curr Chin Affairs 39(3):87–123

Wang KY (2008) The United Nation's Convention on the Rights of Persons with Disabilities: its implication to Taiwanese policy. Community Dev J 123:106–116

Winckler EA (1992) Taiwan's transition. In Cheng TJ, Haggard S (eds) Political change in Taiwan. Lynne Rienner, Boulder, pp 221–259

World Health Organization and World Bank (2011) World report on disability. WHO Press, Geneva

Yeh JR (2016) The constitution of Taiwan: a contextual analysis. Bloomsbury, London

William P. Alford is Jerome A. and Joan L. Cohen Professor of East Asian Legal Studies at Harvard Law School where he also serves as Vice Dean for the Graduate Program and International Legal Studies, Director of East Asian Legal Studies, and Chair of the Harvard Law School Project on Disability. A scholar of Chinese law and society, his books include *To Steal a Book is an Elegant Offense: Intellectual Property Law in Chinese Civilization* (Stanford 1995); *Raising the Bar: The Emerging Legal Profession in East Asia* (Harvard 2007), 残疾人法律保障機制研究 (A Study of Legal Mechanisms to Protect Persons with Disabilities) (Huaxia 2008, with Wang Liming and Ma Yu'er, in Chinese), and *Prospects for the Professions in China* (Routledge 2011, with William Kirby and Kenneth Winston). In addition, he has published dozens of articles concerning China, law and international affairs. Professor Alford's work has been recognized with an honorary doctorate from the University of Geneva in 2010 and honorary professorships at Renmin University of China and Zhejiang University. He is also the recipient of the inaugural O'Melveny & Myers Centennial Award, the Kluwer China Prize, an Abe (Japan) Fellowship, the Harvard Law School Alumni Association Award, an award from Special Olympics International recognizing his work on behalf of persons with intellectual disabilities, and several other fellowships and honors. He is a graduate of Amherst College (B.A.), the University of Cambridge (LL.B.), Yale University (M.A. in History and M.A. in Chinese Studies), and Harvard Law School (J.D.).

Qiongyue Hu is a licensed attorney in California and works at Learning Rights Law Center, a nonprofit law firm that serves children with learning disabilities in low-income families. Qiongyue graduated in 2017 with a J.D. from Harvard Law School, where she took classes in disability law and comparative law. In 2016, she spent three weeks in Taiwan conducting comparative legal research on Taiwan's disability rights movement. Prior to Harvard, Qiongyue graduated from Renmin University of China with a B.A. in law.

Charles Wharton served as Visiting Assistant Professor, then Visiting Associate Professor, at National Taiwan University College of Law from 2014 to 2017, where he taught and researched in the area of international disability rights law. A 2012 graduate of Harvard Law School, he previously worked as an Assistant Professor at Renmin University Law School in Beijing. While there, he supervised the country's first Disability Rights Law Clinic, in which students worked directly with NGOs on projects on access to education and legal capacity building. He has also previously undertaken research on corporate social responsibility and the hiring of workers with disabilities at Chinese companies under the auspices of the Harvard Law School Project on Disability and he has conducted training for stakeholders, including families and government officials, on negotiation skills. In addition to his work related to persons with disabilities, he also contributes research and editorial assistance on environmental law for the UN International Law Commission Special Rapporteur on the Protection of the Atmosphere.

Chapter 37
On the Road to Equal Enjoyment of Human Rights for Persons with Disabilities: The Development of Domestic Laws in Taiwan and Their Dialogue with the CRPD

Nai-Yi Sun

Abstract The fundamental rights and freedoms of persons with disabilities are guaranteed by the Constitution of the Republic of China (Taiwan). Article 155 of the Constitution obliges the state to provide appropriate assistance and relief to the aged and infirm who are unable to earn a living. Paragraph 7, Article 10 of the Additional Articles of the Constitution, amended during the 1990s, further obliges the state to assist persons with disabilities to develop and attain independence. These constitutional state duties are realized mainly in the People with Disabilities Rights Protection Act. Developed over the past 30 years, the Act, through its regulations, provides not only for monetary payments but also for a diverse range of individualized services to be made available to persons with disabilities. Furthermore, there are detailed legal requirements regarding barrier-free public facilities and transport. However, the fundamental rights of persons with disabilities are often restricted or compromised by laws in other fields, while government agencies tend to handle matters related to disability-based discrimination by private persons in a passive manner. In 2014, Taiwan incorporated the Convention on the Rights of Persons with Disabilities (CRPD) into domestic law. The Convention furthers the purpose of equal enjoyment of human rights under the International Covenant on Civil and Political Rights and the International Covenant on Economic, Social and Cultural Rights, and promotes the full and effective participation in society of people with disabilities. The convention is intended to act as a stimulus for the mainstreaming of the human rights of persons with disabilities, a concept that is foreign to our legal system. This chapter aims to describe the development of domestic laws relating to the rights of persons with disabilities in Taiwan while analyzing the continuing discrimination occurring behind the façade of legislative progress. It further compares the distinct concepts of equal enjoyment of human rights between the domestic laws and the CRPD. With regard to the insufficient awareness of the spirit of the

N.-Y. Sun (✉)
National Chengchi University, Taipei, Taiwan
e-mail: naiyisun@nccu.edu.tw

J. A. Cohen et al. (eds.), *Taiwan and International Human Rights*, Economics, Law, and Institutions in Asia Pacific, https://doi.org/10.1007/978-981-13-0350-0_37

CRPD, as presented in the initial state report of the government of Taiwan, this chapter analyzes how the denial of accessibility and reasonable accessibility are defined as discrimination based on disability by the Convention, which challenges and transforms the conventional understanding of equal protection for the rights of persons with disabilities in Taiwan.

Keywords Accessibility · Convention on the rights of people with disabilities
Non-discrimination · People with disabilities rights protection act
Persons with disabilities · Reasonable accommodation · Substantial equality

1 Introduction

The human rights of persons with and without disabilities are protected equally by the Constitution in Taiwan. Article 7 of the Constitution of the Republic of China (Taiwan) enumerates non-discrimination based on sex, religion, race, class and political affiliations and sets out the principle of equal treatment before the law in general.[1] As a result, people with disabilities, although not specifically mentioned in the wording of the article, cannot be unequally treated under the law without justification. In consideration of the poverty and vulnerability that people with disabilities often suffer, Article 155 of the Constitution also obliges the state to provide appropriate assistance and relief in order to ensure a minimum standard of life is maintained. Furthermore, drawing on the concept of substantial equality, Article 10, Paragraph 7 of the Additional Articles of the Constitution, adopted in the 1990s, stipulates that the state shall assist persons with disabilities to develop and attain independence.

The abovementioned constitutional orders have been realized by laws in multiple fields. The Persons with Disabilities Rights Protection Act is regarded as the main statute providing monetary payments and benefits-in-kind to people with disabilities, and sets out certain specific anti-discrimination clauses. In reality, however, people with disabilities are often ignored, regarded as incapable and unqualified, and therefore often excluded from engaging with others in activities on an equal basis by laws and regulations. This exclusion persists due to deeply-rooted cultural and social biases, notwithstanding the promotion of affirmative action in fields such as education and employment. As a result, it remains doubtful that the individual autonomy and independence of persons with disabilities is indeed recognized by law.

In 2014, following the previously adopted model of incorporating fundamental rights and freedoms enshrined in the United Nations Human Rights Conventions by way of Implementing Acts, Taiwan passed the Implementation Act of the Convention on the Rights of Persons with Disabilities (hereinafter Implementation Act). One year later, the Parliament ratified the Convention on the Rights of Persons

[1]Lin (1993), pp. 92–94; Lee (2015), pp. 141–142.

with Disabilities (hereinafter CRPD, or the Convention). Both parliamentary actions carry high expectations for strengthening the legal status of persons with disabilities in domestic law, not only because, by way of the Implementation Act, provisions in the CRPD now have legal status in domestic law, but also because the Implementation Act stipulates in Article 8 the manner in which litigation may be conducted. In cases where the rights protected by the Convention, other ratified conventions or the Act's regulations are infringed, or cannot be implemented or are only implemented with difficulty, persons with disabilities may make an appeal, file a claim or file any other petition to protect their rights. In these situations, the government shall provide legal aid for the appointment of an attorney. This clause is unique to the Implementation Act and demonstrates that there was insufficient legal protection of the rights of persons with disabilities prior to the act.

In order to illustrate the significance of the incorporation of the CRPD in Taiwan, this chapter will first provide a brief overview of the legal framework in Taiwan for protecting the rights of persons with disabilities. It will highlight important conceptual and legislative developments related to the rights of persons with disabilities that have occurred in the past 30 years, under the influence of the relevant international regulations, and analyze the discrimination that has persisted behind this façade of legislative progress. The chapter will go on to compare the concepts of equal protection and non-discrimination within domestic laws and the CRPD, and point out the principal challenges involved in incorporating the Convention in Taiwan's legal system, especially when sufficient awareness about the discrepancies between the domestic and international laws is lacking, as shown by the initial state report by the government of Taiwan.

2 The Development of the Rights of Persons with Disabilities in Domestic Law Under the Influence of International Law

In Taiwan, conventionally, persons with disabilities have had to depend entirely on their families for support. Without such support, they were often confined to their homes or became homeless. Persons with disabilities would very rarely be placed in institutions by the local government. The state duty to provide assistance to maintain their minimum standard of living, as stipulated in the Constitution, was either ignored or only partially realized. The first legislation targeting persons with disabilities, the Disabled Persons Welfare Act (1980), was enacted immediately after the end of diplomatic relations between the United States and the government of ROC (Taiwan) in 1979. Utilizing two other welfare acts, the Public Assistance Act and the Senior Citizen Welfare Act, the legislation aimed to calm the political discontent under the martial regime of the Kuomintang in China.[2]

[2]Lin (1994), p. 184.

In the past 30 years, this Act has been amended and renamed twice: in 1997 as the People with Disabilities Protection Act and in 2007 as the People with Disabilities Rights Protection Act. The rights and freedoms of people with disabilities have also subsequently been considered in other acts. To some extent, the development of these domestic laws in Taiwan has been influenced by the advancement of international human rights. The following section discusses the significant development of Taiwan's legislation in relation to the rights and freedoms of persons with disabilities against the background of international human rights development.

2.1 Persons with Disabilities Under the Persons with Disabilities Rights Protection Act and Its Former Acts

During the 1980s through to the mid-1990s, the Disabled Persons Welfare Act served as no more than a political declaration, owing to its extremely vague provisions. For example, it announced on the one hand that no discrimination against people with disabilities is permitted and that their legal rights shall be protected; but, on the other hand, it provided no legal effects in the event of violation. Furthermore, all benefits given to persons with disabilities, both monetary and in-kind, depended on the discretion of local governments without any national regulations or guidelines. Nevertheless, the Act established a disability policy framework in Taiwan. Only those who were evaluated by physicians as belonging to one of the numerous categories of physical disability or disease, and who had been issued with a disability identification card, could qualify for welfare benefits under the Act. In addition, affirmative action was put in place, including occupational reservation of the massage business for the blind, discounts for public transport fares, and purchasing priority, afforded within the public sector for products and services provided by welfare care facilities that employed people with disabilities.

In 1990, taking into account the UN World Programme of Action Concerning Disabled Persons of 1982 and the UN Decade of Disabled Persons (1983–1992), the Disabled Persons Welfare Act was amended for the first time. The amended Act added administrative fines for violation of the non-discrimination clause and other legal obligations, and expanded the categories of disability and disease. To promote job opportunities for those with working capacity, the Act introduced employment quota policies for people with disabilities in the private and public sectors, however, not beyond a residual level. One change that may be regarded as being in accordance with the core principle of the World Programme of Action that enhances the equalization of opportunities for persons with disabilities was the barrier-free requirement imposed on newly built facilities and public transport. The requirement was enforced by giving competent authorities the power to decline to issue a construction license in the event of non-compliance with the relevant architectural regulations. Further points of ideological progress relate to the provision of subsidies for people with disabilities in relation to their national health insurance contributions, and the wider supply of assistive devices, including accessible educational materials, so that such devices were no longer limited only to recipients of social assistance.

In 1997, the Act was substantially amended and renamed the Disabled Citizens Protection Act. Article 1 explicitly sets out the Act's overall objective—to create equal opportunities for participation in social life for persons with disabilities. The Act's content was extended from 31 provisions to 75, divided into eight chapters. In addition to penalties and supplementary provisions, as well as chapters concerning the regulation of welfare institutions by the government, the Act's essential chapters included provisions relating to the general principles, rights and interests of health and medical care, education, employment promotion and welfare services. An important paradigm-shift in the disability policy in Taiwan also emerged, namely that the duty to realize equal opportunities for persons with disabilities was not limited solely to the competent ministry and social welfare agencies of the local authorities; other departments were also to be engaged if the affairs prescribed in the Act related to their competency. For example, authorities charged with ensuring equal educational opportunities for children with disabilities should at least include the Ministry of the Health and Welfare and the Ministry of Education.

In 2007, this Act was once again amended and renamed for the second time the People with Disabilities Rights Protection Act (PDRPA). This amendment was based on the social model of disability studies and the International Classification of Functioning, Disability and Health (ICF), declared by the World Health Organization (WHO) in 2001 and actively promoted by scholars.[3] Chapters on supportive services, economic security and protection services were accordingly added to the PDRPA. The Act abandoned the categories of disabilities that had been adopted through political lobbying and lacked any theoretical background,[4] shifting instead to an approach that mirrored the WHO-ICF model, with a 5-year transition period. Accordingly, the Act adopted a classification of impairment based on activity limitations and participation restrictions, and also imposed a requirement that assessments of individuals must also take into account the environmental factors affecting how they conduct their lives.[5] The aforementioned assessment is to be evaluated by physicians as a first step, while the assessment of individuals is conducted at a later stage by a committee composed of professionals from social work, special education and employment counseling backgrounds. Services regulated by the Act and provided by competent authorities for people with disabilities shall, based on the needs assessment, be individualized, diversified, integrated and continuous.

[3]Wang and Leu (2004).

[4]*Id.*, at p. 228.

[5]Chou et al. (2015), pp. 24–31.

The other essential issues covered by the Act include: adding non-discrimination clauses in relation to exam opportunities, education, employment, residence in the community and the media; strengthening the benefits-in-kind available for people with disabilities and their family; establishing comprehensive notification systems for suspicious cases of unlawful deprivation of liberty or cruel, inhuman, or degrading treatment; and providing urgent protection or resettlement by competent local authorities in situations where people with disabilities encounter imminent danger to their lives, body or freedom, including a requirement that resettlement exceeding 72 hours shall be approved by the court. In subsequent years, the scope of individualized services has been continuously expanded under the Act, with the aim of promoting the independent living and community integration of disabled persons, while reducing the burden on their families.

During 2014 and 2015, parallel amendments were made to the PDRPA, the Copyright Act and the Library Act to incorporate the principles of the Marrakesh Treaty to Facilitate Access to Published Works for Persons Who Are Blind, Visually Impaired or Otherwise Print Disabled of 2013, and to address matters regarding reasonable use of intellectual property rights in relation to accessible publishing and textbooks for people with disabilities.

2.2 *People with Disabilities Under Other Relevant Laws*

People with disabilities in Taiwan are also supported by other legislation. The Special Education Act is most important in providing support for the education of children with disabilities. Under this Act, students may attend special schools, special centralized classes or be integrated into regular classes in accordance with their educational assessment. Each student shall be supported by an individualized education plan, and schools may be equipped with special education teachers, teacher assistants and/or aides to assist students with special needs, when necessary. In relation to employment, discrimination by employers against job applicants and employees, based on the type of disabilities prescribed under the Employment Services Act, shall be punished by an administrative fine.[6] With respect to the need for barrier-free physical environments, design requirements of accessible buildings, indoor and outdoor facilities, roads, transport and alternative improvement plans, are detailed in the regulations set out in the various administrative rules and legal orders established by the PDRPA, the Building Act, the Urban Road Act and the Road Traffic Management and Penalty Act.

On the other hand, the rights and freedoms of people with disabilities are still broadly restrained by laws in multiple dimensions. At the moment, the most

[6]According to the administrative interpretation announced by the Ministry of Labor on 4 Apr 2017 (勞動部勞動條 4 字第 1060130457 號函), discrimination based on disabilities in the Employment Services Act applies to discrimination against all persons with disabilities, regardless of whether the person holds a disability identification card.

controversial issue is the legitimacy of compulsory full-time hospitalization, under the Mental Health Act, of patients with severe mental disorders to prevent them from harming themselves or others. Orders for compulsory hospitalization are issued by the local government, based on a mandatory evaluation by at least two specialist physicians and with the permission of a review committee composed of professionals under the Ministry of Health and Welfare, without judicial review in advance. The procedure has been abused recently, reflecting the community's unreasonable reaction to some crimes committed by offenders with mental illness. According to the Habeas Corpus Act of 2014, the detained person or any other person may apply to the district court immediately for a writ of habeas corpus, which is akin to the petition process for suspending emergency placement or mandatory hospitalization under the Mental Health Act.

3 Discrimination Behind the Legal System

After decades of legal development, the PDRPA and other legislation have made significant progress towards recognizing the diversity of human beings, including people with disabilities and their right to equal participation in society. However, people with disabilities still confront obstacles and exclusion in their daily lives, and direct and indirect discrimination has not been eliminated. In fact, the legal strategies adopted under the influence of international standards are fragmented. The various values behind the law, including restraint, protection and promotion, have not yet been viewed holistically nor critically reviewed. This observation can be explained through the following legal issues.

3.1 Affirmative Action as Protection or Limitation?

Affirmative action is one of the most popular measures used by the government to promote the employment of people with disabilities. Before 2009, an employment quota for people with disabilities in the public and private sectors, the establishment of a separate civil servants' entrance exam exclusively for people with disabilities and the preservation of the massage business exclusively for the blind, were provided for in the PDRPA. Unlike the first two measures, exclusivity of the massage occupation had historical roots—until the 19th century, most visually impaired people lived by begging, fortune-telling or street performing, or were unskilled. During the Japanese colonial period of 1895–1945, people with visual impairment were trained to become masseurs with acupuncture and electrotherapy skills for the first time.[7]

[7]Chiu (2009).

In consideration of the fact that a significant number of people with visual impairment had long depended on the massage industry for their livelihood, the Disabled Persons Welfare Acts in 1980 and 1990 provided for the visually impaired to have the exclusive right to engage in the massage business. People with visual impairment, whether innately or acquired, accordingly preferred to be vocationally trained as masseurs. To engage in the massage business, a certificate of massage technique had to be obtained, and the certificate was only granted to visually impaired people with vocational training. However, the accessibility of the masseuse occupation for the visually impaired has been gradually restricted through amendments to the Physician Act 1967. According to the opinion of the competent authority, acupuncture and electrotherapy are defined as medical treatments, and cannot be performed without a professional license. People with visual impairment intending to gain an occupational advantage were generally excluded from medical education and all other professions in this field. Under the "de-medicalization" policy, the role of masseurs changed from being a professional, at least to some extent, to being a provider of relaxation and leisure services. In other words, people with visual impairment were "protected" by the law, but in fact they were confined within a disadvantaged boundary without the chance of occupational development as a result.[8]

In 2009, the Constitutional Court (in J.Y. Interpretation No. 649) declared that the provision in the PDRPA of an occupational monopoly for the visually-impaired was unconstitutional. The Justices scrutinized the constitutional justification for unequal treatment based on a physical condition beyond human control. Such a justification requires a substantial nexus between the means and the objectives it intends to accomplish. The Justices held that the measure of a vocational monopoly for the visually-impaired had been legitimate in the past, when there were fewer career options available for vision-impaired individuals. However, it was argued that the talents of people with visual impairment were not limited to massage alone, and with enhanced knowledge and capability, the occupations that are suitable and available for visually impaired people have now been expanded. It was felt that, after nearly 30 years of the statute's promulgation, the measure has contributed no significant improvement to the socioeconomic conditions of the visually-impaired, but disproportionally restricted non-visually impaired people's freedom to choose an occupation, especially when the expansion of the massage business market in response to social development is taken into consideration. The Justices concluded that the disputed provision had no substantial nexus to the purpose of securing employment opportunities for visually impaired people and therefore was no longer justified under the Constitution.

The Constitutional Court's Interpretation presents exactly the limited effect of vocational monopolies. The measure provided the government with an excuse to refrain from eliminating discrimination against persons with disabilities. According to a 2010 survey by the Ministry of Labor, 70% of fully vision-impaired persons with

[8]Sun (2011).

working ability engaged in the massage business, and 67.7% of blind masseurs with a bachelor degree had conducted other vocations before entering the massage business.[9] These statistics prove that people with a visual impairment, even when they had a higher education background, are not being integrated into the competitive labor market and are confined to the massage business by government policy, which was regarded by law-makers as appropriate for the vision-impaired.

After the Constitutional Court's Interpretation, various well-known enterprises in Taiwan claimed that they had employed visually-impaired masseurs to help them face market competition from non-visually-impaired masseurs, after the vocational monopoly had been terminated, and to raise the general public's awareness of people with disabilities' vulnerable status in the labor market. These visually impaired employees were paid the basic wage for providing massage services but were not trained to conduct the services performed by the non-vision-impaired employees. As a strategy, these business enterprises could, on the one hand, fulfill their legal employment quota obligations, and on the other hand, earn the reputation of being socially responsible employers. In fact, the ability of visually impaired people to perform other jobs outside the massage business, and to develop their careers on an equal basis with non-visually-impaired people, has never been recognized by society. The stigma has never been changed. Such difficulties faced by people with disabilities illustrate the discrimination that remains behind the "good-will" of affirmative action.

3.2 *Physical and Mental Disability as a Justification for Exclusion?*

Problems similar to those mentioned above also occur where a physically or mentally disabled person seeks to attain certain professional qualifications, become a technologist or civil service employee, or even apply for admission to certain university courses. For instance, people with color-blindness are not eligible to enroll in the Master's programs at the Central Police University, according to the university's regulations governing graduate school admissions examinations. As mentioned above, the principle of equal protection before the law under Article 7 of the Constitution does not prohibit all unequal treatment, but demands legitimacy for differential treatment, especially when based on physical conditions beyond human control. J.Y. Interpretation No. 626 considered the wide range of police tasks, the complexity of police work, and the frequent transfers that occur in police posts, and accepted the argument that a police officer may be required to distinguish color at

[9]Council of Labor Affair (Ministry of Labor), Executive Yuan (2010), pp. 14–16, 34–35, Table 21.

any given moment. The constitutionality of excluding people with color-blindness from the Master's program was therefore affirmed by the Justices.

This conclusion demonstrates the paradox of constitutional jurisprudence in Taiwan. Constitutional scrutiny should, prima facie, provide greater protection of equality for people with disabilities if their exclusion is based on physical or mental characteristics beyond human control. However, unequal limitations on a disabled person's freedom can be easily justified, because physical or mental disability often results in the non-accomplishment of job requirements. For example, police officers with color-blindness are unable to direct traffic; and judges with visual impairment may not reach the right decision if they are unable to review evidence or observe the behavior of plaintiffs and defendants. The legal argument focuses only on the conditions of individuals, without considering the erosion of equal opportunities that can arise from barriers within the environment and biases in society. The latter consideration falls within the scope of substantial equality, but not the equality of everyone before the law. According to the common opinions of constitutional theories and of the jurisprudence of the Constitutional Court, the fact that the government refrains from fulfilling its constitutional obligation to realize substantial equality for women, people with disabilities and other vulnerable groups does not constitute a violation of the principle of equal protection.[10]

3.3 *Accessibility as a Right for People with Disabilities?*

The same predicament—where the rights of people with disabilities are "considered," but there is no real "entitlement" to them—can also be observed in relation to accessibility. Although the PDRPA and other relevant acts and legal orders explicitly stipulate barrier-free regulations for access to physical environments, an individual with disabilities who is unable to access public facilities or public transport still has no legal standing to file a lawsuit against the owner or administrator of the facilities, the transport carrier or the competent authority.

In cases where plaintiffs with disabilities have sought to eliminate road blocks and barriers on elementary school grounds, sidewalks and sports halls in their residential neighborhoods,[11] the high administrative court has held that people with disabilities are indirectly benefited by legislation aiming to address public interests, but are not individually entitled to exercise any right of request as a rights holder under the law. Furthermore, the Supreme Administrative Court considered the competent authorities' budgeting, and concluded that the decision as to when and

[10]For a general analysis on this issue, see Chen (2007), Hwang (2009), Hwang (2017) and Sun (2016), pp. 1177–1180.

[11]98 Nian Suzi Di 186 Hao Panjue [98 年訴字第 186 號判決] (Kaohsiung Admin. High Ct. [高雄高等行政法院] 17 Aug 2010) (Taiwan); 100 NIan Panzi Di 1454 Hao Panjue [100 年判字第 1454 號判決] (Supreme Admin. Ct. [最高行政法院] 18 Aug 2011) (Taiwan). For an analysis of these cases, see Sun (2017).

how the government is to fulfill its obligation to foster an accessible environment should not be determined by the judiciary, as it would be beyond its authority to examine the legality of an executive decision.

Similarly, even though public transport carriers provide urban buses with access-free equipment, in compliance with relevant regulations, passengers in wheelchairs are often rejected by bus drivers. In such cases, affected passengers may appeal to the competent authority and demand improvement, but they have no legal recourse against the private transport carrier, as no legislation in terms of anti-discrimination mandates extends such a duty beyond the civil law.

The laws, regulations and the practices mentioned above create doubt as to whether and how far people with disabilities are regarded as rights-holders, as opposed to merely people who are subject to protection in the legal system.

4 From a Protected Vulnerable Group to Persons with Supported Autonomy and Equal Participation in Society Through Adoption of the CRPD

4.1 Scope of Rights and Core Values in the CRPD

The incorporation of the CRPD into domestic law brings about several innovations and drives the concept of equality forward in the field of international human rights law. Based on the respect for differences and the acceptance of persons with disabilities as a part of human diversity, the Convention emphasizes that people with disabilities are inherently autonomous and independent agents, and aims to promote, protect and ensure their full enjoyment of all human rights and participation in society, and to promote respect for their inherent dignity. It informs a strengthened vision of substantial equality, fixed in the notion of non-discrimination, in the private sector[12] and in all rights contained in the Convention.

In comparison to the legal doctrine regarding the distinction between equal protection before the law as a fundamental right, and achieving substantial equality as a governmental obligation without any individual entitlement under constitutional jurisprudence in Taiwan, the notion of equality in the CRPD contains both a formal and a substantive dimension. Article 5(2) of the Convention bans all discrimination on the basis of disability, which according to the definition in Article 2, includes exclusion or restriction on the basis of disability with the purpose or effect of impairing or nullifying the enjoyment or exercise of all human rights. This understanding is similar to the notion of equal protection before the law. However,

[12]Office of the United Nation High Commissioner for Human Rights, Equality and non-discrimination under Article 5 of the Convention on the Rights of Persons with Disabilities, para 3, UN Doc. A/HRC/34/26 (9 Dec 2016) [hereinafter Report of the Office of the UN High Commissioner for Human Rights].

Article 2(3) of the Convention extends the content of discrimination on the basis of disability to cover denial of reasonable accommodation. Furthermore, according to the opinion of the Committee on the Rights of Persons with Disabilities, in General Comment No. 2 (2014), the denial of accessibility stipulated in Article 9 of the Convention shall also be viewed in the context of discrimination on the basis of disability.[13] The CRPD introduces multiple forms of protection from discrimination for individuals with disabilities in a number of situations, including exclusion and restriction, denial of accessibility ex ante and denial of reasonable accommodation ex-nunc,[14] that were hitherto alien to domestic law in Taiwan.

With this distinctive vision of equality, the Convention intends to establish a framework that confers legally enforceable rights on individuals with disabilities as opposed to the traditional group-based welfare approach. The state is expected to play an active role in creating the social conditions necessary for the individual with disabilities to be treated with dignity, while the broad state obligation corresponds to the entitlements of the individual, rather than as a question of the state exercising benevolence through social welfare provisions.[15] According to this conception, people with disabilities are seen to be entitled to claim essential support to enable them to live independently and to enhance their autonomy.

4.2 Incorporation of the CRPD by the Parliament

Given the distinctive vision of equality that the CRPD embodies, a comprehensive reform of the domestic legal framework and policy related to the rights of persons with disabilities was expected. The Taiwanese government, however, had no clear view of the changes required in national law in order to avoid conflicts between the Convention and domestic law because there was no deliberative consideration during the ratification and enacting process in Parliament.

At the time the CRPD came into force, and in the years following, incorporating the Convention into domestic law was not a priority for the executive branch under the ruling Kuomintang party. It took the view that the social model embodied in the CRPD had been adopted in the People with Disabilities Rights Protection Act, as amended in 2007, under which the disability assessment was changed from the medical model to the ICF system.[16] Notwithstanding such a passive view, nongovernmental organizations (hereinafter NGOs), actively working to support

---

[13]See Committee on the Rights of Persons with Disabilities, General Comment no. 2 (2014) Article 9: Accessibility, para. 23, UN Doc. CRPD/C/GC/2 (22 May 2014) [hereinafter General Comment no. 2].

[14]See *Id.*, at paras. 25, 26.

[15]O'Cinneide (2009), pp. 163–166.

[16]Li Fa Yuan Gongbao [立法院公報] (Legislative Yuan Gazette) 102, no. 32 (Apr 2014), 460–465; Li Fa Yuan Gongbao [立法院公報] (Legislative Yuan Gazette) 103, no. 50 (Aug 2014), 25–26.

the rights of people with disabilities in Taiwan allied to advocate for the need to reform the current disability policies and laws through a human rights perspective, and to establish an external monitoring mechanism. The NGOs successfully lobbied legislators from the ruling party, as well as the opposition party (the Democratic Progressive Party), for a draft implementation bill, albeit without a commitment from the executive power in advance.[17] Based on a broad consensus among the legislators, the bill passed smoothly without debate.[18]

Although the government was not well prepared for the adoption of the UN Convention when the Implementation Act of the CRPD was enacted in 2014, it is required to submit its initial state report and to formulate, within two years of the promulgation of the Implementation Act, a priority list of legislation and administrative measures that are inconsistent with the Convention. The Executive Yuan was forced by the Act to draft the "Action Plan for Implementation of the CRPD 2014–2019." Unlike the action programs adopted by other countries after ratifying the CRPD,[19] the action plan of the Taiwanese government does not focus on the substantial issues arising from the implementation of the international human rights standard or the key objectives to be achieved or the measures to be engaged. Taiwan's action plan instead focuses on procedures for education and training on the CRPD for relevant civil servants throughout the government, scheduling a review of domestic legislation and administrative measures for compliance with the CRPD, as well as drafting the initial state report and preparation of the state report review by independent international experts.

Ratification of the CRPD took place after the parliamentary election in 2016. By the time of the second parliamentary deliberation, the review by both central and local governments of the compatibility of regulations with the Convention was underway. The impact of the substantial equality concept encapsulated in the CRPD on national laws and policies related to the rights of people with disabilities was still absent from parliamentary discussion.[20]

4.3 *The Key Challenge for Implementing the CRPD*

The lack of awareness of the discrepancies between the CRPD and the national legal system is shown in the initial state report of March 2017, especially when read together with the parallel reports by the NGOs. In reference to the key notion of "discrimination," the state report cites the Constitution and describes the

---

[17]Press conference held by the "League of Welfare Organizations for the Disabled," see http://www.coolloud.org.tw/node/76377.

[18]Li Fa Yuan Gongbao [立法院公報] (Legislative Yuan Gazette) 103, no. 50 (August 2014), 92–96.

[19]Flynn (2011), pp. 101–196.

[20]Li Fa Yuan Gongbao [立法院公報] (Legislative Yuan Gazette) 105, no. 23 (April 2016), part I, 200–256.

development of the PDRPA in general, then indicates that the inaccessibility of public facilities or means of public transport for people with disabilities will constitute discrimination.[21] However, the report fails to mention that current laws and practice in Taiwan do not offer strong protection against differences in treatment on the basis of disability.

With regards to the concept of "reasonable accommodation," pursuant to the report of the Office of the United Nations High Commissioner for Human Rights, national legislation should explicitly set out the government's obligation to provide reasonable accommodation and regard all such rights as immediately enforceable, and state that denial of reasonable accommodation will constitute discrimination on the basis of disability. States also need to develop policy guidelines, training and awareness-rising activities in order to ensure that their governmental agencies and non-state actors are equipped to provide reasonable accommodation.[22] The initial state report of the government of Taiwan recognizes on the one hand that there is no explicit definition in domestic law, yet emphasizes on the other hand that it makes efforts to provide relevant accommodation within its various laws and regulations. It also emphasizes that it provides personalized assistance to meet the needs of people with disabilities in their education, examination, employment and social participation.[23] In fact, denial of reasonable accommodation does not constitute a form of discrimination under the laws of Taiwan.[24] The experts have noted this discrepancy and demanded that the government of Taiwan describe the concrete steps it has taken to amend national legislation and regulations.[25] The government of Taiwan responded that any legislative reform of reasonable accommodation shall be carried out when greater consensuses about its scope are achieved.[26] Behind the official statement, the fact is that the government has not yet taken concrete steps to consider this issue.

Also with regards to accessibility, according to General Comment No. 2, States Parties are obliged to adopt a suitable legal framework, which takes into account the relevant international recommendations for information and communications technology, and to undertake a comprehensive review of the laws on accessibility in order to identify, monitor and address gaps in legislation and implementation. Under the framework, denial of access is to be defined as a prohibited act of

[21]Concluding Observations of the initial report of the Republic of China (Taiwan) on the Convention on the Rights of Persons with Disabilities (CRPD) adopted by the International Review Committee (IRC) on 3 November 2017, paras. 1–6, 14–19 [hereinafter CRPD initial state report of Taiwan].

[22]Report of the Office of the UN High Commissioner for Human Rights, at paras 39, 69.

[23]CRPD initial state report of Taiwan, at para 7.

[24]Covenants Watch (2017), para 24.

[25]International Review Committee (2017) List of Issues, initial state report of Taiwan, para 3 [hereinafter List of Issues]. http://www.sfaa.gov.tw/SFAA/Pages/Detail.aspx?nodeid=834&pid=6358. Accessed 12 Dec 2017.

[26]Replies to Paragraph 3 of the List of Issues (2017). http://www.sfaa.gov.tw/SFAA/Pages/Detail.aspx?nodeid=834&pid=6424. Accessed 12 Dec 2017.

discrimination, and people with disabilities shall have effective legal remedies at their disposal.[27] The initial state report describes precisely the relevant regulations about accessibility in the areas of construction, public information and transport,[28] but fails to mention accessibility requirements in relation to finance, commerce and media, housing, community facilities and public services. These omissions were criticized by NGOs in their parallel reports[29] and questioned by independent experts.[30] The legal remedies available when access has been denied were also not mentioned.

With the interpretations cited above, both notions in the CRPD pose challenges to the ordinary concept of non-discrimination and equal protection in Taiwan's laws and in relevant judicial decisions. In particular, entitlements for persons with disabilities, rather than being a unilateral state obligation, demand a paradigm shift in the legal framework of the equal protection principle. Contrary to the passive attitude of the legislative and executive branches, courts in Taiwan are active in applying the CRPD to certain controversial issues, such as the death penalty and compulsory hospitalization of persons with mental disabilities who are at risk of harming themselves or others.[31] However, without proactive steps by the legislative and executive divisions in all areas of law and public policy, to include persons with disabilities in planning and formulating disability-specific policies, judicial decisions are likely to confront legitimacy issues, especially when applying the concept of substantial equality in cases involving private persons, organizations and private enterprises.[32]

5 Perspective

At the level of international law, Taiwan is isolated and excluded from participating in international human rights conventions. In practice, Taiwan has developed a unique model to incorporate several international human rights conventions into domestic law, including the CRPD. This Convention takes an innovative approach to the principle of equality and non-discrimination, and presents a powerful vision of substantial equality to transform current social structures, systems and

---

[27]General Comment no. 2, at paras 28–29.

[28]CRPD initial state report of Taiwan, paras 42–66.

[29]Covenants Watch (2017), paras 70–84, 150–152, 183–185; League for Persons with Disabilities, R.O.C. (2017), paras 67–68, 77–78; Taiwan Community Living Consortium (2017).

[30]List of Issues, at paras 19–22.

[31]For example, see's decision, 106 Nian Du Weizi Di 4 Hao Min Shi Caiding [106 年度衛字第 4 號民事裁定] (Taoyuan District Ct. [桃園地方法院] [15 Sep 2017]) (Taiwan) about detention of persons with mental disabilities under the Mental Health Act, and decision 105 Nian Du Zhong Su Zi Di 9 Hao Xing Shi Panjue [105 年度重訴字第 9 號刑事判決] (Shih-Lin District Ct. [士林地方法院] [12 May 2017]) (Taiwan) on the death penalty.

[32]Sun (2015).

conceptions. It strengthens the obligations of States Parties in consultation with people with disabilities, to implement and establish monitoring mechanisms. These actions should ensure the exercise of enabling rights, in particular with respect to the entitlements for persons with disabilities in cases involving the denial of access and reasonable accommodation.

In this regard, Taiwan is facing the same challenge as the other States Parties of the CRPD of how to transform international law into domestic law. However, the Convention also presents an opportunity for dialogue between people with disabilities and the Taiwanese government in relation to advanced concepts of human rights. The CRPD provides guidance on the changes required in domestic legislation, policy and jurisprudence. It can be used to broaden the domestic legislative framework, which to date has focused primarily on socio-economic rights, for people with disabilities and the unilateral dimension of governmental obligations, as well as to enable equal enjoyment of civil, political, social, economic and cultural rights with subjective entitlements against the government and the private sectors. In Taiwan, a holistic, and not fragmented, influence of international human rights concepts in all areas of domestic law relating to rights for people with disabilities is to be expected.

References

Chen A-E (2007) Dui Xianfa Pingdengquan Guiding de Jiantao—You Jianshi Sifayuan Dafaguan Xiangguan Jieshi Chufa [對憲法平等權規定的檢討—由檢視司法院大法官相關解釋出發] (Analysis of the right of equal treatment in the Constitution: a review of the relevant constitutional interpretations of the Constitutional Court). In: Tang D T-C and Liao F F-T (eds) Xianfa Jieshi zhi Lilun yu Shiwu (Di 5 Ji) [憲法解釋之理論與實務 (第五輯)] (Constitutional interpretation: Theory and practice, vol. 5). Institutum Iurisprudentiae, Academia Sinica, Taipei, pp 225–260

Chiu T (2009) Bei Hulue de Lishi Shishi: Cong Shizhangzhe Gongzuo Yanbian Kan Dafaguan Shizi Di 649 Hao Jieshi [被忽略的歷史事實: 從視障者工作演變看大法官釋字第六四九號解釋] (The overlooked historical facts: an examination of the Constitutional Court's J.Y. Interpretation No. 649 in light of changes in work by the visually impaired in Taiwan). Soc Policy Soc Work 13(2):55–86

Chou Y-C, Chang H-H, Lee C-J, Chan M-Y (2015) Lianheguo Guoji Weisheng Zuzhi ICF Yuanqi yu Jingshen: Wenxian Jianshi [聯合國國際衛生組織 ICF 緣起與精神: 文獻檢視] (Context and philosophy of the WHO's ICF: literature review). Community Dev Q 150:17–39

Committee on the Rights of Persons with Disabilities, General Comment no. 2 (2014): Article 9: Accessibility, UN Doc. CRPD/C/GC/2 (22 May 2014)

Concluding observations of the initial report of the Republic of China (Taiwan) on the Convention on the Rights of Persons with Disabilities (CRPD) adopted by the International Review Committee (IRC) on 3 Nov 2017

Council of Labor Affairs (Ministry of Labor), Executive Yuan (2010) Shijue Zhang'aizhe Laodong Zhuangkuang Diaocha Baogao [視覺障礙者勞動狀況調查報告] (Survey report of labor conditions of people with visual impairment). Council of Labor Affairs (Ministry of Labor), Executive Yuan, Taipei

Covenants Watch (2017) Parallel paper on the implementation of the Convention of Rights for People with Disabilities

Flynn E (2011) From rhetoric to action: implementing the UN Convention on the Rights of Persons with Disabilities. Cambridge University Press, New York

Hwang J-Y (2009) Pingdengquan Anjian zhi Sifa Shencha Biaozhun—Cong Shizi Di 626 Hao Jieshi Tanqi [平等權案件之司法審查標準—從釋字第 626 號解釋談起] (Judicial standards for review on equal protection cases: before and after J.Y. Interpretation No. 626). In: Liao F F-T (ed) Xianfa Jieshi zhi Lilun yu Shiwu (Di 6 Ji) (Xiace) [憲法解釋之理論與實務 (第六輯) (下冊)] (Constitutional interpretation: theory and practice, vol 6, part II). Institutum Iurisprudentiae, Academia Sinica, Taipei, pp 551–580

Hwang J-Y (2017) Cong Pingdeng Lilun de Yanjin Jiantao Shizhi Pingdengguan zai Xianfa Shiyong Shang de Nanti [從平等理論的演進檢討實質平等觀在憲法適用上的難題] (Evolution of equality theory and difficulties concerning the constitutional application of the conception of substantive equality). In: Lee C-L (ed) Xianfa Jieshi zhi Lilun yu Shiwu (Di 9 Ji) [憲法解釋之理論與實務 (第九輯)] (Constitutional interpretation: theory and practice, vol 9). Institutum Iurisprudentiae, Academia Sinica, Taipei, pp 271–312

International Review Committee (2017) List of issues, initial state report of Taiwan. http://www.sfaa.gov.tw/SFAA/Pages/Detail.aspx?nodeid=834&pid=6358. Accessed 12 Dec 2017

League for Persons with Disabilities, R.O.C. (2017) Parallel paper on the Convention on the Rights of People with Disabilities

Lee H-T (2015) Xianfa Yaoyi [憲法要義] (Constitutional law), 7th edn. Angel Publishing [元照], Taipei

Li Fa Yuan Gongbao [立法院公報] (Legislative Yuan Gazette) 102, no. 32 (Apr 2014)

Li Fa Yuan Gongbao [立法院公報] (Legislative Yuan Gazette) 103, no. 50 (Aug 2014)

Li Fa Yuan Gongbao [立法院公報] (Legislative Yuan Gazette) 105, no. 23 (Apr 2016)

Lin J-D (1993) Zhonghua Minguo Xianfa Zhutiao Shiyi (Yi) [中華民國憲法逐條釋義 (一)] (Commentary on the Constitution of the Republic of China, vol. 1), 7th edn. Wunan Publishing [五南], Taipei

Lin W-Y (1994) Fuli Guojia—Lishi Bijiao de Fenxi [福利國家—歷史比較的分析] (Welfare state—A historical comparative analysis). Chuliu Publishing [巨流], Taipei

O'Cinneide C (2009) Extracting protection for the rights of persons with disabilities from human rights frameworks: established limits and new possibilities. In: Aranrdóttir OM, Quinn G (eds) The UN Convention on the Rights of Persons with Disabilities: European and Scandinavian perspectives. Brill, Leiden, pp 163–198

Office of the United Nation High Commissioner for Human Rights, Equality and Non-discrimination under Article 5 of the Convention on the Rights of Persons with Disabilities, UN Doc. A/HRC/34/26 (9 Dec 2016)

Replies to paragraph 3 of the List of Issues (2017) http://www.sfaa.gov.tw/SFAA/Pages/Detail.aspx?nodeid=834&pid=6424. Accessed 12 Dec 2017

Sun N-Y (2011) Zaitan Shizhang Anmo Baoliu Tiaokuan zhi Hexianxing—Dafaguan Shizi Di 649 Hao Jieshi de Fashishi yu Fashiyi [再探視障按摩保留條款之合憲性—大法官釋字第六四九號解釋的法事實與法釋義] (Rethinking the constitutionality of the vocational monopoly for the vision-impaired masseurs: the legal facts and legal doctrines of J.Y. Interpretation No. 649 of the Constitutional Court). Acad Sinica Law J 9:49–127

Sun N-Y (2015) Shenxin Zhang'aizhe Quanli Gongyue Di 8 Tiao Di 1 Xiang Guiding yu Shenxin Zhang'aizhe Quanli Gongyue Shiyong Wenti Chutan [身心障礙者權利公約第 8 條第 1 項規定與身心障礙者權利公約適用問題初探] (Application issues on the Convention on the Rights of People with Disabilities in conjunction with Article 8 of the Implementation Act of the Convention on the Rights of People with Disabilities). Formosa Transnational Law Rev 204:13–31

Sun N-Y (2016) Wuzhang'ai/Kejixing, Heli Diaozheng yu Pingdeng Buqishi Yuanze: Cong Shenxin Zhang'aizhe Quanli Gongyue Jianshi Woguo Xianfa ji Shenxin Zhangaizhe Quanyi Baozhangfa zhi Pingdeng Yuanze Neihan [無障礙/可及性、合理調整與平等不歧視原則: 從身心障礙者權利公約檢視我國憲法及身心障礙者權益保障法之平原則內涵] (Accessibility, reasonable accommodation and non-discrimination principle: a legal review of consistency between the

CRPD and the equal treatment regulations in the Constitution and the Rights Protection Act for persons with disabilities in Taiwan). Natl Taiwan Univ Law J 45(special edition): 1163–1228

Sun N-Y (2017) Shenxin Zhang'ai Xing Bu Xing—Yi Susong Tujing Qingqiu Gongbumen Luoshi Wuzhang'ai Sheshi Shezhi Yiwu de Kexingxing Pingxi [身心障礙行不行—以訴訟途徑請求公部門落實無障礙設施設置義務的可行性評析] (The right to accessibility for people with disabilities: a legal analysis of enforcing the governmental obligation to construct a barrier-free environment through litigation). In: Lee C-L (ed) Xianfa Jieshi zhi Lilun yu Shiwu (Di 9 Ji) [憲法解釋之理論與實務 (第九輯)] (Constitutional interpretation: theory and practice, vol 9). Institutum Iurisprudentiae, Academia Sinica, Taipei, pp 437–512

Taiwan Community Living Consortium (2017) Shadow report to the UN Convention on the Rights of Persons with Disabilities

Wang K-Y, Leu C-H (2004) Shijie Weisheng Zuzhi Shenxin Zhang'ai Renkou Dingyi Gainian zhi Yanjin: Jianlun Woguo Shenxin Zhang'ai Renkou Dingyi Xitong Wenti yu Weilai Xiuzheng Fangxiang [世界衛生組織身心障礙人口定義概念之演進: 兼論我國身心障礙人口定義系統問題與未來修正方向] (Disability definition system of the WHO: its implications and issues related to the Taiwanese system). Soc Policy Soc Work 8(2):193–235

Nai-Yi Sun is Professor at the College of Law, National Chengchi University, Taipei, Taiwan. She holds a B.A. and M.S. in law from National Taiwan University, and a LL.M. and Ph.D. in Law from Ruprecht-Karls-Universität Heidelberg in Germany. She specializes in constitutional law, administrative law, social security law and disability law. She participated in the establishment of the Taiwan Social Law and Social Policy Society in 2014 and was elected the first president of the council of this society from March 2014 to March 2016. She has also co-edited the first textbook on social law in Taiwan with the core members of the Society. Professor Sun's scholarly peer-reviewed articles focus on the issues of healthcare reform and pension reform in Taiwan, the constitutional issues of the welfare state and the human rights of persons with disabilities. In recent years, she has actively discussed with NGOs legal issues related to implementation of the Convention on the Rights of Persons with Disabilities (CRPD). Prof. Sun has co-edited, with Prof. Fort Fu-Te Liao, a volume of CRPD commentaries published in 2017, which reviews how far the rights in the CRPD have been realized and the challenges confronting further implementation in Taiwan.

Chapter 38
Constitutional Dynamics of Judicial Discourse on the Rights of Non-citizens: The Case of Taiwan

Yi-Li Lee

Abstract The recent developments in global and regional immigration attitudes challenge the constitutionality of policies and regulations on immigrants and foreigners in many countries. Similar demands for such judicial resolutions also occurred in Taiwan while it underwent the successful democratic transition in the 1990s. Its Constitutional Court has rendered several decisions to address the civil, social, and political rights of non-citizens in recent years. Against the backdrop of these vibrant developments, this chapter discusses in what ways and to what extent the Constitutional Court of Taiwan has addressed disputes about the rights of non-citizens in the settings of the democratic transition and globalization and the features and critiques of those judicial decisions are. Having examined those judicial decisions, this chapter finds that the Court's decisions reveal two significant features. First, the Court has increasingly taken an inclusive approach in the civil rights of non-citizens, which has facilitated the subsequent development of migrant regulations. Second, the Court and the individual Justices have actively used international human rights instruments to address the rights of non-citizens while Taiwan incorporates itself into the international human rights regime. However, the Court's decisions on social and political rights drew scholarly critiques when it took a rather deferential approach in reviewing related cases due to concerns of national security and limited social resources. Since non-citizens are usually regarded as "discrete and insular minorities," this chapter argues that the Court should consider applying stricter scrutiny to the legal restrictions on the social and political rights of non-citizens, especially when the issue of national origin classification is sensitive. In addition, to guarantee human rights for non-citizens, the Court should find it necessary to develop diverse criteria to review the disputes that pertain to the social and political rights of non-citizens.

Keywords Active reference of international human rights laws
Constitutional Court of Taiwan · Inclusive approach · Migration
Rights of non-citizens

Y.-L. Lee (✉)
Global Taiwan Institute, Washington, DC, USA
e-mail: r92341036@gmail.com

J. A. Cohen et al. (eds.), *Taiwan and International Human Rights*, Economics, Law, and Institutions in Asia Pacific, https://doi.org/10.1007/978-981-13-0350-0_38

1 Introduction

Driven by global political and economic forces, recent decades have witnessed an increasing number of migration patterns across the world.[1] Dynamic international and regional immigration not only shapes the diverse landscape of citizenship for non-citizen groups but also poses a huge challenge to the traditional concept of sovereignty and the constitutional framework that governs the state-citizen relationship.[2] Similar dramatic developments have also occurred in Taiwan as more and more foreign workers and spouses from South-Asian countries and Mainland China have flocked to Taiwan in the context of its rapid democratic transition and globalization since the late 1990s.[3]

The development of transnational immigration not only shapes dynamic migrant governance but also challenges the existing immigration laws and regulations through constitutional litigation. For example, the Constitutional Court of Taiwan has been forced to consider whether the administrative regulations on the entry of Mainlanders from China violated the freedom of movement, whether the restrictions on the foreign worker compensation scheme violated their right of property and the principle of equal protection, and whether a ten-year waiting period for people from Mainland China in Taiwan violated their right to public services. In addition, the constitutionality of the detention proceedings for illegal foreign nationals and the mandatory deportation system for citizens of Mainland China who legally enter Taiwan were respectively challenged before the Taiwanese Constitutional Court.

Against the backdrop of these developments, this chapter seeks to analyze in what ways and to what extent the Constitutional Court of Taiwan addresses disputes on the rights of foreigners in the context of the country's rapid democratic transition and globalization. Section 2 discusses the development of diverse migrant regulations and policies toward non-citizens. Section 3 analyzes how the Constitutional Court of Taiwan has adjudicated non-citizen disputes in the areas of civil, social and political rights, followed by a discussion of the features and critiques of judicial adjudication on the rights of non-citizens in Section 4. The last Section concludes.

[1] Weissbrodt (2008), p. 1; Kondo and Popovic (2013), p. 349.

[2] Edwards and Ferstman (2010), pp. 3–46.

[3] Yeh (2016), pp. 63–65.

2 Dynamic Migrant Governance Since the Democratic Transition

At the end of World War II, the Nationalist Kuomintang (hereinafter "KMT") government took over Taiwan from the defeated Japanese government in August 1945. Taiwan was immediately incorporated as a province of the Republic of China. Later, due to its defeat in the Chinese Civil War, the KMT government relocated from Mainland China to Taiwan.[4] The Constitution of the Republic of China (hereinafter "ROC Constitution") that had just become effective on the Mainland in 1947 was soon suspended by the "Temporary Provisions Effective during the Period of National Mobilization for the Suppression of Communist Rebellion" (hereinafter "Temporary Provisions") and facilitated the establishment of a one-party regime in 1948.[5] To consolidate its political power, the KMT government imposed martial law on Taiwan, which sanctioned massive human rights infringements. Martial law not only curtailed the freedom of movement guaranteed by the ROC Constitution, but its relevant administrative regulations also heavily restricted travel and immigration in Taiwan. For example, Taiwanese citizens or overseas Chinese citizens were not allowed to enter or exit Taiwan without prior official permission. Martial law was not lifted until July 1987, and the Temporary Provisions were not abolished until May 1991.[6]

After almost forty years of authoritarian rule, Taiwan initiated democratization in the late 1980s.[7] To respond to the outcry of protests from students and the opposition party on the streets, the KMT government undertook large-scale political and constitutional reforms, which were to mark the beginning of democratization.[8] This political democratization gave rise to a much more open society and many legal restrictions on civil and political rights were removed. Since the late 1990s, the sweeping forces of democratization and global economic competition have facilitated the institutional reform of immigration, which not only lifted many previous immigration restrictions but also enacted various laws to manage a diverse range of non-citizens who do not have ROC nationality.[9] Those laws either provide substantive and procedural control over immigration regulatory authorities or recognize different types of migrant rights. Those legal regulations for non-citizens can be divided into three categories. The first category regulates the conditions of foreign workers. Taiwan was experiencing labor shortages and therefore decided to import foreign workers to boost the domestic economy in the late 1980s. Hence, the Legislative Yuan of Taiwan (equivalent to Congress) enacted or revised several

---

[4] *Id.*, at pp. 28–29.

[5] *Id.*, at p. 31.

[6] *Id.*, at pp. 37–38.

[7] *Id.*, at pp. 37–38.

[8] *Id.*, at pp. 38–49.

[9] *Id.*, at pp. 222–224.

laws to accommodate foreign workers in Taiwan. For example, the Legislative Yuan passed the Employment Service Act in 1992, which is the major law to regulate significant foreign labor matters.[10] Later, the Legislative Yuan revised this Act twice to extend the work permits of foreign workers.[11] In addition, the Legislative Yuan revised the Labor Standards Act in early 2000 so that it provides better working condition for foreign workers.

The second category manages mutual exchanges and visits among Taiwan, Mainland China, Hong Kong and Macau. In the early 1990s, decades of overt hostility between Taiwan and Mainland China eased. To resume cross-Strait communications, a coordinating government agency—the Mainland Affairs Council—was established in January 1991 and put in charge of cross-Strait issues. In addition, a nongovernmental institution, the Straits Exchange Foundation, was created to conduct negotiations with its counterpart created by the People's Republic of China (hereinafter 'PRC'), the Association for Relations across the Taiwan Strait.[12] In the same year, a constitutional amendment was passed to moderate the ROC Constitution's strong "one China" ideology and to authorize the enactment of a special law dealing with cross-Strait affairs.[13] In 1992, the Legislative Yuan passed the Act Governing Relations between the People of the Taiwan Area and the Mainland Area (hereinafter Cross-Strait Act). It governs mutual exchanges and visits between Taiwan and the PRC. This Act does not clearly define the legal status of people from Mainland China in Taiwan. The vague status of Mainlanders in Taiwan demands further judicial interpretation. However, the Constitutional Court of Taiwan has not yet made any decision to clarify the status of people from Mainland China in Taiwan,[14] and therefore, there has been some discussion among scholars. The prevailing academic view is that Mainlanders enjoy a special legal status, which is different from the status of foreigners from other countries.[15] Five years later, to respond to the official transfer of sovereignty over Hong Kong from Great Britain to the PRC, the Legislative Yuan passed the Act Governing Relations with Hong Kong and Macau on 1 July 1997. This Act regulates various exchanges between Taiwan, Hong Kong, and Macau.

The last category regulates the movement of foreigners into and out of Taiwan and naturalization. For example, the Legislative Yuan passed the Immigration Act

[10]Wang (2011), pp. 179–180.

[11]Lee (2010), p. 338.

[12]Chen (2016), p. 28.

[13]Yeh (2016), p. 222.

[14]Although the Constitutional Court of Taiwan has not addressed the status of Mainlanders in Taiwan, several Justices of the Taiwanese Constitutional Court have discussed this issue in their individual opinions. For example, to address Constitutional Court Interpretation No. 710, Justice Chun-Sheng Chen, in his opinion of concurring in part and dissenting in part, argued that Mainlanders have a special status under the Taiwanese legal system. In addition, the opinion of concurring in part and dissenting in part issued by Justice Chang-fa Lo argued people from Mainland China shall enjoy the same rights as other foreigners in Taiwan.

[15]Li (2003), p. 162; Lee (2006), pp. 23–34.

and its enforcement rules in 1999 that recognize certain rights of immigrants and regulate significant immigration matters. One year later, to attract more foreign professionals, the Legislative Yuan revised the Nationality Act to lower the threshold of acquiring nationality.[16] In addition, to enhance the administrative efficiency of immigration affairs, the National Immigration Agency was established in 2007.[17] In 2009, the Legislative Yuan revised the Immigration Act, which allows stateless people from India or Nepal to apply for residence permission. In addition, the most important step in the recent immigration reforms has been the passage of the Human Trafficking Prevention and Control Act in 2009, which criminalizes human trafficking and provides legal assistance to the victims of trafficking.[18]

3 Constitutional Litigation on the Rights of Non-citizens

As discussed earlier, driven by democratization and globalization, diverse immigrant laws and regulations were enacted one after another when Taiwan became a migrant-receiving country in the late 1990s. Transnational immigration challenged the constitutionality of existing migrant laws and regulations before the Constitutional Court of Taiwan. In recent decades, the Court has adjudicated several non-citizen cases in the areas of civil, social and political rights. To the Court, the difficult issues are the extent to which non-citizens should enjoy equal rights as citizens and the question of whether or not differential treatments of citizens and non-citizens violates the principles of equality and proportionality.

3.1 Civil Rights

With regard to civil rights, the Constitutional Court of Taiwan was asked to review the following: (1) whether the restrictions on the entry of Chinese citizens violated their freedom of movement; (2) whether the detention proceedings for illegal migrants violated their right to physical freedom and the principle of due process; (3) and whether the mandatory deportation system for Mainlanders who legally enter Taiwan violated their right to physical freedom and the principle of due process.

3.1.1 J.Y. Interpretation No. 497

As mentioned previously, cross-Strait links were reestablished when martial law was lifted in 1987. The Cross-Strait Act took effect on 31 July 1992. Later, authorized by

[16]Momesso and Cheng (2017), p. 230.

[17]Yeh (2016), p. 80.

[18]Momesso and Cheng (2017), pp. 61–99.

Articles 10 and 17 of the Cross-Strait Act, the Ministry of the Interior enacted two administrative regulations—the Regulations Governing the Entry Permission to Taiwan Area for People from Mainland China and the Regulations Governing Permanent or Temporary Residence Permission for People from Mainland China. These regulations impose some limitations on the qualifications, conditions, permission procedures and duration of stay for those who enter Taiwan. Such limitations were challenged before the Constitutional Court of Taiwan for possible violations of the freedom of movement and the proportionality principle guaranteed and enshrined in the ROC Constitution's Article 10 and Article 23, respectively.

In Dec 1999, the Court rendered J.Y. Interpretation No. 497. The Court first indicated the Cross-Strait Act is a special law which regulates mutual exchange between Taiwan and Mainland China that was authorized by Additional Article 11 of the ROC Constitution.[19] Having examined the entire context and legislative content of the Cross-Strait Act, the Court reasoned that the purpose, scope and content of delegation of legislative duty to the executive branch as contained in Cross Strait Act is explicit and concrete. The restrictions in two administrative regulations are in accordance with the legislative content of the Cross-Strait Act and within the scope of legislative delegation.[20] In addition, the Court used Article 23 of the ROC Constitution to justify the restrictions on the freedom of movement as long as they "prevent infringement upon the freedoms of others, to avert an imminent danger, to maintain social order, or to promote public welfare." In the Court's view, the two regulations that place limitations on qualifications, conditions, permission and length of stay for those who enter Taiwan from Mainland China are used to "protect the security and welfare of the people of the Taiwan area." Since the interest in national security is more compelling than the freedom of movement, such regulations do not violate the proportionality principle guaranteed by Article 23 of the ROC Constitution.[21]

3.1.2 J.Y. Interpretation No. 708

As discussed previously, international migration has grown dramatically in Taiwan in the context of the country's rapid democratic transition and globalization since the early 1990s.[22] Also, when Taiwan became a migrant-receiving country and enacted various laws to regulate immigrants and refugees, it fueled a boom in illegal immigration. In the early 1990s, Taiwan established several immigration detention centers to accommodate foreign nationals who were arrested for illegal stays before their deportation. Authorized by Article 38 (1) of the Immigration Act, the National

[19]Si Fa Yuan Da Fa Guan Jie Shi Shizi Di 497 Hao [Justices of the Constitutional Court, Judicial Yuan, Interpretation No. 497] (3 Dec 1999) (R.O.C.) [hereinafter J.Y. Interpretation No. 497 (3 Dec 1999)], Holding and Reasoning.

[20]J.Y. Interpretation No. 497 (3 Dec 1999), Reasoning.

[21]J.Y. Interpretation No. 497 (3 Dec 1999), Reasoning.

[22]Lan (2006), pp. 33–37.

Immigration Agency has sweeping powers to detain and deport foreign nationals, if necessary. According to this provision, the maximum detention period is sixty days. However, the National Immigration Agency can usually extend the period of detention until the foreign national is deported. Hence, illegal foreigners have usually had to endure lengthy detentions without being brought before the courts prior to deportation.

Arguing that the deportation proceedings of illegal immigrants unconstitutionally violated their right to physical freedom, two foreigners who were detained in the immigration detention center for over sixty days petitioned the Constitutional Court of Taiwan. The constitutionality of Article 38 (1) of the Immigration Act was challenged by the petitioners since it did not provide the detained foreigners with a right to an effective remedy by the courts. They argued that the decision to extend the detention without judicial review was unconstitutional. In February 2013, the Court rendered J.Y. Interpretation No. 708, recognizing that foreign nationals have the same physical freedom and protection of due process as ordinary citizens. Thus, the Court invalidated the provisions in the Immigration Act since they did not place clear limitations on the duration of stay in the immigration detention center and provided no judicial remedy to detention decisions.[23]

In this decision, the Court stressed that physical freedom is a core fundamental right and shall be guaranteed without discrimination on the grounds of nationality.[24] According to the Constitutional Court, "physical freedom is a fundamental human right and the foundation of all freedoms and rights of humankind. Protecting physical freedom of each individual, regardless of his nationality, is a common principle upheld by all modern rule-of-law states. Thus, the guarantee of physical freedom under Article 8 of the Constitution extends to foreign nationals, and they shall receive the same protection as domestic nationals."[25] In other words, the Court at the first instance recognized that physical freedom shall extend to foreign nationals in the territory of the ROC.

Having defined the detention of foreign nationals as "a form of deprivation of physical freedom" and "a compulsory measure that severely interferes with physical freedom," the Court required that the principle of due process be applied to detained foreign nationals.[26] Although the Court recognized the immigration agency's power to decide the temporary detention of foreign nationals, foreign nationals shall have the right to a court hearing to challenge any decision to detain them. Hence, the immigration agency shall transfer the detainee to the court within twenty-four hours if the detainee opposes the decision of temporary detention or requests judicial

[23]Si Fa Yuan Da Fa Guan Jie Shi Shizi Di 708 Hao [Justices of the Constitutional Court, Judicial Yuan, Interpretation No. 708] (6 Feb 2013) (R.O.C.) [hereinafter J.Y. Interpretation No. 708 (6 Feb 2013)], Holding.

[24]J.Y. Interpretation No. 708 (6 Feb 2013), Reasoning, para. 1.

[25]J.Y. Interpretation No. 708 (6 Feb 2013), Reasoning, para. 1.

[26]J.Y. Interpretation No. 708 (6 Feb 2013), Reasoning, para. 3.

review of such a decision.[27] In balancing between the practice of deportation and the physical freedom of the detainee, the Court allowed a maximum duration of fifteen days for temporary detention without prior judicial permission.[28] In addition, the Court also emphasized that the decision to extend temporary detention shall be reviewed by judges with due process.[29] Since the provision at issue did not provide foreign nationals with an effective judicial remedy for temporary detention and lacked judicial review for extended temporary detention, the Court ruled that this provision was unconstitutional.

3.1.3 J.Y. Interpretation No. 710

After the ban on cross-Strait visits was lifted in the early 1990s, the number of cross-Strait exchanges dramatically increased. Owing to the consideration of national security, Article 18 (1) of the Cross-Strait Act establishes one mandatory deportation system which provides the police agency with wide authority to deport Mainlanders who have legally entered Taiwan without any hearing. In addition, Section 2 of the same provision allows the police agency to temporarily detain those Mainlanders before their deportation. Article 5 of the Rules Governing Enforced Deportation of People from Mainland China, Hong Kong, and Macau (hereinafter Rules Governing Enforced Deportation) provides reasons for the temporary detention of those who come from Mainland China, Hong and Macau before their deportation. A Chinese citizen who entered Taiwan with official permission was detained by the police and immigration agency and was deported. He then filed a petition to the Constitutional Court of Taiwan to challenge the constitutionality of the mandatory deportation system and the corresponding temporary detention proceedings. In July 2013, the Court rendered J.Y. Interpretation No. 710, invalidating Article 18 (1) of Cross-Strait Act which allowed the people from Mainland China to be detained and deported without due process. It ruled that the mandatory deportation system was unconstitutional since it has violated the freedom of movement guaranteed by Article 10 of the ROC Constitution. The temporary detention before deportation based on Article 18 (2) of the Cross-Strait Act violated the principle of due process enshrined by Article 8 of the ROC Constitution.[30] In addition, Article 5 of the Rules Governing Enforced Deportation, which lacks legislative delegation, was deemed to have lost its legal effect.[31]

[27]J.Y. Interpretation No. 708 (6 Feb 2013), Reasoning, para. 3.

[28]J.Y. Interpretation No. 708 (6 Feb 2013), Reasoning, para. 3.

[29]J.Y. Interpretation No. 708 (6 Feb 2013), Reasoning, para. 4.

[30]Si Fa Yuan Da Fa Guan Jie Shi Shizi Di 710 Hao [Justices of the Constitutional Court, Judicial Yuan, Interpretation No. 710] (5 July 2013) (R.O.C.) [hereinafter J.Y. Interpretation No. 710 (5 July 2013)], Holding, para. 1.

[31]J.Y. Interpretation No. 710 (5 July 2013), Holding, para. 3.

In this decision, the Court referred to Article 12 of the ICCPR and its General Comment No. 15 to recognize that Mainland Chinese citizens who have legally entered Taiwan shall have the same freedom of movement as Taiwanese citizens.[32] Resorting to Article 13 of the ICCPR, the Court stressed the mandatory deportation system should comply with the requirement of due process, except for cases of immediate threats to national security or social order. The Court found that the impugned provision did not provide for court hearings for those who were deported by a police agency; it was, therefore, contradictory to the principle of due process and in violation of the freedom of movement. The Court ultimately decided that the provision should lose effect no later than two years after this decision was issued.[33]

With regard to the constitutionality of temporary detention, the Court again confirmed that temporary detention (before deportation) is a specific form of deprivation of physical freedom and it further emphasized that the requirements for detention shall be prescribed by law. After examining the provision at issue, the Court found that the requirements for deportation proceedings were too vague and did not provide clear legal grounds for temporary detention. Hence, the impugned provision violated the principle of legal clarity.[34] Furthermore, the Court indicated that this provision failed to provide an effective judicial remedy for those who have been detained temporarily or who have had their detention extended. This provision violated the physical freedom guaranteed by Article 8 of the ROC Constitution. Lastly, the Court mentioned that this provision was excessive and disproportional in depriving detainees of their physical freedom since it did not mandate the specific period of detention. Hence, the Court also held that this provision violated the principles of proportionality under Article 23 of the ROC Constitution and of physical freedom guaranteed under Article 8 of the ROC Constitution.[35] In addition, Article 5 of the Rules Governing Enforced Deportation, which did not provide clear legal grounds for a competent agency to decide the temporary detention, was no longer to be effective within two years after this decision was made.[36]

3.2 Political Rights: J.Y. Interpretation No. 618

Article 18 of the ROC Constitution guarantees that "the people shall have the freedom of assembly and association." Those who would like to become public office-holders are required to have successfully taken national public examinations. Due to the hostilities across the Strait and the consideration of China's different political system, some special restrictions have been imposed on recent immigrants

[32]J.Y. Interpretation No. 710 (5 July 2013), Reasoning, para. 2.

[33]J.Y. Interpretation No. 710 (5 July 2013), Reasoning, para. 2.

[34]J.Y. Interpretation No. 710 (5 July 2013), Reasoning, para. 3.

[35]J.Y. Interpretation No. 710 (5 July 2013), Reasoning, para. 3.

[36]J.Y. Interpretation No. 710 (5 July 2013), Reasoning, para. 6.

from Mainland China which affect their right to hold public office.[37] For example, Article 21-I of the Cross-Strait Act provides that people from Mainland China should hold a ten-year household registration in Taiwan if he or she would like to register as a candidate for any public office, serve in any military, governmental or educational organization, or state enterprise, or organize any political party. Arguing that this provision violates the principle of equality, the principle of proportionality and the right to hold public office, a Chinese woman who had married a Taiwanese citizen and had acquired the nationality of the Republic of China petitioned the Constitutional Court of Taiwan. The Court rendered J.Y. Interpretation No. 618 on 3 November 2006.

In the view of the Court, although all citizens of the Republic of China shall enjoy equal rights to take public examinations and hold public office positions irrespective of their gender, religion, race, class, or party affiliation, as guaranteed by Article 7 and Article 18 of the ROC Constitution, differential treatment based on the nature of subjective matters is allowed under the consideration of substantial equality.[38] Using the proportionality principle, the Court emphasized the importance of the duty of loyalty of a public functionary. As a public functionary, he/she shall not only obey the law and social order but also act upon and adopt each policy that he or she considers is in the best and overall interests of the state as the exercising of his/her official duties will involve the state's public authorities.[39] The Court indicated that Taiwan and Mainland China are two separate and antagonistic political entities with significant differences in terms of their political, economic, and social systems. Since "the security of the Taiwan Area, the welfare of the people of Taiwan, as well as the constitutional structure of a free democracy, must be ensured and preserved," the Court concluded the ten-year requirement did not violate Additional Article 11 of the ROC Constitution.[40]

Further, the Court reasoned that those who are from Mainland China have a different view as to the constitutional structure of a free democracy and may need some time to adapt to and settle into Taiwanese society. Furthermore, it may also take a while for the Taiwanese people to place their trust in a person who has come from the Mainland Area when he or she serves as a public functionary. Hence, a ten-year ban is a necessary and reasonable means as it does not violate the principle of proportionality under Article 23 of the Constitution.[41]

[37]Yeh (2016), p. 208.

[38]Si Fa Yuan Da Fa Guan Jie Shi Shizi Di 618 Hao [Justices of the Constitutional Court, Judicial Yuan, Interpretation No. 618] (13 Nov 2006) (R.O.C.) [hereinafter J.Y. Interpretation No. 618 (13 Nov 2006)], Reasoning, para. 2.

[39]J.Y. Interpretation No. 618 (13 Nov 2006), Reasoning, para. 3.

[40]J.Y. Interpretation No. 618 (13 Nov 2006), Reasoning, para. 3.

[41]J.Y. Interpretation No. 618 (13 Nov 2006), Reasoning, para. 3.

3.3 *Social and Economic Rights: J.Y. Interpretation No. 560*

Taiwan has one mandatory standard labor insurance program in which domestic and foreign employees are required to participate. This insurance program provides maternity pay, retirement and other benefits. Article 62 of the Labor Insurance Act provides that an employee with labor insurance is entitled to claim burial compensation in the incidence of the death of his/her parents, spouse, or children. However, Article 43(5) of the Employment Services Act provides a foreign employee no such entitlement to claim burial compensation if his or her family member dies outside the jurisdictional territory of the Labor Insurance Act. The Taiwanese Constitutional Court was requested to review whether such restrictions imposed on foreign workers violate the principle of equality and the right to property. In July 2003, the Court rendered J.Y. Interpretation No. 560.

In the decision, the Court first indicated that the labor insurance is a social welfare program that guarantees workers with a stable livelihood and promotes their social security. The insurance fund is financed by the insurance fees of employers, employees and the government according to different ratios.[42] Article 62 of the Labor Insurance Act allows an employee with insurance to claim burial compensation in the incidence of the death of his/her spouse, child, or parents. In the Court's view, the purpose of the insurance is to "alleviate the burden on the worker's family finances and to help him maintain financial stability by way of making available to him burial compensation to meet his increased expenses incurred as a result of the loss of a member of his family."[43] Since the insurance benefit is conditioned by the insurance incident of an insured person, it can be said that this insurance functions as a social aid. Moreover, this is different from the regular insurance program, which provides insurance benefits to an insured person when the insurance incident occurs. The legislative body is vested with the power to decide which insurance incident should be covered by this social security program and the necessary coverage of such a payment.[44]

Under the consideration of social security, the Court indicated that the restrictions on burial compensation are different from those of regular labor insurance coverage. With regard to eligibility for social aid, the Court mentioned that a foreign worker's dependents living in a foreign country have a different degree of reliance on living expenses from those living in Taiwan. Having considered the function and purpose of the social security system, the restriction on the eligibility for social aid is constitutional.[45]

---

[42]Si Fa Yuan Da Fa Guan Jie Shi Shizi Di 560 Hao [Justices of the Constitutional Court, Judicial Yuan, Interpretation No. 560] (4 July 2003) (R.O.C.) [hereinafter J.Y. Interpretation No. 560 (4 July 2003)], Reasoning, para. 1.

[43]J.Y. Interpretation No. 560 (4 July 2003), Reasoning, para. 1.

[44]J.Y. Interpretation No. 560 (5 July 2003), Reasoning, para. 1.

[45]J.Y. Interpretation No. 560 (4 July 2003), Reasoning, para. 2.

4 Features and Critiques of Judicial Adjudication on Rights of Non-citizens

As previously discussed, the Court has made several decisions in the areas of civil, political and social rights of non-citizens. Its decisions have some interesting features and also draw some critiques. Those features and critiques are analyzed in the following section.

4.1 Features

The Court's recent decisions show two salient features. First, the Court has taken a rather inclusive approach to deal with the civil rights of non-citizens. Secondly, the Court or the individual Justices are more likely to use international human rights laws in addressing non-citizen rights.

4.1.1 Take an Inclusive Approach to Define Non-citizen Rights and Shape Migration Regulation

A national constitution that regulates the relationship between the government and citizens is a symbol of supreme sovereignty. Influenced by a nationalist spirit and a traditional concept of sovereignty, the ROC Constitution does not contain clear provisions relating to the status and rights of non-citizens. Although the title of Chap. II of the ROC Constitution is "the fundamental human rights of the people," this Chapter only has one constitutional clause about the rights of foreigners. Article 22 of the ROC Constitution stipulates that "[a]ll other freedoms and rights of the people that are not detrimental to social order or public welfare shall be guaranteed under the Constitution." However, those words are too vague. The ambiguous constitutional words on the status and rights of foreigners require further judicial interpretation.

In its earlier decisions concerning non-citizen rights, the Constitutional Court of Taiwan has neither addressed whether a foreigner is a subject of constitutional rights nor decided the scope of constitutional guarantees for non-citizens. Taking a rather deferential approach in reviewing these earlier cases, the Court showed due respect to decisions made by the legislative branch and largely maintained the constitutionality of laws that place restrictions on non-citizens.[46] However, using an inclusive approach, the Court made a great leap forward in two recent decisions concerning the civil rights of non-citizens. The Court, in J.Y. Interpretation No. 708, first recognized non-citizens as the subject of constitutional rights, at least

[46]Wu (2012), pp. 143–147.

in the area of civil rights, and then decided that substantive and procedural protections of due process and physical freedoms prescribed in Article 8 of the Constitution should be extended to foreigners, no matter where they are from.[47] Later, the Court, in J.Y. Interpretation No. 710, further confirmed that Mainlanders who lawfully enter Taiwan should enjoy the same freedom of movement as Taiwanese citizens, except where national security is an issue.[48]

In addition, another significant contribution of the court is to safeguard the right of due process to non-citizens when they are detained or face deportation in immigration detention centers. Regarding detention, based on Article 8 of the ROC Constitution, which contains habeas corpus, the Court emphasized that the foreign detainee has a right to a full and fair hearing in detention proceedings. Hence, the foreign detainee is entitled to petition the court to challenge the detention decision made by the immigrant agency during the detention period. In addition, the decision to extend detention shall be reviewed by judges in accordance with due process. Similar substantial requirements of due process also apply to the deportation proceedings of Chinese Mainlanders. In the Court's view, removing a Mainlander from Taiwan without any of the procedural safeguards of a formal hearing may result in a due process violation. These decisions have had a positive impact on subsequent revisions of migrant regulations. For example, the Legislative Yuan added one clause in the Administrative Litigation Act that provides foreign detainees the right to challenge the detention decision of the National Immigration Agency. In addition, this clause also requires the National Immigration Agency to transfer foreign detainees to courts within 24 hours when its detention decision is challenged.[49]

4.1.2 Active Judicial Reference to International Human Rights Laws and Its Corresponding Function

Despite its troubled statehood, Taiwan has made much progress in adopting major international human rights instruments since the late 1990s.[50] For example, the Taiwanese government ratified the Convention on the Elimination of All Forms of Discrimination against Women in 2007. In 2009, the government also ratified the International Covenant on Civil and Political Rights (hereinafter ICCPR) and the International Convenant on Social, Economic and Social Rights (hereinafter ICESCR).[51] The Implementation Acts to those international human rights laws

[47]Chang (2017), p. 614.

[48]J.Y. Interpretation No. 710 (5 July 2013).

[49]Republic of China (2016), para. 123.

[50]Chang (2011), p. 106.

[51]There are two different Chinese-language versions of the ICCPR. One is the original version that the Republic of China signed in the 1960s, and the other is a different translation that has been used in recent years by the UN. The two different versions of the ICCPR have different names. The original Chinese version and the recent Chinese version of the ICCPR have different translations in some parts of the ICCPR. The differences are the translations of "civil and political rights" and

were enacted one after another to guarantee the rights in those laws were directly applicable in the Taiwanese legal system.[52] Those international human rights laws not only provide non-discriminatory principles to the member states, but also obligate the member states to protect and promote the human rights of non-citizens. For example, Article 13 and Article 26 of the ICCPR and its General Comment No. 15 require that States Parties of the ICCPR shall guarantee that non-citizens in its territory enjoy the same rights and protections as citizens.[53] In addition, Article 2 (2) of the ICESCR obliges States Parties to guarantee the economic, social and cultural rights "without discrimination of any kind as to …national or social origin…birth or other status."

The recent active incorporation of international human rights laws into the domestic system facilitates vibrant reference to those human rights laws in the court's decision or a Justice's individual opinion in addressing non-citizen rights. In cases involving aliens, the main function of the use of international human rights laws is to offer persuasive arguments for the protection of alien rights. The use of international human rights standards also helps the courts to define the content of the rights and further to extend the protection of these rights that the national laws fail to provide.[54] For example, the ROC Constitution does not clearly address whether Mainlanders enjoy the same constitutional rights as Taiwanese citizens and which rights they have. The Court in J.Y. Interpretation No. 710 cited Article 13 of the ICCPR to recognize that Mainlanders who lawfully enter Taiwan have the same freedom of movement as citizens in Taiwan.[55] In addition, although the majority opinion in J.Y. Interpretation No. 708 did not invoke any international human rights instruments, several Justices in their individual opinion interpreted the personal freedoms and due process in the ICCPR along with other international human rights instruments.[56] Those interpretations and judicial debates among Justices deepen the understanding of the scope of physical freedom and due process for non-citizens in international human rights laws and domestic constitutional rights.

"covenant." The Taiwanese government adopted the original Chinese version of the ICCPR. The language is traditional Chinese. The Legislative Yuan of Taiwan ratified this version of the ICCPR and enacted the Implementation Act in 2009. Yeh and Chang (2014), pp. 152–153.

[52]Yeh and Chang (2014), pp. 152–153.

[53]General Comment No. 15 emphasizes "that each one of the rights of the Covenant must be guaranteed without discrimination between citizens and aliens."

[54]Chang (2011), p. 117.

[55]J.Y. Interpretation No. 710 (5 July 2013).

[56]Justice Yeong-Chin Su's concurring opinion; Justice Ching-You Tsay's concurring opinion; Justice Pai-Hsiu Yeh's concurring opinion; Justice Dennis Te-Chung Tang's concurring opinion; Justice Chang-fa Lo's opinion of concurring in part and dissenting in part.

4.2 Critiques

The recent decisions of the Taiwanese Constitutional Court represent some progress in the context of improving the rights of non-citizens in Taiwan. However, the decisions have also drawn criticisms from scholars. In the context of the civil rights of non-citizens, J.Y. Interpretation No. 708 emphasized the importance of due process in the detention of non-citizens. However, the Court sanctioned the temporary detention for a maximum duration of fifteen days before the deportation of non-citizens or foreigners. This decision has been criticized by several Justices of the Constitutional Court; they argue that the fifteen-day temporary detention infringes upon the physical freedom of foreign detainees and violates the purpose of the due process enshrined in Article 8 of the ROC Constitution.[57]

Additionally, some scholars have also criticized the Court's decisions on the political and social rights of foreigners. In the context of political rights, the Court in J.Y. Interpretation No. 618 held that the ten-year waiting period did not violate the right to public service for immigrants from Mainland China who had registered their residence in Taiwan in the name of national security. However, scholars have argued that national origin is a sensitive classification of difference and one that needs stricter scrutiny. They have contended that the Court has failed to use stricter scrutiny on the restriction found in Article 21 of the "Cross-Strait Act."[58] In addition, the restrictive measure was criticized for being over-inclusive as it imposed excessive restrictions on some categories of the civil service which do not threaten national security.[59] Moreover, in J.Y. Interpretation No. 560, the Court upheld the limitations imposed on foreigners' social rights due to concerns about the limited social resources available to the country. A similar critique is also raised of the Court's scrutiny on nationality classification.[60] Scholars have criticized the fact that the Court failed to use stricter scrutiny to review such limitations which used national origin as a criterion to deny the right to burial compensation of foreign workers.

Under the power of sovereignty, the legislative branch is typically vested with wider power to make decisions about non-citizens. Hence, the Taiwanese Constitutional Court usually adopts a rather deferential approach to respect legislative power, especially in the domain of national security and the distribution of social resources. Non-citizens usually do not have the right to vote for the representatives of their choice or to be elected as public officials. For them, the judicial review process is the main mechanism available to them to redress human rights violations as they are typically excluded from decision-making processes and the

[57]Justice Chun-Sheng Chen's opinion of concurring in part and dissenting in part; Justice Chang-fa Lo's opinion of concurring in part and dissenting in part; Justice Chen-Shan Li's opinion of concurring in part and dissenting in part; Justice Shin-Min Chen's dissenting opinion.

[58]Hwang (2007), pp. 471–498.

[59]Friedman (2010), pp. 79-83.

[60]Li (2016), pp. 5–6.

mainstream political community. Hence, it is important that the Court shall consider using stricter scrutiny on the legal restrictions on the social and political rights of non-citizens, given that national origin is a sensitive classification.

In recent years, courts in neighboring countries have increasingly held an open position regarding recognizing the social and political rights of non-citizens, which has reshaped the traditional concept of nationalist ideology.[61] For example, the Japanese Supreme Court and the Korean Constitutional Court have admitted that permanent foreign residents have the right to vote in local elections.[62] In addition, the Constitutional Court of Korea and the Supreme Court of Japan have been more inclusive in their approach; this is characterized by their flexible interpretations of the social and economic rights of foreigners.[63] This trend can give the Taiwanese Constitutional Court a chance to reconsider its role by making migrant governance more inclusive, especially when Taiwan has recently actively incorporated international human rights laws. To guarantee human rights for non-citizens, the Court would find it necessary to develop diverse criteria to review disputes that pertain to the social and political rights of non-citizens.[64]

5 Conclusion

Increasing global immigration has challenged the traditional concept of nationalist ideology that has been entrenched in many countries and is gradually transforming the constitutional frameworks governing the state–citizen relationship. Transnational immigration also shapes various immigration policies and regulations through constitutional challenges. Similar demands for judicial resolutions have emerged before the Taiwanese Constitutional Court in recent decades. The Court has rendered several decisions to address the civil, social, and political rights of non-citizens.

Having examined those judicial decisions, this chapter argues that the Court's recent decisions have revealed two significant features. First, the Court has increasingly taken an inclusive approach to the civil rights of non-citizens, which has shaped the subsequent development of migrant governance. Second, the Court and the individual Justices actively use international human rights instruments to address the rights of foreigners. However, the Court's decisions on social and

[61]Kondo and Popovic (2013), pp. 354–358.

[62]*Id.*, at p. 357.

[63]Richards (2014) Japanese Supreme Court Rules Against Foreign Residents on Welfare, The Diplomat, 23 July 2014, http://thediplomat.com/2014/07/supreme-court-makes-foreigners-second-class-citizens/. Accessed 21 Dec 2017; Constitutional Court of Korea, Case on Placing Limitations on the Number of Workplace Transfers by Foreign Workers, 2007 Hun-Ma 1083, 29 Sept 2011 (23-2(A) KCCR 623).

[64]For example, multi-dimensional closeness between non-citizens and the host country can be included in a consideration of the judicial considerations: physical proximity, the legal duties they fulfill (to pay taxes), and their allegiance to the country. Moore (2013), p. 804.

political rights have drawn scholarly critiques when it took a rather deferential approach in reviewing related cases under concerns of national security and limited social resources. Since non-citizens are usually regarded as "discrete and insular minorities," this chapter argues that the Court should consider using stricter scrutiny of the legal restrictions of the social and political rights of non-citizens, especially when the national origin classification is a sensitive issue. In addition, to guarantee human rights for non-citizens, the Court would find it necessary to develop diverse criteria to review the disputes that pertain to the social and political rights of non-citizens.

References

Chang W-C (2011) The convergence of constitutions and international human rights: Taiwan and South Korea in comparison. N C J Int'l L Comp Reg 36(3):101–132

Chang W-C (2017) The Constitutional Court of Taiwan. In: Jakab A, Dyevre A, Itzcovich G (eds) Comparative constitutional reasoning. Cambridge University Press, Cambridge, pp 604–640

Chen L-C (2016) The U.S.-Taiwan-China relationship in international law and policy. Oxford University Press, Oxford

Cheng I, Momesso L (2017) Look, the world is watching how we treat migrants! The making of the anti-trafficking legislation during the Ma administration. J Curr Chin Affairs 46(1):61–99

Edwards A, Ferstman C (2010) Humanising non-citizens: convergence of human rights and human security. In: Edwards A, Ferstman C (eds) Human security and non-citizens: law, policy and international affairs. Cambridge University Press, Cambridge, pp 3–46

Friedman SL (2010) Marital immigration and graduated citizenship: post-naturalization restrictions on Mainland Chinese spouses in Taiwan. Pac Affairs 83(1):73–93

Hwang J-Y (2007) Judicial standard of review for national origin classification: the case of J.Y. interpretation No. 618. In: Chou C-H, Hsu C-H, Tsai M-I (eds) Theory and practice of modern constitution: essays in honor of professor Hong-Hsi Lee. Taipei, Angle, pp 471–498. (In Chinese)

Kondo A, Popovic D (2013) Rights of non-citizens. In: Tushnet M, Fleiner T, Saunders C (eds) Routledge handbook of constitutional law. Routledge, London, pp 349–360

Lan P-C (2006) Global cinderellas: migrant domestics and newly rich employers in Taiwan. Duke University Press, Durham

Lee C-L (2006) Nationality and citizenship: origins and legal analysis on identity linkage between people and state. Paper presented at the Conference on Citizenship and Social Change, held by the Institute of Sociology and the Institute of Political Science, Academia Sinica. Taipei, 26 May 2006 (in Chinese)

Lee SJ (2010) Immigration to Taiwan. In: Segal AU, Elliott D, Nazneen S, Mayadas SN (eds) Immigration worldwide: policies, practices, and trends. Oxford University Press, Oxford, pp 335–351

Li C-S (2003) Immigration system and fundamental rights of foreigners. Police L J 2:159–187 (in Chinese)

Li N-T (2016) Inequality or equality? foreigners on the decisions of the Constitutional Court. Dissent 28:4–7 (in Chinese)

Momesso L, Cheng I (2017) A team player pursuing its own dreams: rights-claim campaign of Chinese migrant spouses in the migrant movement before and after 2008. In: Fell D (ed), Taiwan's social movements under Ma Ying-jeou: from the wild strawberries to the sunflowers. Routledge, London, pp 219–235

Moore KN (2013) Madison lecture: aliens and the constitution. NYU L Rev 88(3):801–877

Republic of China (2016) Implementation of the International Covenant of Civil and Political Rights: second report submitted under Article 40 of the Covenant

Richards C (2014) Japanese Supreme Court rules against foreign residents on welfare, The Diplomat. http://thediplomat.com/2014/07/supreme-court-makes-foreigners-second-class-citizens/. Accessed 21 Dec 2017

Wang H-Z (2011) Immigration trends and policy changes in Taiwan. Asian Pac Migr J 30(2): 169–194

Weissbrodt D (2008) The human rights of non-citizens. Oxford University Press, Oxford

Wu C-H (2012) WTO and the greater China: economic integration and dispute resolution. Martinus Nijhoff Publisher, Leiden

Yeh J-R (2016) The Constitution of Taiwan: a contextual analysis. Hart Publisher, Oxford

Yeh J-R, Chang W-C (2014) A decade of changing constitutionalism in Taiwan: transitional and transnational perspectives. In: Chen AHY (ed) Constitutionalism in Asia in the early twenty-first century. Cambridge University Press, Cambridge, pp 141–168

Yi-Li Lee is currently Visiting Scholar at the Global Taiwan Institute in Washington D.C. She was awarded a Fulbright Scholarship and a scholarship from Taiwan's Ministry of Science and Technology to serve as a Post-doctoral Visiting Fellow in the Human Rights Program and East Asian Legal Studies at Harvard Law School. Dr. Lee received her Ph.D. in law from National Taiwan University College of Law in 2014. Her academic interests cover a variety of topics including transitional justice, comparative constitutions, international human rights, international humanitarian law and international criminal law.

Index

J. A. Cohen et al. (eds.), *Taiwan and International Human Rights*, Economics, Law, and Institutions in Asia Pacific, https://doi.org/10.1007/978-981-13-0350-0

D

CPSIA information can be obtained
at www.ICGtesting.com
Printed in the USA
LVHW051626290519
619458LV00002B/4/P

9 789811 303494